2002

LAW SCHOOLS

The Most Comprehensive Guide to 185 Accredited U.S. Law Schools

PETERSON'S

THOMSON LEARNING

Australia • Canada • Mexico • Singapore • Spain • United Kingdom • United States

About Peterson's

Founded in 1966, Peterson's, a division of Thomson Learning, is the nation's largest and most respected provider of lifelong learning resources, both in print and online. The Education Supersite[SM] at www.petersons.com—the Internet's most heavily traveled education resource—has searchable databases and interactive tools for contacting U.S.-accredited institutions and programs. In addition, Peterson's delivers unmatched financial aid resources and test-preparation tools. Peterson's serves more than 100 million education consumers annually.

Peterson's is a division of Thomson Learning, one of the world's largest providers of lifelong learning. Thomson Learning serves the needs of individuals, learning institutions, and corporations with products and services for both traditional and distributed learning. Headquartered in Stamford, Connecticut, with offices worldwide, Thomson Learning is a division of The Thomson Corporation (www.thomson.com), one of the world's leading e-information and solutions companies in the business, professional, and education marketplaces. For more information, visit www.thomsonlearning.com.

CONTENTS

PREFACE

These articles are designed to give you a comprehensive account of how to go about preparing and applying for law school. Information about deadlines and other procedural matters is important in preventing you from making a fatal mistake, such as not taking the Law School Admissions Test in time to be used in a recruitment season. At the end of the article section, you will find a comprehensive timetable for accomplishing the many tasks associated with applying to law school.

When reading these chapters, keep in mind that the probability of your acceptance at any law school is largely determined by your GPA and LSAT score, and there are only minimal actions you can take to distort that probability to any degree in your favor. So many of the strategies discussed here must be viewed in the context of your comprehensive record. With this caveat out of the way, it is important to add that this does not mean you should not pay attention to these strategies. Sometimes, what separates an offer of admission from a rejection is blessed little.

William Weaver received his J.D. and Ph.D. from the University of Virginia. He has advised prelaw students at three different colleges throughout the last decade and currently teaches at the University of Texas at El Paso, where he is codirector of UTEP's Law School Preparation Institute.

THE ABSOLUTE BASICS

WHAT IS LAW SCHOOL?

Law school is normally three years (six semesters) of full-time classes. There are more than 180 schools that are accredited by the American Bar Association (ABA). Accreditation through this body is extremely demanding and requires a school to have minimum resources in areas such as faculty, materials, and classroom space. In addition, the ABA maintains close supervision over the curriculum requirements of accredited schools. These requirements are most stringent for first-year courses. Today, it is absolutely crucial that you attend an ABA-accredited law school. In many jurisdictions, a law graduate's ability to practice law is severely limited if he or she has not received a law degree from an ABA-accredited law school. And in today's employment climate it may be almost impossible for graduates of non-ABA-accredited schools to find a job.

WHEN DOES LAW SCHOOL START?

Almost all ABA-accredited full-time law programs start in the fall semester. A few schools have programs directed at ethnic minority, nontraditional, or provisional students that begin in the summer prior to the normal first-year fall session. These programs are generally for students who do not meet normal admission requirements for the school and are a way of determining if a student, despite not having strong enough numbers, can still excel in a law school environment. These programs, however, are extraordinary and irrelevant for most law school applicants.

Some schools also allow students to attend full-time twelve months a year. The advantage of such a program is that students graduate in roughly two years rather than the normal three. The disadvantages, though, can be serious. Such a program means that a student will not engage in summer employment—often crucial in obtaining a job offer. Without summer employment, students look less attractive to prospective law firms. In addition, many job offers to law students come from firms and institutions that the students work for in the summer. Again, schools that offer twelve-month programs are few in number, and where they are offered they are optional. Some institutions cater to part-time students and may allow these students to be admitted in the fall or spring or even the summer.

William Weaver, J.D., Ph.D., Department of Political Science, University of Texas at El Paso

Unless you absolutely must attend law school part-time, though, you should enroll in the normal program of study, starting with full-time fall admission.

WHAT DO YOU NEED TO APPLY TO LAW SCHOOL?

In order to apply to law school, you must have a four-year degree from an accredited college or university. No particular undergraduate major or course of study is required, and applicants from the so-called "hard" sciences are welcomed by law schools. Law schools mainly look for students who have taken a rigorous track in undergraduate school and who have demonstrated writing and critical thinking abilities. No law-related courses at the undergraduate level are required in order to apply to law school.

HOW MUCH DOES IT COST TO APPLY?

Registration for the Law School Admission Test, or LSAT, is about $90, and Law School Data Assembly Service, or LSDAS (explanations of these services can be found in the application booklet, which is available from your prelaw adviser or on line; see contact information on page 86) registration for a dozen schools or so costs another couple of hundred dollars. But these expenses are just the beginning. If you intend to take a professionally-administered preparation course for the LSAT, the fee can be up to $1000 or more in a group setting and $2000 or more in a private setting. In addition, law schools charge application fees that can range from $15 to $80. If a person applies to a dozen law schools and takes a professional preparation course for the LSAT, the final bill for the law school application process could easily be more than $2000. Some law schools will waive fees for members of minority groups under certain circumstances, and the Law School Admission Council (LSAC) gives test fee waivers and application fee waivers for participating schools when an applicant is in dire financial need. Talk to your prelaw adviser for information and forms concerning fee waivers, or contact the LSAC on the World Wide Web or by phone at the number found on page 86.

HOW DO LAW SCHOOLS DECIDE WHICH STUDENTS TO ACCEPT?

Law school admissions committees generally make their decisions based on two factors: undergraduate GPA and

LSAT scores. Most schools transform an applicant's GPA and LSAT score into an index score, a single number that is then used to compare the applicant to the rest of the applicant pool. Some schools require extremely high GPAs and LSATs, while other schools are more flexible in their approach. Typically, the highest-ranked law schools require superior performance in terms of both grades and LSAT scores. We will discuss these matters at greater length later in this book.

WHEN SHOULD YOU TALK TO A PRELAW ADVISER?

You should talk to a prelaw adviser as soon as you recognize that you may have an interest in applying to law school. Even your first year of undergraduate school is not too early to talk to an adviser. Many students have strange misconceptions about law school and the applications process, and these should be cleared up as soon as possible. See your prelaw adviser.

HOW MUCH MONEY MIGHT YOU MAKE AS A LAWYER?

Many people imagine that attorneys make vast sums of money and lead endlessly interesting lives. In reality, most attorneys earn a solid middle-class living. Fully one third of attorneys are in solo practice and many times they—like other small business owners—are just barely scraping by. And while lawyers often work on interesting cases or projects, they are just as likely to be laboring away on excruciatingly boring material. Unlike on TV, most attorneys never try a major case in court, and eye strain and back pain are the main hazards of the average attorney's life. Being an attorney usually means extremely long working hours—60 hours a week is not unusual—and sometimes coming into contact with extremely unpleasant people and circumstances.

ARE YOU SMART ENOUGH TO BE A LAWYER?

Of course, law school requires dedication and serious work, but any person of average intelligence and above-average persistence should make it through with little trouble. Perhaps the most important skills you can take to law school are the abilities to analyze and write quickly, clearly, and in a direct and nonelliptical manner. After all, all attorneys have are words. So the better you are at writing and analysis the better you will be prepared for law school. With this in mind, make sure that you take undergraduate courses that require significant amounts of writing and analysis.

HOW CAN YOU AFFORD LAW SCHOOL?

Most law school students survive on student loans, and loan debt can easily exceed $100,000 for undergraduate and law school expenses combined. Do not over worry about this aspect of legal education. At any rate, be assured that if you are admitted to an ABA-approved law school you will be eligible for sufficient loans to pay for school and survive (barely, perhaps)—provided you are not delinquent in any other school loans. Law school is big business, and most schools have a staff that exclusively handles financial aid matters. Some students can get through with filling out a minimal amount of paperwork and a few weeks later being summoned to an office to sign over a chunk of money to the school with a smaller chunk doled out to make rent, etc. The process is relatively painless. Notice, however, that financial aid practices are meant to make things easy for the school, not necessarily the student. A student may not receive financial aid until well after the start of the semester and may receive only two or three disbursements for the entire school year. This requires students to manage their money very carefully. At any rate, you should arrive at law school with enough financial wherewithal to make sure that you can pay rent, buy books, and eat for the first few months of school. With luck, things will go smoothly, but prepare for the worst.

STRATEGIES AND CONSIDERATIONS

SHOULD YOU GO TO LAW SCHOOL?

Law school is a lengthy, arduous, annoying, expensive, and anxiety-inducing experience. Common wisdom would probably dictate that it is something to be withstood only if one has clear reasons and goals for withstanding it. However, on this point, most law students depart a great distance from this assumption. Few law school students end up doing anything remotely resembling what they thought they would be doing before they entered law school. The truth is that before you go to law school you are woefully equipped to make judgments about what areas of law or what types of jobs you will be interested in. Even if a family member or friend is an attorney, it is still difficult to get a grasp of the myriad possibilities in legal practice to make your mind up about what it is you want to do after graduation. If you simply have a generalized, largely unjustified desire to go to law school, do not second-guess yourself. Do it. As long as you know what you are getting into, law school is not such a bad place, even if you do not know what you want to do with your life. Law school is an oftentimes whirlwind experience where you are constantly being exposed to new ideas and new people from many areas of business and law. If you cannot figure out a direction to follow in life from such an environment then you will not have an easy time of it anywhere.

The adventure potential in law school is high. One week you may have convinced yourself that you are not going to be offered summer employment and the next you have been hired by a large law firm to spend the summer in its Salzburg, Austria, office. So do not worry if your life goals are indefinite, and do not mentally strap yourself down before going to law school. Leave all of your options open and do not be afraid to experiment.

WHAT SHOULD YOU DO IN COLLEGE PRIOR TO LAW SCHOOL?

Many students labor under misconceptions about what in their undergraduate record will make them more attractive

---

William Weaver, *J.D.*, *Ph.D.*, *Department of Political Science, University of Texas at El Paso*

law school candidates. These misconceptions generally fall into one of three categories: selection of major, course selection, or extracurricular activities.

Major

Perhaps the most pervasive misconception of potential law school applicants is that majoring in certain disciplines provides an advantage in the law school admissions process. Virtually no school has a "prelaw" undergraduate major, so many students believe that political science is the prelaw major. The actuality is that any rigorous program of study, from anthropology to zoology, is fine. You should major in an area you enjoy, since you are more likely to do better working at a subject you like than working at one you simply think will open a door for you. People in the so-called "hard" sciences should take special note. Engineering or physics majors frequently think that they cannot or should not apply to law school because they lack a liberal arts degree. This perception is dead wrong. Law schools are happy to receive applications from engineers, physics majors, and chemists.

Course Selection

Students often believe that they need to, or should take, law courses in the undergraduate curriculum to prepare for law school. This perception is false. By all means, take courses in public law or business law if you are interested in those areas, but don't feel compelled to take these courses simply because you are applying to law school. In fact, while it is not a crucial point, law schools often frown on student records that show lots of courses in law-related areas. Law schools don't want students coming in with preconceived notions about the law, because such students are less open to the pervasive "world-changing" effects of law school. You cannot "learn" the law in undergraduate school, so don't worry about "preparing" for law school in this substantive way. The best tools to take to law school are the abilities to write and analyze quickly, well, and with economy. If you are a "hard" science major, make sure that you take courses that require sufficient writing so you are not handicapped in law school. Conversely, liberal arts majors should take courses requiring logical analysis. For example, "hard" science majors should consider taking courses in philosophy or critical writing as electives.

Likewise, liberal arts majors should consider taking math all the way through calculus or advanced courses in the physical sciences.

Extracurricular Activities

Evidence of extracurricular activities are useful in the admissions process in that they can tell a story about your commitment to community and those who are friendless and resourceless. But do not undertake these activities merely to have something to put on your application. Do these things because your heart tells you to. The difference that extracurricular activities make in gaining admission to law school is insufficient to warrant undertaking them unless you are really inclined to such activity. Certain types of activities say more than others. It may be nice that you were on the governing board of your social fraternity, but it says more about you from the law school perspective if you spent your weekends as a research volunteer for the Legal Aid Society or helped fix up the local battered spouse's shelter.

IS IT TRUE WHAT THEY SAY ABOUT LAW SCHOOL?

Take some bright, ambitious, inquisitive people. Uproot them from situations in which they were successful and in control. Toss them into an environment in which they're in competition with other intelligent, articulate people and everything is unfamiliar to them—from basic terminology to study habits. Words like "injury" and "agreement" don't mean what they seem. All-nighters before tests that worked in the past become futile. While they're figuring out how to deal with all this change, keep them in the dark about how they compare with other classmates. And for the coup de grace, throw exams at them at the end of each semester upon which their future careers will largely depend.

Give or take a few degrees of reality, the above description of the first year at law school is essentially accurate. Smart people choose to put themselves into circumstances where they must learn how to think differently, learn the foreign language of law, and have little upon which to gauge their progress for the first two semesters except final exams.

TAKE THE SCARE TACTICS WITH A GRAIN OF SALT

If you're contemplating going to law school and haven't already heard all the horror stories, you will. Tom Noble, a second-year law student at Northwestern, did, and he'd been working in law firms since high school. "It's a war-story mentality," he explains. "People like to fill you with dread. It's more glamorous to tell all the bad stories."

However, the alarmists are not too far off. "You are being stretched emotionally and intellectually," points out Dean Frank Newton of the Texas Tech University School of Law. He compares the first year of law school to athletes in training. The initial months are the hardest, after which challenges that seemed insurmountable become routine.

The hurdles are what you're paying for, says Marshall S. Shapo, Professor of Law at Northwestern School of Law. He and his wife, Helene S. Shapo, also a Professor of Law at Northwestern, wrote a book for first-year law students, *Law School Without Fear*. The book began as advice for one of their sons who was entering law school. From his own experience as a first-year law student (called 1Ls for short), Shapo remembers when he and other classmates were preparing for their first set of exams and happened upon a smug upperclassman in the library. Recalls Shapo, "Smirking at us, he said, 'What's the difference between a 1L and a 2L?' We eagerly turned our ears toward him. 'Confidence,' he replied as he strode away." Shapo muses that this incident stuck with him because what he said was accurate. "Once you've been through one set of exams, you've heard live bullets going past and know what it's like."

Noble had heard all the combat legends about professors stomping their feet at supposedly dull-witted remarks by students and competitive students ripping pages from library textbooks to fend off avaricious classmates. However, the more he looked into law schools, visited them, and spoke with current students, his anticipation of a "boot camp" mentality diminished. His report: Club Med it isn't. But for him, that first year of law school was an intellectual blast even though it was crammed with an immense amount of skull-cracking work.

Shelli Soto, Assistant Dean for Admissions at the University of Texas at Austin School of Law, concurs that the first year of law school is often characterized as wild and scary. She agrees that it is an intellectual and social challenge, but the gloom and doom myths are fueled by the fact that it is so different from anything most students have experienced in college or since graduating. Even those who are somewhat familiar with the practice of law are caught off guard, like Noble, or Jeff Kitner, who is going into his second year at the University of Texas at Austin and whose dad is a lawyer.

FEELING INADEQUATE IS THE NORM AT FIRST

One reason most incoming students walk around in a state of shock is that they're used to being at the top of their classes. For ambitious and motivated people, feeling incompetent and out of control is not a familiar state of mind. "All of us think at one time or another during that first year, 'They made a mistake letting me in,'" reflects Amber Garza, who is a second-year law student (called a 2L for short) at Stanford. "You have older students telling you that you'll get through it. Saying that you'll be okay and that it only gets easier. But at the time it's hard to believe."

For Mushtaq Kapasi, a 2L at Yale, the fact that he was admitted kept his head above the waves of doubt. *Someone* thought he could make it. The "everyone is smarter than I am" syndrome hits hard, says Noble, but everyone eventually figures out what the routine is. "Incoming law students should know that most students will be intimidated the first couple of weeks," adds Jennifer Carney, also a 2L at Northwestern. However, most won't admit it, says Kapasi, because it's a sign of weakness, and it's confusing to be in the midst of an amazing intellectual experience and feel lousy about yourself.

Unfortunately, the realization that you are going to get through comes *after* you've gotten through. According to John Malik, a 2L at Stanford, incoming law students have plenty of skills from their undergraduate experience that they can harness. "Keep doing the things that got you into law school in the first place," he says. Carney contributes another positive note. "Law school is humbling, but it's easier to cope if you're not basing your whole life on grades. Who you are is not based on grades."

KILLER EXAMS

However, if the "I'm not smart enough" affliction doesn't get to you, the final exams just might. It seems to be an odd system that gives 1Ls few clues about how they're doing during the semester, as far as grades go. "Most law schools have only one major exam per semester for the substantive courses," says Shapo, though in his classes he goes through reviews of upcoming exams and talks his students through the process. Some have only one final grade, which is given at the end of the second semester. Or as Noble puts it, the powers that determine what direction your law career will likely take are giving out winning medals one third of the way through a three-year experience. What's more, many law schools grade on a curve, and some exams are blind—you aren't a name, you're a number.

A lot rides on those finals. Based on those first-year grades, employers hire 1Ls for the all-important summer job between their first and second year. That first job could influence the second summer job, which often becomes the one students are offered after graduation. "One thing leads to another," says Shapo. "I'm not saying that there's not a lot of room for late bloomers, whatever track they want to get on. But there's no question, if you get a head start on grades, you have a head start at least along conventional law firm career lines." Chris Garofalo, a third-year law student at New York University, saw friends who didn't do well the first year and as a result didn't get into the firms

they wanted, but they did well the second year and have a good shot at getting them now. "The first year can lead to a permanent position, but it's not the be-all and end-all," he concludes.

According to Janet Bolin, Assistant Dean for Admissions and Financial Aid at Washington University in St. Louis School of Law, certain law careers are seen as more prestigious. The higher the grades, the more likelihood of getting them. Understandably, the competition that ensues foments anxiety. "It all comes down to what you put on paper at the end of the semester," says Tracey Holmes, a 2L at the University of Minnesota. "Everyone is doing tons of work, and they don't know if it will pay off." The uncertainty is what causes panic attacks.

STRESS PRODUCES GOOD LAWYERS

But that's the way the system is supposed to work, notes Newton. Lawyers must perform at the highest levels of competence and in competition with others just like them. "When you leave school, you often will be responsible for a client's business and liberty," he says. "We can't release that pressure. What if we allowed students to do less than their best, and it's your business or your son or daughter going to jail that's at stake?"

The competition law students encounter, he continues, prepares them to vehemently argue a case in court, lose or win it, and go out to lunch with the opposing lawyer. "Quite frequently you're dealing with the same lawyers representing different clients. Part of the process of law school is to adjust students to the competition that says, 'You prevailed the first time, now how can I prevail the next?'"

Kitner contends that being ultracompetitive doesn't work that well. "You're in it for the long haul with the same people, so you develop a camaraderie," he observes. Some students let the quest for the top grades consume them. Kitner speculates that they might win, but at what cost?

Adds Carney, "Grades only make a big difference in the ease of getting a job. At my school, 99 percent [\] were employed, but if they had a lower GPA, they had to do more leg work." From the law school's side, Bolin counsels that most law schools are selective enough to choose those students who will do well. "We want them to succeed," she says.

THE LSAT

The LSAT is a half-day long exam given in six parts with a writing sample requirement. The exam is given four times a year, usually in June, September or October, December, and February. By and large, the test carries much more weight in the admissions process than the applicant's GPA. For this reason, all those applying to law school should definitely prepare for the test as throughly as possible. Your preparation for the LSAT should be extensive. Here are a few tips.

TIPS FOR TAKING THE LSAT

- Try to sign up for the June administration of the exam just prior to the fall semester in which you plan to apply to law school.
- Do not prepare for the exam months ahead of time. The LSAT is not a knowledge-based examination, but rather is meant to test the way in which you solve problems. Therefore, the test does not require months and months of preparation. In fact, over preparation is a problem. If you over prepare you lose your edge.
- Devote an intense period of four to six weeks preparing for the exam. Order back examinations from the LSAS corporation (may be ordered using forms in the information and registration booklet or on line) and buy self-help books from reputable publishers.
- Take your practice exams under test conditions. That is, time yourself and take a full examination each time.
- Take one or two practice exams under less-than-ideal conditions. Take an exam in a cafeteria or other location that is likely to be noisy. LSAT test conditions are as quiet as can possibly be achieved under the circumstances, but that does not mean that they are as quiet as a library special collections room. People get up and move around during the exam. Many people are concentrating so hard during the exam that they do not realize that they are making noises by shaking their legs or groaning.
- If you drink coffee, quit. Coffee will only accentuate the anxiety associated with the exam. Further, it may cause you to make a trip to the bathroom during the exam—a catastrophic event—which will make you worry even more about how you are doing.
- Visit the room where the exam will be given before the day of the examination. Select several seats that appear to be satisfactory. Don't sit next to a window or in an aisle seat. Things going on outside the windows might distract you, and if you sit in an aisle seat, anybody who gets up in your row will have to climb past you. The corner seat farthest from the entrance to the room is usually a fine choice.
- Wear loose clothing and after you sit down spend a few seconds taking several deep breaths and think of something restful.
- Prepare for the LSAT as you would prepare yourself for a sporting event—psych yourself up but try to keep yourself controlled at the same time.

Two practice LSAT tests appear on page 11 and 40. For advice and practice to boost your LSAT test scores, *LSAT Success* with diagnostic CD-ROM test feedback is available in your local bookstore or directly through http://www.petersons.com.

William Weaver, J.D., Ph.D., Department of Political Science, University of Texas at El Paso

LSAT PRACTICE TESTS

LAW SCHOOL ADMISSION TEST SIMULATIONS

On the following pages are two examples of what a real LSAT is like. According to the test-taking strategies you have developed during the course of your training, you may use these tests in one of two ways.

First, you could work only on those sections of the tests that you feel require additional practice. Use the individual section-tests of this simulation as if each is a pretest, employing the 9-12-18 system to sharpen your test-taking techniques (Sections 1 and 3 contain Relationships problems, Sections 2 and 5 contain Arguments problems, and Section 4 contains Passages problems). Review the sessions on the particular question type before beginning, and be sure to follow the instructions for each section-test carefully.

The second way to approach these simulated tests is to treat them as if you were taking an actual LSAT. In this case, you would spend 30 minutes on the Writing Sample and 35 minutes on each of the five section-tests, in effect putting the 9-12-18 system through a dry run in preparation for this 3-hour-and-25-minute test. Work only on one section during the 35 minutes allowed, and do not work on or review other sections. Take a 15-minute break between Sections 3 and 4 of the test.

Whichever method of working through the questions you choose, mark the best answers in the book, and, when you have finished a question set, transfer your choices to the answer sheet (on the next page for Practice Test 1; on page 39 for Practice Test 2). For ease of use, you might want to photocopy the answer sheet before working on the questions.

Quick-Score Answers to the two LSAT Practice Tests are found on pages 69 and 70, while Explanatory Answers begin on page 71.

Excerpted from *LSAT Success 2002* © 1996 by Thomas O. White

Law School Admission Test Simulation Answer Sheet

SECTION 1	SECTION 2	SECTION 3	SECTION 4	SECTION 5
1. Ⓐ Ⓑ Ⓒ Ⓓ Ⓔ	1. Ⓐ Ⓑ Ⓒ Ⓓ Ⓔ	1. Ⓐ Ⓑ Ⓒ Ⓓ Ⓔ	1. Ⓐ Ⓑ Ⓒ Ⓓ Ⓔ	1. Ⓐ Ⓑ Ⓒ Ⓓ Ⓔ
2. Ⓐ Ⓑ Ⓒ Ⓓ Ⓔ	2. Ⓐ Ⓑ Ⓒ Ⓓ Ⓔ	2. Ⓐ Ⓑ Ⓒ Ⓓ Ⓔ	2. Ⓐ Ⓑ Ⓒ Ⓓ Ⓔ	2. Ⓐ Ⓑ Ⓒ Ⓓ Ⓔ
3. Ⓐ Ⓑ Ⓒ Ⓓ Ⓔ	3. Ⓐ Ⓑ Ⓒ Ⓓ Ⓔ	3. Ⓐ Ⓑ Ⓒ Ⓓ Ⓔ	3. Ⓐ Ⓑ Ⓒ Ⓓ Ⓔ	3. Ⓐ Ⓑ Ⓒ Ⓓ Ⓔ
4. Ⓐ Ⓑ Ⓒ Ⓓ Ⓔ	4. Ⓐ Ⓑ Ⓒ Ⓓ Ⓔ	4. Ⓐ Ⓑ Ⓒ Ⓓ Ⓔ	4. Ⓐ Ⓑ Ⓒ Ⓓ Ⓔ	4. Ⓐ Ⓑ Ⓒ Ⓓ Ⓔ
5. Ⓐ Ⓑ Ⓒ Ⓓ Ⓔ	5. Ⓐ Ⓑ Ⓒ Ⓓ Ⓔ	5. Ⓐ Ⓑ Ⓒ Ⓓ Ⓔ	5. Ⓐ Ⓑ Ⓒ Ⓓ Ⓔ	5. Ⓐ Ⓑ Ⓒ Ⓓ Ⓔ
6. Ⓐ Ⓑ Ⓒ Ⓓ Ⓔ	6. Ⓐ Ⓑ Ⓒ Ⓓ Ⓔ	6. Ⓐ Ⓑ Ⓒ Ⓓ Ⓔ	6. Ⓐ Ⓑ Ⓒ Ⓓ Ⓔ	6. Ⓐ Ⓑ Ⓒ Ⓓ Ⓔ
7. Ⓐ Ⓑ Ⓒ Ⓓ Ⓔ	7. Ⓐ Ⓑ Ⓒ Ⓓ Ⓔ	7. Ⓐ Ⓑ Ⓒ Ⓓ Ⓔ	7. Ⓐ Ⓑ Ⓒ Ⓓ Ⓔ	7. Ⓐ Ⓑ Ⓒ Ⓓ Ⓔ
8. Ⓐ Ⓑ Ⓒ Ⓓ Ⓔ	8. Ⓐ Ⓑ Ⓒ Ⓓ Ⓔ	8. Ⓐ Ⓑ Ⓒ Ⓓ Ⓔ	8. Ⓐ Ⓑ Ⓒ Ⓓ Ⓔ	8. Ⓐ Ⓑ Ⓒ Ⓓ Ⓔ
9. Ⓐ Ⓑ Ⓒ Ⓓ Ⓔ	9. Ⓐ Ⓑ Ⓒ Ⓓ Ⓔ	9. Ⓐ Ⓑ Ⓒ Ⓓ Ⓔ	9. Ⓐ Ⓑ Ⓒ Ⓓ Ⓔ	9. Ⓐ Ⓑ Ⓒ Ⓓ Ⓔ
10. Ⓐ Ⓑ Ⓒ Ⓓ Ⓔ	10. Ⓐ Ⓑ Ⓒ Ⓓ Ⓔ	10. Ⓐ Ⓑ Ⓒ Ⓓ Ⓔ	10. Ⓐ Ⓑ Ⓒ Ⓓ Ⓔ	10. Ⓐ Ⓑ Ⓒ Ⓓ Ⓔ
11. Ⓐ Ⓑ Ⓒ Ⓓ Ⓔ	11. Ⓐ Ⓑ Ⓒ Ⓓ Ⓔ	11. Ⓐ Ⓑ Ⓒ Ⓓ Ⓔ	11. Ⓐ Ⓑ Ⓒ Ⓓ Ⓔ	11. Ⓐ Ⓑ Ⓒ Ⓓ Ⓔ
12. Ⓐ Ⓑ Ⓒ Ⓓ Ⓔ	12. Ⓐ Ⓑ Ⓒ Ⓓ Ⓔ	12. Ⓐ Ⓑ Ⓒ Ⓓ Ⓔ	12. Ⓐ Ⓑ Ⓒ Ⓓ Ⓔ	12. Ⓐ Ⓑ Ⓒ Ⓓ Ⓔ
13. Ⓐ Ⓑ Ⓒ Ⓓ Ⓔ	13. Ⓐ Ⓑ Ⓒ Ⓓ Ⓔ	13. Ⓐ Ⓑ Ⓒ Ⓓ Ⓔ	13. Ⓐ Ⓑ Ⓒ Ⓓ Ⓔ	13. Ⓐ Ⓑ Ⓒ Ⓓ Ⓔ
14. Ⓐ Ⓑ Ⓒ Ⓓ Ⓔ	14. Ⓐ Ⓑ Ⓒ Ⓓ Ⓔ	14. Ⓐ Ⓑ Ⓒ Ⓓ Ⓔ	14. Ⓐ Ⓑ Ⓒ Ⓓ Ⓔ	14. Ⓐ Ⓑ Ⓒ Ⓓ Ⓔ
15. Ⓐ Ⓑ Ⓒ Ⓓ Ⓔ	15. Ⓐ Ⓑ Ⓒ Ⓓ Ⓔ	15. Ⓐ Ⓑ Ⓒ Ⓓ Ⓔ	15. Ⓐ Ⓑ Ⓒ Ⓓ Ⓔ	15. Ⓐ Ⓑ Ⓒ Ⓓ Ⓔ
16. Ⓐ Ⓑ Ⓒ Ⓓ Ⓔ	16. Ⓐ Ⓑ Ⓒ Ⓓ Ⓔ	16. Ⓐ Ⓑ Ⓒ Ⓓ Ⓔ	16. Ⓐ Ⓑ Ⓒ Ⓓ Ⓔ	16. Ⓐ Ⓑ Ⓒ Ⓓ Ⓔ
17. Ⓐ Ⓑ Ⓒ Ⓓ Ⓔ	17. Ⓐ Ⓑ Ⓒ Ⓓ Ⓔ	17. Ⓐ Ⓑ Ⓒ Ⓓ Ⓔ	17. Ⓐ Ⓑ Ⓒ Ⓓ Ⓔ	17. Ⓐ Ⓑ Ⓒ Ⓓ Ⓔ
18. Ⓐ Ⓑ Ⓒ Ⓓ Ⓔ	18. Ⓐ Ⓑ Ⓒ Ⓓ Ⓔ	18. Ⓐ Ⓑ Ⓒ Ⓓ Ⓔ	18. Ⓐ Ⓑ Ⓒ Ⓓ Ⓔ	18. Ⓐ Ⓑ Ⓒ Ⓓ Ⓔ
19. Ⓐ Ⓑ Ⓒ Ⓓ Ⓔ	19. Ⓐ Ⓑ Ⓒ Ⓓ Ⓔ	19. Ⓐ Ⓑ Ⓒ Ⓓ Ⓔ	19. Ⓐ Ⓑ Ⓒ Ⓓ Ⓔ	19. Ⓐ Ⓑ Ⓒ Ⓓ Ⓔ
20. Ⓐ Ⓑ Ⓒ Ⓓ Ⓔ	20. Ⓐ Ⓑ Ⓒ Ⓓ Ⓔ	20. Ⓐ Ⓑ Ⓒ Ⓓ Ⓔ	20. Ⓐ Ⓑ Ⓒ Ⓓ Ⓔ	20. Ⓐ Ⓑ Ⓒ Ⓓ Ⓔ
21. Ⓐ Ⓑ Ⓒ Ⓓ Ⓔ	21. Ⓐ Ⓑ Ⓒ Ⓓ Ⓔ	21. Ⓐ Ⓑ Ⓒ Ⓓ Ⓔ	21. Ⓐ Ⓑ Ⓒ Ⓓ Ⓔ	21. Ⓐ Ⓑ Ⓒ Ⓓ Ⓔ
22. Ⓐ Ⓑ Ⓒ Ⓓ Ⓔ	22. Ⓐ Ⓑ Ⓒ Ⓓ Ⓔ	22. Ⓐ Ⓑ Ⓒ Ⓓ Ⓔ	22. Ⓐ Ⓑ Ⓒ Ⓓ Ⓔ	22. Ⓐ Ⓑ Ⓒ Ⓓ Ⓔ
23. Ⓐ Ⓑ Ⓒ Ⓓ Ⓔ	23. Ⓐ Ⓑ Ⓒ Ⓓ Ⓔ	23. Ⓐ Ⓑ Ⓒ Ⓓ Ⓔ	23. Ⓐ Ⓑ Ⓒ Ⓓ Ⓔ	23. Ⓐ Ⓑ Ⓒ Ⓓ Ⓔ
24. Ⓐ Ⓑ Ⓒ Ⓓ Ⓔ	24. Ⓐ Ⓑ Ⓒ Ⓓ Ⓔ	24. Ⓐ Ⓑ Ⓒ Ⓓ Ⓔ	24. Ⓐ Ⓑ Ⓒ Ⓓ Ⓔ	24. Ⓐ Ⓑ Ⓒ Ⓓ Ⓔ
25. Ⓐ Ⓑ Ⓒ Ⓓ Ⓔ	25. Ⓐ Ⓑ Ⓒ Ⓓ Ⓔ	25. Ⓐ Ⓑ Ⓒ Ⓓ Ⓔ	25. Ⓐ Ⓑ Ⓒ Ⓓ Ⓔ	25. Ⓐ Ⓑ Ⓒ Ⓓ Ⓔ
26. Ⓐ Ⓑ Ⓒ Ⓓ Ⓔ	26. Ⓐ Ⓑ Ⓒ Ⓓ Ⓔ	26. Ⓐ Ⓑ Ⓒ Ⓓ Ⓔ	26. Ⓐ Ⓑ Ⓒ Ⓓ Ⓔ	26. Ⓐ Ⓑ Ⓒ Ⓓ Ⓔ
27. Ⓐ Ⓑ Ⓒ Ⓓ Ⓔ	27. Ⓐ Ⓑ Ⓒ Ⓓ Ⓔ	27. Ⓐ Ⓑ Ⓒ Ⓓ Ⓔ	27. Ⓐ Ⓑ Ⓒ Ⓓ Ⓔ	27. Ⓐ Ⓑ Ⓒ Ⓓ Ⓔ
28. Ⓐ Ⓑ Ⓒ Ⓓ Ⓔ	28. Ⓐ Ⓑ Ⓒ Ⓓ Ⓔ	28. Ⓐ Ⓑ Ⓒ Ⓓ Ⓔ	28. Ⓐ Ⓑ Ⓒ Ⓓ Ⓔ	28. Ⓐ Ⓑ Ⓒ Ⓓ Ⓔ
29. Ⓐ Ⓑ Ⓒ Ⓓ Ⓔ	29. Ⓐ Ⓑ Ⓒ Ⓓ Ⓔ	29. Ⓐ Ⓑ Ⓒ Ⓓ Ⓔ	29. Ⓐ Ⓑ Ⓒ Ⓓ Ⓔ	29. Ⓐ Ⓑ Ⓒ Ⓓ Ⓔ
30. Ⓐ Ⓑ Ⓒ Ⓓ Ⓔ	30. Ⓐ Ⓑ Ⓒ Ⓓ Ⓔ	30. Ⓐ Ⓑ Ⓒ Ⓓ Ⓔ	30. Ⓐ Ⓑ Ⓒ Ⓓ Ⓔ	30. Ⓐ Ⓑ Ⓒ Ⓓ Ⓔ

Excerpted from *LSAT Success 2002* © 1996 by Thomas O. White

PRACTICE TEST 1

Complete the short writing exercise on the topic that follows. You have only 30 minutes to plan, organize, and write your sample. WRITE ONLY ON THE TOPIC SPECIFIED.

Alice Anderson is a senior at John Paul Jones University. She has been offered two positions as a result of her outstanding record in her major, television and radio broadcasting. As her counselor, you are to write an argument favoring one of the two offers. Two considerations guide your decision:

- Alice has a large student-loan debt that she has to begin to repay immediately upon graduation.
- Alice has as her career goal a position as a network-news anchorperson.

WAND is the only television station serving a large area located some 250 miles north of the capital of the state. The station has offered Alice a job as a reporter whose principal assignments would be to cover the activities of local government, politics, and business. In addition to her assigned stories, Alice would have the opportunity to independently prepare stories for possible broadcast. Because the station is small, has a very stable staff, and has limited growth prospects, Alice's chances for advancement are not good. WAND's owner is a former network executive who purchased the station in order to get away from the pressures of broadcasting in major markets. Alice would get only a modest salary at WAND, and she would have to supplement her income with outside work.

KBSC is one of three television stations located in the state capital. The station has offered Alice a job as a production assistant in the news department. She would primarily do background research and check facts and sources for the producers and reporters. Production assistants who work hard are promoted to positions as special-assignment reporters in about two years. There are many special-assignment reporters competing for assignments, most of which involve covering minor events such as political dinners, award ceremonies, and concerts and writing human-interest stories. Most special-assignment reporters spend at least five years covering minor events before moving into a position as a general report-anchorperson. KBSC would pay Alice a salary in excess of the amount she would need to live comfortably in the city.

Excerpted from *LSAT Success 2002* © 1996 by Thomas O. White

Excerpted from *LSAT Success 2002* © 1996 by Thomas O. White

<table>
<tr><td>

SECTION 1

</td><td>

TIME—35 MINUTES

</td><td>

24 QUESTIONS

</td></tr>
</table>

The questions in this section are based on a set of conditions. A diagram may be helpful in the answer selection process. Select the best answer to each question, and mark the corresponding space on the answer sheet.

Questions 1–6

A student is preparing a report on statehood. The source material is incomplete, but the following is known.

Wyoming became a state before Ohio.
Kansas became a state before Wyoming.
Ohio became a state after Maine.

1. Which of the following CANNOT be true?

(A) Kansas was a state before Maine.
(B) Maine was a state before Wyoming.
(C) Ohio was a state before Kansas.
(D) Wyoming was a state before Maine.
(E) Kansas was a state before Ohio.

2. Which of the following must be true?

(A) Kansas was a state before Maine.
(B) Wyoming was a state before Kansas.
(C) Maine was a state before Kansas.
(D) Ohio was a state before Maine.
(E) Kansas was a state before Ohio.

3. If Texas was a state before Maine, which of the following must be true?

(A) Texas was a state first.
(B) Texas was a state before Kansas.
(C) Wyoming was a state before Texas.
(D) Texas was a state before Ohio.
(E) Maine was a state before Texas.

4. If Kansas became a state before Maine, Wyoming became a state after Maine, and Vermont was last to become a state, which of the following must be the order of statehood, first to last?

(A) Vermont, Wyoming, Maine, Ohio, Kansas
(B) Wyoming, Ohio, Kansas, Vermont, Maine

5. If Utah became a state before Ohio, and Florida became a state after Wyoming, which of the following CANNOT be true if Maine became a state after Utah and before Florida?

(A) Utah was a state before Wyoming.
(B) Florida was a state before Ohio.
(C) Florida was a state before Kansas.
(D) Maine was a state before Ohio.
(E) Wyoming was a state before Florida.

6. If Alaska became a state after Iowa and Wyoming, which of the following must be true?

(A) Alaska was a state before Maine.
(B) Iowa was a state before Wyoming.
(C) Iowa was a state before Ohio.
(D) Alaska was a state before Ohio.
(E) Kansas was a state before Alaska.

(C) Maine, Kansas, Ohio, Vermont, Wyoming
(D) Kansas, Maine, Wyoming, Ohio, Vermont
(E) Ohio, Wyoming, Vermont, Kansas, Maine

Questions 7–12

T lives in a smaller house than her brother.
T lives in a larger house than her parents.
T's children live with T.
T has no other relatives.

7. If four females and two males live in smaller houses than T's brother, how many of T's children are boys and girls, respectively?

(A) 1, 0
(B) 0, 1
(C) 2, 1
(D) 1, 2
(E) 2, 0

8. If T's relative U lives in a larger house than her relative S, and both U and S are the same sex, what relationship could U be to S?

   (A) father to son
   (B) mother to daughter
   (C) daughter to mother
   (D) grandfather to grandson
   (E) son to father

9. If T's relative U lives in a larger house than T's relative S, all of the following may be true EXCEPT

   (A) S is U's son
   (B) S is U's mother
   (C) U is younger than S
   (D) S is younger than U
   (E) U and S are both female

10. If T's relative U is not as old as T, who is not as old as her relative V, what relationship can U NOT be to V?

   (A) grandson
   (B) uncle
   (C) nephew
   (D) son
   (E) granddaughter

11. If, of all T's relatives who could possibly be either older or younger than T, none are the same age or older, how many of T's relatives must be younger than T?

   (A) less than 2
   (B) 2
   (C) 2 or 3
   (D) 3
   (E) more than 3

12. If the number of males related to T equals the number of females related to T, which of the following can be true?

   (A) T has exactly 4 children.
   (B) T has exactly 3 children.
   (C) T has exactly 1 child.
   (D) T has exactly 6 children.
   (E) T has exactly 2 children.

Questions 13–18

Busses 1, 2, and 3 make one trip each day, and they are the only ones that riders A, B, C, D, E, F, and G take to work.

   Neither E nor G takes bus 1 on a day when B does.
   G does not take bus 2 on a day when D does.
   When A and F take the same bus, it is always bus 3.
   C always takes bus 3.

13. Which of the following groups consists of riders who CANNOT take bus 1 to work on the same day?

   (A) A, D, G
   (B) D, E, F
   (C) D, E, G
   (D) E, F, G
   (E) B, D, G

14. Traveling together to work, B, C, and G could take which of the same busses on a given day?

   (A) 1 only
   (B) 2 only
   (C) 3 only
   (D) 2 and 3 only
   (E) 1, 2, and 3

15. The maximum number of riders who could take bus 2 to work on a given day must be

   (A) 3
   (B) 4
   (C) 5
   (D) 6
   (E) 7

16. Traveling together to work, B, D, E, F, and G could take which of the same busses on a given day?

   (A) 1 only
   (B) 2 only
   (C) 3 only
   (D) 1 and 3 only
   (E) 2 and 3 only

Excerpted from *LSAT Success 2002* © 1996 by Thomas O. White

17. On a day when each of the riders takes one of the three busses to work, exactly how many riders CANNOT take any bus other than bus 2?

(A) 0
(B) 1
(C) 2
(D) 3
(E) 4

18. Which of the following could be a group of riders that takes bus 1 to work on a given day?

(A) A, C, E, G
(B) A, D, E, G
(C) A, E, F, G
(D) B, D, E, F
(E) B, D, E, G

Questions 19–24

Angela, Bruce, Cora, Dora, and Elmer live at different points along a straight east-west highway.

Angela lives 5 miles away from Bruce.
Cora lives 7 miles away from Dora.
Elmer lives 2 miles away from Cora.
Bruce lives 3 miles away from Cora.
The distance between houses is measured by straight line only.

19. Which of the following could be true?

(A) Dora lives 9 miles from Elmer.
(B) Dora lives 2 miles from Bruce.
(C) Angela lives 5 miles from Cora.
(D) Elmer lives 2 miles from Bruce.
(E) Angela lives 18 miles from Dora.

20. Which of the following must be true?

(A) The distance between Elmer's and Bruce's houses is greater than the distance between Cora's and Angela's houses.
(B) The distance between Bruce's and Elmer's houses is shorter than the distance between Cora's and Dora's houses.
(C) Of the group, Dora lives farthest from Cora.
(D) Cora lives closer to Dora than she does to Angela.
(E) Elmer lives closer to Cora than Angela does.

21. Which of the following statements must be FALSE?

(A) Angela and Cora live 12 miles apart.
(B) Angela and Dora live 5 miles apart.
(C) Bruce and Dora live 10 miles apart.
(D) Elmer and Dora live 9 miles apart.
(E) Elmer and Bruce live 5 miles apart.

22. If Bruce and Dora live east of Cora, which of the following must be the distance between Bruce's and Dora's houses?

(A) 10 miles
(B) 8 miles
(C) 5 miles
(D) 4 miles
(E) 2 miles

23. If Bruce and Elmer live east of Cora, and Dora lives west of Cora, which of the following must be true?

(A) Dora lives closer to Elmer than Cora does to Bruce.
(B) Cora lives closer to Dora than Elmer does to Bruce.
(C) Elmer lives closer to Cora than Bruce does to Elmer.
(D) Bruce lives closer to Elmer than Cora does to Dora.
(E) Angela lives closer to Bruce than Cora does to Elmer.

24. If Cora, starting from her house, visits Dora, Bruce, and Elmer in that order and then returns home, what is the smallest number of miles she walks?

(A) 14
(B) 15
(C) 16
(D) 17
(E) 18

Excerpted from *LSAT Success 2002* © 1996 by Thomas O. White

<table><tr><td>**SECTION 2**</td><td>**TIME—35 MINUTES**</td><td>**24 QUESTIONS**</td></tr></table>

Evaluate the reasoning contained in the brief statements, and select the best answer. Do not make implausible, superfluous, or incompatible assumptions. Select the best answer to each question, and mark the corresponding space on the answer sheet.

1. Well-designed clothing was once described as the hallmark of a stylish person. We agree, and our clothing is designed for stylish people. Their lifestyles are well-defined. They do everything in good taste. And they search out well-designed clothing as the guarantee of good workmanship.

   This advertisement is intended to suggest which of the following conclusions?

   (A) Well-designed clothing defines a lifestyle.
   (B) Good taste is important in clothing design.
   (C) Workmanship guarantees good design.
   (D) Purchasers of this brand of clothing will be stylish.
   (E) Appearance is the hallmark of purchasers of this brand of clothing.

2. Native American tribes seeking monetary reparations from the government are often told, "There is neither wealth nor wisdom enough in the world to compensate in money for all the wrongs in history."

   Which of the following most weakens the argument above?

   (A) Prior wrongs should not be permitted as a justification for present wrongs.
   (B) Even though all wrongs cannot be compensated for, some wrongs can be.
   (C) Since most people committed wrongs, the government should compensate for wrongs with money.
   (D) Monetary reparations upset social order less than other forms of reparation.
   (E) Since money is the basic cause of the wrongs, should it not be the cure?

3. A mother told her daughter, "You lie too much. You cannot be believed. When you start telling me the truth, I will start believing you."

   Which of the following is assumed by the mother's statement?

   (A) The mother has explained what is wrong about lying.
   (B) The mother has determined that her daughter knows what a lie is.
   (C) The mother knows when the daughter has been truthful.
   (D) The mother is routinely truthful with her daughter.
   (E) The mother believes her daughter ultimately will tell the truth.

4. Manufacturing products using glass made from sand rather than materials made from other natural resources can save energy, despite the fact that the initial cost is high.

   Which of the following, if true, does NOT support the above argument?

   (A) Manufacturing wood and metal products requires energy that could have been more efficiently used to make glass.
   (B) Unlike metal and wood products, those made from glass must be discarded rather than repaired when they break.
   (C) Aluminum products require much more energy to produce than do those made of glass.
   (D) Fiberglass insulation is much more energy efficient than insulation made with other materials.
   (E) Glass cookware transfers heat more efficiently than that made from metal.

Excerpted from *LSAT Success 2002* © 1996 by Thomas O. White

5. The United States gets 5 percent of its oil from Mexico. If Mexico raises the price of its oil by 20 percent, that will result in an increase of 1 percent (5 percent times 20 percent) in the price of oil products in the United States.

Which of the following is an assumption upon which the above argument depends?

(A) Oil prices in the United States are not affected by inflation in Mexico.

(B) Other countries will not increase oil exports to the United States.

(C) The price increase will not result in a decrease in the sales of Mexican oil products.

(D) People will not substitute other products for those made from Mexican oil.

(E) A 1 percent price increase in oil products will not be recognized by the buying public.

6. Historians, by trade, describe events that are confused as to motive and significance. Therefore, historians, however well-intentioned, primarily traffic in half-truths and lies. But novelists are free from such burdens. Even though they relate many things that are untrue, their characterizations are not offered as true and, therefore, are not half-truths or lies.

Which of the following, if true, would be an extension of the argument above?

(A) Historians and novelists, by trade, characterize events and, therefore, are required to deal in half-truths and lies.

(B) Poets offer their writing as truth in perception and, thus, do not deal in half-truths and lies.

(C) Journalists report on motives and the significance of events and, like historians, traffic primarily in half-truths and lies.

(D) Nonfiction writers select information to support their point and, thus, deal in half-truths.

(E) Economists characterize statistics and, therefore, do not deal in half-truths and lies.

7. The policy of equal pay for women continues to erode the importance of the mother's role in society.

The above argument can be criticized for which of the following reasons?

(A) The importance of a role is not related to the pay for that role.

(B) Equal pay for women is unrelated to motherhood.

(C) All women are not mothers.

(D) Society continues to devalue motherhood.

(E) When someone gains in a society, someone else loses.

8. The Earth receives energy in the form of heat from the sun and discharges heat energy into space by its own emissions. The heat energy received undergoes many transformations. But in the long run, no significant amount of heat energy is stored on the Earth, and there is no continuing trend toward higher or lower temperatures.

Which of the following sentences provides the most logical continuation of this paragraph?

(A) It is obvious, therefore, that much of the heat energy that reaches the Earth is transformed by some means not yet understood.

(B) Thus, it is imperative that we develop a way to use solar energy before it is dissipated into outer space.

(C) As a result, the amount of heat energy lost by the Earth must closely approximate the amount gained from the sun.

(D) The Earth would become as hot as the sun without the many transformations of heat energy.

(E) The Earth's slow but persistent receding from the sun prevents it from overheating.

Excerpted from *LSAT Success 2002* © 1996 by Thomas O. White

Questions 9–10

Lecturer: On average, the majority of Americans enjoy the highest standard of living of any people in the world.

Critic: There are thousands of Americans who have annual incomes of less than $3,000 per year.

9. Which of the following best describes the critic's response?

   (A) It is not inconsistent with the lecturer's statement.
   (B) It cites data confirming the lecturer's statement.
   (C) It fails to distinguish between cause and effect.
   (D) It generalizes from too small a number of cases.
   (E) It resorts to emotional language.

10. A logical criticism of the lecturer's statement would focus on the existence of

   (A) a country in which the majority of people enjoy a higher standard of living than that of the American people
   (B) a country with a higher level of employment than America
   (C) poor Americans who receive federal aid
   (D) a higher level of inflation in America than in other countries
   (E) many poor American families that are so isolated that they are not included in statistical surveys

Questions 11–12

The position that the prohibition of morally offensive works is wrong in principle is hardly tenable. There certainly are circumstances in which censorship could be desirable. If it were shown that all or most people of a certain type who saw a film thereafter committed a burglary or murder that they would not otherwise have committed, no one would deny that public exhibition of the film should be prohibited. To admit this is to admit that censorship is not wrong in principle. But to approve the principle of censorship on these grounds does not, of course, commit one to approve censorship in every form.

11. Which of the following can be inferred from the paragraph above?

   (A) No film affects any 2 individuals in the same way.
   (B) The causal connection between specific acts and exposure to specific films is not established.
   (C) We cannot anticipate the abuses to which censorship may lead.
   (D) People not exposed to morally offensive works will commit socially offensive acts.
   (E) There can be no relationship between a general principle and specific practices.

12. The paragraph questions the position that censorship is wrong in principle by

   (A) pointing out the ambiguity of a key term
   (B) rehearsing facts that are not generally known
   (C) questioning the truth of a factual generalization
   (D) exposing a logical inconsistency
   (E) presenting a hypothetical case

13. No Vikings carried watches. Some Vikings were explorers. Therefore, some explorers did not carry watches.

   Which of the following is logically most similar to the argument above?

   (A) Everyone who eats too much candy will be sick. I do not eat too much candy and will, therefore, probably avoid sickness.
   (B) All dogs are excluded from this motel, but many dogs are friendly. Therefore, some friendly animals are kept out of this motel.
   (C) People who want to avoid the pain of dental work will see the dentist twice a year. My children refuse to have their cavities filled. Therefore, my children like pain.
   (D) Some who are athletic are young people, and all young people can run. Therefore, everyone who can run is young.
   (E) Hawaii is a beautiful place. Some Hawaiians emigrate to California. Therefore, California is a beautiful place.

Excerpted from *LSAT Success 2002* © 1996 by Thomas O. White

14. Many people confuse reasons and causes. Any justification for performing an action is a reason. Anything that makes performing an action necessary is a cause—for example, a strong urge, hunger, an intense desire, social pressure, or some brain disorder. Those people who believe that the same thing may be both a reason for performing an action and its cause are clearly mistaken.

Which of the above examples of a cause that makes an action necessary best fits the description of a cause of an action rather than a justification for it?

(A) ''hunger''
(B) ''some brain disorder''
(C) ''social pressure''
(D) ''a strong urge''
(E) ''an intense desire''

15. One form of reasoning holds that by eliminating all possible explanations until only one remains, that one should be accepted. Critics argue that the flaw in this form of reasoning is that one cannot know about all possible explanations.

Which of the following examples best supports this criticism?

(A) the possible causes of heart disease
(B) the possible results of rolling dice
(C) the possible family members who left the house unlocked
(D) the possible candidates running for mayor of Atlanta, Georgia
(E) the possible countries with nuclear weapons

16. Doctor: The law of genetics holds that if both parents have brown eyes, then they can have only brown-eyed children.

Patient: That is not true; my mother has blue eyes, and I have brown eyes.

The patient has misinterpreted the doctor's statement to mean that

(A) only brown-eyed people can have blue-eyed children
(B) brown-eyed people cannot have blue-eyed children
(C) people with blue eyes invariably have blue-eyed children
(D) parents with the same eye color have children with a different eye color
(E) parents with different eye colors have children with the same eye color

17. Certain similarities between prehistoric art and the art of children has led some people to the mistaken conclusion that either early humans had the mentality of children or that they were as unskilled as children. These conclusions assume which of the following?

(A) Art that is considered sophisticated today must always have been considered sophisticated.
(B) What is easy for humans today must always have been easy.
(C) The significance of art is consistent over time.
(D) Prehistoric humans painted in the same way that children now paint.
(E) Modern humans have learned from prehistoric man.

18. During the cultural revolution in China under Chairman Mao, thousands of ''enemies of the republic'' were killed. When Mao's critics accused him of confusing his personal enemies with enemies of the republic, he responded, ''I deny the accusation, and the proof is that you are still alive.''

Which of the following assumptions was Mao making?

(A) All the enemies of the republic are dead.
(B) His critics are his personal enemies.
(C) Some personal enemies are also enemies of the republic.
(D) Enemies of the republic are not personal critics.
(E) Those killed were personal enemies.

Excerpted from *LSAT Success 2002* © 1996 by Thomas O. White

19. Today, neither scientists nor the pharmaceutical companies for which they work are willing to run the risk of being wrong. In the past, these scientists were encouraged to experiment with imaginative hypotheses that had a high probability of failure. If this situation continues, the country's drug-development work will come to a standstill.

The point of the argument above is that

(A) scientists are too concerned about failure

(B) scientists are not concerned about the outcome of experimentation

(C) risk should be an issue in experimental research

(D) scientific advances repay extensive experimentation

(E) support for drug research is vanishing

20. In his latest book, John does some clever writing, but even he might have been encouraged to use more everyday language.

Which of the following has a logical structure most like that of the above statement?

(A) The fertilizer serves some valuable purposes, but the smell of it when it is used is offensive.

(B) The latest sermon was effective as inspirational writing, but it did not offer the path to realizing the objectives it outlined.

(C) The star's last movie contained the usual bit of impressive acting, but her director should have advised her to act more like an average person.

(D) The chef at the resort makes wonderful desserts, but the manager should explain how to portion them more reasonably.

(E) Cage was a brilliant composer, but only a few people are able to understand his music.

21. The end of overcrowding at colleges and universities provides them with the opportunity to improve the quality of the educational services they offer. As enrollment declines, services and campus facilities should better serve student needs.

If true, which of the following statements most weakens the above conclusion?

(A) The quality of educational services does not depend on the variety of services offered.

(B) Fees paid by students are the major source of funding for educational services.

(C) Educational services are a critical factor in a student's choice of school.

(D) As campus facilities grow older, their maintenance becomes more expensive.

(E) Student needs are different than they were when colleges and universities were overcrowded.

22. When pregnant laboratory rats are given caffeine equivalent to the amount a human would consume by drinking six cups of coffee per day, an increase in the incidence of birth defects results. When asked if the government would require warning labels on products containing caffeine, a spokesperson stated that it would not, because if the finding of these studies were to be refuted in the future, the government would lose credibility.

Which of the following is most strongly suggested by the government's statement above?

(A) A warning that applies to a small population is inappropriate.

(B) Very few people drink as many as six cups of coffee a day.

(C) There are doubts about the conclusive nature of studies on animals.

(D) Studies on rats provide little data about human birth defects.

(E) The seriousness of birth defects involving caffeine is not clear.

Excerpted from *LSAT Success 2002* © 1996 by Thomas O. White

23. The Mercers are avid sailors. They have a child who will never be able to accompany them sailing because he is afraid of water.

Upon which of the following assumptions does the conclusion above depend?

(A) The Mercers will not take their child sailing.

(B) Avid sailors are not afraid of water.

(C) The Mercer's child will never want to sail.

(D) Sailors cannot be afraid of water.

(E) The Mercer's child may overcome his fear of water.

24. Sam: Olive oil can help prevent heart attacks, according to physicians.

Betty: It cannot. My mother cooked with olive oil her entire life, and she died of a heart attack last year.

Betty's statement can best be countered by pointing out that

(A) Betty's mother was an exception

(B) other factors could have nullified the influence of the olive oil

(C) Betty does not know that her mother always cooked with olive oil

(D) It has never been scientifically proven that olive oil causes heart attacks

(E) Betty's mother might have used olive oil irregularly

Excerpted from *LSAT Success 2002* © 1996 by Thomas O. White

<table>
<tr><td>SECTION 3</td><td>TIME—35 MINUTES</td><td>23 QUESTIONS</td></tr>
</table>

The questions in this section are based on a set of conditions. A diagram may be helpful in the answer selection process. Select the best answer to each question, and mark the corresponding space on the answer sheet.

Questions 1-6

A restaurant franchise has several locations in Ames County that are designated by the letters A, B, C, D, etc. The restaurants have the following relationships to the Central Office and one another:

A is northwest of the Central Office.
B is northeast of the Central Office.
C is northeast of the Central Office, but C is located farther east than B.
D is south (but not necessarily due south) of the Central Office.
E is southwest of the Central Office.
A is farther north than C and farther west than D.
E is farther west than A.
G is southeast of the Central Office and farther east than B.

1. If a delivery truck travels in a straight line from E to the Central Office and continues in exactly the same direction, it could pass directly by which of the following?

    (A) the northwest corner of D
    (B) the southeast corner of G
    (C) the northwest corner of A
    (D) the west side of A
    (E) the east side of G

2. If F is located due north of the Central Office, which of the following could be true?

    (A) F is located due north of G.
    (B) F is located west of E.
    (C) F is located east of B.
    (D) F is located due west of C.
    (E) F is located due north of E.

3. A restaurant located precisely midway between C and G must be

    (A) farther east than B
    (B) north of the Central Office
    (C) farther south than B
    (D) farther south than A
    (E) south of the Central Office

4. Which of the following CANNOT be the location of D?

    (A) northeast of A
    (B) northeast of C
    (C) southeast of E
    (D) southeast of G
    (E) northwest of G

5. Which of the following CANNOT be true?

    (A) B is precisely midway between E and G.
    (B) B is precisely midway between C and D.
    (C) B is precisely midway between C and E.
    (D) G is precisely midway between C and E.
    (E) D is precisely midway between C and E.

6. If G is southeast of D, and D is farther east than B, which of the following must be true?

    (A) The Central Office is closer to D than to G.
    (B) E is closer to D than to G.
    (C) E is closer to G than to D.
    (D) E is closer to the Central Office than to G.
    (E) C is closer to D than to G.

Questions 7–11

Six college officers—H, I, J, K, L, and M—are seated at equal distances around a circular table according to a list of personal preferences submitted by each officer.

The secretary and the treasurer have no preference as to where they sit.
The president must be seated directly opposite the vice president.
The 2 trustees may not sit together.
H must sit next to either J or K.

Excerpted from LSAT Success 2002 © 1996 by Thomas O. White

While it is unclear who occupies which office,
M is neither the president nor a trustee.
The vice president is either L or J.
Either H or I or both are trustees.

7. If, in satisfying all of the above conditions,
the officers are seated around the table in
the order K, I, J, H, L, and M, all of the
following may be true EXCEPT

(A) J is the vice president
(B) H is a trustee
(C) I is the president
(D) K is the treasurer
(E) M is the secretary

8. If H is seated between K and L, and M is
seated opposite H, what is a complete and
accurate listing of every officer who could
be sitting next to M?

(A) president, vice president
(B) president, vice president, secretary
(C) president, vice president, trustee,
     secretary, treasurer
(D) trustee, secretary, treasurer
(E) vice president, trustee, secretary,
     treasurer

9. If the president has M to her right and H to
her left, which is NOT an acceptable
arrangement for the other three officers,
assuming that their order starts with H and
goes around the table clockwise?

(A) J, K, L
(B) I, J, L
(C) K, J, I
(D) K, L, I
(E) L, J, K

10. If the officers are seated around the table
clockwise in the order J, H, I, K, M, and L,
and I is the treasurer, who are the 2
trustees?

(A) I and K
(B) H and J
(C) H and K
(D) I and J
(E) H and L

11. If the officers are seated around the table
clockwise in the order H, J, K, L, M, and I,
all of the following must be true EXCEPT

(A) M is the secretary
(B) H is not the treasurer
(C) J is not the vice president
(D) I is a trustee
(E) either J or K is a trustee

Questions 12–17

Holly Hauling has six vehicles. The Kenworth,
Mack, and White are trucks; the Chevrolet,
Dodge, and Ford are vans.

Holly always fuels and washes the trucks
before the vans.
Within the respective groups, Holly fuels the
vehicles that hold comparatively more fuel
before she fuels those that hold comparatively less.
Holly washes the vehicles in their respective
groups in the opposite order of their
fueling.

The White holds more fuel than the Chevrolet, and no vehicle holds both more than
the Chevrolet and less than the White.
The Dodge holds more than the Mack, and no
vehicle holds both less than the Dodge and
more than the Mack.
Only the Ford and the Kenworth hold the
same amount of fuel.

12. If the Kenworth is fueled first and the
White third, which of the following must be
true?

(A) The Ford is fueled fifth.
(B) The Ford is fueled last.
(C) The Chevrolet is fueled fifth.
(D) The Chevrolet is fueled last.
(E) The Dodge is fueled fourth.

13. If the White is washed first, which of the
following could NOT be possible?

(A) The Kenworth is fueled before the
     White.
(B) The Mack is fueled before the Ken-
     worth.
(C) The Chevrolet is fueled before the
     Ford.
(D) The Dodge is fueled after the Ford.
(E) The Ford is fueled before the Chevro-
     let.

Excerpted from *LSAT Success 2002* © 1996 by Thomas O. White

14. If the Mack is fueled first and the White third, which of the following must be true?

   (A) The Ford is washed first.
   (B) The Dodge is washed second.
   (C) The Kenworth is washed second.
   (D) The White is washed third.
   (E) The Chevrolet is washed third.

15. Which of the following is NOT a possible order in which the vehicles are washed?

   (A) Kenworth, White, Mack, Ford, Chevrolet, Dodge
   (B) Mack, Kenworth, White, Dodge, Ford, Chevrolet
   (C) Mack, White, Kenworth, Dodge, Chevrolet, Ford
   (D) White, Kenworth, Mack, Chevrolet, Ford, Dodge
   (E) White, Mack, Kenworth, Ford, Dodge, Chevrolet

16. Suppose Holly does not wash the trucks first but alternates by washing a van and then a truck. If the Mack is fueled first, it would NOT be possible for which pair of vehicles to be washed sequentially?

   (A) the Kenworth immediately before the Chevrolet
   (B) the Chevrolet immediately before the White
   (C) the White immediately before the Ford
   (D) the Dodge immediately before the Mack
   (E) the Ford immediately before the Dodge

17. If Holly fuels the trucks after the vans on a day the White is washed second and the Dodge is washed fourth, the order of fueling must be

   (A) Chevrolet, Dodge, Ford, White, Mack, Kenworth
   (B) Chevrolet, Ford, Dodge, White, Kenworth, Mack
   (C) Ford, Chevrolet, Dodge, Kenworth, White, Mack
   (D) Ford, Dodge, Chevrolet, Kenworth, Mack, White
   (E) Dodge, Chevrolet, Ford, Mack, White, Kenworth

Questions 18–23

There are six distinct building groups in a large office complex. From smallest to largest, respectively, the groups are constructed of aluminum, brick, concrete, glass, stone, and wood. The building groups are designated Groups 1 through 6.

   Group 1, which is not stone, is larger than Group 3.
   Group 2 is larger than Group 5 and Group 6.
   Group 2 is smaller than Group 4.
   Group 3 is larger than Group 6.

18. What material must Group 6 be made of if Group 3 is smaller than Group 5?

   (A) aluminum
   (B) brick
   (C) concrete
   (D) glass
   (E) stone

19. From smallest to largest, which of the following is a possible arrangement of the groups?

   (A) 5, 3, 6, 1, 2, 4
   (B) 6, 3, 1, 5, 2, 4
   (C) 6, 3, 1, 2, 5, 4
   (D) 6, 3, 5, 2, 1, 4
   (E) 6, 5, 3, 2, 1, 4

20. If Group 1 is concrete, Group 3 must be which of the following?

   (A) aluminum
   (B) brick
   (C) glass
   (D) stone
   (E) wood

21. Which of the following CANNOT be a possible arrangement of the groups from smallest to largest?

   (A) 5, 6, 3, 1, 2, 4
   (B) 5, 6, 3, 2, 4, 1
   (C) 6, 5, 2, 4, 3, 1
   (D) 6, 5, 3, 1, 2, 4
   (E) 6, 5, 4, 3, 2, 1

Excerpted from *LSAT Success 2002* © 1996 by Thomas O. White

22. If Group 5 is glass, Group 2 could be made
of which of the following materials?

    (A) concrete
    (B) stone
    (C) wood
    (D) brick
    (E) aluminum

23. If Group 4 is stone, Group 1 could be made
of which of the following materials?

    (A) concrete
    (B) glass
    (C) brick
    (D) aluminum
    (E) wood

Excerpted from *LSAT Success 2002* © 1996 by Thomas O. White

<table><tr><td>**SECTION 4**</td><td>**TIME—35 MINUTES**</td><td>**28 QUESTIONS**</td></tr></table>

The questions in this section are based on what is stated or implied in the passage. Select the best answer to each question, and mark the corresponding space on the answer sheet.

Line A. L. Macfie makes the distinction between what he calls the Scottish method, characteristic of Adam Smith's approach to problems of social policy, and the scientific
5 or analytical method, which is more familiar to modern social scientists. In the former, the center of attention lay in the society as observed rather than in the idealized version of the society considered as an
10 abstraction. Smith did have an underlying model or paradigm for social interaction; he could scarcely have discussed reforms without one. But his interest was in making the existing social structure "work better,"
15 in terms of the norms that he laid down, rather than in evaluating the possible limitations of the structure as it might work ideally if organized on specific principles.

    Frank Knight suggested that critics of
20 the free-enterprise system are seldom clear as to whether they object to the system because it does not work in accordance with its idealized principles or because it does, in fact, work in some approximation
25 to these principles. There is no such uncertainty with respect to Adam Smith. He was critical of the economic order of his time because it did not work in accordance with the principles of natural liberty. He
30 was not, and need not have been, overly concerned with some ultimate evaluation of an idealized structure.

    Smith's methodology has been turned on its head by many modern scientists. The
35 post-Pigovian theory of welfare economics has largely, if not entirely, consisted of a search for conceptual flaws in the working of an idealized competitive economic order, conceived independently of the flawed and
40 imperfect order that may be observed to exist. Partial correctives are offered in both the theory of the second-best and in the still-emerging theory of public choice, but the perfect-competition paradigm continues
45 to dominate applied economic policy discussions.

    This methodological distinction is important in our examination of Smith's conception of justice. In one sense, John
50 Rawls's efforts in defining and delineating "a theory of justice" are akin to those of the neoclassical economists who first described the idealized competitive economy. By contrast, Adam Smith saw no
55 need for defining in great detail the idealized operation of a market system and for evaluating this system in terms of strict efficiency criteria. Similarly, he would have seen no need for elaborating in detail a
60 complete "theory of justice" for defining those principles that must be operative in a society that would be adjudged to be "just." In comparing Smith with Rawls, therefore, we must somehow bridge the
65 contrasting methodologies. We can make an attempt to infer from Smith's applied discussion of real problems what his idealized principles of justice might have embodied. Or we can infer from John
70 Rawls's treatment of idealized principles what his particular application of these might be in an institutional context.

1. Which of the following best describes the passage's objective?

  (A) distinguishing between the Scottish and Pigovian theories of justice

  (B) supporting Adam Smith's concept of justice

  (C) comparing Smith's and Rawls's views of a just society

  (D) supporting John Rawls's theory of justice

  (E) analyzing the contrasting methodologies of Smith and Rawls

Excerpted from *LSAT Success 2002* © 1996 by Thomas O. White

2. According to the passage, all of the following are methods used to explain social policy EXCEPT

   (A) the Scottish method
   (B) the theory of welfare economics
   (C) the perfect-competition paradigm
   (D) the scientific method
   (E) the principles of natural liberty

3. According to the passage, John Rawls's "theory of justice" is similar to which of the following?

   (A) the description of the free-enterprise system
   (B) the description of the efficiency of the market system
   (C) the description of the idealized structure of natural liberty
   (D) the description of the idealized competitive economy
   (E) the description of the society considered as an abstraction

4. It can be inferred from the passage that Adam Smith was

   (A) not interested in achieving a just society
   (B) concerned with improving the operation of society
   (C) not worried about efficiency in the operation of society
   (D) indifferent to the economic operation of society
   (E) anxious to achieve an idealized operation of society

5. The author of the passage is presenting which of the following?

   (A) a recitation of methods of approaching social problems

   (B) an analysis of various economic systems
   (C) a comparison of the theories of Knight, Rawls, and Smith
   (D) an exposition of various theories of justice
   (E) an argument supporting idealized versions of social order

6. Which of the following is most likely to be the next sentence of the passage?

   (A) Since Smith planned a book on jurisprudence, there is a reason to develop his theory of justice.
   (B) The practical application of theories of what is "just" is guided by principles of natural justice.
   (C) In what follows, both of these routes will be explored.
   (D) Neither Rawls nor Smith was successful in dealing with real problems.
   (E) Rawls's "theory of justice" is difficult to apply to questions of natural liberty.

7. The author's purpose in finding a bridge between the Rawls and Smith methodologies (lines 63–65) is to

   (A) facilitate understanding of their philosophies
   (B) identify principles that each feels are just
   (C) explore their views toward an idealized market system
   (D) permit comparison of their concepts of justice
   (E) support their attempts to reform society

Excerpted from *LSAT Success 2002* © 1996 by Thomas O. White

Line Many, perhaps most, well-disposed,
practical people would, if they had to
designate a philosophy that comes closest
to expressing their unstated principles, pick
5 utilitarianism. The philosophy that pro-
claims as its sovereign criterion the
procuring of the greatest good for the
greatest number has indeed served as a
powerful engine of legal reform and
10 rationalization. And it is a crucial feature of
utilitarianism that it is consequences that
count. Now it is interesting that some
judgments that are actually made in the law
and elsewhere do not appear to accord
15 with this thoroughgoing consequentialism.
For instance, both in law and morals there
are many instances of a distinction being
made between direct and indirect intention—i.e., the distinction between, on the
20 one hand, the doing of evil as an end in
itself or, on the other hand, bringing about
the same evil result as a consequence of
one's direct ends or means. So also the
distinction is drawn between the conse-
25 quences that we bring about by our actions
and consequences that come about through
our failures to act. Also, when bad consequences ensue from our actions and what
was done was in the exercise of a right or
30 privilege, the law is less likely to lay those
bad consequences at our doorstep. And,
finally, if the only way to prevent some
great harm would be by inflicting a lesser
harm on ourselves or on others, then too
35 the law is inclined to absolve us of responsibility for that avoidable greater harm. It is
as if the net value of the consequences
were not crucial, at least where net benefit
is procured by the intentional infliction of
40 harm.

   Not only are these distinctions drawn
in some moral systems, but there are
numerous places in the law where they are
made regularly. Since in utilitarianism and
45 consequentialism in general the ultimate
questions must always be whether and to
what extent the valued end-state (be it
happiness or possession of true knowledge)
is obtained at a particular moment, it is
50 inevitable that the judgments on the human
agencies that may affect this end-state must
be wholly instrumental: Human actions can
be judged only by their tendency to
produce the relevant end-states.

55   Indeed, it may well be that even the
point and contents of normative judgments—whether legal or moral—are
concerned not just with particular end-
states of the world but also with how
60 end-states are brought about. These kinds
of substantive judgments take the form:
There are some things one should just
never do—kill an innocent person, falsely
accuse a defendant in a criminal proceed-
65 ing, engage in sex for pay. These are to be
contrasted to judgments that this or that is
an unfortunate, perhaps terrible, result that
(other things being equal) one would want
to avoid. The former are—very generally—
70 judgments of right and wrong. It is wrong
to do this or that, even if the balance of
advantages favors it; a person is right to do
some particular thing (help a friend, protect
his client's interests) even though more
good will come if he does not.

8. The author's point in the passage is
primarily that

(A) law and utilitarianism are not always
compatible
(B) utilitarianism is the operating philosophy of most people
(C) consequentialism is the basis for legal
reform
(D) direct and indirect intentions lead to
different end-states
(E) judgments about human actions can
be made only by the resulting end-
states

9. Which of the following is NOT a feature of
utilitarianism?

(A) Results are considered important.
(B) Consequences are considered important.
(C) The valued end-state is considered
important.
(D) The means of achieving results are
considered important.
(E) The net value of consequences is
considered important.

Excerpted from *LSAT Success 2002* © 1996 by Thomas O. White

10. Which of the following is an example of judgments that may conflict with the utilitarian philosophy?

   (A) It is legally acceptable to base judgments on the net consequences of acts.

   (B) It is legally acceptable to act for the greatest good to the greatest number.

   (C) It is legally acceptable for human actions that produce more harm than good to be punished.

   (D) It is legally acceptable for bad consequences to flow from the exercise of an individual's right or privilege.

   (E) It is not legally acceptable to avoid a small harm to oneself, even if the result is a great harm to another.

11. The point of the last paragraph is to

   (A) explain the differences between utilitarianism and consequentialism

   (B) contrast judgments of right and wrong with other types of judgments

   (C) discuss the role of intention in both law and words

   (D) distinguish between the results of actions and inaction

   (E) develop a rationale upon which to judge human actions

12. It can be inferred from the passage that the author is concerned with which of the following?

   (A) legal reform

   (B) false accusations

   (C) results of human inaction

   (D) means used to produce results

   (E) aspirations producing human action

13. The passage suggests that utilitarianism

   (A) explains all legal and moral judgments

   (B) explains only judgments of right and wrong

   (C) explains some judgments in law and morals

   (D) explains judgments of direct and indirect intentions

   (E) explains judgments of right and privilege

14. The author's attitude about utilitarianism as a philosophy is best described as

   (A) somewhat critical

   (B) generally supportive

   (C) mostly accepting

   (D) totally convinced

   (E) nearly convinced

Excerpted from *LSAT Success 2002* © 1996 by Thomas O. White

Line Although lawyers frequently reason in
terms of models, they tend to reason, in
Henry Steiner's terms, in *prose* models. I
think there are some real advantages of the
5 symbolic-logic type of reasoning in the law.
Although lawyers pride themselves on their
method of argumentation and on being
logicians, actually a lot of their arguments
are very flabby. One way of teasing them is
10 to say, "Well, let's write this problem down
in formal terms and abstract systems; let's
agree on a rigorous abstract definition of
this concept or behavioral principle and
derive its logical implications." And then
15 you allege that two situations they consider
as absolutely distinct are really formally
identical. That is what the model says. And
if they are not formally identical, what
really is the distinction? How has the model
20 been misspecified? You ask them whether
they may be making a distinction without a
difference.

I think that the benefit of formal logic
is that it sets out very nakedly, with all of
25 its warts and pimples exposed, whatever
difficulties there are in the argumentation.
By using prose, a lot of that is swept under
the carpet. Lawyers invoke the forces of
"equity" and "fairness" on both sides of
30 precisely the same set of facts. Two
arguments produce equity and fairness
"clearly or obviously," as they put it, while
pointing in different directions.

Formal models can be built assuming
35 that all people act in accord with the
Kantian categorical imperative—or pick any
principle you want. The desirable thing is
to write it down, to define your terms as
well as you can, say what you mean, and
40 then argue about it.

Those of us who have been making
models for a long time realize that all
models are bad, but some models are worse
than others. Part of the seduction of
45 mathematical models is that they look
much more rigorous than they are. They
are always abstractions; there is always
something wrong with them, something left
out of consideration. But I think that this is
50 no less true in the physical sciences, where
the models are supposed to be very good.
My chemist friends tell me that the
fundamental laws of chemistry are contra-
dicted every day in the laboratory. In the

55 last analysis, I think the way one ought to
look at this is as a method of argumentation. I feel that for a lot of uses in the law,
it will demonstrate to you problems you did
not think existed, inconsistencies, and
60 incidences of illogic. Although we are never
going to get all of the answers from formal
models, we would be foolish not to take
them for what they are worth.

And if the Landes and Posner thesis
65 stimulated this argument, that is precisely
what "writing it down" is supposed to
accomplish.

15. The passage can best be summarized as

(A) an analysis of law as a social science
(B) a comparison of formal and flabby
     models
(C) an argument for the use of formal
     models by lawyers
(D) a criticism of the method of argumen-
     tation of lawyers
(E) a challenge to the value of models in
     the sciences

16. According to the passage, which of the
following applies to both prose models and
formal models?

(A) expose all imperfections
(B) require precise definition of terms
(C) appear to be more rigorous than they
     are
(D) not demonstrably useful in the law
(E) a method of argumentation

17. The author contends that all of the following are benefits of using formal models
EXCEPT

(A) determining that an argument is
     making a distinction without a
     difference
(B) locating something left out of consid-
     eration
(C) demonstrating inconsistencies in an
     argument
(D) setting out difficulties with the form of
     argumentation
(E) assisting in the derivation of the
     logical implications of an argument

Excerpted from *LSAT Success 2002* © 1996 by Thomas O. White

18. The author defines a "flabby" argument
    (line 9) as one that

    (A) is not internally contradicted
    (B) is presented in prose
    (C) is too abstract
    (D) is not logically rigorous
    (E) is formally identical to another

19. According to the passage, the primary
    purpose of "writing it down" is to

    (A) avoid contradictions in arguments
    (B) pick the principle for the model
    (C) provide the basis for argumentation
    (D) determine the worth of an argument
    (E) identify distinctions without differ-
        ences

20. The passage indicates that models are used
    as all of the following EXCEPT

    (A) as a method of argumentation
    (B) as a source of answers to problems
    (C) as a form of reasoning used by lawyers
    (D) as a method to identify problems with
        logic
    (E) as a technique to ensure equity

21. Which of the following, if true, most
    weakens the author's argument about
    formal models?

    (A) Abstract symbols are the same as words.
    (B) Behavioral principles are hard to
        reduce to abstract symbols.
    (C) Models are regularly contradicted by facts.
    (D) Formal models are as illogical as prose
        models.
    (E) Prose models are routinely used by
        scientists.

22. Which of the following is implied by the
    author of the passage?

    (A) Symbols are inefficient expressions of
        behavioral principles.
    (B) A lawyer should not use an argument
        on both sides of a set of facts.
    (C) Prose is not a useful form of argumen-
        tation.
    (D) Omissions are a problem with formal
        models.
    (E) Mathematical inconsistencies are a
        problem with formal models.

Excerpted from *LSAT Success 2002* © 1996 by Thomas O. White

Line Applying communications theory to legal discourse has foundered on a lack of clear conception of what the theory means in the context of law and can tell attorneys
5 about the legal process. Communications theory is not a unified body of thought. It has three quite distinct branches. The first, "syntactics," is concerned with the logical arrangement, transmission, and receipt of
10 signals or signs. The second is "semantics," which is concerned with the meaning of signals to people. The third is "pragmatics," which is the study of the impact of signal transmission on human behavior.
15 The key concepts of syntactics are "information," "redundancy," and "feedback," of which the first two are best discussed together. For the telegraphic engineer, information is the content of the
20 signal that could not have been predicted by the receiver; it is a probability concept. The more probable the transmission of a given sign, the less information its actual transmission conveys. "Redundancy" is the
25 opposite of information. It is the introduction of repetition or pattern into the message. If the telegrapher sends each message twice, his second sending is redundant and contains less information
30 than his first.

The ideal transmission, then, in terms of pure "information," would contain no repetition and no pattern. The engineer finds it wise, however, to introduce
35 redundancy at the cost of reducing the information content of the message, because otherwise, any loss of information due to malfunctions in the transmission system would be undetectable and irreme-
40 diable. It is only when we can predict, at least partially, what message we are going to receive that we can spot an erroneous transmission or substitution in the message and call for its correction. The ideal
45 message, then, will contain the highest proportion of information and the lowest proportion of redundancy necessary to identify and correct errors in transmission.

Thus, it will be seen that redundancy
50 and information, in syntactic terms, are reciprocals of each other. But the situation is more complicated when we consider the semantic dimension of communication, for both information and redundancy convey

55 meaning. And the line is even more blurred when we consider the pragmatics of communication. Weakland has said, "There is no redundancy," his point being, of course, that repetitions and patterns in
60 messages do have significance to participants in the communication process. Such redundancies carry a freight of meaning, knowledge, and stimuli to the receiver and in this important sense are not redundant.
65 In the law, the strongest argument that an attorney can make is that the current case is "on all fours" with many previous cases, all of which were decided by repeatedly applying the same legal
70 principle. So it is that, in terms of communications theory, the rules of legal discourse seem to require attorneys to suppress as much information and transmit as much redundancy as possible.

23. The passage can best be characterized as

(A) an explanation of the principles of communications theory
(B) a description of conflict between information and redundancy
(C) an interpretation of syntactics applied to aspects of legal discourse
(D) an exposition of redundancy
(E) a review of the branches of thought in communications theory

24. According to the passage, which of the following describes an ideal transmission in terms of pure information?

(A) A, 2, #, +, s, ?, c, p, %, $
(B) A, C, A, E, A, G, A, I, A, K
(C) 1, 2, 3, 4, 5, 6, 5, 4, 3, 2, 1
(D) @, %, &, @, %, &, @, %, &
(E) 8, 1, 9, 1, 7, 1, 6, 1, 5, 1, 4, 1

Excerpted from *LSAT Success 2002* © 1996 by Thomas O. White

25. According to the passage, which of the following is an unambiguous example of syntactic redundancy?

(A) the transmission of the dash in dot-dot-dash

(B) the transmission of the dash in dot-dot-dash when two dots are always followed by a dash

(C) the transmission of a dot in dot-dot-dash

(D) the transmission of a dot when two dashes are never followed by a dot

(E) the transmission of the dash in dot-dot-dash when two dots are never followed by a dash

26. In the context of the passage, "on all fours" (line 67) most likely refers to

(A) a type of information in terms of communications theory

(B) a legal principle that is applied to many different cases

(C) the most recent example in a series of cases

(D) a type of argument lawyers use to distinguish one case from another

(E) a case that is exactly the same as previous cases

27. According to the passage, which of the following is NOT true?

(A) Patterns in messages are significant to communicating.

(B) Legal discourse requires maximum redundancy.

(C) Information in a message can be predicted by a telegraphic engineer.

(D) Redundancy in a message reduces the information transmitted.

(E) Information is the opposite of redundancy.

28. Which of the following best reflects the author's view about the application of communications theory to legal discourse?

(A) Syntactics tell lawyers very little about the legal process.

(B) Redundancy accounts for the difference between strong and weak legal arguments.

(C) Engineering, not law, has been the profession making use of communications theory.

(D) Communications theory is too difficult for lawyers to understand clearly.

(E) Legal discourse is dominated by the attempt to present pure information.

Excerpted from *LSAT Success 2002* © 1996 by Thomas O. White

SECTION 5　　　　　　**TIME—35 MINUTES**　　　　　　**24 QUESTIONS**

Evaluate the reasoning contained in the brief statements, and select the best answer. Do not make implausible, superfluous, or incompatible assumptions. Select the best answer to each question, and mark the corresponding space on the answer sheet.

1. There are no great writers in Largo because freedom of expression does not exist there.

   The conclusion above depends upon which of the following assumptions?

   (A) In the absence of freedom of expression, great writers do not develop.
   (B) If there is freedom of expression, there will be many great writers.
   (C) Where there is no freedom of expression, great writers turn to politics.
   (D) Great writers leave places that do not have freedom of expression.
   (E) Great writers must express themselves freely.

2. Archaeologists have determined that the bison was the primary source of meat for the cave dwellers, but their caves also contained the bones of birds, snakes, and fish, which indicates that they also liked to eat these animals.

   Which of the following, if true, would weaken the conclusion reached in the statement above?

   (A) Drawings of snakes and fish were made by cave dwellers.
   (B) Cave dwellers were not always able to eat what they liked.
   (C) Birds, rather than cave dwellers, may have brought snakes and fish to the caves to eat.
   (D) Cave dwellers ate grains and berries.
   (E) The bones of birds, snakes, and fish found in the caves were from small animals.

3. Some psychologists believe that humans, like porpoises, are benevolent creatures by nature. These psychologists assume that human nature is essentially disposed to benevolent conduct. To account for social evils, psychologists have to blame institutions that corrupt the native disposition of humans.

   The psychologists' argument described above would be most strengthened if it were to explain how

   (A) a way of life consistent with benevolent ideals is possible in the modern world
   (B) people can be persuaded to abandon technology, urbanization, and mass production
   (C) benevolent conduct can result from humans living in accordance with their own natural dispositions
   (D) benevolent dispositions give rise to evil institutions
   (E) corrupt institutions can be eliminated or reformed

4. Whenever the sky is cloudy and rain is falling, Bob wears his slicker. Whenever the sky is cloudy and rain is not falling, Bob ties his slicker around his waist. Sometimes rain falls when the sky is not cloudy.

   If the statements above are true, and it is true that Bob is not wearing his slicker, which of the following must also be true?

   (A) Bob has tied his slicker around his waist.
   (B) The sky is not overcast.
   (C) The sky is not cloudy, and rain is not falling.
   (D) The sky is cloudy, and/or rain is not falling.
   (E) The sky is not cloudy, and/or rain is not falling.

5. Only excellent musicians can be professors at Juilliard. No insensitive people are great lovers of poetry. No one who is not sensitive can be a lover. There are no excellent musicians who are not great lovers of poetry. Therefore, all Juilliard professors are lovers.

Which of the following inferences leading to the conclusion above is NOT valid?

(A) All Juilliard professors are excellent musicians.
(B) Juilliard professors are sensitive people.
(C) Sensitive people are lovers.
(D) Great lovers of poetry are sensitive people.
(E) Excellent musicians are great lovers of poetry.

6. Since plaznium evaporates in air, and this cube did not evaporate when it was exposed to air, it is not plaznium.

Which of the following is most like the argument above?

(A) Since no cats have hooves, and Fifi is a cat, Fifi does not have hooves.
(B) Since owls feed only at night, the bird feeding in daylight is not an owl.
(C) Since this box is made of brass, and boxes not made of brass are better than brass boxes, this brass box is not as good as a box not made of brass.
(D) Since chicks are never furry, and this animal is not furry, it is not a chick.
(E) Since every Canarbik dog is black or white, and Fido is a Canarbik, Fido cannot be gray.

7. Some ocean-liner captains are alcoholics. Ocean-liner captains who are alcoholics are dangerous. Every captain of an ocean liner is responsible for the care of the passengers.

The above leads to which of the following conclusions?

(A) All ocean-liner passengers are in the care of an alcoholic.
(B) Some ocean-liner passengers are dangerous when they drink.
(C) Some ocean-liner passengers are in the care of a dangerous person.
(D) All ocean-liner captains are dangerous when they drink.

(E) Some ocean-liner captains are dangerous when they drink.

8. Because coal is a nonrenewable resource, states that produce coal will experience problems that will never be faced by the lumber-processing industry.

Which of the following, if true, most weakens this argument?

(A) The resources required to log forests cannot be replenished.
(B) States with economies dominated by coal are trying to develop forest products.
(C) Lumber-producing states must secure much of the food they require from other states.
(D) Renewable resources are a significant part of the economies of coal-producing states.
(E) Coal-producing states depend on money from coal sales to buy lumber.

9. A criminal justice study has found that 82 percent of people presented with eyewitness testimony regarding a crime were willing to convict the accused. However, only 58 percent of the same people were willing to convict the accused when presented with lie-detector, fingerprint, and handwriting evidence from experts.

Which of the following conclusions is most reasonably supported by the above study results?

(A) Most crimes do not involve eyewitness and expert testimony.
(B) An accused can only be convicted by evidence that eliminates all reasonable doubt.
(C) Most people do not understand expert evidence.
(D) Prosecutors can ensure conviction by presenting both eyewitness and expert testimony.
(E) Jurors think eyewitness testimony leaves less room for doubt than does expert testimony.

Excerpted from *LSAT Success 2002* © 1996 by Thomas O. White

10. By 1997, the number of 18-year-olds will be dramatically lower than it was in 1961, when population growth in the United States reached its highest point. This decline in the number of potential college students will result in large enrollment decreases at colleges in the United States.

If true, which of the following would most weaken the conclusion of the above argument?

(A) Colleges prospered in the 1950s with lower enrollments than there are today.

(B) By 1997, there will be more colleges than there are today.

(C) Colleges will compete more aggressively for students when the number of 18-year-olds declines sharply.

(D) In the future, more older students will enter college than ever before.

(E) College enrollments in the 1960s were inflated by students avoiding the draft.

11. The contemporary film is a form of mass entertainment rather than an important art form. It fascinates, amuses, and distracts but fails to elevate the human spirit and deepen awareness. Film can be ignored if one is looking for art rather than escape.

Which of the following is NOT implied by the argument above?

(A) When looking for art, film can be ignored.

(B) Contemporary film is not an important art form.

(C) Film is an amusement.

(D) In the past, film was an important art form.

(E) Film is a form of escape.

Questions 12–13

Critics who claim that the sale of U.S. military equipment to other countries is destabilizing and leads to war take a narrow view of history. War occurs when one country gains a military advantage over another. By selling arms, the United States can ensure that the military balance among countries is maintained and war avoided.

12. The above argument depends on which of the following assumptions?

(A) Arms sales by the United States do not lead to wars between countries.

(B) Critics do not understand military history.

(C) Countries can accurately determine one another's military strength.

(D) Arms imbalances stimulate conflict between countries.

(E) Critics misunderstand the principle of military balance between countries.

13. Which of the following, if true, most weakens the above argument?

(A) Military equipment is usually used to intimidate rather than to actually conduct war.

(B) A country's military strength depends on military equipment rather than on the expertise of military commanders.

(C) The sale and delivery of military equipment is usually known only by the two countries involved.

(D) The military advantages of all countries are well known by the United States.

(E) Military equipment sold by the United States to other countries is less sophisticated than the equipment it produces for itself.

14. A study by the motor-vehicle bureau shows that only 3 percent of all cars fail the annual safety inspection because of defective lights. Consequently, the bureau has decided to discontinue inspecting lights, because the benefit is not worth the expense involved.

Which of the following, if true, is the greatest weakness in the decision of the bureau?

(A) Studies in other states show that a larger percentage of cars have defective lights.

(B) Cars with defective lights often have safety problems that are not part of the inspection.

(C) Lights are maintained in good working order because of the inspection requirement.

(D) Most cars fail inspection for more than one defect.

(E) Inspecting for defective lights costs less than 2 percent of the annual budget of the motor-vehicle bureau.

Excerpted from *LSAT Success 2002* © 1996 by Thomas O. White

Questions 15–16

The public's right to know is an inadequate justification for exposing people's private lives to public scrutiny. Only when the public welfare is involved does the public have a right to know information about a person's private life.

15. Which of the following, if true, most weakens the position taken in the above argument?

   (A) The public seldom knows which activities promote its welfare.

   (B) The public seldom wants much of the information exposed to it.

   (C) It is seldom possible to discover the most intimate details of someone's personal life.

   (D) The public seldom understands the implications of the information exposed to it.

   (E) It is seldom possible to determine which information involves the public welfare.

16. Which of the following best expresses the underlying point of the above argument?

   (A) Public welfare is the greatest good.

   (B) A justification is not a reason.

   (C) Personal privacy is an important right.

   (D) The common good is an insufficient justification.

   (E) Public rights supersede individual privacy.

17. A study shows that there is a strong positive relationship between voting and political involvement.

Which of the following CANNOT be inferred from this finding?

   (A) Political involvement and voting appear to be interrelated.

   (B) People who are not involved in politics are less likely to vote than those who are involved.

   (C) After people become involved in politics, they vote more frequently than before.

   (D) People who vote are more likely to be involved in politics.

   (E) Voting is a form of political involvement.

Questions 18–19

A survey of students concludes that some students prefer physics to history; all students prefer history to geometry; no students prefer history to economics; and all students prefer biology to history.

18. Based on the survey results, which of the following must represent students' preferences?

   (A) Some students prefer geometry to physics.

   (B) Some students prefer physics to geometry.

   (C) Some students prefer biology to economics.

   (D) Some students prefer geometry to economics.

   (E) Some students prefer physics to economics.

19. Based on the survey results, which of the following CANNOT represent students' preferences?

   (A) Some students prefer geometry to physics.

   (B) Some students prefer physics to geometry.

   (C) Some students prefer biology to economics.

   (D) Some students prefer economics to biology.

   (E) Some students prefer physics to economics.

20. Voters who complain about a trusted politician's betrayal remind me of the tale of the man who nursed a starving snake back to health. Afterward, the snake bit the man, who then complained about the snake's ingratitude. The snake responded to the complaint by saying, "You knew I was a snake when you saved me."

Which of the following can be derived from the argument above?

   (A) Don't cut off your nose to spite your face.

   (B) Things are not always what they seem.

   (C) Chickens always come home to roost.

   (D) Nature cannot be changed.

   (E) Take the bitter with the sweet.

21. Representatives of dairy producers say that government subsidies are needed to ensure that milk processors produce sufficient amounts for children. If there are no milk-price subsidies, processors will attempt to meet the demand for cheese and butter before producing milk.

Which of the following can be inferred from the above argument?

(A) The demand for milk is volatile, often leading to underproduction and shortages.

(B) Processors have produced sufficient milk in the past because they understood the needs of hungry children.

(C) Cheese and butter produce greater profits for processors than does milk.

(D) Representatives of dairies have a lobby that is powerful enough to ensure the passage of favorable subsidies.

(E) Dairy representatives are trying to avoid a surplus of cheese and butter.

22. The sculpture of the woman was carved during the early Greek period. The shape of the fingers, the style of hair, and the design of her sandals indicate the early period. The tilt of the chin and the closed eyes are frequently found in early Greek sculpture.

Which of the following is an assumption upon which this argument is based?

(A) The period of a work of art can be established with certainty.

(B) Certain attributes of works of art are typical of specific periods.

(C) Tilted chins and closed eyes always appear together in Greek sculpture.

(D) Sculptures of women first appeared in the early Greek period.

(E) Closed eyes are characteristic of early art.

23. The village is overrun by poisonous snakes. The mayor argues that paying a $10 bounty for each dead snake turned in by a villager will result in ridding the village of snakes.

Which of the following does NOT weaken the mayor's argument?

(A) The bounty ensures that breeding the snakes is in the economic interest of the villagers.

(B) Village taxes will triple if the mayor's proposal is implemented.

(C) The villagers do not trust the mayor.

(D) The snakes control the rat population, so the villagers will not kill the snakes.

(E) A drug company pays villagers $15 for each live snake delivered to it.

24. Spring Lake does not appear to be good for sailing. I have gone to the lake many times this year, and each time the water was too rough for sailing.

Which of the following most closely parallels the above argument?

(A) It appears that we will move to Spring Lake this year. The city is simply too rough for safe living.

(B) Economy-grade gasoline apparently does not prevent my car from running rough. It appears that a good grade of fuel is required.

(C) It appears that the cost of housing at Spring Lake is prohibitive. I looked at a number of houses last month, and they cost much more than I could afford.

(D) I am withdrawing from Spring Lake College. Two months at school was sufficient to prove that college was too rough for me.

(E) It appears that I will never play the clarinet. I began lessons many times, but each time, I quit.

Excerpted from *LSAT Success 2002* © 1996 by Thomas O. White

Law School Admission Test Simulation Answer Sheet

SECTION 1	SECTION 2	SECTION 3	SECTION 4	SECTION 5
1. Ⓐ Ⓑ Ⓒ Ⓓ Ⓔ	1. Ⓐ Ⓑ Ⓒ Ⓓ Ⓔ	1. Ⓐ Ⓑ Ⓒ Ⓓ Ⓔ	1. Ⓐ Ⓑ Ⓒ Ⓓ Ⓔ	1. Ⓐ Ⓑ Ⓒ Ⓓ Ⓔ
2. Ⓐ Ⓑ Ⓒ Ⓓ Ⓔ	2. Ⓐ Ⓑ Ⓒ Ⓓ Ⓔ	2. Ⓐ Ⓑ Ⓒ Ⓓ Ⓔ	2. Ⓐ Ⓑ Ⓒ Ⓓ Ⓔ	2. Ⓐ Ⓑ Ⓒ Ⓓ Ⓔ
3. Ⓐ Ⓑ Ⓒ Ⓓ Ⓔ	3. Ⓐ Ⓑ Ⓒ Ⓓ Ⓔ	3. Ⓐ Ⓑ Ⓒ Ⓓ Ⓔ	3. Ⓐ Ⓑ Ⓒ Ⓓ Ⓔ	3. Ⓐ Ⓑ Ⓒ Ⓓ Ⓔ
4. Ⓐ Ⓑ Ⓒ Ⓓ Ⓔ	4. Ⓐ Ⓑ Ⓒ Ⓓ Ⓔ	4. Ⓐ Ⓑ Ⓒ Ⓓ Ⓔ	4. Ⓐ Ⓑ Ⓒ Ⓓ Ⓔ	4. Ⓐ Ⓑ Ⓒ Ⓓ Ⓔ
5. Ⓐ Ⓑ Ⓒ Ⓓ Ⓔ	5. Ⓐ Ⓑ Ⓒ Ⓓ Ⓔ	5. Ⓐ Ⓑ Ⓒ Ⓓ Ⓔ	5. Ⓐ Ⓑ Ⓒ Ⓓ Ⓔ	5. Ⓐ Ⓑ Ⓒ Ⓓ Ⓔ
6. Ⓐ Ⓑ Ⓒ Ⓓ Ⓔ	6. Ⓐ Ⓑ Ⓒ Ⓓ Ⓔ	6. Ⓐ Ⓑ Ⓒ Ⓓ Ⓔ	6. Ⓐ Ⓑ Ⓒ Ⓓ Ⓔ	6. Ⓐ Ⓑ Ⓒ Ⓓ Ⓔ
7. Ⓐ Ⓑ Ⓒ Ⓓ Ⓔ	7. Ⓐ Ⓑ Ⓒ Ⓓ Ⓔ	7. Ⓐ Ⓑ Ⓒ Ⓓ Ⓔ	7. Ⓐ Ⓑ Ⓒ Ⓓ Ⓔ	7. Ⓐ Ⓑ Ⓒ Ⓓ Ⓔ
8. Ⓐ Ⓑ Ⓒ Ⓓ Ⓔ	8. Ⓐ Ⓑ Ⓒ Ⓓ Ⓔ	8. Ⓐ Ⓑ Ⓒ Ⓓ Ⓔ	8. Ⓐ Ⓑ Ⓒ Ⓓ Ⓔ	8. Ⓐ Ⓑ Ⓒ Ⓓ Ⓔ
9. Ⓐ Ⓑ Ⓒ Ⓓ Ⓔ	9. Ⓐ Ⓑ Ⓒ Ⓓ Ⓔ	9. Ⓐ Ⓑ Ⓒ Ⓓ Ⓔ	9. Ⓐ Ⓑ Ⓒ Ⓓ Ⓔ	9. Ⓐ Ⓑ Ⓒ Ⓓ Ⓔ
10. Ⓐ Ⓑ Ⓒ Ⓓ Ⓔ	10. Ⓐ Ⓑ Ⓒ Ⓓ Ⓔ	10. Ⓐ Ⓑ Ⓒ Ⓓ Ⓔ	10. Ⓐ Ⓑ Ⓒ Ⓓ Ⓔ	10. Ⓐ Ⓑ Ⓒ Ⓓ Ⓔ
11. Ⓐ Ⓑ Ⓒ Ⓓ Ⓔ	11. Ⓐ Ⓑ Ⓒ Ⓓ Ⓔ	11. Ⓐ Ⓑ Ⓒ Ⓓ Ⓔ	11. Ⓐ Ⓑ Ⓒ Ⓓ Ⓔ	11. Ⓐ Ⓑ Ⓒ Ⓓ Ⓔ
12. Ⓐ Ⓑ Ⓒ Ⓓ Ⓔ	12. Ⓐ Ⓑ Ⓒ Ⓓ Ⓔ	12. Ⓐ Ⓑ Ⓒ Ⓓ Ⓔ	12. Ⓐ Ⓑ Ⓒ Ⓓ Ⓔ	12. Ⓐ Ⓑ Ⓒ Ⓓ Ⓔ
13. Ⓐ Ⓑ Ⓒ Ⓓ Ⓔ	13. Ⓐ Ⓑ Ⓒ Ⓓ Ⓔ	13. Ⓐ Ⓑ Ⓒ Ⓓ Ⓔ	13. Ⓐ Ⓑ Ⓒ Ⓓ Ⓔ	13. Ⓐ Ⓑ Ⓒ Ⓓ Ⓔ
14. Ⓐ Ⓑ Ⓒ Ⓓ Ⓔ	14. Ⓐ Ⓑ Ⓒ Ⓓ Ⓔ	14. Ⓐ Ⓑ Ⓒ Ⓓ Ⓔ	14. Ⓐ Ⓑ Ⓒ Ⓓ Ⓔ	14. Ⓐ Ⓑ Ⓒ Ⓓ Ⓔ
15. Ⓐ Ⓑ Ⓒ Ⓓ Ⓔ	15. Ⓐ Ⓑ Ⓒ Ⓓ Ⓔ	15. Ⓐ Ⓑ Ⓒ Ⓓ Ⓔ	15. Ⓐ Ⓑ Ⓒ Ⓓ Ⓔ	15. Ⓐ Ⓑ Ⓒ Ⓓ Ⓔ
16. Ⓐ Ⓑ Ⓒ Ⓓ Ⓔ	16. Ⓐ Ⓑ Ⓒ Ⓓ Ⓔ	16. Ⓐ Ⓑ Ⓒ Ⓓ Ⓔ	16. Ⓐ Ⓑ Ⓒ Ⓓ Ⓔ	16. Ⓐ Ⓑ Ⓒ Ⓓ Ⓔ
17. Ⓐ Ⓑ Ⓒ Ⓓ Ⓔ	17. Ⓐ Ⓑ Ⓒ Ⓓ Ⓔ	17. Ⓐ Ⓑ Ⓒ Ⓓ Ⓔ	17. Ⓐ Ⓑ Ⓒ Ⓓ Ⓔ	17. Ⓐ Ⓑ Ⓒ Ⓓ Ⓔ
18. Ⓐ Ⓑ Ⓒ Ⓓ Ⓔ	18. Ⓐ Ⓑ Ⓒ Ⓓ Ⓔ	18. Ⓐ Ⓑ Ⓒ Ⓓ Ⓔ	18. Ⓐ Ⓑ Ⓒ Ⓓ Ⓔ	18. Ⓐ Ⓑ Ⓒ Ⓓ Ⓔ
19. Ⓐ Ⓑ Ⓒ Ⓓ Ⓔ	19. Ⓐ Ⓑ Ⓒ Ⓓ Ⓔ	19. Ⓐ Ⓑ Ⓒ Ⓓ Ⓔ	19. Ⓐ Ⓑ Ⓒ Ⓓ Ⓔ	19. Ⓐ Ⓑ Ⓒ Ⓓ Ⓔ
20. Ⓐ Ⓑ Ⓒ Ⓓ Ⓔ	20. Ⓐ Ⓑ Ⓒ Ⓓ Ⓔ	20. Ⓐ Ⓑ Ⓒ Ⓓ Ⓔ	20. Ⓐ Ⓑ Ⓒ Ⓓ Ⓔ	20. Ⓐ Ⓑ Ⓒ Ⓓ Ⓔ
21. Ⓐ Ⓑ Ⓒ Ⓓ Ⓔ	21. Ⓐ Ⓑ Ⓒ Ⓓ Ⓔ	21. Ⓐ Ⓑ Ⓒ Ⓓ Ⓔ	21. Ⓐ Ⓑ Ⓒ Ⓓ Ⓔ	21. Ⓐ Ⓑ Ⓒ Ⓓ Ⓔ
22. Ⓐ Ⓑ Ⓒ Ⓓ Ⓔ	22. Ⓐ Ⓑ Ⓒ Ⓓ Ⓔ	22. Ⓐ Ⓑ Ⓒ Ⓓ Ⓔ	22. Ⓐ Ⓑ Ⓒ Ⓓ Ⓔ	22. Ⓐ Ⓑ Ⓒ Ⓓ Ⓔ
23. Ⓐ Ⓑ Ⓒ Ⓓ Ⓔ	23. Ⓐ Ⓑ Ⓒ Ⓓ Ⓔ	23. Ⓐ Ⓑ Ⓒ Ⓓ Ⓔ	23. Ⓐ Ⓑ Ⓒ Ⓓ Ⓔ	23. Ⓐ Ⓑ Ⓒ Ⓓ Ⓔ
24. Ⓐ Ⓑ Ⓒ Ⓓ Ⓔ	24. Ⓐ Ⓑ Ⓒ Ⓓ Ⓔ	24. Ⓐ Ⓑ Ⓒ Ⓓ Ⓔ	24. Ⓐ Ⓑ Ⓒ Ⓓ Ⓔ	24. Ⓐ Ⓑ Ⓒ Ⓓ Ⓔ
25. Ⓐ Ⓑ Ⓒ Ⓓ Ⓔ	25. Ⓐ Ⓑ Ⓒ Ⓓ Ⓔ	25. Ⓐ Ⓑ Ⓒ Ⓓ Ⓔ	25. Ⓐ Ⓑ Ⓒ Ⓓ Ⓔ	25. Ⓐ Ⓑ Ⓒ Ⓓ Ⓔ
26. Ⓐ Ⓑ Ⓒ Ⓓ Ⓔ	26. Ⓐ Ⓑ Ⓒ Ⓓ Ⓔ	26. Ⓐ Ⓑ Ⓒ Ⓓ Ⓔ	26. Ⓐ Ⓑ Ⓒ Ⓓ Ⓔ	26. Ⓐ Ⓑ Ⓒ Ⓓ Ⓔ
27. Ⓐ Ⓑ Ⓒ Ⓓ Ⓔ	27. Ⓐ Ⓑ Ⓒ Ⓓ Ⓔ	27. Ⓐ Ⓑ Ⓒ Ⓓ Ⓔ	27. Ⓐ Ⓑ Ⓒ Ⓓ Ⓔ	27. Ⓐ Ⓑ Ⓒ Ⓓ Ⓔ
28. Ⓐ Ⓑ Ⓒ Ⓓ Ⓔ	28. Ⓐ Ⓑ Ⓒ Ⓓ Ⓔ	28. Ⓐ Ⓑ Ⓒ Ⓓ Ⓔ	28. Ⓐ Ⓑ Ⓒ Ⓓ Ⓔ	28. Ⓐ Ⓑ Ⓒ Ⓓ Ⓔ
29. Ⓐ Ⓑ Ⓒ Ⓓ Ⓔ	29. Ⓐ Ⓑ Ⓒ Ⓓ Ⓔ	29. Ⓐ Ⓑ Ⓒ Ⓓ Ⓔ	29. Ⓐ Ⓑ Ⓒ Ⓓ Ⓔ	29. Ⓐ Ⓑ Ⓒ Ⓓ Ⓔ
30. Ⓐ Ⓑ Ⓒ Ⓓ Ⓔ	30. Ⓐ Ⓑ Ⓒ Ⓓ Ⓔ	30. Ⓐ Ⓑ Ⓒ Ⓓ Ⓔ	30. Ⓐ Ⓑ Ⓒ Ⓓ Ⓔ	30. Ⓐ Ⓑ Ⓒ Ⓓ Ⓔ

Excerpted from *LSAT Success 2002* © 1996 by Thomas O. White

PRACTICE TEST 2

Complete the short writing exercise on the topic that follows. You have only 30 minutes to plan, organize, and write your sample. WRITE ONLY ON THE TOPIC SPECIFIED.

As the director of the Carthage University Press, you must recommend to the board of managers a long-range plan to counteract the Press's financial decline. You must choose between merging with a high-quality publisher or changing your publishing policy in a way that would greatly increase income. Two considerations guide your decision:

- The plan must provide a relatively permanent solution to the financial problems of the Press.
- The Press must maintain its tradition of only publishing work of the highest quality, using the very best paper, printing, and binding.

By merging with Lisle & Fish, Ltd., savings would result from combined sales, advertising, management, and printing, and a strong financial future would be ensured. Lisle & Fish has an impeccable reputation in the industry, and its taste is fastidious. If the companies merged, however, Carthage would lose its autonomy, and Lisle & Fish policies would control, including the use of somewhat lower-quality paper, printing, and binding.

On the other hand, by changing the Carthage publishing policy and introducing a series of annotated works of Shakespeare for use in high school and college courses, a permanently enlarged market would result. Professor Barth, the series' editor, produces popular and effective material but is not a highly respected scholar. And the Shakespeare series would require Carthage to publish in paperback form, which Carthage has refused to do for decades because it felt its reputation would suffer.

Excerpted from *LSAT Success 2002* © 1996 by Thomas O. White

Excerpted from *LSAT Success 2002* © 1996 by Thomas O. White

<table>
<tr><td>

SECTION 1

</td><td>

TIME—35 MINUTES

</td><td>

24 QUESTIONS

</td></tr>
</table>

The questions are based on a set of conditions. A diagram may be helpful in the answer selection process. Select the best answer to each question, and mark the corresponding space on the answer sheet.

Questions 1–6

Five golfers, C, D, E, F, and G, play a series of matches in which the following are always true of the results.

> Either C is last and G is first or C is first and G is last.
> D finishes ahead of E.
> Every golfer plays in and finishes every match.
> There are no ties in any match; that is, no 2 players ever finish in the same position in a match.

1. If exactly 1 golfer finishes between C and D, which of the following must be true?

   (A) C finishes first.
   (B) G finishes first.
   (C) F finishes third.
   (D) D finishes fourth.
   (E) E finishes fourth.

2. Which of the following CANNOT be true?

   (A) E finishes second.
   (B) F finishes second.
   (C) F finishes third.
   (D) E finishes ahead of F.
   (E) F finishes ahead of D.

3. If D finishes third, which of the following must be true?

   (A) G finishes first.
   (B) C finishes first.
   (C) E finishes ahead of F.
   (D) F finishes ahead of E.
   (E) F finishes behind D.

4. If C finishes first, in how many different orders is it possible for the other golfers to finish?

   (A) 1
   (B) 2
   (C) 3
   (D) 4
   (E) 5

5. Which of the following additional conditions makes it certain that F finishes second?

   (A) C finishes ahead of D.
   (B) D finishes ahead of F.
   (C) F finishes ahead of D.
   (D) D finishes behind G.
   (E) G finishes behind F.

6. If a sixth golfer, H, enters a match and finishes ahead of F and behind D, which of the following CANNOT be true?

   (A) D finishes ahead of G.
   (B) H finishes ahead of E.
   (C) E finishes third.
   (D) F finishes fourth.
   (E) H finishes fifth.

Questions 7–12

The state presidents of the Half Century Club are comparing ages at the Club's annual meeting.

> The Kansas president is older than the Wyoming president.
> The Ohio president is younger than the Maine president.

7. If the president from Ohio is younger than the president from Wyoming, which of the following CANNOT be true?

   (A) The Kansas president is younger than the Maine president.
   (B) The Maine president is younger than the Wyoming president.
   (C) The Ohio president is younger than the Kansas president.
   (D) The Wyoming president is younger than the Maine president.
   (E) The Kansas president is younger than the Ohio president.

8. If the president from Wyoming is older than the president from Ohio, which of the following must be true?

    (A) The Kansas president is older than the Maine president.
    (B) The Wyoming president is older than the Kansas president.
    (C) The Maine president is older than the Kansas president.
    (D) The Wyoming president is older than the Maine president.
    (E) The Kansas president is older than the Ohio president.

9. If the Texas president is older than the Maine president, which of the following must be true?

    (A) The Texas president is the oldest president.
    (B) The Texas president is older than the Kansas president.
    (C) The Wyoming president is older than the Texas president.
    (D) The Texas president is older than the Ohio president.
    (E) The Kansas president is older than the Texas president.

10. If the Vermont president is younger than the Maine president, the Wyoming president is older than the Maine president, and the Ohio president is the youngest, which of the following is the second-oldest president?

    (A) Vermont
    (B) Wyoming
    (C) Maine
    (D) Kansas
    (E) Ohio

11. If the Utah president is older than the Ohio president and the Florida president is younger than the Wyoming president, which of the following CANNOT be true if the age of the Maine president is between the ages of the Utah and Florida presidents?

    (A) The Utah president is older than the Wyoming president.
    (B) The Florida president is older than the Ohio president.

    (C) The Florida president is older than the Kansas president.
    (D) The Maine president is older than the Ohio president.
    (E) The Wyoming president is older than the Florida president.

12. If the Alaska president is older than the Iowa, Maine, and Wyoming presidents, which of the following must be true?

    (A) The Iowa president is older than the Maine president.
    (B) The Iowa president is older than the Wyoming president.
    (C) The Iowa president is older than the Ohio president.
    (D) The Alaska president is older than the Ohio president.
    (E) The Kansas president is older than the Alaska president.

Questions 13–18

There are four parallel train tracks at a railroad station, numbered 1 through 4 from left to right. Tracks 1 and 2 are northbound, tracks 3 and 4 are southbound. A train coming from the north will arrive on a southbound track. A train coming from the south will arrive on a northbound track.

A round-trip train must arrive on a track adjacent to a track going the other direction.
A local train can only arrive immediately after either an express or a metroliner.
Two consecutive trains cannot use the same track.

13. If three trains, P, Q, and R, arrive at the station on tracks 2, 4, and 1, respectively, and in that order, what could be true about the trains?

    I. P is an express.

    II. P and R are metroliners.

    III. Q and R are locals.

    (A) I only
    (B) II only
    (C) III only
    (D) I and II only
    (E) I, II, and III

14. If two northbound locals, a southbound express, and a round-trip metroliner coming from the north are all approaching the station, what is the order in which the tracks can be used, from first to last?

(A) 2,3,4,1
(B) 1,2,3,4
(C) 3,2,1,4
(D) 1,3,2,4
(E) 4,1,3,2

15. If five trains arrive on tracks 1,3,1,4, and 2, in that order, and the second train to arrive is not a local, what is the maximum number of trains that could be locals?

(A) 1
(B) 2
(C) 3
(D) 4
(E) 5

16. Train Q, a northbound express; train R, a round-trip express coming from the south; train S, a northbound metroliner; and trains T and U, both southbound locals, are arriving at the station, though not necessarily in that order.

In what order and on what track can each train arrive?

(A) S on track 1, U on track 4, Q on track 2, T on track 4, R on track 3
(B) R on track 2, T on track 3, S on track 1, Q on track 1, U on track 4
(C) R on track 2, U on track 3, S on track 1, T on track 3, Q on track 2
(D) Q on track 2, T on track 4, R on track 3, U on track 4, S on track 1
(E) T on track 3, Q on track 2, S on track 1, U on track 4, R on track 2

17. If six trains arrive on tracks 1,2,1,3,4,3, in that order, and there are two locals, what are the maximum and minimum numbers, respectively, of trains that could be expresses?

(A) 3,0
(B) 3,2
(C) 4,2
(D) 2,1
(E) 4,0

18. If four trains arrive at the station, and none of them arrives on track 3, what must be true about the trains?

(A) None are round-trip trains.
(B) Two of the trains are not northbound locals.
(C) The number of locals equals the number of southbound trains.
(D) There are more northbound trains than there are southbound trains.
(E) The greatest number of locals cannot exceed the greatest number of express trains.

Questions 19–24

Five friends, Carol, Ed, Jenny, Rick, and Walt, go to the beach. Each person either brings something (food, blankets, or umbrella) or does something for the trip (drives or pays the tolls along the route).

Two people are brother and sister. They are the only two of the group of friends who are related to each other.

One person meets the others on the beach when they arrive. This person brings the umbrella. The driver of the group that meets the person on the beach is male.

When Ed brings the food, Walt does not drive.

The brother pays the tolls.

When Carol or Jenny brings the blankets, Rick drives.

19. If Ed brings the food, which of the following must be true?

(A) Carol brings the blankets.
(B) Rick drives.
(C) Jenny does not bring the blankets.
(D) Carol does not bring the umbrella.
(E) Jenny meets the others at the beach.

20. If Rick drives, what CANNOT be true?

(A) Jenny brings the umbrella.
(B) Ed pays the tolls.
(C) Ed brings the food.
(D) Walt is Jenny's brother.
(E) Carol is Rick's sister.

21. If Walt brings the food, Rick CANNOT

(A) drive
(B) be Jenny's brother
(C) bring the umbrella
(D) be Carol's brother
(E) pay the tolls

Excerpted from *LSAT Success 2002* © 1996 by Thomas O. White

22. If Carol brings the umbrella, which of the following CANNOT be true?

    (A) Carol is Rick's sister.
    (B) Ed pays no tolls.
    (C) Jenny brings neither blankets nor food.
    (D) Ed brings the food.
    (E) Jenny does not bring the blankets.

23. If Ed brings the food, Rick must

    (A) drive
    (B) pay tolls
    (C) bring the blankets
    (D) bring the umbrella
    (E) be someone's brother

24. If Jenny brings the blankets, which two people CANNOT be related?

    (A) Carol and Ed
    (B) Carol and Rick
    (C) Jenny and Walt
    (D) Carol and Walt
    (E) Jenny and Ed

Excerpted from *LSAT Success 2002* © 1996 by Thomas O. White

<table><tr><td>**SECTION 2**</td><td>**TIME—35 MINUTES**</td><td>**24 QUESTIONS**</td></tr></table>

Evaluate the reasoning contained in the brief statements, and select the best answer. Do not make implausible, superfluous, or incompatible assumptions. Select the best answer to each question, and mark the corresponding space on the answer sheet.

1. All quiet people are harmless.

   No harmless people are easily identified.

   The premises above lead to which of the following conclusions?

   (A) Quiet people are not easily identified.
   (B) Most people who are easily identified are harmless.
   (C) No harmless people are quiet.
   (D) Some easily identified people are quiet.
   (E) All quiet people are easily identified.

2. I don't believe that ambitious people are good parents. Of course, there are some parents who have successful careers and well-raised children. But these parents are not really ambitious. Were they ambitious, they could not devote the necessary time and energy to raising their children well.

   Which of the following best explains the flawed reasoning in the author's argument?

   (A) It relies on a word with two different meanings.
   (B) It bases an absolute conclusion upon relative evidence.
   (C) It assumes the conclusion.
   (D) It generalizes from inappropriate specifics.
   (E) It depends on a false analogy.

3. Arthritis specialists understand that effective treatment must do more than relieve pain. So, the medicine arthritis specialists prescribe most has both an anti-pain and anti-inflammation ingredient. These same ingredients are found in Arthrelief. Use Arthrelief to combat arthritic pain.

   The advertisement above does NOT assume which of the following?

   (A) Arthritis specialists provide authoritative information on effective medication for arthritis.
   (B) Arthritis specialists use Arthrelief because it contains anti-inflammation medicine.
   (C) A medicine containing ingredients prescribed for arthritis will be effective.
   (D) Arthrelief only combats arthritic pain.
   (E) Arthritis specialists prescribe Arthrelief most.

4. Testing the reasoning abilities of illiterate people has proven to be particularly challenging to psychologists. When illiterate people are given tasks that are designed to require them to reason to a conclusion, they are relatively successful when the mechanical devices used in the test are familiar ones. But if the devices used in the test are unfamiliar to the illiterate person, they are relatively unsuccessful at performing analogous tasks.

   Which of the following conclusions can be reasonably drawn from the information above?

   (A) Reasoning abilities of illiterate people should not be tested using tasks that do not involve familiar devices.
   (B) Literacy is required in order to test the reasoning abilities of people through the use of mechanical devices.
   (C) Testing illiterate people for reasoning abilities is relatively unsuccessful.
   (D) Mechanical devices are a poor substitute for words in reasoning to a conclusion.
   (E) Unfamiliar tasks provide a better measure of reasoning ability than do familiar tasks.

Excerpted from *LSAT Success 2002* © 1996 by Thomas O. White

5. Japanese workers exercise each day in their workplaces. American employers do not require daily exercise, and, as a result, American workers are more overweight and much less fit and suffer more sickness and injuries than their Japanese counterparts. American workers will only become as productive as the Japanese if they are required to exercise on a daily basis.

Which of the following, if true, most weakens the above argument?

(A) Daily exercise does not reduce or prevent incidents of sickness.

(B) Daily exercise does not reduce the severity of on-the-job injuries.

(C) Daily exercise does not contribute greatly to Japanese worker fitness.

(D) Daily exercise does not contribute greatly to Japanese worker productivity.

(E) Daily exercise does not result in significant weight loss.

6. Dictatorships or centralized governments result from the political indifference of a country's people. If people were not politically indifferent, all governments would be democratic or decentralized.

Which of the following could NOT be inferred from the above argument?

(A) Democratic governments result from politically active people.

(B) Dictatorships only exist in countries whose people are politically indifferent.

(C) Politically active people are responsible for decentralized governments.

(D) A country with a democratic government must have politically active people.

(E) Centralized governments are the responsibility of the politically indifferent.

7. Question

I. By reducing its standard of living the United States can conserve energy.

II. Yet, the United States aspires to energy independence.

III. Studies confirm that the only certain path to energy independence is through conservation.

IV. More than 20 percent of the energy consumed by the United States is imported.

Which is the most logical arrangement of the above sentences?

(A) I, II, III, IV
(B) I, III, IV, II
(C) II, III, IV, I
(D) III, IV, I, II
(E) IV, II, III, I

8. Dr. Bartels concludes that governments waste the money they spend in support of higher education. His argument is based on longitudinal research that shows that fewer than 20 percent of persons with college degrees are working in the field of their training five years after receiving their degrees.

Dr. Bartels makes the assumption that

(A) higher education in a field is valuable training only for that field

(B) what is desirable at one time will continue into another

(C) higher education can be valued only in degrees awarded

(D) work areas are directly related to college-degree areas

(E) higher education should not be a governmental concern

Excerpted from *LSAT Success 2002* © 1996 by Thomas O. White

9. Ninety percent of the students taking as few as two Alert tablets daily got better grades in school. Improve your grades, get Alert today!

   Which of the following could be offered as a valid criticism of the advertisement above?

   (A) It does not state that Alert tablets cause grade improvement.
   (B) Using medication to get good grades is cheating.
   (C) Taking more Alert will result in greater grade improvement.
   (D) It suggests that only 10 percent of students do not use Alert daily.
   (E) Being alert in school does not always result in improved grades.

10. According to dog lovers, the principal virtue of the dog is its general friendliness toward all people. According to cat lovers, the principal virtue of the cat is its exclusive friendliness toward its provider.

    Which of the following is true of the claims of both dog and cat lovers?

    (A) Pet friendliness toward a provider is unworthy.
    (B) They come from sources that apply the same standard.
    (C) Animals cannot be judged by standards for human behavior.
    (D) Animal lovers are friendly.
    (E) Friendliness is a virtue.

11. In Canada, a family can stay overnight in a litter-free public campground on a clear lake for less than it costs to spend a day at a filthy public beach in the United States. Why must public beaches in the United States be so expensive and dirty?

Which of the following, if true, most weakens the above argument?

(A) Campgrounds in Canada are little used.
(B) Beaches in the United States are intensely used.
(C) There are more public campgrounds in Canada than there are public beaches in the United States.
(D) There are more public beaches in the United States than there are public campgrounds in Canada.
(E) Public beaches in Canada are no cleaner or cheaper than those in the United States.

12. Computers have been programmed to play poker. Because of the way they are programmed, computers reproduce human strategies, such as bluffing. Apparently, they make decisions for the same reasons as human players.

    The author of this note

    (A) uses scientific evidence to support the conclusion
    (B) proposes a common cause for similar effects
    (C) grounds the argument on the double meaning of the word "reason"
    (D) states a conclusion and then explains how it was reached
    (E) argues from an analogy to reconcile an apparent contradiction

13. The Department of Agriculture will stop inspecting milk processing plants because no citations have been issued in the past two years.

    If true, which of the following most strengthens the decision?

    (A) Processors will cut corners if the threat of inspection is removed.
    (B) Milk processing is very automated.
    (C) The source of milk is known, so compensation can be had for any problem that occurs.
    (D) The Department budget has been cut by 30 percent.
    (E) The industry association has standards that exceed the legal requirements.

Excerpted from *LSAT Success 2002* © 1996 by Thomas O. White

14. Rites of adulthood are more frequently found in societies where the differences between adults and children are not clear. The purpose of such rites is to formally impose adult responsibilities on participants.

The above argument would be most strengthened if it were found that

(A) children do not generally behave as adults prior to the rites

(B) children generally accept the rites without question

(C) adults generally approve of the rites

(D) formal rites are prevalent in such societies

(E) children do not generally accept adult responsibilities prior to the rites

15. Attempts to make public-transportation facilities accessible to physically challenged people are misguided. Only the most athletic of the physically challenged are able to get to the stops and stations where it is possible for them to take advantage of special devices installed on buses and trains.

Which of the following most strengthens the argument above?

(A) It is extremely expensive to install special devices on buses and trains to accommodate the physically challenged.

(B) More physically challenged people have access to motorized wheelchairs than ever before.

(C) Very few physically challenged people use facilities in the places where they have been installed.

(D) Special-access facilities to public buildings have increased their use by physically challenged people.

(E) Physically challenged people on buses and trains are at greater safety risk than others.

Questions 16–17

Every time a business grants financial credit to an individual, the business assumes the risk of the individual not being able to make all the agreed-upon payments. Credit bureaus assist businesses in their efforts to evaluate the risks involved with the extension of credit to individual purchasers. The financial history of individuals is maintained and reported on by credit bureaus. Credit bureaus assist debtors as well as creditors by preventing them from assuming greater debt resulting from the work of credit bureaus, which holds losses and prices down and, thus, benefits consumers generally. The few concerns for individual privacy that have been raised about credit bureaus hardly offset their financial value to business and consumer alike.

16. Which of the following is assumed by the above argument?

(A) Business would have no way to make credit decisions without credit bureaus.

(B) Risk of nonpayment is difficult for most businesses to assess.

(C) Purchasers attempt to secure more credit than they can afford.

(D) Credit bureaus seldom make errors in their reports about individuals' financial histories.

(E) Financial histories are complex and difficult to develop and maintain.

17. According to the above argument, harm that results from the use of credit bureaus by businesses is

(A) offset by the need for individual financial histories

(B) minimal, because so few errors are made in their reports

(C) acceptable, because business requires financial histories

(D) justified by the economic value to business and society

(E) essential to the effective extension of credit to individuals

Excerpted from *LSAT Success 2002* © 1996 by Thomas O. White

18. Harold is a better writer of short stories than Stan and a better novelist, too. Thus, Harold is indubitably a better playwright as well.

    Given the information in the passage, which of the following is a belief about Harold that can be most justifiably attributed to the speaker?

    (A) Harold is more versatile than Stan.
    (B) Harold is a better writer than Stan.
    (C) Harold is altogether more effective than Stan.
    (D) Harold is more cultivated than Stan.
    (E) Harold is more artistically talented than Stan.

19. The average salary of a college graduate is only 22 percent greater than that of a high school graduate. In 1969, the difference was 55 percent. In addition, college graduates' salaries have not kept up with inflation. For most, the rewards of a college education will not justify the cost of tuition and lost income while getting a degree.

    Which of the following, if true, most weakens the above argument?

    (A) Since 1969, the incomes of few groups have kept pace with inflation.
    (B) Since 1969, college education costs have outpaced inflation by nearly 100 percent.
    (C) Since 1969, more high school graduates have decided to seek a college degree.
    (D) Since 1969, the unemployment rate for college graduates is lower than that for high school graduates.
    (E) Since 1969, there has been a steady decline in the number of high school graduates in the job market.

20. Genetic engineering places the nature-versus-nurture argument in stark relief. Not only will physical qualities (nature) of individuals be altered by manufacturing processes, but intellectual, emotional, and spiritual qualities will be modified as well. Those who argue that the altering of human qualities violates the laws of nature ignore the reality that people are already the result of engineering in the form of their manufactured education, socialization, and environment (nurture).

    Which of the following, if true, supports the above argument?

    (A) Manufacturing techniques do not alter spiritual qualities of individuals.
    (B) By definition, the laws of nature cannot be altered.
    (C) Manufacturing of education and intellect are markedly different.
    (D) Engineering of genes and environment are virtually the same.
    (E) Qualities of individuals and societies are virtually the same.

Questions 21–22

There is an inherent fallacy in the reasoning of Shea, who suggests that all of his readers ought to attend the retrospective of Beatles music offered by the Springfield Pops because ''the Beatles have had as great an influence on the musical development of our day as Beethoven had on his.'' Stalin had great influence on the political development of his time, but no one suggests that people should rush to Moscow to pay homage at his tomb.

21. The point of the above argument is that

    (A) Shea confuses influence with merit
    (B) Shea confuses politics with music
    (C) Shea confuses the Beatles with Beethoven
    (D) Shea confuses honor with attendance
    (E) Shea confuses popularity with importance

22. Which of the following is analogous to Stalin's tomb in the argument above?

    (A) the Springfield Pops
    (B) musical influence
    (C) Beethoven
    (D) attendance at the Beatles retrospective
    (E) Shea's readers

Excerpted from *LSAT Success 2002* © 1996 by Thomas O. White

23. Ann has vacationed at three different Florida resorts and has enjoyed each of them very much. Thus, Ann is confident that she will enjoy vacationing at the newly opened resort in the Florida keys.

    Which of the following statements does NOT alter the probability that vacationing at the new Florida resort will be enjoyable?

    (A) All three resorts Ann previously visited are in north Miami Beach, and the new resort is in south Miami Beach.
    (B) The new resort was unfavorably reviewed in a national travel magazine.
    (C) The manager of the new resort was trained at the same hotel-management school as 2 of the 3 managers of the other three resorts.
    (D) The owner of the new resort has been in the resort business for thirty years.
    (E) The architect of the other three resorts did not design the new resort.

24. A recent survey has found that the number of high school students that attend a house of worship regularly has increased 60 percent in the past decade. This increase in religious exposure appears to have significantly reduced cheating on tests and improved class participation.

    Which of the following, if true, most weakens the inference made above?

    (A) Religious leaders frequently speak out for academic honesty.
    (B) Not all students responded to the survey.
    (C) Recently the high school changed from proctored exams to an honor system.
    (D) Social reasons account for the attendance of most students at services.
    (E) Cheating is not considered to be a major problem by most teachers.

Excerpted from *LSAT Success 2002* © 1996 by Thomas O. White

<table><tr><td>**SECTION 3**</td><td>**TIME—35 MINUTES**</td><td>**24 QUESTIONS**</td></tr></table>

The questions are based on a set of conditions. A diagram may be helpful in the answer selection process. Select the best answer to each question, and mark the corresponding space on the answer sheet.

Questions 1–6

Six building contractors—L, M, N, O, P, and Q—bid on the construction of a new school. Each submits one bid stating the total price for constructing the building. The school board must award the job to the lowest bidder.

P bids less than N but more than Q.
O bids less than P but more than M.
Q bids less than N but more than L.
No two bids are equal to each other.

1. Which of the following could be the ranking of the contractors' bids?

(A) M, Q, O, P, L, N
(B) M, L, O, Q, P, N
(C) L, Q, M, P, O, N
(D) Q, M, O, L, P, N
(E) L, M, Q, N, P, O

2. If O submits the third-highest bid, which of the following contractors could get the job?

(A) M only
(B) L only
(C) Q or M
(D) M or L
(E) Q or L

3. If O submits one of the lowest two bids, which of the following must be true?

(A) N submits the second-highest bid.
(B) L submits the third-lowest bid.
(C) P submits the third-highest bid.
(D) Q submits the fourth-highest bid.
(E) L submits the fourth-lowest bid.

4. If L submits the lowest bid, all of the following must be true EXCEPT

(A) M submits a lower bid than O
(B) Q submits a higher bid than M
(C) Q submits a lower bid than P
(D) P submits a higher bid than O
(E) M submits a lower bid than P

5. If M submits the second-lowest bid, which of the following can be a ranking of the contractors' bids?

(A) L, M, Q, O, P, N
(B) Q, M, L, O, P, N
(C) O, M, L, Q, P, N
(D) L, M, Q, P, O, N
(E) L, M, P, O, Q, N

6. Which of the following contractors could submit the lowest bid and the second-lowest bid, respectively?

(A) Q and N
(B) M and Q
(C) Q and L
(D) L and P
(E) Q and M

Questions 7–12

Ten students—L, M, N, O, P, Q, R, S, T, and U—graduated from Naquapaug High School in the years 1971–1975, two students per year.

M graduated the year before Q.
P and R graduated together before 1975.
Q and N did not graduate in the same year S and T graduated together.

7. All of the following are possible orders of graduation, starting with the 1971 pair of graduates EXCEPT

(A) S, T; P, R; M, O; Q, N; L, U
(B) S, T; P, R; M, N; Q, O; L, U
(C) O, U; M, N; Q, L; P, R; S, T
(D) P, R; M, U; Q, L; N, O; S, T
(E) L, U; M, N; Q, O; P, R; S, T

8. Which of the following could be in the pairs that graduated in 1971, 1973, and 1975, respectively?

   (A) O, U, N
   (B) O, L, U
   (C) L, N, S
   (D) S, N, P
   (E) L, O, U

9. If Q, T, and U graduated in 1972, 1973, and 1975, respectively, and O and M graduated together, which of the following must be true?

   (A) L graduated in 1972.
   (B) N graduated in 1974.
   (C) P graduated two years before N.
   (D) R graduated before 1974.
   (E) S graduated the year before O.

10. If O and U graduated together, and Q graduated in 1974, which of the following must be true?

    (A) N graduated in 1974.
    (B) N graduated in 1972.
    (C) L graduated in 1974.
    (D) R graduated in 1972.
    (E) T graduated in 1971.

11. If P graduated in 1973, and L and O graduated together, which of the following are the only years in which N could be one of the pair of graduates?

    (A) 1971 and 1972
    (B) 1971 and 1974
    (C) 1971 and 1975
    (D) 1972 and 1974
    (E) 1972 and 1975

12. If L, O, and U each graduated in an even-numbered year, which of the following must be true?

    (A) P graduated in 1971.
    (B) O graduated in 1972.
    (C) Q graduated in 1972.
    (D) N graduated in 1973.
    (E) S graduated in 1975.

Questions 13–18

On any day their schedules permit, Adam, Beth, Cary, Dana, and Edith each set up a sales table at a flea market.

   Edith will set up only when Cary does not.
   Dana will set up only when Adam does not.
   Cary will set up only when Dana does.
   Beth will set up only when Edith does.
   Adam will always set up.

13. Who will set up on a day when the schedules of only Adam, Beth, and Cary permit them to sell?

    (A) Adam only
    (B) Beth only
    (C) Cary only
    (D) Adam and Beth only
    (E) Beth and Cary only

14. How many will set up on a day when the schedules of only Adam, Beth, and Cary permit them to sell?

    (A) one
    (B) two
    (C) three
    (D) four
    (E) five

15. Which of the following groups of people could set up on the same day?

    (A) Adam, Beth, and Cary
    (B) Adam, Cary, and Dana
    (C) Cary, Dana, and Edith
    (D) Beth, Dana, and Edith
    (E) Beth, Cary, and Edith

16. If a buyer wanted to be certain that both Beth and Cary were set up on the same day, which of the following must be set up also?

    (A) Dana and Edith
    (B) Adam
    (C) Edith
    (D) Adam and Dana
    (E) Adam and Edith

17. Which of the following could set up on a day when the schedules of only Beth, Cary, and Edith permit them to sell?

    (A) Beth only
    (B) Cary only
    (C) Edith only
    (D) Cary and Edith only
    (E) Beth and Edith only

Excerpted from *LSAT Success 2002* © 1996 by Thomas O. White

18. How many will set up on a day when the schedules of only Beth, Cary, and Dana permit them to sell?

   (A) Zero
   (B) One
   (C) Two
   (D) Three
   (E) Four

Questions 19–24

A, B, and C are dentists and S, T, U, and V are hygienists assigned to work for them.

> A and B each have exactly two hygienists assigned to them.
> C sometimes is assigned one hygienist and sometimes two.
> T is assigned to A and one other dentist.
> Each hygienist is assigned to at least one dentist.

19. If S and T are assigned to the same two dentists, V must work for

   (A) both A and B
   (B) both A and C
   (C) either A or B
   (D) either A or C
   (E) either B or C

20. If V is assigned to both B and C, which of the following must be true?

   (A) U is assigned to B.
   (B) S is assigned to A.
   (C) T and U are assigned to the same dentist.
   (D) S and T are assigned to the same dentist.
   (E) U is assigned to only one dentist.

21. If T and V both are assigned to the same two dentists, S must work for

   (A) both A and B
   (B) both A and C
   (C) either A or B
   (D) either A or C
   (E) either B or C

22. If U is assigned to B and C, and V is assigned to B, S must work for

   (A) A only
   (B) B only
   (C) C only
   (D) both A and B
   (E) both A and C

23. Whenever S is assigned to only one dentist and C is assigned only one hygienist, which of the following must be true?

   (A) S is assigned to C.
   (B) V is assigned to two dentists.
   (C) U is assigned to only one dentist.
   (D) T is assigned to C.
   (E) U is assigned to A.

24. If S is assigned to both B and C, which of the following must be true?

   (A) T and V are assigned to the same dentist.
   (B) V is assigned to A.
   (C) U and V are assigned to the same dentist.
   (D) U is assigned to B.
   (E) U is assigned to only one dentist.

Excerpted from *LSAT Success 2002* © 1996 by Thomas O. White

| SECTION **4** | TIME—35 MINUTES | **28 QUESTIONS** |

The questions are based on what is stated or implied in the passage. Select the best answer to each question, and mark the corresponding space on the answer sheet.

Line Without a doubt, the role of firearms in American violence is much greater today than a decade ago. Rates of gun violence and the proportion of violent acts that are
5   committed by guns have increased substantially, even after the Gun Control Act went into effect. Behind these increases lies the probability that handgun ownership has become at least a subcultural institution in
10   the big cities that are the main arena of American violence. During this period, regional differences in gun ownership and use have been moderated as the large Northeastern cities that were traditionally
15   areas of low ownership and use have experienced large increases in handgun use.

The special role of the handgun in urban violence is one of the more obvious
20   lessons of the data that are reported. Over the past ten years, rates of handgun homicide have increased more than three times as much as homicides by all other means. The data reported suggest, but do
25   not compel, other conclusions about patterns of handgun ownership and violence in the United States. First, the sharp rise in the proportion of violence attributable to handguns in Northeastern
30   cities may lead to modification of the hypothesis that general patterns of handgun ownership determine the extent to which handguns are used in violent episodes. While it is still true that those regions with
35   the highest general levels of gun ownership have the highest proportion of gun use in violence, the past decade has produced an increase in handgun use in the Northeast that leaves cities in that region closer to but
40   still below the average handgun share of violence. This could be due to a substantial rise in handgun ownership in the general population in these cities, but that would

45   mean that a vast Northeastern urban handgun arsenal has been accumulating during the past ten years. It is more likely that handgun ownership increased substantially among subcultural groups disproportionately associated with violence without
50   necessarily affecting other parts of the population.

If one adopts a "subcultural" explanation of the relationship between gun ownership and violence, hypotheses about
55   the effect of increases or decreases in handgun ownership on handgun violence should take a slightly more complicated form. One would predict that high levels of handgun ownership produce high levels of
60   handgun violence for two reasons: More handguns are available at a moment of perceived need, and high ownership rates necessarily suggest high levels of handgun availability to all potential consumers. Low
65   general levels of handgun ownership, on the other hand, become the necessary but not sufficient condition of low levels of handgun violence. If the lower-than-average general ownership levels are still high
70   enough to create relatively easy handgun availability and if both handgun ownership and propensity for violence are concentrated in discrete subpopulations, lower-than-average general ownership is an
75   inadequate insurance policy against increases in handgun violence. It is only when ownership levels are low enough to have an impact on handgun availability that low aggregate ownership will depress
80   handgun involvement in rates of subcultural violence. Efforts to limit handgun supply on a national basis by limiting legitimate production, or imports, or both will not require a large federal street police force.
85   At the point when market controls make illicit gun production profitable, some police work will obviously be needed, along the lines of controls on illicit liquor production.

Excerpted from *LSAT Success 2002* © 1996 by Thomas O. White

1. The primary purpose of the passage is to

    (A) criticize the Gun Control Act
    (B) describe the role of the handgun in urban violence
    (C) advocate limiting handgun availability
    (D) explain the growth of handgun violence
    (E) point out the increase in the urban handgun arsenal

2. If true, the "subcultural" explanation of gun ownership and violence means that

    (A) all parts of the population own more guns
    (B) general patterns of gun ownership determine their use in violent episodes
    (C) higher levels of gun ownership produce higher levels of violence
    (D) gun ownership by people associated with violence has greatly increased
    (E) guns are now primarily owned by the violent elements of urban society

3. The author refers to the Gun Control Act to

    (A) dramatize the increase in gun-related violence
    (B) criticize the government for gun-related violence
    (C) point out the statute's total ineffectiveness
    (D) minimize the importance of gun-control legislation
    (E) argue for more enforcement of the statute

4. Which of the following, if true, would most weaken the author's argument concerning handgun ownership in Northeastern cities?

    (A) Handgun ownership among Boston drug dealers has increased 300 percent in the past ten years.
    (B) Handgun ownership among organized crime figures in New Jersey has increased dramatically in the past ten years.
    (C) Handgun ownership among convicted criminals has increased in the past ten years.
    (D) Handgun ownership among middle-class New Yorkers has increased fourfold in the last ten years.
    (E) Handgun ownership among middle-class Philadelphians has increased slightly in the past ten years.

5. Which of the following may be inferred from the passage?

    (A) The rate of growth in gun ownership in the Northeast is greater than that of other regions.
    (B) Gun ownership in the Northeast is greater than that of other regions.
    (C) There is little data available concerning the growth of gun ownership in urban areas.
    (D) High levels of handgun ownership do not necessarily result in increased violence.
    (E) High levels of handgun ownership in urban areas do not necessarily result in increased violence.

6. The passage suggests which of the following?

    (A) High levels of handgun ownership are not related to perceived needs among consumers.
    (B) More violent acts are committed by means other than handguns.
    (C) Urban violence is due to subcultural differences among residents.
    (D) The number of homicides not involving handguns has increased in the past ten years.
    (E) Lower-than-average handgun ownership will result in lower violence.

7. The author would likely disagree that which of the following would reduce handgun violence?

    (A) regulation of handgun imports
    (B) reduction of handgun ownership in certain subcultural groups
    (C) regulation of handgun possession
    (D) reduction of handgun ownership levels
    (E) regulation of handgun production

Excerpted from *LSAT Success 2002* © 1996 by Thomas O. White

Line Software is like hardware in that it causes machines to perform tasks. Software is merely a replacement for hardware components that could otherwise perform
5 the same function. Software is often embedded in hardware and part of an overall hardware system. Like hardware, software can often serve as a tool for creating other items. Like hardware,
10 software needs maintenance work from time to time to operate properly.

Software is unlike hardware, however, in a great many ways. Software is, for example, easy and cheap to replicate as
15 compared with hardware. Once the first copy has been produced, software can be almost endlessly replicated at almost no cost, regardless of how complex it is. One of the consequences of this characteristic is
20 that the government tends to think that additional copies of software ought to be deliverable at a very low cost, whereas industry, which is concerned about recouping its research and development
25 costs and which tends to regard the sale of software as the sale of a production facility (as if one bought a General Motors factory when one bought a truck produced by GM), thinks that sales at higher price levels
30 are necessary to make the software business viable. A second consequence of low-cost replicability is that the software industry, for the most part, tends to make its products available only on a highly
35 restrictive licensing basis, rather than selling copies outright.

Another important difference between software and hardware is that software may be wholly subject to a very lengthy lawful
40 monopoly (i.e., a copyright) as well as being held as a trade secret, whereas hardware may be subject to a much shorter monopoly (i.e., a patent) and most often cannot be held as a trade secret. Moreover,
45 quite often hardware is either not patented at all or only subject to partial patent protection. A high standard of inventiveness is required for patent, while copyright requires only the most minimal originality.
50 Hardware, unlike software, cannot be copyrighted at all. As a result, it tends to be much harder to get competition for software procurements and maintenance than for hardware, which means that it is

55 even easier for the government to find itself in a sole-source position as to software than as to hardware. Moreover, because software engineering is still in the early stages of development, it is generally more difficult
60 to specify how software, as opposed to hardware, should be developed for particular functions and to estimate the cost and development schedule for it.

Software, which consists of a stream
65 of electrical impulses, is also virtually "invisible" as compared with hardware, which means that it is more difficult to detect if someone delivers very similar or nearly identical software on a second
70 development contract. Again, because software engineering is a developing art, software is likely to contain many undetected defects that will need to be corrected while in the user's possession.

75 Unlike hardware, software is readily changeable; that is, new capabilities can be added to software without additional plant or material costs. Often, all that is required is some intellectual labor. All of these
80 factors tend to make software maintenance and enhancement a much bigger part of computer system life-cycle planning than is the case with hardware.

8. The passage is primarily concerned with

(A) correcting misimpressions about hardware and software
(B) explaining the nature of software
(C) minimizing apparent difficulties with software
(D) comparing hardware and software
(E) describing computer system life-cycle planning

9. According to the passage, which of the following is true?

(A) Hardware and software cannot perform the same functions.
(B) Software can make hardware cheaper.
(C) Software can be located within hardware.
(D) Software cannot be copyrighted.
(E) Hardware is readily changeable.

10. According to the passage all of the following is true EXCEPT

    (A) the cost of duplicating software is low
    (B) very little software is sold outright
    (C) hardware is often not patented
    (D) software requires minimal originality
    (E) hardware is readily changeable

11. According to the passage, which of the following characteristics does NOT apply to both hardware and software?

    (A) It can be held as a trade secret.
    (B) It can be copyrighted.
    (C) It can create other items.
    (D) It can be subject to a monopoly.
    (E) It can be maintained.

12. Which of the following can be inferred from the passage?

    (A) Hardware is more expensive than software.
    (B) It is more profitable to sell copies of software than hardware.
    (C) Software maintenance is a relatively competitive business.
    (D) Procurement of hardware is not a competitive business.
    (E) Software is licensed because it is too expensive to buy.

13. Which of the following can be inferred from the passage?

    (A) Ownership rights in software can be better protected than those in hardware.
    (B) Copyrighted software requires greater inventiveness than does hardware.
    (C) Ownership rights in hardware can be better protected than those in software.
    (D) Patented hardware requires greater inventiveness than does software.
    (E) Patented hardware is difficult to specify for particular functions.

14. The argument that one purchased the factory when one purchased a truck made at the factory (lines 27–29) is most like which of the following?

    (A) One purchased the typewriter when one purchased the book that prepared the manuscript.
    (B) One purchased the cruise when one purchased the cruise ship.
    (C) One purchased the restaurant when one purchased the dinner prepared there.
    (D) One purchased the office building when one leased an office located in the building.
    (E) One purchased the health club when one purchased a membership to use the club facilities.

Excerpted from *LSAT Success 2002* © 1996 by Thomas O. White

Line We customarily identify the concept of
status with its conventional indices, such as
wealth, title, and occupation. But there is
nothing sacred about these indices; they are
5 merely the most convenient and concrete
manifestations in everyday life of different
social positions. If every member of society
routinely tested his strength in court several
times each year instead of once or twice a
10 lifetime, we would immediately recognize
court performance as a direct measure of
social position, perhaps even more reveal-
ing of the pecking order than conventional
indices, such as power.

15   Of course, in no society, not even a
litigious one like premodern New Haven,
does the court play so vital a role as this in
the life of the community. Nevertheless, if
other societies show the same positive
20 correlation between status and court
performance found in New Haven, we will
be compelled to admit that individual court
appearances—infrequent though they
are—are revelatory of group status when
25 treated collectively. Of course, one cannot
assume on the basis of this one study of a
single society that court performance is
always and everywhere a reliable index of
status. Only a considerable accumulation of
30 confirmatory studies of other communities
and courts could justify the use of the
voluntary appearance ratio as an independent measure of status. But if, as in the case
of New Haven, it can be shown for a given
35 community that court performance is
strongly correlated with the more conventional indices of status over a long period of
time, then it seems reasonable to treat
court performance itself as an index of
40 status in that community. Doing so may be
extremely advantageous because, unlike
most indices of status, court performance
can be reconstructed on a year-to-year
basis.

45   If court performance can be shown to
reflect the static distribution of power and
advantage in the community—as has been
done for New Haven—then by tracing
court performance through time, on a
50 year-to-year basis, it should be possible to
reveal shifts of power and advantage as
they take place. Court records exploited in
this manner might serve as a weather vane
of social change. The gentry controversy in

55 English history stands as the classic
illustration of the difficulty of reconstructing an account through time of the relative
position of two classes, using only economic and demographic data. Of all the
60 kinds of data relating to group status, none
is more likely to be recorded and be
preserved in as complete a form as court
records. A continuous year-by-year account
of group status would be virtually impos-
65 sible to reconstruct from surviving economic data, but such an account may be
feasible for societies with complete court
records. Such a methodological tool should
be useful to any historian who wants to test
70 hypotheses postulating the rise or fall of a
class or other large group.

15. The author views court records primarily as

   (A) surviving other available records about
       society

   (B) a source of more reliable data about
       society

   (C) reflecting distribution of power in
       society

   (D) a means of tracing changes in group
       status in society

   (E) reporting on tests of strength within a
       society

16. The term ''positive correlation'' in lines
19–20 refers to which of the following?

   (A) the relationship between individual
       and group status

   (B) the relationship between group status
       and frequency of court appearance

   (C) the relationship between individual
       court appearance and social position

   (D) the relationship between the pecking
       order and group status in the commu-
       nity

   (E) the relationship between power shifts
       and frequency of court appearance

17. The passage suggests that which of the
following is an indication of individual
social status?

   (A) wealth
   (B) occupation
   (C) title
   (D) court performance
   (E) power

Excerpted from *LSAT Success 2002* © 1996 by Thomas O. White

18. Which of the following, if true, would most weaken the author's thesis?

(A) There is an inverse relationship between wealth and court appearances.

(B) There is a negative relationship between age and court appearances.

(C) There is a random relationship between occupation and court appearances.

(D) There is a positive relationship between title and court appearances.

(E) There is a direct relationship between land ownership and court appearances.

19. If true, which of the following would best support the author's thesis?

(A) There is little correlation between the New Haven findings and those of other towns.

(B) There is a positive correlation between the New Haven findings and those of other towns.

(C) There is a positive correlation between wealth and court appearances in New Haven and those of other towns.

(D) There is little correlation between occupations and court appearances in New Haven and those of other towns.

(E) There is a direct relationship between land ownership in New Haven and ten surrounding towns.

20. Which of the following is most likely the author of the passage?

(A) a sociologist
(B) a genealogist
(C) a heraldrist
(D) an anthropologist
(E) a legal historian

21. The passage suggests that all of the following would be advantages of using court records and performance as a means of social status determination EXCEPT

(A) court records can be reconstructed over long periods of time

(B) court appearances change with status within the society

(C) court records are generally preserved in most jurisdictions

(D) court appearances can be treated collectively to reflect status

(E) court procedures remain the same over long periods of time

Excerpted from *LSAT Success 2002* © 1996 by Thomas O. White

Line Much advertising is patently uninformative:
Rational consumers should not care what
sort of breakfast cereal is eaten by famous
baseball players. Nonetheless, advertisers
5 spend large sums of money on these sorts
of messages as well as many others of equal
value as information. Rational consumers
should not be influenced by such messages,
and rational advertisers should not spend
10 money on messages without influence.

There are two types of goods: search
goods and experience goods. A search good
is one whose salient characteristics can be
ascertained by presale inspection (e.g., the
15 comfort of a pair of shoes); experience
goods are those that must be consumed to
be evaluated (e.g., the taste of a candy bar).
The role of advertising differs depending on
which type of good is involved. In the case
20 of search goods, where the consumer can
and will easily determine for himself
whether the goods are what he wants,
advertisers have little incentive to misrepre-
sent the quality of their goods. Thus,
25 advertisers simply urge the consumer to
make the inspection, and their message
should be largely informative and truthful.
In the case of the experience good, the
consumer can determine quality only by
30 purchasing and using the good. The
function of advertising, therefore, is to get
the consumer to try the product. Here,
advertisers might have an incentive to
mislead and make false claims.
35 With respect to advertising, then, the
characteristics of goods and services form a
continuum, from those in which it is very
easy to detect the truth or falsity of
advertising claims (search goods: The truth
40 of the claim can be ascertained before
purchase) through experience goods
(where the truth of the claim can be
detected only after purchase and use)
through credence goods (where the validity
45 of advertisements may never be determined).

As we move along this continuum
from search to credence characteristics,
misrepresentation becomes relatively more
50 profitable, since detection by consumers
becomes more expensive. Nonetheless, it is
in the case of credence characteristics that
self-protection becomes most difficult and

in which some legal remedy would seem
55 most important.

For any one purchase where credence
qualities are involved, the consumer cannot
be sure that he is getting a desirable good;
i.e., there is a low probability of his finding
60 out whether claims about any one good are
true or false. However, if the consumer
buys many goods from the same source,
the probability of ascertaining that claims
about one of those goods are false would
65 be increased. In this situation, claims about
individual goods have credence characteristics; but the reputation of the seller of all of
the goods is an experience characteristic. It
may be that consumer trust in the reputa-
70 tion of the intermediary is misplaced in the
situation of mail-order advertisements
carried by magazines. Although the
consumer may rely on the publisher of the
magazine to police their advertisers,
75 Consumers Union claims that in fact such
policing is minimal or nonexistent.

22. Which of the following best states the
primary objective of the passage?

(A) to point out that advertising reliability
varies by type of good
(B) to contrast advertising purposes for
three types of goods
(C) to differentiate between advertising for
two types of goods
(D) to discuss the role of advertising as
information
(E) to question the trustworthiness of
magazine mail-order advertising

23. According to the passage, the consumer can
determine the quality of experience goods
by which of the following?

(A) advertising
(B) inspection
(C) consumption
(D) policing
(E) reputation

Excerpted from *LSAT Success 2002* © 1996 by Thomas O. White

24. According to the passage, each of the
following is true EXCEPT which statement?

(A) Search-goods advertising is likely to be
informative and truthful.
(B) Mail-order advertising in magazines is
not likely to be truthful.
(C) Experience-goods advertisers have
incentive to mislead.
(D) Credence-goods advertisements may
never be determined to be valid.
(E) Advertisers spend large sums of money
on informative messages.

25. Which of the following articles is the most
likely source of the passage?

(A) "The Economics of Advertising"
(B) "The Law of False Advertising"
(C) "Advertising by Type of Good"
(D) "Analysis of the Function of Advertis-
ing"
(E) "Advertising and the Quality of
Goods"

26. It can be inferred from the passage that
which of the following are credence goods?

(A) auto transmission oil
(B) vitamin pills
(C) plant fertilizer
(D) eyeglasses
(E) air conditioner

27. Which of the following best describes the
author's attitude toward advertising?

(A) Many advertisers and consumers do
not act rationally.
(B) Many advertisers spend too much
money on ads.
(C) Many consumers are influenced by
advertising.
(D) Many advertisers are not interested in
informing consumers.
(E) Many consumers use advertising to
determine the quality of goods.

28. The author implies which of the following
in the passage?

(A) Search-goods consumers are easily
misled by advertising.
(B) Experience-goods consumers purchase
by mail order.
(C) Credence-goods consumers require
statutory protection.
(D) Experience-goods consumers ascertain
value by inspection.
(E) Credence-goods consumers depend on
seller credibility.

Excerpted from *LSAT Success 2002* © 1996 by Thomas O. White

<table>
<tr><td>SECTION 5</td><td>TIME—35 MINUTES</td><td>24 QUESTIONS</td></tr>
</table>

Evaluate the reasoning contained in the brief statements, and select the best answer. Do not make implausible, superfluous, or incompatible assumptions. Select the best answer to each question, and mark the corresponding space on the answer sheet.

1. Hitler was born in 1889 and became chancellor of Germany in 1933. On December 7, 1941, he was 52 years old and had been in power for 8 years. Hirohito was born in 1901 and became emperor of Japan in 1926. On December 7, 1941, he was 40 years old and had been in power for 15 years. The four underlined figures for each man total 3,882.

   Which of the following most accurately describes the total 3,882?

   (A) It is significant, but its meaning is not clear.
   (B) It is insignificant and coincidental.
   (C) Important leaders share significant events and figures.
   (D) It is politically significant only.
   (E) There is more significance in figures than is usually acknowledged.

2. It is acceptable to support one corrupt faction in a war against another in Nicaragua. And it is acceptable to send troops to Grenada to oust a Communist leader. But it is unacceptable to use force to get food to thousands of isolated and starving people in Sudan because it would interfere with that nation's internal affairs.

   The author makes a point by

   (A) identifying incongruities in the use of force
   (B) analyzing evidence of the use of force
   (C) attacking proprieties in the use of force
   (D) complaining about irrationality in the use of force
   (E) arguing for a more pervasive use of force

3. "Return my pocket watch!"

   "How did you get it?"

   "My father gave it to me."

   "How did your father get it?"

   "His father gave it to him."

   "How did your grandfather get it?"

   "He won it in a poker game."

   "Good, we will play poker for it."

   Which of the following is best inferred from the statement, "Good, we will play poker for it"?

   (A) Gambling achieves objectives effectively.
   (B) Past practice validates future action.
   (C) Meaningful customs transcend generations.
   (D) Possession is a privilege not a right.
   (E) Wanting another's possessions is instinctive.

4. Kaminski's disparaging reviews of the book call her abilities as a critic into question since the book became an immediate best-seller.

   Which of the following, if true, would most weaken the author's questioning of Kaminski's critical ability?

   (A) Immediate success of books is quickly forgotten.
   (B) Book critics often disagree with each other.
   (C) Sales of a book are not always indicative of its value.
   (D) The significance of a book is not known for years.
   (E) Critics often change their views about books.

Excerpted from *LSAT Success 2002* © 1996 by Thomas O. White

Questions 5–6

If a writer is truly emotional, his writing will comprise his deepest feelings about the world; and one would expect such feelings to appear in his work, if not dominate it. Many societies and people are very emotional, and their writing has as its principal function the expression and integration of deep feeling. This suggests that writing must be either emotional or trivial, that only emotional people can be great writers, and that writing cannot flourish in a technical society.

5. The writing of emotional people demonstrates

   (A) feelings are not integrated in other ways
   (B) only emotional writing can be great
   (C) the expression of deep feeling
   (D) writing cannot flourish in a technical society
   (E) one type of writing is better than another

6. On which of the following assumptions is the author's position based?

   (A) Great writers must be emotional.
   (B) Societies must be emotional or technical.
   (C) Feelings dominate an emotional writer's work.
   (D) Writing is emotional or trivial.
   (E) A writer's purpose is to express emotion.

Questions 7–8

It is almost as safe to assume that an artist of any dignity is against his country, i.e., against the environment in which God hath placed him, as it is to assume that his country is against the artist. He differs from the rest of us mainly because he reacts sharply and in an uncommon manner to phenomena that leave the rest of us unmoved, or, at most, merely annoy us vaguely. Therefore, he takes to artistic endeavor, which is at once a criticism of life and an attempt to escape from life.

   The more the facts are studied, the more they bear out these generalizations. In those fields of art, at all events, which concern themselves with ideas as well as with sensations, it is almost impossible to find any trace of an artist who was not actively hostile to his environ-

ment and, thus, an indifferent patriot. From Dante to Tolstoy and from Shakespeare to Mark Twain, the story is ever the same. Names suggest themselves instantly: Goethe, Shelley, Byron, Balzac, Cervantes, Swift, Dostoevsky, Carlyle, Moliere, and Pope were each a bitter critic of his time and nation.

7. Which of the following, if true, would most strongly refute the author's argument?

   (A) Artists are generally honored by their countries.
   (B) Artists best recognize life's difficulties.
   (C) Artists usually escape from their countries.
   (D) Artists generally venerate their countries.
   (E) Artists are best known in their own countries.

8. The author's argument most depends upon which of the following assumptions?

   (A) Most people are annoyed by phenomena that make an artist hostile.
   (B) Art defines in the abstract events and sensations that are uncommon.
   (C) The purpose of art is to both find fault with and escape from life.
   (D) In order to be an artist of dignity, a person must be an indifferent patriot.
   (E) Life is actively hostile to the artistic endeavors of most artists.

9. In a recent survey, the majority of respondents answered "no" to the question, "Should free hypodermic needles be provided by the government to drug addicts on welfare?"

   The survey results can be best criticized because the question structure

   (A) presented more than one issue to respondents
   (B) presented a choice that suggested a negative reply
   (C) presented respondents an impossible value judgment
   (D) presented an issue to largely unaffected respondents
   (E) presented a controversial issue out of context

10. When it rains, the crops grow; but it hasn't rained recently, so the crops must not be growing.

Which of the following arguments is logically most similar to the one above?

(A) When people are old, they complain about their health; but our town has no health problems, so it must have no old people.

(B) When a town has health problems, so it must also have many old people.

(C) When people are old, they complain about their health; but one can complain about one's health and yet not be old.

(D) When people complain about their health, they get old; but no one is complaining about their health, so we must have no people getting old.

(E) When a town has people complaining about their health, it must also have old people; our town has many people complaining about their health, so it must have many old people.

Questions 11–12

The proposal to divert one third of the flow of the Delaware River to supply New York City with water ought to be a matter of great concern to the people who live in the Delaware Valley. The interests of the people of the Delaware Valley are being put aside so that growth can continue in an already overdeveloped area. Fresh water is a natural resource in the same sense that oil and coal are natural resources. Do Texas and Alaska give away their oil? Does West Virginia give away its coal? Why should Pennsylvania and New Jersey supply New York or any other place with fresh water? If the growth of New York is capped by limited fresh water, so much the better.

11. The author assumes which of the following to be fact rather than opinion?

(A) Diverting the Delaware River is a matter of great concern to people in the Delaware Valley.

(B) Oil, coal, and fresh water are natural resources.

(C) The purpose of diverting the Delaware River is to allow New York City to continue to grow.

(D) The interests of New York and the Delaware Valley conflict.

(E) The Delaware River supplies New York with water.

12. Which of the following, if true, would most weaken the author's argument?

(A) New York City is permanently committed to zero growth.

(B) The diversion will not reduce water availability to people in the Delaware Valley.

(C) New York City will pay Pennsylvania and New Jersey for each gallon of water diverted.

(D) The diversion will reduce the risk of flooding in the Delaware Valley.

(E) New York City will get water from Vermont if the Delaware River is not diverted.

13. If the present moment contains no living and creative choice and is totally and mechanically the product of the matter and moment of the moment before, so, then, was that moment the mechanical effect of the moment that preceded it and so on until we arrive at a single cause of every later event, of every act and suffering of man.

Which of the following would NOT be supported by the above argument?

(A) a theory postulating a mechanistic origin of the universe

(B) a theory postulating suffering as a requisite for creativity

(C) a theory postulating a deterministic explanation of history

(D) a theory postulating that there are no choices in the present moment

(E) a theory postulating a single cause of all events

Excerpted from *LSAT Success 2002* © 1996 by Thomas O. White

14. Baxter defends paternal authority and the preservation of the family in her most recent work. But other aspects of her thinking more convincingly demonstrate that she cannot be considered a feminist. For example, she fails to appreciate that the full realization of a woman's capacities depends on her securing the same political, economic, and civil rights as those afforded me.

Which of the following inferences is NOT supported by the above argument?

(A) Paternal authority is not generally supported by feminists.
(B) The family is not generally supported by feminists.
(C) Baxter feels that women do not need rights equal to men's.
(D) Women's capacities have not been fully realized.
(E) Baxter feels that women and men have unequal capacities.

15. Many children in urban schools are forced to learn in dilapidated classrooms with few modern teaching aids. Compared to children in suburban schools with their computers, labs, and the latest advances in educational resources, the urban student is truly deprived.

The point of the author's argument is best stated by which of the following?

(A) Modern educational aids should be provided for urban children.
(B) Urban and suburban children should be educated in the same schools.
(C) Urban schoolchildren should not be required to compete with suburban schoolchildren.
(D) Unequal resources for urban and suburban children should be investigated.
(E) Suburban school resources should be combined with those of urban schools if an ideal education is to be achieved.

16. A philosopher makes arguments that frequently are not logical in order to demonstrate that rationality is not as valuable as irrationality to us humans. Consequently, the philosopher should not be expected to use the same arguments as those whose positions are rationally based.

The argument above is most similar to which of the following?

(A) A philosopher's arguments focus on the flaws in logical reasoning of those who oppose her.
(B) A writer often uses great restraint when describing mayhem.
(C) A female author was not taken seriously, so she used a male pseudonym when establishing her reputation.
(D) A novel is judged to be boring because it describes a boring situation.
(E) A philosopher's reasoning is complicated because he was trained in a tradition that often uses complicated reasoning.

Question 17–18

United States treaty negotiations with Japan about trade involve the basic question, "Can the Japanese be trusted?" But treaties are based on self-interest rather than on trust. There would be no need to have treaties if countries trusted one another. A treaty is an alternative to trust; one that formally recognizes that each country finds an advantage in the agreement.

17. Which of the following is an argument made above?

(A) If the Japanese can be trusted, the United States should negotiate treaties with Japan.
(B) If the Japanese cannot be trusted, the United States should not negotiate treaties with Japan.
(C) If Japan and the United States have common trade interests, a treaty between the countries should be negotiated.
(D) If Japan and the United States sign a treaty, interests of each will be served by the agreement.
(E) If Japanese and United States interests are different, a treaty dealing with those interests will not be signed.

Excerpted from *LSAT Success 2002* © 1996 by Thomas O. White

18. Which of the following is NOT supported by the author's argument above?

   (A) Treaties are made only between countries that trust one another.

   (B) Treaties further the self-interest of countries.

   (C) Treaties formally recognize an advantage one country has over another.

   (D) Treaties do not serve mutual interests of countries.

   (E) Treaties serve as reasonable alternatives to trust.

19. Tests done on the employees of a chemical plant showed that 28 percent had abnormal chromosome patterns. Chemical fumes, radiation, and airborne particulates are among the causes of abnormal chromosome patterns.

Which of the following would most support the conclusion that chemical fumes were responsible for employees' abnormal chromosome patterns?

   (A) Abnormal chromosome patterns can be altered.

   (B) Nonemployees in the area also develop abnormal chromosome patterns.

   (C) Employees of other chemical plants do not develop abnormal chromosome patterns.

   (D) Abnormal chromosome patterns are not necessarily harmful.

   (E) Employees of most chemical plants develop abnormal chromosome patterns.

20. "None of the legislators we polled are in favor of this bill?"

"That cannot be true. There are six legislators who introduced the bill and support it."

Which of the following can be inferred from the above exchange?

   (A) Legislators who do not favor the bill may support it.

   (B) The only legislators who favor the bill are those who introduced it.

   (C) Only legislators who do not favor the bill were polled.

   (D) Some legislators refused to participate in the poll.

   (E) Legislators might indicate that they favor a bill when they do not.

21. The Audubon Society Falcon Watch reports that there were 2,487 more falcon sightings in 1988 than there were in 1987. This proves that an increase in the falcon population has finally been realized.

Which of the following, if true, most weakens the above argument?

   (A) Falcons regularly move from area to area in search of food.

   (B) Falcons have been introduced into urban environments.

   (C) Development in falcon nesting areas is being restricted.

   (D) The Society intensified its falcon sighting program in 1988.

   (E) The Society database about falcons improved in 1988.

22. The following notice was received by Mary Castle, a scientist.

"We regret that your article cannot be accepted. Page limitations in the *Journal* force the editor to return many worthy and well-written articles."

All of the following may be inferred from the above, EXCEPT

   (A) only well-written articles were accepted for publication

   (B) Castle's article was considered to be well-written

   (C) Castle's article was found to be too long for the *Journal*

   (D) Castle's article was considered to be worthy of publication

   (E) writing was not the only factor in deciding which articles to publish

Questions 23–24

The drug Thalidomide caused unforeseen birth defects in thousands of babies; therefore, thorough testing of the effects of all new drugs should be required before release to the public.

23. Which of the following is an assumption made in the argument above?

(A) Birth defects caused by Thalidomide could have been prevented by testing.

(B) Thalidomide produced more harmful birth defects than any drug before it.

(C) The benefits of Thalidomide are not outweighed by its harmful side effects.

(D) Thalidomide producers acted irresponsibly in putting such a dangerous drug on the market.

(E) Less harmful drugs were available to treat the problems treated by Thalidomide.

24. The argument above is most similar to which of the following?

(A) Exposure to loud music has been shown to be harmful to teenage hearing; therefore, teens should not be permitted to listen to loud music.

(B) The value of research is hard to determine; therefore, amounts spent for research should be reduced.

(C) The Ford Pinto has been found to have a design defect; therefore, it should be replaced by the manufacturer.

(D) Teenage drivers have caused some of the worst auto accidents; therefore, driving tests for teenagers should be more rigorous than for others.

(E) Generic drugs are less expensive than brand-name drugs; therefore, doctors should prescribe only generic drugs.

Excerpted from *LSAT Success 2002* © 1996 by Thomas O. White

QUICK-SCORE ANSWERS

ANSWERS FOR PRACTICE TEST 1

Section 1	*Section 2*	*Section 3*	*Section 4*	*Section 5*
1. C	1. D	1. A	1. C	1. A
2. E	2. B	2. D	2. B	2. C
3. D	3. C	3. A	3. D	3. B
4. D	4. B	4. B	4. B	4. C
5. C	5. C	5. A	5. A	5. C
6. E	6. C	6. A	6. C	6. B
7. D	7. C	7. A	7. D	7. C
8. E	8. C	8. C	8. E	8. A
9. A	9. A	9. A	9. E	9. E
10. B	10. A	10. B	10. D	10. D
11. D	11. E	11. A	11. B	11. D
12. B	12. E	12. C	12. D	12. C
13. E	13. B	13. C	13. C	13. C
14. C	14. C	14. C	14. A	14. C
15. B	15. A	15. E	15. C	15. E
16. C	16. C	16. E	16. E	16. C
17. A	17. C	17. C	17. B	17. E
18. B	18. A	18. A	18. D	18. A
19. A	19. A	19. B	19. C	19. A
20. B	20. C	20. B	20. E	20. D
21. A	21. B	21. E	21. D	21. C
22. D	22. C	22. B	22. D	22. B
23. D	23. D	23. E	23. C	23. C
24. A	24. B		24. A	24. C
			25. B	
			26. E	
			27. D	
			28. B	

Excerpted from *LSAT Success 2002* © 1996 by Thomas O. White

QUICK-SCORE ANSWERS

ANSWERS FOR PRACTICE TEST 2

Section 1	*Section 2*	*Section 3*	*Section 4*	*Section 5*
1. E	1. A	1. B	1. C	1. B
2. A	2. C	2. D	2. D	2. A
3. D	3. A	3. B	3. A	3. B
4. C	4. A	4. B	4. D	4. C
5. C	5. D	5. A	5. A	5. C
6. D	6. D	6. C	6. C	6. B
7. E	7. E	7. A	7. C	7. D
8. E	8. D	8. C	8. D	8. C
9. D	9. A	9. A	9. C	9. A
10. B	10. E	10. D	10. E	10. D
11. C	11. E	11. B	11. B	11. B
12. D	12. B	12. E	12. B	12. C
13. D	13. E	13. A	13. D	13. B
14. E	14. E	14. A	14. C	14. E
15. B	15. C	15. D	15. D	15. A
16. C	16. C	16. A	16. B	16. E
17. E	17. D	17. E	17. D	17. D
18. E	18. B	18. C	18. A	18. D
19. B	19. C	19. E	19. B	19. E
20. E	20. D	20. E	20. E	20. C
21. C	21. A	21. E	21. E	21. D
22. C	22. A	22. A	22. A	22. E
23. A	23. A	23. C	23. C	23. A
24. B	24. D	24. E	24. E	24. D
			25. D	
			26. A	
			27. A	
			28. C	

Excerpted from *LSAT Success 2002* © 1996 by Thomas O. White

EXPLANATORY ANSWERS FOR PRACTICE TESTS 1 AND 2

PRACTICE TEST 1

In the following answer guide, the credited responses appear in bold type and the visualizations that make the credited response clear appear before the answers to each question set. Use the visualization to guide you in determining the credited answer.

Section 1

Questions 1-6

Statehood   A,F,K,M,O,T,V,W

Earlier   Later

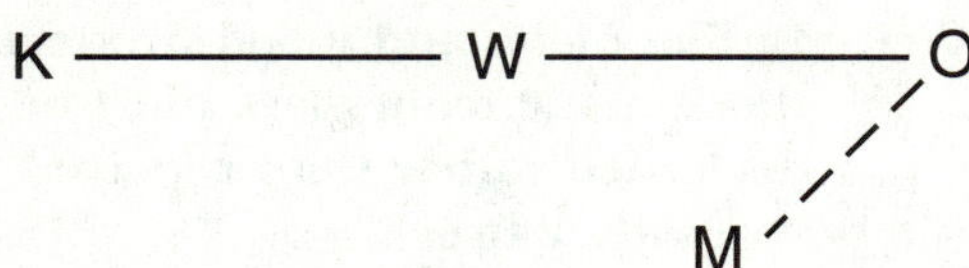

1. **(C) Ohio was a state before Kansas.**

2. **(E) Kansas was a state before Ohio.**

3. **(D) Texas was a state before Ohio.**

4. **(D) Kansas, Maine, Wyoming, Ohio, Vermont**

5. **(C) Florida was a state before Kansas.**

6. **(E) Kansas was a state before Alaska.**

Questions 7-12

Houses   T
                T's Children
                Brother
                Parents

Smaller   Larger

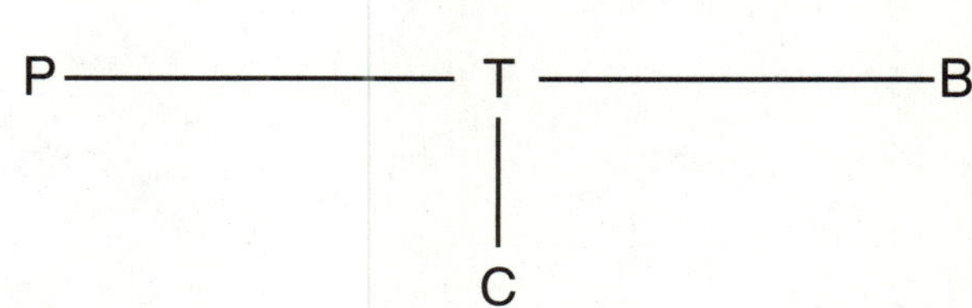

7. **(D) 1, 2**

8. **(E) son to father**

9. **(A) S is U's son.**

10. **(B) uncle**

11. **(D) 3**

12. **(B) T has exactly 3 children.**

Questions 13-18

Riders-A,B,C,D,E,F,G

Busses-1,2,3

Bus

1 if B then no E or G

2 if D then no G

3 C always

3 when A and F take the same bus

13. **(E) B, D, G**
14. **(C) 3 only**
15. **(B) 4**
16. **(C) 3 only**
17. **(A) 0**
18. **(B) A, D, E, G**

Questions 19-24

W ⟵⟶ E

B ⟵5— A —5⟶ B
D ⟵7— C —7⟶ D
E ⟵2— C —2⟶ E
B ⟵3— C —3⟶ B

19. **(A) Dora lives 9 miles from Elmer.**
20. **(B) The distance between Bruce's and Elmer's houses is shorter than the distance between Cora's and Dora's houses.**
21. **(A) Angela and Cora live 12 miles apart.**
22. **(D) 4 miles**
23. **(D) Bruce lives closer to Elmer than Cora does to Dora.**
24. **(A) 14**

Section 2

In the following answer guide, the credited responses appear in bold type and the guide that directs you toward the credited response appears within the answer-choice context. The first reference is to the point of the argument and the second is to the nature of the issue involved.

1. **(D) Purchasers of this brand of clothing will be stylish.**

   Point—Stylish people wear well-designed clothing.

   Issue—Extension question/conclusion

2. **(B) Even though all wrongs cannot be compensated for, some wrongs can be.**

   Point—Money cannot compensate for historic wrongs.

   Issue—Extension question/assumption

3. **(C) The mother knows when the daughter has been truthful.**

   Point—Tell the truth and I will believe you.
   Issue—Extension question/assumption

4. **(B) Unlike metal and wood products, those made from glass must be discarded rather than repaired when they break.**

   Point—Products made from glass can save energy.

   Issue—Extension question/weakening evidence

5. **(C) The price increase will not result in a decrease in the sales of Mexican oil products.**

   Point—Raising oil prices 20 percent will cause a 1 percent increase in the U.S.

   Issue—Extension question/assumption

6. **(C) Journalists report on motives and the significance of events and, like historians, traffic primarily in half-truths and lies.**

   Point—Those who try to describe events engage in half-truths and lies.

   Issue—Extension question/conclusion

Excerpted from *LSAT Success 2002* © 1996 by Thomas O. White

7. **(C)** **All women are not mothers.**

    Point—Equal pay for women detracts from motherhood.

    Issue—Extension question/weakening evidence

8. **(C)** **As a result, the amount of heat energy lost by the Earth must closely approximate the amount gained from the sun.**

    Point—The Earth does not store energy.

    Issue—Extension question/conclusion

9. **(A)** **It is not inconsistent with the lecturer's statement.**

    Point—All Americans do not enjoy a high standard of living.

    Issue—Description question/nature of response

10. **(A)** **a country in which the majority of people enjoy a higher standard of living than that of the American people**

    Point—All Americans do not enjoy a high standard of living.

    Issue—Extension question/weakening evidence

11. **(E)** **There can be no relationship between a general principle and specific practices.**

    Point—Censorship is appropriate in some circumstances.

    Issue—Extension question/conclusion

12. **(E)** **presenting a hypothetical case**

    Point—Censorship is appropriate in some circumstances.

    Issue—Description question/tactic

13. **(B)** **All dogs are excluded from this motel, but many dogs are friendly. Therefore, some friendly animals are kept out of this motel.**

    Point—All have one attribute, some have another attribute; therefore, some have both attributes.

    Issue—Extension question/same point, new context

14. **(C)** **"social pressure"**

    Point—Causes require actions; reasons justify actions.

    Issue—Extension question/conclusion

15. **(A)** **the possible causes of heart disease**

    Point—Accepting the only explanation does not take all possible explanations into account.

    Issue—Description question/example

16. **(C)** **people with blue eyes invariably have blue-eyed children**

    Point—Children have the same color eyes as their parent(s)

    Issue—Extension question/conclusion

17. **(C)** **The significance of art is consistent over time.**

    Point—Similar results connote similar causes, regardless of context.

    Issue—Extension question/assumption

18. **(A)** **All the enemies of the republic are dead.**

    Point—Any living critic proves that Mao did not have personal enemies killed.

    Issue—Extension question/assumption

19. **(A)** **scientists are too concerned about failure**

    Point—Risking failure is no longer tolerated in drug development.

    Issue—Extension question/conclusion

20. **(C)** **The star's last movie contained the usual bit of impressive acting, but her director should have advised her to act more like an average person.**

    Point—Those producing exceptional work should use more common devices.

    Issue—Extension question/same point, new context

Excerpted from *LSAT Success 2002* © 1996 by Thomas O. White

21. **(B) Fees paid by students are the major source of funding for educational services.**

    Point—As demands on resources decrease, services and facilities should improve.

    Issue—Extension question/weakening evidence

22. **(C) There are doubts about the conclusive nature of studies on animals.**

    Point—If the government acts prematurely, it loses credibility.

    Issue—Extension question/conclusion

23. **(D) Sailors cannot be afraid of water.**

    Point—The Mercer child will not sail because of his fear of water.

    Issue—Extension question/conclusion

24. **(B) other factors could have nullified the influence of the olive oil**

    Point—Olive oil did not prevent heart attack in Betty's mother.

    Issue—Extension question/weakening evidence

Section 3

In the following answer guide, the credited responses appear in bold type and the visualizations that make the credited response clear appear before the answers to each question set. Use the visualization to guide you in determining the credited answer.

Questions 1-6

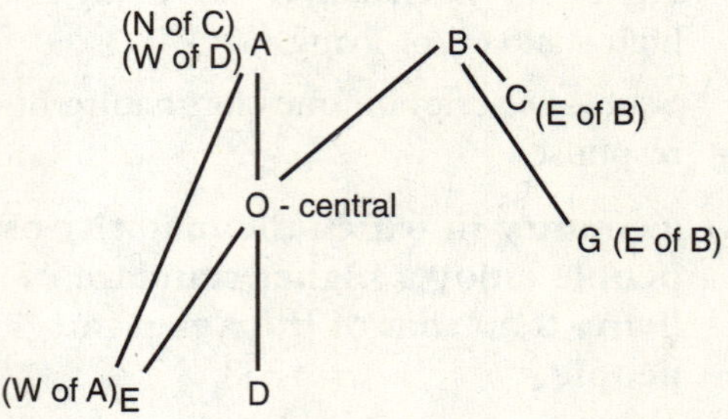

1. **(A) the northwest corner of D**

2. **(D) F is located due west of C.**

3. **(A) farther east than B**

4. **(B) northeast of C**

5. **(A) B is precisely midway between E and G.**

6. **(A) The Central Office is closer to D than to G.**

Excerpted from LSAT Success 2002 © 1996 by Thomas O. White

Questions 7-11

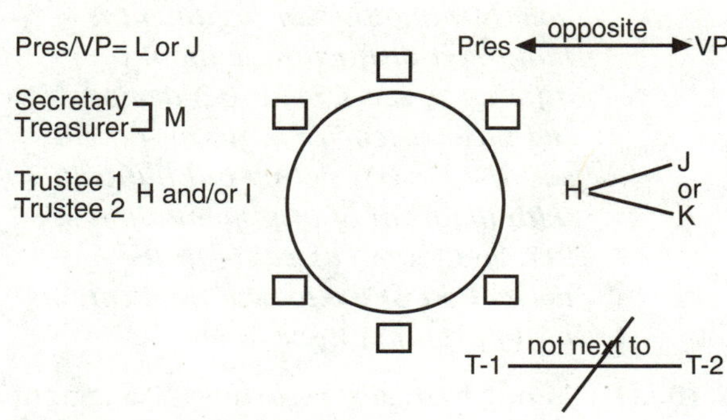

7. **(A) J is the vice president**

8. **(C) president, vice president, trustee, secretary, treasurer**

9. **(A) J, K, L**

10. **(B) H and J**

11. **(A) M is the secretary**

Questions 12-17

Trucks - K, M, W   Fuel and wash - trucks before vans
                          Fuel larger tanks before smaller
Vans - C, D, F   Wash smaller before larger

Tank Size

Larger ———————————————————— Small

K

equals ——— D ——— M ————————— W more than C

F

12. **(C) The Chevrolet is fueled fifth.**

13. **(C) The Chevrolet is fueled before the Ford.**

14. **(C) The Kenworth is washed second.**

15. **(E) White, Mack, Kenworth, Ford, Dodge, Chevrolet**

16. **(E) the Ford immediately before the Dodge**

17. **(C) Ford, Chevrolet, Dodge, Kenworth, White, Mack**

Questions 18-23

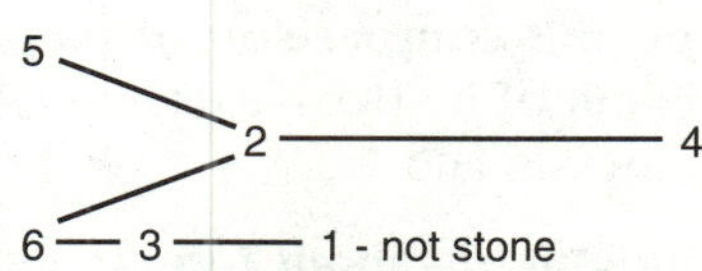

18. **(A) aluminum**

19. **(B) 6, 3, 1, 5, 2, 4**

20. **(B) brick**

21. **(E) 6, 5, 4, 3, 2, 1**

22. **(B) stone**

23. **(E) wood**

Section 4

In the following answer guide, the credited responses appear in bold type and the guide that directs you to the place in the passage that accounts for the credited response appears within the answer-choice context. The first reference is to the paragraph number in the passage that accounts for the credited response and the second number refers to the relevant sentence in the paragraph. The reference will appear as 2/4 for example. This means paragraph 2 and sentence 4 within paragraph 2.

1. **(C) comparing Smith's and Rawls's views of a just society**—Paragraph 4/Sentence 5

2. **(B) the theory of welfare economics** For (A) *the Scottish method* and (D) *the scientific method*, see 1/1; for (C) *the perfect-competition paradigm*, see 3/3; and for (E) *the principles of natural liberty*, see 2/3.

3. **(D) the description of the idealized competitive economy**—Paragraph 4/Sentence 2

4. **(B) concerned with improving the operation of society**—Paragraph 1/Sentence 4

Excerpted from *LSAT Success 2002* © 1996 by Thomas O. White

5. **(A) a recitation of methods of approaching social problems**—Most inclusive of the five answer choices

6. **(C) In what follows, both of these routes will be explored.**—Paragraph 4/Sentence 7

7. **(D) permit comparison of their concepts of justice**—Paragraph 4/Sentences 6 and 7

8. **(E) judgments about human actions can be made only by the resulting end-states**—Paragraph 2/Sentence 2

9. **(E) The net value of consequences is considered important.** Only (A), (B), (C), and (D) are mentioned as features of utilitarianism. See the importance of (A) *results*, 3/3; (B) *consequences*, 1/3; (C) *valued end-state*, 2/2; and (D) *means of achieving results*, 3/1.

10. **(D) It is legally acceptable for bad consequences to flow from the exercise of an individual's right or privilege.**—Paragraph 1/Sentence 8

11. **(B) contrast judgments of right and wrong with other types of judgments**—Paragraph 4/Sentence 5

12. **(D) means used to produce results**—Paragraph 3/Sentence 1 and Paragraph 2/Sentence 2

13. **(C) explains some judgments in law and morals**—Paragraph 1/Sentence 2

14. **(A) somewhat critical**—Paragraph 1/Sentence 4

15. **(C) an argument for the use of formal models by lawyers**—Paragraph 1/Sentence 8

16. **(E) a method of argumentation**—Paragraph 1/Sentence 6

17. **(B) locating something left out of consideration**
Only (A), (C), (D), and (E) are benefits of using formal models. For (A) *determining that an argument is making a distinction without a difference*, see 1/8; for (C) *demonstrating inconsistencies in an argument*, see 4/7; for (D) *setting out difficulties with the form of argumentation*, see 2/1; and for (E) *assisting in the derivation of the logical implications of an argument*, see 1/4.

18. **(D) is not logically rigorous**—Paragraph 1/Sentence 4

19. **(C) provide the basis for argumentation**—Paragraph 3/Sentence 2

20. **(E) as a technique to ensure equity** Only (A), (B), (C), and (D) describe uses for models as argued in the passage. For models used (A) *as a method of argumentation*, see 4/7; (B) *as a source of answers to problems,* see 4/8; (C) *as a form of reasoning used by lawyers*, see 1/1; and (D) *as a method to identify problems with logic*, see 4/7.

21. **(D) Formal models are as illogical as prose models.**—Paragraph 2/Sentences 1 and 2

22. **(D) Omissions are a problem with formal models**.—Paragraph 4/Sentence 3

23. **(C) an interpretation of syntactics applied to aspects of legal discourse**—Paragraph 1/Sentence 1

24. **(A) A, 2, #, +, s, ?, c, p, %, $**—Paragraph 3/Sentence 1

25. **(B) the transmission of the dash in dot-dot-dash when two dots are always followed by a dash**—Paragraph 2/Sentence 6

26. **(E) a case that is exactly the same as previous cases**—Paragraph 5/Sentence 1

Excerpted from *LSAT Success 2002* © 1996 by Thomas O. White

27. **(D) Redundancy in a message reduces the information transmitted.**—Paragraph 4/Sentence 4

28. **(B) Redundancy accounts for the difference between strong and weak legal arguments.**—Paragraph 5/Sentence 2

Section 5

In the following answer guide, the credited responses appear in bold type and the guide that directs you toward the credited response appears within the answer-choice context. The first reference is to the point of the argument and the second is to the nature of the issue involved.

1. **(A) In the absence of freedom of expression, great writers do not develop.**

   Point—Neither great writers nor freedom of expression exist in Largo.

   Issue—Extension question/assumption

2. **(C) Birds, rather than cave dwellers, may have brought snakes and fish to the caves to eat.**

   Point—Cavemen ate bison, birds, snakes, and fish.

   Issue—Extension question/weakening evidence

3. **(B) people can be persuaded to abandon technology, urbanization, and mass production**

   Point—The natural benevolence of people is corrupted by institutions.

   Issue—Extension question/strengthening evidence

4. **(C) The sky is not cloudy, and rain is not falling.**

   Point—Bob is not in the slicker he wears when it is cloudy and rainy.

   Issue—Extension question/conclusion

5. **(C) Sensitive people are lovers.**

   Point—Excellent musicians love poetry.
   Issue—Description question/Sensitivity not involved in argument

6. **(B) Since owls feed only at night, the bird feeding in daylight is not an owl.**

   Point—Reasoning from properties of plazium to a conclusion

   Issue—Description question/structure of argument

7. **(C) Some ocean-liner passengers are in the care of a dangerous person.**

   Point—Captains who care for passengers may be dangerous alcoholics.

   Issue—Extension question/conclusion

8. **(A) The resources required to log forests cannot be replenished.**

   Point—Coal is a nonrenewable resource—trees are a renewable resource.

   Issue—Extension question/weakening evidence

9. **(E) Jurors think eyewitness testimony leaves less room for doubt than does expert testimony.**

   Point—Jurors find expert testimony less persuasive than eyewitness testimony.

   Issue—Extension question/conclusion

10. **(D) In the future, more older students will enter college than ever before.**

    Point—College enrollment will decline when the number of 18-year-olds declines.

    Issue—Extension question/weakening evidence

11. **(D) In the past, film was an important art form.**

    Point—Contemporary film is not an art form.

    Issue—Extension question/unsupported conclusion

Excerpted from *LSAT Success 2002* © 1996 by Thomas O. White

12. **(C)** **Countries can accurately determine one another's military strength.**

    Point—U. S. can assure military balance of power by selling arms to other countries.

    Issue—Extension question/assumption

13. **(C)** **The sale and delivery of military equipment is usually known only by the two countries involved.**

    Point—U. S. can assure military balance of power by selling arms to other countries.

    Issue—Extension question/weakening evidence

14. **(C)** **Lights are maintained in good working order because of the inspection requirement.**

    Point—Turn-signal inspection identifies few defective lights.

    Issue—Extension question/weakening evidence

15. **(E)** **It is seldom possible to determine which information involves the public welfare.**

    Point—Public welfare is the only justification for exposing people's private lives.

    Issue—Extension question/weakening evidence

16. **(C)** **Personal privacy is an important right.**

    Point—Public welfare is the only justification for exposing people's private lives.

    Issue—Extension question/conclusion

17. **(E)** **Voting is a form of political involvement.**

    Point—Voting and political involvement have a strong relationship.

    Issue—Extension question/conclusion

18. **(A)** **Some students prefer geometry to physics.**

    Point—All prefer history to geometry—some prefer physics to history.

    Issue—Extension question/conclusion

19. **(A)** **Some students prefer geometry to physics.**

    Point—All prefer history to geometry—some prefer physics to history.

    Issue—Extension question/conclusion

20. **(D)** **Nature cannot be changed.**

    Point—A snake will bite a hand that fed it.

    Issue—Extension question/conclusion

21. **(C)** **Cheese and butter produce greater profits for processors than does milk.**

    Point—Without government subsidies, more milk would be used for cheese and butter.

    Issue—Extension question/conclusion

22. **(B)** **Certain attributes of works of art are typical of specific periods.**

    Point—Many characteristics differentiate early Greek period sculpture.

    Issue—Extension question/assumption

23. **(C)** **The villagers do not trust the mayor.**

    Point—By paying a bounty for snakes, the mayor will rid the town of them.

    Issue—Extension question/NOT weakening evidence

24. **(C)** **It appears that the cost of housing at Spring Lake is prohibitive. I looked at a number of houses last month, and they cost much more than I could afford.**

    Point—Spring Lake is too rough for sailing.

    Issue—Description question/structure of argument

Excerpted from *LSAT Success 2002* © 1996 by Thomas O. White

PRACTICE TEST 2

In the following answer guide, the credited responses appear in bold type, and the visualization that makes the credited response clear appears before the question set. Use the visualization to guide you in determining the credited answer.

Section 1

Questions 1–6

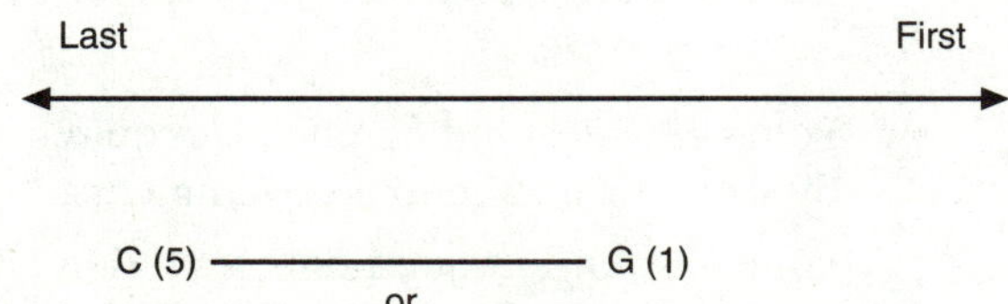

1. **(E) E finishes fourth.**

2. **(A) E finishes second.**

3. **(D) F finishes ahead of E.**

4. **(C) 3**

5. **(C) F finishes ahead of D.**

6. **(D) F finishes fourth.**

Questions 7–12

7. **(E) The Kansas president is younger than the Ohio president.**

8. **(E) The Kansas president is older than the Ohio president.**

9. **(D) The Texas president is older than the Ohio president.**

10. **(B) Wyoming**

11. **(C) The Florida president is older than the Kansas president.**

12. **(D) The Alaska president is older than the Ohio president.**

Questions 13–18

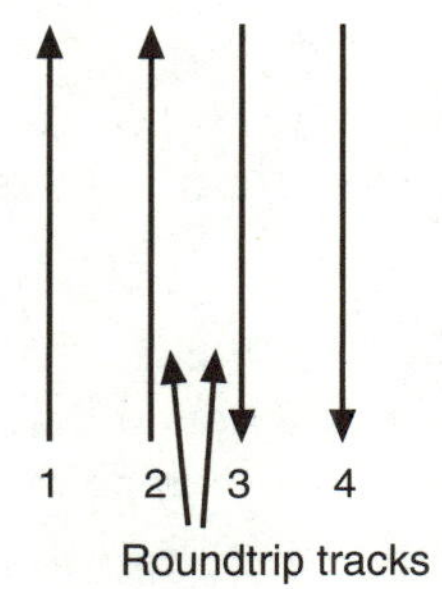

2 consecutive trains cannot use same track

Local after express or metro

13. **(D) I and II only**

14. **(E) 4, 1, 3, 2**

15. **(B) 2**

16. **(C) R on track 2, U on track 3, S on track 1, T on track 3, Q on track 2**

17. **(E) 4, 0**

18. **(E) The greatest number of locals cannot exceed the greatest number of express trains.**

Excerpted from *LSAT Success 2002* © 1996 by Thomas O. White

Questions 19–24

Beach   C, E, J, R, W
             Food, Blankets, Umbrella, Drives, Pays

Brother—Sister
First brings umbrella
Driver = male
Brother pays
When E brings food—W not drive
When C or J brings blankets—R drives

19. **(B) Rick drives.**

20. **(E) Carol is Rick's sister.**

21. **(C) bring the umbrella**

22. **(C) Jenny brings neither blankets nor food.**

23. **(A) drive**

24. **(B) Carol and Rick**

Section 2

In the following answer guide, the credited responses appear in bold type, and the guide that directs you toward the credited response appears within the answer choice context. The first reference is to the point of the argument and the second is to the nature of the issue involved.

1. **(A) Quiet people are not easily identified.**

    Point—All people have one attribute. All with the one attribute have a second attribute.

    Issue—Extension question/conclusion

2. **(C) It assumes the conclusion.**

    Point—Ambitious people are not good parents. Good parents are not ambitious people.

    Issue—Description question/tactic

3. **(A) Arthritis specialists provide authoritative information on effective medication for arthritis.**

    Point—Connect Arthrelief to the most prescribed medicine.

    Issue—Extension question/NOT assumption

4. **(A) Reasoning abilities of illiterate people should not be tested using tasks that do not involve familiar devices.**

    Point—Testing results for illiterates vary by the devices used to test.

    Issue—Extension question/conclusion

5. **(D) Daily exercise does not contribute greatly to Japanese worker productivity.**

    Point—Americans and Japanese vary in terms of daily exercise and productivity.

    Issue—Extension question/weakening evidence

6. **(D) A country with a democratic government must have a politically active people.**

    Point—Political indifference is required by dictators and central governments.

    Issue—Extension question/conclusion

7. **(E) IV, II, III, I**

    Point—The path to follow to U. S. energy independence

    Issue—Extension question/order of evidence to conclusion

8. **(D) work areas are directly related to college degree areas**

    Point—It is wasteful to spend for training that is little used.

    Issue—Extension question/assumption

9. **(A) It does not state that Alert tablets cause grade improvement.**

    Point—Students who use Alert get good grades.

    Issue—Extension question/strengthening conclusion

10. **(E) Friendliness is a virtue.**

    Point—Dogs and cats express friendliness differently.

    Issue—Extension question/conclusion

Excerpted from *LSAT Success 2002* © 1996 by Thomas O. White

11. **(E) Public beaches in Canada are no cleaner or cheaper than those in the United States.**

   Point—Canadian public campgrounds compare favorably with U. S. public beaches.

   Issue—Extension question/weakening evidence

12. **(B) proposes a common cause for similar effects**

   Point—Computers and people play poker in the same way.

   Issue—Description question/tactic

13. **(E) The industry association has standards that exceed the legal requirements.**

   Point—Inspections identify no violations.

   Issue—Extension question/conclusion

14. **(E) children do not generally accept adult responsibilities prior to the rites**

   Point—Rites that formally impose adult responsibilities are found in societies with unclear differences between adults and children.

   Issue—Extension question/strengthening evidence

15. **(C) Very few physically challenged people use facilities in the places where they have been installed.**

   Point—Devices to help the physically impaired use public transportation help only very athletic people.

   Issue—Extension question/strengthening evidence

Questions 16–17

16. **(C) Purchasers attempt to secure more credit than they can afford.**

   Point—Credit bureaus provide valuable services with little personal intrusion by reducing business losses and preventing consumers from overextending their financial obligations.

   Issue—Extension question/assumption of behavior

17. **(D) justified by the economic value to business and society**

   Point—Credit bureaus provide valuable services with little personal intrusion by reducing business losses and preventing consumers from overextending their financial obligations.

   Issue—Extension question/conclusion

18. **(B) Harold is a better writer than Stan.**

   Point—Harold writes better short stories and novels than does Stan.

   Issue—Extension question/conclusion

19. **(C) Since 1969, more high school graduates have decided to seek a college degree.**

   Point—The value of a college education has dropped significantly over time.

   Issue—Extension question/weakening evidence

20. **(D) Engineering of genes and environment are virtually the same.**

   Point—Engineering produces change in many characteristics of people.

   Issue—Extension question/strengthening evidence

Questions 21–22

21. **(A) Shea confuses influence with merit**

   Point—Similar influence requires similar recognition.

   Issue—Extension question/conclusion

22. **(A) the Springfield Pops**

   Point—Similar influence requires similar recognition.

   Issue—Extension question/same structure/new context

23. **(A) All three resorts Ann previously visited are in north Miami Beach, and the new resort is in south Miami Beach.**

   Point—Florida resorts are enjoyable to Ann.

   Issue—Extension question/insignificant evidence

Excerpted from *LSAT Success 2002* © 1996 by Thomas O. White

24. (D) Social reasons account for the attendance of most students at services.

Point—There is an inverse relationship between cheating and religious exposure.

Issue—Extension question/weakening evidence

Section 3

In the following answer guide, the credited responses appear in bold type, and the visualization that makes the credited response clear appears before each question set. Use the visualization to guide you in determining the credited answer.

Questions 1–6

Bids   L, M, N, O, P, Q

Lowest   Highest

K ———— Q ———— P ———— N

M ———— O —— P

1. (B) M, L, O, Q, P, N

2. (D) M or L

3. (B) L submits the third-lowest bid.

4. (B) Q submits a higher bid than M

5. (A) L, M, Q, O, P, N

6. (C) Q and L

Questions 7–12

Graduation   L, M, N, O, P, Q, R, S, T, U

1971 - 1975 - Two per year

1971   1975

M ———1——— Q

P and Q in '71 to '74

S and T together

Q not with N

7. (A) S, T; P, R; M, O; Q, N; L, U

8. (C) L, N, S

9. (A) L graduated in 1972.

10. (D) R graduated in 1972.

11. (B) 1971 and 1974

12. (E) S graduated in 1975.

Questions 13–18

Table set-ups   A,B,C,D,E

B must E
C must D
E not with C
D not with A
A always sets up

13. (A) Adam only

14. (A) one

15. (D) Beth, Dana, and Edith

16. (A) Dana and Edith

17. (E) Beth and Edith only

18. (C) two

Questions 19–24

Dentists - A, B, C   Hygienists all assigned
Hygienists - S, T, U, V

A and B - 2 hygienists each
C - 1 or 2 hygienists
T assign A and B or C

19. (E) either B or C

20. (E) U is assigned to only one dentist.

21. (E) either B or C

22. (A) A only

23. (C) U is assigned to only one dentist.

24. (E) U is assigned to only one dentist.

Excerpted from *LSAT Success 2002* © 1996 by Thomas O. White

Section 4

In the following answer guide, the credited responses appear in bold type, and the guide that directs you to the place in the passage that accounts for the credited response appears within the answer choice context. The first reference is to the paragraph number in the passage that accounts for the credited response and the second number refers to the relevant sentence in the paragraph. The reference will appear as 2/4 for example. This means paragraph 2 and sentence 4 within paragraph 2.

1. **(C) advocate limiting handgun availability—Paragraph 3/Sentence 6**

2. **(D) gun ownership by people associated with violence has greatly increased—Paragraph 2/Sentence 7**

3. **(A) dramatize the increase in gun-related violence—Paragraph 1/Sentence 2**

4. **(D) Handgun ownership among middle-class New Yorkers has increased fourfold in the last ten years.—Paragraph 2/Sentences 6 and 7**

5. **(A) The rate of growth in gun ownership in the Northeast is greater than that of other regions—Paragraph 2/Sentence 5**

6. **(C) Urban violence is due to subcultural differences among residents. —Paragraph 1/Sentences 3 and 4**

7. **(C) regulation of handgun possession—Paragraph 3/Sentence 4**

8. **(D) comparing hardware and software—Paragraph 1/Sentence 1; Paragraph 2/Sentence 1**

9. **(C) Software can be located within hardware.—Paragraph 1/Sentence 3**

10. **(E) hardware is readily changeable** According to the passage, choices (A), (B), (C), and (D) are all true. For (A) the cost of duplicating software is low, see 2/1; for (B) very little software is sold outright, see 2/5; for (C) hardware is often not patented, see 3/2; and for (D) software requires minimal originality, see 3/3.

11. **(B) It can be copyrighted.—Paragraph 3/Sentence 1**

12. **(B) It is more profitable to sell copies of software than hardware.—Paragraph 2/Sentences 2 and 4**

13. **(D) Patented hardware requires greater inventiveness than does software.—Paragraph 3/Sentence 3**

14. **(C) One purchased the restaurant when one purchased the dinner prepared there.—Production Capacity/Production Result**

15. **(D) a means of tracing changes in group status in society—Paragraph 1/Sentence 3**

16. **(B) the relationship between group status and frequency of court appearance—Paragraph 2/Sentence 2**

17. **(D) court performance—Paragraph 2/Sentence 5**

18. **(A) There is an inverse relationship between wealth and court appearances.—Paragraph 2/Sentence 5**

19. **(B) There is a positive correlation between the New Haven findings and those of other towns.—Paragraph 2/Sentence 4**

20. **(E) a legal historian—Paragraph 5/Sentence 6**

21. **(E) court procedures remain the same over long periods of time** According to the passage, choices (A), (B), (C), and (D) are all true. For (A) court records can be constructed over long periods of time, see 3/5; for (B) court appearances change with status within the society, see 3/1; for (C) court records are generally preserved in most jurisdictions, see 3/4; and for (D) court appearances can be treated collectively to reflect status, see 3/5.

22. **(A) to point out that advertising reliability varies by type of good—Paragraph 2/Sentence 3**

23. **(C) consumption—Paragraph 2/Sentence 2**

Excerpted from *LSAT Success 2002* © 1996 by Thomas O. White

24. **(E) Advertisers spend large sums of money on informative messages.** According to the passage, choices (A), (B), (C), and (D) are all true. For (A) Search goods advertising is likely to be informative and truthful, see 2/5; for (B) Mail order advertising in magazines is not likely to be truthful, see 5/4; for (C) Experienced goods advertisers have incentive to mislead, see 3/1; and for (D) Credence goods advertisements may never be determined to be valid, see 3/1.

25. **(D) "Analysis of the Function of Advertising"—Paragraph 1/Sentence 1**

26. **(A) auto transmission oil—Paragraph 3/Sentence 1**

27. **(A) Many advertisers and consumers do not act rationally.—Paragraph 1/Sentence 3**

28. **(C) Credence-goods consumers require statutory protection.—Paragraph 4/Sentence 2**

Section 5

In the following answer guide, the credited responses appear in bold type, and the guide that directs you toward the credited response appears within the answer choice context. The first reference is to the point of the argument and the second is to the nature of the issue involved.

1. **(B) It is insignificant and coincidental.**

    Point—Significant figures in two peoples lives total the same number.
    Issue—Description question/characterize the number

2. **(A) identifying incongruities in the use of force**

    Point—The acceptable use of force varies by context.
    Issue—Description question/tactic

3. **(B) Past practice validates future action.**

    Point—Past is prologue
    Issue—Extension question/conclusion

4. **(C) Sales of a book are not always indicative of its value.**

    Point—Able criticism anticipates the market reaction.
    Issue—Extension question/weakening evidence

Questions 5–6

5. **(C) the expression of deep feeling**

    Point—Emotional societies produce better writing than technical societies.
    Issue—Description question/rephrasing

6. **(B) Societies must be emotional or technical.**

    Point—Emotional societies produce better writing than technical societies.
    Issue—Extension question/assumption

Questions 7–8

7. **(D) Artists generally venerate their countries.**

    Point—Artists oppose their environments.
    Issue—Extension question/weakening evidence

8. **(C) The purpose of art is to both find fault with and escape from life.**

    Point—Artists oppose their environments.
    Issue—Extension question/assumption

9. **(A) presented more than one issue to respondents**

    Point—Drug addicts on welfare should not get free needles.
    Issue—Description question/tactic

10. **(D) When people complain about their health, they get old; but no one is complaining about their health, so we must have no people getting old.**

    Point—If : then—Not if : not then
    Issue—Extension question/same structure/new context

Excerpted from *LSAT Success 2002* © 1996 by Thomas O. White

Questions 11–12

11. (B) Oil, coal, and fresh water are natural resources.

Point—Natural resources should not be given away by a state.

Issue—Extension question/assumption

12. (C) New York City will pay Pennsylvania and New Jersey for each gallon of water diverted.

Point—Natural resources should not be given away by a state.

Issue—Extension question/weakening evidence

13. (B) a theory postulating suffering as a requisite for creativity

Point—Excluding matters of choice, the present is the product of past actions.

Issue—Extension question/NOT conclusion

14. (E) Baxter feels that women and men have unequal capacities.

Point—For various reasons Baxter is not a feminist.

Issue—Extension question/NOT conclusion

15. (A) Modern educational aids should be provided for urban children.

Point—Suburban students have more educational resources than urban students.

Issue—Extension question/conclusion

16. (E) A philosopher's reasoning is complicated because he was trained in a tradition that often uses complicated reasoning.

Point—Because they do not, they should not be expected to.

Issue—Extension question/same structure/new context

Questions 17–18

17. (D) If Japan and the United States sign a treaty, interests of each will be served by the agreement.

Point—Treaties serve self-interest, not trust.

Issue—Extension question/conclusion

18. (D) Treaties do not serve mutual interests of countries.

Point—Treaties serve self-interest, not trust.

Issue—Extension question/NOT conclusion

19. (E) Employees of most chemical plants develop abnormal chromosome patterns.

Point—Plant environment may produce abnormal chromosome patterns in workers.

Issue—Extension question/strengthening evidence

20. (C) Only legislators who do not favor the bill were polled.

Point—Some legislators support the bills and some do not.

Issue—Extension question/conclusion

21. (D) The Society intensified its falcon sighting program in 1988.

Point—More sightings result from more falcons.

Issue—Extension question/weakening evidence

22. (E) writing was not the only factor in deciding which articles to publish

Point—Worthy and well-written articles are not always published.

Issue—Extension question/conclusion

Questions 23–24

23. (A) Birth defects caused by Thalidomide could have been prevented by testing.

Point—Testing will detect unforeseen effects in new drugs.

Issue—Extension question/assumption

24. (D) Teenage drivers have caused some of the worst auto accidents; therefore, driving tests for teenagers should be more rigorous than for others.

Point—Testing will detect unforeseen effects in new drugs.

Issue—Extension question/same structure/new context

Excerpted from *LSAT Success 2002* © 1996 by Thomas O. White

TIMETABLE FOR THE LAW SCHOOL APPLICATION PROCESS

- See your prelaw adviser as soon as you *think you may* be interested in attending law school.

SPRING OF YOUR JUNIOR YEAR

- Collect the LSAC Law School Admissions Test application from your prelaw adviser or request a copy directly from LSAC by phone at 215-968-1001 or on the Web at http://www.lsac. org.
- Register for June LSAT. By taking the June administration you gain three advantages. First, you will know both your GPA and your LSAT before you must select to which schools to apply. This allows you to make a more informed choice about where to apply. Second, if anything goes wrong and you must cancel your test results or wish to retake the exam in October, you are no worse off than the vast majority of other candidates. Third, the June administration does not interfere with normal school time frames, so you are not dealing with both classwork and the LSAT.
- Register with the Law School Data Assembly Service (LSDAS). Registration forms are found in the packet you received from your prelaw adviser.
- After the end of spring semester, begin preparation for the LSAT. Prepare intensely for at least four weeks prior to the test.
- Begin identifying appropriate law schools based on your LSAT practice scores and your GPA.

SUMMER AFTER JUNIOR YEAR

- Take the June LSAT.

- Write law schools for their catalogs and admissions materials (August).
- Receive your LSAT score (four to six weeks after the test).
- Begin receiving law school catalogs (September).
- Review law school choices in light of your LSAT score.
- Register for the October LSAT, if appropriate.
- If appropriate, request official school transcripts be sent to the LSDAS from all higher education institutions you attended.

FALL OF SENIOR YEAR

- Meet with your prelaw adviser to review your selection of schools.
- Request letters of recommendation.
- Take the October LSAT, if appropriate.
- Prepare applications. Applications should be submitted well ahead of the deadlines. Try to have all of your applications submitted by December 1.

SPRING OF SENIOR YEAR

- If you have not received notification, call the law schools to see if your applications are complete (February 1).
- Fill out the required financial aid forms as soon as they become available.

William Weaver, J.D., Ph.D., Department of Political Science, University of Texas at El Paso

THE APPLICATION: INSIDER'S TIPS

THE PERSONAL STATEMENT

All law schools require or allow you to submit some sort of personal statement with your application, and nothing gives students more trouble than this seemingly simple task. People become nervous and disconcerted when asked to write about themselves and tend to make two general types of mistakes when constructing their personal statements. The first is the "why-I'm-so-great" mistake. The brightest, most humble student will end up writing a personal statement that would make people with Napoleon complexes blush in embarrassment. The second type of mistake is the "laundry-list" mistake. Your personal statement should not be a grab bag of all the things you have done in your life. Information about charitable work, club membership, offices held, etc., should appear in the application proper. Nearly all schools have sections for extracurricular activities and charitable work.

Think of the personal statement as a mini-paper or a short story about some feature of your life. It should have a thesis (an implied thesis works better in this situation), a development phase, and a conclusion. It should be no more than 450 words and, if possible, should fit on a single sheet of paper. Do not, however, make the font so small as to be unreadable in trying to reduce it to one page in length. Try to make the opening sentence catchy, but don't make it sound ridiculous or pompous. A short account of some important event in your life is perfectly fine for the personal statement. The idea is to tell the law school a lot about yourself without duplicating information that should be found elsewhere in the application.

The personal statement is usually not a terribly important part of the application, but it is the kind of thing that if very badly done and then read by committee members could result in serious harm. On some occasions, though, a personal statement can be so charming, moving, or painfully forthright that it can make the difference between admission and rejection, so you must give the personal statement careful attention.

LETTERS OF RECOMMENDATION

You should arrange for at least three letters of recommendation. Two of these letters should come from academics, preferably from professors of classes you have done extremely well in. Don't be concerned that the professor won't remember you. Just give her a brief resume, a list of when you took his or her class and the final grade in the class, and any papers you might still have from the course.

It is not required that recommending professors know you well, only that they can comment on your class performance relative to other students. Then ask the professor directly whether or not he or she can write you a good recommendation. If there is some reluctance on the part of the professor, thank him or her and move on.

With rare exceptions, a recommender will write one letter addressed generically to law school admission committees. This letter will then be sent to all of the law schools to which you apply. Tell your professors early that you will be needing a letter of recommendation. This means notifying potential recommenders in September of the year you are applying to law school. Also give your recommenders a deadline for when to have the letters ready. Let them have three or so weeks, but definitely track down for the letters if you have not received them by the middle of October.

Give all of the materials to the professor at the same time; don't string out requests for letters two or three at a time. Include envelopes addressed to either yourself or the law school, depending on what the application requires (explained at the end of this heading). This means that you must have all of your applications by mid-September. Waiver forms allow you to waive your right to see your letters of recommendation. If schools ask, your best course is usually to waive your right to see your letters of recommendation. Make sure any waiver forms are correctly filled in with your signature. Without such a waiver the law school will place less credence in the recommender's statements, believing that the recommender will not be as forthcoming if she thinks the student will have access to her evaluation.

Law schools receive letters of recommendation in one of three ways. First, they may ask the recommender to send the letter directly to the law school. In this case, make sure that the envelopes are correctly made out and that all the forms are attached by a paper clip to the appropriate envelopes. Second, some schools ask that recommenders enclose their letters in an envelope, sign it across the back seal, and then give the envelope back to the student who is to enclose it in the application. Make sure you know which school does things which way and keep the two piles separate when giving them to the recommender. Third, you

William Weaver, *J.D., Ph.D., Department of Political Science, University of Texas at El Paso*

can place your letters on file, for a fee, with the Law School Admission Council (LSAC) and it will send the letters out to schools requesting your test scores. It is important to recognize that very few college professors or employers know how to write an effective letter of recommendation for law school. You should delicately suggest to your recommenders that they approach the letter in the following way. First, they should use specifics rather than rely on generalizations. Rather than saying that "Roger X was a wonderful student who earned an 'A' in my class in American literature" and leaving the matter there, it would make a big difference if we knew, say, that historically only 5 percent of the professor's American literature students receive "A" grades. Also, citing specifics about class performance can be helpful, especially if the student demonstrated exceptional rhetorical skills or helped substantially in making the class successful. Likewise, detailed comments about written work submitted for the course are preferable to general statements about ability. Letters should concentrate on three things. First, they should address the student's dependability in performing the assignments and keeping up with the course readings. Second, the analytical skills of the student should be addressed. And, finally, the student's communication skills should be discussed. Additional comments, where appropriate, about a student's integrity or personal information are welcome.

One additional question that is frequently asked concerns letters of recommendation and whether or not the student should use the recommendation of a famous friend or relative or a family member or friend who is a judge or attorney. Use only recommenders who know you well enough to write intelligently about your character and abilities. If a famous person or judge meets this requirement, then by all means, ask that person to recommend you.

TO HOW MANY SCHOOLS SHOULD YOU APPLY?

One of the worst mistakes a prospective law student can make is to apply to too few schools. As a general rule, apply to no less than twelve institutions. Under certain circumstances, apply to an upward of twenty schools. Those circumstances are discussed below.

If you apply to a dozen schools, divide them up into four groups. Three of the schools you apply to should be institutions where your chances of admission are slim. Obviously, what counts as slim depends on your numbers. If you have a 3.0 GPA and score in the 70th percentile on the LSAT, then UT Austin, Duke, Cornell, Wisconsin, Minnesota, etc., are all slim possibilities for admission. The second three schools should be institutions where you

probably will not be admitted, but stand, say, a 25 percent chance of getting in. The third set of three schools should be institutions where you stand a 40 percent chance or better of admission. Finally, you should have three schools where you stand a very high chance of admission. Many times students get "boxed out," left without an offer of admission because they applied to too few schools or applied only to schools beyond their reach. Bear in mind that at schools such as Stanford, Yale, Harvard, and Columbia you cannot count on admission even if you have a 3.9 GPA and score above the 95th percentile on the LSAT. All applicants should apply to a range of schools. This book contains bar graphs for most schools that show the total enrollment, percentage of students admitted, average LSAT score, average GPA of students, and average student debt upon graduation. You can use the information in these graphs to estimate your chances of admission to a particular school.

There are basically three circumstances where students should apply to up to twenty law schools. The first is when students have extremely low numbers—say a 2.5 GPA and a 30th percentile on the LSAT. In this circumstance, students should apply to fifteen schools that are considered to be in the bottom tier of law schools. Five applications should be directed at third-tier (one tier up from the bottom) law schools. Remember, all ABA-accredited law schools deliver a first-rate education, and whether or not you are a good lawyer often has little to do with grades or where you went to law school. Prospective clients do not ask F. Lee Bailey where he went to law school or what sort of grades he earned.

The second circumstance that justifies higher numbers of applications is when an applicant has very good numbers that are not quite good enough for top-tier institutions. If you are Anglo and have a 3.5 GPA and score in the 80th percentile on the LSAT, you should send twelve applications to schools that seem just beyond your reach—schools ranging in rank from number five to twenty-five.

The final circumstance that justifies increased numbers of applications is when the applicant is a member of a minority group favored by law school admission committees and has "mixed" or good but marginal numbers. For example, a student who has a 3.8 GPA but scores in the 50th percentile on the LSAT may still want to use the four-category approach, but triple the normal number of applications for the first tier or schools where the student perceives he or she has a "slim" chance of admission. The same goes for an applicant who is a member of a minority group favored for admission by law schools and has, say, a 3.2 GPA and scores in the 80th percentile on the LSAT. The reason applicants in these categories should increase the number of applications is because admission of members of minority groups is often idiosyncratic and not measured against the standard applicant pool. These students should risk a few more applications to schools that seem out of their range.

GEOGRAPHIC CONSIDERATIONS

There is a slight admissions edge given to candidates who live farther away from the school to which they applied. Schools seek to formulate a diverse student body that includes representation of as many states as possible. Since most law schools receive the majority of their applications from relatively nearby, candidates from across the country might get a slight break in admissions decisions. This favoring may be the subconscious desire on the part of the evaluator to introduce some degree of novelty in the class, or may even specifically be an item for consideration. Also, you should realize that it is usually more difficult to gain admission to your undergraduate alma mater, simply because the law school receives a very large number of applicants from the "home" school. In addition, a lot of students are under the misconception that they will have to practice law near where they attended law school. After graduating from an ABA-accredited school, you may take the bar in any jurisdiction in the United States. And rarely do people attending law school in the jurisdiction to which you wish to move have any decided advantage in passing the bar. So do not think, for example, that you must go to law school in Texas in order to practice in Texas.

ELECTRONIC APPLICATIONS

As would be expected, more and more schools are allowing candidates to submit applications electronically over the Internet. Obviously, there is no admissions advantage to electronically submitted applications, and until the entire applications process becomes electronically integrated, letters of recommendation and other matter to be appended to the application may be submitted via file attachment, document scanner, or other electronic means. The traditional paper method, in fact, may be preferable because it allows the student to have everything together in one place to be submitted. It is easier to keep track of what is missing from a packet and what further actions need to be taken. If you are applying both online and through the traditional method, you will just have more items to keep track of. You will already have a lot to follow anyway, making sure your letters of recommendation are turned in, your personal statement is included, your LSAT score is requested for each school from the LSDAS, and so forth. Filing with some schools online simply adds another layer—and an avoidable layer—of complexity.

Second, there is a different mind-set when filling out paper forms than that used when submitting information via a computer. There is a penumbra of informality, spontaneity, fuzzy edges, however one wishes to put it, when communicating over the Internet. This can be readily seen in the difference in grammar and syntax found on the Internet when compared to typewriting. You may not be as alert to mistakes, colloquialisms, idiosyncratic phrasing, and syntactical errors when submitting an electronic application as when you must think about answers before committing them to paper.

The LSAC makes and sells a CD-ROM containing applications for all member schools. Core data, such as name and address, need be filled in only once, so you can print your applications and submit them without going through all of the trouble associated with typing up individual applications. This information is also available on their Web site at http://www.lsac.org.

DEAN CERTIFICATION FORMS

Some law schools still require that you have the dean of your school at your undergraduate institution fill out a certification form. This sometimes confuses students, since they often do not know the dean of their school or what a dean even does. Generally, the forms are used to make sure that the student is formally held in good character or integrity by the student's undergraduate college and institution. Disciplinary action for cheating and violation of laws are the sorts of things that the form is meant to elicit from the applicant's dean's office. Just take the form to the dean of your school—ask any professor in your department where that is—and he or she will know what to do with it.

THINGS TO CONSIDER: GENDER, ETHNICITY, AND EXPERIENCE

Law schools look to diversify their classes as much as possible. The most common law student tends to be about 23 years old, white, and male. Many law students have never had full-time jobs, and the first such job they will have will be as a lawyer. Consequently, law schools usually give slightly favorable admission breaks to students who are members of minority groups with favored admission status, nontraditional students, and applicants who have interesting experiences or backgrounds. If you fall into one of these categories, your chances for admission at schools outside the range of your numbers increase, but such decisions become more idiosyncratic. In essence, if you have reasonable numbers you are no longer competing against the entire applicant pool for a school. You may be competing against other members of minority groups or nontraditional students. So, if you are a member of a minority group, a nontraditional student, or someone with unusual life experiences, shoot higher than you normally would.

Applicants who are members of minority groups ought not feel any guilt that they will be trading on their ethnicity to gain admission to law school. Perhaps your first lesson as an attorney is that you use whatever weapons you have available to win your case. Law schools give preferences to veterans, women, nontraditional students, single mothers, and a host of other "classes" of applicants. They do not do this because they are all run by bleeding hearts—they do this because it is the best thing for the school. Think about it. In three years a law school has to take a group of (mostly) young people, who often have never had a full-time job, and prepare them to take responsibility for the property, affairs, and sometimes the lives, of their clients. One aid in this process is to develop a diverse class with students of varying backgrounds and experiences. Preferences in admission are designed to help all law students mature and learn together.

Note that the registration form for the LSAT and LSDAS includes an ethnic identity section. This section contains categories for Hispanic and Chicano applicants. Make sure that you indicate the proper category; do not simply glance and see Hispanic and check it. Also, make sure that you sign up for the Candidate Referral Service (CRS) for ABA-accredited law schools (question 12), but do not bother to sign up for the Candidate Referral Service for non-ABA–approved law schools. The CRS allows schools to access a database looking for specific sorts of potential law applicants. Often as a result of these searches, a student will receive an application from an institution that he or she had not thought of applying to. Further, these invitations to apply often come with an application fee waiver.

Note further that the Fifth Circuit Court of Appeals held in Hopwood v. Texas that being a member of a minority group may not be used as a criterion in admitting students to law school. This decision is law for the states of Texas, Louisiana, and Mississippi.

HOW LAW SCHOOLS EVALUATE APPLICATIONS

Obviously the two most important items in your application are your undergraduate GPA and your LSAT score. All law schools have devised their own unique formula to give varying amounts of weight to these two items. These indexes are calculated by the LSDAS and are available upon demand. Initially, the index score of an applicant is the most crucial item in the application. Based on the index number, many schools will have a score at which the applicant is presumptively admitted and, conversely, a score at which the applicant is presumptively rejected. Except for very unusual situations, it is difficult to get out of the automatic rejection pile. The presumptive admit numbers usually do not come anywhere near the majority of admissions offers to be made. Most of the decisions of admission are made by considering further information in applications. Difficulty of course work, undergraduate institution attended loads taken, full-time work during school, letters of recommendation, life experience, charitable work, and other items may affect decisions. Some evaluators go through each application in depth, while others stick mainly with the numbers.

Usually a file is looked at by a number of evaluators, and a sort of collective "grade" oftentimes determines whether or not to admit a candidate. Recently, some law schools have been moving back to the practice of granting interviews to applicants. For a period of years, few schools were willing to interview applicants. Now, however, schools such as University of Texas School of Law and Texas Tech School of Law are interviewing candidates. The primary reason these two schools moved to an interview method is the Fifth Circuit Court of Appeals decision forbidding the use of ethnic information in the admissions decisions of candidates to school programs. By moving to interviews, these institutions hope to be able to develop information leading to admissions of ethnically diverse candidates without violating the rule in Hopwood.

However, schools outside of the Fifth Circuit that are not governed by Hopwood are also revisiting the interview as an admissions tool. If you are invited to interview at a school that you are very interested in, go on the interview. If you are broke and cannot pay for a trip, do not be bashful; tell the school you have no money to make a trip at the moment but that you would be willing to accept all help in this regard. The school will probably say there is no money available, but at least it knows that you declined the interview for financial reasons rather than for holding a negative opinion of the school. And, you never know, the school might come through with money for the trip. Be aware, though, that an interview is a double-edged sword. It can just as easily assure rejection as can advance the possibility of admission. Make sure you are up on your interview skills and dress appropriately. Your career counseling office will be able to help you in these matters.

LAW SCHOOL RESPONSES TO APPLICATIONS

WHICH OFFER TO ACCEPT

Deciding which offer of admission to accept is a relatively straightforward proposition, so long as you keep a few things in mind. One thing to remember is that you are not shopping for a piece of art. You don't "buy" what you like or what "feels good" to you. You select a law school based on practical considerations. These considerations include the reputation of the school, its success at placing graduates, starting salary of graduates, its effective area of placement, and, if relevant, cost of attendance.

Let us begin by dividing law schools up into three classes: national, regional, and localized institutions. National institutions are law schools that have a reputation that allows their graduates to be competitive for employment almost anywhere in the United States. National institutions are usually, though not exclusively, the top twenty or thirty law schools in rankings lists.

Regional institutions are schools that have strong reputations within some relatively large but limited geographic area. Regional schools generally enjoy strong hiring patterns in their areas, but the further away one gets from these schools the weaker one's placement ability becomes as one encroaches on territory occupied by neighbor regional institutions.

Localized institutions are schools that have a fairly limited placement area. Sometimes these schools can be dramatically hemmed in by more highly ranked schools nearby. Law schools with lesser reputations within 250 miles of a dozen or more "national" law schools may be severely limited in where they can place their graduates.

There is no such thing as a bad ABA-approved law school. They are all high-quality institutions, and there will be little difference between the training at Yale and at Nebraska. However, perhaps unfairly, certain things will hinge on where you attend law school.

Offers from National Schools

If you are lucky enough to have numbers that bring offers of admission from top-thirty institutions, your decision is, or should be, fairly easy: you simply accept admission at the law school that can demonstrate the greatest success in placing its graduates, as measured by high starting salaries, employment in large and prestigious law firms or major corporations, and location of employed graduates in the country's major urban centers. This rule is fairly hard and

fast, but there are a couple of situations that might justify a deviation. Say you are accepted at the University of Texas at Austin and Cornell University, but you are a Texas resident. Even though Cornell can demonstrate a superior track record of placements based on your criteria, Texas has a much better placement record than the average law school. Also, Texas is well regarded by judges and lawyers, and Cornell's record is not significantly better than that of Texas to justify the difference in the cost of tuition. Here you must make your decision based on likelihoods. The likelihood of getting a job offer as a graduate of Texas, which is near or matches a job offer you would get coming out of Cornell, is high enough to warrant sacrificing the slight difference in the rankings between the universities.

For some, the more interesting question might arise when they have been accepted by Texas and, say, Columbia. Generally, one should select Columbia. There may be a $50,000 (or more) difference in educational expenses, but there is a strong likelihood that if you attend Columbia, this difference will quickly be made up by a higher starting salary or by a greater marketability that lets you practice law wherever you want. Do not be contrary just to be contrary. If you are given the opportunity to attend a school whose graduates' beginning salaries are among the top in the country but you would prefer to attend another school that has considerably lower salaries, think about the long-term results of your education first. Although money may not be everything, you are going to be investing a large amount of money, time, and effort in your education, and you will want to be as successful as possible in your new career.

Offers from Regional Schools

If you don't get any offers from national schools, then your best bet is to attend a regional school with a strong placement record and bar passage rate. If you can do it, visit your two best options and try to get a feel for the area and the way the law school operates. Talk to law students and ask the placement office for detailed information on bar passage rates, starting salaries, percent placed in law-related positions within six months of graduation, and

---

William Weaver, J.D., Ph.D., Department of Political Science, University of Texas at El Paso

the number and kind of employers who come to campus to interview students. Just because you go to a regional school does not mean that you cannot get a job outside of the school's region; it just means that the odds are more strongly against it as compared to national institutions. But if you are editor of the law review, no matter where you go to school, you will have opportunities all over the United States. So even if you go to a regional school, superior performance can make you sell like a graduate from a national institution.

Offers from Local Institutions

"Local" schools are those that have a very limited placement area for graduates. If you don't have offers from national or regional schools, then where you choose to go to law school becomes even more important than for the person trying to select from regional institutions. As with the regional choice, visit your most attractive offers, ask questions of students, and obtain the information described above. Again, just because you go to a local institution does not mean that you cannot get a job anywhere in the country practicing law—it simply means you must work harder at such a prospect. And as mentioned previously for regional schools, superior performance can make up for a lot of the differences in marketability between the three divisions.

ACCEPTANCE, REJECTION, AND THE WAITING LIST

Law schools may do one of several things with your application. The two most obvious are that they may either reject you or make you an offer of admission. But law schools may also place you on a waiting list. Waiting lists are strange and obscure items that vary in length and purpose from school to school. Some schools have relatively short waiting lists that yield a high percentage of ultimate offers of admission, while others are tantamount to rejection. If you find yourself on the waiting list of a school you are really interested in attending, you must go on as if you had been rejected by the school. It would be unwise to place any reliance on your position on the waiting list. If you do make it into the school from the waiting list, be prepared to accept the offer and to move quickly. You may not be notified that you are admitted until as late as the first day of class. Though this rarely occurs, the law school must make provisions for acceptees that cancel at the last minute.

POSITION DEPOSITS

Once you receive an acceptance from a law school, the school will ask you to send a specified amount of money to reserve your seat in the entering class—usually a couple of hundred dollars. By sending a deposit, you are not promising to attend the law school. The deposit only reserves your right to attend the school and gives the law school an indication of how serious you might be about attending. These deposits are almost never refundable, but you should not think of them as a commitment to attend a particular school. When you receive your first acceptance, and if you have received no more acceptances from schools you deem more attractive by the time the deadline for deposit comes for the first school, make sure to send in the deposit. As other acceptances arrive, make sure that the deadline for the most attractive school among the acceptances does not pass without submission of a deposit. In the end you may lose some money on deposits, but it is better than being boxed out with no law school to attend in the fall.

WHAT TO DO BEFORE LAW SCHOOL BEGINS

Before beginning law school there are a number of things you can do to make your first semester easier. Do not arrive in town the day before classes or orientations are scheduled to begin. Try to arrive the last week in July or the first week in August to nail down your living quarters. If you have roommates, live with other law students—at least they will understand what you are going through. Avoid living with people who party or talk a lot. Living with nonlaw graduate students is OK, but by no means optimal. If you have the money, live by yourself the first year—the closer to school the better.

Certain things that did not annoy you before will begin to bug you in law school. One of those things is commute time and trying to find a parking space. Your time is so impacted in law school that the frittering away of minutes driving back and forth and looking for a spot to park can cause upset way out of proportion to the inconvenience. Become familiar with the arrangement of the law school. Become especially familiar with the library. Ask for a guide to the location of commonly used resources, and ask about any tours or orientations the library staff might give. Summer is a good time to ask library staff for "special" help. Maintain a good relationship with library staff members—they can be enormously helpful. Most students treat library staff members as their servants and rarely even know their names. Try to be someone who stands out to the staff members in a positive way—they are a tremendous resource that goes largely untapped. Also, most head librarians at law schools are lawyers as well as professional librarians, and they usually like to help students with interesting research problems.

Figure out where and when you will do your weekly shopping in advance. Do not do your shopping during popular shopping hours—as with commuting and other time-wasting endeavors you will just get aggravated. Shop late at night or early in the morning. Make a detailed weekly schedule for everything you do. This includes exercise, movies, study time (allot four hours per day minimum), class note entry, TV, etc. Try to schedule as much homework time as possible during breaks between classes during the day. Too many students talk the days away while they could be freeing up their evenings by studying for next day's assignments at school. Schedule at least one hour for lunch, and try to always have lunch with classmates.

Decide early on who the people are in your class that you really like and want to spend time with. As for the rest, even the ones that you sort of like, don't commit any time to them. If you are already at a function you budgeted time for, such as a class party, by all means be gregarious. But don't schedule your leisure time activities with people you don't really want to be with. Time is too short in law school.

Have a fund of several thousand dollars to see you through the first few months of school. Financial aid disbursements are often slow in coming. If you do not have cash, try to arrange something with relatives or apply for credit cards or a line of credit with a bank.

Try not to fall in love while you are in law school. If you do you can kiss your schedule and orderly life goodbye. Alas, if you must fall in love, try to make sure you fall in love with another law student—at least that way you can study together.

William Weaver, J.D., Ph.D., Department of Political Science, University of Texas at El Paso

WHAT IS FIRST-YEAR LAW SCHOOL LIKE?

First-year law school is a disorienting experience, and it is meant to be that way. In law school, you don't so much learn law as you learn to speak and think like a lawyer—you learn the language of law. The type of logic and thinking that serves lawyers well is often very different from the patterns of thought students have acquired in their previous schooling. So, first-year law school often resembles and feels more like boot camp than a purely intellectual endeavor. This analogy is apt in that law professors try to break down the presuppositions and pretensions of students and then build up the entire class in a singular understanding of a legal subject or area. The important thing to remember is that pretty much everyone feels the same way as you do—lost, somewhat depressed, a bit frightened, and wondering how they could ever have wanted to go to law school in the first place.

Law school is mostly about solving problems through the application of logic. Often, there is no "right" answer to a particular problem; there may be many satisfactory solutions or no satisfactory solutions. If you like playing with problems, often seemingly intractable problems, then you will be deluged to your heart's content in law school. If you don't like to play with such problems, or you find them hopelessly boring or trivial, you may want to talk to a prelaw adviser and dig a bit deeper into what exactly transpires in law school.

The first few weeks of law school are anxiety ridden. It is an uncomfortable time, but it can be made easier if you understand what is going to happen to you in that first semester. Most schools have orientations for new students, but there seems to be mixed reviews about whether these orientations do much good or merely increase anxiety. As with everything else, it depends on how it is done and who is doing it. So you should have a handle on what it is you will be doing and facing before you begin law school. You should find out as much as you can about how the school does things. You might also read some sources on law school education that can put you in the "proper" frame of mind. Two good sources are Scott Turow's *One L* and Karl Llewellyn's classic, *Bramble Bush*. First-semester first-year courses usually meet four times a week for an hour each time. Usually, these first-semester courses are torts, contracts, civil procedure, and criminal law or property. Along with these courses you will be required to take legal writing, a course that meets only a couple of hours a week, but is extremely valuable. Pay close attention to what your legal writing instructors say and, even though such courses are often pass-fail, put in as much effort as possible on the legal writing assignments. Researching is much of a lawyer's stock in trade, so make sure you understand how to use all of the tools you will be exposed to in legal writing.

Law school classes do not begin like undergraduate classes. There is no "slow start" or "class introduction," at least not usually. You will have assigned reading for the first day of class, and the instructor simply will come in and without further pause start grilling various students about the day's reading. In many law schools there is a bulletin board where first-day assignments are posted. Make sure you get off to a good start—do your reading. However, you will not have yet learned how to "read" a case, so you can expect to be somewhat lost and intimidated in class. Expect that several times at the beginning of your first year you will be asking yourself, "Is the instructor talking about the same case that I read last night?" Often it seems as if what you are supposed to get out of a case and what you do get out of a case are hopelessly irreconcilable. After a few weeks, though, you begin to get the hang of reading cases, and things start coming into focus. The important thing is not to panic or come to the conclusion that you just can't make it. You can and will make it.

Students occasionally ask if they should join a study group in their first year of law school. Yes, but do not rely on the group to do any of your work. It's okay to get involved in a group outline (a detailed digest of a course's material and concepts used to prepare for the final exam—some outlines can be quite lengthy) of your courses, but make sure that you do your own outline from your own notes, using the group outline to fill in any gaps and holes in your personal outline. You should be rigorous in your schedule, in that you have a reserved time for entering your class notes into your class outline. If you don't already have one, you should purchase a computer prior to law school. Spend the hour or so it will take each day to enter that day's notes into your personal outlines. Students sometimes ask if they should purchase any commercial outlines for first-year courses. Again, yes, but

William Weaver, J.D., Ph.D., Department of Political Science, University of Texas at El Paso

they should be used only to fill in holes in your personal outlines or to clear up areas of confusion. Buy the expansive, detailed outlines, not the cut-rate jobs. Remember, though, the emphases of your course will differ greatly from what is in the commercial outline since your instructor will tailor the course around his or her interests. There is no substitute for a good personal outline. Usually you will make the best grades in the courses in which you invest the time and effort to make a detailed, extensive outline from your course notes.

Remember to set aside time in your schedule for fun and relaxation. Schedule a movie for Saturday night or an evening walk along a river during the week. Finally, realize that your family might find you insufferable during the holiday season after your first semester. Law will have become your life, but it will not have become the life of your relatives. As hard as it might be, try to avoid talking about law while you are home on vacation.

WHAT'S A TORT AND OTHER THINGS THAT MAKE LAW SCHOOL A DIFFERENT ANIMAL

Heading into your first year of law school, you've probably heard enough scary stories to make you realize that you're in for some heavy-duty pressure. Tips like "You don't know stress until you're briefing cases using nineteenth century trial notes" and "You haven't a clue what they're talking about" throw fuel on the fires of anxiety.

Depending on which law school you attend, the myths about the first year may or may not apply. Though law school is unlike most other educational experiences you've had in the past or will have in the future, what makes it different often goes unexplained.

A DIFFERENT STRUCTURE

In contrast to other graduate degrees, the three-year structure of law school alone makes it unique, says Yale Law School's Associate Dean Toni Davis, who completed her master's in law at Yale. It takes less time than many other graduate studies, which can take from five to six years, thus the curriculum is condensed. It's also more professionally oriented, which means students must make more immediate decisions about a career path, beginning with the choice of summer employment or internship settings between each year of law school.

A DIFFERENT STUDENT BODY

Adding to the list of differences, Dean David Cohen from Pace University School of Law mentions that fellow students, with whom you'll be in intense contact for three years, come from a multitude of disciplines, experiences, and age levels. For younger students, who may have only been out of college for one or two years or who come to law school directly from college, being thrown in with older people who have been in the workplace for years can be unsettling. Turn the tables and the older students with established careers may be nervous about the prospect of studying for exams and writing papers again.

However, the diversity makes for a rich learning environment. Speaking as a second-year Stanford University law student (called 2Ls for short), John Malik characterizes his fellow students as anything but dull, quiet, or subdued. "Classes are comprised of phenomenally interesting personalities," he says.

A DIFFERENT LEARNING PROCESS

Whether or not they've been out of the studying loop for a while, incoming students soon encounter analytical thinking—the rigorous level of this kind of thinking is unfamiliar to most new students. Marshall S. Shapo, a professor at Northwestern University School of Law and co-author of the book, *Law School Without Fear,* explains that along with new subject matter, law students must quickly develop the skill to look at situations most students have never been in, conceptualize them, and derive solutions. Unlike most college courses, there's often no single right answer. The best exam question, according to Shapo, is one that sits right between two good arguments. In a typical law school, the first semester is fourteen weeks long, so students must hop in the saddle and start riding right away, says Shapo.

A DIFFERENT LANGUAGE

But before students can saddle up and canter off into the sunset once they've got the system figured out, they must first learn the peculiar language of law. "You think you know what certain phrases mean, but they mean something else," says Amber Garza, who just completed her first year at Stanford's law school. You could well be reading a judgment written in 1898 for other lawyers of that era and have to make sense of it, points out Cohen.

Janet Bolin, Assistant Dean for Admissions and Financial Aid at Washington University in St. Louis School of Law, notes that it's not so much the volume of reading, but the terminology that is hard to comprehend. "You might have thirty pages of reading, which doesn't sound like much, but the complexity of the cases makes it difficult," she says.

A DIFFERENT WAY OF TEACHING

In addition to grasping unfamiliar concepts in what amounts to a foreign language, students have to deal with the Socratic teaching method that not many know about other than as a footnote in a history book. In a lot of law schools the Socratic method—or variations of it—is alive and well and full of snares to catch the unprepared. Comments Angela D'Agostino, Assistant Dean and Director of Admissions at Pace's law school, professors don't give answers but ask questions that force students to analyze the material and devise the answer themselves. Explains Assistant Dean of Admissions Shelli Soto from the University of Texas at Austin School of Law, this method of teaching leads students to investigate options as a lawyer would—if *this,* then *this.*

"Professors won't be doing most of the talking. It will be the students talking," says Tom Noble, a 2L at Northwestern. Class discussion is where learning takes place, and while students hash out arguments, the professor may or may not point out the best paths for an argument to follow. Shapo elaborates that it's not that there are no correct answers, but law school pushes the mental envelope by requiring students to formulate the most sensible answer, which broadens them in valuable ways.

The Socratic method isn't cut in marble but can be altered according to a professor's inclination. For instance, Garza says Stanford's law professors mostly use a variation of the Socratic method called the panel system, in which students know ahead of time when they will be called on. However, Malik recalls classes at Stanford in which students didn't know what to expect. When called upon, they could choose to pass for that day, says Malik, but he advises against it. Some professors were prone to make mental notes about who spoke up and who didn't and in some cases pursued reluctant students with greater vigor the next day. He has mixed sentiments about the Socratic method. According to him, it works if professors have a good sense of their students. It doesn't work if the professor asks questions that first-year (1L) students can't answer, is condescending, or is on stage to showcase his or her wit.

A DIFFERENT WAY OF RELATING TO PROFESSORS

While students jump through intellectual hoops for professors in class, outside of class they might have little contact with their professors. Unlike other graduate departments, where the ratio of teachers to students can be high, in some law schools chances are that students will not be able to spend a lot of time with professors. At least until the second year, the ability to work closely with faculty members is greatly diminished, says Frank Newton, Dean of the Texas Tech University School of Law.

Jeff Kitner, a 2L at the University of Texas at Austin, notes that the onus on forming relationships with professors is on the student. Though professors have office hours and encourage questions outside of class, the large number of students makes it hard to establish relationships.

Yet taking the time to buck the long lines that often form outside a professor's door can be worthwhile in many ways. Though Garza says she's never had to wait long to talk to Stanford professors, she advises first-year students to talk with professors outside of class and not get so caught up in studying. Getting to know professors can lead to clerkship recommendations and teaching assistantships.

A DIFFERENT WAY OF STUDYING

Other than anticipating having to work harder, Kitner entered law school thinking it wouldn't be that much different than college. He found a night-and-day transition when it came to studying. The amount of hours one puts in is not the key. You have to learn how to study effectively, he says. Garza puts it more bluntly. "Throw any skills you picked up in a lifetime of learning out the window," she warns. Instead of reading material, extracting the main ideas, and memorizing them, professors want you to examine all the ideas and come down strongly with your own opinion of the right answer. Loading up on facts and dates won't necessarily help. Students have to understand the concepts and underlying thought processes.

Quality not quantity definitely applies to law school. From Northwestern, 2L Jennifer Carney notes that unless you are extraordinarily brilliant, you have to work hard, but working hard won't guarantee a top class ranking. At first she would read a case and have no idea what she was looking for or even if she was proceeding in the right direction, until she became fluent in legal reasoning.

Bolin suggests that students often mistakenly equate the amount of time spent studying with future success on exams. While acknowledging that law is a time-driven profession based on billable hours, Bolin comments that the most successful students quickly learn the difference between simply reading volumes and studying smart. Newton, who also has seen law students drag in bleary eyed from hours pouring over case studies, says it's easy to get lost in the forest of details instead of seeing the larger themes that professors are really going for. "We're more concerned that you learn the process and what arguments count so you can use them on behalf of your clients, because the rules change," he states.

A DIFFERENT WAY TO SCOPE OUT WHAT PROFESSORS WANT

Coupled with learning how to study all over again, students will find that each professor has his or her own unique angle on teaching. Study guides or commercial outlines aren't all that helpful, warns Malik. He illustrates this by asking what angle will a criminal law instructor take in his classes after forty years of work in lower Los Angeles? But if study guides aren't much help, 2L students are, advises Tracey Holmes, a 2L at the University of Minnesota. She suggests that students pick upperclassmates' brains about how a professor teaches and what he or she is looking for. Look at old exams and case outlines. Garza goes one step further by suggesting that students research articles written by their professors to analyze their reasoning.

A DIFFERENT WAY TO RELATE TO FELLOW STUDENTS

Despite the legendary competition among law students, study groups are one common antidote to first-year jitters. Malik speculates that non-law graduate students usually work independently and lead a "more monastic existence." On the other hand, he feels that law students who study in total seclusion miss out. Soto agrees that a big part of learning in law school is interacting with other students, many of whom become lifelong friends. There will always be those competitive types who wall themselves off and won't share information, but she observes that a few months into the first semester, students find their niche of people with whom they feel comfortable. Yet she says that some students might be more productive studying alone, especially around exam time, without "ten others going crazy around you."

Noble, who found study groups to be very helpful, says that tossing opinions around with other classmates in the library, in restaurants, and on campus is where a lot of learning takes place and ideas begin to jell. Malik found that the same synergy existed because of articulate and forceful arguments from fellow study group members. "Law school collects personalities who are quite capable of furnishing a persuasive answer at the expense of accuracy," he wryly states.

Explaining a bit more about why law school is so different, Shapo says, "One of the great virtues of a legal education is that it teaches you to be critical. That is actually what you ought to get out of any graduate education, whether it's in math or poetry. Law school has just historically been very good at requiring students to test the logic of someone else's position, including their own."

TAMING THE 1L BEAST WITH 2L TIPS

Perhaps one of the most frustrating aspects of being a first-year law student (1L) is that when the first panic attack hits in the first few months, everyone—from second and third-year students (2L and 3L) to professors to parents and friends—will tell you to not be anxious, you *will* make it to the second year.

Meanwhile, as you tackle your first case and realize you must comprehend totally unfathomable text, the dastardly voice of doubt inside your head will be telling you just the opposite. Thoughts such as "I was a success at what I did before, why do I feel like such a failure now?" run rampant. As 2L Mushtaq Kapasi can attest, those negative thoughts came through when he began law school at Yale. Now, having successfully passed those dreaded exams, he reflects that, yes, he shouldn't have been so dubious about his abilities—nor should other incoming law students.

With hindsight comes confidence. It seems as though the lack of certainty that incoming 1Ls have about this wild beast called law school prevails over any encouragement they get. The first year of law school is an experience one just has to get through. So while incoming students probably won't initially heed any assurances from others that they will succeed, they might find some "insider" tips on other facets of the first year, such as study habits and preparing for exams, helpful.

THERE IS LIFE OUTSIDE OF LAW SCHOOL

You will be told to relax once in a while. Do it.

Amber Garza, a 2L at Stanford, made the startling discovery that those students who devoted all their time to studying with no breaks weren't at the top of the class. It was odd to her that time spent studying didn't equal high rankings. She concludes that success depends on how well students can express themselves, on their understanding of the material, and on their creativity.

You're in this for the long haul, cautions Dean Frank Newton at Texas Tech University School of Law. It's easy for students to get off balance because they concentrate on studying to the exclusion of anything else. Over extended periods of time, that single-mindedness does more harm than good. "At the beginning of the first year, they think they'll fall behind the competition if they take an hour to work out," which is short-term thinking, says Newton.

Jennifer Carney, a 2L at Northwestern, made that mistake. She didn't leave campus for six weeks and studied every weekend. In retrospect, she advises new students to give themselves a few hours to do something fun. "You have time," she says. "If I'd been emotionally confident about what I was doing, I'd have relaxed." Though she learned an immense amount of material, it was a grueling experience that wasn't necessary.

At the University of Texas at Austin School of Law, Assistant Dean of Admissions Shelli Soto has seen many 1Ls completely change lifestyles the minute they enter law school and cease activities they used to enjoy. If you played basketball a few times a week or were into gourmet cooking, she recommends that you continue these activities.

Determine whether you have the sniper or shotgun approach to studying.

According to John Malik, a 2L at Stanford, much of the learning that takes place in law school revolves around each professor's "experience, political inclinations, world views, and social agendas." That's what made his classes interesting and engaging. He counsels that once students discern what points of law each professor considers significant, they are ahead when preparing for exams, which he calls the sniper approach. Shotgun students pick up every word uttered by the professor and every aspect of the course material. The sniper critically analyzes what each instructor is emphasizing in order to intuit the professor's "take" on any given subject and anticipates what will be on the exam. "It can be done either way," says Malik. "I know people who cram everything in, and it works for them." He says he's a sniper.

BRIEFS AND OUTLINES

Strategize how you'll deal with briefing and outlining cases.

New law students must make some decisions about the best way to brief cases, which is breaking down a case to its essential components. Some find that meticulously outlining each case is effective. Others, like Carney, wrote notes about the key issues in the margins of old outlined cases so she was not starting from scratch. Tracey Holmes, a 2L at University of Minnesota, urges students to get the outlines from each of their professors and not to rely on outlines from other professors, as each has a unique focus.

Malik uses his sniper approach in briefing cases, too, by going for the big picture rather than the minutiae. "The tendency for 1Ls is to advocate briefing cases as a panacea for every first year's problem," he says. They scrutinize the circumstances of each case rather than the underlying principles. He feels that most of the time what's in the case is not as important as the instructor's critical approach to the case. "You can't brief that," he comments. "You'll get that from class notes and office visits."

EXAMS

Professors look for your thinking process.

Much of 1L stress strikes as students prepare for exams. Those who got good grades as undergraduates by relying on all-night cram sessions and short-term memory recall are in for a rude awakening. "You have to understand the material, not just regurgitate it," reports Tom Noble, a 2L at Northwestern. Students must glean what the law is and apply what they've learned over a semester to the exam question rather than giving a recitation of facts.

Don't base your success or failure only on the exam.

While top class rankings lead to the first summer job, which leads to the second summer job, which leads to a permanent offer and clerkships, the exam is not the be-all and end-all of the first year. Garza noted that friends who didn't do as well as they'd hoped at the end of their first year often recovered ground later. Maybe they didn't get into the firm they wanted or hit the high salaries, but they were able to make up for it in the second year.

"Who you are is not based on grades," elaborates Carney. Law school can be a humbling experience for students who are not used to getting anything lower than As. And with most exams graded on a curve, some will get Bs. It's easier to cope with that possibility if you're not just focusing on grades.

SUPPORT SYSTEMS

Take advantage of the help and encouragement that will be available.

Realizing that first-year law school is harrowing for even the most brilliant student, law schools have abundant sources of advice and mentoring. For example, Soto points to a University of Texas at Austin student organization of current students who volunteer to talk to entering students about what law school is like and answer their questions, which can range from "Do people really cry?" to "Do you have to study all the time?" Soto has observed how the "urban law school legends" get passed around so that incoming students often mix myth with reality. Most law schools have mentoring groups or other support systems in place.

YOUR FUTURE AS A LAWYER

Be open to learning unfamiliar legal subjects and unexpected career possibilities.

Law is a large area of study, so explore career options you may not have considered, says Yale Law School Assistant Dean Toni Davis. Shop courses you wouldn't necessarily consider and listen in on class sessions to gauge if they pique your interest. Talk to other students about courses they're taking. Kapasi pursued legal journalism for his first summer job and found it fascinating and fun. As a result of going off the beaten path, he says he won't have a top Wall Street position, but he'll have a decent job that will give him a lot of satisfaction.

Malik notes that it's entirely possible for law students to go through three years of school and end up in a private firm in some location where they don't want to be. He cites the rigidity and highly mechanical structure of law school and the process that determines where students go for summer jobs as the reason one's future can take on a momentum of its own. Considering alternatives outside the box during the first year can lead to exciting possibilities.

Once in a while, step off the treadmill and give yourself a well-deserved pat on the back.

In the fast-paced and competitive environment of law school, it's easy to keep your eyes trained on final exams. Garza reminds students that even under the extreme pressure to keep ahead of the pack, they should step aside and look back at what they've accomplished so far. Accept the fact that you probably will not be at the very pinnacle of your class. But you will succeed. You will get a job. And you will have learned a lot.

PREPARING FOR THE UNPREPARABLE

One would think that Jeff Kitner, a second-year law student (2L) at the University of Texas at Austin, would have been amply prepared to begin his first year. His father is a lawyer and had clued him in on what to expect. The same goes for Tom Noble, a 2L at Northwestern, and Tracey Holmes, a 2L at the University of Minnesota. Both had worked in law firms and assumed their legal backgrounds would give them an advantage.

However, the unique reality of law school clobbered them, as forcefully as it did students who had no legal knowledge at all, such as Mushtaq Kapasi. Before entering law school, he had majored in math and philosophy and had worked in management consulting, along with stints in journalism and theater.

"I don't know if you can really anticipate what you're getting into," says Kitner. People warned him it would be the most difficult year of his life. Difficult it was, Kitner admits, but he says there is no way to fully comprehend what is in store for you.

In light of this gloomy prediction, is it really true that there is nothing incoming law students can do to prepare? "You can't duplicate being around that many talented people and the volume of work that exists," says Dean Frank Newton at Texas Tech University School of Law. "How do you do that until you do it?" he questions. Go to a movie and have some fun, he suggests.

Along those lines, Amber Garza, a 2L at Stanford, had the right idea. She watched the movie *Paper Chase* and read novels about lawyers. She also talked to people as she shopped around for law schools. Then, when she had settled on Stanford and was admitted, she made an effort to become familiar with the school and its environs ahead of time. Holmes, too, found it helpful to talk to law school alumni whose names she acquired from admissions. Like soldiers who have survived a battle, practicing attorneys enjoy rehashing the rigors of their first year.

Kapasi wished he had had a little more knowledge of law than cocktail party conversation. He says he should have talked to people already in law school because the professors and students in his beginning classes at Yale assumed he knew the basics. It took a lot of work for him to get up to speed. He did catch up, but for a while he felt as though he was in over his head.

Luckily, law schools are becoming much more compassionate about the hurdles incoming law students must overcome, says Janet Bolin, Assistant Dean for Admissions and Financial Aid at Washington University in St. Louis School of Law. They offer an increasing number of programs for students before the regular semester begins. Incoming first-year law students (1Ls) can become somewhat familiar with briefing and outlining cases and taking notes and exams. Angela D'Agostino, Assistant Dean and Director of Admissions at Pace University School of Law, says the summer programs they have instituted for law students have been well-received.

Bolin recommends that students read books to get a handle on the terminology, which will save them time once the first semester starts. D'Agostino notes that Pace provides a suggested summer reading list. Students entering other schools without established reading lists can ask faculty members and people in admissions offices to suggest materials that will give them a head start.

The undergraduate background students come from can make a difference in how quickly they will grasp legal concepts. Jennifer Carney, a 2L at Northwestern, notes that humanities majors are accustomed to reading text, whereas science and math majors may want to read novels to get into the mode of absorbing written information.

The right mental attitude helps, too, especially if it provides for "the possibility that law school won't be what you thought it would be," remarks John Malik, a 2L at Stanford.

AH YES, MY FIRST YEAR OF LAW SCHOOL . . .

Advice From Lawyers About Law Schools and Your Career Options

Talk to any lawyer and you'll find a former law student with plenty to say—with good reason. To begin with, law school is not an easy academic road to take. Picking the right law school can mean juggling the concerns of reputation, accessibility, and lifestyle, not to mention debt. There are plenty of reasons why people considering a law degree should take some time to figure out what attracts them to the law.

SO, WHAT'S SO HARD ABOUT THE FIRST YEAR?

"For the most part," says William Fay, who left an engineering career to attend Arizona State University's College of Law, "there's a big mystique about law school. Most students go into it not really knowing what they're getting into." What he found was that law school was not all that difficult for him. The hard part was doing well.

GRADES, GRADES, GRADES

When getting his first and second summer jobs and ensuing employment, Jeffrey Hart, a graduate of Duke University's law school and a current employee of Robinson, Bradshaw and Hinson in Charlotte, North Carolina, found his first year to be the yardstick by which he was measured. "First-year grades mean everything," he says, describing how law firms will recruit law students during the spring semester based on their grades in order to lure them to summer jobs after graduation.

The first year is to law school what compound interest is to investing, observes Lance Witcher, who practices law at Blackwell Sanders Peper Martin in St. Louis, Missouri. The more you study or save early on, the easier it will be to reach your goals. Though he had not taken college academics as seriously as he should have, he quickly realized that if he did not do so during his first year at Washington University in St. Louis School of Law, it would be an uphill battle.

YOU'RE IN ANOTHER WORLD

Entering the University of Southern California Law School, Derek Haskew experienced a similar culture shock between what he thought the study of law entailed and its reality. "People are automatically resistant to what upsets them," notes Haskew of those first trying months. He realizes now that his own resistance to the legal culture drained some of the energy he could have used to learn the immense amount of material students are expected to absorb that first year. "There's such an emphasis on learning that if you get sidetracked, you've missed something crucial." While his grades were not stellar, what he learned has served him well since then in his practice at a legal services office on the Navajo Nation in Mexican Hat, Utah.

Mark Wiedman got the same jolt of reality when he entered Yale Law. He describes his first year as "being immediately drenched in an alien universe with a new vocabulary and a fresh and bizarre prestige structure." Tim Swensen, who was making a drastic career switch from child psychologist to lawyer at Vanderbilt University, saw his first year as the discovery of a new intellectual world. He says he was "terrified" because he was a lot older than his fellow students and had much more at stake. But the stimulation of talking with bright students and faculty members soon overcame his misgivings. "I doubt that there are law schools out there that are so miserable students can't derive some enjoyment from them," he adds. He finds tremendous satisfaction in his work in commercial litigation at Blackwell Sanders Peper Martin in Kansas City, Missouri.

WHAT'S IN A NAME?

On the surface, picking a law school seems relatively easy—look at a list and get as near to the top as you can. That's not always the case, say lawyers who have been through the process. As is commonly known, the name recognition of a law school can be and often is a significant factor in obtaining future employment. Many decry this system, but concede its existence, with some prudent advice. "The name of a law school won't get you a job, but it will often get your foot in the door," remarks Hart. You'll be listened to at first, but then you have to get the job.

Class position can be almost as significant. "Where you went to law school matters for about five seconds of a thirty-minute interview," suggests Haskew. "There's more emphasis on whether you're in the top 10 percent of any class. If you are, certain kinds of employers will lay out the red carpet for you. If not, you have to carve another niche for yourself." That's exactly what he did. By going into public interest law rather than into a large private firm, Haskew won grants and prizes over some of his more academically accomplished peers.

Wiedman does not think the "obsession with pedigree" is an admirable side to the legal profession, but he grants that in law firms everyone knows where the top partners went to school. Speaking from the business world's perspective, he says that is seldom the case. In business, what you can do matters more than where you went to school. Adrienne Moss, who got her job at Patterson, Belknap, Webb and Tyler in New York City, went outside of the normal career path that is directed for the most part by school name. Nevertheless, she points out that law firms in major cities do use the applicant's school and grades to weed out interviews. Moss graduated from the University of Maryland School of Law in 1997, but did not expect to land a job in corporate law in New York right after graduating. Through happenstance and hard work, she did.

DEBT CAN PUT A CRIMP IN YOUR CAREER

When Haskew was looking at schools, he assumed that a law degree from a well-known school like the University of Southern California (USC) would be a "go anywhere, do anything" degree. While that might be true to some extent, Haskew, like many other law school applicants, failed to consider the high cost of attending a prestigious school and the consequent debt he would face upon graduating. "It limits your career options," he observes. "That's one of the delusions I had. I thought I'd have this huge high-paying job and figured, 'Oh well, debt doesn't matter because I'm going to be a lawyer.' " Because he went into public interest law, he was able to avoid some of the crushing loan paybacks due to a loan repayment assistance program for graduates who pursue public service careers, but he notes that students at other law schools without such programs might not be so fortunate.

Witcher advises students to seek the best schools they can get into and can afford. He believes that he received an excellent education at Washington University in St. Louis that also gave him a wide selection of attractive career options. Nevertheless, he mentions that colleagues of his

who went to and excelled at less recognized schools are earning the same salary and are on the same partnership track as he is.

PAYING YOUR DUES AFTER HOURS

Before they even get to the point of choosing a law school, Haskew counsels students to take a long, hard look at their motives for studying law. The training and profession demand a great deal, continues Hart. He warns that being a lawyer is not simple, and responsibilities weigh heavily. Regardless of the size of the firm, new lawyers are expected to pay their dues, which can lead to extensive hours—plus the stress and time pressures from clients to get work done quickly, efficiently, correctly, and cheaply. He reports that it is a competitive marketplace with a lot of firms and only so many clients. "If you're apprehensive about being confrontational, don't put yourself in the position where the stakes are high and you're dealing with things that are important to others since that is why they need the services of a lawyer," he explains.

"Law school can subtly change you," says Fay. While in law school, he was shocked at his own reactions to a friend's stress during finals. Instead of sympathizing with her need, he only saw the competitive advantage he had over her. "The monster was so subtle, I didn't see it coming," he confides. "Watch out, law school can burn you."

SMARTS AND MONEY DON'T EQUAL CAREER SATISFACTION

Witcher concurs that law school is not for everyone, even if you see yourself as a great problem-solver. There are other ways to solve problems, he notes, speaking of classmates who got their law degrees and discovered they didn't want to practice law. "Don't make the mistake of choosing to study law because you think you're smart and don't know what else to do," says Moss. If the subject matter of law does not interest you, you will not want to dedicate the necessary amount of time to it. Though it has not been her experience, friends of hers beginning their careers in other law firms tell her they have to work nights and weekends, and vacation plans are routinely canceled. Lawyers make a decent living, she notes, but if you lack the passion for it, it's not worth the money.

"If the only reason you want to go to law school is because you're sharp and want a prominent job, you could find yourself miserable working at a law firm," agrees Neena Chaudhry, whose opinion of her present job is full of idealistic enthusiasm. Working now as staff counsel for the National Women's Law Center in Washington, D.C., the former Yale Law School student urges potential law students to think about what they hope to accomplish with a law degree, which might help direct their choice of a school.

GET OUTSIDE THE BOX

Once you're in law school, there are more ways to get off-track. One way is by specializing too narrowly in one area. Swensen notes that a law degree can lead to many different options. He encourages students to be open-minded about the possibilities that are available to them and which they might pass by if they are not willing to explore unfamiliar intellectual territory. They might discover that an area they thought would be exciting bores them, or that something that seemed mundane at first turns out to be quite stimulating.

Before you get locked into a law school, especially if you're headed there directly from college, Haskew advises students to take a year off or explore a "whimsical minimum-wage job," like river rafting or being a camp counselor. Such diversions from the path into a law career might be just what you need to sort out why you want to study law in the first place. And if you find that a career in law really is for you, you are in for an exceptional time in your life.

WHY LAWYERS PRACTICE LAW

It's Not All About Prestige and Money

Other than what's filtered through television, film, and the experiences of family members, most lawyers will tell you that incoming law students have little grasp of what it is like to be a lawyer. What are the perks from all the hard work students know they are in for? Why do people go through the rigors of getting a law degree in the first place? Some might be dazzled by the money and prestige or the exclusive membership in a club of heady intellectuals. These reasons are valid, but in reality, there is much more.

FOLLOWING SOME FOOTSTEPS

Jeffrey Hart knew more or less what to expect. His father was a lawyer and alumnus of Duke Law School. Though he flirted with history as an undergrad, he grew up knowing he would go to Duke and be a lawyer too. He graduated from Duke in 1997 and was hired by the law firm of Robinson, Bradshaw and Hinson in Charlotte, North Carolina.

LAWYER POWER VS. ENGINEERING POWER

With no idea he would eventually go into law, William Fay saw lawyers in action while representing state agencies as a civil engineer. A former military man, Fay knew clout when he saw it. He observed that people listened more to a lawyer's sharp reasoning rather than an engineer's technical data. He could not help noticing that lawyers drove the projects with which he was involved. He decided to pursue that kind of power and was accepted at Arizona State's College of Law and graduated in 1998. He now wields both his legal and engineering knowledge for the Assistant Attorney General in Arizona in the land and natural resources section.

A FASCINATION WITH LAW

A career switch likewise brought Tim Swensen to law school. He too had worked with lawyers while testifying in court as a child psychologist, and initially wanted to combine psychology and law. However, he became so fascinated with law while at Vanderbilt University Law School that he dropped psychology entirely. After his graduation in 1997, he began practicing commercial litigation at Blackwell Sanders Peper Martin in Kansas City, Missouri.

The reasons for seeking a law degree are as varied as the people who seek them. Whatever the motives, students entering law school have made a unique choice among graduate studies, says Mark Wiedman, a 1996 Yale Law School graduate. According to Wiedman, law students—more than those in business or economics—develop "crisp reasoning skills that prepare them to think about the impact that decisions and policies will have on the real world."

Wiedman's concerns for how law affects human beings stems from his Harvard undergraduate degree in social studies. He parlayed his interest in social organization and the training in "logical rigorous thinking" he received at Yale into a management consulting job at McKinsey and Co. in New York City, where he specializes in international business. "There's no other place in the world of affairs and business where there is such an opportunity for confronting difficult logical problems with direct implications for real people," he says.

HUMDRUM IT ISN'T—WELL, MOST OF THE TIME

Wherever your law career takes you, it will not be boring, assures Adrienne Moss, who practices corporate law at Patterson, Belknap, Webb and Tyler in New York City. Rather than looking for problems, Moss says the fun and creativity of a law career are evident to her when she is looking for answers for clients. She admits that some aspects of being a lawyer, especially a new one, can be "deadly dull;" however, the inevitable roadblocks do not fit that category. Instead of stopping her, problems present the challenge to find solutions and accomplish the goals of her clients.

Surprise was another element in Moss' law career. Having received her law degree from the University of Maryland in 1997, she did not anticipate immediately beginning professional life at a New York law firm. She theorizes it was "pure dumb luck," but it was more likely the combination of her forthright pursuit of the position of editor-in-chief of the law journal and her subsequent networking skills.

PICK UP YOUR PAINTBRUSH AND PRACTICE LAW

Although Hart knew from his father what a law career most likely held for him, he says he is constantly confronted with situations that require both his creativity and logical analysis. Swensen, too, observes that every day he walks in the door he encounters situations that are interesting because of their complexity. "It's rare I go through a day painting by numbers," he says. "I feel I have to stretch myself to come up with different and creative ways to handle all sorts of disputes." He likes the fact that these problems don't have "A-B-C solutions." If he is handling something by rote, he knows he is doing something wrong.

Solving problems is one of the biggest satisfactions of a law career. Lance Witcher, who graduated from Washington University in St. Louis School of Law in 1996 and practices at Blackwell Sanders Peper Martin in St. Louis, Missouri, jokes about the "long hours, demanding clients, loss of appetite and hair" that result from practicing law. But on the serious side, he thinks of his clients' cases and legal matters as problems requiring the solutions that best fit the clients' needs. "It's your job to find and implement those solutions," he explains.

HIGH IDEALS

Idealism is high on the list of career payoffs for lawyers. Derek Haskew took his degree from the University of Southern California's Law School to the Navajo Nation to manage a small legal services office in Mexican Hat, Utah. His determination to "get into life and get his hands dirty changing the world" was realized in public interest law. Fay says he also genuinely enjoys making a difference in people's lives and helping them resolve their problems using the law. Engineers solve dilemmas with science and math. In his new career in law, he is intrigued by how people's lives can be so greatly affected by the outcome of cases. For him, these results can be as far-reaching as the condemnation of one and a half million acres of government land involving thirty lawyers on each side.

Idealism attracted Neena Chaudhry, with an undergraduate degree at the University of Maryland in economics and math, to study law. The social aspect had to be integral to the career she was searching for, and, more specifically, she knew she wanted to help people secure equal educational opportunities. This passion for education is what led her to enter Yale Law School in 1996. She now works as staff counsel for the National Women's Law Center in the area of gender equity in education and women's health/reproductive rights. Noting that Gandhi was a lawyer, she says, "Law offered me the appeal of being analytical and people-oriented and a way for me to pursue social issues." Though she initially worried about the adversarial image of lawyers, she focused on the noble side of practicing law. Above all, she does not feel as though she is working merely for the sake of working, but that her job has a purpose. "Often," she says, "law itself can be dry, but if you know why you're doing it, it's worth it."

ADVICE FOR MEMBERS OF MINORITY GROUPS

As we move into the twenty-first century, the legal profession still offers lifelong opportunities for professional challenge, community service, and professional satisfaction.

BACKGROUND

In 1997, the typical entering law school class was a little more than 20 percent members of minority groups. Thirty years ago, there were fewer than 800 law students nationally who were members of minority groups, accounting for fewer than 10 percent of an entering law school class. This nearly doubling of enrollment of members of minority groups would not have happened without the enhanced commitment of law schools to recruit, admit, retain, and graduate talented students who are members of minority groups into the legal profession. In June 1991, the Association of American Law Schools, the American Bar Association, and the Law School Admission Council issued a joint statement saying that "a student body diverse with respect to sex, ethnicity, race, economic, educational, and experiential backgrounds is essential to a quality legal education. Students must obtain a wide range of perspectives concerning the impact of law on various segments of our population and a deeper understanding of law and justice in an increasingly complex society." According to Carl Monk, the Executive Vice President and Executive Director of the Association of American Law Schools, the learned society representing law professors, "It is not possible in our increasingly diverse society and increasingly global economy to offer quality legal education without the many cultures of our society being adequately represented in the classroom."

Today, nearly forty years after the Supreme Court ruled in Sweatt v. Painter that maintenance of racially segregated law schools violated equal protection and while members of minority groups constitute more than 20 percent of the national population, they are still only 4 percent of all practicing lawyers. A *Personal Reflection on 30 Years in Legal Education* comes to us from Judge Harry Edwards. When he entered Michigan Law School in 1962, he was the only black student in his class and there were no black faculty members until 1970. He reports that the assumption over thirty years ago was that he must be talented and had succeeded despite his race. Today, his son, a summa cum laude and Phi Beta Kappa graduate of Yale with a Ph.D. in comparative literature, frequently encounters people who assume he's made it only because of his race. Judge Edwards continues to support affirmative action efforts, noting that the need is greater than the cost. As law professor Charles E. Daye recently wrote, "the challenges of the 1990s and beyond is best expressed by Native American leader Chief Seattle who observed, 'A great vision is hard to hold.'"

As our society becomes increasingly multicultural, the practice of law becomes increasingly transnational. Educating lawyers for the twenty-first century in an increasingly global economy requires introducing voices of different cultures and perspectives. In choosing lawyers for the future, we must continue to be creative in our search for talent. Admissions professionals must learn about the variety of backgrounds from which future lawyers will come.

We must remember that students of color are still victims of diminished expectations. A recent newspaper article told the story of young Denise Sepulveda. When Denise glowingly told her inner-city high school guidance counselor of her dream of teaching at a university, the guidance counselor rolled her eyes in disbelief. The first African-American astronaut was told by a high school counselor that he was only smart enough for trade school. When I was considering applying to law school nearly twenty years ago, I was told by a college adviser that as a nontraditional student with children, I could never go to law school. I worked hard in school, worked part-time as a paralegal, and found others who believed in me and my ability to handle the difficult work of law school. Your job, as an applicant who is a member of a minority group, is to educate the admissions committee about hurdles that you have to clear before reaching our doors.

HOW TO PREPARE FOR LAW SCHOOL

Ideally, preparation for law school begins with a challenging course of study in undergraduate school. Build a solid academic foundation and do well. If you get off to a weak start, work toward establishing an upward grade trend with

Camille deJorna, Director of Admission and Assistant to the Dean, University of Iowa College of Law

a strong finish. Counter stereotypical expectations by taking rigorous courses, reading scholarly journals, and gaining critical writing experience. Know the academic reputation of your school and your department. This will help you to understand the value of your degree, your major, and your grade point average in the competitive world of law school admissions.

Augment your course work, if possible, with law-related internships that emphasize research and writing assignments, not just by observing trials. Consult with prelaw advisers. Take courses taught by faculty members who regularly teach students who go on to law school. They will be both a good source of advice and an opportunity for learning more about the rigors of law school.

HOW TO APPLY TO LAW SCHOOL

Plan to take the Law School Admission Test (LSAT) in June preceding your senior year or early in the fall of the year you plan to apply. The test is offered four times a year. While you may hear conflicting information on preparing for the LSAT, the best preparation begins with taking undergraduate courses that emphasize reasoning and problem-solving skills. The test is timed, and the more exposure you have to the testing materials prior to the exam and the more intense your preparation, the better you are likely to do. Minority test takers must focus on finishing the exam.

Research shows that people who prepare do better than those who don't. Sample questions and other materials are available from the Law School Admission Council (LSAC), the testing company that produces the test. Treat preparing for the LSAT as you would prepare for a marathon. Take the test under time conditions as often as you can, well in advance of the actual test. Consider investing in low-cost test-prep programs like those sponsored by the Puerto Rican Legal Defense Fund.

Students with poor histories of standardized testing should be prepared to document their claims and to offset them with an outstanding record of academic achievement. Sustained academic excellence with unusually strong letters of recommendation from faculty members who can compare you favorably with former students they have taught and who have done well in law school is the best antidote to less-than-stellar standardized test performance. Students in this situation may also take law school classes, where possible, and do well to establish their ability to handle the demanding work of law school, despite conflicting indicators.

Apply Broadly

Approach the application process for law school in a lawyerly fashion. Begin to gather information well in advance of the year that you plan to apply. Compile a list of law schools, including your dream or reach school, likely schools based on your credentials, and schools that would consider you a sure bet. Determine this strategy by gathering information on how many applicants for admission with your credentials selected by a school in the preceding year. This information is available online and in various publications provided by the ABA and LSAC, for example. Your prelaw adviser may also have this data or may keep his or her own.

Apply broadly and your likelihood of success will improve. Fee waivers, both for the LSAT and for individual school application fees, may be available for students with need. Call the admissions office and ask for the names and telephone numbers of the leaders of the organizations for members of minority groups who may be more candid about the range of credentials at their institution. Ask if there is a minority recruiter for the law school or if a faculty member who is a member of a minority group is available to answer applicant questions about the admissions process and about life for students of color at the school. Schools often keep a directory of alumni who are members of minority groups who are also willing to help future lawyers who are members of minority groups.

Once you know your undergraduate grade point average and LSAT score, plan on attending prelaw conferences and forums sponsored by colleges, LSAC, and others. Make a list of schools that you plan to visit at these events. They are often attended by directors of admission or faculty members from the admissions committee who are available to give you substantive advice about their process. Treat these encounters as mini-interviews. Introduce yourself, give a quick summary of your credentials, and ask about the likelihood of success at their school for admission and for scholarship opportunities.

Determine rationally how competitive you are and proceed accordingly. If you are at the top of the pool, don't just apply to schools that you know. You may get full scholarship opportunities and more overall institutional support at schools with which you are less familiar. If you are in the middle, complete your application early. Distinguish yourself. Describe your accomplishments. Put your performance in a context. If, for example, you worked 40 hours a week while in school to support yourself or your family and still maintained a good record of accomplishment, give the committee that information. If you are the first in your family to attend college, let them know.

Apply Early

Plan to have your personal statement completed by Thanksgiving and to mail your application by mid-December. Schools tend to have more flexibility earlier than later in the process. It also gives you time to gather additional information if the admissions committee requests it. December should also be the latest that you plan to take or retake the LSAT. Once you take the test, you may receive targeted mailings from the Candidate Referral Service. Read these letters carefully, since schools often encourage applications from students to whom they write. These letters may be accompanied by waivers of the school's application fee.

BEYOND THE NUMBERS IN LAW SCHOOL ADMISSIONS

What do we value beyond grade point average and performance on the LSAT? The American Bar Association suggests that in addition to critical-thinking, problem-solving, writing, and researching skills, "each member of the legal profession should be dedicated to serving others and promoting justice." I was recently inspired by Morris Dees, founder of the Southern Poverty Law Center, to consider a "passion for justice" among these criteria. How do we measure a candidate's likelihood to devoting their efforts to others? Many in law school admissions have been encouraging applicants to tell their stories, whether or not there is a box to check indicating your racial background.

For example, at a recent Society of American Law Teachers conference on "Affirming Action and Reconstructing Merit," Julie Su reported that her effective representation of Thai and Latina sweatshop workers required "strategizing with clients, engagement in their lives, and the comfort and flexibility to meet with clients where they lived." Describe your encounters with the legal system that inform your sense of justice. Describe experiences of injustice and remedies you pursued or how you plan to expand access to justice in your community. Describe experiences that will influence the kind of lawyer you are likely to become. Law schools are looking for students who, in addition to being able to handle the work of law school, have overcome and won "personal battles of courage," making them more empathetic advocates for their clients.

FORMULATING PLAN B

If you did not take full advantage of college there are still options remaining. Plan to attend graduate school and aim to reach a GPA of 3.5 or better. Students who enter law school following another career or after a lengthy time away from an academic environment should contact the law school they are interested in to learn what they are likely to put more weight on in their selection process. Often you can think about your work life, think about law school, and establish that you have the skills for law school based on transferable skills that you use in your current professional life. If you interact with lawyers or judges in the course of your employment, get to know them, let

them know of your interest, and see if they might be willing to write a letter of recommendation.

Finally, you can also apply to schools with conditional admission programs. You should also consider conditional admit programs like CLEO, the Council on Legal Education Opportunity. If you are Native American, consider applying to the American Indian Law Center's Pre-Law Summer Institute (PLSI) at the University of New Mexico Law School.

SELECTING A LAW SCHOOL

Select a law school where you are likely to thrive. Find out how many students, faculty members, and alumni are members of minority groups and how involved they all are in campus life. Are there administrators or staff members who are also members of minority groups? Find out what resources are committed to students who are members of minority groups. How extensive is the financial aid budget? Is there an academic support program? What is the retention rate for members of minority groups? The placement rate for members of minority groups? The bar passage rate for members of minority groups? Is there a mentoring program for members of minority groups with the local minority bar association? What's the day-to-day climate at the school like for members of minority groups? Despite our best efforts and progress in the area of diversity, law schools are not sanctuaries from the realities of life for members of minority groups in the U.S. Law school can be an alienating and isolating experience for members of minority groups. Racially insensitive hypotheticals posed by faculty members, the absence of strong numbers of faculty members who are members of minority groups, and a more conservative student body mirror the challenges you can expect in practice.

Once you select a law school, take full advantage of the resources that the school offers to ensure that you do your best. Join the student organizations for members of minority groups as well as other student organizations. Do not become isolated. Share your experiences with others. There is no monolithic minority experience of law school. As critical race scholar Mari Matsuda reminds us, "Issues of identity are not just of our own making, it's part of our history. Speak in your own voice in your professional life. Issues of race and gender in the academy, in legal education, and in the profession are unavoidable."

Work hard, learn as much as you can, and hold onto your dreams so you may join the next generation of lawyers, the women and men who will serve as leaders in the twenty-first century.

PAYING FOR LAW SCHOOL

If you're considering attending law school but fear you don't have enough money, don't despair. Financial support for graduate and professional study does exist, although, admittedly, the information about support sources can be difficult to find.

For those of you who have applied for financial aid as undergraduates, there are some differences for law students you'll notice right away. For one, most aid to undergraduates is based primarily on need (although the number of colleges that now offer undergraduate merit-based aid is increasing). But law school aid is more often based on academic merit. Second, as a law student, you are automatically declared "independent" for federal financial aid purposes, meaning your parents' income and assets information is not required in assessing your need for federal aid. And third, at some law schools, the awarding of aid may be administered by the law school itself, not the financial aid office.

FINANCIAL AID MYTHS

- Financial aid is just for poor people.
- Financial aid is just for smart people.
- Financial aid is mainly for minority students.
- I have a job, so I must not be eligible for aid.
- If I apply for aid, it will affect whether or not I'm admitted.
- Loans are not financial aid.

BE PREPARED

Being prepared for law school means you have to put together a financial plan. Before you enter law school, you should have answers to these questions:

- What should I be doing now to prepare for the cost of my law education?
- What can I do to minimize my costs once I arrive on campus?
- What financial aid programs are available at each of the schools to which I am applying?
- What financial aid programs are available outside the university, at the federal, state, or private level?
- What financing options do I have if I cannot pay the full cost from my own resources and those of my family?
- What should I know about the loans I am being offered?

- What impact will these loans have on me when I complete my program?

You'll find your answers in three guiding principles: think ahead, live within your means, and keep your head above water.

THINK AHEAD

The first step in putting together your financial plan comes from thinking about the future: the loss of your income while you're attending school, your projected income after you graduate, the annual rate of inflation, additional expenses you will incur as a student and after you graduate, and any loss of income you may experience later from unintentional periods of unemployment, pregnancy, or disability. The cornerstone of thinking ahead is following a step-by-step process.

1. *Set your goals.* Decide what and where you want to study, and determine an appropriate level of debt.
2. *Take inventory.* Collect your financial information and add up your assets—bank accounts, stocks, bonds, real estate, business and personal property. Then subtract your liabilities—money owed on your assets, including credit card debt and car loans—to yield your net worth.
3. *Calculate your need.* Compare your net worth with the costs at the schools you are considering to get a rough estimate of how much of your assets you can use for your schooling.
4. *Create an action plan.* Determine how much you'll earn while in school, how much you think you will receive in grants and scholarships, and how much you plan to borrow. Don't forget to consider inflation and possible life changes that could affect your overall financial plan.
5. *Review your plan regularly.* Measure the progress of your plan every year and make adjustments for such things as increases in salary or other changes in your goals or circumstances.

LIVE WITHIN YOUR MEANS

The second step in being prepared is knowing how much you spend now so you can determine how much you'll spend when you're in school. Use the standard cost of attendance budget published by your school as a guide. But don't be surprised if your estimated budget is higher than the one the school provides, especially if you've been out of school for a while. Once you've figured out your budget, see if you can pare down your current costs and financial obligations so the lean years of law school don't come as too large a shock.

KEEP YOUR HEAD ABOVE WATER

Finally, the third step is managing the debt you'll accrue as a law student. Debt is manageable only when considered in terms of five things:

1. Your future income
2. The amount of time it takes to repay the loan
3. The interest rate you are being charged
4. Your personal lifestyle and expenses after graduation
5. Unexpected circumstances that change your income or your ability to repay what you owe

To make sure your educational debt is manageable, you should borrow an amount that requires payments of between 8 and 15 percent of your starting salary.

The approximate monthly installments for repaying borrowed principal at 5, 8–10, 12, and 14 percent are indicated in the following chart.

Estimated Loan Repayment Schedule
Monthly Payments for Every $1000 Borrowed

Rate	5 years	10 years	15 years	20 years	25 years
5%	$18.87	$10.61	$ 7.91	$ 6.60	$ 5.85
8%	20.28	12.13	9.56	8.36	7.72
9%	20.76	12.67	10.14	9.00	8.39
10%	21.74	13.77	10.75	9.65	9.09
12%	22.24	14.35	12.00	11.01	10.53
14%	23.27	15.53	13.32	12.44	12.04

Use this table to estimate your monthly payments on a loan for any of the five repayment periods (5, 10, 15, 20, and 25 years). The amounts listed are the monthly payments for a $1000 loan for each of the interest rates. To estimate your monthly payment, choose the closest interest rate and multiply the amount of the payment listed by the total amount of your loan and then divide by 1,000. For example, for a total loan of $15,000 at 9 percent to be paid back over ten years, multiply $12.67 times 15,000 (190,050) divided by 1,000. This yields $190.05 per month.

If you're wondering just how much of a loan payment you can afford monthly without running into payment problems, consult the chart below.

How Much Can You Afford to Repay?

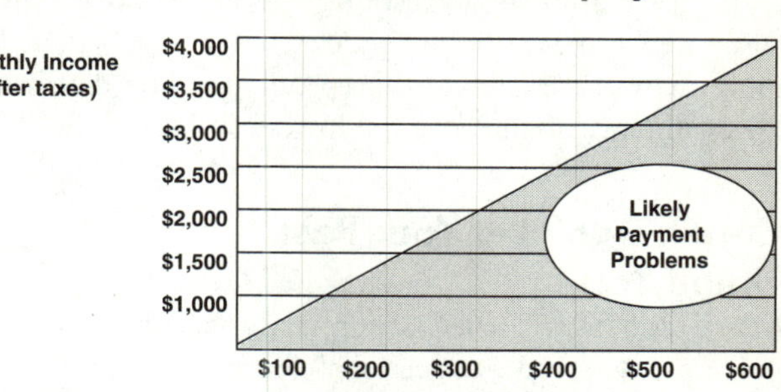

This graph shows the monthly cash-flow outlook based on your total monthly loan payments in comparison with your monthly income earned after taxes. Ideally, to eliminate likely payment problems, your monthly loan payment should be less than 15 percent of your monthly income.

Of course, the best way to manage your debt is to borrow less. While cutting your personal budget may be one option, you also may wish to investigate asking your family for help. Although the federal government considers you "independent," your parents and family may still be willing and able to help pay for your graduate education. If your family is not open to just giving you money, they may be open to making a low-interest (or deferred-interest) loan. Family loans usually have more attractive interest rates and repayment terms than commercial loans. They may also have tax consequences, so you may want to check with a tax adviser.

Roll Your Loans into One

There's a good chance that as a law student you will have two or more loans included in your aid package, plus any money you borrowed as an undergraduate. That means when you start repaying, you could be making loan payments to several different lenders. Not only can the record keeping be a nightmare, but with each loan having a minimum payment, your total monthly payments may be more than you can handle. If you owe more than $7500 in federal loans, you can combine your loans into one consolidated loan at either a flat 9 percent interest rate or a weighted average of the rates on the loans consolidated. Your repayment can also be extended to up to thirty years, depending on the total amount you borrow, which will make your monthly payments lower (of course, you'll also be paying more total interest). With a consolidated loan, some lenders offer graduated or income-sensitive repayment options. Consult with your lender or the U.S. Department of Education about the types of consolidation provisions offered.

Plastic Mania

Any section on managing debt would be incomplete if it didn't mention the responsible use of credit cards. Most law students hold one or more credit cards, and many students find themselves in financial difficulties because of them. Here are two suggestions: use credit cards only for convenience, never for extended credit; and, if you have more than one credit card, keep only the one that has the lowest finance charge and the lowest limit.

Credit: Don't Let Your Past Haunt You

Many schools will check your credit history before they process any private educational loans for you. To make sure your credit rating is accurate, you may want to request a copy of your credit report before you start law school. You can get a copy of your report by sending a signed, written request to one of the three national credit reporting agencies at the addresses listed below. Include your full name, social security number, current address, any previous addresses for the past five years, date of birth, and daytime phone number. Call the agency before you request your report so you know whether there is a fee for this report. Note that you are entitled to a free copy of your credit report if you have been denied credit within the last sixty days. In addition, Experian currently provides complimentary credit reports once every twelve months.

Credit criteria used to review and approve student loans can include the following:
· Absence of negative credit
· No bankruptcies, foreclosures, repossessions, charge-offs, or open judgments
· No prior educational loan defaults, unless paid in full or making satisfactory repayments
· Absence of excessive past due accounts; that is, no 30-, 60-, or 90-day delinquencies on consumer loans or revolving charge accounts within the past two years

Types of Aid Available

There are three types of aid: money given to you (grants, scholarships, and fellowships), money you earn through work, and loans.

GRANTS, SCHOLARSHIPS, AND FELLOWSHIPS

Most grants, scholarships, and fellowships are outright awards that require no service in return. The one major exception for law students is ROTC aid, which can be very generous, but entails a commitment to serve as an officer in the branch providing the aid. Often these gift aid programs provide the cost of tuition and fees plus a stipend to cover living expenses. Some are based exclusively on financial need, some exclusively on academic merit, and some on a combination of need and merit. As a rule, grants are awarded to those with financial need, although they may require the recipient to have expertise in a certain field. Fellowships and scholarships often connote selectivity based on ability—financial need is usually not a factor.

Federal Support

The provision of free federal money in the form of grants and scholarships for the training of future lawyers has never ranked very high as a national priority. This is especially noticeable compared with what is available to prospective doctors, teachers, or scientific researchers. The only notable federal grant program for lawyers is the newly enacted Thurgood Marshall Legal Educational Opportunity Program to aid low-income, minority, or disadvantaged students seeking a law school education. The Marshall program, to be administered by the Department of Education, provides information, preparation, and financial assistance to students so they may gain access to and complete a law school education. The U.S. Department of Education or one of the law schools that you are interested in should have more details about this new program.

State Support

Many states offer grants for graduate study. States grant approximately $64 million per year to graduate students. To qualify for a particular state's aid you must be a resident of that state. Residency is established in most states after you have lived there for at least twelve consecutive months

---

Credit Reporting Agencies

Equifax
P.O. Box 10596
Atlanta, Georgia 30348-5496
800-997-2493
Web site: http://www.equifax.com

Experian
P.O. Box 2104
Allen, Texas 75013-2104
888-397-3742
800-972-0322 (TTY/TDD)
Web site: http://www.experian.com/consumer/

Trans Union Corporation
P.O. Box 2000
Chester, Pennsylvania 19022
800-888-4213
Web site: http://www.transunion.com

prior to enrolling in school. Many states provide funds for in-state students only; that is, funds are not transferable out of state. Contact your state scholarship office to determine what aid it offers.

Institutional Aid

Educational institutions using their own funds provide between $2 and $3 billion in graduate assistance in the form of fellowships, tuition waivers, and assistantships. In the field of law, most scholarship aid comes from the institutions themselves. Consult each school's catalog for information about their aid programs.

Aid from Foundations

Certain foundation grants available to other graduate students, such as the Harry S. Truman Scholarships, are also open to law school students. Most foundations provide support in areas of interest to them. The Association of Trial Lawyers of America and the Harry A. Blackmun Scholarly Foundation are a couple of the national foundations that make awards specifically to law school students. Addresses for these are: Harry S. Truman Scholarship Foundation, 712 Jackson Place, NW, Washington DC 20006; Association of Trial Lawyers of America, 1050 31st Street, NW, Washington DC 20007; Harry A. Blackmun Scholarship Foundation, 118 West Mulberry Street, Baltimore, MD 21201-3600. The Foundation Center of New York publishes several reference books on foundation support for graduate study. For more information, call 212-620-4230 or access their Web site at http://fdncenter.org.

Financial Aid for Minorities and Women

Bureau of Indian Affairs. The Bureau of Indian Affairs (BIA) offers aid to students who are at least one-quarter American Indian or native Alaskan and from a federally recognized tribe. Contact your tribal education officer, BIA area office, or call the Bureau of Indian Affairs at 202-208-4871.

In addition, below are some books available that describe financial aid opportunities for women and minorities.

The Directory of Financial Aids for Women by Gail Ann Schlachter (Reference Service Press, 1999) lists sources of support and identifies foundations and other organizations interested in helping women secure funding for graduate study.

Books such as *Financial Aid for Minorities* (Garrett Park Press, 1998) describe financial aid opportunities for minority students.

Disabled students are eligible to receive aid from a number of organizations. *Financial Aid for the Disabled and Their Families* by Gail Ann Schlachter and R. David Weber (Reference Service Press, 2000) lists aid opportunities for disabled students. The Vocational Rehabilitation Services in your home state can also provide information.

RESEARCHING GRANTS AND FELLOWSHIPS

The books listed below are good sources of information on grant and fellowship support for graduate education and should be consulted before you resort to borrowing. Keep in mind that grant support varies dramatically from field to field.

Annual Register of Grant Support: A Directory of Funding Sources 2000 (R.R. Bowker, 1999). This is a comprehensive guide to grants and awards from government agencies, foundations, and business and professional organizations.

Corporate Foundation Profiles, (Foundation Center, 1998). This is an in-depth, analytical profile of 195 of the largest company-sponsored foundations in the United States. Brief descriptions of an additional 1,000 company-sponsored foundations are also included. There is an index of subjects, types of support, and geographical locations.

The Foundation Directory (Foundation Center, 2000). This directory, with a supplement, gives detailed information on U.S. foundations with brief descriptions of the purpose and activities of each.

The Grants Register 2000, 18th ed. Edited by Ruth Austen (St. Martin's, 1999). This lists grant agencies alphabetically and gives information on awards available to law students, young professionals, and scholars for study and research.

Peterson's Grants for Graduate and Postdoctoral Study, 5th ed. (Peterson's, 1998). This book includes information on 1,400 grants, scholarships, awards, fellowships, and prizes. Originally compiled by the Office of Research Affairs at the Graduate School of the University of Massachusetts at Amherst, this guide is updated periodically by Peterson's.

Graduate schools sometimes publish listings of support sources in their catalogs, and some provide separate publications, such as the *Graduate Guide to Grants,* compiled by the Harvard Graduate School of Arts and Sciences. For more information, call 617-495-1814.

THE INTERNET: A NEW SOURCE OF FUNDING INFORMATION

If you have not explored the financial resources on the World Wide Web, your research is not complete. A wealth of information is now available on the Web, ranging from loan and entrance applications to minority grants and scholarships.

Web Mailing Lists

There is a mailing list, or newsgroup, called GRANTS-L, for announcements of grants and fellowships of interest to law students. To subscribe, send mail to listproc@listproc. gsu.edu with "subscribe GRANTS-L YOUR NAME" in the body of the message.

University-Specific Information on the Web

Universities are now in the process of creating Web financial aid directories. Applications of admission can be downloaded from the Web to start the graduate process. After that, detailed information can be obtained on financial aid processes, forms, and deadlines. University-specific grant and scholarship information can also be found, and more may be learned about financing information by using the Web than by an actual visit to the school. Questions can be answered on line.

Scholarships on the Web

When searching for scholarship opportunities, be sure to search the Web. Many benefactors and other scholarship donors are creating pages on the Web listing pertinent information with regard to their specific scholarship. You can reach this information through a variety of methods. For example, you can find a directory listing minority scholarships, quickly look at the information on line, decide if it applies to you, and then move on. New scholarship pages are being added to the Web daily.

The Web also lists many services that will look for scholarships for you. Some of these services cost money and advertise more scholarships per dollar than any other service. While some of these might be helpful, surfing the Web and using the traditional library resources on available scholarships is often just as productive and free.

Bank and Loan Information on the Web

Banks and loan servicing centers are creating pages on the Web, making it easier to access loan information. Having the information on screen in front of you instantaneously is more convenient than being put on hold on the phone. Any loan information, such as interest rate variations, descriptions of loans, loan consolidation programs, and repayment charts, can be found on the Web.

LOANS

Most needy law students borrow to finance their law programs. There are basically two sources of student loans—the federal government and private loan programs. You should read and understand the terms of these loan programs before submitting your loan application.

FEDERAL LOANS

Federal Stafford Loans. The Federal Stafford Loan Program offers government-sponsored, low-interest loans to students either through the Department of Education or a private lender, such as a bank, credit union, or savings and loan association.

There are two components of the Federal Stafford Loan program. Under the *subsidized* component of the program, the federal government pays the interest accruing on the loan while you are enrolled in law school on at least a half-time basis. Under the *unsubsidized* component of the program, you pay the interest on the loan from the day proceeds are issued. Eligibility for the federal subsidy is based on demonstrated financial need as determined by the financial aid office from the information you provide on the Free Application for Federal Student Aid (FAFSA). A cosigner is not required, since the loan is not based on creditworthiness.

Although Unsubsidized Federal Stafford Loans may not be as desirable as Subsidized Federal Stafford Loans from the consumer's perspective, they are a useful source of support for those who may not qualify for the subsidized loans or who need additional financial assistance.

Eligible borrowers may borrow up to $8500 per year through the Subsidized Stafford Loan Program, up to a maximum of $65,500, including undergraduate borrowing. In addition to loans through the Subsidized Stafford Loan Program, law students may borrow up to an additional $10,000 per year through the unsubsidized component of the Federal Stafford Loan Program. You may borrow up to the cost of the school in which you are enrolled or will attend, minus estimated financial assistance from other federal, state, and private sources, with a maximum of $138,500, including undergraduate borrowing. Graduate students who borrow the maximum allowable amounts each year can receive a total of $18,500; $8500 through the *subsidized* program and an additional $10,000 through the *unsubsidized* program.

The interest rate for the Federal Stafford Loans varies annually and is set every July. The rate during in-school, grace, and deferment periods is based on the 91-Day U.S. Treasury Bill rate plus 2.5 percent, capped at 8.25 percent. The rate in repayment is based on the 91-Day U.S. Treasury Bill rate plus 3.1 percent, capped at 8.25 percent.

Two fees are deducted from the loan proceeds upon disbursement: a guarantee fee of up to 1 percent, which is deposited in an insurance pool to ensure repayment to the lender if the borrower defaults, and a federally mandated 3 percent origination fee, which is used to offset the administrative cost of the Federal Stafford Loan Program.

Under the *subsidized* Federal Loan Program, repayment begins six months after your last enrollment on at least a half-time basis. Under the *unsubsidized* program, repayment of interest begins within thirty days from disbursement of the loan proceeds, and repayment of the principal begins six months after your last enrollment on at least a half-time basis. Some lenders may require that some payments may be made even while you are in school, although most lenders will allow you to defer payments and will add the accrued interest to the loan balance. Under both components of the program, repayment may extend over a maximum of ten years with no prepayment penalty.

Federal Perkins Loans. The Federal Perkins Loan is a long-term loan available to students demonstrating financial need and is administered directly by the school. Not all schools have these funds, and some may award them to undergraduates only. Eligibility is determined from the information you provide on the FAFSA. The school will notify you of your eligibility.

Eligible law students may borrow up to $6,000 per year, up to a maximum of $40,000, including undergraduate borrowing (even if your previous Perkins Loans have been repaid.) The interest rate for Federal Perkins Loans is 5 percent, and no interest accrues while you remain in school at least half-time. There are no guarantee, loan, or disbursement fees. Repayment begins nine months after your last enrollment on at least a half-time basis and may extend over a maximum of ten years with no prepayment penalty.

Deferring Your Federal Loan Repayments. If you borrowed under the Federal Stafford Loan Program or the Federal Perkins Loan Program for previous undergraduate or graduate study, some of your repayments may be deferred (i.e., suspended) when you return to law school, depending on when you borrowed and under which program.

There are other deferment options available if you are temporarily unable to repay your loan. Information about these deferments is provided at your entrance and exit interviews. If you believe you are eligible for a deferment of your loan repayments, you must contact your lender to complete a deferment form. The deferment must be filed prior to the time your repayment is due, and it must be refiled when it expires if you remain eligible for deferment at that time.

Law Access Loan Program

In an effort to ensure that new and continuing law students have an adequate opportunity to finance their legal education at the law school of their choice, the Law School Admission Council (LSAC), in cooperation with other higher education and financial institutions, sponsors student loans. The Law Access program offers a wide range of services to law students attending LSAC member schools approved by the American Bar Association. Through Law Access, students can obtain five types of loans: Federal Stafford Loans; Federal Supplemental Loans for Students; Law Access Loans (LAL); Private Bar Examination Loans (BEL); and private Federal Consolidation Loans. For further information, contact the Law Access Loan Program, Box 2500, Newtown, PA 18940; 800-282-1550.

Supplemental Loans

Many lending institutions offer supplemental loan programs and other financing plans, such as the ones described below, to students seeking assistance in meeting their expected contribution toward educational expenses.

If you are considering borrowing through a supplemental loan program, you should carefully consider the terms of the program and be sure to "read the fine print." Check with the program sponsor for the most current terms that will be applicable to the amounts you intend to borrow for graduate study. Most supplemental loan programs for graduate study offer unsubsidized, credit-based loans. In general, a credit-ready borrower is one who has a satisfactory credit history or no credit history at all. A creditworthy borrower generally must pass a credit test to be eligible to borrow or act as a cosigner for the loan funds.

Many supplemental loan programs have a minimum annual loan limit and a maximum annual loan limit. Some offer amounts equal to the cost of attendance minus any other aid you will receive for graduate study. If you are planning to borrow for several years of graduate study, consider whether there is a cumulative or aggregate limit on the amount you may borrow. Often this cumulative or aggregate limit will include any amounts you borrowed and have not repaid for undergraduate or previous graduate study.

The combination of the annual interest rate, loan fees, and the repayment terms you choose will determine how much the amount is that you will repay over time. Compare these features in combination before you decide which loan program to use. Some loans offer interest rates that are adjusted monthly, some quarterly, some annually. Some offer interest rates that are lower during the in-school, grace, and deferment periods, and then increase when you begin repayment. Most programs include a loan "origination" fee, which is usually deducted from the principal amount you receive when the loan is disbursed, and must be repaid along with the interest and other principal when you graduate, withdraw from school, or drop below half-time study. Sometimes the loan fees are reduced if you borrow with a qualified cosigner. Some programs allow you to defer interest and/or principal payments while you are enrolled in law school. Many programs allow you to capitalize your interest payments; the interest due on your loan is added to the outstanding balance of your loan, so you don't have to repay immediately, but this increases the amount you owe. Other programs allow you to pay the interest as you go, which will reduce the amount you later have to repay.

For more information about supplemental loan programs or to obtain applications, call the customer service phone numbers of the organizations listed below, access the sponsor's site on the World Wide Web, or visit your school's financial aid office.

CitiAssist Loans. An unsubsidized, credit-based loan for graduate students, sponsored by Citibank. Telephone: 800-692-8200; Web site: http://www.studentloan.com.

EXCEL Grad Loan. An unsubsidized, credit-based loan for credit-ready graduate and professional students enrolled at least half-time, sponsored by Nellie Mae. Telephone: 800-367-8848; Web site: http://www.nelliemae.com.

LawAchiever Loan. An unsubsidized, credit-based loan for law students enrolled at least half-time, sponsored by Key Education Resources. Telephone: 800-KEY-LEND; Web site: http://www.keybank.com/educate.

PEP Loan. An unsubsidized, credit-based loan for credit-ready law students enrolled at least half-time, sponsored by the Education Resources Institute. Telephone: 800-255-8374; Web site: http://www.teri.org.

Law Access Loan. An unsubsidized, credit-based loan for creditworthy law students enrolled at least half-time, sponsored by the Access Group. Telephone: 800-282-1550; Web site: http://www.accessgroup.org.

LawLoan. An unsubsidized, credit-based loan for law students enrolled at least half-time, sponsored by Sallie Mae. Telephone: 888-239-4269; Web site: http://www.salliemae.com.

How to Apply

All applicants for federal aid must complete the Free Application for Federal Student Aid (FAFSA). This application must be completed *after* January 1 preceding enrollment in the fall. On this form you report your income and asset information for the preceding calendar year and specify which schools will receive the data. Two to four weeks later you'll receive an acknowledgment on which you can make any corrections. The schools you've designated will also receive the information and may begin asking you to send them documents (usually your U.S. income tax return) that verify what you reported.

In addition to the FAFSA, some law schools want additional information and will ask you to complete the CSS Financial Aid PROFILE. If your school requires this form, it will be listed in the PROFILE registration form available in college financial aid offices. Other schools use their own supplemental application. Check with your financial aid office to confirm which forms they require.

If you have already filed your federal income tax for the year, it will be much easier for you to complete these forms. If not, use estimates, but be certain to notify the financial aid office if your estimated figures differ from the actual ones once you have calculated them.

Application Deadlines

Application deadlines vary. Some schools require you to apply for aid when applying for admission; others require that you be admitted before applying for aid. Aid application instructions and deadlines should be clearly stated in each school's application material. The FAFSA must be filed after January 1 of the year you are applying for aid, but the Financial Aid PROFILE can be completed earlier, in October or November.

Determining Financial Need

Eligibility for need-based financial aid is based on your income during the calendar year prior to the academic year in which you apply for aid. Prior-year income is used because it is a good predictor of current-year income and is verifiable. If you have a significant reduction in income or assets after your aid application is completed, consult a financial aid counselor. If, for example, you are returning to school after working, you should let the financial aid counselor know your projected income for the year you will be in school. Aid counselors may use their "professional judgment" to revise your financial need, based on the actual income you will earn while you are in law school.

Need is determined by examining the difference between the cost of attendance at a given institution and the financial resources you bring to the table. Eligibility for aid is calculated by subtracting your resources from the total cost of attendance budget. These standard student budgets are generally on the low side of the norm. So if your expenses are higher because of graduate bills, higher research travel, or more costly books, for example, a financial aid counselor can make an adjustment. Of course, you'll have to document any unusual expenses. Also, keep in mind that with limited grant and scholarship aid, a higher budget will probably mean either more loan or more working hours for you.

Tax Issues

Since the passage of the Tax Reform Act of 1986, grants, scholarships, and fellowships may be considered taxable income. That portion of the grant used for payment of tuition and course-required fees, books, supplies, and equipment is excludable from taxable income. Grant support for living expenses is taxable. A good rule of thumb for determining the tax liability for grants and scholarships is to view anything that exceeds the actual cost of tuition, required fees, books, supplies related to courses, and required equipment as taxable.

- If you are employed by an educational institution or other organization that gives tuition reimbursement, you must pay tax on the value that exceeds $5250.
- If your tuition is waived in exchange for working at the institution, the tuition waiver is taxable. This includes waivers that come with teaching or research assistantships.
- Other student support, such as stipends and wages paid to research assistants and teaching assistants, is also taxable income. Student loans, however, are not taxable.
- If you are an international student you may or may not owe taxes depending upon the agreement the U.S. has negotiated with your home country. The United States has tax treaties with more than forty countries. You are responsible for making sure that the school you attend follows the terms of the tax treaty. If your country does not have a tax treaty with the U.S., you may have as much as 30 percent withheld from your paycheck.

A Final Note

While amounts and eligibility criteria vary from field to field as well as from year to year, with thorough research you can uncover many opportunities for graduate financial assistance. If you are interested in graduate study, discuss your plans with faculty members and advisers. Explore all options. Plan ahead, complete forms on time, and be tenacious in your search for support. No matter what your financial situation, if you are academically qualified and knowledgeable about the different sources of aid, you should be able to attend the law school of your choice.

Patricia McWade
Dean of Student Financial Services
Georgetown University

HOW TO USE THIS BOOK

Peterson's Law Schools provides detailed information, including more than 3,500 elective and clinical courses, for the 185 law schools that, as of August 2001, are accredited (approved) by the American Bar Association to confer the first degree in law. Law programs are described only for schools that have accreditation with national recognition. In addition to J.D. programs, other advanced degree programs in law, such as the LL.M., combined degree, and postdoctoral programs, are described for relevant institutions. These programs are offered only in the United States and its territories. Fifteen law schools have elected to provide additional information that should prove useful to students who are considering application options.

PROGRAM PROFILES

Profiles begin with the official school name, the name of the law unit (if applicable), and the primary address of the school.

Information Module

The left-hand column of the first page of the profile provides a defined section of basic school contact, student body, and application-related information.

Address and Contact

Address information appears within the first box. All this information is specific to the law school and is the preferred address for applicants to use to request information. Typically provided are the name of the person to whom application queries and applications should be addressed and the law school postal address, telephone and fax numbers, and World Wide Web and e-mail addresses.

Law Student Profile

Following the boxed information is the Law Student Profile. This is immediately appended with the date, in parentheses, for which this information is correct. The profile is segmented into four sections: full-time, part-time, racial or ethnic composition, and applicants and admittees.

The full-time section provides information on the full-time total enrollment in the law school as of the noted date and the percentage of women and men students.

The part-time section provides information on the part-time total enrollment in the law school as of the noted date and the percentage of women and men students.

The racial or ethnic composition section lists the percentage of students reported by the law school as fitting the four minority ethnic categories established by the U.S. Bureau of the Census (African American, Asian/Pacific Islander, Hispanic, American Indian) and the percentage of international students, meaning those students who are not U.S. citizens.

Applicants and Admittees

The applicants and admittees section lists the number of prospective students who applied to the law school, the number admitted, the percentage of those who applied that were accepted, the number of available seats (or openings available) for full-time students (law schools typically fill all their seats), the average LSAT score of entering students, and the average GPA of entering students. All of these figures are for the entering class of fall 2000.

At a Glance

At the bottom of the first page, five bar graphs represent key statistics. Each bar graph has numbers at the top and bottom that represent the ultimate end of each particular range. The bisecting line and figure to the right show the number reported by the institution being profiled. The bottom half of each bar is shaded to make viewing easier. The graphic presentation will help readers quickly zero in on answers to their most frequently asked questions: How large is the school? How hard is it to be accepted? What do I have to pay? The bar graphs also provide an easy way to compare schools in these areas. Total enrollment is the law school enrollment for fall 2000. Percentage admitted is the percentage of applicants accepted for fall 2000. Average LSAT scores and GPA are the averages of the entering class in fall 2000. Average debt on graduation is the figure reported by the schools.

Application Information

This section indicates what forms, fees, scores, or other items are required or recommended of applicants to the law school. Among these items are the **LSAT** (Law School Admissions Test), the **GRE** (Graduate Record Examinations), the **LSDAS** (use of the centralized Law School Data Assembly Service of the Law School Admissions Council), the **application form** specific to the law school, the **application fee**, the **minimum undergraduate GPA**, **letters of recommendation**, the **personal statement**, an **essay**, a **writing sample**, an **interview**, **college transcripts**, and a **resume**. If they are required, minimum LSAT scores, minimum GPA, application fee amount, and the number of letters of recommendation are specified immediately after the item. The application deadline indicates whether this is for fall entrance. If it is not a strict deadline, but a priority deadline, this is indicated. If applications are received and processed continually, the term *rolling* is used to show this.

Costs

Costs normally represent the tuition for the 2000–2001 school year. If a different year is represented, or if the tuition is estimated rather than actual, this is indicated. Other tuition rates for part-time students and for out-of-state residents (where applicable) are specifically indicated.

Financial Aid

Financial aid indicates the percentage of students in the law school who receive some form of financial aid, the number of fellowships awarded through the school to students at all levels and their total dollar value, the number of other types of awards and their total dollar value, and whether law-related internships, federal work-study, or institutionally sponsored loans are available. The average student debt on graduation is also indicated. The types of application forms for financial aid are indicated as is whether or not the law school participates in an LRAP (Loan Repayment Assistance Program), which is a state or institutionally supported low-interest or interest-free loan provided to help make payments on regular loans. The deadline for financial aid forms is indicated, as are the name, title, mailing address, phone and fax numbers, and e-mail address of the party to contact about financial aid.

Law School Library

This paragraph provides the name of the law library; the total number of volumes and number of periodicals in the law library; the number of seats; the availability of WESTLAW, LEXIS-NEXIS, the World Wide Web, other online bibliographic retrieval services, CD-ROM players, and other kinds of resources through the law library; and names of any special law collections.

Degree Options

Highlighted in a box are the degrees offered by the law school. The acronym and name of the degree or joint degree are indicated in the left-hand column. The total credits or range of credits required to complete the degree are shown in the middle column. The usual length, or range, in years is shown in the right-hand column as is an indication of whether the degree program is offered full-time and part-time or full-time only. If the program is

available to part-time students, an indication is made of whether it is scheduled during the day, evenings, weekends, and/or summers.

First-Year Program

This portion of each profile reveals the average class size for first-year courses and what percentage of first-year courses are taught by full-time faculty members.

Upper-Level Program

This section lists the average class size for upper-level (second-and third-year) courses and also lists many of the courses offered to students at this level. A star preceding the course indicates that the school has indicated that this course represents a subject that is given special emphasis or strength.

Clinical Courses

This provides information on clinical courses offered by the law school, whether they are required, how many hours may be required, and what some of the clinical offerings may be.

Internships and Special Programs

The final sentences of the second page of the profile provide information about special programs. The percentage of students who participate in internships is listed. Also, if an international exchange program is offered, this is indicated with the countries that participate.

In-Depth Description

Many of the law schools profiled have chosen to provide two pages of additional information about the special qualities, values, and attractions of their law school for prospective students. This information includes:

- A statement from the Dean of the law school
- The history of the school and a description of its location and physical facilities
- A description of the special qualities of the school
- A description of the integration of electronic and telecommunications into campus life and instruction
- A description of the school's financial aid efforts and of major scholarship and loan programs available through the college
- Special opportunities for students, including law reviews, moot court, extracurricular activities, special opportunities to enhance legal education, aspects of the institution with special interest for women and minorities, and special certificate programs
- Bar passage rates for graduates and states in which the greatest number practice
- Career services provided to graduates and alumni

- Percentages of graduates that placed in specific legal fields and their average salaries or average starting salaries

DATA COLLECTION PROCEDURES

Information contained in the program profile was collected in the spring and summer of 2001 through Peterson's Survey of ABA-Accredited Law Schools and Peterson's Annual Survey of Graduate Institutions. Questionnaires were sent to all institutions approved by the American Bar Association to confer the first degree in law. Information was requested from admissions officers or other appropriate personnel within these institutions in order to ensure accuracy. In some cases, this information was supplemented with data available from school catalogs and brochures, or directly from the institution's Web site, in order to provide as much detail as possible on a particular law school's degree offerings.

The omission of any particular item from a profile, chart, or index entry indicates that the item was either not applicable, not available at the time of publication, or not provided by the institution. Check with specific colleges and universities at the time of application to verify figures such as tuition and fees that may have changed since the publication of this guide.

LAW SCHOOL PROFILES
AND
IN-DEPTH DESCRIPTIONS

SAMFORD UNIVERSITY
CUMBERLAND SCHOOL OF LAW

Birmingham, Alabama

INFORMATION CONTACT

Mitzi S. Davis, Assistant Dean for Admissions
800 Lakeshore Drive
Birmingham, AL 35229

Phone: 205-726-2702   Fax: 205-726-2673
E-mail: msdavis@samford.edu
Web site: http://cumberland.samford.edu/

LAW STUDENT PROFILE [2000–2001]

FULL-TIME   Enrollment: 541
Women: 44%   Men: 56%

PART-TIME   Enrollment: 2
Women: 50%   Men: 50%

RACIAL or ETHNIC COMPOSITION
African American, 6%; Asian/Pacific Islander, 1%; Hispanic, 1%

APPLICANTS and ADMITTEES
Number applied: 870
Admitted: 462
Percentage accepted: 53%
Seats available: 173
Average LSAT score: 151
Average GPA: 3.0

Samford University Cumberland School of Law is a private institution that organizes classes on a semester calendar system. The campus is situated in a suburban setting. Founded in 1847, first ABA approved in 1949, and an AALS member, Samford University Cumberland School of Law offers JD, JD/M Acct, JD/MBA, JD/MDiv, JD/MPA, JD/MPH, JD/MS, LLM, MCL, and SJD degrees.

Faculty consists of 26 full-time and 18 part-time members in 2000–2001. 6 full-time faculty members and 6 part-time faculty members are women. 100% of all faculty members have a JD; 15.6% have advanced law degrees. Of all faculty members, 3.1% are Asian/Pacific Islander, 9.4% are African American, 87.5% are white.

Application Information *Required:* LSAT, LSDAS, application form, application fee of $40, baccalaureate degree, 2 letters of recommendation, personal statement, writing sample, college transcripts. *Application deadline* for fall term is February 28 (priority date). Applications are processed on a rolling basis.

Costs The 2000–2001 tuition was $19,550 full-time; $660 per credit part-time.

Financial Aid In 2000–2001, 84% of all students received some form of financial aid. Loans, merit-based grants/scholarships, and need-based grants/scholarships are available. The average student debt at graduation is $63,000. To apply for financial assistance, students must complete the Free Application for Federal Student Aid. Completed financial aid forms should be received by March 1. Financial aid contact: Ann Peeples, Assistant Director of Financial Aid, 800 Lakeshore Drive, Birming-

AT a GLANCE

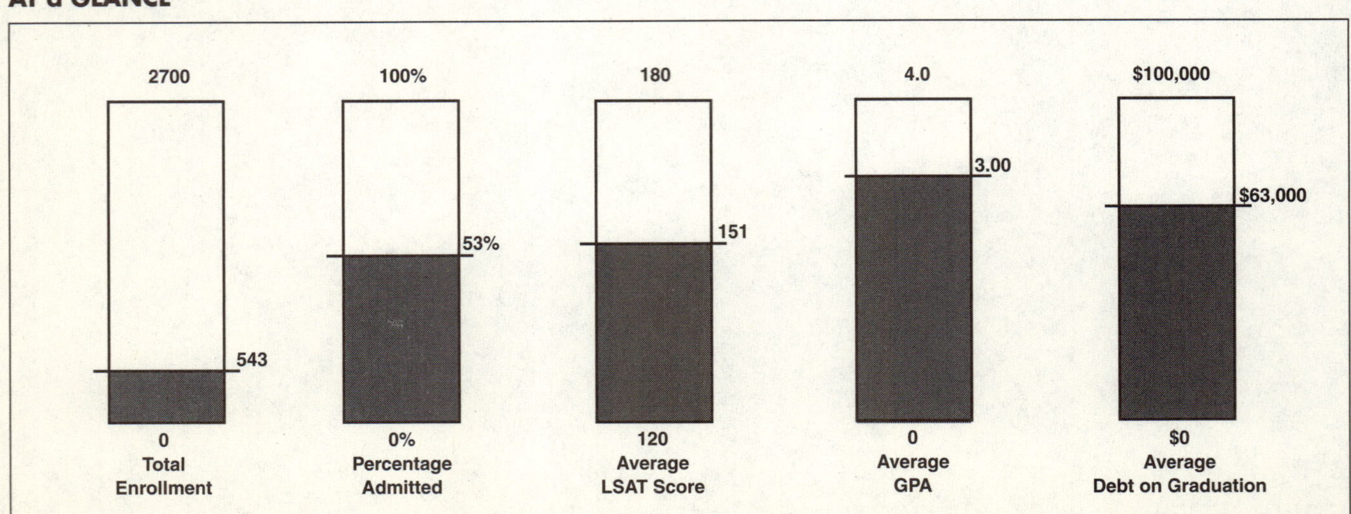

Degree Options

Degree	Total Credits Required	Length of Program
JD–Doctor of Laws	90	3 yrs, full-time or part-time [day, summer]
JD/M Acct–Juris Doctor/Master of Accountancy–Dual-degree Program	99	3–4 yrs, full-time only [day, evening, summer]
JD/MBA–Juris Doctor/Master of Business Administration–Dual-degree Program	99	4 yrs, full-time only [day, evening, summer]
JD/MDiv–Juris Doctor/Master of Divinity–Dual-degree Program	154	5 yrs, full-time only [day, evening, summer]
JD/MPA–Juris Doctor/Master of Professional Accountancy–Dual-degree Program	111	4 yrs, full-time only [day, evening]
JD/MPH–Juris Doctor/Master of Public Health–Dual-degree Program	102	4 yrs, full-time only [day, evening, summer]
JD/MS–Juris Doctor/Master of Science–Environmental Management Dual-degree Program	102	4 yrs, full-time only [day, evening]
LLM–Master of Laws		1 yr, full-time only [day]
MCL–Master of Comparative Law–International Jurists Program	16	full-time only [summer]
SJD–Doctor of Juridical Science		4 yrs, part-time only

ham, AL 35229. Phone: 800-888-7245 or toll free 800-888-7213. Fax: 205-726-2738. E-mail: appeeple@samford.edu

Law School Library Lucille Stewart Beeson Law Library has 7 professional staff members and contains more than 262,282 volumes and 2,959 periodicals. 474 seats are available in the library. When classes are in session, the library is open 107 hours per week.

WESTLAW and LEXIS-NEXIS are available, as are the World Wide Web, online bibliographic services, and CD-ROM players. 32 computer workstations are available to students in the library. Special law collections include the Brantley collection.

First-Year Program Class size in the average section is 56; 100% of the first-year courses are taught by full-time faculty.

Upper-Level Program Class size in the average section is 30. Among the electives are:

- Administrative Law
- ★ Advocacy
- Business and Corporate Law
- Constitutional Law
- Consumer Law
- Corporate Law
- Criminal Law
- Criminal Procedure
- Education Law
- Entertainment Law
- ★ Environmental Law
- Family Law
- Government/Regulation
- ★ Health Care/Human Services
- Intellectual Property
- ★ International/Comparative Law
- Jurisprudence
- Juvenile Law
- Labor Law
- Land Use Law/Natural Resources
- ★ Law and Religion
- ★ Lawyering Skills
- Legal Externship
- Legal History/Philosophy
- ★ Litigation
- Maritime Law
- Mediation
- Probate Law
- Public Interest
- Securities
- ★ Tax Law

(★ *indicates an area of special strength*)

Clinical Courses Students receive degree credit for clinical courses. (Clinical practicum is not required.) Among the clinical areas offered are:

- Administrative Law
- Corporate Law
- Criminal Law
- Criminal Procedure
- Criminal Prosecution
- Family Law
- General Practice
- Government Litigation
- Juvenile Law
- Legal Externship
- Litigation
- Public Interest
- Tax Law

THE UNIVERSITY OF ALABAMA
SCHOOL OF LAW

Tuscaloosa, Alabama

INFORMATION CONTACT

Betty McGinley, Admissions Coordinator
Box 870382
Tuscaloosa, AL 35487

Phone: 205-348-5440   Fax: 205-348-3917
E-mail: admissions@law.ua.edu
Web site: http://www.ua.edu/

LAW STUDENT PROFILE [2000–2001]

FULL-TIME   Enrollment: 524
Women: 37%   Men: 63%

RACIAL or ETHNIC COMPOSITION
African American, 9%; Asian/Pacific Islander, 1%; Hispanic, 1%; Native American, 1%

APPLICANTS and ADMITTEES
Number applied: 931
Admitted: 344
Percentage accepted: 37%
Seats available: 185
Average LSAT score: 159
Average GPA: 3.3

The University of Alabama School of Law is a public institution that organizes classes on a semester calendar system. The campus is situated in a small-town setting. Founded in 1872, first ABA approved in 1926, and an AALS member, The University of Alabama School of Law offers JD, JD/MBA, and LLM degrees.

Faculty consists of 31 full-time and 48 part-time members in 2000–2001. 5 full-time faculty members and 6 part-time faculty members are women. 97% of all faculty members have a JD; 31% have advanced law degrees. Of all faculty members, 1% are Native American, 1% are Asian/Pacific Islander, 7% are African American, 93% are white.

Application Information *Required:* LSAT, LSDAS, application form, application fee of $25, baccalaureate degree, personal statement, essay, college transcripts. *Recommended:* recommendations. *Application deadline* for fall term is March 1. Applications are processed on a rolling basis.

Costs The 2000–2001 tuition was $5112 full-time for state residents. Tuition was $10,798 full-time for nonresidents.

Financial Aid In 2000–2001, 72% of all students received some form of financial aid. 54 research assistantships were awarded. Graduate assistantships, loans, merit-based grants/scholarships, need-based grants/scholarships, and federal work-study loans are also available. To apply for financial assistance, students must complete the Free Application for Federal Student Aid, institutional forms,

AT a GLANCE

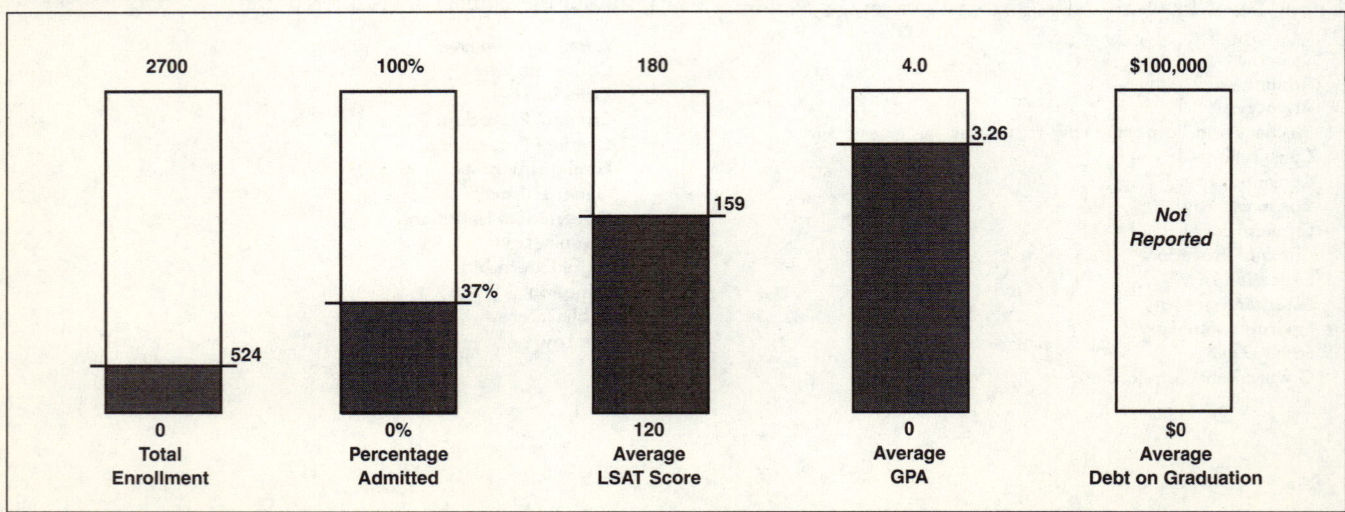

Degree Options

Degree	Total Credits Required	Length of Program
JD–Doctor of Laws	90	3–4 yrs, full-time only [day, summer]
JD/MBA–Juris Doctor/Master of Business Administration–Dual-degree Program	108	4–5 yrs, full-time only [day, summer]
LLM–Master of Laws–Taxation	24	2 yrs, part-time only [evening, weekend]
LLM–Master of Laws–International Graduate Program	24	1 yr, full-time only [day]

scholarship specific applications. Completed financial aid forms should be received by May 15. Financial aid contact: Noah Funderburg, Assistant Dean for Administration, Box 870384, Tuscaloosa, AL 35487. Phone: 205-348-4508. Fax: 205-348-3917. E-mail: nfunderb@law.ua.edu

Law School Library Bounds Law Library has 8 professional staff members and contains more than 388,369 volumes and 3,259 periodicals. 566 seats are available in the library. When classes are in session, the library is open 102 hours per week.

WESTLAW and LEXIS-NEXIS are available, as are the World Wide Web, online bibliographic services, and CD-ROM players. 96 computer workstations are available to students in the library. Special law collections include Howell Heflins papers, Hugo Black papers, John C. Payne Special Collection..

First-Year Program Class size in the average section is 67; 100% of the first-year courses are taught by full-time faculty.

Upper-Level Program Class size in the average section is 31. Among the electives are:

  Administrative Law
★ Advocacy
★ Business and Corporate Law
  Consumer Law
★ Criminal Defense
★ Education
  Education Law

★ Elderly Advocacy
  Entertainment Law
  Environmental Law
  Family Law
  Government/Regulation
  Health Care/Human Services
  Intellectual Property
  International/Comparative Law
  Jurisprudence
  Labor Law
  Land Use Law/Natural Resources
★ Lawyering Skills
  Legal History/Philosophy
★ Litigation
  Maritime Law
  Media Law
  Mediation
★ Pensions
  Probate Law
★ Public Interest
  Securities
★ Tax Law

(★ *indicates an area of special strength*)

Clinical Courses Students receive degree credit for clinical courses. (Clinical practicum is not required.) Among the clinical areas offered are:

  Criminal Defense
  Education
  Elderly Advocacy
  Pensions
  Public Interest

International exchange programs permit students to visit Australia and Switzerland.

DEAN'S STATEMENT . . .

The University of Alabama School of Law combines great traditions with great promise. The University of Alabama offers students a nationally recognized, progressive legal education. For more than 125 years, the law school has educated premier lawyers, business and civic leaders, and state and federal judges. Never content with the law school's past success, the University of Alabama today offers state-of-the-art facilities and technology, an updated curriculum, increased opportunity for skills training, and expanded career services. The School of Law particularly proud that it is recognized as one of the top fifty law schools in the United States. Significant factors in the School of Law's success include externships, clinics, two international programs, trial advocacy teams, public interest opportunities, and high bar-passage and employment rates. Alabama is a thriving and vibrant law school, with outstanding faculty members who bring to the classroom years of experience working with large and small law firms, the courts, government agencies, and public interest groups. Students find the Alabama faculty members collegial, supportive, and accessible outside the classroom. The academic environment at the University of Alabama is nurturing yet consistent with the atmosphere appropriate for the rigors of a high-quality law school. Our student body of approximately 520 students is talented, diverse, and academically strong. Alabama students graduate with a positive attitude about their legal education. Alabama law alumni are some of the most devoted in the country. The faculty and staff members and students at the University of Alabama School of Law invite you to experience our progressive atmosphere and consider receiving your legal education at Alabama.

—*Ken Randall, Dean and Thomas E. McMillan Professor of Law*

HISTORY, CAMPUS, AND LOCATION

The University of Alabama School of Law was established in 1872 on the campus of the University of Alabama in Tuscaloosa and remains the only state-supported law school in Alabama. Law students enjoy the advantages of belonging to a university of more than 19,000 students, as well as the benefits of a self-contained law school facility with its own bookstore, computer lab, administrative offices, and a library of more than 65,000 square feet. The Law Center is a modern, spacious building with plenty of natural light and open spaces. Future construction plans include a new building to house clinical offices, the addition of more classrooms and faculty offices, and increased space for student activities and organizations. An expansion of the Bounds Law Library is also planned. Tuscaloosa is a vibrant city of approximately 100,000 residents and offers a variety of employment, history, sports, and cultural and entertainment opportunities.

SPECIAL QUALITIES OF THE SCHOOL

The law faculty includes nationally known scholars with impressive academic credentials, whose first priority is teaching. The Law School curriculum offers a wide variety of traditional and cutting-edge courses. The breadth of the curriculum allows students the opportunity to undertake a broad or specialized course of study, depending on each student's career goals. The expansive curriculum reflects the Law School's commitment to evolving areas of law, such as international, environmental, and intellectual property law, while providing a traditional course of study that ensures a solid legal foundation.

The University of Alabama School of Law also provides a strong academic support program for students with lower numerical predictors and for students who might face academic difficulties. This program includes offering a summer class that allows first-year students to take a reduced course load in the fall, a smaller section of a spring semester first-year class that includes emphasis on writing and analytical skills, special instruction from faculty members, and extra support tailored to students' needs.

TECHNOLOGY ON CAMPUS

The law school is substantially expanding and enhancing its information services and the technology available to students and faculty members. The Law Center houses a multimedia classroom equipped with distance-learning technology. Portable multimedia equipment allows professors to use state-of-the-art equipment in any classroom. Expansion plans for the Law Center include the use of advanced technology in several new classrooms. Students and faculty and staff members may communicate through the School's network, and they also may access the network from their home computers through the School of Law's dial-in capabilities. The Bounds Law Library houses a large and up-to-date computer lab, and there are carrels in the library connected to the School network for laptop use. The School's LL.M. in taxation program is taught through interactive, distance learning through the University's IITS system.

SCHOLARSHIPS AND LOANS

Though tuition remains reasonable, the Law School provides almost $500,000 a year in student scholarships. Law School applicants are automatically considered for first-year scholarships, which are awarded based on criteria established by the donors and the Scholarship Committee. Criteria include undergraduate grade point average and performance on the LSAT, and may also include other relevant factors, including economic background. Outstanding nonresident students may receive a nonresident tuition grant. Scholarships sometimes are renewable during the second and third years, depending upon funding, the student's need, and whether the recipient maintains stated levels of academic achievement.

Many students obtain loans through the University of Alabama Student Financial Services Office. Upon acceptance, each student receives a financial aid packet from the Financial Aid Office. Further information is available at Student Financial Services, The University of Alabama, Box 870162, Tuscaloosa, Alabama 35487-0162, telephone: 205-348-6756.

STUDENT ACTIVITIES AND OPPORTUNITIES

Law Review Three student-edited law journals–the *Alabama Law Review*, *The Journal of the Legal Profession*, and the *Law and Psychology Review*–provide excellent opportunities in legal research, writing, and editing. Staff members of these journals edit and publish articles on important legal topics written by legal scholars and practitioners throughout the country. Students also write notes and comments for these journals. The *Alabama Law Review* is ranked among the top twenty-five student journals in the country. *The Journal of the Legal Profession* was the nation's first periodical to explore legal ethics and problems confronting the profession. The *Law and Psychology Review* was among the first legal periodicals to combine the discipline of law with the behavioral sciences.

Moot Court Moot court is required in the first year. Many students participate beyond the first year in moot court competitions. The Law School enjoys a history of excellence among its competitors, and the moot court teams have garnered many team and individual awards. The Law School sponsors teams in the Jessup International Moot Court Competition, the National Moot Court Competition, the Frederick Douglass Moot Court Competition, the Pace Environmental Law Moot Court Competition, the Wagner Labor Law Competition, the National Criminal Law Moot Court Competition, the Intellectual Property Moot Court Competition, the National Tax Moot Court Competition, and the Duberstein Bankruptcy Competition.

Special Opportunities The Law School offers extensive, varied, and high-quality clinical programs. Students may participate in the Elder Law Clinic, the Alabama Disabilities Advocacy Clinic, the Children's Rights Clinic, the Student Legal Clinic, the Pension Law Clinic, and the Public Defender Clinic. Externship opportunities are offered during the academic year and during the summer. Many students also participate in the Law School's nationally recognized trial advocacy program. The trial advocacy teams have won numerous individual and team awards.

The Law School's Public Law Institute awards grants to encourage students to perform public interest work during the summer. Students also receive awards for completing an established amount of legal and nonlegal service.

The Law School and the Manderson Graduate School of Business at the University of Alabama offer select students an opportunity to earn a joint J.D./M.B.A. degree in a four-year program of study. Summer programs at the University of Fribourg in Fribourg, Switzerland and the Australian National University in Canberra, Australia allow students to study other legal systems while enjoying a unique cultural experience. Three endowed lecture series bring national judges and scholars to campus. These have included U.S. Supreme Court Justices Anthony Kennedy, Antonin Scalia, and Sandra Day O'Connor.

The LL.M. in Taxation is awarded to qualified graduates of law schools upon completion of 24 graduate hours. This two-year program is part-time and is offered through distance education. Law School faculty members and adjunct faculty members drawn from the top ranks of Alabama's tax bar teach the courses. The Graduate Program for International Students offers a limited number of international lawyers an opportunity to earn an LL.M. upon successful completion of 24 credit hours of course work.

Opportunities for Members of Minority Groups and Women Students who are members of minority groups participate in all extracurricular and clinical programs, law reviews, and student organizations. The Black Law Student Association is very active, sponsoring activities during Black History Month, tutoring at a local elementary school, and providing support for entering first-year students. The Dorbin Association is a student organization interested in the needs, interests, and problems unique to the woman law student, lawyer, and client. Members examine these issues and present various programs at the Law School. Membership is open to all interested law students.

BAR PASSAGE, CAREER SERVICES, AND PLACEMENT

Alabama graduates are successful in passing the Alabama bar exam. The Alabama bar passage rate for Alabama graduates is much higher than the overall state average. The Law School is committed to supporting the career goals of its students and alumni whatever and wherever their jobs. Through individual counseling, speaker programs, seminars on resume writing and interviewing, and library and database resources, the Career Services Office assists students in exploring a wide variety of legal career options, both traditional and nontraditional, and in determining the best methods for pursuing those options. The Law School enjoys a consistently high employment rate (99 percent) among its graduates within nine months of graduation.

Legal Field	Percentage of Graduates	Average Starting Salary
Academic	3%	n/a
Business	10%	$30,000
Government	10%	$37,667
Judicial Clerkships	17%	$34,173
Private Practice	56%	$65,356
Public Interest	3%	$30,000
Other	1%	n/a

CORRESPONDENCE AND INFORMATION

The University of Alabama School of Law
Admissions Office, Box 870382
Tuscaloosa, Alabama 35487-0382
Telephone: 205-348-5440
Fax: 205-348-3917
E-mail: admissions@law.ua.edu
World Wide Web: http://www.law.ua.edu

ARIZONA STATE UNIVERSITY
COLLEGE OF LAW

Tempe, Arizona

INFORMATION CONTACT

Brenda Brock, Assistant Dean and Director of
Admissions
PO Box 877906
Tempe, AZ 85287-7906

Phone: 480-965-6380   Fax: 480-965-5550
E-mail: brenda.brock@asu.edu
Web site: http://www.law.asu.edu/

LAW STUDENT PROFILE [2000–2001]

FULL-TIME   Enrollment: 515
Women: 50%   Men: 50%
PART-TIME   Enrollment: 9
Women: 44%   Men: 56%

RACIAL or ETHNIC COMPOSITION
African American, 4%; Asian/Pacific Islander, 3%; Hispanic,
13%; Native American, 7%; International, 1%

APPLICANTS and ADMITTEES
Number applied: 1,707
Admitted: 462
Percentage accepted: 27%
Seats available: 150
Average LSAT score: 156
Average GPA: 3.3

Arizona State University College of Law is a public
institution that organizes classes on a semester calendar
system. The campus is situated in an urban setting.
Founded in 1966, first ABA approved in 1969, and an
AALS member, Arizona State University College of Law
offers JD, JD/MBA, JD/MHA, and JD/PhD degrees.

Faculty consists of 32 full-time and 24 part-time
members in 2000–2001. 91% of all faculty members have
a JD; 11% have advanced law degrees. Of all faculty
members, 6% are Native American, 4% are African
American, 4% are Hispanic, 86% are white.

Application Information *Required:* LSAT, LSDAS,
application form, application fee of $45, baccalaureate
degree, 2 letters of recommendation, personal statement,
statement of residency form, college transcripts, resume.
Application deadline for fall term is March 1. Applications are processed on a rolling basis.

Costs The 2000–2001 tuition was $5022 full-time for
state residents. Tuition was $12,478 full-time for
nonresidents. Fees: $37 per semester full-time.

Financial Aid In 2000–2001, 68% of all students received
some form of financial aid. 50 research assistantships,
totaling $657; 13 teaching assistantships, totaling $1241,
were awarded. Graduate assistantships, loans, merit-based
grants/scholarships, need-based grants/scholarships, and
federal work-study loans are also available. The average
student debt at graduation is $31,196. To apply for
financial assistance, students must complete the Free
Application for Federal Student Aid. Completed financial
aid forms should be received by March 1. Financial aid

AT a GLANCE

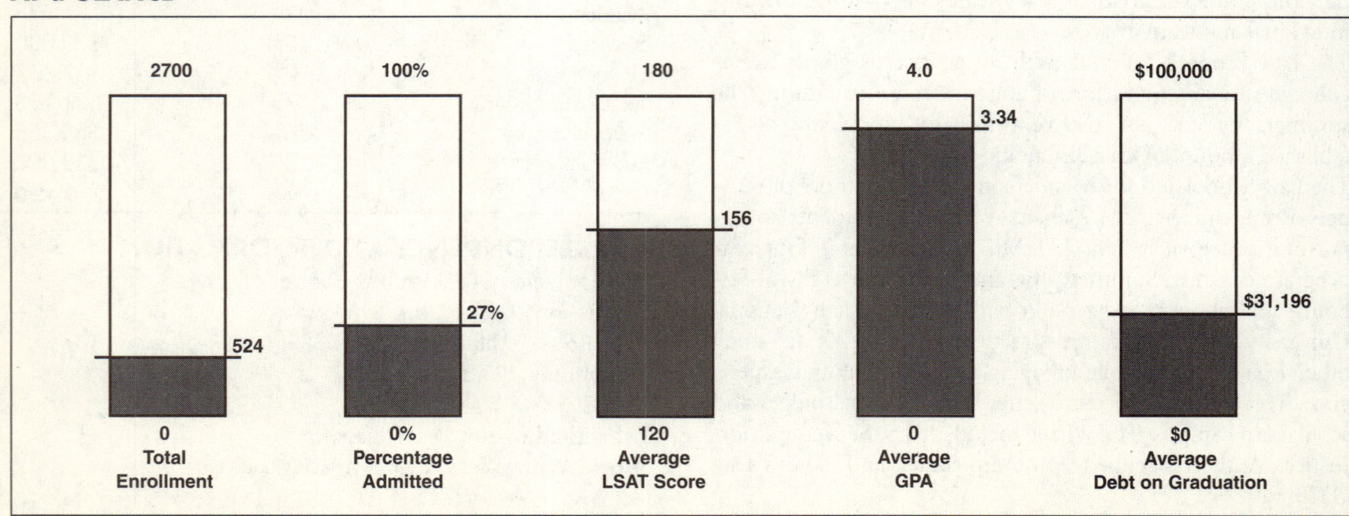

Degree Options

Degree	Total Credits Required	Length of Program
JD–Doctor of Laws	87	3 yrs, full-time only [day, summer]
JD/MBA–Juris Doctor/Master of Business Administration–Dual-degree Program		4 yrs, full-time only [day, summer]
JD/MHA–Juris Doctor/Master of Health Administration–Dual-degree Program Health Services Administration		4 yrs, full-time only [day, summer]
JD/PhD–Juris Doctor/Doctor of Philosophy–Dual-degree Program Justice Studies		full-time only [day, summer]

contact: Michael Bossone, Director Student Developement and Financial Aid, Arizona State University College of Law, Box, 877906, Tempe, AZ 85287-7906. Phone: 480-967-7429. Fax: 480-965-5550. E-mail: michael.bossone@asu.edu

Law School Library John J. Ross - William C. Blakley Law Library has 8 professional staff members and contains more than 386,830 volumes and 3,650 periodicals. 558 seats are available in the library. When classes are in session, the library is open 110 hours per week.

WESTLAW and LEXIS-NEXIS are available, as are the World Wide Web, online bibliographic services, and CD-ROM players. 96 computer workstations are available to students in the library. Special law collections include Native American; Federal Government Depository.

First-Year Program Class size in the average section is 40; 100% of the first-year courses are taught by full-time faculty.

Upper-Level Program Class size in the average section is 30. Among the electives are:

  Business and Corporate Law
★ Civil Litigation
  Civil Rights
  Conflict of Laws
  Constitutional Law
  Criminal Defense
  Criminal Procedure
  Criminal Prosecution
  Environmental Law
  Evidence
  Family Law
  General Practice
  Government/Regulation
  Health Law
★ Indian/Tribal Law
★ Intellectual Property
  International Law
  Labor Law
★ Law and Science
★ Lawyering Skills
  Legal History/Philosophy
  Legislation
★ Mediation
★ Technology Law
  Water Law
(★ *indicates an area of special strength*)

Clinical Courses Students receive degree credit for clinical courses. (Clinical practicum is not required.) Among the clinical areas offered are:

  Civil Litigation
  Criminal Defense
  Criminal Prosecution
  General Practice
  Indian/Tribal Law
  Lawyering Skills
  Mediation

International exchange programs permit students to visit Argentina.

THE UNIVERSITY OF ARIZONA
JAMES E. ROGERS COLLEGE OF LAW

Tucson, Arizona

INFORMATION CONTACT

Terry Sue Holpert, Assistant Dean for Admissions
1201 East Speedway
PO Box 210176
Tucson, AZ 85721-0176

Phone: 520-621-3477   Fax: 520-621-9140
E-mail: holpert@law.arizona.edu
Web site: http://www.law.arizona.edu/

LAW STUDENT PROFILE [2000–2001]

FULL-TIME   Enrollment: *477*
Women: 51%   Men: 49%

RACIAL or ETHNIC COMPOSITION
African American, 3%; Asian/Pacific Islander, 6%; Hispanic, 10%; Native American, 4%; International, 4%

APPLICANTS and ADMITTEES
Number applied: 1,660
Admitted: 430
Percentage accepted: 25%
Average LSAT score: 160
Average GPA: 3.5

The University of Arizona James E. Rogers College of Law is a public institution that organizes classes on a semester calendar system. The campus is situated in an urban setting. Founded in 1915, first ABA approved in 1931, and an AALS member, The University of Arizona James E. Rogers College of Law offers JD, JD/MA, JD/MBA, JD/MPAd, and JD/PhD degrees.

Faculty consists of 30 full-time and 55 part-time members in 2000–2001. 13 full-time faculty members and 23 part-time faculty members are women. 100% of all faculty members have a JD; 40% have advanced law degrees. Of all faculty members, 12% are Native American, 7% are African American, 7% are Hispanic, 78% are white.

Application Information *Required:* LSAT, application form, application fee of $50, baccalaureate degree, 2 letters of recommendation, personal statement, writing sample, college transcripts, resume, LSDAS. *Application deadline* for fall term is February 15. Applications are processed on a rolling basis.

Costs The 1999–2000 tuition was $5014 full-time for state residents. Tuition was $12,166 full-time for nonresidents.

Financial Aid In 2000–2001, 75% of all students received some form of financial aid. Fellowships, loans, merit-based grants/scholarships, need-based grants/scholarships, and federal work-study loans are available. The average student debt at graduation is $35,000. To apply for financial assistance, students must complete the Free Application for Federal Student Aid. Completed financial

AT a GLANCE

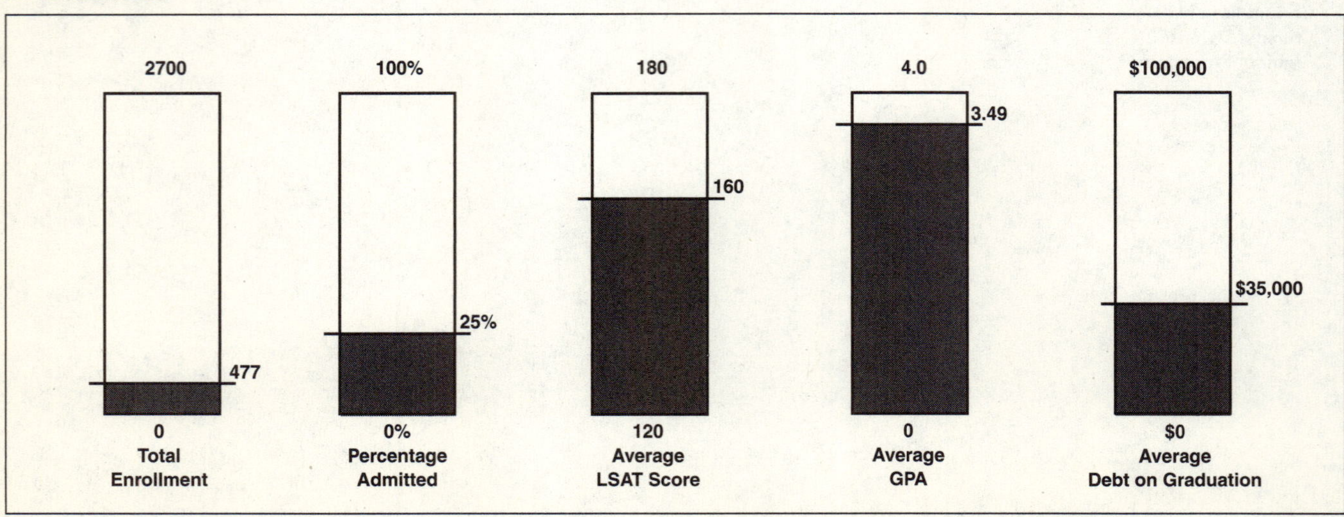

Degree Options

Degree	Total Credits Required	Length of Program
JD–Doctor of Laws	85	3 yrs, full-time only [day, summer]
JD/MA–Juris Doctor/Master of Arts–Economics	103	3 yrs, full-time only [day, summer]
JD/MA–Juris Doctor/Master of Arts–Indian Studies, Women's Studies, and Latin American Studies	106	4 yrs, full-time only [day, summer]
JD/MBA–Juris Doctor/Master of Business Administration–JD/MBA	113	4 yrs, full-time only [day, summer]
JD/MPAd–Juris Doctor/Master of Public Administration–JD/MPA	112	4 yrs, full-time only [day, summer]
JD/PhD–Juris Doctor/Doctor of Philosophy–Psychology, Philosophy, or Economics	133	6 yrs, full-time only [day, summer]

aid forms should be received by March 1. Financial aid contact: Kim Marlow, Financial Aid Counselor, PO Box 210176, Tucson, AZ 85721-0176. Phone: 520-626-8101. Fax: 520-621-9140. E-mail: marlow@law.arizona.edu

Law School Library College of Law Library has 9 professional staff members and contains more than 382,871 volumes and 4,450 periodicals. 368 seats are available in the library. When classes are in session, the library is open 107 hours per week.

WESTLAW and LEXIS-NEXIS are available, as are the World Wide Web, online bibliographic services, and CD-ROM players. 50 computer workstations are available to students in the library. Special law collections include International/Mexican Law Collection, International Commercial Law Collection, Latin American Law Collection, Government Documents Repository.

First-Year Program Class size in the average section is 35; 100% of the first-year courses are taught by full-time faculty.

Upper-Level Program Class size in the average section is 30. Among the electives are:

Accounting
★ Advocacy
Business and Corporate Law
★ Children's Advocacy
Constitutional Law
★ Criminal Defense
★ Criminal Prosecution
★ Domestic Violence
Environmental Law
★ Family Law
Health Care/Human Services
★ Immigration
★ Indian/Tribal Law
★ Indigenous Human Rights
Intellectual Property
★ International Law
★ International/Comparative Law
Juvenile Law
Land Use Law/Natural Resources
Lawyering Skills
★ Legal History/Philosophy
Media Law
Mediation
Probate Law
Public Interest
Sports Law
★ Tax Law
★ Water Law
(★ *indicates an area of special strength*)

Clinical Courses Students receive degree credit for clinical courses. (Clinical practicum is not required.) Among the clinical areas offered are:

Children's Advocacy
Criminal Defense
Criminal Prosecution
Domestic Violence
Immigration
Indian/Tribal Law
Indigenous Human Rights
International Law
Juvenile Law
Lawyering Skills
Mediation

UNIVERSITY OF ARKANSAS
SCHOOL OF LAW

Fayetteville, Arkansas

INFORMATION CONTACT

James K. Miller, Associate Dean for Students
Leflar Law Center
Fayetteville, AR 72701

Phone: 501-575-3102   Fax: 501-575-3320
Web site: http://www.law.uark.edu/

LAW STUDENT PROFILE [2000–2001]

FULL-TIME   Enrollment: 352
Women: 40%   Men: 60%

RACIAL or ETHNIC COMPOSITION
African American, 5%; Asian/Pacific Islander, 2%; Hispanic,
2%; Native American, 5%; International, 1%

APPLICANTS and ADMITTEES
Number applied: 530
Admitted: 280
Percentage accepted: 53%
Seats available: 109
Average LSAT score: 153
Average GPA: 3.3

University of Arkansas School of Law is a public
institution that organizes classes on a semester calendar
system. The campus is situated in a small-town setting.
Founded in 1924, first ABA approved in 1926, and an
AALS member, University of Arkansas School of Law
offers JD, JD/MBA, JD/MPA, and LLM degrees.

Faculty consists of 37 full-time and 5 part-time members
in 2000–2001. 10 full-time faculty members and 1
part-time faculty members are women. 100% of all
faculty members have a JD; 29% have advanced law
degrees. Of all faculty members, 3% are Native American, 9% are African American, 3% are Hispanic, 85% are
white.

Application Information *Required:* LSAT, LSDAS,
application form, baccalaureate degree. *Application
deadline* for fall term is April 1. Applications are
processed on a rolling basis.

Financial Aid In 2000–2001, 30% of all students received
some form of financial aid. Loans, merit-based grants/
scholarships, need-based grants/scholarships, and federal
work-study loans are available. The average student debt
at graduation is $36,483. To apply for financial assis-
tance, students must complete the Free Application for
Federal Student Aid, institutional forms. Completed
financial aid forms should be received by April 1.
Financial aid contact: James K. Miller, Associate Dean for
Students, Leflar Law Center, Fayetteville, AR 72701.
Phone: 501-575-3102. Fax: 501-575-3320.

Law School Library Young Law Library has 13 professional staff members and contains more than 252,000

AT a GLANCE

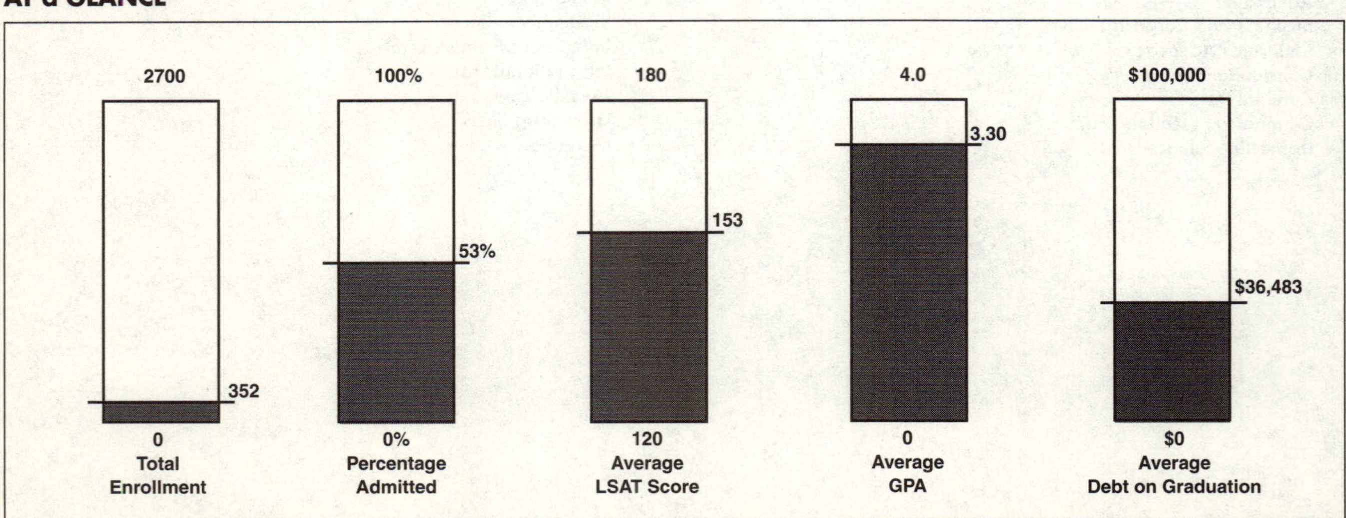

Degree Options

Degree	Total Credits Required	Length of Program
JD–Doctor of Laws	90	3 yrs, full-time only [day, summer]
JD/MBA–Juris Doctor/Master of Business Administration–Joint Program		3 yrs, full-time only [day, summer]
JD/MPA–Juris Doctor/Master of Professional Accountancy		full-time only [day, summer]
LLM–Master of Laws–Agricultural Law	24	1 yr, full-time only [day, summer]

volumes and 2,240 periodicals. 346 seats are available in the library. When classes are in session, the library is open 99 hours per week.

WESTLAW and LEXIS-NEXIS are available, as are the World Wide Web, online bibliographic services, and CD-ROM players. 34 computer workstations are available to students in the library. Special law collections include agricultural law.

First-Year Program 100% of the first-year courses are taught by full-time faculty.

Upper-Level Program Class size in the average section is 30. Among the electives are:

Administrative Law
Advocacy
Business and Corporate Law
Consumer Law
Education Law
Entertainment Law
Environmental Law
Family Law
Government/Regulation
Health Care/Human Services
Indian/Tribal Law

Intellectual Property
International/Comparative Law
Jurisprudence
Labor Law
Land Use Law/Natural Resources
Lawyering Skills
Legal History/Philosophy
Litigation
Media Law
Mediation
Probate Law
Public Interest
Securities
Tax Law

Clinical Courses Students receive degree credit for clinical courses. (Clinical practicum is not required.) Among the clinical areas offered are:

Civil Litigation
Criminal Defense
Criminal Prosecution
General Practice
Government Litigation
Juvenile Law

UNIVERSITY OF ARKANSAS AT LITTLE ROCK
WILLIAM H. BOWEN SCHOOL OF LAW

Little Rock, Arkansas

INFORMATION CONTACT

Jean M. Probasco, Director of Admissions and
Registrar
1201 McAlmont Street
Little Rock, AR 72202-5142

Phone: 501-324-9939   Fax: 501-324-9433
Web site: http://www.ualr.edu/~lawschool/

LAW STUDENT PROFILE [2000–2001]

FULL-TIME   Enrollment: 252
Women: 48%   Men: 52%
PART-TIME   Enrollment: 133
Women: 41%   Men: 59%

RACIAL or ETHNIC COMPOSITION
African American, 7%; Asian/Pacific Islander, 1%; Hispanic,
2%; International, 1%

APPLICANTS and ADMITTEES
Number applied: 408
Admitted: 238
Percentage accepted: 58%
Seats available: 130
Average LSAT score: 151
Average GPA: 3.3

**University of Arkansas at Little Rock William H.
Bowen School of Law** is a public institution that
organizes classes on a semester calendar system. The
campus is situated in an urban setting. Founded in 1975,
first ABA approved in 1969, and an AALS member,
University of Arkansas at Little Rock William H. Bowen
School of Law offers JD, JD/MBA, and JD/MPA degrees.

Faculty consists of 28 full-time and 24 part-time
members in 2000–2001. 12 full-time faculty members
and 8 part-time faculty members are women. 100% of all
faculty members have a JD; 18.18% have advanced law
degrees. Of all faculty members, 2% are Asian/Pacific
Islander, 8% are African American, 90% are white.

Application Information *Required:* LSAT, LSDAS,
application form, application fee of $40, baccalaureate
degree, 2 letters of recommendation, personal statement,
college transcripts. *Application deadline* for fall term is
May 1. Applications are processed on a rolling basis.

Costs The 2000–2001 tuition was $5100 full-time for
state residents; $170 per credit hour part-time for state
residents. Tuition was $11,460 full-time for nonresidents;
$382 per credit hour part-time for nonresidents. Fees:
$406 per term full-time; $3 per credit hour part-time;
$361 per credit hour part-time; $25 full-time (one-time
charge).

Financial Aid In 2000–2001, 72% of all students received
some form of financial aid. 25 research assistantships,
totaling $1250 were awarded. Loans, merit-based

AT a GLANCE

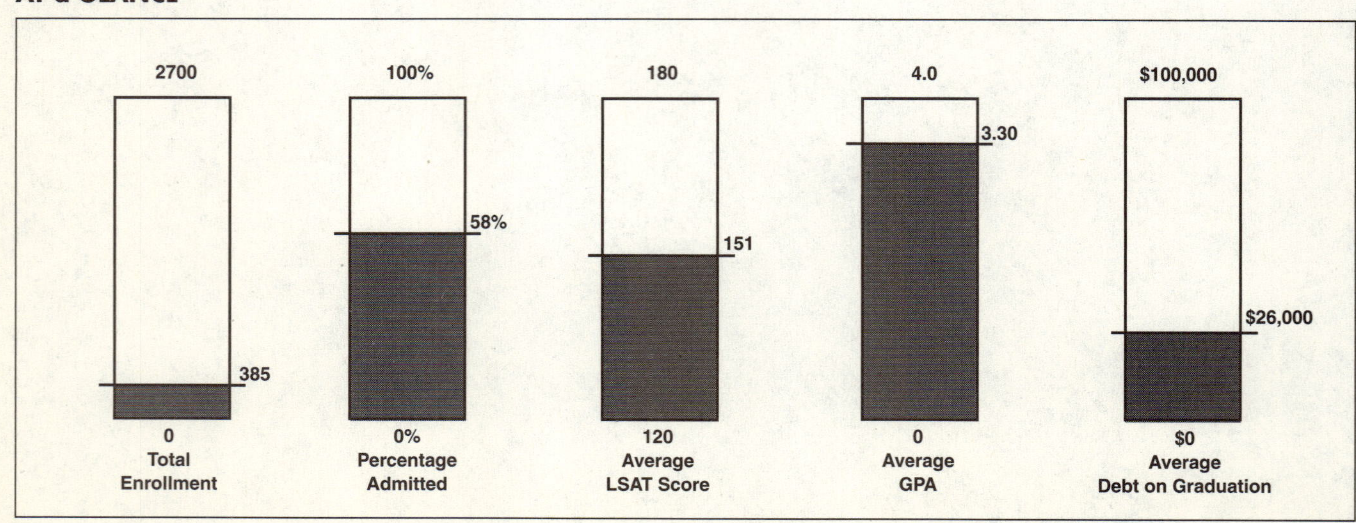

Degree Options

Degree	Total Credits Required	Length of Program
JD–Doctor of Laws	90	3–4 yrs, full-time or part-time [day, evening, summer]
JD/MBA–Juris Doctor/Master of Business Administration–Joint-degree	102	4–6 yrs, full-time or part-time [day, evening, summer]
JD/MPA–Juris Doctor/Master of Professional Accountancy–Joint-degree	111	4–6 yrs, full-time or part-time [day, evening, summer]

grants/scholarships, need-based grants/scholarships, and federal work-study loans are also available. The average student debt at graduation is $26,000. To apply for financial assistance, students must complete the Free Application for Federal Student Aid. Completed financial aid forms should be received by March 1. Financial aid contact: Cari Wickliffe, Director, Financial Aid Office, 2801 South University, Administration South 206, Little Rock, AR 72204. Phone: 501-569-3035. Fax: 501-569-8956. E-mail: kkhusley@ualr.edu

Law School Library UALR/Pulaski Country Law Library has 6 professional staff members and contains more than 270,000 volumes and 3,168 periodicals. 385 seats are available in the library. When classes are in session, the library is open 101 hours per week.

WESTLAW and LEXIS-NEXIS are available, as are the World Wide Web, online bibliographic services, and CD-ROM players. 35 computer workstations are available to students in the library. Special law collections include Archive of Arkansas Supreme Court Records and Briefs.

First-Year Program Class size in the average section is 65; 100% of the first-year courses are taught by full-time faculty.

Upper-Level Program Class size in the average section is 26. Among the electives are:

Admiralty Law
★ Advocacy
Agency
Agricultural Law
Alternative Dispute Resolution
American Legal History
Antitrust Law
Appellate Advocacy
Arkanas Criminal Trial Procedure
Bankruptcy
Bioethics
Business and Corporate Law
Civil Liberties
Civil Procedure
Commercial Transactions
Communications Law
Conflict of Laws
Constitutional Law
Consumer Law
Corporate Restructuring
Corporate Taxation

Corporations
Creditor's Rights
Criminal Law
Criminal Procedure
Debtor Law
Disability Law
Employment Discrimination
Employment Law
Environmental Law
Equity
Estate & Gift Taxation
Estate Planning
Estates & Trusts
Evidence
Family Law
★ Family Practice
Federal Income Tax
Federal Jurisdiction
Film & Criminal Law
First Amendment
Franchising Law
Guns & the Law
★ Health Care/Human Services
Health Law
Immigration
Insurance Law
Intellectual Property
International Business Transactions
International/Comparative Law
Interviewing and Counseling
Jurisprudence
★ Juvenile Law
Labor Law
Land Use Law/Natural Resources
Law and Literature
Law and Medicine
Law and Psychiatry
Law and Religion
Law Office Management
Lawyering Skills
Legal History/Philosophy
Legal Research
Legal Writing
Legislation
Litigation
Local Government
Maritime Law
Media Law
★ Mediation
★ Mental Health and Law
Nonprofit Organizations
Oil and Gas
Partnerships
Pretrial Litigation
Probate Law
Product Liability

Public International Law
Race and Criminal Justice
Real Estate Finance
Real Estate Transactions
Securities
Securities Regulation
Sports Law
State and Local Taxation
★ Tax Law
Tax Policy
Trial Advocacy
Water Law
White Collar Crime
Women and the Law

Workers' Compensation
(★ *indicates an area of special strength*)

Clinical Courses Students receive degree credit for clinical courses. (Clinical practicum is not required.) Among the clinical areas offered are:

Family Practice
Health Care/Human Services
Juvenile Law
Mediation
Mental Health and Law

CALIFORNIA WESTERN SCHOOL OF LAW

San Diego, California

LAW STUDENT PROFILE [2000–2001]

FULL-TIME   Enrollment: 650
Women: 51%   Men: 49%

PART-TIME   Enrollment: 110
Women: 54%   Men: 46%

APPLICANTS and ADMITTEES

Number applied: 1,694
Admitted: 1,102
Percentage accepted: 65%
Seats available: 256
Average LSAT score: 150
Average GPA: 3.1

California Western School of Law is a private nonprofit institution that organizes classes on a trimester calendar system. The campus is situated in an urban setting. Founded in 1924, first ABA approved in 1962, and an AALS member, California Western School of Law offers JD, JD/MSW, JD/PhD, LLM, and MCL degrees.

Faculty 100% of all faculty members have a JD; 21% have advanced law degrees. Of all faculty members, 5% are African American, 11% are Hispanic, 83% are white.

Application Information *Required:* LSAT, LSDAS, application form, application fee of $45, baccalaureate degree, 2 letters of recommendation, personal statement, college transcripts. *Recommended:* resume.

Costs The 2000–2001 tuition was $8100 per trimester part-time.

Financial Aid Loans, merit-based grants/scholarships, need-based grants/scholarships, and federal work-study loans are available. The average student debt at graduation is $87,000. To apply for financial assistance, students must complete the Free Application for Federal Student Aid, institutional forms. Financial aid contact: Kyle C. Poston, Executive Director of Financial Aid, 225 Cedar Street, San Diego, CA 92101. Phone: 619-525-7060. Fax: 619-525-7092. E-mail: financial-aid@cwsl.edu

Law School Library California Western School of Law Library has 9 professional staff members and contains more than 282,000 volumes and 3,750 periodicals. 616 seats are available in the library. When classes are in session, the library is open 119 hours per week.

WESTLAW and LEXIS-NEXIS are available, as are the World Wide Web, online bibliographic services, and

AT a GLANCE

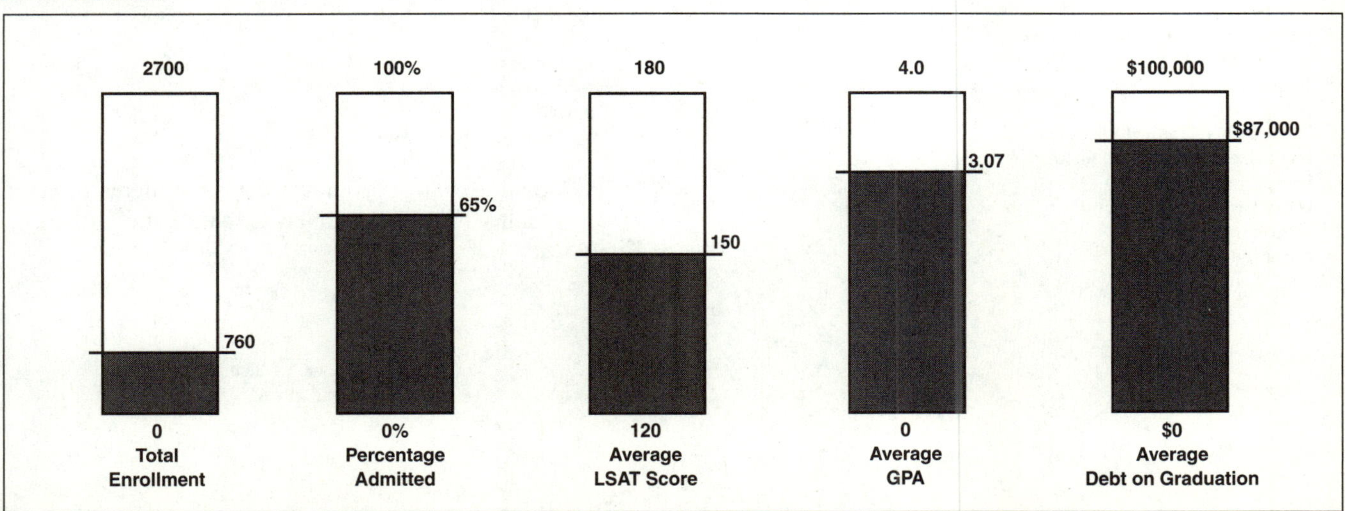

Degree Options

Degree	Total Credits Required	Length of Program
JD–Doctor of Laws	89	2–5 yrs, full-time or part-time [day]
JD/MSW–Juris Doctor/Master of Social Work–Dual-degree Program	149	4 yrs, full-time or part-time [day]
JD/PhD–Juris Doctor/Doctor of Philosophy–Political Science		4–5 yrs, full-time only [day]
JD/PhD–Juris Doctor/Doctor of Philosophy–History		4–5 yrs, full-time only [day]
LLM–Master of Laws–Comparative Law	22	1 yr, full-time or part-time [day]
MCL–Master of Comparative Law–Comparative Law	21	1 yr, full-time or part-time [day]

CD-ROM players. 56 computer workstations are available to students in the library. Special law collections include State Session Laws, CIS Legislative History (complete set), Pacific Island codes, Law of the Sea, Creative Problem Solving, International and Comparative Law..

First-Year Program Class size in the average section is 85; 100% of the first-year courses are taught by full-time faculty.

Upper-Level Program Class size in the average section is 50. Among the electives are:

Administrative Law
★ Advocacy
★ Business and Corporate Law
Civil Rights
Corporate Law
★ Criminal Defense
★ Criminal Prosecution
★ Elderly Advocacy
Entertainment Law
Environmental Law
★ Family Practice
General Practice
Health Care/Human Services
★ Health Law
Immigration
Indian/Tribal Law
★ Intellectual Property
★ International Law
★ International/Comparative Law
Jurisprudence
★ Juvenile Law
★ Labor Law
Land Rights/Natural Resource
Land Use Law/Natural Resources
Lawyering Skills
Legal History/Philosophy
Litigation
Maritime Law

Media Law
★ Mediation
Probate Law
Securities
Sports Law
Tax Law
Telecommunications Law
(★ indicates an area of special strength)

Clinical Courses Students receive degree credit for clinical courses. (Clinical practicum is not required.) Among the clinical areas offered are:

Advocacy
Business and Corporate Law
Civil Litigation
Civil Rights
Corporate Law
Criminal Defense
Criminal Prosecution
Education
Elderly Advocacy
Entertainment Law
Environmental Law
Family Practice
General Practice
Government Litigation
Health Law
Immigration
Indian/Tribal Law
Intellectual Property
International Law
Juvenile Law
Land Rights/Natural Resource
Mediation
Public Interest
Sports Law
Tax Law
Telecommunications Law

International exchange programs permit students to visit Ireland, Malta, Netherlands, New Zealand, and United Kingdom.

CHAPMAN UNIVERSITY
SCHOOL OF LAW

Orange, California

LAW STUDENT PROFILE [2000–2001]

APPLICANTS AND ADMITTEES
Seats available: 120
Average LSAT score: 153
Average GPA: 3.1

Chapman University School of Law is a private institution that organizes classes on a semester calendar system. The campus is situated in a suburban setting. Founded in 1995, first ABA approved in 1998, Chapman University School of Law offers JD and JD/MBA degrees.

Faculty consists of 18 full-time and 4 part-time members in 2000–2001. 9 full-time faculty members are women. 100% of all faculty members have a JD; 25% have advanced law degrees. Of all faculty members, 5% are Asian/Pacific Islander, 5% are African American, 90% are white.

Application Information *Required:* LSAT, LSDAS, application form, application fee of $50, baccalaureate degree, 2 letters of recommendation, personal statement. *Recommended:* resume.

Financial Aid Graduate assistantships, loans, merit-based grants/scholarships, and federal work-study loans are available. The average student debt at graduation is $53,000. To apply for financial assistance, students must complete the Free Application for Federal Student Aid, institutional forms. Completed financial aid forms should be received by March 1. Financial aid contact: Peggy Crawford, Director of Financial Aid, One University Drive, Orange, CA 92866. Phone: 714-628-2500 or toll free 888-242-1913. Fax: 714-628-2501. E-mail: pcrawfor@chapman.edu

Law School Library The Harry and Diane Rinker Law Library has 5 professional staff members and contains

AT a GLANCE

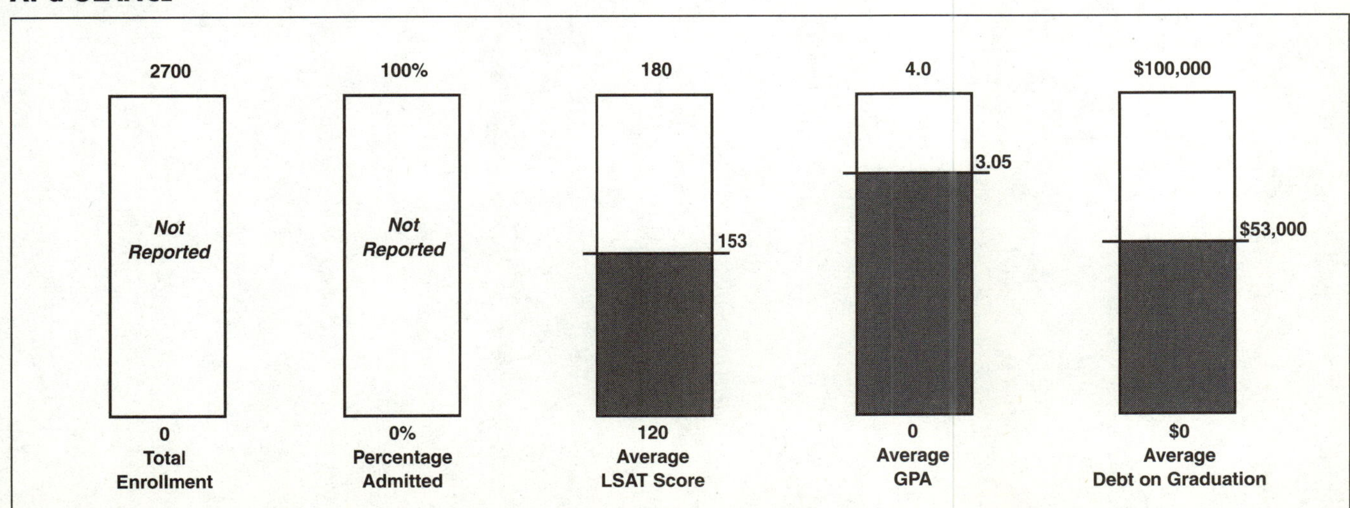

Degree Options		
Degree	**Total Credits Required**	**Length of Program**
JD–Doctor of Laws	88	3–4 yrs, full-time or part-time [day, evening, summer]
JD/MBA–Juris Doctor/Master of Business Administration–JD/MBA Joint Degree	113	4 yrs, full-time only [day, summer]

more than 244,049 volumes and 521 periodicals. 322 seats are available in the library. When classes are in session, the library is open 96 hours per week.

WESTLAW and LEXIS-NEXIS are available, as are the World Wide Web, online bibliographic services, and CD-ROM players. 31 computer workstations are available to students in the library.

First-Year Program Class size in the average section is 40; 100% of the first-year courses are taught by full-time faculty.

Upper-Level Program Class size in the average section is 12. Among the electives are:

  Administrative Law
★ Advocacy
★ Bankruptcy
  Business and Corporate Law
  Capital Punishment
  Constitutional Law
  Consumer Law
★ Dispute Resolution
★ Elder Law
  Entertainment Law
★ Environmental Law
  Estate Planning
  Family Law
  Intellectual Property
  International/Comparative Law
  Internet Law
  Judicial Externship
  Jurisprudence
  Labor Law
★ Land Use Law/Natural Resources
  Lawyering Skills
  Legal History/Philosophy
  Litigation
  Negotiation
  Probate Law
  Public Interest
  Securities
★ Tax Law
(★ *indicates an area of special strength*)

Clinical Courses Students receive degree credit for clinical courses. (Clinical practicum is not required.) Among the clinical areas offered are:

  Advocacy
  Bankruptcy
  Elder Law
  Tax Law

GOLDEN GATE UNIVERSITY
SCHOOL OF LAW

GOLDEN GATE UNIVERSITY
SCHOOL OF LAW

San Francisco, California

INFORMATION CONTACT

Assistant Dean for Admissions and Financial Aid
536 Mission Street
San Francisco, CA 94105

Phone: 415-442-6630   Fax: 415-442-6631
E-mail: lawadmit@ggu.edu
Web site: http://www.ggu.edu/law/

LAW STUDENT PROFILE [2000–2001]

FULL-TIME   Enrollment: 437
Women: 62%   Men: 38%
PART-TIME   Enrollment: 313
Women: 53%   Men: 47%

RACIAL or ETHNIC COMPOSITION
African American, 6%; Asian/Pacific Islander, 16%; Hispanic, 7%; Native American, 1%

APPLICANTS and ADMITTEES
Number applied: 1,677
Admitted: 977
Percentage accepted: 58%
Seats available: 190
Average LSAT score: 151
Average GPA: 3.1

Golden Gate University School of Law is a private institution that organizes classes on a semester calendar system. The campus is situated in an urban setting. Founded in 1901, first ABA approved in 1956, and an AALS member, Golden Gate University School of Law offers JD, JD/MBA, JD/PhD, LLM, and SJD degrees.

Faculty consists of 45 full-time and 129 part-time members in 2000–2001. 19 full-time faculty members and 50 part-time faculty members are women. 100% of all faculty members have a JD; 11% have advanced law degrees. Of all faculty members, 11% are Asian/Pacific Islander, 9% are African American, 2% are Hispanic, 78% are white.

Application Information *Required:* LSAT, LSDAS, application form, application fee of $40, baccalaureate degree, 1 recommendation, personal statement, college transcripts. *Recommended:* writing sample, resume. *Application deadline* for fall term is April 15 (priority date); for spring term is November 15.

Costs The 2000–2001 tuition was $21,808 full-time; $752 per unit part-time. Fees: $120 per semester full-time; $120 per semester part-time. Tuition and fees vary according to course load and degree level.

Financial Aid In 2000–2001, 71% of all students received some form of financial aid. Fellowships, graduate assistantships, loans, loan repayment assistance program (LRAP), merit-based grants/scholarships, need-based grants/scholarships, and federal work-study loans are available. The average student debt at graduation is $60,000. To apply for financial assistance, students must

AT a GLANCE

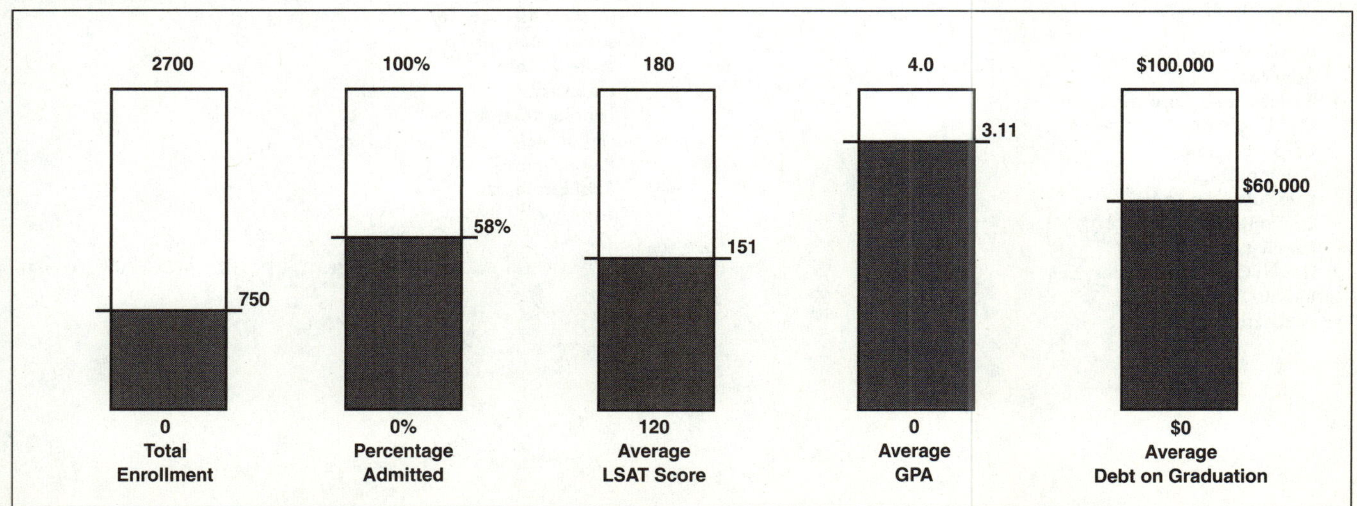

Degree Options

Degree	Total Credits Required	Length of Program
JD–Doctor of Laws	88	3–4 yrs, full-time or part-time [day, evening, summer]
JD/MBA–Juris Doctor/Master of Business Administration–Combined-degree Program	100	3–5 yrs, full-time or part-time [day, evening, summer]
JD/PhD–Juris Doctor/Doctor of Philosophy–Combined-degree Program	232	7 yrs, full-time or part-time [day, evening, summer]
LLM–Master of Laws–US Legal Studies, International Legal Studies	24	1–2 yrs, full-time or part-time [day, evening, summer]
LLM–Master of Laws–Taxation	26	1–2 yrs, full-time or part-time [day, evening, summer]
SJD–Doctor of Juridical Science–International Legal Studies	8	3–5 yrs, full-time or part-time [day, evening, summer]

complete the Free Application for Federal Student Aid, institutional forms. Completed financial aid forms should be received by November 15. Financial aid contact: Assistant Dean for Admissions and Financial Aid, 536 Mission Street, San Francisco, CA 94105. Phone: 415-442-6630. Fax: 415-442-6631. E-mail: lawfao@ggu.edu

Law School Library Golden Gate University School of Law Library has 7 professional staff members and contains more than 230,000 volumes and 3,300 periodicals. 322 seats are available in the library. When classes are in session, the library is open 91 hours per week.

WESTLAW and LEXIS-NEXIS are available, as are the World Wide Web, online bibliographic services, and CD-ROM players. 45 computer workstations are available to students in the library. Special law collections include McDaniel Law and Literature Collection.

First-Year Program Class size in the average section is 49; 75% of the first-year courses are taught by full-time faculty.

Upper-Level Program Class size in the average section is 20. Among the electives are:

  Administrative Law
★ Advocacy
★ Business and Corporate Law
  Civil Litigation
  Corporate Law
★ Criminal Defense
  Entertainment Law
★ Environmental Law
★ Family Law
  Health Care/Human Services
  Indian/Tribal Law
★ Intellectual Property

★ International/Comparative Law
  Judicial Externship
  Jurisprudence
★ Labor Law
  Land Use Law/Natural Resources
  Lawyering Skills
★ Litigation
  Maritime Law
  Media Law
  Mediation
★ Public Interest
★ Real Estate Law
  Securities
  Tax Law
(★ indicates an area of special strength)

Clinical Courses Students receive degree credit for clinical courses. (Clinical practicum is not required.) Among the clinical areas offered are:

  Civil Litigation
  Corporate Law
  Criminal Defense
  Criminal Prosecution
  Environmental Law
  Family Practice
  General Practice
  Government Litigation
  Health Law
  Intellectual Property
  Judicial Externship
  Juvenile Law
  Labor Law
  Landlord/Tenant
  Litigation
  Public Interest
  Real Estate Law
  Tax Law

International exchange programs permit students to visit France.

HISTORY, CAMPUS, AND LOCATION

Golden Gate University School of Law was founded in 1901 and is fully accredited by the American Bar Association (ABA) and the Committee of Bar Examiners of the State of California and is a member of the Association of American Law Schools (AALS). Graduates qualify to take the bar exam in all fifty states and in the District of Columbia.

Golden Gate University School of Law is located in the heart of downtown San Francisco, gateway to the Pacific Rim and one of the most beautiful cities in the world. With the legal and financial district on one side and the bustling South of Market area on the other, the School is a short walk from restaurants, shopping, and downtown plazas.

Golden Gate's 700 full- and part-time law students include working professionals and recent college graduates drawn from more than 100 undergraduate and graduate institutions. They come from across the United States and from a number of other nations and represent a wide spectrum of ethnic, economic, and cultural backgrounds.

SPECIAL QUALITIES OF THE SCHOOL

Golden Gate University is an urban law school that draws on the dynamic environment of the legal/business district of San Francisco. Students can enroll part-time or full-time, and full-time students can begin their studies in August or January. The student-faculty ratio of 18:1 strengthens the bonds of communication between students and teachers. The Law School endowment of $2.9 million allows the School to attract an excellent faculty and provide generous financial aid to incoming and continuing students.

TECHNOLOGY ON CAMPUS

All first-year students complete training in the use of the LEXIS and WESTLAW online databases. The law library maintains online links to consortium law library catalogs. Computer labs in the library provides students access to the Internet, various CD-ROM databases, Computer-Assisted Legal Instruction, word processing and spreadsheet applications, and the Golden Gate University e-mail system, which also provides access to the Internet. Every law student receives an e-mail account.

SCHOLARSHIPS AND LOANS

To attract a highly qualified student body, the School of Law awards entering students a number of full and partial tuition scholarships based solely on academic merit. In addition, scholarships in the amount of $5000 are awarded to entering members of minority groups who have demonstrated leadership qualities.

All eligible first-year students are considered for several endowed scholarships. Entering students who are accepted to the Public Interest Scholars Program may be eligible for scholarship assistance. The School of Law also has a variety of scholarships for continuing students.

STUDENT ACTIVITIES AND OPPORTUNITIES

Law Review The *Golden Gate University Law Review* is written and edited by student members who are selected by academic standing or on the basis of a writing competition. Three issues of the *Law Review* are published annually: a survey of cases from the Ninth Circuit Court of Appeals; a Women's Law Forum; and a Notes and Comments issue on the environment. Students interested in International Legal Studies may work on the *Annual Survey of International and Comparative Law*.

Moot Court All second-year students are required to take Appellate Advocacy, a course in which they prepare appellate briefs and present oral arguments in a moot court program. Tryouts for interscholastic moot court teams are open to all students. Golden Gate regularly participates in the Jessup International Law, American Bar Association Appellate Advocacy, and Roger Traynor California Moot Court Competitions. The School selects additional competitions based on demonstrated student interest.

Extracurricular Activities The Student Bar Association sponsors a variety of activities and events for all law students. In addition, there are more than fifteen other campus organizations that students can join.

Special Opportunities In addition to the standard J.D. program, Golden Gate offers the Honors Lawyering Program (also known as the Integrated Professional Apprenticeship Curriculum, or IPAC). In this innovative honors program, students attend classes with other J.D. students but also participate in two full-time semester-long professional apprenticeships in law offices and other legal settings. These apprenticeships link work in the legal community with the theory, skills, and values learned in the classroom.

Golden Gate University School of Law also has one of the most extensive clinical programs in the country. Three on-site clinics and seven field-placement clinics offer students excellent opportunities to experience hands-on, practical legal training. The law school also has a comprehensive litigation program, with small classes that allow all students full participation in litigation skills training.

Opportunities for Members of Minority Groups and Women These opportunities include the Women's Employment Rights Clinic through which students represent clients in employment disputes and the Environmental Law and Justice Clinic through which students provide direct representation to community groups and environmental organizations in low-income and minority communities. A variety of scholarships are available for new and continuing women and minority students.

Special Certificate Programs J.D. students can earn specialization certificates in business law, criminal law, environmental law, intellectual property, international law, labor and employment law, litigation, public interest law, or real estate law. Students may also earn a combined J.D./M.B.A. with a focus in one of eleven business areas. Other combined degrees include a J.D./M.A. in international relations and a J.D./Ph.D. in clinical psychology.

In recent years, the law school has become a center for graduate legal study, offering four Master of Law (LL.M.) degree programs: international legal studies, environmental law, taxation, and United States legal studies. In addition, students with an LL.M. can earn a Doctor of Laws (S.J.D.) degree in international legal studies.

BAR PASSAGE, CAREER SERVICES, AND PLACEMENT

The first-time bar passage rate for 1998–99 graduates was 65 percent. Most graduates take the California bar exam.

The Golden Gate University Law Career and Alumni Services Office provides comprehensive services and support from the time students enter law school through graduation and beyond. All first-year students receive a one-on-one orientation session, a special resume and cover letter workshop, and a free Job Search Guide. Continuing students have access to print and online job listings, career counseling, job search skills workshops, resume and cover letter review, special programs and job fairs, mock interviews with alumni, alumni mentors, recruitment programs, and many other services. Services and programs for graduates are also available. Recent graduates were employed as shown below.

Legal Field	Percentage of Graduates	Average Salary
Academic	1.8%	$63,750
Business	26.3%	$66,660
Government	11.4%	$42,120
Judicial Clerkship	6.1%	$46,286
Private Practice	49.1%	$58,070
Public Interest	5.3%	$32,100
Other	0.0%	n/a

CORRESPONDENCE AND INFORMATION

Admissions Office
Golden Gate University School of Law
536 Mission Street
San Francisco, California 94105-2968
Telephone: 415-442-6630
Fax: 415-442-6631
E-mail: lawadmit@ggu.edu
World Wide Web: http://www.ggu.edu/law

LOYOLA MARYMOUNT UNIVERSITY
LOYOLA LAW SCHOOL

Los Angeles, California

INFORMATION CONTACT

Anton P. Mack, Assistant Dean for Admissions
919 South Albany Street
Los Angeles, CA 90015

Phone: 213-736-1180   Fax: 213-736-6523
E-mail: admissions@lls.edu
Web site: http://www.lls.edu/

LAW STUDENT PROFILE [2000–2001]

FULL-TIME   Enrollment: 1,017
Women: 52%   Men: 48%

PART-TIME   Enrollment: 377
Women: 42%   Men: 58%

RACIAL or ETHNIC COMPOSITION
African American, 4%; Asian/Pacific Islander, 23%; Hispanic, 11%; Native American, 1%; International, 1%

APPLICANTS and ADMITTEES
Number applied: 3,130
Admitted: 1,259
Percentage accepted: 40%
Seats available: 441
Average LSAT score: 158
Average GPA: 3.3

Loyola Marymount University Loyola Law School is a private institution that organizes classes on a semester calendar system. The campus is situated in an urban setting. Founded in 1920, first ABA approved in 1937, and an AALS member, Loyola Marymount University Loyola Law School offers JD, JD/MBA, and LL M in Tax degrees.

Faculty consists of 64 full-time and 58 part-time members in 2000–2001. 26 full-time faculty members and 15 part-time faculty members are women. 100% of all faculty members have a JD; 7.69% have advanced law degrees. Of all faculty members, 6.15% are Asian/Pacific Islander, 6.15% are African American, 7.69% are Hispanic, 80.01% are white.

Application Information *Required:* LSAT, LSDAS, application form, application fee of $50, baccalaureate degree, 1 recommendation, personal statement, college transcripts. *Application deadline* for fall term is February 1 (priority date). Applications are processed on a rolling basis.

Financial Aid In 2000–2001, 83% of all students received some form of financial aid. 3 fellowships; 50 research assistantships, totaling $3500, were awarded. Loans, loan repayment assistance program (LRAP), merit-based grants/scholarships, and federal work-study loans are also available. The average student debt at graduation is $73,458. To apply for financial assistance, students must complete the Free Application for Federal Student Aid, institutional forms. Completed financial aid forms should be received by March 2. Financial aid contact: Maureen

AT a GLANCE

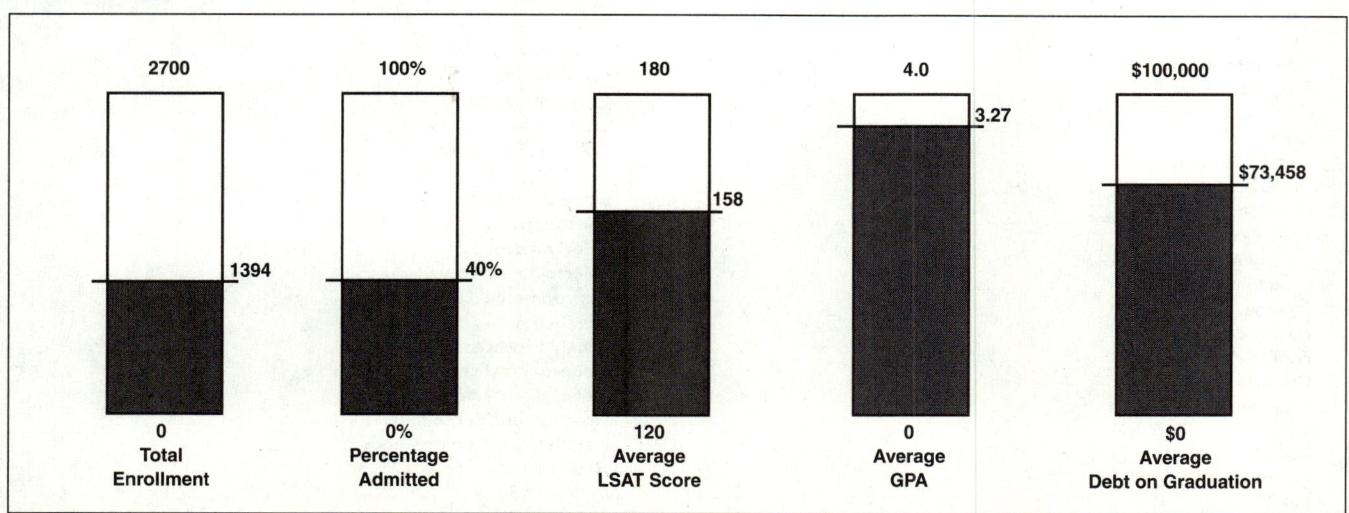

Degree Options

Degree	Total Credits Required	Length of Program
JD–Doctor of Laws	87	3–4 yrs, full-time or part-time [day, evening, summer]
JD/MBA–Juris Doctor/Master of Business Administration–Dual-degree Program		4–5 yrs, full-time only [day, evening, summer]
LL M in Tax–Master of Laws in Taxation–Tax LLM Program	24	1–5 yrs, full-time or part-time [evening, summer]

Hessler, Director of Financial Aid, 919 South Albany Street, Los Angeles, CA 90015. Phone: 213-736-1140. Fax: 213-736-6523. E-mail: maureen.hessler@lls.edu

Law School Library William M. Rains Law Library has 12 professional staff members and contains more than 524,108 volumes and 6,861 periodicals. 604 seats are available in the library. When classes are in session, the library is open 108 hours per week.

WESTLAW and LEXIS-NEXIS are available, as are the World Wide Web, online bibliographic services, and CD-ROM players. 550 computer workstations are available to students in the library. Special law collections include federal and state depositories; foreign collections of European, Latin American and Pacific Rim nations; complete US legislative history (1970-present); complete collection of UN documents; CBS News O.J. Simpson archive.

First-Year Program Class size in the average section is 86; 100% of the first-year courses are taught by full-time faculty.

Upper-Level Program Class size in the average section is 37. Among the electives are:

  Administrative Law
★ Advocacy
  Business and Corporate Law
  Children and the Law
  Civil Litigation
  Civil Rights
  Constitutional Law
  Consumer Law
  Corporate Law
  Criminal Defense
  Criminal Law
  Criminal Prosecution
★ Disability Law
  Domestic Violence
  Education Law
  Elderly Advocacy
★ Entertainment Law
  Environmental Law
  Family Law
  Family Practice
  General Practice
  Government Litigation
  Government/Regulation
  Health Care/Human Services
  Health Law
  Immigration

  Indian/Tribal Law
  Intellectual Property
  International Law
  International/Comparative Law
  Jurisprudence
  Juvenile Law
  Labor Law
  Land Rights/Natural Resource
  Land Use Law/Natural Resources
  Landlord/Tenant
  Law and Society
  Lawyering Skills
  Legal History/Philosophy
  Litigation
  Maritime Law
  Media Law
★ Mediation
  Personal Injury
  Poverty/Welfare Law
  Probate Law
  Property/Real Estate
★ Public Interest
  Securities
★ Tax Law
(★ indicates an area of special strength)

Clinical Courses Students receive degree credit for clinical courses. (Clinical practicum is not required.) Among the clinical areas offered are:

  Administrative Law
  Advocacy
  Business and Corporate Law
  Children and the Law
  Civil Litigation
  Civil Rights
  Constitutional Law
  Consumer Law
  Corporate Law
  Criminal Defense
  Criminal Law
  Criminal Prosecution
  Disability Law
  Domestic Violence
  Education Law
  Elderly Advocacy
  Entertainment Law
  Environmental Law
  Family Law
  Family Practice
  General Practice
  Government Litigation
  Government/Regulation
  Health Care/Human Services
  Health Law
  Immigration

Intellectual Property
International Law
Jurisprudence
Juvenile Law
Labor Law
Land Rights/Natural Resource
Land Use Law/Natural Resources
Landlord/Tenant
Lawyering Skills
Litigation
Media Law

Mediation
Poverty/Welfare Law
Probate Law
Property/Real Estate
Public Interest
Securities
Tax Law

International exchange programs permit students to visit China, Costa Rica, and Italy.

PEPPERDINE UNIVERSITY
SCHOOL OF LAW

Malibu, California

INFORMATION CONTACT

Shannon Phillips, Director of Admissions
24255 Pacific Coast Highway
Malibu, CA 90263

Phone: 310-506-4631   Fax: 310-506-4266
E-mail: sphillip@pepperdine.edu
Web site: http://www.pepperdine.edu/

LAW STUDENT PROFILE [2000–2001]

FULL-TIME   Enrollment: 638
Women: 47%   Men: 53%

PART-TIME   Enrollment: 37
Women: 49%   Men: 51%

RACIAL or ETHNIC COMPOSITION
African American, 5%; Asian/Pacific Islander, 4%; Hispanic, 3%; Native American, 1%; International, 2%

APPLICANTS and ADMITTEES
Number applied: 2,319
Admitted: 1,033
Percentage accepted: 45%
Seats available: 230
Average LSAT score: 156
Average GPA: 3.3

Pepperdine University School of Law is a private institution that organizes classes on a semester calendar system. The campus is situated in a suburban setting. Founded in 1970, first ABA approved in 1972, and an AALS member, Pepperdine University School of Law offers JD, JD/MBA, JD/MDR, JD/MPP, and MDR degrees.

Faculty consists of 35 full-time and 28 part-time members in 2000–2001. 6 full-time faculty members and 12 part-time faculty members are women. 100% of all faculty members have a JD; 18% have advanced law degrees. Of all faculty members, 7% are Asian/Pacific Islander, 3.5% are African American, 3.5% are Hispanic, 86% are white.

Application Information *Required:* LSAT, LSDAS, application form, application fee of $50, baccalaureate degree, 2 letters of recommendation, personal statement, college transcripts, resume. *Application deadline* for fall term is March 1. Applications are processed on a rolling basis.

Costs The 2000–2001 tuition was $24,820 full-time; $915 per credit part-time.

Financial Aid Loans, merit-based grants/scholarships, need-based grants/scholarships, and federal work-study loans are available. The average student debt at graduation is $79,500. To apply for financial assistance, students must complete the Free Application for Federal Student Aid, institutional forms, scholarship specific applications, income tax returns. Completed financial aid forms should be received by April 1. Financial aid contact:

AT a GLANCE

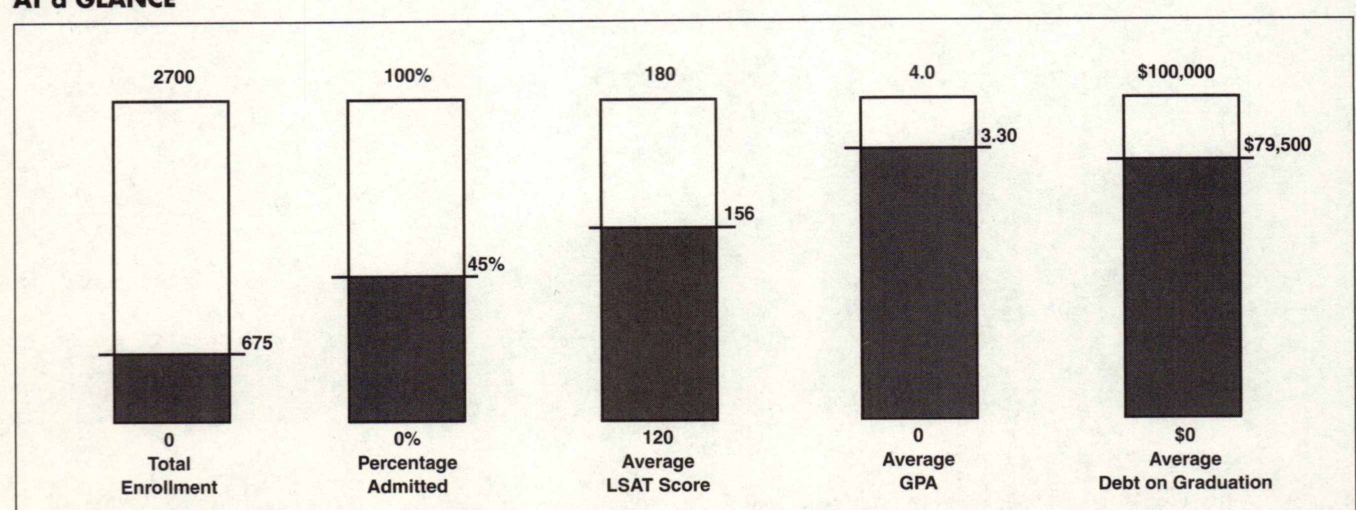

Degree Options

Degree	Total Credits Required	Length of Program
JD–Doctor of Laws	88	3 yrs, full-time only [day]
JD/MBA–Juris Doctor/Master of Business Administration–Joint-degree Program	130	4 yrs, full-time only [day]
JD/MDR–Juris Doctor/Master of Dispute Resolution–Joint-degree Program	106	3–4 yrs, full-time only [day]
JD/MPP–Juris Doctor/Master of Public Planning–Joint-degree Program	120	4 yrs, full-time only [day]
MDR–Master of Dispute Resolution	32	1 yr, full-time or part-time [day, weekend, summer]

Janet Lockhart, Director of Financial Aid, 24255 Pacific Coast Highway, Malibu, CA 90263. Phone: 310-506-4633. Fax: 310-506-4866. E-mail: janet.lockhart@pepperdine.edu

Law School Library Jerene Appleby Harnish Law Library has 4 professional staff members and contains more than 338,157 volumes and 3,551 periodicals. 500 seats are available in the library. When classes are in session, the library is open 99 hours per week.

WESTLAW and LEXIS-NEXIS are available, as are the World Wide Web, online bibliographic services, and CD-ROM players. 49 computer workstations are available to students in the library.

First-Year Program Class size in the average section is 76; 100% of the first-year courses are taught by full-time faculty.

Upper-Level Program Class size in the average section is 60. Among the electives are:

Administrative Law
Advocacy
★ Business and Corporate Law
Criminal Defense
Criminal Prosecution
★ Dispute Resolution
★ Entertainment Law
★ Entrepreneurship Law
Environmental Law
Family Law
Intellectual Property
★ International Law
International/Comparative Law
Judicial Clerkship
Juvenile Law
Labor Law
Land Use Law/Natural Resources
Lawyering Skills
Litigation
★ Mediation
Probate Law
Public Interest
★ Securities
★ Tax Law
★ Technology Law
(★ indicates an area of special strength)

Clinical Courses Students receive degree credit for clinical courses. (Clinical practicum is not required.) Among the clinical areas offered are:

Criminal Defense
Criminal Prosecution
Entertainment Law
International Law
Judicial Clerkship
Juvenile Law
Mediation
Public Interest

International exchange programs permit students to visit United Kingdom.

SANTA CLARA UNIVERSITY
SCHOOL OF LAW

Santa Clara, California

INFORMATION CONTACT

Julia Yaffee, Director of Admissions
500 El Camino Real
Santa Clara, CA 95053

Phone: 408-554-4800   Fax: 408-554-7897
Web site: http://www.scu.edu/law/

LAW STUDENT PROFILE [2000–2001]

FULL-TIME   Enrollment: 868
Women: 56%   Men: 44%

PART-TIME   Enrollment: 40
Women: 48%   Men: 52%

RACIAL or ETHNIC COMPOSITION

African American, 3%; Asian/Pacific Islander, 21%; Hispanic,
8%; Native American, 1%; International, 5%

APPLICANTS and ADMITTEES

Number applied: 2,693
Admitted: 1,322
Percentage accepted: 49%
Seats available: 306
Average LSAT score: 156
Average GPA: 3.2

Santa Clara University School of Law is a private
institution that organizes classes on a semester calendar
system. The campus is situated in an urban setting.
Founded in 1912, first ABA approved in 1937, and an
AALS member, Santa Clara University School of Law
offers JD, JD/MBA, and LLM degrees.

Faculty consists of 38 full-time and 24 part-time
members in 2000–2001. 13 full-time faculty members
and 11 part-time faculty members are women. 98.5% of
all faculty members have a JD; 25% have advanced law
degrees. Of all faculty members, 7.5% are Asian/Pacific
Islander, 10% are African American, 5% are Hispanic,
75% are white, 2.5% are international.

Application Information *Required:* LSAT, LSDAS,
application form, application fee of $40, baccalaureate
degree, college transcripts. *Recommended:* recommendations, personal statement, essay. *Application deadline* for
fall term is March 1.

Financial Aid Fellowships, graduate assistantships, loans,
loan repayment assistance program (LRAP), merit-based
grants/scholarships, need-based grants/scholarships, and
federal work-study loans are available. The average
student debt at graduation is $63,000. To apply for
financial assistance, students must complete the Free
Application for Federal Student Aid, scholarship specific
applications. Completed financial aid forms should be
received by February 1. Financial aid contact: Bryan
Hinkle, Financial Aid Counselor, Santa Clara University
School of Law, Santa Clara, CA 95053. Phone: 408-554-
5048. Fax: 408-554-7897. E-mail: lawadmissions@scu.edu

AT a GLANCE

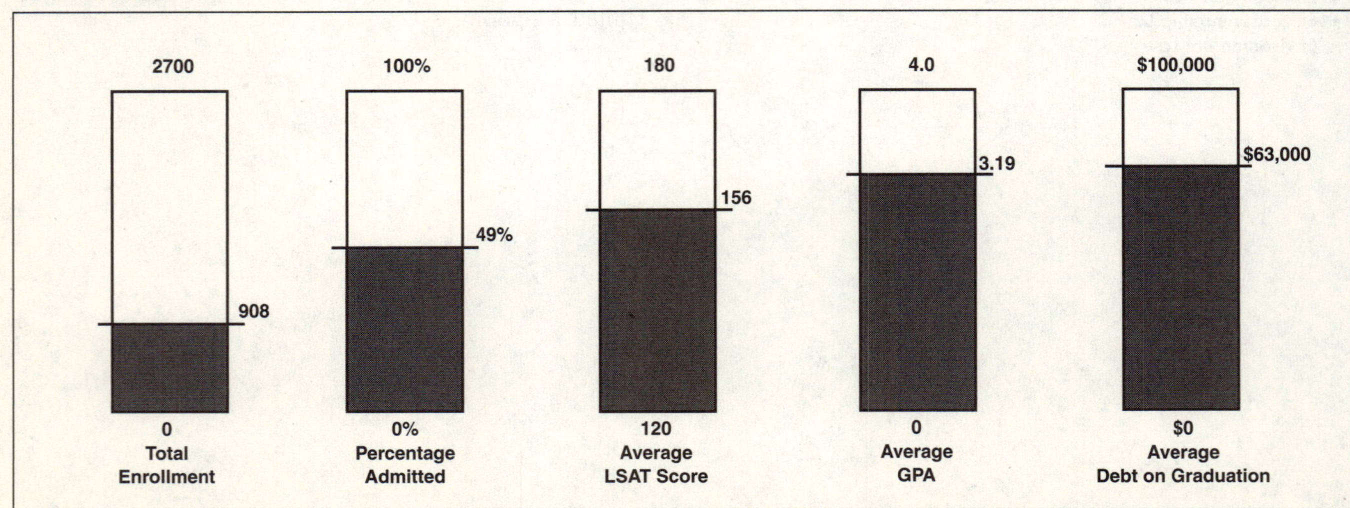

Degree Options

Degree	Total Credits Required	Length of Program
JD–Doctor of Laws	86	3–4 yrs, full-time or part-time [day, evening, summer]
JD/MBA–Juris Doctor/Master of Business Administration–Combined-degree Program		3.5–4 yrs, full-time or part-time [day, evening, summer]
LLM–Master of Laws–US Law for Foreign Lawyers	24	1 yr, full-time or part-time [day, evening, summer]
LLM–Master of Laws–Intellectual Property	24	1–2 yrs, full-time or part-time [day, evening, weekend, summer]
LLM–Master of Laws–International and Comparative Law	24	1–2 yrs, full-time or part-time [day, evening, weekend, summer]

Law School Library Heafey Law Library has 9 professional staff members and contains more than 283,114 volumes and 3,668 periodicals. 476 seats are available in the library. When classes are in session, the library is open 105 hours per week.

WESTLAW and LEXIS-NEXIS are available, as are the World Wide Web, online bibliographic services, and CD-ROM players. 60 computer workstations are available to students in the library. Special law collections include Watergate Hearings.

First-Year Program Class size in the average section is 74; 100% of the first-year courses are taught by full-time faculty.

Upper-Level Program Class size in the average section is 36. Among the electives are:

    Administrative Law
  ★ Advocacy
  ★ Business and Corporate Law
    Consumer Law
    Criminal Defense
    Education Law
    Environmental Law
    Family Law
    Government/Regulation
    Health Care/Human Services
    Indian/Tribal Law
  ★ Intellectual Property
  ★ International/Comparative Law
    Jurisprudence
    Labor Law
    Land Use Law/Natural Resources
  ★ Lawyering Skills
    Legal History/Philosophy
  ★ Litigation
    Maritime Law
    Media Law
    Mediation
    Probate Law
  ★ Public Interest
    Securities
    Tax Law
(★ indicates an area of special strength)

Clinical Courses Students receive degree credit for clinical courses. (Clinical practicum is not required.) Among the clinical areas offered are:

    Civil Litigation
    Criminal Defense
    Environmental Law
    Immigration
    Intellectual Property
    Public Interest

International exchange programs permit students to visit China, France, Hong Kong, Hungary, Malaysia, Japan, Republic of Korea, Singapore, Switzerland, Thailand, United Kingdom, and Viet Nam.

SOUTHWESTERN UNIVERSITY SCHOOL OF LAW

Los Angeles, California

INFORMATION CONTACT

Anne Wilson, Director of Admissions
675 South Westmoreland Avenue
Los Angeles, CA 90005-3992

Phone: 213-738-6717   Fax: 213-383-1688
E-mail: admissions@swlaw.edu
Web site: http://www.swlaw.edu/

LAW STUDENT PROFILE [2000–2001]

FULL-TIME   Enrollment: 572
Women: 54%   Men: 46%

PART-TIME   Enrollment: 254
Women: 53%   Men: 47%

APPLICANTS and ADMITTEES

Number applied: 1,968
Admitted: 1,078
Percentage accepted: 55%
Seats available: 342

Southwestern University School of Law is a private nonprofit institution that organizes classes on a semester calendar system. The campus is situated in an urban setting. Founded in 1911, first ABA approved in 1970, and an AALS member, Southwestern University School of Law offers a JD degree.

Faculty Of all faculty members, 1% are Native American, 5% are Asian/Pacific Islander, 6% are African American, 9% are Hispanic, 79% are white.

Application Information *Required:* LSAT, LSDAS, application form, baccalaureate degree, application fee of $50. *Recommended:* personal statement, 3 letters of recommendation, resume.

Costs The 2000–2001 tuition was $23,310 full-time; $777 per unit part-time. Fees: $100 full-time; $100 per year part-time. Tuition and fees vary according to course load, degree level, and program.

Financial Aid Graduate assistantships, loans, loan repayment assistance program (LRAP), merit-based grants/scholarships, need-based grants/scholarships, and federal work-study loans are available. To apply for financial assistance, students must complete the Free Application for Federal Student Aid, institutional forms. Financial aid contact: Wayne Mahoney, Director of Financial Aid, Room 102, 675 South Westmoreland Avenue, Los Angeles, CA 90005-3992. Phone: 213-738-6719. Fax: 213-383-1688. E-mail: finaid@swlaw.edu

Law School Library has 11 professional staff members and contains more than 415,068 volumes and 5,100

AT a GLANCE

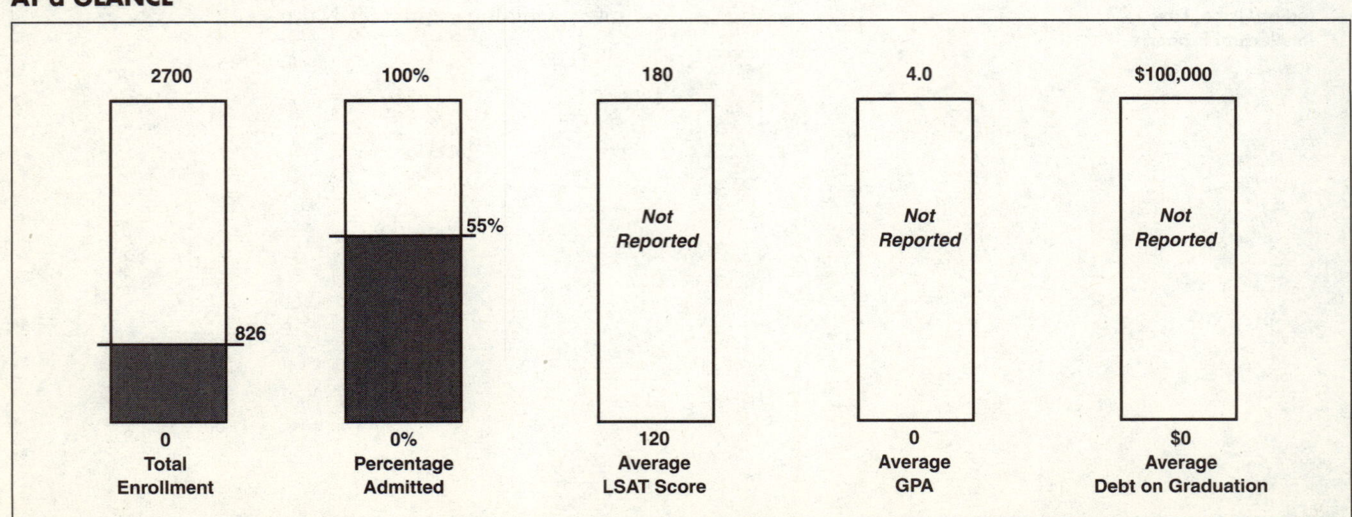

<table>
<tr><td colspan="3">Degree Options</td></tr>
<tr><td>Degree</td><td>Total Credits Required</td><td>Length of Program</td></tr>
<tr><td>JD–Juris Doctor</td><td>87</td><td>2–4 yrs, full-time or part-time [day, evening]</td></tr>
</table>

periodicals. 610 seats are available in the library. When classes are in session, the library is open 103 hours per week.

WESTLAW and LEXIS-NEXIS are available, as are the World Wide Web, online bibliographic services, and CD-ROM players. 82 computer workstations are available to students in the library. Special law collections include constitutional law; entertainment, sports, intellectual property; environmental law; international law; taxation.

First-Year Program Class size in the average section is 75; 100% of the first-year courses are taught by full-time faculty.

Upper-Level Program Among the electives are:

- Accounting
- Administrative Law
- Advocacy
- Bankruptcy
- Business and Corporate Law
- Civil Litigation
- Civil Procedure
- Civil Rights
- Conflict of Laws
- Constitutional Law
- Consumer Law
- Criminal Defense
- Criminal Law
- Criminal Prosecution
- ★ Entertainment Law
- Environmental Law
- Evidence
- Family Law
- Government Litigation
- Government/Regulation
- Health Care/Human Services
- Health Law
- Immigration
- Indian/Tribal Law
- Insurance Law
- Intellectual Property
- International/Comparative Law
- Judicial Clerkship
- Jurisprudence
- Juvenile Law
- Labor Law
- Land Use Law/Natural Resources
- Lawyering Skills
- Legal History/Philosophy
- Maritime Law
- ★ Media Law
- Mediation
- Property/Real Estate
- Race and Law
- Securities
- Sports Law
- Tax Law

(★ *indicates an area of special strength*)

Clinical Courses Students receive degree credit for clinical courses. (Clinical practicum is not required.) Among the clinical areas offered are:

- Civil Litigation
- Civil Rights
- Criminal Defense
- Criminal Prosecution
- Elderly Advocacy
- Entertainment Law
- Family Practice
- General Practice
- Government Litigation
- Health Law
- Intellectual Property
- Judicial Clerkship
- Juvenile Law
- Public Interest
- Tax Law

International exchange programs permit students to visit Argentina, Canada, and Mexico.

STANFORD UNIVERSITY
LAW SCHOOL

Stanford, California

INFORMATION CONTACT

Faye Deal, Director of Admissions
559 Nathan Abbott Way
Stanford, CA 94305-8610

Phone: 650-723-0302   Fax: 650-723-0838
E-mail: law.admissions@stanford.edu
Web site: http://law.stanford.edu/

LAW STUDENT PROFILE [2000–2001]

FULL-TIME   Enrollment: 558
Women: 46%   Men: 54%

PART-TIME   Enrollment: 35
Women: 37%   Men: 63%

RACIAL or ETHNIC COMPOSITION
African American, 7%; Asian/Pacific Islander, 8%; Hispanic, 13%; Native American, 1%; International, 11%

APPLICANTS and ADMITTEES
Number applied: 4,228
Admitted: 529
Percentage accepted: 13%
Seats available: 180
Average LSAT score: 168
Average GPA: 3.8

Stanford University Law School is a private institution that organizes classes on a semester calendar system. The campus is situated in a suburban setting. Founded in 1908, first ABA approved in 1923, and an AALS member, Stanford University Law School offers JD, JD/MBA, JSD, JSM, and MLS degrees.

Faculty consists of 42 full-time members in 2000–2001. 8 full-time faculty members are women. 92% of all faculty members have a JD; 14% have advanced law degrees. Of all faculty members, 2% are Asian/Pacific Islander, 10% are African American, 4% are Hispanic, 80% are white, 4% are international.

Application Information *Required:* LSAT, LSDAS, application form, application fee of $65, baccalaureate degree, 2 letters of recommendation, personal statement. *Recommended:* resume. *Application deadline* for fall term is February 1.

Costs The 2000–2001 tuition was $27,726 full-time. Fees: $72 full-time. Students are required to have their own computers.

Financial Aid Fellowships, graduate assistantships, loans, loan repayment assistance program (LRAP), need-based grants/scholarships, and federal work-study loans are available. The average student debt at graduation is $72,395. To apply for financial assistance, students must complete the Free Application for Federal Student Aid, institutional forms, Need Access disk. Financial aid contact: Ruth Burciaga, Assistant Director of Financial

AT a GLANCE

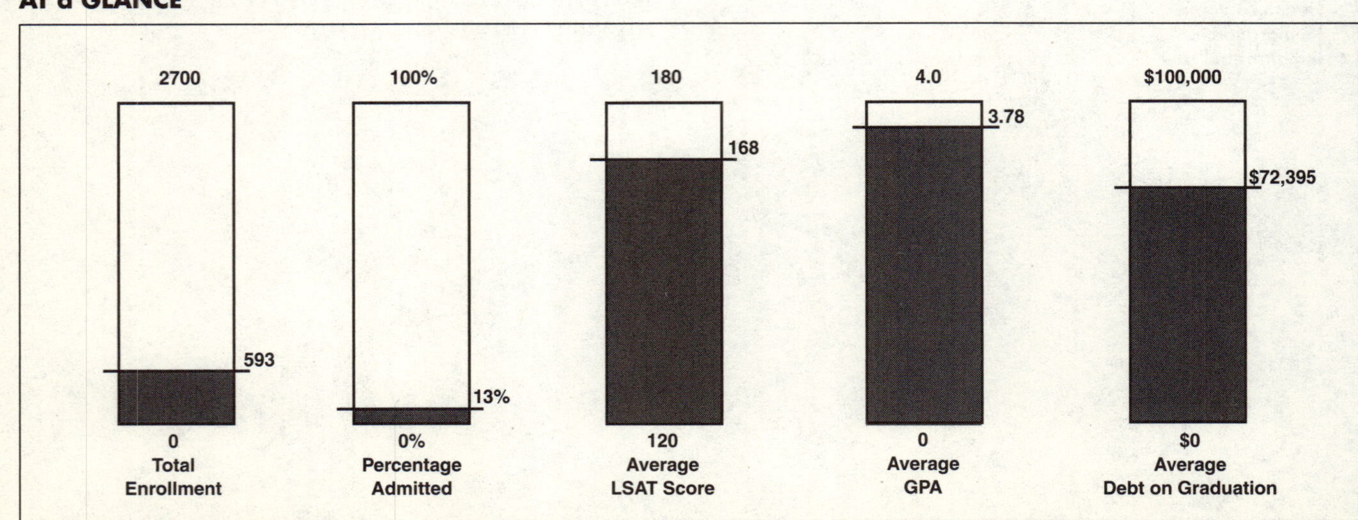

Degree Options		
Degree	**Total Credits Required**	**Length of Program**
JD–Doctor of Laws	86	3 yrs, full-time only [day]
JD/MBA–Juris Doctor/Master of Business Administration–Dual-degree Program	110	4 yrs, full-time only [day]
JSD–Doctor of Juridical Science–Doctor of the Science of the Law	26	1–3 yrs, full-time only [day]
JSM–Master of the Science of Law	26	1 yr, full-time only [day]
MLS–Master of Library Science	30	1 yr, full-time only [day]

Aid, 559 Nathan Abbot Way, Stanford, CA 94305. Phone: 650-723-9247. Fax: 650-725-0838. E-mail: Ruth.Burciaga@leland.stanford.edu

Law School Library Robert Crown Law Library has 25 professional staff members and contains more than 496,103 volumes and 7,282 periodicals. 562 seats are available in the library. When classes are in session, the library is open 96 hours per week.

WESTLAW and LEXIS-NEXIS are available, as are the World Wide Web, online bibliographic services, and CD-ROM players. 90 computer workstations are available to students in the library.

First-Year Program Class size in the average section is 60; 67% of the first-year courses are taught by full-time faculty.

Upper-Level Program Among the electives are:

Administrative Law
Advocacy
Business and Corporate Law
Civil Rights
Consumer Law
Education
Education Law
Entertainment Law
Environmental Law
Family Law
Family Practice
Government/Regulation
Health Care/Human Services
Indian/Tribal Law
Intellectual Property
International Law
International/Comparative Law
Jurisprudence
Labor Law
Land Use Law/Natural Resources
Lawyering Skills
Legal History/Philosophy
Litigation
Media Law
Mediation
Probate Law
Public Interest
Securities
Tax Law

Clinical Courses Students receive degree credit for clinical courses. (Clinical practicum is not required.) Among the clinical areas offered are:

Business and Corporate Law
Education
Environmental Law
Family Practice
Public Interest

THOMAS JEFFERSON SCHOOL OF LAW

San Diego, California

INFORMATION CONTACT

Jennifer M. Keller, Assistant Dean of Admissions
and Registrar
2121 San Diego Avenue
San Diego, CA 92110-2905

Phone: 619-297-9700   Fax: 619-294-4713
     ext. 1472
E-mail: jkeller@tjsl.edu
Web site: http://www.tjsl.edu/

LAW STUDENT PROFILE [2000–2001]

FULL-TIME   Enrollment: 385
Women: 42%   Men: 58%

PART-TIME   Enrollment: 190
Women: 39%   Men: 61%

APPLICANTS and ADMITTEES

Number applied: 1,632
Admitted: 1,047
Percentage accepted: 64%
Seats available: 200
Average LSAT score: 149
Average GPA: 2.9

Thomas Jefferson School of Law is a private institution that organizes classes on a semester calendar system. The campus is situated in an urban setting. Founded in 1969, first ABA approved in 1996, Thomas Jefferson School of Law offers a JD degree.

Faculty consists of 21 full-time and 32 part-time members in 2000–2001. 10 full-time faculty members and 13 part-time faculty members are women. 100% of all faculty members have a JD; 22% have advanced law degrees. Of all faculty members, 2% are Asian/Pacific Islander, 5% are African American, 93% are white.

Application Information *Required:* LSAT, LSDAS, application form, application fee of $35, minimum 2.0 GPA, 2 letters of recommendation, personal statement, college transcripts. *Recommended:* baccalaureate degree.

Costs The 2000–2001 tuition was $21,150 full-time. Fees: $75 per semester full-time; $75 per semester part-time.

Financial Aid Fellowships, loans, merit-based grants/scholarships, and federal work-study loans are available. The average student debt at graduation is $65,661. To apply for financial assistance, students must complete the Free Application for Federal Student Aid, institutional forms. Financial aid contact: Paula Rogers, Associate Director of Financial Assistance, 2121 San Diego Avenue, San Diego, CA 92110. Phone: 619-297-9700 ext. 1353 or toll free 800-936-7529. Fax: 619-294-4713. E-mail: paular@tjsl.edu

Law School Library Thomas Jefferson School of Law Library has 7 professional staff members and contains

AT a GLANCE

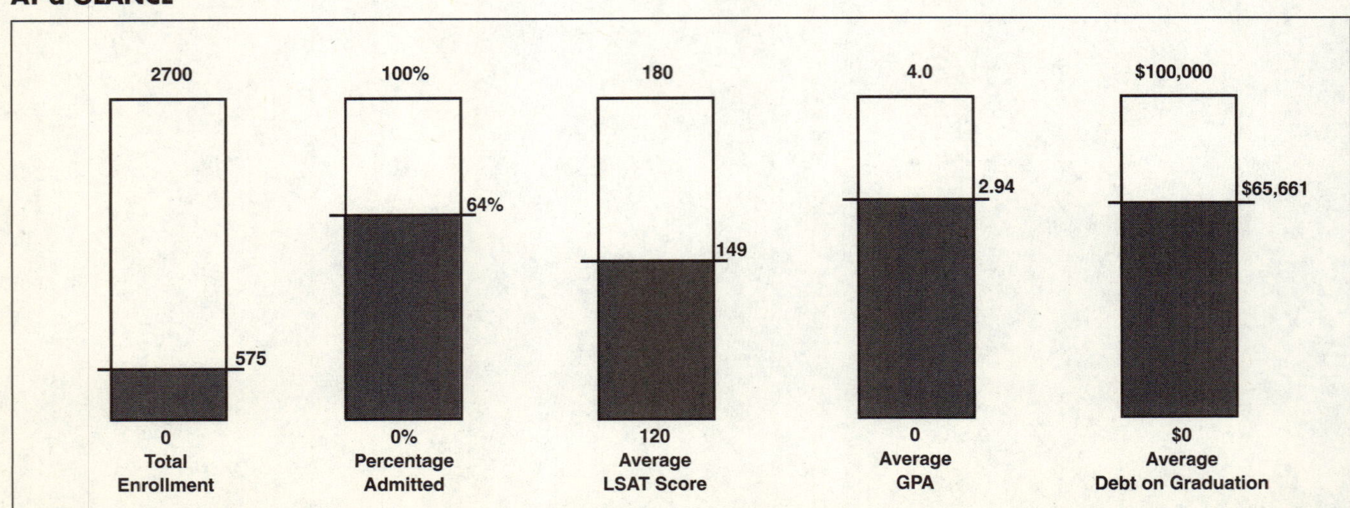

Degree Options

Degree	Total Credits Required	Length of Program
JD–Doctor of Laws	88	3–4 yrs, full-time or part-time [day, evening, summer]

more than 226,394 volumes and 1,493 periodicals. 385 seats are available in the library. When classes are in session, the library is open 115 hours per week.

WESTLAW and LEXIS-NEXIS are available, as are the World Wide Web, online bibliographic services, and CD-ROM players. 42 computer workstations are available to students in the library. Special law collections include The Thomas Jefferson Collection.

First-Year Program Class size in the average section is 33; 100% of the first-year courses are taught by full-time faculty.

Upper-Level Program Class size in the average section is 40. Among the electives are:

- Administrative Law
- ★ Advocacy
- Business and Corporate Law
- Consumer Law
- Entertainment Law
- ★ Environmental Law
- Family Law
- Government/Regulation
- Health Care/Human Services
- Indian/Tribal Law
- ★ Intellectual Property
- ★ International/Comparative Law
- Jurisprudence
- Labor Law
- Land Use Law/Natural Resources
- ★ Lawyering Skills
- Legal History/Philosophy
- ★ Litigation
- Maritime Law
- Media Law
- Mediation
- Probate Law
- Public Interest
- Securities
- Tax Law

(★ *indicates an area of special strength*)

Clinical Courses Students receive degree credit for clinical courses. (Clinical practicum is not required.) Among the clinical areas offered are:

- Civil Litigation
- Civil Rights
- Criminal Defense
- Criminal Prosecution
- Environmental Law
- Government Litigation
- Immigration
- Juvenile Law
- Land Rights/Natural Resource
- Mediation

UNIVERSITY OF CALIFORNIA, BERKELEY
SCHOOL OF LAW

Berkeley, California

LAW STUDENT PROFILE [2000–2001]

FULL-TIME   Enrollment: 873
Women: 55%   Men: 45%

RACIAL or ETHNIC COMPOSITION
African American, 2%; Asian/Pacific Islander, 15%; Hispanic, 6%; Native American, 0.5%; International, 4%

APPLICANTS and ADMITTEES
Number applied: 5,493
Admitted: 938
Percentage accepted: 17%
Seats available: 270
Average LSAT score: 165
Average GPA: 3.8

University of California, Berkeley School of Law is a public institution that organizes classes on a semester calendar system. The campus is situated in an urban setting. Founded in 1894, first ABA approved in 1923, and an AALS member, University of California, Berkeley School of Law offers JD, JD/MA, JD/MBA, JD/MCRP, JD/MJ, JD/MPPo, JD/MSW, JD/PhD, JSD, LLM, MA, and PhD degrees.

Faculty consists of 63 full-time and 100 part-time members in 2000–2001. 18 full-time faculty members and 33 part-time faculty members are women. 93% of all faculty members have a JD degree. Of all faculty members, 1% are Native American, 4% are Asian/Pacific Islander, 2% are African American, 2% are Hispanic, 89% are white, 2% are international.

Application Information *Required:* LSAT, LSDAS, application form, application fee of $40, baccalaureate degree, personal statement, college transcripts. *Recommended:* recommendations, resume. *Application deadline* for fall term is February 1.

Costs The 1999–2000 tuition was $9804 full-time for nonresidents. Fees: $10,865 full-time. Full-time tuition and fees vary according to program.

Financial Aid In 2000–2001, 85% of all students received some form of financial aid. 10 fellowships, totaling $5227; 58 research assistantships, totaling $4010; 8 teaching assistantships, totaling $7383, were awarded. Fellowships, graduate assistantships, loans, loan repayment assistance program (LRAP), merit-based grants/scholarships, need-based grants/scholarships, and federal work-study loans are also available. The average student debt at graduation is $49,580. To apply for financial assistance, students must complete the Free Application for Federal Student Aid, institutional forms. Completed

AT a GLANCE

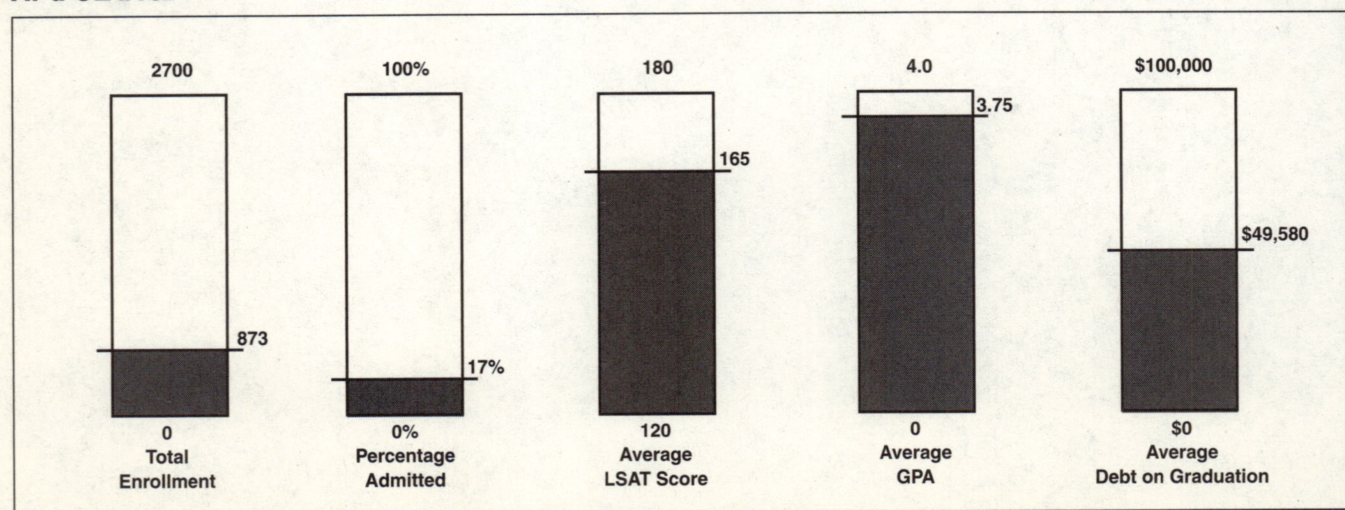

Degree Options		
Degree	**Total Credits Required**	**Length of Program**
JD–Juris Doctor	85	3 yrs, full-time only [day]
JD/MA–Juris Doctor/Master of Arts–Asian Studies, Economics, International and Area Studies, Jurisprudence and Social Policy, School of Information Management and Systems		4 yrs, full-time only [day]
JD/MBA–Juris Doctor/Master of Business Administration		4 yrs, full-time only [day]
JD/MCRP–Juris Doctor/Master of Community and Regional Planning		4 yrs, full-time only [day]
JD/MJ–Juris Doctor/Master of Journalism		4 yrs, full-time only [day]
JD/MPPo–Juris Doctor/Master of Public Policy		4 yrs, full-time only [day]
JD/MSW–Juris Doctor/Master of Social Work–Social Welfare		4 yrs, full-time only [day]
JD/PhD–Juris Doctor/Doctor of Philosophy–Economics, History, Jurisprudence and Social Policy		6 yrs, full-time only [day]
JSD–Doctor of Juridical Science		2 yrs, full-time only [day]
LLM–Master of Laws	20	1 yr, full-time only [day]
MA–Master of Arts–Jurisprudence and Social Policy		4 yrs, full-time only [day]
PhD–Doctor of Philosophy–Jurisprudence and Social Policy		6 yrs, full-time only [day]

financial aid forms should be received by March 2. Financial aid contact: Dennis Tominaga, Director of Financial Aid, 5 Boalt Hall, Berkeley, CA 94720. Phone: 510-642-1563. Fax: 510-643-6222. E-mail: financial_aid@law.berkeley.edu

Law School Library Garret W. McEnerney Law Library has 14 professional staff members and contains more than 629,245 volumes and 8,411 periodicals. 401 seats are available in the library. When classes are in session, the library is open 96 hours per week.

WESTLAW and LEXIS-NEXIS are available, as are the World Wide Web, online bibliographic services, and CD-ROM players. 100 computer workstations are available to students in the library. Special law collections include Robbins Collection of ecclesiastical, civil, comparative, and international law.

First-Year Program Class size in the average section is 60; 83% of the first-year courses are taught by full-time faculty.

Upper-Level Program Class size in the average section is 34. Among the electives are:

Administrative Law
Advocacy
Business and Corporate Law
★ Disability Law
★ Discrimination
★ Domestic Violence
Education Law
Entertainment Law
★ Environmental Law
Family Law
Government/Regulation
Health Care/Human Services
★ Human Rights
★ Immigration
★ Indian/Tribal Law
★ Intellectual Property
★ International Law
★ International/Comparative Law
Jurisprudence
Juvenile Law
Labor Law
Land Use Law/Natural Resources
Lawyering Skills
Legal History/Philosophy
Litigation
Maritime Law
Media Law
Mediation
Probate Law
Public Interest
Securities
Sports Law
Tax Law
★ Technology Law
Telecommunications Law
Trusts and Estates
(★ indicates an area of special strength)

Clinical Courses Students receive degree credit for clinical courses. (Clinical practicum is not required.) Among the clinical areas offered are:

Disability Law
Domestic Violence
Environmental Law
Government/Regulation
Human Rights
Immigration
Indian/Tribal Law
Juvenile Law
Public Interest

International exchange programs permit students to visit France, Hungary, Italy, Netherlands, and Spain.

UNIVERSITY OF CALIFORNIA, DAVIS
SCHOOL OF LAW

Davis, California

INFORMATION CONTACT

Sharon Pinkney, Director, Admissions
400 Mrak Hall Drive
Davis, CA 95616-5201

Phone: 530-752-6477   Fax: 530-752-4704
E-mail: lawadmissions@ucdavis.edu
Web site: http://kinghall.ucdavis.edu/

LAW STUDENT PROFILE [2000–2001]

FULL-TIME   Enrollment: 522
Women: 52%   Men: 48%

RACIAL or ETHNIC COMPOSITION
African American, 3%; Asian/Pacific Islander, 12%; Hispanic, 7%; Native American, 1%; International, 2%

APPLICANTS and ADMITTEES
Number applied: 2,421
Admitted: 841
Percentage accepted: 35%
Seats available: 161
Average LSAT score: 159
Average GPA: 3.4

University of California, Davis School of Law is a public institution that organizes classes on a semester calendar system. The campus is situated in a suburban setting. Founded in 1965, first ABA approved in 1968, and an AALS member, University of California, Davis School of Law offers JD, JD/MA, JD/MBA, JD/MS, and LLM degrees.

Faculty consists of 34 full-time and 21 part-time members in 2000–2001. 14 full-time faculty members and 10 part-time faculty members are women. 100% of all faculty members have a JD; 3% have advanced law degrees. Of all faculty members, 4% are Asian/Pacific Islander, 5% are African American, 10% are Hispanic, 81% are white.

Application Information *Required:* LSAT, LSDAS, application form, application fee of $40, baccalaureate degree, 2 letters of recommendation, personal statement, college transcripts. *Recommended:* minimum GPA. *Application deadline* for fall term is February 1. Applications are processed on a rolling basis.

Costs The 1999–2000 tuition was $9804 full-time for nonresidents. Fees: $10,895 full-time.

Financial Aid In 2000–2001, 77% of all students received some form of financial aid. Loans, loan repayment assistance program (LRAP), merit-based grants/scholarships, need-based grants/scholarships, and federal work-study loans are available. The average student debt at graduation is $41,490. To apply for financial assistance, students must complete the Free Application for Federal Student Aid, scholarship specific applications.

AT a GLANCE

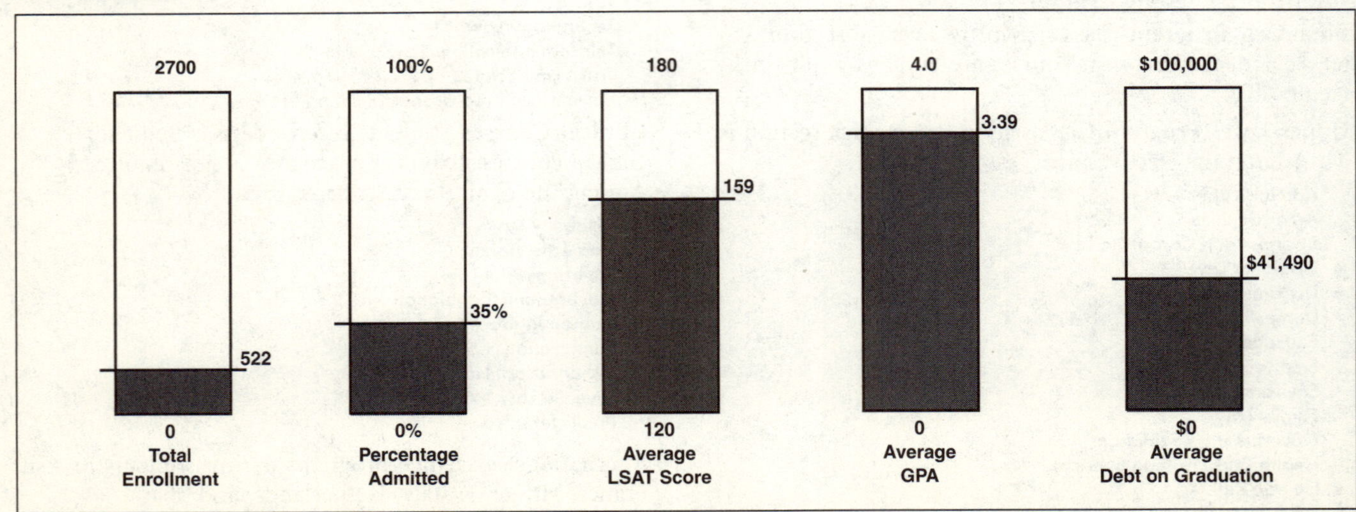

Degree Options

Degree	Total Credits Required	Length of Program
JD–Juris Doctor	88	3 yrs, full-time only [day]
JD/MA–Juris Doctor/Master of Arts–Dual-degree Program	110	3.5–4 yrs, full-time only [day]
JD/MBA–Juris Doctor/Master of Business Administration–Dual-degree Program	110	3.5–4 yrs, full-time only [day]
JD/MS–Juris Doctor/Master of Science–Dual-degree Program	110	3.5–4 yrs, full-time only [day]
LLM–Master of Laws	20	1 yr, full-time only [day]

Completed financial aid forms should be received by March 2. Financial aid contact: Delecia Nunnally, Director, Financial Aid, Financial Aid Office, 400 Mrak Hall Drive, Davis, CA 95616-5201. Phone: 530-752-6573. Fax: 530-752-6125. E-mail: lawfinaid@ucdavis.edu

Law School Library UC Davis Law Library has 5 professional staff members and contains more than 276,361 volumes and 5,043 periodicals. 379 seats are available in the library. When classes are in session, the library is open 78 hours per week.

WESTLAW and LEXIS-NEXIS are available, as are the World Wide Web, online bibliographic services, and CD-ROM players. 51 computer workstations are available to students in the library. Special law collections include federal and California government documents, environmental law, intellectual property, immigration, international law.

First-Year Program Class size in the average section is 72; 100% of the first-year courses are taught by full-time faculty.

Upper-Level Program Class size in the average section is 25. Among the electives are:

   Administrative Law
★ Advocacy
★ Business and Corporate Law
★ Civil Rights
   Consumer Law
   Criminal Prosecution
★ Employment Law
   Entertainment Law
★ Environmental Law
★ Family Law
   Government/Regulation
   Health Care/Human Services
★ Immigration
   Indian/Tribal Law

★ Intellectual Property
★ International/Comparative Law
★ Judicial Process
   Jurisprudence
★ Labor Law
   Land Use Law/Natural Resources
★ Lawyering Skills
   Legal History/Philosophy
   Legislation
★ Litigation
   Media Law
   Mediation
★ Prisoners' Rights
   Probate Law
   Professional Responsibility
★ Public Interest
   Securities
★ Tax Law

(★ indicates an area of special strength)

Clinical Courses Students receive degree credit for clinical courses. (Clinical practicum is not required.) Among the clinical areas offered are:

   Advocacy
   Civil Rights
   Criminal Defense
   Criminal Prosecution
   Employment Law
   Environmental Law
   Family Law
   Family Practice
   Government/Regulation
   Immigration
   Judicial Process
   Labor Law
   Land Use Law/Natural Resources
   Lawyering Skills
   Legislation
   Litigation
   Mediation
   Prisoners' Rights
   Public Interest
   Tax Law

UNIVERSITY OF CALIFORNIA, HASTINGS COLLEGE OF THE LAW

San Francisco, California

INFORMATION CONTACT

Akira Shiroma, Director of Admissions
200 McAllister Street
San Francisco, CA 94102-4978

Phone: 415-565-1885   Fax: 415-565-1863
E-mail: shiroma@uchastings.edu
Web site: http://www.uchastings.edu/

LAW STUDENT PROFILE [2000–2001]

FULL-TIME   Enrollment: 1,201
Women: 51%   Men: 49%

APPLICANTS and ADMITTEES

Number applied: 4,452
Admitted: 1417
Percentage accepted: 32%
Seats available: 433
Average LSAT score: 161
Average GPA: 3.4

University of California, Hastings College of the Law is a public institution that organizes classes on a semester calendar system. The campus is situated in an urban setting. Founded in 1878, first ABA approved in 1939, and an AALS member, University of California, Hastings College of the Law offers a JD degree.

Faculty 100% of all faculty members have a JD degree. Of all faculty members, 12.24% are Asian/Pacific Islander, 6.12% are African American, 4.08% are Hispanic, 75.52% are white, 2.04% are international.

Application Information *Required:* LSAT, LSDAS, application form, application fee of $40, baccalaureate degree, personal statement. *Recommended:* recommendations, resume.

Costs The 2000–2001 tuition was $10,175 full-time for state residents. Tuition was $19,296 full-time for nonresidents. Fees: $1057 full-time.

Financial Aid Loans, loan repayment assistance program (LRAP), merit-based grants/scholarships, need-based grants/scholarships, and federal work-study loans are available. The average student debt at graduation is $51,500. To apply for financial assistance, students must complete the Free Application for Federal Student Aid, institutional forms. Financial aid contact: Linda Bisesi, Director of Financial Aid, 200 McAllister Street, San Francisco, CA 94102. Phone: 415-565-4624. Fax: 415-565-4863.

Law School Library Hastings Law Library has 11 professional staff members and contains more than

AT a GLANCE

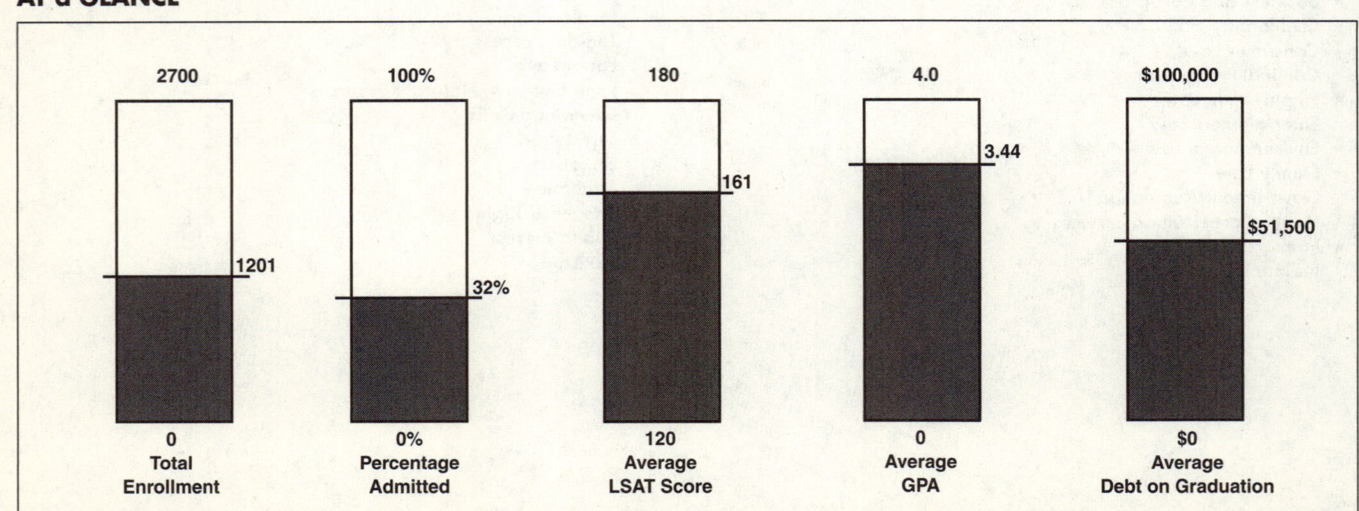

Degree Options		
Degree	**Total Credits Required**	**Length of Program**
JD–Doctor of Laws	86	3 yrs, full-time only [day]

638,059 volumes and 8,273 periodicals. 652 seats are available in the library. When classes are in session, the library is open 102 hours per week.

WESTLAW and LEXIS-NEXIS are available, as are the World Wide Web, online bibliographic services, and CD-ROM players. 202 computer workstations are available to students in the library. Special law collections include federal and California depositories.

First-Year Program Class size in the average section is 85; 99% of the first-year courses are taught by full-time faculty.

Upper-Level Program Class size in the average section is 60. Among the electives are:

Administrative Law
Advocacy
Animal Rights Law
Business and Corporate Law
★ Civil Litigation
Consumer Law
Criminal Defense
Criminal Prosecution
Entertainment Law
Environmental Law
Family Law
Government/Regulation
Health Care/Human Services
Immigration
Indian/Tribal Law
Intellectual Property
★ International/Comparative Law
Judicial Externship
Jurisprudence
Labor Law
Land Use Law/Natural Resources
Lawyering Skills
Legal History/Philosophy
Litigation
Local Government
Maritime Law
Media Law
Mediation
Probate Law
★ Public Interest
Securities
★ Tax Law
(★ indicates an area of special strength)

Clinical Courses Students receive degree credit for clinical courses. (Clinical practicum is not required.) Among the clinical areas offered are:

Civil Litigation
Criminal Defense
Criminal Prosecution
Environmental Law
Immigration
Judicial Externship
Local Government
Mediation
Public Interest

International exchange programs permit students to visit Canada and Netherlands.

UNIVERSITY OF CALIFORNIA, LOS ANGELES
SCHOOL OF LAW

Los Angeles, California

INFORMATION CONTACT

Admissions Office
405 Hilgard Avenue
Los Angeles, CA 90024

Phone: 310-825-2080
Web site: http://www.law.ucla.edu/

LAW STUDENT PROFILE [2000–2001]

FULL-TIME   Enrollment: 896
Women: 55%   Men: 45%

RACIAL or ETHNIC COMPOSITION
African American, 2%; Asian/Pacific Islander, 16%; Hispanic,
8%; Native American, 0.3%; International, 3%

APPLICANTS and ADMITTEES
Number applied: 4,404
Admitted: 856
Percentage accepted: 19%
Seats available: 290
Average LSAT score: 164
Average GPA: 3.7

University of California, Los Angeles School of Law is
a public institution that organizes classes on a semester
calendar system. The campus is situated in an urban
setting. Founded in 1947, first ABA approved in 1950,
and an AALS member, University of California, Los
Angeles School of Law offers JD, JD/MA, JD/MBA,
JD/MPH, JD/MPP, JD/MSW, and LLM degrees.

Faculty 99% of all faculty members have a JD; 15% have
advanced law degrees. Of all faculty members, 1% are
Native American, 3% are Asian/Pacific Islander, 3% are
African American, 1% are Hispanic, 92% are white.

Application Information *Required:* LSAT, LSDAS,
application form, application fee of $40, baccalaureate
degree, 1 recommendation, personal statement, essay,
college transcripts, resume.

Financial Aid In 2000–2001, 97% of all students received
some form of financial aid. 6 research assistantships, 10
teaching assistantships, were awarded. Fellowships, loans,
loan repayment assistance program (LRAP), merit-based
grants/scholarships, need-based grants/scholarships, and
federal work-study loans are also available. The average
student debt at graduation is $48,850. To apply for
financial assistance, students must complete the Free
Application for Federal Student Aid, institutional forms,
Need Access electronic applications for need-based
grants. Completed financial aid forms should be received
by March 1. Financial aid contact: Veronica Wilson,
Director of Financial Aid, Box 951476, Los Angeles, CA
90095-1476. Phone: 310-825-2459. Fax: 310-794-5827.
E-mail: wilsonv@mail.law.ucla.edu

AT a GLANCE

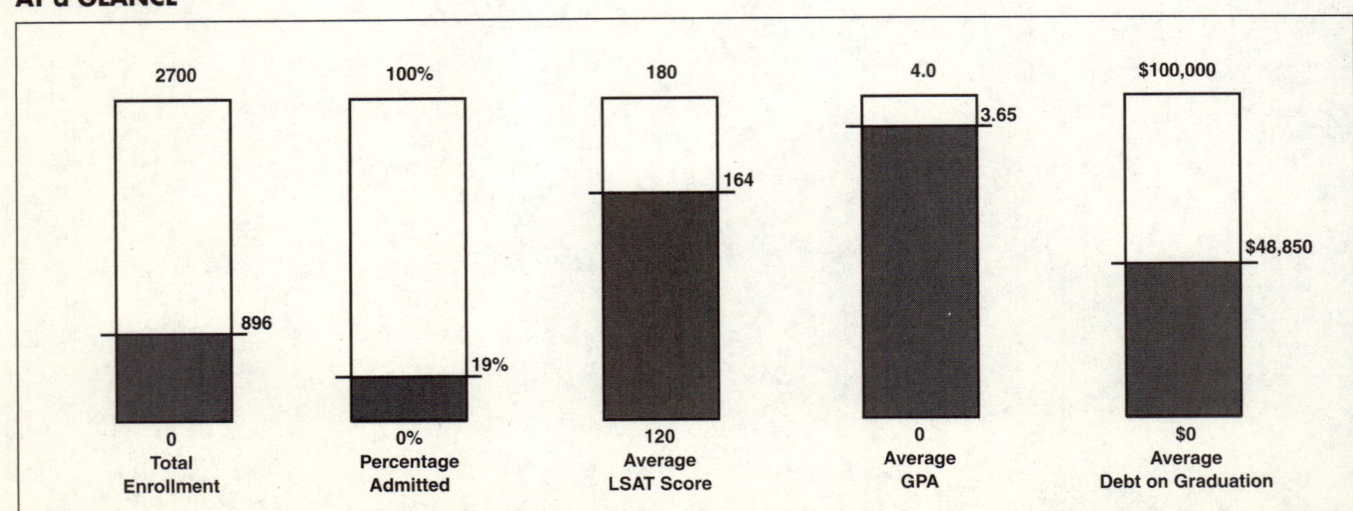

Degree Options

Degree	Total Credits Required	Length of Program
JD–Doctor of Laws	87	3 yrs, full-time only [day]
JD/MA–Juris Doctor/Master of Arts–Law and Urban Planning Program	143	4 yrs, full-time only [day]
JD/MA–Juris Doctor/Master of Arts–Law and Afro-American Studies Joint-Degree Program		4 yrs, full-time only
JD/MA–Juris Doctor/Master of Arts–Law and American Indian Studies Joint-degree Program	87	3.5–4 yrs, full-time only [day]
JD/MBA–Juris Doctor/Master of Business Administration–Law and Management Joint-degree Program	149	4 yrs, full-time only [day]
JD/MPH–Juris Doctor/Master of Public Health–JD/MPH Dual Degree Program	157	full-time only
JD/MPP–Juris Doctor/Master of Public Planning–Law and Public Policy Joint-degree Program	73	4 yrs, full-time only [day]
JD/MSW–Juris Doctor/Master of Social Work–Law Social Welfare Joint-degree Program	141	4 yrs, full-time only [day]
LLM–Master of Laws–Program for Graduates of Foreign Law Schools	20	1 yr, full-time only [day]

Law School Library Hugh and Hazel Darling Law Library has 10 professional staff members and contains more than 560,194 volumes and 7,447 periodicals. 774 seats are available in the library. When classes are in session, the library is open 98 hours per week.

WESTLAW and LEXIS-NEXIS are available, as are the World Wide Web, online bibliographic services, and CD-ROM players. 65 computer workstations are available to students in the library. Special law collections include Aviation Law, Islamic Law.

First-Year Program Class size in the average section is 70; 95% of the first-year courses are taught by full-time faculty.

Upper-Level Program Class size in the average section is 28. Among the electives are:

Administrative Law
Advocacy
Animal Rights Law
★ Business and Corporate Law
Civil Litigation
Criminal Defense
Education Law
Elderly Advocacy
Entertainment Law
★ Environmental Law
Family Law
Family Practice
General Practice
Government/Regulation
Health Care/Human Services
★ Indian/Tribal Law
Intellectual Property
★ International/Comparative Law
Jurisprudence
Juvenile Law
Labor Law
Land Rights/Natural Resource
★ Land Use Law/Natural Resources
Lawyering Skills
Legal History/Philosophy
Litigation
Media Law
Mediation
Probate Law
★ Public Interest
Securities
Tax Law

(★ indicates an area of special strength)

Clinical Courses Students receive degree credit for clinical courses. (Clinical practicum is required.) Among the clinical areas offered are:

Administrative Law
Advocacy
Business and Corporate Law
Civil Litigation
Criminal Defense
Education Law
Elderly Advocacy
Environmental Law
Family Practice
General Practice
Government/Regulation
Health Care/Human Services
Indian/Tribal Law
Jurisprudence
Juvenile Law
Labor Law
Land Rights/Natural Resource
Lawyering Skills
Litigation
Mediation
Public Interest
Securities

International exchange programs permit students to visit Chile, Italy, Spain, and United Kingdom.

UNIVERSITY OF SAN DIEGO
SCHOOL OF LAW

San Diego, California

INFORMATION CONTACT

Carl J. Eging, Director of Admissions and Financial Aid
5998 Alcala Park
San Diego, CA 92110

Phone: 619-260-4528   Fax: 619-260-2218
E-mail: eging@sandiego.edu
Web site: http://www.sandiego.edu/usdlaw/

LAW STUDENT PROFILE [2000–2001]

FULL-TIME   Enrollment: 776
Women: 48%   Men: 52%

PART-TIME   Enrollment: 314
Women: 43%   Men: 57%

RACIAL or ETHNIC COMPOSITION

African American, 3%; Asian/Pacific Islander, 12%; Hispanic, 8%; Native American, 1%; International, 3%

APPLICANTS and ADMITTEES

Number applied: 3,082
Admitted: 1,258
Percentage accepted: 41%
Seats available: 338
Average LSAT score: 160
Average GPA: 3.3

University of San Diego School of Law is a private institution that organizes classes on a semester calendar system. The campus is situated in an urban setting. Founded in 1954, first ABA approved in 1961, and an AALS member, University of San Diego School of Law offers JD, JD/IMBA, JD/MA, JD/MBA, and LLM degrees.

Faculty consists of 53 full-time and 37 part-time members in 2000–2001. 18 full-time faculty members and 5 part-time faculty members are women. 100% of all faculty members have a JD degree. Of all faculty members, 3% are Asian/Pacific Islander, 3% are African American, 7% are Hispanic, 87% are white.

Application Information *Required:* LSAT, LSDAS, application form, application fee of $50, baccalaureate degree, minimum 2.0 GPA, personal statement, college transcripts. *Recommended:* resume. *Application deadline* for fall term is February 1 (priority date). Applications are processed on a rolling basis.

Costs The 2000–2001 tuition was $23,510 full-time; $815 per credit part-time. Fees: $50 full-time; $20 per term part-time.

Financial Aid In 2000–2001, 84% of all students received some form of financial aid. 60 research assistantships, totaling $4000 were awarded. Loans, loan repayment assistance program (LRAP), merit-based grants/scholarships, need-based grants/scholarships, and federal work-study loans are also available. The average student debt at graduation is $68,000. To apply for financial assistance, students must complete the Free Application for Federal Student Aid, institutional forms. Completed

AT a GLANCE

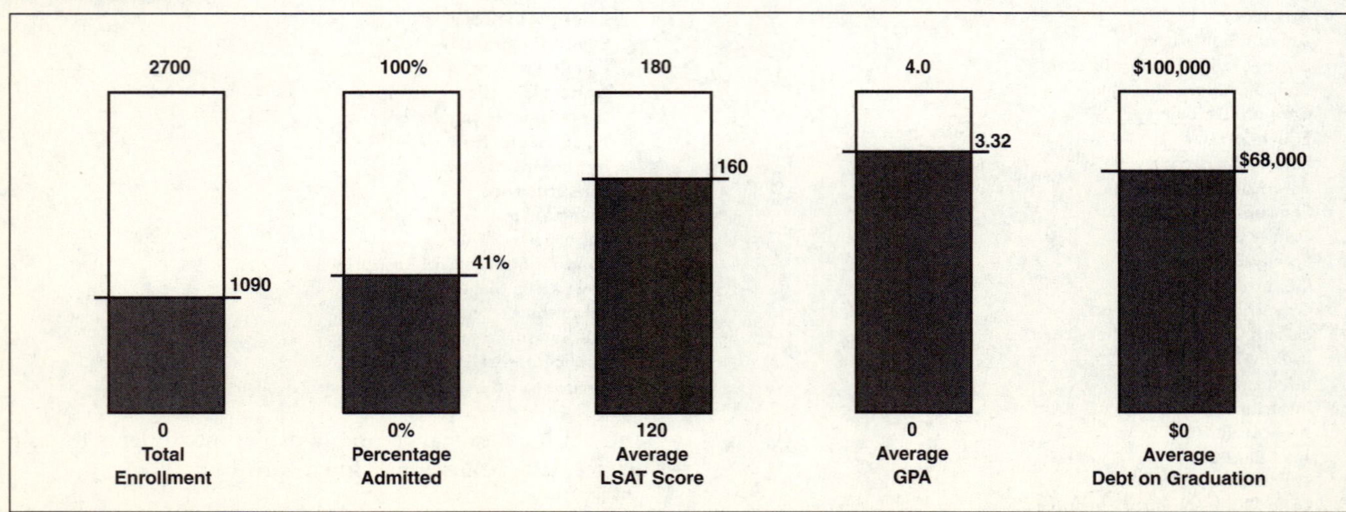

Degree Options

Degree	Total Credits Required	Length of Program
JD–Doctor of Laws	85	3–4 yrs, full-time or part-time [day, evening, summer]
JD/IMBA–Juris Doctor/International Master of Business Administration–Dual-degree Program	133	4–5 yrs, full-time or part-time [day, evening, summer]
JD/MA–Juris Doctor/Master of Arts–International Relations Dual-degree Program	115	4–5 yrs, full-time or part-time [day, evening, summer]
JD/MBA–Juris Doctor/Master of Business Administration–Dual-degree Program	133	4–5 yrs, full-time or part-time [day, evening, summer]
LLM–Master of Laws–Comparative Law for Foreign Attorneys	25	1 yr, full-time or part-time [day, evening, summer]
LLM–Master of Laws–Business and Corporate Law	24	1 yr, full-time or part-time [day, evening, summer]
LLM–Master of Laws–General	24	1 yr, full-time or part-time [day, evening, summer]
LLM–Master of Laws–International Law	24	1 yr, full-time or part-time [day, evening, summer]
LLM–Master of Laws–Taxation	24	1 yr, full-time or part-time [day, evening, summer]

financial aid forms should be received by March 1. Financial aid contact: Carl J. Eging, Director of Admissions and Financial Aid, 5998 Alcala Park, San Diego, CA 92110. Phone: 619-260-4570. Fax: 619-260-2218. E-mail: jdinfo@SanDeigo.edu

Law School Library Legal Research Center has 12 professional staff members and contains more than 471,914 volumes and 5,361 periodicals. 600 seats are available in the library. When classes are in session, the library is open 109 hours per week.

WESTLAW and LEXIS-NEXIS are available, as are the World Wide Web, online bibliographic services, and CD-ROM players. 38 computer workstations are available to students in the library. Special law collections include Taxation, Mexican Law, Law and Popular Culture.

First-Year Program Class size in the average section is 80; 100% of the first-year courses are taught by full-time faculty.

Upper-Level Program Class size in the average section is 30. Among the electives are:

Administrative Law
★ Advocacy
Business and Corporate Law
★ Children and the Law
★ Civil Litigation
Civil Procedure
★ Criminal Defense
★ Criminal Law
Entertainment Law
Entrepreneurship Law
Environmental Law
★ Family Law
Government/Regulation

Health Care/Human Services
★ Immigration
Indian/Tribal Law
Intellectual Property
★ International/Comparative Law
Judicial
Jurisprudence
Labor Law
★ Land Rights/Natural Resource
Lawyering Skills
Legal History/Philosophy
Litigation
Maritime Law
Media Law
Mediation
★ Mental Health and Law
Probate Law
★ Public Interest
Securities
★ Tax Law
(★ indicates an area of special strength)

Clinical Courses Students receive degree credit for clinical courses. (Clinical practicum is not required.) Among the clinical areas offered are:

Children and the Law
Civil Litigation
Criminal Defense
Criminal Law
Entrepreneurship Law
Environmental Law
Immigration
Lawyering Skills
Mental Health and Law
Public Interest
Tax Law

International exchange programs permit students to visit France, Ireland, Italy, Russian Federation, Spain, and United Kingdom.

UNIVERSITY OF SAN FRANCISCO
SCHOOL OF LAW

San Francisco, California

INFORMATION CONTACT

Saralynn T. Ferrara, Director of Admissions
2100 Fulton Street
San Francisco, CA 94117-1080

Phone: 415-422-6586   Fax: 415-422-6433
Web site: http://www.usfca.edu/law/

LAW STUDENT PROFILE [2000–2001]

FULL-TIME   Enrollment: 512
Women: 61%   Men: 39%

PART-TIME   Enrollment: 116
Women: 50%   Men: 50%

RACIAL or ETHNIC COMPOSITION
African American, 4%; Asian/Pacific Islander, 15%; Hispanic, 6%; Native American, 0.5%; International, 0.3%

APPLICANTS and ADMITTEES
Number applied: 1,933
Admitted: 912
Percentage accepted: 47%
Seats available: 225
Median LSAT score: 155
Average GPA: 3.2

University of San Francisco School of Law is a private institution that organizes classes on a semester calendar system. The campus is situated in an urban setting. Founded in 1912, first ABA approved in 1933, and an AALS member, University of San Francisco School of Law offers JD, JD/MBA, and LLM degrees.

Faculty consists of 28 full-time and 34 part-time members in 2000–2001. 9 full-time faculty members and 9 part-time faculty members are women. 100% of all faculty members have a JD; 9% have advanced law degrees. Of all faculty members, 6% are Asian/Pacific Islander, 9% are African American, 6% are Hispanic, 79% are white.

Application Information *Required:* LSAT, LSDAS, application form, application fee of $50, baccalaureate degree, 2 letters of recommendation, personal statement, college transcripts. *Application deadline* for fall term is April 1. Applications are processed on a rolling basis.

Costs The 2000–2001 tuition was $23,636 full-time; $843 per credit part-time.

Financial Aid In 2000–2001, 87% of all students received some form of financial aid. Fellowships, loans, loan repayment assistance program (LRAP), merit-based grants/scholarships, need-based grants/scholarships, and federal work-study loans are available. The average student debt at graduation is $62,390. To apply for financial assistance, students must complete the Free Application for Federal Student Aid. Completed financial aid forms should be received by March 2. Financial aid contact: Gabriela De la Vega, Financial Aid Counselor,

AT a GLANCE

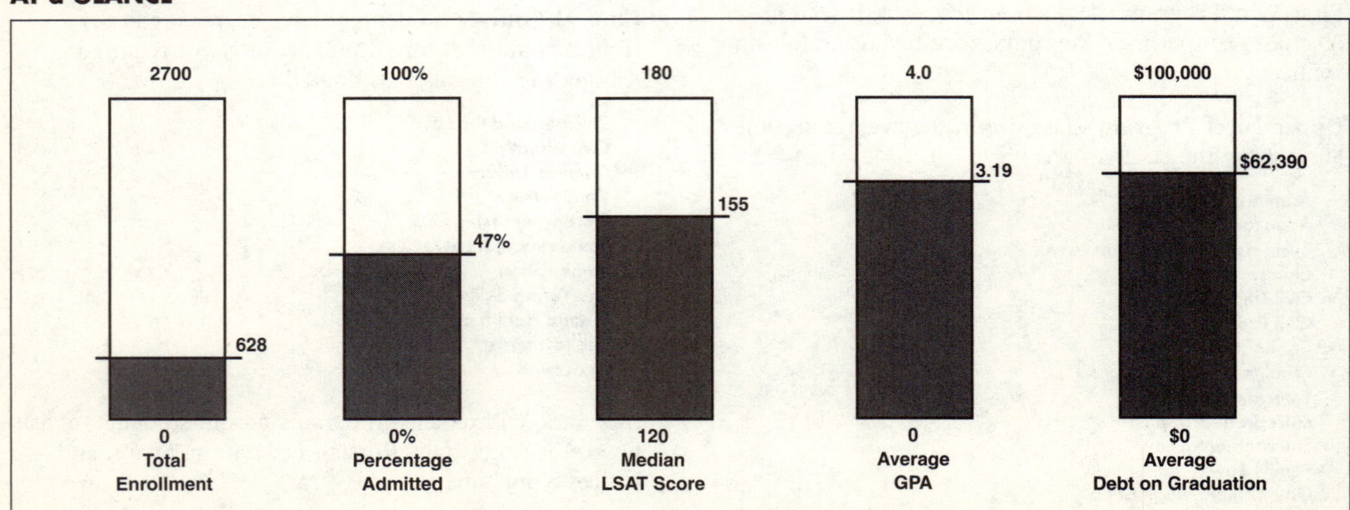

Degree Options

Degree	Total Credits Required	Length of Program
JD–Doctor of Laws	86	3–4 yrs, full-time or part-time [day, evening, summer]
JD/MBA–Juris Doctor/Master of Business Administration–Concurrent Program	116	4 yrs, full-time only [day, evening, summer]
LLM–Master of Laws–Foreign Lawyers in International Transactions and Comparative Law	25	1–2 yrs, full-time or part-time [day]

USF School of Law, San Francisco, CA 94117-1080. Phone: 415-422-6210. Fax: 415-422-6433. E-mail: delavegag@usfca.edu

Law School Library University of San Francisco School of Law Library has 7 professional staff members and contains more than 302,348 volumes and 2,757 periodicals. 471 seats are available in the library. When classes are in session, the library is open 100 hours per week.

WESTLAW and LEXIS-NEXIS are available, as are the World Wide Web, online bibliographic services, and CD-ROM players. 36 computer workstations are available to students in the library. Special law collections include California law, Reserve, Reference.

First-Year Program Class size in the average section is 80; 100% of the first-year courses are taught by full-time faculty.

Upper-Level Program Class size in the average section is 28. Among the electives are:

- Administrative Law
- ★ Advocacy
- Business and Corporate Law
- ★ Civil Litigation
- Consumer Law
- Criminal Defense
- ★ Criminal Law
- ★ Dispute Resolution
- Entertainment Law
- Environmental Law
- Family Law
- Government/Regulation
- Indian/Tribal Law
- ★ Intellectual Property
- ★ International/Comparative Law
- Investigation
- Labor Law
- Law and Democracy
- Lawyering Skills
- ★ Litigation
- Maritime Law
- Media Law
- Mediation
- Probate Law
- ★ Public Interest
- Securities
- Tax Law

(★ *indicates an area of special strength*)

Clinical Courses Students receive degree credit for clinical courses. (Clinical practicum is not required.) Among the clinical areas offered are:

- Civil Litigation
- Criminal Defense
- Intellectual Property
- Investigation
- Mediation

International exchange programs permit students to visit Czech Republic, Indonesia, and Ireland.

UNIVERSITY OF SOUTHERN CALIFORNIA
LAW SCHOOL

Los Angeles, California

LAW STUDENT PROFILE [2000–2001]

FULL-TIME   Enrollment: 560
Women: 49%   Men: 51%

PART-TIME   Enrollment: 16
Women: 50%   Men: 50%

RACIAL or ETHNIC COMPOSITION
African American, 12%; Asian/Pacific Islander, 14%;
Hispanic, 11%; International, 1%

APPLICANTS and ADMITTEES
Seats available: 205
Median LSAT score: 164
Average GPA: 3.6

University of Southern California Law School is a private institution that organizes classes on a semester calendar system. The campus is situated in an urban setting. Founded in 1900, first ABA approved in 1924, and an AALS member, University of Southern California Law School offers JD, JD/MA, JD/MBA, JD/MPAd, JD/MPPo, JD/MRED, JD/MS, JD/MSW, JD/MTAX, and JD/PhD degrees.

Faculty consists of 53 full-time and 38 part-time members in 2000–2001. 15 full-time faculty members and 7 part-time faculty members are women. 98% of all faculty members have a JD; 6% have advanced law degrees.

Application Information *Required:* LSAT, LSDAS, application form, application fee of $60, baccalaureate degree, 2 letters of recommendation, personal statement, college transcripts. *Recommended:* resume. *Application deadline* for fall term is February 1. Applications are processed on a rolling basis.

Financial Aid 273 fellowships, 9 teaching assistantships, were awarded. Fellowships, graduate assistantships, loans, loan repayment assistance program (LRAP), merit-based grants/scholarships, need-based grants/scholarships, and federal work-study loans are also available. To apply for financial assistance, students must complete the Free Application for Federal Student Aid, institutional forms, photocopy of income tax return. Completed financial aid forms should be received by February 15. Financial aid contact: Mary Bingham, Director of Financial Aid,

AT a GLANCE

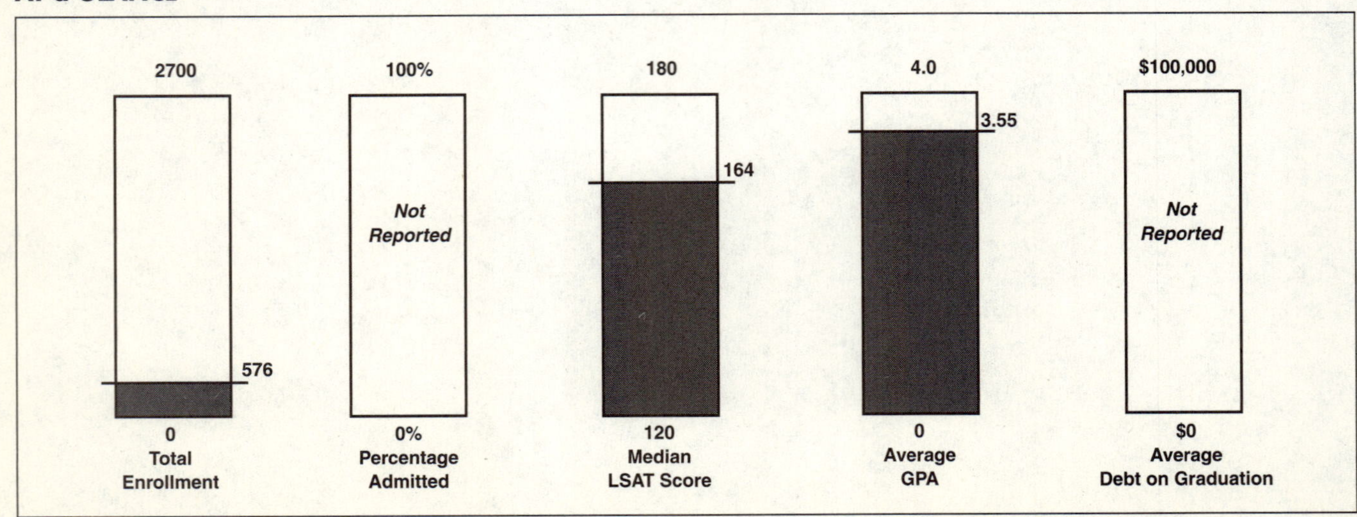

Degree Options

Degree	Total Credits Required	Length of Program
JD–Doctor of Laws	88	3 yrs, full-time only [day]
JD–Juris Doctor–Graduate Certificate in Gender Studies		3 yrs, full-time only [day]
JD/MA–Juris Doctor/Master of Arts–(Economics) Dual-degree	89	3 yrs, full-time only [day]
JD/MA–Juris Doctor/Master of Arts–(Communication, Management) Dual-degree	89	3 yrs, full-time only [day]
JD/MA–Juris Doctor/Master of Arts–(Religion) Dual-degree	91	3 yrs, full-time only [day]
JD/MA–Juris Doctor/Master of Arts–(Political Science) Dual Degree program		full-time only [day]
JD/MA–Juris Doctor/Master of Arts–(Philosophy) Dual-degree	90	3 yrs, full-time only [day]
JD/MA–Juris Doctor/Master of Arts–(International Relations) Dual-degree	95	3.5 yrs, full-time only [day]
JD/MBA–Juris Doctor/Master of Business Administration–Dual-degree	122	4 yrs, full-time only [day]
JD/MPAd–Juris Doctor/Master of Public Administration–Dual-degree	97	3.5 yrs, full-time only [day]
JD/MPPo–Juris Doctor/Master of Public Policy–Dual-degree	112	4 yrs, full-time only [day]
JD/MRED–Juris Doctor/Master of Real Estate Development	108	3.5 yrs, full-time only [day]
JD/MS–Juris Doctor/Master of Science–(Gerontology) Dual-degree	110	4 yrs, full-time only [day]
JD/MSW–Juris Doctor/Master of Social Work–Dual-degree	117	4 yrs, full-time only [day]
JD/MTAX–Juris Doctor/Master of Taxation–Business Tax Dual-degree	118	4 yrs [day]
JD/PhD–Juris Doctor/Doctor of Philosophy–(Economics) California Institute of Technology		full-time only [day]
JD/PhD–Juris Doctor/Doctor of Philosophy–(Political Science) Dual Degree program		full-time only [day]

University Park, Los Angeles, CA 90089-0071. Phone: 213-740-7331. Fax: 213-740-4570. E-mail: mbingham@law.usc.edu

Law School Library Gabriel and Matilda Barnett Information Technology Center and Asa V. Call Law Library has 10 professional staff members and contains more than 373,488 volumes and 4,300 periodicals. 298 seats are available in the library. When classes are in session, the library is open 101 hours per week.

WESTLAW and LEXIS-NEXIS are available, as are the World Wide Web, online bibliographic services, and CD-ROM players. 74 computer workstations are available to students in the library. Special law collections include Client (self-help) Library; Abraham Lincoln Special Books Collection; highly developed collections in many areas, including bioethics, health, bias issues.

First-Year Program Class size in the average section is 65; 100% of the first-year courses are taught by full-time faculty.

Upper-Level Program Class size in the average section is 30. Among the electives are:

Accounting
Administrative Law
★ Advocacy
★ Business and Corporate Law
Civil Litigation
Civil Rights
★ Corporate Law
★ Criminal Defense
Discrimination
Dispute Resolution
★ Entertainment Law
Environmental Law
★ Family Law
Government/Regulation
★ Health Care/Human Services
★ Health Law
★ Immigration
Indian/Tribal Law
★ Intellectual Property
★ International/Comparative Law
Jurisprudence
★ Juvenile Law

       Labor Law
       Land Use Law/Natural Resources
 ★ Law and Economics
 ★ Lawyering Skills
 ★ Legal History/Philosophy
 ★ Litigation
       Maritime Law
 ★ Media Law
       Mediation
       Probate Law
 ★ Public Interest
       Securities
 ★ Tax Law
(★ indicates an area of special strength)

Clinical Courses Students receive degree credit for
clinical courses. (Clinical practicum is not required.)
Among the clinical areas offered are:

       Advocacy

Business and Corporate Law
Civil Litigation
Civil Rights
Corporate Law
Criminal Defense
Discrimination
Dispute Resolution
Family Law
General Practice
Health Care/Human Services
Health Law
Immigration
Juvenile Law
Labor Law
Law and Economics
Lawyering Skills
Litigation
Mediation
Public Interest

UNIVERSITY OF THE PACIFIC
MCGEORGE SCHOOL OF LAW

Sacramento, California

LAW STUDENT PROFILE [2000–2001]

FULL-TIME   Enrollment: 635
Women: 51%   Men: 49%

PART-TIME   Enrollment: 301
Women: 49%   Men: 51%

RACIAL or ETHNIC COMPOSITION
African American, 4%; Asian/Pacific Islander, 11%; Hispanic, 8%; Native American, 1%

APPLICANTS and ADMITTEES
Number applied: 1,680
Admitted: 1,174
Percentage accepted: 70%
Seats available: 360
Median LSAT score: 151
Average GPA: 3.0

University of the Pacific McGeorge School of Law is a private institution that organizes classes on a semester calendar system. The campus is situated in an urban setting. Founded in 1924, first ABA approved in 1969, and an AALS member, University of the Pacific McGeorge School of Law offers JD, JD/MBA, JD/MPPA, and LLM degrees.

Faculty consists of 44 full-time and 64 part-time members in 2000–2001. 14 full-time faculty members and 15 part-time faculty members are women. 100% of all faculty members have a JD; 16% have advanced law degrees. Of all faculty members, 1% are Asian/Pacific Islander, 4% are African American, 1% are Hispanic, 94% are white.

Application Information *Required:* LSAT, LSDAS, application form, application fee of $40, baccalaureate degree, personal statement, college transcripts. *Recommended:* recommendations, resume. *Application deadline* for fall term is May 1 (priority date). Applications are processed on a rolling basis.

Costs The 1999–2000 tuition was $21,656 full-time; $14,396 per year part-time. Fees: $38 full-time; $38 per year part-time.

Financial Aid In 2000–2001, 51% of all students received some form of financial aid. 2 fellowships; 14 teaching assistantships, totaling $5130, were awarded. Loans, loan repayment assistance program (LRAP), merit-based grants/scholarships, need-based grants/scholarships, and federal work-study loans are also available. The average student debt at graduation is $64,500. To apply for

AT a GLANCE

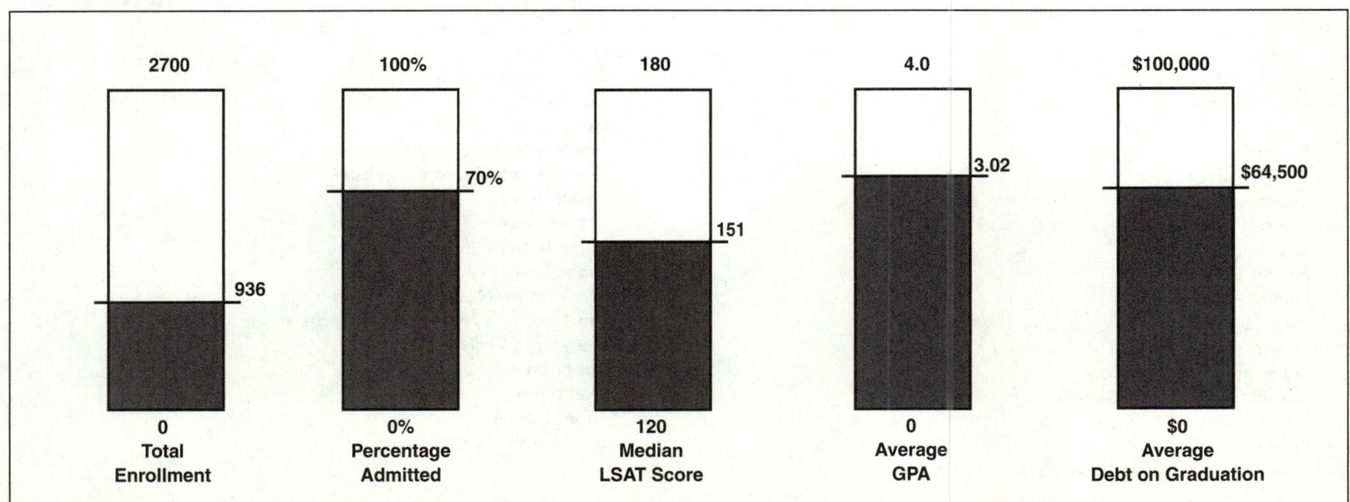

Degree Options

Degree	Total Credits Required	Length of Program
JD–Doctor of Laws	88	3–4 yrs, full-time or part-time [day, evening, summer]
JD/MBA–Juris Doctor/Master of Business Administration–Dual-degree Program	100	4–5 yrs, full-time or part-time [day, evening, summer]
JD/MPPA–Juris Doctor/Master of Public Policy and Administration–Dual-degree Program	100	4–5 yrs, full-time or part-time [day, evening, summer]
LLM–Master of Laws–Transnational Business Practice	24	1 yr, full-time only [day]

financial assistance, students must complete the Free Application for Federal Student Aid, institutional forms. Financial aid contact: Addalou Davis, Director, Financial Aid, 3200 Fifth Avenue, Sacramento, CA 95817. Phone: 916-739-7158. Fax: 916-739-7162. E-mail: finaid@uop.edu

Law School Library Gordon D. Schaber Law Library has 8 professional staff members and contains more than 440,381 volumes and 4,509 periodicals. 615 seats are available in the library. When classes are in session, the library is open 108 hours per week.

WESTLAW and LEXIS-NEXIS are available, as are the World Wide Web, online bibliographic services, and CD-ROM players. 50 computer workstations are available to students in the library. Special law collections include Tax and International Law; California; California and US documents depository.

First-Year Program Class size in the average section is 90; 100% of the first-year courses are taught by full-time faculty.

Upper-Level Program Among the electives are:

- Administrative Law
- ★ Advocacy
- ★ Business and Corporate Law
- ★ Civil Litigation
- Civil Rights
- Constitutional Law
- Consumer Law
- ★ Corporate Law
- Criminal Defense
- ★ Criminal Law
- Criminal Prosecution
- Education
- Elderly Advocacy
- Employment Law
- Entertainment Law
- Environmental Law
- Family Law
- Family Practice
- General Practice
- Government Litigation
- ★ Government/Regulation
- Health Care/Human Services
- Health Law
- ★ Intellectual Property
- ★ International/Comparative Law
- Jurisprudence
- Juvenile Law
- Labor Law
- Land Rights/Natural Resource
- Land Use Law/Natural Resources
- ★ Lawyering Skills
- Legal History/Philosophy
- ★ Litigation
- Maritime Law
- Media Law
- Mediation
- Probate Law
- Public Interest
- Securities
- ★ Tax Law

(★ *indicates an area of special strength*)

Clinical Courses Students receive degree credit for clinical courses. (Clinical practicum is not required.) Among the clinical areas offered are:

- Administrative Law
- Advocacy
- Business and Corporate Law
- Civil Litigation
- Civil Rights
- Constitutional Law
- Consumer Law
- Corporate Law
- Criminal Defense
- Criminal Law
- Criminal Prosecution
- Education
- Elderly Advocacy
- Employment Law
- Environmental Law
- Family Law
- Family Practice
- General Practice
- Government Litigation
- Government/Regulation
- Health Care/Human Services
- Health Law
- Immigration
- Juvenile Law
- Labor Law
- Land Rights/Natural Resource
- Land Use Law/Natural Resources
- Lawyering Skills
- Litigation
- Mediation
- Public Interest
- Tax Law

WESTERN STATE UNIVERSITY COLLEGE OF LAW

Fullerton, California

INFORMATION CONTACT

Joel H. Goodman, Associate Dean
1111 North State College Boulevard
Fullerton, CA 92831-3000

Phone: 714-738-1000   Fax: 714-526-1062
E-mail: adm@wsulaw.edu
Web site: http://www.wsulaw.edu/

LAW STUDENT PROFILE [2000–2001]

FULL-TIME   Enrollment: 233
Women: 48%   Men: 52%

PART-TIME   Enrollment: 268
Women: 44%   Men: 56%

APPLICANTS and ADMITTEES

Number applied: 777
Admitted: 474
Percentage accepted: 61%
Seats available: 173
Average LSAT score: 149
Average GPA: 2.9

Western State University College of Law is a private institution that organizes classes on a semester calendar system. The campus is situated in an urban setting. Founded in 1966, first ABA approved in 1998, Western State University College of Law offers a JD degree.

Faculty consists of 1 full-time faculty member is a woman. 100% of all faculty members have a JD; 14.5% have advanced law degrees. Of all faculty members, 2% are Native American, 5% are African American, 9% are Hispanic, 84% are white.

Application Information *Required:* LSAT, LSDAS, application form, application fee of $50, 2 letters of recommendation, personal statement, college transcripts, baccalaureate degree, writing sample. *Recommended:* resume.

Costs The 2000–2001 tuition was $21,840 full-time. Fees: $70 per semester full-time.

Financial Aid Loans, merit-based grants/scholarships, need-based grants/scholarships, and federal work-study loans are available. The average student debt at graduation is $48,857. To apply for financial assistance, students must complete the Free Application for Federal Student Aid, institutional forms, scholarship specific applications. Financial aid contact: Donna Espinoza, Financial Assistance Director, 1111 North State College Boulevard, Fullerton, CA 92831. Phone: 714-738-1000 ext. 2350. Fax: 714-871-5037. E-mail: fa@wsulaw.edu

Law School Library Western State University Law Library has 7 professional staff members and contains

AT a GLANCE

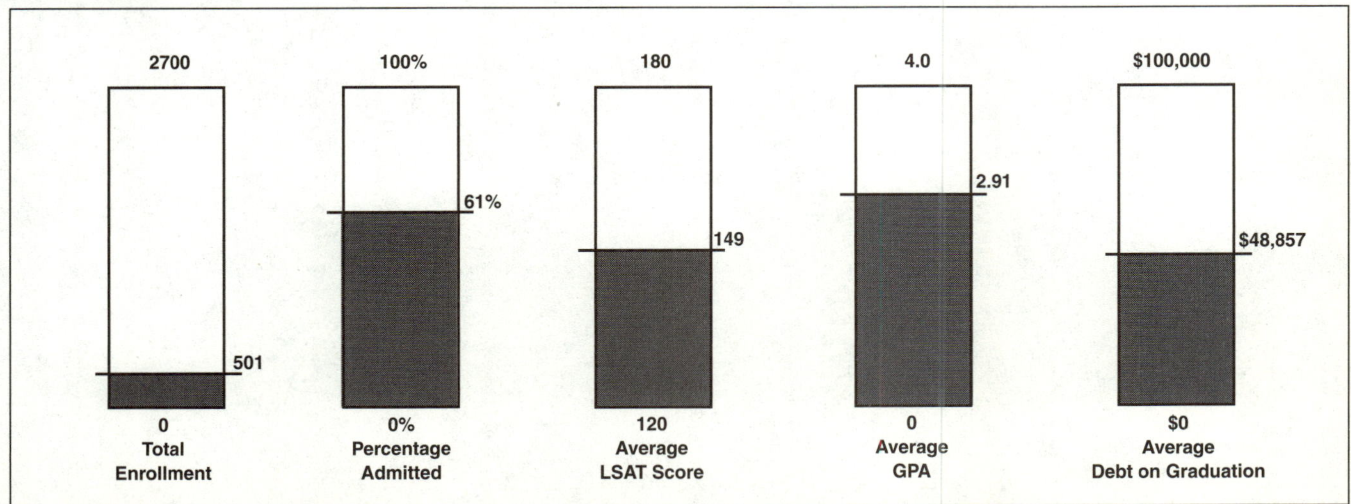

Degree Options		
Degree	**Total Credits Required**	**Length of Program**
JD–Doctor of Laws	88	3–4 yrs, full-time or part-time [day, evening]

more than 164,261 volumes and 2,847 periodicals. 353 seats are available in the library. When classes are in session, the library is open 107 hours per week.

WESTLAW and LEXIS-NEXIS are available, as are the World Wide Web, online bibliographic services, and CD-ROM players. 47 computer workstations are available to students in the library.

First-Year Program Class size in the average section is 37; 100% of the first-year courses are taught by full-time faculty.

Upper-Level Program Class size in the average section is 32. Among the electives are:

Administrative Law
Appellate Litigation

Business and Corporate Law
Civil Litigation
Consumer Law
Criminal Defense
Criminal Prosecution
★ Entrepreneurship Law
Environmental Law
Family Law
General Practice
Intellectual Property
Lawyering Skills
Legal History/Philosophy
Mediation
Probate Law
Tax Law
(★ *indicates an area of special strength*)

DEAN'S STATEMENT . . .

At Western State University, students are introduced to skills that lawyers use in their everyday practice from the day they commence their studies. Our curriculum, stressing "practice-oriented legal studies" is based upon our belief that students in today's world need to enter the professional world armed with the tools necessary to practice law successfully. Our mission is to train students to practice law competently and ethically from the inception of their careers.

"Practice-oriented legal studies" describes a program wherein practical skills training enriches traditional legal education. From the start of a Western State legal education, we expose students to techniques for negotiation, counseling, drafting, litigation, and related skills, as well as critical analysis, research, and basic legal writing. This method of skills integration continues throughout the course of study. In addition to upper-level skills courses taught on the simulation model, we offer extraordinary externships with trial and appellate judges in both federal and state courts, with a broad array of firms and agencies in civil practice, and with the Offices of the Public Defender and the District Attorney.

Western State offers students the opportunity to participate in the Entrepreneurial Law Center (ELC) program. Designed to impart the specialized skills necessary to effectively represent and guide small businesses and entrepreneurs, ELC continues an innovative upper-level curriculum with externships, community involvement and service, and scholarship. Courses are structured to help students develop competence in the transactional matters that lawyers regularly handle such as drafting, negotiating, counseling, and evaluating.

Students who wish to emphasize studies in criminal law may participate in the Criminal Law Practice Center (CLPC). Following the same pattern as ELC, CLPC offers a focused curriculum, externships, community involvement, and scholarship, all designed to prepare the student for effective practice in both criminal prosecution and criminal defense.

Another unique aspect of the Western State academic program is the Academic Support and Enrichment Program, a voluntary program available to all entering students. For no additional charges, students may enroll in this program, which is designed to provide them with extra assistance in making the adjustment to law school. The program includes structured study groups, workshops, and writing assistance.

In addition to "practice-oriented legal studies," one other principle guides us—that the entire program be student friendly. Faculty and staff members recognize that the atmosphere under which students study is as important as what they study.

—*Maryann Jones, Dean*

HISTORY, CAMPUS, AND LOCATION

The history of Western State spans five decades. The law school's growth has paralleled the evolution of Orange County, a region whose vitality is continually fed by the influx of businesses and people from around the nation and the world. The growing number of small start-up companies, the strength of the real estate industry, and the vitality of the country's ethnic diversity are key factors in creating opportunities for new law graduates.

Orange County, California, while part of the greater Los Angeles area, was listed as the most livable community in the U.S. by a recent Places Rated survey. World-class beaches, mountain ski resorts, and dramatic desert panoramas are within an hour of the campus. Cultural and recreational opportunities abound. The campus is located within the university district of Fullerton, a small gem of a city noted for the excellence of its five institutes of higher education and the charm of its "old California" downtown.

SPECIAL QUALITIES OF THE SCHOOL

Western State's cutting-edge curriculum integrates abstract legal concepts with real-world scenarios, making the law relevant to students' lives. The law school's professional skills training helps students develop the combination of analytical ability and finely honed instincts that makes the difference between becoming a great attorney or merely a good one.

The law school has graduated more than 10,000 alumni, who have distinguished themselves as lawmakers, jurists, prosecutors, public defenders, and highly respected private practitioners in every legal specialty, from aviation law to elder law. Opportunities for students to find part-time jobs and supportive legal mentors or to volunteer for rewarding public service assignments in a variety of government and nonprofit environments abound because of the alumni's strong presence here and the school's long-standing relationship with the community.

TECHNOLOGY ON CAMPUS

With the opening of a state-of-the-art library in 1997, Western State's students and faculty members have direct access to highly advanced, technologically sophisticated research materials. Students can plug in their laptops anywhere in the library and access electronic legal resources right at their seats. Professors have that same option thanks to "smart podiums" in new classrooms. A twenty-seven-station computer lab in the library provides users access to tutorial programs, a fifty-six-bay CD-ROM tower, and the Internet, as well as the legal database services. Law students also have the chance to interact with virtual judges on multimedia computers.

SCHOLARSHIPS AND LOANS

Most students finance their education through low-interest federal loans. Students are also eligible for scholarships based on their performance on the Law School Admission Test (LSAT). First-year scholarships range from $2500 to total tuition expense for full-time students and from $1200 to total part-time tuition expense for part-time students. For upper-level students, Trustees' Scholarships are awarded to those with cumulative GPAs that put them in the top 30 percent of upper-division students. Other specialty and need-based scholarships are also available.

STUDENT ACTIVITIES AND OPPORTUNITIES

Law Review Of the fifteen active student organizations, one of the most prestigious venues for law students to showcase their abilities and to refine their research, writing, analytical, and editing skills is by serving on the Western State University Law Review, for which they are also able to earn academic credit.

Moot Court Western State has incorporated moot court into the third course of a 9-unit professional skills sequence in which students learn how to interview a client and develop the facts of a case as they learn the skills of critical thinking, legal writing, and legal research. The third course, advocacy, has students apply these skills in a variety of settings. Students conduct an arbitration and negotiate a settlement. The semester culminates in the Ferguson Moot Court Competition, in which students write an appellate brief and argue orally before a panel of judges.

Extracurricular Activities Active student organizations include students with similar law specialty interests as well as students interested in literature and ethics as they relate to law. Several minority student organizations address the issues and concerns of those who are members of ethnic and racial minorities. Many students engage in public service work through Western State's voluntary public service program. Through their efforts, students make an impact on the world around them. They volunteer at government agencies, legal service organizations, charitable organizations, and private law firms that undertake pro bono cases. The Delta Theta Phi law fraternity and the Student Bar Association sponsor several annual charitable events for underprivileged children. The Volunteer Income Tax Assistance Program (VITA) helps older and indigent taxpayers prepare their returns. In 1999, WSU received the ABA's Student Division award for the best new VITA site. In 2000, WSU was recognized as the best continuing VITA site.

Special Opportunities For students who desire to become particularly knowledgeable about legal practice on behalf of small and entrepreneurial businesses, the Entrepreneurial Law Center (ELC) offers a program of externships, advanced curriculum, and opportunities for community involvement and scholarships, all focused on the needs and practices of this burgeoning and exciting client segment. Similarly, the Criminal Law Practice Center (CLPC) focuses curriculum, externships, scholarship, and community undertakings toward a heightened preparation for the practice of criminal law—both defense and prosecution. While both ELC and CLPC include externships, all students are encouraged to participate in the externship program, which covers a wide variety of legal practices as well as federal and state courts at both trial and appellate levels.

Opportunities for Members of Minority Groups and Women More than 36 percent of the law school's students come from ethnic and minority backgrounds that are underrepresented in the legal profession. About 46 percent of the student body is women. Women constitute 52 percent and members of minority groups constitute 24 percent of Western State's full-time faculty. Western State's minority student leaders champion causes and address concerns of importance to the entire student body. Among the student groups that are active on campus are several that provide forums for their members to discuss the issues facing women and minorities in law school. These include the Asian-Pacific American Law Student, Black Law Student, Latino Law Student, and Women's Law Associations. In 2000, Western State University won the prestigious Henry Ramsey, Jr. Award from the ABA's Law Student Division in recognition of WSU's commitment to diversity.

BAR PASSAGE, CAREER SERVICES, AND PLACEMENT

Western State's Career Services Offices provide new graduates and alumni with attorney, law clerk, and alternative career placement counseling; campus interviews; workshops and seminars; library and computer resources; and career-related brochures and monthly publications. Ninety-two percent of 1999 graduates found legal employment within six months of graduation.

Legal Field	Percentage of Graduates	Average Salary
Academic	3%	$52,300
Business	25%	$97,000
Government	14%	$50,086
Judicial Clerkship	2%	$37,600
Private Practice	52%	$62,500
Public Interest	3%	$52,500
Other	0%	n/a

CORRESPONDENCE AND INFORMATION

Admission Office
Western State University College of Law
1111 North State College Boulevard
Fullerton, California 92831-3000
Telephone: 714-738-1000 ext. 2600 or 800-WSU-4LAW
Fax: 714-441-1748
E-mail: adm@wsulaw.edu
World Wide Web: http://www.wsulaw.edu

WHITTIER COLLEGE
WHITTIER LAW SCHOOL

Costa Mesa, California

INFORMATION CONTACT

Patricia Abracia, Director of Admissions
3333 Harbor Boulevard
Costa Mesa, CA 92626

Phone: 714-444-4141   Fax: 714-444-0250
    ext. 122
E-mail: info@law.whittier.edu
Web site: http://www.law.whittier.edu/

LAW STUDENT PROFILE [2000–2001]

FULL-TIME   Enrollment: 432
Women: 53%   Men: 47%

PART-TIME   Enrollment: 286
Women: 50%   Men: 50%

RACIAL or ETHNIC COMPOSITION

African American, 7%; Asian/Pacific Islander, 19%; Hispanic, 14%; Native American, 1%; International, 1%

APPLICANTS and ADMITTEES

Number applied: 1,313
Admitted: 861
Percentage accepted: 66%
Seats available: 300
Average LSAT score: 148
Average GPA: 2.9

Whittier College Whittier Law School is a private institution that organizes classes on a semester calendar system. The campus is situated in a suburban setting. Founded in 1976, first ABA approved in 1978, and an AALS member, Whittier College Whittier Law School offers JD and LLM degrees.

Faculty consists of 28 full-time and 38 part-time members in 2000–2001. 11 full-time faculty members and 19 part-time faculty members are women. 100% of all faculty members have a JD; 8% have advanced law degrees. Of all faculty members, 9% are Asian/Pacific Islander, 1% are African American, 2% are Hispanic, 88% are white.

Application Information *Required:* LSAT, LSDAS, application form, application fee of $50, baccalaureate degree, minimum 2.0 GPA, personal statement, writing sample, college transcripts. *Recommended:* recommendations, essay, resume. *Application deadline* for fall term is March 15 (priority date); for spring term is November 1. Applications are processed on a rolling basis.

Costs The 2000–2001 tuition was $22,980 full-time; $766 per unit part-time. Fees: $17 per semester full-time; $17 per semester part-time.

Financial Aid In 2000–2001, 83% of all students received some form of financial aid. 24 fellowships, totaling $3500; 14 research assistantships; 74 teaching assistantships, were awarded. Fellowships, graduate assistantships, loans, merit-based grants/scholarships, need-based grants/scholarships, and federal work-study loans are also available. The average student debt at graduation is

AT a GLANCE

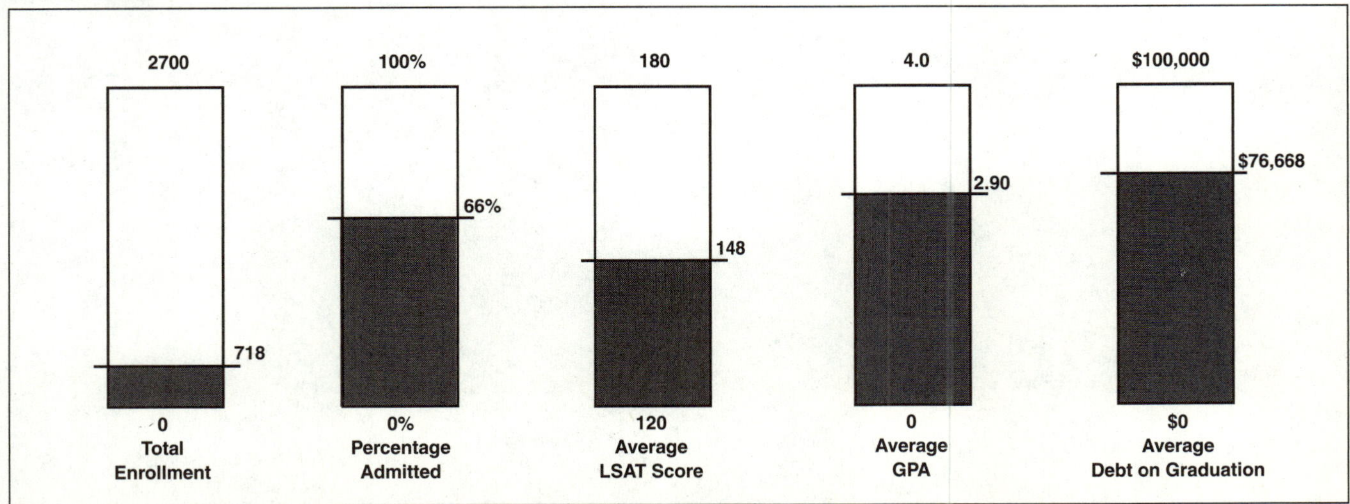

Degree Options

Degree	Total Credits Required	Length of Program
JD–Doctor of Laws	87	3–4 yrs, full-time or part-time [day, evening]
LLM–Master of Laws–US Legal Studies	24	1–2 yrs, full-time or part-time [day, evening, summer]

$76,668. To apply for financial assistance, students must complete the Free Application for Federal Student Aid, institutional forms, scholarship specific applications. Completed financial aid forms should be received by April 15. Financial aid contact: Julie McAllister, Director of Financial Aid, 3333 Harbor Boulevard, Costa Mesa, CA 92626. Phone: 714-444-4141 ext. 205. Fax: 714-444-3458. E-mail: jmcallister@law.whittier.edu

Law School Library has 6 professional staff members and contains more than 341,631 volumes and 5,097 periodicals. 386 seats are available in the library. When classes are in session, the library is open 103 hours per week.

WESTLAW and LEXIS-NEXIS are available, as are the World Wide Web, online bibliographic services, and CD-ROM players. 204 computer workstations are available to students in the library.

First-Year Program Class size in the average section is 49; 100% of the first-year courses are taught by full-time faculty.

Upper-Level Program Class size in the average section is 29. Among the electives are:

 Advocacy
 Business and Corporate Law
★ Children's Rights
 Consumer Law
★ Entertainment Law
 Environmental Law
★ Family Law
 Government/Regulation
★ Health Care/Human Services
 Indian/Tribal Law
★ Intellectual Property
★ International/Comparative Law
 Labor Law
 Land Use Law/Natural Resources
 Lawyering Skills
 Litigation
 Maritime Law
 Mediation
 Probate Law
 Public Interest
 Securities
 Tax Law

(★ indicates an area of special strength)

Clinical Courses Students receive degree credit for clinical courses. (Clinical practicum is not required.) Among the clinical areas offered are:

 Advocacy
 Children's Rights
 Family Law
 Intellectual Property
 Lawyering Skills
 Litigation
 Mediation

International exchange programs permit students to visit France and Spain.

UNIVERSITY OF COLORADO AT BOULDER
SCHOOL OF LAW

Boulder, Colorado

INFORMATION CONTACT

Carol Nelson-Douglas, Director of Admissions and Financial Aid
Fleming Law Building
Campus Box 401
Boulder, CO 80309-0401

Phone: 303-492-7203   Fax: 303-492-1200
E-mail: lawadmin@colorado.edu
Web site: http://www.colorado.edu/Law/

LAW STUDENT PROFILE [2000–2001]

FULL-TIME   Enrollment: 479
Women: 53%   Men: 47%

RACIAL or ETHNIC COMPOSITION
African American, 4%; Asian/Pacific Islander, 4%; Hispanic, 7%; Native American, 2%

APPLICANTS and ADMITTEES
Number applied: 1,944
Admitted: 612
Percentage accepted: 31%
Seats available: 168
Average LSAT score: 160
Average GPA: 3.5

University of Colorado at Boulder School of Law is a public institution that organizes classes on a semester calendar system. The campus is situated in an urban setting. Founded in 1892, first ABA approved in 1923, and an AALS member, University of Colorado at Boulder School of Law offers JD, JD/MBA, JD/MIA, and JD/MPAd degrees.

Faculty consists of 29 full-time members in 2000–2001. 7 full-time faculty members are women. 100% of all faculty members have a JD; 1% have advanced law degrees. Of all faculty members, 1% are Native American, 1% are Asian/Pacific Islander, 5% are African American, 6% are Hispanic, 87% are white.

Application Information *Required:* LSAT, LSDAS, application form, application fee of $45, baccalaureate degree, 1 recommendation, personal statement, college transcripts. *Recommended:* resume. *Application deadline* for fall term is February 15. Applications are processed on a rolling basis.

Financial Aid 1 research assistantship, totaling $3000; 15 teaching assistantships, totaling $2188, were awarded. Fellowships, graduate assistantships, loans, merit-based grants/scholarships, need-based grants/scholarships, and federal work-study loans are also available. The average student debt at graduation is $42,110. To apply for financial assistance, students must complete the Free Application for Federal Student Aid. Completed financial aid forms should be received by March 1. Financial aid contact: Jamy Coulson, Financial Aid Counselor, Fleming

AT a GLANCE

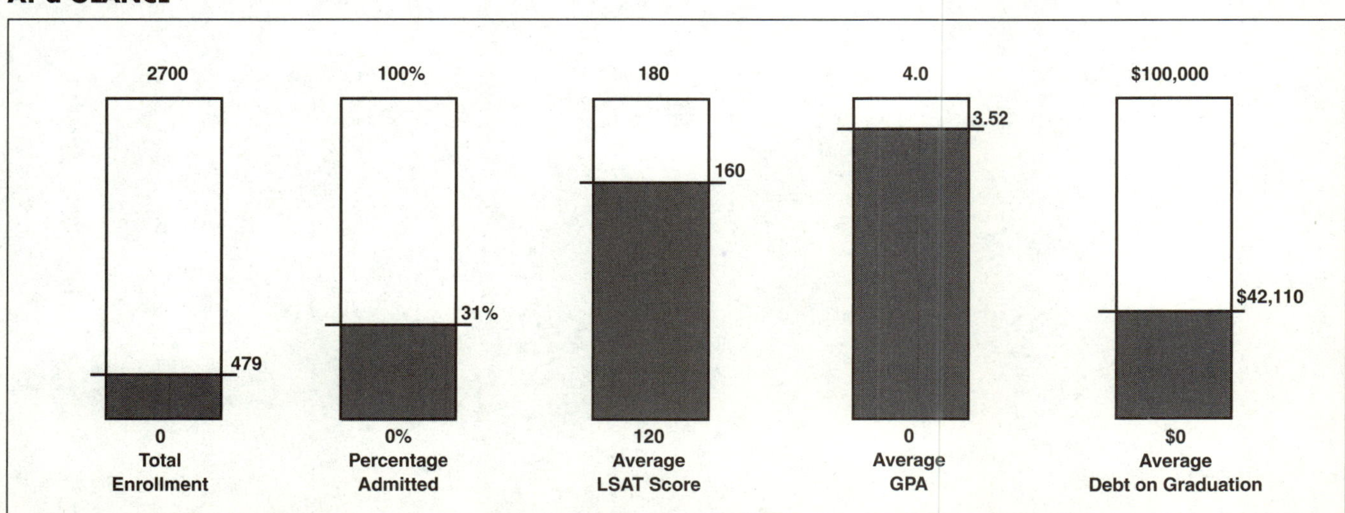

Degree Options

Degree	Total Credits Required	Length of Program
JD–Juris Doctor	89	3 yrs, full-time only [day, summer]
JD/MBA–Juris Doctor/Master of Business Administration		4 yrs, full-time only [day, summer]
JD/MIA–Juris Doctor/Master of International Affairs		4 yrs, full-time only [day]
JD/MPAd–Juris Doctor/Master of Public Administration		4 yrs, full-time only [day, summer]

Law Building, Campus Box 403, Boulder, CO 80309-0403. Phone: 303-492-0647. Fax: 303-492-2542. E-mail: coulson_j@gems.colorado.edu

Law School Library University of Colorado Law Library has 7 professional staff members and contains more than 315,000 volumes and 4,000 periodicals. 333 seats are available in the library. When classes are in session, the library is open 109 hours per week.

WESTLAW and LEXIS-NEXIS are available, as are the World Wide Web, online bibliographic services, and CD-ROM players. 82 computer workstations are available to students in the library. Special law collections include American Indian/Native American Law, water law.

First-Year Program Class size in the average section is 46; 100% of the first-year courses are taught by full-time faculty.

Upper-Level Program Class size in the average section is 25. Among the electives are:

  Administrative Law
  Advocacy
★ Business and Corporate Law
  Civil Litigation
  Consumer Law
★ Criminal Defense
  Education Law
★ Environmental Law
  Family Law
  Family Practice

  Health Care/Human Services
  Health Law
  Immigration
★ Indian/Tribal Law
  Intellectual Property
  International/Comparative Law
  Jurisprudence
  Labor Law
★ Land Use Law/Natural Resources
  Lawyering Skills
  Litigation
  Media Law
  Mediation
  Probate Law
  Securities
★ Tax Law
(★ *indicates an area of special strength*)

Clinical Courses Students receive degree credit for clinical courses. (Clinical practicum is not required.) Among the clinical areas offered are:

  Administrative Law
  Advocacy
  Civil Litigation
  Consumer Law
  Criminal Defense
  Environmental Law
  Family Law
  Family Practice
  Health Law
  Immigration
  Indian/Tribal Law
  Land Use Law/Natural Resources
  Lawyering Skills
  Litigation

UNIVERSITY OF DENVER
COLLEGE OF LAW

Denver, Colorado

LAW STUDENT PROFILE [2000–2001]

FULL TIME   Enrollment: 1,379

APPLICANTS AND ADMITTEES
Number applied: 1,926
Admitted: 1,457
Percentage accepted: 76%
Seats available: 340
Average LSAT score: 154
Average GPA: 3.0

University of Denver College of Law is a private institution that organizes classes on a semester calendar system. The campus is situated in an urban setting. Founded in 1892, first ABA approved in 1928, and an AALS member, University of Denver College of Law offers JD, JD/MBA, LLM, and MS degrees.

Faculty 97% of all faculty members have a JD; 13.4% have advanced law degrees. Of all faculty members, 5% are Asian/Pacific Islander, 5% are African American, 3% are Hispanic, 87% are white.

Application Information *Required:* LSAT, LSDAS, application form, application fee of $45, baccalaureate degree, minimum 2.0 GPA, 2 letters of recommendation, personal statement, college transcripts, resume. *Application deadline* for fall term is May 1. Applications are processed on a rolling basis.

Financial Aid In 2000–2001, 51% of all students received some form of financial aid. Graduate assistantships, loans, merit-based grants/scholarships, need-based grants/scholarships, and federal work-study loans are available. The average student debt at graduation is $60,000. To apply for financial assistance, students must complete the Free Application for Federal Student Aid. Completed financial aid forms should be received by February 15. Financial aid contact: Iain Davis, Director of Financial Aid, 7039 East 18th Avenue, Denver, CO 80220. Phone: 303-871-6136. Fax: 303-871-6358. E-mail: idavis@law.du.edu

Law School Library Westminster Law Library has 10 professional staff members and contains more than

AT a GLANCE

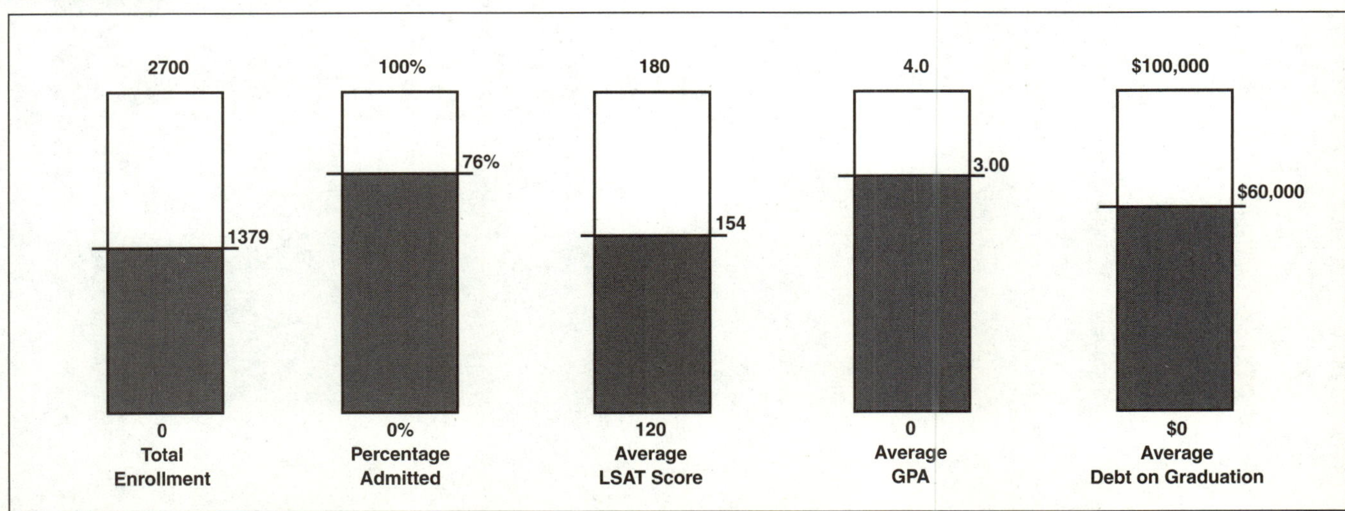

Degree Options

Degree	Total Credits Required	Length of Program
JD–Doctor of Laws	90	4–5 yrs, full-time or part-time [day, evening, summer]
JD/MBA–Juris Doctor/Master of Business Administration–JD/MBA Dual-degree Program	110	4–5 yrs, full-time or part-time [day, evening]
LLM–Master of Laws–American and Comparative Laws	24	1 yr, full-time only [day]
LLM–Master of Laws–Natural Resource Law Graduate Program	24	1 yr, full-time or part-time [day, evening]
LLM–Master of Laws–Taxation	30	1 yr, full-time or part-time [evening]
MS–Master of Science–Natural Resources Law and Policy	24	1 yr, full-time or part-time [day, evening]
MS–Master of Science–Legal Administration		1.5 yrs, full-time or part-time [day, evening]

314,155 volumes and 3,100 periodicals. 624 seats are available in the library. When classes are in session, the library is open 107 hours per week.

WESTLAW and LEXIS-NEXIS are available, as is the World Wide Web. 60 computer workstations are available to students in the library. Special law collections include government document selective depository, Hughes Rare Book Room.

First-Year Program Class size in the average section is 87; 100% of the first-year courses are taught by full-time faculty.

Upper-Level Program Class size in the average section is 40. Among the electives are:

Administrative Law
★ Advocacy
★ Business and Corporate Law
★ Civil Litigation
Criminal Defense
★ Environmental Law
Family Law
Family Practice
Government/Regulation
Health Care/Human Services
Indian/Tribal Law

Intellectual Property
★ International/Comparative Law
Jurisprudence
Labor Law
★ Land Use Law/Natural Resources
★ Lawyering Skills
Legal History/Philosophy
★ Litigation
Media Law
Mediation
Probate Law
★ Public Interest
Securities
★ Tax Law

(★ indicates an area of special strength)

Clinical Courses Students receive degree credit for clinical courses. (Clinical practicum is not required.) Among the clinical areas offered are:

Civil Litigation
Criminal Defense
Environmental Law
Family Law
Family Practice
Land Rights/Natural Resource
Land Use Law/Natural Resources
Mediation
Public Interest

QUINNIPIAC UNIVERSITY
SCHOOL OF LAW

Hamden, Connecticut

INFORMATION CONTACT

John J. Noonan, Dean of Admissions
275 Mt. Carmel Avenue
Hamden, CT 06518

Phone: 203-582-3400   Fax: 203-582-3339
E-mail: ladm@quinnipiac.edu
Web site: http://law.quinnipiac.edu/

LAW STUDENT PROFILE [2000–2001]

FULL-TIME   Enrollment: 473
Women: 48%   Men: 52%

PART-TIME   Enrollment: 274
Women: 47%   Men: 53%

RACIAL or ETHNIC COMPOSITION
African American, 6%; Asian/Pacific Islander, 2%; Hispanic, 5%; Native American, 1%

APPLICANTS and ADMITTEES
Number applied: 1,864
Admitted: 856
Percentage accepted: 46%
Seats available: 225

Quinnipiac University School of Law is a private institution that organizes classes on a semester calendar system. The campus is situated in a suburban setting. Founded in 1974, first ABA approved in 1979, and an AALS member, Quinnipiac University School of Law offers JD, JD/MBA, and JD/MHA degrees.

Faculty consists of 44 full-time and 46 part-time members in 2000–2001. 18 full-time faculty members and 11 part-time faculty members are women. 100% of all faculty members have a JD; 16% have advanced law degrees. Of all faculty members, 1.5% are Asian/Pacific Islander, 3.1% are African American, 95.4% are white.

Application Information *Required:* LSAT, LSDAS, application form, application fee of $40, baccalaureate degree, personal statement, college transcripts. *Recommended:* 2 letters of recommendation, essay, resume. *Application deadline* is rolling.

Costs The 2000–2001 tuition was $23,000 full-time; $870 per credit part-time. Fees: $465 full-time; $465 per year part-time.

Financial Aid Graduate assistantships, loans, merit-based grants/scholarships, need-based grants/scholarships, and federal work-study loans are available. The average student debt at graduation is $65,100. To apply for financial assistance, students must complete the Free Application for Federal Student Aid, institutional forms. Completed financial aid forms should be received by May 1. Financial aid contact: Anne Traverso, Director of

AT a GLANCE

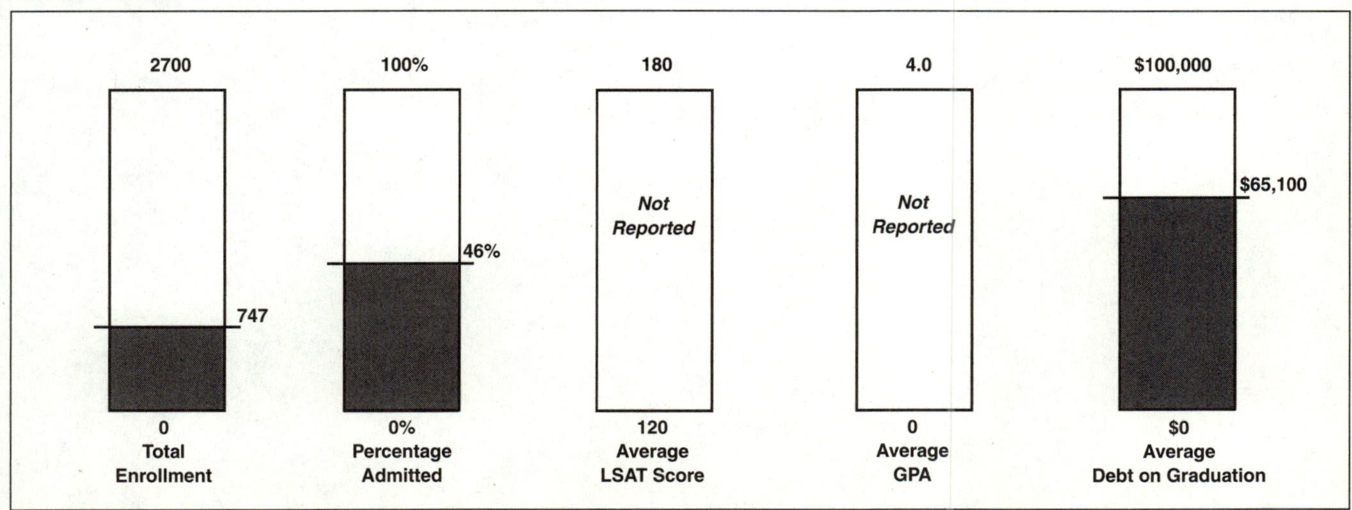

Degree Options

Degree	Total Credits Required	Length of Program
JD–Doctor of Laws	86	3–4 yrs, full-time or part-time [day, evening, summer]
JD/MBA–Juris Doctor/Master of Business Administration–Joint-degree Program	107	3.5–4 yrs, full-time or part-time [day, evening, summer]
JD/MHA–Juris Doctor/Master of Health Administration–Joint-degree Program	107	3.5–4 yrs, full-time or part-time [day, evening, summer]

Financial Aid, 275 Mt. Carmel Avenue, Hamden, CT 06518. Phone: 203-582-3405. Fax: 203-582-3339. E-mail: lawfinaid@quinnipiac.edu

Law School Library Quinnipiac University School of Law Library has 7 professional staff members and contains more than 354,167 volumes and 2,800 periodicals. 400 seats are available in the library. When classes are in session, the library is open 96 hours per week.

WESTLAW and LEXIS-NEXIS are available, as are the World Wide Web, online bibliographic services, and CD-ROM players. 58 computer workstations are available to students in the library. Special law collections include federal tax materials, Connecticut statutes, laws, and historical documents.

First-Year Program Class size in the average section is 75; 100% of the first-year courses are taught by full-time faculty.

Upper-Level Program Class size in the average section is 30. Among the electives are:

    Administrative Law
  ★ Advocacy
    Appellate Litigation
  ★ Business and Corporate Law
    Civil Litigation
    Consumer Law
    Criminal Defense
    Criminal Prosecution
    Education Law
    Environmental Law
  ★ Family Law
  ★ Family Practice
    General Practice
    Government/Regulation

  ★ Health Care/Human Services
  ★ Health Law
    Indian/Tribal Law
    Intellectual Property
  ★ International/Comparative Law
    Jurisprudence
    Labor Law
    Land Use Law/Natural Resources
  ★ Lawyering Skills
    Legal History/Philosophy
  ★ Litigation
    Maritime Law
    Media Law
  ★ Mediation
    Probate Law
    Public Interest
    Securities
  ★ Tax Law
(★ indicates an area of special strength)

Clinical Courses Students receive degree credit for clinical courses. (Clinical practicum is not required.) Among the clinical areas offered are:

    Administrative Law
    Advocacy
    Appellate Litigation
    Civil Litigation
    Consumer Law
    Criminal Defense
    Criminal Prosecution
    Family Law
    Family Practice
    General Practice
    Health Care/Human Services
    Health Law
    Lawyering Skills
    Litigation
    Tax Law

UNIVERSITY OF CONNECTICUT
SCHOOL OF LAW

Hartford, Connecticut

INFORMATION CONTACT

Karen L. DeMeola, Director of Admissions
45 Elizabeth Street
Hartford, CT 06105

Phone: 860-570-5100   Fax: 860-570-5153
E-mail: admit@law.uconn.edu
Web site: http://www.law.uconn.edu/

LAW STUDENT PROFILE [2000–2001]

FULL-TIME   Enrollment: 412
Women: 47%   Men: 53%

PART-TIME   Enrollment: 164
Women: 49%   Men: 51%

RACIAL or ETHNIC COMPOSITION
African American, 4%; Asian/Pacific Islander, 4%; Hispanic,
5%; Native American, 1%

APPLICANTS and ADMITTEES
Number applied: 1,776
Admitted: 529
Percentage accepted: 30%
Seats available: 182
Average LSAT score: 159
Average GPA: 3.3

University of Connecticut School of Law is a public
institution that organizes classes on a semester calendar
system. The campus is situated in a suburban setting.
first ABA approved in 1933, and an AALS member,
University of Connecticut School of Law offers JD,
JD/LLM, JD/MA, JD/MBA, JD/MLS, JD/MPA, JD/MPH,
JD/MSW, and LLM degrees.

Faculty consists of 52 full-time and 74 part-time
members in 2000–2001. 15 full-time faculty members are
women. 100% of all faculty members have a JD degree.
Of all faculty members, 9% are African American, 2%
are Hispanic, 89% are white.

Application Information *Required:* LSAT, LSDAS,
application form, application fee of $30, baccalaureate
degree, 2 letters of recommendation, essay, resume,
college transcripts. *Application deadline* for fall term is
March 15. Applications are processed on a rolling basis.

Costs The 2000–2001 tuition was $11,374 full-time for
state residents; $474 per credit part-time for state
residents. Tuition was $23,992 full-time for nonresidents;
$1000 per credit part-time for nonresidents. Fees: $172
full-time.

Financial Aid In 2000–2001, 72% of all students received
some form of financial aid. Fellowships, loans, merit-
based grants/scholarships, need-based grants/scholarships,
and federal work-study loans are available. The average
student debt at graduation is $45,138. To apply for
financial assistance, students must complete the Free
Application for Federal Student Aid, institutional forms.
Completed financial aid forms should be received by

AT a GLANCE

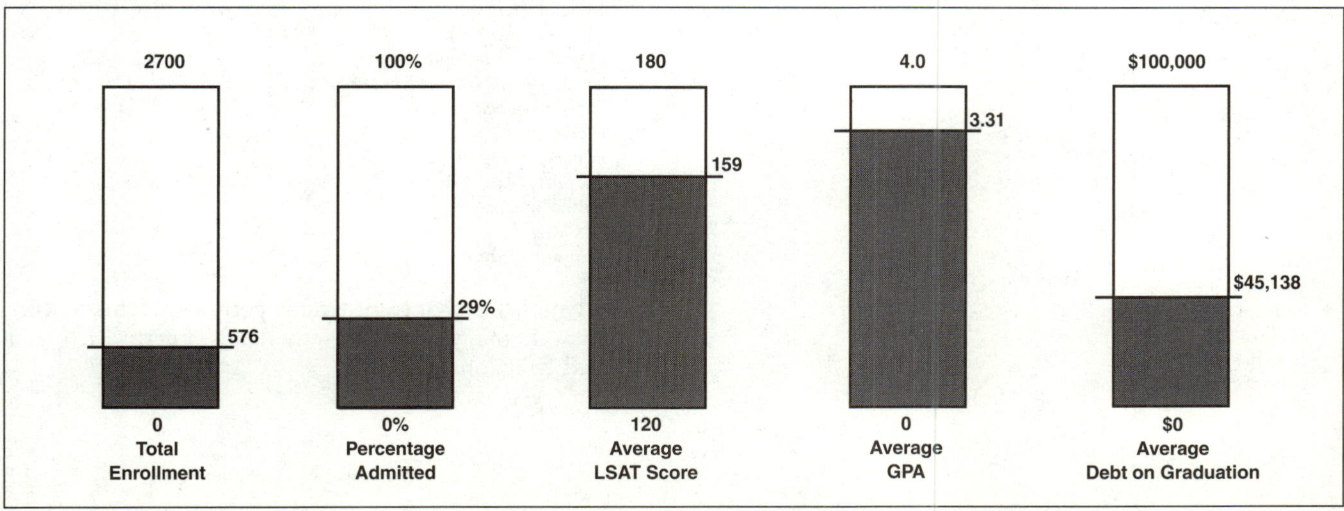

Degree Options

Degree	Total Credits Required	Length of Program
JD–Doctor of Laws	86	full-time or part-time [day, evening]
JD/LLM–Juris Doctor/Master of Laws	98	3.25–5 yrs, full-time or part-time [day, evening]
JD/MA–Juris Doctor/Master of Arts–Public Policy		3.5–5 yrs, full-time or part-time [day, evening]
JD/MBA–Juris Doctor/Master of Business Administration–Dual-degree Program	110	4–5 yrs, full-time or part-time [day, evening]
JD/MLS–Juris Doctor/Master of Library Science–Dual-degree Program		3.5–5 yrs, full-time only [day]
JD/MPA–Juris Doctor/Master of Professional Accountancy–Dual-degree Program		4–5 yrs, full-time only [day]
JD/MPH–Juris Doctor/Master of Public Health–Dual-degree Program		4–5 yrs, full-time only [day]
JD/MSW–Juris Doctor/Master of Social Work–Dual-degree Program		4–5 yrs, full-time only [day]
LLM–Master of Laws–US Legal Studies		1 yr, full-time only [day]

March 15. Financial aid contact: Robyn Alferi, Director of Student Finance, Student Finance Office, 55 Elizabeth Street, Hartford, CT 06105. Phone: 860-570-5147. E-mail: stu_fin_dept@law.uconn.edu

Law School Library University of Connecticut School of Law Library has 15 professional staff members and contains more than 482,696 volumes and 6,342 periodicals. 747 seats are available in the library. When classes are in session, the library is open 92 hours per week.

WESTLAW and LEXIS-NEXIS are available, as are the World Wide Web, online bibliographic services, and CD-ROM players. 48 computer workstations are available to students in the library.

First-Year Program Class size in the average section is 63.

Upper-Level Program Class size in the average section is 20. Among the electives are:

Administrative Law
Children's Advocacy
★ Civil Litigation
★ Civil Rights
★ Corporate Law
★ Criminal Defense
★ Disability Law
★ Environmental Law
General Practice
Government Litigation
★ Health Law
★ Human Rights
★ Intellectual Property
★ International Law
Judicial Clerkship
Juvenile Law
★ Labor and Employment

Land Rights/Natural Resource
Legislative Services
Mediation
★ Poverty/Welfare Law
★ Property/Real Estate
★ Public Interest
★ Tax Law
★ Women's Rights
(★ *indicates an area of special strength*)

Clinical Courses Students receive degree credit for clinical courses. (Clinical practicum is not required.) Among the clinical areas offered are:

Administrative Law
Children's Advocacy
Civil Litigation
Civil Rights
Criminal Defense
Disability Law
Environmental Law
General Practice
Government Litigation
Health Law
Human Rights
Judicial Clerkship
Juvenile Law
Labor and Employment
Land Rights/Natural Resource
Legislative Services
Mediation
Poverty/Welfare Law
Property/Real Estate
Public Interest
Tax Law
Women's Rights

International exchange programs permit students to visit France, Germany, Ireland, Netherlands, Puerto Rico, and United Kingdom.

YALE UNIVERSITY
YALE LAW SCHOOL

New Haven, Connecticut

INFORMATION CONTACT

Jean Webb, Director of Admissions
127 Wall Street
PO Box 208215
New Haven, CT 06520-8215

Phone: 203-432-4995   Fax: 203-436-1235
E-mail: admissions.law@yale.edu
Web site: http://www.law.yale.edu/

LAW STUDENT PROFILE [2000–2001]

FULL-TIME   Enrollment: 637

APPLICANTS and ADMITTEES
Number applied: 3,042
Admitted: 305
Percentage accepted: 10%
Seats available: 185
Average LSAT score: 170
Average GPA: 3.8

Yale University Yale Law School is a private institution that organizes classes on a semester calendar system. The campus is situated in an urban setting. Founded in 1824, first ABA approved in 1923, and an AALS member, Yale University Yale Law School offers JD, JD/MA, JD/MBA, JSD, LLM, and MSL degrees.

Faculty consists of 58 full-time and 33 part-time members in 2000–2001.

Application Information *Required:* LSAT, LSDAS, application form, application fee of $65, baccalaureate degree, 2 letters of recommendation, writing sample, essay, college transcripts. *Recommended:* personal statement, resume. *Application deadline* for fall term is February 15. Applications are processed on a rolling basis.

Costs The 2000–2001 tuition was $28,440 full-time.

Financial Aid Loans, loan repayment assistance program (LRAP), and need-based grants/scholarships are available. The average student debt at graduation is $58,000. To apply for financial assistance, students must complete the Free Application for Federal Student Aid, Need Access diskette. Completed financial aid forms should be received by March 15. Financial aid contact: Zina Shaffer, Registrar and Director of Financial Aid, Yale Law School, PO Box 208215, New Haven, CT 06520. Phone: 203-432-1688. Fax: 203-436-1235.

Law School Library Lillian Goldman Law Library has 18 professional staff members and contains more than 1

AT a GLANCE

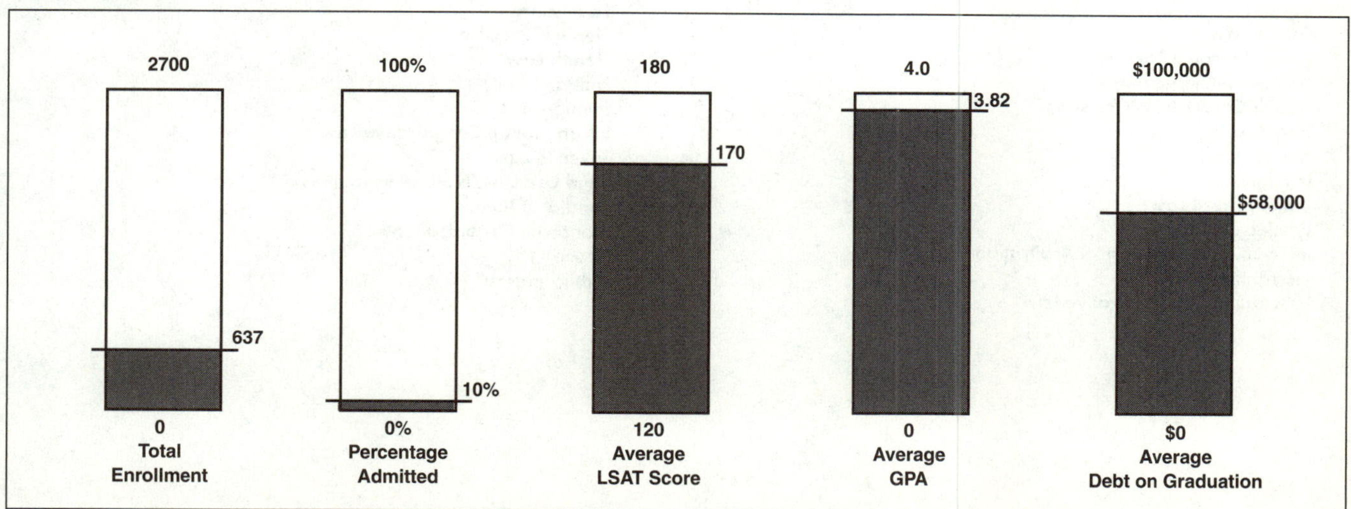

Degree Options

Degree	Total Credits Required	Length of Program
JD–Doctor of Laws	82	3 yrs, full-time only [day]
JD/MA–Juris Doctor/Master of Arts–Joint-degree Program		4 yrs, full-time only [day]
JD/MBA–Juris Doctor/Master of Business Administration–Joint-degree Program	110	4–5 yrs, full-time only [day]
JSD–Doctor of Juridical Science		full-time only [day]
LLM–Master of Laws		1 yr, full-time only [day]
MSL–Master of School Leadership		1 yr, full-time only [day]

million volumes and 9,504 periodicals. 403 seats are available in the library. When classes are in session, the library is open 168 hours per week.

WESTLAW and LEXIS-NEXIS are available, as are the World Wide Web, online bibliographic services, and CD-ROM players. 46 computer workstations are available to students in the library. Special law collections include law and the social sciences, foreign and international law, rare books in English legal history.

Upper-Level Program Among the electives are:

Administrative Law
Advocacy
Bankruptcy
Business and Corporate Law
Business Organizations
Civil Litigation
Civil Rights
Constitutional Law
Constitutional Theory
Consumer Law
Copyright & Trademark Law
Corporate Law
Criminal Law
Criminal Procedure
Education
Education Law
Entertainment Law
Environmental Law
Estate & Gift Taxation
Evidence
Family Law
Federal Income Tax
Government/Regulation
Health Care/Human Services
Health Law
Human Rights
Immigration
Indian/Tribal Law
Intellectual Property
International Commerical Arbitration
International Law
International/Comparative Law

Jurisprudence
Juvenile Law
Labor Law
Land Use Law/Natural Resources
Landlord/Tenant
Law and Economics
Law and Science
Lawyering Skills
Legal History/Philosophy
Legal Writing
Litigation
Maritime Law
Media Law
Mediation
Nonprofit Organizations
Probate Law
Professional Responsibility
Public Interest
Securities
Securities Regulation
Tax Law
Trusts and Estates

Clinical Courses Students receive degree credit for clinical courses. (Clinical practicum is not required.) Among the clinical areas offered are:

Civil Litigation
Civil Rights
Disability Law
Education
Elderly Advocacy
Environmental Law
Family Law
General Practice
Health Law
Human Rights
Immigration
International/Comparative Law
Juvenile Law
Land Use Law/Natural Resources
Landlord/Tenant
Nonprofit Organizations
Prison
Public Interest

WIDENER UNIVERSITY
SCHOOL OF LAW AT WILMINGTON

Wilmington, Delaware

INFORMATION CONTACT

Barbara L. Ayars, Assistant Dean of Admissions
4601 Concord Pike
PO Box 7474
Wilmington, DE 19803-0474

Phone: 302-477-2210   Fax: 302-477-2224
E-mail: barbara.l.ayars@law.widener.edu
Web site: http://www.law.widener.edu/

LAW STUDENT PROFILE [2000–2001]

FULL-TIME   Enrollment: 638
Women: 49%   Men: 51%

PART-TIME   Enrollment: 474
Women: 47%   Men: 53%

RACIAL or ETHNIC COMPOSITION
African American, 6%; Asian/Pacific Islander, 2%; Hispanic, 2%; Native American, 0.1%; International, 0.4%

APPLICANTS and ADMITTEES
Number applied: 305
Seats available: 390
Average LSAT score: 148
Average GPA: 3.0

Widener University School of Law at Wilmington is a private institution that organizes classes on a semester calendar system. The campus is situated in a suburban setting. Founded in 1975, first ABA approved in 1975, and an AALS member, Widener University School of Law at Wilmington offers DL, JD, JD/MBA, JD/MMP, JD/PsyD, LLM, MJ, and SJD degrees.

Faculty consists of 54 full-time and 38 part-time members in 2000–2001. 22 full-time faculty members and 8 part-time faculty members are women. 100% of all faculty members have a JD; 18% have advanced law degrees. Of all faculty members, 4% are African American, 96% are white.

Application Information *Required:* LSAT, LSDAS, application form, application fee of $60, baccalaureate degree, college transcripts. *Recommended:* recommendations, personal statement, resume. *Application deadline* for fall term is May 15; for spring term is December 1. Applications are processed on a rolling basis.

Financial Aid Loans, loan repayment assistance program (LRAP), merit-based grants/scholarships, need-based grants/scholarships, and federal work-study loans are available. The average student debt at graduation is $66,905. To apply for financial assistance, students must complete the Free Application for Federal Student Aid, institutional forms. Completed financial aid forms should be received by February 15. Financial aid contact: Anthony Doyle, Assistant Dean for Financial Aid, 4601 Concord Pike, PO Box 7474, Wilmington, DE 19803-0474. Phone: 302-477-2272. Fax: 302-477-2180. E-mail: anthony.j.doyle@law.widener.edu

AT a GLANCE

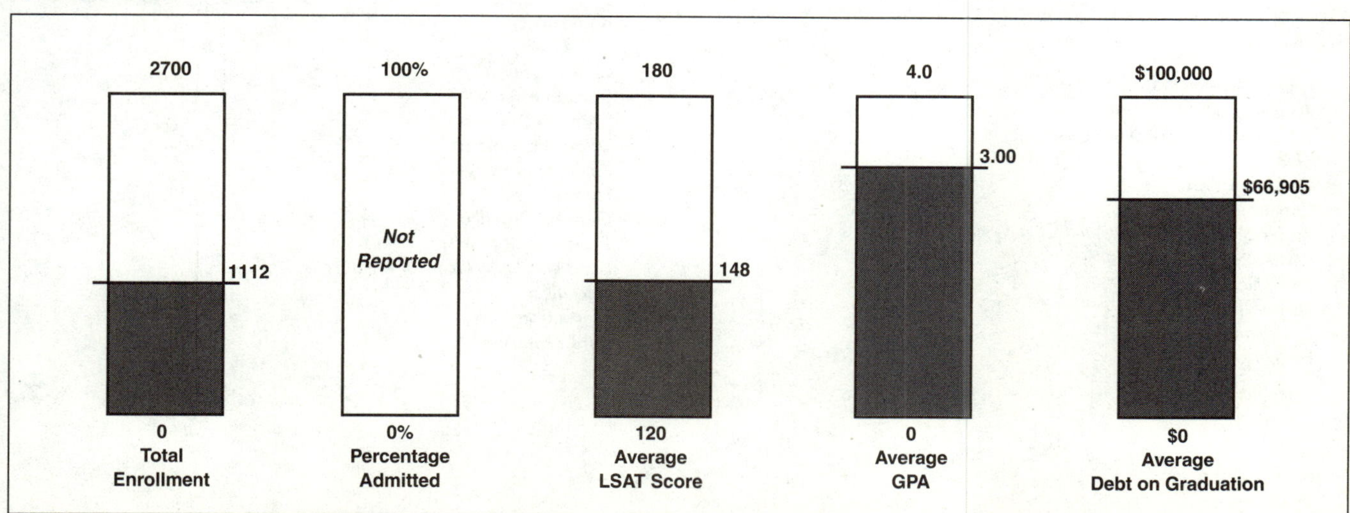

Degree Options

Degree	Total Credits Required	Length of Program
Certificate–Health Law	8	2–4 yrs, full-time or part-time [day, evening, summer]
JD–Doctor of Laws	87	3–4 yrs, full-time or part-time [day, evening, summer]
JD/MBA–Juris Doctor/Master of Business Administration–Dual-degree Program	114	4–5 yrs, full-time or part-time [day, evening, weekend, summer]
Certificate–Dual-degree Program	108	4–5 yrs, full-time or part-time [day, evening, summer]
Certificate–Dual-degree Program	172	6 yrs, full-time or part-time [day, evening, summer]
LLM–Master of Laws–Corporate Laws and Finance	24	1–2 yrs, full-time or part-time [day, evening, summer]
LLM–Master of Laws–Health Law	24	1–4 yrs, full-time or part-time [day, evening, summer]
MJ–Master of Jurisprudence–Health Law	30	1–2 yrs, full-time or part-time [day, evening, summer]
SJD–Doctor of Juridical Science–Health Law	8	2–4 yrs, full-time or part-time [day, evening, summer]

Law School Library Widener University School of Law Legal Information Center has 11 professional staff members and contains more than 413,446 volumes and 5,214 periodicals. 396 seats are available in the library. When classes are in session, the library is open 107 hours per week.

WESTLAW and LEXIS-NEXIS are available, as are the World Wide Web, online bibliographic services, and CD-ROM players. 112 computer workstations are available to students in the library. Special law collections include Public Law, United States Selective Depository for government documents, collections in corporate law, health law, and tax laws..

First-Year Program Class size in the average section is 50; 100% of the first-year courses are taught by full-time faculty.

Upper-Level Program Class size in the average section is 30. Among the electives are:

  Administrative Law
★ Bankruptcy
★ Business and Corporate Law
★ Civil Law
★ Civil Litigation
★ Consumer Law
★ Criminal Defense
★ Domestic Violence
  Education Law
  Entertainment Law
★ Environmental Law
★ Family Law

  General Practice
  Government/Regulation
★ Health Care/Human Services
  Intellectual Property
  International/Comparative Law
★ Judicial Externship
  Jurisprudence
  Labor Law
  Land Use Law/Natural Resources
  Lawyering Skills
  Litigation
  Mediation
  Probate Law
  Public Interest
  Securities
  Tax Law
(★ indicates an area of special strength)

Clinical Courses Students receive degree credit for clinical courses. (Clinical practicum is not required.) Among the clinical areas offered are:

  Bankruptcy
  Civil Law
  Civil Litigation
  Consumer Law
  Criminal Defense
  Domestic Violence
  Environmental Law
  Family Law
  General Practice
  Judicial Externship
  Land Use Law/Natural Resources
  Litigation
  Mediation
  Public Interest

AMERICAN UNIVERSITY
WASHINGTON COLLEGE OF LAW

Washington, District of Columbia

INFORMATION CONTACT

Sandra J. Oakman, Director of Admissions
4801 Massachusetts Avenue, NW, Suite 366
Washington, DC 20016

Phone: 202-274-4101   Fax: 202-274-4107
E-mail: wcladmit@american.edu
Web site: http://www.wcl.american.edu/

LAW STUDENT PROFILE [2000–2001]

FULL-TIME   Enrollment: 1,006
Women: 62%   Men: 38%

PART-TIME   Enrollment: 479
Women: 55%   Men: 45%

RACIAL or ETHNIC COMPOSITION
African American, 7%; Asian/Pacific Islander, 8%; Hispanic, 5%; Native American, 0.5%; International, 12%

APPLICANTS and ADMITTEES
Number applied: 5,514
Admitted: 1,813
Percentage accepted: 33%
Seats available: 370
Average LSAT score: 157
Average GPA: 3.3

American University Washington College of Law is a private institution that organizes classes on a semester calendar system. The campus is situated in an urban setting. Founded in 1896, first ABA approved in 1940, and an AALS member, American University Washington College of Law offers JD, JD/MA, JD/MBA, JD/MS, and LLM degrees.

Faculty consists of 48 full-time and 95 part-time members in 2000–2001. 17 full-time faculty members and 29 part-time faculty members are women. 95% of all faculty members have a JD; 19% have advanced law degrees. Of all faculty members, 2.5% are Asian/Pacific Islander, 15.5% are African American, 3.5% are Hispanic, 78.5% are white.

Application Information *Required:* LSAT, LSDAS, application form, application fee of $55, baccalaureate degree, 1 recommendation, personal statement, college transcripts. *Recommended:* minimum GPA, resume. *Application deadline* is rolling.

Costs The 2000–2001 tuition was $24,904 full-time. Fees: $278 full-time.

Financial Aid In 2000–2001, 26% of all students received some form of financial aid. Graduate assistantships, loans, loan repayment assistance program (LRAP), merit-based grants/scholarships, need-based grants/scholarships, and federal work-study loans are available. The average student debt at graduation is $66,000. To apply for financial assistance, students must complete the Free Application for Federal Student Aid, Need Access diskette. Completed financial aid forms should be

AT a GLANCE

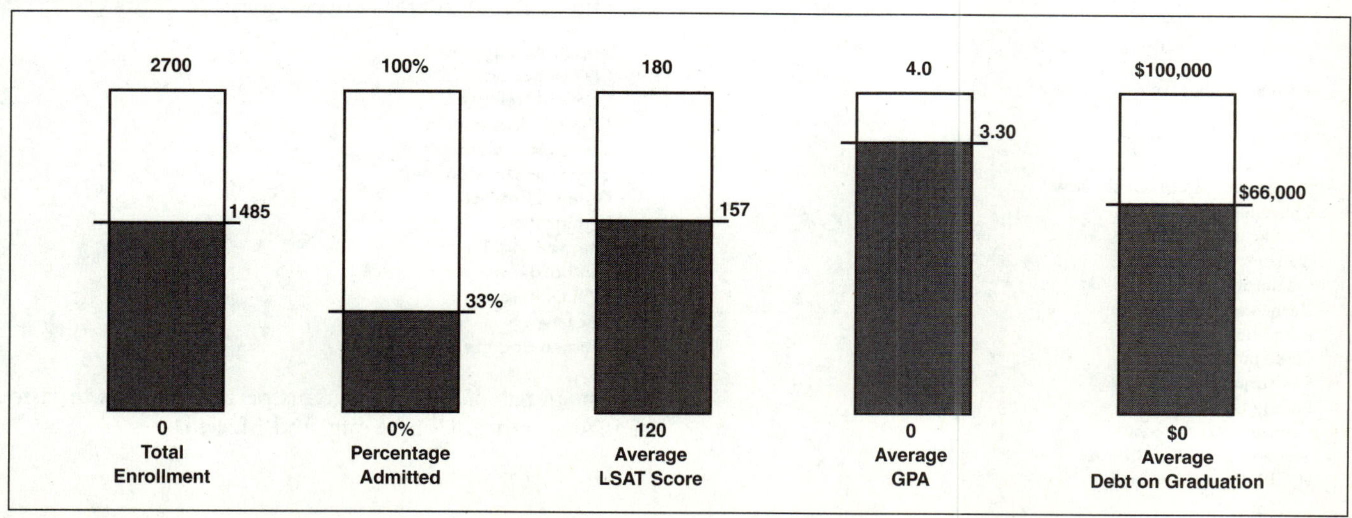

Degree Options

Degree	Total Credits Required	Length of Program
JD–Doctor of Laws	86	3–4 yrs, full-time or part-time [day, evening, summer]
JD/MA–Juris Doctor/Master of Arts–Dual-degree Program in Law and International Affairs	101	3.5–4 yrs, full-time or part-time [day, evening, summer]
JD/MBA–Juris Doctor/Master of Business Administration–Dual-degree Program in Law and Business Administration	112	3.5–4 yrs, full-time or part-time [day, evening, summer]
JD/MS–Juris Doctor/Master of Science–Dual-degree Program-Justice, Law, and Society	107	3.5–4 yrs, full-time or part-time [day, evening, summer]
LLM–Master of Laws–International Legal Studies	24	1–1.5 yrs, full-time or part-time [day, evening, summer]
LLM–Master of Laws–Law and Government	24	1–1.5 yrs, full-time or part-time [day, evening, summer]

received by February 15. Financial aid contact: Barbara Williams, Director, 4801 Massachusetts Avenue, NW, Washington, DC 20016. Phone: 202-274-4040. Fax: 202-274-4107. E-mail: bwilli@wcl.american.edu

Law School Library Washington College of Law Library has 9 professional staff members and contains more than 462,373 volumes and 5,736 periodicals. 549 seats are available in the library. When classes are in session, the library is open 119 hours per week.

WESTLAW and LEXIS-NEXIS are available, as are the World Wide Web, online bibliographic services, and CD-ROM players. 94 computer workstations are available to students in the library. Special law collections include United States Archive, Administrative Conference of the United States, Baxter Collection in International Law, European Union Depository, Goodman Collection of Rare and Semi-rare Law Books, The National Bankruptcy Review Commission Archive.

First-Year Program Class size in the average section is 95; 90% of the first-year courses are taught by full-time faculty.

Upper-Level Program Among the electives are:

Administrative Law
Advocacy
AIDS and the Law
Antitrust Law
★ Business and Corporate Law
Church-State
Civil Rights
Consumer Law
Criminal Law
Domestic Violence
Education Law
Entertainment Law
★ Environmental Law
Family Law
★ Gender and the Law
★ Government/Regulation
Health Care/Human Services

Health Law
★ Human Rights
Immigration
Indian/Tribal Law
Intellectual Property
★ International Environmental Law
★ International/Comparative Law
Jurisprudence
Labor Law
Land Use Law/Natural Resources
★ Lawyering Skills
Legal History/Philosophy
Legislation
Litigation
Maritime Law
Media Law
Mediation
Pensions
Probate Law
Public Interest
Securities
Tax Law
Telecommunications Law
(★ *indicates an area of special strength*)

Clinical Courses Students receive degree credit for clinical courses. (Clinical practicum is not required.) Among the clinical areas offered are:

Appellate Litigation
Civil Litigation
Criminal Defense
Criminal Prosecution
Domestic Violence
Economic Development
General Practice
Immigration
International Law
Landlord/Tenant
Public Interest
Tax Law
Women and the Law

International exchange programs permit students to visit Canada, France, Hong Kong, and Mexico.

THE CATHOLIC UNIVERSITY OF AMERICA
COLUMBUS SCHOOL OF LAW

Washington, District of Columbia

INFORMATION CONTACT

George P. Braxton II, Director of Admissions
Cardinal Station Post Office
Washington, DC 20064

Phone: 202-319-5151   Fax: 202-319-4498
E-mail: braxton@law.edu
Web site: http://law.edu/

LAW STUDENT PROFILE [2000–2001]

FULL-TIME   Enrollment: 654
Women: 54%   Men: 46%

PART-TIME   Enrollment: 278
Women: 46%   Men: 54%

RACIAL or ETHNIC COMPOSITION
African American, 13%; Asian/Pacific Islander, 4%; Hispanic, 5%; Native American, 0.1%; International, 1%

APPLICANTS and ADMITTEES
Number applied: 2,165
Admitted: 1,033
Percentage accepted: 48%
Seats available: 304
Average LSAT score: 154
Average GPA: 3.1

The **Catholic University of America Columbus School of Law** is a private institution that organizes classes on a semester calendar system. The campus is situated in an urban setting. Founded in 1898, first ABA approved in 1925, and an AALS member, The Catholic University of America Columbus School of Law offers JD, JD/JCL, JD/MA, JD/MLS, and JD/MSW degrees.

Faculty consists of 44 full-time and 49 part-time members in 2000–2001. 15 full-time faculty members and 14 part-time faculty members are women. 100% of all faculty members have a JD; 20% have advanced law degrees. Of all faculty members, 10% are African American, 2% are Hispanic, 88% are white.

Application Information *Required:* LSAT, LSDAS, application form, application fee of $55, baccalaureate degree, 2 letters of recommendation, personal statement, college transcripts. *Recommended:* resume. *Application deadline* for fall term is March 1. Applications are processed on a rolling basis.

Costs The 1999–2000 tuition was $24,170 full-time; $880 per credit hour part-time. Fees: $796 full-time; $228 per semester part-time; $126 full-time (one-time charge). Full-time tuition and fees vary according to student level. Part-time tuition and fees vary according to course load, degree level, and student level.

Financial Aid In 2000–2001, 80% of all students received some form of financial aid. Fellowships, loans, merit-based grants/scholarships, need-based grants/scholarships, and federal work-study loans are available. The average student debt at graduation is $75,000. To apply for

AT a GLANCE

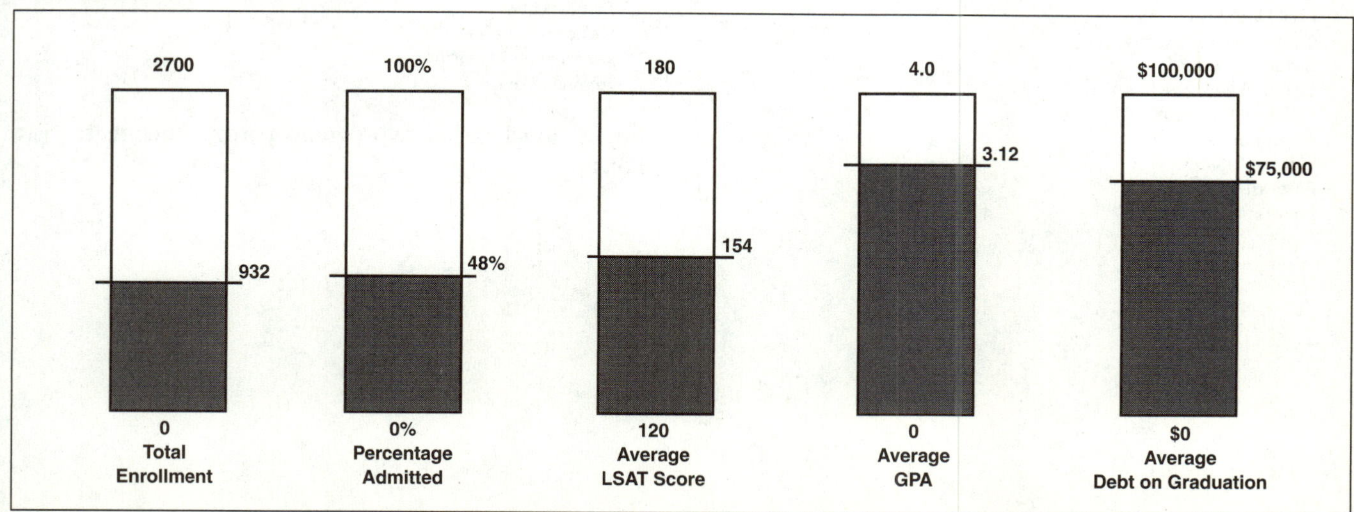

Degree Options

Degree	Total Credits Required	Length of Program
JD–Juris Doctor	84	3–4 yrs, full-time or part-time [day, evening]
JD/JCL–Juris Doctor/Licentiate in Canon Law–Joint-degree with Canon Law	130	4–5 yrs, full-time or part-time [day, evening]
JD/MA–Juris Doctor/Master of Arts–Joint-degree Program	112	3–4 yrs, full-time or part-time [day, evening]
JD/MLS–Juris Doctor/Master of Library Science–Joint-degree with Library Science	112	3–4 yrs, full-time or part-time [day, evening]
JD/MSW–Juris Doctor/Master of Social Work–Joint-degree Program with Social Work	132	4–5 yrs, full-time or part-time [day, evening]

financial assistance, students must complete the Free Application for Federal Student Aid, institutional forms. Completed financial aid forms should be received by March 1. Financial aid contact: Joanna Bader, Acting Director of Financial Aid, CUA-CSL, Cardinal Station, Washington, DC 20064. Phone: 202-319-5143. Fax: 202-319-4462. E-mail: bader@law.edu

Law School Library Kathryn Dufour Law Library has 12 professional staff members and contains more than 322,816 volumes and 5,334 periodicals. 502 seats are available in the library. When classes are in session, the library is open 115 hours per week.

WESTLAW and LEXIS-NEXIS are available, as are the World Wide Web, online bibliographic services, and CD-ROM players. 54 computer workstations are available to students in the library.

First-Year Program Class size in the average section is 70; 100% of the first-year courses are taught by full-time faculty.

Upper-Level Program Class size in the average section is 50. Among the electives are:

  Administrative Law
★ Advocacy
★ Business and Corporate Law
★ Civil Litigation
★ Communications Law
  Consumer Law
  Criminal Defense
  Criminal Prosecution
  Education Law
  Elderly Advocacy
  Entertainment Law
  Environmental Law
  Family Law
  General Practice
  Government Litigation
  Government/Regulation
  Health Care/Human Services
  Indian/Tribal Law
  Intellectual Property
★ International/Comparative Law
  Jurisprudence
  Juvenile Law
  Labor Law
  Land Use Law/Natural Resources
★ Lawyering Skills
  Legal History/Philosophy
★ Litigation
  Maritime Law
  Media Law
  Mediation
  Probate Law
  Public Interest
★ Public Policy
★ Securities
(★ *indicates an area of special strength*)

Clinical Courses Students receive degree credit for clinical courses. (Clinical practicum is not required.) Among the clinical areas offered are:

  Civil Litigation
  Criminal Defense
  Criminal Prosecution
  Elderly Advocacy
  Family Law
  General Practice
  Government Litigation
  Juvenile Law

International exchange programs permit students to visit Poland.

GEORGETOWN UNIVERSITY
LAW CENTER

Washington, District of Columbia

INFORMATION CONTACT

Andy Cornblatt, Assistant Dean for Admissions
600 New Jersey Avenue, NW
Washington, DC 20001

Phone: 202-662-9010   Fax: 202-662-9444
Web site: http://www.law.georgetown.edu/

LAW STUDENT PROFILE [2000–2001]

FULL-TIME   Enrollment: 2,212
Women: 45%   Men: 55%

PART-TIME   Enrollment: 487
Women: 41%   Men: 59%

RACIAL or ETHNIC COMPOSITION

African American, 9%; Asian/Pacific Islander, 8%; Hispanic, 5%; Native American, 1%; International, 6%

APPLICANTS and ADMITTEES

Seats available: 575
Median LSAT score: 167
Average GPA: 3.6

Georgetown University Law Center is a private institution that organizes classes on a semester calendar system. The campus is situated in an urban setting. Founded in 1870, first ABA approved in 1924, and an AALS member, Georgetown University Law Center offers Certificate, JD, JD/MA, JD/MBA, JD/MPH, JD/MPP, JD/MSFS, JD/PhD, LLM, and SJD degrees.

Faculty consists of 92 full-time and 28 part-time members in 2000–2001. 30 full-time faculty members and 4 part-time faculty members are women. 97% of all faculty members have a JD; 15% have advanced law degrees. Of all faculty members, 3% are Asian/Pacific Islander, 8% are African American, 1% are Hispanic, 87% are white, 1% are international.

Application Information *Required:* LSAT, application form, application fee of $65, baccalaureate degree, 1 recommendation, LSDAS. *Recommended:* personal statement, resume. *Application deadline* for fall term is February 1. Applications are processed on a rolling basis.

Financial Aid In 2000–2001, 55% of all students received some form of financial aid. 25 fellowships were awarded. Loans, loan repayment assistance program (LRAP), need-based grants/scholarships, and federal work-study loans are also available. The average student debt at graduation is $80,300. To apply for financial assistance, students must complete the Free Application for Federal Student Aid, institutional forms, Need Access application or CSS Aid Profile. Completed financial aid forms should be received by March 1. Financial aid contact: Ruth Lammert-Reeves, Assistant Dean, Financial Aid, 600 New

AT a GLANCE

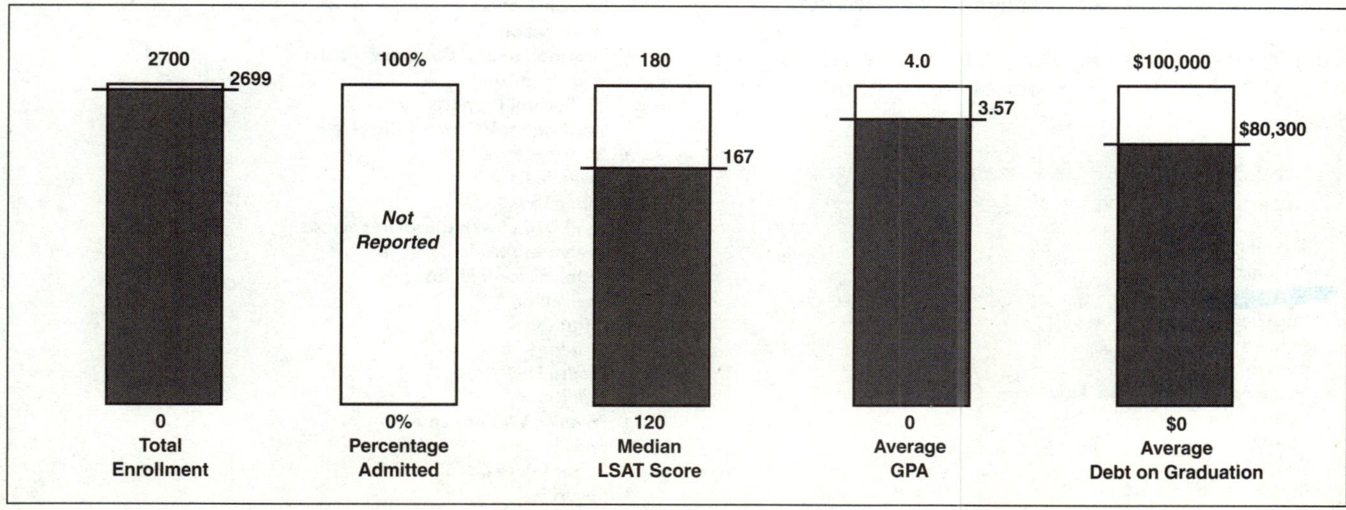

Degree Options

Degree	Total Credits Required	Length of Program
Certificate–Employee Benefits	10	1–3 yrs, part-time only [evening]
JD–Juris Doctor		full-time or part-time [day, evening, summer]
JD/MA–Juris Doctor/Master of Arts–Philosophy Joint-degree Program	98	full-time only [day]
JD/MBA–Juris Doctor/Master of Business Administration–Joint-degree Program in Business Administration	122	4 yrs, full-time only [day]
JD/MPH–Juris Doctor/Master of Public Health–Joint-degree Program in Public Health		4 yrs, full-time only [day]
JD/MPP–Juris Doctor/Master of Public Planning–Public Policy Joint-degree Program	111	4 yrs, full-time or part-time [day, evening]
Certificate–Foreign Service Joint-degree Program	113	4 yrs, full-time only [day]
JD/PhD–Juris Doctor/Doctor of Philosophy–Government Joint-degree Program	116	6 yrs, full-time or part-time [day, evening]
JD/PhD–Juris Doctor/Doctor of Philosophy–Philosophy Joint-degree Program	110	5 yrs, full-time or part-time [day, evening]
LLM–Master of Laws–Taxation, Securities and Financial Regulation, International and Comparative Law, Individual Study	24	1–3 yrs, full-time or part-time [day, evening]
LLM–Master of Laws–International Legal Studies, General Studies	20	1 yr, full-time only [day]
SJD–Doctor of Juridical Science	10	2–4 yrs, full-time only
SJD–Doctor of Juridical Science	10	2–5 yrs, full-time only [day]

Jersey Avenue, NW, Washington, DC 20001. Phone: 202-662-9210. Fax: 202-662-9367. E-mail: finaid@law.georgetown.edu

Law School Library E.B. Williams Law Library has 22 professional staff members and contains more than 995,306 volumes and 12,420 periodicals. 1,075 seats are available in the library. When classes are in session, the library is open 107 hours per week.

WESTLAW and LEXIS-NEXIS are available, as are the World Wide Web, online bibliographic services, and CD-ROM players. 154 computer workstations are available to students in the library. Special law collections include International and Foreign Law Collection.

First-Year Program Class size in the average section is 87; 100% of the first-year courses are taught by full-time faculty.

Upper-Level Program Class size in the average section is 50. Among the electives are:

Accounting
★ Administrative Law
★ Advocacy
★ Appellate Litigation
Aviation Law
Bankruptcy
★ Business and Corporate Law
Canon Law
Church-State
★ Civil Litigation
Civil Procedure

★ Civil Rights
Conflict of Laws
★ Constitutional Law
★ Criminal Defense
★ Criminal Procedure
★ Domestic Violence
Entertainment Law
★ Environmental Law
Evidence
★ Fair Housing
★ Family Law
★ Family Practice
★ Global Legal Studies
★ Government/Regulation
★ Health Care/Human Services
★ Health Law
★ Human Rights
★ Immigration
★ Information and Communications
Insurance Law
★ Intellectual Property
★ International/Comparative Law
★ Jurisprudence
★ Juvenile Law
★ Labor Law
Land Use Law/Natural Resources
★ Lawyering Skills
★ Legal History/Philosophy
★ Legislation
★ Litigation
Maritime Law
Media Law
★ Mediation
★ Poverty/Welfare Law
★ Probate Law
★ Public Interest
★ Securities

Sports Law
★ Street Law
★ Tax Law
Water Law
★ Women's Rights
(★ indicates an area of special strength)

Clinical Courses Students receive degree credit for clinical courses. (Clinical practicum is not required.) Among the clinical areas offered are:

Appellate Litigation
Civil Litigation
Civil Rights
Criminal Defense
Criminal Justice
Domestic Violence
Environmental Law

Fair Housing
Family Practice
General Practice
Government Litigation
Health Law
Human Rights
Immigration
Information and Communications
International/Comparative Law
Juvenile Law
Lawyering Skills
Legislation
Litigation
Poverty/Welfare Law
Public Interest
Street Law
Women's Rights

THE GEORGE WASHINGTON UNIVERSITY
LAW SCHOOL

Washington, District of Columbia

INFORMATION CONTACT

Robert V. Stanek, Assistant Dean of Admissions and
Financial Aid
2000 H Street, NW
Washington, DC 20052

Phone: 202-739-0648   Fax: 202-739-0624
E-mail: jd@admit.nlc.gwu.edu
Web site: http://www.law.gwu.edu/

LAW STUDENT PROFILE [2000–2001]

FULL-TIME   Enrollment: 1,388
Women: 48%   Men: 52%

PART-TIME   Enrollment: 355
Women: 38%   Men: 62%

RACIAL or ETHNIC COMPOSITION
African American, 12%; Asian/Pacific Islander, 10%;
Hispanic, 8%; Native American, 0.5%; International, 4%

APPLICANTS and ADMITTEES
Number applied: 8,400
Admitted: 2,772
Percentage accepted: 33%
Seats available: 450
Average LSAT score: 162
Average GPA: 3.4

The George Washington University Law School is a
private institution that organizes classes on a semester
calendar system. The campus is situated in an urban
setting. Founded in 1865, first ABA approved in 1925,
and an AALS member, The George Washington University Law School offers JD, JD/MA, JD/MBA, JD/MPAd,
JD/MPH, LL M/MA, LLM, LLM/MPH, and SJD degrees.

Faculty consists of 62 full-time and 91 part-time
members in 2000–2001. 15 full-time faculty members
and 30 part-time faculty members are women. 100% of
all faculty members have a JD; 18% have advanced law
degrees. Of all faculty members, 2% are Asian/Pacific
Islander, 6% are African American, 2% are Hispanic,
91% are white.

Application Information *Required:* LSAT, LSDAS,
application form, application fee of $65, baccalaureate
degree, personal statement, college transcripts. *Recommended:* recommendations, resume. *Application deadline*
for fall term is March 1. Applications are processed on a
rolling basis.

Costs The 2000–2001 tuition was $28,045 full-time.

Financial Aid In 2000–2001, 32% of all students received
some form of financial aid. Loans, loan repayment
assistance program (LRAP), merit-based grants/scholar-
ships, need-based grants/scholarships, and federal
work-study loans are available. The average student debt
at graduation is $71,000. To apply for financial assis-
tance, students must complete the Free Application for
Federal Student Aid, institutional forms, CSS PROFILE
form. Completed financial aid forms should be received

AT a GLANCE

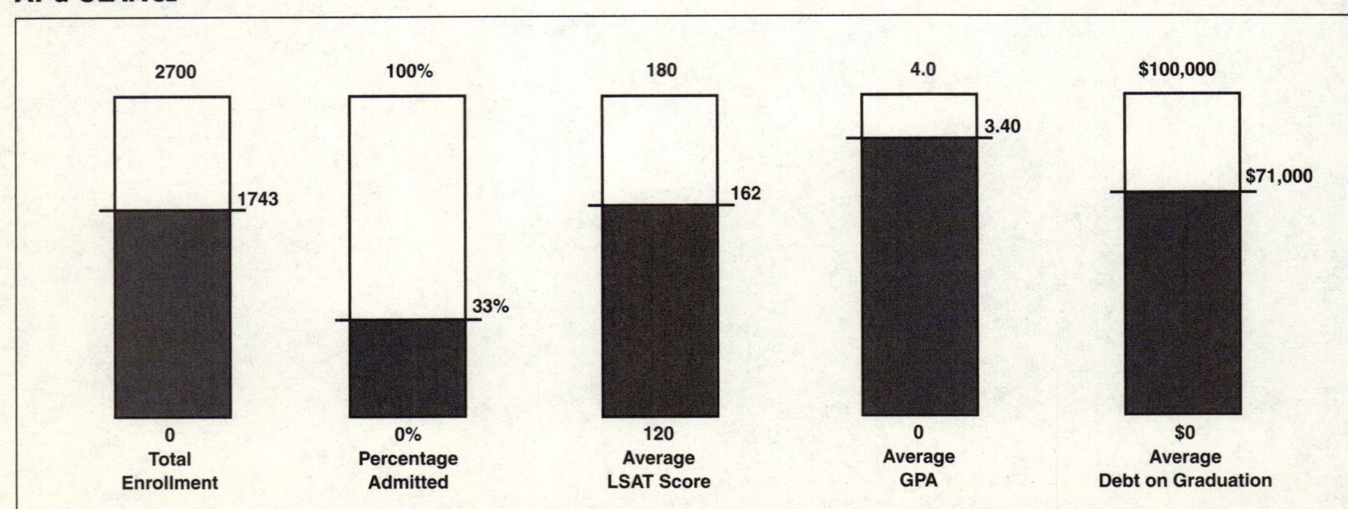

Degree Options

Degree	Total Credits Required	Length of Program
JD–Doctor of Laws	84	3–4 yrs, full-time or part-time [day, evening, summer]
JD/MA–Juris Doctor/Master of Arts–Majors include: Int'l Affairs; Science, Technology & Public Policy; Security Policy Studies; East Asian Studies; Latin American Studies; Russian & East European Studies; European Studies; Int'l Development Studies; Int'l Trade & Investment Policy		4 yrs, full-time or part-time [day, evening, summer]
JD/MA–Juris Doctor/Master of Arts–Joint-degree in Law and Women's studies		4 yrs, full-time or part-time [day, evening, summer]
JD/MA–Juris Doctor/Master of Arts–History Joint-degree Program	96	4 yrs, full-time or part-time [day, evening, summer]
JD/MBA–Juris Doctor/Master of Business Administration–Joint-degree	114	4 yrs, full-time or part-time [day, evening, summer]
JD/MPAd–Juris Doctor/Master of Public Administration–Joint-degree	100	4 yrs, full-time or part-time [day, evening, summer]
JD/MPH–Juris Doctor/Master of Public Health–Joint-degree	93	3–4 yrs, full-time or part-time [day, evening, summer]
LL M/MA–Master of Laws/Master of Arts–History	45	4 yrs, full-time or part-time [day, evening, summer]
LLM–Master of Laws–Government Procurement and Environmental Law	24	1–2 yrs, full-time or part-time [day, evening, summer]
LLM–Master of Laws–Sustainable Growth and Environmental Law	24	1–2 yrs, full-time or part-time [day, evening, summer]
LLM–Master of Laws–International Environmental Law	24	1–2 yrs, full-time or part-time [day, evening, summer]
LLM–Master of Laws–Litigation and Dispute Resolution	24	1–2 yrs, full-time or part-time [day, evening, summer]
LLM–Master of Laws–International and Comparative Law	24	1–2 yrs, full-time or part-time [day, evening, summer]
LLM–Master of Laws–Environmental Law	24	1–2 yrs, full-time or part-time [day, evening, summer]
LLM–Master of Laws–Government Procurement Law	24	1–2 yrs, full-time or part-time [day, evening, summer]
LLM–Master of Laws–Intellectual Property Law	24	1–2 yrs, full-time or part-time [day, evening, summer]
LLM/MPH–Master of Laws/Master in Public Health–Joint-degree Program	45	4 yrs, full-time or part-time [day, evening, summer]
SJD–Doctor of Juridical Science	8	3 yrs, full-time or part-time [day, evening, summer]

by March 1. Financial aid contact: Nancy LaMotta, Financial Aid Director, 1819 H Street, NW, Suite 750, Washington, DC 20052. Phone: 202-739-0641. Fax: 202-739-0624.

Law School Library Jacob Burns Law Library has 18 professional staff members and contains more than 542,674 volumes and 5,660 periodicals. 645 seats are available in the library. When classes are in session, the library is open 110 hours per week.

WESTLAW and LEXIS-NEXIS are available, as are the World Wide Web, online bibliographic services, and CD-ROM players. 127 computer workstations are available to students in the library. Special law collections include Intellectual Property, Environmental Law, International Law.

First-Year Program Class size in the average section is 90; 100% of the first-year courses are taught by full-time faculty.

Upper-Level Program Class size in the average section is 36. Among the electives are:

    Administrative Law
★ Advocacy
    Animal Rights Law
★ Business and Corporate Law
    Civil Litigation

★ Consumer Law
Corporate Law
Criminal Defense
Domestic Violence
Education Law
Elderly Advocacy
Entertainment Law
★ Environmental Law
★ Family Law
Family Practice
Government Litigation
★ Government Procurement
★ Government/Regulation
★ Health Care/Human Services
Health Law
★ Immigration
Indian/Tribal Law
★ Intellectual Property
★ International/Comparative Law
Islamic Law
Jurisprudence
Juvenile Law
Labor Law
Land Use Law/Natural Resources
★ Lawyering Skills
★ Legal History/Philosophy
★ Litigation
Maritime Law
Media Law
★ Mediation
★ Prisoners' Rights
Probate Law
★ Public Interest
Securities
Tax Law
Vaccine Injury
(★ *indicates an area of special strength*)

Clinical Courses Students receive degree credit for clinical courses. (Clinical practicum is not required.) Among the clinical areas offered are:

Administrative Law
Advocacy
Business and Corporate Law
Civil Litigation
Consumer Law
Corporate Law
Criminal Defense
Domestic Violence
Elderly Advocacy
Environmental Law
Family Law
Family Practice
General Practice
Government Litigation
Health Care/Human Services
Health Law
Immigration
Juvenile Law
Lawyering Skills
Litigation
Mediation
Prisoners' Rights
Probate Law
Public Interest
Vaccine Injury

HOWARD UNIVERSITY
SCHOOL OF LAW

Washington, District of Columbia

LAW STUDENT PROFILE [2000–2001]

FULL-TIME Enrollment: 401
Women: 58% Men: 42%

PART-TIME Enrollment: 1
Women: 100%

RACIAL or ETHNIC COMPOSITION
African American, 88%; Asian/Pacific Islander, 3%; Hispanic, 3%

APPLICANTS and ADMITTEES
Number applied: 1,275
Admitted: 413
Percentage accepted: 32%
Seats available: 141
Average LSAT score: 152
Average GPA: 3.0

Howard University School of Law is a private institution that organizes classes on a semester calendar system. The campus is situated in an urban setting. Founded in 1869, first ABA approved in 1931, and an AALS member, Howard University School of Law offers JD, JD/MBA, and LLM degrees.

Faculty consists of 34 full-time and 17 part-time members in 2000–2001. 14 full-time faculty members and 3 part-time faculty members are women. 100% of all faculty members have a JD; 22% have advanced law degrees. Of all faculty members, 6% are Asian/Pacific Islander, 81% are African American, 13% are white.

Application Information *Required:* LSAT, LSDAS, application form, application fee of $60, baccalaureate degree, minimum 3.0 GPA, 2 letters of recommendation, personal statement, college transcripts. *Application deadline* for fall term is March 31. Applications are processed on a rolling basis.

Costs The 2000–2001 tuition was $13,030 full-time; $724 per credit part-time. Fees: $610 full-time; $328 per term part-time.

Financial Aid In 2000–2001, 67% of all students received some form of financial aid. Loans, merit-based grants/scholarships, need-based grants/scholarships, and federal work-study loans are available. The average student debt at graduation is $55,000. To apply for financial assistance, students must complete the Free Application for Federal Student Aid, institutional forms. Completed financial aid forms should be received by March 1.

AT a GLANCE

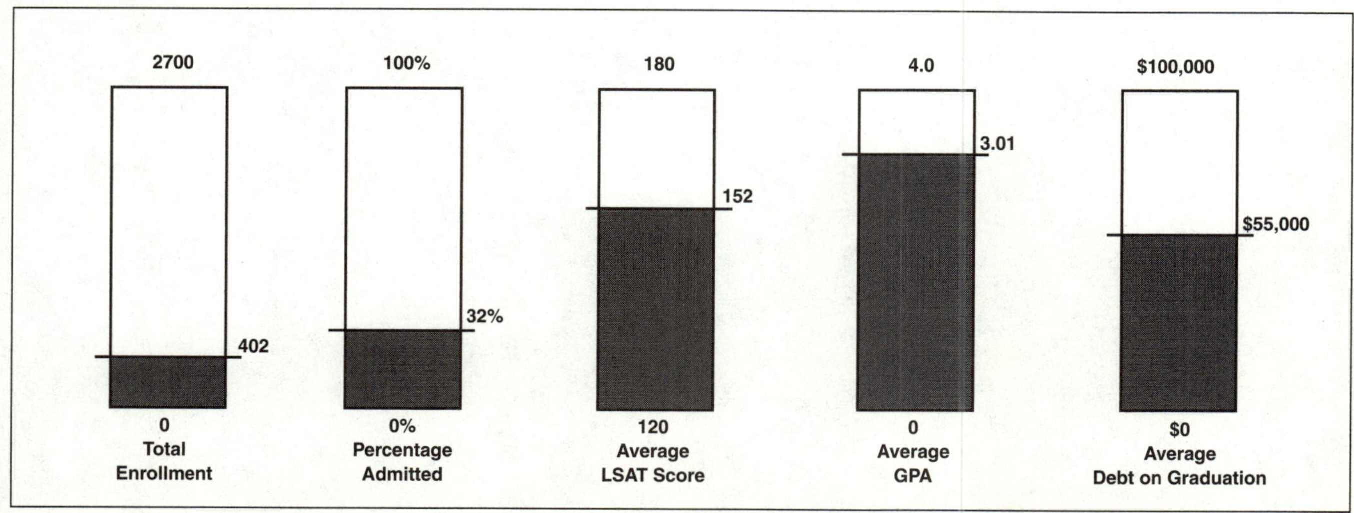

Degree Options

Degree	Total Credits Required	Length of Program
JD–Juris Doctor	88	3 yrs, full-time only [day]
JD/MBA–Juris Doctor/Master of Business Administration		4–5 yrs, full-time only
LLM–Master of Laws	24	1 yr, full-time only [day]

Financial aid contact: Mr. Norman James, Financial Aid Manager, 2900 Van Ness Street, NW, Washington, DC 20008. Phone: 202-806-8005. Fax: 202-806-8564.

Law School Library Allen Mercer Daniel Law Library has 9 professional staff members and contains more than 284,000 volumes and 3,473 periodicals. 173 seats are available in the library. When classes are in session, the library is open 101 hours per week.

WESTLAW and LEXIS-NEXIS are available, as is the World Wide Web. 38 computer workstations are available to students in the library. Special law collections include South Africa laws, the Phineas Indritz Papers, Civil Rights..

First-Year Program Class size in the average section is 45; 100% of the first-year courses are taught by full-time faculty.

Upper-Level Program Class size in the average section is 35. Among the electives are:

Administrative Law
Advocacy
Business and Corporate Law
Church-State
Civil Litigation
Civil Rights
Consumer Law
Elderly Advocacy
Election Law
Entertainment Law
Environmental Law
Family Law
Government/Regulation
Immigration
Intellectual Property
International/Comparative Law
Jurisprudence
Labor Law
Land Use Law/Natural Resources
Law and Medicine
Lawyering Skills
Legal History/Philosophy
Litigation
Media Law
Mediation
Municipal Law
Probate Law
Public Ethics
Public Interest
Securities
Small Business Counseling

Clinical Courses Students receive degree credit for clinical courses. (Clinical practicum is not required.) Among the clinical areas offered are:

Alternative Dispute Resolution
Business and Corporate Law
Civil Litigation
Criminal Defense
Elderly Advocacy
Immigration
Litigation
Small Business Counseling

UNIVERSITY OF THE DISTRICT OF COLUMBIA
DAVID A. CLARKE SCHOOL OF LAW

Washington, District of Columbia

INFORMATION CONTACT

Vivian W. Canty, Director of Admission
4200 Connecticut Avenue, NW
Washington, DC 20008-1175

Phone: 202-274-7336   Fax: 202-274-5583
E-mail: vcanty@law.udc.edu
Web site: http://www.law.udc.edu/

LAW STUDENT PROFILE [2000–2001]

FULL-TIME   Enrollment: 143
Women: 62%   Men: 38%

APPLICANTS and ADMITTEES

Number applied: 375
Admitted: 100
Percentage accepted: 27%
Seats available: 100
Average LSAT score: 145
Average GPA: 2.8

University of the District of Columbia David A. Clarke School of Law is a public institution that organizes classes on a semester calendar system. The campus is situated in an urban setting. Founded in 1988, first ABA approved in 1991, University of the District of Columbia David A. Clarke School of Law offers a JD degree.

Faculty consists of 23 full-time and 17 part-time members in 2000–2001. 14 full-time faculty members and 6 part-time faculty members are women. 100% of all faculty members have a JD; 10% have advanced law degrees. Of all faculty members, 4% are Asian/Pacific Islander, 33% are African American, 63% are white.

Application Information *Required:* LSAT, LSDAS, application form, application fee of $35, baccalaureate degree, 2 letters of recommendation, essay, minimum 2.3 GPA, college transcripts. *Recommended:* personal statement, interview. *Application deadline* for fall term is April 1. Applications are processed on a rolling basis.

Costs The 2000–2001 tuition was $14,000 full-time. Fees: $150 full-time. Students are required to have their own computers.

Financial Aid Fellowships, loans, merit-based grants/scholarships, need-based grants/scholarships, and federal work-study loans are available. The average student debt at graduation is $63,000. To apply for financial assistance, students must complete the Free Application for Federal Student Aid, institutional forms, scholarship specific applications, Need Access application. Completed

AT a GLANCE

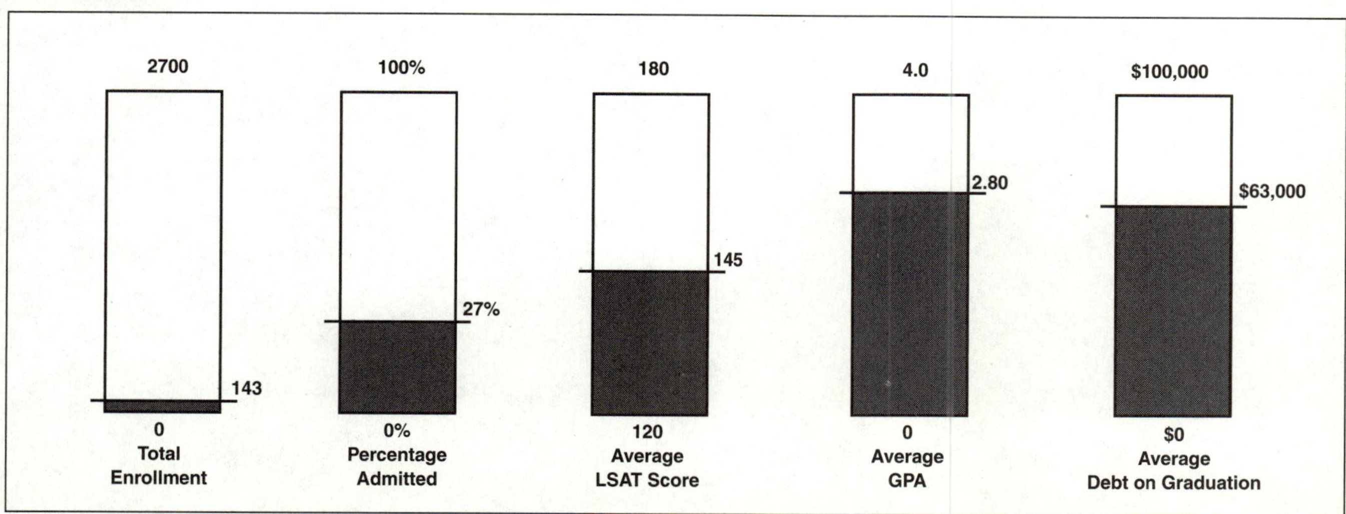

Degree Options		
Degree	**Total Credits Required**	**Length of Program**
JD–Doctor of Laws	90	3 yrs, full-time only [day, summer]

financial aid forms should be received by May 1. Financial aid contact: Anne El Shazli, Financial Aid Officer, 4200 Connecticut Avenue, NW, Washington, DC 20008. Phone: 202-274-7337. Fax: 202-274-5583. E-mail: aelshazli@law.udc.edu

Law School Library University of DC School of Law Library has 6 professional staff members and contains more than 188,000 volumes and 2,486 periodicals. 140 seats are available in the library. When classes are in session, the library is open 104 hours per week.

WESTLAW and LEXIS-NEXIS are available, as are the World Wide Web, online bibliographic services, and CD-ROM players. 9 computer workstations are available to students in the library. Special law collections include Clinical Law Library.

First-Year Program Class size in the average section is 100; 45% of the first-year courses are taught by full-time faculty.

Upper-Level Program Class size in the average section is 25. Among the electives are:

Administrative Law
★ Advocacy
★ AIDS and the Law
Business and Corporate Law
Civil Litigation
★ Consumer Law
Education Law
Environmental Law

Family Law
Family Practice
★ Government/Regulation
Health Care/Human Services
★ Housing Law
International/Comparative Law
Jurisprudence
★ Juvenile Law
Labor Law
★ Lawyering Skills
★ Legislation
★ Litigation
Public Benefits
★ Public Interest
Race and Law
Securities

(★ *indicates an area of special strength*)

Clinical Courses Students receive degree credit for clinical courses. 14 credit hours of clinical practicum are required. Among the clinical areas offered are:

AIDS and the Law
Civil Litigation
Community Development
Consumer Law
Education Law
Government/Regulation
Housing Law
Immigration
Juvenile Law
Legislation
Public Benefits
Public Interest

FLORIDA COASTAL SCHOOL OF LAW

Jacksonville, Florida

INFORMATION CONTACT

Director of Admissions
7555 Beach Boulevard
Jacksonville, FL 32216

Phone: 904-680-7710   Fax: 904-680-7776
E-mail: admissions@fcsl.edu
Web site: http://www.fcsl.edu/

LAW STUDENT PROFILE [2000–2001]

FULL-TIME   Enrollment: 267
Women: 42%   Men: 58%

PART-TIME   Enrollment: 185
Women: 45%   Men: 55%

APPLICANTS and ADMITTEES

Number applied: 2,006
Admitted: 518
Percentage accepted: 26%
Seats available: 150
Average LSAT score: 151
Average GPA: 2.9

Florida Coastal School of Law is a private institution that organizes classes on a semester calendar system. The campus is situated in a suburban setting. Founded in 1994, first ABA approved in 1999, Florida Coastal School of Law offers a JD degree.

Faculty 100% of all faculty members have a JD; 15% have advanced law degrees. Of all faculty members, 4% are Asian/Pacific Islander, 12% are African American, 84% are white.

Application Information *Required:* LSAT, application fee of $50, 2 letters of recommendation, personal statement, application form, LSDAS, baccalaureate degree, minimum 2.0 GPA. *Recommended:* college transcripts, resume.

Costs The 2000–2001 tuition was $18,420 full-time; $14,730 per year part-time. Fees: $435 per semester full-time; $435 per semester part-time.

Financial Aid Fellowships, graduate assistantships, loans, loan repayment assistance program (LRAP), merit-based grants/scholarships, need-based grants/scholarships, and federal work-study loans are available. The average student debt at graduation is $23,152. To apply for financial assistance, students must complete the Free Application for Federal Student Aid. Financial aid contact: Denise Wendle, Director of Admissions, 7555 Beach Boulevard, Jacksonville, FL 32216. Phone: 904-680-7717. Fax: 904-680-7777.

Law School Library Law Library - Information and Technology Center has 6 professional staff members and

AT a GLANCE

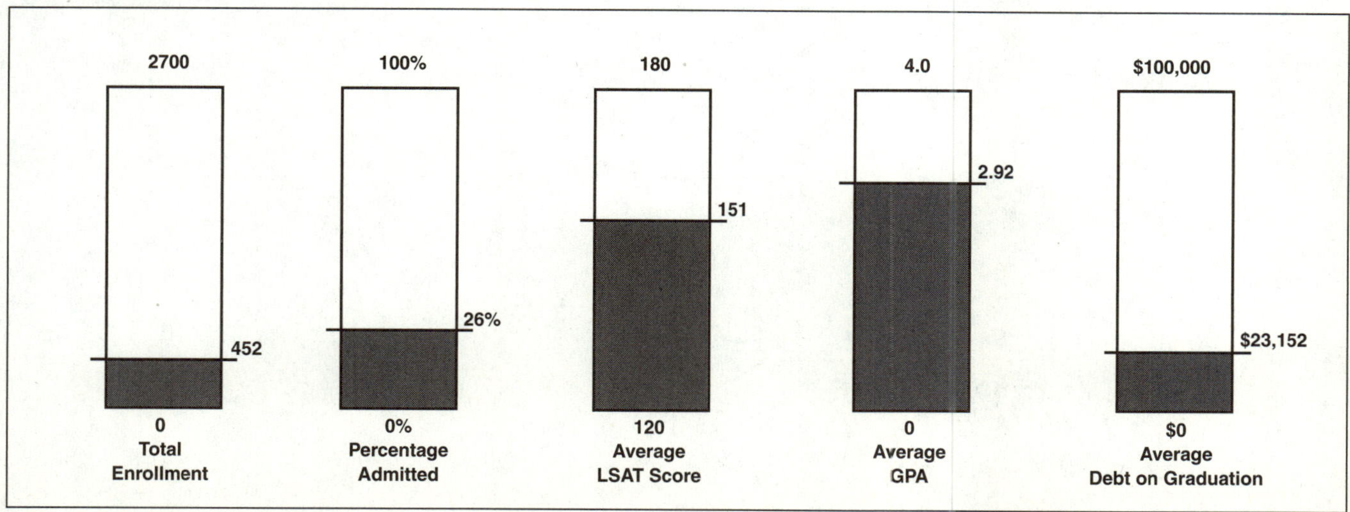

Degree Options		
Degree	**Total Credits Required**	**Length of Program**
JD–Doctor of Laws	87	3–4 yrs, full-time or part-time [day, evening, summer]

contains more than 203,273 volumes and 2,450 periodicals. 387 seats are available in the library. When classes are in session, the library is open 92 hours per week.

WESTLAW and LEXIS-NEXIS are available, as are the World Wide Web, online bibliographic services, and CD-ROM players. 52 computer workstations are available to students in the library.

First-Year Program Class size in the average section is 50; 100% of the first-year courses are taught by full-time faculty.

Upper-Level Program Class size in the average section is 20. Among the electives are:

Advocacy
★ Business and Corporate Law
Consumer Law
Education Law
Entertainment Law
★ Family Law
★ Government/Regulation
★ Health Care/Human Services
Indian/Tribal Law
Intellectual Property
★ International/Comparative Law
★ Jurisprudence
Labor Law
Land Use Law/Natural Resources
★ Lawyering Skills
Legal History/Philosophy
Maritime Law
Media Law
Mediation
Probate Law
★ Public Interest
Securities
Tax Law
(★ *indicates an area of special strength*)

Clinical Courses Students receive degree credit for clinical courses. (Clinical practicum is not required.) Among the clinical areas offered are:

Civil Litigation
Civil Rights
Corporate Law
Criminal Defense
Criminal Prosecution
Education
Elderly Advocacy
Environmental Law
Family Practice
General Practice
Government Litigation
Health Law
Immigration
Indian/Tribal Law
Intellectual Property
International Law
Juvenile Law
Land Rights/Natural Resource
Mediation
Public Interest
Tax Law

FLORIDA STATE UNIVERSITY
COLLEGE OF LAW

Tallahassee, Florida

INFORMATION CONTACT

Sharon J. Booker, Director of Admissions and Records
425 West Jefferson Street
Tallahassee, FL 32306-1601

Phone: 850-644-3787   Fax: 850-644-7284
E-mail: admissions@law.fsu.edu
Web site: http://www.law.fsu.edu/

LAW STUDENT PROFILE [2000–2001]

FULL-TIME   Enrollment: 727
Women: 46%   Men: 54%

RACIAL or ETHNIC COMPOSITION

African American, 8%; Asian/Pacific Islander, 3%; Hispanic, 8%; Native American, 1%; International, 1%

APPLICANTS and ADMITTEES

Number applied: 1,812
Admitted: 741
Percentage accepted: 41%
Seats available: 245
Average LSAT score: 155
Average GPA: 3.3

Florida State University College of Law is a public institution that organizes classes on a semester calendar system. The campus is situated in a small-town setting. Founded in 1966, first ABA approved in 1968, and an AALS member, Florida State University College of Law offers JD, JD/MBA, JD/MEc, JD/MPAd, JD/MPIA, JD/MSW, and JD/MURP degrees.

Faculty consists of 42 full-time and 12 part-time members in 2000–2001. 13 full-time faculty members and 2 part-time faculty members are women. 100% of all faculty members have a JD; 21% have advanced law degrees. Of all faculty members, 2.3% are Native American, 4.7% are African American, 7% are Hispanic, 86% are white.

Application Information *Required:* LSAT, LSDAS, application form, application fee of $20, baccalaureate degree, 2 letters of recommendation, personal statement, college transcripts. *Application deadline* for fall term is February 15 (priority date). Applications are processed on a rolling basis.

Costs The 2000–2001 tuition was $4107 full-time for state residents. Tuition was $10,897 full-time for nonresidents. Fees: $845 full-time. Students are required to have their own computers.

Financial Aid In 2000–2001, 9% of all students received some form of financial aid. 67 fellowships, totaling $1596; 58 research assistantships, totaling $3300; 22 teaching assistantships, totaling $1700, were awarded. Fellowships, graduate assistantships, loans, merit-based grants/scholarships, and need-based grants/scholarships

AT a GLANCE

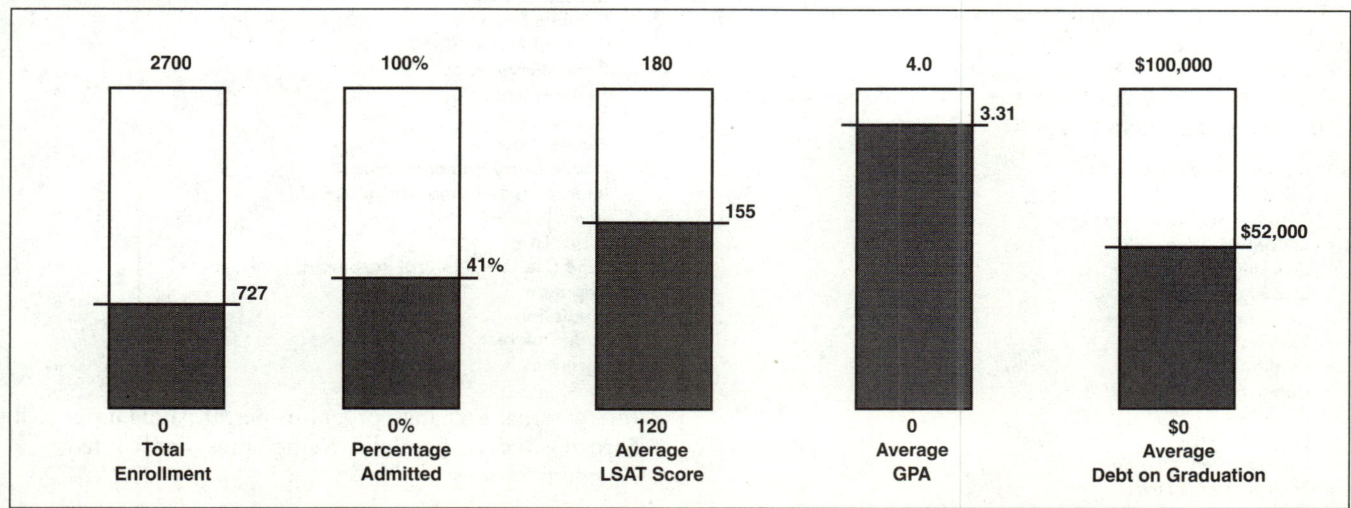

Degree Options

Degree	Total Credits Required	Length of Program
JD–Juris Doctor	88	3 yrs, full-time only [day]
JD/MBA–Juris Doctor/Master of Business Administration–Joint-degree Program	112	4 yrs, full-time only [day]
JD/MEc–Juris Doctor/Master of Economics–Joint-degree Program	104	4 yrs, full-time only [day]
JD/MPAd–Juris Doctor/Master of Public Administration–Joint-degree Program	112	4 yrs, full-time only [day]
JD/MPIA–Juris Doctor/Master of Public and International Affairs–Joint-degree Program	104	4 yrs, full-time only [day]
JD/MSW–Juris Doctor/Master of Social Work–Joint-degree Program	133	4 yrs, full-time only [day]
JD/MURP–Juris Doctor/Masters of Urban and Regional Planning–Joint-degree Program	111	4 yrs, full-time only [day]

are also available. The average student debt at graduation is $52,000. To apply for financial assistance, students must complete the Free Application for Federal Student Aid, scholarship specific applications. Completed financial aid forms should be received by April 1. Financial aid contact: JoAnne Clark, Coordinator for Law Student Financial Aid, Office of Financial Aid, University Center A4423, Tallahassee, FL 32306-2430. Phone: 850-644-5716. Fax: 850-644-6404. E-mail: jclark@admin.fsu.edu

Law School Library FSU College of Law Library has 10 professional staff members and contains more than 428,535 volumes and 5,120 periodicals. 346 seats are available in the library. When classes are in session, the library is open 93 hours per week.

WESTLAW and LEXIS-NEXIS are available, as are the World Wide Web, online bibliographic services, and CD-ROM players. 50 computer workstations are available to students in the library. Special law collections include Commonwealth Caribbean Law Materials.

First-Year Program Class size in the average section is 77; 100% of the first-year courses are taught by full-time faculty.

Upper-Level Program Class size in the average section is 30. Among the electives are:

Administrative Law
Advocacy
Business and Corporate Law
★ Children's Advocacy
Civil Litigation
Civil Rights
Consumer Law
★ Criminal Defense
★ Criminal Prosecution
★ Domestic Violence
Education
Education Law
Entertainment Law
★ Environmental Law
Family Law
Health Care/Human Services
Intellectual Property
★ International/Comparative Law
Jurisprudence
★ Juvenile Law
Labor Law
★ Land Use Law/Natural Resources
Legal History/Philosophy
Litigation
Maritime Law
Media Law
Mediation
★ Public Interest
Securities
★ Tax Law
(★ *indicates an area of special strength*)

Clinical Courses Students receive degree credit for clinical courses. (Clinical practicum is not required.) Among the clinical areas offered are:

Administrative Law
Advocacy
Business and Corporate Law
Children's Advocacy
Civil Litigation
Consumer Law
Criminal Defense
Criminal Prosecution
Domestic Violence
Environmental Law
Family Law
Family Practice
Health Care/Human Services
International/Comparative Law
Juvenile Law
Labor Law
Land Use Law/Natural Resources
Litigation
Mediation
Public Interest
Securities

International exchange programs permit students to visit Barbados, Czech Republic, Netherlands, and United Kingdom.

NOVA SOUTHEASTERN UNIVERSITY
SHEPARD BROAD LAW CENTER

Ft. Lauderdale, Florida

INFORMATION CONTACT

Nancy Kelly Sanguigni, Director of Admissions
3305 College Avenue
Ft. Lauderdale, FL 33314

Phone: 954-262-6120   Fax: 954-262-3844
E-mail: sanguignin@nsu.law.nova.edu
Web site: http://www.nsulaw.nova.edu/

LAW STUDENT PROFILE [2000–2001]

FULL-TIME   Enrollment: 743
Women: 52%   Men: 48%

PART-TIME   Enrollment: 225
Women: 51%   Men: 49%

APPLICANTS and ADMITTEES

Number applied: 1,321
Admitted: 699
Percentage accepted: 53%
Seats available: 330
Average LSAT score: 148
Average GPA: 2.8

Nova Southeastern University Shepard Broad Law Center is a private institution that organizes classes on a semester calendar system. The campus is situated in a suburban setting. Founded in 1974, first ABA approved in 1975, and an AALS member, Nova Southeastern University Shepard Broad Law Center offers JD, JD/MBA, JD/MS, and JD/MURP degrees.

Faculty consists of 46 full-time and 62 part-time members in 2000–2001. 19 full-time faculty members and 16 part-time faculty members are women. 100% of all faculty members have a JD; 50% have advanced law degrees. Of all faculty members, .9% are Asian/Pacific Islander, 7.1% are African American, 8.9% are Hispanic, 83% are white.

Application Information *Required:* LSAT, LSDAS, application form, application fee of $50, baccalaureate degree, personal statement, essay, college transcripts. *Application deadline* for fall term is March 1 (priority date). Applications are processed on a rolling basis.

Costs The 2000–2001 tuition was $20,370 full-time. Students are required to have their own computers.

Financial Aid In 2000–2001, 14% of all students received some form of financial aid. 130 fellowships, totaling $12,800; 125 research assistantships; 18 teaching assistantships, were awarded. Loans, merit-based grants/scholarships, need-based grants/scholarships, and federal work-study loans are also available. The average student debt at graduation is $76,940. To apply for financial assistance, students must complete the Free Application for Federal Student Aid, institutional forms. Completed

AT a GLANCE

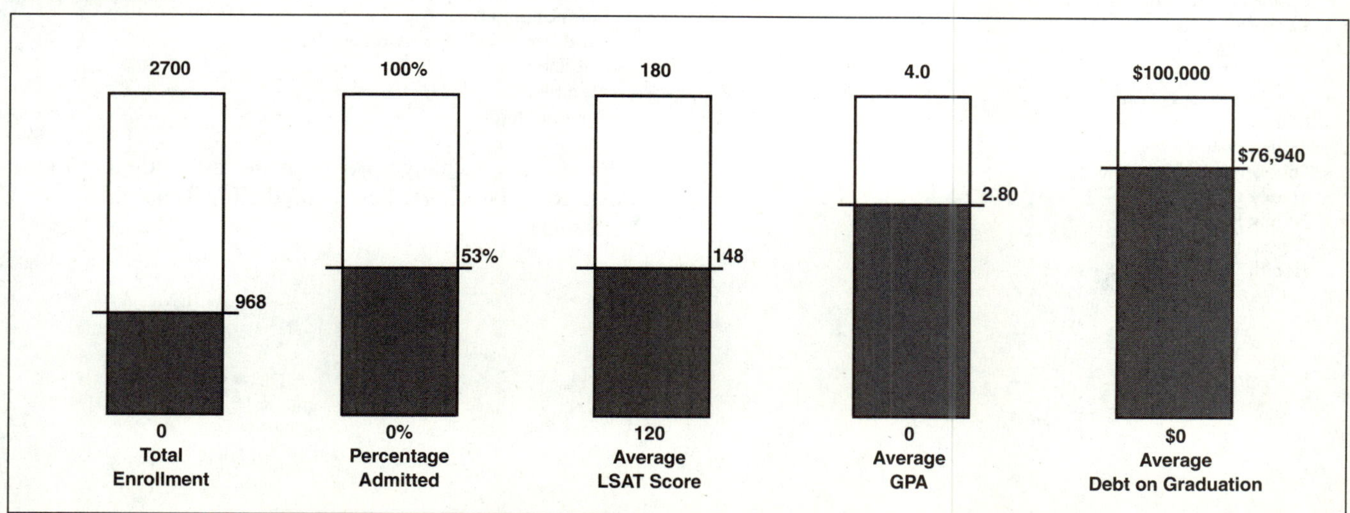

Degree Options

Degree	Total Credits Required	Length of Program
JD–Doctor of Laws	90	3–4 yrs, full-time or part-time [day, evening]
JD/MBA–Juris Doctor/Master of Business Administration		4–5 yrs, full-time or part-time [day, evening, weekend]
JD/MS–Juris Doctor/Master of Science–Dispute Resolution		4–5 yrs, full-time or part-time [day, evening, weekend]
JD/MS–Juris Doctor/Master of Science–Computer Information Technology		4–5 yrs, full-time or part-time [day, evening, weekend]
JD/MURP–Juris Doctor/Masters of Urban and Regional Planning		4–5 yrs, full-time or part-time [day, evening, weekend]

financial aid forms should be received by March 1. Financial aid contact: Lynn Acosta, Financial Aid Counselor, 3305 College Ave, Ft. Lauderdale, FL 33314. Phone: 954-262-7412. Fax: 954-262-3844. E-mail: acostal@nsu.law.nova.edu

Law School Library Law Library and Technology Center has 11 professional staff members and contains more than 340,345 volumes and 5,325 periodicals. 573 seats are available in the library. When classes are in session, the library is open 105 hours per week.

WESTLAW and LEXIS-NEXIS are available, as are the World Wide Web, online bibliographic services, and CD-ROM players. 59 computer workstations are available to students in the library. Special law collections include United Nations Depository, depository for state and federal documents, Children's First.

First-Year Program Class size in the average section is 50; 90% of the first-year courses are taught by full-time faculty.

Upper-Level Program Class size in the average section is 60. Among the electives are:

Administrative Law
★ Advocacy
★ Business and Corporate Law
Consumer Law
★ Corporate Law
★ Criminal Defense
★ Criminal Prosecution
Education Law
Entertainment Law
★ Environmental Law
★ Family Law
Family Practice
Government/Regulation
Health Care/Human Services
Intellectual Property
★ International Law
Jurisprudence
Labor Law
★ Land Use Law/Natural Resources
★ Lawyering Skills
Legal History/Philosophy
★ Litigation
Maritime Law
Media Law
★ Mediation
Probate Law
Public Interest
Securities
Tax Law

(★ indicates an area of special strength)

Clinical Courses Students receive degree credit for clinical courses. (Clinical practicum is not required.) Among the clinical areas offered are:

Alternative Dispute Resolution
Business and Corporate Law
Children and the Law
Civil Litigation
Corporate Law
Criminal Defense
Criminal Prosecution
Environmental Law
Family Law
Family Practice
Intellectual Property
International Law
Land Use Law/Natural Resources
Litigation
Mediation
Personal Injury

International exchange programs permit students to visit Costa Rica, Israel, Turkey, United Kingdom, and Venezuela.

ST. THOMAS UNIVERSITY
SCHOOL OF LAW

Miami, Florida

INFORMATION CONTACT

Lydia Amy, Assistant Dean for Enrollment and
Career Services
16400 Northwest 32nd Avenue
Miami, FL 33054-6459

Phone: 305-623-2310   Fax: 305-623-2357
E-mail: lamy@stu.edu
Web site: http://www.stu.edu/lawschool/

LAW STUDENT PROFILE [2000–2001]

FULL-TIME   Enrollment: 472
Women: 47%   Men: 53%

PART-TIME   Enrollment: 28
Women: 14%   Men: 86%

RACIAL or ETHNIC COMPOSITION
African American, 13%; Asian/Pacific Islander, 2%; Hispanic,
31%; Native American, 0.4%; International, 3%

APPLICANTS and ADMITTEES
Number applied: 1,658
Admitted: 1,103
Percentage accepted: 67%
Seats available: 191
Average LSAT score: 148
Average GPA: 3.0

St. Thomas University School of Law is a public
institution that organizes classes on a semester calendar
system. The campus is situated in an urban setting.
Founded in 1984, first ABA approved in 1995, and an
AALS member, St. Thomas University School of Law
offers JD, JD/MBA, JD/MS, and LL M T degrees.

Faculty consists of 22 full-time and 45 part-time
members in 2000–2001. 8 full-time faculty members and
16 part-time faculty members are women. 100% of all
faculty members have a JD; 32% have advanced law
degrees. Of all faculty members, 16% are African
American, 8% are Hispanic, 76% are white.

Application Information *Required:* LSAT, LSDAS,
application form, application fee of $40, baccalaureate
degree, 1 recommendation, personal statement, college
transcripts. *Recommended:* minimum GPA, resume.
Application deadline for fall term is April 30 (priority
date); for spring term is November 1 (priority date).
Applications are processed on a rolling basis.

Financial Aid Fellowships, graduate assistantships, loans,
merit-based grants/scholarships, and federal work-study
loans are available. The average student debt at graduation is $84,000. To apply for financial assistance, students
must complete the Free Application for Federal Student
Aid, institutional forms. Completed financial aid forms
should be received by May 1. Financial aid contact:
Andres Marrero, Assistant Director of Financial Aid,
16400 NW 32 Avenue, Miami, FL 33054. Phone:
305-628-6547. Fax: 305-628-6754. E-mail:
amarrero@stu.edu

AT a GLANCE

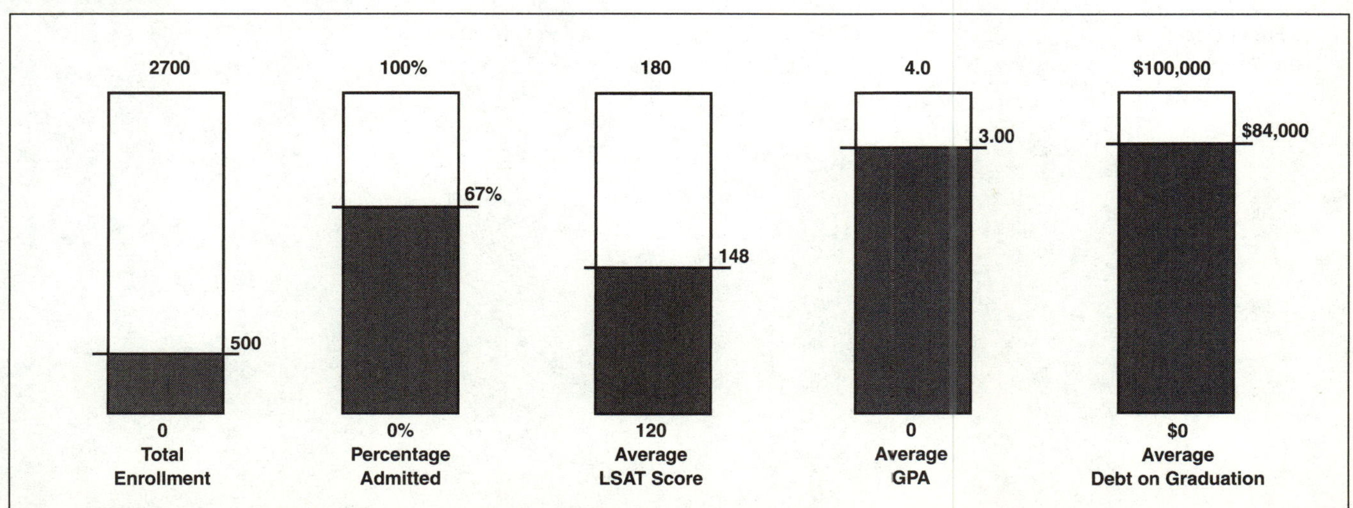

Degree Options

Degree	Total Credits Required	Length of Program
JD–Doctor of Laws	87	3 yrs, full-time only [day, summer]
JD/MBA–Juris Doctor/Master of Business Administration–JD/MBA Joint-degree Program	107	3 yrs, full-time only [day, summer]
JD/MS–Juris Doctor/Master of Science–JD/MS in Sports Management	103	3 yrs, full-time only [day, summer]
JD/MS–Juris Doctor/Master of Science–Joint degree program	109	3 yrs, full-time only [day, summer]
LL M T–Master of Laws in Taxation–LLM in International Taxation	32	2 yrs, part-time only [day, evening, summer]

Law School Library St. Thomas University School of Law Library has 6 professional staff members and contains more than 296,773 volumes and 2,319 periodicals. 302 seats are available in the library. When classes are in session, the library is open 108 hours per week.

WESTLAW and LEXIS-NEXIS are available, as are the World Wide Web and online bibliographic services. 34 computer workstations are available to students in the library. Special law collections include Native Americans, Canon Law, Supreme Court Records and Briefs 1897-present.

First-Year Program Class size in the average section is 60; 100% of the first-year courses are taught by full-time faculty.

Upper-Level Program Class size in the average section is 30. Among the electives are:

  Administrative Law
  Advocacy
  Banking and Finance
★ Bankruptcy
  Business and Corporate Law
  Civil Litigation
  Consumer Law
★ Criminal Defense
★ Criminal Prosecution
  Employment Law
  Entertainment Law
  Environmental Law
★ Family Law
★ Family Practice
  Federal Courts
  Government/Regulation
  Health Care/Human Services
★ Immigration
  Intellectual Property
  International/Comparative Law
  Jurisprudence
  Juvenile Law
  Labor Law
  Land Use Law/Natural Resources
  Lawyering Skills
  Legal History/Philosophy
  Litigation
  Maritime Law
  Media Law
  Mediation
  Probate Law
  Product Liability
  Securities
★ Tax Law
(★ indicates an area of special strength)

Clinical Courses Students receive degree credit for clinical courses. (Clinical practicum is not required.) Among the clinical areas offered are:

  Bankruptcy
  Civil Litigation
  Criminal Defense
  Criminal Prosecution
  Family Law
  Family Practice
  Immigration
  Tax Law

STETSON UNIVERSITY
COLLEGE OF LAW

St. Petersburg, Florida

INFORMATION CONTACT

Jack Huebsch, Director of Admissions and Financial Aid
1401 61st Street South
St. Petersburg, FL 33707

Phone: 727-562-7802   Fax: 727-347-3738
E-mail: lawadmit@law.stetson.edu
Web site: http://www.law.stetson.edu/

LAW STUDENT PROFILE [2000–2001]

FULL-TIME Enrollment: 680
Women: 54%   Men: 46%

PART-TIME Enrollment: 28
Women: 39%   Men: 61%

RACIAL or ETHNIC COMPOSITION
African American, 7%; Asian/Pacific Islander, 2%; Hispanic, 8%; Native American, 0.4%; International, 4%

APPLICANTS and ADMITTEES
Seats available: 140
Average LSAT score: 152
Average GPA: 3.3

Stetson University College of Law is a private institution that organizes classes on a semester calendar system. The campus is situated in a suburban setting. Founded in 1900, first ABA approved in 1930, and an AALS member, Stetson University College of Law offers JD, JD/MBA, and LLM degrees.

Faculty 100% of all faculty members have a JD; 48% have advanced law degrees. Of all faculty members, 2% are Native American, 5% are African American, 3% are Hispanic, 90% are white.

Application Information *Required:* LSAT, LSDAS, application form, application fee of $50, baccalaureate degree, personal statement, college transcripts. *Recommended:* resume. *Application deadline* for fall term is March 1 (priority date); for spring term is September 1.

Costs The 2000–2001 tuition was $21,165 full-time. Students are required to have their own computers.

Financial Aid Fellowships, graduate assistantships, loans, merit-based grants/scholarships, and need-based grants/scholarships are available. The average student debt at graduation is $72,000. To apply for financial assistance, students must complete the Free Application for Federal Student Aid, institutional forms, income tax returns (for need based financial aid applicants). Completed financial aid forms should be received by April 1. Financial aid contact: Emily Schmidt, Assistant Director of Financial Aid, 1401 61st Street South, St. Petersburg, FL 33707. Phone: 727-562-7813. Fax: 727-343-0136.

AT a GLANCE

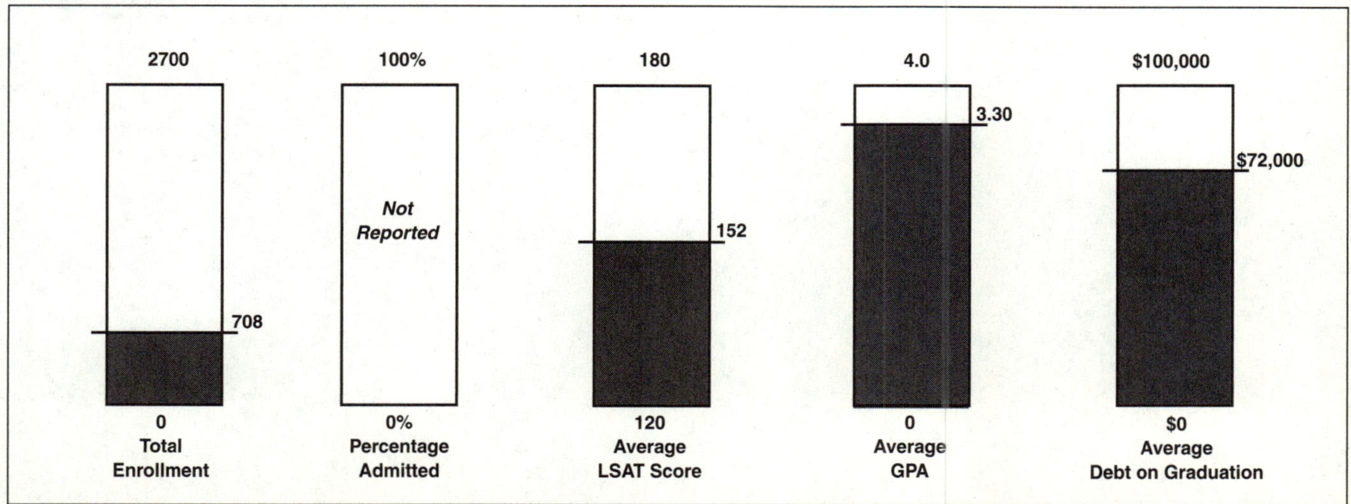

Degree Options

Degree	Total Credits Required	Length of Program
JD–Doctor of Laws	88	3 yrs, full-time only [day, summer]
JD/MBA–Juris Doctor/Master of Business Administration–Joint-degree Program	94	3–4 yrs, full-time only [day, summer]
LLM–Master of Laws–International Law and Business	24	1 yr, full-time or part-time [day, summer]

Law School Library Stetson Law Library has 10 professional staff members and contains more than 366,000 volumes and 5,500 periodicals. 487 seats are available in the library. When classes are in session, the library is open 103 hours per week.

WESTLAW and LEXIS-NEXIS are available, as are the World Wide Web, online bibliographic services, and CD-ROM players. 60 computer workstations are available to students in the library.

First-Year Program Class size in the average section is 68; 100% of the first-year courses are taught by full-time faculty.

Upper-Level Program Class size in the average section is 30. Among the electives are:

Advocacy
Business and Corporate Law
Civil Litigation
★ Criminal Defense
★ Criminal Prosecution
Elderly Advocacy
Employment Law
Entertainment Law
★ Environmental Law
Family Law
Government/Regulation
★ Health Care/Human Services
Intellectual Property
★ International/Comparative Law
Jurisprudence
★ Labor Law
Land Rights/Natural Resource
★ Land Use Law/Natural Resources
★ Lawyering Skills
★ Litigation
Maritime Law
★ Mediation
Probate Law
Public Interest
Securities
Tax Law
(★ *indicates an area of special strength*)

Clinical Courses Students receive degree credit for clinical courses. (Clinical practicum is not required.) Among the clinical areas offered are:

Civil Litigation
Criminal Defense
Criminal Prosecution
Elderly Advocacy
Employment Law
Environmental Law
Government Litigation
Government/Regulation
Labor Law
Land Rights/Natural Resource
Mediation

UNIVERSITY OF FLORIDA
FREDRIC G. LEVIN COLLEGE OF LAW

Gainesville, Florida

INFORMATION CONTACT

J. Michael Patrick, Assistant Dean for Admissions
Box 117622
Gainesville, FL 32611

Phone: 352-392-2087   Fax: 352-392-4087
E-mail: patrick@law.ufl.edu
Web site: http://www.law.ufl.edu/

LAW STUDENT PROFILE [2000–2001]

FULL-TIME   Enrollment: 1,264
Women: 42%   Men: 58%

PART-TIME   Enrollment: 5
Women: 40%   Men: 60%

APPLICANTS and ADMITTEES

Seats available: 200
Average LSAT score: 156
Average GPA: 3.6

University of Florida Fredric G. Levin College of Law is a public institution that organizes classes on a semester calendar system. The campus is situated in a small-town setting. Founded in 1909, first ABA approved in 1925, and an AALS member, University of Florida Fredric G. Levin College of Law offers JD, JD/MA, JD/MAcc, JD/MD, JD/MS, JD/MURP, JD/PhD, LLM, and SJD degrees.

Faculty 100% of all faculty members have a JD; 36% have advanced law degrees. Of all faculty members, 7% are African American, 7% are Hispanic, 86% are white.

Application Information *Required:* LSAT, LSDAS, application form, application fee of $20, baccalaureate degree, personal statement, essay, college transcripts, resume. *Recommended:* 3 letters of recommendation. *Application deadline* is rolling.

Costs The 1999–2000 tuition was $161 per credit hour part-time for state residents. Tuition was $537 per credit hour part-time for nonresidents. Students are required to have their own computers.

Financial Aid In 2000–2001, 3% of all students received some form of financial aid. Fellowships, graduate assistantships, loans, merit-based grants/scholarships, need-based grants/scholarships, and federal work-study loans are available. The average student debt at graduation is $45,000. To apply for financial assistance, students must complete the Free Application for Federal Student Aid. Financial aid contact: Patricia Varnes, Financial Aid

AT a GLANCE

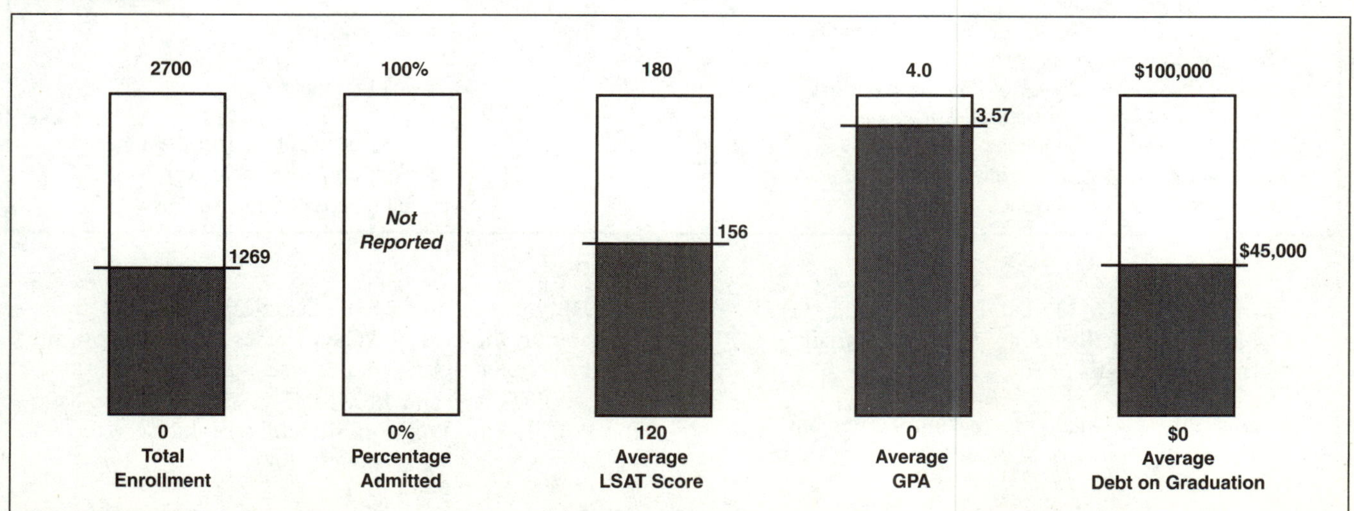

Degree Options

Degree	Total Credits Required	Length of Program
JD–Juris Doctor	88	3 yrs, full-time only [day, summer]
JD/MA–Juris Doctor/Master of Arts–Anthropology Dual-degree Program	103	4 yrs, full-time only
JD/MA–Juris Doctor/Master of Arts–Women's Studies Dual-degree Program	98	4 yrs, full-time only
JD/MA–Juris Doctor/Master of Arts–Sports Sciences Dual-degree Program	98	4 yrs, full-time only
JD/MA–Juris Doctor/Master of Arts–History Dual-degree Program	96	4 yrs, full-time only
JD/MA–Juris Doctor/Master of Arts–Mass Communication Dual-degree Program	100	4 yrs, full-time only
JD/MA–Juris Doctor/Master of Arts–Real Estate Finance Dual-degree Program	96	4 yrs, full-time only
JD/MA–Juris Doctor/Master of Arts–Sociology Dual-degree Program	102	4 yrs, full-time only
JD/MA–Juris Doctor/Master of Arts–Political Science Dual-degree Program	103	4 yrs, full-time only
JD/MA–Juris Doctor/Master of Arts–Latin American Studies Dual-degree Program	100	4 yrs, full-time only
Certificate–Dual-degree Program	102	4 yrs, full-time only
JD/MD–Juris Doctor/Doctor of Medicine–Dual-degree Program		6 yrs, full-time only [day]
JD/MS–Juris Doctor/Master of Science–Environmental Engineering Dual-degree Program	96	4 yrs, full-time only
JD/MS–Juris Doctor/Master of Science–Forest Conservation Dual-degree Program	96	4 yrs, full-time only
JD/MS–Juris Doctor/Master of Science–Medical Science Dual-degree Program	102	4 yrs, full-time only
JD/MURP–Juris Doctor/Masters of Urban and Regional Planning–Dual-degree Program	108	4 yrs, full-time only
JD/PhD–Juris Doctor/Doctor of Philosophy–Anthropology Dual-degree Program	154	5–6 yrs, full-time only [day]
JD/PhD–Juris Doctor/Doctor of Philosophy–Educational Leadership Dual-degree Program	154	5–6 yrs, full-time only
JD/PhD–Juris Doctor/Doctor of Philosophy–History Dual-degree Program	154	5–6 yrs, full-time only
JD/PhD–Juris Doctor/Doctor of Philosophy–Forest Conservation Dual-degree Program	148	5–6 yrs, full-time only
JD/PhD–Juris Doctor/Doctor of Philosophy–Psychology Dual-degree Program	154	5–6 yrs, full-time only
JD/PhD–Juris Doctor/Doctor of Philosophy–Political Science Dual-degree Program	154	5–6 yrs, full-time only
JD/PhD–Juris Doctor/Doctor of Philosophy–Mass Communication Dual-degree Program	153	5–6 yrs, full-time only
LLM–Master of Laws–Taxation	26	1 yr, full-time or part-time [day, summer]
LLM–Master of Laws–Comparative Law	30	1 yr, full-time only [day, summer]
SJD–Doctor of Juridical Science–Taxation	30	1.5 yrs, full-time only [day, summer]

Administrator, PO Box 117620, Gainesville, FL 32611. Phone: 352-392-0421. Fax: 352-392-3800. E-mail: trish-varnes@sfa.ufl.edu

Law School Library Legal Information Center has 26 professional staff members and contains more than 585,930 volumes and 7,838 periodicals. 697 seats are available in the library. When classes are in session, the library is open 100 hours per week.

WESTLAW and LEXIS-NEXIS are available, as are the World Wide Web, online bibliographic services, and

CD-ROM players. 71 computer workstations are available to students in the library. Special law collections include British Commonwealth, Slavery.

First-Year Program Class size in the average section is 100; 100% of the first-year courses are taught by full-time faculty.

Upper-Level Program Class size in the average section is 75. Among the electives are:

  Administrative Law
★ Advocacy
  Business and Corporate Law
  Civil Litigation
  Criminal Defense
★ Criminal Procedure
  Criminal Prosecution
  Entertainment Law
★ Environmental Law
★ Family Law
★ Family Practice
  Government/Regulation
  Health Care/Human Services
  Immigration
★ Intellectual Property
★ International/Comparative Law
  Jurisprudence
★ Juvenile Law
  Labor Law
  Land Use Law/Natural Resources
  Lawyering Skills
  Legal Writing
★ Litigation
  Maritime Law
  Media Law
★ Mediation
  Probate Law
  Public Interest
  Race and Race Relations
  Securities
  Tax Law

(★ *indicates an area of special strength*)

Clinical Courses Students receive degree credit for clinical courses. (Clinical practicum is not required.) Among the clinical areas offered are:

  Advocacy
  Agricultural Law
  Civil Litigation
  Criminal Defense
  Criminal Prosecution
  Family Practice
  Juvenile Law
  Mediation

International exchange programs permit students to visit Costa Rica, France, Germany, Netherlands, and South Africa.

UNIVERSITY OF MIAMI
SCHOOL OF LAW

Coral Gables, Florida

INFORMATION CONTACT

Therese Lambert, Director of Student Recruiting
PO Box 248087
Coral Gables, FL 33124-8087

Phone: 305-284-6746   Fax: 305-284-3084
Web site: http://www.law.miami.edu/

LAW STUDENT PROFILE [2000–2001]

FULL-TIME Enrollment: 946
Women: 46%   Men: 54%

PART-TIME Enrollment: 133
Women: 49%   Men: 51%

RACIAL or ETHNIC COMPOSITION
African American, 7%; Asian/Pacific Islander, 3%; Hispanic,
20%; Native American, 1%; International, 6%

APPLICANTS and ADMITTEES
Number applied: 2,712
Admitted: 1,502
Percentage accepted: 55%
Seats available: 391
Average LSAT score: 153
Average GPA: 3.3

University of Miami School of Law is a private institution that organizes classes on a semester calendar system. The campus is situated in a suburban setting. Founded in 1926, first ABA approved in 1941, and an AALS member, University of Miami School of Law offers JD, JD/MBA, JD/MPH, JD/MS, and LL M degrees.

Faculty consists of 51 full-time and 102 part-time members in 2000–2001. 15 full-time faculty members and 24 part-time faculty members are women. 100% of all faculty members have a JD; 10.8% have advanced law degrees. Of all faculty members, 5.7% are African American, 7% are Hispanic, 87.3% are white.

Application Information *Required:* LSAT, LSDAS, application form, application fee of $50, baccalaureate degree, 2 letters of recommendation. *Recommended:* personal statement, resume. *Application deadline* for fall term is March 9 (priority date). Applications are processed on a rolling basis.

Costs The 2000–2001 tuition was $23,760 full-time; $1037 per credit part-time. Fees: $408 per term full-time; $50 per term part-time.

Financial Aid In 2000–2001, 87% of all students received some form of financial aid. 14 research assistantships, totaling $12,050 were awarded. Loans, loan repayment assistance program (LRAP), merit-based grants/scholarships, need-based grants/scholarships, and federal work-study loans are also available. The average student debt at graduation is $71,707. To apply for financial assistance, students must complete the Free Application for Federal Student Aid, scholarship specific applications.

AT a GLANCE

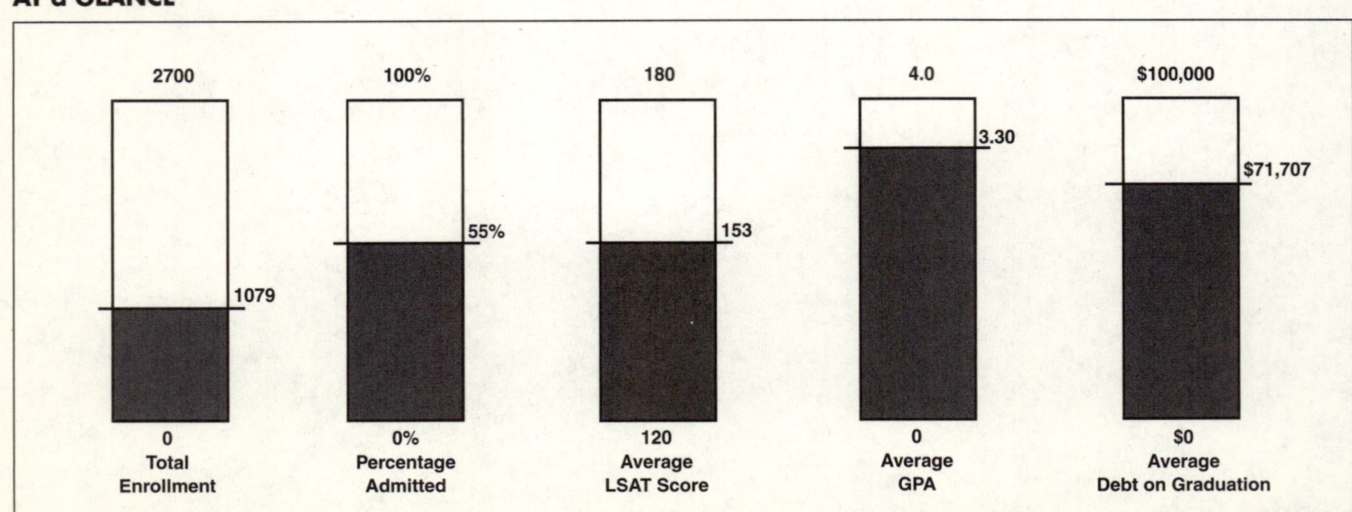

Degree Options

Degree	Total Credits Required	Length of Program
JD–Doctor of Laws	88	3–4 yrs, full-time or part-time [day, evening, summer]
JD/MBA–Juris Doctor/Master of Business Administration–Joint-degree Program	112	3.5–4 yrs, full-time or part-time [day, evening, summer]
JD/MPH–Juris Doctor/Master of Public Health–Joint-degree Program	115	4 yrs, full-time or part-time [day, evening, summer]
JD/MS–Juris Doctor/Master of Science–Joint-degree Program Marine Science	106	3.5–4 yrs, full-time or part-time [day, evening, summer]
LL M–Master of Laws		1–2 yrs, full-time or part-time [day, evening]

Completed financial aid forms should be received by March 1. Financial aid contact: Felicita Colon, Director, Law School Financial Aid, PO Box 248087, Coral Gables, FL 33124. Phone: 305-284-3115. Fax: 305-284-5868. E-mail: fcolon@law.miami.edu

Law School Library University of Miami Law Library has 12 professional staff members and contains more than 533,178 volumes and 6,923 periodicals. 704 seats are available in the library. When classes are in session, the library is open 111 hours per week.

WESTLAW and LEXIS-NEXIS are available, as are the World Wide Web and online bibliographic services. 79 computer workstations are available to students in the library. Special law collections include foreign law, taxation, estate planning, labor law, ocean law, environmental law, Latin American/Caribbean Law, Everglades Collection.

First-Year Program Class size in the average section is 100; 100% of the first-year courses are taught by full-time faculty.

Upper-Level Program Class size in the average section is 55. Among the electives are:

- Administrative Law
- ★ Advocacy
- ★ Business and Corporate Law
- Civil Litigation
- Criminal Defense
- Criminal Prosecution
- Entertainment Law
- Environmental Law
- Family Law
- Health Care/Human Services
- Immigration
- Intellectual Property
- ★ International/Comparative Law
- Jurisprudence
- Labor Law
- Land Use Law/Natural Resources
- ★ Lawyering Skills
- Legal History/Philosophy
- ★ Litigation
- ★ Maritime Law
- Media Law
- Mediation
- Probate Law
- Public Interest
- Securities
- ★ Tax Law

(★ indicates an area of special strength)

Clinical Courses Students receive degree credit for clinical courses. (Clinical practicum is not required.) Among the clinical areas offered are:

- Administrative Law
- Advocacy
- Civil Litigation
- Civil Rights
- Corporate Law
- Criminal Defense
- Criminal Prosecution
- Elderly Advocacy
- Environmental Law
- Family Law
- Family Practice
- General Practice
- Government Litigation
- Health Care/Human Services
- Immigration
- Juvenile Law
- Labor Law
- Land Use Law/Natural Resources
- Lawyering Skills
- Litigation
- Mediation
- Public Interest
- Securities
- Tax Law

EMORY UNIVERSITY
SCHOOL OF LAW

Atlanta, Georgia

INFORMATION CONTACT

Lynell A. Cadray, Assistant Dean for Admissions
Gambrell Hall
1301 Clifton Road
Atlanta, GA 30322-2770

Phone: 404-727-6802   Fax: 404-727-2477
Web site: http://www.emory.edu/

LAW STUDENT PROFILE [2000–2001]

FULL-TIME Enrollment: 649
Women: 53%   Men: 47%

RACIAL or ETHNIC COMPOSITION
African American, 7%; Asian/Pacific Islander, 7%; Hispanic, 3%; Native American, 0.3%; International, 3%

APPLICANTS and ADMITTEES
Number applied: 2,616
Admitted: 1,063
Percentage accepted: 41%
Seats available: 205
Average LSAT score: 159
Average GPA: 3.4

Emory University School of Law is a private institution that organizes classes on a semester calendar system. The campus is situated in a suburban setting. Founded in 1916, first ABA approved in 1923, and an AALS member, Emory University School of Law offers JD, JD/MBA, JD/MDiv, JD/MPH, JD/MTS, and LLM degrees.

Faculty consists of 46 full-time and 62 part-time members in 2000–2001. 12 full-time faculty members and 18 part-time faculty members are women. 100% of all faculty members have a JD; 34% have advanced law degrees. Of all faculty members, 8% are African American, 92% are white.

Application Information *Required:* LSAT, LSDAS, application form, application fee of $50, baccalaureate degree, 2 letters of recommendation, personal statement, college transcripts. *Recommended:* resume. *Application deadline* for fall term is March 1. Applications are processed on a rolling basis.

Costs The 2000–2001 tuition was $25,064 full-time. Fees: $232 full-time; $116 per semester full-time.

Financial Aid In 2000–2001, 93% of all students received some form of financial aid. 12 fellowships, totaling $3000; 78 research assistantships, totaling $530; 12 teaching assistantships, were awarded. Fellowships, loans, merit-based grants/scholarships, need-based grants/scholarships, and federal work-study loans are also available. The average student debt at graduation is $65,000. To apply for financial assistance, students must complete the Free Application for Federal Student Aid,

AT a GLANCE

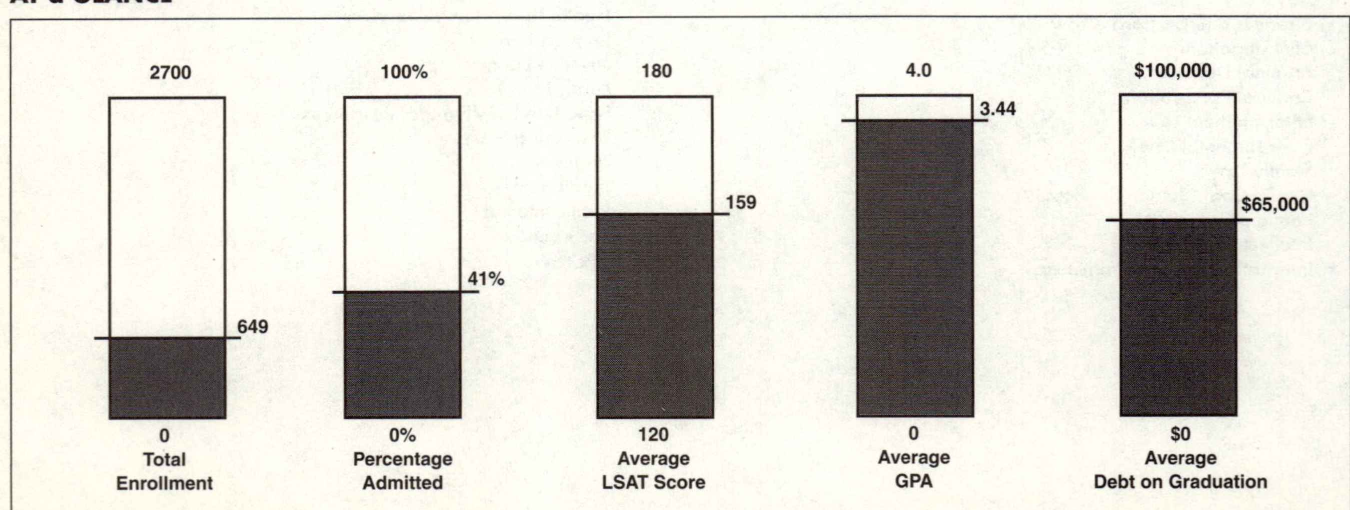

Degree Options

Degree	Total Credits Required	Length of Program
JD–Doctor of Laws	90	3–4 yrs, full-time only [day]
JD/MBA–Juris Doctor/Master of Business Administration–Joint-degree	129	4–8 yrs, full-time only [day]
JD/MDiv–Juris Doctor/Master of Divinity–Joint-degree	149	5 yrs, full-time only [day]
JD/MPH–Juris Doctor/Master of Public Health–Joint-degree	111	3.5 yrs, full-time only [day]
JD/MTS–Juris Doctor/Master of Theological Studies–Joint-degree	118	4 yrs, full-time only [day]
LLM–Master of Laws	24	1 yr, full-time only [day]

institutional forms, scholarship specific applications. Completed financial aid forms should be received by March 1. Financial aid contact: Lynell Cadray, Assistant Dean for Admission, 1301 Clifton Road, Atlanta, GA 30322-2770. Phone: 404-727-6802. Fax: 404-727-2477. E-mail: lcadray@law.emory.edu

Law School Library Hugh F. MacMillan Law Library has 9 professional staff members and contains more than 357,788 volumes and 5,509 periodicals. 489 seats are available in the library. When classes are in session, the library is open 114 hours per week.

WESTLAW and LEXIS-NEXIS are available, as are the World Wide Web, online bibliographic services, and CD-ROM players. 48 computer workstations are available to students in the library. Special law collections include European Union Depository.

First-Year Program Class size in the average section is 75; 100% of the first-year courses are taught by full-time faculty.

Upper-Level Program Class size in the average section is 30. Among the electives are:

Administrative Law
★ Advocacy
★ Business and Corporate Law
★ Capital Punishment
Civil Litigation
Civil Rights
★ Corporate Law
Criminal Defense
Criminal Prosecution
Entertainment Law
★ Environmental Law
Family Law
Government/Regulation
Health Care/Human Services
Health Law
Immigration
Intellectual Property
★ International/Comparative Law
Jurisprudence
Juvenile Law
Labor Law
Land Use Law/Natural Resources
Lawyering Skills
Legal History/Philosophy
★ Litigation
Maritime Law
Mediation
Probate Law
★ Public Interest
Securities
Tax Law

(★ *indicates an area of special strength*)

Clinical Courses Students receive degree credit for clinical courses. (Clinical practicum is not required.) Among the clinical areas offered are:

Administrative Law
Business and Corporate Law
Capital Punishment
Civil Litigation
Civil Rights
Corporate Law
Criminal Defense
Criminal Prosecution
Entertainment Law
Environmental Law
Family Law
General Practice
Government Litigation
Government/Regulation
Health Law
Immigration
Intellectual Property
Juvenile Law
Labor Law
Land Use Law/Natural Resources
Lawyering Skills
Litigation
Mediation
Public Interest
Securities
Tax Law

International exchange programs permit students to visit Germany and Hungary.

GEORGIA STATE UNIVERSITY
COLLEGE OF LAW

Atlanta, Georgia

INFORMATION CONTACT

Dr. Cheryl Jackson, Director of Admissions
PO Box 4037
Atlanta, GA 30302-4037

Phone: 404-651-2048   Fax: 404-651-1244
E-mail: admissions@gsulaw.gsu.edu
Web site: http://law.gsu.edu/

LAW STUDENT PROFILE [2000–2001]

FULL-TIME   Enrollment: 415
Women: 53%   Men: 47%

PART-TIME   Enrollment: 188
Women: 51%   Men: 49%

APPLICANTS and ADMITTEES

Number applied: 1,847
Admitted: 503
Percentage accepted: 27%
Seats available: 200
Average LSAT score: 156
Average GPA: 3.2

Georgia State University College of Law is a public institution that organizes classes on a semester calendar system. The campus is situated in an urban setting. Founded in 1982, first ABA approved in 1984, and an AALS member, Georgia State University College of Law offers JD, JD/MA, JD/MBA, and JD/MPA degrees.

Faculty consists of 42 full-time and 28 part-time members in 2000–2001. 18 full-time faculty members and 8 part-time faculty members are women. 100% of all faculty members have a JD; 14% have advanced law degrees. Of all faculty members, 1% are Native American, 1% are Asian/Pacific Islander, 16% are African American, 82% are white.

Application Information *Required:* LSAT, LSDAS, application form, application fee of $30, baccalaureate degree, 2 letters of recommendation, personal statement, college transcripts. *Application deadline* for fall term is March 15. Applications are processed on a rolling basis.

Costs The 2000–2001 tuition was $3520 full-time for area residents; $147 per hour part-time for area residents. Tuition was $14,080 full-time for nonresidents; $587 per hour part-time for nonresidents. Fees: $360 per semester full-time; $360 per semester part-time. Tuition and fees vary according to course load and degree level.

Financial Aid In 2000–2001, 61% of all students received some form of financial aid. 96 research assistantships, totaling $1000 were awarded. Graduate assistantships, loans, merit-based grants/scholarships, need-based grants/scholarships, and federal work-study loans are also available. The average student debt at graduation is

AT a GLANCE

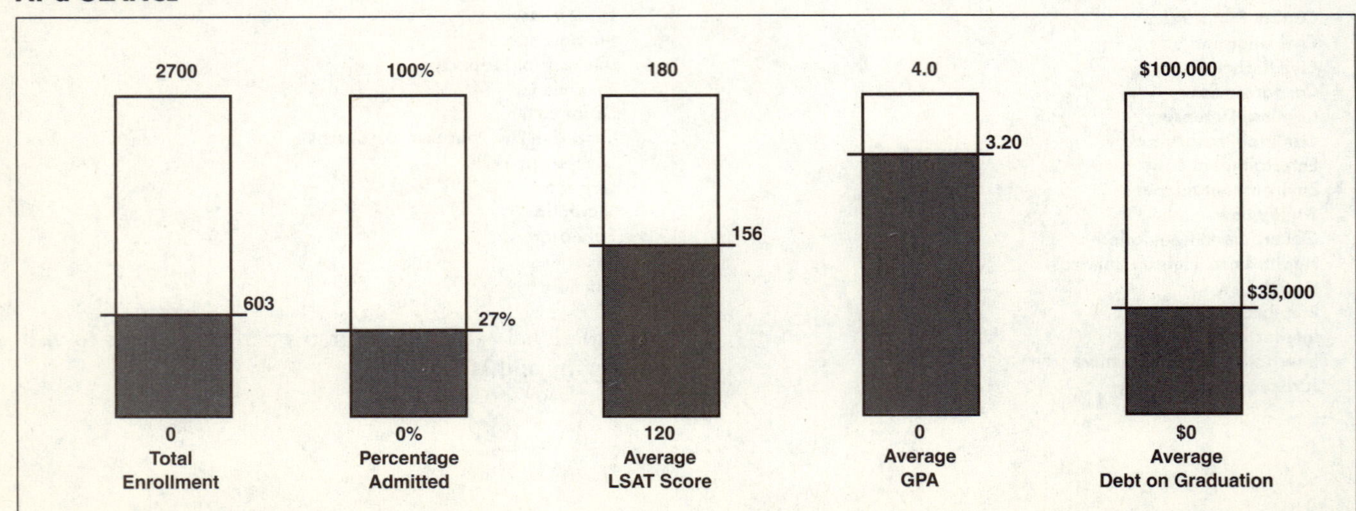

Degree Options

Degree	Total Credits Required	Length of Program
JD–Doctor of Laws	90	3–4.5 yrs, full-time or part-time [day, evening, summer]
JD/MA–Juris Doctor/Master of Arts–Philosophy Dual-degree Program		4–6 yrs, full-time or part-time [day, evening, summer]
JD/MBA–Juris Doctor/Master of Business Administration–Dual-degree Program		4–6 yrs, full-time or part-time [day, evening, summer]
JD/MPA–Juris Doctor/Master of Professional Accountancy–Dual-degree Program		4–6 yrs, full-time or part-time [day, evening, summer]

$35,000. To apply for financial assistance, students must complete the Free Application for Federal Student Aid. Completed financial aid forms should be received by April 1. Financial aid contact: Benita Mathews, Financial Aid Counselor, PO Box 4040, Atlanta, GA 30302-4040. Phone: 404-651-2675. Fax: 404-651-3418. E-mail: fiabms@langate.gsu.edu

Law School Library Georgia State University College of Law Library has 7 professional staff members and contains more than 145,000 volumes and 3,548 periodicals. 335 seats are available in the library. When classes are in session, the library is open 105 hours per week.

WESTLAW and LEXIS-NEXIS are available, as are the World Wide Web, online bibliographic services, and CD-ROM players. 30 computer workstations are available to students in the library. Special law collections include tax law, labor law, health law, and international law.

First-Year Program Class size in the average section is 65; 100% of the first-year courses are taught by full-time faculty.

Upper-Level Program Class size in the average section is 30. Among the electives are:

Administrative Law
Advocacy
Business and Corporate Law
Civil Rights
Consumer Law
★ Criminal Defense
★ Criminal Prosecution
★ Dispute Resolution
Education Law
Elderly Advocacy
Entertainment Law
Environmental Law
Family Law
Family Practice
Government/Regulation

Health Care/Human Services
Health Law
Immigration
Intellectual Property
International/Comparative Law
★ Judicial Clerkship
Jurisprudence
Juvenile Law
Labor Law
Land Rights/Natural Resource
Land Use Law/Natural Resources
★ Lawyering Skills
Legal History/Philosophy
★ Litigation
Maritime Law
Media Law
★ Mediation
Probate Law
Public Interest
Securities
★ Tax Law
(★ *indicates an area of special strength*)

Clinical Courses Students receive degree credit for clinical courses. (Clinical practicum is not required.) Among the clinical areas offered are:

Civil Rights
Criminal Defense
Criminal Prosecution
Dispute Resolution
Elderly Advocacy
Environmental Law
Family Practice
Government/Regulation
Health Law
Immigration
Judicial Clerkship
Juvenile Law
Labor Law
Land Rights/Natural Resource
Mediation
Tax Law

International exchange programs permit students to visit Austria.

MERCER UNIVERSITY
WALTER F. GEORGE SCHOOL OF LAW

Macon, Georgia

INFORMATION CONTACT

Elaine Deaton, Admissions Assistant
1021 Georgia Avenue
Macon, GA 31207

Phone: 478-301-2605   Fax: 478-301-2989
E-mail: deaton_ed@mercer.edu
Web site: http://www.law.mercer.edu/

LAW STUDENT PROFILE [2000–2001]

FULL-TIME   Enrollment: 429
Women: 49%   Men: 51%

PART-TIME   Enrollment: 1
Men: 100%

RACIAL or ETHNIC COMPOSITION
African American, 9%; Asian/Pacific Islander, 4%; Hispanic,
1%; Native American, 0.2%

APPLICANTS and ADMITTEES
Number applied: 896
Admitted: 439
Percentage accepted: 49%
Seats available: 173
Average LSAT score: 153
Average GPA: 3.1

Mercer University Walter F. George School of Law is a
private institution that organizes classes on a semester
calendar system. The campus is situated in a suburban
setting. Founded in 1873, first ABA approved in 1925,
and an AALS member, Mercer University Walter F.
George School of Law offers JD and JD/MBA degrees.

Faculty consists of 29 full-time and 25 part-time
members in 2000–2001. 7 full-time faculty members and
8 part-time faculty members are women. 100% of all
faculty members have a JD; 13% have advanced law
degrees. Of all faculty members, 7.4% are African
American, 92.6% are white.

Application Information *Required:* LSAT, LSDAS,
application form, application fee of $45, baccalaureate
degree, 2 letters of recommendation, personal statement,
college transcripts. *Recommended:* essay, writing sample,
resume. *Application deadline* for fall term is March 15
(priority date). Applications are processed on a rolling
basis.

Financial Aid In 2000–2001, 81% of all students received
some form of financial aid. 1 fellowship, totaling $4000;
45 research assistantships, totaling $1100, were awarded.
Fellowships, loans, merit-based grants/scholarships, and
federal work-study loans are also available. The average
student debt at graduation is $70,410. To apply for
financial assistance, students must complete the Free
Application for Federal Student Aid, institutional forms.
Completed financial aid forms should be received by
April 1. Financial aid contact: Leigh Love, Director of

AT a GLANCE

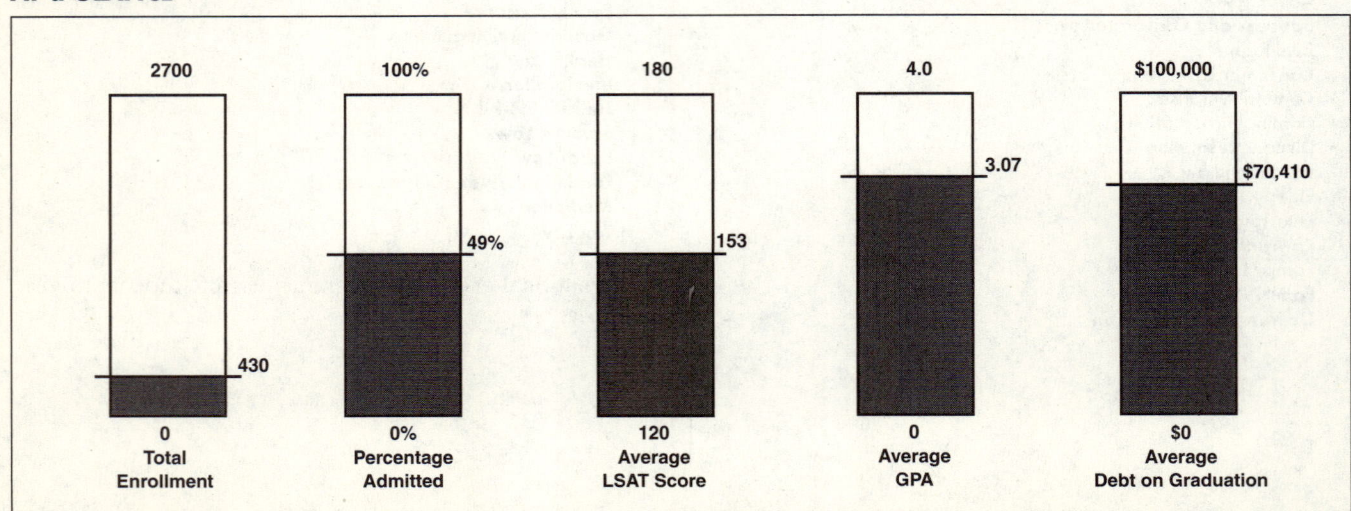

Degree Options

Degree	Total Credits Required	Length of Program
JD–Doctor of Laws	91	3 yrs, full-time only [day]
JD/MBA–Juris Doctor/Master of Business Administration–Dual-degree Program	112	4–7 yrs, full-time only [day]

Financial Aid/Assistant Director of Admissions, 1021 Georgia Avenue, Macon, GA 31207. Phone: 478-301-2064. Fax: 478-301-2989. E-mail: love_sl@mercer.edu

Law School Library Furman Smith Law Library has 7 professional staff members and contains more than 298,039 volumes and 3,200 periodicals. 272 seats are available in the library. When classes are in session, the library is open 70 hours per week.

WESTLAW and LEXIS-NEXIS are available, as are the World Wide Web, online bibliographic services, and CD-ROM players. 78 computer workstations are available to students in the library. Special law collections include law school archives and Griffin Bell Papers.

First-Year Program Class size in the average section is 40; 100% of the first-year courses are taught by full-time faculty.

Upper-Level Program Class size in the average section is 27. Among the electives are:

Administrative Law

Advocacy
Business and Corporate Law
Consumer Law
Entertainment Law
Environmental Law
Family Law
Government/Regulation
Health Care/Human Services
Intellectual Property
International/Comparative Law
Jurisprudence
Labor Law
Land Use Law/Natural Resources
Lawyering Skills
Legal History/Philosophy
Litigation
Media Law
Mediation
Probate Law
Public Interest
Securities
Tax Law

UNIVERSITY OF GEORGIA
SCHOOL OF LAW

Athens, Georgia

LAW STUDENT PROFILE [2000–2001]

APPLICANTS AND ADMITTEES
Seats available: 200
Average LSAT score: 162
Average GPA: 3.6

University of Georgia School of Law is a public institution that organizes classes on a semester calendar system. The campus is situated in a small-town setting. Founded in 1859, first ABA approved in 1930, and an AALS member, University of Georgia School of Law offers JD, JD/MBA, JD/MED, JD/MPA, and LLM degrees.

Faculty 100% of all faculty members have a JD; 26% have advanced law degrees. Of all faculty members, 4% are Asian/Pacific Islander, 4% are African American, 92% are white.

Application Information *Required:* LSAT, LSDAS, application form, application fee of $30, baccalaureate degree, 2 letters of recommendation, essay, personal statement. *Application deadline* for fall term is July 1 (priority date); for spring term is November 15.

Costs The 2000–2001 tuition was $5072 full-time for state residents. Tuition was $17,858 full-time for nonresidents.

Financial Aid Loans, loan repayment assistance program (LRAP), merit-based grants/scholarships, need-based grants/scholarships, and federal work-study loans are available. The average student debt at graduation is $38,000. To apply for financial assistance, students must complete the Free Application for Federal Student Aid, institutional forms. Completed financial aid forms should be received by January 31. Financial aid contact: University of Georgia, Office of Financial Aid, Academic Building, Athens, GA 30602-6114. Phone: 706-542-6147. Fax: 706-542-5556.

AT a GLANCE

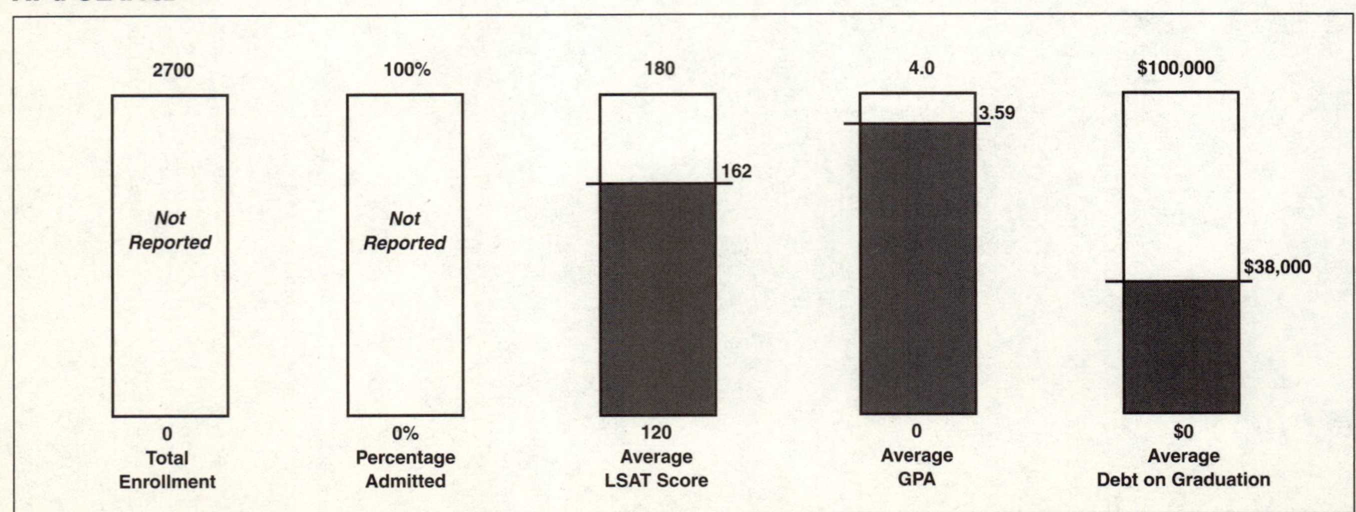

Degree Options

Degree	Total Credits Required	Length of Program
JD–Juris Doctor	88	3 yrs, full-time only [day]
JD/MBA–Juris Doctor/Master of Business Administration–JD/MBA Joint degree program	118	4 yrs, full-time only [day]
JD/MED–Juris Doctor/Master of Education–JD/MED in Sports Studies joint degree program	106	4 yrs, full-time only [day, summer]
JD/MPA–Juris Doctor/Master of Professional Accountancy–JD/MBA Joint degree program	104	4 yrs, full-time only [day, summer]
LLM–Master of Laws	27	1 yr, full-time only [day]

Law School Library Alexander Campbell King Law Library has 10 professional staff members and contains more than 481,110 volumes and 7,097 periodicals. 409 seats are available in the library. When classes are in session, the library is open 115 hours per week.

WESTLAW and LEXIS-NEXIS are available, as is the World Wide Web. 47 computer workstations are available to students in the library. Special law collections include Specialized European Documents, United Nations Documents.

First-Year Program Class size in the average section is 68; 100% of the first-year courses are taught by full-time faculty.

Upper-Level Program Class size in the average section is 27. Among the electives are:

Administrative Law
★ Advocacy
★ Banking and Finance
Bankruptcy
★ Business and Corporate Law
Constitutional Law
★ Criminal Defense
★ Criminal Procedure
Entertainment Law
Environmental Law
Family Law
★ General Practice
Government/Regulation
Health Care/Human Services
Immigration
★ Intellectual Property
★ International/Comparative Law
Jurisprudence
Labor Law
★ Land Use Law/Natural Resources

★ Lawyering Skills
Legal History/Philosophy
★ Litigation
Maritime Law
Mediation
Probate Law
Property/Real Estate
★ Public Interest
Securities
Sports Law
Tax Law
Trusts and Estates

(★ indicates an area of special strength)

Clinical Courses Students receive degree credit for clinical courses. (Clinical practicum is not required.) Among the clinical areas offered are:

Advocacy
Civil Litigation
Constitutional Law
Criminal Defense
Criminal Procedure
Criminal Prosecution
Elderly Advocacy
Environmental Law
Family Law
Family Practice
General Practice
Government/Regulation
Health Care/Human Services
Juvenile Law
Land Use Law/Natural Resources
Lawyering Skills
Litigation
Public Interest

International exchange programs permit students to visit Argentina, Belgium, France, Germany, and United Kingdom.

UNIVERSITY OF HAWAII AT MANOA
WILLIAM S. RICHARDSON SCHOOL OF LAW

Honolulu, Hawaii

INFORMATION CONTACT

Laurie A. Tochiki, Assistant Dean
2515 Dole Street
Honolulu, HI 96822

Phone: 808-956-7966   Fax: 808-956-3813
E-mail: lawadm@hawaii.edu
Web site: http://www.hawaii.edu/law

LAW STUDENT PROFILE [2000–2001]

FULL-TIME   Enrollment: 229
Women: 55%   Men: 45%

RACIAL or ETHNIC COMPOSITION
African American, 2%; Asian/Pacific Islander, 62%; Hispanic, 3%; Native American, 2%; International, 2%

APPLICANTS and ADMITTEES
Number applied: 594
Admitted: 189
Percentage accepted: 32%
Seats available: 75
Average LSAT score: 156
Average GPA: 3.3

University of Hawaii at Manoa William S. Richardson School of Law is a public institution that organizes classes on a semester calendar system. The campus is situated in an urban setting. Founded in 1973, first ABA approved in 1974, and an AALS member, University of Hawaii at Manoa William S. Richardson School of Law offers JD, JD/Certificate, JD/MA, JD/MBA, and JD/MURP degrees.

Faculty consists of 18 full-time and 15 part-time members in 2000–2001. 9 full-time faculty members and 6 part-time faculty members are women. 100% of all faculty members have a JD; 44% have advanced law degrees. Of all faculty members, 32% are Asian/Pacific Islander, 5% are African American, 63% are white.

Application Information *Required:* LSAT, LSDAS, application fee of $45, baccalaureate degree, 2 letters of recommendation, application form, college transcripts, personal statement. *Application deadline* for fall term is March 1.

Costs The 2000–2001 tuition was $9624 full-time for state residents. Tuition was $16,344 full-time for nonresidents. Fees: $59 per semester full-time. Students are required to have their own computers.

Financial Aid In 2000–2001, 59% of all students received some form of financial aid. 20 research assistantships, totaling $2500 were awarded. Fellowships, graduate assistantships, loans, merit-based grants/scholarships, need-based grants/scholarships, and federal work-study loans are also available. The average student debt at graduation is $41,265. To apply for financial assistance,

AT a GLANCE

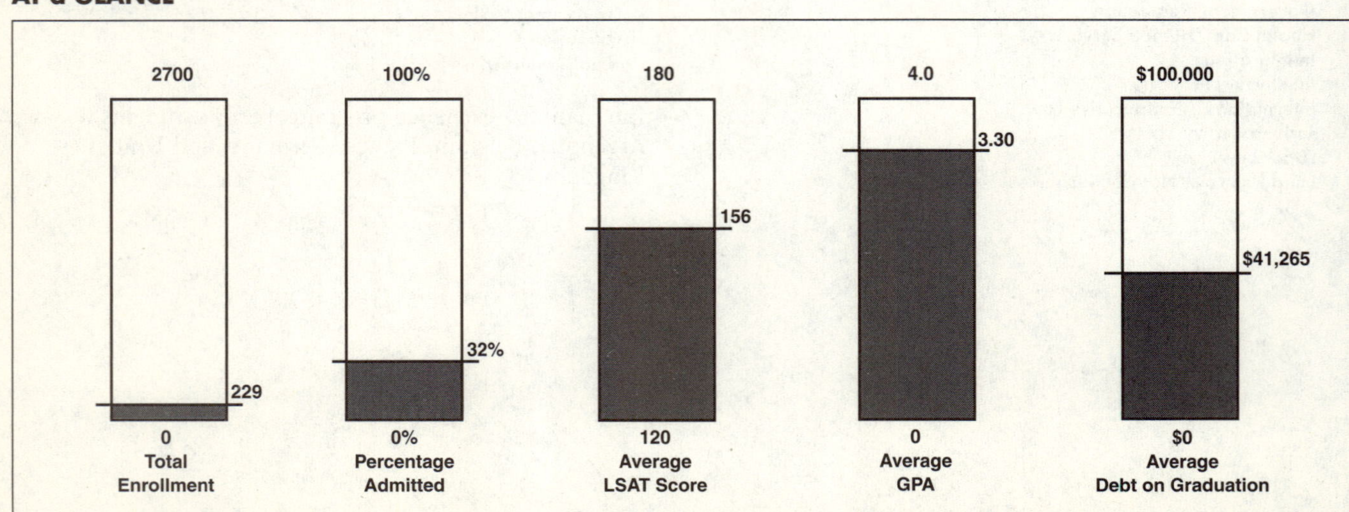

Degree Options

Degree	Total Credits Required	Length of Program
JD–Juris Doctor	89	3 yrs, full-time only [day]
JD/Certificate–Juris Doctor/Certificate–Pacific Assignment Legal Studies	89	3 yrs, full-time only [day]
JD/Certificate–Juris Doctor/Certificate–Environmental Law program	89	3 yrs, full-time only [day]
JD/MA–Juris Doctor/Master of Arts–Asian Studies Joint-degree Program		4 yrs, full-time only [day]
JD/MBA–Juris Doctor/Master of Business Administration–Joint-degree Program	110	4 yrs, full-time only [day]
JD/MURP–Juris Doctor/Masters of Urban and Regional Planning–Joint-degree Program		4 yrs, full-time only [day]

students must complete the Free Application for Federal Student Aid, institutional forms. Completed financial aid forms should be received by March 1. Financial aid contact: Gail Koki, Director of Financial Aid Services, University of Hawaii at Manoa, Student Services Center, Room 112, Honolulu, HI 96822. Phone: 808-956-7251. Fax: 808-956-3985. E-mail: gkoki@kala.ssc.hawaii.edu

Law School Library William S. Richardson School of Law Library has 5 professional staff members and contains more than 283,632 volumes and 3,332 periodicals. 387 seats are available in the library. When classes are in session, the library is open 86 hours per week.

WESTLAW and LEXIS-NEXIS are available, as are the World Wide Web, online bibliographic services, and CD-ROM players. 20 computer workstations are available to students in the library.

First-Year Program Class size in the average section is 75; 90% of the first-year courses are taught by full-time faculty.

Upper-Level Program Class size in the average section is 21. Among the electives are:

Accounting
Administrative Law
Alternative Dispute Resolution
Antitrust Law
Appellate Litigation
Asian Legal Systems
Bankruptcy
Business and Corporate Law
Chinese Law
Civil Law
Civil Rights
Conflict of Laws
Constitutional Law
Consumer Law
Criminal Law
Criminal Procedure
Criminal Prosecution
★ Elder Law
Elderly Advocacy
Employment Law
★ Environmental Law
Estate Planning
Evidence
Extern
Family Law
Health Care/Human Services
Health Law
Immigration
Insurance Law
Intellectual Property
International Environmental Law
International Law
International/Comparative Law
Japanese Law
Jurisprudence
Labor and Employment
Labor Law
Land Use Law/Natural Resources
Lawyering Skills
Legal History/Philosophy
Litigation
Maritime Law
Mediation
Native Hawaiian Rights
Negotiation
★ Pacific/Asian Legal Studies
Pretrial Litigation
Probate Law
Professional Responsibility
Property/Real Estate
Race and Law
Tax Law
Wildlife Law

(★ *indicates an area of special strength*)

Clinical Courses Students receive degree credit for clinical courses. (Clinical practicum is required.) Among the clinical areas offered are:

Criminal Defense
Criminal Prosecution
Elderly Advocacy
Estate Planning
Extern
Family Law
Immigration
Mediation
Native Hawaiian Rights
Wildlife Law

UNIVERSITY OF IDAHO
COLLEGE OF LAW

Moscow, Idaho

INFORMATION CONTACT

Director of Admissions
6th and Rayburn
PO Box 442321
Moscow, ID 83844-2321

Phone: 208-885-6422   Fax: 208-885-5709
Web site: http://www.uidaho.edu/law/

LAW STUDENT PROFILE [2000–2001]

FULL-TIME   Enrollment: 275
Women: 33%   Men: 67%

PART-TIME   Enrollment: 11
Women: 9%   Men: 91%

RACIAL or ETHNIC COMPOSITION
African American, 1%; Asian/Pacific Islander, 2%; Hispanic, 2%; Native American, 1%

APPLICANTS and ADMITTEES
Number applied: 529
Admitted: 294
Percentage accepted: 56%
Seats available: 112
Average LSAT score: 152
Average GPA: 3.2

University of Idaho College of Law is a public institution that organizes classes on a semester calendar system. The campus is situated in a rural setting. Founded in 1909, first ABA approved in 1925, and an AALS member, University of Idaho College of Law offers JD, JD/MBA, and JD/MS degrees.

Faculty consists of 16 full-time and 1 part-time members in 2000–2001. 7 full-time faculty members are women. 100% of all faculty members have a JD; 6% have advanced law degrees. Of all faculty members, .7% are Native American, 1% are Asian/Pacific Islander, .3% are African American, 2% are Hispanic, 95% are white, 1% are international.

Application Information *Required:* LSAT, LSDAS, application form, application fee of $40, baccalaureate degree, college transcripts. *Recommended:* 3 letters of recommendation, personal statement, resume. *Application deadline* for fall term is February 1.

Financial Aid Loans, merit-based grants/scholarships, need-based grants/scholarships, and federal work-study loans are available. The average student debt at graduation is $38,770. To apply for financial assistance, students must complete the Free Application for Federal Student Aid. Completed financial aid forms should be received by February 15. Financial aid contact: Director of Admissions, PO Box 444291, Moscow, ID 83844-4291. Phone: 208-885-6312. Fax: 208-885-5592. E-mail: finaid@uidaho.edu

Law School Library University of Idaho Law Library has 4 professional staff members and contains more than

AT a GLANCE

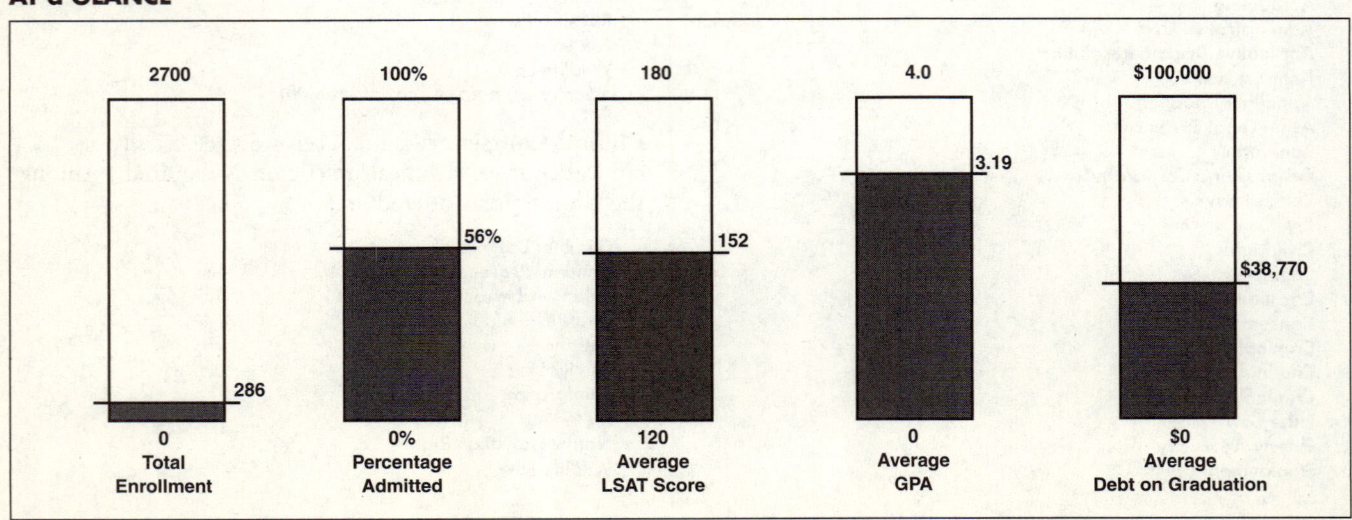

Degree Options

Degree	Total Credits Required	Length of Program
JD–Doctor of Laws	88	3–4 yrs, full-time only [day, summer]
JD/MBA–Juris Doctor/Master of Business Administration–Concurrent Degree Program	110	4–5 yrs, full-time only [day, summer]
JD/MS–Juris Doctor/Master of Science–Environmental Science Concurrent Degree Program		4–5 yrs, full-time only [day, summer]

184,051 volumes and 3,563 periodicals. 366 seats are available in the library. When classes are in session, the library is open 92 hours per week.

WESTLAW and LEXIS-NEXIS are available, as are the World Wide Web, online bibliographic services, and CD-ROM players. 28 computer workstations are available to students in the library. Special law collections include Idaho Supreme Court records and briefs.

First-Year Program Class size in the average section is 55; 100% of the first-year courses are taught by full-time faculty.

Upper-Level Program Among the electives are:

  Administrative Law
★ Advocacy
  Appellate Litigation
★ Business and Corporate Law
  Extern
  Family Law
  General Practice

  Government/Regulation
  International/Comparative Law
  Jurisprudence
  Labor Law
★ Lawyering Skills
  Legal History/Philosophy
  Litigation
  Native American Defense
  Probate Law
  Securities
  Tax Law
(★ indicates an area of special strength)

Clinical Courses Students receive degree credit for clinical courses. (Clinical practicum is not required.) Among the clinical areas offered are:

  Appellate Litigation
  Extern
  General Practice
  Native American Defense
  Tax Law

DEAN'S STATEMENT . . .

I invite you to consider the University of Idaho, where we provide a high-quality legal education in the beautiful inland Northwest. Our campus combines the collegial and intimate feeling of a dignified small college, encircled by natural splendor, with the technological and social advantages of a major state university. Our faculty members have been handpicked over many years to provide you with excellent instruction and mentoring. Our building is a comfortable, well-designed, fully networked facility with all the appropriate amenities, including computer labs, distance learning facilities, recreational space, and dining facilities. Our entering class usually numbers slightly more than 100, providing you with plenty of opportunities to get to know your teachers and your classmates. At Idaho, you will make friendships that will last for the rest of your life while earning an honored degree that has potent market impact.

The University of Idaho's low tuition and the relatively modest cost of living in Moscow mean that our graduates can begin their careers on a firm financial footing. This low tuition, combined with the quality of education and services we provide, makes the University of Idaho College of Law one of the best bargains in legal education in the United States.

For more than ninety years, Idaho has produced high-quality lawyers who have gone on to make a positive difference in the world they inhabit. Numbered among our thousands of graduates are leading lawyers, businesspeople, judges, and other public servants. Our curriculum is well balanced and offers you the opportunity to succeed in a variety of settings after graduation. I invite you to visit our campus, our university, and our community. The Admissions Office will be happy to assist you in scheduling a visit. I look forward to seeing you.

—John A. Miller, Dean

HISTORY, CAMPUS, AND LOCATION

The University of Idaho is located in the northern Idaho town of Moscow, a friendly walking and biking community of 20,000. Located approximately 80 miles from Spokane, Washington, Moscow is the heart of the Palouse, an area of rolling wheat-covered hills and forested mountains. The school's small size and informal atmosphere provide a supportive collegial environment for the study of law.

The University's location, only 8 miles from Washington State University in Pullman, offers numerous cultural, academic, employment, research, athletic, and social opportunities. A free bus service operates between the two universities, and a biking/walking path connects Moscow and Pullman. Recreational opportunities abound, and nearby rivers and mountains offer hiking, white-water rafting, skiing, mountain biking, snowboarding, hunting, and fishing adventures.

Established in 1909, the University of Idaho College of Law has been accredited by the American Bar Association since 1925. It is the only law school in Idaho and has more than 3,000 living alumni.

SPECIAL QUALITIES OF THE SCHOOL

While the University of Idaho College of Law has a strong basic curriculum, there is particular depth in the areas of environmental and natural resources law, business, and professional and litigation skills.

The vast wilderness areas of Idaho create a natural place to study environmental law. The business curriculum is varied, and the faculty has extensive commercial law experience gained in large national firms and through participation in state and national law reform projects. Extensive clinical offerings and externship opportunities allow students to gain practical experience through both actual and simulated trial practice and mediation opportunities.

To complement the broad range of curriculum topics, the Bellwood Lecture Series, funded by an endowment of more than $1 million, brings nationally known speakers on a variety of legal topics to the College each year.

TECHNOLOGY ON CAMPUS

The University of Idaho was listed as the thirteenth "most wired campus" in the country by *Wired* magazine. The College of Law is part of this success (the Law School was ranked twentieth) and continues to provide and enhance the audiovisual, computer, and other technological advances that impact the practice of law. The centerpiece is the College's own interactive video classroom that connects the College with the Idaho Law Center in Boise, Idaho and other locations in the state and region. The courtroom and all classrooms are networked, and the College is moving steadily toward its goal to provide 100 percent network access at all carrel locations. Computers are maintained and upgraded by an in-house technology team, and student labs provide assistants to answer both software- and hardware-related questions.

SCHOLARSHIPS AND LOANS

In addition to assistance that is available to qualified students in the form of grants, loans, and work-study, the College of Law awards a number of scholarships to incoming students. Recipients are selected on the basis of academic ability, need, and professional promise. Highly qualified applicants are eligible for scholarships equal to the entire cost of tuition.

STUDENT ACTIVITIES AND OPPORTUNITIES

Law Review Published three times a year, the *Idaho Law Review* provides scholarly discussion of timely legal issues. The *Idaho Law Review* also sponsors annual symposia to bring regional and national experts together to address topics of current interest.

Moot Court From the McNichols Competition, the College's intramural moot court competition which is held in a student's second year, a student Board of Advocates selects teams to participate in a number of national forensic competitions, including National Moot Court and National Trial Competition.

Extracurricular Activities More than twenty student organizations provide students with diverse opportunities to enhance personal interests and to participate in social and educational activities. Organizations include student divisions of the American Bar Association, the Idaho Trial Lawyer's Association, and the National Lawyers Guild Student Chapter. Several organizations are dedicated to particular types of law, such as environmental law, international law, public interest law, and sports law. There is also a student spouse organization to provide support and to enhance participation between students and their families.

Special Opportunities The College of Law operates four legal aid clinics: a General Clinic that represents clients in civil and criminal cases; an Appellate Clinic that represents clients before the Ninth Circuit Court of Appeals, the Idaho Supreme Court, and the Idaho Court of Appeals; a Native American Legal Clinic, where students function as public defenders for the Nez Perce tribe; and a Tax Clinic, which provides representation of clients in tax disputes.

Opportunities for Members of Minority Groups and WomenThe College of Law has a diverse faculty and student body. Minority and women students are involved in all aspects of the law school community. Students may also participate in the Women's Law Caucus and the Minority Law Students Association. In addition to a regular course on Indian Law, the College maintains a close relationship with the neighboring Nez Perce Indian Tribe, which includes the Native American Legal Clinic. As a result of its small size and location in a small community, students have extensive one-on-one contact with faculty members, including the opportunity to develop unique directed research and seminar opportunities to meet specialized student interests. In the last several years, students and faculty have worked together to offer seminars, including Feminist Jurisprudence; Race, Gender and Justice; and Practicing Law in the Public Interest.

Special Certificate Programs Two concurrent degree programs are offered. The University of Idaho College of Law and College of Graduate Studies/Environmental Science Program offer a concurrent degree program designed to allow students to obtain both a Juris Doctor (J.D.) from the College of Law, as well as a Master in Environmental Science from the College of Graduate Studies, in as few as eight semesters. The University of Idaho College of Law and the Washington State University College of Business and Economics collaboratively offer another concurrent degree program, which is designed to allow participating students to achieve a J.D. degree from the University of Idaho and the Master of Business Administration degree from Washington State University in as few as seven semesters. As concurrent programs, students are required to satisfy the degree requirements of each college separately to receive both degrees. Specific degree requirements for each program can be obtained by contacting each university separately.

BAR PASSAGE, CAREER SERVICES, AND PLACEMENT

Eighty-eight percent of Idaho graduates passed the Idaho state bar examination in 2000. In 1999, the Idaho passage rate was 82 percent.

Career Services arranges on-campus interviews and other appearances by employers and alumni. Students receive information to help define and focus their career goals and job searches. Employment position opportunities are compiled and posted for both permanent employment and contract work opportunities. The office maintains employer files and directories to assist students in networking with alumni and prospective employers.

Ninety-six percent of the 2000 graduates were employed within six months of graduation, or were pursuing an additional law degree.

Legal Field	Percentage of Graduates	Average Starting Salary
Academic	1.0%	n/a
Business	4.3%	$46,250
Government	19.5%	$44,574
Judicial Clerkship	23.0%	$35,385
Private Practice	48.4%	$45,669
Public Interest	3.2%	$42,260
Other	0.6%	n/a

CORRESPONDENCE AND INFORMATION

Admissions
College of Law
University of Idaho
P.O. Box 442321
Moscow, Idaho 83844-2321
Telephone: 208-885-6423
Fax: 208-885-7609
E-mail: lawadmit@uidaho.edu
World Wide Web: http://www.uidaho.edu/law/

DEPAUL UNIVERSITY
COLLEGE OF LAW

Chicago, Illinois

INFORMATION CONTACT

Dennis Shea, Director of Law Admissions
25 East Jackson Boulevard
Chicago, IL 60604-2287

Phone: 312-362-8013   Fax: 312-362-5280
E-mail: dshea@wppost.depaul.edu
Web site: http://www.law.depaul.edu/

LAW STUDENT PROFILE [2000–2001]

FULL-TIME   Enrollment: 785
Women: 54%   Men: 46%

PART-TIME   Enrollment: 323
Women: 50%   Men: 50%

RACIAL or ETHNIC COMPOSITION
African American, 6%; Asian/Pacific Islander, 6%; Hispanic, 8%; Native American, 0.3%

APPLICANTS and ADMITTEES
Number applied: 2,414
Admitted: 1,093
Percentage accepted: 45%
Seats available: 305
Average LSAT score: 153
Average GPA: 3.2

DePaul University College of Law is a private institution that organizes classes on a semester calendar system. The campus is situated in an urban setting. Founded in 1912, first ABA approved in 1925, and an AALS member, DePaul University College of Law offers JD, JD/MAIS, JD/MBA, and LLM degrees.

Faculty consists of 47 full-time and 90 part-time members in 2000–2001. 18 full-time faculty members and 30 part-time faculty members are women. 100% of all faculty members have a JD; 40% have advanced law degrees. Of all faculty members, 2% are Native American, 2% are Asian/Pacific Islander, 6% are African American, 4% are Hispanic, 86% are white.

Application Information *Required:* LSAT, LSDAS, application form, application fee of $40, baccalaureate degree, 1 recommendation, personal statement, essay, writing sample, college transcripts. *Recommended:* resume. *Application deadline* for fall term is April 1. Applications are processed on a rolling basis.

Costs The 1999–2000 tuition was $20,700 full-time; $725 per credit hour part-time. Fees: $30 full-time; $10 per term part-time. Full-time tuition and fees vary according to class time and program.

Financial Aid In 2000–2001, 79% of all students received some form of financial aid. 152 research assistantships, totaling $671 were awarded. Loans, merit-based grants/scholarships, need-based grants/scholarships, and federal work-study loans are also available. The average student debt at graduation is $60,996. To apply for financial assistance, students must complete the Free Application

AT a GLANCE

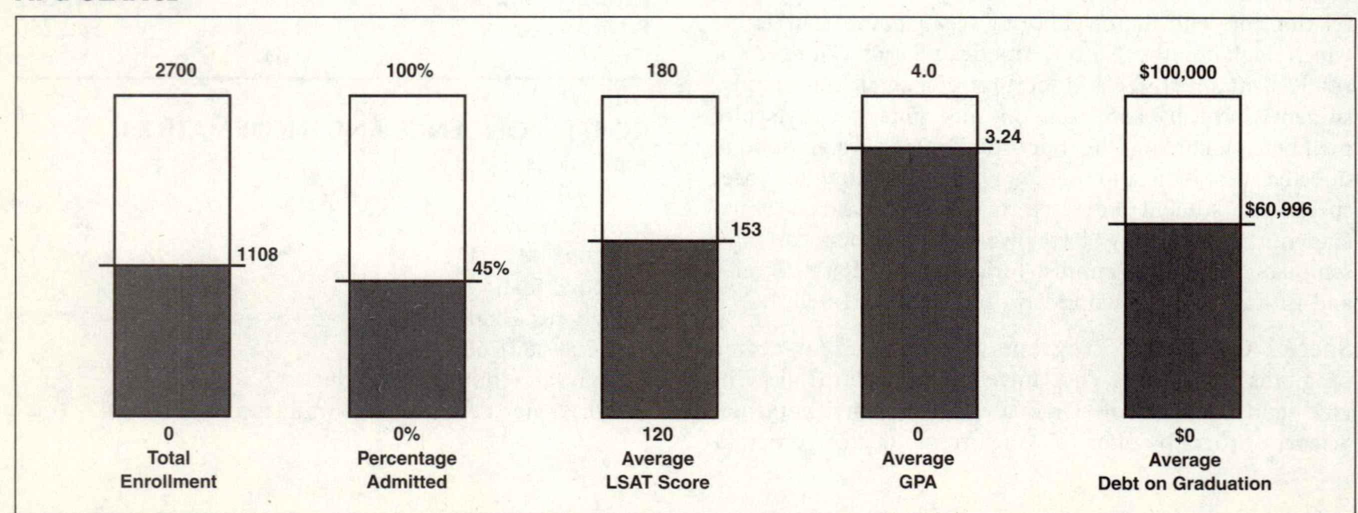

Degree Options

Degree	Total Credits Required	Length of Program
JD–Doctor of Laws	86	3–4 yrs, full-time or part-time [day, evening, summer]
JD/MAIS–Juris Doctor/Master of Arts in International Studies–Joint Program	120	4–5 yrs, full-time or part-time [day, evening, summer]
JD/MBA–Juris Doctor/Master of Business Administration–Joint Program	120	4–5 yrs, full-time or part-time [day, evening, summer]
JD/MBA–Juris Doctor/Master of Business Administration–Dual Degree program	110	4–5 yrs, full-time or part-time [day, evening, summer]
LLM–Master of Laws–Taxation	24	1–5 yrs, full-time or part-time [day, evening, summer]
LLM–Master of Laws–Health	24	1–5 yrs, full-time or part-time [day, evening, summer]

for Federal Student Aid, institutional forms, scholarship specific applications. Completed financial aid forms should be received by April 21. Financial aid contact: Claire Timm, Assistant Director of Financial Aid, 1 East Jackson Boulevard, Suite 9000, Chicago, IL 60604. Phone: 312-362-5024. Fax: 312-362-5748. E-mail: ctimm@wppost.depaul.edu

Law School Library DePaul University College of Law Vincent G. Rinn Law Library has 10 professional staff members and contains more than 346,098 volumes and 4,926 periodicals. 465 seats are available in the library. When classes are in session, the library is open 94 hours per week.

WESTLAW and LEXIS-NEXIS are available, as are the World Wide Web, online bibliographic services, and CD-ROM players. 48 computer workstations are available to students in the library. Special law collections include tax law, health law, international human rights law, church/state relations, constitutional law.

First-Year Program Class size in the average section is 83; 100% of the first-year courses are taught by full-time faculty.

Upper-Level Program Class size in the average section is 50. Among the electives are:

Administrative Law
★ Advocacy
AIDS and the Law
Alternative Dispute Resolution
Antitrust Law
Bankruptcy
Bioethics
★ Business and Corporate Law
Business Organizations
Capital Punishment
Children and the Law
Civil Litigation
Civil Procedure
Civil Rights
Commercial Law
Conflict of Laws

Consumer Law
Correctional Law
★ Criminal Procedure
Democratic Theory
Employment Discrimination
Employment Law
★ Entertainment Law
Environmental Law
Estate & Gift Taxation
European Union Law
Evidence
★ Family Law
Federal Courts
Federal Income Tax
First Amendment
Food & Drug Law
Government/Regulation
★ Health Care Law
★ Health Care/Human Services
★ Immigration
★ Intellectual Property
International Criminal Law
International Human Rights
★ International/Comparative Law
Jewish Law
Jurisprudence
Labor Law
Land Use Law/Natural Resources
Law and Economics
★ Lawyering Skills
Legal History/Philosophy
★ Litigation
★ Media Law
★ Mediation
Medical Malpractice Law
Mental Health and Law
Patent Law
Probate Law
Professional Responsibility
★ Public Interest
Race and Law
Real Estate Transactions
Remedies
★ Securities
Sports Law
★ Tax Law
Trial Advocacy
Trusts and Estates
(★ *indicates an area of special strength*)

Clinical Courses Students receive degree credit for clinical courses. (Clinical practicum is not required.) Among the clinical areas offered are:

- Capital Punishment
- Community Development
- Criminal Defense
- Disability Law

- Immigration
- Intellectual Property
- Patent Law

International exchange programs permit students to visit Ireland.

ILLINOIS INSTITUTE OF TECHNOLOGY
CHICAGO-KENT COLLEGE OF LAW

Chicago, Illinois

LAW STUDENT PROFILE [2000–2001]

FULL-TIME   Enrollment: 794
Women: 49%   Men: 51%

PART-TIME   Enrollment: 347
Women: 51%   Men: 49%

APPLICANTS and ADMITTEES
Number applied: 2,408
Admitted: 1,087
Percentage accepted: 45%
Seats available: 314
Average LSAT score: 155
Average GPA: 3.2

Illinois Institute of Technology Chicago-Kent College of Law is a private institution that organizes classes on a semester calendar system. The campus is situated in an urban setting. Founded in 1888, first ABA approved in 1936, and an AALS member, Illinois Institute of Technology Chicago-Kent College of Law offers JD, JD/LLM, JD/MBA, JD/MPAd, JD/MS, and LLM degrees.

Faculty consists of 74 full-time and 139 part-time members in 2000–2001. 23 full-time faculty members and 34 part-time faculty members are women. 100% of all faculty members have a JD degree. Of all faculty members, 3.2% are African American, 1.6% are Hispanic, 95.2% are white.

Application Information *Required:* application fee of $45, LSAT, LSDAS, baccalaureate degree, 1 recommendation, personal statement, application form, college transcripts. *Application deadline* for fall term is March 1 (priority date). Applications are processed on a rolling basis.

Costs The 2000–2001 tuition was $22,850 full-time; $810 per credit hour part-time. Fees: $100 full-time; $100 per year part-time. Tuition and fees vary according to program. Students are required to have their own computers.

Financial Aid In 2000–2001, 82% of all students received some form of financial aid. 27 research assistantships, 41 teaching assistantships, were awarded. Loans, merit-based grants/scholarships, and need-based grants/scholarships are also available. The average student debt at graduation is $64,643. To apply for financial assistance, students

AT a GLANCE

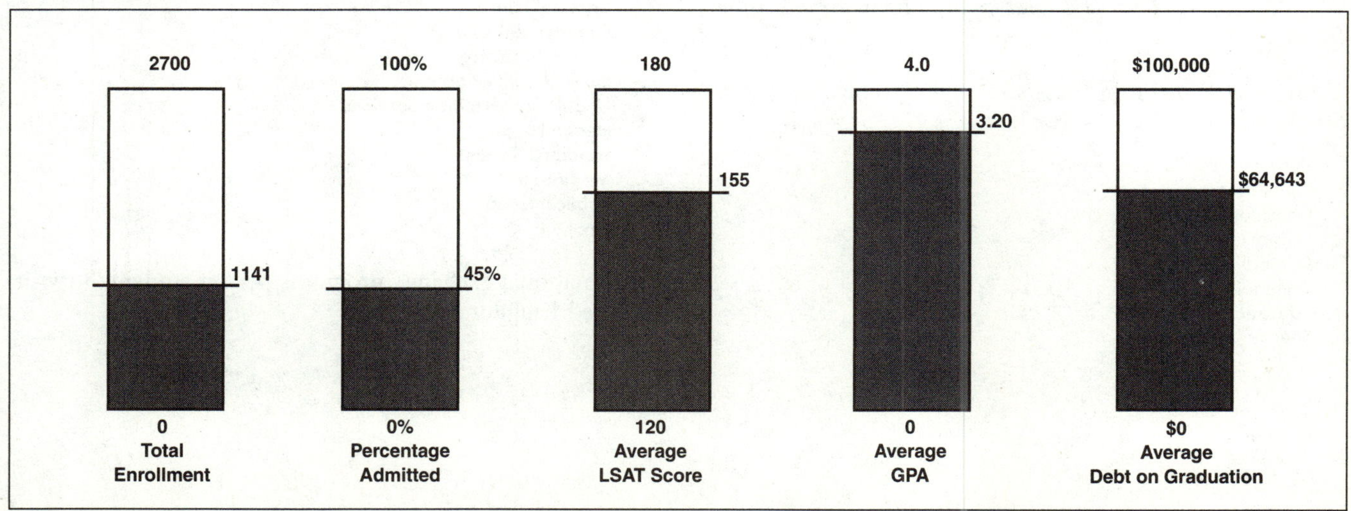

Degree Options

Degree	Total Credits Required	Length of Program
JD–Juris Doctor	87	3–4 yrs, full-time or part-time [day, evening, summer]
JD/LLM–Juris Doctor/Master of Laws–Taxation	99	4–5 yrs, full-time or part-time [day, evening, summer]
JD/LLM–Juris Doctor/Master of Laws–Financial Services	99	4–5 yrs, full-time or part-time [day, evening, summer]
JD/MBA–Juris Doctor/Master of Business Administration	99	4–5 yrs, full-time or part-time [day, evening, summer]
JD/MPAd–Juris Doctor/Master of Public Administration		4–5 yrs, full-time or part-time [day, evening, summer]
JD/MS–Juris Doctor/Master of Science–Financial Markets	113	4–5 yrs, full-time or part-time [day, evening, summer]
JD/MS–Juris Doctor/Master of Science–Environmental Management		
LLM–Master of Laws–International and Comparative Law	24	1 yr, full-time only [day, summer]

must complete the Free Application for Federal Student Aid. Completed financial aid forms should be received by April 16. Financial aid contact: Ada Chin, Office of Financial Aid, 565 West Adams, Chicago, IL 60661. Phone: 302-906-5180. Fax: 312-906-5280. E-mail: finaid@kentlaw.edu

Law School Library has 10 professional staff members and contains more than 558,002 volumes and 7,846 periodicals. 686 seats are available in the library. When classes are in session, the library is open 96 hours per week.

WESTLAW and LEXIS-NEXIS are available, as are the World Wide Web, online bibliographic services, and CD-ROM players. 135 computer workstations are available to students in the library. Special law collections include International relations, intellectual property, labor law, environmental/energy law, UN, EU..

First-Year Program Class size in the average section is 70; 100% of the first-year courses are taught by full-time faculty.

Upper-Level Program Class size in the average section is 50. Among the electives are:

Business and Corporate Law
Civil Procedure
Constitutional Law
Corporate Law
Criminal Defense
Criminal Law
Education Law
Energy Law
Estate Planning
Family Law
Financial Services
Health Care/Human Services
Health Law
★ International/Comparative Law
Jurisprudence
★ Labor Law
Legal History/Philosophy
★ Litigation
Mediation
Personal Injury
Property/Real Estate
Public Interest
Tax Law
(★ *indicates an area of special strength*)

Clinical Courses Students receive degree credit for clinical courses. (Clinical practicum is not required.) Among the clinical areas offered are:

Civil Litigation
Corporate Law
Criminal Defense
Criminal Law
Employment Law
General Practice
Government Litigation
Health Care/Human Services
Health Law
Landlord/Tenant
Mediation
Public Interest
Tax Law

International exchange programs permit students to visit United Kingdom.

JOHN MARSHALL LAW SCHOOL

Chicago, Illinois

INFORMATION CONTACT

William B. Powers, Associate Dean of Admission and Student Affairs
315 South Plymouth Court
Chicago, IL 60604-3968

Phone: 800-537-4280   Fax: 312-427-5136
E-mail: admission@jmls.edu
Web site: http://www.jmls.edu/

LAW STUDENT PROFILE [2000–2001]

FULL-TIME   Enrollment: 898
Women: 45%   Men: 55%

PART-TIME   Enrollment: 480
Women: 50%   Men: 50%

APPLICANTS and ADMITTEES

Number applied: 1,643
Admitted: 875
Percentage accepted: 53%
Seats available: 270
Average LSAT score: 154
Average GPA: 3.2

John Marshall Law School is a private nonprofit institution that organizes classes on a semester calendar system. The campus is situated in an urban setting. Founded in 1899, first ABA approved in 1951, and an AALS member, John Marshall Law School offers JD, LLM, and MS degrees.

Faculty 100% of all faculty members have a JD; 6% have advanced law degrees. Of all faculty members, 2% are Asian/Pacific Islander, 3% are African American, 1% are Hispanic, 81% are white, 5% are international.

Application Information *Required:* LSAT, LSDAS, application form, application fee of $50, baccalaureate degree, personal statement, college transcripts. *Recommended:* recommendations, resume.

Costs The 2000–2001 tuition was $24,300 full-time; $14,580 per year part-time. Fees: $100 full-time; $50 per semester part-time. Tuition and fees vary according to course load, degree level, and program.

Financial Aid Loans, merit-based grants/scholarships, and need-based grants/scholarships are available. The average student debt at graduation is $73,495. To apply for financial assistance, students must complete the Free Application for Federal Student Aid, institutional forms. Financial aid contact: Susan Bogart, Financial Aid Officer, 315 South Plymouth Court, Chicago, IL 60604. Phone: 800-537-4280. Fax: 312-427-5136. E-mail: bogart@jmls.edu

Law School Library The John Marshall Law School Library has 9 professional staff members and contains

AT a GLANCE

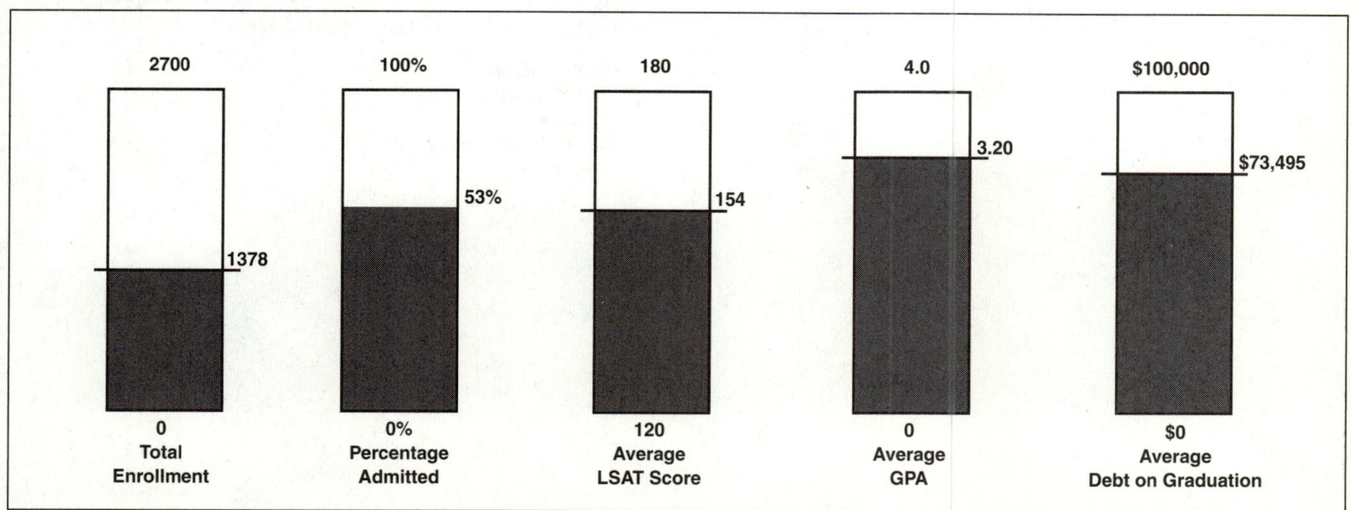

Degree Options

Degree	Total Credits Required	Length of Program
JD–Juris Doctor	90	3–4 yrs, full-time or part-time [day, evening, summer]
LLM–Master of Laws–Intellectual Property	24	1–2 yrs, full-time or part-time [evening, summer]
LLM–Master of Laws–Taxation	24	1–2 yrs, full-time or part-time [evening, summer]
LLM–Master of Laws–Real Estate	24	1–2 yrs, full-time or part-time [evening, summer]
LLM–Master of Laws–Comparative Law	24	1–2 yrs, full-time or part-time [day, evening, summer]
LLM–Master of Laws–Information/Technology Law	22	1–2 yrs, full-time or part-time [evening, summer]
LLM–Master of Laws–International Business and Trade	24	1–2 yrs, full-time or part-time [evening, summer]
LLM–Master of Laws–Employee Benefits	24	1–2 yrs, full-time or part-time [evening, summer]
MS–Master of Science–Information/Technology Law	22	1–2 yrs, full-time or part-time [evening, weekend, summer]

more than 363,836 volumes and 841 periodicals. 624 seats are available in the library. When classes are in session, the library is open 100 hours per week.

WESTLAW and LEXIS-NEXIS are available, as are the World Wide Web, online bibliographic services, and CD-ROM players. 75 computer workstations are available to students in the library. Special law collections include international human rights, animal rights, intellectual rights, taxation.

First-Year Program Class size in the average section is 60; 90% of the first-year courses are taught by full-time faculty.

Upper-Level Program Class size in the average section is 50. Among the electives are:

Administrative Law
★ Advocacy
Business and Corporate Law
Consumer Law
★ Employee Benefit Law
★ Employment Law
Entertainment Law
Environmental Law
★ Fair Housing
Family Law

Government/Regulation
Immigration
★ Information and Communications
★ Intellectual Property
★ International/Comparative Law
Labor Law
Land Use Law/Natural Resources
★ Lawyering Skills
Legal History/Philosophy
★ Litigation
Maritime Law
Media Law
Mediation
Probate Law
Public Interest
Securities
★ Tax Law
Technology Law
(★ *indicates an area of special strength*)

Clinical Courses Students receive degree credit for clinical courses. (Clinical practicum is not required.) Among the clinical areas offered are:

Civil Litigation
Fair Housing
Immigration
Intellectual Property
Litigation

LOYOLA UNIVERSITY CHICAGO
SCHOOL OF LAW

Chicago, Illinois

INFORMATION CONTACT

Pamela A. Bloomquist, Assistant Dean, Law
Admission and Financial Assistance
1 East Pearson Street
Chicago, IL 60611

Phone: 312-915-7170   Fax: 312-915-7906
E-mail: law-admissions@luc.edu
Web site: http://www.luc.edu/schools/law/

LAW STUDENT PROFILE [2000–2001]

FULL-TIME   Enrollment: 535
Women: 61%   Men: 39%

PART-TIME   Enrollment: 179
Women: 56%   Men: 44%

RACIAL or ETHNIC COMPOSITION
African American, 4%; Asian/Pacific Islander, 6%; Hispanic,
4%; International, 1%

APPLICANTS and ADMITTEES
Number applied: 2,296
Admitted: 885
Percentage accepted: 39%
Seats available: 165
Average LSAT score: 158
Median GPA: 3.3

Loyola University Chicago School of Law is a private
institution that organizes classes on a semester calendar
system. The campus is situated in an urban setting.
Founded in 1908, first ABA approved in 1925, and an
AALS member, Loyola University Chicago School of Law
offers JD, JD/MA, JD/MBA, JD/MS, JD/MSW, LLM, MJ,
and SJD degrees.

Faculty consists of 33 full-time and 81 part-time
members in 2000–2001. 13 full-time faculty members
and 33 part-time faculty members are women. 100% of
all faculty members have a JD; 16.6% have advanced law
degrees. Of all faculty members, 3.34% are Asian/Pacific
Islander, 3.34% are African American, 93.32% are white.

Application Information *Required:* LSAT, LSDAS,
application form, application fee of $50, baccalaureate
degree, 2 letters of recommendation, personal statement.
Recommended: resume. *Application deadline* for fall term
is April 1. Applications are processed on a rolling basis.

Costs The 2000–2001 tuition was $23,660 full-time. Fees:
$230 full-time.

Financial Aid In 2000–2001, 88% of all students received
some form of financial aid. Fellowships, graduate
assistantships, loans, loan repayment assistance program
(LRAP), merit-based grants/scholarships, need-based
grants/scholarships, and federal work-study loans are
available. The average student debt at graduation is
$67,000. To apply for financial assistance, students must
complete the Free Application for Federal Student Aid,
scholarship specific applications. Completed financial aid
forms should be received by March 1. Financial aid

AT a GLANCE

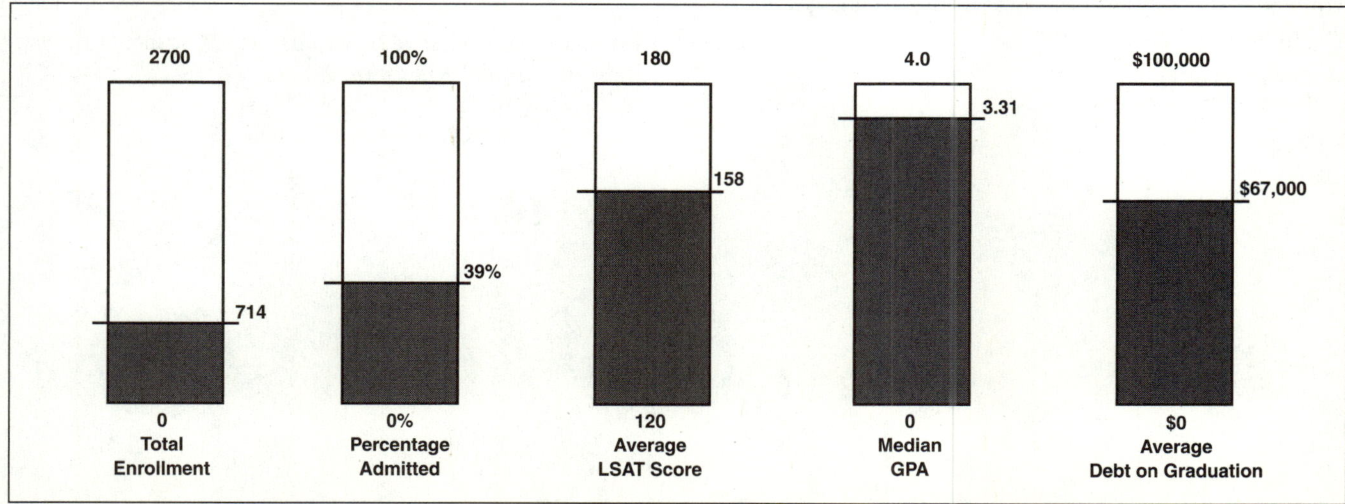

Degree Options

Degree	Total Credits Required	Length of Program
JD–Juris Doctor	86	3–4 yrs, full-time or part-time [day, evening, summer]
JD/MA–Juris Doctor/Master of Arts–Political Science	98	4–5 yrs, full-time or part-time [day, evening, summer]
JD/MBA–Juris Doctor/Master of Business Administration	116	4–5 yrs, full-time or part-time [day, evening, summer]
JD/MS–Juris Doctor/Master of Science–Institute of Human Resources and Industrial Relations	110	4–5 yrs, full-time or part-time [day, evening, summer]
JD/MSW–Juris Doctor/Master of Social Work	123	4–5 yrs, full-time or part-time [day, evening, summer]
LLM–Master of Laws–Health Law	24	1–2 yrs, full-time or part-time
LLM–Master of Laws–Child and Family Law	24	1–2 yrs, full-time or part-time
LLM–Master of Laws–Business Law	24	1–2 yrs, full-time or part-time
MJ–Master of Jurisprudence–Business Law	22	2 yrs, part-time only [evening, summer]
MJ–Master of Jurisprudence–Health Law	22	2 yrs, part-time only [evening, summer]
MJ–Master of Jurisprudence–Child and Family Law	22	2 yrs, part-time only [evening, summer]
SJD–Doctor of Juridical Science–Health Law and Policy	10	2 yrs, full-time only [day]

contact: Michael Minnice, Assistant Director, Law Financial Assistance, 1 East Pearson Street, Chicago, IL 60611. Phone: 312-915-7170. Fax: 312-915-7906. E-mail: law-financial-aid@luc.edu

Law School Library Loyola Law Library has 7 professional staff members and contains more than 346,663 volumes and 3,499 periodicals. 380 seats are available in the library. When classes are in session, the library is open 100 hours per week.

WESTLAW and LEXIS-NEXIS are available, as are the World Wide Web and online bibliographic services. 50 computer workstations are available to students in the library. Special law collections include Health law.

First-Year Program Class size in the average section is 55; 80% of the first-year courses are taught by full-time faculty.

Upper-Level Program Class size in the average section is 26. Among the electives are:

Civil Litigation
Disability Law
Elder Law
★ Family Practice
General Practice
★ Health Law
★ Juvenile Law
Landlord/Tenant
★ Tax Law
Unemployment Compensation

(★ *indicates an area of special strength*)

Clinical Courses Students receive degree credit for clinical courses. (Clinical practicum is not required.) Among the clinical areas offered are:

Civil Litigation
Disability Law
Elder Law
Family Practice
General Practice
Juvenile Law
Landlord/Tenant
Tax Law
Unemployment Compensation

International exchange programs permit students to visit Italy and United Kingdom.

NORTHERN ILLINOIS UNIVERSITY
COLLEGE OF LAW

DeKalb, Illinois

INFORMATION CONTACT

Judith L. Malen, Director of Admissions and
Financial Aid
DeKalb, IL 60115

Phone: 815-753-1420   Fax: 815-753-4501
Web site: http://www.niu.edu/

LAW STUDENT PROFILE [2000–2001]

FULL-TIME   Enrollment: 286
Women: 45%   Men: 55%

PART-TIME   Enrollment: 12
Women: 58%   Men: 42%

RACIAL or ETHNIC COMPOSITION

African American, 8%; Asian/Pacific Islander, 5%; Hispanic,
7%; Native American, 1%; International, 0.3%

APPLICANTS and ADMITTEES

Seats available: 111
Average LSAT score: 153
Average GPA: 3.1

Northern Illinois University College of Law is a public
institution that organizes classes on a semester calendar
system. The campus is situated in a small-town setting.
Founded in 1974, first ABA approved in 1978, and an
AALS member, Northern Illinois University College of
Law offers JD and JD/MBA degrees.

Faculty consists of 22 full-time members in 2000–2001.
11 full-time faculty members are women. 100% of all
faculty members have a JD; 42% have advanced law
degrees. Of all faculty members, 5% are Asian/Pacific
Islander, 20% are African American, 5% are Hispanic,
70% are white.

Application Information *Required:* LSAT, LSDAS,
application form, application fee of $40, baccalaureate
degree, 2 letters of recommendation, personal statement,
college transcripts. *Recommended:* resume. *Application
deadline* for fall term is June 1.

Costs The 1999–2000 tuition was $7219 full-time for
state residents; $289 per credit hour part-time for state
residents. Tuition was $13,106 full-time for nonresidents;
$534 per credit hour part-time for nonresidents. Tuition
and fees vary according to campus/location.

Financial Aid 22 teaching assistantships were awarded.
Graduate assistantships, loans, merit-based grants/
scholarships, need-based grants/scholarships, and federal
work-study loans are also available. To apply for
financial assistance, students must complete the Free
Application for Federal Student Aid, institutional forms,
NIU Financial Aid Application, Federal 1040 and W-2's.
Financial aid contact: Judith L. Malen, Director of

AT a GLANCE

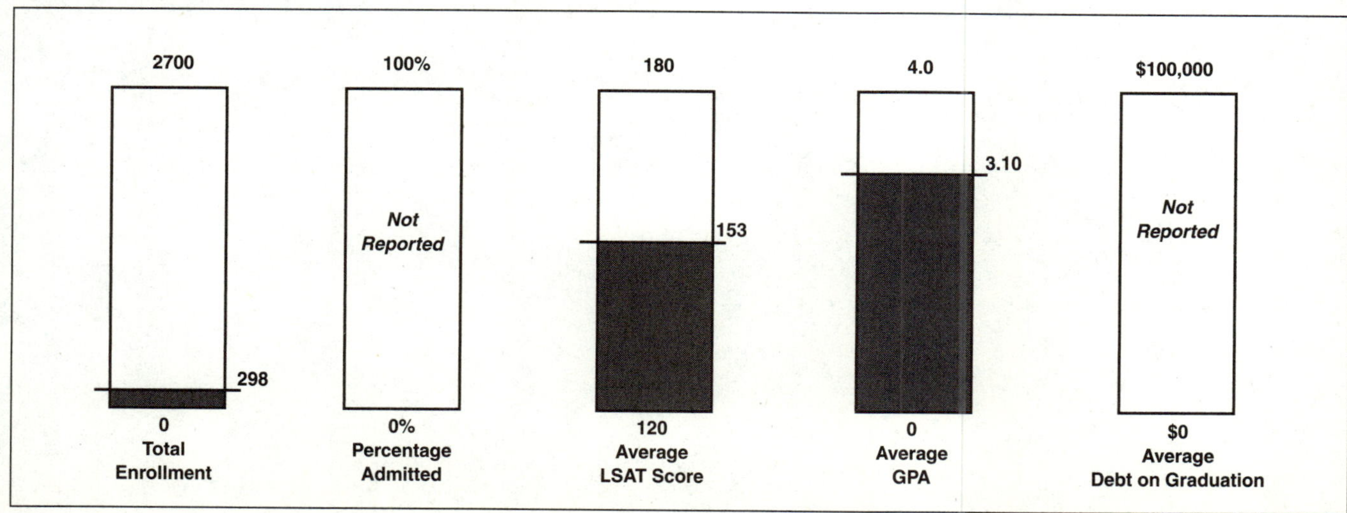

Degree Options

Degree	Total Credits Required	Length of Program
JD–Doctor of Laws	90	3 yrs, full-time only [day]
JD/MBA–Juris Doctor/Master of Business Administration–Dual-degree Program	120	4 yrs, full-time only [day]

Admissions and Financial Aid, DeKalb, IL 60115. Phone: 815-753-9485. Fax: 815-753-4501. E-mail: jmalen@niu.edu

Law School Library David C. Shapiro Memorial Law Library has 5 professional staff members and contains more than 216,863 volumes and 3,240 periodicals. 204 seats are available in the library. When classes are in session, the library is open 97 hours per week.

WESTLAW and LEXIS-NEXIS are available, as are the World Wide Web, online bibliographic services, and CD-ROM players. 30 computer workstations are available to students in the library.

First-Year Program Class size in the average section is 44; 100% of the first-year courses are taught by full-time faculty.

Upper-Level Program Class size in the average section is 25. Among the electives are:

Administrative Law
Advocacy
★ Business and Corporate Law
Civil Litigation
Consumer Law
Criminal Defense
Criminal Prosecution
Education Law
Elderly Advocacy
Entertainment Law

Environmental Law
Family Law
Family Practice
Government/Regulation
Health Care/Human Services
Intellectual Property
International/Comparative Law
Jurisprudence
Juvenile Law
Labor Law
Land Use Law/Natural Resources
★ Lawyering Skills
Legal History/Philosophy
Litigation
Maritime Law
Media Law
★ Mediation
Probate Law
★ Public Interest
Securities
Tax Law

(★ indicates an area of special strength)

Clinical Courses Students receive degree credit for clinical courses. (Clinical practicum is not required.) Among the clinical areas offered are:

Advocacy
Civil Litigation
Criminal Defense
Criminal Prosecution
Elderly Advocacy
Family Practice
Juvenile Law

NORTHWESTERN UNIVERSITY
LAW SCHOOL

Chicago, Illinois

INFORMATION CONTACT

Donald Rebstock, Associate Dean of Enrollment
Management and Career Strategy
357 East Chicago Avenue
Chicago, IL 60611-3069

Phone: 312-503-8465   Fax: 312-503-0179
E-mail: d-rebstock@northwestern.edu
Web site: http://www.law1.northwestern.edu

LAW STUDENT PROFILE [2000–2001]

FULL-TIME   Enrollment: 656
Women: 50%   Men: 50%

RACIAL or ETHNIC COMPOSITION
African American, 8%; Asian/Pacific Islander, 13%; Hispanic,
2%; Native American, 1%

APPLICANTS and ADMITTEES
Number applied: 4,214
Admitted: 785
Percentage accepted: 19%
Seats available: 205
Average LSAT score: 167
Average GPA: 3.5

Northwestern University Law School is a private
institution that organizes classes on a semester calendar
system. The campus is situated in an urban setting.
Founded in 1859, first ABA approved in 1923, and an
AALS member, Northwestern University Law School
offers JD, JD/MBA, JD/MM, JD/PhD, and LLM degrees.

Faculty consists of 64 full-time and 72 part-time
members in 2000–2001. 25 full-time faculty members are
women. 100% of all faculty members have a JD degree.
Of all faculty members, 1% are African American, 99%
are white.

Application Information *Required:* LSAT, LSDAS,
application form, application fee of $80, baccalaureate
degree, 2 letters of recommendation, personal statement,
college transcripts, resume. *Recommended:* essay,
interview. *Application deadline* for fall term is February 15. Applications are processed on a rolling basis.

Costs The 2000–2001 tuition was $28,488 full-time.
Students are required to have their own computers.

Financial Aid In 2000–2001, 78% of all students received
some form of financial aid. 296 fellowships, totaling
$11,000 were awarded. Loans, loan repayment assistance
program (LRAP), merit-based grants/scholarships,
need-based grants/scholarships, and federal work-study
loans are also available. The average student debt at
graduation is $65,000. To apply for financial assistance,
students must complete the Free Application for Federal
Student Aid, institutional forms, parental and student
income tax returns. Completed financial aid forms
should be received by March 1. Financial aid contact:

AT a GLANCE

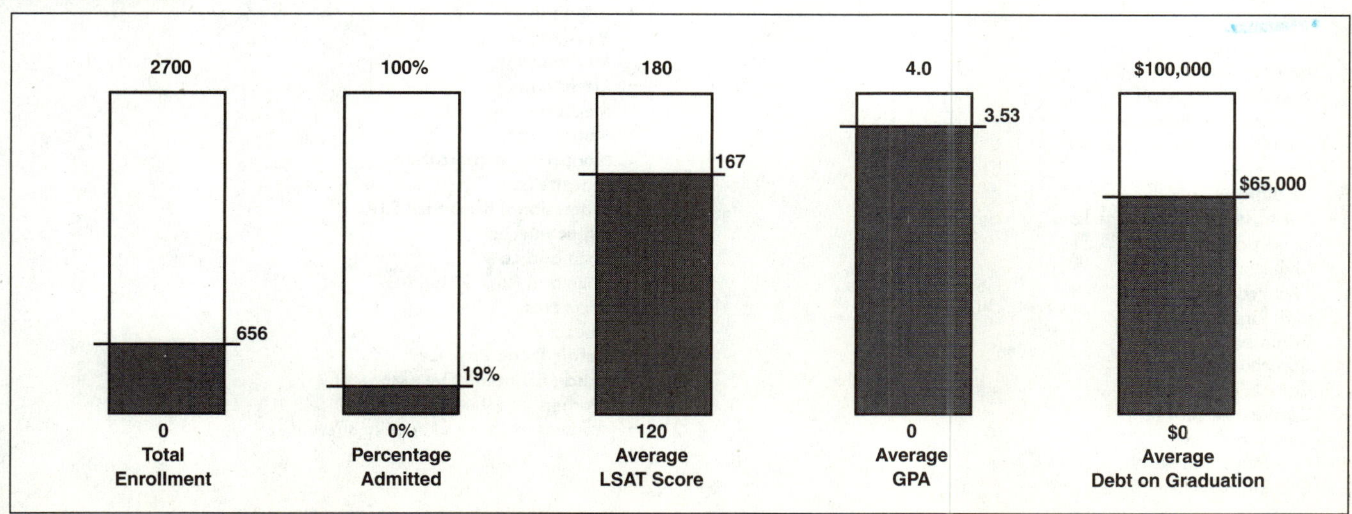

Degree Options

Degree	Total Credits Required	Length of Program
JD–Doctor of Laws	86	3–4 yrs, full-time only [day]
JD/MBA–Juris Doctor/Master of Business Administration–JD/MBA Dual Degree program	110	3 yrs, full-time only [day]
JD/MM–Juris Doctor/Master of Management–Dual-degree Program		3 yrs, full-time only [day]
JD/PhD–Juris Doctor/Doctor of Philosophy–Dual-degree Program		6 yrs, full-time only [day]
LLM–Master of Laws	20	1 yr [day]
LLM–Master of Laws–Management Program		1 yr, full-time only [day, summer]

Sarah Rewerts, Director of Admissions and Financial Aid, 357 East Chicago Avenue, Chicago, IL 60611-3069. Phone: 312-503-8465. Fax: 312-503-0178. E-mail: s-rewerts@law.northwestern.edu

Law School Library Pritzker Legal Research Center has 13 professional staff members and contains more than 670,184 volumes and 8,388 periodicals. 794 seats are available in the library. When classes are in session, the library is open 105 hours per week.

WESTLAW and LEXIS-NEXIS are available, as are the World Wide Web, online bibliographic services, and CD-ROM players. 75 computer workstations are available to students in the library. Special law collections include the United States Supreme Court papers of Justice Arthur J. Goldberg, the Anglo-American Collection.

First-Year Program Class size in the average section is 50; 100% of the first-year courses are taught by full-time faculty.

Upper-Level Program Class size in the average section is 29. Among the electives are:

Accounting
Administrative Law
Admiralty Law
★ Advocacy
American Legal History
Antitrust Law
Appellate Litigation
Banking and Finance
Banking Law & Regulation
Bankruptcy
Bioethics
★ Business and Corporate Law
Children's Rights
★ Civil Litigation
Civil Procedure
Civil Rights
Commercial Law
Constitutional Law
Consumer Law
Corporate Finance
★ Corporate Law
★ Criminal Defense
Criminal Law
Criminal Procedure
★ Criminal Prosecution
Democratic Theory
Economic Development
Education Law
Employment Law
Entertainment Law
Environmental Law
Ethics
Evidence
Family Law
Family Practice
Feminist Jurisprudence
Government/Regulation
★ Health Care/Human Services
Immigration
Indian/Tribal Law
Insurance Law
Intellectual Property
★ International Law
★ International/Comparative Law
Japanese Law
Jewish Law
Judicial Externship
Jurisdiction
Jurisprudence
★ Juvenile Law
Labor Law
Land Use Law/Natural Resources
Lawyering Skills
Legal History/Philosophy
Legal Writing
★ Litigation
Maritime Law
Media Law
★ Mediation
Medicine
Negotiation
Nonprofit Organizations
Probate Law
Professional Responsibility
★ Public Interest
Race and Law
Race and Race Relations
Securities
Tax Law
Unfair Trade Practices
Urban Economic Development
Women and the Law
(★ *indicates an area of special strength*)

Clinical Courses Students receive degree credit for clinical courses. (Clinical practicum is not required.) Among the clinical areas offered are:

- Advocacy
- Business and Corporate Law
- Civil Litigation
- Civil Rights
- Corporate Law
- Criminal Defense
- Criminal Prosecution
- Domestic Violence
- Family Law
- Family Practice
- Human Rights
- Immigration
- International Law
- Judicial
- Juvenile Law
- Public Interest
- Social Security
- Special Education Law

International exchange programs permit students to visit Argentina, Australia, Belgium, Israel, and Netherlands.

SOUTHERN ILLINOIS UNIVERSITY CARBONDALE
SCHOOL OF LAW

Carbondale, Illinois

INFORMATION CONTACT

Michael P. Ruiz, Assistant Dean for Admissions and
Student Affairs
Lesar Law Building
Carbondale, IL 62901-6804

Phone: 618-453-8768   Fax: 618-453-8769
E-mail: mikeruiz@siu.edu
Web site: http://www.siu.edu/~lawsch/

LAW STUDENT PROFILE [2000–2001]

FULL-TIME   Enrollment: 369
Women: 29%   Men: 71%

APPLICANTS and ADMITTEES

Number applied: 563
Admitted: 329
Percentage accepted: 58%
Seats available: 130
Average LSAT score: 152
Average GPA: 3.1

Southern Illinois University Carbondale School of Law
is a public institution that organizes classes on a semester
calendar system. The campus is situated in a rural
setting. Founded in 1973, first ABA approved in 1980,
and an AALS member, Southern Illinois University
Carbondale School of Law offers JD, JD/MBA, JD/MD,
JD/MPA, JD/MPAd, JD/MSW, and JD/PhD degrees.

Faculty consists of 23 full-time and 6 part-time members
in 2000–2001. 8 full-time faculty members and 4
part-time faculty members are women. 98% of all faculty
members have a JD; 27% have advanced law degrees. Of
all faculty members, 1% are Asian/Pacific Islander, 1%
are African American, 98% are white.

Application Information *Required:* minimum 145 LSAT
score, LSDAS, application form, application fee of $40,
baccalaureate degree, college transcripts. *Recommended:*
minimum 2.0 GPA, recommendations, personal statement, resume. *Application deadline* for fall term is March
1 (priority date). Applications are processed on a rolling
basis.

Costs The 2000–2001 tuition was $5028 full-time for
area residents. Fees: $1097 full-time.

Financial Aid In 2000–2001, 100% of all students
received some form of financial aid. Loans, merit-based
grants/scholarships, need-based grants/scholarships, and
federal work-study loans are available. The average
student debt at graduation is $24,000. To apply for
financial assistance, students must complete the Free

AT a GLANCE

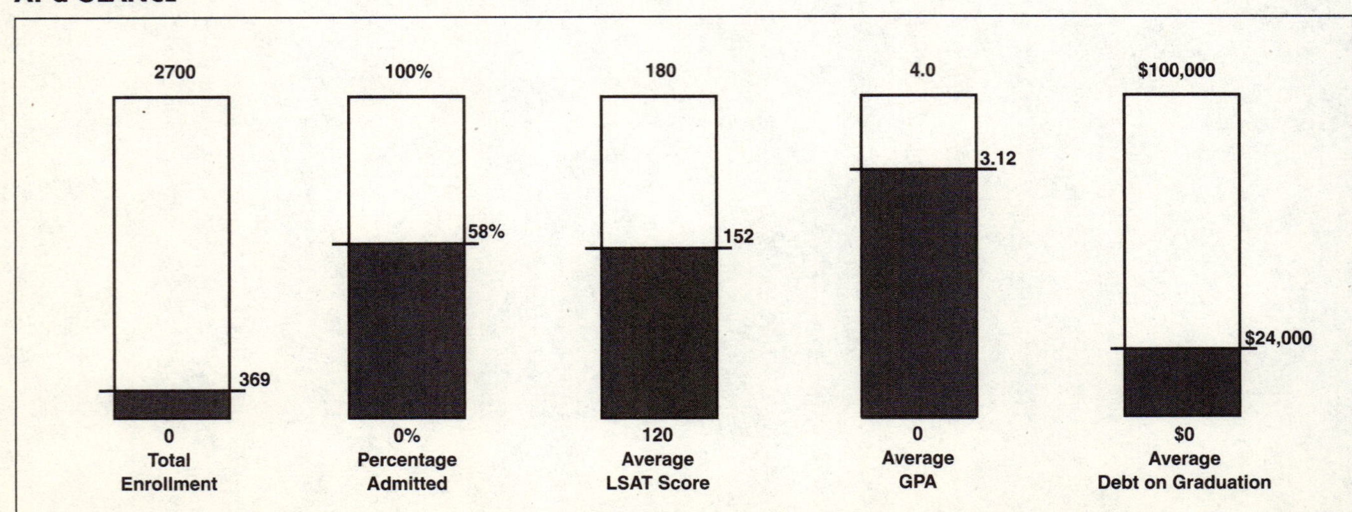

Degree Options

Degree	Total Credits Required	Length of Program
JD–Doctor of Laws	90	3 yrs, full-time only [day, summer]
JD/MBA–Juris Doctor/Master of Business Administration–Dual-degree Program	120	4 yrs, full-time only [day, summer]
JD/MD–Juris Doctor/Doctor of Medicine–Dual-degree Program		6 yrs, full-time only [day, summer]
JD/MPA–Juris Doctor/Master of Professional Accountancy–Dual-degree Program	120	4 yrs, full-time only [day, summer]
JD/MPAd–Juris Doctor/Master of Public Administration–Dual-degree Program		4 yrs, full-time only [day, summer]
JD/MSW–Juris Doctor/Master of Social Work–Dual-degree Program		4 yrs, full-time only [day, summer]
JD/PhD–Juris Doctor/Doctor of Philosophy–Political Science		4–6 yrs, full-time only [day, summer]

Application for Federal Student Aid. Financial aid contact: Pat Caporale, Admissions Assistant, School of Law, Mailcode 6804, Carbondale, IL 62901-6804. Phone: 618-453-8767 or toll free 800-739-9187. Fax: 618-453-8769. E-mail: lawadmit@siu.edu

Law School Library Southern Illinois University School of Law Library has 7 professional staff members and contains more than 358,972 volumes and 4,218 periodicals. 340 seats are available in the library. When classes are in session, the library is open 78 hours per week.

WESTLAW and LEXIS-NEXIS are available, as are the World Wide Web, online bibliographic services, and CD-ROM players. 29 computer workstations are available to students in the library.

First-Year Program Class size in the average section is 60; 100% of the first-year courses are taught by full-time faculty.

Upper-Level Program Class size in the average section is 27. Among the electives are:

Administrative Law
Advocacy
★ Bioethics
Business and Corporate Law
Commercial Law
Domestic Violence
Education Law
★ Elderly Advocacy
Environmental Law
Family Law
Federal Courts
★ Health Care/Human Services
★ Health Law
Intellectual Property
International/Comparative Law
Jurisprudence
Labor Law
★ Land Use Law/Natural Resources
Lawyering Skills
★ Legal Externship
Legal History/Philosophy
Litigation
★ Mediation
Probate Law
Property/Real Estate
Public Interest
Securities
Tax Law
(★ indicates an area of special strength)

Clinical Courses Students receive degree credit for clinical courses. (Clinical practicum is not required.) Among the clinical areas offered are:

Civil Litigation
Domestic Violence
Elderly Advocacy
Family Law
Legal Externship
Mediation
Public Interest

UNIVERSITY OF CHICAGO
THE LAW SCHOOL

Chicago, Illinois

INFORMATION CONTACT

Genita Robinson, Dean of Admissions
1111 East 60th Street
Chicago, IL 60637

Phone: 773-702-9484   Fax: 773-834-0942
E-mail: admissions@law.uchicago.edu
Web site: http://www.law.uchicago.edu/

LAW STUDENT PROFILE [2000–2001]

FULL-TIME   Enrollment: 583
Women: 37%   Men: 63%

RACIAL or ETHNIC COMPOSITION
African American, 3%; Asian/Pacific Islander, 9%; Hispanic, 8%; Native American, 0.3%; International, 1%

APPLICANTS and ADMITTEES
Number applied: 3,562
Admitted: 824
Percentage accepted: 23%
Seats available: 175
Median LSAT score: 169
Average GPA: 3.6

University of Chicago The Law School is a private institution that organizes classes on a semester calendar system. The campus is situated in an urban setting. Founded in 1902, first ABA approved in 1923, and an AALS member, University of Chicago The Law School offers DCL, JD, JD/AM, JD/MBA, JD/MPP, JD/PhD, JSD, LLM, and MCL degrees.

Faculty consists of 47 full-time and 64 part-time members in 2000–2001. 98% of all faculty members have a JD degree. Of all faculty members, 4.5% are African American, 1.8% are Hispanic, 92.7% are white.

Application Information *Required:* LSAT, LSDAS, application form, application fee of $60, baccalaureate degree, 2 letters of recommendation, personal statement, college transcripts, resume. *Application deadline* for fall term is February 1 (priority date). Applications are processed on a rolling basis.

Costs The 1999–2000 tuition was $26,406 full-time. Fees: $390 full-time. Students are required to have their own computers.

Financial Aid In 2000–2001, 48% of all students received some form of financial aid. Loans, loan repayment assistance program (LRAP), merit-based grants/scholarships, and need-based grants/scholarships are available. To apply for financial assistance, students must complete the Free Application for Federal Student Aid, Need Access diskette. Completed financial aid forms should be received by March 15. Financial aid contact: Joyce Wilson, Admissions & Financial Aid, LBQ A100C, 1111

AT a GLANCE

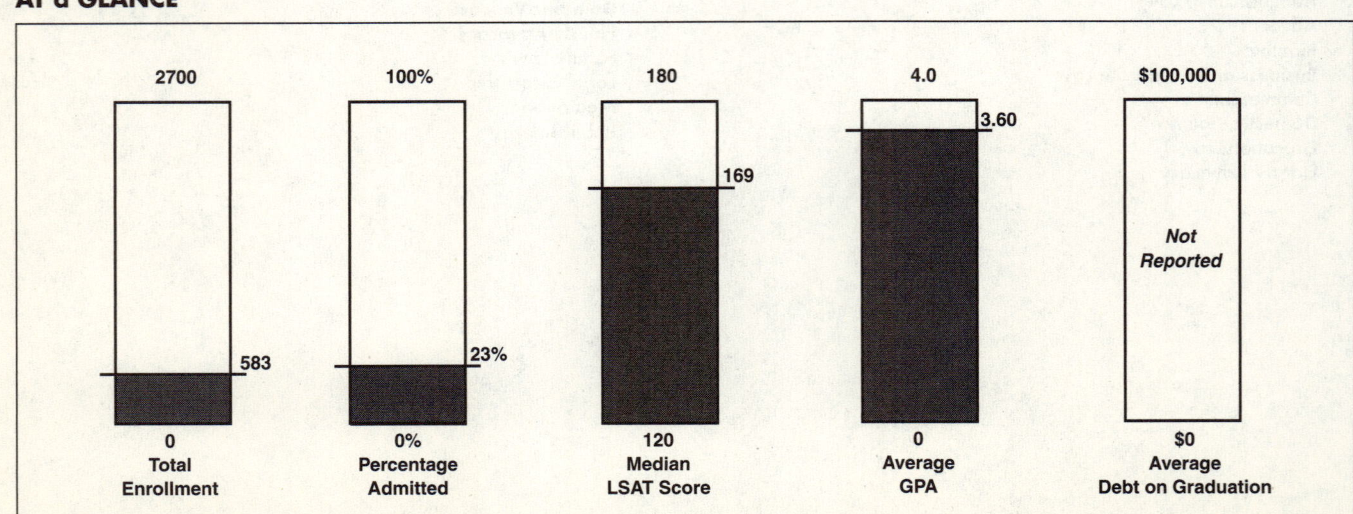

Degree Options

Degree	Total Credits Required	Length of Program
DCL–Doctor of Comparative Law		full-time only [day]
JD–Doctor of Law	105	3 yrs, full-time only [day]
JD/AM–Juris Doctor/Master of Arts–History Joint-degree		full-time only [day]
JD/AM–Juris Doctor/Master of Arts–International Relations		full-time only [day]
JD/AM–Juris Doctor/Master of Arts–Economics Joint-degree		full-time only [day]
JD/MBA–Juris Doctor/Master of Business Administration–Joint-degree	135	4 yrs, full-time only [day]
JD/MPP–Juris Doctor/Master of Public Planning–Public Policy	49	4 yrs, full-time only [day]
JD/PhD–Juris Doctor/Doctor of Philosophy–History Joint-degree		full-time only [day]
JD/PhD–Juris Doctor/Doctor of Philosophy–Economics Joint-degree		full-time only [day]
JSD–Doctor of Juridical Science		full-time only [day]
LLM–Master of Laws	27	1 yr, full-time only [day]
MCL–Master of Comparative Law	27	1 yr

East 60th Street, Chicago, IL 60637. Phone: 773-834-4428. Fax: 773-834-0942. E-mail: jwilson@midway.uchicago.edu

Law School Library D'Angelo Law Library has 8 professional staff members and contains more than 651,822 volumes and 8,429 periodicals. 445 seats are available in the library. When classes are in session, the library is open 90 hours per week.

WESTLAW and LEXIS-NEXIS are available, as are the World Wide Web and CD-ROM players. 38 computer workstations are available to students in the library.

First-Year Program Class size in the average section is 90; 100% of the first-year courses are taught by full-time faculty.

Upper-Level Program Class size in the average section is 50. Among the electives are:

- Administrative Law
- Advocacy
- Bankruptcy
- Business and Corporate Law
- Civil Rights
- Constitutional Law
- Criminal Defense
- Education Law
- Employment Law
- Environmental Law
- Family Law
- Feminist Jurisprudence
- Government/Regulation
- Health Care/Human Services
- Health Law
- Intellectual Property
- International/Comparative Law
- Jurisprudence
- Juvenile Law
- Labor Law
- Land Use Law/Natural Resources
- Lawyering Skills
- Legal History/Philosophy
- Litigation
- Maritime Law
- Mediation
- Mental Health and Law
- Poverty/Welfare Law
- Public Interest
- Securities
- Small Business Counseling
- Tax Law
- Trusts and Estates

Clinical Courses Students receive degree credit for clinical courses. (Clinical practicum is not required.) Among the clinical areas offered are:

- Business and Corporate Law
- Civil Rights
- Criminal Defense
- Employment Law
- Health Law
- Juvenile Law
- Mental Health and Law
- Poverty/Welfare Law
- Small Business Counseling

UNIVERSITY OF ILLINOIS AT URBANA–CHAMPAIGN
COLLEGE OF LAW

Champaign, Illinois

INFORMATION CONTACT

Ann Kay Perry, Assistant Dean
504 East Pennsylvania Avenue
Champaign, IL 61820

Phone: 217-333-1097   Fax: 217-244-1478
E-mail: ak_perry@uiuc.edu
Web site: http://www.law.uiuc.edu/

LAW STUDENT PROFILE [2000–2001]

APPLICANTS AND ADMITTEES
Number applied: 1,855
Admitted: 59
Percentage accepted: 3%
Seats available: 205
Average LSAT score: 161
Average GPA: 3.4

University of Illinois at Urbana–Champaign College of Law is a public institution that organizes classes on a semester calendar system. The campus is situated in a small-town setting. Founded in 1897, first ABA approved in 1923, and an AALS member, University of Illinois at Urbana–Champaign College of Law offers JD, JD/DVM, JD/MA, JD/MBA, JD/MD, JD/MED, JD/MES, JD/MS, JD/MUP, and JD/PhD degrees.

Faculty 97% of all faculty members have a JD degree. Of all faculty members, 4% are Asian/Pacific Islander, 10% are African American, 6% are Hispanic, 80% are white.

Application Information *Required:* LSAT, LSDAS, application form, application fee of $40, baccalaureate degree, 2 letters of recommendation, personal statement, college transcripts, resume. *Application deadline* for fall term is March 15. Applications are processed on a rolling basis.

Costs The 1999–2000 tuition was $8024 full-time for state residents. Tuition was $18,814 full-time for nonresidents. Fees: $637 per semester full-time. Full-time tuition and fees vary according to course load and degree level. Students are required to have their own computers.

Financial Aid 4 research assistantships were awarded. Fellowships, graduate assistantships, loans, merit-based grants/scholarships, need-based grants/scholarships, and federal work-study loans are also available. The average student debt at graduation is $36,000. To apply for financial assistance, students must complete the Free

AT a GLANCE

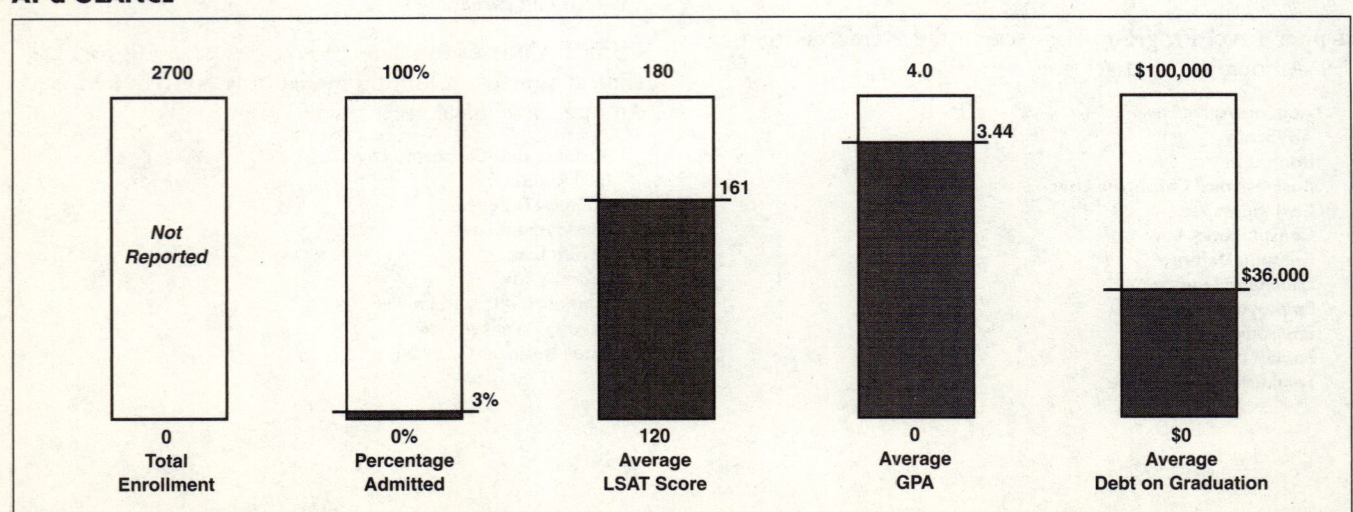

Degree Options

Degree	Total Credits Required	Length of Program
JD–Juris Doctor	90	3–4 yrs, full-time only [day]
JD/DVM–Juris Doctor/Doctor of Veterinary Medicine–Veterinary Medicine Joint-degree Program	219	6 yrs, full-time only [day]
JD/MA–Juris Doctor/Master of Arts–Labor and Industrial Relations Joint-degree Program	98	3.5 yrs, full-time only [day]
JD/MBA–Juris Doctor/Master of Business Administration–Joint-degree Program	119	4 yrs, full-time only [day]
JD/MD–Juris Doctor/Doctor of Medicine–Joint-degree Program	210	6 yrs, full-time only [day]
JD/MED–Juris Doctor/Master of Education–Joint-degree Program	96	3.5 yrs, full-time only [day]
JD/MES–Juris Doctor/Master of Environmental Studies–Natural Resource & Environmental Science Joint-degree Program	96	3.5 yrs, full-time only [day]
JD/MS–Juris Doctor/Master of Science–Journalism Joint-degree Program	96	3.5 yrs, full-time only [day]
JD/MS–Juris Doctor/Master of Science–Chemistry Joint-degree Program	96	3.5 yrs, full-time only
JD/MUP–Juris Doctor/Masters of Urban Planning–Joint-degree Program	104	4 yrs, full-time only [day]
JD/PhD–Juris Doctor/Doctor of Philosophy–Education Joint-degree Program	114	5–6 yrs, full-time only [day]

Application for Federal Student Aid, institutional forms, scholarship specific applications. Financial aid contact: Ann Killian Perry, Assistant Dean for Student Affairs and Financial Aid, 504 East Pennsylvania Avenue, Champaign, IL 61820. Phone: 217-333-1097. Fax: 217-244-1478. E-mail: akperry@law.uiuc.edu

Law School Library Albert E. Jenner, Jr. Memorial Law Library has 10 professional staff members and contains more than 696,332 volumes and 8,450 periodicals. 398 seats are available in the library. When classes are in session, the library is open 102 hours per week.

WESTLAW and LEXIS-NEXIS are available, as are the World Wide Web, online bibliographic services, and CD-ROM players. 77 computer workstations are available to students in the library.

First-Year Program Class size in the average section is 70; 80% of the first-year courses are taught by full-time faculty.

Upper-Level Program Class size in the average section is 24. Among the electives are:

Administrative Law
★ Advocacy
★ Business and Corporate Law
★ Civil Litigation
Consumer Law
★ Corporate Law
★ Criminal Defense
Education Law
★ Environmental Law
★ Family Law
★ Family Practice
Government Litigation
Government/Regulation
Health Care/Human Services
Indian/Tribal Law
★ Intellectual Property
★ International/Comparative Law
Jurisprudence
★ Labor Law
Land Use Law/Natural Resources
★ Lawyering Skills
Legal History/Philosophy
★ Litigation
Media Law
Mediation
★ Probate Law
★ Public Interest
★ Securities
★ Tax Law
(★ indicates an area of special strength)

Clinical Courses Students receive degree credit for clinical courses. (Clinical practicum is not required.) Among the clinical areas offered are:

Civil Litigation
Corporate Law
Criminal Defense
Environmental Law
Family Law
Family Practice
Government Litigation
Intellectual Property
Public Interest
Tax Law

INDIANA UNIVERSITY SCHOOL OF LAW-BLOOMINGTON

Bloomington, Indiana

INFORMATION CONTACT

Kevin Robling, Assistant Dean for Admissions
211 South Indiana Avenue
Bloomington, IN 47405

Phone: 812-855-4765   Fax: 812-855-0555
E-mail: lawadmis@indiana.edu
Web site: http://www.law.indiana.edu/

LAW STUDENT PROFILE [2000–2001]

FULL-TIME   Enrollment: 609
Women: 37%   Men: 63%

PART-TIME   Enrollment: 52
Women: 40%   Men: 60%

RACIAL or ETHNIC COMPOSITION

African American, 8%; Asian/Pacific Islander, 5%; Hispanic, 4%; Native American, 0.2%; International, 7%

APPLICANTS and ADMITTEES

Seats available: 200
Average LSAT score: 157
Average GPA: 3.3

Indiana University School of Law-Bloomington is a public institution that organizes classes on a semester calendar system. The campus is situated in a small-town setting. Founded in 1842, first ABA approved in 1937, and an AALS member, Indiana University School of Law-Bloomington offers JD, JD/MA, JD/MBA, JD/MES, JD/MLS, JD/MPA, JD/MPAf, JD/MS/MA, LLM, MCL, PhD, and SJD degrees.

Faculty consists of 44 full-time and 6 part-time members in 2000–2001. 13 full-time faculty members and 3 part-time faculty members are women. 96% of all faculty members have a JD; 23% have advanced law degrees. Of all faculty members, 7% are African American, 89% are white, 4% are international.

Application Information *Required:* LSAT, LSDAS, application form, application fee of $35, baccalaureate degree, college transcripts. *Recommended:* 3 letters of recommendation, personal statement. *Application deadline* for fall term is March 1 (priority date). Applications are processed on a rolling basis.

Costs The 1999–2000 tuition was $6850 full-time for state residents; $236 per credit hour part-time for state residents. Tuition was $17,568 full-time for nonresidents; $606 per credit hour part-time for nonresidents. Fees: $360 full-time. Tuition and fees vary according to student level. Students are required to have their own computers.

Financial Aid Fellowships, graduate assistantships, loans, loan repayment assistance program (LRAP), merit-based

AT a GLANCE

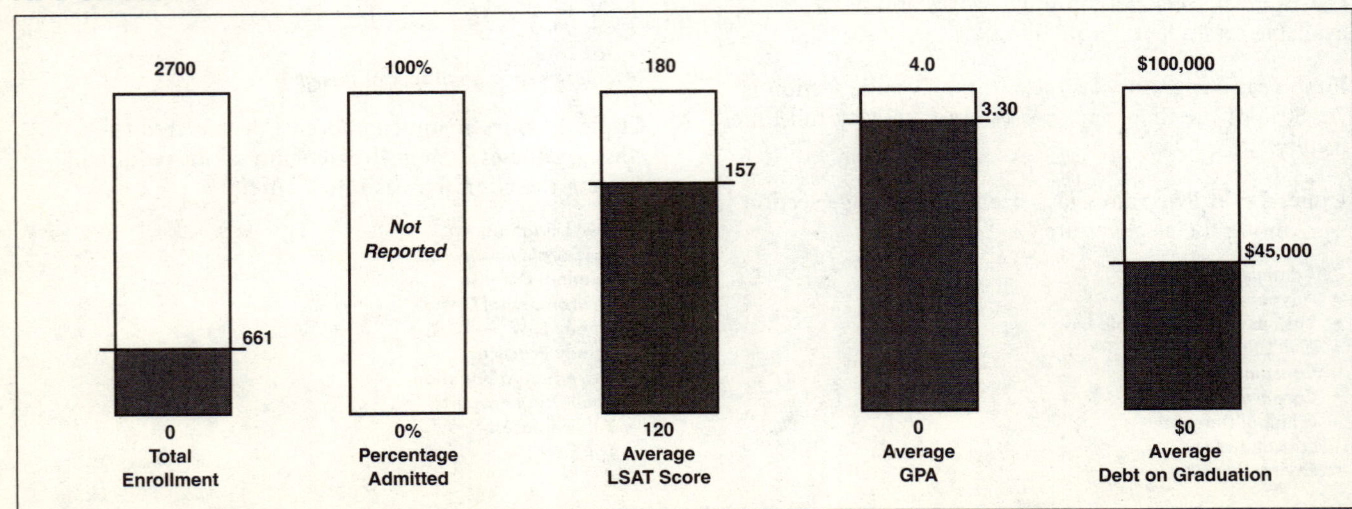

Degree Options

Degree	Total Credits Required	Length of Program
JD–Juris Doctor	86	3 yrs, full-time only [day, summer]
JD–Juris Doctor–Business Minor	92	3 yrs, full-time only [day, summer]
JD–Juris Doctor–Women's Studies Minor	86	3 yrs, full-time only [day, summer]
JD/MA–Juris Doctor/Master of Arts–Journalism Dual-degree Program	104	4 yrs, full-time only [day, summer]
JD/MBA–Juris Doctor/Master of Business Administration–Dual-degree Program	119	4 yrs, full-time only [day, summer]
JD/MES–Juris Doctor/Master of Environmental Studies–Dual-degree Program	113	4 yrs, full-time only [day, summer]
JD/MLS–Juris Doctor/Master of Library Science–Dual-degree Program	110	4 yrs, full-time only [day, summer]
JD/MPA–Juris Doctor/Master of Professional Accountancy–Dual-degree Program	107	4 yrs, full-time only [day, summer]
JD/MPAf–Juris Doctor/Master of Public Affairs–Dual-degree program	113	4 yrs, full-time only [day, summer]
JD/MS/MA–Juris Doctor/Master of Science or Master of Arts–Telecommunications Dual-degree Program	104	4 yrs, full-time only [day, summer]
LLM–Master of Laws	27	1 yr, full-time only [day, summer]
MCL–Master of Comparative Law	24	1 yr, full-time only [day, summer]
PhD–Doctor of Philosophy–Law and Social Science		[day, summer]
SJD–Doctor of Juridical Science	30	1 yr, full-time only [day, summer]

grants/scholarships, need-based grants/scholarships, and federal work-study loans are available. The average student debt at graduation is $45,000. To apply for financial assistance, students must complete the Free Application for Federal Student Aid, institutional forms, internal application. Completed financial aid forms should be received by March 1. Financial aid contact: Patricia Clark, Director of Admissions, Indiana University School of Law, 211 South Indiana Avenue, Bloomington, IN 47405. Phone: 812-855-4765. Fax: 812-855-0555. E-mail: lawadmis@indiana.edu

Law School Library Indiana University School of Law - Bloomington Law Library has 11 professional staff members and contains more than 631,475 volumes and 8,000 periodicals. 700 seats are available in the library. When classes are in session, the library is open 115 hours per week.

WESTLAW and LEXIS-NEXIS are available, as are the World Wide Web, online bibliographic services, and CD-ROM players. 79 computer workstations are available to students in the library. Special law collections include depository for records and briefs of the United States Supreme Court, Seventh Circuit Court of Appeals, and Indiana Supreme and Appellate Courts.

First-Year Program Class size in the average section is 70; 100% of the first-year courses are taught by full-time faculty.

Upper-Level Program Class size in the average section is 50. Among the electives are:

- Administrative Law
- ★ Advocacy
- ★ Business and Corporate Law
- Civil Litigation
- Consumer Law
- Education Law
- Entertainment Law
- ★ Environmental Law
- Family Law
- Family Practice
- General Practice
- ★ Global Legal Studies
- Government/Regulation
- Health Care/Human Services
- Indian/Tribal Law
- ★ Information and Communications
- Intellectual Property
- ★ International/Comparative Law
- Jurisprudence
- Labor Law
- Land Rights/Natural Resource
- Land Use Law/Natural Resources
- ★ Law and Society
- Lawyering Skills
- Legal History/Philosophy
- ★ Legal Writing
- Litigation
- Media Law
- Mediation
- Probate Law
- Public Interest
- Securities
- Tax Law

(★ indicates an area of special strength)

Clinical Courses Students receive degree credit for clinical courses. (Clinical practicum is not required.) Among the clinical areas offered are:

Civil Litigation
Environmental Law
Family Law
Family Practice
General Practice
Government Litigation
Juvenile Law

Land Rights/Natural Resource
Mediation
Public Interest

International exchange programs permit students to visit France, Spain, and United Kingdom.

INDIANA UNIVERSITY SCHOOL OF LAW-INDIANAPOLIS

Indianapolis, Indiana

INFORMATION CONTACT

Angela M. Espada, Assistant Dean for Admissions
530 West New York Street
Indianapolis, IN 46202-3225

Phone: 317-274-2459   Fax: 317-274-3955
E-mail: amespada@iupui.edu
Web site: http://www.iulaw.indy.indiana.edu/

LAW STUDENT PROFILE [2000–2001]

FULL-TIME   Enrollment: 601
Women: 47%   Men: 53%

PART-TIME   Enrollment: 262
Women: 45%   Men: 55%

RACIAL or ETHNIC COMPOSITION
African American, 7%; Asian/Pacific Islander, 2%; Hispanic, 2%; Native American, 0.5%; International, 2%

APPLICANTS and ADMITTEES
Number applied: 945
Admitted: 504
Percentage accepted: 53%
Seats available: 260
Average LSAT score: 156
Average GPA: 3.2

Indiana University School of Law-Indianapolis is a public institution that organizes classes on a semester calendar system. The campus is situated in an urban setting. Founded in 1895, first ABA approved in 1936, and an AALS member, Indiana University School of Law-Indianapolis offers JD, JD/MBA, JD/MHA, JD/MPAf, and JD/MSPH degrees.

Faculty consists of 41 full-time and 38 part-time members in 2000–2001. 14 full-time faculty members and 8 part-time faculty members are women. 100% of all faculty members have a JD; 17% have advanced law degrees. Of all faculty members, 1% are Asian/Pacific Islander, 4% are African American, 95% are white.

Application Information *Required:* LSAT, LSDAS, application form, application fee of $35, baccalaureate degree, personal statement, college transcripts. *Recommended:* 2 letters of recommendation, resume. *Application deadline* for fall term is March 1 (priority date). Applications are processed on a rolling basis.

Costs The 2000–2001 tuition was $7404 full-time for state residents; $245 per credit hour part-time for state residents. Tuition was $17,982 full-time for nonresidents; $599 per credit hour part-time for nonresidents. Fees: $310 full-time. Tuition and fees vary according to course load and degree level.

Financial Aid Fellowships, loans, merit-based grants/scholarships, need-based grants/scholarships, and federal work-study loans are available. The average student debt at graduation is $52,000. To apply for financial assis-

AT a GLANCE

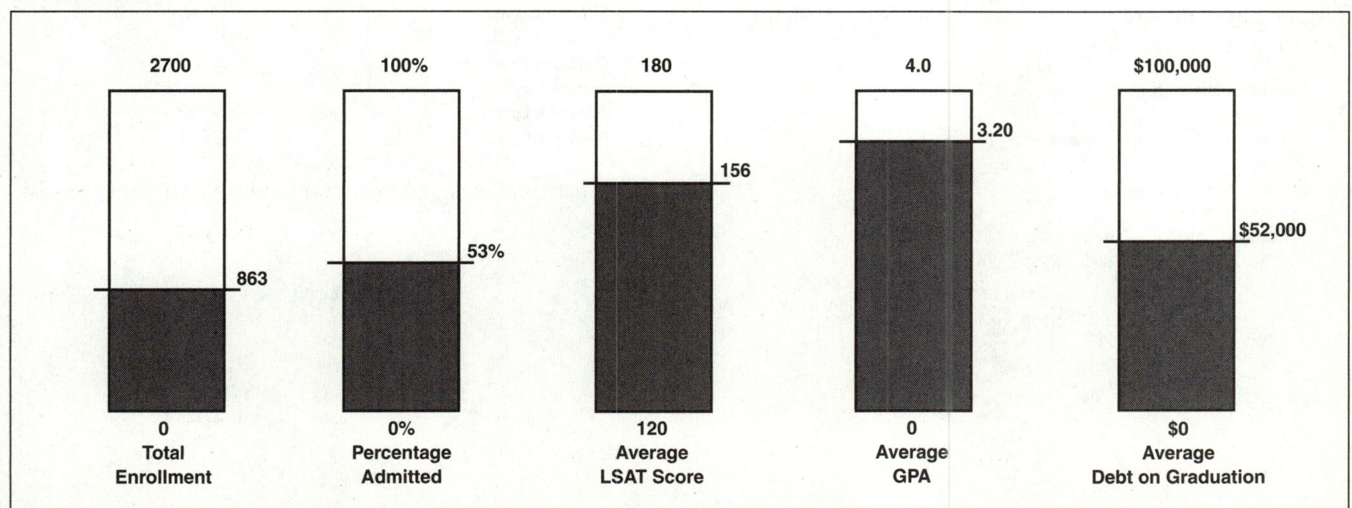

Degree Options

Degree	Total Credits Required	Length of Program
JD–Juris Doctor	90	3–4 yrs, full-time or part-time [day, evening, summer]
JD/MBA–Juris Doctor/Master of Business Administration	119	4–5 yrs, full-time or part-time [day, evening, summer]
JD/MHA–Juris Doctor/Master of Health Administration	130	4–5 yrs, full-time or part-time [day, evening, summer]
JD/MPAf–Juris Doctor/Master of Public Affairs	118	4–5 yrs, full-time or part-time [day, evening, summer]
JD/MSPH–Juris Doctor/Master of Science in Public Health	119	4–5 yrs, full-time or part-time [day, evening, summer]

tance, students must complete the Free Application for Federal Student Aid, institutional forms, scholarship specific applications. Financial aid contact: Jim Schutter, Assistant Director Graduate Programs, 425 University Boulevard, CA103, Indianapolis, IN 46202-5145. Phone: 317-278-GRAD. Fax: 317-274-5930. E-mail: finaid5@iupui.edu

Law School Library Indiana University School of Law - Indianapolis law library has 8 professional staff members and contains more than 530,312 volumes and 9,448 periodicals. 578 seats are available in the library. When classes are in session, the library is open 101 hours per week.

WESTLAW and LEXIS-NEXIS are available, as are the World Wide Web, online bibliographic services, and CD-ROM players. 96 computer workstations are available to students in the library. Special law collections include selective United States depository, United Nations depository, European community legal publications.

First-Year Program Class size in the average section is 85; 100% of the first-year courses are taught by full-time faculty.

Upper-Level Program Class size in the average section is 40. Among the electives are:

Administrative Law
Advocacy
Business and Corporate Law
Civil Litigation
Consumer Law
Criminal Defense
Education Law

Elderly Advocacy
Entertainment Law
Environmental Law
Family Law
Government/Regulation
★ Health Care/Human Services
Health Law
Intellectual Property
International/Comparative Law
Jurisprudence
Labor Law
Land Use Law/Natural Resources
Law and Economics
★ Lawyering Skills
Legal History/Philosophy
Litigation
Media Law
Mediation
Probate Law
Property/Real Estate
Public Interest
Securities
Tax Law
(★ *indicates an area of special strength*)

Clinical Courses Students receive degree credit for clinical courses. (Clinical practicum is not required.) Among the clinical areas offered are:

Civil Litigation
Criminal Defense
Elderly Advocacy
Family Practice
General Practice
Health Law
Juvenile Law
Public Interest

International exchange programs permit students to visit France.

UNIVERSITY OF NOTRE DAME
LAW SCHOOL

Notre Dame, Indiana

INFORMATION CONTACT

Director of Admissions
Notre Dame, IN 46556

Phone: 219-631-6626   Fax: 219-631-3980
E-mail: law.bulletin.1@nd.edu
Web site: http://www.law.nd.edu/

LAW STUDENT PROFILE [2000–2001]

FULL-TIME   Enrollment: 553
Women: 42%   Men: 58%

RACIAL or ETHNIC COMPOSITION

African American, 3%; Asian/Pacific Islander, 7%; Hispanic,
6%; Native American, 1%; International, 1%

APPLICANTS and ADMITTEES

Number applied: 1,859
Admitted: 514
Percentage accepted: 28%
Seats available: 180
Average LSAT score: 161
Average GPA: 3.4

University of Notre Dame Law School is a private
institution that organizes classes on a semester calendar
system. The campus is situated in a suburban setting.
Founded in 1869, first ABA approved in 1925, and an
AALS member, University of Notre Dame Law School
offers JD, JD/MA, JD/MBA, JD/MS, JSD, LLM, and MA
degrees.

Faculty consists of 39 full-time and 34 part-time
members in 2000–2001. 10 full-time faculty members
and 7 part-time faculty members are women. 94% of all
faculty members have a JD; 12% have advanced law
degrees. Of all faculty members, 4% are African American, 2% are Hispanic, 94% are white.

Application Information *Required:* LSAT, LSDAS,
application form, application fee of $55, baccalaureate
degree, 2 letters of recommendation, personal statement,
college transcripts. *Recommended:* resume. *Application
deadline* for fall term is March 1. Applications are
processed on a rolling basis.

Costs The 2000–2001 tuition was $23,780 full-time. Fees:
$142 full-time.

Financial Aid In 2000–2001, 45% of all students received
some form of financial aid. 249 fellowships, totaling
$7500; 20 research assistantships, totaling $3000; 10
teaching assistantships, totaling $6000, were awarded.
Fellowships, graduate assistantships, loans, merit-based
grants/scholarships, need-based grants/scholarships, and
federal work-study loans are also available. The average
student debt at graduation is $61,568. To apply for
financial assistance, students must complete the Free

AT a GLANCE

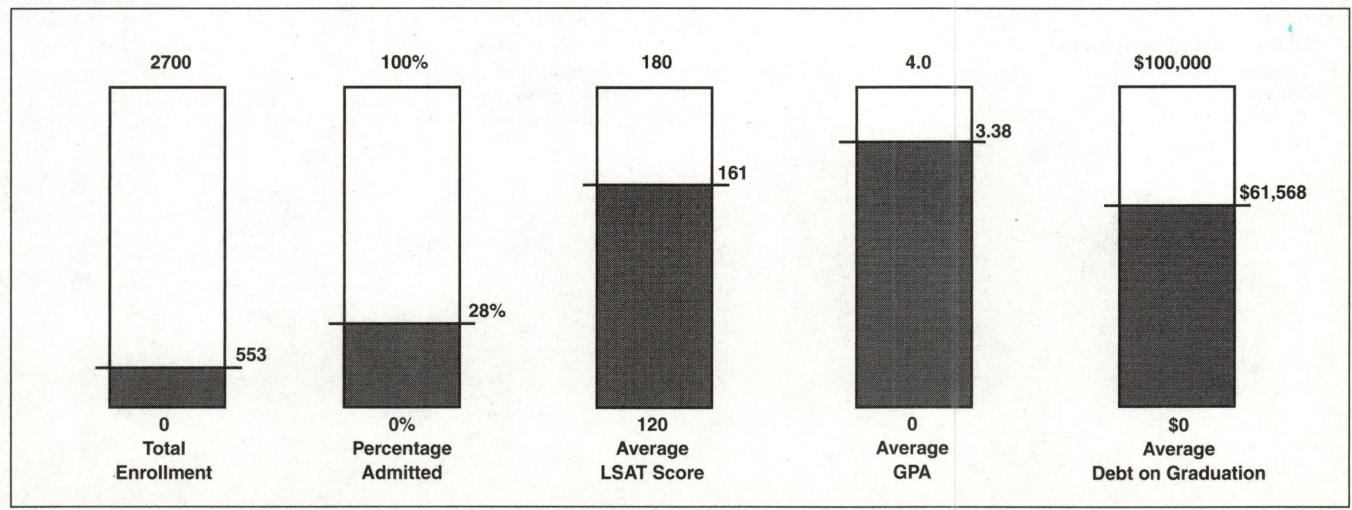

Degree Options

Degree	Total Credits Required	Length of Program
JD–Doctor of Laws	90	3 yrs, full-time only [day]
JD/MA–Juris Doctor/Master of Arts–Peace Studies	111	4 yrs, full-time only
JD/MBA–Juris Doctor/Master of Business Administration–Dual-degree Program	123	4 yrs, full-time only [day]
JD/MS–Juris Doctor/Master of Science–Engineering and Law	99	4 yrs, full-time only [day]
JSD–Doctor of Juridical Science–Civil and Human Rights		full-time or part-time [day]
LLM–Master of Laws–Civil and Human Rights	24	1 yr, full-time only [day]
LLM–Master of Laws–International and Comparative Law	24	1 yr, full-time only [day]
MA–Master of Arts–English and Law	99	4 yrs, full-time only [day]

Application for Federal Student Aid, institutional forms. Completed financial aid forms should be received by March 1. Financial aid contact: Heather Moriconi, Assistant Director, Admissions, PO Box 959, Notre Dame, IN 46556-0959. Phone: 219-631-6626. Fax: 219-631-3980. E-mail: law.bulletin.1@nd.edu

Law School Library Kresge Law Library has 12 professional staff members and contains more than 519,477 volumes and 4,041 periodicals. 484 seats are available in the library. When classes are in session, the library is open 168 hours per week.

WESTLAW and LEXIS-NEXIS are available, as are the World Wide Web, online bibliographic services, and CD-ROM players. 60 computer workstations are available to students in the library.

First-Year Program Class size in the average section is 97; 100% of the first-year courses are taught by full-time faculty.

Upper-Level Program Class size in the average section is 25. Among the electives are:

Administrative Law
★ Advocacy
Business and Corporate Law
Civil Litigation
Consumer Law
Cyberspace Law
Education Law
Elderly Advocacy
Environmental Law
Family Law
Family Practice
Health Care/Human Services
Human Rights
Immigration
Intellectual Property
International/Comparative Law
★ Jurisprudence
Labor Law
Land Use Law/Natural Resources
★ Lawyering Skills
Legal History/Philosophy
Litigation
Maritime Law
Mediation
Public Interest
Securities
Tax Law

(★ indicates an area of special strength)

Clinical Courses Students receive degree credit for clinical courses. (Clinical practicum is not required.) Among the clinical areas offered are:

Civil Litigation
Criminal Defense
Elderly Advocacy
Family Law
Family Practice
Immigration
Mediation
Public Interest

VALPARAISO UNIVERSITY
SCHOOL OF LAW

Valparaiso, Indiana

INFORMATION CONTACT

Marilyn Olson, Director of Admissions and Student Relations/Assistant Dean for Admissions and Student Services
Weseman Hall
Valparaiso, IN 46383

Phone: 219-465-7829   Fax: 219-465-7872
E-mail: marilyn.olson@valpo.edu
Web site: http://www.valpo.edu/law/

LAW STUDENT PROFILE [2000–2001]

FULL-TIME   Enrollment: 381
Women: 47%   Men: 53%

PART-TIME   Enrollment: 54
Women: 41%   Men: 59%

RACIAL or ETHNIC COMPOSITION
African American, 5%; Asian/Pacific Islander, 1%; Hispanic, 3%; Native American, 0.2%; International, 1%

APPLICANTS and ADMITTEES
Number applied: 853
Admitted: 530
Percentage accepted: 62%
Seats available: 160
Average LSAT score: 152
Average GPA: 3.1

Valparaiso University School of Law is a private institution that organizes classes on a semester calendar system. The campus is situated in a small-town setting. Founded in 1879, first ABA approved in 1929, and an AALS member, Valparaiso University School of Law offers JD, JD/AMBA, JD/MA, and LLM degrees.

Faculty consists of 32 full-time and 32 part-time members in 2000–2001. 13 full-time faculty members and 11 part-time faculty members are women. 100% of all faculty members have a JD; 20% have advanced law degrees. Of all faculty members, 12% are African American, 88% are white.

Application Information *Required:* LSAT, LSDAS, application form, application fee of $30, baccalaureate degree, personal statement, essay, college transcripts. *Recommended:* recommendations, resume. *Application deadline* for fall term is April 15 (priority date). Applications are processed on a rolling basis.

Financial Aid 32 research assistantships, totaling $500; 1 teaching assistantship, totaling $2000, were awarded. Loans, loan repayment assistance program (LRAP), merit-based grants/scholarships, need-based grants/scholarships, and federal work-study loans are also available. The average student debt at graduation is $56,916. To apply for financial assistance, students must complete the Free Application for Federal Student Aid. Completed financial aid forms should be received by May 1. Financial aid contact: Ann Weitgenant, Financial Aid Counselor, Wesemann Hall, Valparaiso, IN 46383. Phone: 219-465-7818. Fax: 219-465-7808. E-mail: ann.weitgenant@valpo.edu

AT a GLANCE

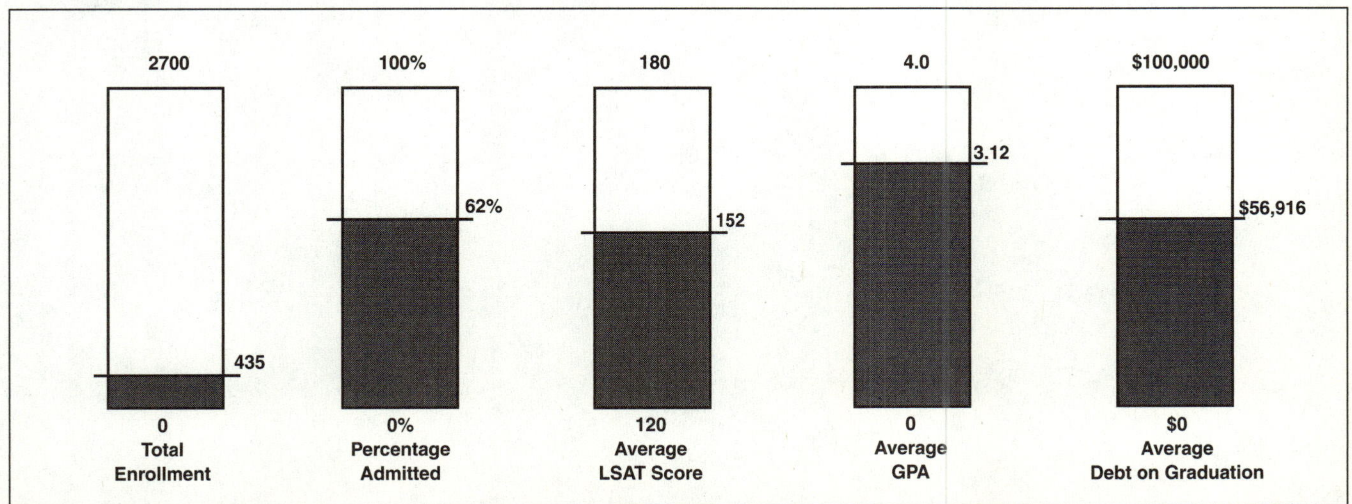

Degree Options

Degree	Total Credits Required	Length of Program
JD–Juris Doctor	90	3–5 yrs, full-time or part-time [day]
JD/AMBA–Juris Doctor/Master of Business Administration with Accounting Major	108	4 yrs, full-time or part-time [day]
JD/MA–Juris Doctor/Master of Arts–Joint-degree Psychology	108	4–5 yrs, full-time or part-time [day]
LLM–Master of Laws	24	1–2 yrs, full-time or part-time [day]

Law School Library School of Law Library has 6 professional staff members and contains more than 283,803 volumes and 2,806 periodicals. 347 seats are available in the library. When classes are in session, the library is open 110 hours per week.

WESTLAW and LEXIS-NEXIS are available, as are the World Wide Web, online bibliographic services, and CD-ROM players. 39 computer workstations are available to students in the library. Special law collections include Indiana Supreme Court and Indiana Court of Appeals briefs.

First-Year Program Class size in the average section is 55; 100% of the first-year courses are taught by full-time faculty.

Upper-Level Program Class size in the average section is 35. Among the electives are:

Administrative Law
Advocacy
★ Alternative Dispute Resolution
Business and Corporate Law
★ Civil Litigation
★ Criminal Defense
★ Elder Law
★ Entertainment Law
★ Environmental Law
Family Law
Government/Regulation
★ Health Care/Human Services

★ Intellectual Property
★ International/Comparative Law
Jurisprudence
Juvenile Law
★ Labor Law
Land Use Law/Natural Resources
Lawyering Skills
Legal History/Philosophy
Litigation
Maritime Law
Media Law
★ Mediation
Probate Law
Public Interest
Securities
Tax Law

(★ indicates an area of special strength)

Clinical Courses Students receive degree credit for clinical courses. (Clinical practicum is not required.) Among the clinical areas offered are:

Civil Litigation
Criminal Defense
Domestic Violence
Environmental Law
Juvenile Law
Mediation
Public Interest
Tax Law

International exchange programs permit students to visit United Kingdom.

DRAKE UNIVERSITY
LAW SCHOOL

Des Moines, Iowa

INFORMATION CONTACT

J. Kara Blanchard, Director of Admission and
Financial Aid
Cartwright Hall, 2507 University Avenue
Des Moines, IA 50311-4505

Phone: 800-44-   Fax: 515-271-2530
       DRAKE ext.
       2782
E-mail: lawadmit@drake.edu
Web site: http://www.law.drake.edu/

LAW STUDENT PROFILE [2000–2001]

FULL-TIME   Enrollment: 372
Women: 49%   Men: 51%

PART-TIME   Enrollment: 12
Women: 50%   Men: 50%

RACIAL or ETHNIC COMPOSITION

African American, 4%; Asian/Pacific Islander, 2%; Hispanic,
2%; International, 2%

APPLICANTS and ADMITTEES

Number applied: 673
Admitted: 509
Percentage accepted: 76%
Seats available: 135
Average LSAT score: 151
Average GPA: 3.2

Drake University Law School is a private institution that
organizes classes on a semester calendar system. The
campus is situated in an urban setting. Founded in 1865,
first ABA approved in 1923, and an AALS member,
Drake University Law School offers JD, JD/MA, JD/MBA,
JD/MPAd, JD/MS, JD/MSW, and JD/PharmD degrees.

Faculty consists of 29 full-time and 24 part-time
members in 2000–2001. 9 full-time faculty members and
5 part-time faculty members are women. 100% of all
faculty members have a JD; 20.6% have advanced law
degrees. Of all faculty members, 5.9% are African
American, 94.1% are white.

Application Information *Required:* LSAT, LSDAS,
application form, application fee of $40, baccalaureate
degree, personal statement, college transcripts. *Recommended:* recommendations, resume. *Application deadline*
for fall term is April 1 (priority date). Applications are
processed on a rolling basis.

Costs The 2000–2001 tuition was $18,800 full-time; $625
per credit part-time.

Financial Aid In 2000–2001, 93% of all students received
some form of financial aid. 19 research assistantships,
totaling $2400; 6 teaching assistantships, totaling $1800,
were awarded. Graduate assistantships, loans, merit-based
grants/scholarships, need-based grants/scholarships, and
federal work-study loans are also available. The average
student debt at graduation is $58,800. To apply for
financial assistance, students must complete the Free
Application for Federal Student Aid, institutional forms,
scholarship specific applications. Completed financial aid

AT a GLANCE

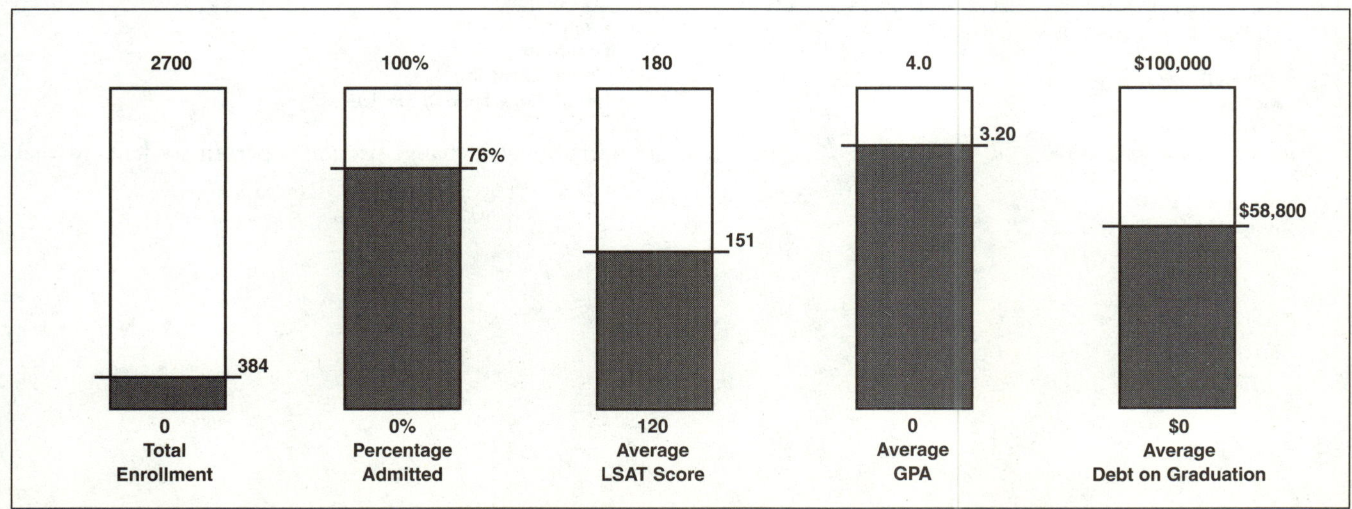

Degree Options

Degree	Total Credits Required	Length of Program
JD–Juris Doctor	90	3 yrs, full-time or part-time [day, evening, summer]
JD/MA–Juris Doctor/Master of Arts–Mass Communication, Political Science		full-time only [day, evening, summer]
JD/MBA–Juris Doctor/Master of Business Administration–Joint-degree Program		full-time only [day, evening, summer]
JD/MPAd–Juris Doctor/Master of Public Administration–Joint-degree Program		full-time only [day, evening, summer]
JD/MS–Juris Doctor/Master of Science–Agricultural Economics Joint-degree Program		full-time only [day, evening, summer]
JD/MSW–Juris Doctor/Master of Social Work–Joint-degree Program		full-time only [day, evening, summer]
JD/PharmD–Juris Doctor/Doctor of Pharmacy–Joint-degree Program		full-time only [day, evening, summer]

forms should be received by March 1. Financial aid contact: Kara Blanchard, Director of Admission and Financial Aid, 2507 University Avenue, Des Moines, IA 50311. Phone: 800-44-DRAKE ext. 2782 or toll free 800-44DRAKE ext. 2782 (in-state), ext. 2782 (out-of-state). Fax: 515-271-1990. E-mail: lawadmit@drake.edu

Law School Library Drake University Law Library has 5 professional staff members and contains more than 281,815 volumes and 3,177 periodicals. 705 seats are available in the library. When classes are in session, the library is open 109 hours per week.

WESTLAW and LEXIS-NEXIS are available, as are the World Wide Web, online bibliographic services, and CD-ROM players. 104 computer workstations are available to students in the library. Special law collections include agricultural law, Iowa law, constitutional law.

First-Year Program Class size in the average section is 61; 100% of the first-year courses are taught by full-time faculty.

Upper-Level Program Class size in the average section is 21. Among the electives are:

Administrative Law
Advocacy
★ Agricultural Law
Business and Corporate Law
Civil Litigation
★ Constitutional Law
Consumer Law
★ Criminal Defense
Education Law
Family Law
★ General Practice
Health Care/Human Services
Intellectual Property
★ International/Comparative Law
Jurisprudence
Labor Law
Land Use Law/Natural Resources
Lawyering Skills
Legal History/Philosophy
Litigation
Media Law
Mediation
Probate Law
Securities
Tax Law

(★ indicates an area of special strength)

Clinical Courses Students receive degree credit for clinical courses. (Clinical practicum is not required.) Among the clinical areas offered are:

Administrative Law
Children's Rights
Civil Litigation
Criminal Defense
Family Law
General Practice
Health Care/Human Services

International exchange programs permit students to visit France.

THE UNIVERSITY OF IOWA
COLLEGE OF LAW

Iowa City, Iowa

INFORMATION CONTACT

Camille de Jorna, Admissions Director
Boyd Law Building
Iowa City, IA 52242

Phone: 319-335-9095   Fax: 319-335-9019
E-mail: law-admissions@uiowa.edu
Web site: http://www.uiowa.edu/

LAW STUDENT PROFILE [2000–2001]

FULL-TIME   Enrollment: 682
Women: 42%   Men: 58%

RACIAL or ETHNIC COMPOSITION
African American, 6%; Asian/Pacific Islander, 4%; Hispanic, 4%; Native American, 1%; International, 4%

APPLICANTS and ADMITTEES
Number applied: 1,119
Admitted: 537
Percentage accepted: 48%
Seats available: 231
Median LSAT score: 158
Average GPA: 3.5

The University of Iowa College of Law is a public institution that organizes classes on a semester calendar system. The campus is situated in a small-town setting. Founded in 1865, first ABA approved in 1923, and an AALS member, The University of Iowa College of Law offers JD, JD/MA, JD/MSW, JD/PhD, and LLM degrees.

Faculty consists of 44 full-time and 41 part-time members in 2000–2001. 14 full-time faculty members and 7 part-time faculty members are women. 100% of all faculty members have a JD; 25% have advanced law degrees. Of all faculty members, 2% are Asian/Pacific Islander, 6% are African American, 4% are Hispanic, 88% are white.

Application Information *Required:* LSAT, LSDAS, application form, application fee of $30, baccalaureate degree, personal statement, essay, college transcripts. *Recommended:* recommendations. *Application deadline* for fall term is March 1. Applications are processed on a rolling basis.

Costs The 1999–2000 tuition was $6822 full-time for state residents. Tuition was $17,384 full-time for nonresidents. Fees: $143 per semester full-time. Full-time tuition and fees vary according to course load and degree level.

Financial Aid In 2000–2001, 91% of all students received some form of financial aid. 130 fellowships; 121 research assistantships, totaling $1653, were awarded. Fellowships, graduate assistantships, loans, loan repayment assistance program (LRAP), merit-based grants/scholarships, need-based grants/scholarships, and federal work-study

AT a GLANCE

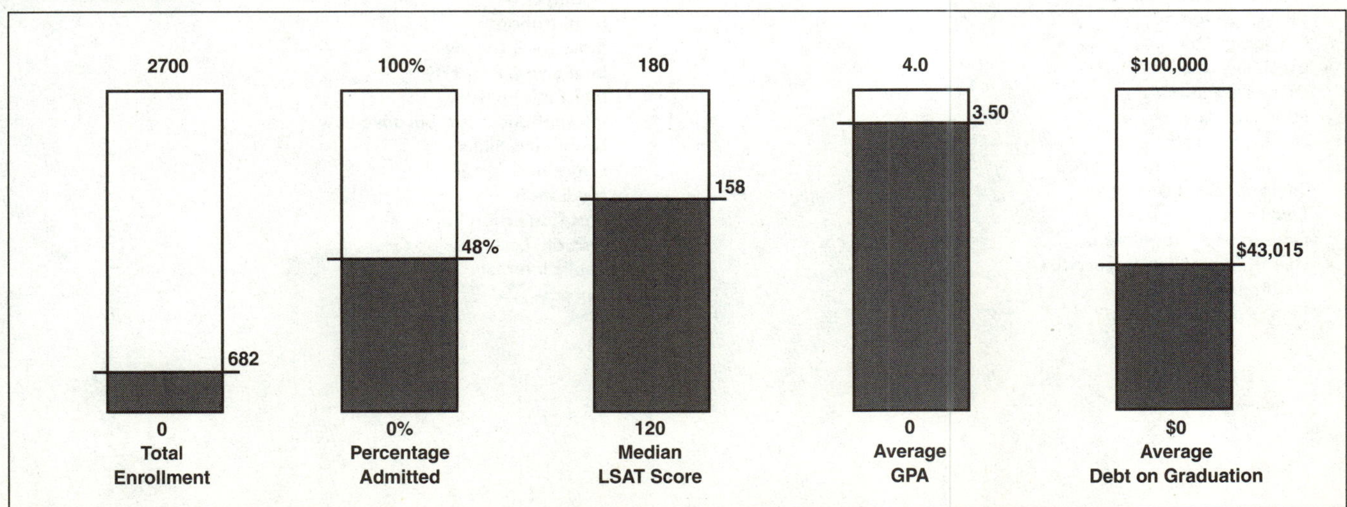

Degree Options

Degree	Total Credits Required	Length of Program
JD–Juris Doctor	90	3 yrs, full-time only [day]
JD/MA–Juris Doctor/Master of Arts		full-time only [day]
JD/MSW–Juris Doctor/Master of Social Work	126	full-time only [day]
JD/PhD–Juris Doctor/Doctor of Philosophy		full-time only [day]
LLM–Master of Laws	24	1 yr, full-time only [day]

loans are also available. The average student debt at graduation is $43,015. To apply for financial assistance, students must complete the Free Application for Federal Student Aid, institutional forms, federal income tax return (student only). Financial aid contact: Susan Palmer, Director of Financial Aid, College of Law, 276 Boyd Law Building, Iowa City, IA 52242. Phone: 319-335-9095. Fax: 319-335-9019. E-mail: law-admissions@uiowa.edu

Law School Library University of Iowa Law Library has 14 professional staff members and contains more than 961,377 volumes and 8,663 periodicals. 700 seats are available in the library. When classes are in session, the library is open 106 hours per week.

WESTLAW and LEXIS-NEXIS are available, as are the World Wide Web, online bibliographic services, and CD-ROM players. 62 computer workstations are available to students in the library. Special law collections include United Nations collection, records and briefs, NAACP papers.

First-Year Program Class size in the average section is 60; 100% of the first-year courses are taught by full-time faculty.

Upper-Level Program Among the electives are:

- Administrative Law
- Advocacy
- AIDS and the Law
- ★ Business and Corporate Law
- Civil Litigation
- Consumer Law
- ★ Disability Law
- Domestic Violence
- Education Law
- Employment Law
- Entertainment Law
- Environmental Law
- Family Law
- Government/Regulation
- ★ Health Care/Human Services
- Health Law
- Immigration
- ★ Indian/Tribal Law
- ★ Intellectual Property
- International Law
- ★ International/Comparative Law
- Jurisprudence
- Labor Law
- Land Use Law/Natural Resources
- ★ Lawyering Skills
- ★ Legal History/Philosophy
- Litigation
- ★ Media Law
- ★ Mediation
- Post-Conviction Relief
- Probate Law
- Public Interest
- Securities
- Tax Law

(★ *indicates an area of special strength*)

Clinical Courses Students receive degree credit for clinical courses. (Clinical practicum is not required.) Among the clinical areas offered are:

- Administrative Law
- Advocacy
- AIDS and the Law
- Business and Corporate Law
- Civil Litigation
- Civil Rights
- Consumer Law
- Disability Law
- Domestic Violence
- Employment Law
- Family Law
- Government/Regulation
- Health Care/Human Services
- Health Law
- Immigration
- Indian/Tribal Law
- Intellectual Property
- International Law
- International/Comparative Law
- Lawyering Skills
- Litigation
- Mediation
- Post-Conviction Relief
- Probate Law
- Public Interest
- Tax Law

UNIVERSITY OF KANSAS
SCHOOL OF LAW

Lawrence, Kansas

LAW STUDENT PROFILE [2000–2001]

FULL-TIME   Enrollment: 494
Women: 44%   Men: 56%

RACIAL or ETHNIC COMPOSITION
African American, 3%; Asian/Pacific Islander, 1%; Hispanic, 3%; Native American, 1%; International, 1%

APPLICANTS and ADMITTEES
Number applied: 728
Admitted: 395
Percentage accepted: 54%
Seats available: 180
Average LSAT score: 155
Average GPA: 3.3

University of Kansas School of Law is a public institution that organizes classes on a semester calendar system. The campus is situated in a small-town setting. Founded in 1878, first ABA approved in 1923, and an AALS member, University of Kansas School of Law offers JD, JD/MA, JD/MBA, JD/MHA, JD/MPAd, JD/MSW, and JD/MUP degrees.

Faculty consists of 35 full-time and 14 part-time members in 2000–2001. 10 full-time faculty members and 3 part-time faculty members are women. 100% of all faculty members have a JD; 2.7% have advanced law degrees. Of all faculty members, 2.7% are Native American, 5.5% are African American, 5.5% are Hispanic, 86.3% are white.

Application Information *Required:* LSAT, LSDAS, application form, application fee of $40, baccalaureate degree, 1 recommendation, personal statement, writing sample, college transcripts. *Recommended:* resume. *Application deadline* for fall term is March 15. Applications are processed on a rolling basis.

Costs The 2000–2001 tuition was $7182 full-time for state residents. Tuition was $14,866 full-time for nonresidents.

Financial Aid In 2000–2001, 51% of all students received some form of financial aid. 187 fellowships, totaling $3700; 56 research assistantships, totaling $540; 7 teaching assistantships, totaling $2440, were awarded. Graduate assistantships, loans, merit-based grants/scholarships, need-based grants/scholarships, and federal work-study loans are also available. The average student

AT a GLANCE

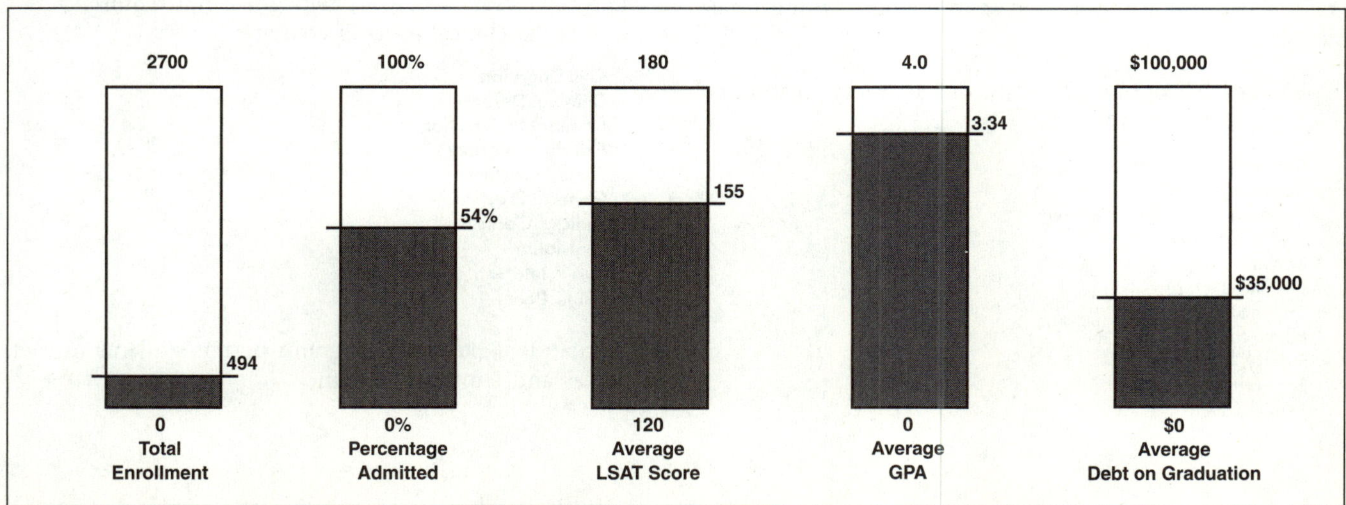

Degree Options

Degree	Total Credits Required	Length of Program
JD–Juris Doctor	90	3 yrs, full-time only [day, summer]
JD/MA–Juris Doctor/Master of Arts–Economics Joint-degree Program	120	3 yrs, full-time only [day, summer]
JD/MA–Juris Doctor/Master of Arts–Philosophy Joint-degree Program	102	3 yrs, full-time only [day, summer]
JD/MBA–Juris Doctor/Master of Business Administration–Joint-degree Program	118	4 yrs, full-time only [day, summer]
JD/MHA–Juris Doctor/Master of Health Administration–Joint-degree Program	127	4 yrs, full-time only [day, summer]
JD/MPAd–Juris Doctor/Master of Public Administration–Joint-degree Program	115	4 yrs, full-time only [day, summer]
JD/MSW–Juris Doctor/Master of Social Work–Joint-degree Program	131	4 yrs, full-time only [day, summer]
JD/MUP–Juris Doctor/Masters of Urban Planning–Joint-degree Program	115	4 yrs, full-time only [day, summer]

debt at graduation is $35,000. To apply for financial assistance, students must complete the Free Application for Federal Student Aid. Completed financial aid forms should be received by March 1. Financial aid contact: Rachel Reitz, Director of Admissions, University of Kansas School of Law, Lawrence, KS 66045. Phone: 866-220-3654. Fax: 785-864-5054. E-mail: admit@law.wpo.ukans.edu

Law School Library University of Kansas School of Law Library has 5 professional staff members and contains more than 331,393 volumes and 4,345 periodicals. 276 seats are available in the library. When classes are in session, the library is open 103 hours per week.

WESTLAW and LEXIS-NEXIS are available, as are the World Wide Web, online bibliographic services, and CD-ROM players. 50 computer workstations are available to students in the library. Special law collections include Kansas State Law, Indian Law.

First-Year Program Class size in the average section is 45; 100% of the first-year courses are taught by full-time faculty.

Upper-Level Program Class size in the average section is 28. Among the electives are:

Administrative Law
Advocacy
Business and Corporate Law
Civil Litigation
Consumer Law
★ Criminal Defense
★ Criminal Prosecution
Education Law
★ Elderly Advocacy
Environmental Law
Family Law

★ Family Practice
General Practice
Government/Regulation
Health Care/Human Services
★ Indian/Tribal Law
Intellectual Property
International/Comparative Law
★ Judicial Clerkship
Jurisprudence
Labor Law
Land Use Law/Natural Resources
Lawyering Skills
Legal History/Philosophy
★ Legislation
Litigation
★ Media Law
Mediation
Probate Law
★ Public Interest
★ Public Policy
Securities
★ Tax Law
(★ *indicates an area of special strength*)

Clinical Courses Students receive degree credit for clinical courses. (Clinical practicum is not required.) Among the clinical areas offered are:

Civil Litigation
Criminal Defense
Criminal Prosecution
Elderly Advocacy
Family Practice
General Practice
Judicial Clerkship
Legislation
Public Interest
Public Policy

International exchange programs permit students to visit Turkey and United Kingdom.

WASHBURN UNIVERSITY OF TOPEKA
SCHOOL OF LAW

Topeka, Kansas

INFORMATION CONTACT

Janet K. Kerr, Director of Admissions
1700 College
Topeka, KS 66621

Phone: 785-231-1185   Fax: 785-232-8087
E-mail: zzkerr@washburn.edu
Web site: http://washburnlaw.edu/

LAW STUDENT PROFILE [2000–2001]

FULL-TIME   Enrollment: 407
Women: 43%   Men: 57%

APPLICANTS and ADMITTEES

Number applied: 560
Admitted: 364
Percentage accepted: 65%
Seats available: 149
Average LSAT score: 148
Average GPA: 3.1

Washburn University of Topeka School of Law is a public institution that organizes classes on a semester calendar system. The campus is situated in an urban setting. Founded in 1903, first ABA approved in 1923, and an AALS member.

Faculty consists of 29 full-time and 36 part-time members in 2000–2001. 9 full-time faculty members and 7 part-time faculty members are women. 100% of all faculty members have a JD; 40.6% have advanced law degrees. Of all faculty members, 6.25% are Asian/Pacific Islander, 6.25% are African American, 6.25% are Hispanic, 81.25% are white.

Application Information *Required:* LSAT, LSDAS, application form, application fee of $30, baccalaureate degree, 1 recommendation, personal statement, college transcripts. *Recommended:* resume. *Application deadline* for fall term is March 15 (priority date); for spring term is September 15 (priority date). Applications are processed on a rolling basis.

Costs The 1999–2000 tuition was $7530 full-time for state residents; $251 per credit hour part-time for state residents. Tuition was $11,340 full-time for nonresidents; $378 per credit hour part-time for nonresidents. Tuition was $11,340 full-time for international students. Fees: $20 per semester full-time; $20 per semester part-time. Tuition and fees vary according to course load and degree level.

Financial Aid In 2000–2001, 91% of all students received some form of financial aid. 15 research assistantships, totaling $2570; 27 teaching assistantships, totaling $2570,

AT a GLANCE

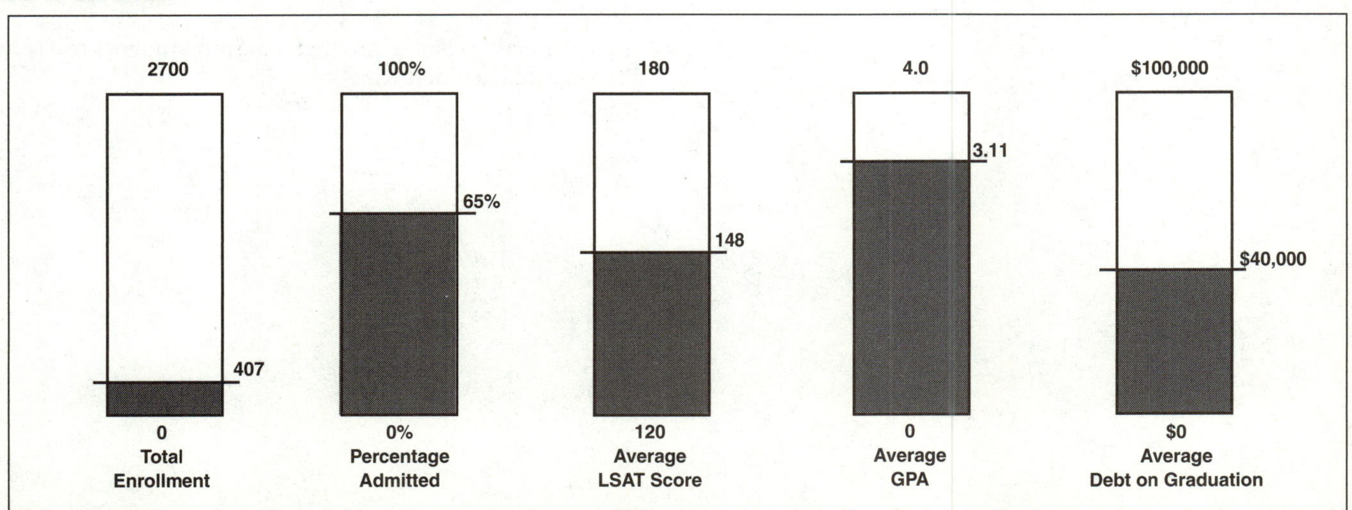

were awarded. Graduate assistantships, loans, merit-based grants/scholarships, need-based grants/scholarships, and federal work-study loans are also available. The average student debt at graduation is $40,000. To apply for financial assistance, students must complete the Free Application for Federal Student Aid, institutional forms, scholarship specific applications, CSS PROFILE form. Completed financial aid forms should be received by April 1. Financial aid contact: Janell Harris, Assistant Director, Financial Aid, 1700 College, Topeka, KS 66621. Phone: 800-524-8447. Fax: 785-231-1079. E-mail: zzharr@washburn.edu

Law School Library Washburn University School of Law Library has 9 professional staff members and contains more than 321,470 volumes and 3,861 periodicals. 381 seats are available in the library. When classes are in session, the library is open 99 hours per week.

WESTLAW and LEXIS-NEXIS are available, as are the World Wide Web, online bibliographic services, and CD-ROM players. 105 computer workstations are available to students in the library. Special law collections include US Government Documents, Kansas Government Documents, Wolf Creek Collection (Nuclear Regulatory Commission Depository).

First-Year Program Class size in the average section is 57; 100% of the first-year courses are taught by full-time faculty.

Upper-Level Program Class size in the average section is 42. Among the electives are:

- Administrative Law
- ★ Advocacy
- ★ Agricultural Law
- ★ Bankruptcy
- Business and Corporate Law
- Civil Litigation
- Civil Rights
- ★ Consumer Law
- ★ Criminal Defense
- Criminal Prosecution
- Education Law
- ★ Elderly Advocacy
- Entertainment Law
- ★ Environmental Law
- ★ Family Law
- ★ Family Practice

- ★ General Practice
- Government/Regulation
- Health Care/Human Services
- Health Law
- Indian/Tribal Law
- Intellectual Property
- ★ International/Comparative Law
- Jurisprudence
- Juvenile Law
- Labor Law
- ★ Land Use Law/Natural Resources
- ★ Lawyering Skills
- Legal History/Philosophy
- ★ Litigation
- Maritime Law
- Media Law
- ★ Mediation
- ★ Mental Health and Law
- Probate Law
- ★ Public Interest
- Securities
- ★ Tax Law

(★ indicates an area of special strength)

Clinical Courses Students receive degree credit for clinical courses. (Clinical practicum is not required.) Among the clinical areas offered are:

- Administrative Law
- Advocacy
- Bankruptcy
- Civil Litigation
- Civil Rights
- Consumer Law
- Criminal Defense
- Criminal Prosecution
- Elderly Advocacy
- Family Law
- Family Practice
- General Practice
- Health Care/Human Services
- Health Law
- Indian/Tribal Law
- Juvenile Law
- Labor Law
- Lawyering Skills
- Litigation
- Mediation
- Mental Health and Law
- Public Interest
- Tax Law

International exchange programs permit students to visit Paraguay and United Kingdom.

NORTHERN KENTUCKY UNIVERSITY
SALMON P. CHASE COLLEGE OF LAW

Highland Heights, Kentucky

INFORMATION CONTACT

Gina Bray, Admissions Specialist
Nunn Hall
Highland Heights, KY 41099

Phone: 859-572-5384   Fax: 859-572-6081
Web site: http://www.nku.edu/~chase/

LAW STUDENT PROFILE [2000–2001]

FULL-TIME   Enrollment: 210
Women: 48%   Men: 52%

PART-TIME   Enrollment: 161
Women: 42%   Men: 58%

RACIAL or ETHNIC COMPOSITION
African American, 4%; Asian/Pacific Islander, 1%; Hispanic, 1%; Native American, 1%

APPLICANTS and ADMITTEES
Seats available: 120
Average LSAT score: 152
Average GPA: 3.2

Northern Kentucky University Salmon P. Chase College of Law is a public institution that organizes classes on a semester calendar system. The campus is situated in a suburban setting. Founded in 1893, first ABA approved in 1954, and an AALS member, Northern Kentucky University Salmon P. Chase College of Law offers JD and JD/MBA degrees.

Faculty consists of 26 full-time members in 2000–2001. 8 full-time faculty members are women. 100% of all faculty members have a JD; 31% have advanced law degrees. Of all faculty members, 4% are Asian/Pacific Islander, 8% are African American, 88% are white.

Application Information *Required:* LSAT, LSDAS, application form, application fee of $30, baccalaureate degree, 2 letters of recommendation, personal statement, essay, writing sample. *Application deadline* for fall term is May 15. Applications are processed on a rolling basis.

Costs The 2000–2001 tuition was $6846 full-time for state residents; $252 per credit hour part-time for state residents. Tuition was $14,798 full-time for nonresidents; $584 per credit hour part-time for nonresidents.

Financial Aid Graduate assistantships, loans, merit-based grants/scholarships, need-based grants/scholarships, and federal work-study loans are available. The average student debt at graduation is $57,511. To apply for financial assistance, students must complete the Free Application for Federal Student Aid. Completed financial aid forms should be received by April 1. Financial aid

AT a GLANCE

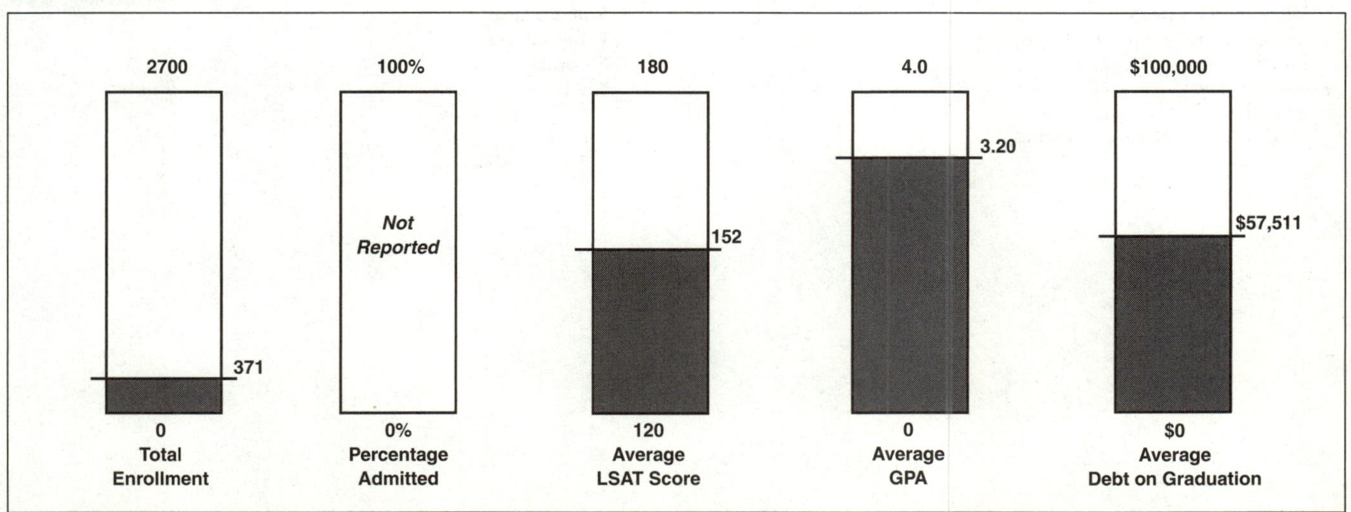

Degree Options

Degree	Total Credits Required	Length of Program
JD–Doctor of Laws	90	3–4 yrs, full-time or part-time [day, evening, summer]
JD/MBA–Juris Doctor/Master of Business Administration–JD/MBA Dual-degree	110	4–5 yrs, full-time or part-time [day, evening, summer]

contact: Penny Parsons, Assistant Director of Financial Aid, AC 419, Nunn Drive, Highland Heights, KY 41099. Phone: 606-572-6434. Fax: 606-572-6997. E-mail: parsonsp@nku.edu

Law School Library Salmon P. Chase College of Law Library has 7 professional staff members and contains more than 246,832 volumes and 1,899 periodicals. 240 seats are available in the library. When classes are in session, the library is open 80 hours per week.

WESTLAW and LEXIS-NEXIS are available, as are the World Wide Web, online bibliographic services, and CD-ROM players. 43 computer workstations are available to students in the library. Special law collections include Siebenthaler Rare Book Collection and United States Supreme Court records and briefs on microfiche.

First-Year Program Class size in the average section is 60; 100% of the first-year courses are taught by full-time faculty.

Upper-Level Program Class size in the average section is 25. Among the electives are:

- Administrative Law
- ★ Advocacy
- ★ Business and Corporate Law
- Consumer Law
- Education Law
- Entertainment Law
- ★ Environmental Law
- Family Law
- Government/Regulation
- Health Care/Human Services
- Intellectual Property
- International/Comparative Law
- Jurisprudence
- ★ Juvenile Law
- Labor Law
- Land Use Law/Natural Resources
- ★ Lawyering Skills
- Legal History/Philosophy
- Litigation
- ★ Local Government
- Media Law
- Mediation
- Probate Law
- Public Interest
- Securities
- Tax Law

(★ *indicates an area of special strength*)

Clinical Courses Students receive degree credit for clinical courses. (Clinical practicum is not required.) Among the clinical areas offered are:

- Administrative Law
- Advocacy
- Business and Corporate Law
- Consumer Law
- Education Law
- Entertainment Law
- Environmental Law
- Family Law
- Government/Regulation
- Health Care/Human Services
- Intellectual Property
- Judicial Process
- Jurisprudence
- Juvenile Law
- Labor Law
- Land Use Law/Natural Resources
- Lawyering Skills
- Legal History/Philosophy
- Litigation
- Local Government
- Media Law
- Mediation
- Probate Law
- Public Interest
- Securities
- Tax Law

UNIVERSITY OF KENTUCKY
COLLEGE OF LAW

Lexington, Kentucky

INFORMATION CONTACT

Drusilla V. Bakert, Associate Dean
209 Law Building
Lexington, KY 40506-0048

Phone: 859-257-6770   Fax: 859-323-1061
E-mail: dbakert@pop.uky.edu
Web site: http://www.uky.edu/Law/

LAW STUDENT PROFILE [2000–2001]

FULL-TIME Enrollment: 379
Women: 44%   Men: 56%

RACIAL or ETHNIC COMPOSITION
African American, 4%; Hispanic, 1%; Native American, 0.3%;
International, 0.3%

APPLICANTS and ADMITTEES
Number applied: 881
Admitted: 340
Percentage accepted: 39%
Seats available: 135
Average LSAT score: 158
Average GPA: 3.5

University of Kentucky College of Law is a public institution that organizes classes on a semester calendar system. The campus is situated in an urban setting. Founded in 1908, first ABA approved in 1925, and an AALS member, University of Kentucky College of Law offers JD, JD/MBA, and JD/MPAd degrees.

Faculty consists of 29 full-time and 22 part-time members in 2000–2001. 9 full-time faculty members and 8 part-time faculty members are women. 100% of all faculty members have a JD; 24% have advanced law degrees. Of all faculty members, 10% are African American, 90% are white.

Application Information *Required:* LSAT, LSDAS, application form, application fee of $35, baccalaureate degree, personal statement. *Recommended:* recommendations. *Application deadline* for fall term is March 1 (priority date). Applications are processed on a rolling basis.

Costs The 2000–2001 tuition was $5876 full-time for state residents. Tuition was $15,450 full-time for nonresidents. Fees: $350 full-time.

Financial Aid In 2000–2001, 69% of all students received some form of financial aid. 160 fellowships, totaling $2500 were awarded. Fellowships, loans, merit-based grants/scholarships, need-based grants/scholarships, and federal work-study loans are also available. The average student debt at graduation is $38,000. To apply for financial assistance, students must complete the Free Application for Federal Student Aid, scholarship specific applications. Completed financial aid forms should be

AT a GLANCE

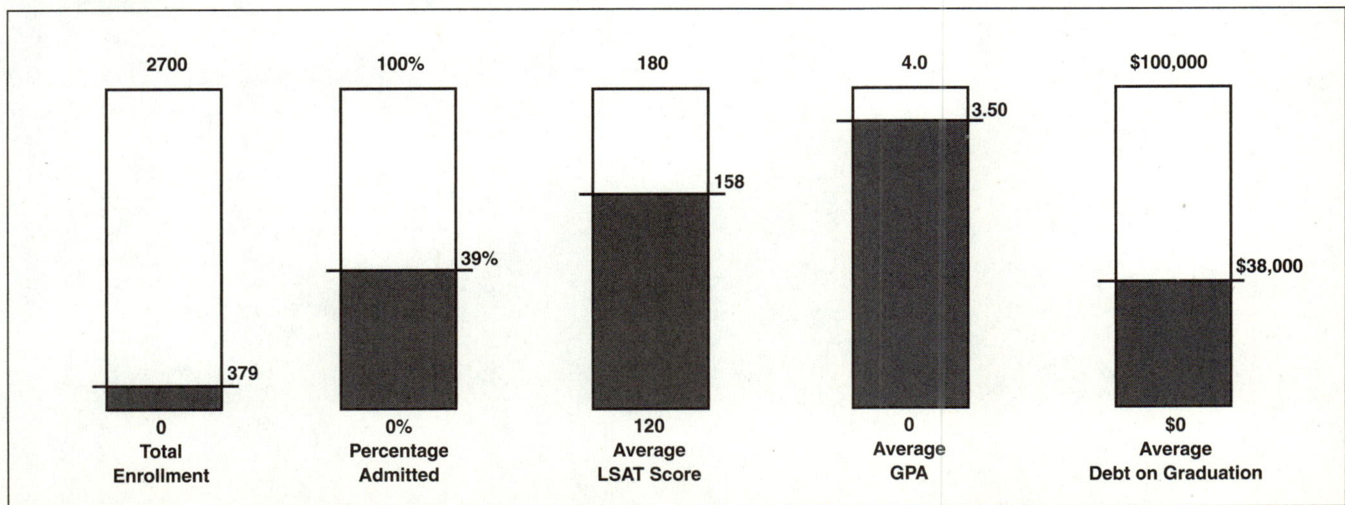

Degree Options

Degree	Total Credits Required	Length of Program
JD–Juris Doctor	90	2.5–3 yrs, full-time only [day, summer]
JD/MBA–Juris Doctor/Master of Business Administration–Dual-degree Program	111	3.5–4 yrs, full-time only [day, summer]
JD/MPAd–Juris Doctor/Master of Public Administration–Dual-degree Program	111	3.5–4 yrs, full-time only [day, summer]

received by April 1. Financial aid contact: Drusilla V. Bakert, Associate Dean, 209 Law Building, Lexington, KY 40506-0048. Phone: 859-257-6770. Fax: 859-323-1061. E-mail: dbakert@pop.uky.edu

Law School Library Alvin E. Evans Law Library has 8 professional staff members and contains more than 421,154 volumes and 3,926 periodicals. 279 seats are available in the library. When classes are in session, the library is open 106 hours per week.

WESTLAW and LEXIS-NEXIS are available, as are the World Wide Web, online bibliographic services, and CD-ROM players. 104 computer workstations are available to students in the library.

First-Year Program Class size in the average section is 60; 100% of the first-year courses are taught by full-time faculty.

Upper-Level Program Class size in the average section is 40. Among the electives are:

- Administrative Law
- Advocacy
- Business and Corporate Law
- Consumer Law
- Criminal Prosecution
- Elderly Advocacy
- Environmental Law
- Family Law
- Government/Regulation
- Health Care/Human Services
- Intellectual Property
- International/Comparative Law
- Judicial Clerkship
- Jurisprudence
- Labor Law
- Land Use Law/Natural Resources
- Legal History/Philosophy
- Litigation
- Mediation
- Prisoners' Rights
- Probate Law
- Public Interest
- Securities
- Tax Law

Clinical Courses Students receive degree credit for clinical courses. (Clinical practicum is not required.) Among the clinical areas offered are:

- Criminal Prosecution
- Elderly Advocacy
- Environmental Law
- Family Law
- Judicial Clerkship
- Litigation
- Mediation
- Prisoners' Rights

UNIVERSITY OF LOUISVILLE
LOUIS D. BRANDEIS SCHOOL OF LAW

Louisville, Kentucky

INFORMATION CONTACT

Connie C. Shumake, Dean of Admissions
Wilson W. Wyatt Hall
Louisville, KY 40292

Phone: 502-852-6364   Fax: 502-852-0862
E-mail: lawadmissions@louisville.edu
Web site: http://www.louisville.edu/brandeislaw/

LAW STUDENT PROFILE [2000–2001]

FULL-TIME   Enrollment: 262
Women: 49%   Men: 51%

PART-TIME   Enrollment: 106
Women: 53%   Men: 47%

RACIAL or ETHNIC COMPOSITION
African American, 6%; Asian/Pacific Islander, 2%; Hispanic, 1%; Native American, 0.3%; International, 1%

APPLICANTS and ADMITTEES
Number applied: 850
Admitted: 310
Percentage accepted: 36%
Seats available: 120
Average LSAT score: 156
Average GPA: 3.3

University of Louisville Louis D. Brandeis School of Law is a public institution that organizes classes on a semester calendar system. The campus is situated in an urban setting. Founded in 1846, first ABA approved in 1933, and an AALS member, University of Louisville Louis D. Brandeis School of Law offers JD, JD/MA, JD/MBA, JD/MDiv, and JD/MSW degrees.

Faculty consists of 27 full-time and 9 part-time members in 2000–2001. 9 full-time faculty members and 2 part-time faculty members are women. 100% of all faculty members have a JD; 30% have advanced law degrees. Of all faculty members, 12% are African American, 3% are Hispanic, 85% are white.

Application Information *Required:* LSAT, LSDAS, application form, application fee of $40, baccalaureate degree. *Recommended:* recommendations, personal statement, resume. *Application deadline* for fall term is March 1 (priority date). Applications are processed on a rolling basis.

Costs The 2000–2001 tuition was $5977 full-time for area residents; $249 per credit hour part-time for area residents. Tuition was $16,050 full-time for nonresidents; $669 per credit hour part-time for nonresidents. Fees: $298 full-time; $25 per credit hour part-time.

Financial Aid In 2000–2001, 35% of all students received some form of financial aid. 24 research assistantships, totaling $826 were awarded. Fellowships, loans, merit-based grants/scholarships, and federal work-study loans are also available. The average student debt at graduation is $30,000. To apply for financial assistance, students

AT a GLANCE

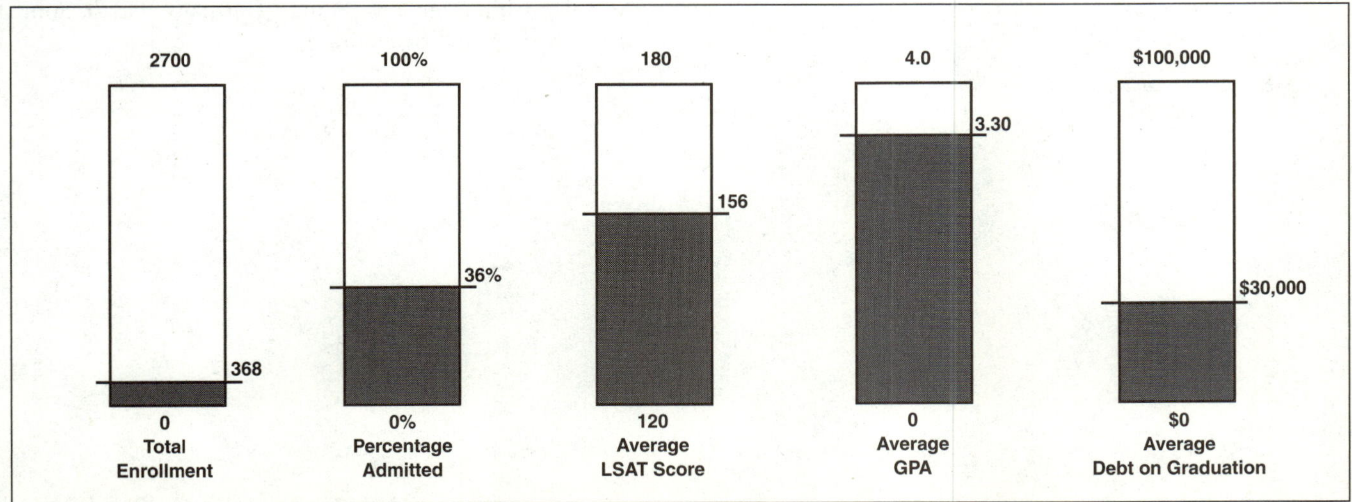

Degree Options

Degree	Total Credits Required	Length of Program
JD–Juris Doctor	90	3–4 yrs, full-time or part-time [day, evening]
JD/MA–Juris Doctor/Master of Arts–Dual-degree		4–5 yrs, full-time or part-time [day, evening]
JD/MBA–Juris Doctor/Master of Business Administration–Dual-degree	108	4–5 yrs, full-time or part-time [day, evening]
JD/MDiv–Juris Doctor/Master of Divinity–Dual-degree		4–5 yrs, full-time only [day, evening]
JD/MSW–Juris Doctor/Master of Social Work–Dual-degree	129	4–5 yrs, full-time or part-time [day, evening]

must complete the Free Application for Federal Student Aid. Completed financial aid forms should be received by June 1. Financial aid contact: Ms. Connie C. Shumake, Assistant Dean, Brandeis School of Law, University of Louisville, Louisville, KY 40292. Phone: 502-852-6096. Fax: 502-852-0862. E-mail: connie.chumake@louisville.edu

Law School Library Brandeis School of Law Library has 5 professional staff members and contains more than 358,620 volumes and 5,300 periodicals. 391 seats are available in the library. When classes are in session, the library is open 88 hours per week.

WESTLAW and LEXIS-NEXIS are available, as are the World Wide Web, online bibliographic services, and CD-ROM players. 40 computer workstations are available to students in the library. Special law collections include the papers of Justice Louis D. Brandeis and of Justice John Marshall Harlan.

First-Year Program Class size in the average section is 40; 100% of the first-year courses are taught by full-time faculty.

Upper-Level Program Class size in the average section is 35. Among the electives are:

  Administrative Law
  Advocacy
★ Business and Corporate Law
  Consumer Law
★ Criminal Law
  Education Law
  Entertainment Law

★ Environmental Law
  Ethics
  Family Law
★ Government/Regulation
★ Health Care/Human Services
  Indian/Tribal Law
  Intellectual Property
★ International/Comparative Law
  Judicial Process
  Jurisprudence
★ Labor Law
  Land Use Law/Natural Resources
★ Lawyering Skills
  Legal History/Philosophy
  Litigation
  Media Law
  Mediation
  Probate Law
  Professional Responsibility
★ Public Interest
★ Securities
  Tax Law

(★ *indicates an area of special strength*)

Clinical Courses Students receive degree credit for clinical courses. (Clinical practicum is not required.) Among the clinical areas offered are:

  Criminal Law
  Family Law
  Judicial Process
  Tax Law

International exchange programs permit students to visit Australia, China, Finland, France, Germany, Japan, South Africa, and United Kingdom.

LOUISIANA STATE UNIVERSITY AND AGRICULTURAL AND MECHANICAL COLLEGE
PAUL M. HEBERT LAW CENTER

Baton Rouge, Louisiana

INFORMATION CONTACT

Michelle Forbes, Director of Admissions and Student Affairs
210 Law Center
Baton Rouge, LA 70803

Phone: 225-578-8646   Fax: 225-578-8647
E-mail: mforbe1@lsu.edu
Web site: http://www.law.lsu.edu/

LAW STUDENT PROFILE [2000–2001]

FULL-TIME Enrollment: 655
Women: 44%   Men: 56%

RACIAL or ETHNIC COMPOSITION

African American, 6%; Asian/Pacific Islander, 1%; Hispanic, 2%; Native American, 0.2%; International, 2%

APPLICANTS and ADMITTEES

Number applied: 819
Admitted: 503
Percentage accepted: 61%
Seats available: 233
Average LSAT score: 153
Average GPA: 3.3

Louisiana State University and Agricultural and Mechanical College Paul M. Hebert Law Center is a public institution that organizes classes on a semester calendar system. The campus is situated in an urban setting. Founded in 1907, first ABA approved in 1926, and an AALS member, Louisiana State University and Agricultural and Mechanical College Paul M. Hebert Law Center offers JD, JD/MBA, JD/MPAd, LLM, and MCl degrees.

Faculty consists of 32 full-time and 19 part-time members in 2000–2001. 5 full-time faculty members are women. 100% of all faculty members have a JD; 22% have advanced law degrees. Of all faculty members, 3% are African American, 3% are Hispanic, 94% are white.

Application Information *Required:* LSAT, LSDAS, application form, application fee of $25, baccalaureate degree, 2 letters of recommendation, personal statement, college transcripts. *Recommended:* resume, writing sample. *Application deadline* for fall term is February 1 (priority date). Applications are processed on a rolling basis.

Costs The 2000–2001 tuition was $6586 full-time for state residents. Tuition was $12,428 full-time for nonresidents. Fees: $435 full-time.

AT a GLANCE

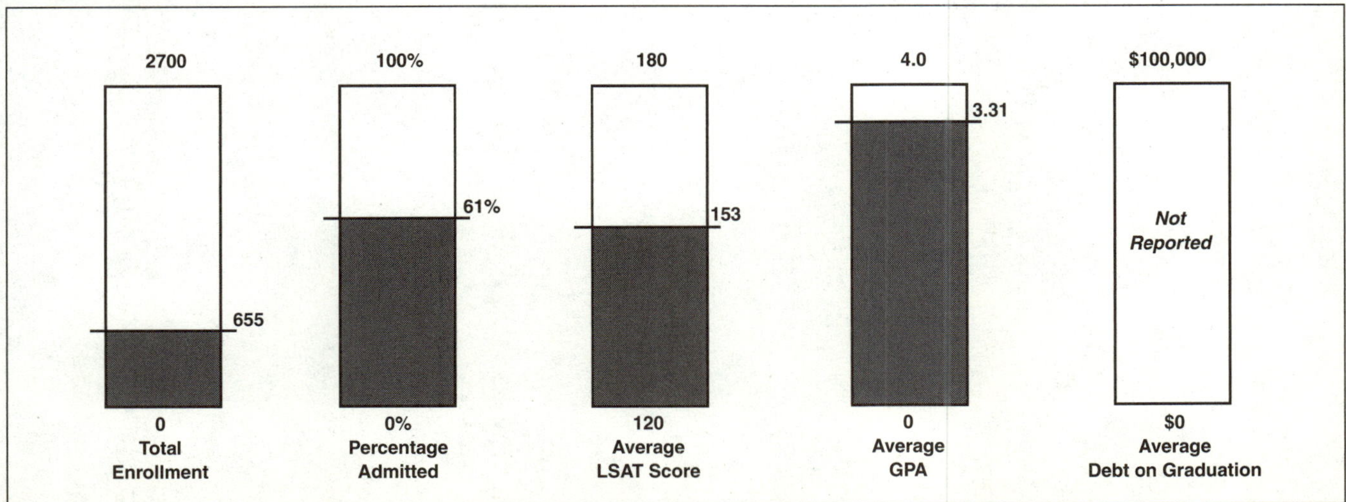

Degree Options

Degree	Total Credits Required	Length of Program
JD–Juris Doctor	97	3–4 yrs, full-time only [day]
JD/MBA–Juris Doctor/Master of Business Administration		4 yrs, full-time only [day]
JD/MPAd–Juris Doctor/Master of Public Administration–Joint-degree Program		3 yrs, full-time only [day]
LLM–Master of Laws	24	1–1.5 yrs, full-time only [day]
MCl–Master of Civil Law	24	1–1.5 yrs, full-time only [day]

Financial Aid 4 fellowships were awarded. Loans, merit-based grants/scholarships, and need-based grants/scholarships are also available. To apply for financial assistance, students must complete the Free Application for Federal Student Aid. Financial aid contact: Kathy Sciacchetano, Director of Student Aid & Scholarships, Office of Student Aid and Scholarships, 202 Himes Hall, Baton Rouge, LA 70803-3701. Phone: 225-388-3103.

Law School Library Louisiana State University Law Library has 10 professional staff members and contains more than 406,308 volumes and 2,571 periodicals. 464 seats are available in the library. When classes are in session, the library is open 99 hours per week.

WESTLAW and LEXIS-NEXIS are available, as are the World Wide Web, online bibliographic services, and CD-ROM players. 30 computer workstations are available to students in the library. Special law collections include US government documents depository, Louisiana state documents depository, records and briefs of Louisiana Supreme Court and Courts of Appeals.

First-Year Program Class size in the average section is 75; 100% of the first-year courses are taught by full-time faculty.

Upper-Level Program Class size in the average section is 50. Among the electives are:

Administrative Law
Advocacy
Banking and Finance
Business and Corporate Law
Constitutional Law
Consumer Law
Environmental Law
Family Law
French Law
Government/Regulation
Insurance Law
Intellectual Property
International/Comparative Law
Jurisprudence
Labor Law
Land Use Law/Natural Resources
Lawyering Skills
Legal History/Philosophy
Litigation
Media Law
Mediation
Mineral Rights
Probate Law
Securities

Clinical Courses

International exchange programs permit students to visit France.

LOYOLA UNIVERSITY NEW ORLEANS
SCHOOL OF LAW

New Orleans, Louisiana

INFORMATION CONTACT

Michele K. Allison-Davis, Assistant Dean, Admissions
7214 St. Charles Avenue
New Orleans, LA 70118

Phone: 504-861-5575   Fax: 504-861-5772
E-mail: maldavis@loyno.edu
Web site: http://www.loyno.edu/law

LAW STUDENT PROFILE [2000–2001]

FULL-TIME   Enrollment: 653
Women: 49%   Men: 51%

PART-TIME   Enrollment: 67
Women: 52%   Men: 48%

RACIAL or ETHNIC COMPOSITION
African American, 4%; Asian/Pacific Islander, 2%; Hispanic, 2%; Native American, 0.1%; International, 1%

APPLICANTS and ADMITTEES
Number applied: 1,235
Admitted: 760
Percentage accepted: 62%
Seats available: 250
Average LSAT score: 151
Average GPA: 3.0

Loyola University New Orleans School of Law is a private institution that organizes classes on a semester calendar system. The campus is situated in an urban setting. Founded in 1914, first ABA approved in 1931, and an AALS member, Loyola University New Orleans School of Law offers Certificate, JD, JD/MA, JD/MBA, JD/MPA, and JD/MURP degrees.

Faculty consists of 30 full-time and 1 part-time members in 2000–2001. 10 full-time faculty members and 1 part-time faculty members are women. 100% of all faculty members have a JD; 25% have advanced law degrees. Of all faculty members, 20% are African American, 8% are Hispanic, 72% are white.

Application Information *Required:* LSAT, LSDAS, application form, application fee of $40, college transcripts. *Recommended:* recommendations, personal statement, resume. *Application deadline* for fall term is May 1 (priority date). Applications are processed on a rolling basis.

Costs The 2000–2001 tuition was $728 per credit hour part-time.

Financial Aid 31 research assistantships, totaling $1000; 53 teaching assistantships, totaling $1000, were awarded. Graduate assistantships, loans, loan repayment assistance program (LRAP), merit-based grants/scholarships, need-based grants/scholarships, and federal work-study loans are also available. The average student debt at graduation is $67,157. To apply for financial assistance, students must complete the Free Application for Federal Student Aid. Completed financial aid forms should be

AT a GLANCE

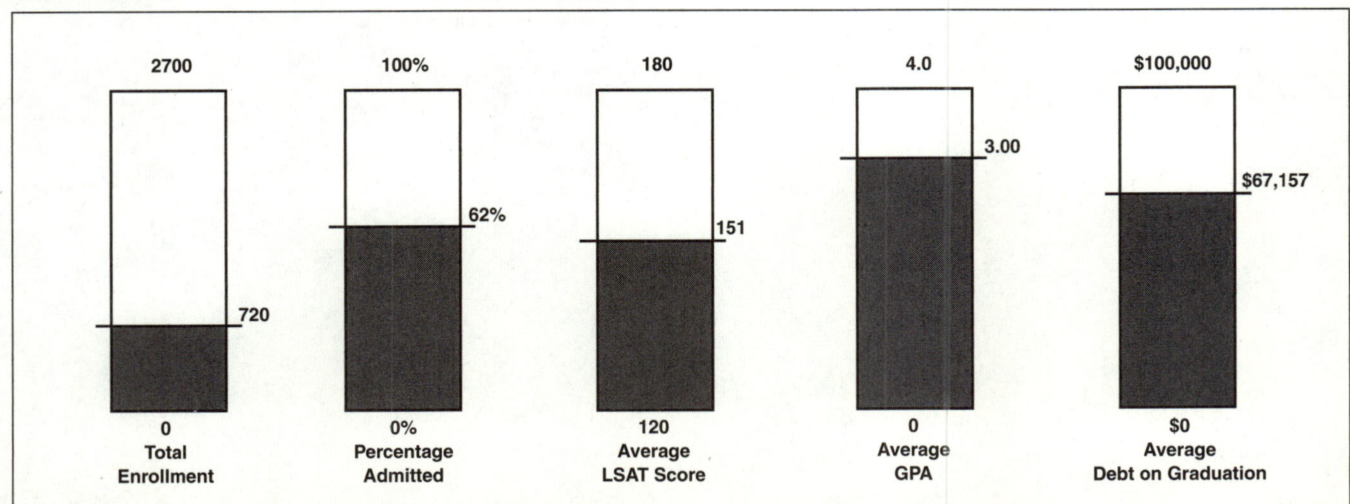

Degree Options

Degree	Total Credits Required	Length of Program
Certificate–International Legal Studies		
JD–Doctor of Laws	90	3–4 yrs, full-time or part-time [day, evening]
JD/MA–Juris Doctor/Master of Arts–Religious Studies Dual-degree Program	108	3.5–5 yrs, full-time or part-time [day, evening]
JD/MA–Juris Doctor/Master of Arts–Mass Communication Dual-degree Program	102	3.5–5 yrs, full-time or part-time [day, evening]
JD/MBA–Juris Doctor/Master of Business Administration–Joint-degree Program	102	3.5–5 yrs, full-time or part-time [day]
JD/MPA–Juris Doctor/Master of Professional Accountancy–Joint-degree Program	114	4–5 yrs, full-time or part-time [day, evening]
JD/MURP–Juris Doctor/Masters of Urban and Regional Planning–Joint-degree Program	117	4–5 yrs, full-time or part-time [day, evening]

received by May 1. Financial aid contact: Catherine M. Simoneaux, Director of Financial Aid, 6363 St. Charles Avenue, New Orleans, LA 70118. Phone: 504-865-3231. Fax: 504-865-3233. E-mail: cmsimone@loyno.edu

Law School Library Loyola Law Library has 8 professional staff members and contains more than 293,852 volumes. 519 seats are available in the library. When classes are in session, the library is open 104 hours per week.

WESTLAW and LEXIS-NEXIS are available, as are the World Wide Web, online bibliographic services, and CD-ROM players. 71 computer workstations are available to students in the library. Special law collections include Civil Law collections, Federal and State depository, Tim O'Brien Supreme Court/ABC News correspondent papers.

First-Year Program Class size in the average section is 90; 100% of the first-year courses are taught by full-time faculty.

Upper-Level Program Class size in the average section is 41. Among the electives are:

Advocacy
Business and Corporate Law
★ Civil Law
Civil Litigation
Civil Rights
★ Common Law
Criminal Defense

★ Criminal Prosecution
Education Law
Entertainment Law
Environmental Law
Family Law
★ Immigration
Intellectual Property
★ International/Comparative Law
Jurisprudence
Juvenile Law
Labor Law
★ Lawyering Skills
Legal History/Philosophy
★ Litigation
Maritime Law
★ Mediation
Probate Law
Public Interest
Securities
Tax Law
(★ indicates an area of special strength)

Clinical Courses Students receive degree credit for clinical courses. (Clinical practicum is not required.) Among the clinical areas offered are:

Civil Litigation
Civil Rights
Criminal Defense
Criminal Prosecution
Family Law
Immigration
Juvenile Law
Litigation
Mediation
Tax Law

SOUTHERN UNIVERSITY AND AGRICULTURAL AND MECHANICAL COLLEGE
SOUTHERN UNIVERSITY LAW CENTER

Baton Rouge, Louisiana

INFORMATION CONTACT

Velma Wilkerson, Coordinator of Admissions
PO Box 9294
Baton Rouge, LA 70813

Phone: 504-771-5341   Fax: 504-771-2121
E-mail: vwilkerson@sus.edu
Web site: http://www.sus.edu/sulc/

LAW STUDENT PROFILE [2000–2001]

FULL-TIME   Enrollment: 317
Women: 52%   Men: 48%

APPLICANTS and ADMITTEES

Number applied: 589
Admitted: 198
Percentage accepted: 34%
Seats available: 140
Average LSAT score: 146
Average GPA: 2.7

Southern University and Agricultural and Mechanical College Southern University Law Center is a public institution that organizes classes on a semester calendar system. The campus is situated in an urban setting. Founded in 1947, first ABA approved in 1953, Southern University and Agricultural and Mechanical College Southern University Law Center offers a JD degree.

Faculty consists of 30 full-time and 14 part-time members in 2000–2001. 12 full-time faculty members and 3 part-time faculty members are women. 100% of all faculty members have a JD; 16% have advanced law degrees. Of all faculty members, 3% are Asian/Pacific Islander, 64% are African American, 33% are white.

Application Information *Required:* LSAT, LSDAS, application form, application fee of $25, baccalaureate degree, 2 letters of recommendation, college transcripts, minimum 2.0 GPA, personal statement. *Application deadline* for fall term is March 31 (priority date).

Costs The 1999–2000 tuition was $3288 full-time for state residents. Tuition was $7888 full-time for nonresidents.

Financial Aid In 2000–2001, 85% of all students received some form of financial aid. 29 research assistantships, 24 teaching assistantships, were awarded. Graduate assistantships, loans, merit-based grants/scholarships, need-based

AT a GLANCE

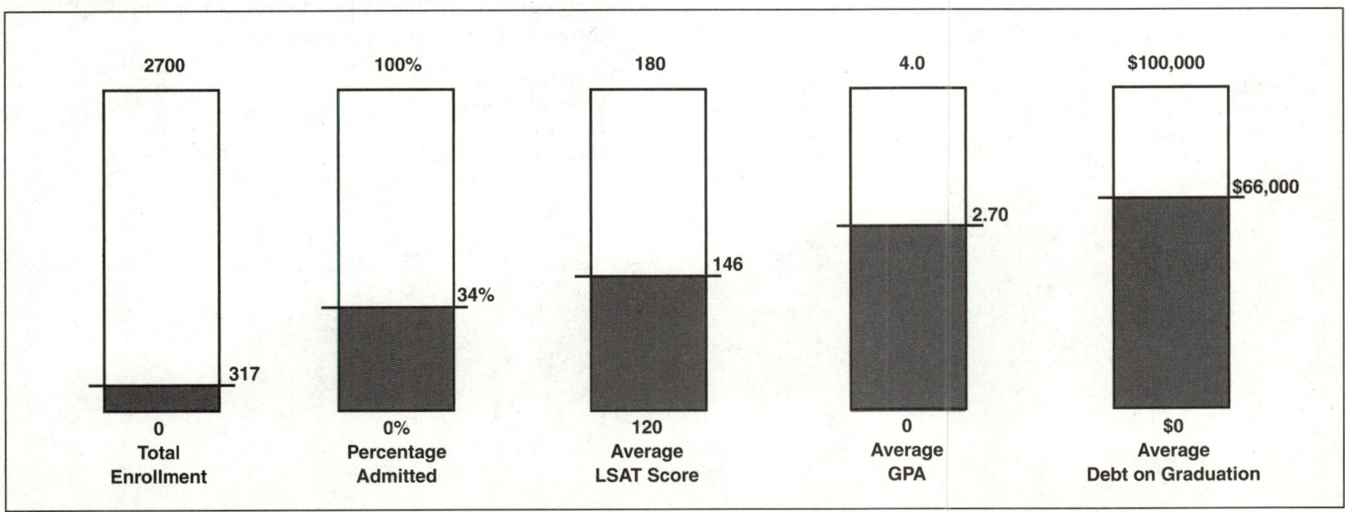

Degree Options		
Degree	**Total Credits Required**	**Length of Program**
JD–Juris Doctor	96	3–4 yrs, full-time or part-time [day, summer]

grants/scholarships, and federal work-study loans are also available. The average student debt at graduation is $66,000. To apply for financial assistance, students must complete the Free Application for Federal Student Aid, institutional forms, scholarship specific applications. Completed financial aid forms should be received by April 15. Financial aid contact: Jerome Harris, Director of Financial Aid, PO Box 9294, Baton Rouge, LA 70813. Phone: 225-771-2141 or toll free 800-537-1135. Fax: 225-771-5890. E-mail: jharris@sus.edu

Law School Library Southern University Law Library has 7 professional staff members and contains more than 426,386 volumes and 4,402 periodicals. 284 seats are available in the library. When classes are in session, the library is open 96 hours per week.

WESTLAW and LEXIS-NEXIS are available, as are the World Wide Web, online bibliographic services, and CD-ROM players. 52 computer workstations are available to students in the library. Special law collections include civil law, civil rights, human rights, South African law.

First-Year Program Class size in the average section is 45; 100% of the first-year courses are taught by full-time faculty.

Upper-Level Program Class size in the average section is 40. Among the electives are:

Administrative Law
Admiralty Law
Advocacy
African Law
Alternative Dispute Resolution
Appellate Advocacy
Bankruptcy
Business and Corporate Law
Civil Law
Civil Rights
Commercial Law
Constitutional Law
Consumer Law
Criminal Justice
Education Law
Elder Law
Employment Discrimination
Environmental Law
Equity
Immigration
Income Tax Law
Insurance Law
Intellectual Property
International Human Rights
International Law
International Trade
International/Comparative Law
Interviewing and Counseling
Jurisprudence
Juvenile Law
Labor Law
Law and Medicine
Law and Technology
Lawyering Skills
Legal Drafting
Legal Research
Legislation
Local Government
Matrimonial Regimes
Mineral Rights
Negotiation
Offshore Personal Injury
Poverty/Welfare Law
Product Liability
Property/Real Estate
Public Interest
Public Office Law
Securities
Sports Law
Tax Law
Trusts and Estates
Urban Legal Problems
Workers' Compensation

Clinical Courses Students receive degree credit for clinical courses. (Clinical practicum is not required.) Among the clinical areas offered are:

Administrative Law
Criminal Defense
Elder Law
Juvenile Law

TULANE UNIVERSITY
SCHOOL OF LAW

New Orleans, Louisiana

INFORMATION CONTACT

Susan Krinsky, Associate Dean
Weinmann Hall
6329 Freret Street
New Orleans, LA 70118

Phone: 504-865-5930   Fax: 504-865-6710
E-mail: skrinsky@law.tulane.edu
Web site: http://www.law.tulane.edu/

LAW STUDENT PROFILE [2000–2001]

FULL-TIME   Enrollment: 1,045
Women: 50%   Men: 50%

PART-TIME   Enrollment: 8
Women: 38%   Men: 62%

RACIAL or ETHNIC COMPOSITION
African American, 10%; Asian/Pacific Islander, 3%; Hispanic, 5%; Native American, 0.1%; International, 9%

APPLICANTS and ADMITTEES
Number applied: 3,013
Admitted: 1,419
Percentage accepted: 47%
Seats available: 315
Average LSAT score: 158
Average GPA: 3.3

Tulane University School of Law is a private institution that organizes classes on a semester calendar system. The campus is situated in an urban setting. Founded in 1847, first ABA approved in 1925, and an AALS member, Tulane University School of Law offers JD, JD/MA, JD/MAC, JD/MBA, JD/MHA, JD/MPH, JD/MSW, and LLM degrees.

Faculty consists of 53 full-time and 105 part-time members in 2000–2001. 12 full-time faculty members and 18 part-time faculty members are women. 100% of all faculty members have a JD; 32% have advanced law degrees. Of all faculty members, 2% are Asian/Pacific Islander, 8% are African American, 2% are Hispanic, 88% are white.

Application Information *Required:* LSAT, LSDAS, application form, application fee of $50, personal statement, college transcripts. *Recommended:* baccalaureate degree, recommendations. *Application deadline* for fall term is March 15 (priority date). Applications are processed on a rolling basis.

Costs The 1999–2000 tuition was $22,664 full-time. Fees: $1152 full-time.

Financial Aid In 2000–2001, 61% of all students received some form of financial aid. 3 fellowships were awarded. Loans, loan repayment assistance program (LRAP), merit-based grants/scholarships, need-based grants/scholarships, and federal work-study loans are also available. The average student debt at graduation is $75,000. To apply for financial assistance, students must complete the Free Application for Federal Student Aid,

AT a GLANCE

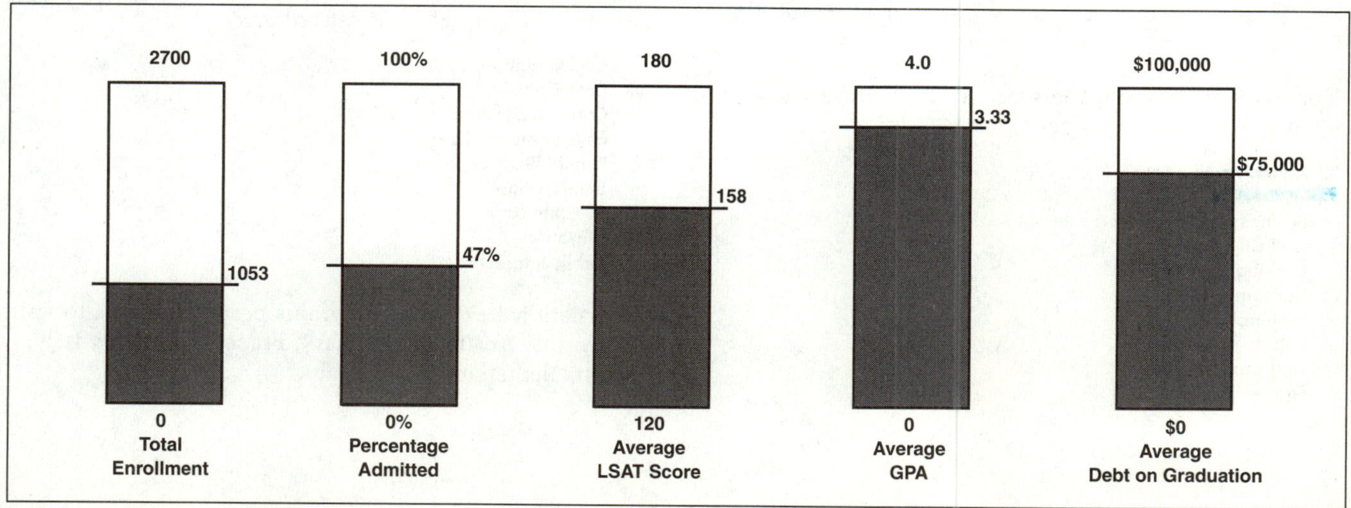

Degree Options

Degree	Total Credits Required	Length of Program
JD–Juris Doctor	88	3–4 yrs, full-time only [day]
JD/MA–Juris Doctor/Master of Arts–Political Science–International Affairs	94	3–4 yrs, full-time only [day]
JD/MA–Juris Doctor/Master of Arts–Latin American Studies	103	3–4 yrs, full-time only [day]
JD/MAC–Juris Doctor/Master of Accounting	106	3.5–4 yrs, full-time only [day]
JD/MBA–Juris Doctor/Master of Business Administration	128	4 yrs, full-time only [day]
JD/MHA–Juris Doctor/Master of Health Administration	127	4 yrs, full-time only [day]
JD/MPH–Juris Doctor/Master of Public Health–Environmental Sciences	107	3 yrs, full-time only [day]
JD/MSW–Juris Doctor/Master of Social Work	132	4 yrs, full-time only
LLM–Master of Laws–General	24	1 yr, full-time only [day]
LLM–Master of Laws–Admiralty	24	1–2 yrs, full-time or part-time [day, evening]
LLM–Master of Laws–Energy and Environment	24	1–2 yrs, full-time or part-time [day, evening]
LLM–Master of Laws–International and Comparative Law	24	1 yr, full-time only [day]

institutional forms. Completed financial aid forms should be received by February 15. Financial aid contact: Ms. Georgia Whiddon, Associate Director of Financial Aid, Weinmann Hall, New Orleans, LA 70118. Phone: 504-865-5931. Fax: 504-865-6710. E-mail: finaid@law.tulane.edu

Law School Library Tulane Law School Library has 19 professional staff members and contains more than 500,000 volumes and 5,517 periodicals. 587 seats are available in the library. When classes are in session, the library is open 112 hours per week.

WESTLAW and LEXIS-NEXIS are available, as are the World Wide Web, online bibliographic services, and CD-ROM players. 56 computer workstations are available to students in the library. Special law collections include canon law, civil law, maritime law.

First-Year Program Class size in the average section is 80; 100% of the first-year courses are taught by full-time faculty.

Upper-Level Program Class size in the average section is 30. Among the electives are:

Administrative Law
★ Advocacy
★ Business and Corporate Law
Civil Litigation
Civil Rights
Consumer Law
Criminal Defense
Entertainment Law
★ Environmental Law
Family Law

Government/Regulation
Health Care/Human Services
Immigration
★ Intellectual Property
★ International/Comparative Law
Jurisprudence
Juvenile Law
Labor Law
Land Use Law/Natural Resources
Lawyering Skills
Legal History/Philosophy
Litigation
★ Maritime Law
Media Law
Mediation
★ Public Interest
Securities
★ Sports Law
Tax Law
(★ *indicates an area of special strength*)

Clinical Courses Students receive degree credit for clinical courses. (Clinical practicum is not required.) Among the clinical areas offered are:

Civil Litigation
Civil Rights
Criminal Defense
Environmental Law
Family Practice
Immigration
Juvenile Law
Litigation
Public Interest

International exchange programs permit students to visit Argentina, Australia, Denmark, France, Germany, Italy, Japan, Netherlands, and Spain.

UNIVERSITY OF SOUTHERN MAINE
UNIVERSITY OF MAINE SCHOOL OF LAW

Portland, Maine

INFORMATION CONTACT

Barbara Gauditz, Assistant Dean
246 Deering Avenue
Portland, ME 04102

Phone: 207-780-4341   Fax: 207-780-4239
E-mail: gauditz@usm.maine.edu
Web site: http://www.usm.edu/~law/index2.html

LAW STUDENT PROFILE [2000–2001]

FULL-TIME Enrollment: 235
Women: 46%   Men: 54%

PART-TIME Enrollment: 8
Women: 50%   Men: 50%

RACIAL or ETHNIC COMPOSITION
African American, 1%; Asian/Pacific Islander, 0.4%; Hispanic, 1%; Native American, 1%; International, 0.4%

APPLICANTS and ADMITTEES
Number applied: 568
Admitted: 280
Percentage accepted: 49%
Seats available: 80
Average LSAT score: 154
Average GPA: 3.2

University of Southern Maine University of Maine School of Law is a public institution that organizes classes on a semester calendar system. The campus is situated in an urban setting. Founded in 1962, first ABA approved in 1962, and an AALS member, University of Southern Maine University of Maine School of Law offers a JD degree.

Faculty consists of 16 full-time and 8 part-time members in 2000–2001. 5 full-time faculty members and 2 part-time faculty members are women. 100% of all faculty members have a JD; 20% have advanced law degrees. Of all faculty members, 100% are white.

Application Information *Required:* LSDAS, LSAT, application form, application fee of $50, baccalaureate degree, 1 recommendation, personal statement. *Recommended:* resume. *Application deadline* for fall term is February 15. Applications are processed on a rolling basis.

Costs The 2000–2001 tuition was $9990 full-time for state residents; $333 per credit part-time for state residents. Tuition was $17,790 full-time for nonresidents; $693 per credit part-time for nonresidents. Fees: $47 per term full-time; $14 per credit part-time.

Financial Aid In 2000–2001, 99% of all students received some form of financial aid. Loans, merit-based grants/scholarships, need-based grants/scholarships, and federal work-study loans are available. The average student debt at graduation is $30,000. To apply for financial assistance, students must complete the Free Application for Federal Student Aid. Completed financial aid forms

AT a GLANCE

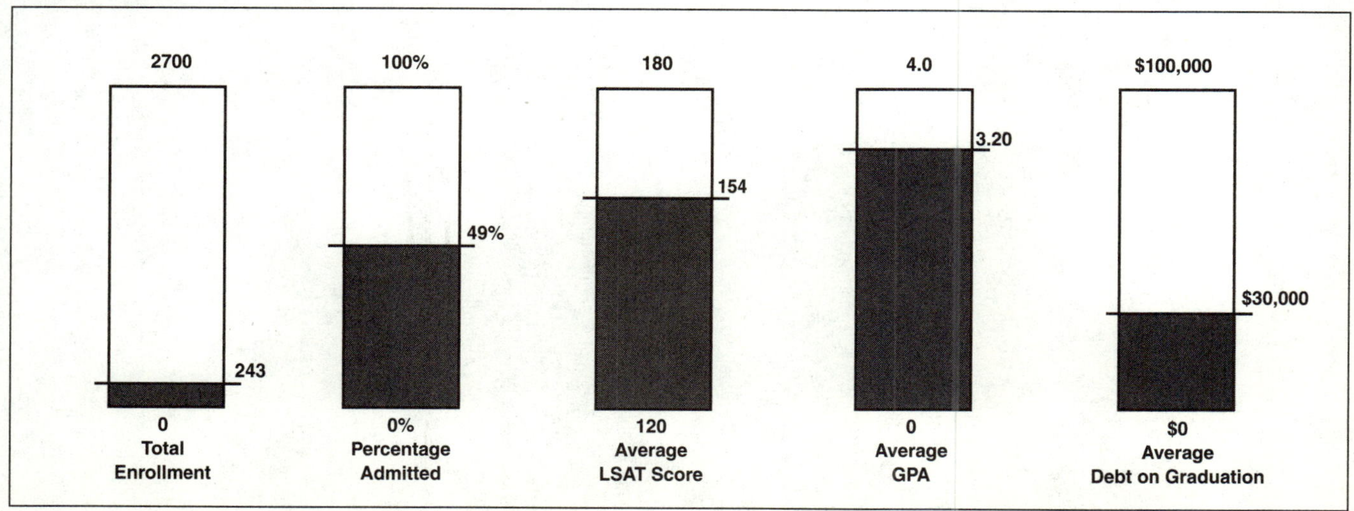

Degree Options

Degree	Total Credits Required	Length of Program
JD–Juris Doctor	89	3–4 yrs, full-time or part-time [day, summer]

should be received by February 1. Financial aid contact: Barbara Gauditz, Assistant Dean, 246 Deering Avenue, Portland, ME 04102. Phone: 207-780-4345. Fax: 207-780-4239. E-mail: gauditz@usm.maine.edu

Law School Library Donald L. Garbrecht Law Library has 7 professional staff members and contains more than 325,000 volumes and 3,605 periodicals. 172 seats are available in the library. When classes are in session, the library is open 99 hours per week.

WESTLAW and LEXIS-NEXIS are available, as are the World Wide Web, online bibliographic services, and CD-ROM players. 14 computer workstations are available to students in the library. Special law collections include Canadian, Commonwealth, European Union, Judge Gignoux Rare Bookroom.

First-Year Program Class size in the average section is 85; 100% of the first-year courses are taught by full-time faculty.

Upper-Level Program Class size in the average section is 35. Among the electives are:

- Administrative Law
- Advocacy
- Business and Corporate Law
- Civil Litigation
- Commercial Law
- Constitutional Law
- Consumer Law
- Criminal Defense
- Criminal Procedure
- Education Law
- Environmental Law
- Family Law
- Family Practice
- General Practice
- Government/Regulation
- Health Care/Human Services
- Intellectual Property
- International/Comparative Law
- Jurisprudence
- Labor Law
- Land Use Law/Natural Resources
- Lawyering Skills
- Legal History/Philosophy
- Litigation
- Maritime Law
- Mediation
- Ocean and Coastal Law
- Probate Law
- Public Interest
- Securities
- Tax Law

Clinical Courses Students receive degree credit for clinical courses. (Clinical practicum is not required.) Among the clinical areas offered are:

- Civil Litigation
- Criminal Defense
- Environmental Law
- Family Practice
- General Practice
- Ocean and Coastal Law
- Public Interest

International exchange programs permit students to visit Canada, France, Ireland, and United Kingdom.

UNIVERSITY OF BALTIMORE
SCHOOL OF LAW

Baltimore, Maryland

INFORMATION CONTACT

Lisa Lawler, Assistant Director of Law Admissions
1420 North Charles Street
Baltimore, MD 21201

Phone: 410-837-4459   Fax: 410-837-4450
E-mail: llawler@ubmail.ubalt.edu
Web site: http://lawschool.ubalt.edu/

LAW STUDENT PROFILE [2000–2001]

FULL TIME   Enrollment: 889

RACIAL OR ETHNIC COMPOSITION
African American, 15%; Asian/Pacific Islander, 3%; Hispanic, 3%; Native American, 0.5%; International, 1%

APPLICANTS and ADMITTEES
Number applied: 1,463
Admitted: 657
Percentage accepted: 45%
Seats available: 303
Median LSAT score: 149
Average GPA: 2.9

University of Baltimore School of Law is a public institution that organizes classes on a semester calendar system. The campus is situated in an urban setting. Founded in 1925, first ABA approved in 1972, and an AALS member, University of Baltimore School of Law offers JD, JD/LLM, JD/MBA, JD/MPAd, JD/MS, and JD/PhD degrees.

Faculty consists of 35 full-time and 70 part-time members in 2000–2001. 12 full-time faculty members and 16 part-time faculty members are women. 100% of all faculty members have a JD; 25% have advanced law degrees. Of all faculty members, 6% are African American, 94% are white.

Application Information *Required:* LSAT, LSDAS, application form, application fee of $35, baccalaureate degree, 2 letters of recommendation, personal statement, college transcripts, resume. *Application deadline* for fall term is April 1 (priority date). Applications are processed on a rolling basis.

Costs The 2000–2001 tuition was $10,116 full-time for state residents. Tuition was $17,552 full-time for nonresidents.

Financial Aid In 2000–2001, 73% of all students received some form of financial aid. 27 teaching assistantships were awarded. Loans, merit-based grants/scholarships, need-based grants/scholarships, and federal work-study loans are also available. The average student debt at graduation is $38,000. To apply for financial assistance, students must complete the Free Application for Federal Student Aid, institutional forms, scholarship specific

AT a GLANCE

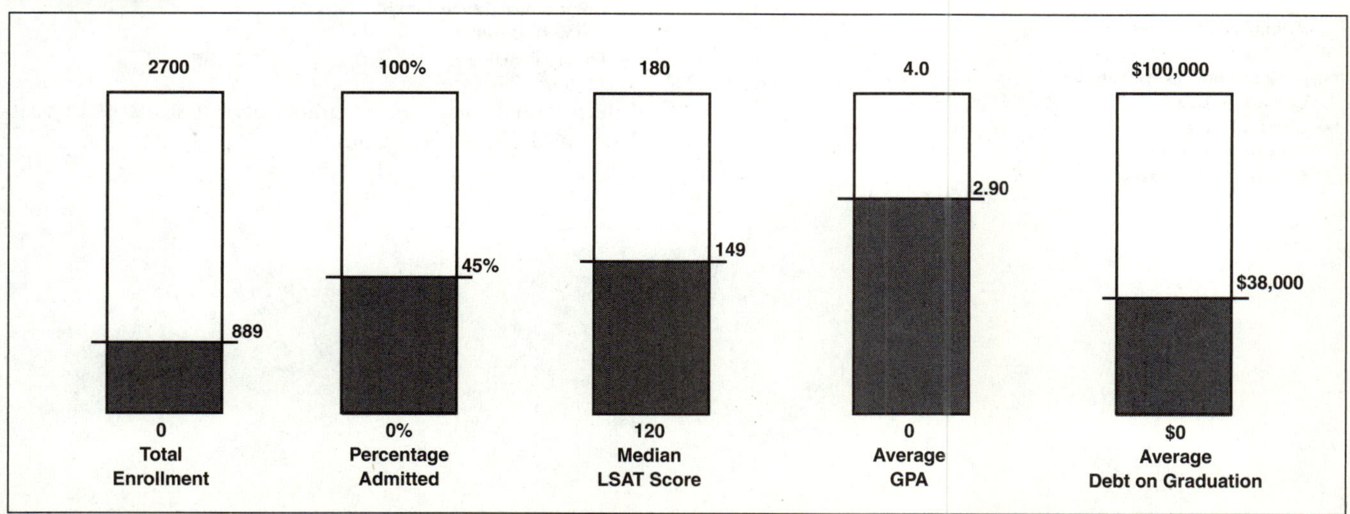

Degree Options

Degree	Total Credits Required	Length of Program
JD–Doctor of Laws	90	3–4 yrs, full-time or part-time [day, evening, summer]
JD/LLM–Juris Doctor/Master of Laws–Dual Program in Taxation	105	4–5 yrs, full-time or part-time [day, evening, summer]
JD/MBA–Juris Doctor/Master of Business Administration–Dual-degree Program	110	4–5 yrs, full-time or part-time [day, evening, summer]
JD/MPAd–Juris Doctor/Master of Public Administration–Dual Program	110	4–5 yrs, full-time or part-time [day, evening, summer]
JD/MS–Juris Doctor/Master of Science–Dual Program in Criminal Justice	110	4–5 yrs, full-time or part-time [day, evening, weekend, summer]
JD/MS–Juris Doctor/Master of Science–Dual Program in Conflict Management and Negotiation	110	4–5 yrs, full-time or part-time [day, evening, summer]
JD/PhD–Juris Doctor/Doctor of Philosophy–Dual Program in Policy Science	110	4–6 yrs, full-time or part-time [day, evening, summer]

applications, loan papers. Completed financial aid forms should be received by April 1. Financial aid contact: Deborah Harry-Walker, Director of Financial Aid, 1420 North Charles Street, Baltimore, MD 21201. Phone: 410-837-4763. Fax: 410-837-4450. E-mail: dharry@ubmail.ubalt.edu

Law School Library has 7 professional staff members and contains more than 287,125 volumes and 3,306 periodicals. 314 seats are available in the library. When classes are in session, the library is open 110 hours per week.

WESTLAW and LEXIS-NEXIS are available, as is the World Wide Web. 75 computer workstations are available to students in the library.

First-Year Program Class size in the average section is 75; 100% of the first-year courses are taught by full-time faculty.

Upper-Level Program Class size in the average section is 40. Among the electives are:

Administrative Law
★ Advocacy
★ Business and Corporate Law
Consumer Law
★ Criminal Law
Entertainment Law
★ Environmental Law

★ Estate Planning
★ Family Law
Government/Regulation
Health Care/Human Services
★ Intellectual Property
★ International/Comparative Law
Jurisprudence
Labor Law
Land Use Law/Natural Resources
★ Lawyering Skills
★ Legal History/Philosophy
Litigation
Maritime Law
Media Law
Mediation
★ Property/Real Estate
★ Public Interest
Securities
★ Tax Law
(★ indicates an area of special strength)

Clinical Courses Students receive degree credit for clinical courses. (Clinical practicum is not required.) Among the clinical areas offered are:

Civil Litigation
Community Development
Criminal Defense
Family Practice

International exchange programs permit students to visit Israel and United Kingdom.

UNIVERSITY OF MARYLAND
SCHOOL OF LAW

Baltimore, Maryland

INFORMATION CONTACT

Patricia Scott, Director of Admissions Progarms
500 West Baltimore Street
Baltimore, MD 21201

Phone: 410-706-3492   Fax: 410-706-4045
E-mail: admissions@law.umaryland.edu
Web site: http://www.law.maryland.edu/

LAW STUDENT PROFILE [2000–2001]

FULL-TIME   Enrollment: 597
Women: 55%   Men: 45%

PART-TIME   Enrollment: 245
Women: 50%   Men: 50%

RACIAL or ETHNIC COMPOSITION
African American, 14%; Asian/Pacific Islander, 8%; Hispanic, 2%; Native American, 0.4%; International, 1%

APPLICANTS and ADMITTEES
Number applied: 2,298
Admitted: 914
Percentage accepted: 40%
Seats available: 260
Average LSAT score: 155
Average GPA: 3.5

University of Maryland School of Law is a public institution that organizes classes on a semester calendar system. The campus is situated in an urban setting. Founded in 1816, first ABA approved in 1930, and an AALS member, University of Maryland School of Law offers JD, JD/MA, JD/MBA, JD/MSW, JD/PhD, and JD/PharmD degrees.

Faculty consists of 52 full-time and 43 part-time members in 2000–2001. 24 full-time faculty members and 10 part-time faculty members are women. 100% of all faculty members have a JD; 17% have advanced law degrees. Of all faculty members, 5.2% are Asian/Pacific Islander, 12.1% are African American, 1.7% are Hispanic, 81% are white.

Application Information *Required:* LSAT, LSDAS, application form, application fee of $60, baccalaureate degree, 2 letters of recommendation, personal statement, college transcripts. *Recommended:* essay, resume. *Application deadline* for fall term is March 1 (priority date). Applications are processed on a rolling basis.

Financial Aid Loans, loan repayment assistance program (LRAP), merit-based grants/scholarships, need-based grants/scholarships, and federal work-study loans are available. The average student debt at graduation is $55,101. To apply for financial assistance, students must complete the Free Application for Federal Student Aid, scholarship specific applications. Completed financial aid forms should be received by March 15. Financial aid contact: Mary S. Vansickle, Director of Financial Aid,

AT a GLANCE

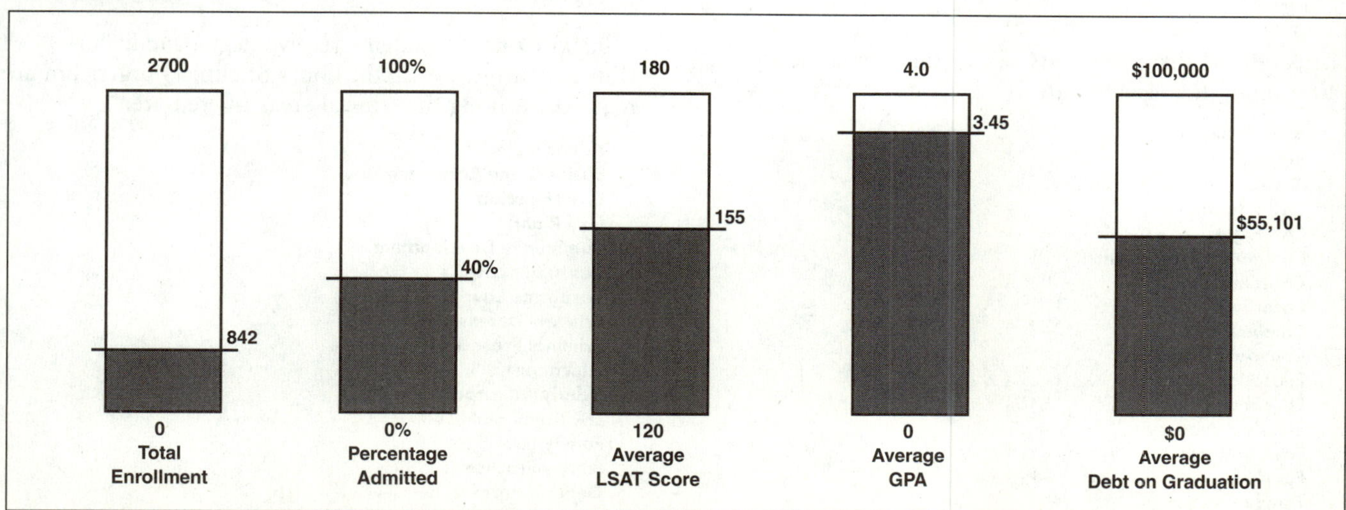

Degree Options

Degree	Total Credits Required	Length of Program
JD–Doctor of Laws	85	3–4 yrs, full-time or part-time [day, evening, summer]
JD/MA–Juris Doctor/Master of Arts–Criminal Justice Dual-degree		4–5 yrs, full-time or part-time [day, evening, summer]
JD/MA–Juris Doctor/Master of Arts–Liberal Education Dual-degree		4–5 yrs, full-time or part-time [day, evening, summer]
JD/MA–Juris Doctor/Master of Arts–Applied and Professional Ethics		3–5 yrs, full-time or part-time [day, evening, summer]
JD/MA–Juris Doctor/Master of Arts–Public Management Dual-degree		4–5 yrs, full-time or part-time [day, evening, summer]
JD/MA–Juris Doctor/Master of Arts–Community Planning		3–5 yrs, full-time or part-time [day, evening, summer]
JD/MBA–Juris Doctor/Master of Business Administration–Dual-degree		4–5 yrs, full-time or part-time [day, evening, summer]
JD/MSW–Juris Doctor/Master of Social Work–Dual-degree		4–5 yrs, full-time or part-time [day, evening, summer]
JD/PhD–Juris Doctor/Doctor of Philosophy–Dual-degree		5–6 yrs, full-time or part-time [day, evening, summer]
JD/PharmD–Juris Doctor/Doctor of Pharmacy–Pharmacy Dual-degree		4–5 yrs, full-time or part-time [day, evening, summer]

624 West Lombard Street, Baltimore, MD 21201. Phone: 410-706-7347. Fax: 410-706-0824. E-mail: aidtalk@umabnet.umaryland.edu

Law School Library Thurgood Marshall Law Library has 10 professional staff members and contains more than 428,342 volumes and 4,037 periodicals. 503 seats are available in the library. When classes are in session, the library is open 98 hours per week.

WESTLAW and LEXIS-NEXIS are available, as are the World Wide Web and online bibliographic services. 47 computer workstations are available to students in the library.

First-Year Program Class size in the average section is 50; 99% of the first-year courses are taught by full-time faculty.

Upper-Level Program Class size in the average section is 40. Among the electives are:

Administrative Law
Advocacy
Business and Corporate Law
Civil Litigation
Civil Rights
Community Development
Consumer Law
Corporate Law
Criminal Defense
Criminal Prosecution
Education
Education Law
Elderly Advocacy
Environmental Law
Family Law
Family Practice
General Practice
Government/Regulation
Health Care/Human Services
Health Law
Immigration
Intellectual Property
International Law
International/Comparative Law
Jurisprudence
Juvenile Law
Labor Law
Land Use Law/Natural Resources
Lawyering Skills
Legal History/Philosophy
Litigation
Mediation
Probate Law
Public Interest
Securities
Tax Law

Clinical Courses Students receive degree credit for clinical courses. 7-8 credit hours of clinical practicum are required. Among the clinical areas offered are:

Advocacy
Business and Corporate Law
Civil Litigation
Civil Rights
Community Development
Consumer Law
Corporate Law
Criminal Defense
Criminal Prosecution
Education
Elderly Advocacy
Environmental Law
Family Law
Family Practice
General Practice

Government Litigation
Health Care/Human Services
Health Law
Immigration
Intellectual Property
Juvenile Law
Land Use Law/Natural Resources
Lawyering Skills

Litigation
Mediation
Public Interest
Tax Law

International exchange programs permit students to visit South Africa and United Kingdom.

BOSTON COLLEGE
LAW SCHOOL

Newton, Massachusetts

> ### INFORMATION CONTACT
>
> Elizabeth Rosselot, Director of Admissions and Financial Aid
> 885 Centre Street
> Newton, MA 02459
>
> Phone: 617-552-4350   Fax: 617-552-2917
> Web site: http://www.bc.edu/lawschool/

LAW STUDENT PROFILE [2000–2001]

FULL-TIME   Enrollment: 805
Women: 51%   Men: 49%

APPLICANTS and ADMITTEES
Number applied: 5,363
Admitted: 1,263
Percentage accepted: 24%
Seats available: 289
Median LSAT score: 162
Average GPA: 3.4

Boston College Law School is a private institution that organizes classes on a semester calendar system. The campus is situated in an urban setting. Founded in 1929, first ABA approved in 1932, and an AALS member, Boston College Law School offers JD, JD/MBA, JD/MED, and JD/MSW degrees.

Faculty consists of 47 full-time and 27 part-time members in 2000–2001. 17 full-time faculty members and 5 part-time faculty members are women. 100% of all faculty members have a JD; 20% have advanced law degrees. Of all faculty members, 5.7% are Asian/Pacific Islander, 7.5% are African American, 1.9% are Hispanic, 84.9% are white.

Application Information *Required:* LSAT, LSDAS, application form, application fee of $55, baccalaureate degree, 2 letters of recommendation, personal statement. *Application deadline* for fall term is March 1. Applications are processed on a rolling basis.

Costs The 2000–2001 tuition was $27,080 full-time. Fees: $64 full-time.

Financial Aid In 2000–2001, 50% of all students received some form of financial aid. Loans, loan repayment assistance program (LRAP), merit-based grants/scholarships, need-based grants/scholarships, and federal work-study loans are available. The average student debt at graduation is $62,000. To apply for financial assistance, students must complete the Free Application for Federal Student Aid, Need Access diskette or College Scholarship Service Profile form, federal income tax forms. Completed financial aid forms should be received

AT a GLANCE

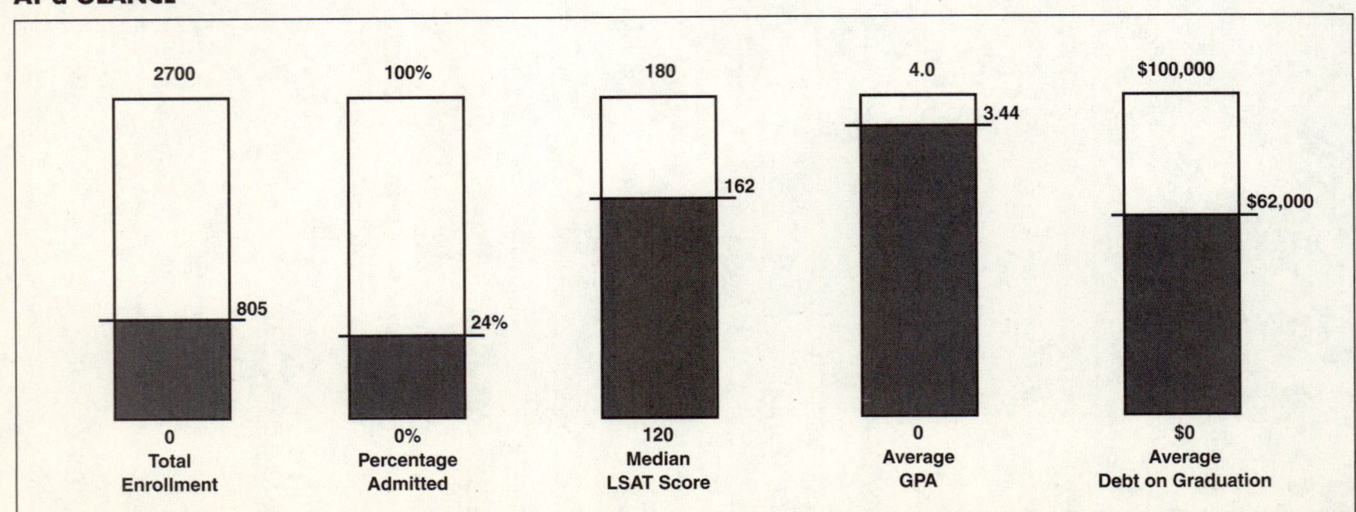

Degree Options

Degree	Total Credits Required	Length of Program
JD–Juris Doctor	85	3 yrs
JD/MBA–Juris Doctor/Master of Business Administration		4 yrs
JD/MED–Juris Doctor/Master of Education		
JD/MSW–Juris Doctor/Master of Social Work		4 yrs

by March 1. Financial aid contact: Elizabeth A. Rosselot, Director of Admissions and Financial Aid, 885 Centre Street, Newtown, MA 02459. Phone: 617-552-4350 or toll free 617-552-2917 (in-state). Fax: 617-552-2917. E-mail: bclawadm@bc.edu

Law School Library Boston College Law Library has 22 professional staff members and contains more than 350,000 volumes and 6,133 periodicals. 560 seats are available in the library. When classes are in session, the library is open 106 hours per week.

WESTLAW and LEXIS-NEXIS are available, as are the World Wide Web and CD-ROM players. 64 computer workstations are available to students in the library. Special law collections include US Government Documents Collection.

First-Year Program Class size in the average section is 90; 100% of the first-year courses are taught by full-time faculty.

Upper-Level Program Class size in the average section is 40. Among the electives are:

Accounting
★ Administrative Law
★ Advocacy
African Law
★ Alternative Dispute Resolution
American Legal History
Antitrust Law
Appellate Advocacy
Arbitration
Asian Legal Systems
Bankruptcy
Business and Corporate Law
Business Planning
Civil Practice
★ Civil Procedure
Civil Rights
Civil Rights Litigation
★ Commercial Law
Communications Law
Conflict of Laws
★ Constitutional Law
Consumer Law
Copyright & Trademark Law
★ Corporate Law
Corporations
★ Criminal Law
Criminal Procedure
Disability Law
Domestic Violence

Drafting Commercial Documents
Education
Education Law
Employment Discrimination
English Legal History
Entertainment Law
Environmental and Toxic Torts
★ Environmental Law
Estate & Gift Taxation
Estate Planning
European Union Law
Evidence
★ Family Law
Federal Courts
Fiduciary Administration
Financial Institutions
First Amendment
Food & Drug Law
Gender and the Law
Government/Regulation
Health Care Law
Health Care/Human Services
Housing Law
Immigration
Income Tax Law
Intellectual Property
International Business Transactions
International Economic Relations
International Environmental Law
International Human Rights
International Income Tax
International Trade
★ International/Comparative Law
Interviewing and Counseling
Judicial Process
Jurisprudence
★ Juvenile Law
★ Labor Law
Land Use Law/Natural Resources
Law and Culture
Law and Medicine
Law and Society
Law, Values, and Professional Identity
★ Lawyering Skills
Legal History/Philosophy
Legal Research
Legal Writing
★ Legislation
Life and Death Decision Making
★ Litigation
Mediation
Mental Health and Law
National Security and the Law
Negotiation
Patent Law
Pretrial Litigation
Product Liability

Professional Responsibility
★ Property/Real Estate
★ Public Interest
Remedies
Russian Constitutionalism
Scientific Evidence
Securities
Securities Regulation
Sports Law
State Constitutional Law
Supreme Court
Tax Law
Trusts and Estates
Women and the Law
Women and the Law
(★ *indicates an area of special strength*)

Clinical Courses Students receive degree credit for clinical courses. (Clinical practicum is not required.) Among the clinical areas offered are:

Administrative Law
Civil Litigation
Criminal Defense
Criminal Prosecution
Elderly Advocacy
Family Practice
General Practice
Government Litigation
Immigration
Judicial
Juvenile Law
Litigation
Public Interest
Women and the Law

International exchange programs permit students to visit United Kingdom.

BOSTON UNIVERSITY
SCHOOL OF LAW

Boston, Massachusetts

INFORMATION CONTACT

Joan Horgan, Director of Admissions and Financial Aid
765 Commonwealth Avenue
Boston, MA 02215

Phone: 617-353-3100   Fax: 617-353-7400
E-mail: bulawadm@bu.edu
Web site: http://www.bu.edu/law/

LAW STUDENT PROFILE [2000–2001]

FULL-TIME   Enrollment: 1,065
Women: 51%   Men: 49%

PART-TIME   Enrollment: 167
Women: 44%   Men: 56%

RACIAL or ETHNIC COMPOSITION
African American, 3%; Asian/Pacific Islander, 9%; Hispanic, 6%; Native American, 0.1%; International, 12%

APPLICANTS and ADMITTEES
Number applied: 5,318
Admitted: 1,727
Percentage accepted: 32%
Seats available: 312
Average LSAT score: 161
Average GPA: 3.4

Boston University School of Law is a private institution that organizes classes on a semester calendar system. The campus is situated in an urban setting. Founded in 1872, first ABA approved in 1925, and an AALS member, Boston University School of Law offers JD, JD/LLM, JD/MA, JD/MBA, JD/MPH, JD/MS, JD/MSW, and LLM degrees.

Faculty consists of 67 full-time and 141 part-time members in 2000–2001. 23 full-time faculty members and 40 part-time faculty members are women. 97.9% of all faculty members have a JD; 11.6% have advanced law degrees. Of all faculty members, 2% are Asian/Pacific Islander, 3.4% are African American, 2.7% are Hispanic, 91.9% are white.

Application Information *Required:* LSAT, LSDAS, application form, application fee of $60, baccalaureate degree, 3 letters of recommendation, personal statement, college transcripts. *Recommended:* resume. *Application deadline* for fall term is March 1. Applications are processed on a rolling basis.

Financial Aid In 2000–2001, 67% of all students received some form of financial aid. 3 fellowships were awarded. Loans, merit-based grants/scholarships, need-based grants/scholarships, and federal work-study loans are also available. The average student debt at graduation is $72,067. To apply for financial assistance, students must complete the Free Application for Federal Student Aid, institutional forms, CSS PROFILE form. Completed financial aid forms should be received by March 1. Financial aid contact: Joan Horgan, Director of Admissions and Financial Aid, Boston University School of

AT a GLANCE

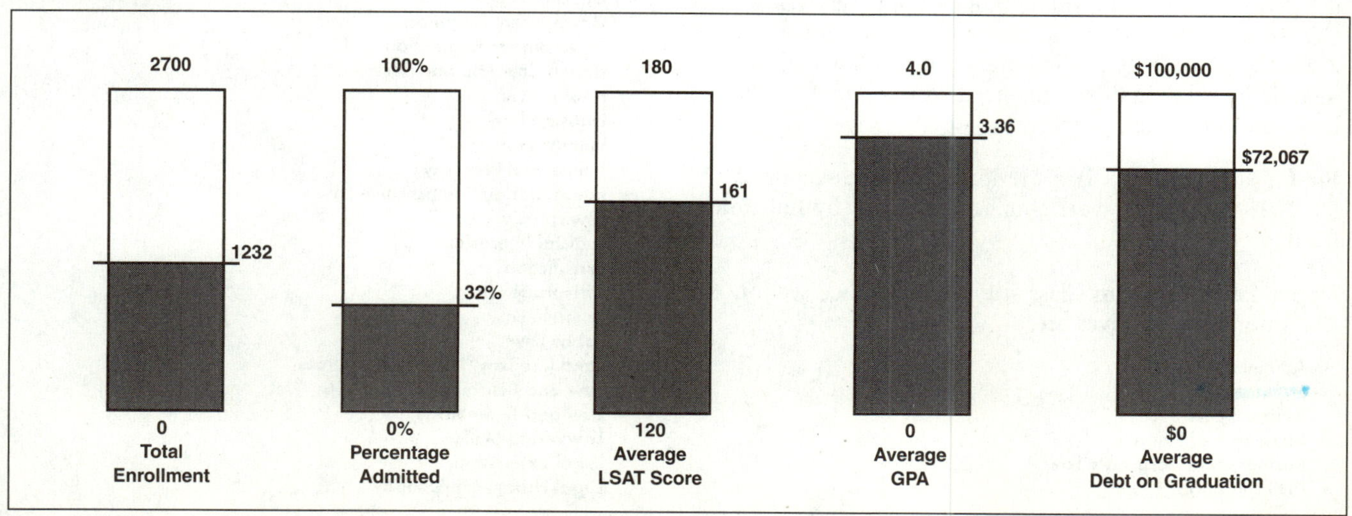

Degree Options

Degree	Total Credits Required	Length of Program
JD–Doctor of Laws	84	3 yrs, full-time only [day]
JD/LLM–Juris Doctor/Master of Laws–Program in Law and Taxation	96	3.5 yrs, full-time only [day, evening]
JD/LLM–Juris Doctor/Master of Laws–Program in Law and Banking	94	3.5 yrs, full-time only [evening]
JD/MA–Juris Doctor/Master of Arts–Program in Law and International Relations	92	3.5–4 yrs, full-time or part-time [day, evening, summer]
JD/MA–Juris Doctor/Master of Arts–Program in Law and Preservation Studies	120	3.5–4 yrs, full-time or part-time [day, evening, summer]
JD/MA–Juris Doctor/Master of Arts–Program in Law and Philosophy	100	3 yrs, full-time only [day]
JD/MBA–Juris Doctor/Master of Business Administration–Program in Law and Health Care Management	136	4 yrs, full-time or part-time [day, evening, summer]
JD/MBA–Juris Doctor/Master of Business Administration–Program in Law and Management	124	4 yrs, full-time or part-time [day, evening]
JD/MPH–Juris Doctor/Master of Public Health–Program in Law and Public Health	132	3.5–4 yrs, full-time or part-time [day, evening, summer]
JD/MS–Juris Doctor/Master of Science–Program in Law and Mass Communication	116	3.5–4 yrs, full-time or part-time [day, evening, summer]
JD/MSW–Juris Doctor/Master of Social Work–Program in Law and Social Work	129	4 yrs, full-time or part-time [day, evening]
LLM–Master of Laws–Graduate Tax Program	24	1–4 yrs, full-time or part-time [evening]
LLM–Master of Laws–Graduate Program in Banking Law Studies/American and International	20	1–3 yrs, full-time or part-time [evening]
LLM–Master of Laws–American Law	24	1 yr, full-time only [day]

Law, 765 Commonwealth Avenue, Boston, MA 02215.
Phone: 617-353-3100. Fax: 617-353-0578. E-mail:
bulawadm@bu.edu; bulawaid@bu.edu

Law School Library Pappas Law Library has 12 professional staff members and contains more than 586,490 volumes and 5,888 periodicals. 777 seats are available in the library. When classes are in session, the library is open 102 hours per week.

WESTLAW and LEXIS-NEXIS are available, as are the World Wide Web, online bibliographic services, and CD-ROM players. 76 computer workstations are available to students in the library. Special law collections include international law, financial services, tax, health law, and intellectual property.

First-Year Program Class size in the average section is 50; 100% of the first-year courses are taught by full-time faculty.

Upper-Level Program Class size in the average section is 27. Among the electives are:

Administrative Law
★ Advocacy
Antitrust Law
★ Banking and Finance
★ Business and Corporate Law
★ Civil Litigation

Communications Law
Conflict of Laws
Constitutional Law
Consumer Law
★ Corporate Law
★ Criminal Defense
Criminal Law
Criminal Procedure
★ Criminal Prosecution
★ Environmental Law
Evidence
Family Law
General Practice
Government Litigation
Government/Regulation
★ Health Care/Human Services
★ Health Law
Housing Law
Immigration
★ Intellectual Property
★ International/Comparative Law
★ Jewish Law
Judicial Internship
Jurisdiction
Jurisprudence
Juvenile Law
Labor Law
Land Use Law/Natural Resources
★ Law and Disability
★ Law and Technology
★ Lawyering Skills
Legal Externship
Legal History/Philosophy

★ Legislative Services
★ Litigation
  Mediation
  Professional Responsibility
  Securities
★ Tax Law
★ Technology Law
(★ *indicates an area of special strength*)

Clinical Courses Students receive degree credit for clinical courses. (Clinical practicum is not required.) Among the clinical areas offered are:

Administrative Law
Advocacy
Civil Litigation
Corporate Law
Criminal Defense
Criminal Procedure
Criminal Prosecution
Elderly Advocacy
Environmental Law
Evidence
Family Law
Family Practice
General Practice

Government Litigation
Health Care/Human Services
Health Law
Housing Law
Immigration
Intellectual Property
Judicial Internship
Juvenile Law
Labor Law
Law and Disability
Law and Technology
Lawyering Skills
Legal Externship
Legislative Services
Litigation
Mediation
Professional Responsibility
Public Interest
Securities
Tax Law
Technology Law

International exchange programs permit students to visit Argentina, China, France, Israel, Italy, Netherlands, and United Kingdom.

4 HARVARD UNIVERSITY
LAW SCHOOL

Cambridge, Massachusetts

INFORMATION CONTACT

Joyce Curll, Assistant Dean for Admissions and
Financial Aid
1563 Massachusetts Avenue
Cambridge, MA 02138

Phone: 617-495-3109   Fax: 617-495-1110
E-mail: jdamiss@law.harvard.edu
Web site: http://www.law.harvard.edu/

LAW STUDENT PROFILE [2000–2001]

FULL-TIME   Enrollment: 1,880

APPLICANTS and ADMITTEES

Number applied: 5,714
Admitted: 842
Percentage accepted: 15%
Seats available: 555

Harvard University Law School is a private institution
that organizes classes on a semester calendar system. The
campus is situated in an urban setting. Founded in 1817,
first ABA approved in 1923, and an AALS member,
Harvard University Law School offers JD, JD/MALD,
JD/MBA, JD/MPPo, LLM, and SJD degrees.

Faculty consists of 79 full-time and 118 part-time
members in 2000–2001. 13 full-time faculty members are
women. 96% of all faculty members have a JD; 4% have
advanced law degrees. Of all faculty members, 1% are
Native American, 9% are African American, 1% are
Hispanic, 89% are white.

Application Information *Required:* LSAT, LSDAS,
application form, application fee of $65, baccalaureate
degree, 2 letters of recommendation, personal statement,
essay. *Application deadline* is rolling.

Costs The 1999–2000 tuition was $25,000 full-time. Fees:
$1272 full-time. Full-time tuition and fees vary according
to program.

Financial Aid In 2000–2001, 69% of all students received
some form of financial aid. Fellowships, graduate
assistantships, loans, loan repayment assistance program
(LRAP), need-based grants/scholarships, and federal
work-study loans are available. The average student debt
at graduation is $69,397. To apply for financial assis-
tance, students must complete the Free Application for
Federal Student Aid, institutional forms, CSS PROFILE
form or Need Access diskette. Financial aid contact:

AT a GLANCE

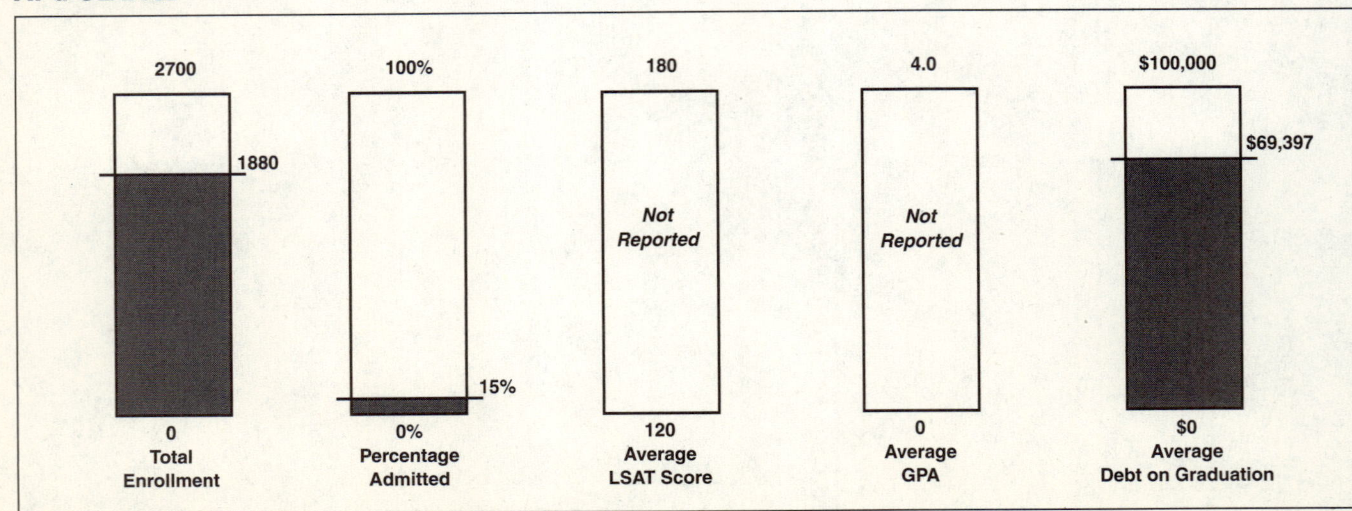

Degree Options

Degree	Total Credits Required	Length of Program
JD–Doctor of Laws	80	3 yrs, full-time only [day]
JD/MALD–Juris Doctor/Master of Arts in Law and Diplomacy		
JD/MBA–Juris Doctor/Master of Business Administration		4 yrs, full-time only [day]
JD/MPPo–Juris Doctor/Master of Public Policy		4 yrs, full-time only [day]
LLM–Master of Laws	18	1 yr, full-time only [day]
SJD–Doctor of Juridical Science	8	4 yrs, full-time only [day]

Elizabeth Rankin, Director of Financial Aid, 1563 Massachusetts Avenue, Cambridge, MA 02138. Phone: 617-495-4606. Fax: 617-495-1110.

Law School Library Harvard Law Library has 32 professional staff members and contains more than 2 million volumes and 15,336 periodicals. 761 seats are available in the library. When classes are in session, the library is open 99 hours per week.

WESTLAW and LEXIS-NEXIS are available, as are the World Wide Web, online bibliographic services, and CD-ROM players. 167 computer workstations are available to students in the library. Special law collections include Anglo-American collection, special collections, Foreign and International law collection.

First-Year Program Class size in the average section is 79; 100% of the first-year courses are taught by full-time faculty.

Upper-Level Program Among the electives are:

Administrative Law
Advocacy
Alternative Dispute Resolution
American Legal History
Animal Rights Law
Antitrust Law
Arbitration
★ Asian Legal Systems
Banking Law & Regulation
Bankruptcy
Biblical Law
Business and Corporate Law
Business Planning
Capital Markets Regulation
Capital Punishment
Chinese Law
Church-State
Civil Litigation
Civil Procedure
★ Civil Rights
Commercial Law
Comparative Civil Litigation
Comparative Taxation
Complex Litigation
Conflict of Laws
Constitutional Interpretation
Constitutional Law
Constitutional Rights
Constitutional Theory
Consumer Finance
Consumer Law
Copyright & Trademark Law
Corporate Finance
Corporate Governance
Corporate Law
Corporate Restructuring
Corporate Taxation
Corporations
★ Criminal Defense
Criminal Procedure
Criminal Prosecution
Democratic Theory
Disability Law
Employment Discrimination
Employment Law
Entertainment Law
Environmental Law
Estate & Gift Taxation
European Community Law
European Union Law
Evidence
Family Law
Family Practice
Federal Budget Law
Federal Courts
Federal Jurisdiction
Feminist Jurisprudence
Financial Institutions
First Amendment
Food & Drug Law
Foreign Investment Law
Gender and Sexuality
General Practice
Government/Regulation
Health Care/Human Services
Health Law
Housing Law
Human Rights
★ Immigration
Indian/Tribal Law
Intellectual Property
Intellectual Property Litigation
International Civil Litigation
International Commerical Arbitration
International Economic Relations
International Environmental Law
International Finance Markets
International Law
International Litigation & Arbitration
International Trade
★ International/Comparative Law
★ Internet Law

Investigation
★ Islamic Law
Judeo-Christian Ethics & the Law
Jurisprudence
★ Juvenile Law
Labor Law
Land Use Law/Natural Resources
Law and Development
Law and Economics
Law and Medicine
Law and Psychology
Law and Society
Lawyering Skills
★ Legal History/Philosophy
Legal Interpretation
Litigation
Local Government
★ Mediation
Mergers & Acquisitions
Multinational Business Enterprises
Natural Resources
★ Negotiation
Nonprofit Organizations
Partnerships
Probate Law
Professional Responsibility
★ Public Interest
★ Race and Law
Race and Race Relations
Roman Law
Secured Transactions
Securities
Securities Regulation
Separation of Powers
Social Security
Sports Law
Supreme Court
Supreme Court Litigation
★ Tax Law
Telecommunications Law
Trial Advocacy
Urban Economic Development

Western Legal Thought & Traditions
Wills & Trusts
(★ *indicates an area of special strength*)

Clinical Courses Students receive degree credit for clinical courses. (Clinical practicum is not required.) Among the clinical areas offered are:

Administrative Law
Advocacy
Business Planning
Civil Litigation
Civil Rights
Corporate Law
Criminal Defense
Criminal Prosecution
Elderly Advocacy
Environmental Law
Family Law
Family Practice
General Practice
Government Litigation
Government/Regulation
Health Care/Human Services
Health Law
Human Rights
Immigration
Indian/Tribal Law
International Law
International/Comparative Law
Juvenile Law
Labor Law
Lawyering Skills
Legal History/Philosophy
Litigation
Mediation
Negotiation
Public Interest
Race and Law
Tax Law
Urban Economic Development

NEW ENGLAND SCHOOL OF LAW

Boston, Massachusetts

INFORMATION CONTACT
Pamela Jorgensen, Director of Admissions
154 Stuart Street
Boston, MA 02116-5687

Phone: 617-422-7210   Fax: 617-422-7200
E-mail: admit@admin.nesl.edu
Web site: http://www.nesl.edu/

LAW STUDENT PROFILE [2000–2001]

FULL-TIME   Enrollment: 616
Women: 60%   Men: 40%

PART-TIME   Enrollment: 365
Women: 52%   Men: 48%

APPLICANTS and ADMITTEES
Number applied: 2,301
Admitted: 1,554
Percentage accepted: 68%
Seats available: 330

New England School of Law is a private nonprofit institution that organizes classes on a semester calendar system. The campus is situated in an urban setting. Founded in 1908, first ABA approved in 1969, and an AALS member, New England School of Law offers a JD degree.

Faculty consists of 30 full-time and 67 part-time members in 2000–2001. 10 full-time faculty members and 17 part-time faculty members are women. 100% of all faculty members have a JD; 14% have advanced law degrees. Of all faculty members, 2.8% are Asian/Pacific Islander, 2.8% are African American, 5.6% are Hispanic, 88.8% are white.

Application Information *Required:* LSAT, LSDAS, application form, application fee of $50, baccalaureate degree, minimum 2.0 GPA, 2 letters of recommendation. *Recommended:* personal statement.

Costs The 2000–2001 tuition was $17,350 full-time; $705 per credit part-time. Fees: $150 full-time; $150 per year part-time.

Financial Aid Loans, merit-based grants/scholarships, need-based grants/scholarships, and federal work-study loans are available. The average student debt at graduation is $60,270. To apply for financial assistance, students must complete the Free Application for Federal Student Aid, institutional forms. Financial aid contact: Douglas Leman, Director of Financial Aid, 154 Stuart Street, Boston, MA 02116. Phone: 617-422-7232. Fax: 617-422-7200. E-mail: finaid@admin.nesl.edu

Law School Library New England School of Law Library has 10 professional staff members and contains more

AT a GLANCE

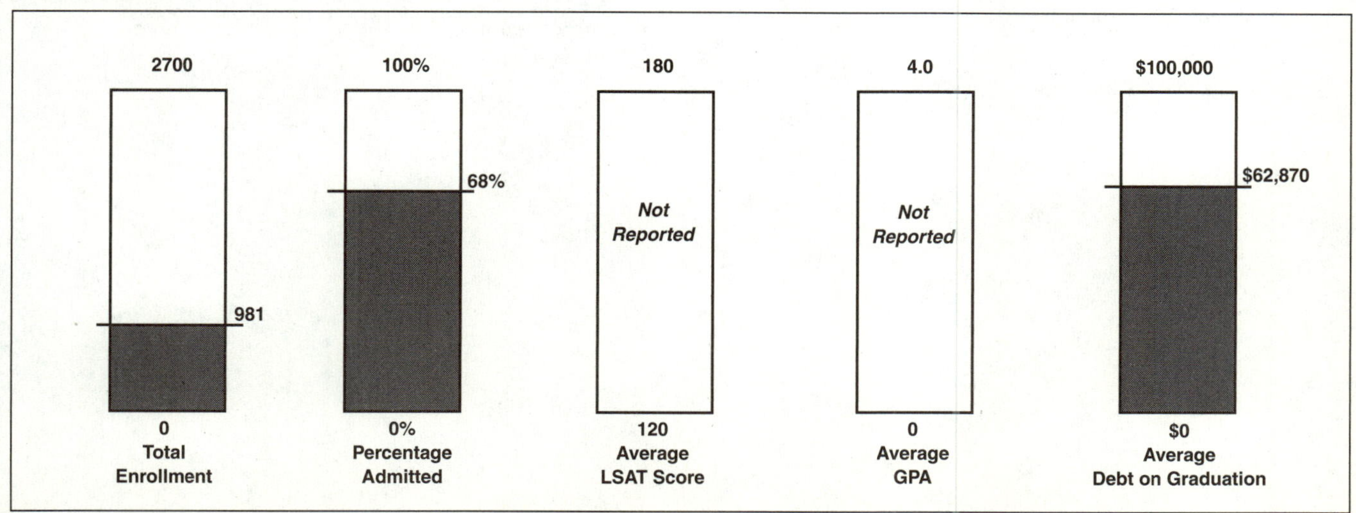

Degree Options		
Degree	**Total Credits Required**	**Length of Program**
JD–Juris Doctor–Law Program	84	3–4 yrs, full-time or part-time [day, evening]

than 309,423 volumes and 3,104 periodicals. 357 seats are available in the library. When classes are in session, the library is open 101 hours per week.

WESTLAW and LEXIS-NEXIS are available, as are the World Wide Web, online bibliographic services, and CD-ROM players. 87 computer workstations are available to students in the library. Special law collections include Women and the Law, Massachusetts Law.

First-Year Program Class size in the average section is 110; 100% of the first-year courses are taught by full-time faculty.

Upper-Level Program Class size in the average section is 47. Among the electives are:

- Administrative Law
- ★ Advocacy
- ★ Business and Corporate Law
- ★ Civil Litigation
- Consumer Law
- Criminal Defense
- ★ Criminal Prosecution
- Domestic Violence
- Education Law
- Employment Law
- Entertainment Law
- ★ Environmental Law
- Family Law
- ★ Family Practice
- Federal Courts
- General Practice
- Government Litigation
- Government/Regulation
- Health Care/Human Services
- Health Law
- ★ Immigration
- Indian/Tribal Law
- ★ Intellectual Property
- ★ International/Comparative Law
- Jurisprudence
- Labor Law
- Land Rights/Natural Resource
- ★ Land Use Law/Natural Resources
- ★ Lawyering Skills
- Legal History/Philosophy
- ★ Litigation
- Maritime Law
- Media Law
- Mediation
- ★ Probate Law
- ★ Public Interest
- Securities
- ★ Tax Law

(★ indicates an area of special strength)

Clinical Courses Students receive degree credit for clinical courses. (Clinical practicum is not required.) Among the clinical areas offered are:

- Administrative Law
- AIDS and the Law
- Business and Corporate Law
- Civil Litigation
- Consumer Law
- Criminal Defense
- Criminal Prosecution
- Domestic Violence
- Employment Law
- Environmental Law
- Family Law
- Family Practice
- Federal Courts
- General Practice
- Government Litigation
- Government/Regulation
- Health Care/Human Services
- Health Law
- Immigration
- International/Comparative Law
- Labor Law
- Land Rights/Natural Resource
- Land Use Law/Natural Resources
- Lawyering Skills
- Mediation
- Public Interest
- Tax Law

DEAN'S STATEMENT . . .

Iwelcome your interest in New England School of Law. We are a community characterized by rigorous study, practical instruction, and a cooperative learning environment. Located in the heart of the intellectually and culturally vibrant city of Boston, we are able to offer our students access to the legal and professional community that they will enter as attorneys.

Founded nearly a century ago as the only law school in the nation exclusively for women, New England School of Law has a proud heritage as an institution that is accessible to bright and motivated students who might otherwise not have the opportunity to study law. Coeducational since 1938, the Law School remains an independent institution, not affiliated with a university, and, therefore, we are able to commit all our resources to developing and improving our educational program.

We are particularly proud of our full-time faculty, who are an energetic and accomplished group of scholars and teachers. Nearly all members of the faculty have practiced in their fields of law before joining academia. They are dedicated teachers who are accessible to students and maintain a high level of scholarly publication. The full-time faculty is supplemented by an outstanding adjunct faculty of practicing attorneys and judges.

We provide our students with an extensive selection of electives, twenty clinical programs that offer real-world lawyering experience, and opportunities to participate on scholarly publications and moot court teams. Our graduates leave school knowledgeable about the law and well-equipped for practice. Our active and dedicated career services staff works with students beginning in their first year to direct and support their search for academic-year internships, summer clerkships, and post-graduate positions.

Please read our description here and then contact our admissions office for additional information. The faculty, administration, and students at New England School of Law are eager to assist you in accomplishing your goals.

—John F. O'Brien, Dean and Professor of Law

HISTORY, CAMPUS, AND LOCATION

New England School of Law was founded in 1908 as Portia Law School, the only law school in the nation exclusively for women. Coeducational since 1938, the Law School is accredited by the American Bar Association (ABA) and is a member of the Association of American Law Schools.

Located in the heart of Boston's theater district and a block from the famous Public Garden, New England School of Law occupies two buildings within walking distance of state and federal courthouses, government agencies, and prominent law firms. This central location opens extensive possibilities for clinical placements, clerkships, and part-time employment.

Relying on a good public transportation system, residents can take advantage of the city's neighborhoods, historic sights, fine cultural institutions, and professional sports teams. With nearly three dozen colleges, universities, and professional schools in the city, Boston has a large population of students and young professionals.

SPECIAL QUALITIES OF THE SCHOOL

In addition to required courses, students at New England School of Law can choose from approximately 120 electives. Courses and co-curricular activities can be combined to focus on areas such as tax, international, business, public interest, criminal, family, and environmental law. The clinical program allows students to combine field work with classroom study in twenty subject areas.

The Law School is a pioneer in incorporating relevant international law into domestic law courses throughout the curriculum. Students in Business Organizations, Contracts, Criminal Law, Family Law, Tax Law, and other classes learn about applicable international law, laws of other nations that impact Americans, and American laws that affect foreign nationals.

New England School of Law is also home to the Center for International Law and Policy, which sponsors an annual conference on a current issue on international law; a seminar series for Boston area law faculty; and the International War Crimes Project through which students provide research and analysis to the prosecutor of the International Criminal Tribunal for the Former Yugoslavia and Rwanda.

The Law School's Center for Law and Social Responsibility supports faculty, students, and alumni in projects and other activities focusing on social problems that can be addressed through the law and those that are products of inequities in the legal system itself. Current projects under the Center's auspices include the Criminal Justice Project, Domestic Violence Project, and Environmental Justice Project, which involve students in legal research and writing projects for practicing lawyers. The Center's Public Service Project identifies and coordinates public service work by faculty, students, and alumni.

Students at New England School of Law may enroll in the full-time day division, the part-time evening division, or the Special Part-time Program, a unique arrangement for parents with primary childrearing responsibilities.

TECHNOLOGY ON CAMPUS

All classrooms are wired for presentation technology and two have computer network connections at each seat. Computer workstations in the library support word processing, WESTLAW and LEXIS, tutorial programs including materials from the Center for Computer Assisted Legal Instruction, Internet access, and an extensive, networked CD-ROM collection.

Each student is issued an e-mail account. The Law School's Web site includes a Web board that faculty use to post materials and answer student questions. Students conduct on-line discussions on class topics.

The library's collection of approximately 300,000 volumes and volume equivalents is supplemented by audio and video collections, microform materials, CD-ROMs, and online research services.

SCHOLARSHIPS AND LOANS

Financial aid consists of a combination of federal loan programs, private loans, and institutional grants and scholarships. Most grants are need-based; however, the Law School awards several academic and merit scholarships. Federal work-study grants are also available.

STUDENT ACTIVITIES AND OPPORTUNITIES

Law Review The Law School has two nationally-distributed scholarly journals: the *New England Law Review* and the *New England Journal on Criminal and Civil Confinement*. The *Journal* is the only publication produced by law school students that is devoted solely to prison and incarceration issues. Students are selected for the editorial boards of both publications based on academic rank or performance in a writing competition. A third publication, the *New England International and Comparative Law Annual*, is published on the Internet.

Moot Court The required Legal Research and Writing Program includes a moot-court component. The Law School also sponsors five advocacy teams: Mock Trial, National Moot Court, Philip C. Jessup International Law Moot Court, National Tax Moot Court, and Environmental Moot Court. In recent regional and national competitions, all teams have advanced at least to semifinal rounds or have won brief or oralist awards.

Extracurricular Activities New England School of Law has a Student Bar Association, which oversees nearly two dozen student groups. Many of those organizations sponsor speakers, social events, and volunteer activities. Student representatives sit on most faculty committees.

Special Opportunities Three programs provide various types of judicial clerkship opportunities. The School's Academic Skills Program offers optional academic support and supervised skills practice for first-year students. Five study-abroad programs are available through the Law School's participation in the Consortium for Innovative Legal Education, Inc. Students may study in Galway, Ireland; London; or Malta in the summer, or they may take courses for a semester in New Zealand or The Netherlands.

Opportunities for Members of Minority Groups and Women In keeping with its history as a school for women, New England School of Law provides a supportive learning environment for women. Sixty percent of the 1999 entering class were women and there is an active Women's Law Caucus. The Law School also boasts a strong minority student community. The Charles Hamilton Houston Enrichment Program, founded to foster a comfortable and supportive atmosphere for students of color, is open to all students. It sponsors student-faculty discussions on race and ethnicity, a speaker series, social events, and an honor society. Four student organizations represent students of color, who made up 20 percent of the 1999 entering class. Several scholarships are earmarked for students of color.

BAR PASSAGE, CAREER SERVICES, AND PLACEMENT

Most students take the Massachusetts bar examination, but significant numbers also take the exam in New York, the District of Columbia, Florida, New Hampshire, and New Jersey.

The Career Services Office provides students with individual counseling, networking information, and programs on job-related issues. The office maintains an extensive resource library of directories of lawyers and legal organizations, books on practice areas, and periodicals, which are available to students and alumni. The career services site on the Law School's Web page features a searchable job-posting database, more than 2,600 career-related links, a student resume bank, and an e-mail service that communicates updated job postings to students. The office also organizes an alumni networking and mentoring program. As a member of the Massachusetts Law School Consortium, New England School of Law participates in recruitment programs with the state's six other ABA-accredited law schools.

Within nine months of graduation, 93 percent of the Class of 2000 were employed.

Legal Field	Percentage of Graduates	Average Starting Salary
Academic	0.5%	$29,750
Business	25.0%	$73,176
Government	19.0%	$40,753
Judicial Clerkship	8.0%	$39,760
Private Practice	38.3%	$45,664
Public Interest	1.1%	n/a
Other	0.9%	n/a

CORRESPONDENCE AND INFORMATION

New England School of Law
154 Stuart Street
Boston, Massachusetts 02116
Telephone: 617-422-7210
Fax: 617-422-7200
E-mail: admit@admin.nesl.edu
World Wide Web: http://www.nesl.edu/

NORTHEASTERN UNIVERSITY
SCHOOL OF LAW

Boston, Massachusetts

INFORMATION CONTACT

Carol Figueroa, Information Contact
400 Huntington Avenue
Boston, MA 02115-5005

Phone: 617-373-2395   Fax: 617-373-8865
Web site: http://www.slaw.neu.edu/

LAW STUDENT PROFILE [2000–2001]

FULL-TIME   Enrollment: 598
Women: 57%   Men: 43%

RACIAL or ETHNIC COMPOSITION
African American, 8%; Asian/Pacific Islander, 9%; Hispanic,
8%; Native American, 1%; International, 2%

APPLICANTS and ADMITTEES
Number applied: 1,979
Admitted: 840
Percentage accepted: 42%
Seats available: 185
Median LSAT score: 157
Average GPA: 3.3

Northeastern University School of Law is a private
nonprofit institution that organizes classes on a semester
calendar system. The campus is situated in an urban
setting. Founded in 1898, first ABA approved in 1969,
and an AALS member, Northeastern University School of
Law offers JD, JD/MBA, JD/MPH, JD/MS/MBA, and
JD/PhD degrees.

Faculty consists of 30 full-time and 36 part-time
members in 2000–2001. 15 full-time faculty members
and 12 part-time faculty members are women. 96.7% of
all faculty members have a JD; 13% have advanced law
degrees. Of all faculty members, 6.3% are Asian/Pacific
Islander, 9.3% are African American, 6.3% are Hispanic,
78.1% are white.

Application Information *Required:* LSAT, LSDAS,
application form, application fee of $65, baccalaureate
degree, 2 letters of recommendation, personal statement,
college transcripts, resume. *Recommended:* essay,
interview. *Application deadline* for fall term is March 1.
Applications are processed on a rolling basis.

Financial Aid In 2000–2001, 85% of all students received
some form of financial aid. 18 research assistantships,
totaling $10,950 were awarded. Loans, loan repayment
assistance program (LRAP), merit-based grants/scholar-
ships, need-based grants/scholarships, and federal
work-study loans are also available. The average student
debt at graduation is $62,000. To apply for financial
assistance, students must complete the Free Application
for Federal Student Aid, institutional forms. Completed
financial aid forms should be received by March 1.
Financial aid contact: Lori Moore, Associate Director of

AT a GLANCE

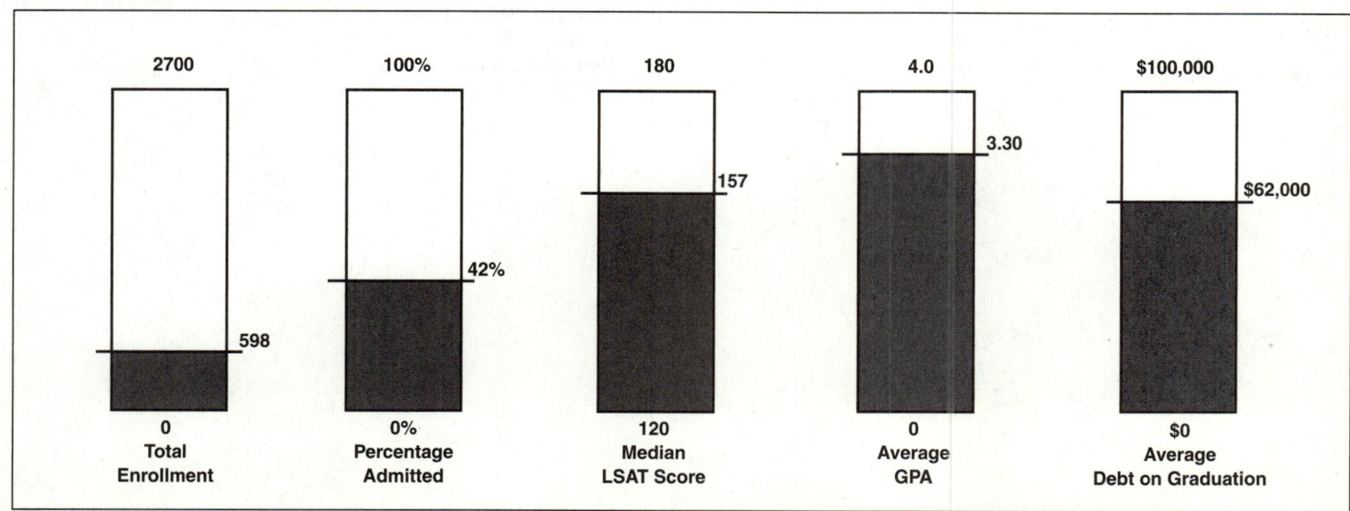

Degree Options

Degree	Total Credits Required	Length of Program
JD–Doctor of Laws	99	3 yrs, full-time only [day, summer]
JD/MBA–Juris Doctor/Master of Business Administration–Concurrent Degree Program	164	3.9 yrs, full-time only [day, summer]
JD/MPH–Juris Doctor/Master of Public Health–Dual-degree Program	123	3.5 yrs, full-time only [day, summer]
JD/MS/MBA–Juris Doctor/Master of Science/Master of Business Administration–Concurrent Degree Program	187	3.75 yrs, full-time only [day, summer]
JD/PhD–Juris Doctor/Doctor of Philosophy–Law, Policy, and Society	135	4–6 yrs, full-time only [day, summer]

Financial Aid, 400 Huntington Avenue, Boston, MA 02115. Phone: 617-373-4620. Fax: 617-373-8793. E-mail: l.moore@nunet.neu.edu

Law School Library The Berkowitz Law Library has 9 professional staff members and contains more than 295,704 volumes and 3,187 periodicals. 388 seats are available in the library. When classes are in session, the library is open 95 hours per week.

WESTLAW and LEXIS-NEXIS are available, as are the World Wide Web, online bibliographic services, and CD-ROM players. 58 computer workstations are available to students in the library. Special law collections include Pappas Public Interest Law Collection.

First-Year Program Class size in the average section is 85; 82.3% of the first-year courses are taught by full-time faculty.

Upper-Level Program Class size in the average section is 26. Among the electives are:

Administrative Law
★ Advocacy
Business and Corporate Law
Constitutional Law
★ Criminal Defense
Criminal Law
★ Diversity in the Legal Profession
★ Domestic Violence
Entertainment Law

Environmental Law
Family Law
Government/Regulation
Health Care/Human Services
Intellectual Property
International/Comparative Law
Jurisprudence
Labor Law
Land Use Law/Natural Resources
Lawyering Skills
Legal History/Philosophy
Litigation
Media Law
Mediation
★ Poverty/Welfare Law
★ Prisoners' Rights
Probate Law
★ Public Interest
Securities
Tax Law
★ Tobacco Control
Urban Economic Development
(★ indicates an area of special strength)

Clinical Courses Students receive degree credit for clinical courses. (Clinical practicum is not required.) Among the clinical areas offered are:

Certiorari Criminal Appeals
Criminal Defense
Domestic Violence
Poverty/Welfare Law
Prisoners' Rights
Tobacco Control

SUFFOLK UNIVERSITY
LAW SCHOOL

Boston, Massachusetts

INFORMATION CONTACT

Judith Reynolds, Director of Graduate Admissions
120 Tremont Street
Boston, MA 02108

Phone: 617-573-8302   Fax: 617-523-0116
E-mail: grad.admission@suffolk.edu
Web site: http://www.law.suffolk.edu/

LAW STUDENT PROFILE [2000–2001]

FULL-TIME   Enrollment: 997
Women: 53%   Men: 47%

PART-TIME   Enrollment: 711
Women: 46%   Men: 54%

RACIAL or ETHNIC COMPOSITION

African American, 4%; Asian/Pacific Islander, 4%; Hispanic,
2%; Native American, 0.1%

APPLICANTS and ADMITTEES

Seats available: 540
Average LSAT score: 153
Average GPA: 3.2

Suffolk University Law School is a private institution
that organizes classes on a semester calendar system. The
campus is situated in an urban setting. Founded in 1906,
first ABA approved in 1953, and an AALS member,
Suffolk University Law School offers JD, JD/MBA,
JD/MPA, and JD/MS degrees.

Faculty consists of 60 full-time and 90 part-time
members in 2000–2001. 10 full-time faculty members
and 22 part-time faculty members are women. 100% of
all faculty members have a JD; 38% have advanced law
degrees.

Application Information *Required:* LSAT, LSDAS,
application form, application fee of $50, baccalaureate
degree, 1 recommendation, personal statement, college
transcripts. *Recommended:* minimum 3.0 GPA, interview,
resume. *Application deadline* for fall term is March 1
(priority date). Applications are processed on a rolling
basis.

Costs The 1999–2000 tuition was $21,750 full-time; $750
per credit part-time. Fees: $40 full-time. Tuition and fees
vary according to class time and program.

Financial Aid In 2000–2001, 47% of all students received
some form of financial aid. Fellowships, loans, loan
repayment assistance program (LRAP), merit-based
grants/scholarships, need-based grants/scholarships, and
federal work-study loans are available. The average
student debt at graduation is $59,600. To apply for
financial assistance, students must complete the Free
Application for Federal Student Aid, institutional forms,
Profile form. Completed financial aid forms should be
received by March 1. Financial aid contact: Jocelyn Allen,

AT a GLANCE

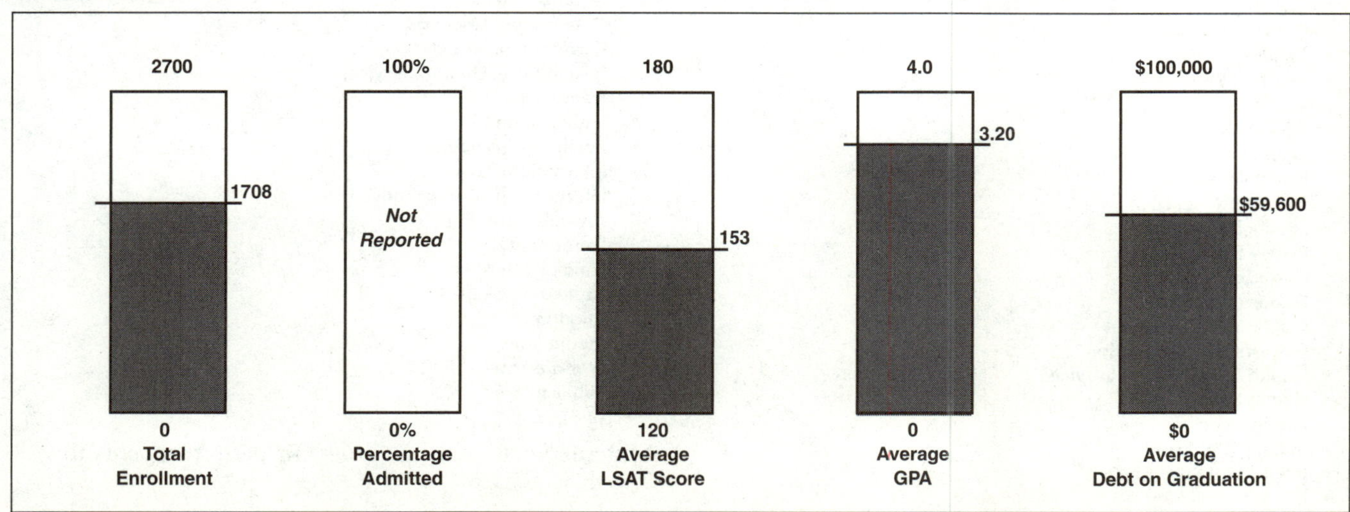

Degree Options

Degree	Total Credits Required	Length of Program
JD–Doctor of Laws	84	3–4 yrs, full-time or part-time [day, evening]
JD/MBA–Juris Doctor/Master of Business Administration–Dual-degree Program	111	4–5 yrs, full-time only [day, evening]
JD/MPA–Juris Doctor/Master of Professional Accountancy	110	4–5 yrs, full-time or part-time [day, evening]
JD/MS–Juris Doctor/Master of Science–International Economics	110	4–5 yrs, full-time or part-time [day, evening]
JD/MS–Juris Doctor/Master of Science–Finance	117	4–5 yrs, full-time only [day, evening]
JD/MS–Juris Doctor/Master of Science–Criminal Justice		

Director of Financial Aid, 120 Tremont Street, Boston, MA 02108-4977. Phone: 617-573-8147. Fax: 617-573-9869. E-mail: jallen@admin.suffolk.edu

Law School Library John Joseph Moakley Library has 11 professional staff members and contains more than 316,000 volumes and 5,300 periodicals. 880 seats are available in the library. When classes are in session, the library is open 98 hours per week.

WESTLAW and LEXIS-NEXIS are available, as are the World Wide Web, online bibliographic services, and CD-ROM players. 156 computer workstations are available to students in the library. Special law collections include collections in high technology/intellectual property, biomedical law, financial services law, and civil litigation.

First-Year Program Class size in the average section is 90; 100% of the first-year courses are taught by full-time faculty.

Upper-Level Program Class size in the average section is 40. Among the electives are:

Administrative Law
★ Advocacy
AIDS and the Law
★ Business and Corporate Law
★ Civil Litigation
Civil Rights
Consumer Law
★ Criminal Defense
★ Criminal Prosecution
Disability Law
Education Law
Employment Law
Entertainment Law
Environmental Law
★ Family Law
Family Practice
★ Financial Services
General Practice
Government Litigation
★ Government/Regulation
★ Health Care/Human Services
★ Health Law
Immigration
Indian/Tribal Law
★ Intellectual Property
★ International Law
★ International/Comparative Law
Jurisprudence
★ Juvenile Law
Labor Law
Land Use Law/Natural Resources
★ Landlord/Tenant
★ Lawyering Skills
Legal History/Philosophy
★ Litigation
Maritime Law
Media Law
Mediation
Probate Law
★ Public Interest
★ Securities
★ Tax Law
★ Technology Law
(★ *indicates an area of special strength*)

Clinical Courses Students receive degree credit for clinical courses. (Clinical practicum is not required.) Among the clinical areas offered are:

Accounting
AIDS and the Law
Civil Litigation
Civil Rights
Criminal Defense
Criminal Prosecution
Employment Law
Family Law
Family Practice
General Practice
Government Litigation
Government/Regulation
Health Care/Human Services
Health Law
Immigration
Intellectual Property
International Law
International/Comparative Law
Juvenile Law
Labor Law
Landlord/Tenant
Lawyering Skills
Litigation
Media Law
Probate Law
Public Interest
Tax Law

International exchange programs permit students to visit Sweden.

DEAN'S STATEMENT . . .

This is an extremely exciting time for the Suffolk University Law School community. In September 1999, we dedicated our new state-of-the-art building, Sargent Hall, which is located in the legal and business center of Boston. Suffolk was founded on the premise that capable men and women should have the opportunity to study law regardless of their backgrounds or circumstances. While it has grown to be one of the largest law schools in the country, with thriving day and evening programs, it has remained true to its historic mission of providing excellent education and training for a diverse student body. Our academic program integrates legal theory and practical skills in developing highly skilled, ethically sensitive, and service-oriented lawyers. The core curriculum provides a strong legal foundation for more than 200 upper-level elective courses in the full range of legal subjects and skills areas.

For these, and many other reasons, we are very proud of Suffolk University Law School. We encourage you to learn more about us by visiting our Web site, reading our literature, or visiting us in person.

—*Robert H. Smith, Dean and Professor of Law*

HISTORY, CAMPUS, AND LOCATION

Suffolk University Law School was founded by Gleason Archer in 1906, whose mission was to make Suffolk a welcoming portal for all who wished to study the law, regardless of economic status, education, or place of birth. In a city where the cobblestones and gas lamps of Beacon Hill coexist with cutting-edge companies of high technology and finance, Suffolk University Law School is woven into Boston's rich past and bright future. Boston offers the authenticity of what was, with the very best of what is—and Sargent Hall is a grand and visible extension of the city's two faces. Our students are steps away from city, state, and federal courthouses. Together, Boston's most prestigious law firms and Beacon Hill create an icon for political leadership and achievement throughout the world.

SPECIAL QUALITIES OF THE SCHOOL

In addition to a very diverse and broad scope of elective courses in all areas of specialization, the Law School offers concentrated programs in high technology/intellectual property, financial services, civil litigation, and health-care/biotechnology law. In addition, students may enroll in one of our joint degree programs, which combine a J.D. degree with any of the following: Masters in Business Administration, Masters in Public Administration, Master of Science in International Economics, Master of Science in Finance, or a Master of Science in Criminal Justice.

Additionally, students may enroll in our clinical programs such as the Voluntary Defenders Program, Voluntary Prosecutors Program, Suffolk University Legal Services Family Law Program, SU Clinical Legal, Landlord-Tenant Clinic, Intensive Civil Clinic, Juvenile Justice Center, or Battered Women's Advocacy Program. More than 200 internship opportunities also exist in the following areas: AIDS and the Law, Children and the Law, Government Lawyer, Immigration Law, Judicial, Labor and Employment Law, Legal Profession, Prosecutors, The Reflective Lawyer–Peace Training for Lawyers, and International Human Rights Project.

TECHNOLOGY ON CAMPUS

Suffolk University Law School opened a new state-of-the-art law school building, Sargent Hall, in June 1999, making the school one of the most technologically advanced law schools in the country. The technology includes a high-speed data network with 2,600 data nodes, gigabit ethernet capability, and a fiber optic cable backbone linking the entire law school building. Each classroom is equipped with a Pentium-based computer installed in the professor's station with Internet and local area network access. Every seat in each classroom, the library, and faculty offices has direct access to the high-speed network. The multimedia classrooms contain a data projector, electric screens, LCD projector, lighting controls, wireless microphones, hearing assistance, advanced speaker systems, and auxiliary computer connections for laptop computer presentations, equipped for teleconferencing/distance learning.

SCHOLARSHIPS AND LOANS

The financial aid program at Suffolk University Law School is designed to help fill the gap between the cost of a legal education and a student's own resources. Suffolk University Law School participates in a number of student financial aid programs in order to assist students in financing the costs of their legal education. Both need-based and merit-based aid is available. Financial aid awards (scholarships, grants, loans, and employment awards) are made to assist students in financing educational costs when their personal and family resources may not be sufficient. Merit scholarships are awarded by the Law School Admissions Committee at the time a candidate is admitted to the Law School. Scholarships are awarded to students based on outstanding academic achievement.

Academic Leadership Awards are awarded to students in the day and evening divisions who are about to enter their second year, and who, at that time, are ranked one through five in their respective sections. The day division has four sections and the evening division has two sections.

Suffolk University Law School also has a Loan Repayment Assistance Program for students who, upon graduation, pursue low-income, public service, law-related employment. The Committee selects two recent graduates each year for this program.

There are also a number of other academic scholarships awarded to worthy students each year.

STUDENT ACTIVITIES AND OPPORTUNITIES

Law Review Suffolk students have a number of opportunities to develop legal skills outside of the classroom through participation in *The Suffolk University Law Review, The Suffolk Transnational Law Review, The Suffolk Journal of Trial and Appellate Advocacy*, and *The Journal of High Technology Law.*

Moot Court Students may participate in various Moot Court competitions, such as the National Trial Competition, ATLA Trial Team, Constitutional Law Team, Information Technology and Privacy Law Team, Intellectual Property Law Team, Jessup International Law Team, National Invitational and Trial Tournament of Champions, National Moot Court Team, Securities Law Team, Sports Law Team, and Tax Law Team.

Extracurricular Activities Students may join one of thirty student organizations or participate in the Student Bar Association.

Special Opportunities A notable opportunity at Suffolk University is The STRIVE Program: Success, Training, and Resources for Inclusion and Validating Excellence. This program was specifically developed to meet the needs of nontraditional students in a diverse educational environment. STRIVE acquaints the nontraditional student with a myriad of possible pressures and hurdles that he or she may face during the integration into the law school community, and the potential academic consequences. STRIVE is a five-day program held one week prior to Orientation. It is available to all students enrolled in the first year class.

The Academic Support Program offers skills evaluation, exam skills training, and writing guidance to both upper-level and first-year students. Students are introduced to the technology that accommodates the learning styles and needs of all students.

Opportunities for Members of Minority Groups and Women The Law School is a supporting member of CLEO and hosted a CLEO Institute in summer 2000. The Law School offers an English as a Second Language (ESL) program for students whose primary language is not English.

BAR PASSAGE, CAREER SERVICES, AND PLACEMENT

Suffolk Law School is committed to preparing students for the increasingly complex and rapidly changing world in which they will serve their clients and communities. Suffolk's balanced curriculum provides a solid foundation essential for a successful practitioner and also offers ample opportunities for individual concentration in specialized areas of the law. The School is proud of its rich diversity. Almost 30 percent of the student body speaks a foreign language. More than 17,000 graduates practice law throughout the United States, as well as in seven countries. They can be found in private practice, corporations, public interest organizations, the military, and the executive, judicial, and legislative branches of government.

The Office of Career Development coordinates the fall recruiting program, resume collection, Web page links to job postings, and national employment information. The Office arranges an off-campus interview program and hosts, in conjunction with other law schools, several placement programs that serve students with special interests or special needs.

Legal Field	Percentage of Graduates	Average Starting Salary
Academic	3.2%	n/a
Business	28.3%	n/a
Government	16.8%	n/a
Judicial Clerkship	8.5%	n/a
Private Practice	40.0%	n/a
Public Interest	0.5%	n/a
Other	2.7%	n/a

CORRESPONDENCE AND INFORMATION

Suffolk University Law School
120 Tremont Street
Boston, Massachusetts 02108-4977
Telephone: 617-573-8144
Fax: 617-523-1367
E-mail: lawadm@admin.suffolk.edu
World Wide Web: http://www.law.suffolk.edu

WESTERN NEW ENGLAND COLLEGE
SCHOOL OF LAW

Springfield, Massachusetts

INFORMATION CONTACT

Eric J. Eden, Assistant Dean and Director of Admissions
1215 Wilbraham Road
Springfield, MA 01119

Phone: 413-782-1406   Fax: 413-796-2067
E-mail: eeden@wnec.edu
Web site:

LAW STUDENT PROFILE [2000–2001]

FULL-TIME Enrollment: 280
Women: 52%   Men: 48%

PART-TIME Enrollment: 238
Women: 54%   Men: 46%

APPLICANTS and ADMITTEES

Number applied: 1,406
Admitted: 881
Percentage accepted: 63%
Seats available: 174
Average LSAT score: 151
Average GPA: 3.1

Western New England College School of Law is a private institution that organizes classes on a semester calendar system. The campus is situated in a suburban setting. Founded in 1919, first ABA approved in 1978, and an AALS member, Western New England College School of Law offers JD, JD/MBA, JD/MRP, and JD/MSW degrees.

Faculty consists of 19 full-time and 37 part-time members in 2000–2001. 6 full-time faculty members and 15 part-time faculty members are women. 100% of all faculty members have a JD; 13.3% have advanced law degrees. Of all faculty members, 5% are African American, 2% are Hispanic, 93% are white.

Application Information *Required:* LSAT, LSDAS, application form, application fee of $45, baccalaureate degree, 2 letters of recommendation, personal statement, college transcripts. *Recommended:* resume. *Application deadline* for fall term is March 15 (priority date). Applications are processed on a rolling basis.

Costs The 1999–2000 tuition was $19,064 full-time; $14,297 per year part-time. Fees: $787 full-time; $373 per year part-time.

Financial Aid Loans, merit-based grants/scholarships, need-based grants/scholarships, and federal work-study loans are available. The average student debt at graduation is $69,013. To apply for financial assistance, students must complete the Free Application for Federal Student Aid, institutional forms. Completed financial aid forms

AT a GLANCE

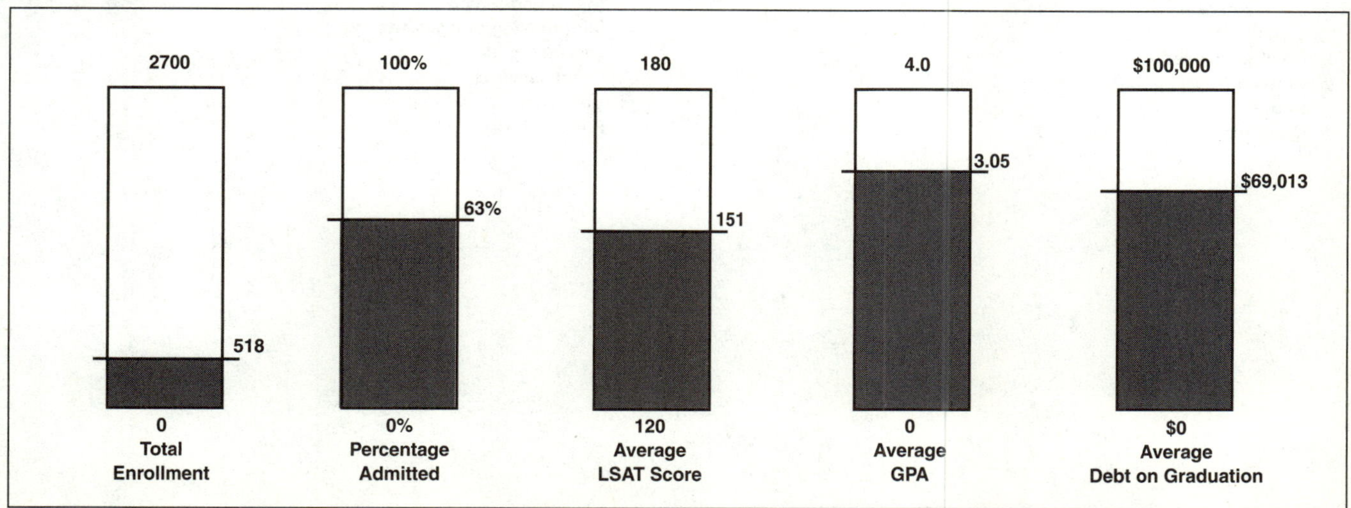

Degree Options

Degree	Total Credits Required	Length of Program
JD–Doctor of Laws	90	3–4.5 yrs, full-time or part-time [day, evening, summer]
JD/MBA–Juris Doctor/Master of Business Administration–JD/MBA Dual Degree program	115	4–5 yrs, full-time or part-time [day, evening, summer]
JD/MRP–Juris Doctor/Master of Regional Planning–Combined-degree Program	124	4 yrs, full-time only [day]
JD/MSW–Juris Doctor/Master of Social Work–Combined-degree Program	124	4 yrs, full-time or part-time [day]

should be received by April 1. Financial aid contact: Sandra Belanger, Financial Aid Specialist, 1215 Wilbraham Road, Student Administrative Services, Springfield, MA 01119. Phone: 413-796-2080. Fax: 413-796-2081.

Law School Library Western New England College School of Law Library has 6 professional staff members and contains more than 366,376 volumes and 5,091 periodicals. 400 seats are available in the library. When classes are in session, the library is open 103 hours per week.

WESTLAW and LEXIS-NEXIS are available, as are the World Wide Web, online bibliographic services, and CD-ROM players. 40 computer workstations are available to students in the library. Special law collections include federal government document depository, law and popular fiction (print and video).

First-Year Program Class size in the average section is 49; 100% of the first-year courses are taught by full-time faculty.

Upper-Level Program Class size in the average section is 30. Among the electives are:

Administrative Law
Advocacy
Bankruptcy
Business and Corporate Law
★ Civil Litigation
Civil Rights
★ Criminal Procedure
★ Criminal Prosecution
Cyberspace Law
★ Discrimination
Education Law
Employment Law
Environmental Law
Family Law
Gender and the Law
Government/Regulation
Health Care/Human Services
Intellectual Property
International/Comparative Law
Interviewing and Counseling
Jurisprudence
Labor Law
Land Use Law/Natural Resources
Lawyering Skills
Legal History/Philosophy
★ Legal Services
★ Litigation
Media Law
Mediation
Probate Law
Public Interest
Securities
Tax Law

(★ indicates an area of special strength)

Clinical Courses Students receive degree credit for clinical courses. (Clinical practicum is not required.) Among the clinical areas offered are:

Advocacy
Civil Litigation
Criminal Procedure
Criminal Prosecution
Discrimination
Interviewing and Counseling
Lawyering Skills
Legal Services
Litigation
Public Interest

DEAN'S STATEMENT . . .

The quality and vibrancy of your legal education is of greatest importance to your success as a law student and a practicing lawyer. So where can you get the best education, a most enjoyable experience, and the greatest chance of success?

Western New England College School of Law offers a full, well-rounded curriculum taught by experts and scholars in their respective fields, faculty who are interested in helping you to learn and understand the law to your fullest ability. Students work with faculty in a close community of learning. Our faculty members have an open-door policy and are available for your educational and professional development. We pride ourselves on being a school where you and your fellow students can obtain a fundamental understanding of the philosophy of the law, as well as a practical application of that law to everyday issues you will experience as an attorney. Our clinics, externships, and vast array of skills courses will allow you the opportunity to develop classroom knowledge into genuine professional skills.

An enjoyable law school experience comes not only from the classroom, but also from the learning environment. Everyone here—the faculty, staff, administrators, and other students—work with you to provide a supportive atmosphere. The law school building is comfortable and equipped with the latest educational technology. Western New England is ideally located on a beautiful, open campus. Its buildings evoke the history and culture in which our American legal system first began to develop.

But don't take my word for it; come and visit us. We look forward to meeting each of you personally. Visit one of our forums for persons interested in attending law school. Talk with our students and alumni. Visit a class and talk with faculty. You'll find a learning environment that will excite you and challenge you.

—Arthur R. Gaudio, Dean

HISTORY, CAMPUS, AND LOCATION

Founded in 1919, Western New England College is the only law school in western Massachusetts. A member of the Association of American Law Schools (AALS), the School of Law is private and has been accredited by the American Bar Association (ABA) since 1978.

Students are drawn to Western New England College by a combination of location—Springfield is a peaceful, small, and inexpensive city—and flexibility—the law school supplements its traditional curriculum with simulation and clinical programs.

Western New England's dedication to the practical aspects of lawyering is demonstrated by the fact that every one of its 63 full- and part-time faculty members has practiced law. The faculty and administration seek to foster a collaborative atmosphere that is virtually devoid of cutthroat competitiveness.

Springfield is a city of approximately 157,000 residents, 19 percent of whom are African American and 16 percent of whom are Hispanic. Along with distinguished museums, a symphony orchestra, and the Basketball Hall of Fame, the nearby five colleges—Amherst, Hampshire, Mt. Holyoke, Smith, and the University of Massachusetts—contribute to the recreational and cultural life of Springfield and the Pioneer Valley.

SPECIAL QUALITIES OF THE SCHOOL

A student-faculty ratio of 16:1 and a variety of social events combine to form an intimate, stimulating environment in which to study law. Throughout the semester there are Dean's Teas, which provide opportunities for students and faculty members to get together. "WNEC Week," a series of receptions hosted by alumni, occurs during spring break.

These receptions are an invaluable opportunity for current students to network with alumni.

Every spring there is an inter–law school basketball tournament hosted by the law school. A number of law schools field men's and women's teams and make their way to the Alumni Healthful Living Center, Western New England College's state-of-the-art athletic facility.

TECHNOLOGY ON CAMPUS

There are numerous computer workstations available in the law school library, including thirty-one IBM and Macintosh machines and six laptops for use. In addition, the library is equipped with WESTLAW, LEXIS-NEXIS, and online cataloging stations. There is ready access from the library to the World Wide Web. Each student is issued an Internet e-mail account, and several classrooms are wired for computer use.

SCHOLARSHIPS AND LOANS

Most student aid is in the form of government and privately sponsored loans. In a typical year, more than one third of incoming students receive scholarship support. Award amounts generally range from $4000 to $15,000. Full-tuition scholarships are also awarded. Most awards are based on academic merit, although some scholarships are designed to assist students who have overcome hardships.

STUDENT ACTIVITIES AND OPPORTUNITIES

Law Review The School publishes the *Western New England Law Review* twice a year. Thirty full- and part-time students participated in the publication in 2000–01.

Moot Court Participation in moot court is elective and allows the participant to practice and refine legal writing and advocacy skills. The law school participates in inter–law school competitions, including the National Moot Court, the ABA National Trial, the ABA Negotiation Moot Court, the Securities Law Moot Court, and the Jessup International Moot Court Competitions. Recent moot court teams have placed as high as first regionally and fifth nationally, and in 2001 the Negotiation Team won its national competition.

Extracurricular Activities Students sit with faculty members on the Admissions and the Academic Standards Committees, and two students attend regular faculty meetings. Student organizations include the Student Bar Association, the Multi-Cultural Law Students Association, the Women's Law Association, the Environmental Law Coalition, the Jewish Law Students Association, Phi Alpha Delta, the Lesbian/Gay/Bisexual Alliance, the Christian Legal Society, the National Lawyers Guild, the International Law Society, the Sports and Entertainment Law Society, the Computer Law Society, the Criminal Law Society, the Business Law Society, the Federalist Society, the American Bar Association's Law Student Division, the Student Animal Defense, Students for the Equal Access to Justice, a newspaper (*Lex Brevis*), and the yearbook.

Special Opportunities Clinics allow students to work with actual clients under the supervision of a faculty member. The School of Law offers four clinical programs: the Criminal Law, Discrimination Law, and Legal Services Clinics. Such internships allow students to work in the office of an attorney, judge, or magistrate to acquire substantive legal knowledge and practical skills.

In conjunction with the University of Massachusetts Amherst, the School of Law offers a combined Juris Doctor/Master of Regional Planning (J.D./M.R.P.) degree program. Students have the opportunity to study how regions develop from economic and environmental standpoints. Combining the two degrees is invaluable, especially for those interested in environmental law issues.

In conjunction with Springfield College, the School of Law offers a combined Juris Doctor/Master of Social Work (J.D./M.S.W.) degree program. Combining law and social work enables professionals to better serve their clients by helping them to understand their clients' concerns from both a legal and social perspective. The School of Law also offers the opportunity to obtain both a J.D. and M.B.A. degree from Western New England College.

Opportunities for Members of Minority Groups and Women The School of Law believes strongly that its student body should mirror society and, as such, actively encourages qualified women and members of minority groups to apply. The Multi-Cultural Law Students Association, the Women's Law Association, and the Lesbian/Gay/Bisexual Alliance host numerous activities throughout the academic year.

BAR PASSAGE, CAREER SERVICES, AND PLACEMENT

Western New England students pass various state bar examinations at or above the state averages. Most students sit for the bar exam in Massachusetts, Connecticut, or New York. The School of Law's Career Services Office provides continuous support to law students and alumni in their professionalization. The Office of Alumni Relations also plays an important role in the professionalization of students.

Legal Field	Percentage of Graduates	Average Starting Salary
Academic	3.2%	n/a
Business	30.2%	n/a
Government	20.6%	n/a
Judicial Clerkship	14.3%	n/a
Private Practice	24.6%	n/a
Public Interest	4.0%	n/a
Other	3.1%	n/a

CORRESPONDENCE AND INFORMATION

Office of Admissions
Western New England College School of Law
1215 Wilbraham Road
Springfield, Massachusetts 01119
Telephone: 800-782-6665 (toll-free)
Fax: 413-796-2067
E-mail: lawadmis@wnec.edu
World Wide Web: http://www.law.wnec.edu

MICHIGAN STATE UNIVERSITY-DETROIT COLLEGE OF LAW

East Lansing, Michigan

LAW STUDENT PROFILE [2000–2001]

FULL-TIME Enrollment: 543
Women: 38%   Men: 62%

PART-TIME Enrollment: 161
Women: 48%   Men: 52%

APPLICANTS and ADMITTEES

Number applied: 1,074
Admitted: 621
Percentage accepted: 58%
Seats available: 240
Average LSAT score: 152
Average GPA: 3.1

Michigan State University-Detroit College of Law is a private nonprofit institution that organizes classes on a semester calendar system. The campus is situated in a suburban setting. Founded in 1891, first ABA approved in 1941, and an AALS member, Michigan State University-Detroit College of Law offers JD, JD/MA, JD/MBA, JD/MILR, JD/MPAd, and JD/MS degrees.

Faculty 100% of all faculty members have a JD; 43% have advanced law degrees. Of all faculty members, 1% are African American, 1% are Hispanic, 98% are white.

Application Information *Required:* LSAT, LSDAS, application form, application fee of $50, baccalaureate degree, personal statement, essay, writing sample, college transcripts. *Recommended:* recommendations, interview.

Costs The 2000–2001 tuition was $17,024 full-time; $587 per credit part-time.

Financial Aid Fellowships, loans, merit-based grants/scholarships, need-based grants/scholarships, and federal work-study loans are available. The average student debt at graduation is $59,381. To apply for financial assistance, students must complete the Free Application for Federal Student Aid, scholarship specific applications. Financial aid contact: Pam Shaw, Director of Financial Aid, 316 Law College Building, East Lansing, MI 48824. Phone: 517-432-6810. Fax: 517-432-0098. E-mail: heatleya@pilot.msu.edu

Law School Library Michigan State University- Detroit College of Law Library has 7 professional staff members and contains more than 237,432 volumes and 3,428

AT a GLANCE

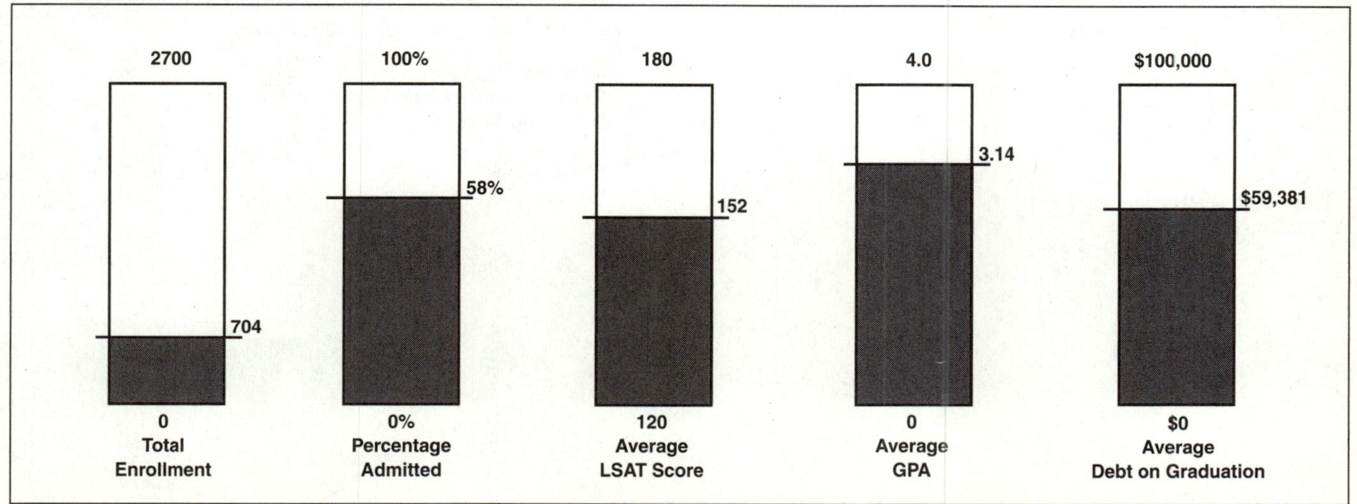

Degree Options

Degree	Total Credits Required	Length of Program
JD–Doctor of Laws	89	3–4 yrs, full-time or part-time [day, evening, summer]
JD/MA–Juris Doctor/Master of Arts–Dual-degree Program		4 yrs, full-time or part-time [day, summer]
JD/MA–Juris Doctor/Master of Arts–Communication		
JD/MBA–Juris Doctor/Master of Business Administration–Dual-degree Program	115	4–5 yrs, full-time or part-time [day, evening, summer]
JD/MILR–Juris Doctor/Master of Industrial and Labor Relations–Dual-degree Program		4 yrs, full-time or part-time [day, evening, summer]
JD/MPAd–Juris Doctor/Master of Public Administration–Dual-degree Program	127	4–5 yrs, full-time or part-time [day, evening, summer]
JD/MS–Juris Doctor/Master of Science–Dual-degree Program Forestry		4–5 yrs, full-time or part-time [day, summer]
JD/MS–Juris Doctor/Master of Science–Fisheries and Wildlife		4 yrs, full-time or part-time [day, evening]
JD/MS–Juris Doctor/Master of Science–Resource Development		4 yrs, full-time or part-time [day, evening, summer]
JD/MS–Juris Doctor/Master of Science–Forestry-Urban Studies		4 yrs, full-time or part-time
JD/MS–Juris Doctor/Master of Science–Park, Recreation, Tourism		4 yrs, full-time or part-time

periodicals. 455 seats are available in the library. When classes are in session, the library is open 109 hours per week.

WESTLAW and LEXIS-NEXIS are available, as are the World Wide Web, online bibliographic services, and CD-ROM players. 49 computer workstations are available to students in the library.

First-Year Program Class size in the average section is 70; 100% of the first-year courses are taught by full-time faculty.

Upper-Level Program Class size in the average section is 20. Among the electives are:

Administrative Law
★ Advocacy
★ Business and Corporate Law
Consumer Law
Education Law
Entertainment Law
★ Environmental Law
★ Family Law
Government/Regulation
★ Health Care/Human Services
Indian/Tribal Law

Intellectual Property
★ International/Comparative Law
Jurisprudence
Labor Law
Land Use Law/Natural Resources
Lawyering Skills
Legal History/Philosophy
★ Litigation
Maritime Law
Media Law
Mediation
Probate Law
Public Interest
Securities
★ Tax Law
(★ indicates an area of special strength)

Clinical Courses Students receive degree credit for clinical courses. (Clinical practicum is not required.) Among the clinical areas offered are:

Administrative Law
Government/Regulation
Lawyering Skills
Litigation
Public Interest
Tax Law

THOMAS M. COOLEY LAW SCHOOL

Lansing, Michigan

INFORMATION CONTACT

Stephanie Gregg, Dean of Admissions
300 South Capitol Ave, PO Box 13038
Lansing, MI 48901-3038

Phone: 517-371-5140   Fax: 517-334-5718
E-mail: greggs@cooley.edu
Web site: http://www.cooley.edu/

LAW STUDENT PROFILE [2000–2001]

FULL-TIME   Enrollment: 454
Women: 46%   Men: 54%

PART-TIME   Enrollment: 1,234
Women: 47%   Men: 53%

APPLICANTS and ADMITTEES

Number applied: 3,006
Admitted: 2,068
Percentage accepted: 69%
Seats available: 732
Average LSAT score: 152
Average GPA: 2.9

Thomas M. Cooley Law School is a private nonprofit institution that organizes classes on a trimester calendar system. The campus is situated in an urban setting. Founded in 1972, first ABA approved in 1975, Thomas M. Cooley Law School offers a JD degree.

Faculty 100% of all faculty members have a JD; 15.5% have advanced law degrees. Of all faculty members, 9% are African American, 91% are white.

Application Information *Required:* minimum 140 LSAT score, LSDAS, application form, college transcripts.

Costs The 2000–2001 tuition was $19,500 full-time; $650 per credit hour part-time. Fees: $20 per term full-time; $20 per term part-time. Tuition and fees vary according to course load and degree level.

Financial Aid Merit-based grants/scholarships, need-based grants/scholarships, and federal work-study loans are available. The average student debt at graduation is $68,000. To apply for financial assistance, students must complete the Free Application for Federal Student Aid. Financial aid contact: Richard Boruszewski, Director of Financial Aid, Financial Aid Office, 507 South Grand Avenue, PO Box 13038, Lansing, MI 48901. Phone: 517-371-5140 ext. 5420. Fax: 517-334-5716. E-mail: finaid@cooley.edu

Law School Library Thomas Cooley Law School Library has 17 professional staff members and contains more than 395,151 volumes and 5,229 periodicals. 530 seats are available in the library. When classes are in session, the library is open 120 hours per week.

WESTLAW and LEXIS-NEXIS are available, as are the World Wide Web and online bibliographic services.

AT a GLANCE

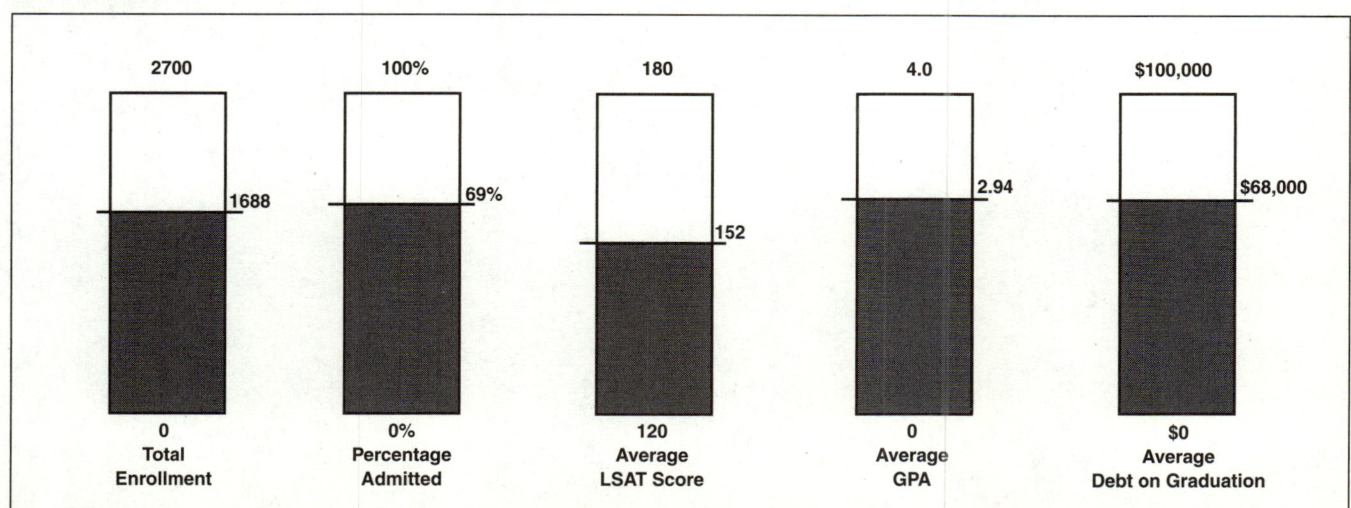

Degree Options

Degree	Total Credits Required	Length of Program
JD–Juris Doctor	90	2–4 yrs, full-time or part-time [day, evening, weekend, summer]

69 computer workstations are available to students in the library. Special law collections include selected United States government document depository.

First-Year Program Class size in the average section is 50; 100% of the first-year courses are taught by full-time faculty.

Upper-Level Program Class size in the average section is 70. Among the electives are:

 Civil Litigation
★ Criminal Defense
★ Criminal Prosecution
★ Elderly Advocacy
 Family Practice
★ General Practice
 Health Law

(★ indicates an area of special strength)

Clinical Courses Students receive degree credit for clinical courses. 3 credit hours of clinical practicum are required. Among the clinical areas offered are:

 Civil Litigation
 Criminal Defense
 Criminal Prosecution
 Elderly Advocacy
 Family Practice
 General Practice
 Health Law
 Nonprofit Organizations

International exchange programs permit students to visit Australia.

UNIVERSITY OF DETROIT MERCY
SCHOOL OF LAW

Detroit, Michigan

INFORMATION CONTACT

Joseph S. Daly, Assistant Dean
651 East Jefferson Avenue
Detroit, MI 48226

Phone: 313-596-0200   Fax: 313-596-0280
Web site: http://www.udmercy.edu/

LAW STUDENT PROFILE [2000–2001]

FULL-TIME   Enrollment: 685
Women: 48%   Men: 52%

PART-TIME   Enrollment: 114
Women: 41%   Men: 59%

RACIAL or ETHNIC COMPOSITION
African American, 12%; Asian/Pacific Islander, 3%; Hispanic, 1%; Native American, 0.4%; International, 5%

APPLICANTS and ADMITTEES
Seats available: 130
Average LSAT score: 147
Average GPA: 3.0

University of Detroit Mercy School of Law is a private institution that organizes classes on a semester calendar system. The campus is situated in an urban setting. Founded in 1912, first ABA approved in 1933, and an AALS member, University of Detroit Mercy School of Law offers JD and JD/MBA degrees.

Faculty consists of 27 full-time members in 2000–2001. 4 full-time faculty members are women. 100% of all faculty members have a JD; 8% have advanced law degrees. Of all faculty members, 10% are African American, 90% are white.

Application Information *Required:* LSAT, LSDAS, application form, application fee of $50, baccalaureate degree, minimum GPA, 2 letters of recommendation, personal statement, college transcripts. *Application deadline* for fall term is April 15.

Financial Aid Loans, merit-based grants/scholarships, and federal work-study loans are available. The average student debt at graduation is $55,540. To apply for financial assistance, students must complete the Free Application for Federal Student Aid, institutional forms, scholarship-specific applications for private scholarships only; not required for financial aid application. Financial aid contact: Denise M. Daniel, Financial Aid Coordinator School of Law, 651 East Jefferson Avenue, Detroit, MI 48226. Phone: 313-596-0214. Fax: 313-596-0280. E-mail: udmlawfa@udmercy.edu

Law School Library University of Detroit Mercy School of Law Library has 5 professional staff members and

AT a GLANCE

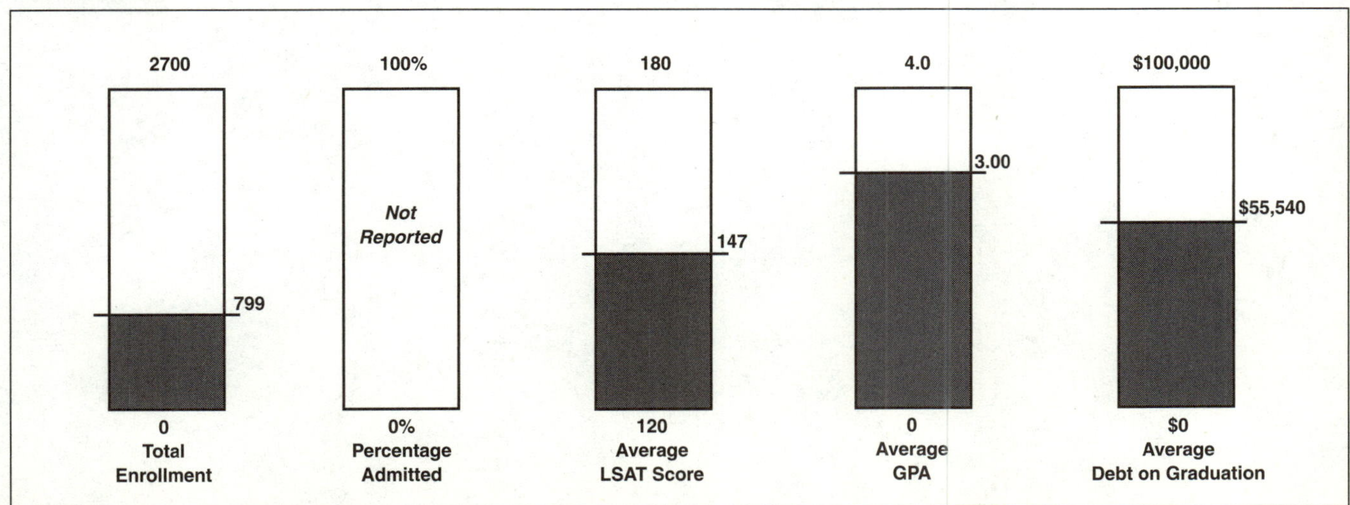

Degree Options

Degree	Total Credits Required	Length of Program
JD–Doctor of Laws	90	3–4 yrs, full-time or part-time [day, evening]
JD/MBA–Juris Doctor/Master of Business Administration–Dual-degree Program	110	4–5 yrs, full-time or part-time [day, evening]

contains more than 317,366 volumes and 3,549 periodicals. 406 seats are available in the library. When classes are in session, the library is open 92 hours per week.

WESTLAW and LEXIS-NEXIS are available, as are the World Wide Web, online bibliographic services, and CD-ROM players. 50 computer workstations are available to students in the library. Special law collections include Canadian, Labor, Tax.

First-Year Program Class size in the average section is 85; 100% of the first-year courses are taught by full-time faculty.

Upper-Level Program Class size in the average section is 30. Among the electives are:

Business and Corporate Law
Civil Rights
Criminal Defense
Criminal Prosecution
Elderly Advocacy
Entertainment Law
Environmental Law
★ Ethics
Health Care/Human Services
★ Immigration
★ Intellectual Property
International Law
★ International/Comparative Law
Labor Law
★ Lawyering Skills
★ Legal Writing
Litigation
★ Tax Law
(★ indicates an area of special strength)

Clinical Courses Students receive degree credit for clinical courses. (Clinical practicum is not required.) Among the clinical areas offered are:

Business and Corporate Law
Civil Rights
Criminal Defense
Criminal Prosecution
Elderly Advocacy
Environmental Law
Government Litigation
Health Care/Human Services
Immigration
International Law
International/Comparative Law
Litigation
Tax Law

International exchange programs permit students to visit France.

UNIVERSITY OF MICHIGAN
LAW SCHOOL

Ann Arbor, Michigan

INFORMATION CONTACT

Sarah C. Zearfoss, Assistant Dean and Director of Admissions
625 South State Street
Ann Arbor, MI 48109-1215

Phone: 734-764-0537   Fax: 734-647-3218
E-mail: law.jd.admissions@umich.edu
Web site: http://www.umich.edu/

LAW STUDENT PROFILE [2000–2001]

FULL TIME   Enrollment: 1,101

RACIAL OR ETHNIC COMPOSITION
African American, 8%; Asian/Pacific Islander, 9%; Hispanic, 4%; Native American, 2%; International, 0.3%

APPLICANTS and ADMITTEES
Number applied: 3,373
Admitted: 1,190
Percentage accepted: 35%
Seats available: 367
Median LSAT score: 166
Average GPA: 3.5

University of Michigan Law School is a public institution that organizes classes on a semester calendar system. The campus is situated in an urban setting. Founded in 1859, first ABA approved in 1923, and an AALS member, University of Michigan Law School offers JD, JD/MA, JD/MBA, JD/MHSA, JD/MPH, JD/MPP, JD/MS, JD/MSW, JD/PhD, LLM, MCL, and SJD degrees.

Faculty consists of 71 full-time members in 2000–2001. 19 full-time faculty members are women. 96% of all faculty members have a JD; 40% have advanced law degrees. Of all faculty members, 3% are African American, 89% are white, 8% are international.

Application Information *Required:* LSAT, LSDAS, application form, application fee of $70, baccalaureate degree, 1 recommendation, personal statement, college transcripts. *Recommended:* essay, writing sample, resume. *Application deadline* for fall term is February 15. Applications are processed on a rolling basis.

Costs The 2000–2001 tuition was $20,956 full-time for area residents. Tuition was $26,956 full-time for nonresidents. Fees: $186 full-time.

Financial Aid Graduate assistantships, loans, loan repayment assistance program (LRAP), merit-based grants/scholarships, need-based grants/scholarships, and federal work-study loans are available. The average student debt at graduation is $65,000. To apply for financial assistance, students must complete the Free Application for Federal Student Aid, institutional forms, scholarship specific applications, Need Access diskette, tax returns. Financial aid contact: Katherine Gottschalk,

AT a GLANCE

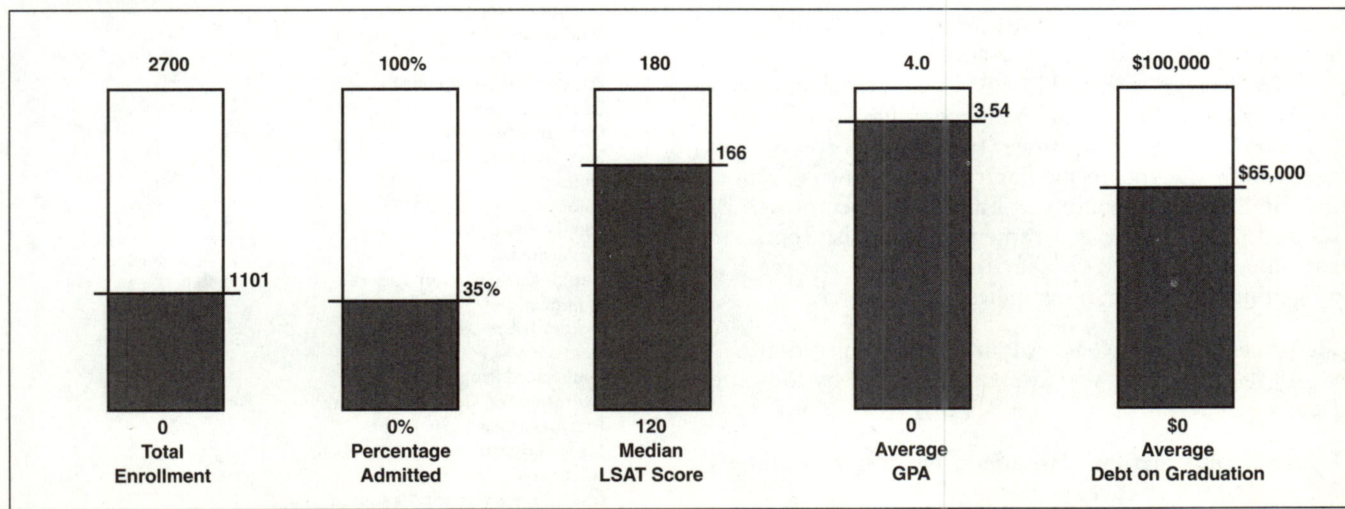

Degree Options

Degree	Total Credits Required	Length of Program
JD–Doctor of Laws	83	3 yrs, full-time only [day, summer]
JD/MA–Juris Doctor/Master of Arts–Law and World Politics Joint-degree Program		3.5 yrs, full-time only [day, summer]
JD/MA–Juris Doctor/Master of Arts–Law and Russian and East European Studies Joint-degree program		3.5 yrs, full-time only [day]
JD/MA–Juris Doctor/Master of Arts–Japanese Studies Joint-degree Program		4 yrs, full-time only [day, summer]
JD/MA–Juris Doctor/Master of Arts–Modern Middle Eastern and North African Studies Joint-degree Program		3.5 yrs, full-time only [day]
JD/MBA–Juris Doctor/Master of Business Administration–Joint-degree Program		4 yrs, full-time only [day, summer]
JD/MHSA–Juris Doctor/Master of Health Service Administration–Joint-degree Program		4 yrs, full-time only [day, summer]
JD/MPH–Juris Doctor/Master of Public Health–Law and Public Health		4 yrs, full-time only
JD/MPP–Juris Doctor/Master of Public Planning–Joint-degree Program		4 yrs, full-time only [day, summer]
JD/MS–Juris Doctor/Master of Science–Natural Resources Joint-degree Program		4 yrs, full-time only [day, summer]
JD/MS–Juris Doctor/Master of Science–Law and Information Joint-degree		4 yrs, full-time only [day, summer]
JD/MSW–Juris Doctor/Master of Social Work–Joint-degree Program		4 yrs, full-time only [day, summer]
JD/PhD–Juris Doctor/Doctor of Philosophy–Joint-degree Program in Economics		5 yrs, full-time only [day, summer]
LLM–Master of Laws	24	1 yr, full-time only [day, summer]
MCL–Master of Comparative Law	20	1 yr, full-time only [day]
SJD–Doctor of Juridical Science	24	1 yr, full-time only [day]

Assistant Dean and Director of Financial Aid, 308 Hutchins Hall, Ann Arbor, MI 48109-1215. Phone: 734-764-5289. Fax: 734-763-7761. E-mail: lawfinaid@umich.edu

Law School Library University of Michigan Law School Library has 12 professional staff members and contains more than 862,197 volumes and 7,055 periodicals. 843 seats are available in the library. When classes are in session, the library is open 112 hours per week.

WESTLAW and LEXIS-NEXIS are available, as are the World Wide Web, online bibliographic services, and CD-ROM players. 48 computer workstations are available to students in the library. Special law collections include European Economic Community documents, selected United States government documents, Roman law, international law, comparative law, trial records, biographies, and legal biographies.

First-Year Program Class size in the average section is 90; 100% of the first-year courses are taught by full-time faculty.

Upper-Level Program Class size in the average section is 50. Among the electives are:

Administrative Law
Advocacy
Appellate Litigation
Blood Feuds
Business and Corporate Law
Civil Litigation
Civil Rights
Consumer Law
Criminal Defense
Criminal Prosecution
Democratic Theory
Domestic Violence
Economic Development
Education Law
Entertainment Law
Environmental Law
Ethics
Family Law
Family Practice
Government/Regulation
Health Care/Human Services
Immigration
Indian/Tribal Law
Insurance Law
Intellectual Property
International/Comparative Law
Japanese Law
Jurisprudence
Labor Law
Land Rights/Natural Resource

Land Use Law/Natural Resources
Lawyering Skills
Legal History/Philosophy
Litigation
Mediation
Medicine
Poverty/Welfare Law
Probate Law
Public Interest
Securities
Tax Law

Clinical Courses Students receive degree credit for clinical courses. (Clinical practicum is not required.) Among the clinical areas offered are:

Appellate Litigation
Civil Litigation
Civil Rights
Criminal Defense

Criminal Prosecution
Domestic Violence
Economic Development
Environmental Law
Family Law
Family Practice
General Practice
Housing Law
Immigration
Juvenile Law
Land Rights/Natural Resource
Mediation
Poverty/Welfare Law
Public Interest
Refugee & Asylum Law

International exchange programs permit students to visit Belgium, Cambodia, France, Germany, Netherlands, South Africa, Switzerland, and United Kingdom.

WAYNE STATE UNIVERSITY
LAW SCHOOL

Detroit, Michigan

INFORMATION CONTACT

Linda Fowler Sims, Assistant Dean for Recruitment and Admissions
471 West Palmer
Detroit, MI 48202

Phone: 313-577-3937   Fax: 313-577-9049
E-mail: ab2594@wayne.edu
Web site: http://www.law.wayne.edu/

LAW STUDENT PROFILE [2000–2001]

FULL-TIME   Enrollment: 554
Women: 47%   Men: 53%

PART-TIME   Enrollment: 321
Women: 42%   Men: 58%

RACIAL or ETHNIC COMPOSITION
African American, 8%; Asian/Pacific Islander, 5%; Hispanic, 1%; Native American, 0.5%

APPLICANTS and ADMITTEES
Number applied: 958
Admitted: 539
Percentage accepted: 55%
Seats available: 260
Average LSAT score: 154
Average GPA: 3.3

Wayne State University Law School is a public institution that organizes classes on a semester calendar system. The campus is situated in an urban setting. Founded in 1927, first ABA approved in 1936, and an AALS member, Wayne State University Law School offers JD, JD/MA, JD/MADR, JD/MBA, and LLM degrees.

Faculty consists of 36 full-time and 38 part-time members in 2000–2001. 15 full-time faculty members and 8 part-time faculty members are women. 97.6% of all faculty members have a JD; 16% have advanced law degrees. Of all faculty members, 2% are Asian/Pacific Islander, 7% are African American, 90% are white.

Application Information *Required:* LSAT, LSDAS, application form, application fee of $20, baccalaureate degree, recommendations, personal statement, college transcripts. *Application deadline* for fall term is April 15.

Financial Aid In 2000–2001, 53% of all students received some form of financial aid. Loans, merit-based grants/scholarships, need-based grants/scholarships, and federal work-study loans are available. The average student debt at graduation is $40,565. To apply for financial assistance, students must complete the Free Application for Federal Student Aid, institutional forms, scholarship specific applications. Completed financial aid forms should be received by April 30. Financial aid contact: Mr. Michael Jones, Assistant Director, Room 1215, Law School Building, Detroit, MI 48202. Phone: 313-577-5142. Fax: 313-577-5498. E-mail: m.jones@wayne.edu

Law School Library Arthur Neef Law Library has 5 professional staff members and contains more than

AT a GLANCE

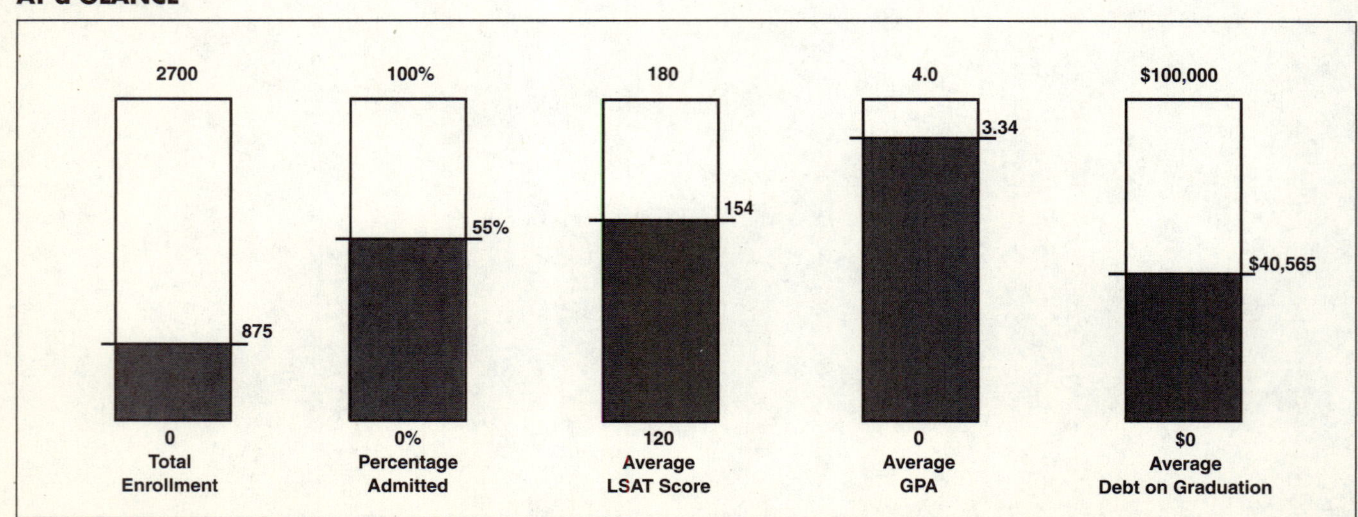

Degree Options

Degree	Total Credits Required	Length of Program
JD–Doctor of Laws	86	3–6 yrs, full-time or part-time [day, evening, summer]
JD/MA–Juris Doctor/Master of Arts–History Dual-degree Program	121	3–6 yrs, full-time or part-time [day, evening, summer]
JD/MA–Juris Doctor/Master of Arts–Political Science Dual-degree Program	122	3–6 yrs, full-time or part-time [day, evening, summer]
JD/MADR–Juris Doctor/Master of Arts in Dispute Resolution	102	4–5 yrs, full-time or part-time [day, evening, summer]
JD/MBA–Juris Doctor/Master of Business Administration–Dual-degree Program	122	3–6 yrs, full-time or part-time [day, evening, summer]
LLM–Master of Laws–Corporate and Finance Law	26	1–6 yrs, full-time or part-time [day, evening]
LLM–Master of Laws–Labor Law	26	1–6 yrs, full-time or part-time [day, evening]
LLM–Master of Laws–Taxation	26	1–6 yrs, full-time or part-time [day, evening]

583,446 volumes and 4,767 periodicals. 449 seats are available in the library. When classes are in session, the library is open 97 hours per week.

WESTLAW and LEXIS-NEXIS are available, as are the World Wide Web, online bibliographic services, and CD-ROM players. 35 computer workstations are available to students in the library. Special law collections include Michigan Probate Opinions, Michigan Environmental Law Collection, Michigan/U.S. Supreme Court Records and Briefs, Jewish Law Collection, Alvyn Freeman International Law Collection, The Driker Antitrust Law Collection, Michigan Superfun site documents.

First-Year Program Class size in the average section is 90; 100% of the first-year courses are taught by full-time faculty.

Upper-Level Program Class size in the average section is 40. Among the electives are:

Administrative Law
Advocacy
Business and Corporate Law
Civil Litigation
Civil Rights
Corporate Law
Criminal Defense
Education Law
Elderly Advocacy
Entertainment Law
Environmental Law
Family Law
Government/Regulation
Health Care/Human Services
Health Law
Immigration
★ Intellectual Property
★ International Law
★ International/Comparative Law
Jurisprudence
Labor Law
Land Rights/Natural Resource
Land Use Law/Natural Resources
Lawyering Skills
Legal History/Philosophy
Litigation
Media Law
Mediation
Probate Law
Public Interest
Securities
Tax Law
(★ indicates an area of special strength)

Clinical Courses Students receive degree credit for clinical courses. (Clinical practicum is not required.) Among the clinical areas offered are:

Business and Corporate Law
Civil Litigation
Civil Rights
Corporate Law
Criminal Defense
Criminal Prosecution
Elderly Advocacy
Environmental Law
Family Practice
General Practice
Government Litigation
Health Care/Human Services
Health Law
Immigration
Intellectual Property
International Law
Juvenile Law
Labor Law
Land Rights/Natural Resource
Mediation
Public Interest
Tax Law

International exchange programs permit students to visit Netherlands and United Kingdom.

HAMLINE UNIVERSITY
SCHOOL OF LAW

St. Paul, Minnesota

INFORMATION CONTACT

Michael J. States, Director of Admissions
1536 Hewitt Avenue
St. Paul, MN 55104

Phone: 800-388-3688   Fax: 651-523-3064
E-mail: mstates@gw.hamline.edu
Web site: http://www.hamline.edu/law/

LAW STUDENT PROFILE [2000–2001]

FULL-TIME   Enrollment: 503
Women: 55%   Men: 45%

PART-TIME   Enrollment: 42
Women: 74%   Men: 26%

RACIAL or ETHNIC COMPOSITION
African American, 4%; Asian/Pacific Islander, 6%; Hispanic,
2%; Native American, 1%; International, 3%

APPLICANTS and ADMITTEES
Number applied: 800
Admitted: 538
Percentage accepted: 67%
Seats available: 188
Average LSAT score: 151
Average GPA: 3.2

Hamline University School of Law is a private institution that organizes classes on a semester calendar system. The campus is situated in an urban setting. Founded in 1972, first ABA approved in 1975, and an AALS member, Hamline University School of Law offers JD, JD/AMBA, JD/MAM, JD/MANM, JD/MAPA, JD/MBA, and LLM degrees.

Faculty consists of 32 full-time and 62 part-time members in 2000–2001. 14 full-time faculty members and 21 part-time faculty members are women. 100% of all faculty members have a JD; 25.7% have advanced law degrees. Of all faculty members, 2.1% are Native American, 1% are Asian/Pacific Islander, 1% are African American, 2.1% are Hispanic, 92.8% are white, 1% are international.

Application Information *Required:* LSAT, LSDAS, application form, application fee of $40, baccalaureate degree, personal statement, college transcripts. *Recommended:* recommendations, resume. *Application deadline* for fall term is May 15 (priority date). Applications are processed on a rolling basis.

Costs The 1999–2000 tuition was $18,150 full-time; $6534 per semester part-time. Fees: $180 full-time. Students are required to have their own computers.

Financial Aid 10 fellowships, totaling $3000 were awarded. Fellowships, loans, merit-based grants/scholarships, need-based grants/scholarships, and federal work-study loans are also available. The average student debt at graduation is $65,000. To apply for financial assistance, students must complete the Free Application

AT a GLANCE

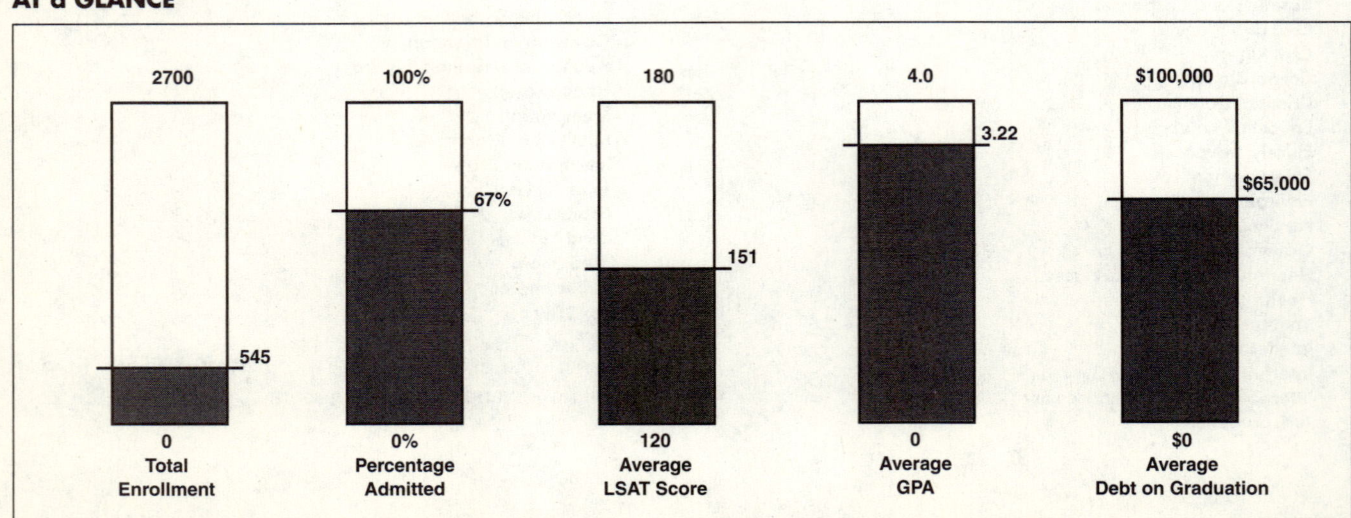

Degree Options

Degree	Total Credits Required	Length of Program
JD–Doctor of Laws	88	3–6 yrs, full-time or part-time [day, weekend, summer]
JD/AMBA–Juris Doctor/Master of Business Administration with Accounting Major–Joint-degree Program	129	4 yrs, full-time only [day, summer]
JD/MAM–Juris Doctor/Master of Arts Management–Dual-degree Program	109	4 yrs, full-time or part-time [day, evening, weekend, summer]
JD/MANM–Juris Doctor/Master of Arts in Nonprofit Management–Dual-degree Program	109	full-time or part-time [day, evening, weekend, summer]
JD/MAPA–Juris Doctor/Master of Arts in Public Administration–Dual-degree Program	109	4 yrs, full-time or part-time [day, evening, weekend, summer]
JD/MBA–Juris Doctor/Master of Business Administration–Joint-degree Program	106	4–6 yrs, full-time or part-time [day, evening, weekend, summer]
LLM–Master of Laws–for Foreign Lawyers	29	1 yr, full-time only [day]

for Federal Student Aid, institutional forms, income tax return. Financial aid contact: Lynette M. Wahl, Senior Associate Director of Financial Aid, 1536 Hewitt Avenue, Saint Paul, MN 55104-1284. Phone: 651-523-2280. Fax: 651-523-2585. E-mail: lwahl@gw.hamline.edu

Law School Library Hamline University Law Library has 6 professional staff members and contains more than 254,595 volumes and 979 periodicals. 374 seats are available in the library. When classes are in session, the library is open 107 hours per week.

WESTLAW and LEXIS-NEXIS are available, as are the World Wide Web, online bibliographic services, and CD-ROM players. 36 computer workstations are available to students in the library.

First-Year Program Class size in the average section is 66; 100% of the first-year courses are taught by full-time faculty.

Upper-Level Program Class size in the average section is 45. Among the electives are:

- Administrative Law
- Advocacy
- ★ Business and Corporate Law
- ★ Children and the Law
- ★ Consumer Law
- ★ Corporate Law
- ★ Criminal Law
- Education
- Education Law
- Entertainment Law
- Environmental Law
- Family Practice
- General Practice
- ★ Government/Regulation
- Health Care/Human Services
- Indian/Tribal Law
- ★ Intellectual Property
- ★ International/Comparative Law
- Jurisprudence
- ★ Juvenile Law
- ★ Labor Law
- Land Use Law/Natural Resources
- Lawyering Skills
- Legal Assistance to Minnesota Prisoners (LAMP)
- Legal History/Philosophy
- Litigation
- Maritime Law
- Media Law
- ★ Mediation
- Probate Law
- ★ Public Interest
- Securities
- Tax Law

(★ indicates an area of special strength)

Clinical Courses Students receive degree credit for clinical courses. (Clinical practicum is not required.) Among the clinical areas offered are:

- Children and the Law
- Corporate Law
- Education
- Family Practice
- General Practice
- Juvenile Law
- Legal Assistance to Minnesota Prisoners (LAMP)
- Mediation
- Nonprofit Organizations
- Small Business Representation

International exchange programs permit students to visit Hungary, Israel, Italy, and Norway.

UNIVERSITY OF MINNESOTA, TWIN CITIES CAMPUS
LAW SCHOOL

Minneapolis, Minnesota

LAW STUDENT PROFILE [2000–2001]

FULL-TIME   Enrollment: 744
Women: 48%   Men: 52%

RACIAL or ETHNIC COMPOSITION
African American, 2%; Asian/Pacific Islander, 8%; Hispanic, 2%; Native American, 1%; International, 9%

APPLICANTS and ADMITTEES
Number applied: 1,800
Admitted: 675
Percentage accepted: 38%
Seats available: 240
Median LSAT score: 162
Average GPA: 3.6

University of Minnesota, Twin Cities Campus Law School is a public institution that organizes classes on a semester calendar system. The campus is situated in an urban setting. Founded in 1888, first ABA approved in 1923, and an AALS member, University of Minnesota, Twin Cities Campus Law School offers JD, JD/MA, JD/MBA, JD/MPP, JD/MS, JD/PhD, and LLM degrees.

Faculty consists of 44 full-time and 97 part-time members in 2000–2001. 14 full-time faculty members and 35 part-time faculty members are women. 100% of all faculty members have a JD; 15% have advanced law degrees. Of all faculty members, 2.5% are Native American, 2.5% are Asian/Pacific Islander, 7.5% are African American, 87.5% are white.

Application Information *Required:* LSAT, LSDAS, application form, application fee of $50, baccalaureate degree, 2 letters of recommendation, personal statement. *Application deadline* for fall term is March 1. Applications are processed on a rolling basis.

Costs The 2000–2001 tuition was $9780 full-time for state residents. Tuition was $16,628 full-time for nonresidents. Fees: $756 full-time. Students are required to have their own computers.

Financial Aid In 2000–2001, 87% of all students received some form of financial aid. Graduate assistantships, loans, loan repayment assistance program (LRAP), merit-based grants/scholarships, need-based grants/scholarships, and federal work-study loans are available.

AT a GLANCE

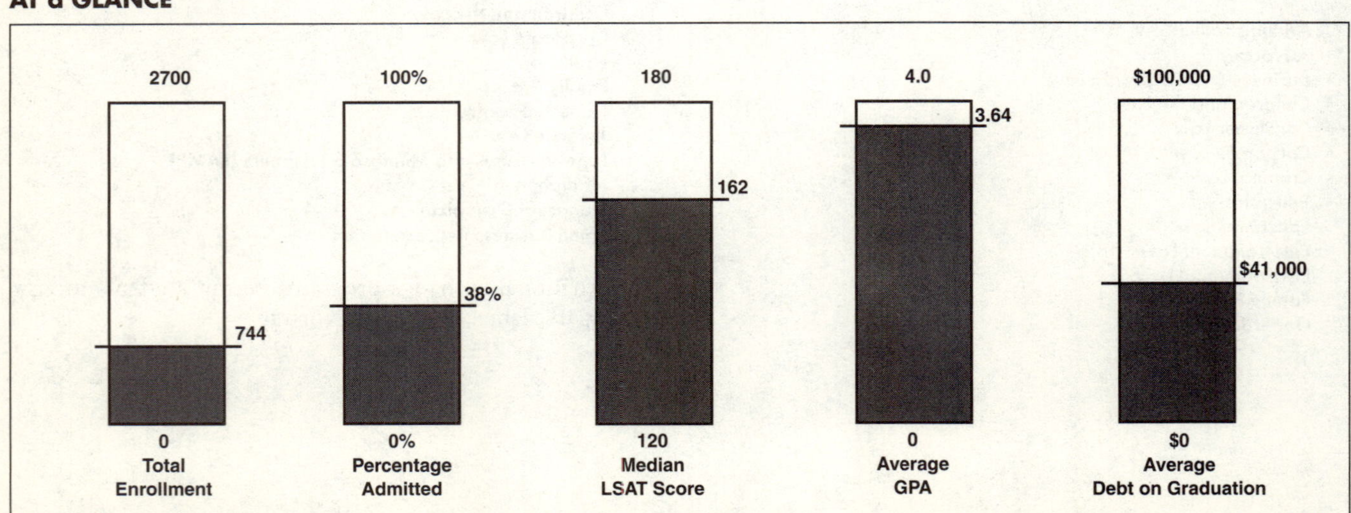

<table>
<tr><td colspan="3">Degree Options</td></tr>
<tr><td>Degree</td><td>Total Credits
Required</td><td>Length of Program</td></tr>
<tr><td>JD–Doctor of Laws</td><td>88</td><td>3 yrs, full-time only [day]</td></tr>
<tr><td>JD/MA–Juris Doctor/Master of Arts–Joint-degree
Program</td><td></td><td>4 yrs, full-time only [day]</td></tr>
<tr><td>JD/MBA–Juris Doctor/Master of Business
Administration–Joint-degree Program</td><td></td><td>4 yrs, full-time only [day]</td></tr>
<tr><td>JD/MPP–Juris Doctor/Master of Public Planning–Joint-
degree Program</td><td></td><td>4 yrs, full-time only [day]</td></tr>
<tr><td>JD/MS–Juris Doctor/Master of Science–Molecular,
Cellular, Developmental Biology and Genetics
Ecology; Conservation Biology; Environmental
Health; Health Services Research Policy and
Administration; Science Technology and
Environmental Policy; Pharmacology</td><td></td><td>4 yrs, full-time only [day]</td></tr>
<tr><td>JD/PhD–Juris Doctor/Doctor of Philosophy–Molecular,
Cellular, Developmental Biology and Genetics
Ecology; Conservation Biology; Environmental
Health; Health Services Research Policy and
Administration; Pharmacology</td><td></td><td>full-time only [day]</td></tr>
<tr><td>LLM–Master of Laws–American Studies for Graduates
of Foreign Law Schools</td><td>24</td><td>1 yr, full-time only [day]</td></tr>
</table>

The average student debt at graduation is $41,000. To apply for financial assistance, students must complete the Free Application for Federal Student Aid. Completed financial aid forms should be received by March 15. Financial aid contact: Collins Byrd, Director of Admissions, University of Minnesota Law School, 229 19 Avenue South, Minneapolis, MN 55455. Phone: 612-625-3487. E-mail: byrdj001@tc.umn.edu

Law School Library has 14 professional staff members and contains more than 906,000 volumes and 10,252 periodicals. 934 seats are available in the library. When classes are in session, the library is open 81 hours per week.

WESTLAW and LEXIS-NEXIS are available, as are the World Wide Web, online bibliographic services, and CD-ROM players. 68 computer workstations are available to students in the library. Special law collections include international law, human rights law, government.

First-Year Program 100% of the first-year courses are taught by full-time faculty.

Upper-Level Program Among the electives are:

Advocacy
Agricultural Law
Bankruptcy
Business and Corporate Law
Children's Advocacy
Civil Litigation
Civil Procedure
Civil Rights
Constitutional Law
Criminal Defense
Criminal Prosecution

Education Law
Environmental Law
Estate Planning
Family Law
General Practice
Government/Regulation
Health Care/Human Services
Immigration
Indian/Tribal Law
International/Comparative Law
Jurisprudence
Labor Law
Land Use Law/Natural Resources
Lawyering Skills
Legal History/Philosophy
Legislation
Litigation
Prisoners' Rights
Probate Law
Property/Real Estate
Public Interest
Sports Law
Tax Law

Clinical Courses Students receive degree credit for clinical courses. (Clinical practicum is not required.) Among the clinical areas offered are:

Advocacy
Bankruptcy
Business and Corporate Law
Children's Advocacy
Civil Litigation
Civil Procedure
Civil Rights
Criminal Defense
Criminal Prosecution
Family Law
Family Practice
General Practice

Immigration
Indian/Tribal Law
Labor Law
Litigation
Prisoners' Rights
Public Interest
Tax Law

International exchange programs permit students to visit France, Germany, Ireland, Netherlands, Spain, and Sweden.

WILLIAM MITCHELL COLLEGE OF LAW

St. Paul, Minnesota

INFORMATION CONTACT

James H. Brooks Jr., Dean of Students
875 Summit Avenue
St. Paul, MN 55105-3076

Phone: 651-290-6362   Fax: 651-290-7535
E-mail: admissions@wmitchell.edu
Web site: http://www.wmitchell.edu/

LAW STUDENT PROFILE [2000–2001]

FULL-TIME   Enrollment: 520
Women: 57%   Men: 43%

PART-TIME   Enrollment: 479
Women: 51%   Men: 49%

APPLICANTS and ADMITTEES

Number applied: 939
Admitted: 623
Percentage accepted: 66%
Seats available: 314
Median LSAT score: 153
Average GPA: 3.3

William Mitchell College of Law is a private nonprofit institution that organizes classes on a semester calendar system. The campus is situated in an urban setting. Founded in 1900, first ABA approved in 1938, and an AALS member, William Mitchell College of Law offers a JD degree.

Faculty consists of 34 full-time and 218 part-time members in 2000–2001. 10 full-time faculty members and 76 part-time faculty members are women. 100% of all faculty members have a JD degree. Of all faculty members, 1% are Native American, 3% are Asian/Pacific Islander, 5% are African American, 2% are Hispanic, 89% are white.

Application Information *Required:* LSAT, LSDAS, application form, application fee of $45, baccalaureate degree, 2 letters of recommendation, personal statement, college transcripts, resume.

Costs The 2000–2001 tuition was $19,030 full-time; $13,800 per year part-time. Fees: $30 full-time; $30 per year part-time.

Financial Aid Loans, loan repayment assistance program (LRAP), merit-based grants/scholarships, need-based grants/scholarships, and federal work-study loans are available. The average student debt at graduation is $57,000. To apply for financial assistance, students must complete the Free Application for Federal Student Aid, institutional forms. Financial aid contact: Ms. Jeanette Maynard Nelson, Assistant Director, Financial Aid, 875 Summit Avenue, St. Paul, MN 55105. Phone: 612-290-6403. Fax: 612-290-6414. E-mail: dvelasco@wmitchell.edu

AT a GLANCE

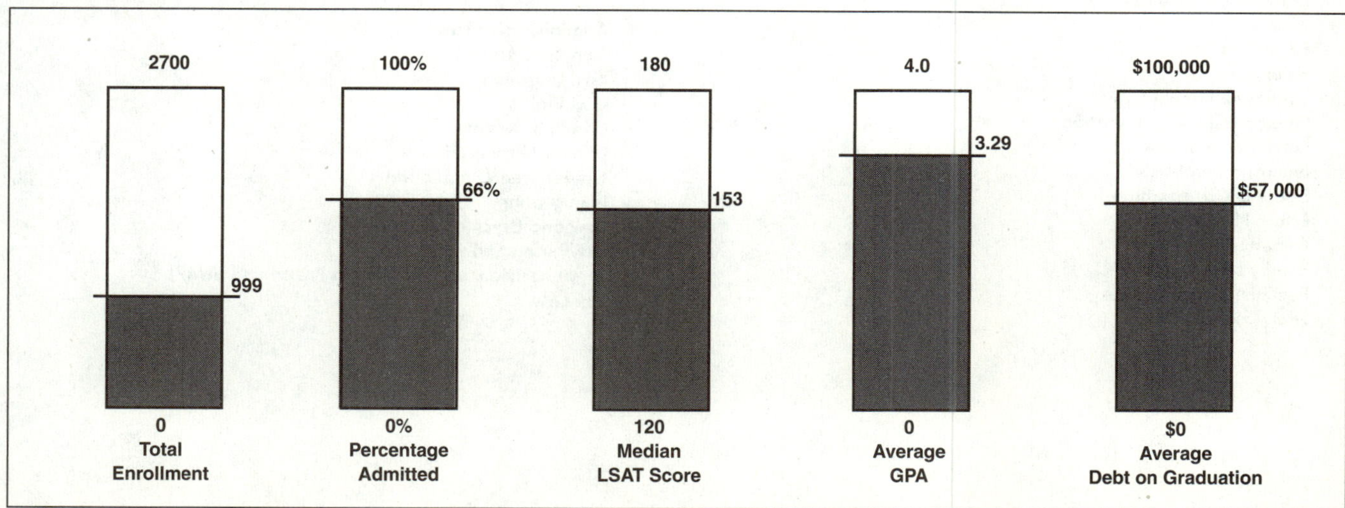

Degree Options		
Degree	**Total Credits Required**	**Length of Program**
JD–Doctor of Laws	86	3–4 yrs, full-time or part-time [day, evening, summer]

Law School Library Warren E. Burger Library has 9 professional staff members and contains more than 305,891 volumes and 4,532 periodicals. 674 seats are available in the library. When classes are in session, the library is open 106 hours per week.

WESTLAW and LEXIS-NEXIS are available, as are the World Wide Web, online bibliographic services, and CD-ROM players. 85 computer workstations are available to students in the library.

First-Year Program Class size in the average section is 45; 100% of the first-year courses are taught by full-time faculty.

Upper-Level Program Class size in the average section is 45. Among the electives are:

  Accounting
★ Administrative Law
★ Advocacy
  Agricultural Law
  American Legal History
  Antitrust Law
  Bioethics
★ Business and Corporate Law
  Business Planning
  Business Torts
  Civil Litigation
  Civil Procedure
  Civil Rights
  Comparative Constitutional Law
  Computer Law
  Constitutional Criminal Procedure
  Corporate Criminal Liability
  Corporate Finance
  Creditor's Rights
★ Criminal Defense
★ Criminal Prosecution
  Debtor Law
  Education Law
  Elder Law
  Employee Benefit Law
  Employment Discrimination
  Entertainment Law
  Environmental Law
  Estate & Gift Taxation
  Estate Planning
  Evidence
★ Family Law
  Feminist Jurisprudence
  First Amendment
  Government/Regulation
  Health Care Law
  Health Care/Human Services
  Immigration
  Indian/Tribal Law
  Insurance Law
★ International/Comparative Law
  Internet Law
  Jurisprudence
  Juvenile Law
  Labor Law
  Land Use Law/Natural Resources
★ Lawyering Skills
  Legal History/Philosophy
★ Litigation
  Media Law
★ Mediation
  Medical Malpractice Law
  Mental Health and Law
  Natural Resources
  Patent Law
★ Poverty/Welfare Law
  Probate Law
  Product Liability
  Professional Responsibility
  Public International Law
  Race and Law
  Real Estate Transactions
  Remedies
  Securities
  Street Law
  Supreme Court
★ Tax Law
  Tort Litigation
  White Collar Crime
(★ *indicates an area of special strength*)

Clinical Courses Students receive degree credit for clinical courses. (Clinical practicum is not required.) Among the clinical areas offered are:

  Administrative Law
  Appellate Law
  Civil Litigation
  Civil Rights
  Criminal Defense
  Criminal Prosecution
  Government/Regulation
  Immigration
  Law and Psychiatry
  Lawyering Skills
  Legal Assistance to Minnesota Prisoners (LAMP)
  Tax Law

MISSISSIPPI COLLEGE
SCHOOL OF LAW

Jackson, Mississippi

INFORMATION CONTACT

Patricia H. Evans, Director of Admissions
151 East Griffith Street
Jackson, MS 39201

Phone: 601-925-7150   Fax: 601-925-7185
E-mail: pevans@mc.edu
Web site: http://www.law.mc.edu

LAW STUDENT PROFILE [2000–2001]

FULL-TIME   Enrollment: 379
Women: 43%   Men: 57%

APPLICANTS and ADMITTEES

Number applied: 609
Admitted: 383
Percentage accepted: 63%
Seats available: 141
Average LSAT score: 149
Average GPA: 3.0

Mississippi College School of Law is a private institution that organizes classes on a semester calendar system. The campus is situated in an urban setting. Founded in 1975, first ABA approved in 1980, and an AALS member, Mississippi College School of Law offers JD and JD/MBA degrees.

Faculty consists of 15 full-time and 15 part-time members in 2000–2001. 5 full-time faculty members and 2 part-time faculty members are women. 100% of all faculty members have a JD; 35% have advanced law degrees. Of all faculty members, 6% are African American, 94% are white.

Application Information *Required:* LSAT, LSDAS, application form, application fee of $25, baccalaureate degree, college transcripts, personal statement. *Recommended:* recommendations. *Application deadline* for fall term is May 1 (priority date). Applications are processed on a rolling basis.

Costs The 2000–2001 tuition was $14,970 full-time.

Financial Aid In 2000–2001, 90% of all students received some form of financial aid. Loans, merit-based grants/scholarships, and federal work-study loans are available. The average student debt at graduation is $67,000. To apply for financial assistance, students must complete the Free Application for Federal Student Aid, school's law financial aid application. Completed financial aid forms should be received by May 1. Financial aid contact: Larry Blankenship, Director of Financial Aid, 151 East Griffith Street, Jackson, MS 39201. Phone: 601-925-7110. Fax: 601-925-7117. E-mail: lblankenship@mc.edu

AT a GLANCE

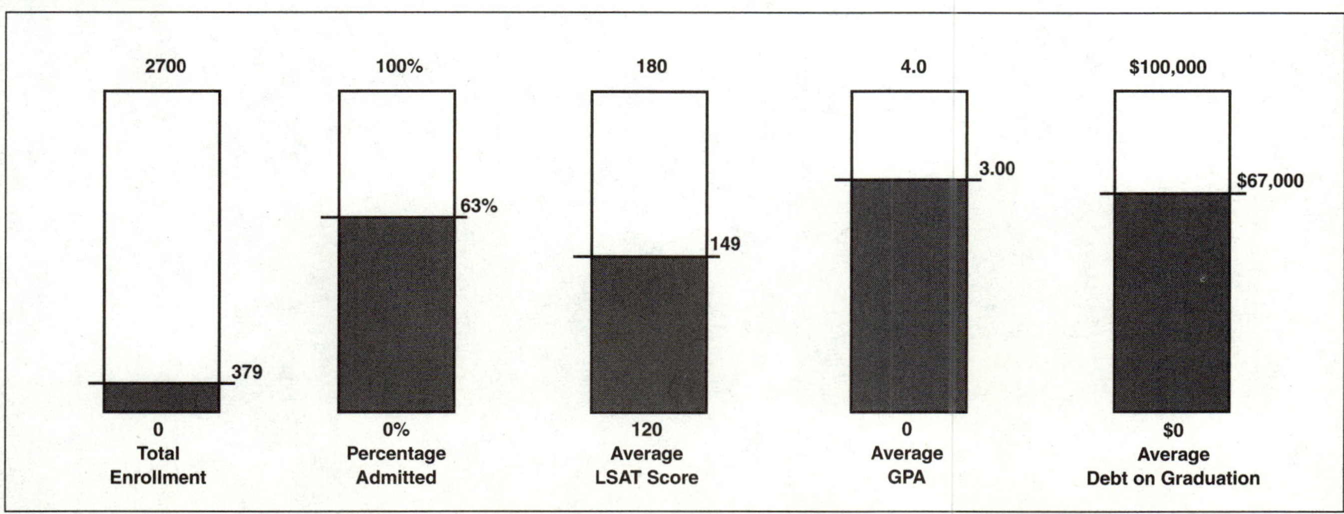

Degree Options

Degree	Total Credits Required	Length of Program
JD–Juris Doctor	88	3 yrs, full-time only [day]
JD/MBA–Juris Doctor/Master of Business Administration	103	3.5 yrs, full-time only [day]

Law School Library The Law Library of the Mississippi College School of Law has 6 professional staff members and contains more than 300,000 volumes and 3,438 periodicals. 207 seats are available in the library. When classes are in session, the library is open 100 hours per week.

WESTLAW and LEXIS-NEXIS are available, as is the World Wide Web. 28 computer workstations are available to students in the library. Special law collections include United States Federal Government Document Selective Depository.

First-Year Program Class size in the average section is 75; 100% of the first-year courses are taught by full-time faculty.

Upper-Level Program Class size in the average section is 50. Among the electives are:

Advocacy
★ Business and Corporate Law
Consumer Law
Education Law
Environmental Law
Family Law
Intellectual Property
International/Comparative Law
Jurisprudence
Labor Law
Land Use Law/Natural Resources
Maritime Law
Public Interest
(★ indicates an area of special strength)

UNIVERSITY OF MISSISSIPPI
SCHOOL OF LAW

University, Mississippi

LAW STUDENT PROFILE [2000–2001]

FULL-TIME   Enrollment: 472
Women: 37%   Men: 63%

RACIAL or ETHNIC COMPOSITION
African American, 10%; Asian/Pacific Islander, 1%; Hispanic,
0.4%; Native American, 1%; International, 1%

APPLICANTS and ADMITTEES
Seats available: 179
Average LSAT score: 153
Average GPA: 3.5

University of Mississippi School of Law is a public
institution that organizes classes on a semester calendar
system. The campus is situated in a small-town setting.
Founded in 1854, first ABA approved in 1930, and an
AALS member, University of Mississippi School of Law
offers JD and JD/MBA degrees.

Faculty consists of 27 full-time members in 2000–2001. 5
full-time faculty members are women. 100% of all
faculty members have a JD; 25% have advanced law
degrees. Of all faculty members, 4% are Native American, 11% are African American, 85% are white.

Application Information *Required:* LSAT, LSDAS,
application form, application fee of $25, baccalaureate
degree, college transcripts. *Recommended:* recommendations, personal statement. *Application deadline* for fall
term is March 1.

Financial Aid Fellowships, loans, merit-based grants/
scholarships, need-based grants/scholarships, and federal
work-study loans are available. The average student debt
at graduation is $43,800. To apply for financial assis-
tance, students must complete the Free Application for
Federal Student Aid. Completed financial aid forms
should be received by March 1. Financial aid contact:
Mr. Larry Ridgeway, Director, PO Box 1848, University,
MS 38677. Phone: 662-915-7175. Fax: 662-915-1164.
E-mail: 1ridgewa@olemiss.edu

Law School Library University of Mississippi Law
Library has 7 professional staff members and contains

AT a GLANCE

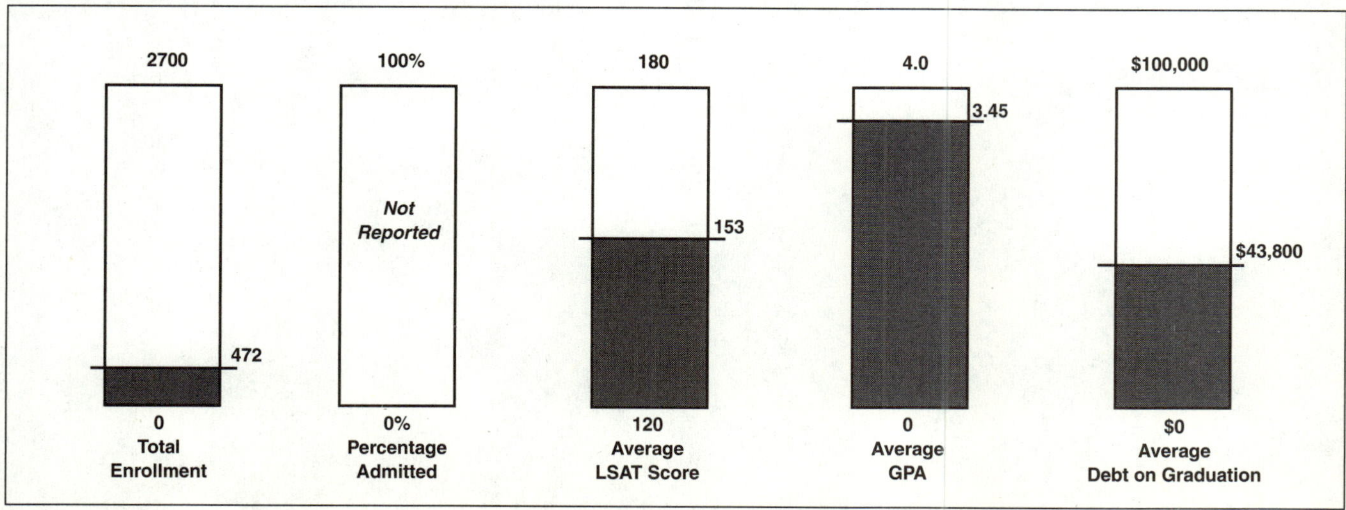

Degree Options		
Degree	**Total Credits Required**	**Length of Program**
JD–Doctor of Laws	90	3 yrs, full-time only [day, summer]
JD/MBA–Juris Doctor/Master of Business Administration–Concurrent Degree Program	133	4–5 yrs, full-time only [day, summer]

more than 296,871 volumes and 2,844 periodicals. 363 seats are available in the library. When classes are in session, the library is open 102 hours per week.

WESTLAW and LEXIS-NEXIS are available, as are the World Wide Web, online bibliographic services, and CD-ROM players. 32 computer workstations are available to students in the library.

First-Year Program Class size in the average section is 63; 100% of the first-year courses are taught by full-time faculty.

Upper-Level Program Class size in the average section is 34. Among the electives are:

- Administrative Law
- Advocacy
- Business and Corporate Law
- Entertainment Law
- Environmental Law
- Family Law
- Intellectual Property
- International/Comparative Law
- Jurisprudence
- Labor Law
- Land Use Law/Natural Resources
- Lawyering Skills
- Legal History/Philosophy
- Litigation
- Maritime Law
- Mediation
- Probate Law
- Securities
- Tax Law

Clinical Courses Students receive degree credit for clinical courses. (Clinical practicum is not required.)

SAINT LOUIS UNIVERSITY
SCHOOL OF LAW

St. Louis, Missouri

INFORMATION CONTACT

Michael J. Kolnik, Director of Admissions
3700 Lindell Boulevard
St. Louis, MO 63108

Phone: 314-977-2800   Fax: 314-977-3333
E-mail: kolnikmj@slu.edu
Web site: http://law.slu.edu/

LAW STUDENT PROFILE [2000–2001]

FULL-TIME   Enrollment: 578
Women: 49%   Men: 51%

PART-TIME   Enrollment: 190
Women: 48%   Men: 52%

RACIAL or ETHNIC COMPOSITION
African American, 7%; Asian/Pacific Islander, 3%; Hispanic, 2%; Native American, 1%; International, 2%

APPLICANTS and ADMITTEES
Number applied: 985
Admitted: 646
Percentage accepted: 66%
Seats available: 255
Average LSAT score: 154
Average GPA: 3.3

Saint Louis University School of Law is a private institution that organizes classes on a semester calendar system. The campus is situated in an urban setting. Founded in 1818, first ABA approved in 1924, and an AALS member, Saint Louis University School of Law offers JD, JD/MA, JD/MBA, JD/MHA, JD/MPAd, JD/MPH, and LLM degrees.

Faculty consists of 37 full-time and 8 part-time members in 2000–2001. 11 full-time faculty members and 4 part-time faculty members are women. 100% of all faculty members have a JD; 23% have advanced law degrees. Of all faculty members, 5% are African American, 95% are white.

Application Information *Required:* LSAT, LSDAS, application form, application fee of $55, baccalaureate degree, 2 letters of recommendation. *Recommended:* personal statement, college transcripts, resume. *Application deadline* for fall term is March 1 (priority date). Applications are processed on a rolling basis.

Financial Aid In 2000–2001, 93% of all students received some form of financial aid. Fellowships, loans, merit-based grants/scholarships, and federal work-study loans are available. To apply for financial assistance, students must complete the Free Application for Federal Student Aid, scholarship specific applications. Completed financial aid forms should be received by April 1. Financial aid contact: Michael J. Kolnik, Assistant Dean and Director of Admissions, 3700 Lindell Boulevard, St. Louis, MO 63108. Phone: 314-977-2800. Fax: 314-977-3966.

AT a GLANCE

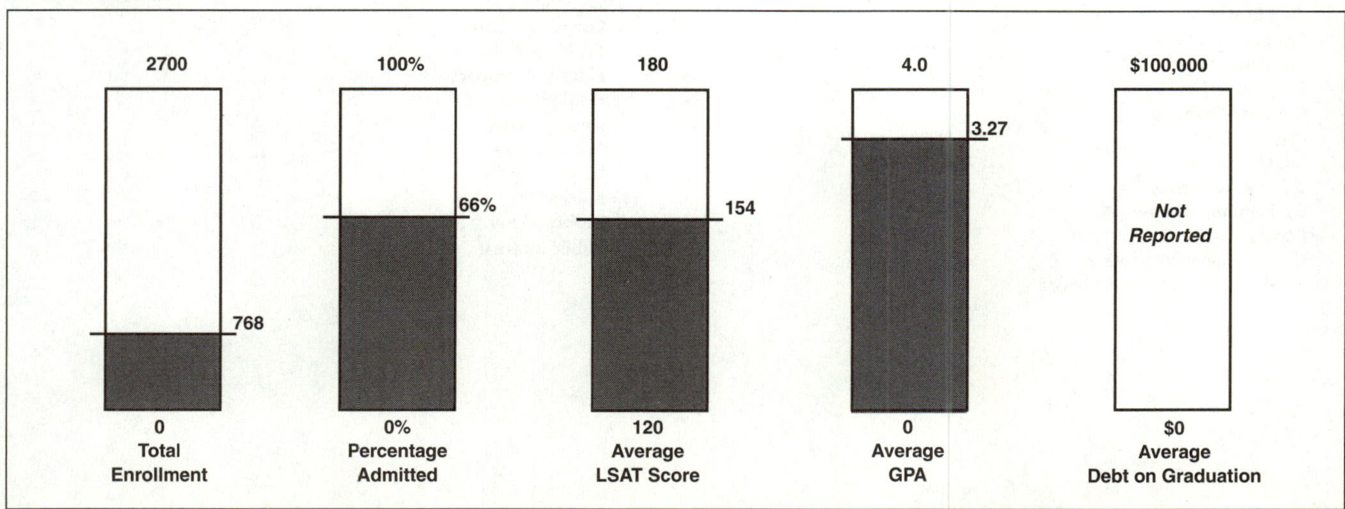

Degree Options

Degree	Total Credits Required	Length of Program
JD–Doctor of Laws	88	3–5 yrs, full-time or part-time [day, evening]
JD/MA–Juris Doctor/Master of Arts–Urban Affairs Joint-degree	103	3.5–4 yrs, full-time only [day, evening]
JD/MBA–Juris Doctor/Master of Business Administration–Joint-degree		4 yrs, full-time or part-time [day, evening]
JD/MHA–Juris Doctor/Master of Health Administration–Joint-degree		4 yrs, full-time or part-time [day, evening]
JD/MPAd–Juris Doctor/Master of Public Administration–Joint-degree	103	3.5–4 yrs, full-time only [day, evening]
JD/MPH–Juris Doctor/Master of Public Health–Joint-degree		4 yrs, full-time only [day, evening]
LLM–Master of Laws–Health Law	24	1–2 yrs, full-time or part-time [day, evening]
LLM–Master of Laws–Foreign Lawyers	24	1–2 yrs, full-time only [day]

Law School Library Omer Poos Law Library has 9 professional staff members and contains more than 565,000 volumes and 6,341 periodicals. 487 seats are available in the library. When classes are in session, the library is open 110 hours per week.

WESTLAW and LEXIS-NEXIS are available, as are the World Wide Web, online bibliographic services, and CD-ROM players. 48 computer workstations are available to students in the library. Special law collections include constitutional law, Smurfit Irish Law Center, Polish law, international and comparative law, Missouri and Illinois law, law journals, health law, employment law, Leonor K. Sullivan papers.

First-Year Program Class size in the average section is 85; 100% of the first-year courses are taught by full-time faculty.

Upper-Level Program Class size in the average section is 40. Among the electives are:

Administrative Law
Advocacy
Business and Corporate Law
Civil Rights
Commercial Law
Consumer Law
Corporate Law
Criminal Defense
Criminal Law
Education Law
Elderly Advocacy
Environmental Law
Family Law
Government/Regulation
★ Health Care/Human Services
★ Health Law
Housing Law
Intellectual Property
★ International/Comparative Law
Jurisprudence
Juvenile Law
★ Labor Law
Land Use Law/Natural Resources
Lawyering Skills
Legal History/Philosophy
Litigation
Maritime Law
Media Law
Mediation
Probate Law
Public Interest
Securities
Tax Law

(★ indicates an area of special strength)

Clinical Courses Students receive degree credit for clinical courses. (Clinical practicum is not required.) Among the clinical areas offered are:

Advocacy
Business and Corporate Law
Civil Litigation
Civil Rights
Corporate Law
Criminal Defense
Elderly Advocacy
Health Law
Housing Law
Juvenile Law
Lawyering Skills
Mediation
Probate Law
Public Interest

UNIVERSITY OF MISSOURI–COLUMBIA
SCHOOL OF LAW

Columbia, Missouri

LAW STUDENT PROFILE [2000–2001]

FULL-TIME   Enrollment: 511
Women: 44%   Men: 56%

PART-TIME   Enrollment: 13
Women: 77%   Men: 23%

RACIAL or ETHNIC COMPOSITION
African American, 8%; Asian/Pacific Islander, 2%; Hispanic,
1%; Native American, 1%; International, 0.2%

APPLICANTS and ADMITTEES
Number applied: 727
Admitted: 413
Percentage accepted: 57%
Seats available: 197
Average LSAT score: 154
Average GPA: 3.3

University of Missouri–Columbia School of Law is a public institution that organizes classes on a semester calendar system. The campus is situated in a small-town setting. Founded in 1872, first ABA approved in 1923, and an AALS member, University of Missouri–Columbia School of Law offers JD, JD/MA ELPA, JD/MA Econ, JD/MA HDFS, JD/MBA, JD/MHA, JD/MJ, and JD/MPAd degrees.

Faculty consists of 33 full-time members in 2000–2001. 11 full-time faculty members are women. 100% of all faculty members have a JD; 13% have advanced law degrees. Of all faculty members, 3% are Asian/Pacific Islander, 5% are African American, 5% are Hispanic, 87% are white.

Application Information *Required:* LSAT, LSDAS, application form, application fee of $40, baccalaureate degree, college transcripts. *Recommended:* recommendations, personal statement. *Application deadline* for fall term is March 1 (priority date). Applications are processed on a rolling basis.

Costs The 1999–2000 tuition was $7320 full-time for state residents; $305 per hour part-time for state residents. Tuition was $14,638 full-time for nonresidents; $610 per hour part-time for nonresidents. Fees: $553 full-time; $18 per hour part-time.

Financial Aid In 2000–2001, 91% of all students received some form of financial aid. Fellowships, graduate assistantships, loans, merit-based grants/scholarships, need-based grants/scholarships, and federal work-study loans are available. The average student debt at gradua-

AT a GLANCE

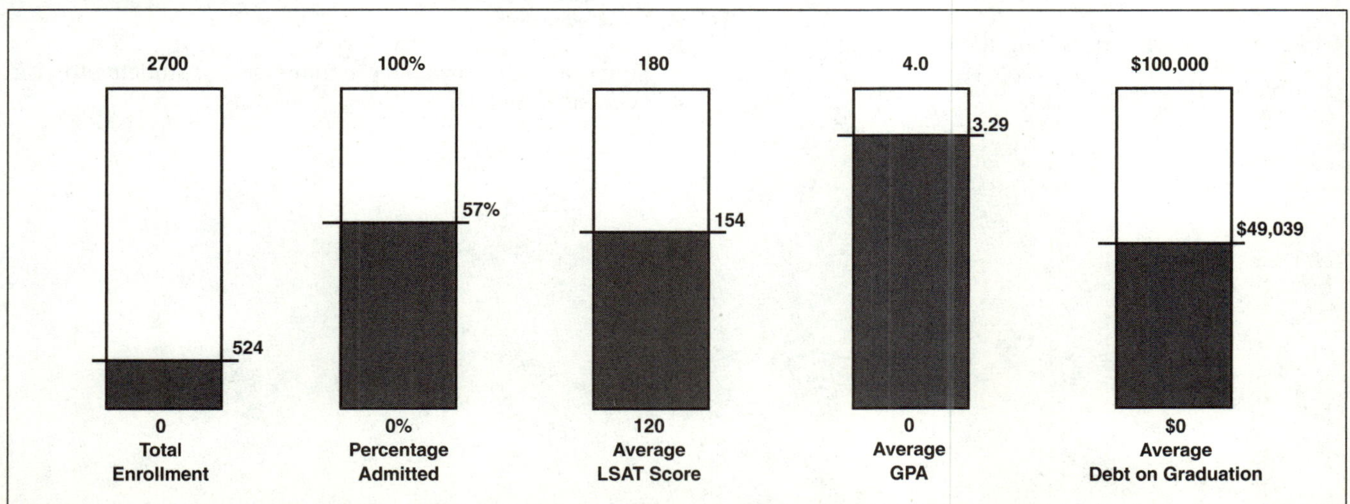

Degree Options

Degree	Total Credits Required	Length of Program
JD–Doctor of Laws	89	3 yrs, full-time only [day, summer]
Certificate–Dual-degree	122	4 yrs, full-time only [day, summer]
Certificate–Dual-degree	119	4 yrs, full-time only [day, summer]
Certificate–Dual-degree	128	4 yrs, full-time only [day, summer]
JD/MBA–Juris Doctor/Master of Business Administration–Dual-degree	119	4 yrs, full-time only [day, summer]
JD/MHA–Juris Doctor/Master of Health Administration–Dual-degree	140	4 yrs, full-time only [day, summer]
JD/MJ–Juris Doctor/Master of Journalism–Dual-degree	119	4 yrs, full-time only [day]
JD/MPAd–Juris Doctor/Master of Public Administration–Dual-degree	113	4 yrs, full-time only [day, summer]

tion is $49,039. To apply for financial assistance, students must complete the Free Application for Federal Student Aid, scholarship specific applications. Completed financial aid forms should be received by March 1. Financial aid contact: Jeff Turnbull, Financial Aid Officer, 105 Hulston Hall, Columbia, MO 65211. Phone: 573-882-1383. Fax: 573-882-9625. E-mail: turnbullj@missouri.edu

Law School Library University of Missouri-Columbia School of Law Library has 7 professional staff members and contains more than 326,693 volumes and 3,138 periodicals. 382 seats are available in the library. When classes are in session, the library is open 89 hours per week.

WESTLAW and LEXIS-NEXIS are available, as are the World Wide Web, online bibliographic services, and CD-ROM players. 46 computer workstations are available to students in the library. Special law collections include John O. Lawson Library of Criminal Law and Criminology.

First-Year Program Class size in the average section is 60; 100% of the first-year courses are taught by full-time faculty.

Upper-Level Program Among the electives are:

Administrative Law
Advocacy

Business and Corporate Law
★ **Criminal Prosecution**
★ **Dispute Resolution**
★ **Domestic Violence**
Education Law
Environmental Law
Family Law
Government/Regulation
Health Care/Human Services
Intellectual Property
International/Comparative Law
Jurisprudence
Labor Law
Land Use Law/Natural Resources
Lawyering Skills
Legal History/Philosophy
Litigation
Media Law
★ **Mediation**
Probate Law
Securities
Tax Law
(★ indicates an area of special strength)

Clinical Courses Students receive degree credit for clinical courses. (Clinical practicum is not required.) Among the clinical areas offered are:

Criminal Prosecution
Domestic Violence
Mediation

International exchange programs permit students to visit United Kingdom.

UNIVERSITY OF MISSOURI–KANSAS CITY
SCHOOL OF LAW

Kansas City, Missouri

LAW STUDENT PROFILE [2000–2001]

FULL-TIME Enrollment: 457
Women: 49%   Men: 51%

PART-TIME Enrollment: 38
Women: 58%   Men: 42%

APPLICANTS and ADMITTEES

Number applied: 696
Admitted: 452
Percentage accepted: 65%
Seats available: 160
Average LSAT score: 152
Average GPA: 3.2

University of Missouri–Kansas City School of Law is a public institution that organizes classes on a semester calendar system. The campus is situated in an urban setting. Founded in 1895, first ABA approved in 1936, and an AALS member, University of Missouri–Kansas City School of Law offers JD, JD/LLM, JD/MBA, and LLM degrees.

Faculty consists of 24 full-time and 16 part-time members in 2000–2001. 5 full-time faculty members and 3 part-time faculty members are women. 100% of all faculty members have a JD; 34% have advanced law degrees. Of all faculty members, 6% are African American, 94% are white.

Application Information *Required:* LSAT, LSDAS, application form, application fee of $25, baccalaureate degree, 2 letters of recommendation, personal statement, college transcripts. *Application deadline* for fall term is April 1 (priority date). Applications are processed on a rolling basis.

Costs The 2000–2001 tuition was $337 per credit part-time for area residents. Tuition was $652 per credit part-time for nonresidents. Fees: $60 full-time; $30 per semester part-time.

Financial Aid In 2000–2001, 88% of all students received some form of financial aid. 1 fellowship, totaling $1500; 25 research assistantships, totaling $1000; 35 teaching assistantships, totaling $1350, were awarded. Graduate assistantships, loans, merit-based grants/scholarships, need-based grants/scholarships, and federal work-study loans are also available. To apply for financial assistance,

AT a GLANCE

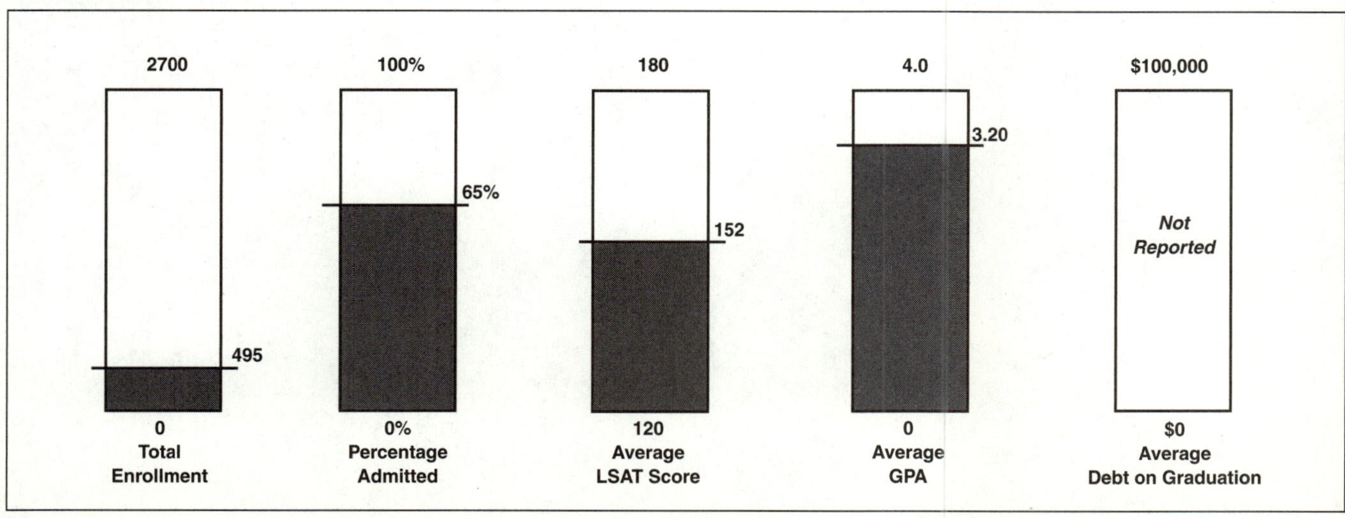

Degree Options

Degree	Total Credits Required	Length of Program
JD–Doctor of Laws	91	3 yrs, full-time or part-time [day]
JD/LLM–Juris Doctor/Master of Laws–Taxation Combined-Degree Program	105	3.5 yrs, full-time or part-time [day, evening]
JD/MBA–Juris Doctor/Master of Business Administration–Dual-degree Program	109	3–4 yrs, full-time or part-time [day, evening]
LLM–Master of Laws–General and Taxation	24	1 yr, full-time or part-time [day, evening]

students must complete the Free Application for Federal Student Aid, scholarship specific applications. Financial aid contact: Jean Klosterman, Director of Admissions, 5100 Rockhill Road, Kansas City, MO 64110. Phone: 816-235-1644. Fax: 816-235-5276. E-mail: klostermanm@umkc.edu

Law School Library Leon E. Bloch Law Library has 5 professional staff members and contains more than 277,843 volumes and 3,830 periodicals. 310 seats are available in the library. When classes are in session, the library is open 109 hours per week.

WESTLAW and LEXIS-NEXIS are available, as are the World Wide Web, online bibliographic services, and CD-ROM players. 45 computer workstations are available to students in the library.

First-Year Program Class size in the average section is 56; 100% of the first-year courses are taught by full-time faculty.

Upper-Level Program Among the electives are:

Administrative Law
Advocacy

Business and Corporate Law
Consumer Law
Education Law
Entertainment Law
Environmental Law
Family Law
Government/Regulation
Health Care/Human Services
Indian/Tribal Law
Intellectual Property
International/Comparative Law
Jurisprudence
Labor Law
Land Use Law/Natural Resources
Lawyering Skills
Legal History/Philosophy
Litigation
Mediation
Probate Law
Public Interest
Securities
Tax Law

Clinical Courses Students receive degree credit for clinical courses. (Clinical practicum is not required.) The clinical area offered includes:

Tax Law

WASHINGTON UNIVERSITY IN ST. LOUIS
SCHOOL OF LAW

St. Louis, Missouri

INFORMATION CONTACT

Janet Bolin, Assistant Dean for Admissions and
Financial Aid
One Brookings Drive
Campus Box 1120
St. Louis, MO 63130-4899

Phone: 314-935-4525   Fax: 314-935-6959
E-mail: admiss@wulaw.wustl.edu
Web site: http://ls.wustl.edu/

LAW STUDENT PROFILE [2000–2001]

FULL-TIME   Enrollment: 649
Women: 43%   Men: 57%

PART-TIME   Enrollment: 29
Women: 38%   Men: 62%

RACIAL or ETHNIC COMPOSITION
African American, 6%; Asian/Pacific Islander, 7%; Hispanic,
2%; Native American, 1%; International, 6%

APPLICANTS and ADMITTEES
Number applied: 1,961
Admitted: 813
Percentage accepted: 41%
Seats available: 213
Average LSAT score: 161
Average GPA: 3.4

Washington University in St. Louis School of Law is a
private institution that organizes classes on a semester
calendar system. The campus is situated in a suburban
setting. first ABA approved in 1923, and an AALS
member, Washington University in St. Louis School of
Law offers JD, JD/MA, JD/MBA, JD/MHA, JD/MS,
JD/MSW, JSD, and LLM degrees.

Faculty consists of 47 full-time and 77 part-time
members in 2000–2001. 19 full-time faculty members
and 24 part-time faculty members are women. 100% of
all faculty members have a JD; 15% have advanced law
degrees. Of all faculty members, 1% are Asian/Pacific
Islander, 2% are African American, 97% are white.

Application Information *Required:* LSAT, LSDAS,
application form, application fee of $60, baccalaureate
degree, personal statement, college transcripts. *Recommended:* 2 letters of recommendation, resume. *Application deadline* for fall term is March 1 (priority date).
Applications are processed on a rolling basis.

Financial Aid Fellowships, loans, merit-based grants/
scholarships, and federal work-study loans are available.
The average student debt at graduation is $65,000. To
apply for financial assistance, students must complete the
Free Application for Federal Student Aid, institutional
forms. Completed financial aid forms should be received
by March 1. Financial aid contact: Jo Ann Eckrich,
Associate Director of Financial Aid, One Brookings
Drive, Campus Box 1120, St. Louis, MO 63130. Phone:
314-935-4605. Fax: 314-935-6959. E-mail:
eckrich@wulaw.wustl.edu

AT a GLANCE

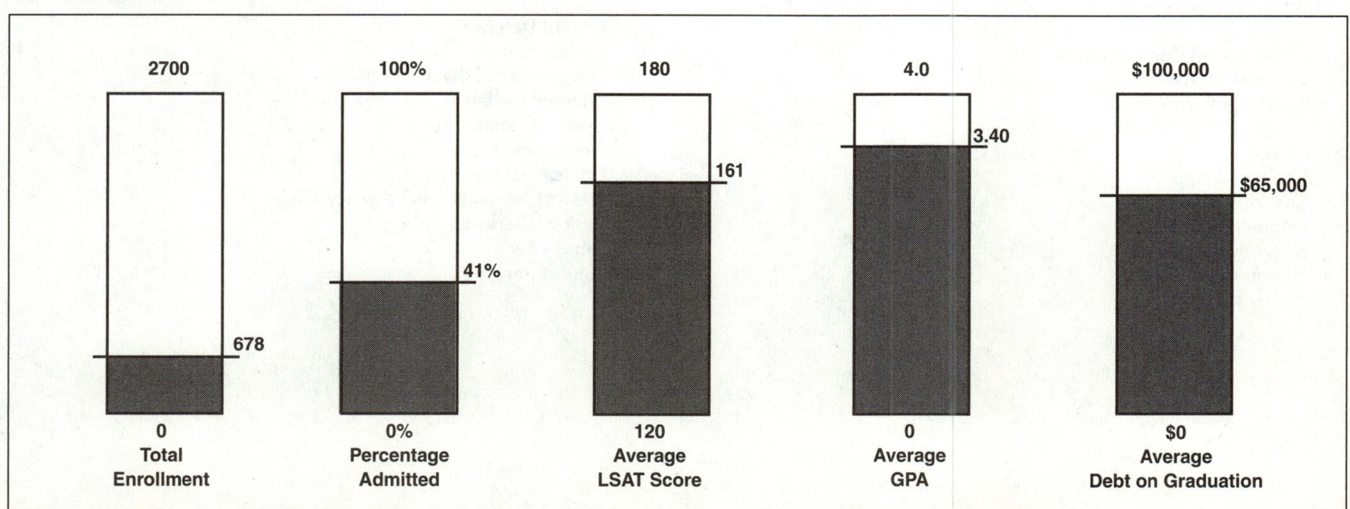

Degree Options

Degree	Total Credits Required	Length of Program
JD–Doctor of Laws	85	3 yrs, full-time only [day]
JD/MA–Juris Doctor/Master of Arts–East Asian Studies		
JD/MA–Juris Doctor/Master of Arts–Economics		
JD/MA–Juris Doctor/Master of Arts–Political Science		
JD/MA–Juris Doctor/Master of Arts–European Studies		
JD/MBA–Juris Doctor/Master of Business Administration–Business		
JD/MHA–Juris Doctor/Master of Health Administration–Health Administration		
JD/MS–Juris Doctor/Master of Science–Engineering and Policy		
JD/MSW–Juris Doctor/Master of Social Work–Social Work		
JSD–Doctor of Juridical Science–Graduate Research Degree		
LLM–Master of Laws–Taxation	24	4 yrs, full-time or part-time [day]
LLM–Master of Laws–International Students		

Law School Library Washington University Law Library has 8 professional staff members and contains more than 584,197 volumes and 6,488 periodicals. 517 seats are available in the library. When classes are in session, the library is open 120 hours per week.

WESTLAW and LEXIS-NEXIS are available, as are the World Wide Web, online bibliographic services, and CD-ROM players. 38 computer workstations are available to students in the library. Special law collections include United States Depository Program, Rare Book Collection, Bryce Collection.

First-Year Program Class size in the average section is 47; 100% of the first-year courses are taught by full-time faculty.

Upper-Level Program Class size in the average section is 25. Among the electives are:

Administrative Law
Advocacy
Business and Corporate Law
★ Capital Defense
★ Civil Litigation
★ Congressional Clinic
Consumer Law
★ Criminal Defense
★ Criminal Prosecution
★ Employment Law
Entertainment Law
★ Environmental Law
Family Law
★ Federal Administrative Agency Clinic
Government/Regulation
Health Care/Human Services
★ Intellectual Property
★ International/Comparative Law
★ Judicial Clerkship
Jurisprudence
Labor Law
Land Use Law/Natural Resources
Lawyering Skills
Legal History/Philosophy
Litigation
Mediation
Probate Law
Public Interest
Securities
Tax Law

(★ *indicates an area of special strength*)

Clinical Courses Students receive degree credit for clinical courses. (Clinical practicum is not required.) Among the clinical areas offered are:

Capital Defense
Civil Litigation
Congressional Clinic
Criminal Defense
Criminal Prosecution
Employment Law
Environmental Law
Federal Administrative Agency Clinic
Judicial Clerkship
Labor Law
Public Interest

THE UNIVERSITY OF MONTANA–MISSOULA
SCHOOL OF LAW

Missoula, Montana

INFORMATION CONTACT

Heidi Fanslow, Admissions Office
Missoula, MT 59812

Phone: 406-243-2698   Fax: 406-243-2576
E-mail: hid314@selway.umt.edu
Web site: http://www.umt.edu/law/

LAW STUDENT PROFILE [2000–2001]

FULL-TIME   Enrollment: 253
Women: 42%   Men: 58%

RACIAL or ETHNIC COMPOSITION

African American, 0.4%; Asian/Pacific Islander, 1%; Hispanic,
2%; Native American, 5%; International, 2%

APPLICANTS and ADMITTEES

Number applied: 409
Admitted: 227
Percentage accepted: 56%
Seats available: 90
Average LSAT score: 153
Average GPA: 3.2

The University of Montana–Missoula School of Law is
a public institution that organizes classes on a semester
calendar system. The campus is situated in a small-town
setting. Founded in 1911, first ABA approved in 1923,
and an AALS member, The University of Montana–
Missoula School of Law offers JD, JD/Certificate,
JD/MBA, JD/MPA, and JD/MS degrees.

Faculty consists of 15 full-time and 14 part-time
members in 2000–2001. 7 full-time faculty members and
6 part-time faculty members are women. 100% of all
faculty members have a JD; 22% have advanced law
degrees. Of all faculty members, 6% are Native American, 94% are white.

Application Information *Required:* LSAT, LSDAS,
application form, application fee of $60, baccalaureate
degree, 3 letters of recommendation, personal statement,
college transcripts, resume, writing sample. *Application
deadline* for fall term is March 1.

Costs The 2000–2001 tuition was $7064 full-time for
state residents. Tuition was $12,907 full-time for
nonresidents.

Financial Aid In 2000–2001, 87% of all students received
some form of financial aid. 22 research assistantships; 16
teaching assistantships, totaling $2640, were awarded.
Graduate assistantships, loans, merit-based grants/
scholarships, need-based grants/scholarships, and federal
work-study loans are also available. To apply for
financial assistance, students must complete the Free

AT a GLANCE

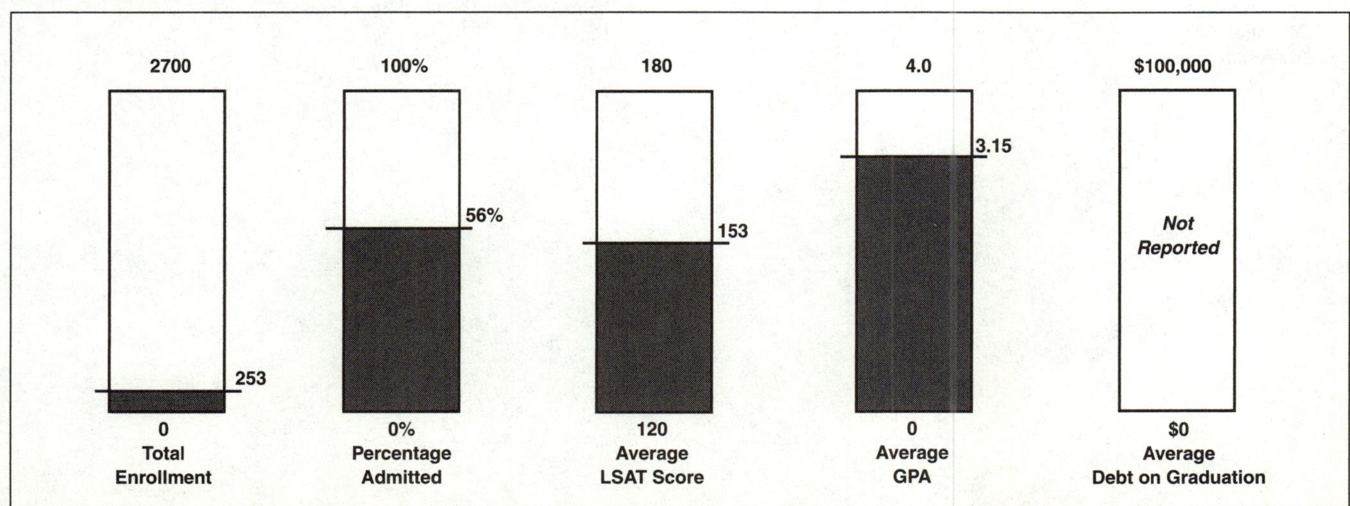

Degree Options

Degree	Total Credits Required	Length of Program
JD–Juris Doctor	90	3 yrs, full-time only [day, summer]
JD/Certificate–Juris Doctor/Certificate–Environmental Law	95	3 yrs, full-time only [day]
JD/MBA–Juris Doctor/Master of Business Administration	90	4 yrs, full-time only [day, summer]
JD/MPA–Juris Doctor/Master of Professional Accountancy–Joint-degree Program	120	4 yrs, full-time only [day, summer]
JD/MS–Juris Doctor/Master of Science–Joint-degree Program in Environmental Studies	120	4 yrs, full-time only [day, summer]

Application for Federal Student Aid. Completed financial aid forms should be received by March 1. Financial aid contact: Connie Bowman, Financial Aid Office, University of Montana Financial Aid Office, Missoula, MT 59812. Phone: 406-243-5524. Fax: 406-243-2576. E-mail: connie@selway.umt.edu

Law School Library Jameson Law Library has 3 professional staff members and contains more than 108,599 volumes and 1,868 periodicals. 212 seats are available in the library. When classes are in session, the library is open 93 hours per week.

WESTLAW and LEXIS-NEXIS are available, as are the World Wide Web, online bibliographic services, and CD-ROM players. 44 computer workstations are available to students in the library.

First-Year Program Class size in the average section is 45; 100% of the first-year courses are taught by full-time faculty.

Upper-Level Program Class size in the average section is 29. Among the electives are:

Administrative Law
Advocacy
Business and Corporate Law
Civil Litigation
Consumer Law
Education Law
★ Environmental Law
Family Law
Government/Regulation
★ Indian/Tribal Law
Intellectual Property
International/Comparative Law
Labor Law
Land Rights/Natural Resource
★ Land Use Law/Natural Resources
Lawyering Skills
Legal History/Philosophy
Litigation
Mediation
Probate Law
Securities
Tax Law
★ Trial Advocacy
(★ indicates an area of special strength)

Clinical Courses Students receive degree credit for clinical courses. 4 credit hours of clinical practicum are required. Among the clinical areas offered are:

Civil Litigation
Criminal Defense
Criminal Prosecution
Disability Law
Education Law
Environmental Law
Family Law
Indian/Tribal Law
Judicial Clerkship
Land Rights/Natural Resource
Land Use Law/Natural Resources
Mediation

CREIGHTON UNIVERSITY
SCHOOL OF LAW

Omaha, Nebraska

INFORMATION CONTACT

Andrea D. Bashara, Assistant Dean
2500 California Plaza
Omaha, NE 68178

Phone: 402-280-2872   Fax: 402-280-3161
E-mail: bashara@culaw.creighton.edu
Web site: http://culaw.creighton.edu/

LAW STUDENT PROFILE [2000–2001]

FULL-TIME   Enrollment: 429
Women: 45%   Men: 55%

PART-TIME   Enrollment: 24
Women: 58%   Men: 42%

RACIAL or ETHNIC COMPOSITION

African American, 3%; Asian/Pacific Islander, 1%; Hispanic,
5%; Native American, 1%

APPLICANTS and ADMITTEES

Number applied: 680
Admitted: 464
Percentage accepted: 68%
Seats available: 150
Median LSAT score: 150
Average GPA: 3.1

Creighton University School of Law is a private
institution that organizes classes on a semester calendar
system. The campus is situated in an urban setting.
Founded in 1904, first ABA approved in 1924, and an
AALS member, Creighton University School of Law
offers JD, JD/MBA, and JD/MS degrees.

Faculty consists of 24 full-time and 41 part-time
members in 2000–2001. 100% of all faculty members
have a JD; 39% have advanced law degrees. Of all faculty
members, 4.3% are African American, 95.7% are white.

Application Information *Required:* LSAT, LSDAS,
application form, application fee of $45, baccalaureate
degree, 2 letters of recommendation, personal statement,
college transcripts. *Application deadline* for fall term is
May 1 (priority date). Applications are processed on a
rolling basis.

Costs The 1999–2000 tuition was $16,548 full-time; $555
per hour part-time. Fees: $566 full-time.

Financial Aid In 2000–2001, 85% of all students received
some form of financial aid. Loans and merit-based
grants/scholarships are available. The average student
debt at graduation is $66,218. To apply for financial
assistance, students must complete the Free Application
for Federal Student Aid, scholarship specific applications.
Completed financial aid forms should be received by
July 1. Financial aid contact: Dean Obenauer, Associate
Director of Financial Aid for Graduate / Professional
Students, 2500 California Plaza, Omaha, NE 68178.
Phone: 402-280-2731. Fax: 402-280-2895. E-mail:
obenauer@creighton.edu

AT a GLANCE

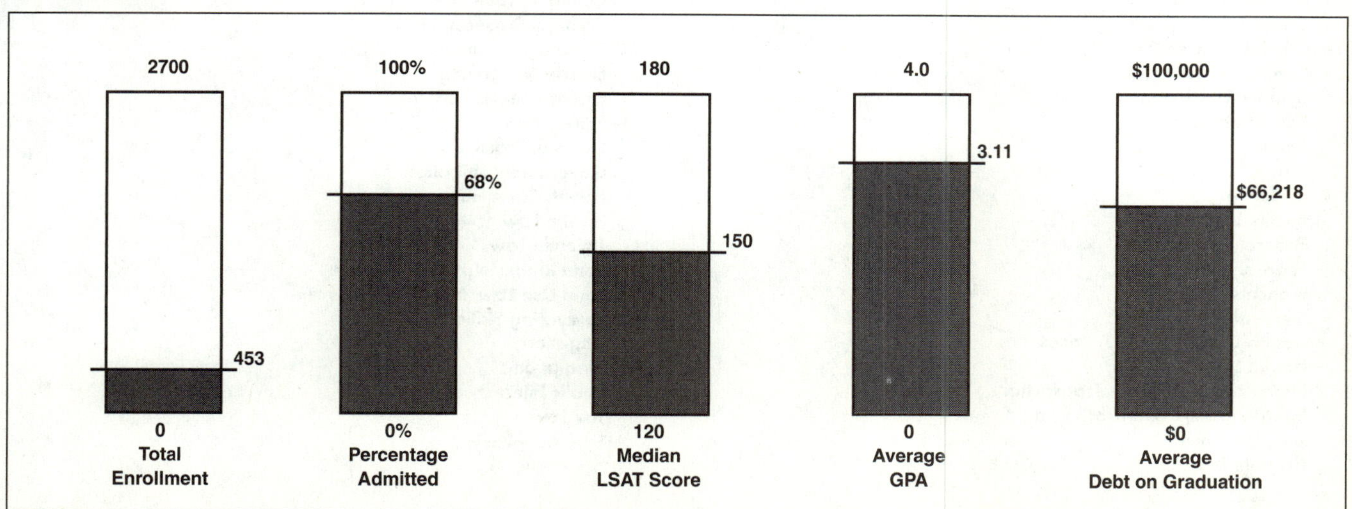

Degree Options

Degree	Total Credits Required	Length of Program
JD–Doctor of Laws	94	3–6 yrs, full-time or part-time [day, summer]
JD/MBA–Juris Doctor/Master of Business Administration–Combined-degree Program	109	3–6 yrs, full-time or part-time [day, evening, summer]
JD/MS–Juris Doctor/Master of Science–Electronic Commerce	109	3–6 yrs, full-time or part-time [day, evening, summer]

Law School Library Klutznick Law Library has 6 professional staff members and contains more than 265,056 volumes and 1,468 periodicals. 418 seats are available in the library. When classes are in session, the library is open 104 hours per week.

WESTLAW and LEXIS-NEXIS are available, as are the World Wide Web, online bibliographic services, and CD-ROM players. 49 computer workstations are available to students in the library. Special law collections include Rare law book collection.

First-Year Program Class size in the average section is 68; 100% of the first-year courses are taught by full-time faculty.

Upper-Level Program Class size in the average section is 30. Among the electives are:

Accounting
Administrative Law
★ Advocacy
Alternative Dispute Resolution
Banking Law & Regulation
★ Business and Corporate Law
★ Civil Litigation
Civil Rights
Commercial Law
Complex Litigation
Conflict of Laws
Consumer Law
Copyright & Trademark Law
Corporate Finance
★ Corporate Law
★ Criminal Defense
★ Criminal Law
★ Criminal Procedure
★ Criminal Prosecution
★ Dispute Resolution
Education Law
Environmental Law
Estate Planning
★ Evidence
Family Law
Federal Courts
Federal Income Tax
Franchising Law
★ General Practice
Health Care/Human Services
Health Law
International Business Transactions
International/Comparative Law
Jurisprudence
Juvenile Law

Labor Law
Land Rights/Natural Resource
Land Use Law/Natural Resources
★ Lawyering Skills
Legal History/Philosophy
★ Litigation
★ Mediation
Negotiable Intruments
Patent Law
Post-Conviction Relief
Pretrial Litigation
Probate Law
★ Public Interest
Real Estate Law
Remedies
Scientific Evidence
Secured Transactions
★ Securities
Securities Regulation
State and Local Taxation
★ Tax Law
★ Trial Advocacy
White Collar Crime
(★ *indicates an area of special strength*)

Clinical Courses Students receive degree credit for clinical courses. (Clinical practicum is not required.) Among the clinical areas offered are:

Administrative Law
Advocacy
Civil Litigation
Civil Rights
Consumer Law
Criminal Defense
Criminal Law
Criminal Procedure
Criminal Prosecution
Dispute Resolution
Elderly Advocacy
Environmental Law
Family Law
General Practice
Government Litigation
Health Care/Human Services
Health Law
Juvenile Law
Land Rights/Natural Resource
Land Use Law/Natural Resources
Lawyering Skills
Litigation
Mediation
Public Interest
Tax Law
Trial Advocacy

UNIVERSITY OF NEBRASKA–LINCOLN
COLLEGE OF LAW

Lincoln, Nebraska

INFORMATION CONTACT

Glenda Pierce, Assistant Dean
PO Box 830902
Lincoln, NE 68583-0902

Phone: 402-472-2161   Fax: 402-472-5185
E-mail: lawadm@unl.edu
Web site: http://www.unl.edu/lawcoll/

LAW STUDENT PROFILE [2000–2001]

FULL-TIME   Enrollment: 371
Women: 43%   Men: 57%

PART-TIME   Enrollment: 1
Women: 100%

RACIAL or ETHNIC COMPOSITION

African American, 2%; Asian/Pacific Islander, 2%; Hispanic, 2%; International, 1%

APPLICANTS and ADMITTEES

Number applied: 647
Admitted: 366
Percentage accepted: 57%
Seats available: 150
Average LSAT score: 153
Average GPA: 3.6

University of Nebraska–Lincoln College of Law is a public institution that organizes classes on a semester calendar system. The campus is situated in a suburban setting. Founded in 1888, first ABA approved in 1923, and an AALS member, University of Nebraska–Lincoln College of Law offers JD/MA, JD/MBA, JD/MCRP, JD/MPA, JD/Maitrise en Driot, and JD/PhD degrees.

Faculty consists of 16 full-time and 2 part-time members in 2000–2001. 2 full-time faculty members are women. 100% of all faculty members have a JD; 21% have advanced law degrees. Of all faculty members, 7.1% are African American, 92.9% are white.

Application Information *Required:* LSAT, LSDAS, application form, application fee of $25, baccalaureate degree, personal statement, writing sample, college transcripts. *Recommended:* 2 letters of recommendation. *Application deadline* for fall term is March 1.

Financial Aid Loans, merit-based grants/scholarships, need-based grants/scholarships, and federal work-study loans are available. The average student debt at graduation is $35,000. To apply for financial assistance, students must complete the Free Application for Federal Student Aid, need-based grant application. Financial aid contact: Glenda Pierce, Assistant Dean, PO Box 830902, Lincoln, NE 68583-0902. Phone: 402-472-2161. Fax: 402-472-5185. E-mail: gpierce1@unl.edu

Law School Library Marvin and Virginia Schmid Law Library has 6 professional staff members and contains

AT a GLANCE

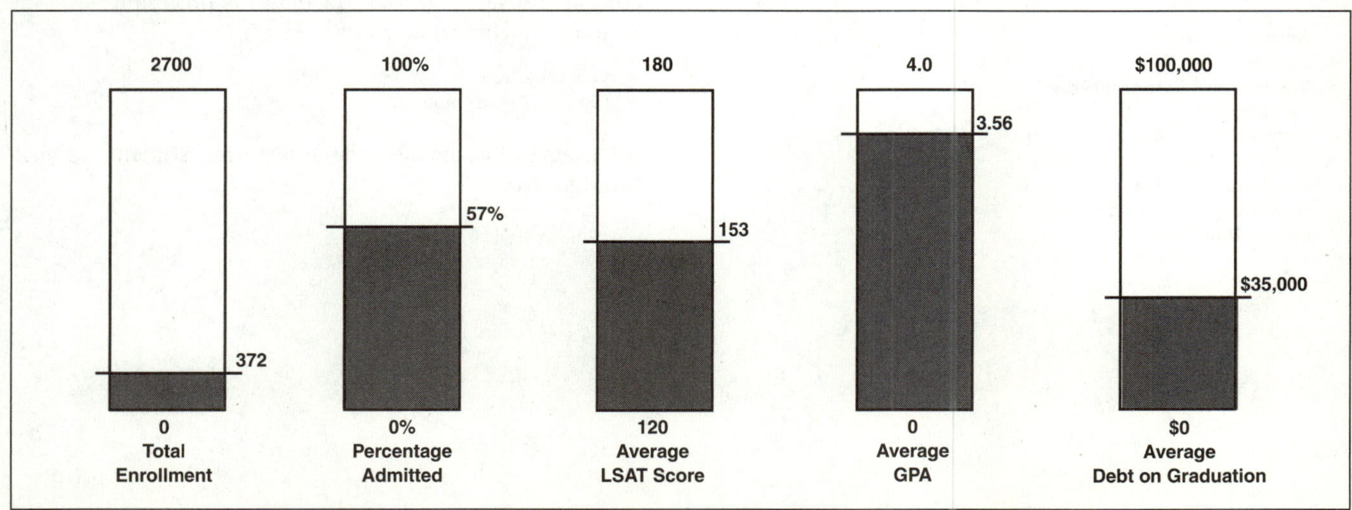

Degree Options

Degree	Total Credits Required	Length of Program
JD/MA–Juris Doctor/Master of Arts–Joint-degree Program in Law and Psychology	132	4 yrs, full-time only [day, summer]
JD/MA–Juris Doctor/Master of Arts–Joint-degree Program in Law and Economics	114	4 yrs, full-time only [day, summer]
JD/MA–Juris Doctor/Master of Arts–Joint-degree Program in Law and International Affairs	114	4 yrs, full-time only [day, summer]
JD/MA–Juris Doctor/Master of Arts–Joint-degree Program in Law and Political Science	108	4 yrs, full-time only [day, summer]
JD/MBA–Juris Doctor/Master of Business Administration–Joint-degree Program in Law and Business	120	4 yrs, full-time only [day, summer]
JD/MCRP–Juris Doctor/Master of Community and Regional Planning–Joint-degree in Law and Community/Regional Planning	117	4 yrs, full-time only [day, summer]
JD/MPA–Juris Doctor/Master of Professional Accountancy–Joint-degree Program in Law and Accounting	126	4 yrs, full-time only [day, summer]
JD/Maitrise en Driot–Juris Doctor	96	3 yrs, full-time only [day, summer]
JD/PhD–Juris Doctor/Doctor of Philosophy–Joint-degree Program in Law and Psychology	168	6 yrs, full-time only [day, summer]
JD/PhD–Juris Doctor/Doctor of Philosophy–Dual-degree Program for Law and Education	144	5 yrs, full-time only [day, summer]

more than 360,816 volumes and 2,779 periodicals. 339 seats are available in the library. When classes are in session, the library is open 109 hours per week.

WESTLAW and LEXIS-NEXIS are available, as are the World Wide Web, online bibliographic services, and CD-ROM players. 57 computer workstations are available to students in the library. Special law collections include tax, selected federal government depository.

First-Year Program Class size in the average section is 65; 100% of the first-year courses are taught by full-time faculty.

Upper-Level Program Class size in the average section is 25. Among the electives are:

Administrative Law
★ Advocacy
★ Business and Corporate Law
Civil Litigation
Criminal Prosecution
★ Environmental Law
Family Law
Health Care/Human Services
Indian/Tribal Law

★ Intellectual Property
International/Comparative Law
Jurisprudence
★ Labor Law
★ Land Use Law/Natural Resources
Lawyering Skills
Legal History/Philosophy
★ Litigation
Media Law
Mediation
Probate Law
Public Interest
Securities
Tax Law
(★ *indicates an area of special strength*)

Clinical Courses Students receive degree credit for clinical courses. (Clinical practicum is not required.) Among the clinical areas offered are:

Civil Litigation
Criminal Prosecution

International exchange programs permit students to visit Montenegro.

UNIVERSITY OF NEVADA, LAS VEGAS
WILLIAM S. BOYD SCHOOL OF LAW

Las Vegas, Nevada

INFORMATION CONTACT

Director of Admissions
4505 Maryland Parkway
Box 451003
Las Vegas, NV 89154-1003

Phone: 702-895-3671   Fax: 702-895-1095
Web site: http://www.law/unlv.edu/

LAW STUDENT PROFILE [2000–2001]

FULL-TIME   Enrollment: 245
Women: 49%   Men: 51%

PART-TIME   Enrollment: 155
Women: 46%   Men: 54%

RACIAL or ETHNIC COMPOSITION
African American, 4%; Asian/Pacific Islander, 3%; Hispanic, 8%; Native American, 3%

APPLICANTS and ADMITTEES
Number applied: 530
Admitted: 227
Percentage accepted: 43%
Seats available: 140
Average LSAT score: 152
Average GPA: 3.2

University of Nevada, Las Vegas William S. Boyd School of Law is a public institution that organizes classes on a semester basis. The campus is situated in an urban setting. first ABA approved in 2000, University of Nevada, Las Vegas William S. Boyd School of Law offers a JD degree.

Faculty consists of 26 full-time and 8 part-time members in 2000–2001. 13 full-time faculty members and 2 part-time faculty members are women. 100% of all faculty members have a JD; 8% have advanced law degrees. Of all faculty members, 4% are Native American, 8% are African American, 8% are Hispanic, 80% are white.

Application Information *Required:* LSAT, LSDAS, application form, application fee of $40, baccalaureate degree, 1 recommendation, personal statement, college transcripts, resume. *Application deadline* for fall term is March 15 (priority date). Applications are processed on a rolling basis.

Financial Aid In 2000–2001, 75% of all students received some form of financial aid. Loans, merit-based grants/scholarships, need-based grants/scholarships, and federal work-study loans are available. The average student debt at graduation is $38,005. To apply for financial assistance, students must complete the Free Application for Federal Student Aid. Completed financial aid forms should be received by February 1. Financial aid contact: Christopher Kypuros, Financial Aid Counselor, 4505 Maryland Parkway, Box 452016, Las Vegas, NV 89154-2016. Phone: 702-895-0630. Fax: 702-895-1353. E-mail: ckypuros@ccmail.nevada.edu

AT a GLANCE

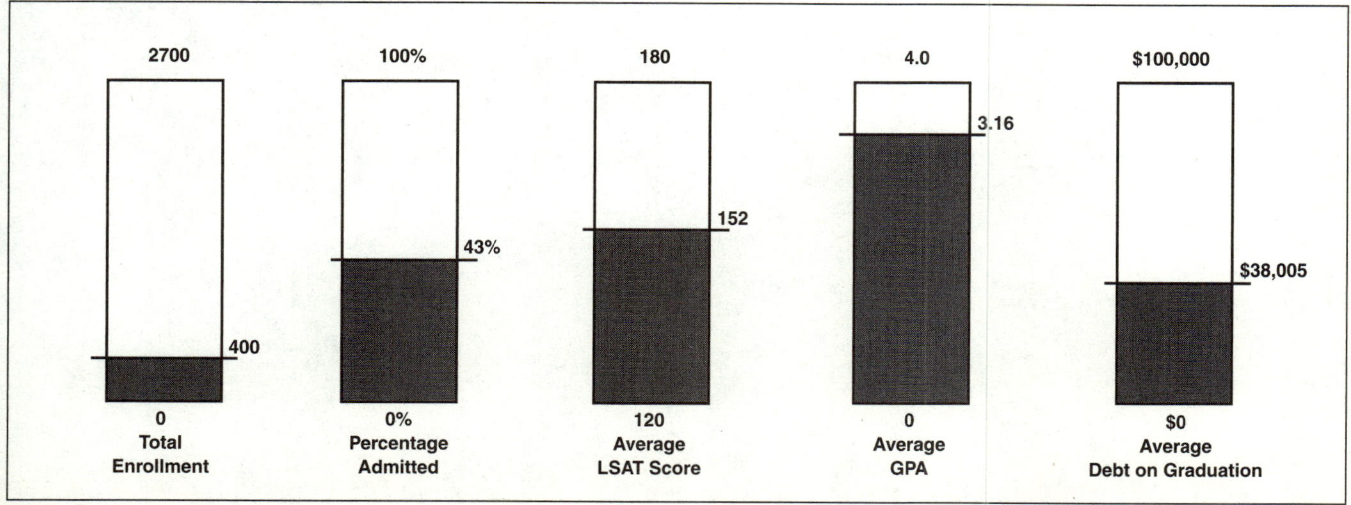

Law School Library has 6 professional staff members and contains more than 199,703 volumes and 1,253 periodicals. 195 seats are available in the library. When classes are in session, the library is open 106 hours per week.

WESTLAW and LEXIS-NEXIS are available, as are the World Wide Web, online bibliographic services, and CD-ROM players. 33 computer workstations are available to students in the library.

Upper-Level Program Among the electives are:

Advocacy
Business and Corporate Law
Entertainment Law
Family Law
Government/Regulation

Health Care/Human Services
Indian/Tribal Law
Intellectual Property
Land Use Law/Natural Resources
Lawyering Skills
Legal History/Philosophy
Probate Law
Public Interest
Securities
Tax Law

Clinical Courses Students receive degree credit for clinical courses. (Clinical practicum is not required.) Among the clinical areas offered are:

Child Welfare Policy
Juvenile Law

FRANKLIN PIERCE LAW CENTER

Concord, New Hampshire

INFORMATION CONTACT

Lory Attalla, Director of Admissions
2 White Street
Concord, NH 03301-4197

Phone: 603-228-9217   Fax: 603-228-1074
E-mail: lattalla@fplc.edu
Web site: http://www.fplc.edu/

LAW STUDENT PROFILE [2000–2001]

FULL-TIME   Enrollment: 445
Women: 43%   Men: 57%

PART-TIME   Enrollment: 21
Women: 57%   Men: 43%

APPLICANTS and ADMITTEES

Number applied: 768
Admitted: 464
Percentage accepted: 60%
Seats available: 132
Average LSAT score: 150
Average GPA: 3.0

Franklin Pierce Law Center is a private nonprofit institution that organizes classes on a semester calendar system. The campus is situated in an urban setting. Founded in 1973, first ABA approved in 1980, Franklin Pierce Law Center offers CAGS, JD, LLM, ME, and MIP degrees.

Faculty 100% of all faculty members have a JD; 14% have advanced law degrees. Of all faculty members, 90% are white, 10% are international.

Application Information *Required:* LSAT, LSDAS, application form, application fee of $45, baccalaureate degree, personal statement, resume. *Recommended:* 2 letters of recommendation.

Costs The 2000–2001 tuition was $18,500 full-time; $617 per credit part-time. Fees: $25 full-time; $25 per year part-time. Part-time tuition and fees vary according to course load and degree level.

Financial Aid Loans, loan repayment assistance program (LRAP), merit-based grants/scholarships, need-based grants/scholarships, and federal work-study loans are available. The average student debt at graduation is $72,180. To apply for financial assistance, students must complete the Free Application for Federal Student Aid, institutional forms. Financial aid contact: Clinton A. Hanson Jr., Director of Financial Aid, 2 White Street, Concord, NH 03301. Phone: 603-228-1541 ext. 1104. Fax: 603-228-1074. E-mail: chanson@fplc.edu

Law School Library Franklin Pierce Law Center has 7 professional staff members and contains more than

AT a GLANCE

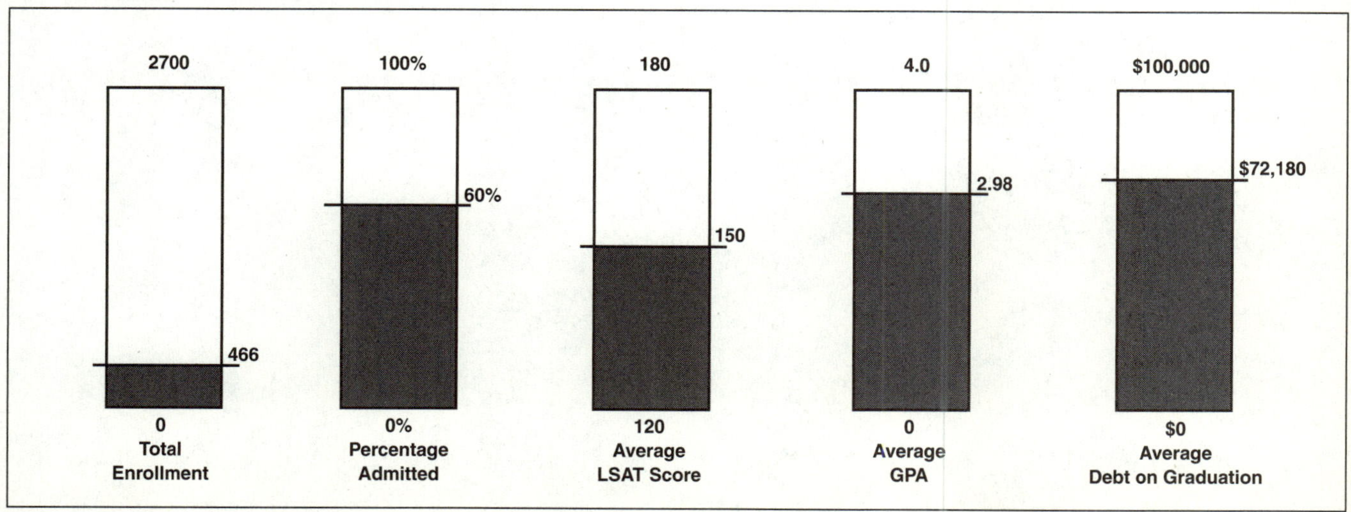

Degree Options

Degree	Total Credits Required	Length of Program
CAGS–Certificate of Advanced Graduate Study– Education Law	40	6 yrs, full-time or part-time [day, summer]
JD–Doctor of Laws	84	3 yrs, full-time or part-time [day]
LLM–Master of Laws–Intellectual Property	30	1 yr, full-time or part-time [day]
ME–Master of Engineering–Education Law	32	5 yrs, full-time or part-time [day, summer]
MIP–Master of Intellectual Property–Intellectual Property	30	1 yr, full-time or part-time [day]

221,745 volumes and 1,434 periodicals. 247 seats are available in the library. When classes are in session, the library is open 104 hours per week.

WESTLAW and LEXIS-NEXIS are available, as are the World Wide Web, online bibliographic services, and CD-ROM players. 44 computer workstations are available to students in the library. Special law collections include intellectual property law.

First-Year Program Class size in the average section is 135; 100% of the first-year courses are taught by full-time faculty.

Upper-Level Program Class size in the average section is 26. Among the electives are:

  Administrative Law
★ Advocacy
★ Business and Corporate Law
★ Education Law
  Entertainment Law
  Environmental Law
★ Family Law
  Government/Regulation
★ Health Care/Human Services
★ Intellectual Property
  International/Comparative Law
  Land Use Law/Natural Resources
  Lawyering Skills
★ Litigation
  Media Law
★ Mediation
  Property/Real Estate
★ Public Interest
★ Tax Law
(★ *indicates an area of special strength*)

Clinical Courses Students receive degree credit for clinical courses. (Clinical practicum is not required.) Among the clinical areas offered are:

  Children's Advocacy
  Civil Litigation
  Criminal Defense
  Family Practice
  Intellectual Property
  Juvenile Law
  Mediation
  Nonprofit Organizations
  Public Interest

RUTGERS, THE STATE UNIVERSITY OF NEW JERSEY, CAMDEN
SCHOOL OF LAW

Camden, New Jersey

INFORMATION CONTACT

Camille Spinello Andrews, Associate Dean of
Enrollment, Law Admissions
217 North Fifth Street
Camden, NJ 08102

Phone: 856-225-6102   Fax: 856-225-6537
E-mail: csa@crab.rutgers.edu
Web site: http://www-camlaw.rutgers.edu/

LAW STUDENT PROFILE [2000–2001]

FULL-TIME   Enrollment: 593
Women: 48%   Men: 52%

PART-TIME   Enrollment: 169
Women: 47%   Men: 53%

RACIAL or ETHNIC COMPOSITION
African American, 7%; Asian/Pacific Islander, 6%; Hispanic,
5%; Native American, 0.4%; International, 2%

APPLICANTS and ADMITTEES
Number applied: 1,910
Admitted: 595
Percentage accepted: 31%
Seats available: 205
Average LSAT score: 158
Average GPA: 3.2

**Rutgers, The State University of New Jersey, Camden
School of Law** is a public institution that organizes
classes on a semester calendar system. The campus is
situated in an urban setting. Founded in 1926, first ABA
approved in 1951, and an AALS member, Rutgers, The
State University of New Jersey, Camden School of Law
offers JD, JD/MBA, JD/MCRP, JD/MD, JD/MPAd,
JD/MS, and JD/MSW degrees.

Faculty consists of 62 full-time and 50 part-time
members in 2000–2001. 20 full-time faculty members
and 12 part-time faculty members are women. 99% of all
faculty members have a JD; 20% have advanced law
degrees. Of all faculty members, 1% are Asian/Pacific
Islander, 5% are African American, 1% are Hispanic,
93% are white.

Application Information *Required:* LSAT, LSDAS,
application form, application fee of $50, baccalaureate
degree, 2 letters of recommendation, personal statement,
college transcripts. *Recommended:* minimum 3.2 GPA,
resume. *Application deadline* for fall term is March 1
(priority date). Applications are processed on a rolling
basis.

Financial Aid In 2000–2001, 79% of all students received
some form of financial aid. Loans, merit-based grants/
scholarships, need-based grants/scholarships, and federal
work-study loans are available. The average student debt
at graduation is $48,500. To apply for financial assis-
tance, students must complete the Free Application for

AT a GLANCE

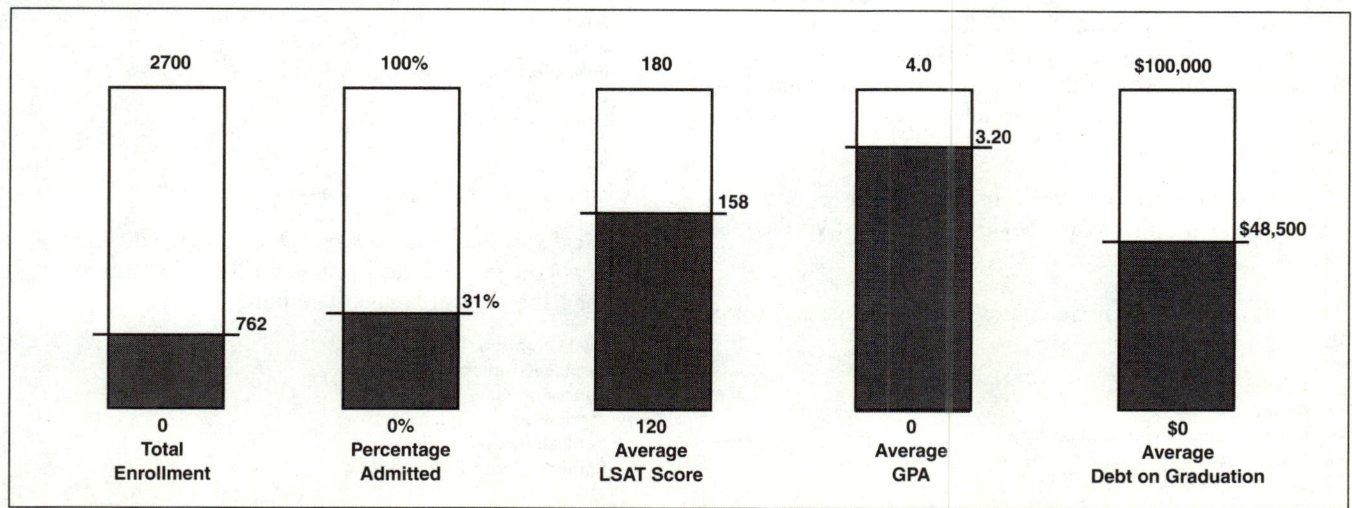

Degree Options

Degree	Total Credits Required	Length of Program
JD–Doctor of Laws	84	3–4 yrs, full-time or part-time [day, evening, summer]
JD/MBA–Juris Doctor/Master of Business Administration–Dual-degree Program	120	3.5–4 yrs, full-time or part-time [day, evening, summer]
JD/MBA–Juris Doctor/Master of Business Administration–Dual-degree Program with Graduate School of Management - Camden	121	4 yrs, full-time or part-time [day, evening, summer]
JD/MCRP–Juris Doctor/Master of Community and Regional Planning–Dual-degree Program		4 yrs, full-time or part-time [day, evening, summer]
JD/MD–Juris Doctor/Doctor of Medicine–Dual-degree Program Robert Wood Johnson Medical School - Camden		6 yrs, full-time only [day, evening, summer]
JD/MPAd–Juris Doctor/Master of Public Administration–Dual-degree Program		4 yrs, full-time or part-time [day, evening, summer]
JD/MPAd–Juris Doctor/Master of Public Administration–Dual-degree Program in Health Care Management with Graduate School-Camden and UMDNJ School of Osteopathic Medicine	102	3.5 yrs, full-time or part-time [day, evening, summer]
JD/MS–Juris Doctor/Master of Science–Dual-degree Program in Public Policy with Eagleton Institute of Politics, Rutgers, New Brunswick	102	3.5 yrs, full-time only [day, evening]
JD/MSW–Juris Doctor/Master of Social Work–Dual-degree Program	120	4 yrs, full-time or part-time [day, evening, summer]

Federal Student Aid. Completed financial aid forms should be received by April 1. Financial aid contact: Richard Woodland, Director of Financial Aid, Office of Financial Aid, Rutgers State University of New Jersey, 401 Cooper Street, Camden, NJ 08102. Phone: 856-225-6103 or toll free 800-466-7561. Fax: 856-225-6470. E-mail: rwoodlan@crab.rutgers.edu

Law School Library Rutgers University School of Law Library - Camden has 7 professional staff members and contains more than 413,548 volumes and 1,400 periodicals. 403 seats are available in the library. When classes are in session, the library is open 100 hours per week.

WESTLAW and LEXIS-NEXIS are available, as are the World Wide Web, online bibliographic services, and CD-ROM players. 51 computer workstations are available to students in the library. Special law collections include Ginsburgs collection - collection of Soviet legal materials.

First-Year Program Class size in the average section is 75; 100% of the first-year courses are taught by full-time faculty.

Upper-Level Program Class size in the average section is 40. Among the electives are:

Administrative Law
★ Advocacy
★ Business and Corporate Law
★ Civil Litigation
★ Commercial Law
★ Constitutional Law
Domestic Violence
Education
★ Environmental Law
★ Family Law
★ Government/Regulation
★ Health Care/Human Services
Indian/Tribal Law
★ Intellectual Property
★ International/Comparative Law
Jurisprudence
Labor Law
Land Use Law/Natural Resources
★ Lawyering Skills
Legal History/Philosophy
★ Litigation
Maritime Law
★ Mediation
Probate Law
★ Public Interest
Securities
Small Business Counseling
Sports Law
★ Tax Law
(★ *indicates an area of special strength*)

Clinical Courses Students receive degree credit for clinical courses. (Clinical practicum is not required.) Among the clinical areas offered are:

Civil Litigation
Domestic Violence
Education
Mediation
Public Interest
Small Business Counseling

HISTORY, CAMPUS, AND LOCATION

Rutgers School of Law at Camden is part of Rutgers, the State University of New Jersey, one of the nation's oldest and most esteemed universities. Chartered in 1766, Rutgers University is the eighth-oldest institution of higher education in the nation. The law school at Camden was founded in 1926 by Arthur E. Armitage Sr. A member of the Association of American Law Schools (AALS) and approved by the American Bar Association (ABA), the law school is known for excellence in scholarship and rigor in the training of new lawyers.

The law school offers a safe, attractive urban campus located on 25 tree-lined acres. The main law school building houses research facilities, seminar and reading rooms, student lounges, a study area, a cafeteria, classrooms, and faculty and administration offices. Law students have access to the other facilities on campus, including the gymnasium with squash and tennis courts and a swimming pool, a fine arts building, a theater, a campus center and dining hall, the Walt Whitman International Poetry Center, and the Paul Robeson Library. The campus is part of the ongoing development of the Camden waterfront. The Blockbuster-Sony Music Entertainment Center, the New Jersey State Aquarium, and new federal and state courthouses are located adjacent to or within a few blocks of the law school.

Just minutes from the Liberty Bell and Independence Hall in Philadelphia, this urban campus is just 1 hour from the famous New Jersey shore and its miles of beaches and Atlantic City. In just under 2 hours students can venture to New York City, Baltimore, Annapolis, Bucks County, and the Pine Barrens. Washington, D.C., can be reached in just 3 hours.

SPECIAL QUALITIES OF THE SCHOOL

Emerging as one of the top public law schools in the nation, Rutgers University School of Law at Camden is known for its eminent faculty and prestigious alumni. Faculty members are ranked among the most accomplished producers of scholarly articles in eminent journals, and their scholarship has been cited by numerous courts, including the United States Supreme Court and the New Jersey Supreme Court. Faculty members also serve as consultants and reporters for the ABA, the American Law Institute, and federal and state commissions and are counsel in important public interest litigation.

An overwhelming number of students choose the School because of its national reputation, geographic location, and reasonable tuition. The law school is deeply committed to the enrichment of the law school community and educational experiences created by a diverse student body. Students are drawn from more than 300 undergraduate institutions, forty-four states and Puerto Rico, and seven other countries. Approximately 20 percent of the total enrollment are students of color, and almost 50 percent are women. Admission is highly competitive; last year, more than half of the class had LSAT scores of 158 to 171 and GPAs of 3.2 to 4.0. However, the Admissions Committee considers each applicant's file individually, and special qualities may occasionally overcome lower numbers. Admission is rolling, but priority is given to applications received by March 1 of each year.

TECHNOLOGY ON CAMPUS

The law school is a leader in the use of computers. Four computer labs, e-mail accounts, Internet connections, and online research, including individual WESTLAW and LEXIS-NEXIS accounts, online nutshells, hornbooks, and restatements, are available to students. Students residing on campus have direct Internet access from their apartments. Professors utilize Web sites for their courses, thus creating an exciting opportunity for students to raise issues, ask questions, and exchange ideas about the substantive course materials outside the classroom.

SCHOLARSHIPS AND LOANS

Rutgers is a direct student loan university. As such, a vast majority of students receive aid in the form of government-sponsored loans. The law school also awards numerous merit-based scholarships, including prestigious Dean's Merit Scholarships and the William G. Bischoff Scholarship without regard to financial need. These awards are the highest forms of recognizing academic achievements.

STUDENT ACTIVITIES AND OPPORTUNITIES

Law Review The *Rutgers Law Journal* is a professional publication devoted to critical discussions of current legal problems. One issue of the journal each year is devoted to a survey of state constitutional law. Invitations for staff positions are extended to a limited number of first-year students on the basis of their academic achievement in the first year of law school and a writing competition. Other students may compete for *Rutgers Law Journal* membership through subsequent open writing competitions. Approximately 60 students participate in the publication. Students may also compete for positions on the *Rutgers Journal on Law and Religion*.

Moot Court All first-year students are required to take moot court. A highlight of the upper-level curriculum is the Judge James A. Hunter III Advanced Moot Court program. Most second-year students participate in this competition to represent the School in the National Moot Court Competition. Students also compete in many other national competitions, including Jessup International Moot Court, Gibbons National Criminal Procedure Moot Court, National Black Law Students Association Frederick Douglass Moot Court, National Latino Law Students Association Moot Court, and the Environmental Moot Court.

Extracurricular Activities Law students participate in a wide range of activities that enhance their academic experience. Student organizations are numerous and include the Student Bar Association and Women's Law Caucus, along with associations for every major interest group and most nationalities. Student activity offices and a student lounge are located adjacent to the main law school building. Rutgers students also participate in intramural sports programs for men and women.

Special Opportunities An outstanding externship program offers third-year students an opportunity to gain academic credit while working in federal and state judicial chambers, public agencies, and public interest organizations, including the United States Court of Appeals for the Third Circuit, U.S. District Courts, the U.S. Attorney's office, legal services and public defender offices, and the Internal Revenue Service. Other third-year students participate in the Civil Practice Clinic, a live-client clinic housed in the law school that represents elderly and disabled clients as well as children and their families who seek free education and related services. The law school supports an active pro bono program that provides opportunities for students to represent clients in a wide range of pro bono activities, including domestic violence, mediation, bankruptcy, legal education, and income tax assistance. Law students also have the opportunity to serve in prestigious judicial clerkships. Rutgers places more than twice the national average and ranks third in the nation in placing its graduates in these highly desirable federal and state clerkships.

Opportunities for Members of Minority Groups and Women With a national reputation for academic excellence, the law school is committed to increasing diversity within the legal profession. Its African-American, Asian, Hispanic, and women graduates are practicing law throughout the United States as federal and state judges, as corporate counsel, in prestigious large and small firms, in corporations, in government agencies, and in legal service organizations. The diverse student body is reflected in the law school's community. Women and members of minority groups may participate in numerous student organizations, such as the Women's Law Caucus, the Domestic Violence Project, the Black Law Students Association (BLSA), the Hispanic Law Student Association (ALIANZA), and the Asian/Pacific American Law Students Association (APALSA). BLSA also participates in a law-related education and mentoring pro bono project in the Camden City public schools. From the moment students arrive on campus, the law school provides academic support by assigning academic advisers to each student and providing tutorial sessions. Special scholarships, such as the C. Clyde Ferguson Scholarship, also encourage women and minorities to excel in the study of law.

BAR PASSAGE, CAREER SERVICES, AND PLACEMENT

Bar passage rates for Rutgers–Camden graduates typically exceed state averages. The most popular states in which the bar exams were taken were New York, New Jersey, and Pennsylvania.

Located at the base of the Benjamin Franklin Bridge leading to Philadelphia, Rutgers–Camden sits in the fifth-largest legal job market in the country. All major Philadelphia, New Jersey, and Delaware firms recruit from Rutgers, as do prestigious firms from New York City, California, and Washington, D.C. As a direct result of the quality of legal education at Rutgers, more than 96 percent of last year's class is working in the following fields.

The average starting salary for private practice is in excess of $76,000, with many students starting in positions that pay in excess of $100,000.

Legal Field	Percentage of Graduates	Average Starting Salary
Academic	1%	n/a
Business	9%	$60,000
Government	9%	$41,000
Judicial Clerkships	53%	$32,000
Private Practice	26%	$66,000
Public Interest	1%	$45,000
Other	n/a	n/a

CORRESPONDENCE AND INFORMATION

Admissions Office
Rutgers School of Law at Camden
406 Penn Street, Third Floor
Camden, New Jersey 08102
Telephone: 800-466-7561 (toll-free)
Fax: 609-225-6537
E-mail: admissions@camlaw.rutgers.edu
World Wide Web: http://www.camden.rutgers.edu/

RUTGERS, THE STATE UNIVERSITY OF NEW JERSEY, NEWARK
SCHOOL OF LAW

Newark, New Jersey

INFORMATION CONTACT

Anita T. Walton, Director of Admissions
123 Washington Street
Newark, NJ 07102-3094

Phone: 973-353-5557   Fax: 973-353-1445
E-mail: awalton@andromeda.rutgers.edu
Web site: http://law.newark.rutgers.edu/

LAW STUDENT PROFILE [2000–2001]

FULL-TIME   Enrollment: 534
Women: 51%   Men: 49%

PART-TIME   Enrollment: 179
Women: 45%   Men: 55%

RACIAL or ETHNIC COMPOSITION
African American, 15%; Asian/Pacific Islander, 14%;
Hispanic, 12%; Native American, 0.3%; International, 1%

APPLICANTS and ADMITTEES
Number applied: 2,001
Admitted: 721
Percentage accepted: 36%
Seats available: 230
Average LSAT score: 157
Average GPA: 3.2

Rutgers, The State University of New Jersey, Newark School of Law is a public institution that organizes classes on a semester calendar system. The campus is situated in an urban setting. Founded in 1908, first ABA approved in 1941, and an AALS member, Rutgers, The State University of New Jersey, Newark School of Law offers JD, JD/MA, JD/MBA, JD/MCRP, JD/MD, and JD/PhD degrees.

Faculty consists of 44 full-time and 58 part-time members in 2000–2001. 14 full-time faculty members and 19 part-time faculty members are women. 100% of all faculty members have a JD; 3.5% have advanced law degrees. Of all faculty members, 2.5% are Asian/Pacific Islander, 19% are African American, 2.5% are Hispanic, 76% are white.

Application Information *Required:* LSAT, LSDAS, application form, application fee of $50, baccalaureate degree, 1 recommendation, personal statement. *Application deadline* for fall term is March 15. Applications are processed on a rolling basis.

Costs The 1999–2000 tuition was $10,106 full-time for state residents; $418 per credit hour part-time for state residents. Tuition was $14,828 full-time for nonresidents; $617 per credit hour part-time for nonresidents. Fees: $560 per semester full-time; $234 per semester part-time. Part-time tuition and fees vary according to course load and degree level.

AT a GLANCE

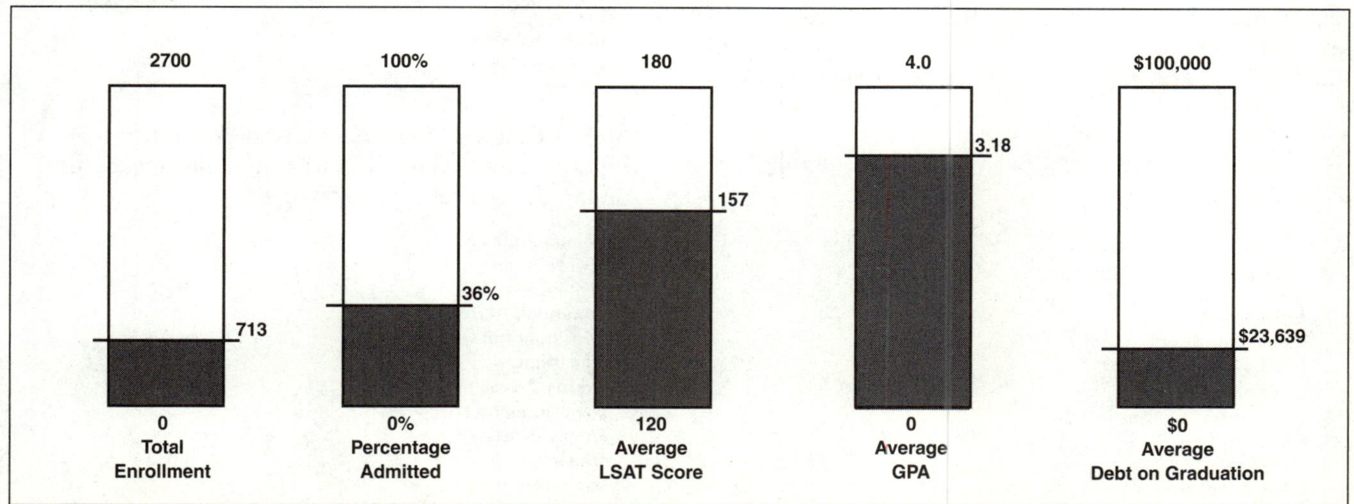

Degree Options

Degree	Total Credits Required	Length of Program
JD–Juris Doctor	84	3–4 yrs, full-time or part-time [day, evening] full-time only [day, evening]
JD/MA–Juris Doctor/Master of Arts–Joint-degree Program Criminal Science		
JD/MA–Juris Doctor/Master of Arts–Joint-degree Program Political Science		full-time only [day, evening]
JD/MBA–Juris Doctor/Master of Business Administration–Joint-degree Program	120	4 yrs, full-time or part-time [day, evening]
JD/MCRP–Juris Doctor/Master of Community and Regional Planning–Joint-degree Program		4 yrs, full-time only [day, evening]
JD/MD–Juris Doctor/Doctor of Medicine–6 Year Program in Law and Medicine		6 yrs, full-time only [day, evening]
JD/PhD–Juris Doctor/Doctor of Philosophy–5 Year Program in Jurisprudence		5 yrs, full-time only [day, evening]

Financial Aid In 2000–2001, 82% of all students received some form of financial aid. 13 fellowships, totaling $3800; 20 research assistantships, totaling $1900; 23 teaching assistantships, totaling $750, were awarded. Fellowships, loan repayment assistance program (LRAP), merit-based grants/scholarships, need-based grants/scholarships, and federal work-study loans are also available. The average student debt at graduation is $23,639. To apply for financial assistance, students must complete the Free Application for Federal Student Aid, institutional forms. Completed financial aid forms should be received by March 1. Financial aid contact: Nancy Fornarotto, Assistant to the Director of Financial Aid, 123 Washington Street, University Heights, Newark, NJ 07102-3192. Phone: 973-353-1702. Fax: 973-353-1717. E-mail: nfornarotto@kinoy.rutgers.edu

Law School Library The Library for the Center for Law and Justice has 8 professional staff members and contains more than 488,100 volumes and 3,500 periodicals. 425 seats are available in the library. When classes are in session, the library is open 107 hours per week.

WESTLAW and LEXIS-NEXIS are available, as is the World Wide Web. 64 computer workstations are available to students in the library. Special law collections include State and Federal Documents Depository.

First-Year Program Class size in the average section is 60; 100% of the first-year courses are taught by full-time faculty.

Upper-Level Program Class size in the average section is 35. Among the electives are:

Administrative Law
Advertising Law
Animal Rights Law
Bankruptcy
★ Business and Corporate Law
Civil Litigation
★ Civil Rights
★ Commercial Law

★ Community Advocacy
Conflict of Laws
★ Constitutional Law
★ Criminal Procedure
Education
Employment Law
Entertainment Law
★ Environmental Law
Evidence
★ Family Law
★ Health Care/Human Services
Immigration
★ Intellectual Property
International/Comparative Law
★ Jurisprudence
Labor Law
Land Use Law/Natural Resources
Lawyering Skills
Legal History/Philosophy
Legislation
Litigation
Media Law
★ Mediation
Probate Law
Property/Real Estate
Public Interest
Race and Law
★ Securities
★ Tax Law
Trusts and Estates
Women's Rights
(★ indicates an area of special strength)

Clinical Courses Students receive degree credit for clinical courses. (Clinical practicum is not required.) Among the clinical areas offered are:

Animal Rights Law
Civil Litigation
Civil Rights
Community Advocacy
Constitutional Law
Education
Elderly Advocacy
Environmental Law
Family Practice
General Practice
Immigration

Litigation
Nonprofit Organizations
Property/Real Estate
Public Interest
Special Education Law
Tax Law
Women's Rights

International exchange programs permit students to visit Netherlands.

SETON HALL UNIVERSITY
SCHOOL OF LAW

Newark, New Jersey

INFORMATION CONTACT

William Perez, Dean for Admissions and Financial Resource Management
1 Newark Center
Newark, NJ 07102-5210

Phone: 973-642-8747   Fax: 973-642-8876
E-mail: admitme@shu.edu
Web site: http://law.shu.edu/

LAW STUDENT PROFILE [2000–2001]

FULL-TIME   Enrollment: 768
Women: 48%   Men: 52%

PART-TIME   Enrollment: 361
Women: 47%   Men: 53%

RACIAL or ETHNIC COMPOSITION
African American, 5%; Asian/Pacific Islander, 5%; Hispanic, 5%; Native American, 0.2%

APPLICANTS and ADMITTEES
Number applied: 2,184
Admitted: 979
Percentage accepted: 45%
Seats available: 381
Average LSAT score: 155
Average GPA: 3.2

Seton Hall University School of Law is a private institution that organizes classes on a semester calendar system. The campus is situated in an urban setting. Founded in 1951, first ABA approved in 1951, and an AALS member, Seton Hall University School of Law offers JD, JD/MA, JD/MBA, LLM, MD/JD, MD/MSJ, and MSJ degrees.

Faculty consists of 46 full-time and 104 part-time members in 2000–2001. 15 full-time faculty members and 26 part-time faculty members are women. 100% of all faculty members have a JD; 23% have advanced law degrees. Of all faculty members, 6% are Asian/Pacific Islander, 10% are African American, 3% are Hispanic, 81% are white.

Application Information *Required:* LSAT, LSDAS, application form, application fee of $50, baccalaureate degree, 2 letters of recommendation, personal statement, writing sample. *Application deadline* for fall term is April 2. Applications are processed on a rolling basis.

Costs The 2000–2001 tuition was $21,700 full-time; $802 per credit part-time. Fees: $190 full-time; $90 per term part-time.

Financial Aid In 2000–2001, 67% of all students received some form of financial aid. 47 research assistantships were awarded. Loans, merit-based grants/scholarships, need-based grants/scholarships, and federal work-study loans are also available. The average student debt at graduation is $66,425. To apply for financial assistance, students must complete the Free Application for Federal Student Aid, institutional forms, signed copy of federal

AT a GLANCE

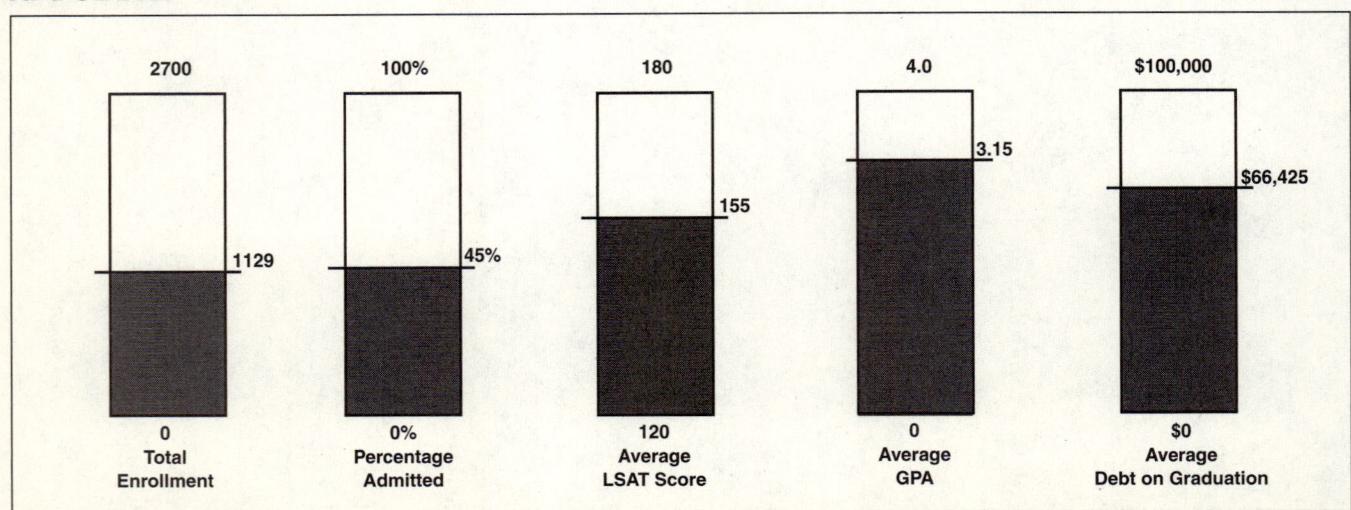

Degree Options

Degree	Total Credits Required	Length of Program
JD–Doctor of Laws	85	3–4 yrs, full-time or part-time [day, evening]
JD/MA–Juris Doctor/Master of Arts–Dual degree in Diplomacy and International Relations	115	4 yrs, full-time only [summer]
JD/MBA–Juris Doctor/Master of Business Administration–Dual-degree Program	110	4 yrs, full-time only [day]
LLM–Master of Laws–Health Law	24	2 yrs
MD/JD–Doctor of Medicine/Juris Doctor–Dual degree		6 yrs
MD/MSJ–Doctor of Medicine/Master of Science in Jurisprudence–Dual degree		5 yrs
MSJ–Master of Science in Journalism–Health Law	30	1–2 yrs

income tax return of student and/or Student Aid Report (SAR). Completed financial aid forms should be received by April 20. Financial aid contact: Sharon Williams, Director of Financial Resource Management, Office of Financial Resource Management, 1 Newark Center, Newark, NJ 07102-5210. Phone: 973-642-8850 ext. 8744 or toll free 888-415-7271. Fax: 973-642-8956. E-mail: williash@shu.edu

Law School Library Peter W. Rodino, Jr. Law Library has 10 professional staff members and contains more than 412,100 volumes and 5,815 periodicals. 600 seats are available in the library. When classes are in session, the library is open 95 hours per week.

WESTLAW and LEXIS-NEXIS are available. 235 computer workstations are available to students in the library. Special law collections include Government (Federal and State) Documents, the Rodino Collection, Rare Book collection.

First-Year Program Class size in the average section is 80; 55% of the first-year courses are taught by full-time faculty.

Upper-Level Program Class size in the average section is 24. Among the electives are:

Accounting
Administrative Law
Advocacy
Bankruptcy
Business and Corporate Law
Civil Litigation
Commercial Law
Consumer Law
Criminal Defense
Criminal Procedure
Entertainment Law
Environmental Law

Family Law
Government/Regulation
Health Care/Human Services
Health Law
Immigration
Insurance Law
★ Intellectual Property
★ International/Comparative Law
Jurisprudence
★ Labor Law
Land Use Law/Natural Resources
Lawyering Skills
Legal History/Philosophy
Litigation
Media Law
Mediation
Probate Law
Public Interest
Securities
Tax Law
(★ *indicates an area of special strength*)

Clinical Courses Students receive degree credit for clinical courses. (Clinical practicum is not required.) Among the clinical areas offered are:

Administrative Law
Appellate Litigation
Bankruptcy
Civil Litigation
Consumer Law
Criminal Defense
Fair Housing
Family Law
Family Practice
General Practice
Health Law
Immigration
Juvenile Law

International exchange programs permit students to visit Egypt and Italy.

UNIVERSITY OF NEW MEXICO
SCHOOL OF LAW

Albuquerque, New Mexico

INFORMATION CONTACT

Susan L. Mitchell, Director of Admissions and
Financial Aid
1117 Stanford NE
Albuquerque, NM 87131-1431

Phone: 505-277-0959   Fax: 505-277-9958
E-mail: mitchell@law.unm.edu
Web site: http://lawschool.unm.edu/

LAW STUDENT PROFILE [2000–2001]

FULL-TIME   Enrollment: 345
Women: 59%   Men: 41%

RACIAL or ETHNIC COMPOSITION
African American, 3%; Asian/Pacific Islander, 3%; Hispanic,
23%; Native American, 6%; International, 1%

APPLICANTS and ADMITTEES
Admitted: 251
Percentage accepted: 35%
Seats available: 105
Average LSAT score: 154
Average GPA: 3.1

University of New Mexico School of Law is a public
institution that organizes classes on a semester calendar
system. The campus is situated in an urban setting.
Founded in 1947, first ABA approved in 1948, and an
AALS member, University of New Mexico School of Law
offers JD, JD/MALAS, JD/MAPA, and JD/MBA degrees.

Faculty consists of 33 full-time and 16 part-time
members in 2000–2001. 14 full-time faculty members
and 7 part-time faculty members are women. 100% of all
faculty members have a JD; 17% have advanced law
degrees. Of all faculty members, 6% are Native American, 6% are African American, 17% are Hispanic, 71%
are white.

Application Information *Required:* LSAT, LSDAS,
application form, application fee of $40, baccalaureate
degree, 1 recommendation, personal statement. *Application deadline* for fall term is February 15 (priority date).
Applications are processed on a rolling basis.

Financial Aid Fellowships, loans, merit-based grants/
scholarships, need-based grants/scholarships, and federal
work-study loans are available. To apply for financial
assistance, students must complete the Free Application
for Federal Student Aid, Access application for grant aid
only.. Completed financial aid forms should be received
by March 1. Financial aid contact: Susan Mitchell,
University of New Mexico, 1117 Stanford Drive N.E.,
Albuquerque, NM 87131-1431. Phone: 505-277-0959.
Fax: 505-277-9958. E-mail: mitchell@law.unm.edu

Law School Library UNM Law Library has 4 professional staff members and contains more than 399,579

AT a GLANCE

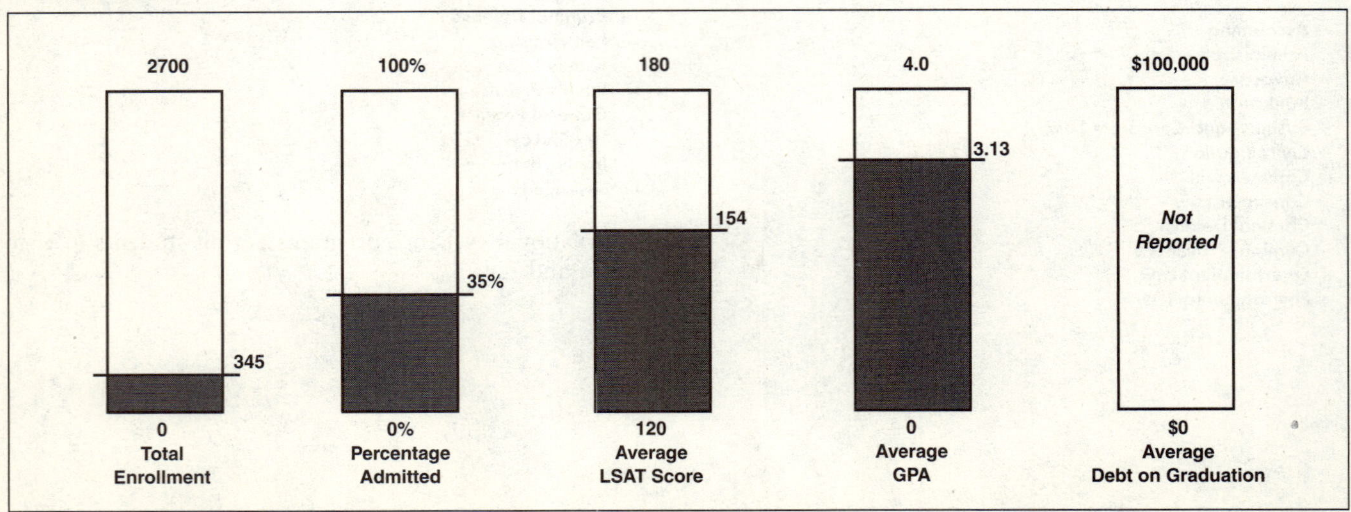

Degree Options

Degree	Total Credits Required	Length of Program
JD–Juris Doctor	86	3–4.5 yrs, full-time only [day]
JD/MALAS–Juris Doctor/Master of Arts in Latin American Studies	107	4 yrs
JD/MAPA–Juris Doctor/Master of Arts in Public Administration		4 yrs
JD/MBA–Juris Doctor/Master of Business Administration		4 yrs

volumes and 3,262 periodicals. 371 seats are available in the library. When classes are in session, the library is open 103 hours per week.

WESTLAW and LEXIS-NEXIS are available, as is the World Wide Web. 32 computer workstations are available to students in the library. Special law collections include New Mexico Appellate Briefs and Records, American Indian Law, Land Grants, Natural Resources Law, Mexican and Latin American Law.

First-Year Program 100% of the first-year courses are taught by full-time faculty.

Upper-Level Program Among the electives are:

   Client Representation
 ★ Community Advocacy
 ★ District Attorney Clinic
 ★ Environmental Law

 ★ General Practice
 ★ Health Care/Human Services
 ★ Indian/Tribal Law
(★ *indicates an area of special strength*)

Clinical Courses Students receive degree credit for clinical courses. 6 credit hours of clinical practicum are required. Among the clinical areas offered are:

   Client Representation
   Community Advocacy
   Criminal Prosecution
   District Attorney Clinic
   General Practice
   Indian/Tribal Law

International exchange programs permit students to visit Australia, Canada, and Mexico.

ALBANY LAW SCHOOL OF UNION UNIVERSITY

Albany, New York

INFORMATION CONTACT

Dawn M. Chamberlaine, Assistant Dean of
Admissions and Financial Aid
80 New Scotland Avenue
Albany, NY 12208-3494

Phone: 518-445-2326   Fax: 518-445-2369
E-mail: admissions@mail.als.edu
Web site: http://www.als.edu/

LAW STUDENT PROFILE [2000–2001]

FULL-TIME Enrollment: 691
Women: 51%   Men: 49%

PART-TIME Enrollment: 53
Women: 57%   Men: 43%

APPLICANTS and ADMITTEES

Number applied: 1,543
Admitted: 943
Percentage accepted: 61%
Seats available: 250
Average LSAT score: 150
Average GPA: 3.2

Albany Law School of Union University is a private nonprofit institution that organizes classes on a semester calendar system. The campus is situated in an urban setting. Founded in 1851, first ABA approved in 1930, and an AALS member, Albany Law School of Union University offers JD, JD/MBA, JD/MPAd, JD/MRP, JD/MSW, and MLS degrees.

Faculty 100% of all faculty members have a JD; 24% have advanced law degrees. Of all faculty members, 2% are Asian/Pacific Islander, 6% are African American, 92% are white.

Application Information *Required:* LSAT, LSDAS, application form, application fee of $50, baccalaureate degree, 2 letters of recommendation. *Recommended:* personal statement, resume.

Costs The 2000–2001 tuition was $21,495 full-time; $16,121 per year part-time. Fees: $130 full-time; $130 per year part-time.

Financial Aid Fellowships, loans, merit-based grants/scholarships, need-based grants/scholarships, and federal work-study loans are available. The average student debt at graduation is $67,000. To apply for financial assistance, students must complete the Free Application for Federal Student Aid, institutional forms, federal income tax return. Financial aid contact: Dawn M. Chamberlaine, Assistant Dean Admissions and Financial Aid, 80 New Scotland Avenue, Albany, NY 12208. Phone: 518-445-2357. Fax: 518-445-2369. E-mail: finaid@mail.als.edu

AT a GLANCE

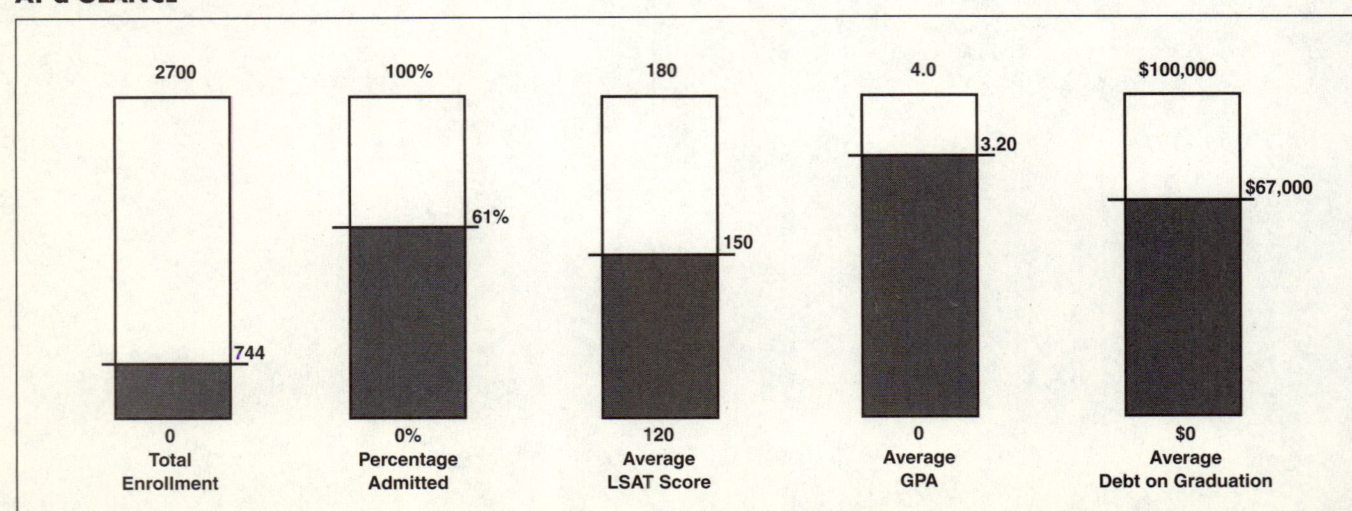

Degree Options

Degree	Total Credits Required	Length of Program
JD–Doctor of Laws	87	3–4.5 yrs, full-time or part-time [day, summer]
JD/MBA–Juris Doctor/Master of Business Administration–Joint-degree		3.5–4.5 yrs, full-time or part-time [day, summer]
JD/MPAd–Juris Doctor/Master of Public Administration–Joint-degree		3.5–4.5 yrs, full-time or part-time [day, summer]
JD/MRP–Juris Doctor/Master of Regional Planning–Joint-degree Program		3.5–4.5 yrs, full-time or part-time [day, summer]
JD/MSW–Juris Doctor/Master of Social Work–Joint-degree Program		3.5–4.5 yrs, full-time or part-time [day, summer]
MLS–Master of Library Science	30	1–4 yrs, full-time or part-time [summer]

Law School Library Schaffer Law Library has 7 professional staff members and contains more than 591,782 volumes and 1,493 periodicals. 482 seats are available in the library. When classes are in session, the library is open 104 hours per week.

WESTLAW and LEXIS-NEXIS are available, as are the World Wide Web, online bibliographic services, and CD-ROM players. 37 computer workstations are available to students in the library. Special law collections include videotapes of New York Court of Appeals oral arguments.

First-Year Program Class size in the average section is 80; 100% of the first-year courses are taught by full-time faculty.

Upper-Level Program Class size in the average section is 40. Among the electives are:

   Administrative Law
★ Advocacy
★ Business and Corporate Law
★ Civil Litigation
   Civil Rights
   Constitutional Law
   Consumer Law
   Criminal Law
★ Domestic Violence
   Education Law
★ Environmental Law
   Estate Planning
★ Family Law
★ General Practice

★ Government/Regulation
★ Health Care/Human Services
★ Intellectual Property
★ International/Comparative Law
   Jurisprudence
★ Labor Law
   Land Use Law/Natural Resources
★ Lawyering Skills
   Legal History/Philosophy
★ Litigation
★ Mediation
★ Probate Law
   Public Interest
   Securities
★ Tax Law

(★ *indicates an area of special strength*)

Clinical Courses Students receive degree credit for clinical courses. (Clinical practicum is not required.) Among the clinical areas offered are:

   Administrative Law
   Advocacy
   Civil Litigation
   Domestic Violence
   Education
   Family Law
   Family Practice
   General Practice
   Government Litigation
   Health Care/Human Services
   Health Law
   Intellectual Property
   Litigation
   Mediation
   Public Interest

BROOKLYN LAW SCHOOL

Brooklyn, New York

INFORMATION CONTACT

Henry W. Haverstick III, Dean of Admissions and Financial Aid
250 Joralemon Street
Brooklyn, NY 11201-3798

Phone: 718-780-7906   Fax: 718-780-0395
E-mail: admitq@brooklaw.edu
Web site: http://www.brooklaw.edu/

LAW STUDENT PROFILE [2000–2001]

FULL-TIME Enrollment: 1,027
Women: 51% Men: 49%

PART-TIME Enrollment: 475
Women: 48% Men: 52%

APPLICANTS and ADMITTEES

Number applied: 2,802
Admitted: 1,376
Percentage accepted: 53%
Seats available: 290
Median LSAT score: 158
Average GPA: 3.4

Brooklyn Law School is a private nonprofit institution that organizes classes on a semester calendar system. The campus is situated in an urban setting. Founded in 1901, first ABA approved in 1937, and an AALS member, Brooklyn Law School offers JD, JD/MA, JD/MBA, JD/MPAd, JD/MS, and JD/MUP degrees.

Faculty 100% of all faculty members have a JD; 10% have advanced law degrees. Of all faculty members, 4% are Asian/Pacific Islander, 3% are African American, 3% are Hispanic, 90% are white.

Application Information *Required:* LSAT, LSDAS, application form, application fee of $60, baccalaureate degree, personal statement, college transcripts. *Recommended:* recommendations, essay, writing sample, resume.

Costs The 2000–2001 tuition was $26,745 full-time.

Financial Aid Fellowships, graduate assistantships, loans, loan repayment assistance program (LRAP), merit-based grants/scholarships, need-based grants/scholarships, and federal work-study loans are available. The average student debt at graduation is $65,530. To apply for financial assistance, students must complete the Free Application for Federal Student Aid, institutional forms, Need Access diskette. Financial aid contact: Gerard N. Anderson, Director of Financial Aid, Brooklyn Law School, 250 Joralemon Street, Brooklyn, NY 11201. Phone: 718-780-7915. Fax: 718-780-0391. E-mail: ganders@brooklaw.edu

Law School Library Brooklyn Law School Library has 11 professional staff members and contains more than

AT a GLANCE

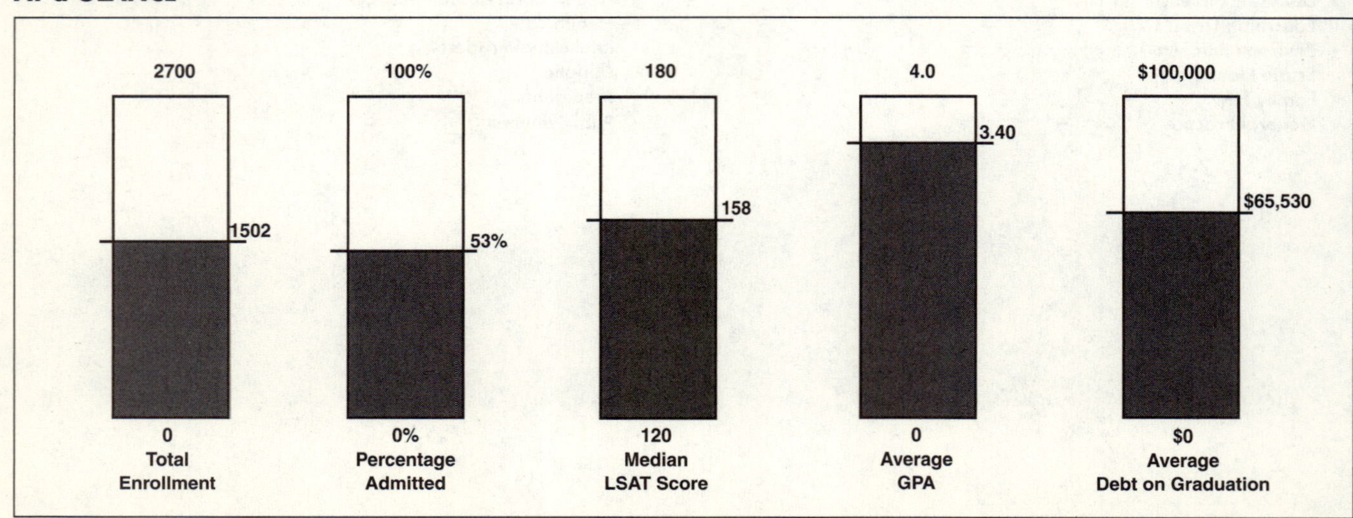

Degree Options

Degree	Total Credits Required	Length of Program
JD–Doctor of Laws	86	3–4 yrs, full-time or part-time [day, evening, summer]
JD/MA–Juris Doctor/Master of Arts–JD/MA in Political Science	119	4–5 yrs, full-time or part-time [day, evening, summer]
JD/MBA–Juris Doctor/Master of Business Administration–Dual-degree Program	122	4–5 yrs, full-time or part-time [day, evening, summer]
JD/MPAd–Juris Doctor/Master of Public Administration–Dual-degree Program	110	4–5 yrs, full-time or part-time [day, evening, summer]
JD/MS–Juris Doctor/Master of Science–City Regional Planning Dual-degree Program	125	4–5 yrs, full-time or part-time [day, evening, summer]
JD/MS–Juris Doctor/Master of Science–Library Science Dual-degree Program	104	4–5 yrs, full-time or part-time [day, evening, summer]
JD/MUP–Juris Doctor/Masters of Urban Planning–Dual-degree Program	121	4–5 yrs, full-time or part-time [day, evening, summer]

500,000 volumes and 1,000 periodicals. 665 seats are available in the library. When classes are in session, the library is open 108 hours per week.

WESTLAW and LEXIS-NEXIS are available, as are the World Wide Web, online bibliographic services, and CD-ROM players. 83 computer workstations are available to students in the library. Special law collections include International Law; Women & the Law.

First-Year Program Class size in the average section is 97; 100% of the first-year courses are taught by full-time faculty.

Upper-Level Program Class size in the average section is 33. Among the electives are:

Administrative Law
★ Advocacy
★ Business and Corporate Law
★ Civil Litigation
★ Consumer Law
★ Criminal Defense
★ Criminal Prosecution
Elderly Advocacy
Entertainment Law
Environmental Law
Family Law
General Practice
Government Litigation
★ Government/Regulation
Health Care/Human Services
Immigration
★ Intellectual Property
★ International/Comparative Law
Jurisprudence
Juvenile Law
Labor Law

Land Use Law/Natural Resources
★ Lawyering Skills
Legal History/Philosophy
★ Litigation
Maritime Law
Media Law
★ Mediation
Probate Law
★ Public Interest
Securities
Tax Law

(★ *indicates an area of special strength*)

Clinical Courses Students receive degree credit for clinical courses. (Clinical practicum is not required.) Among the clinical areas offered are:

Administrative Law
Advocacy
Business and Corporate Law
Civil Litigation
Consumer Law
Criminal Defense
Criminal Prosecution
Elderly Advocacy
Entertainment Law
Environmental Law
Family Law
General Practice
Government Litigation
Government/Regulation
Immigration
Intellectual Property
Juvenile Law
Lawyering Skills
Mediation
Probate Law
Public Interest
Securities

CITY UNIVERSITY OF NEW YORK SCHOOL OF LAW AT QUEENS COLLEGE

Flushing, New York

INFORMATION CONTACT

William D. Perez, Director of Admissions
65-21 Main Street
Flushing, NY 11367-1358

Phone: 718-340-4210   Fax: 718-340-4372
E-mail: perez@mail.law.cuny.edu
Web site: http://www.law.cuny.edu/

LAW STUDENT PROFILE [2000–2001]

FULL-TIME   Enrollment: 389
Women: 59%   Men: 41%

PART-TIME   Enrollment: 3
Women: 33%   Men: 67%

APPLICANTS and ADMITTEES

Number applied: 1,411
Admitted: 547
Percentage accepted: 39%
Seats available: 160

City University of New York School of Law at Queens College is a public institution that organizes classes on a semester calendar system. The campus is situated in an urban setting. Founded in 1983, first ABA approved in 1985, City University of New York School of Law at Queens College offers a JD degree.

Faculty 100% of all faculty members have a JD; 20% have advanced law degrees. Of all faculty members, 12% are Asian/Pacific Islander, 10% are African American, 14% are Hispanic, 64% are white.

Application Information *Required:* LSAT, LSDAS, application form, application fee of $40, baccalaureate degree, 2 letters of recommendation, personal statement, resume.

Costs The 1999–2000 tuition was $5700 full-time for state residents. Tuition was $8930 full-time for nonresidents. Fees: $1052 full-time.

Financial Aid Loans, loan repayment assistance program (LRAP), need-based grants/scholarships, and federal work-study loans are available. The average student debt at graduation is $39,000. To apply for financial assistance, students must complete the Free Application for Federal Student Aid, institutional forms. Financial aid contact: Angela M. Joseph, Director of Financial Aid, 65-21 Main Street, Flushing, NY 11367. Phone: 718-340-4284. Fax: 718-340-4218. E-mail: joseph@mail.law.cuny.edu

Law School Library City University of New York School of Law Library has 9 professional staff members and

AT a GLANCE

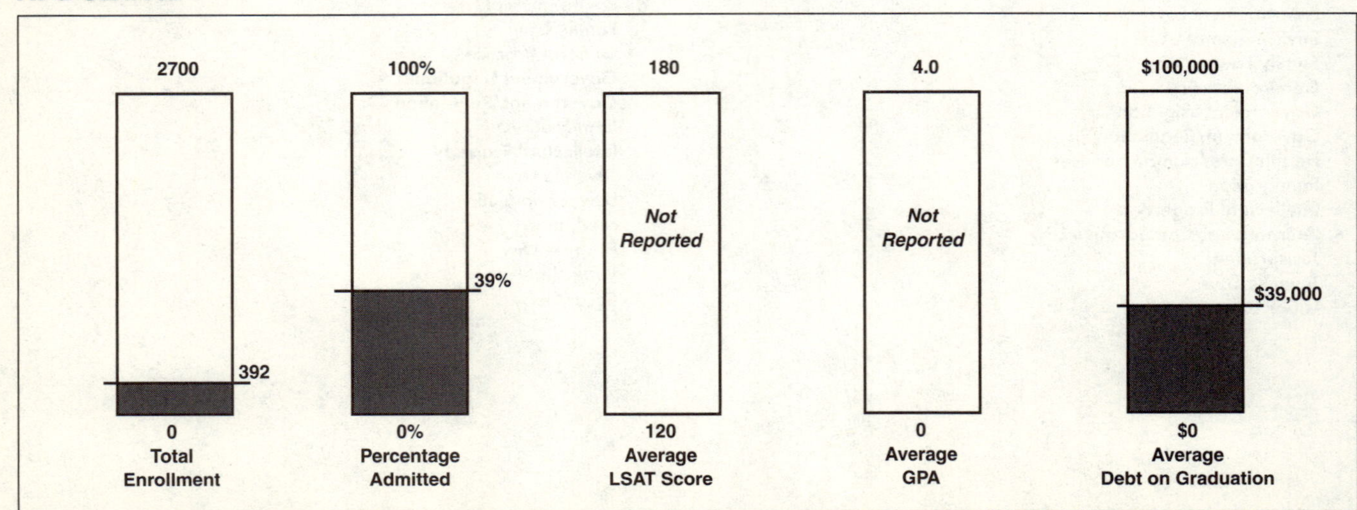

<table>
<tr><td colspan="3">Degree Options</td></tr>
<tr><td>Degree</td><td>Total Credits
Required</td><td>Length of Program</td></tr>
<tr><td>JD–Juris Doctor</td><td>91</td><td>3 yrs, full-time only [day]</td></tr>
</table>

contains more than 250,000 volumes and 2,619 periodicals. 397 seats are available in the library. When classes are in session, the library is open 119 hours per week.

WESTLAW and LEXIS-NEXIS are available, as are the World Wide Web, online bibliographic services, and CD-ROM players. 65 computer workstations are available to students in the library.

First-Year Program Class size in the average section is 40; 100% of the first-year courses are taught by full-time faculty.

Upper-Level Program Class size in the average section is 40. Among the electives are:

Advocacy
★ Battered Women
Business and Corporate Law
★ Criminal Defense
★ Elderly Advocacy
Entertainment Law
Environmental Law
★ Family Law
First Amendment
★ Government/Regulation
★ Health Care/Human Services
★ Human Rights
★ Immigration

Intellectual Property
International Law
★ International/Comparative Law
Jurisprudence
Juvenile Law
★ Labor Law
★ Lawyering Skills
Legal History/Philosophy
Litigation
★ Mediation
Probate Law
Property/Real Estate
Securities
Tax Law
(★ *indicates an area of special strength*)

Clinical Courses Students receive degree credit for clinical courses. 12 credit hours of clinical practicum are required. Among the clinical areas offered are:

Battered Women
Criminal Defense
Elderly Advocacy
Human Rights
Immigration
International Law
Mediation

COLUMBIA UNIVERSITY
SCHOOL OF LAW

New York, New York

LAW STUDENT PROFILE [2000–2001]

FULL-TIME   Enrollment: 1,129
Women: 48%   Men: 52%

RACIAL or ETHNIC COMPOSITION
African American, 10%; Asian/Pacific Islander, 15%;
Hispanic, 7%; Native American, 1%; International, 6%

APPLICANTS and ADMITTEES
Number applied: 6,743
Seats available: 367
Median LSAT score: 169
Average GPA: 3.6

Columbia University School of Law is a private
institution that organizes classes on a semester calendar
system. The campus is situated in an urban setting.
Founded in 1858, first ABA approved in 1923, and an
AALS member, Columbia University School of Law
offers JD, JD/MA, JD/MBA, JD/MPA, JD/MS, JD/PhD,
and LLM degrees.

Faculty consists of 87 full-time and 49 part-time
members in 2000–2001. 20 full-time faculty members
and 7 part-time faculty members are women. 99% of all
faculty members have a JD; 19% have advanced law
degrees.

Application Information *Required:* LSAT, LSDAS,
application form, application fee of $65, 2 letters of
recommendation, personal statement, writing sample,
college transcripts, baccalaureate degree. *Recommended:*
resume. *Application deadline* for fall term is February 15.
Applications are processed on a rolling basis.

Costs The 2000–2001 tuition was $29,396 full-time. Fees:
$666 full-time; $45 full-time (one-time charge for
full-time students).

Financial Aid In 2000–2001, 49% of all students received
some form of financial aid. 70 research assistantships
were awarded. Loans, loan repayment assistance program
(LRAP), merit-based grants/scholarships, need-based
grants/scholarships, and federal work-study loans are also
available. The average student debt at graduation is
$83,000. To apply for financial assistance, students must
complete the Free Application for Federal Student Aid,
institutional forms, Need Access application. Completed

AT a GLANCE

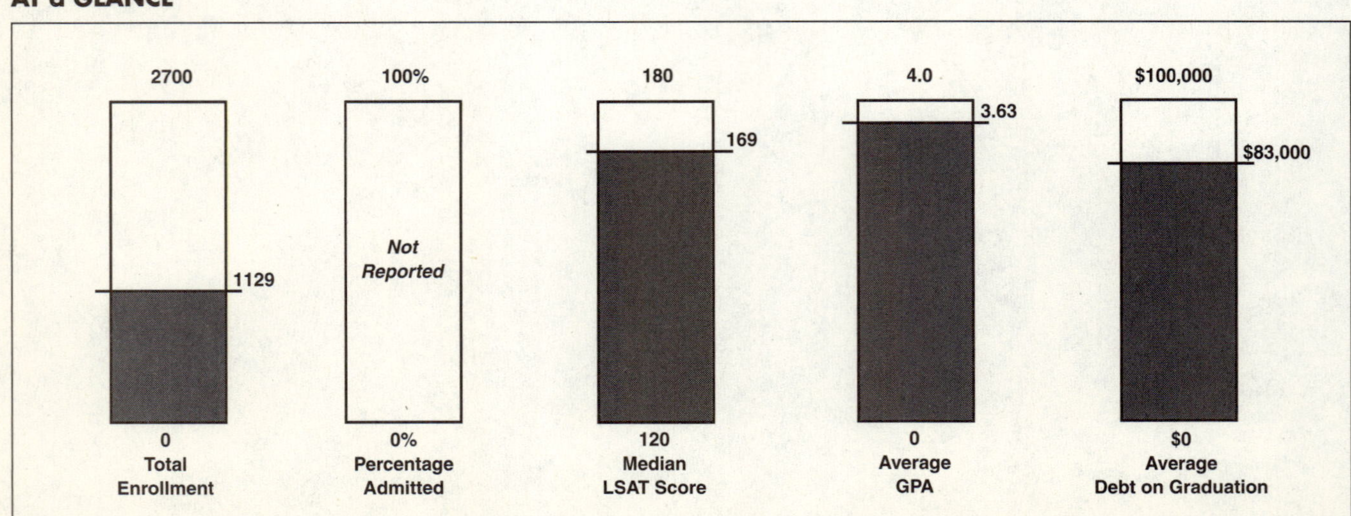

Degree Options

Degree	Total Credits Required	Length of Program
JD–Juris Doctor	83	3 yrs, full-time only [day]
JD/MA–Juris Doctor/Master of Arts–Anthropology, Economics, History, Policy Science, Psychology, or Sociology Joint-degree		4 yrs, full-time only [day]
JD/MBA–Juris Doctor/Master of Business Administration–Joint-degree		3–4 yrs, full-time only [day]
JD/MPA–Juris Doctor/Master of Professional Accountancy–Joint-degree Public Administration with Woodrow Wilson School at Princeton University		4 yrs, full-time only [day]
JD/MPA–Juris Doctor/Master of Professional Accountancy–Joint-degree with Columbia School of International and Public Affairs		4 yrs, full-time only [day]
JD/MS–Juris Doctor/Master of Science–Joint-degree Journalism		3.5 yrs, full-time only [day]
JD/MS–Juris Doctor/Master of Science–Joint-degree Social Work		4 yrs, full-time only [day]
JD/MS–Juris Doctor/Master of Science–Joint-degree Urban Planning		4 yrs, full-time only [day]
JD/PhD–Juris Doctor/Doctor of Philosophy–Anthropology, Economics, History, Political Science, Psychology, Sociology Joint-degree Program and all other doctoral granting divisions of Columbia University.		7 yrs, full-time only
LLM–Master of Laws	24	1 yr, full-time only [day]

financial aid forms should be received by March 1. Financial aid contact: Director of Admissions, Columbia Law School, 435 West 116th Street, New York, NY 10027. Phone: 212-854-7730. Fax: 212-854-7445. E-mail: financial_aid@law.columbia.edu

Law School Library Arthur W. Diamond Law Library has 17 professional staff members and contains more than 1 million volumes and 7,055 periodicals. 417 seats are available in the library. When classes are in session, the library is open 102 hours per week.

WESTLAW and LEXIS-NEXIS are available, as are the World Wide Web, online bibliographic services, and CD-ROM players. 90 computer workstations are available to students in the library. Special law collections include foreign law, Roman law, Nuremberg Trial papers (including a gift from Telford Taylor)' South African Treason Trial papers.

First-Year Program 100% of the first-year courses are taught by full-time faculty.

Upper-Level Program Class size in the average section is 50. Among the electives are:

Accounting
Administrative Law
Admiralty Law
★ Alternative Dispute Resolution
American Legal History
Antitrust Law
Bankruptcy
Bioethics
★ Business and Corporate Law
Campaign Finance Law
★ Capital Markets Regulation
Capital Punishment
Child Abuse
Children and the Law
Children's Advocacy
Chinese Law
Church-State
★ Civil Procedure
★ Civil Rights
★ Commercial Law
Commercial Transactions
Common Law
Complex Litigation
Conflict of Laws
Constitution & Foreign Affairs
Constitution & the Economy
★ Constitutional Law
★ Constitutional Rights
Consumer Law
Contract Theory
★ Copyright & Trademark Law
Corporate Finance
Corporate Governance
Corporate Restructuring
Corporate Taxation
★ Corporations
Creditor's Rights
Criminal Adjudication
Criminal Investigation
★ Criminal Law

Criminal Law Theory
Criminology and Penology
Debtor Law
★ Democratic Theory
★ Education Law
Election Law
Employment Discrimination
★ Employment Law
English Legal History
★ Entertainment Law
★ Environmental Law
★ European Community Law
Evidence
★ Family Law
Federal Courts
Federal Income Tax
★ Feminist Jurisprudence
Fifth Amendment
★ First Amendment
Food & Drug Law
Foreign Investment Law
Fourth Amendment
★ Government/Regulation
★ Health Care/Human Services
★ Human Rights
Immigration
Indian/Tribal Law
Insurance Law
★ Intellectual Property
International Business Transactions
International Commercial Contracts
International Criminal Law
★ International Environmental Law
International Income Tax
International Law
International Organizations
★ International Trade
★ International/Comparative Law
★ Internet Law
Islamic Law
Japanese Law
Jewish Law
Jurisdiction
★ Jurisprudence
★ Labor Law
Land Use Law/Natural Resources
Latin American Law
Law and Anthropology
★ Law and Economics
Law and Literature
Law and Philosophy
★ Law and Social Science
★ Law and the Arts
Lawyering Skills
★ Legal History/Philosophy
Legal Interpretation

Legal Methods
★ Legal Research
Legal Writing
★ Legislation
★ Litigation
Maritime Law
Media Law
★ Mediation
Mental Health and Law
Mergers & Acquisitions
★ Negotiation
Nonprofit Organizations
Organized Crime
Patent Law
Policing
Poverty/Welfare Law
Prisoners' Rights
Probate Law
Product Liability
★ Professional Responsibility
★ Property/Real Estate
★ Public Interest
Real Estate Transactions
Sales
Secured Transactions
★ Securities
Separation of Powers
Sixth Amendment
Sports Law
Supreme Court
★ Tax Law
Taxation of Financial Instruments
Telecommunications Law
Trade Regulation
★ Trusts and Estates
(★ *indicates an area of special strength*)

Clinical Courses Students receive degree credit for clinical courses. (Clinical practicum is not required.) Among the clinical areas offered are:

Children's Advocacy
Environmental Law
Human Rights
Intellectual Property
Law and the Arts
Mediation
Nonprofit Organizations
Prisoners' Rights

International exchange programs permit students to visit Argentina, France, Germany, Hungary, Israel, Italy, Japan, Netherlands, Singapore, South Africa, and United Kingdom.

CORNELL UNIVERSITY
LAW SCHOOL

Ithaca, New York

LAW STUDENT PROFILE [2000–2001]

FULL-TIME   Enrollment: 552
Women: 48%   Men: 52%

APPLICANTS and ADMITTEES

Number applied: 3,520
Admitted: 774
Percentage accepted: 22%
Seats available: 184
Average LSAT score: 165
Average GPA: 3.6

Cornell University Law School is a private institution that organizes classes on a semester calendar system. The campus is situated in a small-town setting. Founded in 1887, first ABA approved in 1923, and an AALS member, Cornell University Law School offers JD, JD/LLM, JD/MA, JD/MBA, JD/MCRP, JD/MILR, JD/MPAd, JD/Maitrise en Driot, JD/PhD, and LLM degrees.

Faculty consists of 38 full-time and 15 part-time members in 2000–2001. 13 full-time faculty members and 3 part-time faculty members are women. 98.2% of all faculty members have a JD; 8.8% have advanced law degrees. Of all faculty members, 7.9% are African American, 87.5% are white, 2.6% are international.

Application Information *Required:* LSAT, LSDAS, application form, application fee of $65, baccalaureate degree, 2 letters of recommendation, personal statement, college transcripts. *Recommended:* resume. *Application deadline* for fall term is February 1.

Costs The 2000–2001 tuition was $27,350 full-time. Fees: $25 per semester full-time.

Financial Aid In 2000–2001, 49% of all students received some form of financial aid. Fellowships, loans, loan repayment assistance program (LRAP), merit-based grants/scholarships, need-based grants/scholarships, and federal work-study loans are available. To apply for financial assistance, students must complete the Free Application for Federal Student Aid, Need Access diskette. Completed financial aid forms should be received by March 15. Financial aid contact: Jane Deathe,

AT a GLANCE

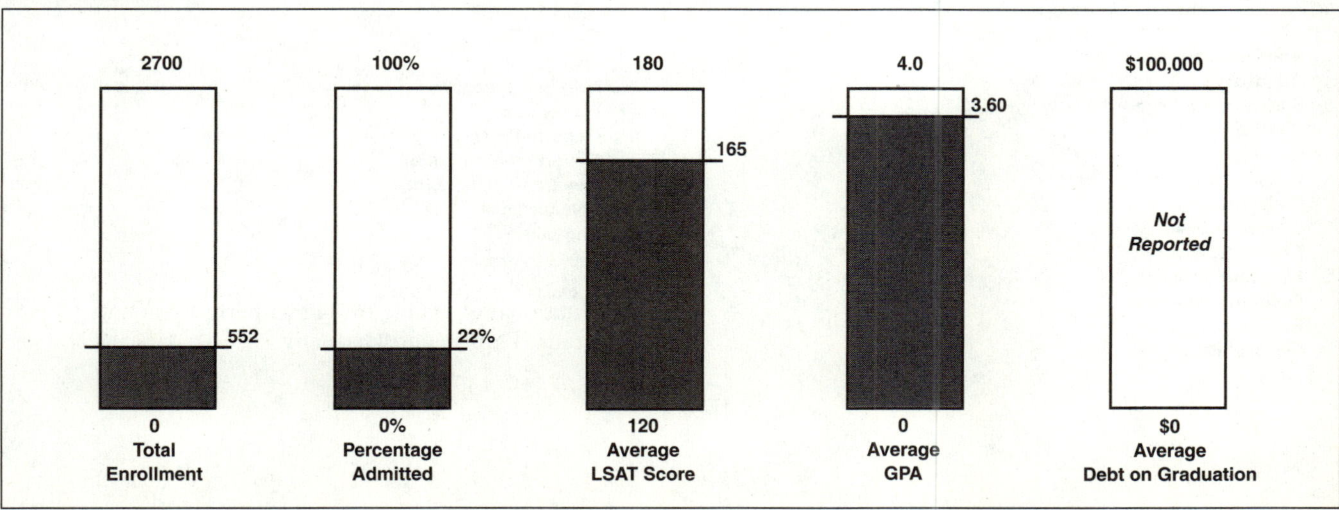

Degree Options

Degree	Total Credits Required	Length of Program
JD–Juris Doctor	84	3 yrs, full-time only
JD/LLM–Juris Doctor/Master of Laws–International Legal Studies	104	3 yrs, full-time only [day]
JD/MA–Juris Doctor/Master of Arts		4 yrs, full-time only [day]
JD/MBA–Juris Doctor/Master of Business Administration–JD/MBA Dual Degree program	110	4–5 yrs, full-time only
JD/MCRP–Juris Doctor/Master of Community and Regional Planning		4 yrs, full-time only [day]
JD/MILR–Juris Doctor/Master of Industrial and Labor Relations		4 yrs, full-time only [day]
JD/MPAd–Juris Doctor/Master of Public Administration		4 yrs, full-time only [day]
JD/Maitrise en Driot–Juris Doctor–American and French Law Degrees		4 yrs, full-time only [day]
JD/PhD–Juris Doctor/Doctor of Philosophy–Philosophy		7 yrs, full-time only [day]
LLM–Master of Laws		1–2 yrs, full-time only [day]

Director of Financial Aid, 240A Myron Taylor Hall, Ithaca, NY 14853. Phone: 607-255-5141. Fax: 607-255-7193. E-mail: jgd4@cornell.edu

Law School Library Cornell Law Library has 7 professional staff members and contains more than 632,922 volumes and 6,349 periodicals. 408 seats are available in the library. When classes are in session, the library is open 85 hours per week.

WESTLAW and LEXIS-NEXIS are available, as are the World Wide Web, online bibliographic services, and CD-ROM players. 59 computer workstations are available to students in the library. Special law collections include Bennett Collection, trials collection, foreign law collection, rare books.

First-Year Program Class size in the average section is 90; 100% of the first-year courses are taught by full-time faculty.

Upper-Level Program Class size in the average section is 50. Among the electives are:

Administrative Law
★ Advocacy
★ Business and Corporate Law
Civil Litigation
Civil Rights
Constitutional Law
Consumer Law
Education Law
Elderly Advocacy
Entertainment Law
Environmental Law
Family Law
★ General Practice
Government Litigation
Government/Regulation
Health Care/Human Services
Indian/Tribal Law
Intellectual Property
International/Comparative Law
Jurisprudence
Juvenile Law
Labor Law
Lawyering Skills
Legal History/Philosophy
Litigation
Media Law
Mediation
Probate Law
Public Interest
Securities
Tax Law

(★ *indicates an area of special strength*)

Clinical Courses Students receive degree credit for clinical courses. (Clinical practicum is not required.) Among the clinical areas offered are:

Administrative Law
Advocacy
Civil Litigation
Civil Rights
Elderly Advocacy
Family Law
General Practice
Government Litigation
Government/Regulation
Juvenile Law
Litigation
Public Interest

International exchange programs permit students to visit Australia, France, and Germany.

FORDHAM UNIVERSITY
SCHOOL OF LAW

New York, New York

LAW STUDENT PROFILE [2000–2001]

FULL-TIME   Enrollment: 1,173
Women: 50%   Men: 50%

PART-TIME   Enrollment: 360
Women: 44%   Men: 56%

RACIAL or ETHNIC COMPOSITION
African American, 8%; Asian/Pacific Islander, 9%; Hispanic, 8%; Native American, 0.1%

APPLICANTS and ADMITTEES
Number applied: 5,237
Admitted: 1,570
Percentage accepted: 30%
Seats available: 463
Average LSAT score: 164
Average GPA: 3.4

Fordham University School of Law is a private institution that organizes classes on a semester calendar system. The campus is situated in an urban setting. Founded in 1905, first ABA approved in 1936, and an AALS member, Fordham University School of Law offers JD, JD/MA, JD/MBA, JD/MSW, and LL M degrees.

Faculty consists of 66 full-time and 112 part-time members in 2000–2001. 21 full-time faculty members and 32 part-time faculty members are women. 100% of all faculty members have a JD; 35% have advanced law degrees. Of all faculty members, 1% are Asian/Pacific Islander, 8% are African American, 1% are Hispanic, 90% are white.

Application Information *Required:* LSAT, LSDAS, application form, application fee of $60, baccalaureate degree, personal statement, essay, college transcripts. *Application deadline* for fall term is March 1. Applications are processed on a rolling basis.

Costs The 1999–2000 tuition was $25,075 full-time. Full-time tuition and fees vary according to class time.

Financial Aid In 2000–2001, 33% of all students received some form of financial aid. Loans, loan repayment assistance program (LRAP), merit-based grants/scholarships, and need-based grants/scholarships are available. The average student debt at graduation is $71,200. To apply for financial assistance, students must complete the Free Application for Federal Student Aid, CSS PROFILE form. Completed financial aid forms should be received by February 28. Financial aid contact: Financial Aid

AT a GLANCE

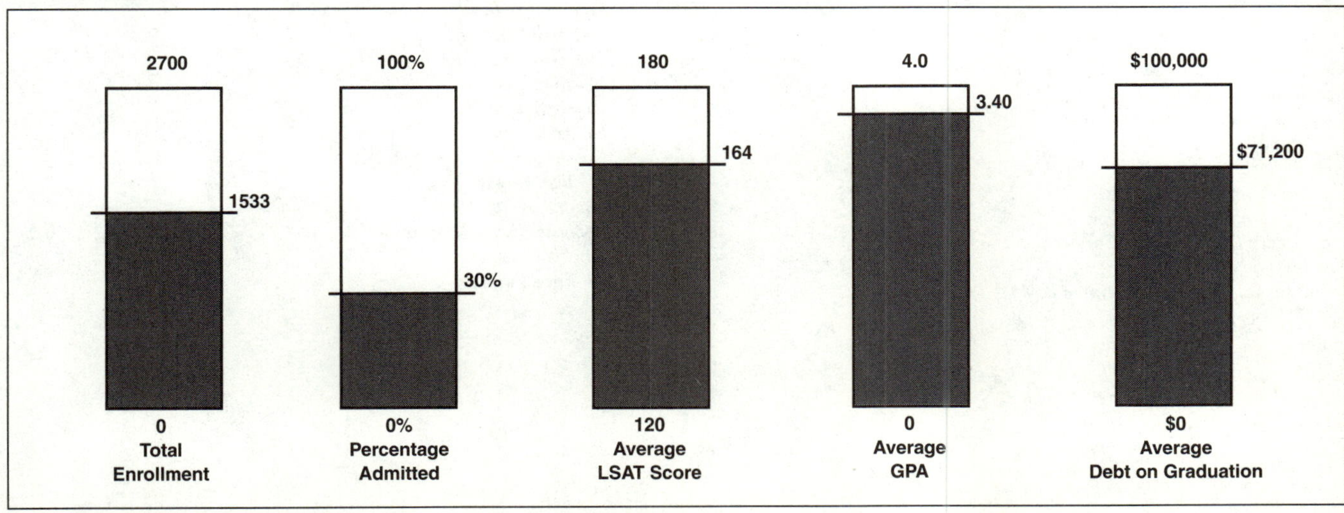

Degree Options

Degree	Total Credits Required	Length of Program
JD–Doctor of Laws	83	3–4 yrs, full-time or part-time [day, evening]
JD/MA–Juris Doctor/Master of Arts–Joint-program	94	3.5–5 yrs, full-time or part-time [day, evening]
JD/MBA–Juris Doctor/Master of Business Administration–Joint Program	115	3.5–6.5 yrs, full-time or part-time [day, evening]
JD/MSW–Juris Doctor/Master of Social Work–Joint Program	133	4–5 yrs, full-time or part-time [day, evening]
LL M–Master of Laws–Masters in Banking, Corporate, and Finance	24	1–3 yrs, full-time or part-time [day]
LL M–Master of Laws–International Business and Trade Law	24	1–3 yrs, full-time or part-time [day]

Office, Fordham Law School, 140 West 62 Street, New York, NY 10023. Phone: 212-636-6815. Fax: 212-636-6899.

Law School Library Leo T. Kissam Memorial Library has 17 professional staff members and contains more than 560,877 volumes and 6,212 periodicals. 473 seats are available in the library. When classes are in session, the library is open 122 hours per week.

WESTLAW and LEXIS-NEXIS are available, as are the World Wide Web, online bibliographic services, and CD-ROM players. 192 computer workstations are available to students in the library. Special law collections include European Community Law.

First-Year Program Class size in the average section is 74; 97% of the first-year courses are taught by full-time faculty.

Upper-Level Program Class size in the average section is 40. Among the electives are:

Advocacy
★ Business and Corporate Law
★ Civil Litigation
★ Civil Rights
Consumer Law
★ Criminal Defense
Criminal Prosecution
Education Law
Entertainment Law
Environmental Law
★ European Community Law
Family Law
General Practice
Government Litigation
Government/Regulation
Health Care/Human Services
★ Intellectual Property
International/Comparative Law
Jurisprudence
Juvenile Law
Labor Law
Land Use Law/Natural Resources
★ Lawyering Skills
Legal History/Philosophy
Litigation
Maritime Law
Media Law
★ Mediation
Probate Law
Public Interest
Securities
Securities Law Arbitration
★ Tax Law
Welfare Rights
(★ indicates an area of special strength)

Clinical Courses Students receive degree credit for clinical courses. (Clinical practicum is not required.) Among the clinical areas offered are:

Advocacy
Business and Corporate Law
Civil Litigation
Civil Rights
Consumer Law
Criminal Defense
Criminal Prosecution
Education
Elderly Advocacy
Environmental Law
Family Practice
General Practice
Government Litigation
Juvenile Law
Lawyering Skills
Litigation
Mediation
Public Interest
Securities
Securities Law Arbitration
Tax Law
Welfare Rights

HOFSTRA UNIVERSITY
SCHOOL OF LAW

Hempstead, New York

INFORMATION CONTACT

Amy L. Engle, Assistant Dean for Admissions
121 Hofstra University
Hempstead, NY 11549

Phone: 516-463-5916   Fax: 516-463-6091
E-mail: lawaee@hofstra.edu
Web site: http://www.hofstra.edu/

LAW STUDENT PROFILE [2000–2001]

FULL-TIME   Enrollment: 812
Women: 44%   Men: 56%

PART-TIME   Enrollment: 8
Women: 50%   Men: 50%

APPLICANTS and ADMITTEES

Seats available: 270
Average LSAT score: 155
Average GPA: 3.3

Hofstra University School of Law is a private institution that organizes classes on a semester calendar system. The campus is situated in a suburban setting. Founded in 1971, first ABA approved in 1973, and an AALS member, Hofstra University School of Law offers JD, JD/MBA, and LLM degrees.

Faculty consists of 40 full-time and 19 part-time members in 2000–2001. 9 full-time faculty members and 3 part-time faculty members are women. 100% of all faculty members have a JD; 23% have advanced law degrees. Of all faculty members, 6% are African American, 6% are Hispanic, 88% are white.

Application Information *Required:* LSAT, LSDAS, application form, application fee of $60, baccalaureate degree, 1 recommendation, personal statement, college transcripts. *Recommended:* resume. *Application deadline* for fall term is April 15 (priority date). Applications are processed on a rolling basis.

Costs The 2000–2001 tuition was $23,956 full-time. Fees: $410 full-time.

Financial Aid Loans, loan repayment assistance program (LRAP), merit-based grants/scholarships, need-based grants/scholarships, and federal work-study loans are available. To apply for financial assistance, students must complete the Free Application for Federal Student Aid, institutional forms, Need Access diskette, student and parent federal tax return. Completed financial aid forms should be received by May 15. Financial aid contact:

AT a GLANCE

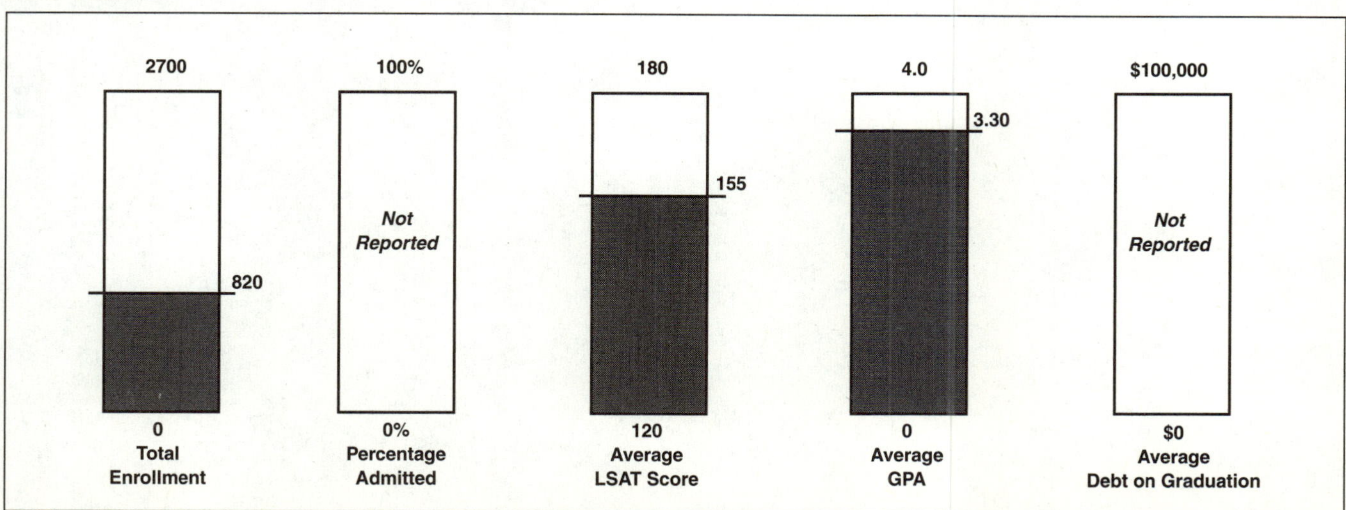

Degree Options

Degree	Total Credits Required	Length of Program
JD–Juris Doctor	87	3–4 yrs, full-time or part-time [day]
JD/MBA–Juris Doctor/Master of Business Administration–Dual-degree Program	123	4 yrs, full-time or part-time [day]
LLM–Master of Laws	24	1 yr, full-time or part-time [day]

Tina Sneed, Assistant Dean for Enrollment, 121 Hofstra University, Hempstead, NY 11549-1210. Phone: 516-463-5929. Fax: 516-463-6338. E-mail: lawtnz@hofstra.edu

Law School Library Barbara and Maurice A. Deane Law Library has 10 professional staff members and contains more than 472,423 volumes and 5,484 periodicals. 595 seats are available in the library. When classes are in session, the library is open 98 hours per week.

WESTLAW and LEXIS-NEXIS are available, as are the World Wide Web, online bibliographic services, and CD-ROM players. 52 computer workstations are available to students in the library. Special law collections include records/briefs of United States Supreme Court 1832 to date, records/briefs of New York Court of Appeals and Appellate Division of Supreme Court, federal depository materials, United Nations documents 1976 to date, ABA archival collection 1878 to date.

First-Year Program Class size in the average section is 100; 100% of the first-year courses are taught by full-time faculty.

Upper-Level Program Class size in the average section is 40. Among the electives are:

- Administrative Law
- ★ Advocacy
- ★ Business and Corporate Law
- Children's Advocacy
- Criminal Defense
- Criminal Prosecution
- Cyberspace Law
- Dispute Resolution
- Entertainment Law
- Environmental Law
- ★ Family Law
- General Practice
- Government/Regulation
- Health Care/Human Services
- Intellectual Property
- ★ International/Comparative Law
- Jurisprudence
- ★ Labor Law
- Lawyering Skills
- Litigation
- Mediation
- Public Interest
- Securities
- Tax Law

(★ indicates an area of special strength)

Clinical Courses Students receive degree credit for clinical courses. (Clinical practicum is not required.) Among the clinical areas offered are:

- Children's Advocacy
- Criminal Defense
- Criminal Prosecution
- General Practice
- Housing Law
- Public Interest

International exchange programs permit students to visit France.

NEW YORK LAW SCHOOL

New York, New York

INFORMATION CONTACT

Thomas Matos, Director of Admissions
57 Worth Street
New York, NY 10013-2959

Phone: 212-431-2888   Fax: 212-966-1522
E-mail: admissions@nyls.edu
Web site: http://www.nyls.edu/

LAW STUDENT PROFILE [2000–2001]

FULL-TIME   Enrollment: 921
Women: 55%   Men: 45%

PART-TIME   Enrollment: 458
Women: 44%   Men: 56%

APPLICANTS and ADMITTEES

Number applied: 3,487
Admitted: 1,826
Percentage accepted: 52%
Seats available: 470
Average LSAT score: 152
Average GPA: 3.4

New York Law School is a private nonprofit institution that organizes classes on a semester calendar system. The campus is situated in an urban setting. Founded in 1891, first ABA approved in 1954, and an AALS member, New York Law School offers JD and JD/MBA degrees.

Faculty consists of 50 full-time and 65 part-time members in 2000–2001. 13 full-time faculty members and 25 part-time faculty members are women. 100% of all faculty members have a JD; 18.6% have advanced law degrees. Of all faculty members, 5.7% are Asian/Pacific Islander, 5.7% are African American, 1.9% are Hispanic, 86.7% are white.

Application Information *Required:* LSAT, LSDAS, application form, application fee of $50, baccalaureate degree, college transcripts. *Recommended:* recommendations, personal statement, essay, writing sample.

Costs The 2000–2001 tuition was $24,274 full-time; $18,210 per year part-time. Fees: $404 full-time (one-time charge for full-time students); $304 full-time (one-time charge for part-time students).

Financial Aid Fellowships, graduate assistantships, loans, loan repayment assistance program (LRAP), merit-based grants/scholarships, need-based grants/scholarships, and federal work-study loans are available. The average student debt at graduation is $56,423. To apply for financial assistance, students must complete the Free Application for Federal Student Aid, institutional forms. Financial aid contact: Eileen Doyle, Director of Financial Aid, New York Law School, 57 Worth Street, New York, NY 10013. Phone: 212-431-2828. Fax: 212-966-1522.

AT a GLANCE

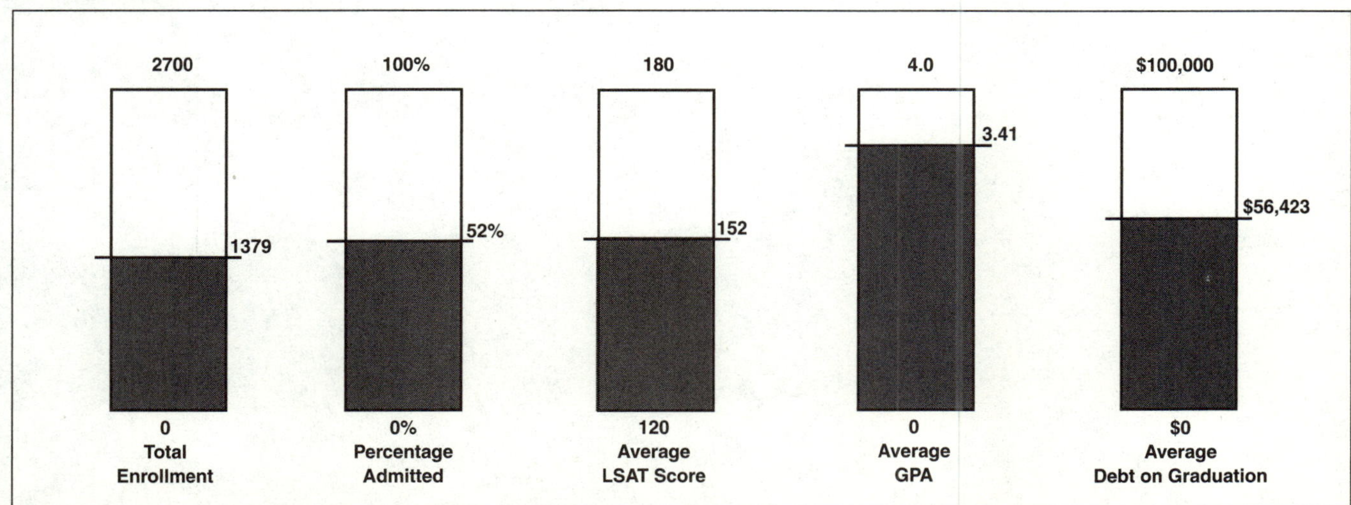

Degree Options

Degree	Total Credits Required	Length of Program
JD–Doctor of Laws	86	3–4 yrs, full-time or part-time [day, evening]
JD/MBA–Juris Doctor/Master of Business Administration–Joint-degree Program		4 yrs, full-time or part-time [day, evening]

Law School Library Mendik Library has 15 professional staff members and contains more than 475,188 volumes and 5,329 periodicals. 616 seats are available in the library. When classes are in session, the library is open 98 hours per week.

WESTLAW and LEXIS-NEXIS are available, as are the World Wide Web, online bibliographic services, and CD-ROM players. 120 computer workstations are available to students in the library. Special law collections include US Government documents depository and special collections in communications rights law, alternative dispute resolution, and labor law..

First-Year Program Class size in the average section is 110; 100% of the first-year courses are taught by full-time faculty.

Upper-Level Program Class size in the average section is 50. Among the electives are:

  Administrative Law
  Advocacy
  Business and Corporate Law
★ Civil Liberties
★ Civil Rights
★ Communications Law
  Consumer Law
★ Dispute Resolution
  Education Law
  Entertainment Law
  Environmental Law
  Family Law
★ Government/Regulation
  Health Care/Human Services
★ Immigration
  Intellectual Property
★ International Human Rights
★ International Trade
★ International/Comparative Law
  Judicial Externship
  Jurisprudence
★ Labor Law
  Land Use Law/Natural Resources
★ Lawyering Skills
  Legal History/Philosophy
  Litigation
  Maritime Law
★ Media Law
  Mediation
★ New York City Law
  Probate Law
★ Public Interest
  Securities
  Tax Law

(★ *indicates an area of special strength*)

Clinical Courses Students receive degree credit for clinical courses. (Clinical practicum is not required.) Among the clinical areas offered are:

  Civil Rights
  Judicial Externship
  Mediation

NEW YORK UNIVERSITY
SCHOOL OF LAW

New York, New York

INFORMATION CONTACT

Kenneth Kleinrock, Assistant Dean for Admissions
40 Washington Square South
Vanderbilt Hall
New York, NY 10012-1019

Phone: 212-998-6060   Fax: 212-995-3156
Web site: http://www.law.nyu.edu/

LAW STUDENT PROFILE [2000–2001]

FULL-TIME   Enrollment: 1,368
Women: 51%   Men: 49%

RACIAL or ETHNIC COMPOSITION
African American, 7%; Asian/Pacific Islander, 11%; Hispanic, 8%; Native American, 0.1%; International, 4%

APPLICANTS and ADMITTEES
Number applied: 6,954
Admitted: 1,547
Percentage accepted: 22%
Seats available: 424
Median LSAT score: 169
Average GPA: 3.7

New York University School of Law is a private institution that organizes classes on a semester calendar system. The campus is situated in an urban setting. Founded in 1835, first ABA approved in 1930, and an AALS member, New York University School of Law offers JD, JD/MA, JD/MBA, JD/MPAd, JD/MPAf, JD/MSW, JD/MUP, JSD, and LLM degrees.

Faculty consists of 116 full-time and 56 part-time members in 2000–2001. 42 full-time faculty members and 15 part-time faculty members are women.

Application Information *Required:* LSAT, LSDAS, application form, application fee of $65, baccalaureate degree, 1 recommendation, personal statement, essay, college transcripts. *Recommended:* resume. *Application deadline* for fall term is February 1. Applications are processed on a rolling basis.

Costs The 2000–2001 tuition was $29,050 full-time. Fees: $955 full-time.

Financial Aid In 2000–2001, 86% of all students received some form of financial aid. Graduate assistantships, loans, loan repayment assistance program (LRAP), merit-based grants/scholarships, need-based grants/scholarships, and federal work-study loans are available. The average student debt at graduation is $81,500. To apply for financial assistance, students must complete the Free Application for Federal Student Aid, institutional forms. Completed financial aid forms should be received by May 1. Financial aid contact: Stephen Brown,

AT a GLANCE

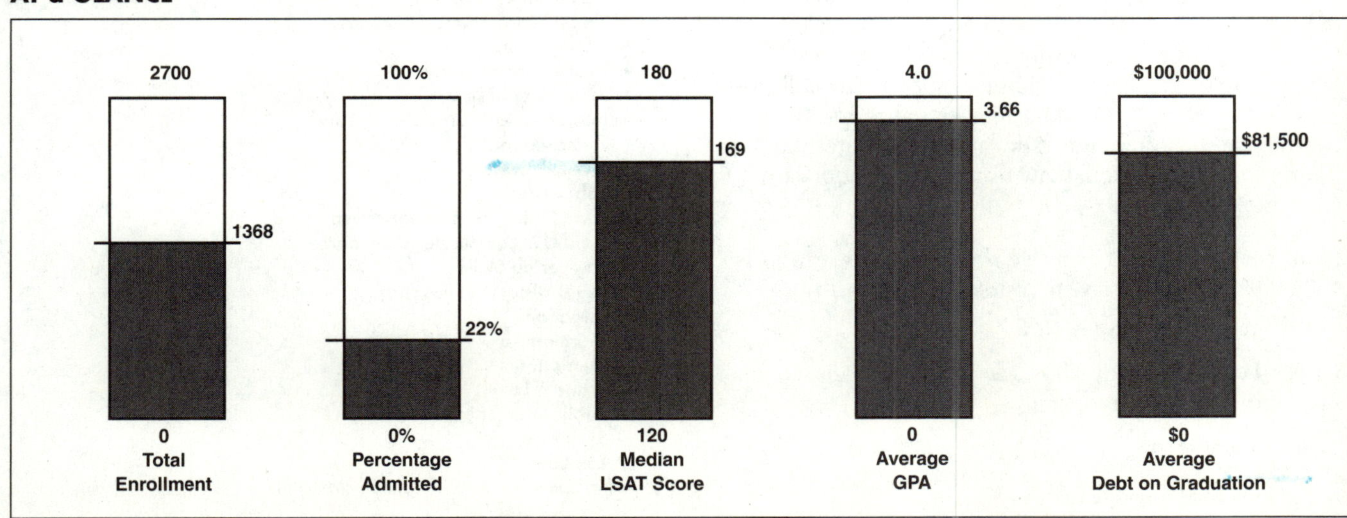

Degree Options

Degree	Total Credits Required	Length of Program
JD–Doctor of Laws	82	3 yrs, full-time only [day]
JD/MA–Juris Doctor/Master of Arts–Dual-degree Programs in Economics, French Studies, Law and Philosophy, Politics, Law and Society	94	3 yrs, full-time only [day]
JD/MA–Juris Doctor/Master of Arts–Dual-degree Program (Latin American and Caribbean Studies)	94	3 yrs, full-time only [day]
JD/MBA–Juris Doctor/Master of Business Administration–Dual-degree Program	131	4 yrs, full-time only [day, evening]
JD/MPAd–Juris Doctor/Master of Public Administration–Dual-degree Program with Wagner School at NYU	114	4 yrs, full-time only [day]
JD/MPAd–Juris Doctor/Master of Public Administration–Dual-degree with Woodrow Wilson School of Public and International Affairs	106	4 yrs, full-time only [day]
JD/MPAf–Juris Doctor/Master of Public Affairs–Dual-degree with Woodrow Wilson School of Public and International Affairs	114	4 yrs, full-time only [day]
JD/MSW–Juris Doctor/Master of Social Work–Dual-degree Program	125	4 yrs, full-time only [day]
JD/MUP–Juris Doctor/Masters of Urban Planning–Dual-degree Program	114	4 yrs, full-time only [day]
JSD–Doctor of Juridical Science		4–5 yrs, full-time only [day]
LLM–Master of Laws–Comparative Jurisprudence, Corporation Law, General Studies, International Legal Studies, International Taxation, Labor and Employment Law, Public Service Law, Taxation, Trade Regulation	24	1 yr, full-time or part-time [day, evening]

Director of Financial Aid, 110 West Third Street, New York, NY 10012. Phone: 212-998-6050. Fax: 212-995-4525. E-mail: law.finaid@nyu.edu

Law School Library NYU Law Library has 13 professional staff members and contains more than 1 million volumes and 6,987 periodicals. 880 seats are available in the library. When classes are in session, the library is open 101 hours per week.

WESTLAW and LEXIS-NEXIS are available, as are the World Wide Web, online bibliographic services, and CD-ROM players. 225 computer workstations are available to students in the library. Special law collections include Gruss, tax collection, intellectual property, commercial banking and trade law, public international law, private international law, foreign law, labor law, environmental law.

First-Year Program Class size in the average section is 100; 100% of the first-year courses are taught by full-time faculty.

Upper-Level Program Class size in the average section is 25. Among the electives are:

Administrative Law
★ Advocacy
★ Business and Corporate Law
Civil Litigation
★ Civil Rights
Consumer Law
★ Criminal Defense
★ Criminal Law
★ Criminal Prosecution
Education Law
Entertainment Law
★ Environmental Law
★ Family Law
Family Practice
★ Government/Regulation
Health Care/Human Services
★ Immigration
★ Intellectual Property
★ International Law
★ International/Comparative Law
Jurisprudence
★ Juvenile Law
★ Labor Law
★ Land Rights/Natural Resource
Land Use Law/Natural Resources
★ Lawyering Skills
★ Legal History/Philosophy
★ Litigation
Maritime Law
Mediation
Probate Law
★ Public Interest
Securities
★ Tax Law
(★ *indicates an area of special strength*)

Clinical Courses Students receive degree credit for clinical courses. (Clinical practicum is not required.) Among the clinical areas offered are:

- Advocacy
- Civil Litigation
- Civil Rights
- Criminal Defense
- Criminal Law
- Criminal Prosecution
- Elderly Advocacy
- Environmental Law
- Family Law
- Family Practice
- Government Litigation
- Government/Regulation
- Immigration
- International Law
- Juvenile Law
- Land Rights/Natural Resource
- Lawyering Skills
- Litigation
- Mediation
- Public Interest

International exchange programs permit students to visit Denmark, France, Italy, Netherlands, and South Africa.

DEAN'S STATEMENT . . .

Legal education has changed dramatically in recent decades. The study of doctrine through the decisions of appellate courts has long been the staple of law school, but it is now generally recognized that this traditional method does not prepare students adequately to practice law. First, the law is not a closed system of rules but an instrument of social policy and moral values, so an interdisciplinary dimension is necessary. Second, the stage on which our leading lawyers act has expanded to include the entire world, so the law must be studied in a global context. Third, because law is a practice, students benefit greatly by confronting law and legal practice in the context of actual and simulated transactions and cases in progress; hence, the addition of a clinical dimension to the curriculum.

At the New York University (NYU) School of Law, our goal has been to chart the future course for American legal education in each of these directions—to develop and refine programs of genuine excellence that encompass the strengths of the traditional curriculum while incorporating the interdisciplinary, global, and clinical dimensions. We are a work in progress, not a final product; but our success to date is remarkably encouraging. The breadth of advanced interdisciplinary work occurring at NYU School of Law is unmatched. Thus, for example, there is no law school in the world with NYU's philosophical sophistication; our faculty is on the cutting edge of work in law and economics, game theory, and rational choice theory; the School is an important center of research in legal history; and studies in law and society are flourishing. Our groundbreaking Global Law School Program has placed in residence on a permanent basis legal scholars and outstanding graduate students from every corner of the world; no other law school has implemented a program of this scope. In addition, NYU's clinical program's reputation as the premier program in clinical studies is seldom questioned and well deserved.

NYU is a law school with the extraordinary diversity, enterprise, and excellence that characterize New York City itself. We take pride in being a community of ideas, a community in which orthodoxy is challenged and invention is celebrated. We ask of our students that they share in and act on these commitments.

—John Sexton, Dean

HISTORY, CAMPUS, AND LOCATION

The School of Law is located at Washington Square in Greenwich Village, one of the most historic and best-preserved neighborhoods of New York City. Surrounding the School is an inexhaustible array of cultural and countercultural activity. As home to the United Nations and many of the world's major nongovernmental agencies, it is a hub of a global public law network. Leaders of the private and public bar regularly participate in classes at the law school, many as adjunct professors, and research and internship opportunities flow from these interactions. The intellectual life at the School is enriched as experts from around the world assemble at the School of Law for conferences on important and emerging issues.

SPECIAL QUALITIES OF THE SCHOOL

On any given day, NYU students may choose from a wide array of activities. Major events occur at the law school each week that would be the event of the year on other campuses. For example, students attended question-and-answer sessions with any of five sitting United States Supreme Court Justices, with justices from the highest courts of several other countries, or the Attorney General of the United States. In addition, they attended a cocktail party to celebrate the King and Queen of Spain or held conversations with the former First Lady of the United States. They also participated in a panel discussion on legal services or one about amending the Federal Constitution. Campus life complements and extends the intellectual dialogue that begins in the more formal setting of the classroom.

TECHNOLOGY ON CAMPUS

The School of Law has invested heavily in state-of-the-art technology. It is fully wired with the latest equipment—in its faculty offices, student residences, classrooms (podiums and seats), library, and administrators' offices. The School's public computing network consists of public-use networked computers at more than 100 sites. These computers use a Windows operating system, but a Macintosh operating system is also supported. On both platforms, there are word processing programs, a spreadsheet application, presentation software, LEXIS-NEXIS and WESTLAW legal research software, Internet browsers, and e-mail. A CD-ROM LAN is accessible in various locations in the library to provide easy access to automated indices. There is a laptop roaming network in the library, classrooms, and the student lounge.

SCHOLARSHIPS AND LOANS

Both need-based and merit-based aid is available. Need-based aid is met first by money available from federal and private lending agencies. Grants are available to students with exceptional need. The Root-Tilden-Kern Program awards merit scholarships based on such attributes as outstanding intellectual potential and demonstrated commitment to public service. The Dean's Merit Scholarships are offered to several outstanding students annually. The School also has an array of generously funded fellowships. The Loan Repayment Assistance Program (LRAP) is designed to pay the costs of law school for graduates who pursue low-paying law-related careers.

STUDENT ACTIVITIES AND OPPORTUNITIES

Law Review One of the most important cocurricular aspects available at NYU School of Law is the opportunity to work on one of the nine student-edited journals, some of which are the leading journals in the field.

Moot Court The NYU Moot Court Board is a student-run honorary organization that combines legal scholarship with oral advocacy. Staff members are selected from the first-year class on the basis of a writing competition held in early spring. Each year, between 30 and 35 students are offered positions on the board.

Extracurricular Activities Many activities are available. For example, with funding from the School, students organize their own lecture series to bring faculty from around the country to present additional perspectives on the law. Students have also created outreach and community projects that enable students to put their nascent legal skills to work. There are daylong symposia on current legal issues, sessions with Supreme Court Justices, and workshops with judges and practitioners. Currently, there are about sixty student organizations, as well as athletic and social program opportunities.

Special Opportunities Throughout the year, the School of Law offers an array of exciting events. There is a set of distinguished lecture series. There are ten colloquiums, in which the distinction between teacher and student is abandoned in favor of joint pursuit of advanced study of the law and other disciplines. There are seventeen institutes and centers involving interaction among faculty members, leading judges and practitioners, and students in a conference, seminar, or course format. Many clinical opportunities are available, including the Public Interest Internship Program, which selects more than 170 first- and second-year students each year to receive grants from the School to pursue public interest work during the summer.

Opportunities for Members of Minority Groups and Women NYU has a historic commitment of seeking the best students from a broad range of backgrounds. For example, in 1890, NYU was one of a small handful of schools that offered legal education to women. In 1967, the National Black Allied Law Students Association (BALSA) was founded at NYU.

Special Certificate Programs In addition to the J.D., NYU offers the Master of Laws (LL.M.) and Doctor of Juridical Science (J.S.D.) degree programs. The LL.M. degree program offers specializations in comparative jurisprudence, corporate law, labor and employment law, public service law, trade regulation, taxation, international taxation, and international legal studies. The LL.M. may also be pursued as a General Studies degree, in which a candidate develops an individualized program of study with an adviser. Joint-degree programs are offered with a master's or Ph.D. in economics, French studies, Latin American/Caribbean studies, legal history, philosophy, and sociology. NYU also offers a joint degree (J.D./master's or J.D./Ph.D.) in its multidisciplinary program in law and society. The J.D. may also be earned simultaneously with a master's degree in business administration, urban planning, public administration, social work, and public affairs (at Princeton's Woodrow Wilson School). The School of Law also offers a joint J.D./Master of Law (LL.M.) degree program in taxation. Finally, the law school has joint-degree programs with the Kennedy School of Government at Harvard University in public administration, international development, public policy, and urban planning.

BAR PASSAGE, CAREER SERVICES, AND PLACEMENT

NYU Law posted a 94% bar passage rate in New York state. NYU students are assisted in their job search by the most extensive placement program in the country. The Office of Career Counseling and Placement begins working with students in the fall of their first year. Together with the Public Interest Law Center, the office organizes panels and workshops on all aspects of job hunting, provides a videotaped simulated interview program, and offers individual counseling. Ninety-six percent of the J.D. class of 2000 reported that they got their first or second choice of jobs.

On-campus interviews are scheduled on the basis of students' preference selections. During 2000–01, more than 600 private law firms, public interest organizations, government agencies, corporations, and public accounting firms visited the law school. Two thirds of these employers were from outside New York. The placement office also arranges off-campus interview programs, and the law school hosts or participates with other schools in several placement programs that serve students with special interests or special needs.

Legal Field	Percentage of Graduates	Average Salary
Academic	n/a	n/a
Business	3.4%	$86,250
Government	2.0%	$37,102
Judicial Clerkship	15.1%	$37,906
Private Practice	70.3%	$96,701
Public Interest	9.0%	$32,211
Other	n/a	n/a

CORRESPONDENCE AND INFORMATION

New York University School of Law
110 West 3rd Street, 2nd floor
New York, New York 10012
Telephone: 212-998-6060
Fax: 212-995-4527
E-mail: law.moreinfo@nyu.edu
World Wide Web: http://www.law.nyu.edu

PACE UNIVERSITY
SCHOOL OF LAW

White Plains, New York

INFORMATION CONTACT

Cathy Alexander, Director of Law Admissions
78 North Broadway
White Plains, NY 10603

Phone: 914-422-4210   Fax: 914-422-4010
E-mail: calexander@law.pace.edu
Web site: http://www.law.pace.edu/

LAW STUDENT PROFILE [2000–2001]

FULL-TIME   Enrollment: 437
Women: 57%   Men: 43%

PART-TIME   Enrollment: 334
Women: 52%   Men: 48%

RACIAL or ETHNIC COMPOSITION

African American, 7%; Asian/Pacific Islander, 4%; Hispanic,
6%

APPLICANTS and ADMITTEES

Number applied: 1,805
Admitted: 866
Percentage accepted: 48%
Seats available: 230
Average LSAT score: 152
Average GPA: 3.2

Pace University School of Law is a private institution that organizes classes on a semester calendar system. The campus is situated in a suburban setting. Founded in 1976, first ABA approved in 1978, and an AALS member, Pace University School of Law offers JD, JD/MBA, JD/MPAd, LLM, and SJD degrees.

Faculty consists of 37 full-time and 60 part-time members in 2000–2001. 100% of all faculty members have a JD; 27% have advanced law degrees. Of all faculty members, 8% are African American, 92% are white.

Application Information *Required:* LSAT, LSDAS, application form, application fee of $55, baccalaureate degree, minimum 2.0 GPA, 2 letters of recommendation, personal statement, college transcripts. *Recommended:* resume. *Application deadline* for fall term is February 15 (priority date). Applications are processed on a rolling basis.

Costs The 2000–2001 tuition was $24,020 full-time. Fees: $40 per semester full-time; $40 per semester part-time.

Financial Aid Loans, loan repayment assistance program (LRAP), merit-based grants/scholarships, need-based grants/scholarships, and federal work-study loans are available. The average student debt at graduation is $60,000. To apply for financial assistance, students must complete the Free Application for Federal Student Aid. Completed financial aid forms should be received by February 1. Financial aid contact: Cathy Alexander, Director of Admissions, 78 North Broadway, White Plains, NY 10603. Phone: 914-422-4210. Fax: 914-422-4010. E-mail: calexander@law.pace.edu

AT a GLANCE

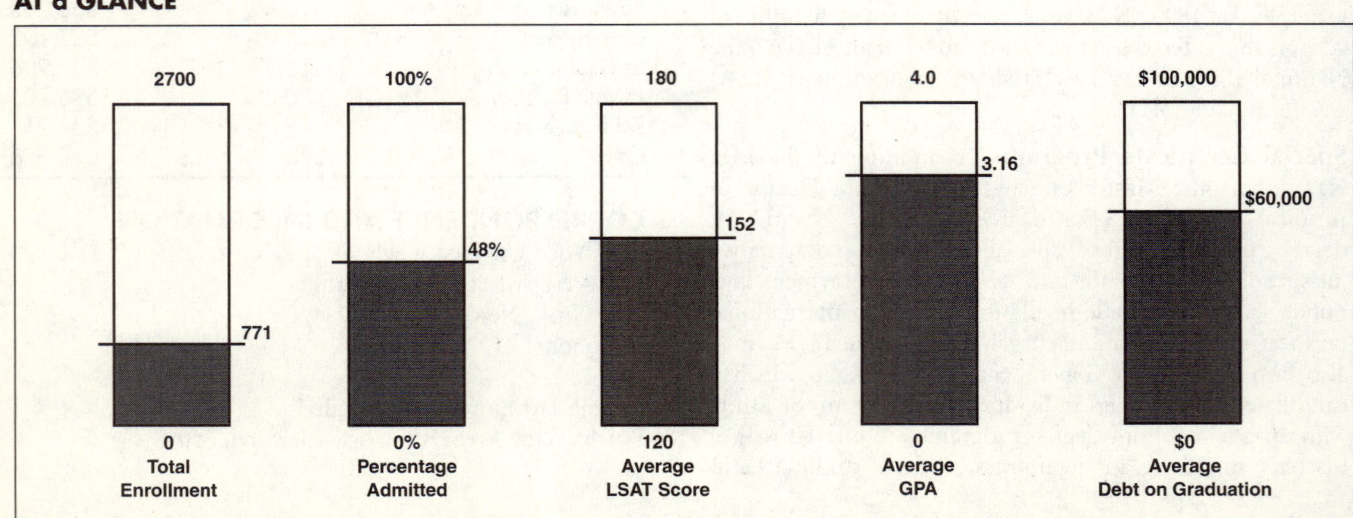

Degree Options

Degree	Total Credits Required	Length of Program
JD–Doctor of Laws	90	3–4 yrs, full-time or part-time [day, evening, summer]
JD/MBA–Juris Doctor/Master of Business Administration–Dual-degree Program	129	4–6 yrs, full-time or part-time [day, evening, summer]
JD/MPAd–Juris Doctor/Master of Public Administration–Dual-degree Program	116	4–6 yrs, full-time or part-time [day, evening, summer]
LLM–Master of Laws–Environmental Law	24	1–2 yrs, full-time or part-time [day, evening, summer]
LLM–Master of Laws–Comparative Legal Studies	24	1 yr, full-time or part-time [day, summer]
SJD–Doctor of Juridical Science–Environmental Law	12	1 yr, full-time only [day, evening, summer]

Law School Library The Pace Law Library has 8 professional staff members and contains more than 343,610 volumes and 3,718 periodicals. 252 seats are available in the library. When classes are in session, the library is open 102 hours per week.

WESTLAW and LEXIS-NEXIS are available, as are the World Wide Web, online bibliographic services, and CD-ROM players. 72 computer workstations are available to students in the library. Special law collections include environmental law, United States Government Depository Collection.

First-Year Program Class size in the average section is 70; 100% of the first-year courses are taught by full-time faculty.

Upper-Level Program Class size in the average section is 40. Among the electives are:

- Administrative Law
- Advocacy
- Appellate Litigation
- Business and Corporate Law
- Civil Procedure
- Constitutional Law
- Criminal Defense
- Criminal Law
- Criminal Procedure
- Criminal Prosecution
- Domestic Violence
- Education Law
- Elderly Advocacy
- Entertainment Law
- ★ Environmental Law
- Family Law
- Government/Regulation
- ★ Health Care/Human Services
- Health Law
- Intellectual Property
- ★ International/Comparative Law
- Labor Law
- ★ Land Use Law/Natural Resources
- ★ Lawyering Skills
- Legal History/Philosophy
- Litigation
- Maritime Law
- Mediation
- Municipal Law
- Property/Real Estate
- Public Interest
- Securities
- Securities Law Arbitration
- ★ Social Justice
- Tax Law
- Trusts and Estates

(★ indicates an area of special strength)

Clinical Courses Students receive degree credit for clinical courses. (Clinical practicum is not required.) Among the clinical areas offered are:

- Appellate Litigation
- Criminal Defense
- Criminal Prosecution
- Disability Law
- Domestic Violence
- Elderly Advocacy
- Environmental Law
- Health Law
- Lawyering Skills
- Litigation
- Securities Law Arbitration

International exchange programs permit students to visit Australia and United Kingdom.

DEAN'S STATEMENT . . .

As members of a learned profession, lawyers owe a duty to society to participate in public life, and therefore they must equip themselves to deal with important matters of public policy. Legal education at Pace Law School is designed to develop in our students the qualities that are unique to the proud tradition of lawyering. This philosophy is manifest in everything at Pace. Our goal is to create complete lawyers, practitioners who are deeply educated in the law, practice-ready, and devoted to service to their communities. Because of this, you—our law students—are the focus of all our decisions regarding curriculum, the library, use of technology, student services, and the new classroom building. We focus on the welfare of the 750 individual students who choose to enter the legal profession through our doors. This means that Pace is also a community, a place where you will spend three or four of the most rewarding years of your life working in an environment that asks that you contribute to each other's learning and leave the law school a better place than it was when you arrived.

At Pace, we deeply believe that students should practice and develop the leadership qualities that are expected of lawyers in our society. Leaders must know the law—it is the starting point for so many public decisions on matters of great import. Pace prides itself as a law school in which learning and teaching count—indeed, it is the reason for our being.

But as leaders, you must know more than the law. You must know how to use the law to further the ends of your respective communities—your schools, your law firms, your advocacy groups, your client companies, and your governments. Pace is dedicated to teaching not only legal knowledge but also the skills necessary to take that knowledge and apply it effectively in practice. And at our law school, we take pride in offering you the widest possible array of programs from which you may choose to design a rich and varied law school program that will help you achieve your goal of becoming a complete lawyer.

But Pace law graduates, while excellent young lawyers, are much more than that. During their years here, our students develop the global vision, a moral compass, and, ultimately, the values that will enable them to help shape the goals of the communities that they join upon graduation. Pace Law School embodies the finest values of legal education—a deeply held respect for the beliefs, ideas, and traditions of others; an unending search for the fullest understanding of law; and a dedication to the pursuit of environmental, social, and legal justice.

—David Cohen, Dean

HISTORY, CAMPUS, AND LOCATION

Pace University is a comprehensive, independent, urban, and suburban New York institution of higher education that offers a wide range of academic and professional programs at the graduate and undergraduate levels in the following six colleges and schools: the Dyson College of Arts and Sciences, the Lubin School of Business, the School of Computer Science and Information Systems, the School of Education, the School of Law, and the Lienhard School of Nursing. Pace University considers teaching and learning to be its highest principles. In recognizing that its educational leadership implies broadening obligations, the University has become increasingly attentive to the integration of scholarship and service with excellent teaching. Faculty members engage in theoretical and applied research as well as other scholarly and professional activities. As part of the teaching role, faculty members often involve undergraduate as well as graduate students in research. Pace University's commitment to the individual needs of students is at the heart of its teaching mission. By offering access and opportunity to qualified men and women, Pace embraces persons of diverse talents, interests, experiences, and origins who have the will to learn and the desire to participate in university life. As a multicampus institution that provides programmatic richness at urban and suburban locations, Pace offers pluralistic, interdependent, collegial environments that foster individual growth, human dignity, civil discourse, and the free exchange of ideas. The White Plains campus on historic North Broadway is the home of the School of Law, which satisfies a community need as the only law school between New York City and Albany. White Plains, the county seat of Westchester County, is an attractive and lively city of about 50,000. Located in White Plains is a new United States Court House that provides a permanent location for the operations of the federal courts in Westchester County.

SPECIAL QUALITIES OF THE SCHOOL

The curriculum at Pace is devoted to preparing graduates to become able and ethical lawyers, to become employable, and to make a difference in improving society. Pace has a strong dedication to excellence in teaching and outstanding training in specialized areas where the need for skilled lawyers is greatest. The majority of classes have less than 25 students, which enables close faculty-student relationships. Deans, other administrators, and faculty members maintain an open-door policy for students. Students participate actively in formulating law school policy through the Student Bar Association and by serving on all faculty committees.

TECHNOLOGY ON CAMPUS

First-year students receive 3 to 4 hours of formal instruction in online research. Additional instruction on advanced research techniques and on research in specialized areas of law is always available to groups of second- and third-year students on request. The Law Library's many computer terminals give students free access to all the information in the LEXIS/NEXIS, WESTLAW/Dialog databases, CALI, networked

CD-roms, and on the World Wide Web; and also provide access to word processing and e-mail.

SCHOLARSHIPS AND LOANS

The School of Law assists students with financial need to the extent that funds are available. A comprehensive aid program has been developed that includes grants, employment, scholarships, and loans, which may be available on the basis of financial need, academic merit, educational costs, or credit considerations.

STUDENT ACTIVITIES AND OPPORTUNITIES

Law Review Pace Law School publishes three law reviews, the *Pace Law Review*, the *Pace Environmental Law Review*, and the *Pace International Law Review*. Admission to the reviews is based upon academic standing and a writing competition. Approximately 50 students participate in each law review.

Moot Court A mandatory first-year moot court competition is part of the Criminal Law Analysis and Writing curriculum. The Law School also competes in interscholastic moot court competitions and hosts the National Environmental Moot Court Competition, the largest environmental moot court competition in the country. Moot team members are selected by professors and chosen based on writing ability and oral presentation skills.

Extracurricular Activities Pace Law School offers more than thirty organizations in which students can participate. Available activities include professional organizations, minority student groups, issue-centered organizations, political groups, social action groups, religious groups, a student bar association, and a student newspaper.

Special Opportunities Pace offers three types of clinical courses. Direct representation clinics are clinics in which students, permitted to practice under a Student Practice Order, take full responsibility for their own caseload under the direct supervision of a full-time faculty member. These include the Appellate Litigation Clinic, the Criminal Defense Clinic, the Disability Rights/Health Law Clinic, the Environmental Litigation Clinic, the Prosecution of Domestic Violence Clinic, and the Securities Arbitration Clinic. Externship programs are clinical courses in which fieldwork is conducted under the supervision of practicing attorneys who are not full-time members of the faculty and include Criminal Justice Defense; Criminal Justice Prosecution; the Environmental Externship in Washington, D.C.; Environmental Law; Family Court Externship; Health Law; International Trade; Judicial Clerkship; and Legal Services. Simulation courses simulate specific components of lawyering work and include Advanced Appellate Advocacy, Interviewing, and Counseling and Negotiating. Pretrial Civil Litigation and Trial Advocacy. The Social Justice Center, the Battered Women's Justice Center, the Land Use Law Center, and the Energy Project all offer opportunities for Pace law students to assist in legal research and discovery, to draft motions, and to attend trials.

Opportunities for Members of Minority Groups and Women A special program for students who are members of minority groups is held annually during the fall semester. This program includes a guest speaker and discussion of the enrollment and placement experiences of alumni who are members of minority groups, current students, and faculty members.

Special Certificate Programs Pace offers Certificates of Concentration in environmental law, health law, and international law. These certificates are awarded upon graduation to students who have successfully completed 12–15 credits with satisfactory grades. A Master of Laws (LL.M.) degree is offered for lawyers in the fields of environmental law and comparative law. Pace also offers a Doctor of Juridical Science (S.J.D.) in environmental law. This program prepares legal scholars for the teaching of environmental law in the United States or abroad.

BAR PASSAGE, CAREER SERVICES, AND PLACEMENT

The first-time bar passage rate for the 2000 graduates was 65 percent. In the survey of the Class of 2000, 92% of the respondents reported employment within nine months of graduation. The Center for Career Development actively solicits law job listings for part-time, summer, and permanent positions for after graduation, as well as for full-time jobs for evening students while they are in school. All job listings for students and alumni, as well as important career information, are maintained on the web site, accessible twenty-four hours a day. The Center for Career Development administers career panels and programs, such as the mock interview program and an alumni mentor program for first-year students, designed to inform students about career opportunities for lawyers and to assist them in their job searches.

Legal Field	Percentage of Graduates	Average Starting Salary
Academic	n/a	n/a
Business	22.2%	$57,719
Government	16.5%	$41,278
Judicial Clerkship	8.2%	$38,779
Private Practice	47.4%	$64,734
Public Interest	2.6%	$32,875
Other	3.1%	n/a

CORRESPONDENCE AND INFORMATION

Office of Admissions
Pace Law School
78 North Broadway
White Plains, New York 10603
Telephone: 914-422-4210
Fax: 914-422-4010
E-mail: admissions@law.pace.edu
World Wide Web: http://www.law.pace.edu

ST. JOHN'S UNIVERSITY
SCHOOL OF LAW

Jamaica, New York

LAW STUDENT PROFILE [2000–2001]

FULL-TIME   Enrollment: 704
Women: 47%   Men: 53%

PART-TIME   Enrollment: 236
Women: 38%   Men: 62%

RACIAL or ETHNIC COMPOSITION
African American, 6%; Asian/Pacific Islander, 6%; Hispanic, 7%; Native American, 0.3%; International, 1%

APPLICANTS and ADMITTEES
Number applied: 2,450
Admitted: 1,058
Percentage accepted: 43%
Seats available: 275
Average LSAT score: 156
Average GPA: 3.2

St. John's University School of Law is a private institution that organizes classes on a semester calendar system. The campus is situated in a suburban setting. Founded in 1925, first ABA approved in 1937, and an AALS member, St. John's University School of Law offers JD, JD/MA, JD/MBA, and LLM degrees.

Faculty consists of 51 full-time and 34 part-time members in 2000–2001. 14 full-time faculty members and 5 part-time faculty members are women. 100% of all faculty members have a JD; 28% have advanced law degrees. Of all faculty members, 2% are Asian/Pacific Islander, 5.5% are African American, 5.5% are Hispanic, 87% are white.

Application Information *Required:* LSAT, LSDAS, application form, application fee of $50, baccalaureate degree, personal statement, college transcripts. *Recommended:* recommendations. *Application deadline* for fall term is March 1; for spring term is November 1.

Costs The 2000–2001 tuition was $23,800 full-time; $850 per credit part-time. Fees: $150 full-time; $75 per term full-time; $75 per term part-time. Tuition and fees vary according to class time and student level.

Financial Aid In 2000–2001, 98% of all students received some form of financial aid. Merit-based grants/scholarships, need-based grants/scholarships, and federal work-study loans are available. The average student debt at graduation is $56,548. To apply for financial assistance, students must complete the Free Application for Federal Student Aid, scholarship specific applications, TAP (if applicable). Completed financial aid forms

AT a GLANCE

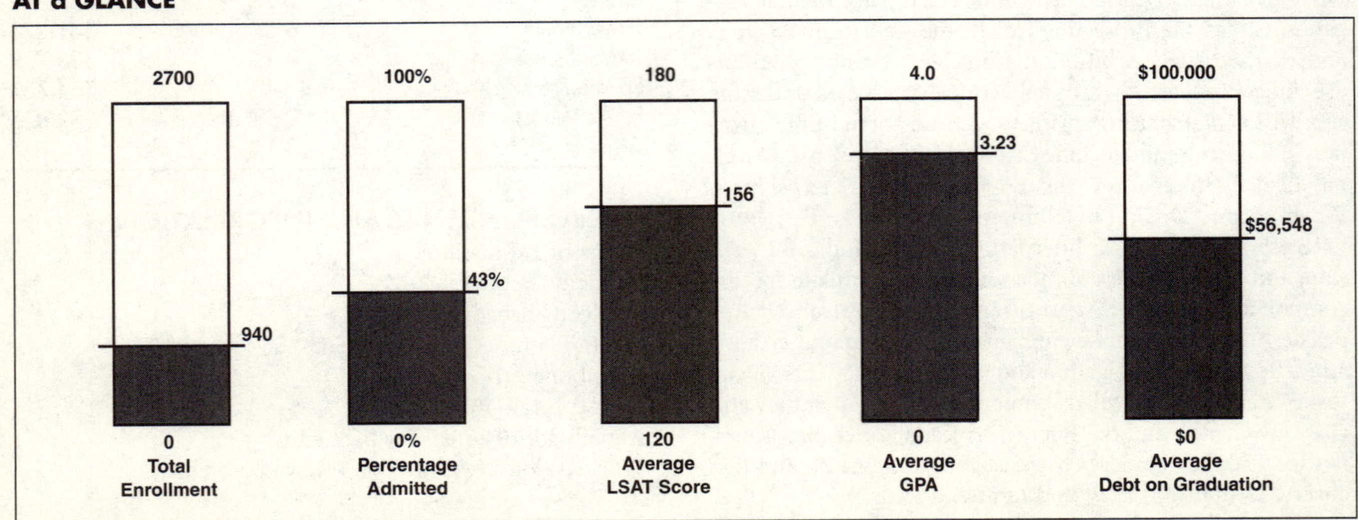

<table>
<tr><td colspan="3">Degree Options</td></tr>
<tr><td>Degree</td><td>Total Credits Required</td><td>Length of Program</td></tr>
<tr><td>JD–Doctor of Laws</td><td>85</td><td>3–4 yrs, full-time or part-time [day, evening, weekend, summer]</td></tr>
<tr><td>JD/MA–Juris Doctor/Master of Arts–Dual-degree Program</td><td>109</td><td>3 yrs, full-time only [day]</td></tr>
<tr><td>JD/MBA–Juris Doctor/Master of Business Administration–Dual-degree Program</td><td>115</td><td>3 yrs, full-time only [day]</td></tr>
<tr><td>LLM–Master of Laws–Bankruptcy</td><td>30</td><td>1–3 yrs, full-time or part-time [day, evening, weekend, summer]</td></tr>
</table>

should be received by March 1. Financial aid contact: Jorge Rodriguez, Assistant Vice President and Executive Director of Financial Aid, 8000 Utopia Parkway, Jamaica, NY 11439. Phone: 718-990-6403. Fax: 718-990-5945. E-mail: rodriguj@stjohns.edu

Law School Library Rittenberg Law Library has 9 professional staff members and contains more than 500,000 volumes and 2,000 periodicals. 601 seats are available in the library. When classes are in session, the library is open 110 hours per week.

WESTLAW and LEXIS-NEXIS are available, as are the World Wide Web, online bibliographic services, and CD-ROM players. 42 computer workstations are available to students in the library. Special law collections include United Nations Depository, Federal and New York State Depository.

First-Year Program Class size in the average section is 70; 100% of the first-year courses are taught by full-time faculty.

Upper-Level Program Class size in the average section is 45. Among the electives are:

- Administrative Law
- Advocacy
- Business and Corporate Law
- Civil Litigation
- Civil Procedure
- Consumer Law
- Criminal Defense
- Criminal Procedure
- ★ Criminal Prosecution
- ★ Domestic Violence
- Education Law
- Elderly Advocacy
- Entertainment Law
- Environmental Law
- Family Law
- Government/Regulation
- Health Care/Human Services
- Immigration
- Indian/Tribal Law
- Intellectual Property
- International Law
- International/Comparative Law
- Judicial Process
- Jurisprudence
- Labor Law
- Land Use Law/Natural Resources
- Lawyering Skills
- Legal History/Philosophy
- Litigation
- Maritime Law
- Media Law
- Mediation
- Probate Law
- Professional Responsibility
- Property/Real Estate
- Public Interest
- Securities
- Tax Law

(★ indicates an area of special strength)

Clinical Courses Students receive degree credit for clinical courses. (Clinical practicum is not required.) Among the clinical areas offered are:

- Civil Litigation
- Criminal Defense
- Criminal Prosecution
- Domestic Violence
- Elderly Advocacy
- Environmental Law
- Government Litigation
- Judicial
- Judicial Process

SYRACUSE UNIVERSITY
COLLEGE OF LAW

Syracuse, New York

INFORMATION CONTACT

Patricia K. Golla, Director of Admissions
Syracuse, NY 13244-1030

Phone: 315-443-1962   Fax: 315-443-9568
E-mail: admissions@law.syr.edu
Web site: http://www.law.syr.edu/

LAW STUDENT PROFILE [2000–2001]

FULL-TIME   Enrollment: 772
Women: 48%   Men: 52%

PART-TIME   Enrollment: 5
Women: 40%   Men: 60%

RACIAL or ETHNIC COMPOSITION

African American, 7%; Asian/Pacific Islander, 7%; Hispanic, 5%; Native American, 1%; International, 3%

APPLICANTS and ADMITTEES

Seats available: 265
Average LSAT score: 151
Average GPA: 3.3

Syracuse University College of Law is a private institution that organizes classes on a semester calendar system. The campus is situated in an urban setting. Founded in 1895, first ABA approved in 1923, and an AALS member, Syracuse University College of Law offers JD, JD/MA, JD/MBA, JD/MLS, JD/MPAd, JD/MS, JD/MSW, and JD/PhD degrees.

Faculty consists of 47 full-time and 42 part-time members in 2000–2001. 20 full-time faculty members and 4 part-time faculty members are women. 97% of all faculty members have a JD; 41% have advanced law degrees. Of all faculty members, 1% are Asian/Pacific Islander, 8% are African American, 91% are white.

Application Information *Required:* LSAT, LSDAS, application form, application fee of $50, baccalaureate degree, 2 letters of recommendation, college transcripts. *Recommended:* personal statement, resume. *Application deadline* for fall term is April 1 (priority date). Applications are processed on a rolling basis.

Costs The 2000–2001 tuition was $24,500 full-time; $1072 per credit part-time. Fees: $459 full-time; $84 per year part-time; $70 full-time (one-time charge). Full-time tuition and fees vary according to course load, degree level, and student level. Part-time tuition and fees vary according to program and student level.

Financial Aid In 2000–2001, 81% of all students received some form of financial aid. Fellowships, graduate assistantships, loans, merit-based grants/scholarships, need-based grants/scholarships, and federal work-study loans are available. The average student debt at gradua-

AT a GLANCE

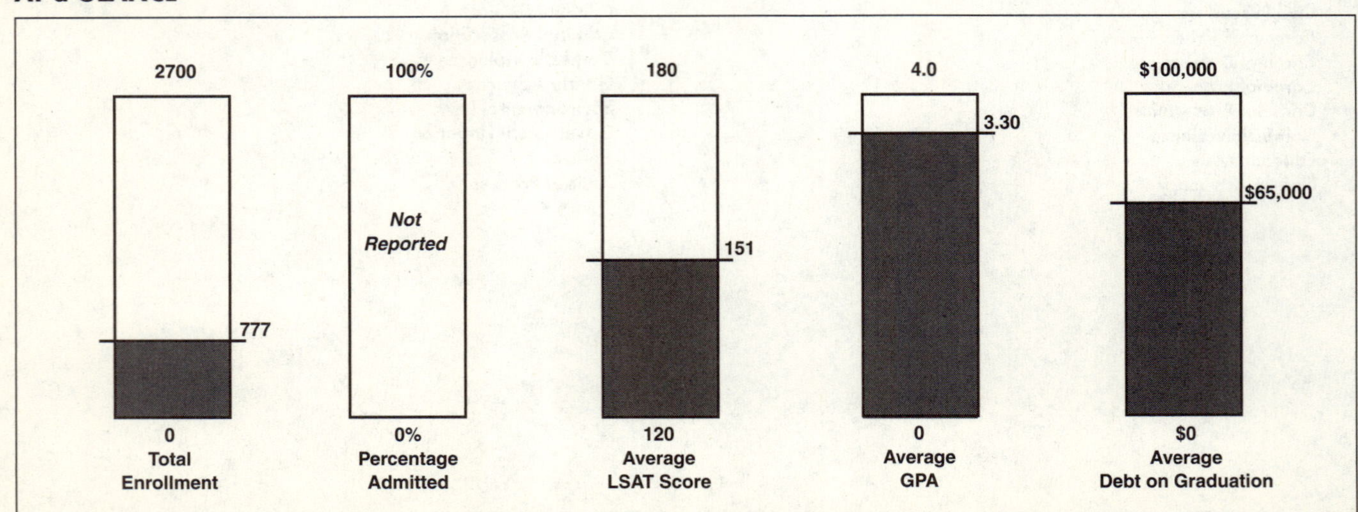

Degree Options

Degree	Total Credits Required	Length of Program
JD–Doctor of Laws	87	3–4 yrs, full-time or part-time [day]
JD/MA–Juris Doctor/Master of Arts–Economics, History, Political Science, International Relations		
JD/MBA–Juris Doctor/Master of Business Administration–Joint-degree Program		4 yrs, full-time only [day, summer]
JD/MLS–Juris Doctor/Master of Library Science	102	3 yrs, full-time only [day, summer]
JD/MPAd–Juris Doctor/Master of Public Administration	97	3.5 yrs, full-time only [day, summer]
JD/MS–Juris Doctor/Master of Science–Accounting		3–4 yrs, full-time only [day, summer]
JD/MS–Juris Doctor/Master of Science–Communications	102	3 yrs
JD/MS–Juris Doctor/Master of Science–Engineering and Computer Science, Environmental Science, Information Resources Management	102	3 yrs, full-time only [day, summer]
JD/MSW–Juris Doctor/Master of Social Work		full-time only [day, summer]
JD/PhD–Juris Doctor/Doctor of Philosophy–History		full-time only [day, summer]

tion is $65,000. To apply for financial assistance, students must complete the Free Application for Federal Student Aid, institutional forms, federal income tax returns, W-2 forms. Completed financial aid forms should be received by February 1. Financial aid contact: Gina M. Soliz, Director of Financial Aid, Office of Admissions and Financial Aid, Suite 340, Syracuse, NY 13244-1030. Phone: 315-443-1963. Fax: 315-443-9568.

Law School Library H. Douglas Barclay Law Library has 8 professional staff members and contains more than 383,605 volumes and 2,884 periodicals. 476 seats are available in the library. When classes are in session, the library is open 105 hours per week.

WESTLAW and LEXIS-NEXIS are available, as are the World Wide Web, online bibliographic services, and CD-ROM players. 110 computer workstations are available to students in the library. Special law collections include International human rights, United States constitutional law and its legal history, trial practice video collection, civil rights, women and the law.

First-Year Program Class size in the average section is 50; 99% of the first-year courses are taught by full-time faculty.

Upper-Level Program Class size in the average section is 50. Among the electives are:

Administrative Law
★ Advocacy
★ Business and Corporate Law

Consumer Law
★ Criminal Law
Entertainment Law
Environmental Law
★ Family Law
Government/Regulation
★ Housing and Finance
Indian/Tribal Law
★ Intellectual Property
★ International/Comparative Law
Jurisprudence
Labor Law
Land Use Law/Natural Resources
★ Law and Economics
★ Law and Technology
★ Lawyering Skills
Legal History/Philosophy
★ Litigation
Media Law
Mediation
Probate Law
★ Public Interest
Securities
Tax Law
(★ *indicates an area of special strength*)

Clinical Courses Students receive degree credit for clinical courses. (Clinical practicum is not required.) Among the clinical areas offered are:

Advocacy
Criminal Defense
Criminal Law
Family Practice
Housing and Finance
Public Interest

TOURO COLLEGE
JACOB D. FUCHSBERG LAW CENTER

Huntington, New York

INFORMATION CONTACT

Office of Admissions
300 Nassau Road
Huntington, NY 11743

Phone: 516-421-2244   Fax: 631-421-2675
    ext. 314
Web site: http://www.tourolaw.edu/

LAW STUDENT PROFILE [2000–2001]

FULL TIME   Enrollment: 776

APPLICANTS AND ADMITTEES
Seats available: 220

Touro College Jacob D. Fuchsberg Law Center is a
private institution that organizes classes on a semester
calendar system. The campus is situated in a suburban
setting. Founded in 1980, first ABA approved in 1983,
and an AALS member, Touro College Jacob D. Fuchsberg Law Center offers JD, JD/MBA, JD/MPA, JD/MSW,
and LLM degrees.

Faculty consists of 37 full-time and 14 part-time
members in 2000–2001. 100% of all faculty members
have a JD; 35% have advanced law degrees. Of all faculty
members, 7% are African American, 93% are white.

Application Information *Required:* LSAT, LSDAS,
application form, application fee of $50, baccalaureate
degree, personal statement, college transcripts. *Recommended:* recommendations, resume. *Application deadline*
for fall term is May 1. Applications are processed on a
rolling basis.

Financial Aid Fellowships, graduate assistantships, loans,
loan repayment assistance program (LRAP), merit-based
grants/scholarships, need-based grants/scholarships, and
federal work-study loans are available. The average
student debt at graduation is $65,000. To apply for
financial assistance, students must complete the Free
Application for Federal Student Aid, institutional forms.
Completed financial aid forms should be received by
May 1. Financial aid contact: Lydia Marcantonio,
Associate Director of Financial Aid, 300 Nassau Road,
Huntington, NY 11743. Phone: 631-421-2244 ext. 322.
Fax: 631-421-0271. E-mail: lydiam@tourolaw.edu

AT a GLANCE

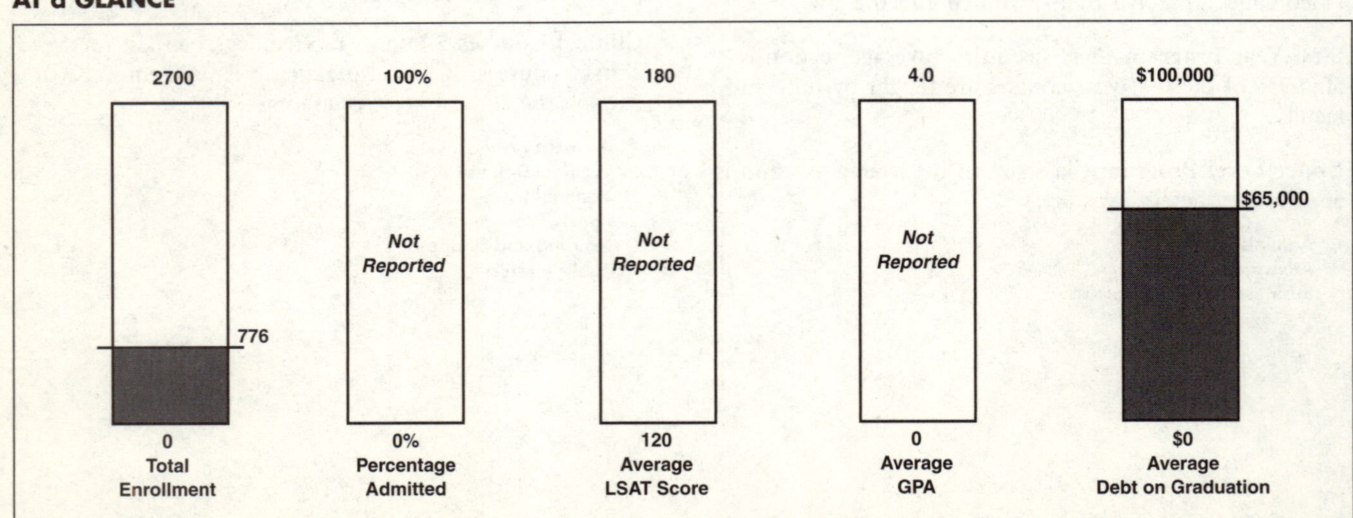

Degree Options

Degree	Total Credits Required	Length of Program
JD–Doctor of Laws	87	3–4 yrs, full-time or part-time [day, evening, summer]
JD/MBA–Juris Doctor/Master of Business Administration–Dual-degree Program	102	3.5–5 yrs, full-time or part-time [day, evening, summer]
JD/MPA–Juris Doctor/Master of Professional Accountancy–Health Law Dual-degree Program	105	3.5–5 yrs, full-time or part-time [day, evening, summer]
JD/MSW–Juris Doctor/Master of Social Work–Dual-degree Program	121	4–6 yrs, full-time or part-time [day, evening, summer]
LLM–Master of Laws–U.S. Legal Studies for Foreign Lawyers	27	1–2 yrs, full-time or part-time [day, evening, summer]
LLM–Master of Laws–General Studies	24	1.5–3 yrs, part-time only [day, evening, summer]

Law School Library Touro College Jacob D. Fuchsberg Law Center Library has 9 professional staff members and contains more than 408,000 volumes and 1,200 periodicals. 350 seats are available in the library. When classes are in session, the library is open 86 hours per week.

WESTLAW and LEXIS-NEXIS are available, as are the World Wide Web, online bibliographic services, and CD-ROM players. 47 computer workstations are available to students in the library. Special law collections include The Judiaca Collection, The Scholar's Collection, The British Collection.

First-Year Program Class size in the average section is 52; 100% of the first-year courses are taught by full-time faculty.

Upper-Level Program Class size in the average section is 42. Among the electives are:

Accounting
Administrative Law
Admiralty Law
Advocacy
Alternative Dispute Resolution
American Legal History
Antitrust Law
Appellate Advocacy
Arbitration
Bioethics
★ Business and Corporate Law
Children's Rights
Civil Rights Litigation
Commercial Transactions
Computer Law
Conflict of Laws
Consumer Law
Corporate Finance
Corporate Law
Creditor's Rights
Criminal Law
Criminal Procedure
Disability Law
Domestic Violence
Drafting Commercial Documents
Education Law
Elder Law

Employment Discrimination
Employment Law
English Legal History
Entertainment Law
Environmental Law
Estate & Gift Taxation
Estate Administration
Estate Planning
Evidence
★ Family Law
Federal Courts
Federal Income Tax
First Amendment
★ General Practice
Government/Regulation
Health Care/Human Services
Housing Law
★ Immigration
Insurance Law
★ Intellectual Property
International Business Transactions
International Criminal Law
★ International Law
★ International/Comparative Law
Interviewing and Counseling
Jewish Law
Judicial Clerkship
★ Jurisprudence
Labor Arbitration
Labor Law
Land Use Law/Natural Resources
Law and Literature
Law and Medicine
Law Practice Management
★ Lawyering Skills
Legal History/Philosophy
Legal Research
Legislation
★ Litigation
Local Government
Mediation
Medical Malpractice Law
New York Practice
★ Nonprofit Organizations
Patent Law
Patient's Rights
Pretrial Litigation
Probate Law
Product Liability

Race and Law
Real Estate Transactions
Remedies
Rights of the Poor
Russian Legal System
Secured Transactions
Securities
Securities Regulation
Sex-based Discrimination
Small Business Counseling
Social Security
Sociology of Law
Sports Law
State Constitutional Law
Supreme Court Litigation
Tax Law
Torts & Product Liability

(★ *indicates an area of special strength*)

Clinical Courses Students receive degree credit for clinical courses. (Clinical practicum is not required.) Among the clinical areas offered are:

Criminal Law
Domestic Violence
Elder Law
Family Law
General Practice
Housing Law
Immigration
Judicial Clerkship
Nonprofit Organizations

UNIVERSITY AT BUFFALO, THE STATE UNIVERSITY OF NEW YORK
SCHOOL OF LAW

Buffalo, New York

INFORMATION CONTACT

Jack D. Cox, Associate Dean and Director of
Admissions and Financial Aid
310 OBrian Hall
Buffalo, NY 14260

Phone: 716-645-6233   Fax: 716-645-5940
E-mail: law-admissions@buffalo.edu
Web site: http://www.law.buffalo.edu/

LAW STUDENT PROFILE [2000–2001]

FULL-TIME   Enrollment: 712
Women: 46%   Men: 54%

PART-TIME   Enrollment: 4
Women: 75%   Men: 25%

RACIAL or ETHNIC COMPOSITION
African American, 8%; Asian/Pacific Islander, 3%; Hispanic,
3%; Native American, 1%; International, 2%

APPLICANTS and ADMITTEES
Number applied: 1,175
Admitted: 555
Percentage accepted: 47%
Seats available: 237
Median LSAT score: 154
Average GPA: 3.2

University at Buffalo, The State University of New York School of Law is a public institution that organizes classes on a semester calendar system. The campus is situated in a suburban setting. Founded in 1887, first ABA approved in 1936, and an AALS member, University at Buffalo, The State University of New York School of Law offers JD, JD/LLM, JD/MA, JD/MBA, JD/MLS, JD/MPH, JD/MSW, JD/PhD, and LLM degrees.

Faculty consists of 54 full-time and 97 part-time members in 2000–2001. 19 full-time faculty members and 24 part-time faculty members are women. 100% of all faculty members have a JD; 24% have advanced law degrees. Of all faculty members, 1.5% are Asian/Pacific Islander, 12% are African American, 86.5% are white.

Application Information *Required:* LSAT, LSDAS, application form, application fee of $50, baccalaureate degree, 2 letters of recommendation, personal statement, college transcripts. *Application deadline* for fall term is March 15 (priority date). Applications are processed on a rolling basis.

Costs The 1999–2000 tuition was $8450 full-time for state residents; $352 per credit hour part-time for state residents. Tuition was $14,000 full-time for nonresidents; $584 per credit hour part-time for nonresidents. Fees: $900 full-time; $85 per semester part-time.

Financial Aid In 2000–2001, 71% of all students received some form of financial aid. 20 fellowships, totaling $10,000; 39 research assistantships, totaling $1150, were

AT a GLANCE

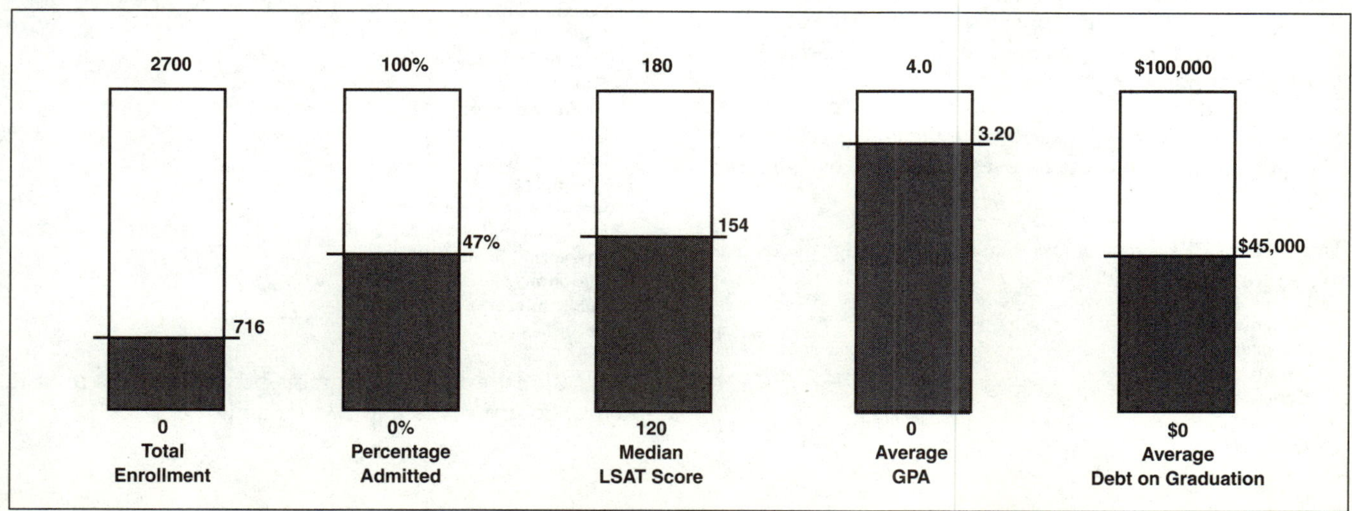

Degree Options

Degree	Total Credits Required	Length of Program
JD–Juris Doctor	89	3 yrs, full-time only [day, summer]
JD/LLM–Juris Doctor/Master of Laws–Master of Laws in Criminal Law	24	1 yr, full-time only
JD/MA–Juris Doctor/Master of Arts–Dual-Degree	120	4 yrs, full-time only
JD/MBA–Juris Doctor/Master of Business Administration–Dual-degree Program	123	4 yrs, full-time only [day, summer]
JD/MLS–Juris Doctor/Master of Library Science–Dual-Degree	114	4 yrs, full-time only
JD/MPH–Juris Doctor/Master of Public Health–Dual-Degree	139	4 yrs, full-time only
JD/MSW–Juris Doctor/Master of Social Work–Dual-degree Program	131	4 yrs, full-time only [day, summer]
JD/PhD–Juris Doctor/Doctor of Philosophy–Dual-Degree		full-time only
LLM–Master of Laws–Program in Criminal Law	24	1 yr, full-time only [day, summer]

awarded. Fellowships, loans, merit-based grants/scholarships, need-based grants/scholarships, and federal work-study loans are also available. The average student debt at graduation is $45,000. To apply for financial assistance, students must complete the Free Application for Federal Student Aid, financial aid transcripts, Tuition Assistance Program (TAP) application. Completed financial aid forms should be received by March 1. Financial aid contact: Brezetta Steverson, Financial Aid Counselor, 306 O'Brian Hall, Buffalo, NY 14260. Phone: 716-645-6676. Fax: 716-645-6676. E-mail: bns@acsu.buffalo.edu

Law School Library The Charles B. Sears Law Library has 9 professional staff members and contains more than 517,227 volumes and 6,769 periodicals. 508 seats are available in the library. When classes are in session, the library is open 93 hours per week.

WESTLAW and LEXIS-NEXIS are available, as are the World Wide Web and CD-ROM players. 32 computer workstations are available to students in the library. Special law collections include The M. Robert Koren AV Center, the papers of John Lord O'Brian, Howard Berman collection.

First-Year Program Class size in the average section is 75; 100% of the first-year courses are taught by full-time faculty.

Upper-Level Program Class size in the average section is 40. Among the electives are:

Administrative Law
★ Advocacy
Bankruptcy
★ Commercial Law
★ Criminal Defense
★ Criminal Law
★ Criminal Prosecution
★ Education
★ Elderly Advocacy
★ Environmental Law
★ Family Law
Family Practice
★ Financial Services
★ Government/Regulation
★ Health Care/Human Services
★ Human Rights
★ International/Comparative Law
★ Labor Law
★ Lawyering Skills
★ Litigation
★ Local Government
★ Public Interest
★ Securities
Tax Law
(★ *indicates an area of special strength*)

Clinical Courses Students receive degree credit for clinical courses. (Clinical practicum is not required.) Among the clinical areas offered are:

Community Development
Criminal Defense
Criminal Law
Criminal Prosecution
Education
Elderly Advocacy
Environmental Law
Family Law
Family Practice
Government/Regulation
Health Care/Human Services
Lawyering Skills
Litigation
Public Interest
Securities

International exchange programs permit students to visit Kenya, South Africa, and Switzerland.

YESHIVA UNIVERSITY
BENJAMIN N. CARDOZO SCHOOL OF LAW

New York, New York

INFORMATION CONTACT

Robert L. Schwartz, Assistant Dean for Admissions
55 Fifth Avenue
New York, NY 10003-4301

Phone: 212-790-0274   Fax: 212-790-0482
E-mail: lawinfo@ymail.yu.edu
Web site: http://www.cardozo.yu.edu/

LAW STUDENT PROFILE [2000–2001]

FULL-TIME   Enrollment: 932
Women: 50%   Men: 50%

PART-TIME   Enrollment: 18
Women: 72%   Men: 28%

APPLICANTS and ADMITTEES

Number applied: 2,768
Admitted: 1,071
Percentage accepted: 39%
Seats available: 250
Median LSAT score: 159
Average GPA: 3.4

Yeshiva University Benjamin N. Cardozo School of Law is a private institution that organizes classes on a semester calendar system. The campus is situated in an urban setting. Founded in 1976, first ABA approved in 1978, and an AALS member, Yeshiva University Benjamin N. Cardozo School of Law offers JD, JD/LLM, JD/MSW, and LLM degrees.

Faculty consists of 43 full-time and 49 part-time members in 2000–2001. 14 full-time faculty members and 14 part-time faculty members are women. 98% of all faculty members have a JD; 13% have advanced law degrees. Of all faculty members, 8% are African American, 92% are white.

Application Information *Required:* LSAT, LSDAS, application form, application fee of $60, baccalaureate degree, 2 letters of recommendation, personal statement, essay, writing sample, college transcripts. *Recommended:* resume. *Application deadline* for fall term is April 1 (priority date); for spring term is December 1. Applications are processed on a rolling basis.

Costs The 2000–2001 tuition was $25,133 full-time. Fees: $150 per term full-time; $75 full-time (one-time charge for full-time students). Full-time tuition and fees vary according to program.

Financial Aid In 2000–2001, 65% of all students received some form of financial aid. 60 research assistantships were awarded. Loans, loan repayment assistance program (LRAP), merit-based grants/scholarships, need-based grants/scholarships, and federal work-study loans are also available. The average student debt at graduation is

AT a GLANCE

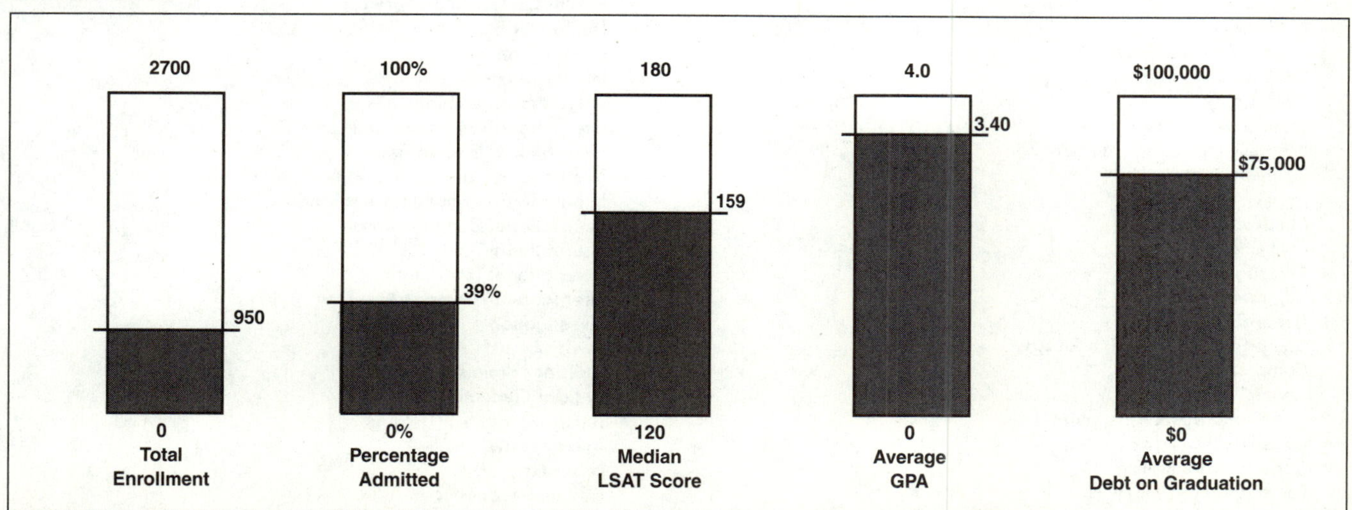

Degree Options

Degree	Total Credits Required	Length of Program
JD–Doctor of Laws	84	3 yrs, full-time only [day, summer]
JD/LLM–Juris Doctor/Master of Laws–Intellectual Property joint degree program	96	3.5 yrs, full-time only [day]
JD/MSW–Juris Doctor/Master of Social Work–Joint-degree Program	124	5 yrs, full-time only [day, summer]
LLM–Master of Laws–Intellectual Property	24	1 yr, full-time or part-time [day]
LLM–Master of Laws–General Studies	24	1 yr, full-time or part-time [day]

$75,000. To apply for financial assistance, students must complete the Free Application for Federal Student Aid, Need Access diskette. Completed financial aid forms should be received by April 15. Financial aid contact: Tom Curtin, Assistant Director of Student Finance, 55 Fifth Avenue, New York, NY 10003. Phone: 212-790-0392. Fax: 212-790-0366. E-mail: tcurtin@ymail.yu.edu

Law School Library Dr. Lillian and Dr. Rebecca Chutick Law Library has 6 professional staff members and contains more than 450,894 volumes and 5,973 periodicals. 472 seats are available in the library. When classes are in session, the library is open 88 hours per week.

WESTLAW and LEXIS-NEXIS are available, as are the World Wide Web, online bibliographic services, and CD-ROM players. 62 computer workstations are available to students in the library. Special law collections include Israeli and Jewish Law, Arts and Entertainment Law, Alternative Dispute Resolution.

First-Year Program Class size in the average section is 50; 91% of the first-year courses are taught by full-time faculty.

Upper-Level Program Class size in the average section is 25. Among the electives are:

- Administrative Law
- ★ Advocacy
- ★ Alternative Dispute Resolution
- Antitrust Law
- Appellate Advocacy
- Banking and Finance
- Bankruptcy
- Bioethics
- ★ Business and Corporate Law
- Business Torts
- Capital Punishment
- Children and the Law
- Civil Litigation
- Civil Rights
- ★ Commercial Law
- ★ Communications Law
- Comparative Constitutional Law
- Complex Litigation
- Conflict of Laws
- Constitutional Interpretation
- ★ Constitutional Law
- ★ Constitutional Rights
- Constitutional Theory
- Contract Drafting
- Copyright & Trademark Law
- Corporate Law
- Corporate Taxation
- Correctional Law
- ★ Criminal Defense
- ★ Criminal Law
- Criminal Liability Theory
- Criminal Prosecution
- Critical Theory
- Cultural Property
- Cyberspace Law
- Divorce Mediation
- Economic Development
- Elder Law
- ★ Elderly Advocacy
- Employment Discrimination
- Employment Law
- ★ Entertainment Law
- Environmental Law
- Environmental Litigation
- Estate Planning
- European Union Law
- Evidence
- ★ Family Law
- Feminist Jurisprudence
- First Amendment
- Food & Drug Law
- Franchising Law
- Gender and Sexuality
- General Litigation
- ★ Government/Regulation
- Habeas Corpus
- Hazardous Waste Law
- Health Care/Human Services
- Human Rights
- ★ Immigration
- Insurance Law
- International Criminal Law
- International Environmental Law
- International Income Tax
- ★ International Law
- International Litigation & Arbitration
- International Organizations
- International Trade
- International Trademark
- ★ International/Comparative Law
- Investigation
- ★ Jewish Law
- Judicial Administration
- ★ Judicial Clerkship
- ★ Jurisprudence
- Juvenile Law
- Labor Law
- Law and Economics

Law and Literature
Law and Religion
★ Lawyering Skills
Legal History/Philosophy
Legislation
★ Litigation
Maritime Law
★ Media Law
★ Mediation
Mergers & Acquisitions
Negotiation
New York Practice
Organized Crime
Partnerships
Patent Law
Pretrial Litigation
Prisoners' Rights
Probate Law
★ Property/Real Estate
Public Benefits
★ Public Interest
Race and Law
Remedies
Secured Transactions
Securities
Securities Regulation
Social Welfare Litigation
State and Local Government
State and Local Taxation
Supreme Court

★ Tax Law
Tax Policy
Taxation of Property Transactions
Taxation of Property Transfers
Telecommunications Law
★ Trial Advocacy
White Collar Crime

(★ *indicates an area of special strength*)

Clinical Courses Students receive degree credit for clinical courses. (Clinical practicum is not required.) Among the clinical areas offered are:

Alternative Dispute Resolution
Appellate Law
Civil Litigation
Corporate Law
Criminal Defense
Criminal Law
Criminal Prosecution
Elderly Advocacy
Family Law
Immigration
International Law
Judicial Clerkship
Legal Services
Mediation
Tax Law
Trial Advocacy

CAMPBELL UNIVERSITY
NORMAN ADRIAN WIGGINS SCHOOL OF LAW

Buies Creek, North Carolina

INFORMATION CONTACT

Alan D. Woodlief Jr., Associate Dean for Admissions
PO Box 158
Buies Creek, NC 27506

Phone: 910-893-1754 Fax: 910-893-1780
E-mail: woodlief@webster.campbell.edu
Web site: http://www.law.campbell.edu/

LAW STUDENT PROFILE [2000–2001]

FULL-TIME Enrollment: 307
Women: 49% Men: 51%

RACIAL or ETHNIC COMPOSITION
African American, 3%; Asian/Pacific Islander, 1%; Hispanic, 1%; Native American, 0.3%; International, 0.3%

APPLICANTS and ADMITTEES
Number applied: 647
Admitted: 197
Percentage accepted: 30%
Seats available: 120
Median LSAT score: 153
Average GPA: 3.3

Campbell University Norman Adrian Wiggins School of Law is a private institution that organizes classes on a semester calendar system. The campus is situated in a rural setting. Founded in 1976, first ABA approved in 1979, Campbell University Norman Adrian Wiggins School of Law offers JD and JD/MBA degrees.

Faculty consists of 20 full-time and 17 part-time members in 2000–2001. 3 full-time faculty members and 4 part-time faculty members are women. 100% of all faculty members have a JD; 25% have advanced law degrees. Of all faculty members, 3% are African American, 97% are white.

Application Information *Required:* LSAT, LSDAS, application form, application fee of $50, 2 letters of recommendation, personal statement, interview, baccalaureate degree, college transcripts. *Recommended:* resume. *Application deadline* for fall term is March 31 (priority date). Applications are processed on a rolling basis.

Costs The 2000–2001 tuition was $18,750 full-time. Fees: $235 full-time.

Financial Aid In 2000–2001, 97% of all students received some form of financial aid. 34 research assistantships; 6 teaching assistantships, totaling $2000, were awarded. Graduate assistantships, loans, merit-based grants/scholarships, need-based grants/scholarships, and federal work-study loans are also available. The average student debt at graduation is $64,500. To apply for financial assistance, students must complete the Free Application for Federal Student Aid. Completed financial aid forms

AT a GLANCE

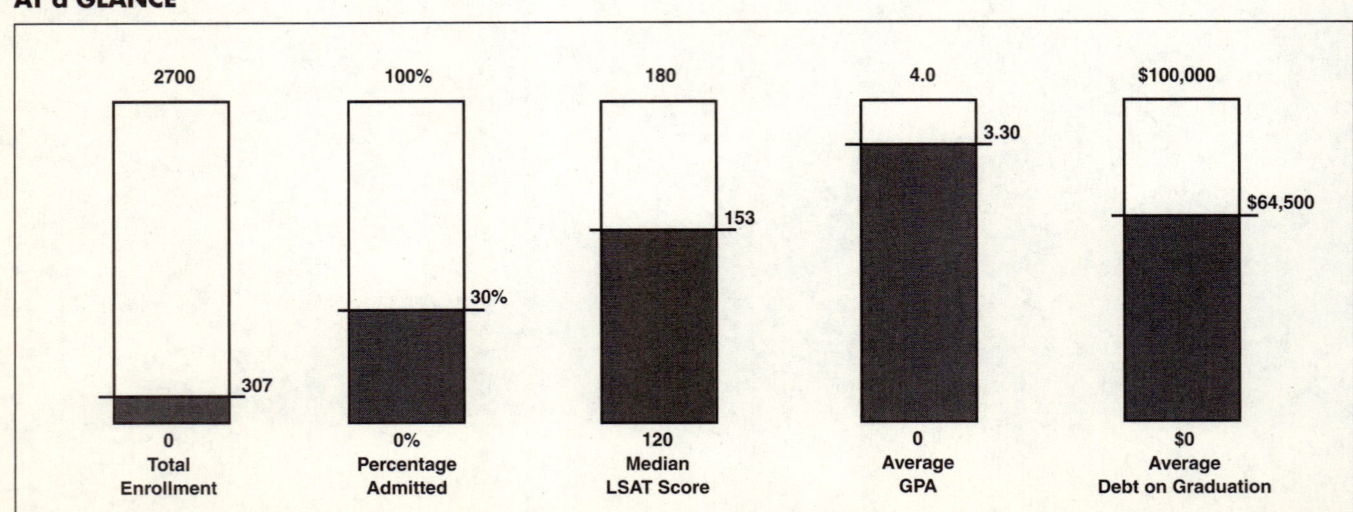

Degree Options

Degree	Total Credits Required	Length of Program
JD–Doctor of Laws	90	3 yrs, full-time only [day]
JD/MBA–Juris Doctor/Master of Business Administration–JD/MBA Dual-Degree Program	120	4–5 yrs, full-time only [day]

should be received by April 15. Financial aid contact: Mrs. Peggy Mason, Director of Financial Aid, PO Box 158, Buies Creek, NC 27506. Phone: 910-893-1310. Fax: 910-893-1780.

Law School Library Campbell Law Library has 5 professional staff members and contains more than 174,160 volumes and 2,559 periodicals. 411 seats are available in the library. When classes are in session, the library is open 106 hours per week.

WESTLAW and LEXIS-NEXIS are available, as are the World Wide Web, online bibliographic services, and CD-ROM players. 42 computer workstations are available to students in the library. Special law collections include trial advocacy, ethics and jurisprudence, public interest law, church-state resources, federal taxation.

First-Year Program Class size in the average section is 78; 100% of the first-year courses are taught by full-time faculty.

Upper-Level Program Class size in the average section is 25. Among the electives are:

Administrative Law
Advocacy
Business and Corporate Law
Education
Environmental Law
Family Law
Health Care/Human Services
Intellectual Property
International/Comparative Law
Jurisprudence
Labor Law
Land Use Law/Natural Resources
Lawyering Skills
Legal History/Philosophy
Litigation
Maritime Law
Media Law
Securities
Tax Law

DUKE UNIVERSITY
SCHOOL OF LAW

Durham, North Carolina

INFORMATION CONTACT

Dennis J. Shields, Assistant Dean for Admissions
and Financial Aid
Science Drive and Towerview Road
Box 90393
Durham, NC 27708

Phone: 919-613-7020   Fax: 919-613-7257
E-mail: admissions@law.duke.edu
Web site: http://www.law.duke.edu/

LAW STUDENT PROFILE [2000–2001]

FULL TIME   Enrollment: 648

APPLICANTS AND ADMITTEES

Number applied: 3,348
Admitted: 831
Percentage accepted: 25%
Seats available: 200
Median LSAT score: 165
Average GPA: 3.5

Duke University School of Law is a private institution that organizes classes on a semester calendar system. The campus is situated in a suburban setting. Founded in 1924, first ABA approved in 1931, and an AALS member, Duke University School of Law offers JD, JD/LLM, JD/MA, JD/MBA, JD/MD, JD/MEM, JD/MPPo, JD/MS, JD/MTS, and JD/PhD degrees.

Faculty consists of 36 full-time and 36 part-time members in 2000–2001. 53% have advanced law degrees. Of all faculty members, 2% are Asian/Pacific Islander, 6% are African American, 86% are white, 6% are international.

Application Information *Required:* LSAT, LSDAS, application form, application fee of $65, baccalaureate degree, 2 letters of recommendation, personal statement, resume. *Recommended:* essay. *Application deadline* for fall term is January 1 (priority date). Applications are processed on a rolling basis.

Costs The 1999–2000 tuition was $25,500 full-time. Fees: $573 full-time. Students are required to have their own computers.

Financial Aid In 2000–2001, 57% of all students received some form of financial aid. Loans, loan repayment assistance program (LRAP), merit-based grants/scholarships, need-based grants/scholarships, and federal work-study loans are available. The average student debt at graduation is $61,000. To apply for financial assistance, students must complete the Free Application for Federal Student Aid, institutional forms. Completed financial aid forms should be received by April 15.

AT a GLANCE

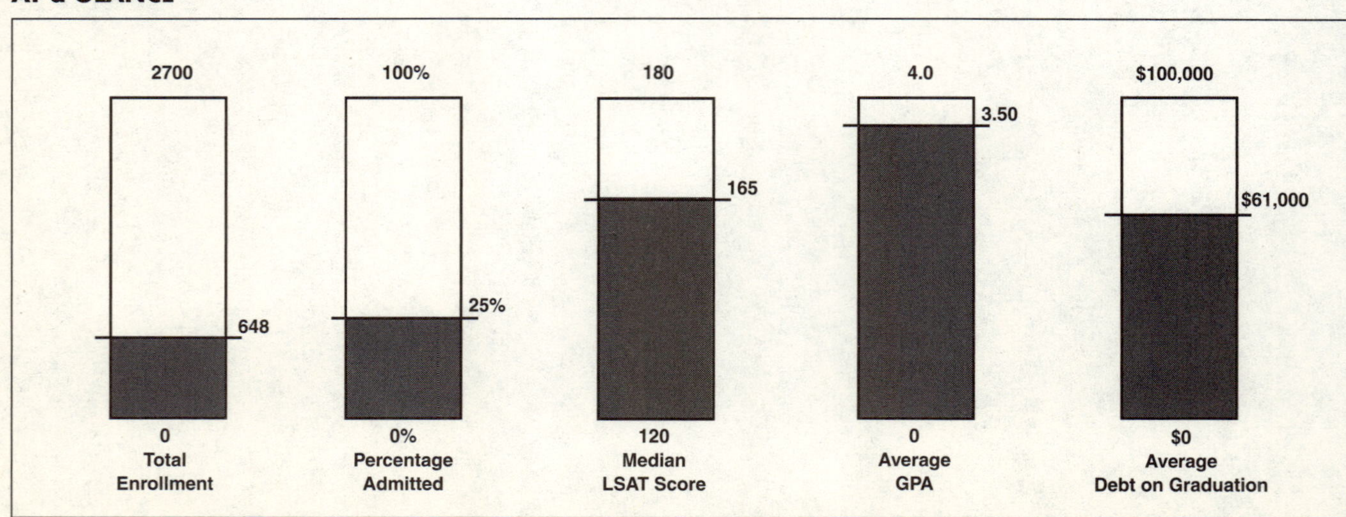

Degree Options

Degree	Total Credits Required	Length of Program
JD–Doctor of Laws	84	3 yrs, full-time only [day]
JD/LLM–Juris Doctor/Master of Laws–International and Comparative Law	104	3 yrs, full-time only [day]
JD/MA–Juris Doctor/Master of Arts–Cultural Anthropology, Economics, English, Forestry & Environmental Studies, History, Humanities, Philosophy, Political Science, Psychology, Public Policy Studies, Romance Studies		3 yrs, full-time only [day]
JD/MBA–Juris Doctor/Master of Business Administration		4 yrs, full-time only [day]
JD/MD–Juris Doctor/Doctor of Medicine		6 yrs, full-time only [day]
JD/MEM–Juris Doctor/Master of Environmental Management		4 yrs, full-time only [day]
JD/MPPo–Juris Doctor/Master of Public Policy		4 yrs, full-time only [day]
JD/MS–Juris Doctor/Master of Science–Mechanical Engineering		3 yrs, full-time only [day]
JD/MTS–Juris Doctor/Master of Theological Studies		4 yrs, full-time only [day]
JD/PhD–Juris Doctor/Doctor of Philosophy–English, Political Science, Literature, and others		7 yrs, full-time only [day]

Financial aid contact: Kochie Richardson, Assistant Director of Financial Aid, Box 90363, Durham, NC 27708. Phone: 919-613-7026. Fax: 919-613-7231. E-mail: krichardson@law.duke.edu

Law School Library Duke Law School Library has 25 professional staff members and contains more than 535,000 volumes and 6,843 periodicals. 451 seats are available in the library. When classes are in session, the library is open 168 hours per week.

WESTLAW and LEXIS-NEXIS are available, as are the World Wide Web, online bibliographic services, and CD-ROM players. 155 computer workstations are available to students in the library. Special law collections include Christie Collection in Jurisprudence, Riddick Collection on Parliamentary Procedure, Cox Collection in Legal Fiction.

First-Year Program Class size in the average section is 90; 100% of the first-year courses are taught by full-time faculty.

Upper-Level Program Class size in the average section is 75. Among the electives are:

Administrative Law
Advocacy
AIDS and the Law
Business and Corporate Law
Capital Punishment
Civil Litigation
Criminal Defense
Criminal Prosecution
Education Law
Entertainment Law
Environmental Law
Family Law
Government/Regulation
Health Care/Human Services
Intellectual Property
International Development
International/Comparative Law
Jurisprudence
Labor Law
Land Use Law/Natural Resources
Lawyering Skills
Legal History/Philosophy
Litigation
Maritime Law
Media Law
Mediation
Probate Law
Public Interest
Securities
Tax Law

Clinical Courses Students receive degree credit for clinical courses. (Clinical practicum is not required.) Among the clinical areas offered are:

AIDS and the Law
Capital Punishment
Civil Litigation
Criminal Defense
Criminal Prosecution
International Development
Public Interest

International exchange programs permit students to visit Australia, Belgium, Chile, China, France, Germany, Japan, Russia, Argentina, Denmark, Hong Kong, Singapore, South Africa, and Switzerland.

NORTH CAROLINA CENTRAL UNIVERSITY
SCHOOL OF LAW

Durham, North Carolina

INFORMATION CONTACT

Adrienne Meddock, Assistant Dean
1512 South Alston Avenue
Durham, NC 27707

Phone: 919-560-5249   Fax: 919-560-6339
Web site: http://www.nccu.edu/law

LAW STUDENT PROFILE [2000–2001]

FULL-TIME   Enrollment: 331
Women: 58%   Men: 42%

PART-TIME   Enrollment: 10
Women: 50%   Men: 50%

RACIAL or ETHNIC COMPOSITION
African American, 49%; Asian/Pacific Islander, 1%; Hispanic, 1%; Native American, 2%

APPLICANTS and ADMITTEES
Number applied: 897
Admitted: 249
Percentage accepted: 28%
Seats available: 125
Average LSAT score: 151
Average GPA: 3.0

North Carolina Central University School of Law is a public institution that organizes classes on a semester calendar system. The campus is situated in an urban setting. Founded in 1939, first ABA approved in 1950, North Carolina Central University School of Law offers JD, JD/MBA, and JD/MLS degrees.

Faculty consists of 21 full-time and 7 part-time members in 2000–2001. 11 full-time faculty members and 1 part-time faculty members are women. 100% of all faculty members have a JD; 14.28% have advanced law degrees. Of all faculty members, 47.62% are African American, 52.38% are white.

Application Information *Required:* LSAT, LSDAS, application form, application fee of $30, baccalaureate degree, 2 letters of recommendation, personal statement, college transcripts. *Recommended:* resume. *Application deadline* for fall term is April 15.

Costs The 2000–2001 tuition was $1022 full-time for state residents; $128 per hour part-time for state residents. Tuition was $10,500 full-time for nonresidents; $1266 per hour part-time for nonresidents. Fees: $900 full-time; $60 per credit part-time.

Financial Aid Fellowships, loans, merit-based grants/scholarships, need-based grants/scholarships, and federal work-study loans are available. The average student debt at graduation is $25,500. To apply for financial assistance, students must complete the Free Application for Federal Student Aid, institutional forms, scholarship specific applications. Completed financial aid forms should be received by May 1. Financial aid contact:

AT a GLANCE

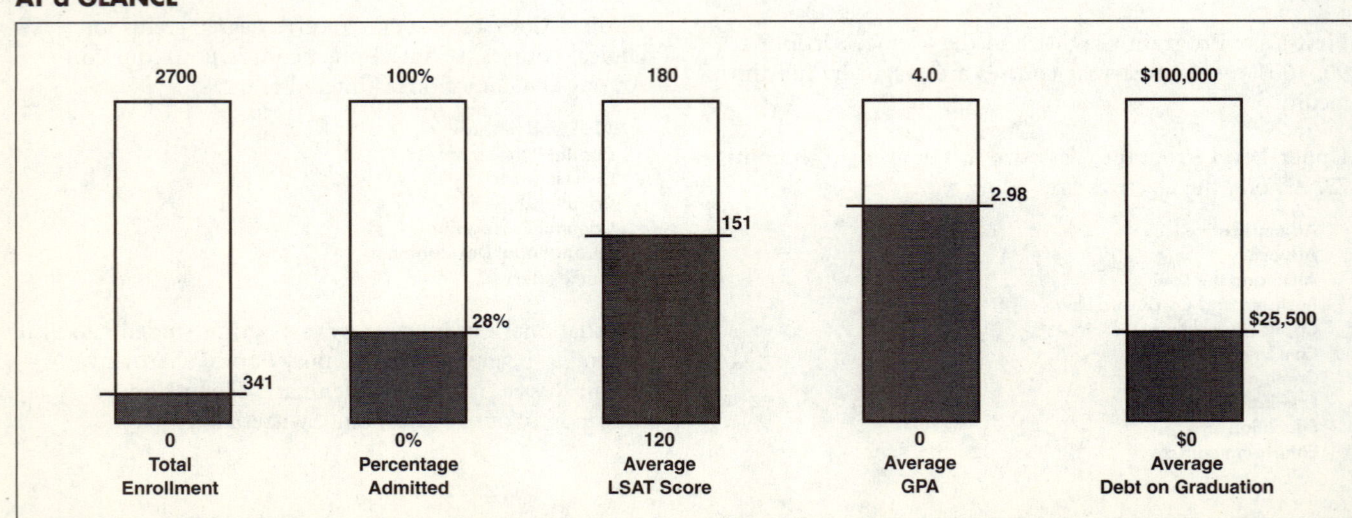

Degree Options

Degree	Total Credits Required	Length of Program
JD–Juris Doctor	88	3–4 yrs, full-time or part-time [day, evening, summer]
JD/MBA–Juris Doctor/Master of Business Administration–Dual-degree Program	121	4–5 yrs, full-time or part-time [day, evening, summer]
JD/MLS–Juris Doctor/Master of Library Science–Dual-degree Program	112	3–4 yrs, full-time or part-time [day, summer]

Ronald Steven Douglas, Assistant Dean, Day Program, 1512 South Alston Avenue, Durham, NC 27707. Phone: 919-560-6333. Fax: 919-560-6339.

Law School Library North Carolina Central University School of Law Library has 6 professional staff members and contains more than 292,173 volumes and 3,328 periodicals. 334 seats are available in the library. When classes are in session, the library is open 97 hours per week.

WESTLAW and LEXIS-NEXIS are available, as are the World Wide Web, online bibliographic services, and CD-ROM players. 46 computer workstations are available to students in the library. Special law collections include The McKissick Collection (Civil Rights).

First-Year Program Class size in the average section is 56; 100% of the first-year courses are taught by full-time faculty.

Upper-Level Program Class size in the average section is 50. Among the electives are:

- Administrative Law
- Advocacy
- Business and Corporate Law
- Civil Litigation
- Consumer Law
- Criminal Defense
- Education Law
- Entertainment Law
- Environmental Law
- Family Law
- Health Care/Human Services
- Intellectual Property
- International/Comparative Law
- Labor Law
- Land Rights/Natural Resource
- Litigation
- Mediation
- Probate Law
- Public Interest
- Tax Law

Clinical Courses Students receive degree credit for clinical courses. (Clinical practicum is not required.) Among the clinical areas offered are:

- Child Protection Center
- Civil Litigation
- Criminal Defense
- Land Rights/Natural Resource

THE UNIVERSITY OF NORTH CAROLINA AT CHAPEL HILL
SCHOOL OF LAW

Chapel Hill, North Carolina

INFORMATION CONTACT

M. Victoria Taylor, Assistant Dean for Admissions
Campus Box 3380
Van Hecke-Wettach Hall
Chapel Hill, NC 27599-3380

Phone: 919-962-5109   Fax: 919-962-1170
E-mail: law_admission@unc.edu
Web site: http://www.law.unc.edu/

LAW STUDENT PROFILE [2000–2001]

FULL-TIME   Enrollment: 781
Women: 50%   Men: 50%

RACIAL or ETHNIC COMPOSITION
African American, 9%; Asian/Pacific Islander, 4%; Hispanic, 2%; Native American, 0.4%

APPLICANTS and ADMITTEES
Number applied: 2,649
Admitted: 718
Percentage accepted: 27%
Seats available: 235
Median LSAT score: 160
Average GPA: 3.6

The University of North Carolina at Chapel Hill School of Law is a public institution that organizes classes on a semester calendar system. The campus is situated in a small-town setting. Founded in 1843, first ABA approved in 1925, and an AALS member, The University of North Carolina at Chapel Hill School of Law offers JD, JD/MBA, JD/MCRP, JD/MPAd, JD/MPH, and JD/MSW degrees.

Faculty consists of 48 full-time and 48 part-time members in 2000–2001. 21 full-time faculty members and 21 part-time faculty members are women. 100% of all faculty members have a JD degree. Of all faculty members, 6.8% are African American, 1% are Hispanic, 92.2% are white.

Application Information *Required:* LSAT, LSDAS, application form, application fee of $60, baccalaureate degree, 2 letters of recommendation, personal statement, essay, college transcripts, resume. *Application deadline* for fall term is February 1. Applications are processed on a rolling basis.

Costs The 2000–2001 tuition was $2966 full-time for area residents. Tuition was $15,066 full-time for nonresidents. Fees: $2065 full-time.

Financial Aid In 2000–2001, 69% of all students received some form of financial aid. 40 research assistantships, totaling $2100 were awarded. Fellowships, graduate assistantships, loans, loan repayment assistance program (LRAP), merit-based grants/scholarships, need-based

AT a GLANCE

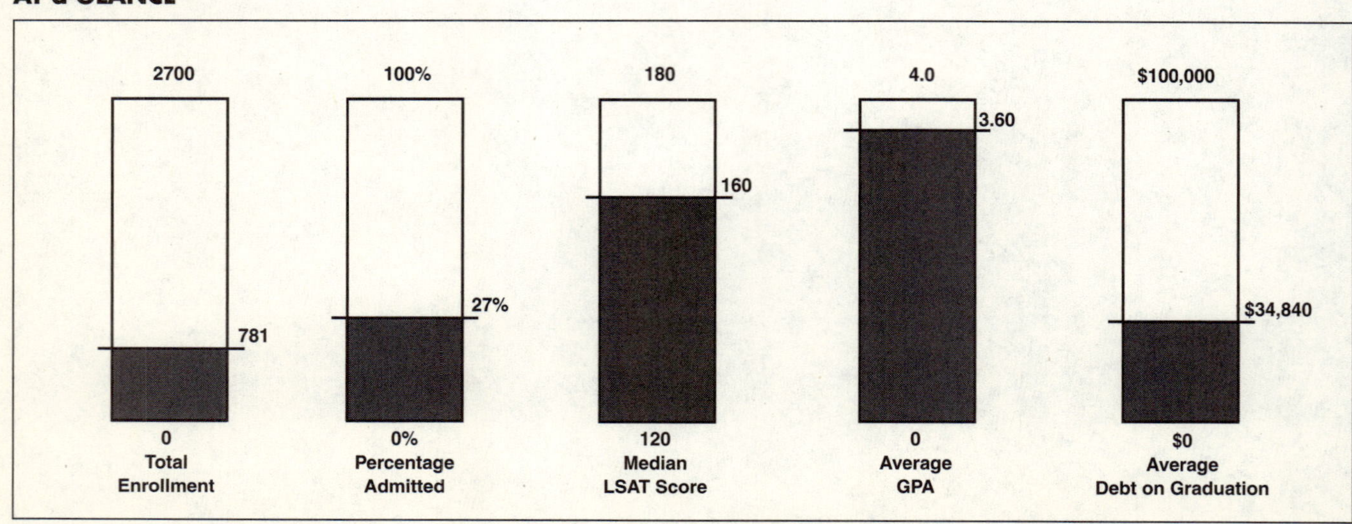

<table>
<tr><th colspan="3">Degree Options</th></tr>
<tr><th>Degree</th><th>Total Credits
Required</th><th>Length of Program</th></tr>
<tr><td>JD–Juris Doctor</td><td>86</td><td>3 yrs, full-time only [day, summer]</td></tr>
<tr><td>JD/MBA–Juris Doctor/Master of Business
Administration</td><td>123</td><td>4 yrs, full-time only [day, summer]</td></tr>
<tr><td>JD/MCRP–Juris Doctor/Master of Community and
Regional Planning</td><td>110</td><td>4 yrs, full-time only [day]</td></tr>
<tr><td>JD/MPAd–Juris Doctor/Master of Public Administration</td><td>128</td><td>4 yrs, full-time only [day, summer]</td></tr>
<tr><td>JD/MPH–Juris Doctor/Master of Public Health</td><td>116</td><td>4 yrs, full-time only</td></tr>
<tr><td>JD/MSW–Juris Doctor/Master of Social Work</td><td>124</td><td>4 yrs, full-time only [day, summer]</td></tr>
</table>

grants/scholarships, and federal work-study loans are also available. The average student debt at graduation is $34,840. To apply for financial assistance, students must complete the Free Application for Federal Student Aid. Completed financial aid forms should be received by March 1. Financial aid contact: Sue Burdick, Assistant Director, University of North Carolina Student Aid Office, CB#2300 Vance Hall, Chapel Hill, NC 27599-2300. Phone: 919-962-8396. Fax: 919-962-2716.

Law School Library Kathrine R. Everett Law Library has 19 professional staff members and contains more than 500,000 volumes and 5,946 periodicals. 407 seats are available in the library. When classes are in session, the library is open 84 hours per week.

WESTLAW and LEXIS-NEXIS are available, as are the World Wide Web, online bibliographic services, and CD-ROM players. 48 computer workstations are available to students in the library. Special law collections include federal government document depository.

First-Year Program Class size in the average section is 75; 95% of the first-year courses are taught by full-time faculty.

Upper-Level Program Class size in the average section is 75. Among the electives are:

- Administrative Law
- Advocacy
- ★ Business and Corporate Law
- Constitutional Law
- Consumer Law
- Corporate Finance
- ★ Criminal Defense
- Disability Law
- Education
- Education Law
- Employment Law
- Environmental Law
- Estate Planning
- Evidence
- Family Law
- First Amendment
- Gender and the Law
- General Practice
- Government/Regulation
- ★ Health Care/Human Services
- Health Law
- Intellectual Property
- ★ International/Comparative Law
- Jurisprudence
- Juvenile Law
- Labor and Employment
- Labor Law
- ★ Land Use Law/Natural Resources
- ★ Lawyering Skills
- Legal History/Philosophy
- ★ Litigation
- ★ Mediation
- Nonprofit Organizations
- Poverty/Welfare Law
- Probate Law
- Professional Responsibility
- ★ Public Interest
- Race and Law
- Securities
- Sports Law
- Tax Law
- Trial Advocacy

(★ indicates an area of special strength)

Clinical Courses Students receive degree credit for clinical courses. (Clinical practicum is not required.) Among the clinical areas offered are:

- Civil Litigation
- Consumer Law
- Criminal Defense
- General Practice
- Juvenile Law
- Landlord/Tenant
- Lawyering Skills
- Mediation
- Public Benefits
- Public Interest
- Social Security

International exchange programs permit students to visit Australia, France, Mexico, Netherlands, and United Kingdom.

WAKE FOREST UNIVERSITY
SCHOOL OF LAW

Winston-Salem, North Carolina

INFORMATION CONTACT

Melanie E. Nutt, Director of Admissions and
Financial Aid
PO Box 7206, Reynolda Station
Winston-Salem, NC 27109

Phone: 336-758-5437   Fax: 336-758-4632
E-mail: admissions@law.wfu.edu
Web site: http://www.law.wfu.edu/

LAW STUDENT PROFILE [2000–2001]

FULL-TIME   Enrollment: 442
Women: 44%   Men: 56%

PART-TIME   Enrollment: 22
Women: 45%   Men: 55%

RACIAL or ETHNIC COMPOSITION
African American, 6%; Asian/Pacific Islander, 2%; Hispanic,
1%; Native American, 0.2%; International, 1%

APPLICANTS and ADMITTEES
Number applied: 1,421
Admitted: 521
Percentage accepted: 37%
Seats available: 160
Median LSAT score: 160
Average GPA: 3.3

Wake Forest University School of Law is a private
institution that organizes classes on a semester calendar
system. The campus is situated in an urban setting.
Founded in 1894, first ABA approved in 1937, and an
AALS member, Wake Forest University School of Law
offers JD, JD/MBA, and LLM degrees.

Faculty consists of 39 full-time and 28 part-time
members in 2000–2001. 100% of all faculty members
have a JD degree. Of all faculty members, 4% are
Asian/Pacific Islander, 7% are African American, 89% are
white.

Application Information *Required:* LSAT, LSDAS,
application form, application fee of $60, baccalaureate
degree, 2 letters of recommendation, personal statement,
essay, writing sample, college transcripts. *Recommended:*
resume. *Application deadline* for fall term is March 15.
Applications are processed on a rolling basis.

Financial Aid Loans, loan repayment assistance program
(LRAP), merit-based grants/scholarships, need-based
grants/scholarships, and federal work-study loans are
available. The average student debt at graduation is
$66,600. To apply for financial assistance, students must
complete the Free Application for Federal Student Aid.
Completed financial aid forms should be received by
April 30. Financial aid contact: Melanie E. Nutt, Director
of Admissions and Financial Aid, PO Box 7206, Reynolda Station, Winston-Salem, NC 27109. Phone:
336-758-5437. Fax: 336-758-4632. E-mail:
admissions@law.wfu.edu

AT a GLANCE

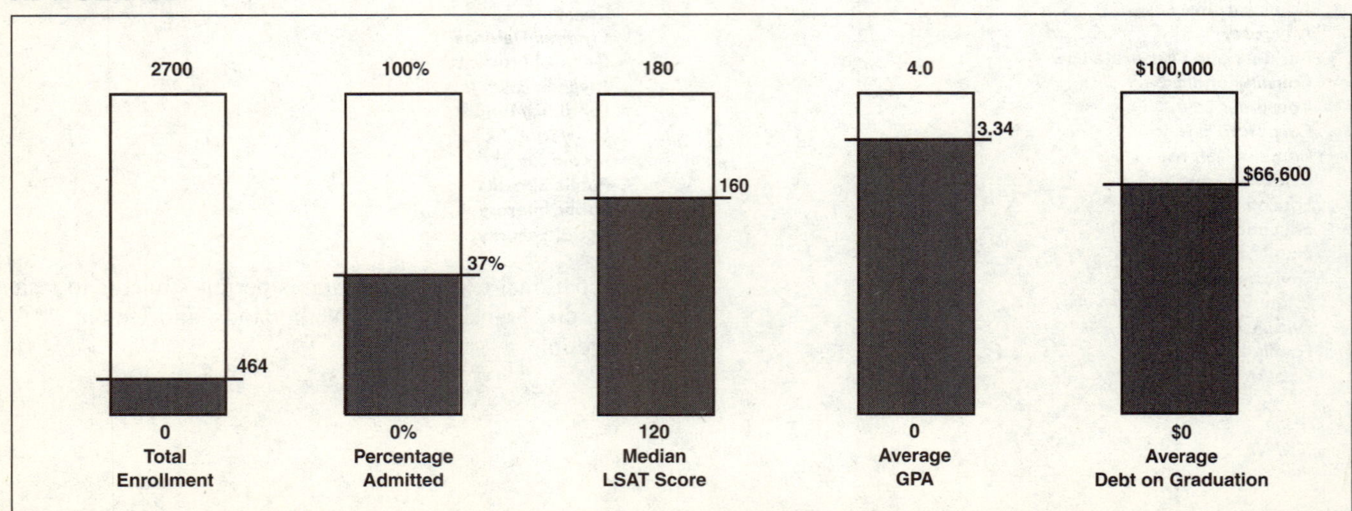

Degree Options

Degree	Total Credits Required	Length of Program
JD–Doctor of Laws	89	3–4 yrs, full-time only [day]
JD/MBA–Juris Doctor/Master of Business Administration–Dual-degree Program	110	4–5 yrs, full-time only [day]
LLM–Master of Laws–American Law	24	1 yr, full-time only [day]

Law School Library Worrell Professional Center for Law and Management has 6 professional staff members and contains more than 341,653 volumes and 5,308 periodicals. 552 seats are available in the library. When classes are in session, the library is open 109 hours per week.

WESTLAW and LEXIS-NEXIS are available, as are the World Wide Web, online bibliographic services, and CD-ROM players. 104 computer workstations are available to students in the library.

First-Year Program Class size in the average section is 40; 100% of the first-year courses are taught by full-time faculty.

Upper-Level Program Among the electives are:

Administrative Law
★ Advocacy
★ Business and Corporate Law
★ Civil Litigation
Constitutional Law
Consumer Law
Elderly Advocacy
Family Law
General Practice
Government/Regulation
Health Care/Human Services
Intellectual Property
International/Comparative Law
Jurisprudence
Labor Law
Land Use Law/Natural Resources
Lawyering Skills
Legal History/Philosophy
★ Litigation
Maritime Law
Media Law
Mediation
Probate Law
Securities
★ Tax Law
(★ *indicates an area of special strength*)

Clinical Courses Students receive degree credit for clinical courses. (Clinical practicum is not required.) Among the clinical areas offered are:

Advocacy
Civil Litigation
Consumer Law
Criminal Defense
Criminal Prosecution
Elderly Advocacy
Family Law
General Practice
Intellectual Property
Labor Law
Litigation

International exchange programs permit students to visit Italy and United Kingdom.

UNIVERSITY OF NORTH DAKOTA
SCHOOL OF LAW

Grand Forks, North Dakota

INFORMATION CONTACT

Linda Kohoutek, Admissions and Records Officer
Centennial Drive
PO Box 9003
Grand Forks, ND 58202

Phone: 701-777-2104   Fax: 701-777-2217
E-mail: linda_kohoutek@thor.law.und.nodak.edu
Web site: http://www.law.und.nodak.edu/

LAW STUDENT PROFILE [2000–2001]

FULL-TIME   Enrollment: 194
Women: 46%   Men: 54%

APPLICANTS and ADMITTEES
Number applied: 216
Admitted: 143
Percentage accepted: 66%
Seats available: 65
Median LSAT score: 152
Average GPA: 3.1

University of North Dakota School of Law is a public institution that organizes classes on a semester calendar system. The campus is situated in an urban setting. Founded in 1899, first ABA approved in 1923, and an AALS member, University of North Dakota School of Law offers a JD degree.

Faculty consists of 13 full-time and 8 part-time members in 2000–2001. 4 full-time faculty members and 3 part-time faculty members are women.

Application Information *Required:* LSAT, LSDAS, application form, application fee of $35, baccalaureate degree, recommendations. *Application deadline* for fall term is April 1 (priority date). Applications are processed on a rolling basis.

Costs The 1999–2000 tuition was $4376 full-time for state residents. Tuition was $9220 full-time for nonresidents. Full-time tuition and fees vary according to program and reciprocity agreements.

Financial Aid 4 teaching assistantships were awarded. Fellowships, loans, merit-based grants/scholarships, need-based grants/scholarships, and federal work-study loans are also available. To apply for financial assistance, students must complete the Free Application for Federal Student Aid. Completed financial aid forms should be received by April 15. Financial aid contact: University of North Dakota Law School, Financial Aid Office, PO Box 8371, Grand Forks, ND 58202-8371. Phone: 701-777-3121.

AT a GLANCE

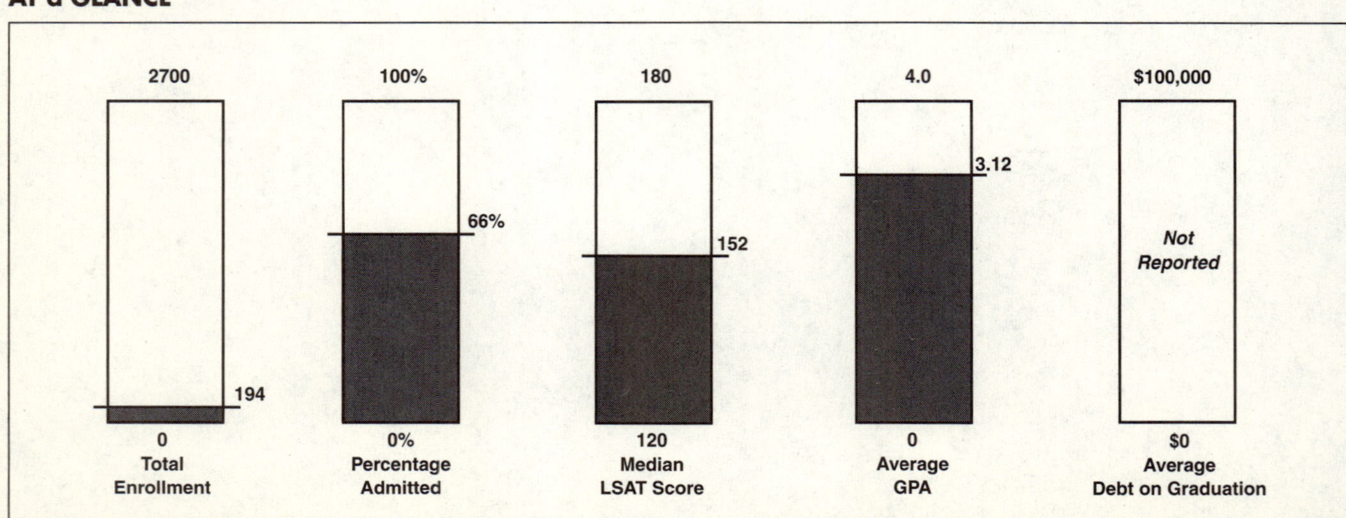

<table>
<tr><td colspan="3">Degree Options</td></tr>
<tr><td>Degree</td><td>Total Credits
Required</td><td>Length of Program</td></tr>
<tr><td>JD–Juris Doctor</td><td>90</td><td>full-time only</td></tr>
</table>

Law School Library Thormodsgard Law Library has 2 professional staff members and contains more than 400,000 volumes and 2,710 periodicals. 279 seats are available in the library. When classes are in session, the library is open 106 hours per week.

WESTLAW and LEXIS-NEXIS are available, as is the World Wide Web. 17 computer workstations are available to students in the library.

First-Year Program Class size in the average section is 72.

Upper-Level Program Among the electives are:

Accounting
Administrative Law
Advocacy
Agricultural Law
Banking and Finance
Business and Corporate Law
Commercial Law
Criminal Procedure
Environmental Law
Evidence
Family Law
Government/Regulation
Indian/Tribal Law
Insurance Law
Intellectual Property
International/Comparative Law
Labor Law
Land Use Law/Natural Resources
Lawyering Skills
Legal History/Philosophy
Legislation
Litigation
Probate Law
Tax Law
Trusts and Estates
Water Law

Clinical Courses Students receive degree credit for clinical courses. Among the clinical areas offered are:

Civil Litigation
Criminal Defense
Family Practice
General Practice
Indian/Tribal Law
Juvenile Law

International exchange programs permit students to visit Norway.

CAPITAL UNIVERSITY
LAW SCHOOL

Columbus, Ohio

INFORMATION CONTACT

Linda J. Mihely, Assistant Dean of Admissions and
Financial Aid
303 East Broad Street
Columbus, OH 43215-3200

Phone: 614-236-6310   Fax: 614-236-6972
E-mail: admissions@law.capital.edu
Web site: http://www.law.capital.edu/

LAW STUDENT PROFILE [2000–2001]

FULL-TIME   Enrollment: 403
Women: 47%   Men: 53%

PART-TIME   Enrollment: 333
Women: 47%   Men: 53%

RACIAL or ETHNIC COMPOSITION
African American, 8%; Asian/Pacific Islander, 1%; Hispanic,
2%; Native American, 0.1%

APPLICANTS and ADMITTEES
Number applied: 957
Admitted: 598
Percentage accepted: 62%
Seats available: 255
Average LSAT score: 150
Average GPA: 3.1

Capital University Law School is a private institution
that organizes classes on a semester calendar system. The
campus is situated in an urban setting. Founded in 1903,
first ABA approved in 1950, and an AALS member,
Capital University Law School offers JD, JD/LLM,
JD/MBA, JD/MSA, JD/MSN, and LLM degrees.

Faculty consists of 29 full-time and 36 part-time
members in 2000–2001. 6 full-time faculty members and
7 part-time faculty members are women. 100% of all
faculty members have a JD; 35.5% have advanced law
degrees. Of all faculty members, 12.9% are African
American, 87.1% are white.

Application Information *Required:* LSAT, LSDAS,
application form, application fee of $35, baccalaureate
degree, 2 letters of recommendation, personal statement,
college transcripts. *Recommended:* essay. *Application
deadline* for fall term is May 1 (priority date). Applications are processed on a rolling basis.

Costs The 2000–2001 tuition was $16,248 full-time; $677
per credit hour part-time. Fees: $677 per credit hour
full-time; $677 per credit hour part-time.

Financial Aid In 2000–2001, 82% of all students received
some form of financial aid. 17 research assistantships,
totaling $2800; 20 teaching assistantships, totaling $4000,
were awarded. Graduate assistantships, loans, merit-based
grants/scholarships, need-based grants/scholarships, and
federal work-study loans are also available. The average
student debt at graduation is $44,000. To apply for
financial assistance, students must complete the Free
Application for Federal Student Aid, institutional forms.

AT a GLANCE

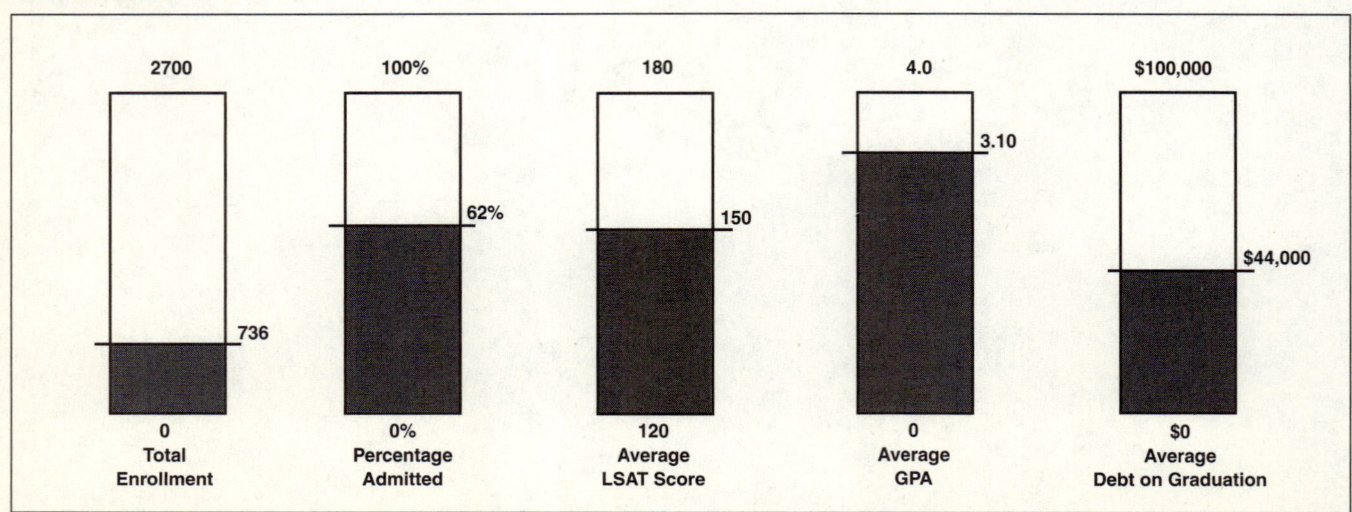

Degree Options

Degree	Total Credits Required	Length of Program
JD–Doctor of Laws	86	3–4 yrs, full-time or part-time [day, evening, summer]
JD/LLM–Juris Doctor/Master of Laws	98	3.5–4.5 yrs, full-time or part-time [day, evening, summer]
JD/MBA–Juris Doctor/Master of Business Administration	118	4–5 yrs, full-time or part-time [day, evening, summer]
JD/MSA–Juris Doctor/Master of Sports Administration	106	3.5–4.5 yrs, full-time or part-time [day, evening, summer]
JD/MSN–Juris Doctor/Master of Science in Nursing	101	4–5 yrs, full-time or part-time [day, evening, summer]
LLM–Master of Laws–Business	24	1–2 yrs, full-time or part-time [day, evening, summer]
LLM–Master of Laws–Taxation	24	1–2 yrs, full-time or part-time [day, evening, summer]

Completed financial aid forms should be received by April 1. Financial aid contact: Samantha Stalnaker, Assistant Director of Admission and Financial Aid, 303 East Broad Street, Columbus, OH 43215-3200. Phone: 614-236-6350. Fax: 614-236-6972. E-mail: b.birk@law.capital.edu

Law School Library Capital University Law School Library has 6 professional staff members and contains more than 252,145 volumes and 2,240 periodicals. 460 seats are available in the library. When classes are in session, the library is open 168 hours per week.

WESTLAW and LEXIS-NEXIS are available, as are the World Wide Web, online bibliographic services, and CD-ROM players. 100 computer workstations are available to students in the library.

First-Year Program Class size in the average section is 85; 100% of the first-year courses are taught by full-time faculty.

Upper-Level Program Class size in the average section is 40. Among the electives are:

Administrative Law
Advocacy
★ Business and Corporate Law
★ Civil Litigation
Corporate Finance
Criminal Defense

★ Dispute Resolution
★ Environmental Law
★ Family Law
★ Government/Regulation
Health Care/Human Services
Indian/Tribal Law
Intellectual Property
★ International/Comparative Law
Jurisprudence
★ Labor Law
Land Use Law/Natural Resources
Lawyering Skills
Legal History/Philosophy
★ Litigation
★ Local Government
Media Law
Mediation
Probate Law
★ Securities
★ Sports Law
★ Tax Law
(★ indicates an area of special strength)

Clinical Courses Students receive degree credit for clinical courses. (Clinical practicum is not required.) Among the clinical areas offered are:

Civil Litigation
Criminal Defense
Mediation

International exchange programs permit students to visit Canada, Germany, and United Kingdom.

CASE WESTERN RESERVE UNIVERSITY
SCHOOL OF LAW

Cleveland, Ohio

INFORMATION CONTACT

Barbara Andelman, Associate Dean for Student Services
11075 East Boulevard
Cleveland, OH 44106

Phone: 216-368-3600   Fax: 216-368-1042
E-mail: lawadmissions@po.cwru.edu
Web site: http://lawwww.cwru.edu/

LAW STUDENT PROFILE [2000–2001]

FULL-TIME   Enrollment: 665
Women: 44%   Men: 56%

PART-TIME   Enrollment: 51
Women: 39%   Men: 61%

RACIAL or ETHNIC COMPOSITION

African American, 5%; Asian/Pacific Islander, 5%; Hispanic, 1%; International, 7%

APPLICANTS and ADMITTEES

Number applied: 1,461
Admitted: 982
Percentage accepted: 67%
Median LSAT score: 155
Average GPA: 3.2

Case Western Reserve University School of Law is a private institution that organizes classes on a semester calendar system. The campus is situated in an urban setting. Founded in 1892, first ABA approved in 1923, and an AALS member, Case Western Reserve University School of Law offers JD, JD/MA, JD/MBA, JD/MD, JD/MNO, JD/MPH, JD/MSN, JD/MSW, and LLM degrees.

Faculty consists of 41 full-time and 39 part-time members in 2000–2001. 10 full-time faculty members and 11 part-time faculty members are women. 100% of all faculty members have a JD; 15.5% have advanced law degrees. Of all faculty members, 6.5% are African American, 93.5% are white.

Application Information *Required:* LSAT, LSDAS, application form, application fee of $40, baccalaureate degree, personal statement, resume. *Recommended:* recommendations. *Application deadline* for fall term is April 1 (priority date). Applications are processed on a rolling basis.

Costs The 2000–2001 tuition was $22,200 full-time; $825 per credit hour part-time. Fees: $60 full-time; $60 per year part-time.

Financial Aid In 2000–2001, 68% of all students received some form of financial aid. Loans, loan repayment assistance program (LRAP), merit-based grants/scholarships, and federal work-study loans are available. The average student debt at graduation is $51,700. To apply for financial assistance, students must complete the Free Application for Federal Student Aid, institutional forms.

AT a GLANCE

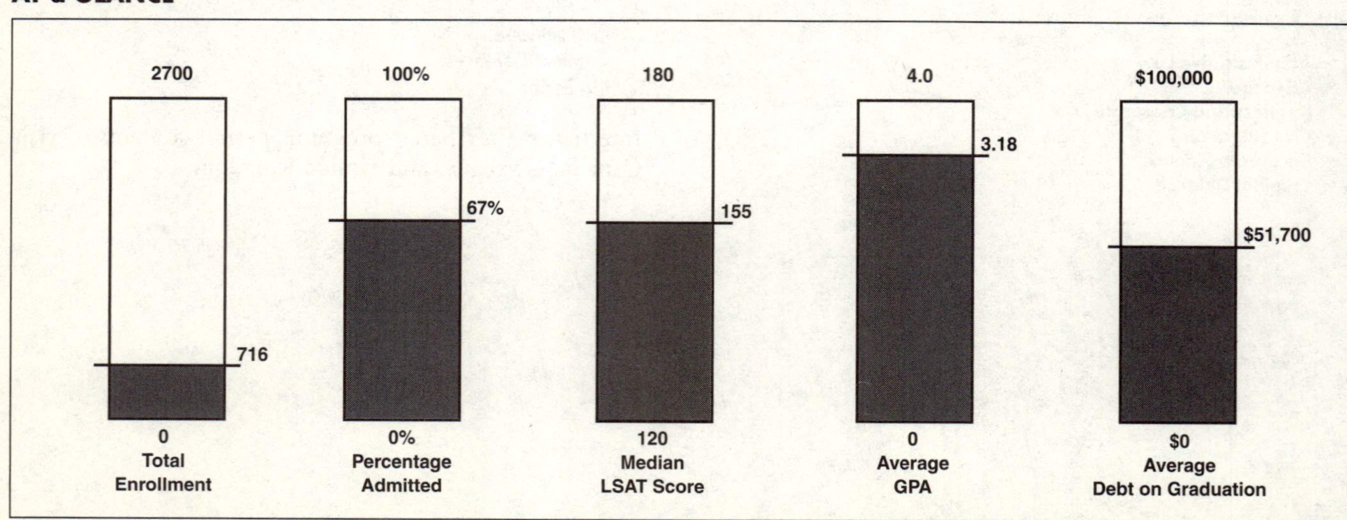

Degree Options

Degree	Total Credits Required	Length of Program
JD–Doctor of Laws	88	3 yrs, full-time or part-time [day]
JD/MA–Juris Doctor/Master of Arts–Legal History	100	3–4 yrs, full-time only [day]
JD/MA–Juris Doctor/Master of Arts–Bioethics	97	4 yrs, full-time only [day]
JD/MBA–Juris Doctor/Master of Business Administration–Management	126	4 yrs, full-time only [day]
JD/MD–Juris Doctor/Doctor of Medicine		6 yrs, full-time only [day, summer]
JD/MNO–Juris Doctor/Master of Nonprofit Organizations–Nonprofit Management	106	4 yrs, full-time only [day]
JD/MPH–Juris Doctor/Master of Public Health–Public Health		4.5 yrs, full-time only [day]
JD/MSN–Juris Doctor/Master of Science in Nursing–Nursing	112	4.5 yrs, full-time only
JD/MSW–Juris Doctor/Master of Social Work–Social Work	112	4 yrs, full-time only [day]
LLM–Master of Laws–US Legal Studies	24	1 yr, full-time only [day]
LLM–Master of Laws–Taxation	24	1 yr, full-time or part-time [evening]

Completed financial aid forms should be received by March 15. Financial aid contact: Jay Ruffner, Student Finances Administrator, 11075 East Boulevard, Cleveland, OH 44106. Phone: 877-889-4279 or toll free 800-756-0036. Fax: 216-368-6144. E-mail: lawmoney@po.cwru.edu

Law School Library CWRU School of Law Library has 10 professional staff members and contains more than 372,438 volumes and 4,917 periodicals. 411 seats are available in the library. When classes are in session, the library is open 108 hours per week.

WESTLAW and LEXIS-NEXIS are available, as are the World Wide Web and CD-ROM players. 78 computer workstations are available to students in the library. Special law collections include British Collection, taxation, labor law, foreign investments, law-medicine, international law.

First-Year Program Class size in the average section is 72; 100% of the first-year courses are taught by full-time faculty.

Upper-Level Program Class size in the average section is 30. Among the electives are:

Administrative Law
Advocacy
★ Business and Corporate Law
★ Civil Litigation
Consumer Law
Criminal Defense
Criminal Prosecution
Environmental Law
Family Law
Government/Regulation

Health Care/Human Services
★ Health Law
★ Intellectual Property
★ International/Comparative Law
Jurisprudence
Juvenile Law
Labor Law
Land Use Law/Natural Resources
★ Law and Technology
★ Lawyering Skills
Legal History/Philosophy
★ Litigation
Media Law
Mediation
Probate Law
★ Public Interest
★ Securities
★ Tax Law
(★ indicates an area of special strength)

Clinical Courses Students receive degree credit for clinical courses. (Clinical practicum is not required.) Among the clinical areas offered are:

Civil Litigation
Community Development
Criminal Defense
Criminal Prosecution
Family Practice
General Practice
Government Litigation
Health Law
Juvenile Law
Mediation

International exchange programs permit students to visit Canada and Mexico.

CLEVELAND STATE UNIVERSITY
CLEVELAND-MARSHALL COLLEGE OF LAW

Cleveland, Ohio

INFORMATION CONTACT

Margaret McNally, Assistant Dean for Admissions
1801 Euclid Avenue
Cleveland, OH 44115

Phone: 216-687-2304   Fax: 216-687-6881
E-mail: admissions@law.csuohio.edu
Web site: http://www.law.csuohio.edu/

LAW STUDENT PROFILE [2000–2001]

FULL-TIME   Enrollment: 474
Women: 50%   Men: 50%

PART-TIME   Enrollment: 315
Women: 50%   Men: 50%

RACIAL or ETHNIC COMPOSITION
African American, 8%; Asian/Pacific Islander, 2%; Hispanic, 2%; Native American, 0.1%; International, 1%

APPLICANTS and ADMITTEES
Number applied: 1,158
Admitted: 636
Percentage accepted: 55%
Seats available: 278
Average LSAT score: 151
Average GPA: 3.1

Cleveland State University Cleveland-Marshall College of Law is a public institution that organizes classes on a semester calendar system. The campus is situated in an urban setting. Founded in 1897, first ABA approved in 1957, and an AALS member, Cleveland State University Cleveland-Marshall College of Law offers JD, JD/MBA, JD/MES, JD/MPAd, and JD/MUP degrees.

Faculty consists of 54 full-time and 19 part-time members in 2000–2001. 24 full-time faculty members and 6 part-time faculty members are women. 100% of all faculty members have a JD; 18% have advanced law degrees. Of all faculty members, 1.8% are Asian/Pacific Islander, 7.2% are African American, 89.2% are white, 1.8% are international.

Application Information *Required:* LSAT, LSDAS, application form, application fee of $35, baccalaureate degree, 2 letters of recommendation, personal statement, writing sample, college transcripts. *Recommended:* resume. *Application deadline* for fall term is April 1. Applications are processed on a rolling basis.

Costs The 2000–2001 tuition was $7579 full-time for state residents; $319 per credit part-time for state residents. Tuition was $15,736 full-time for nonresidents; $633 per credit part-time for nonresidents. Fees: $734 full-time; $282 per term part-time. Tuition and fees vary according to course load and degree level.

Financial Aid In 2000–2001, 89% of all students received some form of financial aid. 281 fellowships, totaling $2683; 40 research assistantships, were awarded. Loans, merit-based grants/scholarships, need-based grants/

AT a GLANCE

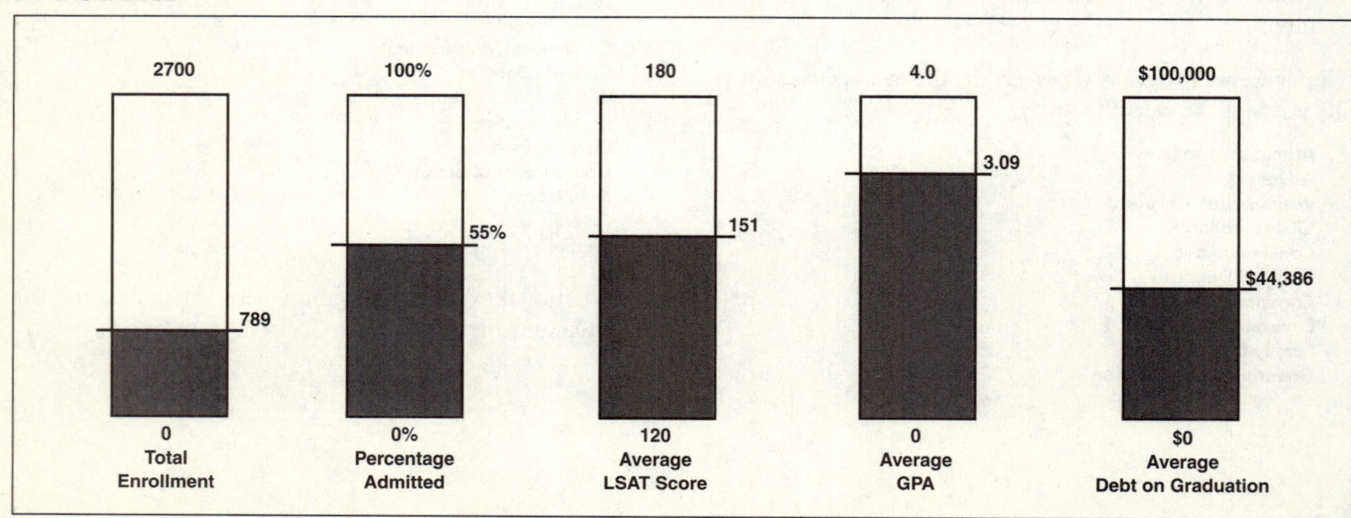

Degree Options

Degree	Total Credits Required	Length of Program
JD–Doctor of Laws	90	3–4 yrs, full-time or part-time [day, evening, summer]
JD/MBA–Juris Doctor/Master of Business Administration–Dual-degree Program	103	4–6 yrs, full-time or part-time [day, evening, summer]
JD/MES–Juris Doctor/Master of Environmental Studies–Dual-degree	110	4–6 yrs, full-time or part-time [day, evening, summer]
JD/MPAd–Juris Doctor/Master of Public Administration–Dual-degree	114	4–6 yrs, full-time or part-time [day, evening, summer]
JD/MUP–Juris Doctor/Masters of Urban Planning–Dual-degree	122	4–6 yrs, full-time or part-time [day, evening, summer]

scholarships, and federal work-study loans are also available. The average student debt at graduation is $44,386. To apply for financial assistance, students must complete the Free Application for Federal Student Aid, institutional forms, scholarship specific applications, loan application. Completed financial aid forms should be received by April 1. Financial aid contact: Catherine Buzanski, Financial Aid Administrator, Cleveland-Marshall College of Law, CSU, 1801 Euclid Avenue, Cleveland, OH 44115. Phone: 216-687-6887. Fax: 216-687-6881. E-mail: catherine.buzanski@law.csuohio.edu

Law School Library Cleveland-Marshall College of Law Library has 13 professional staff members and contains more than 463,106 volumes and 3,483 periodicals. 396 seats are available in the library. When classes are in session, the library is open 95 hours per week.

WESTLAW and LEXIS-NEXIS are available, as are the World Wide Web, online bibliographic services, and CD-ROM players. 53 computer workstations are available to students in the library. Special law collections include federal government depository.

First-Year Program Class size in the average section is 57; 100% of the first-year courses are taught by full-time faculty.

Upper-Level Program Class size in the average section is 40. Among the electives are:

Administrative Law
Admiralty Law
★ Advocacy
Agency
AIDS and the Law
Alternative Dispute Resolution
American Legal History
Antitrust Law
Appellate Advocacy
Arbitration
Banking and Finance
Banking Law & Regulation
Bankruptcy
Bioethics
★ Business and Corporate Law

Business Organizations
Canon Law
Capital Punishment
Children and the Law
Chinese Law
Church-State
Civil Liberties
Civil Procedure
Civil Rights
Commercial Law
Common Law
★ Community Advocacy
Comparative Constitutional Law
Computer Law
Computer/Cyberspace Law
Constitutional Law
Contract Theory
Copyright & Trademark Law
Corporate Restructuring
Corporate Taxation
Criminal Defense
★ Criminal Law
Criminal Procedure
Elder Law
Employment Discrimination
★ Employment Law
Entertainment Law
★ Environmental Law
Estate & Gift Taxation
Estate Planning
Estates & Trusts
Ethics
European Community Law
European Union Law
Evidence
Extern
★ Fair Housing
Family Law
Federal Courts
Federal Income Tax
Federal Jurisdiction
First Amendment
Health Care Law
Health Care/Human Services
Housing Law
Immigration
Indian/Tribal Law
Injury Law
Intellectual Property
International Business Transactions
International Criminal Law
International Environmental Law

International Human Rights
International Income Tax
International Intellectual Property
International Law
International Trade
International Trademark
International/Comparative Law
Interviewing and Counseling
Islamic Law
Jewish Law
Judicial Externship
Jurisprudence
Juvenile Law
Labor Arbitration
Labor Law
Land Use Law/Natural Resources
Landlord/Tenant
Law and Economics
Law and Medicine
Law and Psychiatry
Law and Social Science
Law and the Arts
Law Practice Management
Lawyering Skills
Legal Ethics
Legal History/Philosophy
Legal Methods
Legal Research
Legal Services
Litigation
Local Government
Media Law
Mediation
Mental Health and Law
Nonprofit Organizations

Partnerships
Patent Law
Pensions
Poverty/Welfare Law
Pretrial Litigation
Product Liability
Professional Responsibility
Property/Real Estate
Psychiatry and Law
Race and Law
Real Estate Transactions
Remedies
Secured Transactions
Securities
Securities Regulation
Sexual Orientation and the Law
Small Business Representation
State and Local Government
Tax Law
Tax Policy
Trial Advocacy
Women and the Law
Workers' Compensation

(★ *indicates an area of special strength*)

Clinical Courses Students receive degree credit for clinical courses. (Clinical practicum is not required.) Among the clinical areas offered are:

Community Advocacy
Employment Law
Environmental Law
Fair Housing

OHIO NORTHERN UNIVERSITY
CLAUDE W. PETTIT COLLEGE OF LAW

Ada, Ohio

INFORMATION CONTACT

Sandy Reid, Secretary in Law Admissions
Ohio Northern University of Law
525 South Main Street
Ada, OH 45810-1599

Phone: 419-772-2211   Fax: 419-772-1487
E-mail: s-reid@onu.edu
Web site: http://www.law.onu.edu/

LAW STUDENT PROFILE [2000–2001]

FULL-TIME   Enrollment: 287
Women: 41%   Men: 59%

RACIAL or ETHNIC COMPOSITION
African American, 4%; Asian/Pacific Islander, 3%; Hispanic, 4%; Native American, 1%

APPLICANTS and ADMITTEES
Number applied: 990
Admitted: 659
Percentage accepted: 67%
Seats available: 115

Ohio Northern University Claude W. Pettit College of Law is a private institution that organizes classes on a semester calendar system. The campus is situated in a small-town setting. Founded in 1885, first ABA approved in 1939, and an AALS member, Ohio Northern University Claude W. Pettit College of Law offers a JD degree.

Faculty consists of 17 full-time and 12 part-time members in 2000–2001. 6 full-time faculty members and 5 part-time faculty members are women. 100% of all faculty members have a JD; 33.3% have advanced law degrees. Of all faculty members, 5% are African American, 95% are white.

Application Information *Required:* LSAT, LSDAS, application form, application fee of $40, baccalaureate degree, 2 letters of recommendation, personal statement, college transcripts. *Recommended:* minimum 2.0 GPA, resume. *Application deadline* is rolling.

Costs The 2000–2001 tuition was $19,740 full-time. Fees: $60 full-time (one-time charge for full-time students). Full-time tuition and fees vary according to course load, degree level, and program.

Financial Aid 25 research assistantships were awarded. Graduate assistantships, loans, merit-based grants/scholarships, need-based grants/scholarships, and federal work-study loans are also available. The average student debt at graduation is $50,000. To apply for financial assistance, students must complete the Free Application for Federal Student Aid, institutional forms. Completed financial aid forms should be received by May 1. Financial aid contact: Wendell Schick, Director of

AT a GLANCE

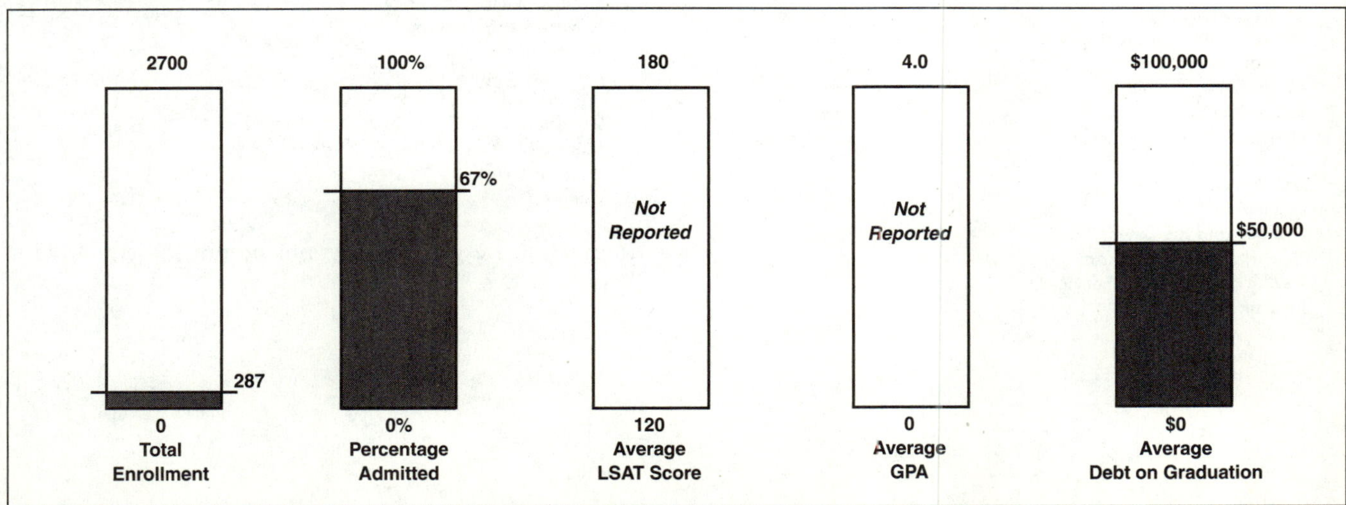

Degree Options

Degree	Total Credits Required	Length of Program
JD–Doctor of Laws	87	3–4 yrs, full-time only [day, summer]

Financial Aid Services, Ohio Northern University, Ada, OH 45810-1599. Phone: 419-772-2272. Fax: 419-772-2313. E-mail: w-schick@onu.edu

Law School Library Tagart Law Library has 4 professional staff members and contains more than 275,000 volumes and 3,000 periodicals. 310 seats are available in the library. When classes are in session, the library is open 108 hours per week.

WESTLAW and LEXIS-NEXIS are available, as are the World Wide Web and CD-ROM players. 40 computer workstations are available to students in the library. Special law collections include federal government depository.

First-Year Program Class size in the average section is 50; 87% of the first-year courses are taught by full-time faculty.

Upper-Level Program Class size in the average section is 20. Among the electives are:

 Administrative Law
★ Advocacy
 Alternative Dispute Resolution
 Antitrust Law
★ Business and Corporate Law
★ Civil Litigation
 Civil Rights
 Commercial Transactions
 Comparative Constitutional Law
 Complex Litigation
 Conflict of Laws
 Consumer Law
 Corporate Law
 Corporate Taxation
★ Criminal Defense
★ Criminal Prosecution
 Elderly Advocacy
 Environmental and Toxic Torts
 Environmental Law
 Estate & Gift Taxation
 Estate Planning
 Estates & Trusts
★ Family Law
★ Family Practice
 Federal Courts
 Gender and the Law
 Government/Regulation
 Health Care/Human Services
 Insurance Law

 International Law
 International/Comparative Law
 Jurisprudence
 Juvenile Law
 Labor Law
 Land Use Law/Natural Resources
 Law and Literature
 Law and Medicine
★ Lawyering Skills
 Legal History/Philosophy
★ Litigation
 Mediation
 Probate Law
 Public Interest
 Real Estate Transactions
 Remedies
 Securities
 Securities Regulation
 Sports Law
 Street Law
★ Tax Law
 Torts & Product Liability
 Trial Advocacy
 Workers' Compensation
(★ *indicates an area of special strength*)

Clinical Courses Students receive degree credit for clinical courses. (Clinical practicum is not required.) Among the clinical areas offered are:

 Administrative Law
 Bankruptcy
 Civil Litigation
 Civil Rights
 Corporate Law
 Criminal Defense
 Criminal Prosecution
 Education
 Elderly Advocacy
 Environmental Law
 Family Law
 Family Practice
 Government/Regulation
 Juvenile Law
 Lawyering Skills
 Legislation
 Litigation
 Mediation
 Public Interest
 Tax Law

International exchange programs permit students to visit Iceland.

THE OHIO STATE UNIVERSITY
COLLEGE OF LAW

Columbus, Ohio

INFORMATION CONTACT

Kathy S. Northern, Associate Dean
55 West 12th Avenue
Columbus, OH 43210

Phone: 614-292-8810   Fax: 614-292-1492
E-mail: lawadmit@osu.edu
Web site: http://www.osu.edu/law/

LAW STUDENT PROFILE [2000–2001]

FULL-TIME   Enrollment: 653
Women: 46%   Men: 54%

PART-TIME   Enrollment: 2
Women: 50%   Men: 50%

RACIAL or ETHNIC COMPOSITION
African American, 10%; Asian/Pacific Islander, 6%; Hispanic, 3%; Native American, 0.3%; International, 2%

APPLICANTS and ADMITTEES
Number applied: 1,499
Admitted: 594
Percentage accepted: 40%
Seats available: 210
Average LSAT score: 157
Average GPA: 3.5

The Ohio State University College of Law is a public institution that organizes classes on a semester calendar system. The campus is situated in an urban setting. Founded in 1891, first ABA approved in 1923, and an AALS member, The Ohio State University College of Law offers JD, JD/MA, JD/MBA, JD/MHA, JD/MPAd, and JD/PhD degrees.

Faculty consists of 53 full-time and 33 part-time members in 2000–2001. 22 full-time faculty members and 16 part-time faculty members are women. 100% of all faculty members have a JD; 10% have advanced law degrees. Of all faculty members, 2% are Asian/Pacific Islander, 12% are African American, 2% are Hispanic, 84% are white.

Application Information *Required:* LSAT, LSDAS, application form, application fee of $30, baccalaureate degree, 2 letters of recommendation, personal statement, college transcripts. *Recommended:* resume. *Application deadline* for fall term is March 15 (priority date). Applications are processed on a rolling basis.

Costs The 2000–2001 tuition was $9984 full-time for area residents. Tuition was $20,342 full-time for nonresidents. Fees: $27 full-time; $25 full-time (one-time charge for full-time students). Full-time tuition and fees vary according to program.

Financial Aid In 2000–2001, 64% of all students received some form of financial aid. Fellowships, loans, loan repayment assistance program (LRAP), merit-based grants/scholarships, need-based grants/scholarships, and federal work-study loans are available. The average

AT a GLANCE

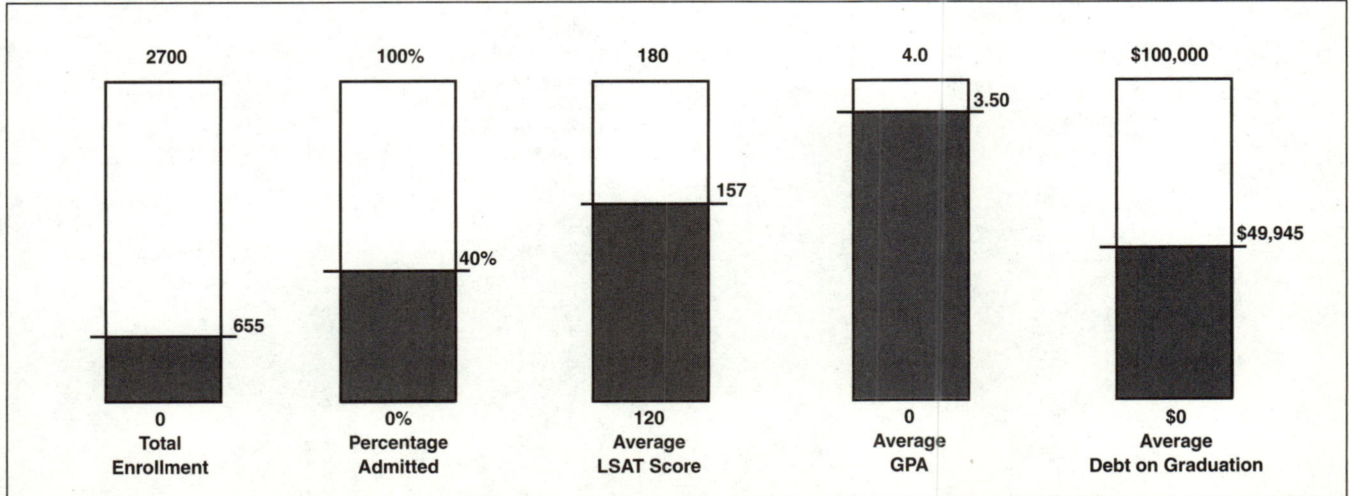

Degree Options

Degree	Total Credits Required	Length of Program
JD–Doctor of Laws	88	3 yrs, full-time only [day, summer]
JD/MA–Juris Doctor/Master of Arts–Dual-degree Program		4 yrs, full-time only [day, summer]
JD/MBA–Juris Doctor/Master of Business Administration–Dual-degree Program		4 yrs, full-time only [day, summer]
JD/MHA–Juris Doctor/Master of Health Administration–Dual-degree Program		4 yrs, full-time only [day, summer]
JD/MPAd–Juris Doctor/Master of Public Administration–Dual-degree Program		4 yrs, full-time only [day, summer]
JD/PhD–Juris Doctor/Doctor of Philosophy–Dual Degree program		5 yrs, full-time only [day, summer]

student debt at graduation is $49,945. To apply for financial assistance, students must complete the Free Application for Federal Student Aid, institutional forms. Completed financial aid forms should be received by March 1. Financial aid contact: Assistant Dean, 55 West 12th Avenue, Columbus, OH 43210. Phone: 614-292-8810. Fax: 614-292-1492. E-mail: lawfinaid@osu.edu

Law School Library The Ohio State University Moritz Law Library has 9 professional staff members and contains more than 691,723 volumes and 8,374 periodicals. 660 seats are available in the library. When classes are in session, the library is open 107 hours per week.

WESTLAW and LEXIS-NEXIS are available, as are the World Wide Web, online bibliographic services, and CD-ROM players. 55 computer workstations are available to students in the library. Special law collections include dispute resolution, labor law, health care policy, foreign and international law.

First-Year Program Class size in the average section is 75; 100% of the first-year courses are taught by full-time faculty.

Upper-Level Program Class size in the average section is 39. Among the electives are:

- Administrative Law
- Advocacy
- ★ Arbitration
- Business and Corporate Law
- ★ Civil Litigation
- Consumer Law
- ★ Criminal Defense
- ★ Criminal Law
- ★ Criminal Prosecution
- Education Law
- Entertainment Law
- Environmental Law
- Family Law
- Government/Regulation
- ★ Health Care/Human Services
- ★ Intellectual Property
- ★ International/Comparative Law
- Jurisprudence
- ★ Juvenile Law
- Labor Law
- Land Use Law/Natural Resources
- ★ Lawyering Skills
- Legal History/Philosophy
- ★ Legislation
- Litigation
- Media Law
- ★ Mediation
- ★ Negotiation
- Probate Law
- Public Interest
- Securities
- Tax Law

(★ indicates an area of special strength)

Clinical Courses Students receive degree credit for clinical courses. (Clinical practicum is not required.) Among the clinical areas offered are:

- Civil Litigation
- Criminal Defense
- Criminal Prosecution
- Juvenile Law
- Legislation
- Mediation

THE UNIVERSITY OF AKRON
SCHOOL OF LAW

Akron, Ohio

LAW STUDENT PROFILE [2000–2001]

FULL-TIME   Enrollment: 311
Women: 47%   Men: 53%

PART-TIME   Enrollment: 212
Women: 48%   Men: 52%

RACIAL or ETHNIC COMPOSITION
African American, 8%; Asian/Pacific Islander, 2%; Hispanic, 2%

APPLICANTS and ADMITTEES
Number applied: 1,273
Admitted: 426
Percentage accepted: 33%
Seats available: 173
Average LSAT score: 153
Average GPA: 3.2

The University of Akron School of Law is a public institution that organizes classes on a semester calendar system. The campus is situated in an urban setting. Founded in 1921, first ABA approved in 1961, and an AALS member, The University of Akron School of Law offers JD, JD/MBA, JD/MPAd, and JD/MTAX degrees.

Faculty consists of 20 full-time and 27 part-time members in 2000–2001. 7 full-time faculty members and 15 part-time faculty members are women. 100% of all faculty members have a JD degree. Of all faculty members, 3% are Asian/Pacific Islander, 12% are African American, 85% are white.

Application Information *Required:* LSAT, LSDAS, application form, application fee of $35, baccalaureate degree, minimum 2.0 GPA, personal statement, college transcripts. *Recommended:* recommendations, resume. *Application deadline* for fall term is March 1 (priority date).

Costs The 2000–2001 tuition was $7873 full-time for state residents; $246 per credit part-time for state residents. Tuition was $13,648 full-time for nonresidents; $426 per credit part-time for nonresidents. Tuition was $13,648 full-time for international students. Fees: $1176 full-time; $588 per semester full-time; $50 per course part-time; $326 per semester part-time.

Financial Aid In 2000–2001, 59% of all students received some form of financial aid. Graduate assistantships, loans, merit-based grants/scholarships, and need-based grants/scholarships are available. The average student debt at graduation is $41,340. To apply for financial

AT a GLANCE

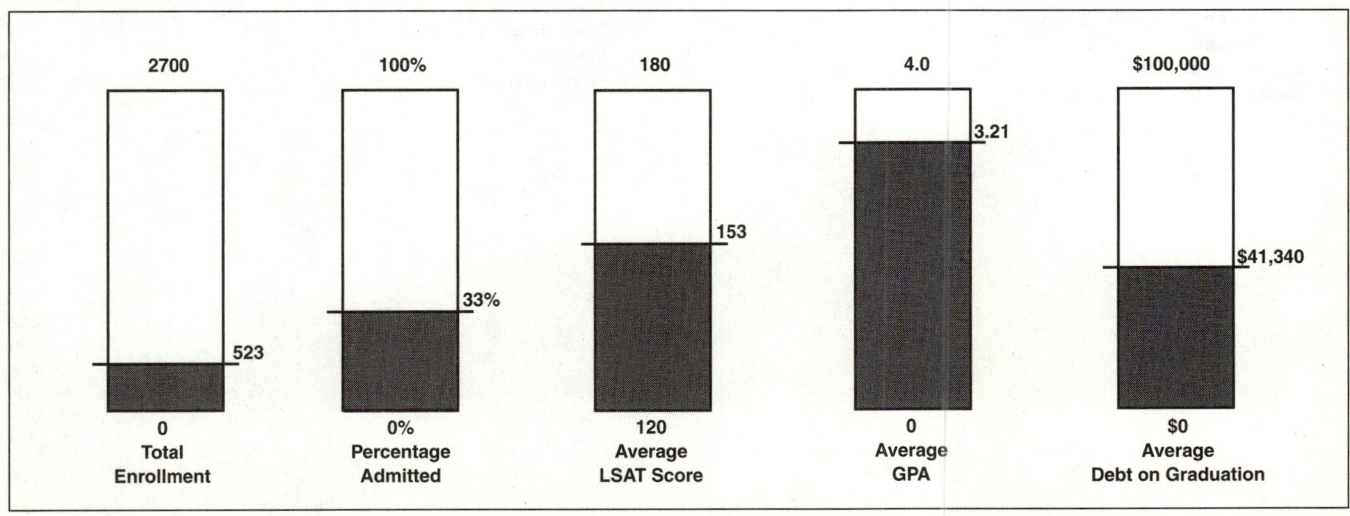

Degree Options

Degree	Total Credits Required	Length of Program
JD–Juris Doctor	88	3–4.5 yrs, full-time or part-time [day, evening, summer]
JD/MBA–Juris Doctor/Master of Business Administration–Dual-degree Program	103	3–4.5 yrs, full-time or part-time [day, evening, summer]
JD/MPAd–Juris Doctor/Master of Public Administration–Dual-degree Program	109	3–4.5 yrs, full-time or part-time [day, evening, summer]
JD/MTAX–Juris Doctor/Master of Taxation–Dual-degree Program	98	3–4.5 yrs, full-time or part-time [day, evening, summer]

assistance, students must complete the Free Application for Federal Student Aid. Completed financial aid forms should be received by May 1. Financial aid contact: Lauri S. File, Director of Admissions and Financial Assistance, Assistant to the Dean, The University of Akron School of Law, Akron, OH 44325-2901. Phone: 330-972-7331 or toll free 800-4-AKRONU. Fax: 330-258-2343. E-mail: lawadmissions@uakron.edu

Law School Library The University of Akron School of Law Library has 5 professional staff members and contains more than 262,766 volumes and 3,325 periodicals. 300 seats are available in the library. When classes are in session, the library is open 95 hours per week.

WESTLAW and LEXIS-NEXIS are available, as are the World Wide Web, online bibliographic services, and CD-ROM players. 60 computer workstations are available to students in the library. Special law collections include intellectual property.

First-Year Program Class size in the average section is 42; 95% of the first-year courses are taught by full-time faculty.

Upper-Level Program Class size in the average section is 28. Among the electives are:

  Administrative Law
★ Advocacy
★ Business and Corporate Law
  Civil Litigation
★ Constitutional Law
  Consumer Law
★ Criminal Defense
  Criminal Prosecution
  Education Law
  Entertainment Law
  Environmental Law
  Family Law
  Government/Regulation
  Health Care/Human Services
★ Intellectual Property
  International/Comparative Law
  Juvenile Law
  Labor Law
  Land Use Law/Natural Resources
  Lawyering Skills
★ Litigation
  Media Law
  Mediation
  Probate Law
  Securities
★ Tax Law
(★ *indicates an area of special strength*)

Clinical Courses Students receive degree credit for clinical courses. (Clinical practicum is not required.) Among the clinical areas offered are:

  Advocacy
  Civil Litigation
  Civil Rights
  Constitutional Law
  Criminal Defense
  Criminal Prosecution
  Family Practice
  Juvenile Law
  Lawyering Skills
  Mediation
  Public Interest

UNIVERSITY OF CINCINNATI
COLLEGE OF LAW

Cincinnati, Ohio

INFORMATION CONTACT

Al Watson, Assistant Dean and Director of Admissions
PO Box 210040
Cincinnati, OH 45221-0040

Phone: 513-556-0077   Fax: 513-556-2391
E-mail: al.watson@uc.edu
Web site: http://www.law.uc.edu/

LAW STUDENT PROFILE [2000–2001]

FULL-TIME   Enrollment: 392
Women: 54%   Men: 46%

RACIAL or ETHNIC COMPOSITION
African American, 11%; Asian/Pacific Islander, 4%; Hispanic, 4%; Native American, 1%

APPLICANTS and ADMITTEES
Number applied: 1,066
Admitted: 475
Percentage accepted: 45%
Seats available: 128
Average LSAT score: 158
Average GPA: 3.5

University of Cincinnati College of Law is a public institution that organizes classes on a semester calendar system. The campus is situated in an urban setting. Founded in 1833, first ABA approved in 1923, and an AALS member, University of Cincinnati College of Law offers JD, JD/MA, JD/MBA, and JD/MCP degrees.

Faculty consists of 29 full-time and 52 part-time members in 2000–2001. 13 full-time faculty members and 14 part-time faculty members are women. 100% of all faculty members have a JD; 32% have advanced law degrees. Of all faculty members, 5% are Asian/Pacific Islander, 11% are African American, 84% are white.

Application Information *Required:* LSAT, LSDAS, application form, application fee of $35, baccalaureate degree, 2 letters of recommendation. *Recommended:* personal statement, essay, writing sample, college transcripts, resume. *Application deadline* for fall term is April 1 (priority date). Applications are processed on a rolling basis.

Costs The 2000–2001 tuition was $7730 full-time for area residents. Tuition was $15,562 full-time for nonresidents. Fees: $870 full-time.

Financial Aid In 2000–2001, 75% of all students received some form of financial aid. 203 fellowships, totaling $5159; 74 research assistantships, were awarded. Fellowships, loans, merit-based grants/scholarships, need-based grants/scholarships, and federal work-study loans are also available. The average student debt at graduation is $42,800. To apply for financial assistance, students must complete the Free Application for Federal Student Aid,

AT a GLANCE

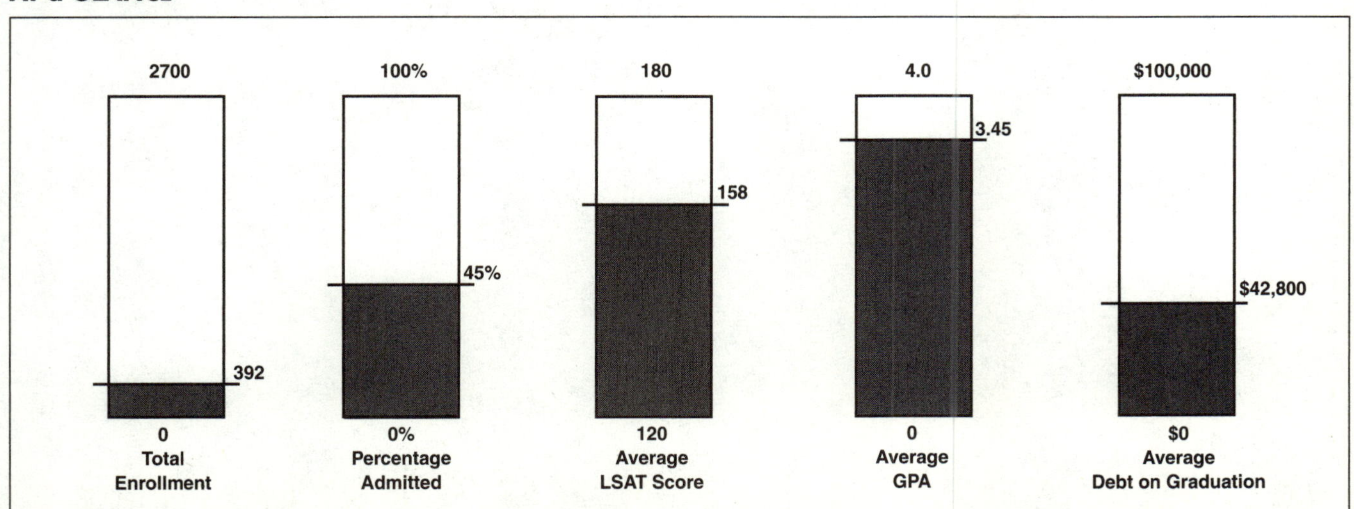

Degree Options

Degree	Total Credits Required	Length of Program
JD–Doctor of Laws	90	3 yrs, full-time only [day]
JD/MA–Juris Doctor/Master of Arts–Women's Studies Joint-degree Program	118	4 yrs, full-time only [day]
JD/MBA–Juris Doctor/Master of Business Administration–Dual-degree	110	4 yrs, full-time only [day]
JD/MCP–Juris Doctor/Master of City Planning–Joint-degree Program	118	4 yrs, full-time only [day]

institutional forms, scholarship specific applications. Completed financial aid forms should be received by March 1. Financial aid contact: Al Watson, Assistant Dean for Admission and Financial Aid, PO Box 210040, Cincinnati, OH 45221-0040. Phone: 513-556-6805. Fax: 513-556-2391. E-mail: admissions@law.uc.edu

Law School Library Robert S. Marx Law Library has 10 professional staff members and contains more than 385,111 volumes and 785 periodicals. 401 seats are available in the library. When classes are in session, the library is open 110 hours per week.

WESTLAW and LEXIS-NEXIS are available, as are the World Wide Web, online bibliographic services, and CD-ROM players. 56 computer workstations are available to students in the library. Special law collections include land use planning, church and state law, international human rights..

First-Year Program Class size in the average section is 47; 100% of the first-year courses are taught by full-time faculty.

Upper-Level Program Class size in the average section is 21. Among the electives are:

Accounting
Administrative Law
Advocacy
★ Business and Corporate Law
Consumer Law
Education
Entertainment Law
Environmental Law
Family Law
Government/Regulation
Health Care/Human Services
★ Human Rights
★ Intellectual Property
International/Comparative Law
Jurisprudence
Labor Law
Land Use Law/Natural Resources
Lawyering Skills
Legal History/Philosophy
Litigation
Maritime Law
Media Law
Mediation
Probate Law
Public Interest
Securities
Tax Law
(★ indicates an area of special strength)

UNIVERSITY OF DAYTON
SCHOOL OF LAW

Dayton, Ohio

INFORMATION CONTACT

Janet L. Hein, Director of Admissions and Financial Aid

300 College Park
Dayton, OH 45469-2760

Phone: 937-229-3555   Fax: 937-229-2469
E-mail: lawinfo@udayton.edu
Web site: http://www.law.udayton.edu

LAW STUDENT PROFILE [2000–2001]

FULL-TIME   Enrollment: 449
Women: 43%   Men: 57%

RACIAL or ETHNIC COMPOSITION

African American, 9%; Asian/Pacific Islander, 2%; Hispanic, 4%; Native American, 1%

APPLICANTS and ADMITTEES

Number applied: 1,334
Admitted: 741
Percentage accepted: 56%
Seats available: 167
Median LSAT score: 152
Average GPA: 3.1

University of Dayton School of Law is a private institution that organizes classes on a semester calendar system. The campus is situated in a suburban setting. Founded in 1974, first ABA approved in 1977, and an AALS member, University of Dayton School of Law offers JD and JD/MBA degrees.

Faculty consists of 27 full-time and 26 part-time members in 2000–2001. 9 full-time faculty members and 7 part-time faculty members are women. 100% of all faculty members have a JD; 19% have advanced law degrees. Of all faculty members, 7% are African American, 3% are Hispanic, 90% are white.

Application Information *Required:* LSAT, LSDAS, application form, application fee of $50, baccalaureate degree, 2 letters of recommendation, personal statement, college transcripts. *Recommended:* resume. *Application deadline* for fall term is May 1 (priority date). Applications are processed on a rolling basis.

Costs The 2000–2001 tuition was $20,756 full-time. Fees: $130 full-time.

Financial Aid Loans and merit-based grants/scholarships are available. The average student debt at graduation is $51,000. To apply for financial assistance, students must complete the Free Application for Federal Student Aid. Completed financial aid forms should be received by March 1. Financial aid contact: Janet Hein, Director of Admission and Financial Aid, 300 College Park, Dayton, OH 45469-2760. Phone: 937-229-3555. Fax: 937-229-4194. E-mail: hein@udayton.edu

AT a GLANCE

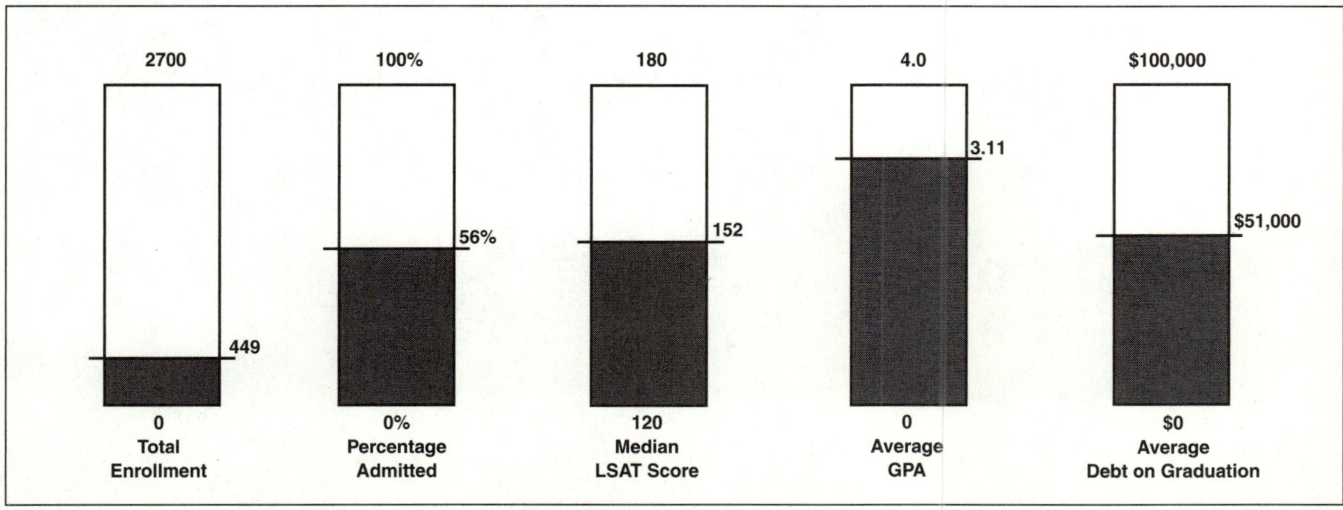

Degree Options

Degree	Total Credits Required	Length of Program
JD–Doctor of Laws	87	3–4 yrs, full-time or part-time [day, summer]
JD/MBA–Juris Doctor/Master of Business Administration–Dual-degree Program	109	4–5 yrs [day, evening]

Law School Library Zimmerman Law Library has 5 professional staff members and contains more than 277,115 volumes and 4,516 periodicals. 501 seats are available in the library. When classes are in session, the library is open 102 hours per week.

WESTLAW and LEXIS-NEXIS are available, as are the World Wide Web and CD-ROM players. 43 computer workstations are available to students in the library.

First-Year Program Class size in the average section is 83; 100% of the first-year courses are taught by full-time faculty.

Upper-Level Program Class size in the average section is 48. Among the electives are:

Administrative Law
★ Advocacy
Alternative Dispute Resolution
Appellate Litigation
Business and Corporate Law
Children and the Law
Computer Law
Computer/Cyberspace Law
Computers, Society, and the Law
Conflict of Laws
Consumer Law
Copyright & Trademark Law
★ Criminal Law
Criminology and Penology
Cyberspace Law

Employment Discrimination
Environmental Law
Evidence
Family Law
Health Care/Human Services
Human Rights
★ Intellectual Property
International/Comparative Law
Interviewing and Counseling
Judeo-Christian Ethics & the Law
Judicial Clerkship
Labor Law
Land Use Law/Natural Resources
Landlord/Tenant
★ Lawyering Skills
★ Litigation
Mediation
Medical Malpractice Law
Negotiation
Patent Law
Probate Law
Public Interest
Securities
Sports Law
★ Tax Law
Trusts and Estates
(★ *indicates an area of special strength*)

Clinical Courses Students receive degree credit for clinical courses. (Clinical practicum is not required.) The clinical area offered includes:

Civil Litigation

UNIVERSITY OF TOLEDO
COLLEGE OF LAW

Toledo, Ohio

INFORMATION CONTACT

Carol E. Frendt, Assistant Dean of Law Admissions
2801 West Bancroft Street
Toledo, OH 43606

Phone: 419-530-4131   Fax: 419-530-4345
E-mail: law.admissions@utoledo.edu
Web site: http://www.law.utoledo.edu/

LAW STUDENT PROFILE [2000–2001]

FULL-TIME   Enrollment: 327
Women: 47%   Men: 53%

PART-TIME   Enrollment: 134
Women: 43%   Men: 57%

RACIAL or ETHNIC COMPOSITION
African American, 5%; Asian/Pacific Islander, 0.4%; Hispanic, 2%; Native American, 0.4%; International, 1%

APPLICANTS and ADMITTEES
Number applied: 757
Admitted: 386
Percentage accepted: 51%
Seats available: 140
Average LSAT score: 152
Average GPA: 3.2

University of Toledo College of Law is a public institution that organizes classes on a semester calendar system. The campus is situated in a suburban setting. Founded in 1906, first ABA approved in 1939, and an AALS member, University of Toledo College of Law offers JD, JD/MBA, JD/MSE, and JD/PhD degrees.

Faculty consists of 32 full-time and 12 part-time members in 2000–2001. 12 full-time faculty members and 5 part-time faculty members are women. 100% of all faculty members have a JD; 50% have advanced law degrees. Of all faculty members, 7% are African American, 93% are white.

Application Information *Required:* LSAT, application form, baccalaureate degree, minimum 2.0 GPA, 2 letters of recommendation, college transcripts, LSDAS. *Recommended:* personal statement. *Application deadline* for fall term is June 1 (priority date). Applications are processed on a rolling basis.

Costs The 2000–2001 tuition was $8314 full-time for area residents; $336 per hour part-time for area residents. Tuition was $16,085 full-time for nonresidents; $660 per hour part-time for nonresidents.

Financial Aid In 2000–2001, 87% of all students received some form of financial aid. 19 research assistantships, totaling $425; 39 teaching assistantships, totaling $750, were awarded. Graduate assistantships, loans, merit-based grants/scholarships, need-based grants/scholarships, and federal work-study loans are also available. The average student debt at graduation is $43,383. To apply for financial assistance, students must complete the Free

AT a GLANCE

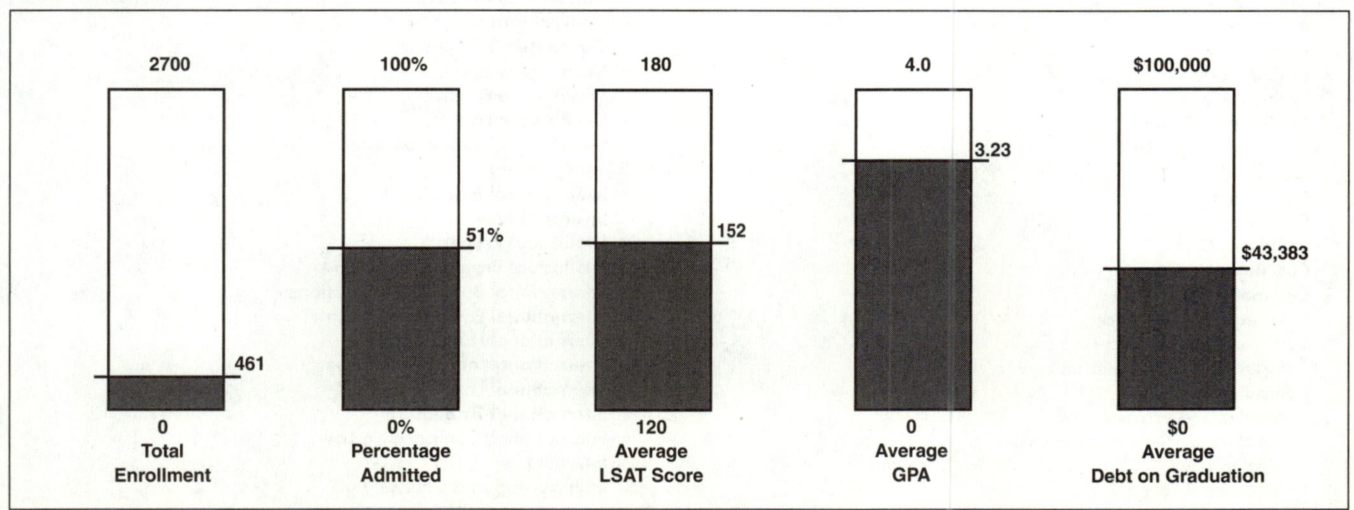

Degree Options

Degree	Total Credits Required	Length of Program
JD–Juris Doctor	89	3–4 yrs, full-time or part-time [day, evening, summer]
JD/MBA–Juris Doctor/Master of Business Administration–Joint-degree	107	3–3.5 yrs, full-time or part-time [day, summer]
Certificate–Dual-degree	107	3.5–4 yrs, full-time or part-time [day, evening, summer]
JD/PhD–Juris Doctor/Doctor of Philosophy		

Application for Federal Student Aid. Financial aid contact: Beth Solo, Assistant Director, University of Toledo College of Law, Toledo, OH 43606. Phone: 419-530-7929. Fax: 419-530-2821. E-mail: bsolo@utnet.utoledo.edu

Law School Library University of Toledo College of Law Library has 13 professional staff members and contains more than 321,650 volumes and 3,263 periodicals. 496 seats are available in the library. When classes are in session, the library is open 113 hours per week.

WESTLAW and LEXIS-NEXIS are available, as are the World Wide Web, online bibliographic services, and CD-ROM players. 50 computer workstations are available to students in the library. Special law collections include the Great Lakes law collection.

First-Year Program Class size in the average section is 37; 100% of the first-year courses are taught by full-time faculty.

Upper-Level Program Class size in the average section is 23. Among the electives are:

Accounting
Administrative Law
★ Advocacy
Alternative Dispute Resolution
American Legal History
Antitrust Law
Appellate Advocacy
Arbitration
Bankruptcy
★ Business and Corporate Law
Business Planning
Capital Punishment
Children and the Law
Civil Law
Civil Litigation
Civil Practice
Civil Procedure
Civil Rights
Commercial Law
Commercial Transactions
Communications Law
Comparative Constitutional Law
Computer Law
Computer/Cyberspace Law
Computers, Society, and the Law
Conflict of Laws
Constitutional Law

Copyright & Trademark Law
Corporate Criminal Liability
Corporate Finance
Corporate Law
Corporate Taxation
Corporations
Creditor's Rights
Criminal Adjudication
Criminal Law
Criminal Procedure
★ Criminal Prosecution
Cyberspace Law
Debtor Law
Dispute Resolution
District Attorney Clinic
Employee Benefit Law
Employment Discrimination
Employment Law
English Legal History
Entertainment Law
★ Environmental Law
Environmental Litigation
Estate & Gift Taxation
Estate Planning
Estates & Trusts
Ethics
European Community Law
European Union Law
Evidence
Extern
Family Law
Federal Courts
Federal Income Tax
Federal Jurisdiction
Gender and the Law
★ General Practice
Government/Regulation
★ Great Lakes Law
Health Care Finance
Health Care Law
Health Care/Human Services
Immigration
Indian/Tribal Law
Insurance Law
★ Intellectual Property
Intellectual Property Litigation
International Business Transactions
International Environmental Law
International Human Rights
International Intellectual Property
International Law
International Trademark
★ International/Comparative Law
Internet Law
Interviewing and Counseling

Jewish Law
Judicial Externship
Jurisprudence
Juvenile Law
Labor and Employment
Labor Arbitration
Labor Law
Land Rights/Natural Resource
★ Land Use Law/Natural Resources
Law and Economics
Law and Literature
Law Office Management
Law Practice Management
Lawyering Skills
Legal Drafting
Legal Ethics
Legal Externship
Legal History/Philosophy
Legal Research
Legal Writing
Legislation
Life and Death Decision Making
★ Litigation
Local Government
Media Law
★ Mediation
Medical Malpractice Law
Medicine
Mental Health and Law
NAFTA Law
Native American Law
Natural Resources
Negotiable Intruments
Patent Law
Probate Law
Professional Responsibility
Property/Real Estate
Public International Law
Real Estate Finance

Real Estate Transactions
Refugee & Asylum Law
Religion and the Law
Sales
Secured Transactions
★ Securities
Securities Regulation
Sex-based Discrimination
Sports Law
State and Local Government
State and Local Taxation
★ Tax Law
Telecommunications Law
Torts & Product Liability
Trial Advocacy
Trusts and Estates
Unfair Trade Practices
Water Law
White Collar Crime
Wills & Trusts

(★ indicates an area of special strength)

Clinical Courses Students receive degree credit for
clinical courses. (Clinical practicum is not required.)
Among the clinical areas offered are:

Accounting
Administrative Law
Advocacy
Alternative Dispute Resolution
Civil Litigation
Civil Rights
Criminal Prosecution
Domestic Violence
General Practice
Juvenile Law
Mediation

OKLAHOMA CITY UNIVERSITY
SCHOOL OF LAW

Oklahoma City, Oklahoma

INFORMATION CONTACT

Peter Storandt, Director of Law School Admissions
2501 North Blackwelder Avenue
Oklahoma City, OK 73106

Phone: 800-633-7242   Fax: 405-521-5814
    ext. 2
E-mail: pstorandt@okcu.edu
Web site: http://www.okcu.edu/law/

LAW STUDENT PROFILE [2000–2001]

FULL-TIME   Enrollment: 365
Women: 42%   Men: 58%

PART-TIME   Enrollment: 128
Women: 38%   Men: 62%

RACIAL or ETHNIC COMPOSITION

African American, 10%; Asian/Pacific Islander, 4%; Hispanic, 4%; Native American, 5%

APPLICANTS and ADMITTEES

Number applied: 1,028
Admitted: 720
Percentage accepted: 70%
Seats available: 200
Median LSAT score: 147
Median GPA: 2.9

Oklahoma City University School of Law is a private institution that organizes classes on a semester calendar system. The campus is situated in an urban setting. Founded in 1907, first ABA approved in 1964, Oklahoma City University School of Law offers JD and JD/MBA degrees.

Faculty consists of 30 full-time and 41 part-time members in 2000–2001. 10 full-time faculty members and 12 part-time faculty members are women. 100% of all faculty members have a JD; 34% have advanced law degrees. Of all faculty members, 1.6% are Native American, 3.4% are Asian/Pacific Islander, 5% are African American, 90% are white.

Application Information *Required:* LSAT, LSDAS, application form, application fee of $35, baccalaureate degree, 2 letters of recommendation, personal statement, college transcripts. *Recommended:* resume. *Application deadline* for fall term is June 1.

Costs The 1999–2000 tuition was $12,720 full-time; $530 per credit hour part-time. Fees: $198 full-time. Tuition and fees vary according to program.

Financial Aid Loans, merit-based grants/scholarships, and federal work-study loans are available. The average student debt at graduation is $45,000. To apply for financial assistance, students must complete the Free Application for Federal Student Aid. Completed financial aid forms should be received by August 1. Financial aid contact: Fran Strange, Director of Financial Aid, 2501 North Blackwelder Avenue, Oklahoma City, OK 73105-1493. Phone: 405-521-5211. Fax: 405-521-5814.

AT a GLANCE

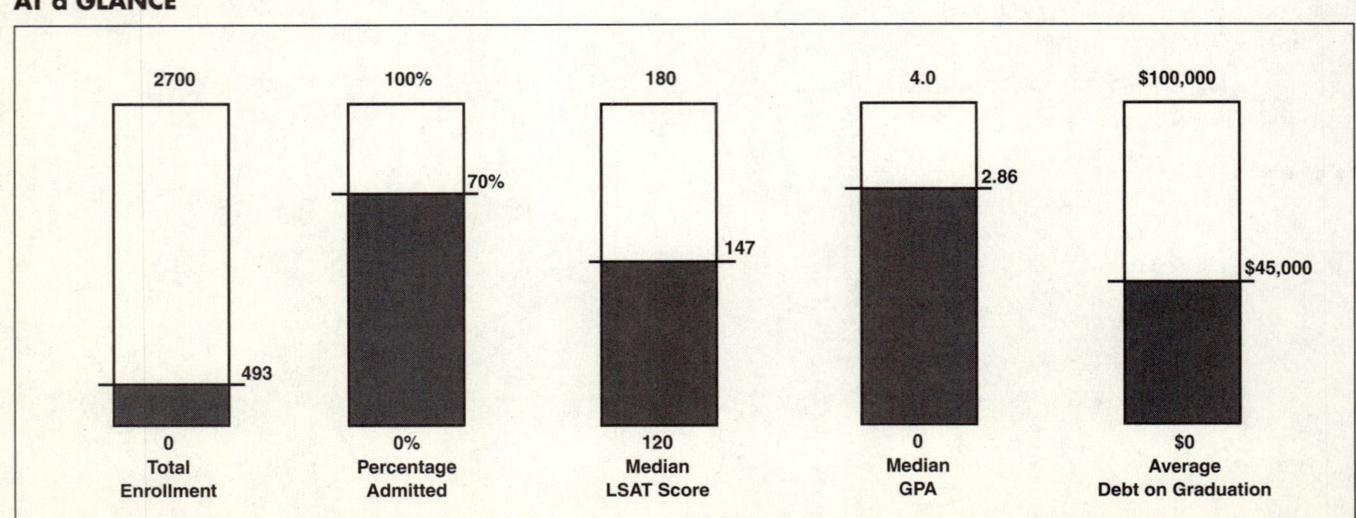

Degree Options

Degree	Total Credits Required	Length of Program
JD–Doctor of Laws	90	3–4 yrs, full-time or part-time [day, evening, summer]
JD/MBA–Juris Doctor/Master of Business Administration–Joint-degree Program	124	4 yrs, full-time or part-time [day, evening, summer]

Law School Library Oklahoma City University Law Library has 8 professional staff members and contains more than 278,000 volumes and 3,940 periodicals. 364 seats are available in the library. When classes are in session, the library is open 102 hours per week.

WESTLAW and LEXIS-NEXIS are available, as are the World Wide Web, online bibliographic services, and CD-ROM players. 70 computer workstations are available to students in the library. Special law collections include Native American Collection.

First-Year Program Class size in the average section is 75; 100% of the first-year courses are taught by full-time faculty.

Upper-Level Program Class size in the average section is 35. Among the electives are:

Administrative Law
Admiralty Law
Advocacy
Agency
Alternative Dispute Resolution
American Legal History
Antitrust Law
Arbitration
Aviation Law
Banking and Finance
Bankruptcy
Business and Corporate Law
Capital Punishment
Civil Rights
Complex Litigation
Conflict of Laws
Constitutional Law
Consumer Law
Corporate Taxation
Creditor's Rights
Criminal Defense
Criminal Law
Criminal Procedure
Criminal Prosecution
Debtor Law
Education Law
Elder Law
Employee Benefit Law
Employment Law
English Legal History
Entertainment Law
Environmental Law
Estate & Gift Taxation
Estate Planning
Evidence
Family Law
Government/Regulation
Health Care Finance

Health Care/Human Services
Immigration
Income Tax Law
Indian/Tribal Law
Insurance Law
Intellectual Property
International Business Transactions
International Law
International/Comparative Law
Jurisprudence
Juvenile Law
Labor and Employment
Labor Law
Land Use Law/Natural Resources
Law and Medicine
Law and Philosophy
Lawyering Skills
Legal History/Philosophy
Legal Methods
Legal Research
Legal Writing
Legislation
Litigation
Mass Torts
Mediation
Mergers & Acquisitions
Natural Resources
Oil and Gas
Partnerships
Patent Law
Post-Conviction Relief
Pretrial Litigation
Probate Law
Product Liability
Professional Responsibility
Property/Real Estate
Public Interest
Remedies
Sales
Secured Transactions
Securities
Securities Regulation
Sports Law
State and Local Government
Tax Law
Water Law
Wills & Trusts
Workers' Compensation

Clinical Courses Students receive degree credit for clinical courses. (Clinical practicum is not required.) Among the clinical areas offered are:

Criminal Defense
Criminal Prosecution
Government Litigation
Indian/Tribal Law
Mediation

UNIVERSITY OF OKLAHOMA
COLLEGE OF LAW

Norman, Oklahoma

INFORMATION CONTACT

Kathie Madden, Admissions and Recruitment Adviser
300 Timberdell Road
Norman, OK 73019

Phone: 405-325-4728   Fax: 405-325-0502
E-mail: kmadden@ou.edu
Web site: http://www.law.ou.edu/

LAW STUDENT PROFILE [2000–2001]

FULL-TIME   Enrollment: 515
Women: 43%   Men: 57%

PART-TIME   Enrollment: 6
Women: 67%   Men: 33%

RACIAL or ETHNIC COMPOSITION

African American, 2%; Asian/Pacific Islander, 2%; Hispanic, 2%; Native American, 7%; International, 0.2%

APPLICANTS and ADMITTEES

Number applied: 737
Admitted: 269
Percentage accepted: 36%
Seats available: 160
Average LSAT score: 155
Average GPA: 3.5

University of Oklahoma College of Law is a public institution that organizes classes on a semester calendar system. The campus is situated in a suburban setting. Founded in 1909, first ABA approved in 1923, and an AALS member, University of Oklahoma College of Law offers JD, JD/MBA, and JD/MPH degrees.

Faculty consists of 4 full-time and 1 part-time members in 2000–2001. 1 full-time faculty members and 1 part-time faculty members are women. 100% of all faculty members have a JD; 36% have advanced law degrees. Of all faculty members, 3% are African American, 3% are Hispanic, 94% are white.

Application Information *Required:* LSAT, LSDAS, application form, application fee of $50, baccalaureate degree, 2 letters of recommendation, personal statement, college transcripts, resume. *Application deadline* for fall term is March 15. Applications are processed on a rolling basis.

Costs The 2000–2001 tuition was $4785 full-time for state residents. Tuition was $13,000 full-time for nonresidents. Fees: $775 full-time.

Financial Aid In 2000–2001, 80% of all students received some form of financial aid. 1 research assistantship, totaling $5400 was awarded. Graduate assistantships, loans, merit-based grants/scholarships, and need-based grants/scholarships are also available. To apply for financial assistance, students must complete the Free Application for Federal Student Aid. Completed financial aid forms should be received by March 1. Financial aid

AT a GLANCE

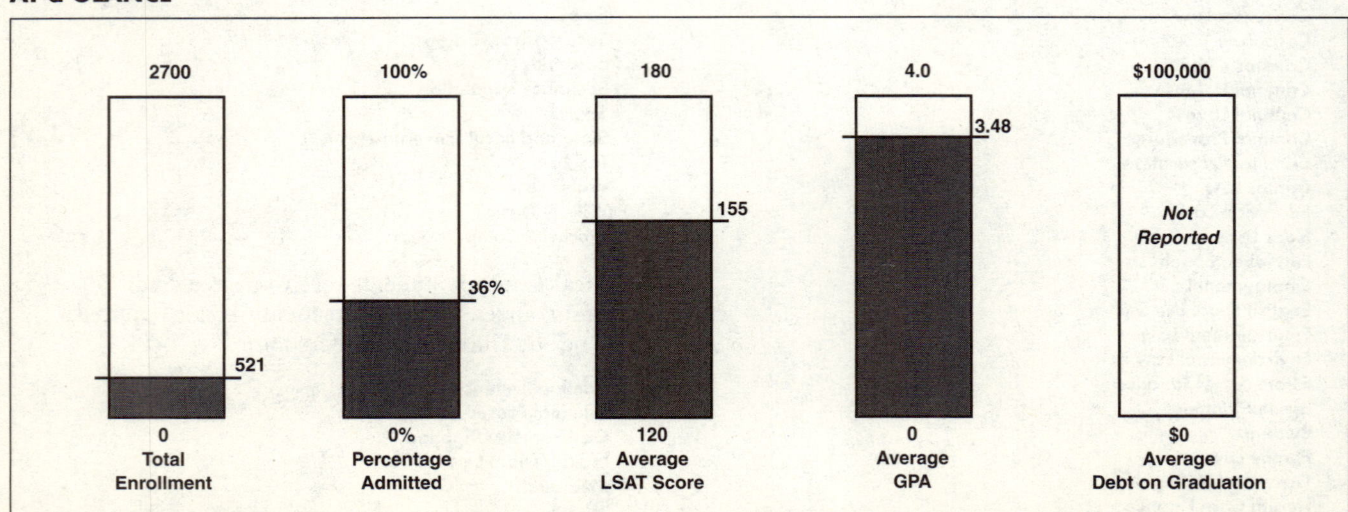

<table>
<tr><td colspan="3">Degree Options</td></tr>
<tr><td>Degree</td><td>Total Credits
Required</td><td>Length of Program</td></tr>
<tr><td>JD–Doctor of Laws</td><td>90</td><td>3–4 yrs, full-time only [day, summer]</td></tr>
<tr><td>JD/MBA–Juris Doctor/Master of Business Administration–Dual-degree</td><td>124</td><td>4 yrs, full-time only [day, summer]</td></tr>
<tr><td>JD/MPH–Juris Doctor/Master of Public Health–Dual-degree</td><td>108</td><td>4 yrs, full-time only [day, summer]</td></tr>
</table>

contact: Financial Aid Services, 731 Elm, Robertson Hall, Norman, OK 73019. Phone: 405-325-4521. Fax: 405-325-0502. E-mail: financialaid@ou.edu

Law School Library John N. Singletary Law Library has 7 professional staff members and contains more than 355,318 volumes and 4,466 periodicals. 375 seats are available in the library. When classes are in session, the library is open 99 hours per week.

WESTLAW and LEXIS-NEXIS are available, as are the World Wide Web, online bibliographic services, and CD-ROM players. 35 computer workstations are available to students in the library. Special law collections include Native Peoples.

First-Year Program Class size in the average section is 40; 100% of the first-year courses are taught by full-time faculty.

Upper-Level Program Class size in the average section is 35. Among the electives are:

Administrative Law
★ Advocacy
Business and Corporate Law
Civil Litigation
Consumer Law
Education Law
Entertainment Law
Family Law
Government/Regulation
Health Care/Human Services
★ Indian/Tribal Law
Intellectual Property
International/Comparative Law
Jurisprudence
★ Land Use Law/Natural Resources
★ Lawyering Skills
Legal History/Philosophy
★ Litigation
Media Law
Mediation
Probate Law
Public Interest
Securities
Tax Law

(★ *indicates an area of special strength*)

Clinical Courses Students receive degree credit for clinical courses. (Clinical practicum is not required.) Among the clinical areas offered are:

Advocacy
Civil Litigation
Criminal Defense
General Practice
Indian/Tribal Law
Lawyering Skills

International exchange programs permit students to visit France, Mexico, Netherlands, and United Kingdom.

UNIVERSITY OF TULSA
COLLEGE OF LAW

Tulsa, Oklahoma

INFORMATION CONTACT

George A. Justice, Assistant Dean of Admissions and Financial Aid
3120 East 4th Place
Tulsa, OK 74104

Phone: 918-631-2709   Fax: 918-631-3630
E-mail: george-justice@utulsa.edu
Web site: http://www.utulsa.edu/law/

LAW STUDENT PROFILE [2000–2001]

FULL-TIME Enrollment: 397
Women: 39% Men: 61%

PART-TIME Enrollment: 129
Women: 50% Men: 50%

RACIAL or ETHNIC COMPOSITION

African American, 6%; Asian/Pacific Islander, 3%; Hispanic, 4%; Native American, 9%; International, 1%

APPLICANTS and ADMITTEES

Number applied: 701
Admitted: 486
Percentage accepted: 69%
Seats available: 175
Average LSAT score: 148
Average GPA: 3.1

University of Tulsa College of Law is a private institution that organizes classes on a semester calendar system. The campus is situated in a suburban setting. Founded in 1923, first ABA approved in 1953, and an AALS member, University of Tulsa College of Law offers JD, JD/MA, JD/MBA, JD/MPA, and JD/MS degrees.

Faculty consists of 33 full-time and 27 part-time members in 2000–2001. 15 full-time faculty members and 5 part-time faculty members are women. 100% of all faculty members have a JD; 33% have advanced law degrees. Of all faculty members, 5% are Native American, 5% are Asian/Pacific Islander, 5% are African American, 5% are Hispanic, 80% are white.

Application Information *Required:* LSAT, LSDAS, application form, application fee of $30, baccalaureate degree, college transcripts. *Recommended:* 2 letters of recommendation, personal statement, resume. *Application deadline* is rolling.

Costs The 2000–2001 tuition was $17,750 full-time; $12,000 per year part-time. Tuition and fees vary according to course load and degree level.

Financial Aid Graduate assistantships, loans, merit-based grants/scholarships, need-based grants/scholarships, and federal work-study loans are available. The average student debt at graduation is $69,021. To apply for financial assistance, students must complete the Free Application for Federal Student Aid, institutional forms, scholarship specific applications. Financial aid contact: George A. Justice Jr., Assistant Dean of Admissions and

AT a GLANCE

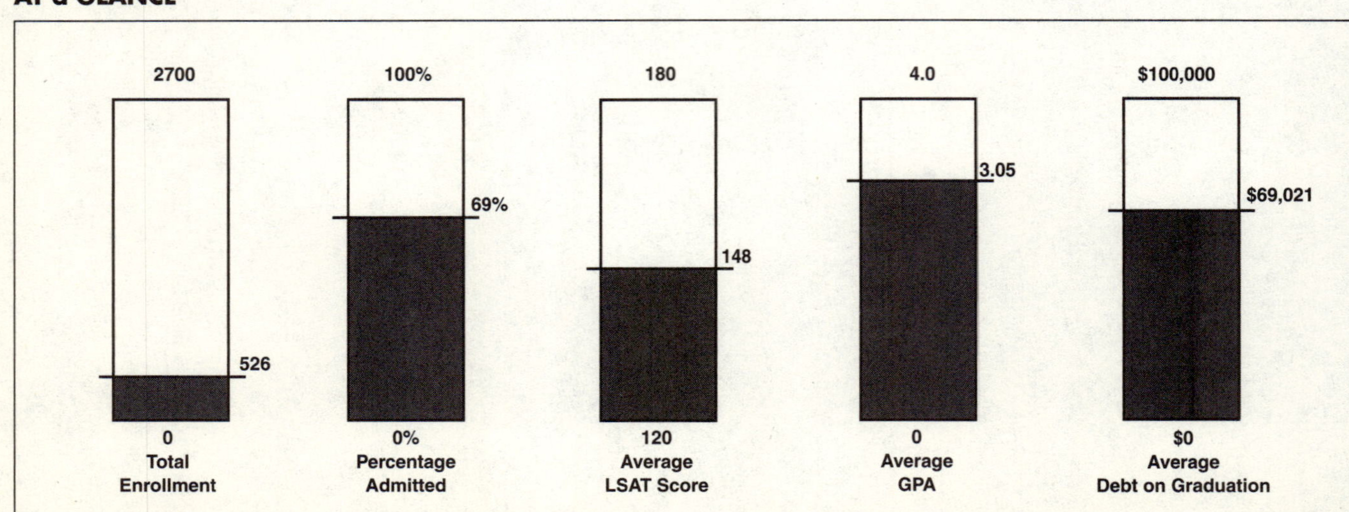

Degree Options

Degree	Total Credits Required	Length of Program
JD–Doctor of Laws	88	3–5 yrs, full-time or part-time [day, evening, weekend, summer]
JD/MA–Juris Doctor/Master of Arts–History	102	4–5 yrs, full-time only [day, evening, summer]
JD/MA–Juris Doctor/Master of Arts–Industrial Psychology/Organizational Psychology	105	4–5 yrs, full-time only [day, evening, summer]
JD/MA–Juris Doctor/Master of Arts–Clinical Psychology	114	4–5 yrs, full-time only [day, evening, summer]
JD/MA–Juris Doctor/Master of Arts–English	105	4–5 yrs, full-time only [day, evening, summer]
JD/MA–Juris Doctor/Master of Arts–Taxation	102	4–5 yrs, full-time only [day, evening, summer]
JD/MA–Juris Doctor/Master of Arts–Anthropology Dual-degree Program	102	4–5 yrs, full-time only [day, evening, summer]
JD/MBA–Juris Doctor/Master of Business Administration–Dual-degree Program	102	4–5 yrs, full-time only [day, evening, summer]
JD/MPA–Juris Doctor/Master of Professional Accountancy	102	4–5 yrs, full-time only [day, evening]
JD/MS–Juris Doctor/Master of Science–Biological Sciences	105	4–5 yrs, full-time only [day, evening, summer]
JD/MS–Juris Doctor/Master of Science–Geosciences	105	4–5 yrs, full-time only [day, evening, summer]

Financial Aid, 3120 East 4th Place, Tulsa, OK 74104. Phone: 918-631-2709. Fax: 918-631-3630. E-mail: george_justice@utulsa.edu

Law School Library Mabee Legal Information Center has 9 professional staff members and contains more than 293,099 volumes and 4,375 periodicals. 704 seats are available in the library. When classes are in session, the library is open 102 hours per week.

WESTLAW and LEXIS-NEXIS are available, as are the World Wide Web, online bibliographic services, and CD-ROM players. 97 computer workstations are available to students in the library. Special law collections include energy law and policy, Native American law, tax law, international law, environmental law, alternative dispute resolution.

First-Year Program Class size in the average section is 35; 100% of the first-year courses are taught by full-time faculty.

Upper-Level Program Class size in the average section is 20. Among the electives are:

- Administrative Law
- ★ Advocacy
- Business and Corporate Law
- Consumer Law
- Elderly Advocacy
- Entrepreneurship Law
- ★ Environmental Law
- Family Law
- ★ General Practice
- ★ Government/Regulation
- ★ Health Care/Human Services
- ★ Health Law
- ★ Indian/Tribal Law
- Intellectual Property
- ★ International/Comparative Law
- Jurisprudence
- Labor Law
- ★ Land Use Law/Natural Resources
- ★ Lawyering Skills
- Legal History/Philosophy
- Litigation
- ★ Mediation
- Probate Law
- ★ Public Interest
- Securities
- Sports Law
- Tax Law

(★ *indicates an area of special strength*)

Clinical Courses Students receive degree credit for clinical courses. (Clinical practicum is not required.) Among the clinical areas offered are:

- Elderly Advocacy
- General Practice
- Health Care/Human Services
- Health Law
- Labor Law
- Probate Law

International exchange programs permit students to visit Argentina, Ireland, and United Kingdom.

LEWIS & CLARK COLLEGE
NORTHWESTERN SCHOOL OF LAW

Portland, Oregon

INFORMATION CONTACT

Martha Spence, Associate Dean
10015 SW Terwilliger Boulevard
Portland, OR 97219-7799

Phone: 503-768-6634   Fax: 503-768-6671
E-mail: spence@lclark.edu
Web site: http://www.lclark.edu/LAW/

LAW STUDENT PROFILE [2000–2001]

FULL-TIME   Enrollment: 508
Women: 48%   Men: 52%

PART-TIME   Enrollment: 171
Women: 48%   Men: 52%

RACIAL or ETHNIC COMPOSITION
African American, 1%; Asian/Pacific Islander, 7%; Hispanic,
4%; Native American, 2%; International, 3%

APPLICANTS and ADMITTEES
Number applied: 1,568
Admitted: 1,030
Percentage accepted: 66%
Seats available: 233
Average LSAT score: 156
Average GPA: 3.2

Lewis & Clark College Northwestern School of Law is a
private institution that organizes classes on a semester
calendar system. The campus is situated in an urban
setting. Founded in 1885, first ABA approved in 1970,
and an AALS member, Lewis & Clark College Northwestern School of Law offers JD and LLM degrees.

Faculty consists of 38 full-time and 23 part-time
members in 2000–2001. 12 full-time faculty members
and 8 part-time faculty members are women. 100% of all
faculty members have a JD; 8% have advanced law
degrees. Of all faculty members, 1% are Native American, 1% are Asian/Pacific Islander, 1% are African
American, 1% are Hispanic, 95% are white.

Application Information *Required:* LSAT, LSDAS,
application form, application fee of $50, 1 recommenda-
tion, essay, baccalaureate degree, college transcripts.
Recommended: resume. *Application deadline* for fall term
is March 15 (priority date). Applications are processed
on a rolling basis.

Costs The 2000–2001 tuition was $21,290 full-time;
$15,970 per year part-time.

Financial Aid 20 research assistantships, totaling $1750
were awarded. Fellowships, loans, loan repayment
assistance program (LRAP), merit-based grants/scholar-
ships, and federal work-study loans are also available.
The average student debt at graduation is $64,124. To
apply for financial assistance, students must complete the
Free Application for Federal Student Aid. Completed
financial aid forms should be received by March 1.
Financial aid contact: Diane Meyer, Assistant Director of

AT a GLANCE

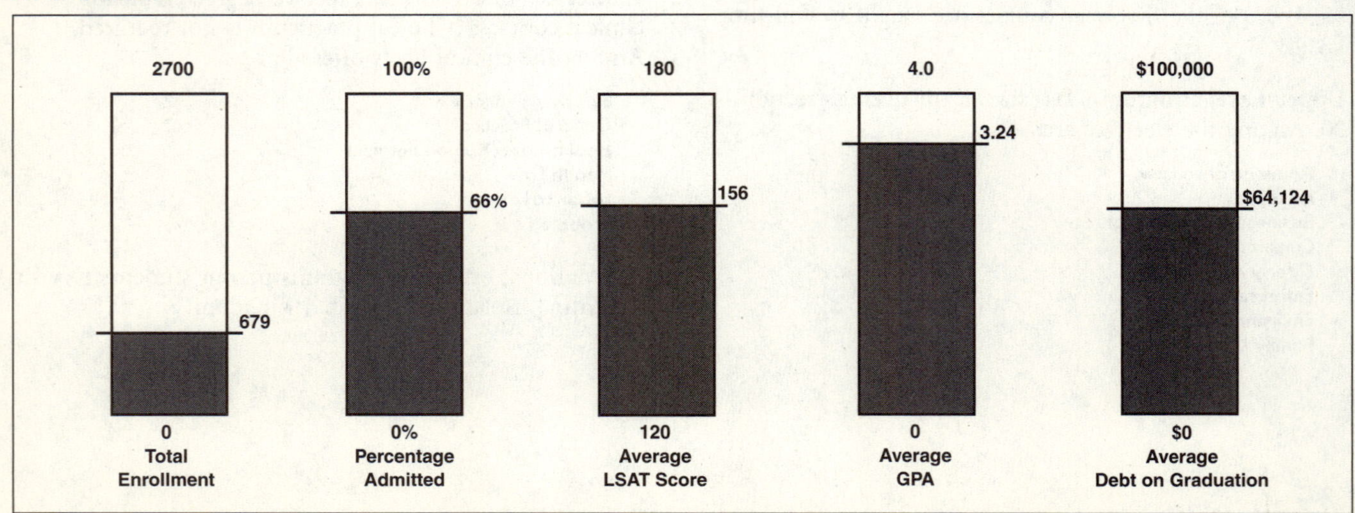

Degree Options

Degree	Total Credits Required	Length of Program
JD–Juris Doctor	86	3–4 yrs, full-time or part-time [day, evening, summer]
LLM–Master of Laws–Environmental and Natural Resources	26	1–2 yrs, full-time or part-time [day, evening, summer]

Financial Services for Law Students, 0615 SW Palatine Hill Road, Portland, OR 97219-7899. Phone: 503-768-7090. Fax: 503-768-7074. E-mail: sfs@lclark.edu

Law School Library Boley Law Library has 8 professional staff members and contains more than 463,019 volumes and 4,816 periodicals. 194 seats are available in the library. When classes are in session, the library is open 113 hours per week.

WESTLAW and LEXIS-NEXIS are available, as are the World Wide Web, online bibliographic services, and CD-ROM players. 52 computer workstations are available to students in the library. Special law collections include United States Patent and Trademark Depository, The Pearl Environmental Law Library, The Johnson Public Land Law Collection.

First-Year Program Class size in the average section is 57; 100% of the first-year courses are taught by full-time faculty.

Upper-Level Program Class size in the average section is 35. Among the electives are:

Administrative Law
Advocacy
Agricultural Law
Animal Rights Law
Bankruptcy
★ Business and Corporate Law
Civil Litigation
Constitutional Law
★ Criminal Defense
Entertainment Law
★ Environmental Law
Family Law
Government/Regulation
Health Care/Human Services
Immigration
Indian/Tribal Law
★ Intellectual Property
International/Comparative Law
Jurisprudence
Labor Law
★ Land Use Law/Natural Resources
Lawyering Skills
Legal History/Philosophy
Litigation
Maritime Law
Mediation
Ocean and Coastal Law
Probate Law
Public Interest
Sports Law
Street Law
★ Tax Law
(★ indicates an area of special strength)

Clinical Courses Students receive degree credit for clinical courses. (Clinical practicum is not required.) Among the clinical areas offered are:

Administrative Law
Advocacy
Bankruptcy
Business and Corporate Law
Civil Litigation
Criminal Defense
Environmental Law
Family Law
Family Practice
Intellectual Property
Labor Law
Land Use Law/Natural Resources
Lawyering Skills
Litigation
Public Interest
Tax Law

UNIVERSITY OF OREGON
SCHOOL OF LAW

Eugene, Oregon

INFORMATION CONTACT

Teresa Specht, Information Contact, Office of
Admissions
Eugene, OR 97403

Phone: 541-346-1810   Fax: 541-346-1564
E-mail: tspect@law.uoregon.edu
Web site: http://www.law.uoregon.edu/

LAW STUDENT PROFILE [2000–2001]

FULL-TIME   Enrollment: 507
Women: 49%   Men: 51%

PART-TIME   Enrollment: 4
Women: 25%   Men: 75%

RACIAL or ETHNIC COMPOSITION

African American, 3%; Asian/Pacific Islander, 6%; Hispanic,
4%; Native American, 1%; International, 1%

APPLICANTS and ADMITTEES

Number applied: 1,134
Admitted: 181
Percentage accepted: 16%
Seats available: 170
Median LSAT score: 157
Average GPA: 3.4

University of Oregon School of Law is a public
institution that organizes classes on a semester calendar
system. The campus is situated in a small-town setting.
Founded in 1884, first ABA approved in 1923, and an
AALS member, University of Oregon School of Law
offers JD and JD/MBA degrees.

Faculty consists of 27 full-time and 4 part-time members
in 2000–2001. 10 full-time faculty members and 1
part-time faculty members are women. 100% of all
faculty members have a JD degree.

Application Information *Required:* LSAT, LSDAS,
application form, application fee of $50, baccalaureate
degree, resume, personal statement, 2 letters of recommendation, college transcripts, writing sample. *Application deadline* for fall term is February 15 (priority date).

Costs The 1999–2000 tuition was $10,898 full-time for
state residents. Tuition was $14,844 full-time for
nonresidents. Students are required to have their own
computers.

Financial Aid 27 teaching assistantships were awarded.
Fellowships, loans, merit-based grants/scholarships, and
need-based grants/scholarships are also available. The
average student debt at graduation is $48,000. To apply
for financial assistance, students must complete the Free
Application for Federal Student Aid. Completed financial
aid forms should be received by February 1. Financial aid
contact: University of Oregon, Office of Financial Aid,
1278 University of Oregon, Eugene, OR 97403-1278.
Phone: 800-760-6953.

AT a GLANCE

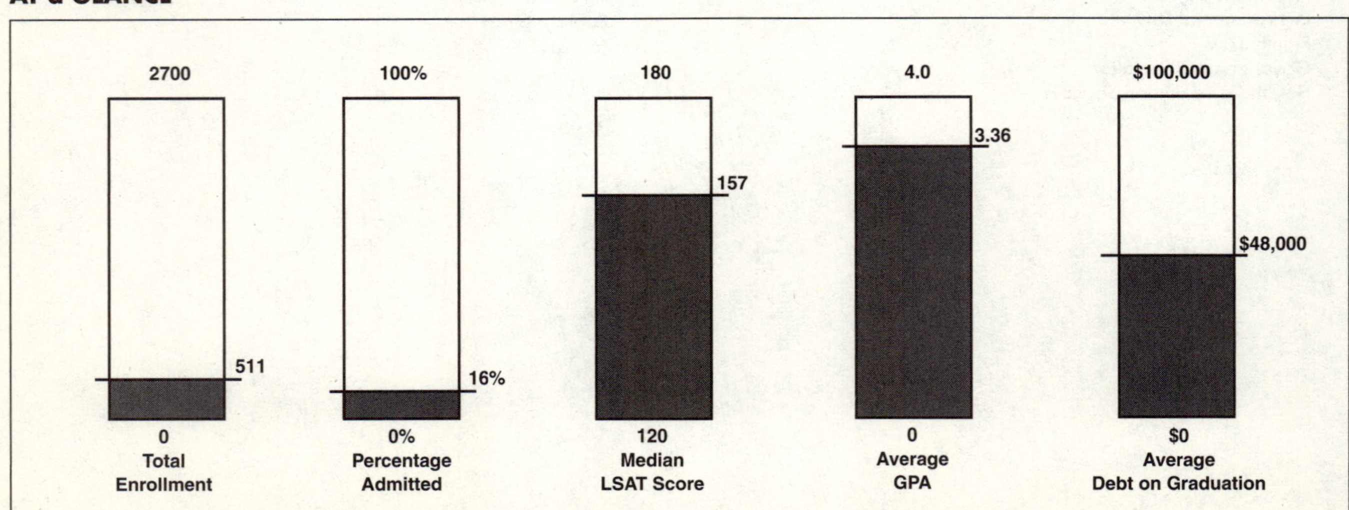

Degree Options

Degree	Total Credits Required	Length of Program
JD–Juris Doctor–Doctor of Jurisprudence	85	full-time only [day]
JD–Doctor of Laws	90	3–4 yrs, full-time or part-time [day, summer]
JD/MBA–Juris Doctor/Master of Business Administration–JD/MBA Dual Degree Program	110	4–5 yrs, full-time only [day]

Law School Library John E. Jaqua Law Library has 6 professional staff members and contains more than 360,000 volumes and 3,314 periodicals. 297 seats are available in the library. When classes are in session, the library is open 111 hours per week.

WESTLAW and LEXIS-NEXIS are available, as are the World Wide Web, online bibliographic services, and CD-ROM players. Special law collections include Ocean and Coastal Law collection.

First-Year Program Class size in the average section is 53.

Upper-Level Program Among the electives are:

- Administrative Law
- Admiralty Law
- Advocacy
- ★ Alternative Dispute Resolution
- American Legal History
- Antitrust Law
- Bankruptcy
- ★ Business and Corporate Law
- Child Welfare Policy
- ★ Children and the Law
- ★ Children's Rights
- Civil Contract Law
- Civil Procedure
- Civil Rights Litigation
- Commercial Law
- Common Law
- Comparative Constitutional Law
- Comparative Federalism
- Comparative Taxation
- Computer Law
- Conflict of Laws
- Constitutional Criminal Procedure
- Constitutional Interpretation
- Constitutional Law
- Constitutional Theory
- Consumer Law
- Contract Theory
- Copyright & Trademark Law
- Corporate Criminal Liability
- Corporate Finance
- Corporate Governance
- Corporate Law
- Corporate Taxation
- Creditor's Rights
- Criminal Adjudication
- Criminal Investigation
- Criminal Law
- Criminal Law Theory
- Criminal Procedure
- Criminology and Penology
- Critical Theory
- Cyberspace Law
- Debtor Law
- Disability Law
- Elder Law
- Employee Benefit Law
- Employment Discrimination
- Employment Law
- Energy Law
- Entertainment Law
- Entrepreneurship Law
- Estate Planning
- European Business Regulation
- European Community Law
- European Economic Law
- Evidence
- Family Law
- Federal Courts
- Federal Income Tax
- Federal Jurisdiction
- ★ Feminist Jurisprudence
- Financial Institutions
- Financial Intruments Tax
- First Amendment
- Food & Drug Law
- Foreign Policy Law
- Fourteenth Amendment
- Futures Markets
- Gender and Sexuality
- Government & Media
- Government/Regulation
- ★ Hazardous Waste Law
- Immigration
- Income Tax Law
- ★ Indian/Tribal Law
- Injury Law
- Insurance Law
- Intellectual Property
- International Agreements
- International Antitrust
- ★ International Business Transactions
- International Criminal Law
- International Economic Relations
- ★ International Environmental Law
- International Finance Markets
- ★ International Human Rights
- International Income Tax
- International Intellectual Property
- International Law
- ★ International Litigation & Arbitration
- International Trade
- International/Comparative Law
- Judging
- Judicial Internship
- Judicial Process
- Juries
- Jurisprudence
- Juvenile Law
- Labor and Employment
- Labor Arbitration

Labor Law
★ Land Use Law/Natural Resources
Law and Economics
Law and Psychology
Law and Social Science
Law and Society
Law of the Sea
Law, Mass Media, and Race
Legal Ethics
Legal History/Philosophy
Legal Research
Legal Writing
Legislation
Litigation
Local Government
Maritime Law
Mediation
Medicine
★ Mergers & Acquisitions
Multinational Business Enterprises
★ Native American Law
★ Natural Resources
Negotiation
Nonprofit Organizations
★ Ocean and Coastal Law
Oregon Practice & Procedure
Patent Law
Pretrial Litigation
Prisoners' Rights
Professional Responsibility
Property/Real Estate
Psychiatry and Law
Psychology, Forensic Science, and the Law
Public Choice & Law
★ Public Interest
★ Public Lands
Race and Law
Refugee & Asylum Law
Regulation & Competition
Regulation of the Political Process
Religion and the Law
Scientific Evidence

Second Amendment
Secure Transactions
Securities
Securities Enforcement
Securities Litigation
Securities Regulation
Separation of Powers
Sexual Orientation and the Law
Small Business Representation
Sociology of Law
State Constitutional Law
Statistics & Law
Supreme Court Litigation
Sustainability
★ Tax Law
★ Technology & Lawyering
★ Technology Law
Tort Reform Law
Torts & Product Liability
Trial Advocacy
Trusts and Estates
Unfair Trade Practices
Urban Economic Development
★ Water Law
White Collar Crime
★ Wildlife Law
Women and the Law
Women's Legal History

(★ *indicates an area of special strength*)

Clinical Courses Students receive degree credit for clinical courses. (Clinical practicum is not required.) Among the clinical areas offered are:

Alternative Dispute Resolution
Juvenile Law
Mediation

International exchange programs permit students to visit Australia.

WILLAMETTE UNIVERSITY
COLLEGE OF LAW

Salem, Oregon

INFORMATION CONTACT

Lawrence Seno Jr., Director of Admission
245 Winter Street, SE
Salem, OR 97301-3922

Phone: 503-370-6282   Fax: 503-370-6375
E-mail: law-admission@willamette.edu
Web site: http://www.willamette.edu/wucl/

LAW STUDENT PROFILE [2000–2001]

FULL-TIME   Enrollment: 426
Women: 48%   Men: 52%

PART-TIME   Enrollment: 8
Women: 25%   Men: 75%

RACIAL or ETHNIC COMPOSITION

African American, 2%; Asian/Pacific Islander, 8%; Hispanic,
2%; Native American, 1%; International, 1%

APPLICANTS and ADMITTEES

Number applied: 645
Admitted: 403
Percentage accepted: 62%
Seats available: 170
Average LSAT score: 154
Average GPA: 3.2

Willamette University College of Law is a private institution that organizes classes on a semester calendar system. The campus is situated in a small-town setting. Founded in 1883, first ABA approved in 1938, and an AALS member, Willamette University College of Law offers JD and JD/MBA degrees.

Faculty consists of 22 full-time and 8 part-time members in 2000–2001. 8 full-time faculty members and 2 part-time faculty members are women. 100% of all faculty members have a JD; 15% have advanced law degrees. Of all faculty members, 5% are Hispanic, 95% are white.

Application Information *Required:* LSAT, LSDAS, application form, application fee of $50, baccalaureate degree, 2 letters of recommendation, personal statement, college transcripts. *Application deadline* for fall term is April 1 (priority date). Applications are processed on a rolling basis.

Costs The 2000–2001 tuition was $19,000 full-time; $633 per hour part-time. Fees: $80 full-time.

Financial Aid In 2000–2001, 42% of all students received some form of financial aid. Loans, loan repayment assistance program (LRAP), merit-based grants/scholarships, and federal work-study loans are available. The average student debt at graduation is $67,000. To apply for financial assistance, students must complete the Free Application for Federal Student Aid. Completed financial aid forms should be received by March 1. Financial aid

AT a GLANCE

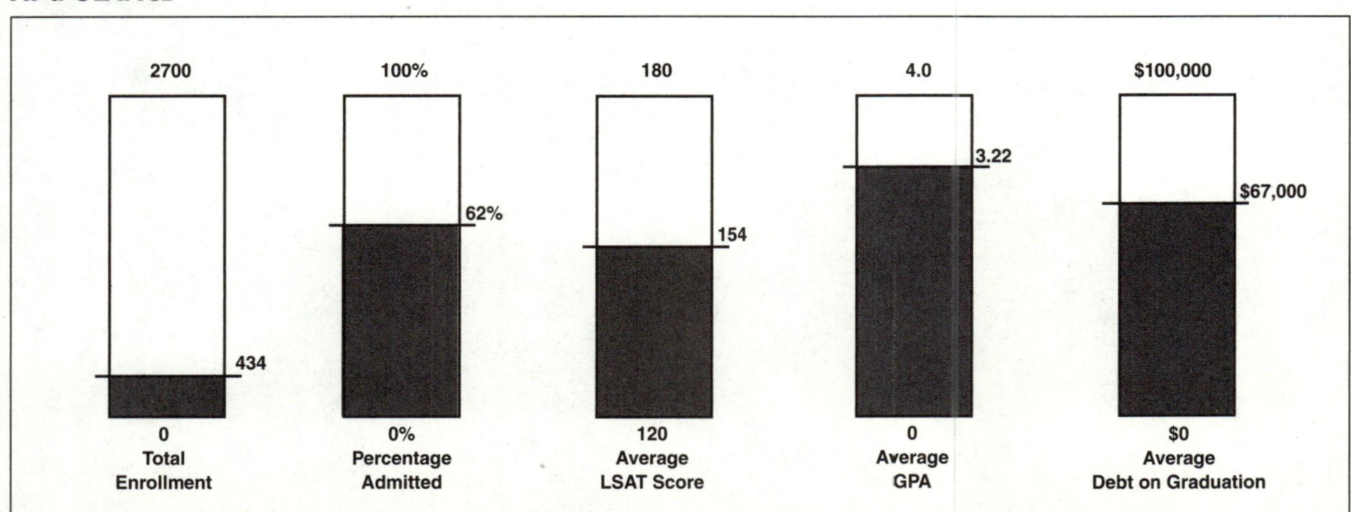

Degree Options

Degree	Total Credits Required	Length of Program
JD–Doctor of Laws	88	3 yrs, full-time or part-time [day]
JD/MBA–Juris Doctor/Master of Business Administration–Joint-degree Program		4 yrs, full-time only [day]

contact: Zophia Miller, Assistant Director of Financial Aid, 900 State Street, Salem, OR 97301. Phone: 503-370-6273. Fax: 503-370-6588. E-mail: zmiller@willamette.edu

Law School Library J. W. Long Law Library has 5 professional staff members and contains more than 286,946 volumes and 2,451 periodicals. 491 seats are available in the library. When classes are in session, the library is open 113 hours per week.

WESTLAW and LEXIS-NEXIS are available, as are the World Wide Web, online bibliographic services, and CD-ROM players. 44 computer workstations are available to students in the library. Special law collections include Public International Law, Tax collection, Labor collection.

First-Year Program Class size in the average section is 65; 100% of the first-year courses are taught by full-time faculty.

Upper-Level Program Class size in the average section is 50. Among the electives are:

Administrative Law
Advocacy
★ Business and Corporate Law
★ Dispute Resolution
Education Law
Environmental Law
Family Law
Family Practice
General Practice

★ Government/Regulation
Health Care/Human Services
Indian/Tribal Law
Intellectual Property
★ International/Comparative Law
Jurisprudence
Labor Law
Land Use Law/Natural Resources
Litigation
Maritime Law
Mediation
Probate Law
Public Interest
Securities
Tax Law
(★ indicates an area of special strength)

Clinical Courses Students receive degree credit for clinical courses. (Clinical practicum is not required.) Among the clinical areas offered are:

Consumer Law
Dispute Resolution
Elder Law
Family Law
Family Practice
General Practice
Government/Regulation
Indian/Tribal Law
Litigation
Mediation
Public Interest

International exchange programs permit students to visit Ecuador.

THE DICKINSON SCHOOL OF LAW OF THE PENNSYLVANIA STATE UNIVERSITY

Carlisle, Pennsylvania

INFORMATION CONTACT

Barbara W. Guillaume, Director, Law Admissions
150 South College Street
Carlisle, PA 17013-2899

Phone: 717-240-5207   Fax: 717-241-3503
E-mail: dsladmit@psu.edu
Web site: http://www.dsl.edu/

LAW STUDENT PROFILE [2000–2001]

FULL-TIME   Enrollment: 536
Women: 42%   Men: 58%

PART-TIME   Enrollment: 2
Women: 100%

APPLICANTS and ADMITTEES

Number applied: 1,320
Admitted: 691
Percentage accepted: 52%
Seats available: 185
Average LSAT score: 154
Average GPA: 3.3

The Dickinson School of Law of The Pennsylvania State University is a public institution that organizes classes on a semester calendar system. The campus is situated in a small-town setting. Founded in 1834, first ABA approved in 1931, and an AALS member, The Dickinson School of Law of The Pennsylvania State University offers JD, JD/MBA, JD/ME, JD/MED, JD/MPAd, JD/MS, JD/MSIS, LLM, and MEPC degrees.

Faculty 100% of all faculty members have a JD; 22% have advanced law degrees. Of all faculty members, 3% are Asian/Pacific Islander, 6% are African American, 3% are Hispanic, 88% are white.

Application Information *Required:* LSAT, LSDAS, application form, application fee of $50, baccalaureate degree, 2 letters of recommendation, personal statement, college transcripts, resume.

Costs The 1999–2000 tuition was $15,850 full-time. Fees: $250 full-time.

Financial Aid Loans, merit-based grants/scholarships, need-based grants/scholarships, and federal work-study loans are available. The average student debt at graduation is $60,094. To apply for financial assistance, students must complete the Free Application for Federal Student Aid, institutional forms, scholarship specific applications, Need Access form. Financial aid contact: Joyce E. James, Financial Aid Director, 150 South College Street, Carlisle, PA 17013. Phone: 717-241-3524. Fax: 717-243-4366. E-mail: jej8@psu.edu

AT a GLANCE

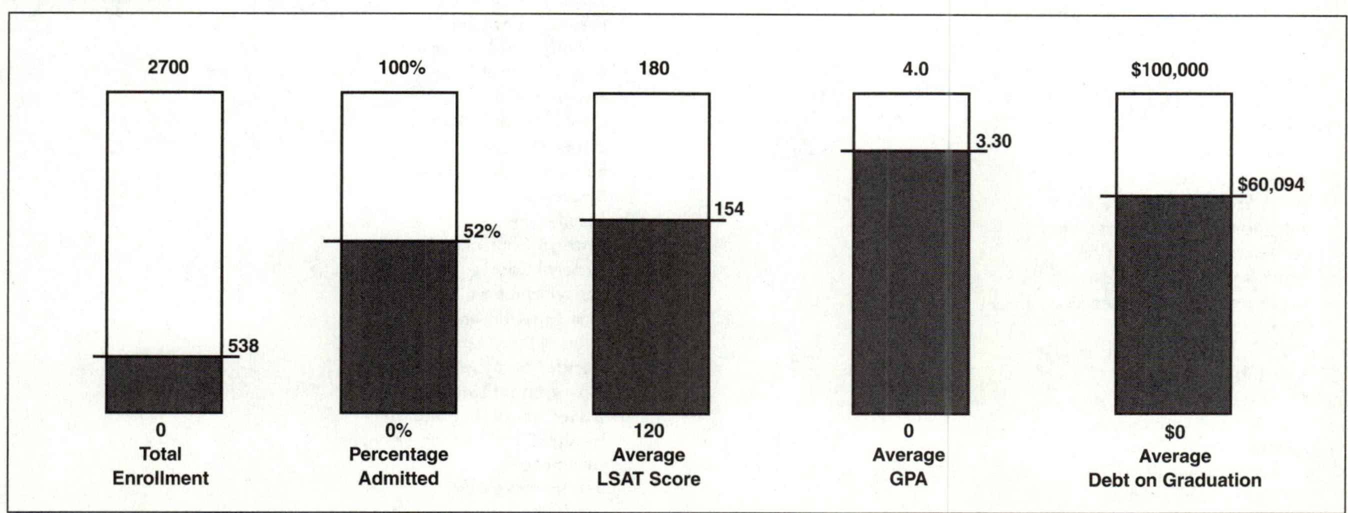

Degree Options

Degree	Total Credits Required	Length of Program
JD–Juris Doctor	88	3 yrs, full-time only [day]
JD/MBA–Juris Doctor/Master of Business Administration–Dual-degree Program	112	4 yrs, full-time only [day]
JD/MBA–Juris Doctor/Master of Business Administration–Dual-degree Program	99	3–4 yrs, full-time or part-time [day, evening]
JD/ME–Juris Doctor/Master of Engineering–Dual-degree Program in Environmental Pollution Control	98	4.5–5 yrs, full-time or part-time [day, evening, summer]
JD/MED–Juris Doctor/Master of Education–Dual-Degree program in Counseling	118	4.5–5 yrs, full-time or part-time [day, evening, summer]
JD/MPAd–Juris Doctor/Master of Public Administration–Dual-degree Program	106	4–5 yrs, full-time or part-time [day, evening, summer]
JD/MS–Juris Doctor/Master of Science–Dual-degree Program in Environmental Pollution Control	98	4.5–5.5 yrs, full-time or part-time [day, evening, summer]
JD/MS–Juris Doctor/Master of Science–Dual-Degree program in Counseling	124	4.5–6 yrs, full-time or part-time [day, evening, summer]
Certificate–Information Systems Dual-degree Program	99	3–4 yrs, full-time or part-time [day, evening, summer]
LLM–Master of Laws–Comparative Law	24	1 yr, full-time only [day]
MEPC–Master of Environmental Pollution Control–Dual-degree Program in Pollution Control	94	4.5 yrs, full-time or part-time [day, evening]

Law School Library Sheely-Lee Law Library has 7 professional staff members and contains more than 440,000 volumes and 1,800 periodicals. 405 seats are available in the library. When classes are in session, the library is open 168 hours per week.

WESTLAW and LEXIS-NEXIS are available, as are the World Wide Web, online bibliographic services, and CD-ROM players. 101 computer workstations are available to students in the library. Special law collections include human rights, European Community Law, International Law.

First-Year Program Class size in the average section is 50; 100% of the first-year courses are taught by full-time faculty.

Upper-Level Program Class size in the average section is 30. Among the electives are:

Accounting
Administrative Law
★ Advocacy
Agency
Agricultural Law
Air & Space Law
★ Alternative Dispute Resolution
American Legal History
Banking Law & Regulation
Business and Corporate Law
Business Planning
Civil Rights
Civil Rights Litigation
Commercial Law
Commercial Transactions
Common Law
Communications Law
Comparative Taxation

Conflict of Laws
Constitutional Law
Constitutional Rights
Constitutional Theory
Consumer Law
Copyright & Trademark Law
Corporate Governance
Corporate Law
Corporate Taxation
Creditor's Rights
★ Criminal Defense
Criminal Law
Criminal Procedure
Debtor Law
★ Disability Law
Education Law
Elder Law
★ Elderly Advocacy
Election Law
Employee Benefit Law
Employment Law
English Legal History
★ Entertainment Law
★ Environmental Law
Estate & Gift Taxation
Estate Planning
European Union Law
Evidence
★ Family Law
Federal Contract Law
Federal Courts
Federal Income Tax
First Amendment
Food & Drug Law
Gender and the Law
Government Litigation
★ Government/Regulation
★ Health Care/Human Services
Health Law
Immigration

Indian/Tribal Law
Insurance Law
Intellectual Property
International Environmental Law
International Human Rights
International Income Tax
International Law
International Trade
★ International/Comparative Law
Interviewing and Counseling
Juries
Jurisprudence
Juvenile Law
Labor Law
Land Rights/Natural Resource
Land Use Law/Natural Resources
Law and Religion
Lawyering Skills
Legal History/Philosophy
Legal Research
★ Legal Writing
Legislation
★ Litigation
Maritime Law
Media Law
Mergers & Acquisitions
Multinational Business Enterprises
Natural Resources
Negotiable Intruments
Ocean and Coastal Law
Patent Law
Pennsylvania Constitutional Law
Pennsylvania Criminal Law
Pensions
Post-Conviction Process
Poverty/Welfare Law
Pretrial Litigation
Probate Law
Probate Practice
Product Liability
Professional Responsibility
★ Public Interest
Race and Law
Real Estate Finance
Real Estate Transactions
Remedies
Sales
Secured Transactions
Securities Regulation
State and Local Government
State and Local Taxation
Supreme Court
Tax Law

Trade Regulation
Trusts and Estates
White Collar Crime
(★ *indicates an area of special strength*)

Clinical Courses Students receive degree credit for clinical courses. (Clinical practicum is not required.) Among the clinical areas offered are:

Administrative Law
Advocacy
Alternative Dispute Resolution
Civil Rights
Communications Law
Constitutional Law
Consumer Law
Copyright & Trademark Law
Creditor's Rights
Criminal Defense
Criminal Law
Criminal Procedure
Criminal Prosecution
Debtor Law
Disability Law
Education Law
Elder Law
Elderly Advocacy
Entertainment Law
Environmental Law
Family Law
Government Litigation
Government/Regulation
Health Care/Human Services
Health Law
Immigration
Intellectual Property
Interviewing and Counseling
Land Rights/Natural Resource
Land Use Law/Natural Resources
Legislation
Litigation
Local Government
Media Law
Natural Resources
Pennsylvania Criminal Law
Poverty/Welfare Law
Public Interest
Sports Law
Trade Regulation
Trusts and Estates
White Collar Crime

DUQUESNE UNIVERSITY
SCHOOL OF LAW

Pittsburgh, Pennsylvania

LAW STUDENT PROFILE [2000–2001]

FULL-TIME   Enrollment: 356
Women: 44%   Men: 56%

PART-TIME   Enrollment: 331
Women: 45%   Men: 55%

RACIAL or ETHNIC COMPOSITION
African American, 4%; Asian/Pacific Islander, 1%; Hispanic,
0.4%; International, 0.4%

APPLICANTS and ADMITTEES
Seats available: 264
Median LSAT score: 155
Median GPA: 3.2

Duquesne University School of Law is a private
institution that organizes classes on a semester calendar
system. The campus is situated in an urban setting.
Founded in 1911, first ABA approved in 1960, and an
AALS member, Duquesne University School of Law
offers JD, JD/BS, JD/MBA, JD/MDiv, and JD/MS degrees.

Faculty consists of 23 full-time and 38 part-time
members in 2000–2001. 5 full-time faculty members and
14 part-time faculty members are women.

Application Information *Required:* LSAT, LSDAS,
application form, application fee of $50, baccalaureate
degree, 2 letters of recommendation. *Application deadline*
for fall term is April 1. Applications are processed on a
rolling basis.

Costs The 1999–2000 tuition was $15,764 full-time; $572
per credit part-time. Fees: $660 full-time; $330 per
semester part-time. Full-time tuition and fees vary
according to class time.

Financial Aid In 2000–2001, 39% of all students received
some form of financial aid. Merit-based grants/scholar-
ships, need-based grants/scholarships, and federal
work-study loans are available. To apply for financial
assistance, students must complete the Free Application
for Federal Student Aid. Completed financial aid forms
should be received by May 31. Financial aid contact:
Duquesne University, Office of Financial Aid, Administration Building, Ground Floor, Pittsburgh, PA 15282-
0299. Phone: 412-396-6607. Fax: 412-396-6283.

AT a GLANCE

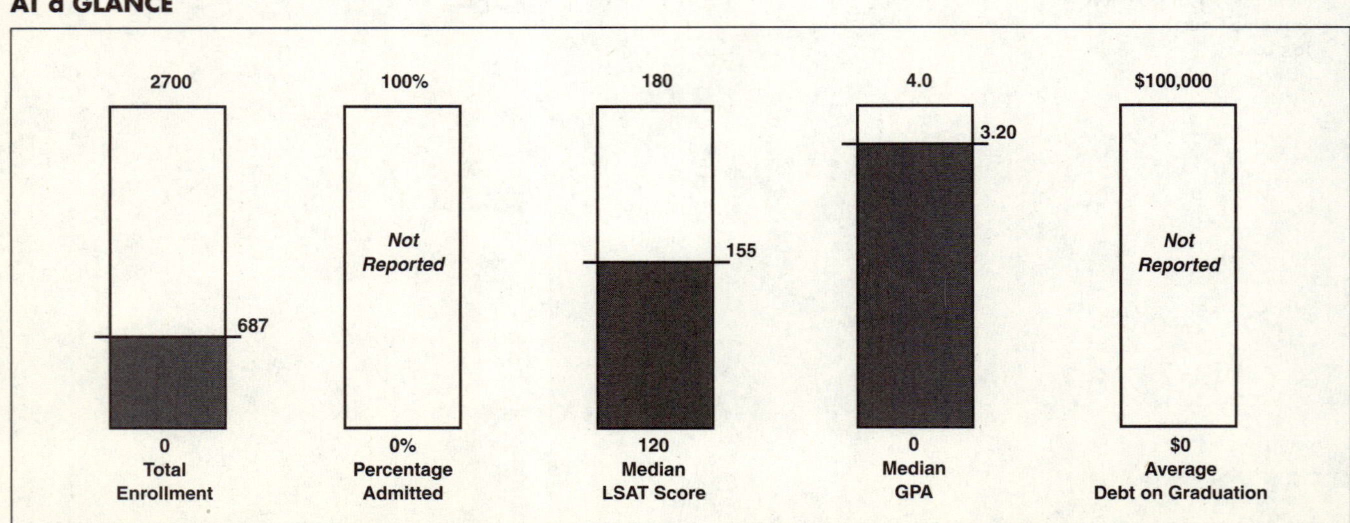

<table>
<tr><td colspan="3">Degree Options</td></tr>
<tr><td>Degree</td><td>Total Credits
Required</td><td>Length of Program</td></tr>
<tr><td>JD–Juris Doctor</td><td></td><td>3–5 yrs, full-time or part-time [day, evening]</td></tr>
<tr><td>JD/BS–Juris Doctor/Bachelor of Science–Joint-degree</td><td></td><td></td></tr>
<tr><td>JD/MBA–Juris Doctor/Master of Business
   Administration–Joint-degree</td><td></td><td>4 yrs [day]</td></tr>
<tr><td>JD/MDiv–Juris Doctor/Master of Divinity–Joint-degree</td><td></td><td>5 yrs, full-time only [day]</td></tr>
<tr><td>JD/MS–Juris Doctor/Master of Science–Environmental
   Science and Management Joint-degree</td><td></td><td>4 yrs, full-time only</td></tr>
</table>

Law School Library Duquesne University Law Library has 6 professional staff members and contains more than 225,668 volumes and 4,586 periodicals. 325 seats are available in the library. When classes are in session, the library is open 102 hours per week.

WESTLAW and LEXIS-NEXIS are available. 31 computer workstations are available to students in the library. Special law collections include federal depository for government documents collection, microform collection.

First-Year Program Class size in the average section is 57.

Upper-Level Program Among the electives are:

Accounting
Administrative Law
Advocacy
Agency
Air Pollution & Waste Management
Alternative Dispute Resolution
American Legal History
Antitrust Law
Bankruptcy
Bioethics
Business and Corporate Law
Business Planning
Civil Rights
★ Commercial Law
Commercial Transactions
Computer Law
Conflict of Laws
Constitutional Criminal Procedure
Constitutional Jurisprudence
★ Constitutional Law
Construction Law
Consumer Law
Copyright & Trademark Law
★ Corporate Law
Corporate Taxation
Corporations
★ Criminal Law
★ Elder Law
Employee Benefit Law
Employment Discrimination
Environmental and Toxic Torts
★ Environmental Law
Estate Planning
Estates & Trusts
European Union Law
Evidence
Family Law

Federal Courts
Federal Income Tax
Fiduciary Administration
★ Government/Regulation
Health Care Finance
★ Health Care Law
Health Care/Human Services
Immigration
Insurance Law
★ Intellectual Property
International Business Regulation
International Environmental Law
International Intellectual Property
International Law
★ International/Comparative Law
Jewish Law
Jurisprudence
Juvenile Law
★ Labor and Employment
★ Labor Law
Land Use Law/Natural Resources
Law and Medicine
Law and Psychiatry
Law and Psychology
Law and Religion
★ Law and Technology
Law of Presidential Power
Lawyering Skills
Legal History/Philosophy
Legal Research
Legal Writing
★ Litigation
Local Government
Mediation
Negotiable Intruments
Patent Law
Pennsylvania Civil Procedure
Pennsylvania Constitutional Law
Philosophy of Law
Probate Law
Professional Responsibility
Property/Real Estate
Remedies
Roman Law
Secured Transactions
Securities
Securities Regulation
Tax Exempt Organizations
★ Tax Law
Trial Advocacy
(★ *indicates an area of special strength*)

Clinical Courses Students receive degree credit for clinical courses. (Clinical practicum is not required.) Among the clinical areas offered are:

Alternative Dispute Resolution
Civil Litigation
Civil Rights
Criminal Prosecution
Economic Development
Environmental Law
Estate Planning
Family Law

General Practice
Pennsylvania Civil Procedure
Trial Advocacy

International exchange programs permit students to visit China and Russian Federation.

TEMPLE UNIVERSITY
JAMES E. BEASLEY SCHOOL OF LAW

Philadelphia, Pennsylvania

INFORMATION CONTACT

Marylouise C. Esten, Assistant Dean for Admissions, Financial Aid, and Student Affairs
1719 North Broad Street
Philadelphia, PA 19122

Phone: 800-560-1428   Fax: 215-204-1185
E-mail: law@astro.ocis.temple.edu
Web site: http://www.temple.edu/lawschool/

LAW STUDENT PROFILE [2000–2001]

FULL-TIME   Enrollment: 765
Women: 50%   Men: 50%

PART-TIME   Enrollment: 310
Women: 44%   Men: 56%

RACIAL or ETHNIC COMPOSITION
African American, 10%; Asian/Pacific Islander, 6%; Hispanic, 4%; Native American, 0.3%

APPLICANTS and ADMITTEES
Number applied: 3,032
Admitted: 1,211
Percentage accepted: 40%
Seats available: 343
Average LSAT score: 155
Average GPA: 3.2

Temple University James E. Beasley School of Law is a public institution that organizes classes on a semester calendar system. The campus is situated in an urban setting. Founded in 1895, first ABA approved in 1933, and an AALS member, Temple University James E. Beasley School of Law offers JD, JD/LLM, JD/MBA, and LLM degrees.

Faculty consists of 56 full-time and 174 part-time members in 2000–2001. 19 full-time faculty members and 41 part-time faculty members are women. 100% of all faculty members have a JD; 28% have advanced law degrees. Of all faculty members, 5% are Asian/Pacific Islander, 16% are African American, 4% are Hispanic, 75% are white.

Application Information *Required:* LSAT, LSDAS, application form, application fee of $50, baccalaureate degree, minimum 2.4 GPA, personal statement, college transcripts. *Recommended:* recommendations, essay, resume. *Application deadline* for fall term is March 1. Applications are processed on a rolling basis.

Costs The 2000–2001 tuition was $9688 full-time for state residents; $374 per credit hour part-time for state residents. Tuition was $16,790 full-time for nonresidents; $685 per credit hour part-time for nonresidents. Fees: $340 full-time.

Financial Aid In 2000–2001, 77% of all students received some form of financial aid. Loans, loan repayment assistance program (LRAP), merit-based grants/scholarships, need-based grants/scholarships, and federal work-study loans are available. The average student debt

AT a GLANCE

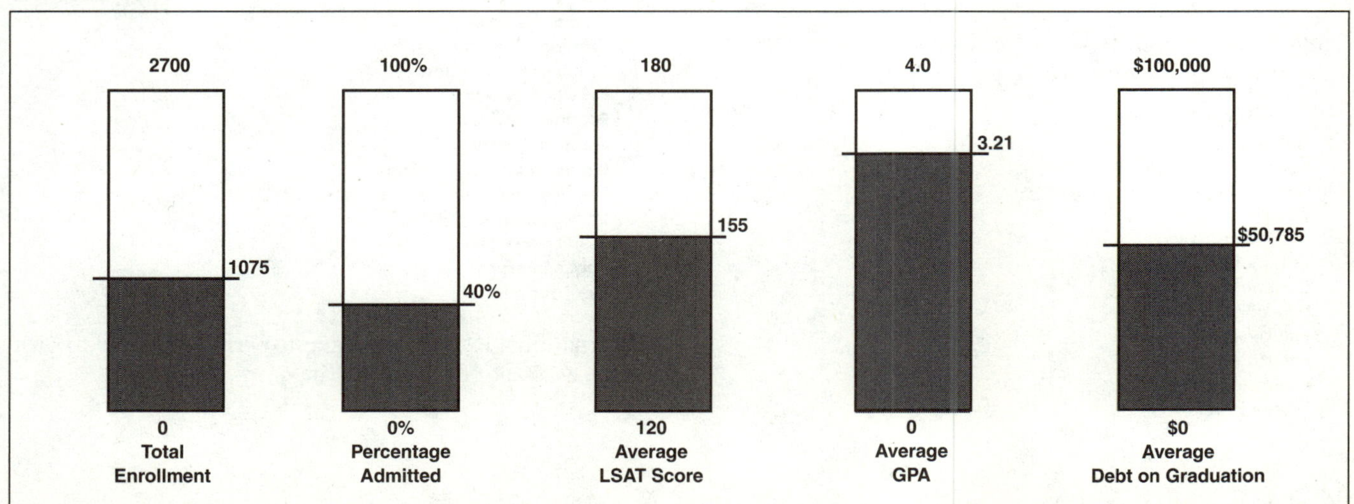

Degree Options

Degree	Total Credits Required	Length of Program
JD–Doctor of Laws	86	3–4 yrs, full-time or part-time [day, evening, summer]
JD/LLM–Juris Doctor/Master of Laws–Transnational Law	98	3.5–4.5 yrs, full-time or part-time [day, evening, summer]
JD/LLM–Juris Doctor/Master of Laws–Taxation	98	3.5–4.5 yrs, full-time or part-time [day, evening, summer]
JD/MBA–Juris Doctor/Master of Business Administration–Dual-degree Program	110	3–4 yrs, full-time or part-time [day, evening, summer]
LLM–Master of Laws–Trial Advocacy	24	1 yr, part-time only [evening, weekend, summer]
LLM–Master of Laws–Foreign Graduate Program	24	1 yr, full-time only [day]
LLM–Master of Laws–Graduate Teaching Fellowship		2 yrs, full-time only [day]

at graduation is $50,785. To apply for financial assistance, students must complete the Free Application for Federal Student Aid, institutional forms. Completed financial aid forms should be received by March 1. Financial aid contact: Johanne Johnston, Director of Financial Aid, 1719 North Broad Street, Philadelphia, PA 19122. Phone: 215-204-8943 or toll free 800-560-1428. Fax: 215-204-1185. E-mail: jjohnsto@vm.temple.edu

Law School Library Charles Klein Law Library has 15 professional staff members and contains more than 511,226 volumes and 3,453 periodicals. 644 seats are available in the library. When classes are in session, the library is open 98 hours per week.

WESTLAW and LEXIS-NEXIS are available, as are the World Wide Web, online bibliographic services, and CD-ROM players. 145 computer workstations are available to students in the library. Special law collections include William Rawle collection of 17th, 18th, and 19th century law books.

First-Year Program Class size in the average section is 66; 90% of the first-year courses are taught by full-time faculty.

Upper-Level Program Class size in the average section is 23. Among the electives are:

Administrative Law
★ Advocacy
★ Business and Corporate Law
★ Civil Litigation
Consumer Law
Corporate Law
Criminal Defense
Criminal Prosecution
Education Law
Elderly Advocacy
Entertainment Law
Environmental Law
Family Practice

Government/Regulation
★ Health Care/Human Services
Health Law
Immigration
Indian/Tribal Law
★ Intellectual Property
★ International/Comparative Law
Jurisprudence
Labor Law
Land Use Law/Natural Resources
★ Lawyering Skills
Legal History/Philosophy
★ Litigation
Maritime Law
Mediation
Probate Law
★ Public Interest
Securities
★ Tax Law
★ Technology Law
(★ indicates an area of special strength)

Clinical Courses Students receive degree credit for clinical courses. (Clinical practicum is not required.) Among the clinical areas offered are:

Advocacy
Business and Corporate Law
Civil Litigation
Corporate Law
Criminal Defense
Criminal Prosecution
Elderly Advocacy
Family Practice
General Practice
Government/Regulation
Health Law
Immigration
Mediation
Public Interest
Tax Law

International exchange programs permit students to visit Greece, Israel, Italy, and Japan.

UNIVERSITY OF PENNSYLVANIA
LAW SCHOOL

Philadelphia, Pennsylvania

INFORMATION CONTACT

Janice L. Austin, Assistant Dean of Admissions
3400 Chestnut Street
Philadelphia, PA 19104

Phone: 215-898-7743   Fax: 215-573-2025
E-mail: admissions@law.upenn.edu
Web site: http://www.law.upenn.edu/

LAW STUDENT PROFILE [2000–2001]

FULL-TIME   Enrollment: 834
Women: 46%   Men: 54%

PART-TIME   Enrollment: 12
Women: 33%   Men: 67%

RACIAL or ETHNIC COMPOSITION
African American, 8%; Asian/Pacific Islander, 7%; Hispanic,
7%; Native American, 0.2%; International, 12%

APPLICANTS and ADMITTEES
Number applied: 3,391
Admitted: 936
Percentage accepted: 28%
Seats available: 240
Average LSAT score: 166
Average GPA: 3.6

University of Pennsylvania Law School is a private
institution that organizes classes on a semester calendar
system. The campus is situated in an urban setting.
Founded in 1790, first ABA approved in 1923, and an
AALS member, University of Pennsylvania Law School
offers JD, JD/BS, JD/BSE, JD/MA, JD/MBA, JD/MBE,
JD/MCP, JD/MSW, JD/PhD, LL.C.M., LLM, and SJD
degrees.

Faculty consists of 61 full-time and 54 part-time
members in 2000–2001. 17 full-time faculty members
and 18 part-time faculty members are women. 96% of all
faculty members have a JD degree. Of all faculty
members, 2.1% are Asian/Pacific Islander, 5.2% are
African American, 3.1% are Hispanic, 85.6% are white,
3.1% are international.

Application Information *Required:* LSAT, LSDAS,
application form, application fee of $70, baccalaureate
degree, 2 letters of recommendation, personal statement,
college transcripts, resume. *Application deadline* for fall
term is March 1. Applications are processed on a rolling
basis.

Costs The 2000–2001 tuition was $26,650 full-time. Fees:
$1710 full-time.

Financial Aid In 2000–2001, 72% of all students received
some form of financial aid. 21 teaching assistantships,
totaling $1750 were awarded. Fellowships, graduate
assistantships, loans, loan repayment assistance program
(LRAP), merit-based grants/scholarships, need-based
grants/scholarships, and federal work-study loans are also
available. The average student debt at graduation is

AT a GLANCE

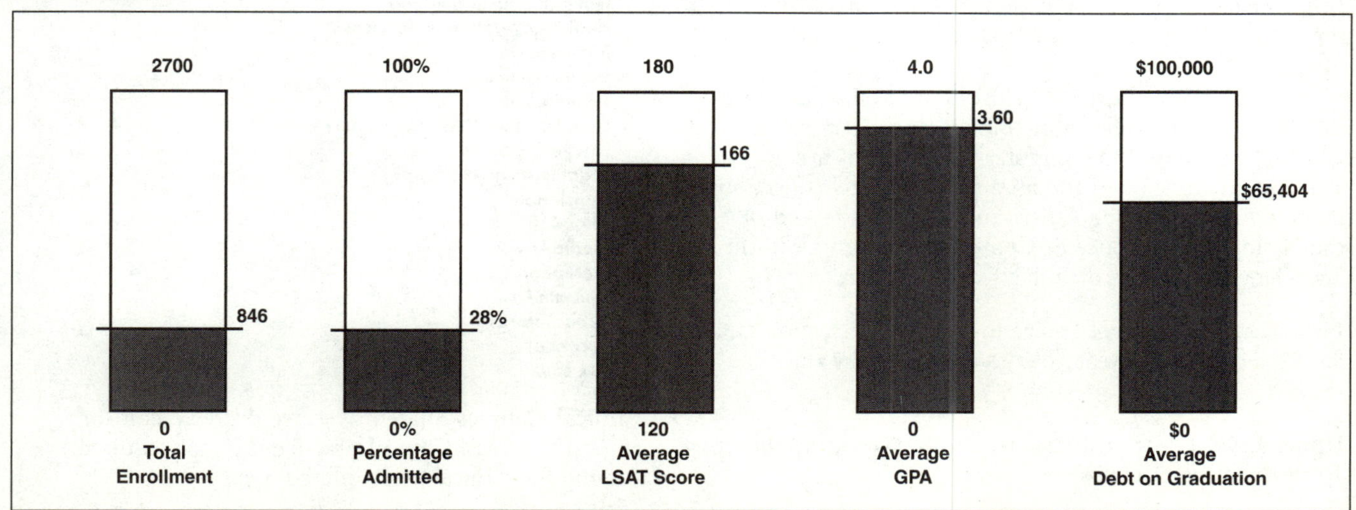

Degree Options

Degree	Total Credits Required	Length of Program
JD–Doctor of Laws	89	3 yrs, full-time only [day]
JD/BS–Juris Doctor/Bachelor of Science–Law/ Economics Dual-degree		6 yrs, full-time only [day]
JD/BS–Juris Doctor/Bachelor of Science–Law/Nursing Dual-degree		6 yrs, full-time only [day]
Certificate–Law/Engineering Dual-degree		6 yrs, full-time only [day]
JD/MA–Juris Doctor/Master of Arts–Law/Islamic Studies Dual-degree		4 yrs, full-time only [day]
JD/MA–Juris Doctor/Master of Arts–Law/Economics Dual-degree		3–4 yrs, full-time only [day]
JD/MBA–Juris Doctor/Master of Business Administration–Law/Business Dual-degree	134	4 yrs, full-time only [day]
Certificate–Law/Bioethics Dual-degree		3 yrs, full-time only [day]
JD/MCP–Juris Doctor/Master of City Planning–Law/ City Planning Dual-degree		4 yrs, full-time only [day]
JD/MSW–Juris Doctor/Master of Social Work–Law/ Social Work Dual-degree		4 yrs, full-time only [day]
JD/PhD–Juris Doctor/Doctor of Philosophy–Law/ Economics Dual-degree		6 yrs, full-time only [day]
JD/PhD–Juris Doctor/Doctor of Philosophy–Law/ Philosophy Dual-degree		6 yrs, full-time only [day]
JD/PhD–Juris Doctor/Doctor of Philosophy–Law/ American Legal History Dual-degree		7 yrs, full-time only [day]
Certificate–Comparative Law	16	1 yr, full-time only [day]
LLM–Master of Laws	23	1 yr, full-time only [day]
SJD–Doctor of Juridical Science		2–5 yrs, full-time only [day]

$65,404. To apply for financial assistance, students must complete the Free Application for Federal Student Aid, institutional forms. Completed financial aid forms should be received by March 1. Financial aid contact: Janice Austin, Assistant Dean of Admissions, 3400 Chestnut Street, Philadelphia, PA 19104. Phone: 215-898-7400. Fax: 215-573-2025. E-mail: admissions@law.upenn.edu

Law School Library Biddle Law Library has 16 professional staff members and contains more than 725,000 volumes and 8,411 periodicals. 525 seats are available in the library. When classes are in session, the library is open 111 hours per week.

WESTLAW and LEXIS-NEXIS are available, as are the World Wide Web, online bibliographic services, and CD-ROM players. 130 computer workstations are available to students in the library. Special law collections include Archives of the American Law Institute and of the National Conference of Commissioners on Uniform State Law, the papers of Judge David Bazelon.

First-Year Program Class size in the average section is 85; 92% of the first-year courses are taught by full-time faculty.

Upper-Level Program Class size in the average section is 70. Among the electives are:

Administrative Law
Advocacy
Business and Corporate Law
Civil Litigation
Civil Rights
Consumer Law
Corporate Law
Criminal Defense
Education Law
Entertainment Law
Environmental Law
Family Law
Government/Regulation
Health Care/Human Services
Immigration
Jurisprudence
Juvenile Law
Land Use Law/Natural Resources
Lawyering Skills
Legal History/Philosophy
Legislation
Litigation
Media Law
Mediation
Probate Law
Public Interest
Securities
Tax Law

Clinical Courses Students receive degree credit for clinical courses. (Clinical practicum is not required.) Among the clinical areas offered are:

Advocacy
Business and Corporate Law
Civil Litigation
Civil Rights
Corporate Law
Criminal Defense
Criminal Prosecution
Elderly Advocacy
Family Law
Family Practice

General Practice
Immigration
Juvenile Law
Lawyering Skills
Legislation
Litigation
Mediation
Public Interest
Tax Law

DEAN'S STATEMENT . . .

The mission of the University of Pennsylvania Law School is to generate intellectual and human capital for the leadership of the legal profession in the twenty-first century through research and teaching. We foresee that in the coming century lawyers will be called upon to integrate the findings of an ever wider array of human knowledge, change specialties, update substantive knowledge more frequently and rapidly, move readily across professional boundaries, and devote increasing energy to building, maintaining, and leading organizations. Leaders of the profession will require not only conventional doctrinal and institutional knowledge and skills in analytical reasoning, research, and written and oral communications, but also skills in integrations and synthesis of knowledge, strategic and tactical thinking, and the capacity of continuous self-criticism and self-education.

Two centuries after our founding, Penn Law School takes the lead by making the study of law central to the education of the new generation of leaders—the "interprofessional professionals" of the next century. Among elite, research-oriented American law schools, Penn has long been known for its strengths in such traditional doctrinal fields as administrative law, civil procedure, commercial law, criminal law, and labor law; its interdisciplinary research in fields such as economics, history, and philosophy; its contributions to law reform through its relationship with organizations like the American Law Institute and the National Constitutional Center; and its commitment to integrating theory and practice in such experiential learning contexts as clinical and public service programs. Creative and selective partnerships with those resources will enable Penn Law to re-create a national model for the study and teaching of leadership in law. I strongly encourage you to consider Penn Law as an institution to pursue your legal education.

—*Michael A. Fitts, Dean* and *Bernard G. Segal Professor of Law*

HISTORY, CAMPUS, AND LOCATION

The University of Pennsylvania traces its roots to Benjamin Franklin's founding of the Academe and Charitable School of the Province of Pennsylvania in 1740. In 1790, the institution (reconstituted during the Revolutionary War as the College of Philadelphia) named as its first Professor of Law James Wilson (a signer of the Declaration of Independence, architect with James Madison of the Constitution, and one of the six original justices of the United States Supreme Court), who presented a series of lectures offering a wide-ranging comparative and critical analysis of legal systems past and present.

In 1900 the Law School moved into Lewis Hall at 34th and Chestnut Streets on the University campus. The Law School's location on the campus of a major research university is ideal because it combines the best of a small school environment with the resources of a large university. In many ways—academically, socially, philosophically, and professionally—Penn Law students benefit greatly from the dynamic communities that surround Penn Law, the University of Pennsylvania, University City, and Philadelphia. Students are fortunate in having easy access to all the amenities of a major metropolis at the School's doorstep.

Philadelphia's Center City is less than 2 miles from the University's campus on the west bank of the Schuylkill River, which provides law students with access to local, state, and federal judiciaries and government agencies; law firms; and public services organizations.

SPECIAL QUALITIES OF THE SCHOOL

The University of Pennsylvania Law School provides a hospitable and rigorous environment for learning. Each year it selects a small, able, and diverse class of approximately 240 individuals and combines an excellent student body with outstanding faculty members who have varied educational backgrounds and a wide spectrum of experience.

There is a certain quality of life at Penn Law that is not often found in law schools. These academically gifted individuals come together to tackle the rigorous curriculum, but do so in a way that is more collegial than is the norm in legal education. Students cooperate with each other, they share notes, and they help and support each other. Because there is no rank in class, a student competes against himself or herself rather than against other students.

TECHNOLOGY ON CAMPUS

The Law School maintains a Virtual Lab environment in which hundreds of network connections provide every student access to electronic resources within the library, classrooms, and University housing. Most commonly students use e-mail, Netnews, and the World Wide Web for classes and to keep informed of developments in the School and beyond. Students also use LEXIS-NEXIS, WESTLAW, CD-ROM databases, and the World Wide Web for legal research; word processing for class assignments; spreadsheets for classes with heavy quantitative content; and databases, provided by Career Planning and Services for employment searches.

SCHOLARSHIPS AND LOANS

It has long been the policy of the Law School that every admitted applicant who wishes to enroll should not be prevented from doing so by lack of funds. In recent years the necessary financial aid support has been provided by a combination of student and parental contributions, government guaranteed loans, grants, merit awards, and University loans, appropriate to the circumstances of each individual student.

STUDENT ACTIVITIES AND OPPORTUNITIES

Law Review The nation's oldest continuous law journal is the *University of Pennsylvania Law Review*. Other journals include the *Journal of Constitutional Law*, the *Journal of International Economic Law*, and the *Journal of Labor and Employment Law*. Admission to the reviews are based on academic standing and a writing competition. Approximately 90 students participate in the publications.

Moot Court Appellate Advocacy II is the Law School's second-year intramural moot court competition. The students research and write briefs and then present their case in one or perhaps two rounds of oral argument before a panel of students, faculty members, and judges. In recent years, Penn students have participated in the National Moot Court Competition, the Merna B. Marshall Moot Court Competition, the Frederick B. Douglass Moot Court Competition, and the Jessup Cup Competition.

Extracurricular Activities Students at the Law School do not merely come to get an education and leave without giving something back to the school and the community. They actively participate in the daily operations of the Law School by serving on every standing committee. Student organizations provide opportunities for activities from intellectual and scholarly engagement to social and public service requirements.

Special Opportunities One of the hallmarks of Penn Law is the array of extraordinary interdisciplinary studies available at the University. Students can draw upon the vast resources of the University to pursue studies and joint degrees in many different disciplines, thus achieving a diverse and intensive education.

Since 1990, the Law School, in keeping with the ethical tenets of the legal profession to render public services, has adopted a public service requirement where all second- and third-year law students perform a total of 70 hours of law-related public service as a condition of graduation. Placements also increase the students' lawyering skills and expose them to new areas of the law. The Law School operates a state-of-the-art teaching law clinical program. Students have the opportunity to obtain valuable learning experiences for academic credit while at the same time providing much needed legal assistance to clients in the following clinics: the Civil Practice Clinic, the Mediation Clinic, the Small Business Clinic, and the Legislative Clinical Seminar.

Opportunities for Members of Minority Groups and Women Traditionally, the enrollment of minority students has been approximately 25 percent of each entering class. Members of minority groups actively participate in the entire life of the Law School. In addition to ethnic student organizations, the Women's Law Group, OWLS (Older, Wiser Law Students), and Lambda Law (gay and lesbian law student group) are examples of the opportunities for all students to have vital roles in the law school community.

Special Certificate Programs There are two unique certificate programs: Certificate of Study in Public Policy and Management with the Wharton School and a Certificate in Women's Studies.

BAR PASSAGE, CAREER SERVICES, AND PLACEMENT

The majority of Penn Law students take the New York and Pennsylvania bar exams.

A wide range of programs to provide balance between practical, how-to sessions with broader programming that will expose students to the great wealth of opportunity and variety are available to the law graduate. Services include assistance to improve presentation skills with resume writing workshops and interviewing programs and, in the upperclass years, in-depth assistance for the clerkship application process.

In addition to the Career Services staff, expertise in conducting a successful job search is provided by hiring partners, recruiting coordinators, fellowships program directors, judges, law clerks, career planning experts, and particularly alumni.

Legal Field	Percentage of Graduates	Average Salary
Academic	1%	n/a
Business	4-6%	$ 87,500
Government	2-5%	$ 41,500
Judicial Clerkship	15-18%	$ 41,500
Private Practice	65-70%	$100,000
Public Interest	2-5%	$ 35,750
Other	n/a	n/a

CORRESPONDENCE AND INFORMATION

Law School
University of Pennsylvania
3400 Chestnut Street
Philadelphia, Pennsylvania 19104-6204
Telephone: 215-898-7400
Fax: 215-573-2025
E-mail: admissions@law.upenn.edu
World Wide Web: http://www.law.upenn.edu

UNIVERSITY OF PITTSBURGH
SCHOOL OF LAW

Pittsburgh, Pennsylvania

LAW STUDENT PROFILE [2000–2001]

FULL-TIME   Enrollment: 713
Women: 47%   Men: 53%

PART-TIME   Enrollment: 4
Women: 50%   Men: 50%

RACIAL or ETHNIC COMPOSITION
African American, 6%; Asian/Pacific Islander, 2%; Hispanic, 1%

APPLICANTS and ADMITTEES
Number applied: 1,276
Admitted: 857
Percentage accepted: 67%
Seats available: 250
Average LSAT score: 156
Average GPA: 3.2

University of Pittsburgh School of Law is a public institution that organizes classes on a semester calendar system. The campus is situated in an urban setting. Founded in 1895, first ABA approved in 1923, and an AALS member, University of Pittsburgh School of Law offers JD, JD/MA, JD/MBA, JD/MPAd, JD/MPH, JD/MPIA, JD/MS, LLM, and MSL degrees.

Faculty consists of 38 full-time and 1 part-time members in 2000–2001. 13 full-time faculty members are women. 100% of all faculty members have a JD; 21% have advanced law degrees. Of all faculty members, 5% are Asian/Pacific Islander, 7% are African American, 88% are white.

Application Information *Required:* LSAT, LSDAS, application form, application fee of $50, baccalaureate degree, personal statement, college transcripts. *Recommended:* recommendations. *Application deadline* is rolling.

Financial Aid In 2000–2001, 33% of all students received some form of financial aid. 7 fellowships, totaling $8000 were awarded. Loans, loan repayment assistance program (LRAP), merit-based grants/scholarships, and need-based grants/scholarships are also available. The average student debt at graduation is $60,000. To apply for financial assistance, students must complete the Free Application for Federal Student Aid, institutional forms, scholarship specific applications. Financial aid contact: Fredi G. Miller, Assistant Dean for Admissions and Financial Aid, 3900 Forbes Avenue, Pittsburgh, PA 15260. Phone: 412-648-1415. Fax: 412-648-2647. E-mail: admissions@law.pitt.edu

AT a GLANCE

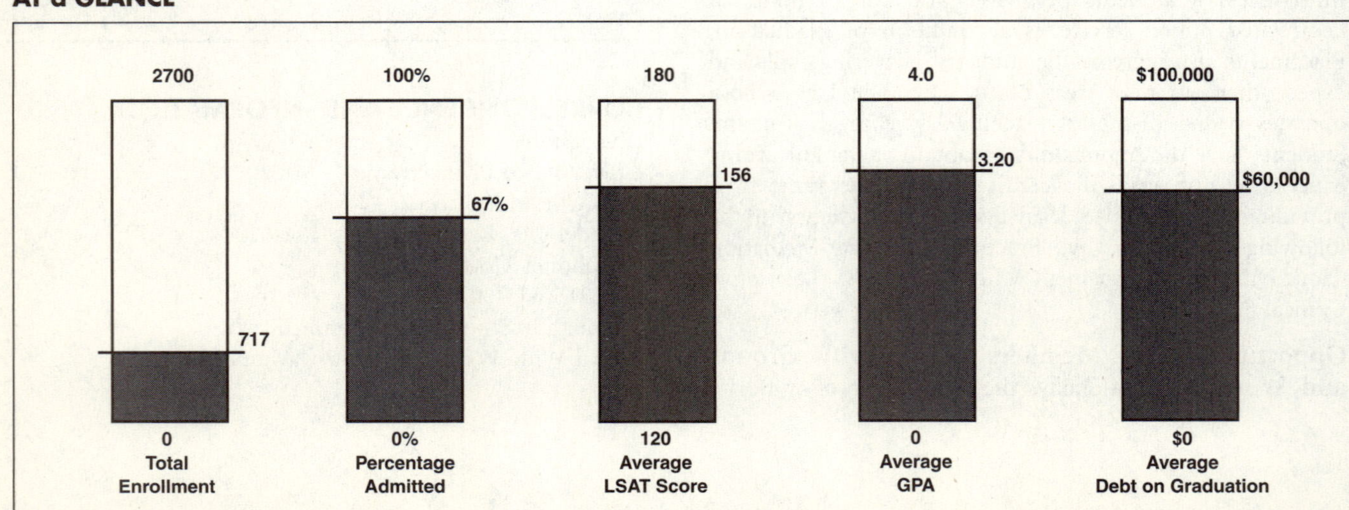

Degree Options

Degree	Total Credits Required	Length of Program
JD–Juris Doctor	88	3 yrs, full-time only [day]
JD/MA–Juris Doctor/Master of Arts–Joint-degree in Medical Ethics	100	4 yrs, full-time only [day]
JD/MBA–Juris Doctor/Master of Business Administration–Joint-degree	115	3.5 yrs, full-time only [day]
JD/MPAd–Juris Doctor/Master of Public Administration–Joint-degree	115	4 yrs, full-time only [day]
JD/MPH–Juris Doctor/Master of Public Health–Joint-degree	118	4 yrs, full-time only [day]
JD/MPIA–Juris Doctor/Master of Public and International Affairs–Joint-degree	115	4 yrs, full-time only [day]
JD/MS–Juris Doctor/Master of Science–Joint-degree in Arts Management	118	4 yrs, full-time only [day]
JD/MS–Juris Doctor/Master of Science–Industrial Administration	118	4 yrs, full-time only [day]
LLM–Master of Laws	24	1 yr, full-time only [day]
MSL–Master of School Leadership	30	1–4 yrs, full-time or part-time [day]

Law School Library Barco Law Library has 7 professional staff members and contains more than 371,606 volumes and 4,747 periodicals. 453 seats are available in the library. When classes are in session, the library is open 102 hours per week.

WESTLAW and LEXIS-NEXIS are available, as are the World Wide Web, online bibliographic services, and CD-ROM players. 72 computer workstations are available to students in the library. Special law collections include rare book collection.

First-Year Program Class size in the average section is 84; 100% of the first-year courses are taught by full-time faculty.

Upper-Level Program Class size in the average section is 28. Among the electives are:

Administrative Law
Advocacy
Business and Corporate Law
Commercial Law
Constitutional Law
Corporate Law
Criminal Law
★ Disability Law
Education Law
★ Elder Law
★ Elderly Advocacy
★ Environmental Law
★ Family Law
★ Health Care/Human Services
★ Health Law
★ Intellectual Property
★ International/Comparative Law
Jurisprudence
Juvenile Law
Labor Law
★ Land Use Law/Natural Resources
Lawyering Skills
Legal History/Philosophy
★ Litigation
Mediation
Personal Injury
Probate Law
Public Interest
Securities
★ Tax Law
(★ indicates an area of special strength)

Clinical Courses Students receive degree credit for clinical courses. (Clinical practicum is not required.) Among the clinical areas offered are:

Business and Corporate Law
Corporate Law
Criminal Law
Disability Law
Education Law
Elder Law
Elderly Advocacy
Environmental Law
Family Law
Health Care/Human Services
Health Law
Immigration
Juvenile Law
Land Use Law/Natural Resources
Lawyering Skills
Litigation
Mediation
Public Interest
Tax Law

VILLANOVA UNIVERSITY
SCHOOL OF LAW

Villanova, Pennsylvania

INFORMATION CONTACT

David P. Pallozzi, Assistant Dean of Admissions
299 North Spring Mill Road
Villanova, PA 19085

Phone: 610-519-7010   Fax: 610-519-6291
E-mail: admissions@law.villanova.edu
Web site: http://vls.law.vill.edu/

LAW STUDENT PROFILE [2000–2001]

FULL-TIME   Enrollment: 769
Women: 47%   Men: 53%

PART-TIME   Enrollment: 102
Women: 35%   Men: 65%

RACIAL or ETHNIC COMPOSITION
African American, 3%; Asian/Pacific Islander, 5%; Hispanic, 2%; Native American, 0.2%; International, 0.1%

APPLICANTS and ADMITTEES
Number applied: 1,663
Admitted: 1,000
Percentage accepted: 60%
Seats available: 230
Average LSAT score: 156
Average GPA: 3.3

Villanova University School of Law is a private institution that organizes classes on a semester calendar system. The campus is situated in a suburban setting. Founded in 1953, first ABA approved in 1953, and an AALS member, Villanova University School of Law offers JD, JD/MBA, JD/PhD, and LLM degrees.

Faculty consists of 43 full-time and 44 part-time members in 2000–2001. 14 full-time faculty members and 16 part-time faculty members are women. 100% of all faculty members have a JD; 29% have advanced law degrees. Of all faculty members, 1% are Native American, 1% are Asian/Pacific Islander, 4% are African American, 1% are Hispanic, 93% are white.

Application Information *Required:* LSAT, LSDAS, application form, application fee of $75, baccalaureate degree, college transcripts. *Recommended:* recommendations, personal statement, resume. *Application deadline* for fall term is March 1. Applications are processed on a rolling basis.

Costs The 2000–2001 tuition was $21,700 full-time. Fees: $80 full-time.

Financial Aid In 2000–2001, 23% of all students received some form of financial aid. 107 research assistantships were awarded. Fellowships, graduate assistantships, loans, merit-based grants/scholarships, need-based grants/scholarships, and federal work-study loans are also available. The average student debt at graduation is $72,846. To apply for financial assistance, students must complete the Free Application for Federal Student Aid, institutional forms. Completed financial aid forms should

AT a GLANCE

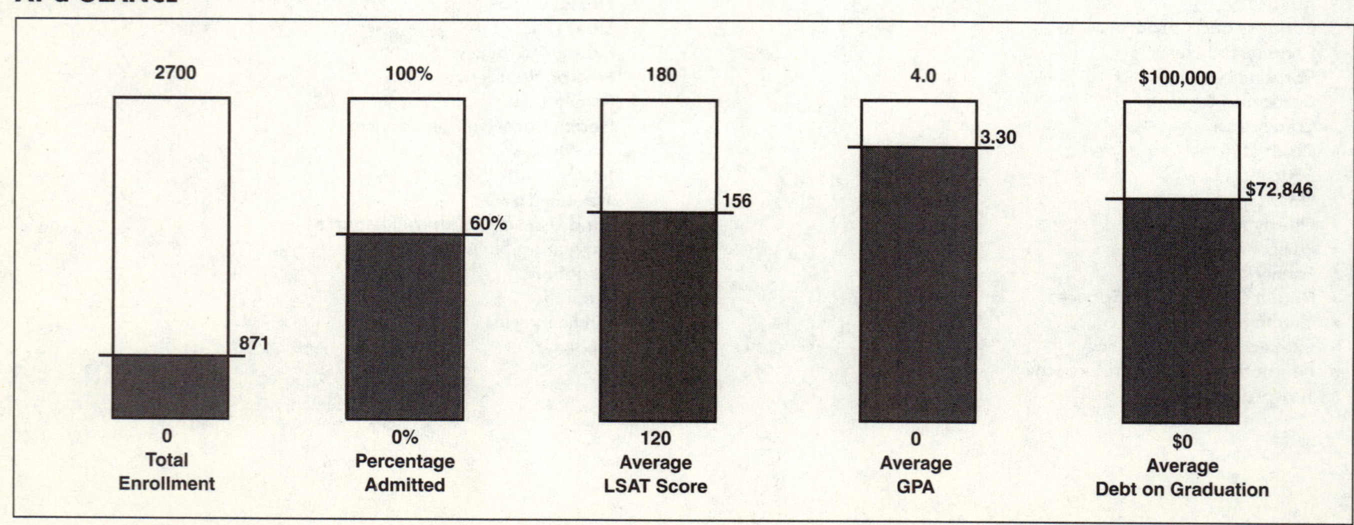

Degree Options

Degree	Total Credits Required	Length of Program
JD–Doctor of Laws	87	3 yrs, full-time only [day]
JD/MBA–Juris Doctor/Master of Business Administration–Dual-degree Program	135	3–4 yrs, full-time only [day, evening, summer]
JD/PhD–Juris Doctor/Doctor of Philosophy–Joint Program in Law and Psychology	199	6–7 yrs, full-time only [day]
LLM–Master of Laws–Taxation	24	1 yr, full-time or part-time [evening]

be received by March 15. Financial aid contact: Wendy Barron, Director of Financial Aid, 299 North Spring Mill Road, Villanova, PA 19085. Phone: 610-519-7015. Fax: 610-519-6291. E-mail: barron@law.vill.edu

Law School Library Arthur Clement Pulling Library has 10 professional staff members and contains more than 458,470 volumes and 3,369 periodicals. 368 seats are available in the library. When classes are in session, the library is open 168 hours per week.

WESTLAW and LEXIS-NEXIS are available, as are the World Wide Web, online bibliographic services, and CD-ROM players. 150 computer workstations are available to students in the library.

First-Year Program Class size in the average section is 117; 100% of the first-year courses are taught by full-time faculty.

Upper-Level Program Among the electives are:

Civil Litigation
Education
Environmental Law
Health Law
Juvenile Law
Public Interest
Tax Law

Clinical Courses Students receive degree credit for clinical courses. (Clinical practicum is not required.) Among the clinical areas offered are:

Civil Litigation
Education
Elderly Advocacy
Immigration
Information and Communications
Juvenile Law
Public Interest
Tax Law

WIDENER UNIVERSITY
WIDENER UNIVERSITY SCHOOL OF LAW

Harrisburg, Pennsylvania

INFORMATION CONTACT

Barbara L. Ayars, Assistant Dean of Admissions
3800 Vartan Way
PO Box 69381
Harrisburg, PA 17106-9381

Phone: 302-477-2210   Fax: 302-477-2224
E-mail: barbara.l.ayars@law.widener.edu
Web site: http://www.law.widener.edu/

LAW STUDENT PROFILE [2000–2001]

FULL-TIME   Enrollment: 235
Women: 46%   Men: 54%

PART-TIME   Enrollment: 156
Women: 44%   Men: 56%

RACIAL or ETHNIC COMPOSITION
African American, 3%; Asian/Pacific Islander, 4%; Hispanic, 3%

APPLICANTS and ADMITTEES
Number applied: 607
Admitted: 354
Percentage accepted: 58%
Seats available: 145
Average LSAT score: 147
Average GPA: 3.0

Widener University Widener University School of Law is a private institution that organizes classes on a semester calendar system. The campus is situated in a suburban setting. Founded in 1988, first ABA approved in 1975, and an AALS member, Widener University Widener University School of Law offers a JD degree.

Faculty consists of 21 full-time and 16 part-time members in 2000–2001. 8 full-time faculty members and 7 part-time faculty members are women. 100% of all faculty members have a JD; 24% have advanced law degrees. Of all faculty members, 5% are African American, 95% are white.

Application Information *Required:* LSAT, LSDAS, application form, application fee of $60, baccalaureate degree, college transcripts. *Recommended:* recommendations, personal statement, resume. *Application deadline* for fall term is May 15. Applications are processed on a rolling basis.

Costs The 1999–2000 tuition was $19,500 full-time. Full-time tuition and fees vary according to campus/location. Part-time tuition and fees vary according to program.

Financial Aid Loans, loan repayment assistance program (LRAP), merit-based grants/scholarships, need-based grants/scholarships, and federal work-study loans are available. The average student debt at graduation is $65,849. To apply for financial assistance, students must complete the Free Application for Federal Student Aid, institutional forms. Completed financial aid forms should be received by February 15. Financial aid contact: James

AT a GLANCE

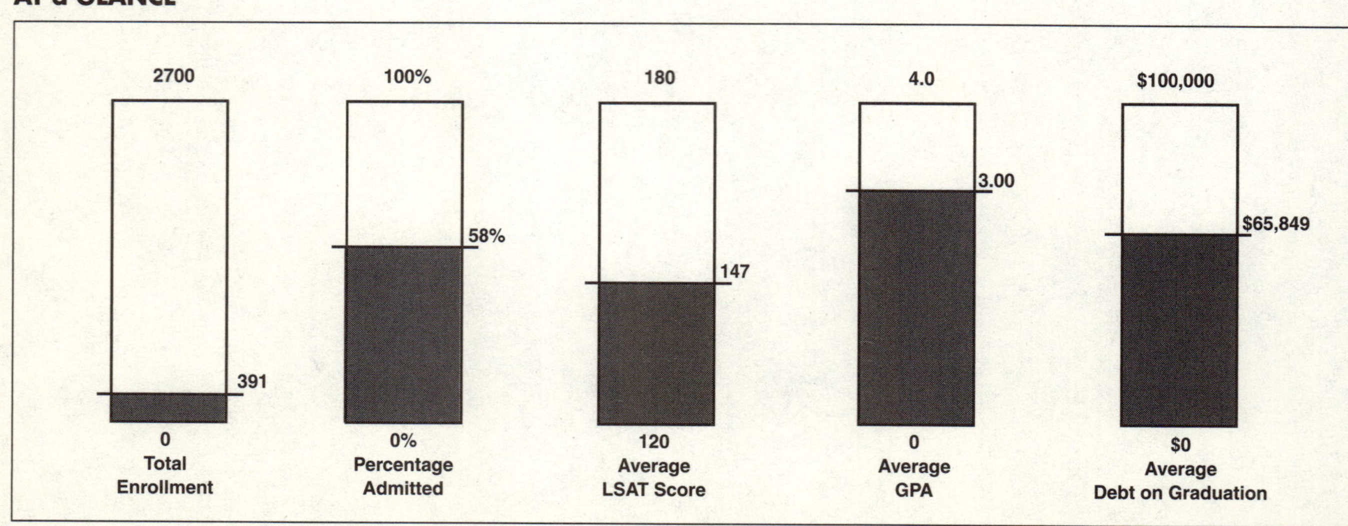

<table>
<tr><td colspan="3">Degree Options</td></tr>
<tr><td>Degree</td><td>Total Credits Required</td><td>Length of Program</td></tr>
<tr><td>JD–Doctor of Laws</td><td>87</td><td>3–4 yrs, full-time or part-time [day, evening, summer]</td></tr>
</table>

Snyder, Assistant Director for Financial Aid, 3800 Vartan Way, PO Box 69381, Harrisburg, PA 17106-9381. Phone: 717-541-1924. Fax: 717-541-3999. E-mail: james.a.snyder@law.widener.edu

Law School Library Widener University School of Law Legal Information Center has 5 professional staff members and contains more than 187,372 volumes and 3,430 periodicals. 358 seats are available in the library. When classes are in session, the library is open 107 hours per week.

WESTLAW and LEXIS-NEXIS are available, as are the World Wide Web, online bibliographic services, and CD-ROM players. 61 computer workstations are available to students in the library. Special law collections include public law, United States selective depository for government documents.

First-Year Program Class size in the average section is 50; 100% of the first-year courses are taught by full-time faculty.

Upper-Level Program Class size in the average section is 25. Among the electives are:

  Administrative Law
★ Bankruptcy
  Business and Corporate Law
★ Civil Law
★ Civil Litigation
★ Consumer Law
★ Criminal Defense
★ Domestic Violence
  Education Law
  Entertainment Law
★ Environmental Law
★ Family Law
  General Practice
★ Government/Regulation
★ Health Care/Human Services
  Intellectual Property
  International/Comparative Law
★ Judicial Externship
  Jurisprudence
  Labor Law
  Land Use Law/Natural Resources
  Lawyering Skills
  Litigation
  Mediation
  Probate Law
★ Public Interest
  Securities
  Tax Law

(★ indicates an area of special strength)

Clinical Courses Students receive degree credit for clinical courses. (Clinical practicum is not required.) Among the clinical areas offered are:

  Administrative Law
  Bankruptcy
  Civil Law
  Civil Litigation
  Consumer Law
  Criminal Defense
  Domestic Violence
  Environmental Law
  Family Law
  General Practice
  Government/Regulation
  Judicial Externship
  Mediation
  Public Interest

ROGER WILLIAMS UNIVERSITY
RALPH R. PAPITTO SCHOOL OF LAW

Bristol, Rhode Island

INFORMATION CONTACT

Christel L. Ertel, Dean of Admissions
10 Metacom Avenue
Bristol, RI 02809-5171

Phone: 401-254-4515   Fax: 401-254-4516
E-mail: cle@rwulaw.rwu.edu
Web site: http://law.rwu.edu

LAW STUDENT PROFILE [2000–2001]

FULL-TIME   Enrollment: 234
PART-TIME   Enrollment: 131

RACIAL or ETHNIC COMPOSITION
African American, 4%; Asian/Pacific Islander, 2%; Hispanic, 4%

APPLICANTS and ADMITTEES
Number applied: 711
Admitted: 392
Percentage accepted: 55%
Seats available: 150
Average LSAT score: 149
Average GPA: 3.0

Roger Williams University Ralph R. Papitto School of Law is a private institution that organizes classes on a semester calendar system. The campus is situated in a small-town setting. Founded in 1992, first ABA approved in 1997, Roger Williams University Ralph R. Papitto School of Law offers JD, JD/MBA, JD/MCP, JD/MMA, and JD/MS degrees.

Faculty consists of 23 full-time and 16 part-time members in 2000–2001. 8 full-time faculty members and 7 part-time faculty members are women. 100% of all faculty members have a JD; 20% have advanced law degrees. Of all faculty members, 1% are African American, 99% are white.

Application Information *Required:* LSAT, LSDAS, application form, application fee of $60, baccalaureate degree, personal statement, college transcripts. *Recommended:* minimum GPA, 2 letters of recommendation. *Application deadline* for fall term is May 15 (priority date). Applications are processed on a rolling basis.

Financial Aid In 2000–2001, 96% of all students received some form of financial aid. 26 research assistantships were awarded. Loans, merit-based grants/scholarships, and need-based grants/scholarships are also available. The average student debt at graduation is $74,557. To apply for financial assistance, students must complete the Free Application for Federal Student Aid, institutional forms. Completed financial aid forms should be received by May 15. Financial aid contact: Amanda Zusman, Assistant Director of Financial Aid, 10 Metacom Avenue, Bristol, RI 02809. Phone: 401-254-4510. Fax: 401-254-4516. E-mail: axz@rwulaw.rwu.edu

AT a GLANCE

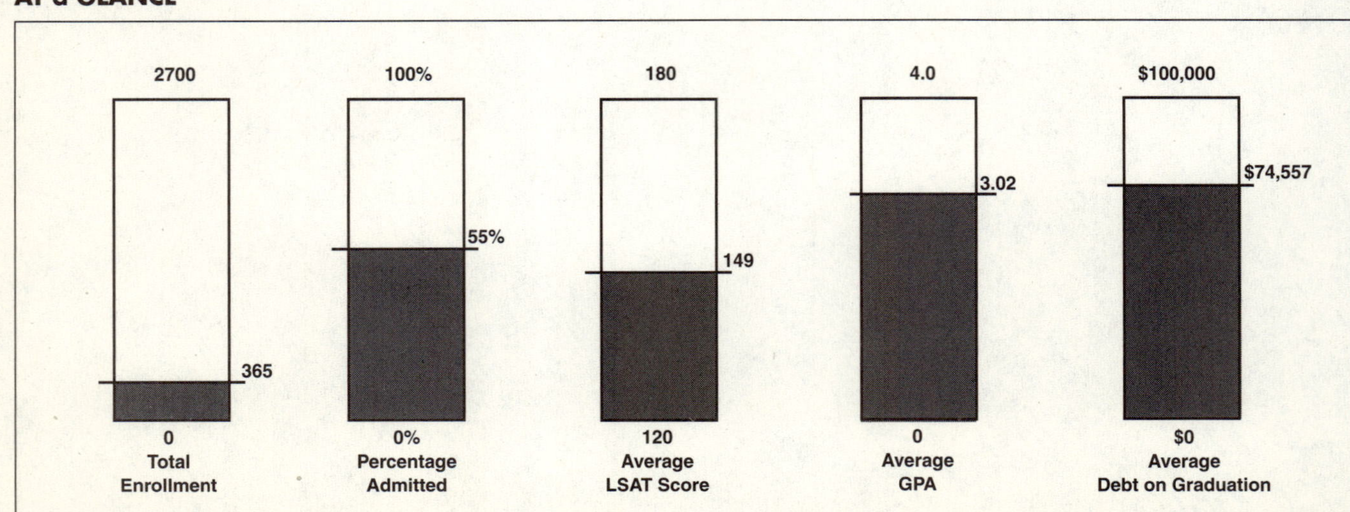

Degree Options

Degree	Total Credits Required	Length of Program
JD–Doctor of Laws	90	3–4 yrs, full-time or part-time [day, evening, summer]
JD/MBA–Juris Doctor/Master of Business Administration–JD/MBA Dual Degree program	110	4–5 yrs, full-time or part-time [day, summer]
JD/MCP–Juris Doctor/Master of City Planning–Joint-degree Program	115	4 yrs, full-time or part-time [day, evening, weekend, summer]
JD/MMA–Juris Doctor/Master of Marine Affairs–Joint-degree Program	105	3.5 yrs, full-time or part-time [day, evening, weekend, summer]
JD/MS–Juris Doctor/Master of Science–Juris Doctor/Master of Science in Labor Relations and Human Resources	105	4 yrs, full-time or part-time [day, evening, summer]

Law School Library Law Library has 7 professional staff members and contains more than 253,000 volumes and 3,718 periodicals. 383 seats are available in the library. When classes are in session, the library is open 110 hours per week.

WESTLAW and LEXIS-NEXIS are available, as are the World Wide Web, online bibliographic services, and CD-ROM players. 63 computer workstations are available to students in the library. Special law collections include Rhode Island Law, Maritime Law, and the State Justice Institute Depository..

First-Year Program Class size in the average section is 75; 100% of the first-year courses are taught by full-time faculty.

Upper-Level Program Class size in the average section is 40. Among the electives are:

  Administrative Law
★ Advocacy
★ Business and Corporate Law
★ Community Development
  Consumer Law
★ Criminal Law
  Entertainment Law
★ Environmental Law
★ Family Law
  Government/Regulation
  Health Care/Human Services
★ Intellectual Property
★ International/Comparative Law
  Jurisprudence
★ Labor Law
  Land Use Law/Natural Resources
★ Lawyering Skills
  Legal History/Philosophy
★ Litigation
★ Maritime Law
  Mediation
  Probate Law
★ Public Interest
  Securities
★ Tax Law

(★ *indicates an area of special strength*)

Clinical Courses Students receive degree credit for clinical courses. (Clinical practicum is not required.) Among the clinical areas offered are:

  Criminal Law
  Family Law
  Family Practice

International exchange programs permit students to visit Portugal and United Kingdom.

DEAN'S STATEMENT . . .

The hallmark of the Roger Williams experience is the intellectual community that we have created. It is a community of rigorous analysis, spirited debate, and relevant scholarship. The key to this environment is our outstanding faculty, which is drawn from the leading universities and law schools in North America. Productivity, breadth of subject matter, large firm experience, and mastery of the issues characterize and mark their interests and law review subjects. This enthusiasm for the study of law is reflected in the faculty's dedication to teaching and the energy brought to the classroom.

Much is happening on our campus. Our Honors Program, which offers a merit scholarship, features a three year curriculum of special seminars, study abroad, judicial internships, and a legislative practicum. This year, we are introducing a new Disability Representation Clinic, in addition to our well-known and established Criminal Defense Clinic. The overall number of clerkships and externships available to our students continues to increase. Recently, we approved a joint Juris Doctor/Master's Program in Labor Relations and Human Resources, which expands on our existing joint J.D./M.A. programs for Marine Affairs and Community Planning with the University of Rhode Island. Roger Williams students also have the opportunity to study abroad at our international programs in London, England and Lisbon, Portugal. We have also connected with the bench and bar to develop the Rhode Island Minority Mentor Program for our students of color.

If you are looking for a school that will prepare you for the practice of law in a supportive, dynamic, exciting, and challenging atmosphere with outstanding faculty, please read on.

—Harvey Rishikof, Dean and Professor of Law

HISTORY, CAMPUS, AND LOCATION

Roger Williams University's (RWU) Ralph R. Papitto School of Law is a young, dynamic institution that has made its mark in the professional and legal communities in an unprecedented short period of time. The School of Law was founded in 1992 and earned full accreditation approval from the American Bar Association (ABA) in February 1997, the earliest possible time under ABA rules and procedures. As the first and only law school in the state of Rhode Island, the School of Law maintains a very close and supportive relationship with the bench and bar.

The Law School is situated on a modern 140-acre campus overlooking Mt. Hope Bay in the historic seaport town of Bristol, Rhode Island. Students enjoy our proximity to Providence, the state capitol, the resort city of Newport, and nearby Boston. The School of Law is self-contained in its own multimillion-dollar building.

SPECIAL QUALITIES OF THE SCHOOL

The School of Law functions as the Law Center for the state of Rhode Island, running programs for the bench and bar. The School of Law holds a unique franchise on student clerkship opportunities with federal and state judges and state offices and agencies. The Law School has established itself as a respected institution within the tradition of legal education, as a highly regarded center for the exploration and evaluation of pertinent legal issues, and as a valued contributor of public service.

The community approach of the Law School fosters personalized attention for students from accessible faculty members in an environment that is cooperative rather than competitive.

TECHNOLOGY ON CAMPUS

The Law Library provides access to computers in the stack areas and contains three computer labs, each complete with access to online research systems, word processing, the Internet, e-mail, the CD-ROM network, and computer-assisted legal instruction. Additional research assistance is available online through the law school Web site (http://law.rwu.edu/LawLib/index.html).

All first-year law students are trained to use LEXIS and WESTLAW, computer-assisted legal research systems which can be accessed either at the School of Law or from home.

Microphones and cameras are installed in the moot courtrooms and many class and seminar rooms. The library contains video playback rooms where faculty and students critique skills and improve techniques.

SCHOLARSHIPS AND LOANS

The School of Law provides generous financial assistance in the way of merit-based and need-based aid. Special programs include the Papitto Scholarships (full tuition and enrollment in the Honors Program), the Presidential Scholarships (half tuition and enrollment in the Honors Program), Roger Williams University School of Law Scholarships (up to half tuition), and Dean's Scholarships (up to $5,000). Awards are renewable provided a particular grade point average is maintained. No special application is required. To apply for need-based financial aid, students should file the FAFSA by the stated deadlines.

STUDENT ACTIVITIES AND OPPORTUNITIES

Law Review Advanced students publish the *Roger Williams University Law Review* twice annually. The fall edition is national in its scholarly scope, while the spring issue features an annual *Survey of Rhode Island Law*. Students are selected to the Law Review in recognition of superior writing skills and academic performance.

Moot Court The Moot Court Honor Society sponsors a broad range of appellate advocacy programs. This society organizes and administers the intrascholastic competition from which students are selected to compete in interscholastic tournaments with other regional and national law schools. The society participates in the National Moot Court Competition and the American Trial Lawyers Association Regional Mock Trial Competition.

Extracurricular Activities Law students can exercise leadership and organizational skills with practical application of academic knowledge in student-run associations. Many groups have direct involvement from faculty advisors, host guest speakers, and organize issue-oriented symposia and mock-trial competitions.

Special Opportunities The Honors Program, an enrichment program coupled with merit-based scholarships, involves a three-year program of seminars, clinics, international training, and externships. Scholarships of half to full tuition are awarded to qualified students.

The School of Law believes that lawyers should serve the communities that support them; therefore, all law students are required to complete twenty hours of community service. Many students satisfy this requirement by counseling indigent clients in either the criminal defense or disability law clinics, which are run from our Louis Feinstein Legal Clinic in Providence. Students advise clients in a law office setting, prepare cases for trial, negotiate settlements, and try and appeal cases before courts and administrative tribunals.

Advanced students may enhance their practical lawyering skills in supervised clerkships in a judge's chambers or in a public interest or governmental law office. Clerkships include placements with trial and appellate judges in southeastern New England and with Rhode Island state offices and agencies, such as the Governor's Office, the Attorney General, and Public Defender, and state departments including Elderly Affairs and Children, Youth, and Families.

The RWU Marine Affairs Institute is recognized as a distinguished focal point for the exploration of legal, economic, and policy issues raised by the development of the oceans and coastal zones. Students interested in acquiring a specialty in marine affairs take the Institute's elective course offerings.

Opportunities for Members of Minority Groups and Women Traditionally, enrollment of women has been 50 percent and enrollment of minorities has been 11 percent of the student body. Women and students of color are an integral part of the Law School–in the classroom, in student organizations, and as part of our community. In collaboration with the Rhode Island bench and bar, RWU has recently established a mentor program for students of color.

BAR PASSAGE, CAREER SERVICES, AND PLACEMENT

The Office of Career Services provides assistance to students beginning in their first year and continuing through graduation and beyond. It offers group workshops as well as individual counseling appointments on the legal job search, cover letter and resume writing, and interviewing skills. In addition to hosting on-campus interviews, Career Services maintains a listing of job openings. For the 2000 class, 68 percent were employed within six months of graduation. (See chart below.) Graduates from the Law School take and pass bar exams all over the country. In 2000, the bar passage rate for 2000 graduates who were first-time takers of the Rhode Island Bar Examination was 57 percent.

Legal Field	Percentage of Graduates	Average Starting Salary
Academic	2%	n/a
Business	13%	n/a
Government	8%	n/a
Judicial Clerkship	13%	n/a
Private Practice	56%	n/a
Public Interest	1%	n/a
Other	n/a	n/a

CORRESPONDENCE AND INFORMATION

Roger Williams University School of Law
Office of Admissions
Ten Metacom Avenue
Bristol, Rhode Island 02809-5171
Telephone: 401-254-4555 or 1-800-633-2727 (toll-free)
Fax: 401-254-4516
E-mail: admissions@rwulaw.rwu.edu
World Wide Web: http://law.rwu.edu

UNIVERSITY OF SOUTH CAROLINA
SCHOOL OF LAW

Columbia, South Carolina

INFORMATION CONTACT

John S. Benfield, Assistant Dean of Admissions
Main and Grove Streets
Columbia, SC 29208

Phone: 803-777-6606   Fax: 803-777-7751
E-mail: johnb@law.law.sc.edu
Web site: http://www.law.sc.edu/

LAW STUDENT PROFILE [2000–2001]

FULL-TIME   Enrollment: 669
Women: 44%   Men: 56%

RACIAL or ETHNIC COMPOSITION
African American, 9%; Asian/Pacific Islander, 1%; Hispanic, 1%; International, 0.4%

APPLICANTS and ADMITTEES
Number applied: 1,195
Admitted: 416
Percentage accepted: 35%
Seats available: 225
Average LSAT score: 156
Average GPA: 3.3

University of South Carolina School of Law is a public institution that organizes classes on a semester calendar system. The campus is situated in an urban setting. Founded in 1867, first ABA approved in 1925, and an AALS member, University of South Carolina School of Law offers JD, JD/MBA, JD/MCJ, JD/MEER, JD/MEc, JD/MHR, JD/MPA, JD/MPAd, JD/MS, and JD/MSW degrees.

Faculty consists of 45 full-time and 24 part-time members in 2000–2001. 2 full-time faculty members and 1 part-time faculty members are women. 100% of all faculty members have a JD; 85% have advanced law degrees. Of all faculty members, 4% are African American, 96% are white.

Application Information *Required:* LSAT, LSDAS, application form, application fee of $40, 2 letters of recommendation, personal statement, baccalaureate degree, college transcripts. *Application deadline* for fall term is February 15. Applications are processed on a rolling basis.

Costs The 2000–2001 tuition was $7990 full-time for area residents. Tuition was $16,530 full-time for nonresidents. Fees: $50 per term full-time; $25 full-time (one-time charge for full-time students).

Financial Aid 15 fellowships were awarded. Graduate assistantships, loans, merit-based grants/scholarships, and need-based grants/scholarships are also available. The average student debt at graduation is $40,000. To apply for financial assistance, students must complete the Free Application for Federal Student Aid, scholarship specific

AT a GLANCE

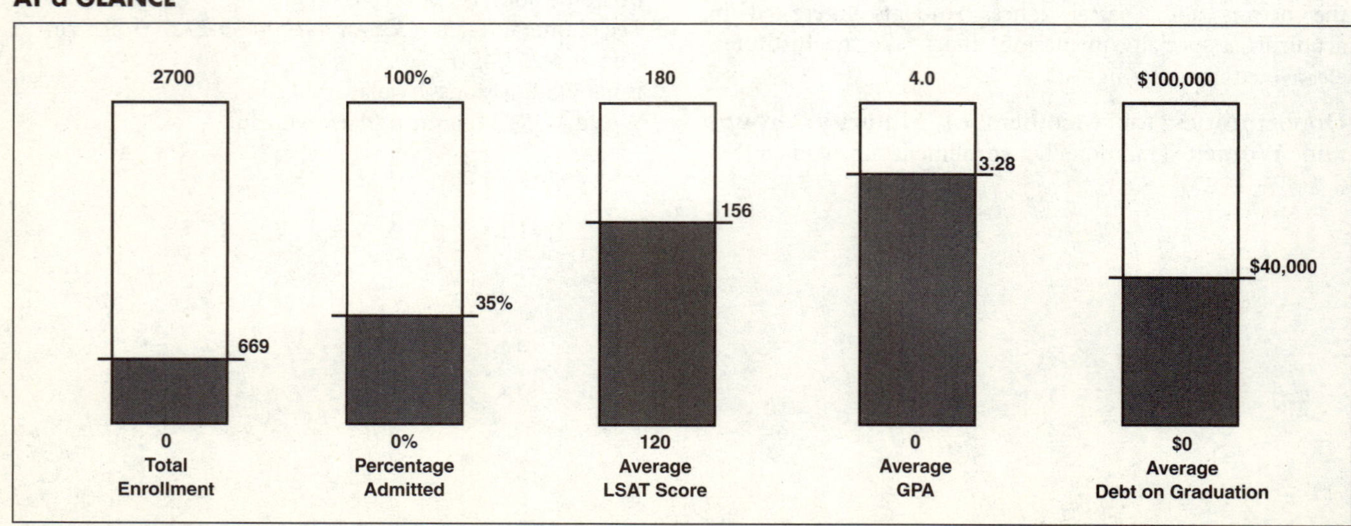

Degree Options

Degree	Total Credits Required	Length of Program
JD–Doctor of Laws	90	3–4 yrs, full-time or part-time [day]
JD/MBA–Juris Doctor/Master of Business Administration–JD/MBA Dual Degree program	110	4–5 yrs, full-time only [day]
JD/MCJ–Juris Doctor/Master of Criminal Justice–Joint-degree Program		4 yrs, full-time only [day]
Certificate–Environmental and Earth Sciences		4 yrs, full-time only [day]
JD/MEc–Juris Doctor/Master of Economics–Joint-degree Program		4 yrs, full-time only [day]
JD/MHR–Juris Doctor/Master of Human Resources		4 yrs, full-time only [day]
JD/MPA–Juris Doctor/Master of Professional Accountancy–Joint-degree Program		4 yrs, full-time only [day]
JD/MPAd–Juris Doctor/Master of Public Administration–Joint-degree Program		4 yrs, full-time only [day]
JD/MS–Juris Doctor/Master of Science–Joint-degree Program International Business		4 yrs, full-time only [day]
JD/MSW–Juris Doctor/Master of Social Work–Joint-degree Program		4 yrs, full-time only [day]

applications. Completed financial aid forms should be received by April 15. Financial aid contact: John S. Benfield, Assistant Dean, USC School of Law, Columbia, SC 29208. Phone: 803-777-6605. Fax: 803-777-7751. E-mail: uscfaid@sc.edu

Law School Library Coleman Karesh Law Library has 14 professional staff members and contains more than 412,406 volumes and 3,043 periodicals. 642 seats are available in the library. When classes are in session, the library is open 95 hours per week.

WESTLAW and LEXIS-NEXIS are available, as are the World Wide Web and CD-ROM players. 50 computer workstations are available to students in the library. Special law collections include South Carolina Legal History collection, rare books, microform collection.

First-Year Program Class size in the average section is 72; 100% of the first-year courses are taught by full-time faculty.

Upper-Level Program Class size in the average section is 70. Among the electives are:

Administrative Law
Advocacy
★ Business and Corporate Law
Criminal Defense
Criminal Prosecution
Education Law

Entertainment Law
Environmental Law
★ Family Law
Government/Regulation
Health Care/Human Services
Intellectual Property
International/Comparative Law
Jurisprudence
Labor Law
Land Use Law/Natural Resources
Lawyering Skills
Legal History/Philosophy
★ Litigation
Maritime Law
Media Law
Mediation
Probate Law
Public Interest
Securities
★ Tax Law
Unfair Trade Practices
(★ *indicates an area of special strength*)

Clinical Courses Students receive degree credit for clinical courses. (Clinical practicum is not required.) Among the clinical areas offered are:

Criminal Defense
Criminal Prosecution
Environmental Law
Family Law
Juvenile Law
Lawyering Skills
Litigation
Mediation

UNIVERSITY OF SOUTH DAKOTA
SCHOOL OF LAW

Vermillion, South Dakota

INFORMATION CONTACT

Jean Henriques, Admissions Officer/Registrar
414 East Clark Street
Vermillion, SD 57069-2390

Phone: 605-677-5443   Fax: 605-677-5417
E-mail: lawreq@usd.edu
Web site: http://www.usd.edu/law/

LAW STUDENT PROFILE [2000–2001]

FULL-TIME   Enrollment: 167
PART-TIME   Enrollment: 1

RACIAL or ETHNIC COMPOSITION
African American, 2%; Asian/Pacific Islander, 1%; Hispanic, 1%; Native American, 6%; International, 1%

APPLICANTS and ADMITTEES
Number applied: 239
Admitted: 168
Percentage accepted: 70%
Seats available: 70
Average LSAT score: 148
Average GPA: 3.2

University of South Dakota School of Law is a public institution that organizes classes on a semester calendar system. The campus is situated in a small-town setting. Founded in 1901, first ABA approved in 1923, and an AALS member, University of South Dakota School of Law offers JD, JD/MA, JD/MBA, JD/MPA, JD/MPAd, and JD/MS degrees.

Faculty consists of 15 full-time and 2 part-time members in 2000–2001. 3 full-time faculty members are women. 100% of all faculty members have a JD; 38% have advanced law degrees. Of all faculty members, 6% are Native American, 94% are white.

Application Information *Required:* LSAT, LSDAS, application form, application fee of $15, baccalaureate degree, 2 letters of recommendation, personal statement, college transcripts. *Application deadline* for fall term is March 1 (priority date). Applications are processed on a rolling basis.

Costs The 1999–2000 tuition was $3210 full-time for state residents. Tuition was $9305 full-time for nonresidents. Fees: $2400 full-time. Full-time tuition and fees vary according to course load, degree level, and reciprocity agreements.

Financial Aid In 2000–2001, 51% of all students received some form of financial aid. 21 research assistantships, totaling $3940 were awarded. Graduate assistantships, loans, merit-based grants/scholarships, need-based grants/scholarships, and federal work-study loans are also available. The average student debt at graduation is $63,700. To apply for financial assistance, students must

AT a GLANCE

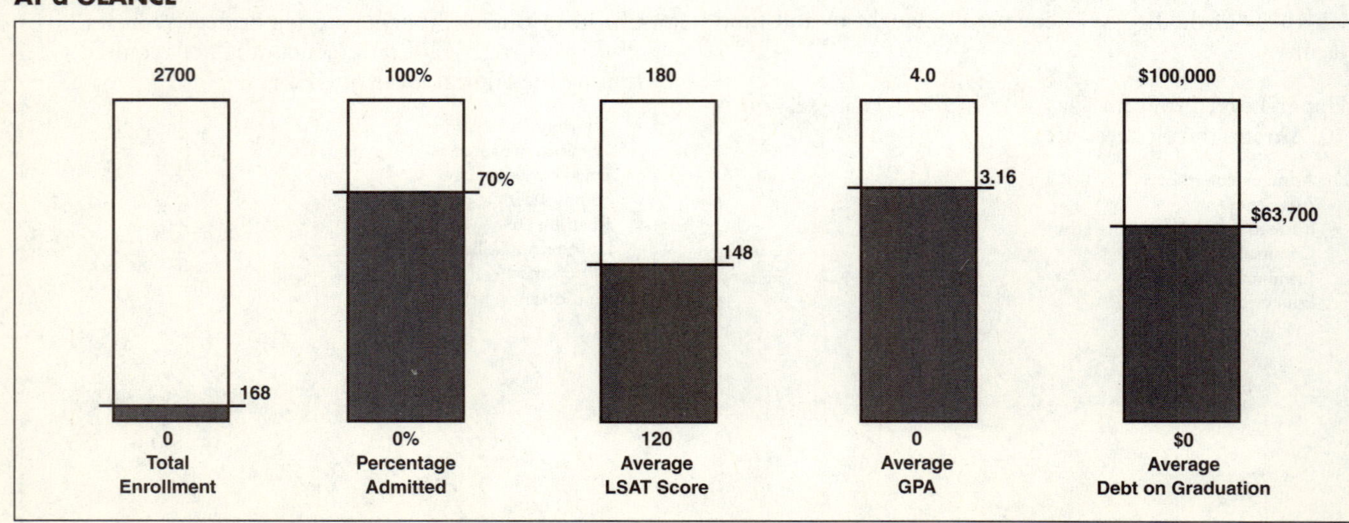

Degree Options

Degree	Total Credits Required	Length of Program
JD–Juris Doctor	90	3 yrs, full-time only [day, summer]
JD–Juris Doctor–Flex-Time	90	5 yrs, part-time only [day]
JD/MA–Juris Doctor/Master of Arts–Joint-degree in Education Administration (without certificate)		3 yrs, full-time only [day, summer]
JD/MA–Juris Doctor/Master of Arts–Joint-degree in English		3 yrs, full-time only [day, summer]
JD/MA–Juris Doctor/Master of Arts–Joint-degree in History		3 yrs, full-time only [day, summer]
JD/MA–Juris Doctor/Master of Arts–Joint-degree in Political Science		3 yrs, full-time only [day, summer]
JD/MA–Juris Doctor/Master of Arts–Joint-degree in Psychology (without certificate)		3 yrs, full-time only [day, summer]
JD/MBA–Juris Doctor/Master of Business Administration–Joint-degree		3 yrs, full-time only [day, summer]
JD/MPA–Juris Doctor/Master of Professional Accountancy–Joint-degree		3 yrs, full-time only [day, summer]
JD/MPAd–Juris Doctor/Master of Public Administration–Joint-degree		3 yrs, full-time only [day, summer]
JD/MS–Juris Doctor/Master of Science–Joint-degree in Administrative Studies		3 yrs, full-time only [day, summer]

complete the Free Application for Federal Student Aid. Completed financial aid forms should be received by April 1. Financial aid contact: Grace Bick, Assistant Director of Financial Aid, University of South Dakota, 414 East Clark, Vermillion, SD 57069-2390. Phone: 605-677-5446. Fax: 605-677-5417.

Law School Library McKusick Law Library has 6 professional staff members and contains more than 191,363 volumes and 750 periodicals. 227 seats are available in the library. When classes are in session, the library is open 168 hours per week.

WESTLAW and LEXIS-NEXIS are available, as are the World Wide Web and online bibliographic services. 40 computer workstations are available to students in the library.

First-Year Program Class size in the average section is 65; 85% of the first-year courses are taught by full-time faculty.

Upper-Level Program Class size in the average section is 25. Among the electives are:

Administrative Law
★ Business and Corporate Law
Commercial Law
Constitutional Law
Education Law
★ Environmental Law
Evidence
Family Law
Health Care/Human Services
★ Indian/Tribal Law
International/Comparative Law
Jurisprudence
Land Use Law/Natural Resources
Legal History/Philosophy
Probate Law
Professional Responsibility
Secure Transactions
Securities
Tax Law
Water Law
(★ indicates an area of special strength)

THE UNIVERSITY OF MEMPHIS
CECIL C. HUMPHREYS SCHOOL OF LAW

Memphis, Tennessee

INFORMATION CONTACT

Dr. Sue Ann McClellan, Assistant Dean for Law
Admissions
207 Law School
Memphis, TN 38152-3140

Phone: 901-678-5403   Fax: 901-678-5210
E-mail: lawadmissions@spc75.law.memphis.edu
Web site: http://www.law.memphis.edu

LAW STUDENT PROFILE [2000–2001]

FULL-TIME   Enrollment: 399
Women: 46%   Men: 54%

PART-TIME   Enrollment: 32
Women: 59%   Men: 41%

RACIAL or ETHNIC COMPOSITION
African American, 12%; Asian/Pacific Islander, 1%; Hispanic,
1%; Native American, 0.5%

APPLICANTS and ADMITTEES
Number applied: 880
Admitted: 404
Percentage accepted: 46%
Seats available: 150
Average LSAT score: 153
Average GPA: 3.2

**The University of Memphis Cecil C. Humphreys
School of Law** is a public institution that organizes
classes on a semester calendar system. The campus is
situated in an urban setting. Founded in 1962, first ABA
approved in 1965, and an AALS member, The University
of Memphis Cecil C. Humphreys School of Law offers
JD and JD/MBA degrees.

Faculty consists of 19 full-time and 27 part-time
members in 2000–2001. 7 full-time faculty members and
9 part-time faculty members are women. 100% of all
faculty members have a JD; 54% have advanced law
degrees. Of all faculty members, 6% are African American, 94% are white.

Application Information *Required:* LSAT, LSDAS,
application form, application fee of $25, baccalaureate
degree, 1 recommendation, personal statement. *Recommended:* resume. *Application deadline* for fall term is
February 15 (priority date). Applications are processed
on a rolling basis.

Costs The 1999–2000 tuition was $4922 full-time for
state residents; $226 per credit hour part-time for state
residents. Tuition was $13,078 full-time for nonresidents;
$580 per credit hour part-time for nonresidents.

Financial Aid In 2000–2001, 83% of all students received
some form of financial aid. 22 fellowships, totaling
$3000; 10 research assistantships, totaling $1200, were
awarded. Fellowships, graduate assistantships, loans,
merit-based grants/scholarships, and federal work-study
loans are also available. The average student debt at
graduation is $49,621. To apply for financial assistance,

AT a GLANCE

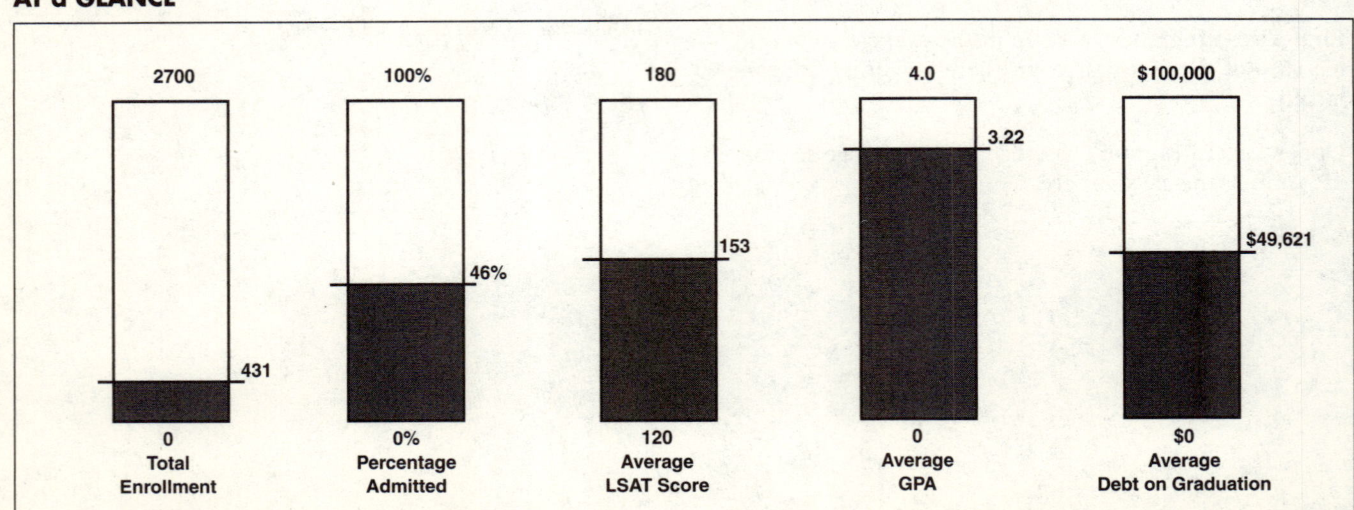

Degree Options		
Degree	**Total Credits Required**	**Length of Program**
JD–Doctor of Laws	90	3–4 yrs, full-time or part-time [day, summer]
JD/MBA–Juris Doctor/Master of Business Administration–Dual-degree Program	110	4–5 yrs, full-time or part-time [day, summer]

students must complete the Free Application for Federal Student Aid, institutional forms. Completed financial aid forms should be received by April 1. Financial aid contact: Ms. Karen Smith, Assistant Director, Student Financial Aid, 312 Scates Hall, Memphis, TN 38152. Phone: 901-678-3687. Fax: 901-678-3590. E-mail: kasmith@memphis.edu

Law School Library has 6 professional staff members and contains more than 279,886 volumes and 2,513 periodicals. 280 seats are available in the library. When classes are in session, the library is open 105 hours per week.

WESTLAW and LEXIS-NEXIS are available, as are the World Wide Web, online bibliographic services, and CD-ROM players. 58 computer workstations are available to students in the library.

First-Year Program Class size in the average section is 75; 100% of the first-year courses are taught by full-time faculty.

Upper-Level Program Class size in the average section is 50. Among the electives are:

Administrative Law
★ Advocacy
★ Business and Corporate Law
★ Children's Advocacy
★ Civil Litigation
Civil Rights
Consumer Law
★ Elderly Advocacy
Environmental Law
★ Family Law
★ Federal Courts
Insurance Law
Intellectual Property
International/Comparative Law
Jurisprudence
Labor Law
Land Use Law/Natural Resources
★ Lawyering Skills
Legal History/Philosophy
★ Litigation
★ Mediation
Probate Law
Securities
★ Tax Law
(★ indicates an area of special strength)

Clinical Courses Students receive degree credit for clinical courses. (Clinical practicum is not required.) Among the clinical areas offered are:

Bankruptcy
Children's Advocacy
Civil Litigation
Domestic Violence
Elderly Advocacy
Labor Law

International exchange programs permit students to visit China.

THE UNIVERSITY OF TENNESSEE
COLLEGE OF LAW

Knoxville, Tennessee

INFORMATION CONTACT

Janet S. Hatcher, Admissions and Financial Aid
Adviser
1505 West Cumberland Avenue
Knoxville, TN 37996-1810

Phone: 865-974-4131   Fax: 865-974-1572
E-mail: hatcher@libra.law.utk.edu
Web site: http://www.law.utk.edu/

LAW STUDENT PROFILE [2000–2001]

FULL-TIME   Enrollment: 478
Women: 46%   Men: 54%

RACIAL or ETHNIC COMPOSITION
African American, 11%; Asian/Pacific Islander, 1%; Hispanic,
1%; Native American, 0.4%

APPLICANTS and ADMITTEES
Number applied: 1,063
Admitted: 383
Percentage accepted: 36%
Seats available: 150
Average LSAT score: 156
Average GPA: 3.5

The University of Tennessee College of Law is a public
institution that organizes classes on a semester calendar
system. The campus is situated in an urban setting.
Founded in 1890, first ABA approved in 1926, and an
AALS member, The University of Tennessee College of
Law offers JD and JD/MBA degrees.

Faculty consists of 29 full-time and 34 part-time
members in 2000–2001. 11 full-time faculty members
and 11 part-time faculty members are women. 100% of
all faculty members have a JD; 10% have advanced law
degrees. Of all faculty members, 10% are African
American, 90% are white.

Application Information *Required:* LSAT, LSDAS,
application form, application fee of $15, baccalaureate
degree, 2 letters of recommendation, personal statement,
essay, college transcripts. *Application deadline* for fall
term is February 15 (priority date).

Costs The 2000–2001 tuition was $5320 full-time for
state residents. Tuition was $14,872 full-time for
nonresidents. Fees: $550 full-time. Full-time tuition and
fees vary according to course load, degree level, and
program.

Financial Aid In 2000–2001, 73% of all students received
some form of financial aid. 121 fellowships, totaling
$5500 were awarded. Loans, merit-based grants/scholar-
ships, need-based grants/scholarships, and federal
work-study loans are also available. The average student
debt at graduation is $38,831. To apply for financial
assistance, students must complete the Free Application
for Federal Student Aid, scholarship specific applications.

AT a GLANCE

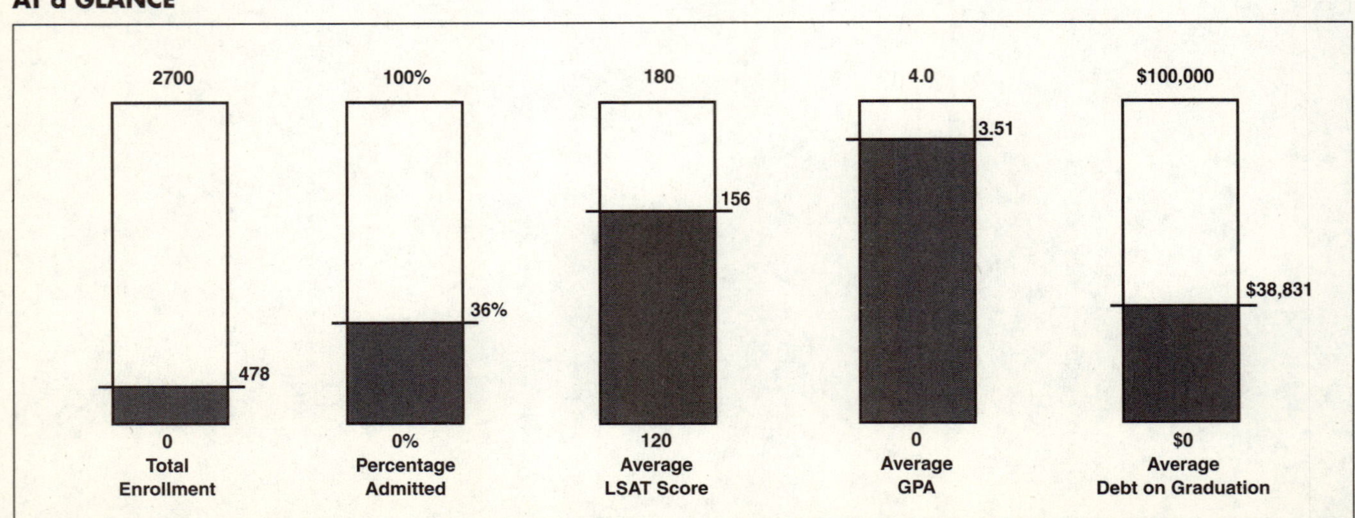

Degree Options

Degree	Total Credits Required	Length of Program
JD–Juris Doctor–Doctor of Jurisprudence	89	3–5 yrs, full-time only [day]
JD/MBA–Juris Doctor/Master of Business Administration–Dual-degree Program		4–5 yrs, full-time only [day]

Completed financial aid forms should be received by March 1. Financial aid contact: Janet S. Hatcher, Admissions and Financial Aid Advisor, 1505 West Cumberland Avenue, Suite 161, Knoxville, TN 37996-1810. Phone: 865-974-4131. Fax: 865-974-1572. E-mail: hatcher@libra.law.utk.edu

Law School Library University of Tennessee College of Law Library has 9 professional staff members and contains more than 483,372 volumes and 6,363 periodicals. 455 seats are available in the library. When classes are in session, the library is open 112 hours per week.

WESTLAW and LEXIS-NEXIS are available, as are the World Wide Web, online bibliographic services, and CD-ROM players. 100 computer workstations are available to students in the library. Special law collections include Special Collection of Rare and Autographed Books, Tennessee Collection, Audiovisual Collection, Microforms Collection.

First-Year Program Class size in the average section is 55; 90% of the first-year courses are taught by full-time faculty.

Upper-Level Program Class size in the average section is 40. Among the electives are:

Administrative Law
★ Advocacy
★ Business and Corporate Law
Entertainment Law
Environmental Law
Family Law
Intellectual Property
International/Comparative Law
Jurisprudence
Labor Law
Land Use Law/Natural Resources
Lawyering Skills
Litigation
Mediation
Probate Law
Public Interest
Securities
Tax Law
(★ indicates an area of special strength)

Clinical Courses Students receive degree credit for clinical courses. (Clinical practicum is not required.) Among the clinical areas offered are:

Advocacy
Criminal Prosecution
Mediation
Nonprofit Organizations

VANDERBILT UNIVERSITY
LAW SCHOOL

Nashville, Tennessee

INFORMATION CONTACT

Sonya G. Smith, Assistant Dean of Admissions
Nashville, TN 37203

Phone: 615-322-6452   Fax: 615-322-6631
Web site: http://www.vanderbilt.edu/Law/

LAW STUDENT PROFILE [2000–2001]

FULL-TIME   Enrollment: 561
Women: 47%   Men: 53%

RACIAL or ETHNIC COMPOSITION

African American, 12%; Asian/Pacific Islander, 6%; Hispanic,
2%; Native American, 0.2%; International, 5%

APPLICANTS and ADMITTEES

Seats available: 180
Median LSAT score: 162
Median GPA: 3.6

Vanderbilt University Law School is a private institution that organizes classes on a semester calendar system. The campus is situated in an urban setting. Founded in 1874, first ABA approved in 1925, and an AALS member, Vanderbilt University Law School offers JD, JD/MA, JD/MBA, JD/MDiv, JD/MTS, and JD/PhD degrees.

Faculty consists of 41 full-time and 52 part-time members in 2000–2001. 13 full-time faculty members and 17 part-time faculty members are women. 98% of all faculty members have a JD degree. Of all faculty members, 2% are Asian/Pacific Islander, 3% are African American, 2% are Hispanic, 93% are white.

Application Information *Required:* LSAT, LSDAS, application form, application fee of $50, baccalaureate degree, 2 letters of recommendation, personal statement, college transcripts. *Application deadline* for fall term is March 1. Applications are processed on a rolling basis.

Financial Aid Fellowships, loans, loan repayment assistance program (LRAP), merit-based grants/scholarships, need-based grants/scholarships, and federal work-study loans are available. The average student debt at graduation is $63,000. To apply for financial assistance, students must complete the Free Application for Federal Student Aid, institutional forms, scholarship specific applications, CSS PROFILE form. Completed financial aid forms should be received by February 28. Financial aid contact: Sonya Smith, Assistant Dean, Vanderbilt Law School, Nashville, TN 37240. Phone: 615-322-6452. Fax: 615-322-6631. E-mail: admissions@law.vanderbilt.edu

AT a GLANCE

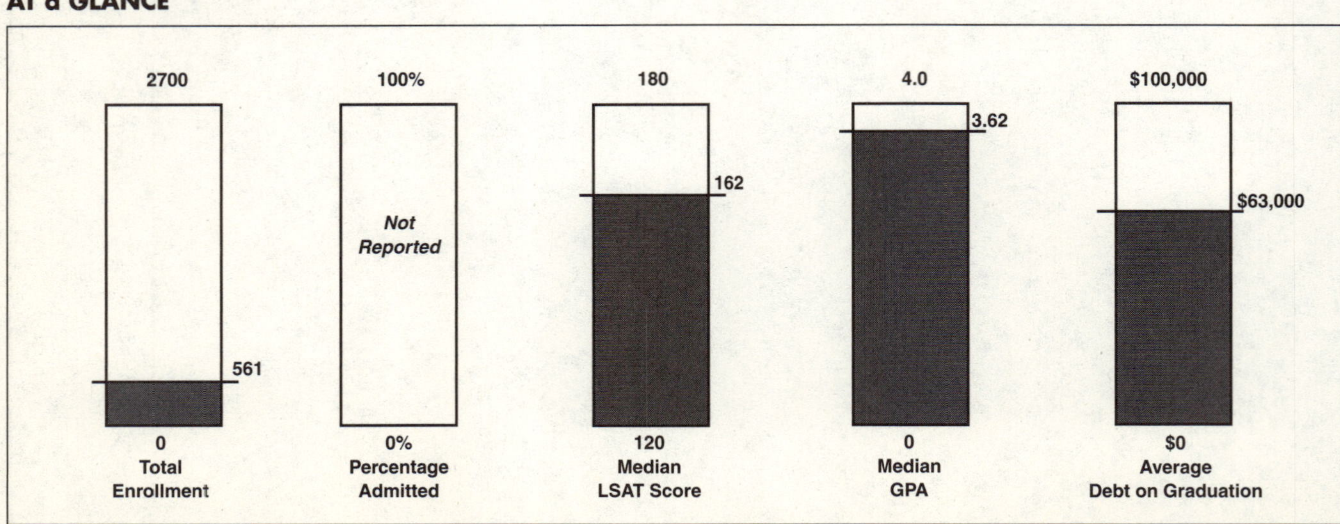

Degree Options

Degree	Total Credits Required	Length of Program
JD–Juris Doctor	88	3 yrs
JD/MA–Juris Doctor/Master of Arts–Joint-degree Program		4 yrs, full-time only [day]
JD/MBA–Juris Doctor/Master of Business Administration–Joint-degree Program		4 yrs, full-time only [day]
JD/MDiv–Juris Doctor/Master of Divinity–Joint-degree Program		5 yrs, full-time only [day]
JD/MTS–Juris Doctor/Master of Theological Studies–Joint-degree Program		4 yrs, full-time only [day]
JD/PhD–Juris Doctor/Doctor of Philosophy–Joint-degree Program		full-time only [day]

Law School Library Alyne Queener Massey Law Library has 9 professional staff members and contains more than 521,151 volumes and 6,139 periodicals. 431 seats are available in the library. When classes are in session, the library is open 111 hours per week.

WESTLAW and LEXIS-NEXIS are available, as are the World Wide Web, online bibliographic services, and CD-ROM players. 64 computer workstations are available to students in the library. Special law collections include intellectual property, medico-legal, foreign/international law.

First-Year Program Class size in the average section is 90; 89% of the first-year courses are taught by full-time faculty.

Upper-Level Program Among the electives are:

Administrative Law
Advocacy
Business and Corporate Law
Civil Litigation
Consumer Law
Criminal Defense
Education Law
Entertainment Law
Environmental Law
Family Law
Government/Regulation
Health Care/Human Services
Intellectual Property
International/Comparative Law
Jurisprudence
Juvenile Law
Labor Law
Land Use Law/Natural Resources
Lawyering Skills
Legal History/Philosophy
Litigation
Media Law
Mediation
Probate Law
Public Interest
Securities
Tax Law

Clinical Courses Students receive degree credit for clinical courses. (Clinical practicum is not required.) Among the clinical areas offered are:

Children and the Law
Civil Litigation
Criminal Defense
Family Law
Juvenile Law

BAYLOR UNIVERSITY
SCHOOL OF LAW

Waco, Texas

INFORMATION CONTACT

Becky Beck, Admissions Director
PO Box 97288
Waco, TX 76798-7288

Phone: 254-710-1911   Fax: 254-710-2316
E-mail: becky_beck@baylor.edu
Web site: http://law.baylor.edu/

LAW STUDENT PROFILE [2000–2001]

FULL-TIME   Enrollment: 371
Women: 39%   Men: 61%

PART-TIME   Enrollment: 8
Women: 50%   Men: 50%

RACIAL or ETHNIC COMPOSITION
African American, 1%; Asian/Pacific Islander, 3%; Hispanic, 6%; International, 1%

APPLICANTS and ADMITTEES
Number applied: 1,259
Admitted: 461
Percentage accepted: 37%
Seats available: 65
Average LSAT score: 161
Average GPA: 3.6

Baylor University School of Law is a private institution that organizes classes on a quarter calendar system. The campus is situated in an urban setting. Founded in 1849, first ABA approved in 1931, and an AALS member, Baylor University School of Law offers JD, JD/MBA, JD/MPPA, and JD/MTAX degrees.

Faculty consists of 20 full-time and 38 part-time members in 2000–2001. 5 full-time faculty members and 4 part-time faculty members are women. 100% of all faculty members have a JD; 14% have advanced law degrees. Of all faculty members, 2% are African American, 2% are Hispanic, 96% are white.

Application Information *Required:* LSAT, LSDAS, application form, application fee of $40, baccalaureate degree, 2 letters of recommendation, personal statement, college transcripts. *Recommended:* resume. *Application deadline* for fall term is March 1; for spring term is November 1. Applications are processed on a rolling basis.

Costs The 2000–2001 tuition was $15,078 full-time. Fees: $802 full-time.

Financial Aid In 2000–2001, 100% of all students received some form of financial aid. Loans, merit-based grants/scholarships, need-based grants/scholarships, and federal work-study loans are available. The average student debt at graduation is $46,457. To apply for financial assistance, students must complete the Free Application for Federal Student Aid. Financial aid

AT a GLANCE

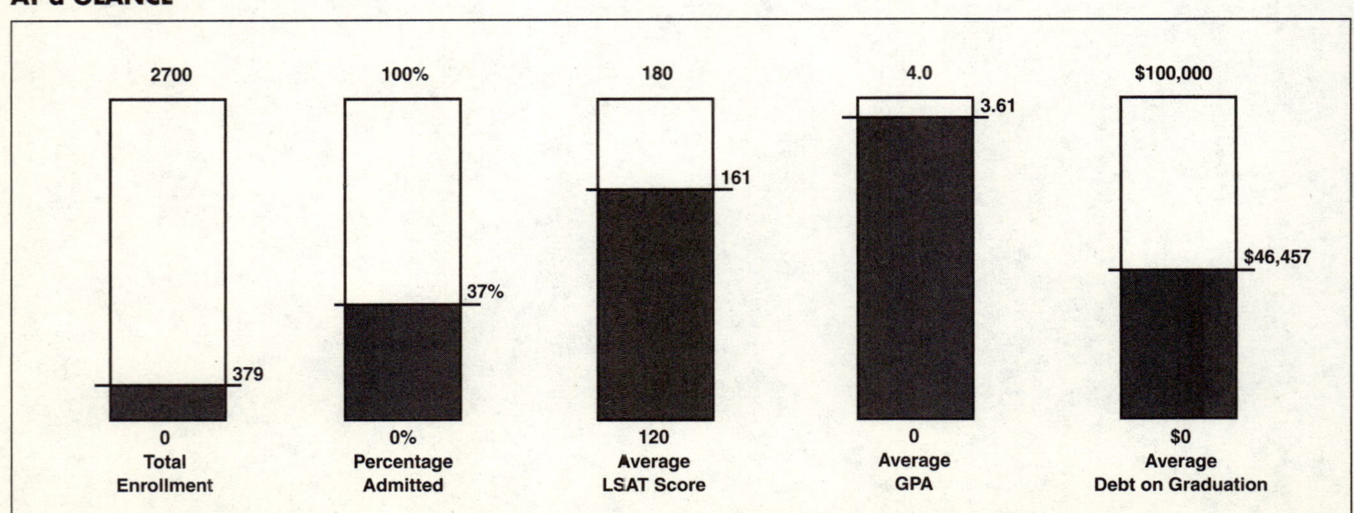

Degree Options

Degree	Total Credits Required	Length of Program
JD–Doctor of Laws	126	3 yrs, full-time only [day, summer]
JD/MBA–Juris Doctor/Master of Business Administration–Joint-degree Program		4 yrs, full-time only [day, summer]
JD/MPPA–Juris Doctor/Master of Public Policy and Administration–Joint-degree Program		4 yrs, full-time only [day, summer]
JD/MTAX–Juris Doctor/Master of Taxation–Joint-degree Program		4 yrs, full-time only [day, summer]

contact: Ms. Pat Lucas, Assistant Director of Loans, PO Box 97028, Waco, TX 76798-7028. Phone: 800-BAY-LORU. Fax: 254-710-2695. E-mail: pat_lucas@baylor.edu

Law School Library Sheridan and John Eddie Williams Legal Research and Technology Center has 8 professional staff members and contains more than 194,787 volumes and 2,161 periodicals. 400 seats are available in the library. When classes are in session, the library is open 112 hours per week.

WESTLAW and LEXIS-NEXIS are available, as are the World Wide Web, online bibliographic services, and CD-ROM players. 57 computer workstations are available to students in the library. Special law collections include Rare Bookroom.

First-Year Program Class size in the average section is 50; 100% of the first-year courses are taught by full-time faculty.

Upper-Level Program Class size in the average section is 33. Among the electives are:

- Administrative Law
- ★ Business and Corporate Law
- Consumer Law
- ★ Criminal Defense
- ★ Criminal Law
- Entertainment Law
- Environmental Law
- Family Law
- Family Practice
- ★ Government/Regulation
- Health Care/Human Services
- Intellectual Property
- International/Comparative Law
- Jurisprudence
- Labor Law
- Lawyering Skills
- ★ Litigation
- Mediation
- ★ Probate Law
- Securities
- Tax Law

(★ *indicates an area of special strength*)

Clinical Courses Students receive degree credit for clinical courses. 2 credit hours of clinical practicum are required. Among the clinical areas offered are:

- Administrative Law
- Advocacy
- Business and Corporate Law
- Criminal Defense
- Criminal Law
- Family Law
- Family Practice
- Health Care/Human Services
- Litigation
- Probate Law

ST. MARY'S UNIVERSITY OF SAN ANTONIO
SCHOOL OF LAW

San Antonio, Texas

LAW STUDENT PROFILE [2000–2001]

FULL-TIME   Enrollment: 739
Women: 48%   Men: 52%

RACIAL or ETHNIC COMPOSITION
African American, 4%; Asian/Pacific Islander, 3%; Hispanic,
38%; Native American, 0.4%

APPLICANTS and ADMITTEES
Number applied: 1,022
Admitted: 660
Percentage accepted: 65%
Seats available: 240
Median LSAT score: 149
Average GPA: 3.0

St. Mary's University of San Antonio School of Law is a private institution that organizes classes on a semester calendar system. The campus is situated in a suburban setting. Founded in 1927, first ABA approved in 1948, and an AALS member, St. Mary's University of San Antonio School of Law offers JD, JD/MA, JD/MAcc, JD/MBA, JD/ME, JD/MPAd, JD/MS, and LLM degrees.

Faculty consists of 46 full-time and 51 part-time members in 2000–2001. 16 full-time faculty members and 17 part-time faculty members are women. 97.7% of all faculty members have a JD; 31.8% have advanced law degrees. Of all faculty members, 6.8% are African American, 22.7% are Hispanic, 68.2% are white, 2.3% are international.

Application Information *Required:* LSAT, LSDAS, application form, application fee of $45, baccalaureate degree, 3 letters of recommendation, personal statement, college transcripts. *Recommended:* essay, resume, minimum 2.2 GPA. *Application deadline* for fall term is March 1 (priority date).

Financial Aid In 2000–2001, 87% of all students received some form of financial aid. 59 research assistantships, totaling $1000; 35 teaching assistantships, totaling $1250, were awarded. Loans, merit-based grants/scholarships, need-based grants/scholarships, and federal work-study loans are also available. The average student debt at graduation is $74,662. To apply for financial assistance, students must complete the Free Application for Federal

AT a GLANCE

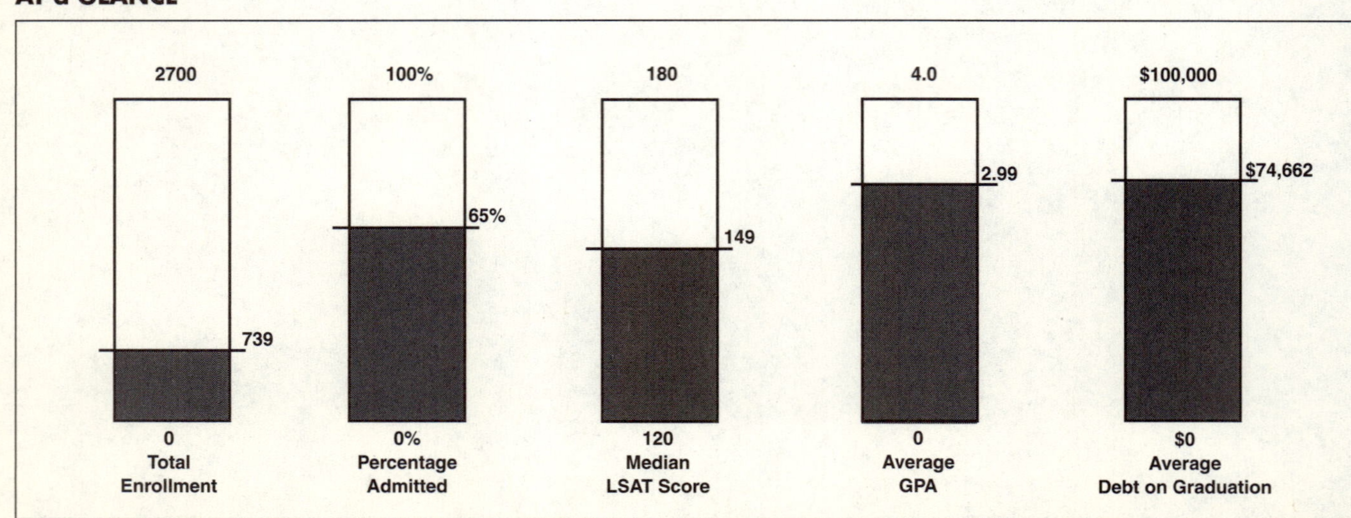

Degree Options

Degree	Total Credits Required	Length of Program
JD–Juris Doctor	90	full-time only [day, summer]
JD/MA–Juris Doctor/Master of Arts–Theology	108	4–5 yrs, full-time only [day, summer]
JD/MA–Juris Doctor/Master of Arts–Economics	108	4–5 yrs, full-time only [day, summer]
JD/MA–Juris Doctor/Master of Arts–Communication Arts	108	4–5 yrs, full-time only [day, summer]
JD/MA–Juris Doctor/Master of Arts–Justice Administration	108	4–5 yrs, full-time only [day, summer]
JD/MA–Juris Doctor/Master of Arts–International Relations	108	4–5 yrs, full-time only [day, summer]
Certificate–Accounting	108	4–5 yrs, full-time only [day, summer]
JD/MBA–Juris Doctor/Master of Business Administration	108	4–5 yrs, full-time only [day, summer]
JD/ME–Juris Doctor/Master of Engineering	108	4–5 yrs, full-time only [day, summer]
JD/MPAd–Juris Doctor/Master of Public Administration	108	4–5 yrs, full-time only [day, summer]
JD/MS–Juris Doctor/Master of Science–Computer Science	108	4–5 yrs, full-time only [day, summer]
LLM–Master of Laws–International and Comparative Law	24	1 yr, full-time only [day, summer]
LLM–Master of Laws–American Legal Studies	24	1 yr, full-time only [day, summer]

Student Aid. Completed financial aid forms should be received by April 1. Financial aid contact: Diana M. Perez, Coordinator, Law Financial Assistance, 1 Camino Santa Maria, San Antonio, TX 78228-8602. Phone: 210-431-6743. Fax: 210-431-6781. E-mail: perezd@law.stmarytx.edu

Law School Library Sarita Kenedy East Law Library has 9 professional staff members and contains more than 335,724 volumes and 3,529 periodicals. 446 seats are available in the library. When classes are in session, the library is open 110 hours per week.

WESTLAW and LEXIS-NEXIS are available, as are the World Wide Web and online bibliographic services. 47 computer workstations are available to students in the library. Special law collections include United Nations documents collection, Mexican legal materials.

First-Year Program Class size in the average section is 40; 100% of the first-year courses are taught by full-time faculty.

Upper-Level Program Class size in the average section is 50. Among the electives are:

- Civil Litigation
- ★ Criminal Defense
- Environmental Law
- Family Practice
- General Practice
- Immigration
- International Law
- NAFTA Law

(★ indicates an area of special strength)

Clinical Courses Students receive degree credit for clinical courses. (Clinical practicum is not required.) Among the clinical areas offered are:

- Civil Litigation
- Criminal Defense
- Family Practice
- General Practice
- Human Rights
- Immigration
- International Law

SOUTHERN METHODIST UNIVERSITY
SCHOOL OF LAW

Dallas, Texas

INFORMATION CONTACT

Lynn Bozalis, Assistant Dean for Admissions
PO Box 750110
Dallas, TX 75275-0110

Phone: 214-768-2550   Fax: 214-768-2549
Web site: http://www.law.smu.edu/

LAW STUDENT PROFILE [2000–2001]

FULL-TIME Enrollment: 776
Women: 45%   Men: 55%

PART-TIME Enrollment: 66
Women: 41%   Men: 59%

RACIAL or ETHNIC COMPOSITION
African American, 2%; Asian/Pacific Islander, 4%; Hispanic, 4%; Native American, 1%; International, 5%

APPLICANTS and ADMITTEES
Number applied: 1,538
Admitted: 650
Percentage accepted: 42%
Seats available: 250
Median LSAT score: 158
Average GPA: 3.4

Southern Methodist University School of Law is a private institution that organizes classes on a semester calendar system. The campus is situated in an urban setting. Founded in 1925, first ABA approved in 1927, and an AALS member, Southern Methodist University School of Law offers JD, JD/MA, JD/MBA, JSD, and LLM degrees.

Faculty consists of 39 full-time members in 2000–2001. 13 full-time faculty members are women. 100% of all faculty members have a JD degree. Of all faculty members, 6% are African American, 8% are Hispanic, 86% are white.

Application Information *Required:* LSAT, LSDAS, application form, application fee of $50, 2 letters of recommendation, personal statement, resume, baccalaureate degree, college transcripts. *Recommended:* essay, interview. *Application deadline* for fall term is February 15 (priority date). Applications are processed on a rolling basis.

Costs The 1999–2000 tuition was $20,850 full-time; $695 per credit hour part-time. Fees: $2088 full-time; $88 per credit hour part-time.

Financial Aid Loans, loan repayment assistance program (LRAP), merit-based grants/scholarships, need-based grants/scholarships, and federal work-study loans are available. The average student debt at graduation is $65,000. To apply for financial assistance, students must complete the Free Application for Federal Student Aid, scholarship specific applications. Completed financial aid forms should be received by February 1. Financial aid

AT a GLANCE

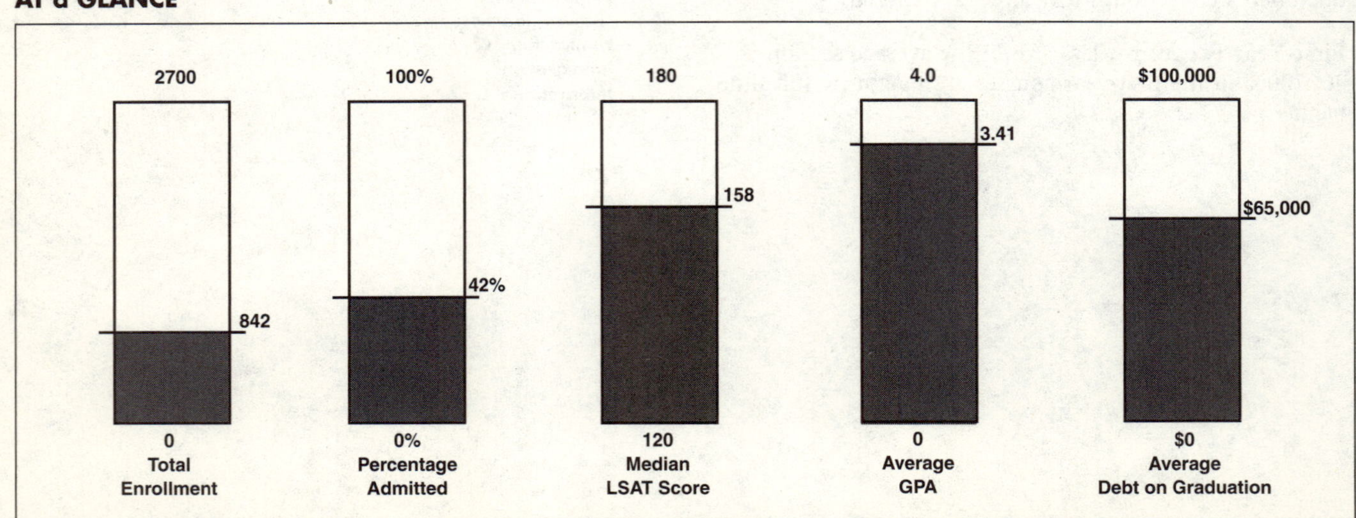

Degree Options

Degree	Total Credits Required	Length of Program
JD–Juris Doctor	90	3 yrs, full-time only [day, summer]
JD/MA–Juris Doctor/Master of Arts–Dual-degree Program in Economics	111	4 yrs, full-time or part-time [day, summer]
JD/MBA–Juris Doctor/Master of Business Administration–Joint-degree program	137	4.5 yrs, full-time only [day, summer]
JSD–Doctor of Juridical Science		2–5 yrs, full-time only [day]
LLM–Master of Laws–Taxation	24	full-time or part-time [day]
LLM–Master of Laws–General	24	1–2 yrs, full-time or part-time [day]
LLM–Master of Laws–Comparative and International Law	24	full-time only [day]

contact: Lynn Switzer Bozalis, Assistant Dean, Admissions, School of Law, PO Box 750110, Dallas, TX. Phone: 214-768-2540. Fax: 214-768-2549. E-mail: lawadmit@mail.smu.edu

Law School Library Underwood Law Library has 11 professional staff members and contains more than 541,971 volumes and 5,293 periodicals. 750 seats are available in the library. When classes are in session, the library is open 102 hours per week.

WESTLAW and LEXIS-NEXIS are available, as is the World Wide Web. 55 computer workstations are available to students in the library.

First-Year Program Class size in the average section is 80; 100% of the first-year courses are taught by full-time faculty.

Upper-Level Program Class size in the average section is 25. Among the electives are:

Administrative Law
Advocacy
Alternative Dispute Resolution
American Legal History
Antitrust Law
Aviation Law
Bankruptcy
Business and Corporate Law
Business Planning
Capital Punishment
Civil Litigation
Civil Procedure
Civil Rights
Commercial Law
Comparative Constitutional Law
Complex Litigation
Constitutional Criminal Procedure
Constitutional Law
Copyright & Trademark Law
Corporate Finance
Corporate Taxation
Creditor's Rights
Criminal Defense
Criminal Law
Criminal Procedure
Criminal Prosecution
Cultural Property
Disability Law
Dispute Resolution
Domestic Violence
Education
Education Law
Employee Benefit Law
Employment Discrimination
Employment Law
Entertainment Law
Environmental Ethics
Environmental Law
Estate & Gift Taxation
Estate Planning
Evidence
Family Law
Family Practice
Federal Courts
Federal Income Tax
Gender and Sexuality
General Practice
Government/Regulation
Health Care/Human Services
Immigration
Indian/Tribal Law
Insurance Law
Insurance Litigation
Intellectual Property
International Business Transactions
International Commerical Arbitration
International Criminal Law
International Finance Markets
International Human Rights
International Income Tax
International Law
International Litigation & Arbitration
International/Comparative Law
Internet Law
Interviewing and Counseling
Japanese Law
Jurisprudence
Juvenile Law
Labor and Employment
Labor Law
Land Use Law/Natural Resources
Law and Economics
Law and Human Nature
Law and Literature
Law and Medicine
Lawyering Skills
Legal History/Philosophy
Legal Research
Legal Writing

Legislation
Litigation
Local Government
Maritime Law
Mass Torts
Mediation
Medical Malpractice Law
Mental Health and Law
Mergers & Acquisitions
Negotiable Intruments
Oil and Gas
Partnerships
Patent Law
Poverty/Welfare Law
Privacy Law
Probate Law
Product Liability
Professional Responsibility
Property/Real Estate
Psychology, Forensic Science, and the Law
Real Estate Transactions
Remedies
Secured Transactions
Securities
Securities Regulation
Software Licensing
Sports Law
State and Local Taxation
Tax Fraud
Tax Law

Texas Criminal Procedure
Texas Matrimonial Property
Texas Pre-Trial Procedure
Texas Trials and Appeals
Trial Advocacy
White Collar Crime
Wills & Trusts
Women and the Law

Clinical Courses Students receive degree credit for clinical courses. (Clinical practicum is not required.) Among the clinical areas offered are:

Civil Litigation
Criminal Defense
Criminal Prosecution
Dispute Resolution
Domestic Violence
Environmental Law
Family Practice
General Practice
Juvenile Law
Legislation
Poverty/Welfare Law
Tax Law

International exchange programs permit students to visit United Kingdom.

SOUTH TEXAS COLLEGE OF LAW

Houston, Texas

INFORMATION CONTACT

Alicia K. Cramer, Director of Admissions
1303 San Jacinto Street
Houston, TX 77002-7000

Phone: 713-646-1810   Fax: 713-646-2929
E-mail: acramer@stcl.edu
Web site: http://www.stcl.edu/

LAW STUDENT PROFILE [2000–2001]

FULL-TIME   Enrollment: 859
Women: 47%   Men: 53%

PART-TIME   Enrollment: 372
Women: 49%   Men: 51%

APPLICANTS and ADMITTEES

Number applied: 1,432
Admitted: 981
Percentage accepted: 69%
Seats available: 384
Average LSAT score: 150
Average GPA: 3.0

South Texas College of Law is a private nonprofit institution that organizes classes on a semester calendar system. The campus is situated in an urban setting. Founded in 1923, first ABA approved in 1959, and an AALS member, South Texas College of Law offers a JD degree.

Faculty 100% of all faculty members have a JD; 30.4% have advanced law degrees. Of all faculty members, 1.8% are Native American, 1.8% are Asian/Pacific Islander, 5.4% are African American, 3.5% are Hispanic, 87.5% are white.

Application Information *Required:* LSAT, LSDAS, application form, application fee of $50, baccalaureate degree, 2 letters of recommendation, personal statement, resume. *Recommended:* minimum 2.9 GPA.

Costs The 2000–2001 tuition was $16,260 full-time; $10,840 per year part-time. Fees: $600 full-time. Tuition and fees vary according to course load and degree level.

Financial Aid Loans, merit-based grants/scholarships, need-based grants/scholarships, and federal work-study loans are available. The average student debt at graduation is $61,399. To apply for financial assistance, students must complete the Free Application for Federal Student Aid, institutional forms, scholarship specific applications, prior year income tax returns with attachments. Financial aid contact: Jennifer N. Pham, Director of Scholarships and Financial Aid, 1303 San Jacinto Street, Houston, TX 77002-7000. Phone: 713-646-1820. Fax: 713-659-3807. E-mail: jpham@stcl.edu

Law School Library South Texas College of Law Library has 9 professional staff members and contains more than

AT a GLANCE

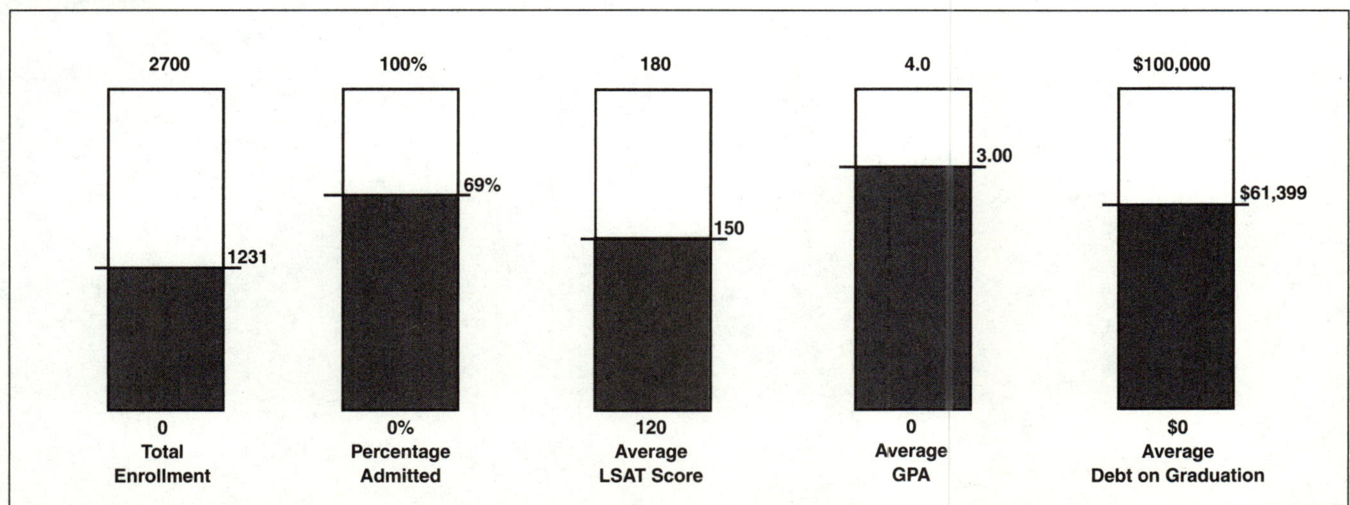

Degree Options

Degree	Total Credits Required	Length of Program
JD–Doctor of Laws	90	2.5–6 yrs, full-time or part-time [day, evening, weekend, summer]

401,778 volumes and 4,439 periodicals. 776 seats are available in the library. When classes are in session, the library is open 108 hours per week.

WESTLAW and LEXIS-NEXIS are available, as are the World Wide Web, online bibliographic services, and CD-ROM players. 77 computer workstations are available to students in the library. Special law collections include maritime, Islamic law, and Mexican Law in the Spanish language.

First-Year Program Class size in the average section is 58; 100% of the first-year courses are taught by full-time faculty.

Upper-Level Program Class size in the average section is 33. Among the electives are:

Administrative Law
Advocacy
Business and Corporate Law
Civil Litigation
Consumer Law
Criminal Defense
Criminal Prosecution
Education Law
Entertainment Law
★ Environmental Law
Family Law
Family Practice
General Practice
Government/Regulation
★ Health Care/Human Services
Health Law
Intellectual Property
★ International/Comparative Law
Jurisprudence
Labor Law
Land Use Law/Natural Resources
★ Lawyering Skills
Legal History/Philosophy
Litigation
Maritime Law
Media Law
★ Mediation
Probate Law
Public Interest
Securities
Tax Law

(★ *indicates an area of special strength*)

Clinical Courses Students receive degree credit for clinical courses. (Clinical practicum is not required.) Among the clinical areas offered are:

Administrative Law
Advocacy
Civil Litigation
Criminal Defense
Criminal Prosecution
Family Law
Family Practice
General Practice
Government/Regulation
Health Law
Lawyering Skills
Litigation
Mediation
Probate Law
Public Interest

International exchange programs permit students to visit Denmark.

TEXAS SOUTHERN UNIVERSITY
THURGOOD MARSHALL SCHOOL OF LAW

Houston, Texas

INFORMATION CONTACT

Edward Rene, Director of Admissions
3100 Cleburne Avenue
Houston, TX 77004

Phone: 713-313-7115   Fax: 713-313-1049
    ext. 1004
E-mail: erene@tsulaw.edu
Web site: http://www.tsulaw.edu/

LAW STUDENT PROFILE [2000–2001]

FULL-TIME   Enrollment: 623
Women: 48%   Men: 52%

RACIAL or ETHNIC COMPOSITION
African American, 60%; Asian/Pacific Islander, 5%; Hispanic,
18%; Native American, 0.3%; International, 0.3%

APPLICANTS and ADMITTEES
Number applied: 932
Admitted: 512
Percentage accepted: 55%
Seats available: 250
Average LSAT score: 143
Average GPA: 2.8

Texas Southern University Thurgood Marshall School of Law is a public institution that organizes classes on a semester calendar system. The campus is situated in an urban setting. Founded in 1947, first ABA approved in 1949, Texas Southern University Thurgood Marshall School of Law offers a JD degree.

Faculty consists of 31 full-time and 15 part-time members in 2000–2001. 10 full-time faculty members and 6 part-time faculty members are women. 100% of all faculty members have a JD; 35% have advanced law degrees. Of all faculty members, 3% are Asian/Pacific Islander, 58% are African American, 13% are Hispanic, 26% are white.

Application Information *Required:* LSAT, LSDAS, application form, application fee of $40, baccalaureate degree, 2 letters of recommendation, personal statement, interview. *Recommended:* resume. *Application deadline* for fall term is April 1 (priority date). Applications are processed on a rolling basis.

Costs The 1999–2000 tuition was $420 per credit hour part-time for area residents. Tuition was $544 per credit hour part-time for nonresidents.

Financial Aid In 2000–2001, 100% of all students received some form of financial aid. 24 research assistantships, totaling $4500 were awarded. Fellowships, loans, merit-based grants/scholarships, need-based grants/scholarships, and federal work-study loans are also available. The average student debt at graduation is $52,285. To apply for financial assistance, students must complete the Free Application for Federal Student Aid,

AT a GLANCE

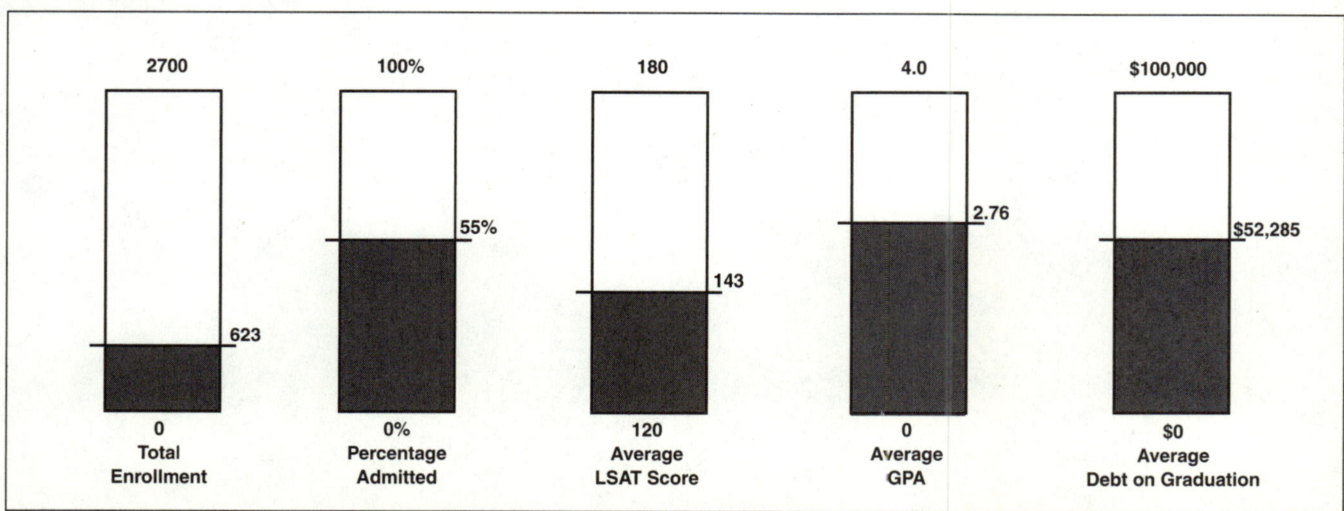

<table>
<tr><td colspan="3">Degree Options</td></tr>
<tr><td>Degree</td><td>Total Credits
Required</td><td>Length of Program</td></tr>
<tr><td>JD–Doctor of Laws</td><td>90</td><td>3 yrs, full-time only [day]</td></tr>
</table>

institutional forms. Completed financial aid forms should be received by May 1. Financial aid contact: Bruce Ware, Student Records Coordinator, 3100 Cleburne Street, Houston, TX 77004. Phone: 713-313-7243. Fax: 713-313-1049. E-mail: bware@tsulaw.edu

Law School Library Law Library has 7 professional staff members and contains more than 300,000 volumes and 2,463 periodicals. 348 seats are available in the library. When classes are in session, the library is open 108 hours per week.

WESTLAW and LEXIS-NEXIS are available, as are the World Wide Web, online bibliographic services, and CD-ROM players. 23 computer workstations are available to students in the library.

First-Year Program Class size in the average section is 60; 92% of the first-year courses are taught by full-time faculty.

Upper-Level Program Class size in the average section is 30. Among the electives are:

Administrative Law
Advocacy
Business and Corporate Law
Consumer Law
Education Law
★ Environmental Law

Family Law
Intellectual Property
International/Comparative Law
Jurisprudence
Labor Law
Lawyering Skills
Litigation
Maritime Law
Media Law
Mediation
Probate Law
Securities
Tax Law

(★ *indicates an area of special strength*)

Clinical Courses Students receive degree credit for clinical courses. (Clinical practicum is not required.) Among the clinical areas offered are:

AIDS and the Law
Civil Law
Criminal Law
Elderly Advocacy
Environmental Law
Family Law
Family Practice
Housing Law
Immigration
Judicial Externship
Juvenile Law
Mediation
Street Law

TEXAS TECH UNIVERSITY
SCHOOL OF LAW

Lubbock, Texas

INFORMATION CONTACT

Graduate Adviser
Box 40004
Lubbock, TX 79409-0004

Phone: 806-742-3990   Fax: 806-742-1629
Web site: http://www.law.ttu.edu/

LAW STUDENT PROFILE [2000–2001]

FULL-TIME   Enrollment: 641
Women: 44%   Men: 56%

PART-TIME   Enrollment: 10
Women: 60%   Men: 40%

RACIAL or ETHNIC COMPOSITION
African American, 2%; Asian/Pacific Islander, 1%; Hispanic, 11%; Native American, 1%; International, 0.3%

APPLICANTS and ADMITTEES
Number applied: 1,030
Admitted: 603
Percentage accepted: 59%
Seats available: 269
Average LSAT score: 153
Average GPA: 3.3

Texas Tech University School of Law is a public institution that organizes classes on a semester calendar system. The campus is situated in a small-town setting. Founded in 1967, first ABA approved in 1970, and an AALS member, Texas Tech University School of Law offers JD, JD/MBA, JD/MPAd, JD/MS, and JD/MSET degrees.

Faculty consists of 30 full-time and 19 part-time members in 2000–2001. 10 full-time faculty members and 4 part-time faculty members are women. 100% of all faculty members have a JD; 36% have advanced law degrees. Of all faculty members, 2% are Native American, 2% are Asian/Pacific Islander, 10% are Hispanic, 84% are white.

Application Information *Required:* LSAT, LSDAS, application form, application fee of $50, baccalaureate degree, personal statement, college transcripts, resume. *Recommended:* 3 letters of recommendation. *Application deadline* for fall term is February 1 (priority date). Applications are processed on a rolling basis.

Costs The 1999–2000 tuition was $5940 full-time for state residents; $198 per hour part-time for state residents. Tuition was $11,010 full-time for nonresidents; $367 per hour part-time for nonresidents. Fees: $827 per semester full-time. Tuition and fees vary according to course load and degree level.

Financial Aid In 2000–2001, 53% of all students received some form of financial aid. 22 research assistantships, totaling $5607; 11 teaching assistantships, totaling $12,886, were awarded. Loans, merit-based grants/

AT a GLANCE

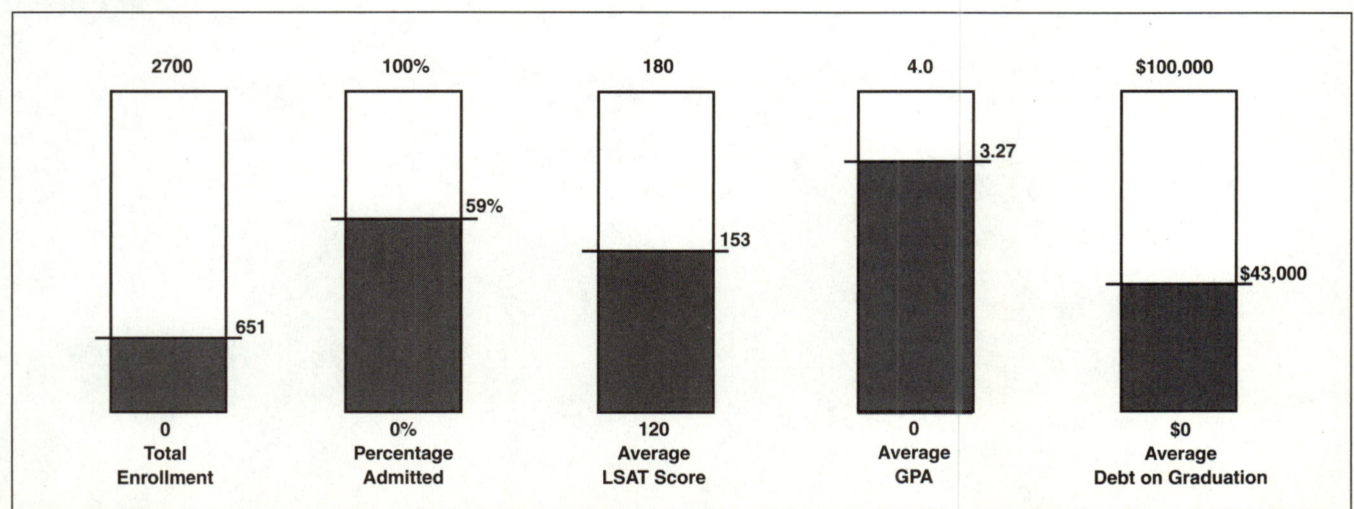

Degree Options

Degree	Total Credits Required	Length of Program
JD–Doctor of Laws	90	3 yrs, full-time only [day, summer]
JD/MBA–Juris Doctor/Master of Business Administration	102	4 yrs, full-time only [day, summer]
JD/MPAd–Juris Doctor/Master of Public Administration	111	4 yrs, full-time only [day, summer]
JD/MS–Juris Doctor/Master of Science–Taxation	102	4 yrs, full-time only [day, summer]
Certificate–Environmental Toxicology	111	4 yrs, full-time only [day]

scholarships, need-based grants/scholarships, and federal work-study loans are also available. The average student debt at graduation is $43,000. To apply for financial assistance, students must complete the Free Application for Federal Student Aid, institutional forms. Completed financial aid forms should be received by May 1. Financial aid contact: Donna Williams, Assistant Supervisor Admissions and Records, 1802 Hartford Avenue, Lubbock, TX 79409. Phone: 802-742-3791. Fax: 802-742-1629. E-mail: donna.williams@ttu.edu

Law School Library Texas Tech Law School Library has 5 professional staff members and contains more than 285,294 volumes and 1,988 periodicals. 380 seats are available in the library. When classes are in session, the library is open 92 hours per week.

WESTLAW and LEXIS-NEXIS are available, as are the World Wide Web, online bibliographic services, and CD-ROM players. 350 computer workstations are available to students in the library.

First-Year Program Class size in the average section is 70; 100% of the first-year courses are taught by full-time faculty.

Upper-Level Program Class size in the average section is 79. Among the electives are:

Administrative Law

★ Advocacy
Business and Corporate Law
Consumer Law
Education Law
Entertainment Law
★ Environmental Law
Family Law
Government/Regulation
Health Care/Human Services
Indian/Tribal Law
Intellectual Property
International/Comparative Law
Jurisprudence
Labor Law
Land Use Law/Natural Resources
Lawyering Skills
Legal History/Philosophy
Litigation
Media Law
Mediation
Probate Law
Public Interest
Tax Law

(★ *indicates an area of special strength*)

Clinical Courses Students receive degree credit for clinical courses. (Clinical practicum is not required.) The clinical area offered includes:

Tax Law

International exchange programs permit students to visit Mexico.

TEXAS WESLEYAN UNIVERSITY
SCHOOL OF LAW

Fort Worth, Texas

INFORMATION CONTACT

Sonel Y. Shropshire, Assistant Dean/Director of Admissions
1515 Commerce Street
Fort Worth, TX 76102

Phone: 817-212-4045   Fax: 817-212-4002
E-mail: law_admissions@law.txwes.edu
Web site: http://www.law.txwes.edu/

LAW STUDENT PROFILE [2000–2001]

FULL-TIME   Enrollment: 279
Women: 56%   Men: 44%

PART-TIME   Enrollment: 294
Women: 45%   Men: 55%

RACIAL or ETHNIC COMPOSITION
African American, 7%; Asian/Pacific Islander, 2%; Hispanic, 8%; Native American, 2%; International, 0.2%

APPLICANTS and ADMITTEES
Seats available: 198
Average LSAT score: 150
Average GPA: 3.1

Texas Wesleyan University School of Law is a private institution that organizes classes on a semester calendar system. The campus is situated in an urban setting. Founded in 1989, first ABA approved in 1994, Texas Wesleyan University School of Law offers a JD degree.

Faculty consists of 25 full-time and 28 part-time members in 2000–2001. 8 full-time faculty members and 11 part-time faculty members are women.

Application Information *Required:* LSAT, LSDAS, application form, application fee of $50, baccalaureate degree, 2 letters of recommendation, personal statement, college transcripts. *Application deadline* for fall term is May 1 (priority date). Applications are processed on a rolling basis.

Costs The 2000–2001 tuition was $15,370 full-time; $530 per hour part-time. Fees: $500 per term full-time.

Financial Aid In 2000–2001, 76% of all students received some form of financial aid. Merit-based grants/scholarships, need-based grants/scholarships, and federal work-study loans are available. The average student debt at graduation is $55,000. To apply for financial assistance, students must complete the Free Application for Federal Student Aid, institutional forms. Completed financial aid forms should be received by March 15. Financial aid contact: Doug Akins, Director of Admissions, Financial Aid Office, 1515 Commerce Street, Fort Worth, TX 76102. Phone: 817-212-4090 or toll free 800-733-9529. Fax: 817-212-4002.

AT a GLANCE

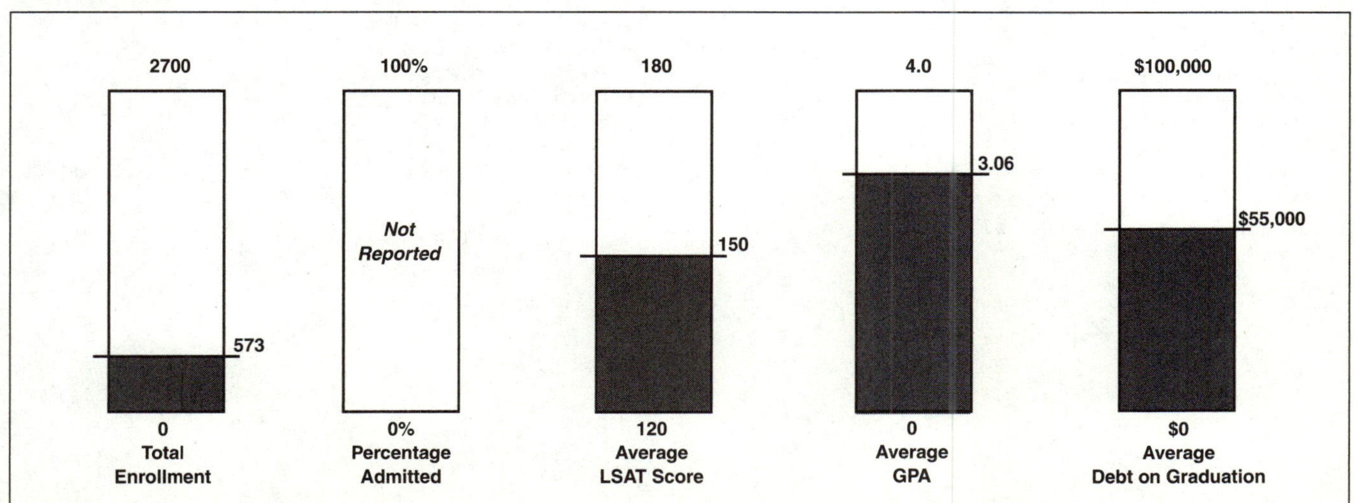

Degree Options

Degree	Total Credits Required	Length of Program
JD–Juris Doctor	88	full-time or part-time [day, evening]

Law School Library Texas Weselyan University Law Library has 7 professional staff members and contains more than 160,420 volumes and 2,515 periodicals. 254 seats are available in the library. When classes are in session, the library is open 102 hours per week.

WESTLAW and LEXIS-NEXIS are available, as are CD-ROM players. 12 computer workstations are available to students in the library. Special law collections include congressional hearings transcripts from 1970 to present.

First-Year Program Class size in the average section is 60; 12% of the first-year courses are taught by full-time faculty.

Upper-Level Program Class size in the average section is 40. Among the electives are:

Accounting
Administrative Law
Advocacy
Alternative Dispute Resolution
American Legal History
Antitrust Law
Banking Law & Regulation
Bankruptcy
Business and Corporate Law
Capital Punishment
Common Law
Computer Law
Conflict of Laws
Constitutional Law
Consumer Law
Copyright & Trademark Law
Corporate Taxation
Creditor's Rights
Criminal Procedure
Debtor Law
Education
Education Law
Elder Law
Employment Discrimination
Employment Law
English Legal History
Entertainment Law
Environmental Law
Estate & Gift Taxation

Estate Planning
Evidence
Family Law
Federal Courts
Feminist Jurisprudence
First Amendment
Government Contracts
Government/Regulation
Immigration
Insurance Law
Intellectual Property
International Business Transactions
International Law
International Litigation & Arbitration
International/Comparative Law
Jurisprudence
Juvenile Law
Labor and Employment
Labor Law
Land Use Law/Natural Resources
Law and Literature
Law and Psychology
Legal History/Philosophy
Legislation
Litigation
Marital Property
Mediation
Medical Malpractice Law
Oil and Gas
Patent Law
Pretrial Litigation
Product Liability
Property/Real Estate
Race and Law
Real Estate Transactions
Remedies
Securities
Securities Regulation
Sports Law
State Constitutional Law
Tax Law
Texas Criminal Procedure
Texas Law
Texas Pre-Trial Procedure
Texas Trials and Appeals
Unfair Trade Practices
White Collar Crime
Women and the Law

UNIVERSITY OF HOUSTON
LAW CENTER

Houston, Texas

> ### INFORMATION CONTACT
>
> Sondra B. Tennessee, Assistant Dean for Admissions
> 4800 Calhoun Street
> Houston, TX 77204-2163
>
> Phone: 713-743-2181   Fax: 713-743-2194
> Web site: http://www.law.uh.edu/

LAW STUDENT PROFILE [2000–2001]

FULL-TIME   Enrollment: 889
Women: 48%   Men: 52%

PART-TIME   Enrollment: 182
Women: 40%   Men: 60%

RACIAL or ETHNIC COMPOSITION
African American, 2%; Asian/Pacific Islander, 5%; Hispanic, 5%; Native American, 0.2%; International, 2%

APPLICANTS and ADMITTEES
Number applied: 2,349
Admitted: 823
Percentage accepted: 35%
Average LSAT score: 158
Average GPA: 3.3

University of Houston Law Center is a public institution that organizes classes on a semester calendar system. The campus is situated in an urban setting. Founded in 1947, first ABA approved in 1950, and an AALS member, University of Houston Law Center offers JD, JD/MA, JD/MBA, JD/MPH, and JD/PhD degrees.

Faculty consists of 34 full-time and 55 part-time members in 2000–2001. 8 full-time faculty members and 16 part-time faculty members are women. 97% of all faculty members have a JD; 33% have advanced law degrees. Of all faculty members, 7.3% are African American, 4.9% are Hispanic, 87.8% are white.

Application Information *Required:* LSAT, LSDAS, application form, application fee of $50, baccalaureate degree, personal statement, college transcripts, resume. *Recommended:* recommendations. *Application deadline* for fall term is February 15 (priority date). Applications are processed on a rolling basis.

Costs The 2000–2001 tuition was $4960 full-time for state residents; $160 per hour part-time for state residents. Tuition was $10,540 full-time for nonresidents; $340 per hour part-time for nonresidents. Tuition was $11,272 full-time for international students. Fees: $2154 full-time; $72 per hour full-time; $339 per hour part-time; $100 per hour part-time. Tuition and fees vary according to course load, degree level, and program.

Financial Aid In 2000–2001, 65% of all students received some form of financial aid. 1 research assistantship was awarded. Loans, merit-based grants/scholarships, need-based grants/scholarships, and federal work-study

AT a GLANCE

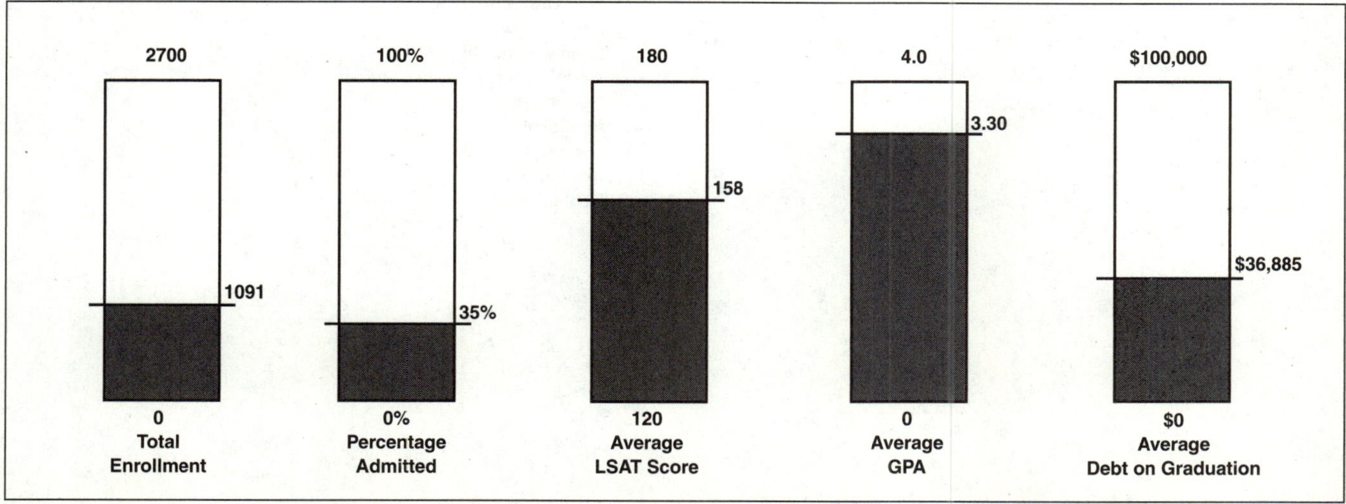

Degree Options

Degree	Total Credits Required	Length of Program
JD–Doctor of Laws	90	3–4 yrs, full-time or part-time [day, evening, summer]
JD/MA–Juris Doctor/Master of Arts–Dual-degree Program in History		3–4 yrs, full-time or part-time [day, evening, summer]
JD/MBA–Juris Doctor/Master of Business Administration–Dual-degree Program	117	4–5 yrs, full-time or part-time [day, evening, summer]
JD/MPH–Juris Doctor/Master of Public Health–Dual-degree Program in Public Health		3–4 yrs, full-time or part-time [day, evening, summer]
JD/PhD–Juris Doctor/Doctor of Philosophy–Dual-degree Program in Medical Humanities		5–6 yrs, full-time or part-time [day, evening, summer]

loans are also available. The average student debt at graduation is $36,885. To apply for financial assistance, students must complete the Free Application for Federal Student Aid. Completed financial aid forms should be received by April 1. Financial aid contact: Laura Neal, Financial Aid Coordinator, 4800 Calhoun, Houston, TX 77204-6391. Phone: 713-743-2269. Fax: 713-743-2194. E-mail: finaid@law.uh.edu/

Law School Library O. Quinn Law Library has 13 professional staff members and contains more than 466,082 volumes and 2,552 periodicals. 347 seats are available in the library. When classes are in session, the library is open 105 hours per week.

WESTLAW and LEXIS-NEXIS are available, as are the World Wide Web, online bibliographic services, and CD-ROM players. 65 computer workstations are available to students in the library.

First-Year Program Class size in the average section is 80; 100% of the first-year courses are taught by full-time faculty.

Upper-Level Program Class size in the average section is 30. Among the electives are:

Administrative Law
★ Advocacy
★ Business and Corporate Law
★ Constitutional Law
★ Consumer Law
Criminal Defense
Criminal Law
Criminal Prosecution
★ Education Law
Entertainment Law
★ Environmental Law
Family Law
Family Practice
Government/Regulation
★ Health Care/Human Services
★ Health Law
Immigration
Indian/Tribal Law
★ Intellectual Property
★ International/Comparative Law
Judicial Internship
Jurisprudence
★ Labor Law
★ Land Use Law/Natural Resources
Lawyering Skills
Legal History/Philosophy
Litigation
Maritime Law
Mediation
Probate Law
Public Interest
Securities
★ Tax Law
(★ *indicates an area of special strength*)

Clinical Courses Students receive degree credit for clinical courses. (Clinical practicum is not required.) Among the clinical areas offered are:

Advocacy
Criminal Defense
Criminal Prosecution
Environmental Law
Family Law
Family Practice
Health Care/Human Services
Health Law
Immigration
Judicial Internship
Mediation
Public Interest

THE UNIVERSITY OF TEXAS AT AUSTIN
SCHOOL OF LAW

Austin, Texas

INFORMATION CONTACT

Shelli D. Soto, Assistant Dean for Admissions
727 East Dean Keeton Street
Austin, TX 78705

Phone: 512-232-1200   Fax: 512-471-6988
E-mail: admissions@mail.law.utexas.edu
Web site: http://www.utexas.edu/law/

LAW STUDENT PROFILE [2000–2001]

FULL-TIME   Enrollment: 1,408
Women: 47%   Men: 53%

RACIAL or ETHNIC COMPOSITION
African American, 2%; Asian/Pacific Islander, 6%; Hispanic,
9%; Native American, 1%; International, 1%

APPLICANTS and ADMITTEES
Number applied: 3,885
Admitted: 1,031
Percentage accepted: 27%
Seats available: 475
Average LSAT score: 161
Average GPA: 3.6

The University of Texas at Austin School of Law is a public institution that organizes classes on a semester calendar system. The campus is situated in an urban setting. Founded in 1883, first ABA approved in 1923, and an AALS member, The University of Texas at Austin School of Law offers JD, JD/MA, JD/MBA, JD/MPAf, JD/MS, and LLM degrees.

Faculty consists of 73 full-time and 66 part-time members in 2000–2001. 19 full-time faculty members and 20 part-time faculty members are women. 97.5% of all faculty members have a JD; 13% have advanced law degrees. Of all faculty members, 1% are Asian/Pacific Islander, 4% are African American, 8% are Hispanic, 81% are white, 7% are international.

Application Information *Required:* LSAT, LSDAS, application form, application fee of $65, baccalaureate degree, minimum 2.2 GPA, personal statement, writing sample, college transcripts, resume. *Recommended:* recommendations. *Application deadline* for fall term is February 1.

Costs The 2000–2001 tuition was $6060 full-time for area residents. Tuition was $15,060 full-time for nonresidents. Fees: $2083 full-time.

Financial Aid In 2000–2001, 85% of all students received some form of financial aid. Loans, merit-based grants/scholarships, need-based grants/scholarships, and federal work-study loans are available. The average student debt at graduation is $50,000. To apply for financial assistance, students must complete the Free Application for Federal Student Aid, scholarship specific applications.

AT a GLANCE

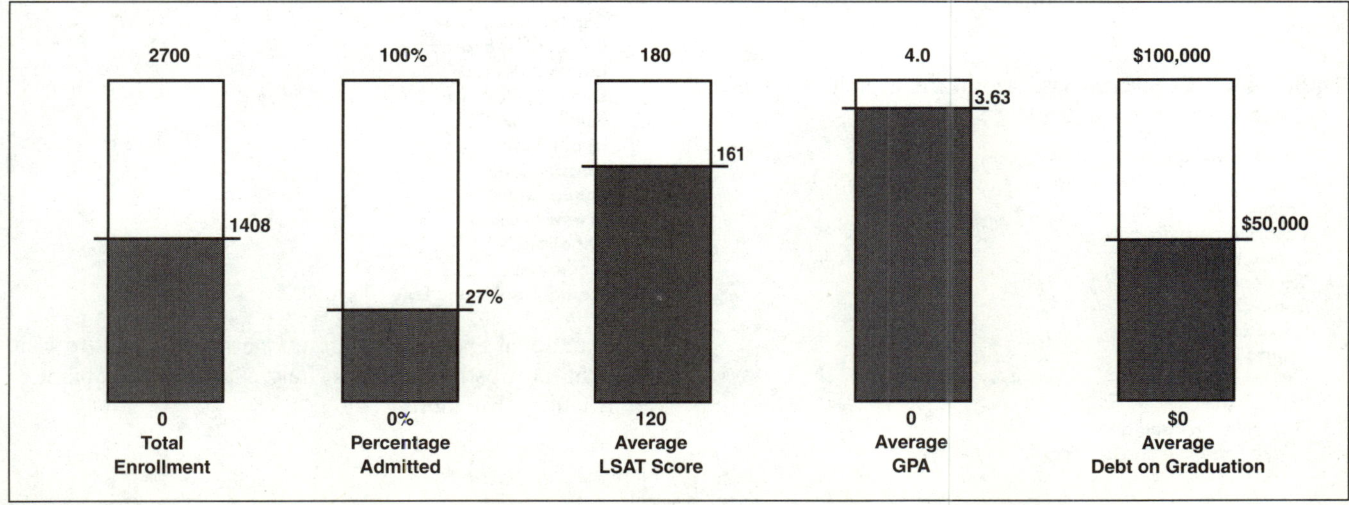

Degree Options

Degree	Total Credits Required	Length of Program
JD–Doctor of Laws	86	3 yrs, full-time only [day, summer]
JD/MA–Juris Doctor/Master of Arts–Joint-degrees Program Latin American Studies	116	4 yrs, full-time only [day, summer]
JD/MA–Juris Doctor/Master of Arts–Joint-degrees Program Middle Eastern Studies	119	4 yrs, full-time only [day, summer]
JD/MA–Juris Doctor/Master of Arts–Joint-degrees Program Russian, East European, and Eurasian Studies	116	4 yrs, full-time only [day, summer]
JD/MBA–Juris Doctor/Master of Business Administration–JD/MBA Joint-degrees Program	134	4–5 yrs, full-time only [day, summer]
JD/MPAf–Juris Doctor/Master of Public Affairs–JD/MPA Joint-degrees Program	109	4 yrs, full-time only [day, summer]
JD/MS–Juris Doctor/Master of Science–Joint-degrees Program in Community and Regional Planning	116	4 yrs, full-time only [day, summer]
LLM–Master of Laws	24	1 yr, full-time only [day, summer]

Completed financial aid forms should be received by March 31. Financial aid contact: Linda A. Alba, Financial Aid Counselor/Director, 727 East Dean Keeton Street, Austin, TX 78705. Phone: 512-232-1130. Fax: 512-471-6988. E-mail: lawfinaid@mail.law.utexas.edu

Law School Library Jamail Center for Legal Research has 20 professional staff members and contains more than 971,727 volumes and 8,700 periodicals. 1,321 seats are available in the library. When classes are in session, the library is open 102 hours per week.

WESTLAW and LEXIS-NEXIS are available, as are the World Wide Web, online bibliographic services, and CD-ROM players. 98 computer workstations are available to students in the library. Special law collections include European Union Documents Depository, Law in Popular Culture Collection, ABA Gavel Awards Archive, United States Supreme Court Justice Tom C. Clark Archives, Canadian Government Publications Depository.

First-Year Program Class size in the average section is 68; 96% of the first-year courses are taught by full-time faculty.

Upper-Level Program Class size in the average section is 44. Among the electives are:

Administrative Law
Business and Corporate Law
★ Capital Punishment
★ Children's Advocacy
Consumer Law
★ Criminal Defense
★ Domestic Violence
Education Law
Entertainment Law
Environmental Law
Family Law
Government/Regulation
Health Care/Human Services
Health Law
★ Housing Law
★ Immigration
Indian/Tribal Law
Intellectual Property
International/Comparative Law
Jurisprudence
★ Juvenile Law
Labor Law
Land Use Law/Natural Resources
Lawyering Skills
Legal History/Philosophy
Litigation
Maritime Law
Media Law
★ Mediation
★ Mental Health and Law
Probate Law
Securities
Tax Law
(★ *indicates an area of special strength*)

Clinical Courses Students receive degree credit for clinical courses. (Clinical practicum is not required.) Among the clinical areas offered are:

Capital Punishment
Children's Advocacy
Criminal Defense
Domestic Violence
Family Law
Health Law
Housing Law
Immigration
Juvenile Law
Litigation
Mediation
Mental Health and Law

International exchange programs permit students to visit Argentina, Australia, France, Italy, Netherlands, Spain, and United Kingdom.

BRIGHAM YOUNG UNIVERSITY
J. REUBEN CLARK LAW SCHOOL

Provo, Utah

INFORMATION CONTACT

Lola Wilcock, Admissions Director
PO Box 28000
Provo, UT 84602-8000

Phone: 801-378-4277   Fax: 801-378-5897
E-mail: wilcockl@lawgate.byu.edu
Web site: http://www.byu.edu/

LAW STUDENT PROFILE [2000–2001]

FULL-TIME   Enrollment: 481
Women: 31%   Men: 69%

PART-TIME   Enrollment: 10
Women: 50%   Men: 50%

RACIAL or ETHNIC COMPOSITION

African American, 1%; Asian/Pacific Islander, 4%; Hispanic, 4%; Native American, 1%; International, 3%

APPLICANTS and ADMITTEES

Number applied: 646
Admitted: 232
Percentage accepted: 36%
Seats available: 161
Average LSAT score: 161
Average GPA: 3.6

Brigham Young University J. Reuben Clark Law School is a private institution that organizes classes on a semester calendar system. The campus is situated in a suburban setting. Founded in 1973, first ABA approved in 1975, and an AALS member, Brigham Young University J. Reuben Clark Law School offers JD, JD/EdD, JD/MBA, JD/MED, JD/MOB, JD/MPA, and LLM degrees.

Faculty consists of 25 full-time and 39 part-time members in 2000–2001. 5 full-time faculty members and 13 part-time faculty members are women. 97% of all faculty members have a JD; 3% have advanced law degrees. Of all faculty members, 3% are Native American, 3% are African American, 6% are Hispanic, 87% are white.

Application Information *Required:* minimum 146 LSAT score, LSDAS, application form, application fee of $50, baccalaureate degree, 3 letters of recommendation, personal statement, writing sample, college transcripts. *Application deadline* for fall term is February 1. Applications are processed on a rolling basis.

Costs The 1999–2000 tuition was $5330 full-time; $296 per credit hour part-time. Fees: $20 per semester full-time. Tuition and fees vary according to student's religious affiliation. Students are required to have their own computers.

Financial Aid In 2000–2001, 41% of all students received some form of financial aid. Graduate assistantships, loans, loan repayment assistance program (LRAP), merit-based grants/scholarships, and need-based grants/scholarships are available. The average student debt at

AT a GLANCE

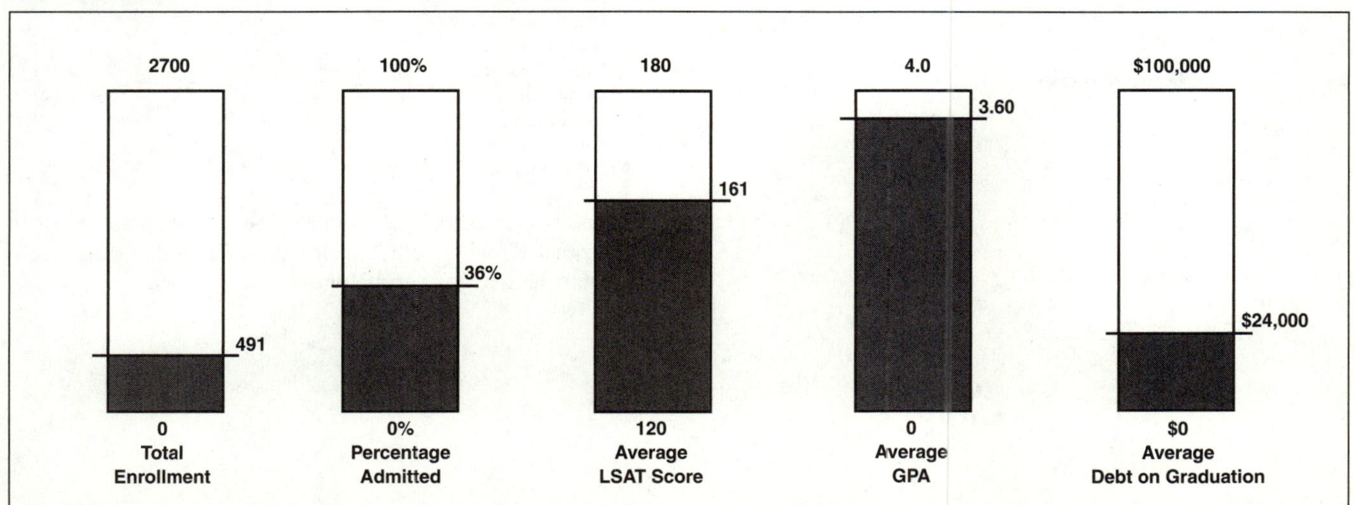

Degree Options

Degree	Total Credits Required	Length of Program
JD–Doctor of Laws	90	3–4 yrs, full-time only [day]
JD/EdD–Juris Doctor/Doctor of Education–Joint-degree	165	5 yrs, full-time only [day]
JD/MBA–Juris Doctor/Master of Business Administration–Joint-degree	131	4 yrs, full-time only [day]
JD/MED–Juris Doctor/Master of Education–Joint-degree	115	4 yrs, full-time only [day]
JD/MOB–Juris Doctor/Master of Organizational Behavior–Joint-degree	131	4 yrs, full-time only [day]
JD/MPA–Juris Doctor/Master of Professional Accountancy–Joint-degree	126	4 yrs, full-time only [day]
LLM–Master of Laws		1 yr, full-time only [day]

graduation is $24,000. To apply for financial assistance, students must complete the Free Application for Federal Student Aid, institutional forms. Completed financial aid forms should be received by June 1. Financial aid contact: Carl Hernandez, Assistant Dean, 342 JRCB Brigham Young University, Provo, UT 84602-8000. Phone: 801-378-6386. Fax: 801-378-5897.

Law School Library Howard W. Hunter Law Library has 11 professional staff members and contains more than 439,259 volumes and 5,616 periodicals. 883 seats are available in the library. When classes are in session, the library is open 105 hours per week.

WESTLAW and LEXIS-NEXIS are available, as are the World Wide Web, online bibliographic services, and CD-ROM players. 47 computer workstations are available to students in the library. Special law collections include Biblical, Feminist, and Native American Law.

First-Year Program Class size in the average section is 110; 100% of the first-year courses are taught by full-time faculty.

Upper-Level Program Class size in the average section is 50. Among the electives are:

Administrative Law
Advocacy
Business and Corporate Law
Civil Litigation
★ Constitutional Law
Consumer Law
Criminal Defense
Criminal Prosecution
Education Law
Elderly Advocacy
Entertainment Law
Environmental Law
Family Law

Family Practice
Government/Regulation
Health Care/Human Services
Immigration
Indian/Tribal Law
★ Intellectual Property
★ International/Comparative Law
Jurisprudence
Labor Law
Land Use Law/Natural Resources
Lawyering Skills
Legal History/Philosophy
Litigation
Maritime Law
Media Law
Mediation
Probate Law
Public Interest
Securities
Tax Law
(★ *indicates an area of special strength*)

Clinical Courses Students receive degree credit for clinical courses. (Clinical practicum is not required.) Among the clinical areas offered are:

Children's Advocacy
Civil Litigation
Criminal Defense
Criminal Prosecution
Elderly Advocacy
Family Law
Family Practice
Immigration
Mediation
Poverty/Welfare Law
Public Interest

International exchange programs permit students to visit Australia, Czech Republic, Hungary, Poland, Romania, Russian Federation, and Yugoslavia.

UNIVERSITY OF UTAH
COLLEGE OF LAW

Salt Lake City, Utah

INFORMATION CONTACT

Reyes Aguilar, Associate Dean for Admission and Financial Aid
332 South 1400 Room 101
Salt Lake City, UT 84112-0730

Phone: 801-581-7479   Fax: 801-581-6897
E-mail: aguilarr@law.utah.edu
Web site: http://www.utah.edu/

LAW STUDENT PROFILE [2000–2001]

FULL-TIME   Enrollment: 386
Women: 39%   Men: 61%

APPLICANTS and ADMITTEES
Number applied: 818
Admitted: 323
Percentage accepted: 39%
Seats available: 130
Average LSAT score: 158
Average GPA: 3.5

University of Utah College of Law is a public institution that organizes classes on a semester calendar system. The campus is situated in an urban setting. Founded in 1919, first ABA approved in 1927, and an AALS member, University of Utah College of Law offers JD, JD/MBA, LLM, and MPA degrees.

Faculty consists of 27 full-time and 21 part-time members in 2000–2001. 8 full-time faculty members and 6 part-time faculty members are women. 100% of all faculty members have a JD; 17.6% have advanced law degrees. Of all faculty members, 4.1% are Native American, 4.1% are Asian/Pacific Islander, 12.5% are Hispanic, 79.3% are white.

Application Information *Required:* LSAT, LSDAS, application form, application fee of $50, baccalaureate degree, 1 recommendation, personal statement, college transcripts, resume. *Application deadline* for fall term is February 1. Applications are processed on a rolling basis.

Costs The 2000–2001 tuition was $5702 full-time for state residents. Tuition was $18,136 full-time for nonresidents. Fees: $225 full-time (one-time charge for full-time students).

Financial Aid 41 fellowships, totaling $3700; 2 research assistantships, totaling $3500, were awarded. Fellowships, loans, loan repayment assistance program (LRAP), merit-based grants/scholarships, need-based grants/scholarships, and federal work-study loans are also available. The average student debt at graduation is $42,000. To apply for financial assistance, students must complete the Free Application for Federal Student Aid,

AT a GLANCE

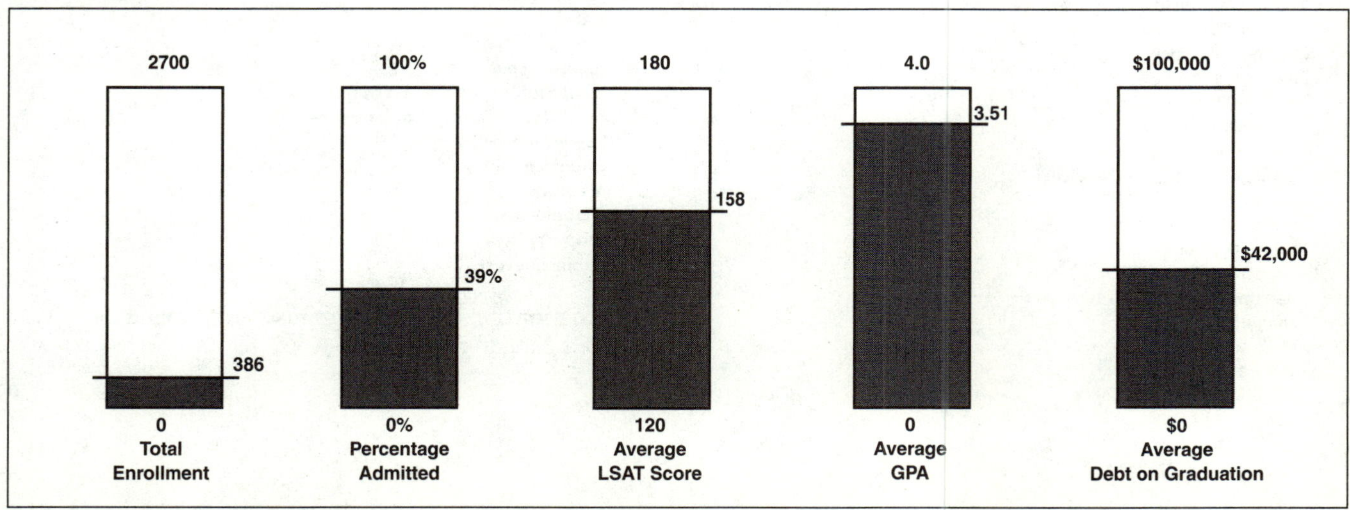

Degree Options

Degree	Total Credits Required	Length of Program
JD–Juris Doctor	88	3 yrs, full-time only [day, summer]
JD/MBA–Juris Doctor/Master of Business Administration–Joint-degree Program	137	3–5 yrs, full-time only [day, evening, summer]
LLM–Master of Laws–Environmental Law	24	1 yr, full-time only [day, summer]
MPA–Master of Public Administration–Joint-degree Program	119	3–4 yrs, full-time only [day, evening, summer]

institutional forms, scholarship specific applications. Completed financial aid forms should be received by March 15. Financial aid contact: Marie McQuiddy, Financial Aid Manager, 105 Student Services Building, Salt Lake City, UT 84112. Phone: 801-585-5828. Fax: 801-585-6350. E-mail: mmcquiddy@ssb2.saff.utah.edu

Law School Library S. J. Quinney Law Library has 7 professional staff members and contains more than 312,000 volumes and 4,698 periodicals. 381 seats are available in the library. When classes are in session, the library is open 100 hours per week.

WESTLAW and LEXIS-NEXIS are available, as are the World Wide Web, online bibliographic services, and CD-ROM players. 15 computer workstations are available to students in the library. Special law collections include state and federal government documents, gaming law, environmental and natural resources.

First-Year Program Class size in the average section is 45; 100% of the first-year courses are taught by full-time faculty.

Upper-Level Program Class size in the average section is 30. Among the electives are:

Administrative Law
Advocacy
★ Business and Corporate Law
Civil Litigation
Consumer Law
Criminal Defense
Criminal Prosecution
Elderly Advocacy
★ Environmental Law
Estate Planning
Family Law
Government/Regulation
Health Care/Human Services
Health Law
Immigration
Indian/Tribal Law
Intellectual Property
★ International/Comparative Law
★ Judicial
Judicial Process
Jurisprudence
Juvenile Law
Labor Law
★ Land Rights/Natural Resource
★ Land Use Law/Natural Resources
★ Lawyering Skills
Legal History/Philosophy
Litigation
Mediation
Probate Law
Property/Real Estate
Public Interest
Securities
Tax Law
(★ indicates an area of special strength)

Clinical Courses Students receive degree credit for clinical courses. (Clinical practicum is not required.) Among the clinical areas offered are:

Administrative Law
Advocacy
Bankruptcy
Civil Litigation
Consumer Law
Criminal Defense
Criminal Prosecution
Education
Elderly Advocacy
Environmental Law
Family Law
Family Practice
Government Litigation
Government/Regulation
Health Care/Human Services
Health Law
Immigration
Indian/Tribal Law
Judicial
Judicial Process
Juvenile Law
Land Rights/Natural Resource
Land Use Law/Natural Resources
Lawyering Skills
Litigation
Mediation
Probate Law
Property/Real Estate
Public Interest

International exchange programs permit students to visit United Kingdom.

VERMONT LAW SCHOOL

South Royalton, Vermont

INFORMATION CONTACT

Michelle D. Mason, Assistant Dean for Admissions
Chelsea Street, PO Box 96
South Royalton, VT 05068-0096

Phone: 802-763-8303   Fax: 802-763-7071
     ext. 2239
E-mail: admiss@vermontlaw.edu
Web site: http://www.vermontlaw.edu/

LAW STUDENT PROFILE [2000–2001]

FULL-TIME   Enrollment: 554
Women: 48%   Men: 52%

APPLICANTS and ADMITTEES
Number applied: 814
Admitted: 565
Percentage accepted: 69%
Seats available: 165
Median LSAT score: 151
Average GPA: 3.0

Vermont Law School is a private nonprofit institution that organizes classes on a semester calendar system. The campus is situated in a small-town setting. Founded in 1973, first ABA approved in 1975, and an AALS member, Vermont Law School offers JD, JD/MSEL, LLM, and MSEL degrees.

Faculty 97% of all faculty members have a JD; 16% have advanced law degrees. Of all faculty members, 6% are Native American, 3% are Asian/Pacific Islander, 91% are white.

Application Information *Required:* LSAT, LSDAS, application form, application fee of $50, baccalaureate degree, 2 letters of recommendation, essay, college transcripts, resume. *Recommended:* interview.

Costs The 2000–2001 tuition was $20,958 full-time. Fees: $75 full-time.

Financial Aid Fellowships, loans, loan repayment assistance program (LRAP), merit-based grants/scholarships, need-based grants/scholarships, and federal work-study loans are available. The average student debt at graduation is $76,550. To apply for financial assistance, students must complete the Free Application for Federal Student Aid, institutional forms. Financial aid contact: Laura McClay, Director of Financial Aid, Chelsea Street, PO Box 96, South Royalton, VT 05068-0096. Phone: 802-763-8303 ext. 2235. Fax: 802-763-7071. E-mail: finaid@vermontlaw.edu

Law School Library Julien and Virginia Cornell Library has 6 professional staff members and contains more than

AT a GLANCE

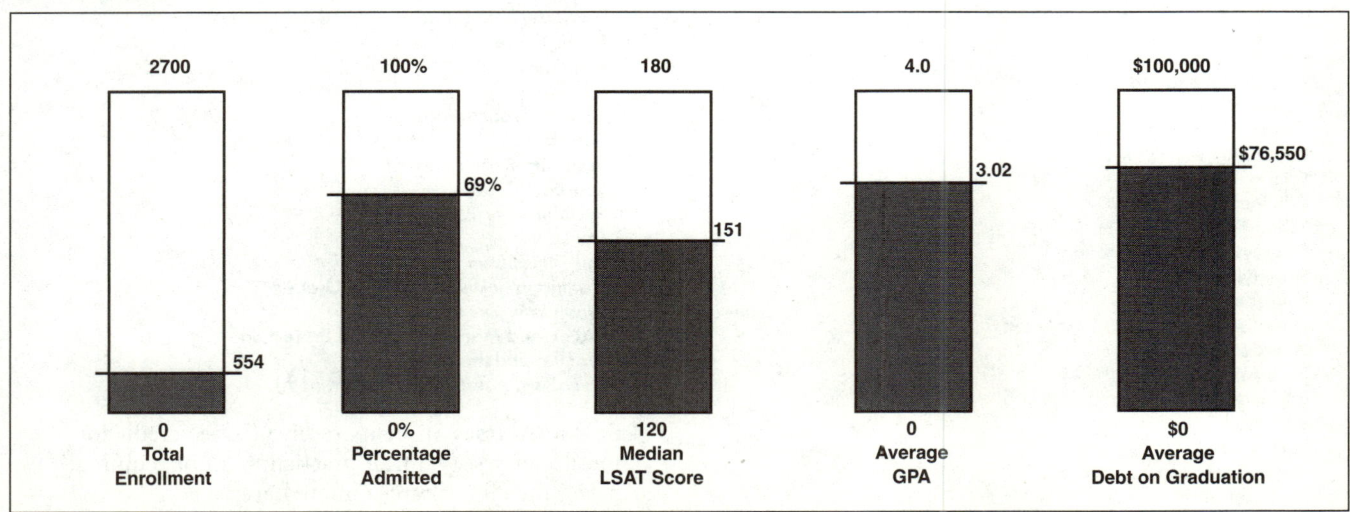

Degree Options

Degree	Total Credits Required	Length of Program
JD–Doctor of Laws	84	3 yrs, full-time only [day]
JD/MSEL–Juris Doctor/Master of Studies in Environmental Law–Joint-degree Program	105	3–4 yrs, full-time only [day, summer]
LLM–Master of Laws–Environmental Law	30	1 yr, full-time or part-time [day, summer]
MSEL–Master of Studies in Environmental Law	30	1.5 yrs, full-time or part-time [day, summer]

230,000 volumes and 2,650 periodicals. 350 seats are available in the library. When classes are in session, the library is open 110 hours per week.

WESTLAW and LEXIS-NEXIS are available, as are the World Wide Web, online bibliographic services, and CD-ROM players. 20 computer workstations are available to students in the library. Special law collections include environmental law.

First-Year Program Class size in the average section is 65; 100% of the first-year courses are taught by full-time faculty.

Upper-Level Program Class size in the average section is 35. Among the electives are:

Accounting
Administrative Law
Advocacy
Air Pollution & Waste Management
Alternative Dispute Resolution
American Legal History
Appellate Advocacy
★ Business and Corporate Law
Canadian Law
Capital Punishment
Children's Rights
Civil Litigation
Civil Procedure
Civil Rights
Civil Rights Litigation
Commercial Law
Conflict of Laws
Constitutional Criminal Procedure
Constitutional Law
Consumer Law
Corporate Law
Corporate Taxation
Corporations
Criminal Defense
Criminal Law
Criminal Procedure
Criminal Prosecution
Economic Development
Employment Discrimination
Employment Law
Entertainment Law
Environmental Dispute Resolution
Environmental Ethics
★ Environmental Law
Estate & Gift Taxation
Evidence
Family Law
Family Practice
Federal Courts

Federal Income Tax
Fourth Amendment
Gender and Sexuality
★ General Practice
Government Litigation
Government/Regulation
Health Care/Human Services
Health Law
★ Indian/Tribal Law
Intellectual Property
International Business Transactions
★ International Law
★ International/Comparative Law
Jurisprudence
★ Labor Law
Land Rights/Natural Resource
★ Land Use Law/Natural Resources
Law and Anthropology
Law and Economics
Law and Literature
Law and Medicine
Law and Philosophy
Law and Population
Law and Science
Lawyering Skills
★ Legal History/Philosophy
Legal Research
Legal Writing
Legislation
Litigation
★ Mediation
Mental Health and Law
National Security and the Law
Natural Resources
Negotiation
Nonprofit Organizations
Probate Law
Property/Real Estate
★ Public Interest
Remedies
Sales
Secured Transactions
Securities
Securities Regulation
Supreme Court
Sustainability
Tax Law
Tort Litigation
★ Traditionally Disadvantaged Groups
Water Law
Watershed Management and Protection
Women and the Law
(★ *indicates an area of special strength*)

Clinical Courses Students receive degree credit for clinical courses. (Clinical practicum is not required.) Among the clinical areas offered are:

Advocacy
Civil Litigation
Civil Rights
Consumer Law
Corporate Law
Criminal Defense
Criminal Law
Criminal Prosecution
Elderly Advocacy
Environmental Law
Family Law
Family Practice
General Practice
Government Litigation
Government/Regulation
Health Care/Human Services
Indian/Tribal Law
Intellectual Property

International Law
International/Comparative Law
Jurisprudence
Juvenile Law
Labor Law
Land Rights/Natural Resource
Land Use Law/Natural Resources
Litigation
Mediation
Probate Law
Public Interest
Securities
Tax Law
Traditionally Disadvantaged Groups

International exchange programs permit students to visit Canada, Italy, and Russian Federation.

APPALACHIAN SCHOOL OF LAW

Grundy, Virginia

INFORMATION CONTACT

Director of Admissions
PO Box 2825
Grundy, VA 24614

Phone: 540-935-4349   Fax: 540-935-8261
Web site: http://www.asl.edu/

LAW STUDENT PROFILE [2000–2001]

FULL-TIME   Enrollment: 166
Women: 42%   Men: 58%

PART-TIME   Enrollment: 4
Women: 50%   Men: 50%

APPLICANTS and ADMITTEES

Number applied: 359
Admitted: 326
Percentage accepted: 91%
Seats available: 125
Average LSAT score: 145
Average GPA: 2.9

Appalachian School of Law is a private nonprofit institution that organizes classes on a semester calendar system. The campus is situated in a small-town setting. Founded in 1994, first ABA approved in 2001, Appalachian School of Law offers a JD degree.

Faculty 100% of all faculty members have a JD; 36% have advanced law degrees. Of all faculty members, 9% are African American, 91% are white.

Application Information *Required:* LSAT, application form, application fee of $40, baccalaureate degree, 2 letters of recommendation, personal statement, college transcripts. *Recommended:* LSDAS, resume.

Costs The 2000–2001 tuition was $16,000 full-time; $525 per credit hour part-time. Fees: $100 per semester full-time. Tuition and fees vary according to course load, degree level, and student level.

Financial Aid Loans, merit-based grants/scholarships, and need-based grants/scholarships are available. To apply for financial assistance, students must complete the Free Application for Federal Student Aid, institutional forms. Financial aid contact: Veronica Keene, Director of Student Services, P.O. Box 2825, Grundy, VA 24614. Phone: 560-935-4349 or toll free 800-895-7411. Fax: 560-935-8261. E-mail: vkeene@asl.edu

Law School Library Appalachian School of Law Library has 5 professional staff members and contains more than 153,070 volumes and 2,322 periodicals. 218 seats are available in the library. When classes are in session, the library is open 74 hours per week.

WESTLAW and LEXIS-NEXIS are available, as are the World Wide Web, online bibliographic services, and

AT a GLANCE

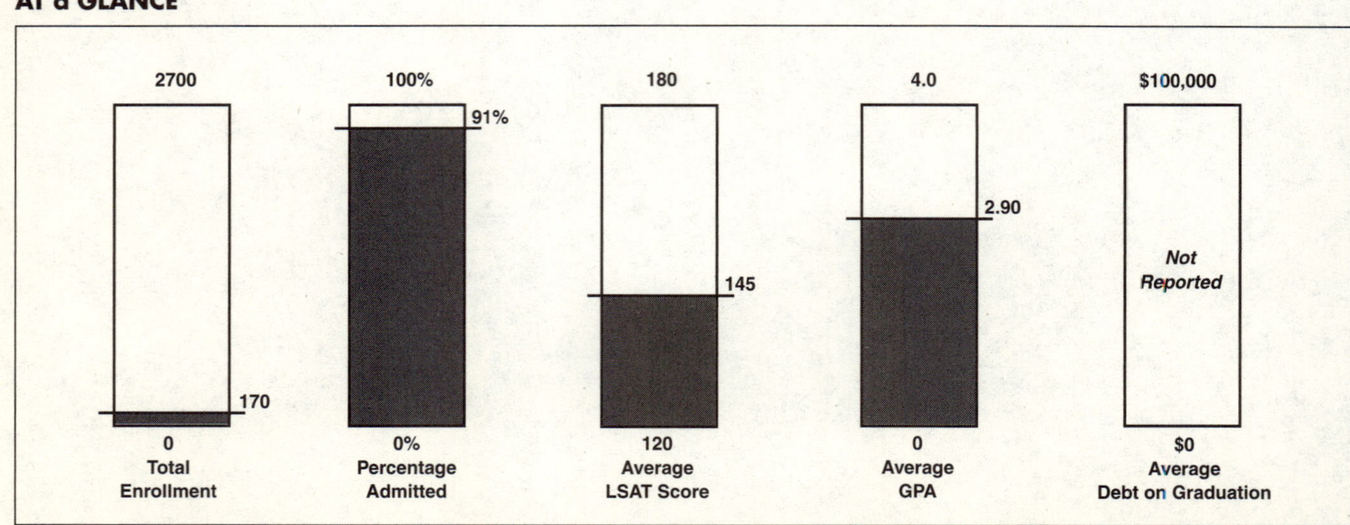

CD-ROM players. 13 computer workstations are available to students in the library. Special law collections include Appalachian Collection.

Upper-Level Program Among the electives are:

Advocacy
★ Alternative Dispute Resolution
Business and Corporate Law
Environmental Law
Family Law
Government/Regulation
Intellectual Property
Labor Law
Lawyering Skills
★ Mediation
Probate Law
★ Professional Responsibility
★ Public Interest
Tax Law
(★ indicates an area of special strength)

THE COLLEGE OF WILLIAM AND MARY
WILLIAM & MARY LAW SCHOOL

Williamsburg, Virginia

INFORMATION CONTACT

Faye F. Shealy, Associate Dean for Admissions
PO Box 8795
Williamsburg, VA 23187-8795

Phone: 757-221-3785   Fax: 757-221-3261
E-mail: ffshea@wm.edu
Web site: http://www.wm.edu/law/

LAW STUDENT PROFILE [2000–2001]

FULL-TIME   Enrollment: 525
Women: 43%   Men: 57%

RACIAL or ETHNIC COMPOSITION
African American, 10%; Asian/Pacific Islander, 4%; Hispanic, 2%; Native American, 1%; International, 2%

APPLICANTS and ADMITTEES
Number applied: 2,479
Admitted: 727
Percentage accepted: 29%
Seats available: 175
Average LSAT score: 161
Average GPA: 3.3

The College of William and Mary William & Mary Law School is a public institution that organizes classes on a semester calendar system. The campus is situated in a small-town setting. Founded in 1779, first ABA approved in 1932, and an AALS member, The College of William and Mary William & Mary Law School offers JD, JD/MA, JD/MBA, JD/MPPo, and LLM degrees.

Faculty consists of 30 full-time and 28 part-time members in 2000–2001. 8 full-time faculty members and 9 part-time faculty members are women. 100% of all faculty members have a JD; 20% have advanced law degrees. Of all faculty members, 3% are Asian/Pacific Islander, 7% are African American, 90% are white.

Application Information *Required:* LSAT, LSDAS, application form, application fee of $40, baccalaureate degree, 2 letters of recommendation, personal statement, writing sample, college transcripts. *Recommended:* essay. *Application deadline* for fall term is March 1 (priority date).

Costs The 2000–2001 tuition was $6750 full-time for state residents; $300 per hour part-time for state residents. Tuition was $15,968 full-time for nonresidents; $611 per hour part-time for nonresidents. Fees: $2841 full-time. Full-time tuition and fees vary according to program.

Financial Aid In 2000–2001, 81% of all students received some form of financial aid. 64 research assistantships, totaling $4000; 24 teaching assistantships, totaling $6000, were awarded. Fellowships, graduate assistantships, loans, merit-based grants/scholarships, need-based grants/

AT a GLANCE

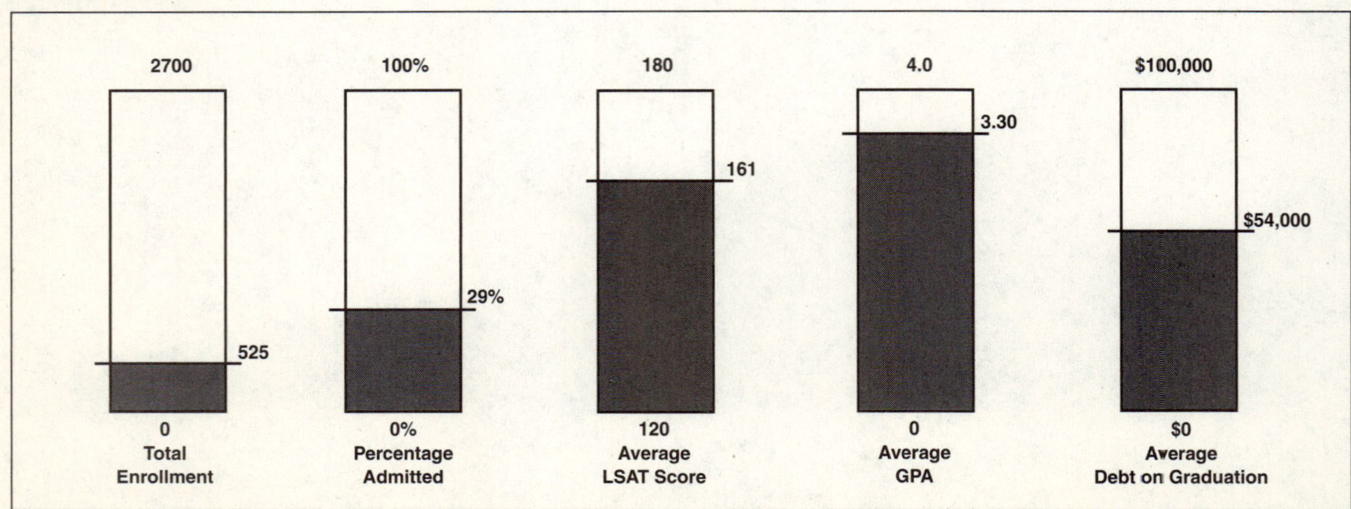

Degree Options

Degree	Total Credits Required	Length of Program
JD–Juris Doctor	90	3 yrs, full-time only [day, summer]
JD/MA–Juris Doctor/Master of Arts–Dual-degree Program in American Studies	108	3–4 yrs, full-time only [day, summer]
JD/MBA–Juris Doctor/Master of Business Administration–Dual-degree Program	125	4 yrs, full-time only [day, summer]
JD/MPPo–Juris Doctor/Master of Public Policy–Dual-degree Program	111	4 yrs, full-time only [day, summer]
LLM–Master of Laws–American Legal System	24	1 yr, full-time only [day]

scholarships, and federal work-study loans are also available. The average student debt at graduation is $54,000. To apply for financial assistance, students must complete the Free Application for Federal Student Aid. Completed financial aid forms should be received by February 15. Financial aid contact: Faye Shealy, Associate Dean, William & Mary Law School, PO Box 8795, Williamsburg, VA 23187-8795. Phone: 757-221-3785. Fax: 757-221-3261. E-mail: lawadm@wm.edu

Law School Library Marshall-Wythe Law Library has 7 professional staff members and contains more than 364,066 volumes and 5,000 periodicals. 433 seats are available in the library. When classes are in session, the library is open 168 hours per week.

WESTLAW and LEXIS-NEXIS are available, as are the World Wide Web, online bibliographic services, and CD-ROM players. 46 computer workstations are available to students in the library. Special law collections include Roman Law, US Constitutional Law and Bill of Rights, Environmental Law, Taxation.

First-Year Program Class size in the average section is 70; 67% of the first-year courses are taught by full-time faculty.

Upper-Level Program Class size in the average section is 25. Among the electives are:

Administrative Law
★ Advocacy
Consumer Law
Entertainment Law
★ Environmental Law
Family Law
Government/Regulation
Health Care/Human Services
Intellectual Property
International/Comparative Law
Jurisprudence
Labor Law
Land Use Law/Natural Resources
★ Lawyering Skills
Legal History/Philosophy
Litigation
Maritime Law
Media Law
Mediation
Probate Law
★ Professional Responsibility
Public Interest
Securities
Tax Law
(★ *indicates an area of special strength*)

Clinical Courses Students receive degree credit for clinical courses. (Clinical practicum is not required.) Among the clinical areas offered are:

Civil Litigation
Environmental Law
Family Practice
General Practice
Public Interest
Tax Law

International exchange programs permit students to visit United Kingdom.

GEORGE MASON UNIVERSITY
SCHOOL OF LAW

Arlington, Virginia

INFORMATION CONTACT

Director of Admissions
3401 North Fairfax Drive
Arlington, VA 22201-4498

Phone: 703-993-8010   Fax: 703-993-8088
Web site: http://www.gmu.edu/departments/law/

LAW STUDENT PROFILE [2000–2001]

FULL-TIME Enrollment: 675
Women: 42% Men: 58%

PART-TIME Enrollment: 39
Women: 36% Men: 64%

RACIAL or ETHNIC COMPOSITION
African American, 2%; Asian/Pacific Islander, 6%; Hispanic, 2%; Native American, 0.4%; International, 0.3%

APPLICANTS and ADMITTEES
Number applied: 1,965
Admitted: 699
Percentage accepted: 36%
Seats available: 204
Average LSAT score: 158
Average GPA: 3.2

George Mason University School of Law is a public institution that organizes classes on a semester calendar system. The campus is situated in a suburban setting. Founded in 1979, first ABA approved in 1980, and an AALS member, George Mason University School of Law offers JD and JM degrees.

Faculty consists of 38 full-time and 43 part-time members in 2000–2001. 9 full-time faculty members and 9 part-time faculty members are women. 97% of all faculty members have a JD; 34% have advanced law degrees. Of all faculty members, 3% are Asian/Pacific Islander, 3% are African American, 94% are white.

Application Information *Required:* LSAT, LSDAS, application form, application fee of $35, baccalaureate degree, 2 letters of recommendation, personal statement. *Recommended:* resume. *Application deadline* for fall term is May 1; for spring term is November 1.

Costs The 2000–2001 tuition was $7938 full-time for state residents; $284 per credit hour part-time for state residents. Tuition was $18,452 full-time for nonresidents; $659 per credit hour part-time for nonresidents.

Financial Aid Fellowships, graduate assistantships, loans, and merit-based grants/scholarships are available. The average student debt at graduation is $39,914. To apply for financial assistance, students must complete the Free Application for Federal Student Aid. Financial aid contact: Jevita De Freitas, Financial Aid Counselor, George Mason University, Fairfax, VA 22030-4444. Phone: 703-993-2353. Fax: 703-993-2350. E-mail: finaid@gmu.edu

AT a GLANCE

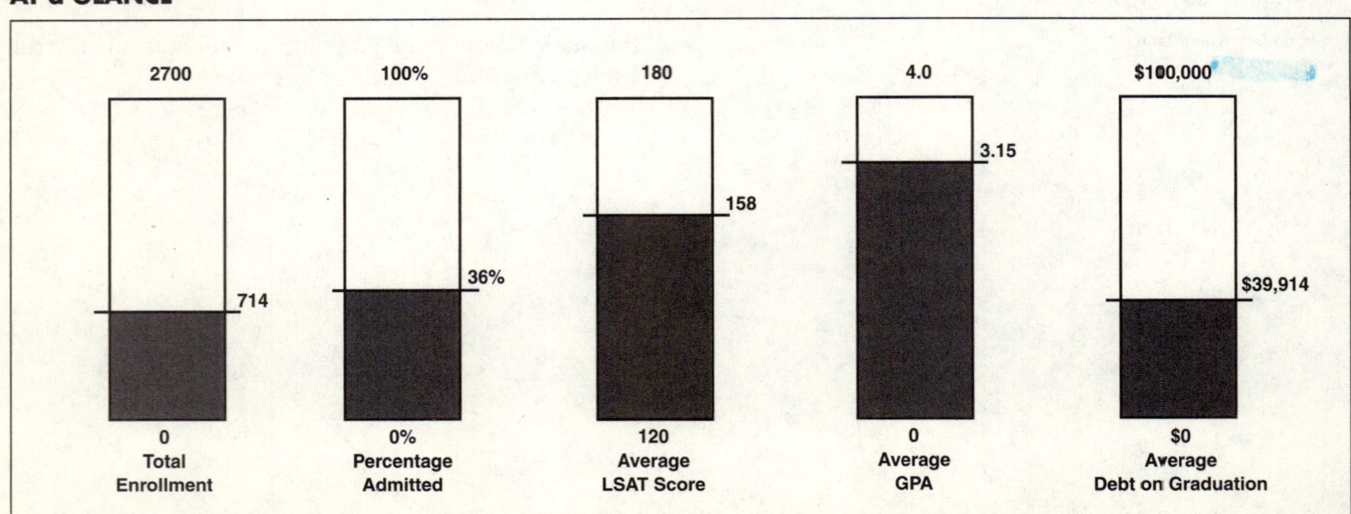

<table>
<tr><td colspan="3">Degree Options</td></tr>
<tr><td>Degree</td><td>Total Credits
Required</td><td>Length of Program</td></tr>
<tr><td>JD–Doctor of Laws</td><td>84</td><td>3–4 yrs, full-time or part-time [day, evening]</td></tr>
<tr><td>Certificate–Concentration in Policy Analysis</td><td>34</td><td>2 yrs, part-time only [evening]</td></tr>
</table>

Law School Library George Mason University Law Library has 8 professional staff members and contains more than 382,334 volumes and 5,300 periodicals. 320 seats are available in the library. When classes are in session, the library is open 94 hours per week.

WESTLAW and LEXIS-NEXIS are available, as are the World Wide Web, online bibliographic services, and CD-ROM players. 75 computer workstations are available to students in the library. Special law collections include federal government documents depository.

First-Year Program Class size in the average section is 102; 100% of the first-year courses are taught by full-time faculty.

Upper-Level Program Among the electives are:

  Administrative Law
  Advocacy
  Bankruptcy
★ Business and Corporate Law
★ Civil Litigation
  Consumer Law
  Criminal Defense
  Criminal Prosecution
  Environmental Law
  Family Law
★ Government/Regulation
  Health Care/Human Services

  Insurance Law
★ Intellectual Property
★ International/Comparative Law
  Jurisprudence
  Labor Law
  Land Use Law/Natural Resources
  Lawyering Skills
  Legal History/Philosophy
★ Litigation
  Mental Health and Law
  Probate Law
  Public Interest
★ Securities
  Tax Law
  Trusts and Estates
  Virginia Practice
(★ indicates an area of special strength)

Clinical Courses Students receive degree credit for clinical courses. (Clinical practicum is not required.) Among the clinical areas offered are:

  Civil Litigation
  Criminal Defense
  Criminal Prosecution
  Litigation
  Mental Health and Law
  Public Interest
  Virginia Practice

REGENT UNIVERSITY
SCHOOL OF LAW

Virginia Beach, Virginia

INFORMATION CONTACT

Bonnie Creef, Director of Law Admissions
1000 Regent University Drive
Virginia Beach, VA 23464

Phone: 757-226-4584   Fax: 757-226-4139
E-mail: lawschool@regent.edu
Web site: http://www.regent.edu/law

LAW STUDENT PROFILE [2000–2001]

FULL-TIME   Enrollment: 489
Women: 46%   Men: 54%

PART-TIME   Enrollment: 69
Women: 26%   Men: 74%

RACIAL or ETHNIC COMPOSITION

African American, 14%; Asian/Pacific Islander, 6%; Hispanic, 3%; Native American, 1%; International, 0.2%

APPLICANTS and ADMITTEES

Number applied: 869
Admitted: 336
Percentage accepted: 39%
Seats available: 200
Average LSAT score: 149
Average GPA: 3.1

Regent University School of Law is a private institution that organizes classes on a semester calendar system. The campus is situated in a suburban setting. Founded in 1986, first ABA approved in 1989, Regent University School of Law offers JD, JD/MA, JD/MBA, and LLM degrees.

Faculty consists of 26 full-time and 31 part-time members in 2000–2001. 5 full-time faculty members and 9 part-time faculty members are women. 100% of all faculty members have a JD; 13.3% have advanced law degrees. Of all faculty members, 3.22% are Native American, 6.45% are Asian/Pacific Islander, 9.67% are African American, 3.22% are Hispanic, 77.41% are white.

Application Information *Required:* minimum 144 LSAT score, LSDAS, application form, application fee of $40, baccalaureate degree, minimum 2.8 GPA, 3 letters of recommendation, personal statement, college transcripts, resume. *Recommended:* essay. *Application deadline* for fall term is March 1. Applications are processed on a rolling basis.

Financial Aid In 2000–2001, 81% of all students received some form of financial aid. Graduate assistantships, loans, merit-based grants/scholarships, and need-based grants/scholarships are available. The average student debt at graduation is $68,029. To apply for financial assistance, students must complete the Free Application for Federal Student Aid, institutional forms, scholarship specific applications. Completed financial aid forms should be received by September 1. Financial aid contact: Militza Lyden, Admissions and Financial Aid Counselor,

AT a GLANCE

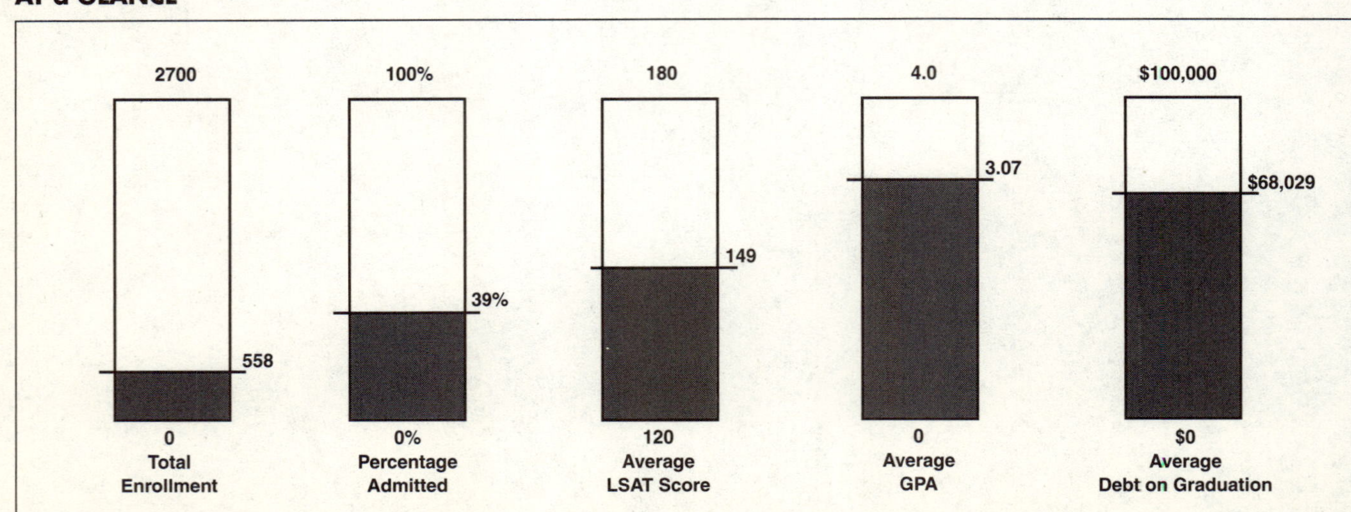

Degree Options

Degree	Total Credits Required	Length of Program
JD–Doctor of Laws	90	3–4 yrs, full-time or part-time [day, evening, weekend, summer]
JD/MA–Juris Doctor/Master of Arts–Public Policy or Public Administration	120	4 yrs, full-time or part-time [day, evening, summer]
JD/MA–Juris Doctor/Master of Arts–Communication Joint-degree Program	120	4 yrs, full-time or part-time [day, evening, summer]
JD/MBA–Juris Doctor/Master of Business Administration–Joint-degree Program	120	4 yrs, full-time or part-time [day, evening, weekend, summer]
LLM–Master of Laws–International Taxation	32	2 yrs, part-time only [day, evening, weekend, summer]

1000 Regent University Drive, Virginia Beach, VA 23464. Phone: 757-226-4559. Fax: 757-226-4139. E-mail: mililyd@regent.edu

Law School Library Law Library has 9 professional staff members and contains more than 354,351 volumes and 1,803 periodicals. 336 seats are available in the library. When classes are in session, the library is open 98 hours per week.

WESTLAW and LEXIS-NEXIS are available, as are the World Wide Web, online bibliographic services, and CD-ROM players. 11 computer workstations are available to students in the library. Special law collections include The Founder's Collection, Civil Right First Amendment Collection, Ralph W. Bunche Personal Library, John Brabner-Smith Library and Papers.

First-Year Program Class size in the average section is 70; 100% of the first-year courses are taught by full-time faculty.

Upper-Level Program Class size in the average section is 35. Among the electives are:

Biblical Law
Business and Corporate Law

★ Common Law
Education
Entertainment Law
Environmental Law
★ Family Law
Health Care/Human Services
Intellectual Property
International/Comparative Law
Jurisprudence
Land Use Law/Natural Resources
Lawyering Skills
Legal History/Philosophy
★ Litigation
Maritime Law
Media Law
★ Mediation
Public Interest
Securities
★ Tax Law
(★ indicates an area of special strength)

Clinical Courses Students receive degree credit for clinical courses. (Clinical practicum is not required.) Among the clinical areas offered are:

Family Law
Litigation
Mediation

UNIVERSITY OF RICHMOND
SCHOOL OF LAW

University of Richmond, Virginia

INFORMATION CONTACT

Michelle L. Rahman, Director of Admissions
University of Richmond, VA 23173

Phone: 804-289-8189   Fax: 804-287-6516
E-mail: mrahman@richmond.edu
Web site: http://law.richmond.edu/

LAW STUDENT PROFILE [2000–2001]

FULL-TIME   Enrollment: 460
Women: 48%   Men: 52%

PART-TIME   Enrollment: 1
Men: 100%

RACIAL or ETHNIC COMPOSITION
African American, 5%; Asian/Pacific Islander, 6%; Hispanic,
2%; Native American, 2%; International, 0.4%

APPLICANTS and ADMITTEES
Number applied: 1,450
Admitted: 533
Percentage accepted: 37%
Seats available: 161
Average LSAT score: 159
Average GPA: 3.1

University of Richmond School of Law is a private
institution that organizes classes on a semester calendar
system. The campus is situated in a suburban setting.
Founded in 1830, first ABA approved in 1928, and an
AALS member, University of Richmond School of Law
offers JD, JD/MBA, JD/MHA, JD/MPA, JD/MSW, and
JD/MUP degrees.

Faculty consists of 28 full-time and 54 part-time
members in 2000–2001. 7 full-time faculty members and
19 part-time faculty members are women. 100% of all
faculty members have a JD; 63% have advanced law
degrees. Of all faculty members, 7% are African American, 93% are white.

Application Information *Required:* LSAT, LSDAS,
application form, application fee of $35, baccalaureate
degree, personal statement, essay, college transcripts.
Recommended: recommendations, resume. *Application
deadline* for fall term is January 15 (priority date).
Applications are processed on a rolling basis. Students
are required to have their own computers.

Financial Aid In 2000–2001, 90% of all students received
some form of financial aid. Loans, merit-based grants/
scholarships, need-based grants/scholarships, and federal
work-study loans are available. The average student debt
at graduation is $62,200. To apply for financial assis-
tance, students must complete the Free Application for
Federal Student Aid, scholarship specific applications,
Merit Scholarships. Completed financial aid forms should
be received by February 25. Financial aid contact: Cindy
Bolger, Director of Financial Aid, Financial Aid Office,

AT a GLANCE

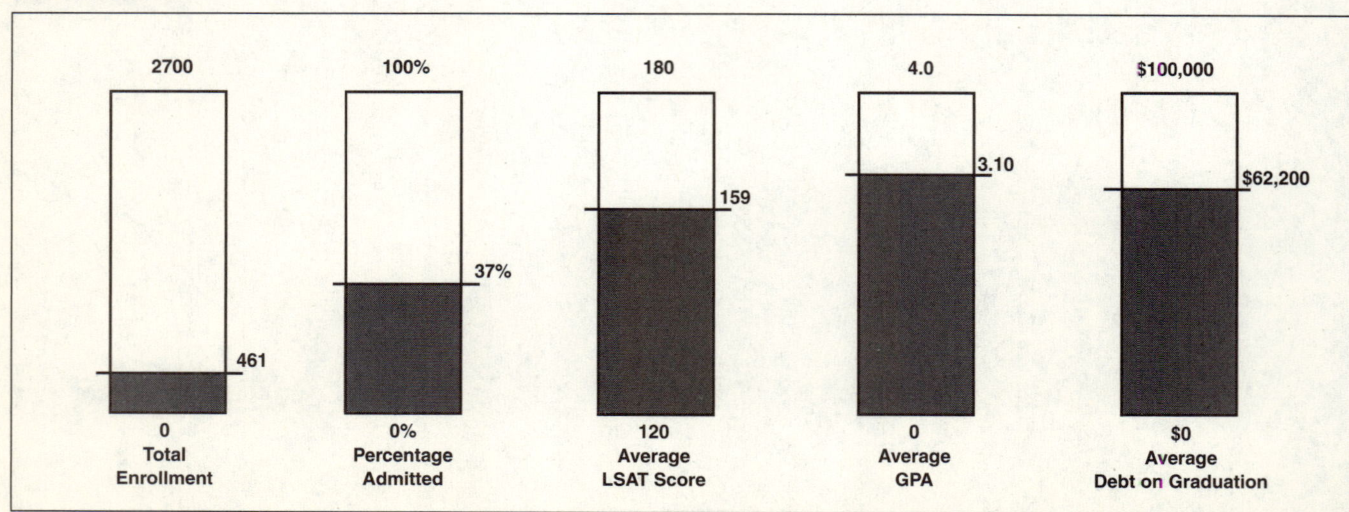

<table>
<tr><td colspan="3">Degree Options</td></tr>
<tr><td>Degree</td><td>Total Credits
Required</td><td>Length of Program</td></tr>
<tr><td>JD–Doctor of Laws</td><td>86</td><td>3–5 yrs, full-time only [day, summer]</td></tr>
<tr><td>JD/MBA–Juris Doctor/Master of Business
   Administration</td><td></td><td>4 yrs, full-time only [day]</td></tr>
<tr><td>JD/MHA–Juris Doctor/Master of Health Administration</td><td></td><td>4 yrs, full-time only [day]</td></tr>
<tr><td>JD/MPA–Juris Doctor/Master of Professional
   Accountancy</td><td>86</td><td>4 yrs, full-time only [day]</td></tr>
<tr><td>JD/MSW–Juris Doctor/Master of Social Work</td><td></td><td>4 yrs, full-time only [day]</td></tr>
<tr><td>JD/MUP–Juris Doctor/Masters of Urban Planning</td><td></td><td>4 yrs, full-time only [day]</td></tr>
</table>

Sarah Brunet Hall, 2700 Sterncroft Drive, Richmond, VA 23173. Phone: 804-289-8438. Fax: 804-289-8992. E-mail: cbogger@richmond.edu

Law School Library William Taylor Muse Law Library has 8 professional staff members and contains more than 294,542 volumes and 4,279 periodicals. 627 seats are available in the library. When classes are in session, the library is open 106 hours per week.

WESTLAW and LEXIS-NEXIS are available, as are the World Wide Web, online bibliographic services, and CD-ROM players. 450 computer workstations are available to students in the library. Special law collections include legal history, taxation, environmental law.

First-Year Program Class size in the average section is 60; 100% of the first-year courses are taught by full-time faculty.

Upper-Level Program Class size in the average section is 30. Among the electives are:

- Administrative Law
- ★ Advocacy
- Business and Corporate Law
- Criminal Defense
- Criminal Prosecution
- Education
- Education Law
- Entertainment Law
- ★ Environmental Law
- ★ Family Law
- Family Practice
- Government Litigation
- Government/Regulation
- Health Care/Human Services
- Intellectual Property
- International Law
- International/Comparative Law
- Jurisprudence
- Juvenile Law
- Labor and Employment
- Labor Law
- Land Rights/Natural Resource
- Land Use Law/Natural Resources
- ★ Lawyering Skills
- Legal History/Philosophy
- Litigation
- Maritime Law
- Mediation
- Probate Law
- ★ Public Interest
- Securities
- Sexual Orientation and the Law
- Tax Law

(★ indicates an area of special strength)

Clinical Courses Students receive degree credit for clinical courses. (Clinical practicum is not required.) Among the clinical areas offered are:

- Administrative Law
- Advocacy
- Civil Litigation
- Criminal Defense
- Criminal Prosecution
- Education
- Education Law
- Environmental Law
- Family Law
- Family Practice
- Government Litigation
- Government/Regulation
- Health Care/Human Services
- Intellectual Property
- International Law
- International/Comparative Law
- Juvenile Law
- Labor and Employment
- Labor Law
- Land Rights/Natural Resource
- Land Use Law/Natural Resources
- Litigation
- Public Interest
- Tax Law

International exchange programs permit students to visit France, Netherlands, Spain, and United Kingdom.

UNIVERSITY OF VIRGINIA
SCHOOL OF LAW

Charlottesville, Virginia

INFORMATION CONTACT

Albert R. Turnbull, Associate Dean
PO Box 400405
Charlottesville, VA 22904-4405

Phone: 804-924-7351   Fax: 804-924-7536
Web site: http://www.law.virginia.edu/

LAW STUDENT PROFILE [2000–2001]

FULL-TIME Enrollment: 1,101
Women: 44%   Men: 56%

PART-TIME Enrollment: 2
Women: 50%   Men: 50%

RACIAL or ETHNIC COMPOSITION
African American, 6%; Asian/Pacific Islander, 5%; Hispanic, 2%; Native American, 1%; International, 4%

APPLICANTS and ADMITTEES
Number applied: 3,755
Admitted: 1,071
Percentage accepted: 29%
Seats available: 340
Average LSAT score: 166
Average GPA: 3.6

University of Virginia School of Law is a public institution that organizes classes on a semester calendar system. The campus is situated in a suburban setting. Founded in 1826, first ABA approved in 1945, and an AALS member, University of Virginia School of Law offers JD, JD/MA, JD/MBA, JD/MPP, JD/MS, JD/PhD, LLM, and SJD degrees.

Faculty consists of 67 full-time and 3 part-time members in 2000–2001. 13 full-time faculty members are women. 100% of all faculty members have a JD degree. Of all faculty members, 3% are Asian/Pacific Islander, 7% are African American, 90% are white.

Application Information *Required:* LSAT, LSDAS, application form, application fee of $65, baccalaureate degree, 2 letters of recommendation, personal statement, college transcripts. *Application deadline* for fall term is January 15.

Costs The 2000–2001 tuition was $14,655 full-time for state residents. Tuition was $22,536 full-time for nonresidents. Fees: $1148 full-time. Students are required to have their own computers.

Financial Aid Loans, loan repayment assistance program (LRAP), merit-based grants/scholarships, need-based grants/scholarships, and federal work-study loans are available. To apply for financial assistance, students must complete the Free Application for Federal Student Aid, institutional forms. Completed financial aid forms should be received by February 15. Financial aid contact: Jerome W. D. Stokes, Senior Assistant Dean for Admissions and

AT a GLANCE

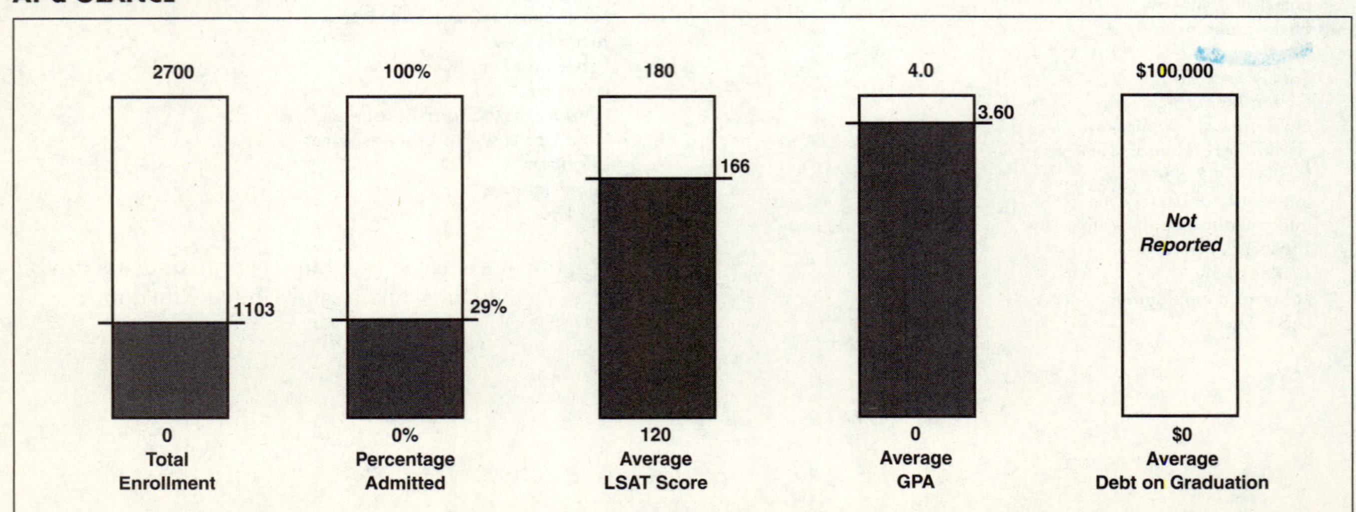

Degree Options

Degree	Total Credits Required	Length of Program
JD–Juris Doctor	86	3 yrs, full-time only [day]
JD/MA–Juris Doctor/Master of Arts–available in history, government, economics, English, philosophy, sociology, marine affairs, and bioethics		
JD/MBA–Juris Doctor/Master of Business Administration		4 yrs, full-time only [day]
JD/MPP–Juris Doctor/Master of Public Planning		
JD/MS–Juris Doctor/Master of Science–Accounting		
JD/PhD–Juris Doctor/Doctor of Philosophy–Government		
LLM–Master of Laws	24	1 yr, full-time only [day]
SJD–Doctor of Juridical Science		

Financial Aid, 580 Massie Road, Charlottesville, VA 22903-1789. Phone: 804-924-7805. Fax: 804-982-2128. E-mail: lawadmit@virginia.edu

Law School Library Morris Law Library has 13 professional staff members and contains more than 813,160 volumes and 13,198 periodicals. 742 seats are available in the library. When classes are in session, the library is open 110 hours per week.

WESTLAW and LEXIS-NEXIS are available, as are the World Wide Web, online bibliographic services, and CD-ROM players. 70 computer workstations are available to students in the library. Special law collections include oceans law, commonwealth law.

First-Year Program Class size in the average section is 60; 100% of the first-year courses are taught by full-time faculty.

Upper-Level Program Among the electives are:

Administrative Law
Advocacy
★ Appellate Litigation
★ Business and Corporate Law
★ Children's Advocacy
Consumer Law
★ Criminal Defense
Criminal Prosecution
★ Employment Law
Entertainment Law
★ Environmental Law
Evidence
Family Law
Feminist Jurisprudence
★ First Amendment
Government/Regulation
Health Care/Human Services

★ Housing Law
★ Human Rights
Indian/Tribal Law
Insurance Law
Intellectual Property
★ International/Comparative Law
Jurisprudence
Labor Law
Land Use Law/Natural Resources
Lawyering Skills
Legal History/Philosophy
Legislation
Litigation
★ Local Government
★ Maritime Law
Media Law
Mediation
Probate Law
★ Public Interest
Race and Law
Securities
Tax Law
(★ *indicates an area of special strength*)

Clinical Courses Students receive degree credit for clinical courses. (Clinical practicum is not required.) Among the clinical areas offered are:

Advocacy
Appellate Litigation
Criminal Defense
Criminal Prosecution
Employment Law
Environmental Law
Family Law
Family Practice
First Amendment
Housing Law
Human Rights
Intellectual Property
Local Government

WASHINGTON AND LEE UNIVERSITY
SCHOOL OF LAW

Lexington, Virginia

INFORMATION CONTACT

Sidney Evans, Director of Admissions
Sydney Lewis Hall
Lexington, VA 24450

Phone: 540-463-8503   Fax: 540-463-8488
Web site: http://www.wlu.edu/

LAW STUDENT PROFILE [2000–2001]

FULL-TIME Enrollment: 363
Women: 41%   Men: 59%

RACIAL or ETHNIC COMPOSITION
African American, 6%; Asian/Pacific Islander, 3%; Hispanic,
1%; Native American, 1%; International, 0.3%

APPLICANTS and ADMITTEES
Number applied: 1,791
Admitted: 514
Percentage accepted: 29%
Seats available: 120
Median LSAT score: 164
Average GPA: 3.4

Washington and Lee University School of Law is a
private institution that organizes classes on a semester
calendar system. The campus is situated in a small-town
setting. Founded in 1849, first ABA approved in 1933,
and an AALS member, Washington and Lee University
School of Law offers a JD degree.

Faculty consists of 33 full-time and 4 part-time members
in 2000–2001. 8 full-time faculty members are women.
100% of all faculty members have a JD; 18.18% have
advanced law degrees. Of all faculty members, 3.03% are
Asian/Pacific Islander, 6.06% are African American,
90.91% are white.

Application Information *Required:* LSAT, LSDAS,
application form, application fee of $40, baccalaureate
degree, 2 letters of recommendation. *Application deadline*
for fall term is February 1 (priority date). Applications
are processed on a rolling basis.

Financial Aid In 2000–2001, 95% of all students received
some form of financial aid. Fellowships, graduate
assistantships, loans, merit-based grants/scholarships,
need-based grants/scholarships, and federal work-study
loans are available. The average student debt at graduation is $60,305. To apply for financial assistance, students
must complete the Free Application for Federal Student
Aid. Completed financial aid forms should be received by
February 15. Financial aid contact: Cynthia Hintze,
Associate Director of Financial Aid, Gilliam House 110,
Washington and Lee University, Lexington, VA 24450.
Phone: 540-463-8032. Fax: 540-463-8062. E-mail:
chintze@wlu.edu

AT a GLANCE

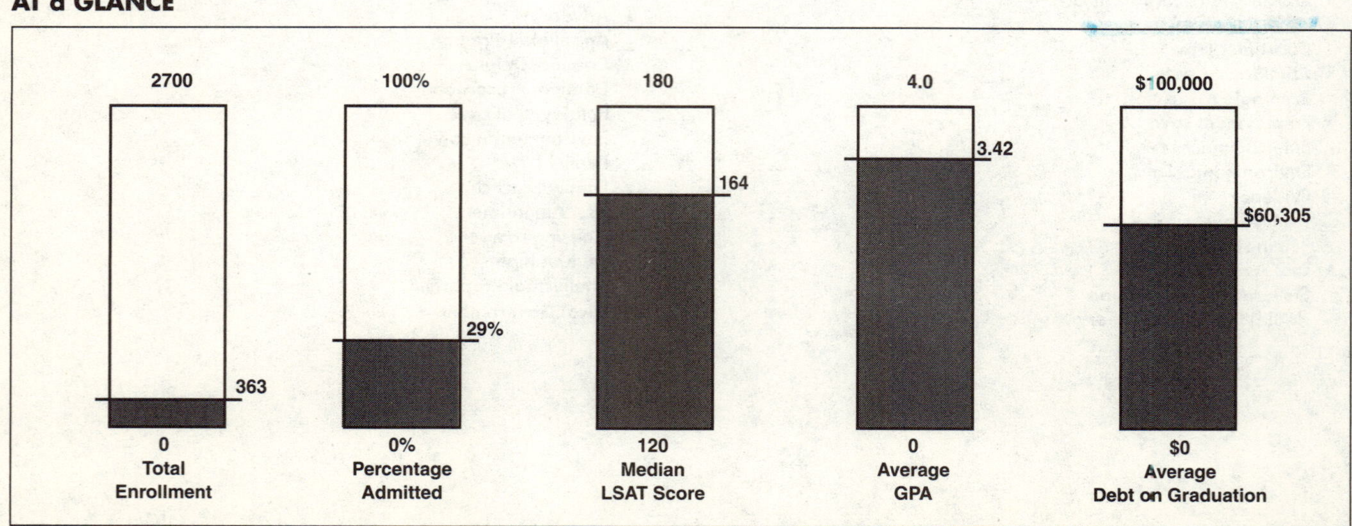

Degree Options		
Degree	**Total Credits Required**	**Length of Program**
JD–Doctor of Laws	85	3 yrs, full-time only [day]

Law School Library Wilbur C. Hall Law Library has 7 professional staff members and contains more than 382,913 volumes and 4,349 periodicals. 551 seats are available in the library. When classes are in session, the library is open 168 hours per week.

WESTLAW and LEXIS-NEXIS are available, as are the World Wide Web and online bibliographic services. 80 computer workstations are available to students in the library. Special law collections include United States Document Depository, papers of Lewis F. Powell, Jr., papers of M. Caldwell Butler (Bankruptcy Reform and Impeachment of Richard M. Nixon).

First-Year Program Class size in the average section is 35; 100% of the first-year courses are taught by full-time faculty.

Upper-Level Program Class size in the average section is 23. Among the electives are:

Administrative Law
★ Advocacy
★ Black Lung
Business and Corporate Law
★ Capital Defense
Civil Litigation
Consumer Law
★ Criminal Defense
★ Criminal Prosecution
Education Law
Entertainment Law
Environmental Law
Family Law
General Practice

Government/Regulation
Health Care/Human Services
Indian/Tribal Law
Intellectual Property
International/Comparative Law
★ Judicial Clerkship
Jurisprudence
Labor Law
Land Use Law/Natural Resources
★ Lawyering Skills
Legal History/Philosophy
★ Litigation
Maritime Law
Media Law
Mediation
★ Prison
Probate Law
Public Interest
Securities
Tax Law
(★ *indicates an area of special strength*)

Clinical Courses Students receive degree credit for clinical courses. (Clinical practicum is not required.) Among the clinical areas offered are:

Advocacy
Black Lung
Capital Defense
Civil Litigation
Criminal Defense
Criminal Prosecution
General Practice
Judicial Clerkship
Mental Health and Law
Prison
Public Interest

GONZAGA UNIVERSITY
SCHOOL OF LAW

Spokane, Washington

LAW STUDENT PROFILE [2000–2001]

FULL-TIME   Enrollment: 446
Women: 48%   Men: 52%

PART-TIME   Enrollment: 26
Women: 46%   Men: 54%

RACIAL or ETHNIC COMPOSITION
African American, 3%; Asian/Pacific Islander, 6%; Hispanic, 4%; Native American, 3%

APPLICANTS and ADMITTEES
Number applied: 1,002
Admitted: 600
Percentage accepted: 60%
Seats available: 180
Average LSAT score: 150
Average GPA: 3.1

Gonzaga University School of Law is a private institution that organizes classes on a semester calendar system. The campus is situated in a suburban setting. Founded in 1912, first ABA approved in 1955, and an AALS member, Gonzaga University School of Law offers JD, JD/MAC, and JD/MBA degrees.

Faculty consists of 30 full-time and 35 part-time members in 2000–2001. 12 full-time faculty members and 7 part-time faculty members are women. 100% of all faculty members have a JD; 23% have advanced law degrees. Of all faculty members, 100% are white.

Application Information *Required:* LSAT, LSDAS, application form, application fee of $40, baccalaureate degree, personal statement, college transcripts, resume. *Recommended:* 3 letters of recommendation. *Application deadline* for fall term is April 1 (priority date). Applications are processed on a rolling basis.

Costs The 2000–2001 tuition was $19,740 full-time; $658 per credit part-time. Fees: $90 full-time; $25 per semester part-time. Tuition and fees vary according to course load and degree level.

Financial Aid In 2000–2001, 90% of all students received some form of financial aid. Loans, merit-based grants/scholarships, need-based grants/scholarships, and federal work-study loans are available. The average student debt at graduation is $69,000. To apply for financial assistance, students must complete the Free Application for Federal Student Aid, scholarship specific applications. Completed financial aid forms should be received by March 15. Financial aid contact: Joan Henning, Coordi-

AT a GLANCE

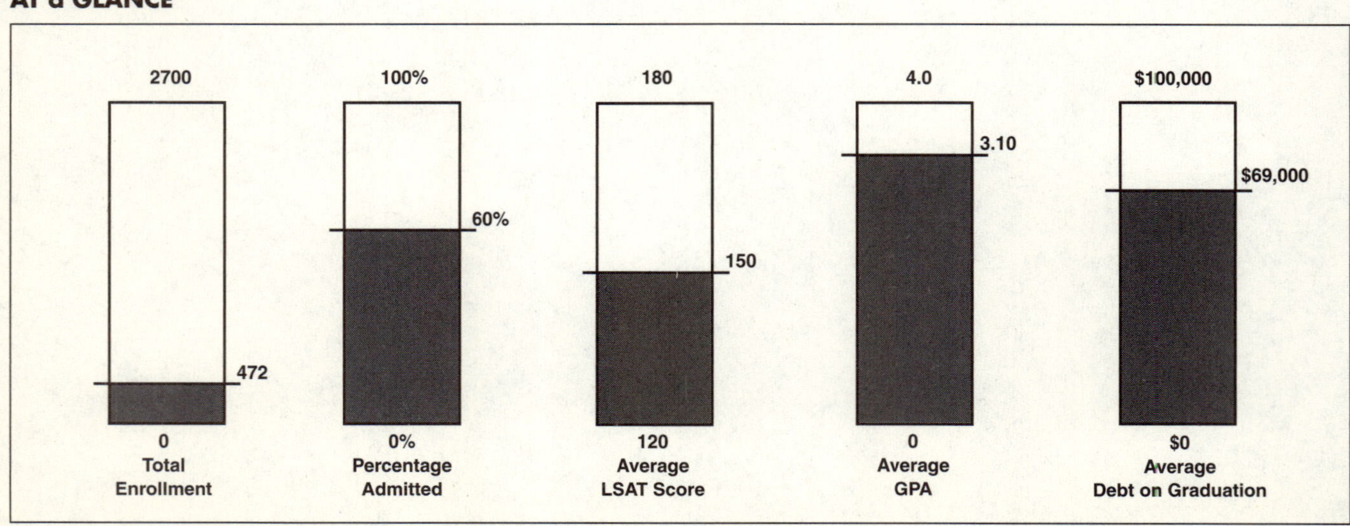

Degree Options

Degree	Total Credits Required	Length of Program
JD–Doctor of Law	90	3–4 yrs, full-time or part-time [day, summer]
JD/MAC–Juris Doctor/Master of Accounting–Dual-degree Program	120	4–4.5 yrs, full-time or part-time [day, evening, summer]
JD/MBA–Juris Doctor/Master of Business Administration–Dual-degree Program	123	4–4.5 yrs, full-time or part-time [day, evening, summer]

nator of Financial Services, PO Box 3528, Spokane, WA 99220. Phone: 509-323-3859. Fax: 509-323-5710. E-mail: jhenning@lawschool.gonzaga.edu

Law School Library Gonzaga University Chasteck School of Law Library has 11 professional staff members and contains more than 257,667 volumes and 2,784 periodicals. 476 seats are available in the library. When classes are in session, the library is open 108 hours per week.

WESTLAW and LEXIS-NEXIS are available, as are the World Wide Web, online bibliographic services, and CD-ROM players. 85 computer workstations are available to students in the library. Special law collections include ABA Archive Files; American Law Institute Collection; Native American Legal Materials; Hein's Federal Legislative History; Hein's Legal Thesis; Selective 19th Century Legal Treatises; Canon Law Collection; Karl Llewellyn Papers.

First-Year Program Class size in the average section is 90; 100% of the first-year courses are taught by full-time faculty.

Upper-Level Program Class size in the average section is 35. Among the electives are:

Administrative Law
Admiralty Law
Advocacy
Alternative Dispute Resolution
Antitrust Law
Appellate Law
Bankruptcy
★ Business and Corporate Law
Business Organizations
Business Planning
City and Town Law
Civil Procedure
Civil Rights
Commercial Law
Community Property
Conflict of Laws
Constitutional Law
Consumer Law
Corporate Taxation
Creditor's Rights
Criminal Law
Criminal Procedure
Deferred Compensation
Education Law
Elder Law
Employment Law
★ Environmental Law

Estate & Gift Taxation
Estate Planning
Evidence
Family Law
Federal Income Tax
Federal Jurisdiction
Government/Regulation
Indian/Tribal Law
Insurance Law
Intellectual Property
International Business Transactions
International Law
International/Comparative Law
Jurisprudence
Juvenile Law
Labor Law
★ Land Use Law/Natural Resources
Landlord/Tenant
Law and Philosophy
Lawyering Skills
Legal Research
Legal Writing
Litigation
Maritime Law
Media Law
Mediation
NAFTA Law
Natural Resources
Negotiation
Oil and Gas
Probate Law
Product Liability
Professional Responsibility
Property/Real Estate
Public Benefits
★ Public Interest
Public Lands
Real Estate Transactions
Remedies
Securities
Securities Regulation
Separation of Powers
Sports Law
State Constitutional Law
Tax Law
Trial Advocacy
Water Law
Wills & Trusts
Women and the Law
Workers' Compensation
(★ *indicates an area of special strength*)

Clinical Courses Students receive degree credit for clinical courses. (Clinical practicum is not required.) Among the clinical areas offered are:

Administrative Law

Bankruptcy
Civil Rights
Criminal Defense
Disability Law
Elder Law
Elderly Advocacy
Environmental Law
Family Law
Family Practice

General Practice
Immigration
Indian/Tribal Law
International Criminal Law
International Law
Litigation
Public Interest

SEATTLE UNIVERSITY
SCHOOL OF LAW

Seattle, Washington

INFORMATION CONTACT

Carol Cochran, Director of Admissions
900 Broadway
Seattle, WA 98122-4340

Phone: 206-398-4200   Fax: 206-398-4058
E-mail: ccochran@seattleu.edu
Web site: http://www.law.seattleu.edu/

LAW STUDENT PROFILE [2000–2001]

FULL-TIME   Enrollment: 716
Women: 57%   Men: 43%

PART-TIME   Enrollment: 215
Women: 50%   Men: 50%

RACIAL or ETHNIC COMPOSITION
African American, 5%; Asian/Pacific Islander, 11%; Hispanic, 4%; Native American, 2%; International, 1%

APPLICANTS and ADMITTEES
Number applied: 1,266
Admitted: 799
Percentage accepted: 63%
Seats available: 320
Average LSAT score: 155
Average GPA: 3.2

Seattle University School of Law is a private institution that organizes classes on a semester calendar system. The campus is situated in an urban setting. Founded in 1972, first ABA approved in 1975, and an AALS member, Seattle University School of Law offers JD, JD/MBA, JD/MIB, and JD/MS degrees.

Faculty consists of 42 full-time and 34 part-time members in 2000–2001. 21 full-time faculty members and 9 part-time faculty members are women. 99.9% of all faculty members have a JD; 10% have advanced law degrees. Of all faculty members, 2.6% are Native American, 7.7% are Asian/Pacific Islander, 5.1% are African American, 2.6% are Hispanic, 82% are white.

Application Information *Required:* LSAT, LSDAS, application form, application fee of $50, baccalaureate degree, 2 letters of recommendation, personal statement, college transcripts, resume. *Application deadline* for fall term is April 1. Applications are processed on a rolling basis.

Costs The 2000–2001 tuition was $20,190 full-time; $673 per credit part-time. Students are required to have their own computers.

Financial Aid In 2000–2001, 93% of all students received some form of financial aid. Loans, loan repayment assistance program (LRAP), merit-based grants/scholarships, need-based grants/scholarships, and federal work-study loans are available. The average student debt at graduation is $66,700. To apply for financial assistance, students must complete the Free Application for Federal Student Aid. Completed financial aid forms

AT a GLANCE

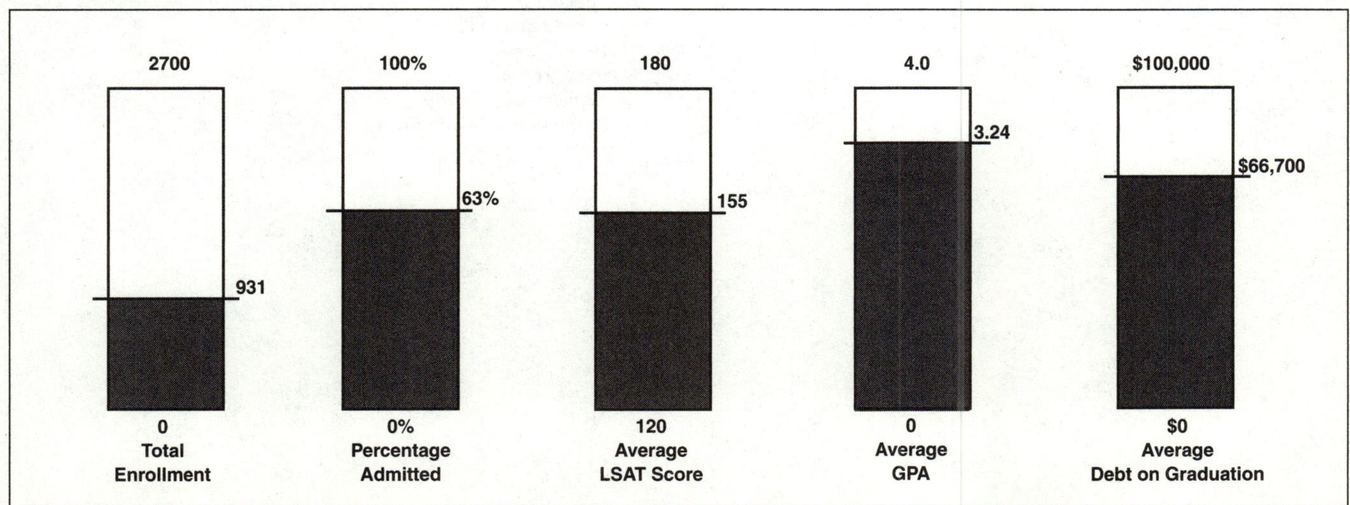

Degree Options

Degree	Total Credits Required	Length of Program
JD–Juris Doctor	90	3–4 yrs, full-time or part-time [day, evening, summer]
JD/MBA–Juris Doctor/Master of Business Administration		4–5 yrs, full-time or part-time [day, evening, summer]
JD/MIB–Juris Doctor/Master of International Business		4–5 yrs, full-time or part-time [day, evening, summer]
JD/MS–Juris Doctor/Master of Science–Finance		4–5 yrs, full-time or part-time [day, evening, summer]

should be received by April 1. Financial aid contact: Kathleen D. Koch, Director of Financial Aid, 900 Broadway, Seattle, WA 98122. Phone: 206-398-4250. Fax: 206-398-4058. E-mail: lawfa@seattleu.edu

Law School Library Seattle University Law Library has 6 professional staff members and contains more than 325,128 volumes and 3,806 periodicals. 313 seats are available in the library. When classes are in session, the library is open 119 hours per week.

WESTLAW and LEXIS-NEXIS are available, as are the World Wide Web, online bibliographic services, and CD-ROM players. 20 computer workstations are available to students in the library.

First-Year Program Class size in the average section is 83; 100% of the first-year courses are taught by full-time faculty.

Upper-Level Program Class size in the average section is 65. Among the electives are:

- Administrative Law
- ★ Advocacy
- Bankruptcy
- ★ Business and Corporate Law
- ★ Civil Litigation
- ★ Commercial Law
- Constitutional Law
- Consumer Law
- ★ Criminal Law
- Education
- Education Law
- Entertainment Law
- ★ Environmental Law
- ★ Estate Planning

- Family Law
- Feminist Jurisprudence
- Government/Regulation
- Health Care/Human Services
- ★ Health Law
- Immigration
- Indian/Tribal Law
- ★ Intellectual Property
- ★ International/Comparative Law
- ★ Jurisprudence
- ★ Labor Law
- ★ Land Use Law/Natural Resources
- Lawyering Skills
- Legal History/Philosophy
- Litigation
- Maritime Law
- Media Law
- Mediation
- Probate Law
- Professional Responsibility
- ★ Public Interest
- ★ Securities
- ★ Tax Law

(★ indicates an area of special strength)

Clinical Courses Students receive degree credit for clinical courses. (Clinical practicum is not required.) Among the clinical areas offered are:

- Administrative Law
- Bankruptcy
- Civil Litigation
- Criminal Defense
- Education
- Entertainment Law
- Health Law
- Immigration
- Intellectual Property
- Professional Responsibility

UNIVERSITY OF WASHINGTON
SCHOOL OF LAW

Seattle, Washington

LAW STUDENT PROFILE [2000–2001]

FULL-TIME   Enrollment: 593
Women: 49%   Men: 51%

PART-TIME   Enrollment: 44
Women: 36%   Men: 64%

RACIAL or ETHNIC COMPOSITION
African American, 2%; Asian/Pacific Islander, 13%; Hispanic, 6%; Native American, 1%; International, 5%

APPLICANTS and ADMITTEES
Number applied: 1,643
Admitted: 487
Percentage accepted: 30%
Seats available: 165
Median LSAT score: 162
Average GPA: 3.6

University of Washington School of Law is a public institution that organizes classes on a quarter calendar system. The campus is situated in an urban setting. Founded in 1899, first ABA approved in 1924, and an AALS member, University of Washington School of Law offers JD, JD/MA, JD/MBA, LLM, and PhD degrees.

Faculty consists of 43 full-time and 19 part-time members in 2000–2001. 18 full-time faculty members and 7 part-time faculty members are women. 96% of all faculty members have a JD; 19% have advanced law degrees. Of all faculty members, 4% are Asian/Pacific Islander, 6% are African American, 90% are white.

Application Information *Required:* LSAT, LSDAS, application form, application fee of $50, 2 letters of recommendation, baccalaureate degree, personal statement, college transcripts. *Application deadline* for fall term is January 15.

Costs The 2000–2001 tuition was $6216 full-time for state residents. Tuition was $15,326 full-time for nonresidents. Fees: $12,432 full-time.

Financial Aid In 2000–2001, 75% of all students received some form of financial aid. 4 fellowships; 10 research assistantships, totaling $4640, were awarded. Fellowships, loans, loan repayment assistance program (LRAP), merit-based grants/scholarships, need-based grants/scholarships, and federal work-study loans are also available. The average student debt at graduation is $50,000. To apply for financial assistance, students must complete the Free Application for Federal Student Aid. Completed financial aid forms should be received by

AT a GLANCE

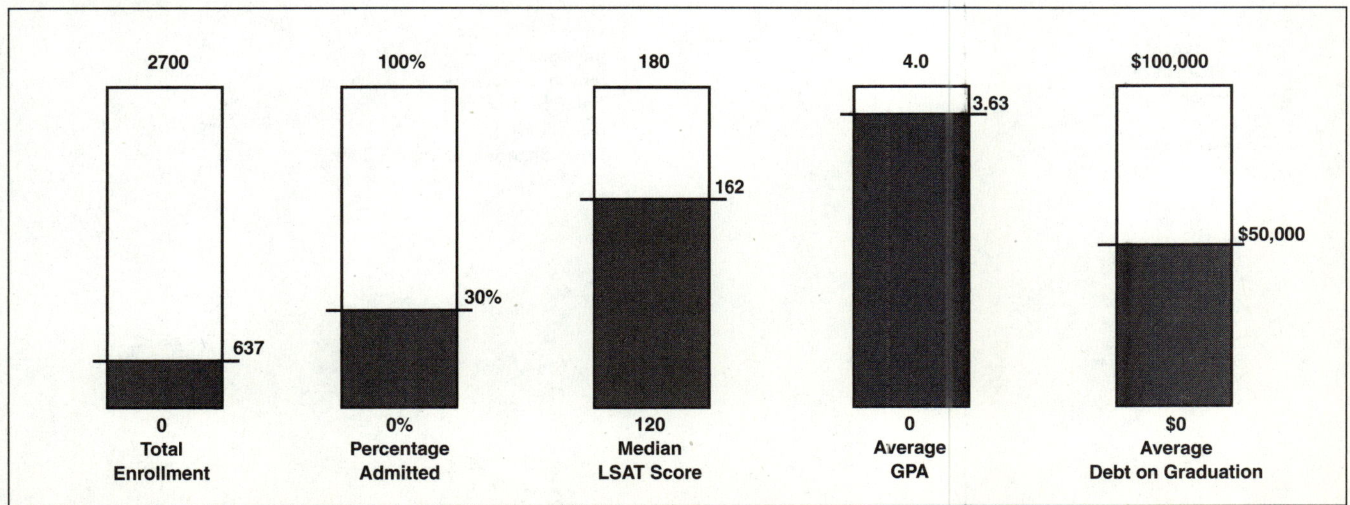

Degree Options

Degree	Total Credits Required	Length of Program
JD–Doctor of Laws	135	3 yrs, full-time only [day]
JD/MA–Juris Doctor/Master of Arts–International Studies	180	4 yrs, full-time only [day]
JD/MBA–Juris Doctor/Master of Business Administration–Business	180	4 yrs, full-time only [day]
LLM–Master of Laws–Taxation	36	1 yr, full-time or part-time [day, evening]
LLM–Master of Laws–Asian and Comparative Law	36	1 yr, full-time only [day]
PhD–Doctor of Philosophy–Asian and Comparative Law	60	2–3 yrs, full-time only [day]

February 28. Financial aid contact: Catherine Schaeffer, Financial Aid Coordinator, 1100 Northeast Campus Parkway, Seattle, WA 98105-6617. Phone: 206-543-4552. Fax: 206-546-5671. E-mail: uwlawaid@u.washington.edu

Law School Library Marian Gould Gallagher Law Library has 14 professional staff members and contains more than 518,686 volumes and 8,041 periodicals. 372 seats are available in the library. When classes are in session, the library is open 89 hours per week.

WESTLAW and LEXIS-NEXIS are available, as are the World Wide Web, online bibliographic services, and CD-ROM players. 22 computer workstations are available to students in the library. Special law collections include East Asian Law collection.

First-Year Program Class size in the average section is 105; 100% of the first-year courses are taught by full-time faculty.

Upper-Level Program Class size in the average section is 23. Among the electives are:

  Administrative Law
  Advocacy
  Appellate Litigation
  Asian Legal Systems
  Business and Corporate Law
  Conflict of Laws
  Constitutional Law
  Criminal Defense
  Criminal Procedure
  Dispute Resolution
  Education Law
  Employment Law
★ Environmental Law
  Estate Planning
  Family Law
  Government/Regulation
★ Health Care/Human Services
  Immigration
  Indian/Tribal Law
  Insurance Law
  Intellectual Property
★ International/Comparative Law
  Jurisprudence
  Juvenile Law
  Labor Law
  Land Use Law/Natural Resources
  Lawyering Skills
  Legal History/Philosophy
  Litigation
  Maritime Law
  Mediation
  Public Interest
  Securities
  Tax Law
  Unemployment Compensation
(★ *indicates an area of special strength*)

Clinical Courses Students receive degree credit for clinical courses. (Clinical practicum is not required.) Among the clinical areas offered are:

  Appellate Litigation
  Criminal Defense
  Employment Law
  Family Law
  Family Practice
  General Practice
  Immigration
  Indian/Tribal Law
  Juvenile Law
  Mediation
  Unemployment Compensation

WEST VIRGINIA UNIVERSITY
COLLEGE OF LAW

Morgantown, West Virginia

INFORMATION CONTACT

Janet Long Armistead, Assistant Dean for
Admissions and Student Affairs
PO Box 6130
Morgantown, WV 26506-6130

Phone: 304-293-7320   Fax: 304-293-6891
E-mail: janet.armistead@mail.wvu.edu
Web site: http://www.wvu.edu/~law/

LAW STUDENT PROFILE [2000–2001]

FULL-TIME   Enrollment: 420
Women: 42%   Men: 58%

PART-TIME   Enrollment: 19
Women: 53%   Men: 47%

RACIAL or ETHNIC COMPOSITION
African American, 4%; Asian/Pacific Islander, 1%; Hispanic, 1%; Native American, 0.2%; International, 1%

APPLICANTS and ADMITTEES
Number applied: 511
Admitted: 255
Percentage accepted: 50%
Seats available: 145
Average LSAT score: 153
Average GPA: 3.3

West Virginia University College of Law is a public institution that organizes classes on a semester calendar system. The campus is situated in a small-town setting. Founded in 1894, first ABA approved in 1923, and an AALS member, West Virginia University College of Law offers JD, JD/MBA, and JD/MPA degrees.

Faculty consists of 24 full-time and 18 part-time members in 2000–2001. 8 full-time faculty members and 4 part-time faculty members are women. 100% of all faculty members have a JD; 34% have advanced law degrees.

Application Information *Required:* LSAT, LSDAS, application form, application fee of $45, baccalaureate degree, 3 letters of recommendation, personal statement, writing sample, college transcripts. *Recommended:* resume. *Application deadline* for fall term is March 1. Applications are processed on a rolling basis.

Costs The 1999–2000 tuition was $5652 full-time for state residents. Tuition was $13,162 full-time for nonresidents.

Financial Aid In 2000–2001, 81% of all students received some form of financial aid. 3 research assistantships, 9 teaching assistantships, were awarded. Fellowships, graduate assistantships, loans, loan repayment assistance program (LRAP), merit-based grants/scholarships, need-based grants/scholarships, and federal work-study loans are also available. To apply for financial assistance, students must complete the Free Application for Federal Student Aid. Completed financial aid forms should be received by March 1. Financial aid contact: Joanna

AT a GLANCE

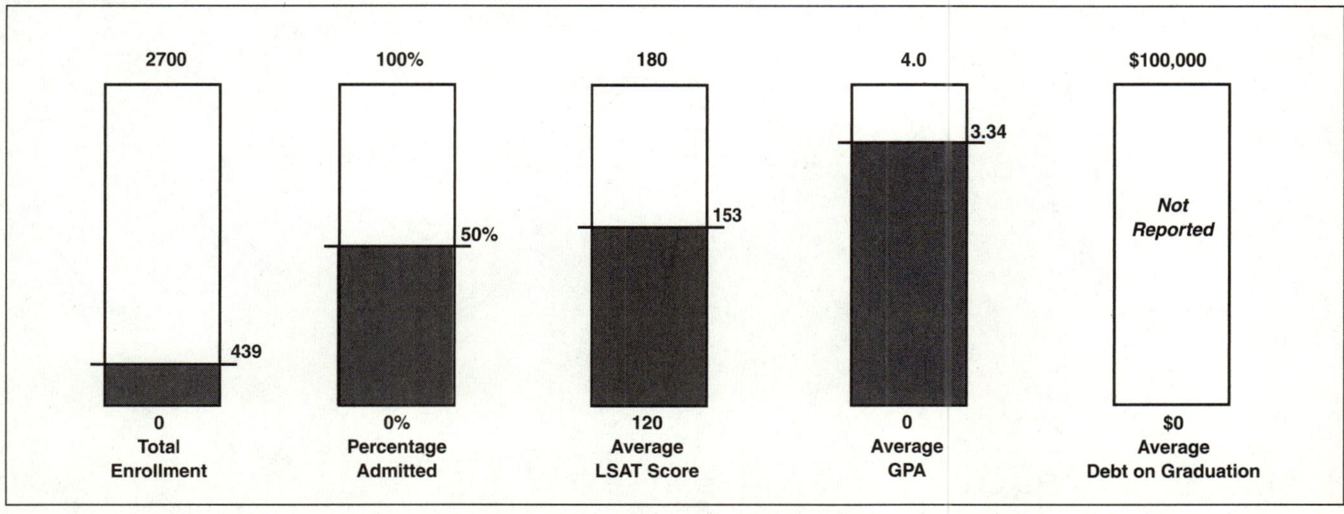

Degree Options

Degree	Total Credits Required	Length of Program
JD–Juris Doctor–Doctor of Jurisprudence JD/MBA–Juris Doctor/Master of Business Administration–Joint-degree Program JD/MPA–Juris Doctor/Master of Professional Accountancy–Joint-degree Program	93	3–4 yrs, full-time or part-time [day]

Hastings, Financial Aid Counselor, PO Box 6130, Morgantown, WV 26506-6130. Phone: 304-293-5302. Fax: 304-293-6891. E-mail: jhasting@wvu.edu

Law School Library West Virginia University College of Law Library has 4 professional staff members and contains more than 265,000 volumes and 2,940 periodicals. 296 seats are available in the library. When classes are in session, the library is open 100 hours per week.

WESTLAW and LEXIS-NEXIS are available, as are the World Wide Web, online bibliographic services, and CD-ROM players. 35 computer workstations are available to students in the library. Special law collections include Andrew J. Colborn and Harry B. Colborn Rare book Room.

First-Year Program Class size in the average section is 70; 100% of the first-year courses are taught by full-time faculty.

Upper-Level Program Class size in the average section is 50. Among the electives are:

Administrative Law
★ Advocacy
Appellate Advocacy
Bankruptcy
Business and Corporate Law
Civil Procedure
Conflict of Laws
Consumer Law
Energy Law
Entertainment Law
Environmental Law
Family Law
Government/Regulation
Health Care/Human Services
Intellectual Property
International/Comparative Law
Jurisprudence
Labor Law
Land Use Law/Natural Resources
★ Lawyering Skills
Legal History/Philosophy
★ Litigation
Media Law
Mediation
Probate Law
Public Interest
Securities
Tax Law

(★ indicates an area of special strength)

Clinical Courses Students receive degree credit for clinical courses. (Clinical practicum is not required.) Among the clinical areas offered are:

Civil Litigation
Family Practice
General Practice
Government Litigation
Immigration
Public Interest

International exchange programs permit students to visit France and Russian Federation.

MARQUETTE UNIVERSITY
LAW SCHOOL

Milwaukee, Wisconsin

INFORMATION CONTACT

Edward A. Kawczynski, Assistant Dean for
Admissions
Sensenbrenner Hall
1103 West Wisconsin Avenue
PO Box 1881
Milwaukee, WI 53201-1881

Phone: 414-288-6767   Fax: 414-288-0676
E-mail: edward.kawczynski@marquette.edu
Web site: http://www.marquette.edu/law/

LAW STUDENT PROFILE [2000–2001]

FULL-TIME   Enrollment: 447
Women: 44%   Men: 56%

PART-TIME   Enrollment: 169
Women: 47%   Men: 53%

APPLICANTS and ADMITTEES

Number applied: 868
Admitted: 438
Percentage accepted: 50%
Seats available: 160
Average LSAT score: 155
Average GPA: 3.3

Marquette University Law School is a private institution
that organizes classes on a semester calendar system. The
campus is situated in an urban setting. Founded in 1892,
first ABA approved in 1925, and an AALS member,
Marquette University Law School offers JD, JD/MA, and
JD/MBA degrees.

Faculty consists of 32 full-time and 63 part-time
members in 2000–2001. 11 full-time faculty members
and 18 part-time faculty members are women. 100% of
all faculty members have a JD; 9% have advanced law
degrees. Of all faculty members, 6.5% are African
American, 3.2% are Hispanic, 90.3% are white.

Application Information *Required:* LSAT, LSDAS,
application form, application fee of $40, baccalaureate
degree, 2 letters of recommendation, personal statement,
essay, college transcripts, resume. *Application deadline* for
fall term is April 1. Applications are processed on a
rolling basis.

Financial Aid In 2000–2001, 78% of all students received
some form of financial aid. Loans, merit-based grants/
scholarships, and federal work-study loans are available.
The average student debt at graduation is $62,000. To
apply for financial assistance, students must complete the
Free Application for Federal Student Aid. Completed
financial aid forms should be received by March 1.
Financial aid contact: Carla Smith-Liebich, Assistant
Director of Student Financial Aid, 1212 Building, Room
415, Milwaukee, WI 53201. Phone: 414-288-0200. Fax:
414-288-1718. E-mail: financialaid@marquette.edu

AT a GLANCE

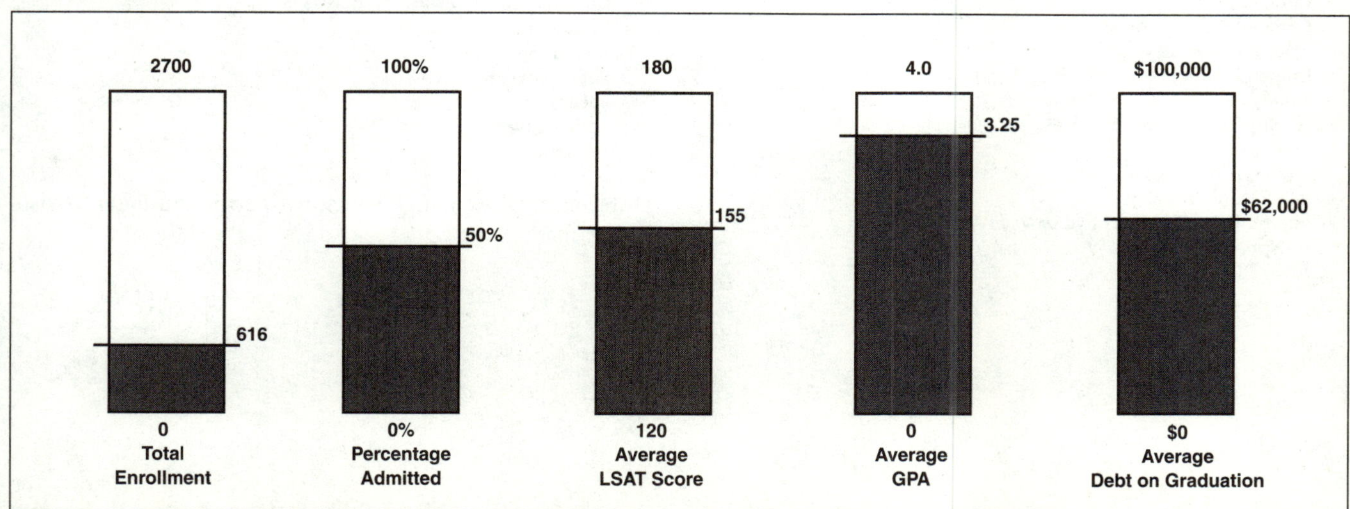

Degree Options

Degree	Total Credits Required	Length of Program
JD–Doctor of Laws	90	3–6 yrs, full-time or part-time [day, evening, summer]
JD/MA–Juris Doctor/Master of Arts–Political Science		4 yrs, full-time or part-time [day, evening, summer]
JD/MA–Juris Doctor/Master of Arts–International Affairs		4 yrs, full-time or part-time [day, evening, summer]
JD/MA–Juris Doctor/Master of Arts–Social & Applied Philosophy		4 yrs, full-time or part-time [day, evening, summer]
JD/MA–Juris Doctor/Master of Arts–History of Philosophy		4 yrs, full-time or part-time [day, evening, summer]
JD/MA–Juris Doctor/Master of Arts–Bioethics		4 yrs, full-time or part-time [day, evening, summer]
JD/MBA–Juris Doctor/Master of Business Administration		4 yrs, full-time or part-time [day, evening, summer]

Law School Library Legal Research Center has 9 professional staff members and contains more than 281,871 volumes and 3,435 periodicals. 368 seats are available in the library. When classes are in session, the library is open 106 hours per week.

WESTLAW and LEXIS-NEXIS are available, as are the World Wide Web, online bibliographic services, and CD-ROM players. 31 computer workstations are available to students in the library. Special law collections include Japanese Language Legal Materials.

First-Year Program Class size in the average section is 80; 99% of the first-year courses are taught by full-time faculty.

Upper-Level Program Class size in the average section is 28. Among the electives are:

 Administrative Law
 Advocacy
★ Business and Corporate Law
★ Commercial Law
 Criminal Defense
★ Criminal Law
 Criminal Prosecution
★ Environmental Law
★ Estate Planning
★ Family Law
★ Health Care/Human Services
 Immigration
 Indian/Tribal Law
★ Intellectual Property
★ International/Comparative Law
 Jurisprudence
 Juvenile Law

★ Labor Law
 Land Use Law/Natural Resources
★ Lawyering Skills
 Legal History/Philosophy
★ Litigation
★ Mediation
★ Public Interest
★ Real Estate Law
★ Securities
★ Sports Law
★ Tax Law

(★ *indicates an area of special strength*)

Clinical Courses Students receive degree credit for clinical courses. (Clinical practicum is not required.) Among the clinical areas offered are:

 Business and Corporate Law
 Criminal Defense
 Criminal Prosecution
 Environmental Law
 Family Law
 Health Care/Human Services
 Immigration
 Juvenile Law
 Labor Law
 Land Use Law/Natural Resources
 Litigation
 Mediation
 Public Interest
 Securities
 Sports Law
 Tax Law

International exchange programs permit students to visit Australia.

UNIVERSITY OF WISCONSIN–MADISON
LAW SCHOOL

Madison, Wisconsin

INFORMATION CONTACT

Director of Admissions
975 Bascom Mall
Madison, WI 53706-1399

Phone: 608-262-5914   Fax: 608-262-5485
Web site: http://www.law.wisc.edu/

LAW STUDENT PROFILE [2000–2001]

FULL-TIME   Enrollment: 813
Women: 46%   Men: 54%

PART-TIME   Enrollment: 50
Women: 48%   Men: 52%

RACIAL or ETHNIC COMPOSITION
African American, 9%; Asian/Pacific Islander, 9%; Hispanic,
6%; Native American, 3%

APPLICANTS and ADMITTEES
Number applied: 1,639
Admitted: 708
Percentage accepted: 43%
Seats available: 310
Average LSAT score: 157
Average GPA: 3.4

University of Wisconsin–Madison Law School is a
public institution that organizes classes on a semester
calendar system. The campus is situated in an urban
setting. Founded in 1868, first ABA approved in 1923,
and an AALS member, University of Wisconsin–Madison
Law School offers JD, JD/MA, JD/MAcc, JD/MBA,
JD/MLS, JD/MPA, JD/MPAd, JD/MS, JD/PhD, LLM, and
SJD degrees.

Faculty consists of 50 full-time members in 2000–2001.
100% of all faculty members have a JD; 21% have
advanced law degrees. Of all faculty members, 2% are
Native American, 6% are African American, 4% are
Hispanic, 88% are white.

Application Information *Required:* LSAT, LSDAS,
application form, application fee of $45, baccalaureate
degree, statement of residency form, personal statement.
Recommended: 3 letters of recommendation. *Application
deadline* is rolling. Students are required to have their
own computers.

Financial Aid Fellowships, graduate assistantships, loans,
merit-based grants/scholarships, need-based grants/
scholarships, and federal work-study loans are available.
The average student debt at graduation is $47,821. To
apply for financial assistance, students must complete the
Free Application for Federal Student Aid, institutional
forms. Completed financial aid forms should be received
by March 1. Financial aid contact: Dorothy Davis,
Financial Aid Officer, 975 Bascom Mall, Room 4314,
Madison, WI 53706. Phone: 608-262-1815. Fax: 608-262-
5485. E-mail: finaid@law.wisc.edu

AT a GLANCE

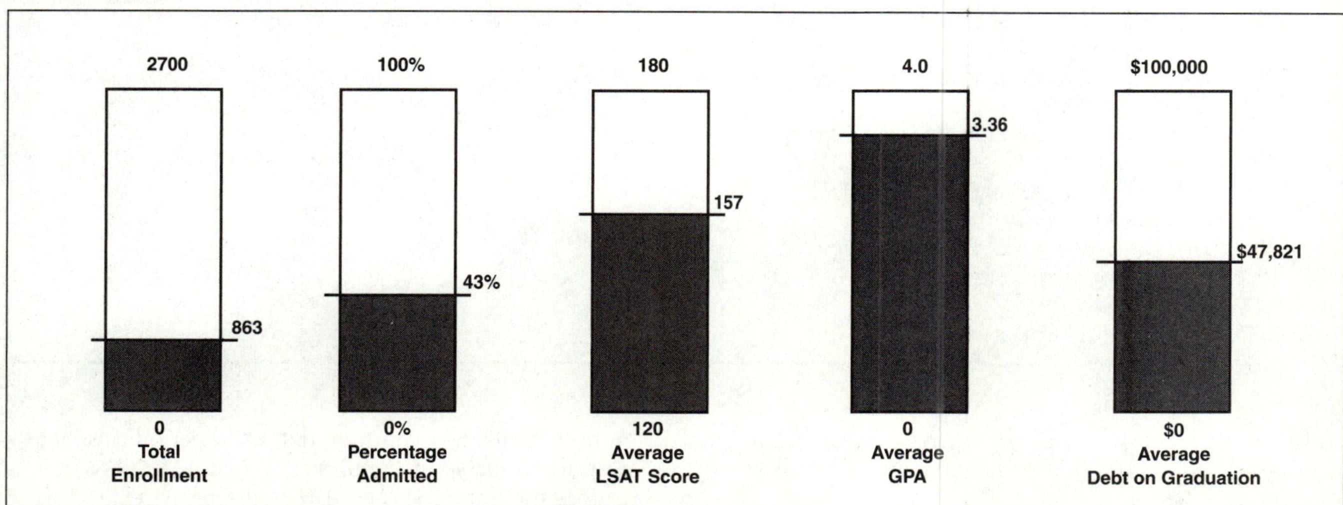

Degree Options

Degree	Total Credits Required	Length of Program
JD–Juris Doctor	90	
JD/MA–Juris Doctor/Master of Arts–Dual-degree: Public Affairs and Public Administration		3–6 yrs, full-time or part-time
JD/MA–Juris Doctor/Master of Arts–Dual-degree: Public Affairs and Policy Analysis		3–6 yrs, full-time or part-time
JD/MA–Juris Doctor/Master of Arts–Dual-degree: Latin American & Iberian Studies		
JD/MA–Juris Doctor/Master of Arts–Dual-degree: Business		
JD/MA–Juris Doctor/Master of Arts–Dual-degree: Public Policy and Administration		3–6 yrs, full-time or part-time
Certificate–Dual-degree: Accounting		
JD/MBA–Juris Doctor/Master of Business Administration		
JD/MBA–Juris Doctor/Master of Business Administration–Dual-degree: Business Administration		
JD/MLS–Juris Doctor/Master of Library Science–Dual-degree: Library Science		
JD/MPA–Juris Doctor/Master of Professional Accountancy–Dual-degree: Public Affairs Analysis		
JD/MPAd–Juris Doctor/Master of Public Administration–Dual-degree: Public Affairs Administration		
JD/MS–Juris Doctor/Master of Science–Dual-degree: Educational Administration		3–6 yrs, full-time or part-time
JD/MS–Juris Doctor/Master of Science–Dual-degree: Sociology		3–6 yrs, full-time or part-time
JD/MS–Juris Doctor/Master of Science–Dual-degree: Environmental Studies		3–6 yrs, full-time or part-time
JD/MS–Juris Doctor/Master of Science–Dual-degree: Water Resources Management		
JD/MS–Juris Doctor/Master of Science–Dual-degree: Business		
JD/MS–Juris Doctor/Master of Science–Dual-degree: Conservation Biology and Sustainable Development		
JD/MS–Juris Doctor/Master of Science–Dual-degree: Land Resources		3–6 yrs, full-time or part-time
JD/MS–Juris Doctor/Master of Science–Dual-degree: Social Work		3–6 yrs, full-time or part-time
JD/MS–Juris Doctor/Master of Science–Dual-degree: Industrial Relations		3–6 yrs, full-time or part-time
JD/PhD–Juris Doctor/Doctor of Philosophy–Dual-degree: Land Resources		
JD/PhD–Juris Doctor/Doctor of Philosophy–Dual-degree: Philosophy		
JD/PhD–Juris Doctor/Doctor of Philosophy–Dual-degree: Sociology		
JD/PhD–Juris Doctor/Doctor of Philosophy–Dual-degree: Rural Sociology		
LLM–Master of Laws		
SJD–Doctor of Juridical Science		

Law School Library The University of Wisconsin Law Library has 13 professional staff members and contains more than 480,846 volumes and 4,876 periodicals. 565 seats are available in the library. When classes are in session, the library is open 104 hours per week.

WESTLAW and LEXIS-NEXIS are available, as are the World Wide Web, online bibliographic services, and CD-ROM players. 43 computer workstations are available to students in the library.

First-Year Program Class size in the average section is 75; 94% of the first-year courses are taught by full-time faculty.

Upper-Level Program Among the electives are:

Accounting
Administrative Law
Advocacy
Appellate Litigation
Business and Corporate Law
Constitutional Law
★ Consumer Law
★ Criminal Defense
★ Criminal Prosecution
Environmental Law
Evidence
★ Family Law
★ General Practice
Government/Regulation
Health Care/Human Services
Health Law
Immigration
Indian/Tribal Law
Intellectual Property
★ International/Comparative Law
Jurisprudence
★ Labor Law
★ Land Rights/Natural Resource
★ Lawyering Skills
Legal History/Philosophy
Litigation
Maritime Law
Mediation
Probate Law
Property/Real Estate
Securities
Tax Law

(★ *indicates an area of special strength*)

Clinical Courses Students receive degree credit for clinical courses. Among the clinical areas offered are:

Consumer Law
Criminal Defense
Criminal Prosecution
Family Law
Family Practice
General Practice
Health Law
Immigration
Indian/Tribal Law

International exchange programs permit students to visit Brazil, Chile, Germany, Italy, Netherlands, and Peru.

UNIVERSITY OF WYOMING
COLLEGE OF LAW

Laramie, Wyoming

INFORMATION CONTACT

Robyn F. Kuiffen, Director of Admission-College of law
PO Box 3035
Laramie, WY 82071-3035

Phone: 307-766-6416   Fax: 307-766-6417
E-mail: awadmis@wyo.edu
Web site: http://www.uwyo.edu/law/law.htm

LAW STUDENT PROFILE [2000–2001]

FULL-TIME   Enrollment: 229
Women: 44%   Men: 56%

APPLICANTS and ADMITTEES
Number applied: 371
Admitted: 245
Percentage accepted: 66%
Seats available: 75
Average LSAT score: 149
Average GPA: 3.2

University of Wyoming College of Law is a public institution that organizes classes on a semester calendar system. The campus is situated in a small-town setting. Founded in 1920, first ABA approved in 1923, and an AALS member, University of Wyoming College of Law offers JD, JD/MBA, and JD/MPAd degrees.

Faculty consists of 14 full-time and 8 part-time members in 2000–2001. 6 full-time faculty members and 5 part-time faculty members are women. 100% of all faculty members have a JD; 13% have advanced law degrees. Of all faculty members, 100% are white.

Application Information *Required:* LSAT, LSDAS, application form, application fee of $35, baccalaureate degree, personal statement, college transcripts, essay. *Recommended:* recommendations, resume. *Application deadline* for fall term is March 15. Applications are processed on a rolling basis.

Costs The 2000–2001 tuition was $2708 full-time for area residents; $150 per credit hour part-time for area residents. Tuition was $433 per credit hour part-time for nonresidents. Tuition was $7790 full-time for international students. Fees: $10 per credit hour part-time.

Financial Aid 97 fellowships, totaling $1665; 7 teaching assistantships, were awarded. Graduate assistantships, loans, merit-based grants/scholarships, need-based grants/scholarships, and federal work-study loans are also available. The average student debt at graduation is $32,000. To apply for financial assistance, students must complete the Free Application for Federal Student Aid, institutional forms. Completed financial aid forms should

AT a GLANCE

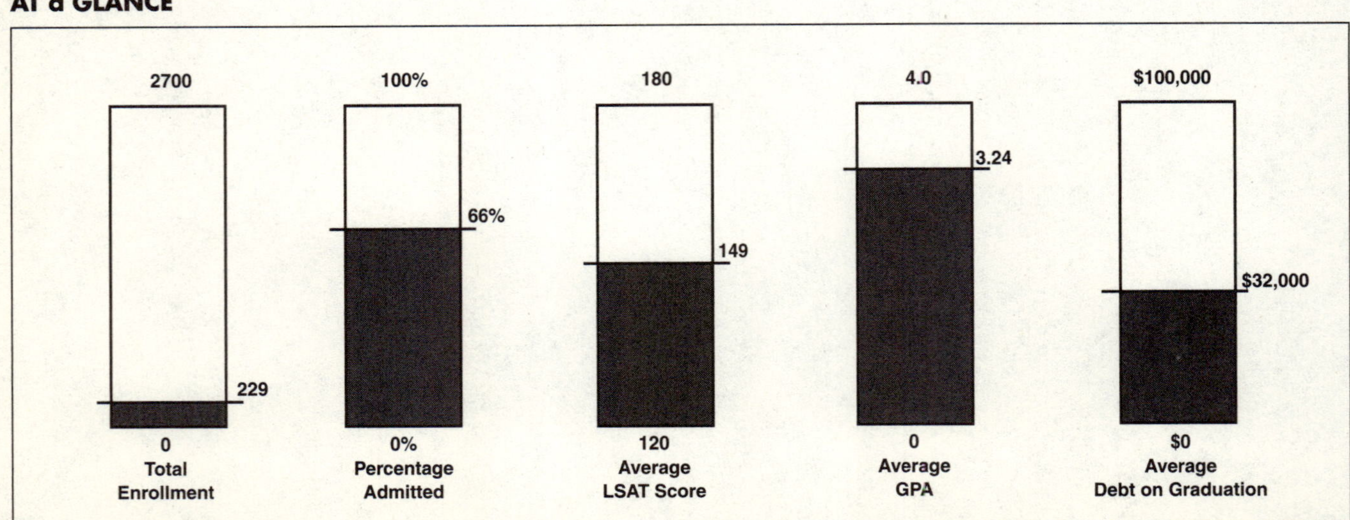

Degree Options

Degree	Total Credits Required	Length of Program
JD–Juris Doctor	88	3 yrs, full-time only [day]
JD/MBA–Juris Doctor/Master of Business Administration–Joint-degree	103	4–5 yrs, full-time only [day]
JD/MPAd–Juris Doctor/Master of Public Administration–Joint-degree	100	3–4 yrs, full-time only [day]

be received by March 1. Financial aid contact: Kathleen Bobbitt, Assistant Director, Student Financial Aid, PO Box 3335, Room 174, Knight Hall West Wing, Laramie, WY 82071-3335. Phone: 307-766-3827. Fax: 307-766-3800. E-mail: bobbitt1@uwy.edu

Law School Library The George William Hopper Law Library has 3 professional staff members and contains more than 273,738 volumes and 2,084 periodicals. 250 seats are available in the library. When classes are in session, the library is open 107 hours per week.

WESTLAW and LEXIS-NEXIS are available, as is online bibliographic services. 29 computer workstations are available to students in the library. Special law collections include Blume Collection of Roman Law.

First-Year Program Class size in the average section is 80; 100% of the first-year courses are taught by full-time faculty.

Upper-Level Program Class size in the average section is 30. Among the electives are:

- Administrative Law
- Advocacy
- Agricultural Law
- Business and Corporate Law
- Civil Litigation
- Consumer Law
- Criminal Defense
- Criminal Law
- Criminal Prosecution
- Domestic Violence
- Education Law
- Employment Law
- Environmental Law
- Estate Planning
- Family Law
- General Practice
- Government/Regulation
- Indian/Tribal Law
- International/Comparative Law
- Jurisprudence
- Labor Law
- Land Use Law/Natural Resources
- Lawyering Skills
- Legal History/Philosophy
- Litigation
- Mineral Rights
- Oil and Gas
- Probate Law
- Public Lands
- Real Estate Finance
- Securities
- Tax Law
- Water Law

Clinical Courses Students receive degree credit for clinical courses. (Clinical practicum is not required.) Among the clinical areas offered are:

- Advocacy
- Civil Litigation
- Criminal Defense
- Criminal Prosecution
- Family Practice
- General Practice
- Juvenile Law
- Litigation

INTER AMERICAN UNIVERSITY OF PUERTO RICO, METROPOLITAN CAMPUS
SCHOOL OF LAW

San Juan, Puerto Rico

INFORMATION CONTACT

Julio Fontanet, Dean of Student Affairs
PO Box 70351
San Juan, PR 00936-8351

Phone: 787-751-1912   Fax: 787-751-2975
       ext. 2011
E-mail: jfontane@inter.edu
Web site: http://www.inter.edu/law.html

LAW STUDENT PROFILE [2000–2001]

FULL-TIME   Enrollment: 336
Women: 58%   Men: 42%
PART-TIME   Enrollment: 380
Women: 45%   Men: 55%

RACIAL or ETHNIC COMPOSITION
Hispanic, 100%

APPLICANTS and ADMITTEES
Number applied: 1,058
Admitted: 331
Percentage accepted: 31%
Seats available: 225
Average LSAT score: 140
Average GPA: 3.2

Inter American University of Puerto Rico, Metropolitan Campus School of Law is a private institution that organizes classes on a semester calendar system. The campus is situated in an urban setting. Founded in 1961, first ABA approved in 1978, Inter American University of Puerto Rico, Metropolitan Campus School of Law offers a JD degree.

Faculty consists of 30 full-time and 30 part-time members in 2000–2001. 13 full-time faculty members and 12 part-time faculty members are women. 100% of all faculty members have a JD; 67% have advanced law degrees. Of all faculty members, 100% are Hispanic.

Application Information *Required:* LSAT, LSDAS, application form, application fee of $63, baccalaureate degree, minimum 2.5 GPA, college transcripts. *Recommended:* personal statement, essay. *Application deadline* for fall term is March 31 (priority date).

Costs The 1999–2000 tuition was $10,500 full-time; $350 per credit part-time. Fees: $452 full-time; $226 per semester part-time; $6 full-time (one-time charge).

Financial Aid In 2000–2001, 83% of all students received some form of financial aid. Loans, loan repayment assistance program (LRAP), merit-based grants/scholarships, need-based grants/scholarships, and federal work-study loans are available. The average student debt at graduation is $28,000. To apply for financial assistance, students must complete the Free Application for Federal Student Aid. Completed financial aid forms

AT a GLANCE

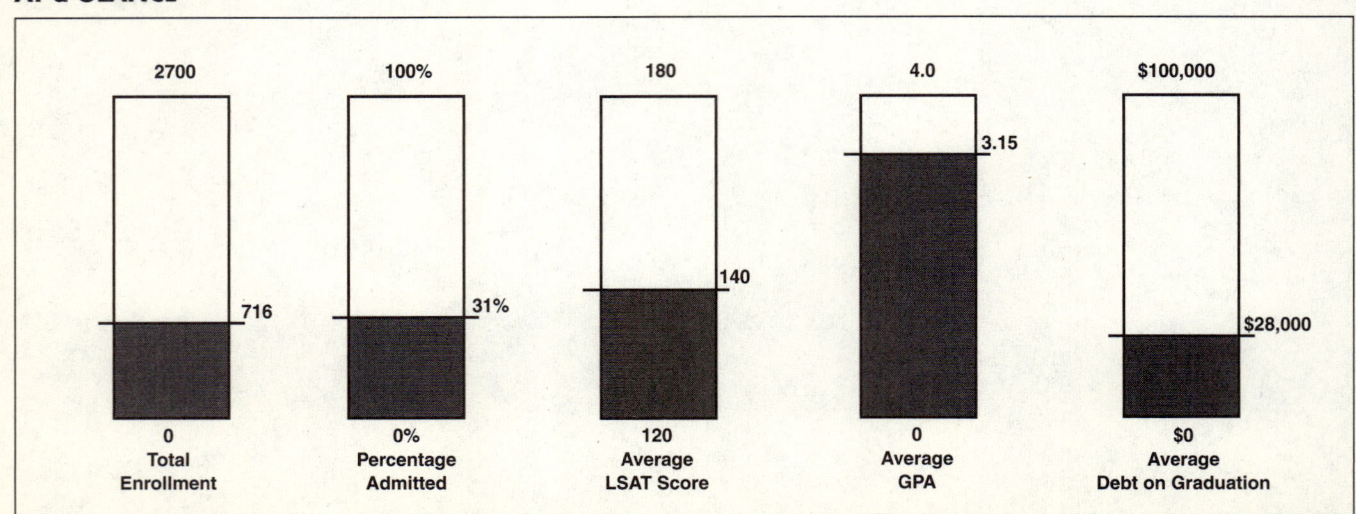

Degree Options		
Degree	**Total Credits Required**	**Length of Program**
JD–Juris Doctor	92	3–4 yrs, full-time or part-time [day, evening]

should be received by April 28. Financial aid contact: Ricardo Crespo, Director of Financial Aid, PO Box 70351, San Juan, PR 00936-8351. Phone: 787-751-1912 ext. 2014. Fax: 787-751-2975. E-mail: rcrespo@inter.edu

Law School Library Domingo Toledo-Alamo has 16 professional staff members and contains more than 174,935 volumes and 435 periodicals. 329 seats are available in the library. When classes are in session, the library is open 102 hours per week.

WESTLAW and LEXIS-NEXIS are available, as are the World Wide Web, online bibliographic services, and CD-ROM players. 39 computer workstations are available to students in the library. Special law collections include Hipolito Marcano, Jose Velez-Torres, Jose Echeverria-Yanez.

First-Year Program Class size in the average section is 60; 65% of the first-year courses are taught by full-time faculty.

Upper-Level Program Class size in the average section is 45. Among the electives are:

Administrative Law
Advocacy
Business and Corporate Law

★ Civil Rights
★ Environmental Law
Family Law
Intellectual Property
International/Comparative Law
Juvenile Law
Labor Law
★ Lawyering Skills
Legal History/Philosophy
Litigation
Maritime Law
Mediation
★ Public Interest
(★ *indicates an area of special strength*)

Clinical Courses Students receive degree credit for clinical courses. (Clinical practicum is not required.) Among the clinical areas offered are:

Civil Litigation
Civil Rights
Criminal Defense
Environmental Law
Family Practice
General Practice
Juvenile Law
Mediation
Public Interest

PONTIFICAL CATHOLIC UNIVERSITY OF PUERTO RICO
SCHOOL OF LAW

Ponce, Puerto Rico

INFORMATION CONTACT

Ana O. Bonilla, Director of Admissions
2250 Las Americas Avenue
Suite 633
Ponce, PR 00717-0777

Phone: 787-841-2000   Fax: 787-840-4295
     ext. 1000

Web site:

LAW STUDENT PROFILE [2000–2001]

FULL-TIME   Enrollment: 560
Women: 53%   Men: 47%

PART-TIME   Enrollment: 6
Women: 67%   Men: 33%

RACIAL or ETHNIC COMPOSITION
Hispanic, 100%

APPLICANTS and ADMITTEES
Number applied: 484
Admitted: 211
Percentage accepted: 44%
Seats available: 147
Average LSAT score: 135
Average GPA: 3.1

Pontifical Catholic University of Puerto Rico School of Law is a private institution that organizes classes on a semester calendar system. The campus is situated in an urban setting. Founded in 1961, first ABA approved in 1967, Pontifical Catholic University of Puerto Rico School of Law offers JD and JD/MBA degrees.

Faculty consists of 28 full-time and 24 part-time members in 2000–2001. 9 full-time faculty members and 1 part-time faculty members are women. 100% of all faculty members have a JD degree. Of all faculty members, 100% are Hispanic.

Application Information *Required:* minimum 130 LSAT score, application form, baccalaureate degree, minimum 2.5 GPA, interview, application fee of $75, 3 letters of recommendation. *Application deadline* for fall term is April 30 (priority date). Applications are processed on a rolling basis.

Costs The 1999–2000 tuition was $265 per credit part-time. Fees: $268 per semester part-time. Tuition and fees vary according to class time and student level.

Financial Aid Loans, merit-based grants/scholarships, need-based grants/scholarships, and federal work-study loans are available. To apply for financial assistance, students must complete the Free Application for Federal Student Aid, institutional forms, federal income tax returns. Completed financial aid forms should be received by July 15. Financial aid contact: Margie Alustiza, Financial Aid Office Director, 2292250 Avenue

AT a GLANCE

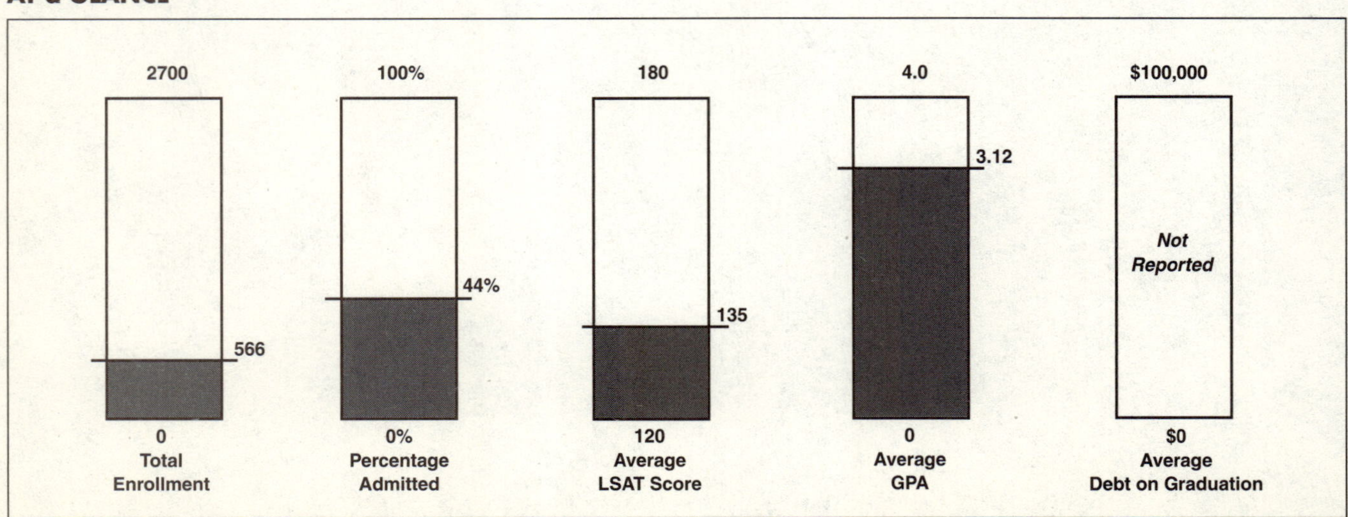

<table>
<tr><th colspan="3">Degree Options</th></tr>
<tr><th>Degree</th><th>Total Credits
Required</th><th>Length of Program</th></tr>
<tr><td>JD–Juris Doctor–Doctor of Laws</td><td>94</td><td>3–4 yrs, full-time or part-time [day, evening]</td></tr>
<tr><td>JD/MBA–Juris Doctor/Master of Business Administration–JD/MBA Dual degree program</td><td>137</td><td>4–5 yrs, full-time only</td></tr>
</table>

Las Americas, Suite 549, Ponce, PR 00717-0777. Phone: 787-841-2000 ext. 1065. Fax: 787-651-2041. E-mail: malustiza@pucpr.edu

Law School Library Monsieur Fremiot Torres Oliver Library has 4 professional staff members and contains more than 193,714 volumes and 2,413 periodicals. 169 seats are available in the library. When classes are in session, the library is open 100 hours per week.

WESTLAW and LEXIS-NEXIS are available, as are the World Wide Web and CD-ROM players. Special law collections include Federal Public Document Depository of he U.S.; Collection of U.N. (General Assembly & Security Council) official documents, resolutions and transcripts; Human Rights materials; a collection of Roman Law and Canon Law..

First-Year Program Class size in the average section is 50.

Clinical Courses Students receive degree credit for clinical courses. 6 credit hours of clinical practicum are required. Among the clinical areas offered are:

Criminal Defense
Criminal Prosecution
Government Litigation
Judicial Clerkship
Tax Law

International exchange programs permit students to visit Spain.

UNIVERSITY OF PUERTO RICO, RÍO PIEDRAS
SCHOOL OF LAW

San Juan, Puerto Rico

INFORMATION CONTACT

Lic. Inés Nieves, Admissions Officer
PO Box 23349
San Juan, PR 00931-3349

Phone: 787-764-2675   Fax: 787-764-2675
     ext. 3843
Web site:

LAW STUDENT PROFILE [2000–2001]

FULL-TIME   Enrollment: 421
Women: 58%   Men: 42%

PART-TIME   Enrollment: 154
Women: 50%   Men: 50%

APPLICANTS and ADMITTEES

Number applied: 196
Admitted: 194
Percentage accepted: 99%
Seats available: 150
Average LSAT score: 148
Average GPA: 3.5

University of Puerto Rico, Río Piedras School of Law is a public institution that organizes classes on a semester calendar system. The campus is situated in an urban setting. Founded in 1913, first ABA approved in 1945, and an AALS member, University of Puerto Rico, Río Piedras School of Law offers JD, JD/Lic, JD/MBA, JD/MD, and JD/MPP degrees.

Faculty 100% of all faculty members have a JD; 55% have advanced law degrees. Of all faculty members, 100% are Hispanic.

Application Information *Required:* LSAT, LSDAS, application form, application fee of $15, baccalaureate degree, personal statement, writing sample, college transcripts. *Application deadline* for fall term is February 1.

Financial Aid Graduate assistantships, loans, need-based grants/scholarships, and federal work-study loans are available. The average student debt at graduation is $6000. To apply for financial assistance, students must complete the Free Application for Federal Student Aid, institutional forms. Completed financial aid forms should be received by May 31. Financial aid contact: Mickel Ayala, Director of Financial Aid Program, University of Puerto Rico, PO Box 23349, San Juan, PR 00931-2349. Phone: 787-764-2675 ext. 5561. Fax: 787-764-2675.

Law School Library University of Puerto Rico Law Library has 10 professional staff members and contains

AT a GLANCE

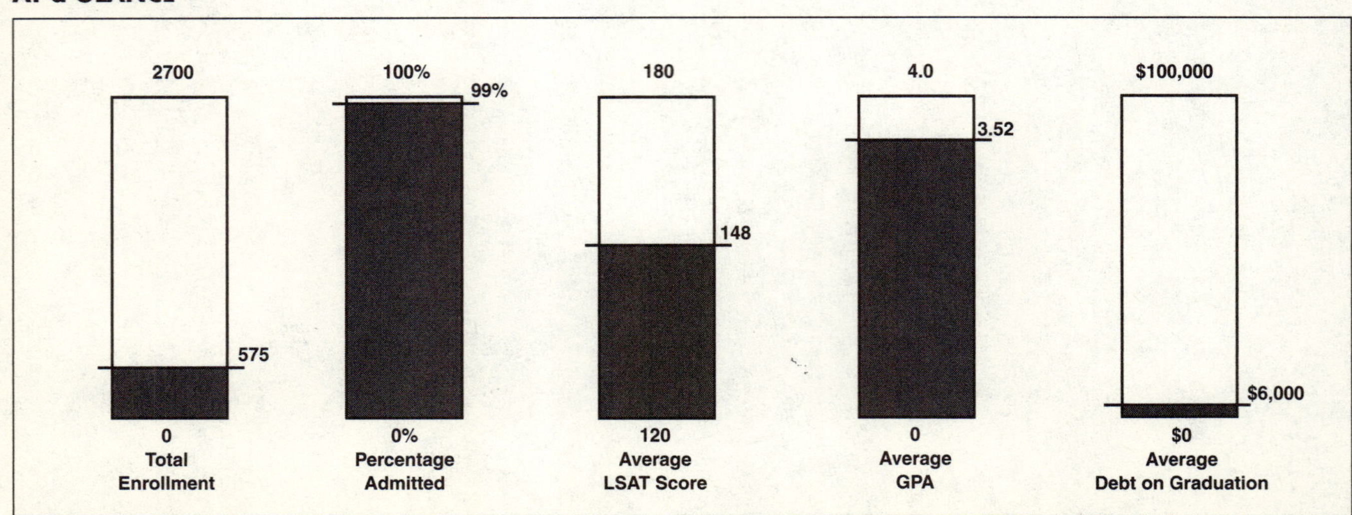

Degree Options

Degree	Total Credits Required	Length of Program
JD–Juris Doctor	92	3–4 yrs, full-time or part-time [day, evening]
JD/Lic–Juris Doctor/Licenciatura–Dual-degree Program	138	4 yrs, full-time only [day]
JD/MBA–Juris Doctor/Master of Business Administration–Dual-degree Program	122	4 yrs, full-time only [day]
JD/MD–Juris Doctor/Doctor of Medicine–Dual Degree Program		6 yrs, full-time only [day]
JD/MPP–Juris Doctor/Master of Public Planning–Dual Degree Program	104	4 yrs, full-time only [day]

more than 358,828 volumes and 4,669 periodicals. 407 seats are available in the library. When classes are in session, the library is open 112 hours per week.

WESTLAW and LEXIS-NEXIS are available, as are the World Wide Web, online bibliographic services, and CD-ROM players. 24 computer workstations are available to students in the library. Special law collections include Caribbean Law Collection.

First-Year Program Class size in the average section is 45; 90% of the first-year courses are taught by full-time faculty.

Upper-Level Program Class size in the average section is 30. Among the electives are:

Administrative Law
Advocacy
Business and Corporate Law
Civil Litigation
Civil Rights
Consumer Law
Criminal Defense
Education Law
Entertainment Law
Environmental Law
Family Law
Family Practice
General Practice
Government/Regulation
Immigration
Intellectual Property
International/Comparative Law
Jurisprudence
Juvenile Law
Labor Law
Land Use Law/Natural Resources
★ Lawyering Skills
Legal History/Philosophy
★ Litigation
Maritime Law
Mediation
Probate Law
Public Interest
Securities
Tax Law

(★ *indicates an area of special strength*)

Clinical Courses Students receive degree credit for clinical courses. 6 credit hours of clinical practicum are required. Among the clinical areas offered are:

Civil Litigation
Civil Rights
Criminal Defense
Environmental Law
Family Practice
General Practice
Immigration
Juvenile Law
Lawyering Skills

International exchange programs permit students to visit Chile and Spain.

INDEXES

SCHOOL NAME INDEX

The following index lists all of the law schools profiled in this book. The schools are listed alphabetically, with the page number of the school's profile appearing to the right of the school name. Those schools that also have an in-depth description appear in **bold type.**

EMPHASIZED UPPER-LEVEL COURSE INDEX

This index lists those upper-level courses that the schools have indicated are areas of special strength. The course titles are listed alphabetically, with the names of the schools that list that course as an area of special strength listed alphabetically under the course title, followed by the school's profile page number to the right of the school name.

Capital Defense

Capital Markets Regulation

Capital Punishment

Children and the Law

Children's Advocacy

Children's Rights

Civil Law

Civil Liberties

Estate Planning

Ethics

European Community Law

Evidence

Legal Externship

Legal History/Philosophy

Legal Research

Public Lands

Public Policy

Race and Law

Real Estate Law

Securities

Social Justice

Sports Law

Street Law

Tax Law

Technology and Lawyering

Technology Law

Tobacco Control

Traditionally Disadvantaged Groups

Trial Advocacy

Trusts and Estates

Water Law

Wildlife Law

Women's Rights

CLINICAL COURSE INDEX

This index lists clinical course areas offered by the schools. The clinical course areas are listed alphabetically, with the names of the schools that offer those courses listed alphabetically, followed by the school's profile page number to the right of the school name.

Civil Procedure

Civil Rights

Client Representation

Communications Law

Community Advocacy

Community Development

Congressional Clinic

Constitutional Law

Debtor Law

Disability Law

Discrimination

Dispute Resolution

District Attorney Clinic

Domestic Violence

Economic Development

Education

Education Law

Elder Law

Elderly Advocacy

Employment Law

Entertainment Law

Health Law

Housing and Finance

Housing Law

Indigenous Human Rights

Information and Communications

Intellectual Property

International Criminal Law

International Development

International Law

International/Comparative Law

Labor and Employment

Labor Law

Local Government

Media Law

Mediation

Mental Health and Law

Native American Defense

Native Hawaiian Rights

Natural Resources

Negotiation

Nonprofit Organizations

Public Policy